1000 Recipes Indian, Chinese Thai and Asian

1000 Recipes : Indian, Chinese Thai and Asian

Presenting all the best-loved dishes, from irresistible appetizers and sizzling hot curries to superb stir-fries, sambals and desserts

Create authentic Asian food at home with easy-to-follow recipes and more than 1000 fabulous photographs

RAFI FERNANDEZ

HERMES HOUSE

This edition is published by Hermes House, an imprint of Anness Publishing Ltd, Blaby Road, Wigston, Leicestershire LE18 4SE
Email: info@anness.com

Web: www.hermeshouse.com; www.annesspublishing.com

Publisher: Joanna Lorenz
Editorial Director: Helen Sudell
Project Editors: Catherine Stuart and Rosie Gordon
Design: SMI and Diane Pullen
Production Manager: Don Campaniello
Recipes: Shehzad Husain, Rafi Fernandez, Mridula Baljekar, Manisha Kanani, Deh-Ta Hsiung, Steven Wheeler, Kathy Man, Terry Tan and Ghillie Basan

Front cover: Duck with Pineapple & Ginger, see page 217

Notes

Bracketed terms are intended for American readers.

For all recipes, quantities are given in both metric and imperial measures and, where appropriate, in standard cups and spoons. Follow one set, but not a mixture, because they are not interchangeable. Standard spoon and cup measures are level. 1 tsp = 5ml, 1 tbsp = 15ml, 1 cup = 250ml/8fl oz. Australian standard tablespoons are 20ml. Australian readers should use 3 tsp in place of 1 tbsp for measuring small quantities of gelatine, flour, salt etc. American pints are 16fl oz/2 cups. American readers should use 20fl oz/2.5 cups in place of 1 pint when measuring liquids.

Electric oven temperatures in this book are for conventional ovens. When using a fan oven, the temperature will probably need to be reduced by about 10–20°C/20–40°F. Since ovens vary, you should check your manufacturer's instruction book for guidance.

The nutritional analysis given for each recipe is calculated per portion (i.e. serving or item), unless otherwise stated. If the recipe gives a range, such as Serves 4–6, then the nutritional analysis will be for the smaller portion size, i.e. 6 servings. Measurements for sodium do not include salt added to taste. Medium (US large) eggs are used unless otherwise stated.

Important: pregnant women, the elderly, the ill and very young children should avoid recipes using raw or lightly cooked eggs.

Contents

Introduction

Some of the world's favourite cuisines come from India, China, Thailand and South-east Asia. The popularity of their many famous dishes is well-deserved: tender vegetables in rich sauces; succulent meat and poultry; flavour-infused seafood; hearty beans and lentils; and, of course, the array of spices, epitomize these dishes that delight the senses.

Most of us live within delivery distance of an Indian, Chinese or Thai takeaway, and evenings with friends often feature a meal at an Asian restaurant. However, if you enjoy creating your own Asian food, look no further than this unique and exciting collection of 1000 recipes. There are quick-and-easy dishes as well as a huge and imaginative variety of recipes that involve blending aromatic spices and flavourings to achieve a truly authentic taste of the East.

The beauty of Asian cooking is in its variety. Different areas and traditions have developed their own specialities, and recipes have often been handed down through families as various combinations of spices and ingredients have been explored.

Indian cuisines

Although Indian dishes are famous for being fiery with chillies, there are many dishes that are mellow and will appeal to more delicate palates. Balti cuisine, which is Kashmiri cooking from the area that is now north Pakistan, is beautifully aromatic, but does not use chillies excessively, so it is not too hot. Many of the most familiar Indian dishes we enjoy come from the north of the country. These include koftas, mild kormas and tandoori recipes. The most fiery spice blends, however, such as the famous vindaloo, come from southern India, as well as an abundance of vegetarian dishes using lentils, beans and chickpeas. Since many Indian people are vegetarian, there is no shortage of delectable meat-free Indian recipes to choose from that utilize nuts, beans, peas and lentils, making nutritious meals that are bound to appeal to vegetarians and meat-eaters alike.

Below: Pickled ginger and other spicy preserves often feature in Asian food, and are particuarly popular in Japan.

Above: Exotic fruits such as papaya feature in many Asian desserts.

Chinese and South-east Asian flavours

China is a vast country with many different regional styles of cooking. The cuisine of the north is light and elegant, with Peking Duck being the best-known speciality. Cantonese cuisine in the south is based on abundant fresh vegetables, fish and shellfish. Stir-frying was perfected here, and Canton is the home of dim sum. Eastern China is famous for noodles and dumplings, while the southern provinces are known for their plentiful fish and rice. All the classic dishes of China share a balance of flavours, colours and textures.

Coconut plays a very important role in Thai cooking. Coconut milk, flavoured with ginger, lemon grass, pungent local chillies and basil leaves, forms the basis of most Thai curries. Many desserts are also made with coconut and palm sugar. Whatever the dish, there is always a fine balance and complexity of taste, texture and colour.

Rice is highly important to Indonesian culture and is eaten at least twice a day there. Fried rice is one of the most popular national dishes. In Malaysia, the cuisine is distinguished by its tremendous variety, influenced by settlers from Indonesia, China, India, Arabia, Holland and elsewhere, while the Spanish influence is very evident in the cooking of the Philippines.

All of these fabulous cuisines, with their diverse cooking styles and creative combinations of herbs, spices and flavourings, are brought together here in one collection of recipes.

Rice culture

The staple grain for the whole of the region is rice. Cultivated in southern Asia for more than five thousand years, it is eaten at every meal, including breakfast, and is the basis of both sweet and savoury snack foods, as well as being a source for both wine and vinegar. There are many varieties of rice but you will generally find it best to stock up on basmati for your Indian meals – it actually has a cooling effect on spicy food – and jasmine or Thai fragrant rice for your Chinese and South-east Asian cooking. If you decide to opt for the brown varieties, which are healthier and high in fibre, you will need to increase the cooking time and amount of water. Glutinous rice is another very useful variety, as it is used for sticky rice and rice cakes, and is a common ingredient in many delicious desserts.

The Asian kitchen

To add an authentic touch to your Asian meal, try cooking and serving it using the traditional pots and utensils, as detailed on the following pages. The karahi is very useful for cooking Indian curries: a little like a wok but made of heavier metal. Another item that is useful for Indian cooking is a heat diffuser which allows curries to simmer at the lowest possible temperature. Most modern kitchens have a wok, and this is the essential item for cooking Thai, Chinese, Indonesian and other Asian dishes – not only for stir-fries and curries but for deep frying and steaming.

Preparing the spices

Many recipes are quick to prepare using the simplest of spice combinations, whereas others call for a more varied store of spices and flavourings, including some lesser-known ingredients, such as mango powder (amchur) and compressed tamarind. Today, however, most of these ingredients are easily available from supermarkets, Asian stores and markets. For the best flavour, buy whole spices and grind them just before you use them. It is now possible to order small quantities of spice via the internet, which makes it very easy to source all the authentic flavours that you want. The recipes in this book feature ingredients that cooks should be able to find quite easily, and give ideas for alternatives to use in case you cannot source certain flavourings. Then, all you need is a reasonably large mortar and pestle in which you can pound all those delicious aromatics – the first step of many of these recipes.

Condiments for the store cupboard

Dried fish and shellfish are perhaps the least familiar area of the Asian diet to Western cooks. However, without the condiments and sauces made from them, we would think many of our favourite Asian dishes were 'lacking something'. Dried fish and shellfish furnish the raw material for fish sauce and shrimp paste, which are used all over south-east Asia under various names. Do aim to keep these in your store, but be cautious with them at first – a little goes a long way.

Below: Some recipes, such as sesame prawn toasts, are quick and easy to make but a guaranteed hit with party guests.

Above: Fresh herbs and spices are essential elements of most of the curry recipes in this book.

Fish sauce is not the only condiment to play a seminal role in Asian cooking. Even more important is soy sauce, which was invented by the Chinese nearly three thousand years ago. A fermented blend made from soy beans, grains (usually wheat), water and salt, it is used at the table and during cooking. Again, different regions have different types of soy sauce under different names. Keeping a light soy sauce and a Japanese soy sauce in your store cupboard may be a good start.

Apart from these 'basics', you will discover how to make a wide range of dips, sambals and condiments in this book. Asian food is never bland – even a snack consisting of a simple dish of rice will probably be spiced up with a lively chilli sambal.

Harmonious presentation

One of the elements that the Far East and South-east Asia have in common is the Chinese principle of fan-cai. The 'fan' is the main part of the meal, usually rice, while the 'cai' includes the supplementary protein and vegetables. These elements must be balanced in every meal, so that the aromas, colours, textures and tastes are all in perfect harmony. Harmony also dictates that the dishes are all served together, including soup, which is enjoyed throughout the meal. Presentation is essential too, especially in Japan. Throughout Asia beautifully carved fruits and vegetables are used to decorate all sorts of dishes.

Using this book

The book is divided into sections that offer everything a fan of Indian, Chinese and South-east Asian cuisines could ask for; from soups and appetizers to fish and shellfish dishes, meat, poultry and vegetable dishes. It also includes a variety of side dishes, salads, relishes and chutneys, as well as breads, desserts and drinks – in fact everything you need to create perfect meals time after time. Cook's Tips throughout the book explain some of the more unusual ingredients and how to prepare them, and the step-by-step instructions are easy to follow.

Once you have shopped for your ingredients, you are ready to create some of the tantalizing dishes contained in this collection. Whether it's a speedy weekday meal or a special dinner, your family and friends are in for a gastronomic treat.

Equipment & Utensils

The equipment in the average Western kitchen will be perfectly adequate for most of the recipes in this book, particularly now that the wok has become an indispensable item in many households. There are some items, however, that will make cooking Asian food easier and more fun. The best way to build up your store of specialist items is to start slowly, with a few basics such as a cleaver, bamboo steamer and wok, then gradually add extra pieces as you experiment with the different styles of cooking that are explored within these pages. If you enjoy making sushi, for instance, you will need a mat for rolling, and moulds for shaping the rice; if Thai curries are your current favourite, you'll be glad of a rough mortar and a pestle for grinding wet spice mixtures.

The design of many utensils has not changed in centuries, and items made from basic materials are often more effective than modern equivalents.

Below: A medium-weight cleaver is a multi-purpose tool.

Cleaver

To Western cooks, a cleaver can seem rather intimidating. In reality, cleavers are among the most useful pieces of kitchen equipment ever invented. The blade of a heavy cleaver is powerful enough to cut through bone, yet delicate enough in the hands of a master chef to create paper-thin slices of raw fish for sushi. The flat of the broad blade is ideal for crushing garlic or ginger.

Cleavers come in several sizes and weights. Number one is the heaviest. The blade is about 23cm/9in long and 10cm/4in wide. It can weigh as much as 1kg/2¼lb and resembles a chopper

Above: A karahi

more than a knife. At the other end of the scale, number three has a shorter, narrower blade and is only half as heavy as the larger cleaver. It is mainly used for slicing, rather than chopping. Number two is the cook's favourite. This medium-weight cleaver is used for both slicing and chopping. The Chinese name translates as 'civil and military knife' because the lighter, front half of the blade is used for slicing, shredding, filleting and scoring (civil work), while the heavier rear half is used for chopping with force (military work). The back of the blade is used for pounding and tenderizing, and the flat for crushing and transporting. Even the handle has more than one purpose – the end can be used as a pestle.

Cleavers are made of several types of material. They can be made of carbonized steel with wooden handles, or of stainless steel with metal or wooden handles. Choose the one you are comfortable with. Hold it in your hand and feel the weight; it should be neither too heavy nor too light. One point to remember is that while a stainless steel cleaver may look good, it will require frequent sharpening if it is to stay razor-sharp. To prevent a carbonized steel blade from rusting and getting stained, wipe it dry after every use, then give it a thin coating of

Right: A grinding stone, or sil padi, mortar and pestle and metal tongs.

Above: Chapati griddle with a rolling pin

vegetable oil. Cleavers should always be sharpened on a fine-grained whetstone, never with a regular steel knife sharpener.

Chapatti griddle

This heavy wrought iron frying pan is perfect for making chapatis and other breads and will not burn them. The pan can also be used for cooking spices.

Chapati rolling board

Generally these boards are round with stubby legs. They are designed to help you shape different-sized breads, and the added height helps disperse excess dry flour.

Chapati spoon
The square-shaped flat head of this spatula assists in roasting breads on the hot griddle.

Chopping block
The traditional chopping block in the East is simply a cross-section of a tree trunk, usually hardwood. The ideal size for use in a domestic kitchen is about 30cm/12in in diameter and about 5cm/2in thick, although you will see much larger blocks being used in restaurants. Season a new block with a liberal dose of vegetable oil on both sides to prevent it from splitting. Let it absorb as much oil as it will take, then clean the block with salt and water and dry it thoroughly. After each use, scrape the surface with the back of your cleaver, then wipe it with a cloth. Never immerse a wooden block in water.

A large rectangular cutting board of hardwood can be used instead, but make sure it is at least 5cm/2in thick or it may not be able to take a hard blow from a cleaver.

Acrylic boards can obviously be used if preferred, but they will not have the same aesthetic appeal as a traditional wooden one.

Below: A traditional Asian grater made of wood.

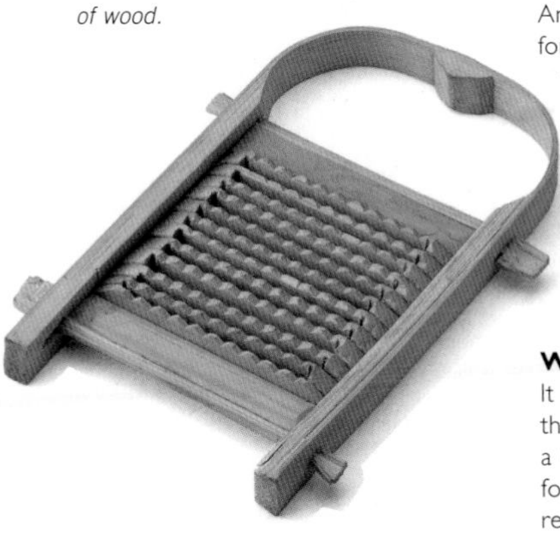

Grater
Traditional graters, used for preparing ginger, galangal and mooli (daikon), are made from wood or bamboo, but a metal cheese grater makes a satisfactory substitute.

Right: The rough surface of a stone mortar and pestle helps grip the ingredients that are being pounded.

Heat diffuser
Many curries are simmered over a low heat, and a heat diffuser helps prevent burning on the base.

Indian frying pan
The karahi is similar to a wok but heavier. It is the traditional cooking vessel for balti dishes.

Grinding stone
The sil padi is a traditional Indian 'food processor', consisting of a heavy slate marked with notches and a rolling pin, used to pulverize the ingredients against the stone.

Mortar and pestle
Oriental cooks prefer granite or stone mortars and pestles, since these have rough surfaces which help to grip the ingredients that are being chopped or pounded. Bigger, flat-bowled mortars are good for making spice pastes that contain large amounts of fresh spices, onion, herbs and garlic.

Spice mill
If you are going to grind a lot of spices, a spice mill will prove useful. An electric coffee grinder works well for this purpose, but it is a good idea to reserve the mill for spices, unless you like to have your coffee flavoured with cardamom or cloves.

Wok
It is not surprising that the wok has become a universal favourite, for it is a remarkably versatile utensil. The rounded bottom was originally designed to fit snugly on a traditional Chinese brazier or stove. It conducts and retains heat evenly and because of its shape, the food always returns to the centre where the heat is most intense. This makes it ideally suited for stir-frying, braising, steaming, boiling and even for deep-frying.

Although the wok might not at first glance appear to be the best utensil for deep-frying, it is actually ideal, requiring far less oil than a flat-bottomed deep-fryer. It has more depth and a greater frying surface, so more food can be cooked more quickly. It is also much safer than a pan. As a wok has a larger capacity at the top than at the base, there is

Below: A double-handled wok is useful for all types of cooking; those with a single handle are particularly good for stir-frying.

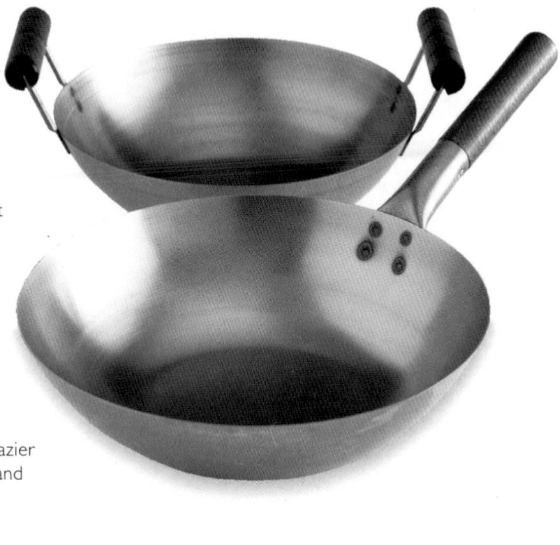

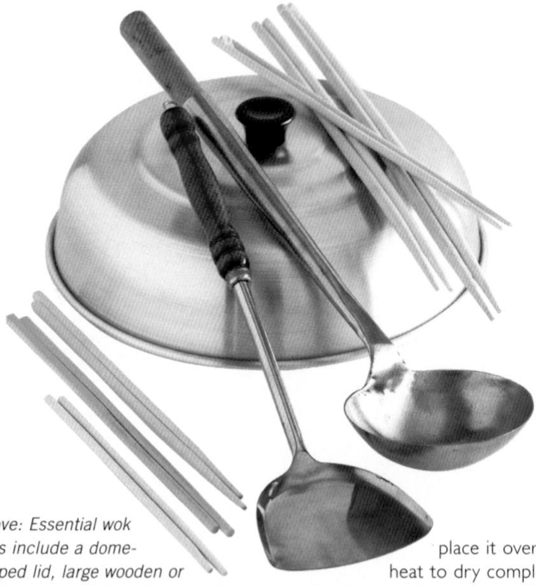

Above: Essential wok tools include a dome-shaped lid, large wooden or bamboo chopsticks, a long-handled spatula and a large ladle.

Above : A perforated metal scoop and a wire skimmer.

plenty of room to accommodate the oil, even when extra ingredients are added, and it is not likely to overflow and catch fire.

There are two basic types of wok available in the West. The most common type, the double-handled wok, is suitable for all types of cooking. The single-handled wok is particularly suitable for quick stir-frying, as it can easily be shaken during cooking. Both types are available with flattened bases for use on electric cookers or gas cookers with burners that would not accommodate a round base.

The best woks are made from lightweight carbonized steel. Cast iron woks are too heavy for all but the strongest cooks to handle, and woks made from other materials, such as stainless steel or aluminium, are not as good for Asian cooking. They also tend to be a great deal more expensive than the standard carbonized steel wok.

A new carbonized steel wok must be seasoned before use. The best way to do this is to place the wok over a high heat until the surface blackens, then wash it in warm, soapy water. Use a stiff brush to get the wok clean, then rinse it well in clean water and place it over a medium heat to dry completely. Finally, wipe the surface with a pad of kitchen paper soaked in vegetable oil. After each use, wash the wok under the hot water tap, but never use detergent as this would remove the 'seasoning' and cause the wok to rust. Any food that sticks should be scraped off the wok with a stiff brush or with a non-metal scourer, and the wok should then be rinsed and dried over a low heat. Before being put away, a little oil should be rubbed into the (inner) surface of the wok.

Wok tools

Some wok sets come with a spatula and ladle made from cast iron or stainless steel. These are very useful, particularly the ladle. In addition to its obvious purpose as a stirrer, it can be used to measure small quantities of liquid. A standard ladle holds about 175ml/6fl oz/ ¾ cup. A dome-shaped lid is also useful, as is a metal draining rack that fits over the wok. Small items such as deep-fried foods can be placed on the rack to keep warm while successive batches are cooked. Other accessories include wooden or bamboo chopsticks. Short ones can be used at the table or in the kitchen – they are ideal for beating eggs – and the long pair are used for deep-frying, as stirrers or tongs – ideal for keeping your hands away from the heat while dealing with food. Finally, a wok stand is handy for protecting your table when serving.

Below: Bamboo steamers come in several sizes.

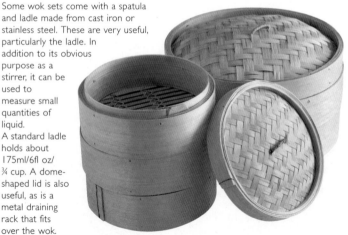

Above: An authentic clay pot can be used in the oven or on top of the stove.

Strainers
Several types of strainer are available, but the two most useful are the perforated metal scoop or slotted spoon, and the coarse-mesh, wire skimmer, preferably with a long bamboo handle. Wire skimmers come in a variety of sizes and are useful for removing food from hot oil when deep-frying.

Steamers
The traditional Chinese steamer is made from bamboo and has a tight-fitting lid. Several sizes are available, and you can stack as many tiers as you like over a wok of boiling water. The modern steamer is free-standing and made of aluminium, but food cooked in a metal steamer lacks the subtle fragrance that a bamboo steamer imparts. If you do not have a steamer, you can improvise with a wok and a trivet. Having placed the trivet in the wok, fill it one-third full of water and bring this to the boil. Place the food in a heatproof bowl on the trivet, cover the wok with the dome-shaped lid and steam the food until it is cooked.

Below: A large pan with a tight-fitting lid is ideal for cooking rice.

Clay pot
Also known as the sand pot or Chinese casserole, this earthenware cooking utensil must have preceded the cast iron pot by thousands of years. Several shapes and sizes are available, and most are glazed on the inside only. They are not expensive and can be bought in Asian or Chinese stores. With care, the pots can be used on top of the stove, where they retain an even heat. They are fairly fragile, and are prone to crack easily.

Rice cooker
Electric rice cookers work extremely well and are worth investing in if you cook a lot of rice. However, a good-sized, deep, heavy pan with a tight-fitting lid is just as suitable for this purpose.

Mongolian fire pot
Also known as a Chinese hot pot or steamboat (in Singapore), this is not unlike a fondue pot, in that it allows food to be cooked at the table. The design is different from that of a fondue, however, as it consists of a wide vessel with a central funnel, which is filled with burning charcoal, surrounded by a moat in which hot stock is placed. The pot is placed in the centre of the table and guests cook small pieces of meat and vegetables in the hot stock. Once these are all cooked and eaten, the stock is served as a soup. There are several different models available, the most expensive being made of brass, while the cheaper ones are made of aluminium or stainless steel.

Below: A Mongolian fire pot or steamboat is used for cooking at the table. The central funnel is filled with burning charcoal, and this heats the stock in the surrounding moat.

Japanese omelette pan
To make the rolled omelettes that are so widely used in Japanese cooking, a rectangular omelette pan or makiyaki-nabe is useful, but not essential: a large non-stick, heavy frying pan or a flat, heavy griddle could be used instead.

Sushi equipment
If you are going to make sushi properly, you will need a *makisu*, also known as a *sushimaki sudare*. This is the bamboo mat (shown below) that is used for rolling sheets of nori (seaweed) around fillings when making norimaki.

Sushi chefs spread the rice on the nori with their fingers, but a rice paddle or *shamoji* makes the job easier. For pressed sushi, shaped moulds made from wood or plastic are very useful.

Tomato & Coriander Soup

Although soups are not often eaten in India or Pakistan, tomato soup bucks the trend and is very popular. It is excellent on a cold winter's day.

Serves 4

675g/1½lb tomatoes, peeled and chopped
15ml/1 tbsp oil
1 bay leaf
4 spring onions (scallions), chopped
5ml/1 tsp salt
2.5ml/½ tsp crushed garlic
5ml/1 tsp crushed black peppercorns
30ml/2 tbsp chopped fresh coriander (cilantro)
750ml/1¼ pints/3 cups water
15ml/1 tbsp cornflour (cornstarch)
30ml/2 tbsp single (light) cream, to garnish (optional)

1 To peel the tomatoes, plunge them in very hot water, leave for 30 seconds, then take them out. The skin should now peel off easily. If not, put the tomatoes back in the water for a little longer. Once they have been peeled, roughly chop the tomatoes.

2 In a medium, heavy pan, heat the oil and fry the tomatoes, bay leaf and spring onions for a few minutes until soft.

3 Gradually add the salt, garlic, peppercorns and coriander. Pour in the water. Stir, then simmer gently over a low heat for 15–20 minutes.

4 Meanwhile, dissolve the cornflour in a little cold water to form a thick creamy paste.

5 Remove the soup from the heat and leave to cool slightly for a few minutes. Press through a sieve (strainer), or purée in a blender or food processor.

6 Return the puréed soup to the pan, add the cornflour mixture and stir over a gentle heat for about 3 minutes until thickened.

7 Pour the soup into individual serving dishes and garnish with a swirl of cream, if using. Serve hot.

Curried Carrot & Apple Soup

The combination of carrot, curry powder and apple is a highly successful one. Curried fruit is delicious.

Serves 4

10ml/2 tsp sunflower oil
15ml/1 tbsp mild korma curry powder
500g/1¼lb carrots, chopped
1 large onion, chopped
1 tart cooking apple, chopped
750ml/1¼ pints/3 cups chicken stock
salt and ground black pepper
plain yogurt and carrot curls, to garnish

1 Heat the oil in a large, heavy pan. Add the curry powder and fry for 2–3 minutes.

2 Add the carrots, onion and cooking apple and stir well until coated with the curry powder. Cover the pan.

3 Cook over low heat for about 15 minutes, shaking the pan occasionally, until soft. Spoon the vegetable mixture into a food processor or blender, then add half the stock and process until the mixture is smooth.

4 Return to the pan and pour in the remaining stock. Bring the soup to the boil and adjust the seasoning before serving in bowls, garnished with a swirl of yogurt and a few curls of raw carrot.

Variations

- *Parsnips also taste great in a curried soup. Simply replace the carrots with chopped parsnips, or, if you prefer, use half the amount of carrots and half of parsnips.*
- *If you don't have any korma powder you can make up your own with 5ml/1 tsp each ground turmeric, cumin, coriander and cinnamon. Add 10ml/2 tsp grated fresh root ginger if you want to give your soup a little more kick.*

tomato & coriander soup Energy 63kcal/267kJ; Protein 2g; Carbohydrate 9.5g, of which sugars 6g; Fat 2.2g, of which saturates 1.1g; Cholesterol 4mg; Calcium 48mg; Fibre 2.5g; Sodium 24mg.
curried carrot & apple soup Energy 90kcal/376kJ; Protein 1.7g; Carbohydrate 17.3g, of which sugars 15g; Fat 2.1g, of which saturates 0.3g; Cholesterol 0mg; Calcium 51mg; Fibre 4.3g; Sodium 34mg.

Spiced Cauliflower Soup

Light and tasty, this creamy, mildly spicy vegetable soup is multi-purpose. It makes a wonderful warming first course, an appetizing quick meal and is delicious chilled.

Serves 4–6

1 large potato, diced
1 small cauliflower, chopped
1 onion, chopped
15ml/1 tbsp oil
1 garlic clove, crushed
15ml/1 tbsp grated fresh root ginger
10ml/2 tsp ground turmeric
5ml/1 tsp cumin seeds
5ml/1 tsp black mustard seeds
10ml/2 tsp ground coriander
1 litre/1¾ pints/4 cups vegetable stock
300ml/½ pint/1¼ cups natural (plain) low-fat yogurt
salt and ground black pepper
fresh coriander (cilantro) or parsley, to garnish

1 Put the potato, cauliflower and onion into a large, heavy pan with the oil and 45ml/3 tbsp water. Heat until hot and bubbling, then stir well, cover the pan and turn the heat down. Continue cooking the mixture for about 10 minutes.

2 Add the garlic, ginger and spices. Stir well, and cook for another 2 minutes, stirring occasionally. Pour in the stock and season well. Bring to the boil, then cover and simmer for about 20 minutes. Purée in a food processor and return to the pan. Stir in the yogurt, adjust the seasoning, and serve garnished with coriander or parsley.

Cook's Tip

A freshly made stock always tastes best. To make home-made vegetable stock, add to 3.5 litres/6 pints/15 cups of water: 2 sliced leeks, 3 chopped celery sticks, 1 chopped onion, 1 chopped parsnip, 1 seeded and chopped yellow (bell) pepper, 3 crushed garlic cloves, fresh herbs and 45ml/3 tbsp light soy sauce. Season, then slowly bring to the boil. Lower the heat and simmer for 30 minutes, stirring from time to time. Leave to cool. Strain, discard the vegetables, and use the stock as indicated in the recipe.

Fiery Hot Yogurt & Chilli Soup

Hot chillies, cool yogurt – this is an unusual and tasty soup with a real punch.

Serves 2–3

450ml/¾ pint/scant 2 cups natural (plain) low-fat yogurt, beaten
60ml/4 tbsp gram flour
2.5ml/½ tsp chilli powder
2.5ml/½ tsp ground turmeric
2 fresh green chillies, finely chopped
30ml/2 tbsp vegetable oil
4 whole dried red chillies
5ml/1 tsp cumin seeds
3 or 4 curry leaves
3 garlic cloves, crushed
5cm/2in piece fresh root ginger, crushed
salt
fresh coriander (cilantro) leaves, chopped, or coriander relish, to garnish

1 Mix the yogurt, gram flour, chilli powder, turmeric and salt to taste in a bowl. Press the mixture through a strainer into a pan. Add the green chillies and simmer for 10 minutes, stirring occasionally.

2 Heat the vegetable oil in a heavy pan and fry the remaining spices, crushed garlic and fresh ginger until the dried chillies turn black.

3 Pour the oil and the spices over the yogurt soup, cover the pan and leave to rest for 5 minutes off the heat. Mix well and gently reheat for a further 5 minutes. Ladle into warmed soup bowls and serve hot, garnished with the coriander leaves.

Cook's Tips

- *For a lower fat version drain off some of the oil before adding the spices to the yogurt.*
- *Adjust the amount of chilli according to how hot you want the soup to be.*

spiced cauliflower soup Energy 122kcal/504kJ; Protein 3.7g; Carbohydrate 7.4g, of which sugars 3.3g; Fat 8.8g, of which saturates 1.2g; Cholesterol 0mg; Calcium 34mg; Fibre 1.4g; Sodium 41mg.
yogurt & chilli soup Energy 226kcal/942kJ; Protein 15.8g; Carbohydrate 9.1g, of which sugars 5.9g; Fat 14.4g, of which saturates 2.3g; Cholesterol 29mg; Calcium 177mg; Fibre 0.5g; Sodium 90mg.

Lentil Soup

This is a simple, mildly spiced lentil soup, which is a good accompaniment to heavily spiced meat dishes.

Serves 4–6

15g/½oz/1 tbsp ghee
1 large onion, finely chopped
2 garlic cloves, crushed
1 fresh green chilli, chopped
2.5ml/½ tsp turmeric
75g/3oz/⅓ cup split red lentils (masoor dhal)
250ml/8fl oz/1 cup water
400g/14oz canned tomatoes, chopped
2.5ml/½ tsp sugar
lemon juice, to taste
200g/7oz/1¾ cups plain boiled rice or 2 boiled potatoes (optional)
salt
fresh coriander (cilantro), chopped, to garnish (optional)

1 Heat the ghee in a large pan and fry the onion, garlic, chilli and turmeric until the onion is translucent.

2 Add the lentils and water, and bring to the boil. Reduce the heat, cover and cook until all the water is absorbed.

3 Mash the lentils with the back of a wooden spoon until you have a smooth paste. Add salt to taste and mix well.

4 Add the tomatoes, sugar and lemon, and reheat the soup. To provide extra texture, fold in the plain boiled rice or potatoes cut into small cubes. Garnish with coriander, if you like, and serve hot.

Cook's Tips

- *When using lentils, first rinse them in cold water and pick over to remove any small stones or loose skins.*
- *Fresh coriander (cilantro) is used in so many dishes that it is worth growing some in a window box or in several pots on your kitchen windowsill. If you have a garden you could grow some in a raised well-drained bed, so that you have a good supply.*

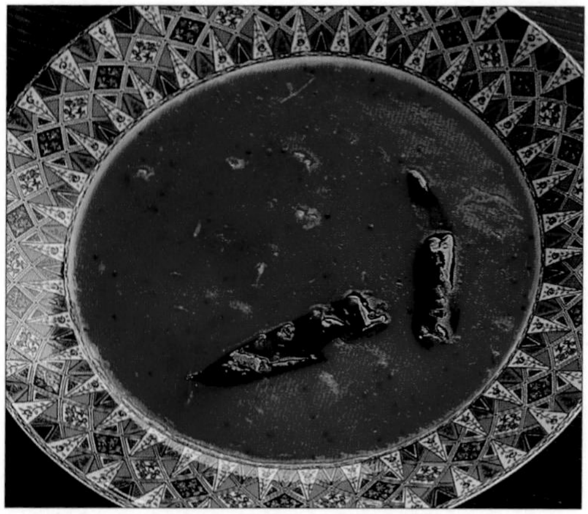

South Indian Pepper Water

This soothing broth is perfect for winter evenings.

Serves 4–6

30ml/2 tbsp vegetable oil
2.5ml/½ tsp black pepper
5ml/1 tsp cumin seeds
2.5ml/½ tsp mustard seeds
1.5ml/¼ tsp asafoetida
2.5ml/½ tsp ground turmeric
2 dried red chillies
4–6 curry leaves
2 garlic cloves, crushed
300ml/½ pint/1¼ cups tomato juice
juice of 2 lemons
120ml/4fl oz/½ cup water
salt
fresh coriander (cilantro), chopped, to garnish

1 Heat the oil in a pan and fry the pepper, spices, curry leaves and garlic until the chillies are just black and the garlic is golden.

2 Lower the heat and pour in the tomato juice, lemon juice and water. Bring to the boil, then simmer for 10 minutes. Season to taste with salt. Pour into heated bowls, garnish with the chopped coriander, if you like, and serve.

Indian Pea Soup

This is a delicate and tasty creamy vegetable soup.

Serves 6

115g/4oz potato, chopped
75g/3oz onion, chopped
1.2 litres/2 pints/5 cups chicken stock
2cm/¾in piece fresh root ginger
2.5ml/½ tsp ground cumin
75ml/5 tbsp chopped fresh coriander (cilantro)
½ green chilli
275g/10oz fresh or frozen peas
15ml/1 tbsp lemon juice
150ml/¼ pint/⅔ cup double (heavy) cream
salt

1 Put the potato, onion, stock, ginger and cumin in a pan and bring to the boil. Simmer for 30 minutes. Remove the ginger.

2 Add the coriander, chilli, peas and lemon juice, and salt to taste. Simmer for 2–3 minutes. Purée in a food processor or blender, then reheat. Add the cream and heat before serving.

lentil soup Energy 195kcal/816kJ; Protein 7.6g; Carbohydrate 17g, of which sugars 3g; Fat 11.2g, of which saturates 1.6g; Cholesterol 0mg; Calcium 28mg; Fibre 3.4g; Sodium 14mg.
pepper water Energy 63kcal/262kJ; Protein 0.7g; Carbohydrate 2.6g, of which sugars 2.3g; Fat 5.6g, of which saturates 0.7g; Cholesterol 0mg; Calcium 16mg; Fibre 0.7g; Sodium 178mg.
Indian pea soup Energy 180kcal/744kJ; Protein 4g; Carbohydrate 9.7g, of which sugars 2.4g; Fat 14.2g, of which saturates 8.5g; Cholesterol 34mg; Calcium 26mg; Fibre 2.5g; Sodium 9mg.

Cellophane Noodle Soup

The noodles used in this soup go by various names: glass, cellophane, mung bean, thread or transparent.

Serves 4

4 large dried shiitake mushrooms
15g/½oz dried lily buds
½ cucumber, coarsely chopped
2 garlic cloves, halved
90g/3½oz white cabbage, coarsely chopped
1.2 litres/2 pints/5 cups boiling water
115g/4oz cellophane noodles
30ml/2 tbsp soy sauce
15ml/1 tbsp palm sugar (jaggery) or light muscovado (brown) sugar
90g/3½oz block silken tofu, diced
fresh coriander (cilantro) leaves, to garnish

1 Soak the shiitake mushrooms in warm water for 30 minutes. In a separate bowl, soak the dried lily buds in warm water, also for 30 minutes.

2 Meanwhile, put the cucumber, garlic and cabbage in a food processor and process to a smooth paste. Scrape the mixture into a large pan and add the measured boiling water.

3 Bring to the boil. Reduce the heat and cook for 2 minutes, stirring occasionally. Strain this stock into another pan, return to a low heat and bring to simmering point.

4 Drain the lily buds, rinse under cold running water, then drain again. Cut off any hard ends. Add the lily buds to the stock with the noodles, soy sauce and sugar and cook for 5 minutes more.

5 Strain the mushroom soaking liquid into the soup. Discard the mushroom stems, then slice the caps. Divide them and the tofu among four bowls. Pour the soup over, garnish, and serve.

Cook's Tip
Tough and brittle, it is better not to try to break or chop cellophane noodles before adding to a hot stock, soup or stew.

Sour Noodle Soup

The sour notes in this classic soup emanate from the tamarind and salted soya beans.

Serves 4

vegetable oil, for deep-frying
225g/8oz firm tofu, rinsed, drained and cut into cubes
60ml/4 tbsp dried prawns (shrimp), soaked until rehydrated
5ml/1 tsp shrimp paste
4 garlic cloves, chopped
4–6 dried red chillies, soaked to soften, drained, seeded and the pulp scraped out
90g/3½oz/¾ cup roasted peanuts, ground
50g/2oz salted soya beans
2 lemon grass stalks, trimmed, halved and bruised
30ml/2 tbsp sugar
15–30ml/1–2 tbsp tamarind paste
150g/5oz dried rice vermicelli, soaked in hot water until pliable
a handful of beansprouts, rinsed and drained
4 quail's eggs, hard-boiled, shelled and halved
2 spring onions (scallions), sliced
salt and ground black pepper
fresh coriander (cilantro) leaves, finely chopped, to garnish

1 In a wok, heat enough vegetable oil for deep-frying. Drop in the tofu and deep-fry until golden. Drain on kitchen paper. Grind the soaked dried prawns with the shrimp paste, garlic and chilli pulp to form a paste.

2 Heat 30ml/2 tbsp vegetable oil in a wok and fry the paste for 1 minute. Add the peanuts, soya beans and lemon grass. Fry for another minute and stir in the sugar and tamarind paste, followed by 900ml/1½ pints/3¾ cups water. Mix well.

3 Bring to the boil, then simmer gently for 10 minutes. Season with salt and pepper.

4 Drain the noodles and heat through in the broth. Divide among individual bowls, sprinkle over the beansprouts and add the tofu, quail's eggs and spring onions. Garnish with the coriander and serve.

cellophane noodle Energy 148kcal/618kJ; Protein 4.1g; Carbohydrate 29.7g, of which sugars 5.7g; Fat 1.1g, of which saturates 0.1g; Cholesterol 0mg; Calcium 139mg; Fibre 0.7g; Sodium 546mg.
sour noodle Energy 477kcal/1993kJ; Protein 27.5g; Carbohydrate 44.8g, of which sugars 10.7g; Fat 21.2g, of which saturates 3.6g; Cholesterol 71mg; Calcium 376mg; Fibre 2.9g; Sodium 83mg.

Miso Broth with Mushrooms

Shiitake mushrooms give this soup superb flavour.

Serves 4

1.2 litres/2 pints/5 cups boiling water
45ml/3 tbsp light miso paste
3 fresh shiitake mushrooms, sliced
115g/4oz tofu, cubed
1 spring onion (scallion), green part only, sliced

1 Mix the boiling water and miso in a pan. Add the mushrooms and simmer for 5 minutes.

2 Divide the tofu among four warmed soup bowls, ladle in the soup, scatter with sliced spring onions and serve.

Miso Broth with Tofu

This nutritious soup is standard breakfast fare, and the tofu adds great texture.

Serves 4

5 baby leeks
15g/½oz fresh coriander (cilantro), including the stalks
3 thin slices fresh root ginger
2 star anise
1 small dried red chilli
1.2 litres/2 pints/5 cups dashi stock or vegetable stock
225g/8oz pak choi (bok choy), thickly sliced
200g/7oz firm tofu, cubed
60ml/4 tbsp red miso
30–45ml/2–3 tbsp shoyu (Japanese soy sauce)

1 Cut the tops off the leeks and slice the rest finely. Place the tops in a large pan. Chop the coriander leaves and set aside. Add the coriander stalks, ginger, star anise and chilli to the pan. Pour in the dashi or vegetable stock. Bring to the boil, then simmer for 10 minutes. Strain, return to the pan and reheat.

2 Add the sliced leeks to the pan with the pak choi and tofu. Cook for 2 minutes, then mix 45ml/3 tbsp of the miso with a little of the hot soup and stir it into the mixture. Taste, and add more miso and shoyu as preferred. Stir in the chopped coriander, cook for a further minute, and serve.

Miso Broth with Noodles

This delicate, fragrant soup is flavoured with just a hint of chilli.

Serves 4

45ml/3 tbsp light miso paste
200g/7oz/scant 2 cups udon, soba or Chinese noodles
30ml/2 tbsp sake or dry sherry
15ml/1 tbsp rice or wine vinegar
45ml/3 tbsp soy sauce
115g/4oz asparagus tips or mangetouts (snow peas), sliced
50g/2oz/scant 1 cup shiitake mushrooms, stalks removed and thinly sliced
1 carrot, sliced into julienne strips
3 spring onions (scallions), thinly sliced diagonally
salt and ground black pepper
5ml/1 tsp dried chilli flakes, to serve

1 Bring 1 litre/1¾ pints/4 cups water to the boil in a pan. Pour 150ml/¼ pint/⅔ cup of the boiling water over the miso and stir until dissolved, then set aside.

2 Meanwhile, bring another large pan of lightly salted water to the boil, add the noodles and cook according to the packet instructions until just tender.

3 Drain the noodles in a colander. Rinse under cold running water, then drain again.

4 Add the sake or sherry, rice or wine vinegar and soy sauce to the pan of boiling water. Boil gently for 3 minutes or until the alcohol has evaporated, then reduce the heat and stir in the miso mixture.

5 Add the asparagus or mangetouts, mushrooms, carrot and spring onions, and simmer for about 2 minutes until the vegetables are just tender. Season to taste.

6 Divide the noodles among four warm bowls and pour the soup over the top. Serve, sprinkled with the chilli flakes, supplying diners with chopsticks and spoons.

miso broth w. mushrooms Energy 25kcal/103kJ; Protein 2.4g; Carbohydrate 2.6g, of which sugars 2.4g; Fat 0.6g, of which saturates 0.1g; Cholesterol 0mg; Calcium 107mg; Fibre 1.6g; Sodium 882mg.
miso broth w. tofu Energy 71kcal/297kJ; Protein 7.2g; Carbohydrate 4.2g, of which sugars 3.5g; Fat 2.9g, of which saturates 0.4g; Cholesterol 0mg; Calcium 372mg; Fibre 2.6g; Sodium 884mg.
miso broth w. noodles Energy 230kcal/973kJ; Protein 7.7g; Carbohydrate 42.6g, of which sugars 5.1g; Fat 3.5g, of which saturates 0.1g; Cholesterol 0mg; Calcium 34mg; Fibre 2.9g; Sodium 809mg.

Red Onion & Vermicelli Laksa

Sliced red onions mimic flour noodles in this soup.

Serves 6

150g/5oz/2½ cups dried shiitake mushrooms
1.2 litres/2 pints/5 cups boiling vegetable stock
30ml/2 tbsp tamarind paste
250ml/8fl oz/1 cup hot water
6 large dried red chillies, stems removed and seeded
2 lemon grass stalks, finely sliced
5ml/1 tsp ground turmeric
15ml/1 tbsp grated fresh galangal
1 onion, chopped
5ml/1 tsp dried shrimp paste
30ml/2 tbsp oil
10ml/2 tsp palm sugar (jaggery)
175g/6oz rice vermicelli
1 red onion, very finely sliced
1 small cucumber, seeded and cut into strips
handful of fresh mint leaves, to garnish

1 Place the mushrooms in a bowl and pour in enough boiling stock to cover them, then leave to soak for 30 minutes. Put the tamarind paste into a bowl and pour in the hot water. Mash, then strain and reserve the liquid, discarding the pulp.

2 Soak the chillies in hot water to cover for 5 minutes, then drain, reserving the liquid. Place in a food processor and blend with the lemon grass, turmeric, galangal, onion and shrimp paste, adding a little soaking water to form a paste.

3 Heat the oil in a large, heavy pan and cook the paste over a low heat for 4–5 minutes. Add the tamarind liquid and bring to the boil, then simmer for 5 minutes. Remove from the heat.

4 Drain the mushrooms and reserve the stock. Discard the stems, then halve or quarter the mushrooms, if large. Add the mushrooms to the pan with their soaking liquid, the remaining stock and the sugar. Simmer for 25–30 minutes or until tender.

5 Put the rice vermicelli into a large bowl and cover with boiling water, then leave to soak for 4 minutes until softened. Drain well, then divide among six bowls. Top with onion and cucumber, then ladle in the boiling shiitake soup. Add a few mint leaves to each bowl and serve.

Noodle Soup with Tofu

This light and refreshing soup is an excellent pick-me-up. The aromatic, spicy broth is simmered first, and then the tofu, beansprouts and noodles are added.

Serves 4

150g/5oz dried thick rice noodles
1 litre/1¾ pints/4 cups vegetable stock
1 fresh red chilli, seeded and thinly sliced
15ml/1 tbsp light soy sauce
juice of ½ lemon
10ml/2 tsp sugar
5ml/1 tsp finely sliced garlic
5ml/1 tsp finely chopped fresh root ginger
200g/7oz firm tofu
90g/3½oz/scant 1 cup beansprouts
50g/2oz/½ cup peanuts
15ml/1 tbsp chopped fresh coriander (cilantro)
spring onion (scallion) slivers and red chilli slivers, to garnish

1 Spread out the noodles in a shallow dish and pour over boiling water to cover. Soak according to the packet instructions until they are just tender. Drain, rinse and set aside.

2 Meanwhile, place the stock, red chilli, soy sauce, lemon juice, sugar, garlic and ginger in a wok over high heat. Bring to the boil, cover, reduce to low heat and simmer the mixture gently for 10–12 minutes.

3 Cut the tofu into cubes. Add it to the wok with the drained noodles and the beansprouts. Cook the mixture gently for 2–3 minutes.

4 Roast the peanuts in a dry non-stick wok, then chop them. Stir the coriander into the soup. Serve in warm bowls with peanuts, spring onions and chilli on top.

Cook's Tip
It is important to use vegetable stock with plenty of flavour for this simple soup.

red onion & vermicelli Energy 161kcal/671kJ; Protein 4.1g; Carbohydrate 26.6g, of which sugars 2.7g; Fat 4.3g, of which saturates 0.6g; Cholesterol 4mg; Calcium 32mg; Fibre 0.2g; Sodium 41mg.
noodle soup w. tofu Energy 261kcal/1092kJ; Protein 10g; Carbohydrate 36.4g, of which sugars 4.3g; Fat 8g, of which saturates 1.4g; Cholesterol 0mg; Calcium 275mg; Fibre 1.2g; Sodium 97mg.

Tom Yam Gung

This fragrant dish would make an ideal light lunch or supper.

Serves 4

30ml/2 tbsp groundnut (peanut) oil
300g/11oz firm tofu, diced
1.2 litres/2 pints/5 cups good vegetable stock
15ml/1 tbsp chilli jam
grated rind of 1 kaffir lime
1 shallot, finely sliced
1 garlic clove, finely chopped
2 kaffir lime leaves, shredded
3 fresh red chillies, seeded and shredded
1 lemon grass stalk, finely chopped
6 shiitake mushrooms, thinly sliced
4 spring onions (scallions), shredded
45ml/3 tbsp fish sauce
45ml/3 tbsp lime juice
5ml/1 tsp sugar
45ml/3 tbsp chopped fresh coriander (cilantro)
salt and ground black pepper

1 Heat the oil in a wok and fry the tofu for 4–5 minutes until it is golden brown, turning occasionally. Use a slotted spoon to remove it and set aside. Tip the oil from the wok into a large, heavy pan.

2 Add the stock, chilli jam, kaffir lime rind, shallot, garlic, lime leaves, two-thirds of the chillies and the lemon grass to the pan. Bring to the boil, reduce the heat and simmer for 20 minutes.

3 Strain the stock into a clean pan. Stir in the remaining chilli, the shiitake mushrooms, spring onions, fish sauce, lime juice and sugar. Simmer for 3 minutes.

4 Add the fried tofu and heat through for 1 minute. Mix in the chopped coriander and season with salt and pepper to taste. Serve at once in warmed bowls.

Cook's Tip
Fresh kaffir limes and leaves are available from South-east Asian stores. If you cannot find them, use freeze dried leaves, which are widely available, or ordinary lime rind.

Hot & Sour Soup

This spicy, warming soup really whets the appetite and is the perfect introduction to a simple Chinese meal.

Serves 4

10g/¼oz dried cloud ear (wood ear) mushrooms
8 fresh shiitake mushrooms
900ml/1½ pints/3¾ cups vegetable stock
75g/3oz firm tofu, cubed
50g/2oz/½ cup shredded, drained, canned bamboo shoots
15ml/1 tbsp caster (superfine) sugar
45ml/3 tbsp rice vinegar
15ml/1 tbsp light soy sauce
1.5ml/¼ tsp chilli oil
2.5ml/½ tsp salt
large pinch of ground white pepper
15ml/1 tbsp cornflour (cornstarch)
15ml/1 tbsp cold water
1 egg white
5ml/1 tsp sesame oil
2 spring onions (scallions), cut into fine rings

1 Cover the dried cloud ear mushrooms in hot water and soak for 20 minutes or until they are soft. Drain, trim off and discard the hard base from each cloud ear and then chop the mushrooms roughly.

2 Remove and discard the stems from the shiitake mushrooms. Cut the caps into thin strips.

3 Place the stock, shiitake mushrooms, tofu, bamboo shoots and cloud ear mushrooms in a large pan. Bring the stock to the boil, lower the heat and simmer for about 5 minutes.

4 Stir in the sugar, vinegar, soy sauce, chilli oil, salt and pepper. Mix the cornflour to a paste with the water. Add to the soup, stirring constantly until it thickens slightly.

5 Lightly beat the egg white, then pour it slowly into the soup in a steady stream, stirring constantly until it forms threads. Add the sesame oil, ladle into heated bowls and garnish with spring onion rings.

tom yam gung Energy 122kcal/506kJ; Protein 7.1g; Carbohydrate 3.6g, of which sugars 2.9g; Fat 8.9g, of which saturates 1.5g; Cholesterol 0mg; Calcium 395mg; Fibre 0.7g; Sodium 273mg.
hot & sour soup Energy 102kcal/429kJ; Protein 7.3g; Carbohydrate 7.3g, of which sugars 0.3g; Fat 5.1g, of which saturates 1g; Cholesterol 44mg; Calcium 135mg; Fibre 0g; Sodium 208mg.

Spicy Tomato & Egg Drop Soup

Served on its own with chunks of crusty bread, or accompanied by jasmine or ginger rice, this is a tasty dish for a light supper.

Serves 4

30ml/2 tbsp vegetable oil
3 shallots, finely sliced
2 garlic cloves, finely chopped
2 fresh red chillies, seeded and finely sliced
25g/1oz galangal, shredded
8 large, ripe tomatoes, skinned, seeded and finely chopped
15ml/1 tbsp sugar
30ml/2 tbsp fish sauce
4 lime leaves
900ml/1½ pints/3¾ cups chicken stock
15ml/1 tbsp wine vinegar
2.5ml/½ tsp salt
4 eggs
sea salt and ground black pepper, to taste

For the garnish

chilli oil, for drizzling
1 small bunch fresh coriander (cilantro), finely chopped
1 small bunch fresh mint leaves, finely chopped

1 Heat the oil in a wok or heavy pan. Stir in the shallots, garlic, chillies and galangal and cook until golden and fragrant. Add the tomatoes with the sugar, fish sauce and lime leaves. Stir until it resembles a sauce. Pour in the stock and bring to the boil. Reduce the heat and simmer for 30 minutes. Season.

2 Just before serving, bring a wide pan of water to the boil. Add the vinegar and half a teaspoon of salt. Break the eggs into individual cups or small bowls.

3 Stir the water rapidly to create a swirl and drop an egg into the centre of the swirl. Follow immediately with the others, or poach two at a time, and keep the water boiling to throw the whites up over the yolks. Turn off the heat, cover the pan and leave to poach until firm enough to lift. Poached eggs are traditional, but you could use lightly fried eggs instead.

4 Using a slotted spoon, lift the eggs out of the water and slip them into the hot soup. Drizzle a little chilli oil over the eggs, sprinkle with the coriander and mint, and serve.

Egg Flower Soup

This simple, healthy soup is flavoured with fresh root ginger and Chinese five-spice powder. It is quick and delicious and can be made at the last minute.

Serves 4

1.2 litres/2 pints/5 cups fresh chicken or vegetable stock
10ml/2 tsp peeled, fresh root ginger, grated
10ml/2 tsp light soy sauce
5ml/1 tsp sesame oil
5ml/1 tsp Chinese five-spice powder
15–30ml/1–2 tbsp cornflour (cornstarch)
2 eggs
salt and ground black pepper
1 spring onion (scallion), very finely sliced and 15ml/1 tbsp roughly chopped coriander (cilantro) to garnish

1 Put the chicken or vegetable stock into a large pan with the ginger, soy sauce, oil and five-spice powder. Bring to the boil and allow to simmer gently for about 10 minutes.

2 Blend the cornflour in a measuring jug (cup) with 60–75ml/4–5 tbsp water and stir into the stock. Cook, stirring constantly, until slightly thickened. Season to taste with salt and pepper.

3 In a jug (pitcher), beat the eggs with 30ml/2 tbsp cold water until the mixture becomes frothy.

4 Bring the soup back just to the boil and drizzle in the egg mixture, stirring vigorously with chopsticks. Serve at once in warmed individual serving bowls sprinkled with the sliced spring onions and chopped coriander.

Cook's Tip

This soup is a good way of using up leftover egg yolks or whites, which have been stored in the freezer and then thawed. When adding the egg to the soup, use a jug with a fine spout to form a very thin drizzle.

tomato & egg drop Energy 181kcal/756kJ; Protein 8g; Carbohydrate 12.3g, of which sugars 11.5g; Fat 11.7g, of which saturates 2.4g; Cholesterol 190mg; Calcium 52mg; Fibre 2.3g; Sodium 284mg.
egg flower soup Energy 58kcal/244kJ; Protein 3.3g; Carbohydrate 3.8g, of which sugars 0.3g; Fat 3.6g, of which saturates 0.9g; Cholesterol 95mg; Calcium 16mg; Fibre 0g; Sodium 304mg.

Omelette Soup

A very satisfying soup that is quick and easy to prepare. It is versatile, too, in that you can vary the vegetables according to what is available in the season.

Serves 4

1 egg
15ml/1 tbsp groundnut (peanut) oil
900ml/1½ pints/3¾ cups well-flavoured vegetable stock
2 large carrots, finely diced
4 outer leaves Savoy cabbage or pak choi (bok choy), shredded
30ml/2 tbsp soy sauce
2.5ml/½ tsp sugar
2.5ml/½ tsp ground black pepper
fresh coriander (cilantro) leaves, to garnish

1 Break the egg into a bowl and beat lightly with a fork. Heat the oil in a small frying pan until it is hot, but not smoking. Pour in the egg and swirl the pan so that it coats the base evenly. Cook over a medium heat until the omelette has set and the underside is golden.

2 Slide the omelette out of the pan and roll it up like a pancake. Slice into 5mm/¼in rounds and set aside for the garnish.

3 Put the stock into a large pan. Add the carrots and cabbage or pak choi and bring to the boil. Reduce the heat and simmer for 5 minutes, then add the soy sauce, sugar and pepper to season.

4 Stir well, then pour into warmed bowls. Lay a few omelette rounds on the surface of each portion and complete the garnish with the coriander leaves.

Variation
Use thinly sliced green beans or mangetouts (snow peas) instead of Savoy cabbage. Simmer for just 2 minutes.

Egg Knot Soup

Omelettes are often used to add protein to light Oriental soups like this one.

Serves 4

1 spring onion (scallion), thinly shredded
800ml/1⅓ pints/3½ cups well-flavoured stock or instant dashi
5ml/1 tsp soy sauce
dash of sake or dry white wine
pinch of salt

For the prawn balls

200g/7oz/generous 1 cup raw large prawns (shrimp), shelled and deveined
65g/2½ oz cod fillet, skinned
5ml/1 tsp egg white
5ml/1 tsp sake or dry white wine, plus a dash extra
22.5ml/4½ tsp cornflour (cornstarch)
2–3 drops soy sauce
pinch of salt

For the omelette

1 egg, beaten
dash of mirin
pinch of salt
oil, for cooking

1 To make the prawn balls, place the prawns, cod, egg white, sake or dry white wine, cornflour, soy sauce and a pinch of salt in a food processor and process to a thick, sticky paste. Shape the mixture into four balls, place in a steaming basket and steam over a pan of vigorously boiling water for about 10 minutes.

2 To make the garnish, soak the spring onion in iced water for about 5 minutes, until the shreds curl, then drain.

3 To make the omelette, mix the egg with the mirin and salt. Heat a little oil in a frying pan and pour in the egg mixture, coating the pan evenly. When the omelette has set, turn it over and cook for 30 seconds. Leave to cool.

4 Cut the omelette into strips and tie each in a knot. Heat the stock or dashi, then add the soy sauce, sake or wine and salt.

5 Divide the prawn balls and knots of omelette among four bowls and add the soup. Garnish with the spring onion.

omelette soup Energy 64kcal/264kJ; Protein 2.3g; Carbohydrate 4.3g, of which sugars 4.1g; Fat 4.3g, of which saturates 0.7g; Cholesterol 48mg; Calcium 27mg; Fibre 1.1g; Sodium 560mg.
egg knot soup Energy 98kcal/412kJ; Protein 13.6g; Carbohydrate 7.1g, of which sugars 0.2g; Fat 1.9g, of which saturates 0.5g; Cholesterol 153mg; Calcium 51mg; Fibre 0.1g; Sodium 218mg.

Chinese Tofu & Lettuce Soup

This delicious, clear soup is brimming with nourishing, tasty vegetables.

Serves 4

30ml/2 tbsp groundnut (peanut) or sunflower oil
200g/7oz smoked or marinated tofu, cubed
3 spring onions (scallions), sliced diagonally
2 garlic cloves, cut in thin strips
1 carrot, thinly sliced in rounds
1 litre/1¾ pints/4 cups vegetable stock
30ml/2 tbsp soy sauce
15ml/1 tbsp dry sherry or vermouth
5ml/1 tsp sugar
115g/4oz cos or romaine lettuce, shredded
salt and ground black pepper

1 Heat the oil in a preheated wok, then stir-fry the tofu cubes until browned. Drain and set aside on kitchen paper.

2 Add the onions, garlic and carrot to the wok and stir-fry for 2 minutes. Pour in the stock, soy sauce, dry sherry or vermouth, sugar and lettuce. Heat through gently for 1 minute, season to taste and serve hot.

Cook's Tip
Also known as beancurd, tofu is a white substance made from soya beans. Popular with vegetarians, tofu is quite soft with a consistency similar to solid jelly and a smooth, silky texture. Plain, smoked or ready marinated tofu are available. Plain tofu will take on any strong flavours from ingredients it is cooked with.

Peppery Vegetable Soup

This soup sharpens the taste buds without being too filling and is ideal as a starter in a meal featuring spicy meat or fish dishes.

Serves 4

100g/3¾oz carrots, peeled
100g/3¾oz cucumber
100g/3¾oz French or long beans
5ml/1 tsp black peppercorns
2 shallots
2 garlic cloves
25g/1oz fresh root ginger
30ml/2 tbsp vegetable oil
700ml/24fl oz/2¾ cups water or vegetable stock
salt
fried shallots, to garnish

1 Cut the carrots into 1cm/½in cubes. Trim the beans and slice them into rounds of a size similar to the carrots.

2 Peel the cucumber and scoop the seeds out, then dice it into 1cm/½in cubes.

3 Grind the peppercorns, shallots, garlic and ginger to a paste. Heat the oil and fry the paste for 3 minutes. Add the water or stock and bring to the boil.

4 Add the vegetables and simmer for 15 minutes, until tender. Taste the soup and add salt as necessary. Serve in individual bowls, garnished with fried shallots.

Thai-style Corn Soup

This is a very quick and easy soup. If you are using frozen prawns, thaw them before adding to the soup.

Serves 4

2.5ml/½ tsp sesame or sunflower oil
2 spring onions (scallions), thinly sliced
1 garlic clove, crushed
600ml/1 pint/2½ cups chicken stock
425g/15oz can creamed-style corn
225g/8oz/2 cups cooked, peeled prawns (shrimp)
5ml/1 tsp green chilli paste or chilli sauce (optional)
salt and ground black pepper
fresh coriander (cilantro) leaves, to garnish

1 Heat the oil in a large, heavy pan over medium heat. Add the spring onions and garlic and cook for about 1 minute, until softened but not browned.

2 Stir in the chicken stock, creamed-style corn, prawns and chilli paste or sauce, if using. Bring the soup just to the boil, stirring occasionally, then remove the pan from the heat.

3 Season the soup to taste with salt and pepper, ladle it into warmed soup bowls, sprinkle with fresh coriander leaves to garnish and serve immediately.

Variations
• *For a Chinese version of this soup add 5ml/1 tsp grated fresh root ginger to the pan with the spring onions (scallions) and garlic in step 1 and substitute finely shredded, cooked chicken for the prawns (shrimp) in step 2. Garnish the soup with rings of spring onion, using the green part only.*
• *For a more pungent version add 10ml/2 tsp grated galangal or fresh root ginger and 1 lemon grass stalk, cut into 2.5cm/1in lengths, to the pan with the spring onions and garlic in step 1. Remove and discard the pieces of lemon grass before ladling the soup into bowls. Serve with a sweet chilli sauce or a chilli relish handed separately.*

tofu & lettuce soup Energy 106kcal/439kJ; Protein 4.8g; Carbohydrate 3.2g, of which sugars 2.8g; Fat 7.8g, of which saturates 1g; Cholesterol 0mg; Calcium 272mg; Fibre 0.8g; Sodium 543mg.
vegetable soup Energy 72kcal/297kJ; Protein 1.1g; Carbohydrate 4.3g, of which sugars 3.6g; Fat 5.8g, of which saturates 0.7g; Cholesterol 0mg; Calcium 24mg; Fibre 1.5g; Sodium 117mg.
Thai-style corn soup Energy 177kcal/751kJ; Protein 13.1g; Carbohydrate 28.4g, of which sugars 10.4g; Fat 2g, of which saturates 0.3g; Cholesterol 110mg; Calcium 51mg; Fibre 1.6g; Sodium 394mg.

Clear Vegetable Soup

In China and Central Asia, this type of clear soup is usually made in large quantities, then stored as appropriate and reheated for consumption over a number of days. If you would like to do the same, double or treble the quantities listed below. Chill leftover soup rapidly and always reheat thoroughly before serving.

Serves 4

30ml/2 tbsp groundnut (peanut) oil
15ml/1 tbsp magic paste (see Cook's Tip)
100g/3½oz Savoy cabbage or Chinese leaves (Chinese cabbage), finely shredded
100g/3½oz mooli (daikon), finely diced
1 medium cauliflower, coarsely chopped
4 celery sticks, coarsely chopped
1.2 litres/2 pints/5 cups vegetable stock
130g/4½oz fried tofu, cut into 2.5cm/1in cubes
5ml/1 tsp palm sugar (jaggery) or light muscovado (brown) sugar
45ml/3 tbsp light soy sauce

1 Heat the groundnut oil in a large, heavy pan or wok. Add the magic paste and cook over a low heat, stirring frequently, until it gives off its aroma. Add the shredded Savoy cabbage or Chinese leaves, mooli, cauliflower and celery.

2 Pour in the vegetable stock, increase the heat to medium and bring to the boil, stirring occasionally. Gently stir in the tofu cubes.

3 Add the sugar and soy sauce. Reduce the heat and simmer for 15 minutes, until the vegetables are cooked and tender. Taste and add a little more soy sauce if needed. Serve hot.

Cook's Tip
Magic paste is a mixture of crushed garlic, white pepper and coriander (cilantro). Look for it at Thai markets.

Bean & Beansprout Soup

This popular soup is based on beans, but any seasonal vegetables can be added or substituted.

Serves 8

225g/8oz green beans
1.2 litres/2 pints/5 cups lightly salted water
1 garlic clove, roughly chopped
2 macadamia nuts or 4 almonds, finely chopped
1cm/½ in cube shrimp paste
10–15ml/2–3 tsp coriander seeds, dry-fried
30ml/2 tbsp vegetable oil
1 onion, finely sliced
400ml/14fl oz can coconut milk
2 bay leaves
225g/8oz/1 cup beansprouts
8 thin lemon wedges
30ml/2 tbsp lemon juice
salt and ground black pepper

1 Trim the beans, then cut them into small, even-sized pieces, reserving a few whole beans for garnishing, if you wish. Bring the water to the boil, add the beans and cook for 3–4 minutes. Drain, reserving the cooking water. Set the beans aside.

2 Finely grind the chopped garlic, macadamia nuts or almonds, shrimp paste and the coriander seeds to a paste using a pestle and mortar or in a food processor.

3 Heat the vegetable oil in a wok, and fry the sliced onion until transparent. Remove with a slotted spoon. Add the nut paste to the wok and fry it for 2 minutes, stirring constantly, without allowing it to brown.

4 Pour in the reserved vegetable water. Spoon off 45–60ml/3–4 tbsp of the cream from the top of the coconut milk and set it aside. Add the remaining coconut milk to the wok, bring to the boil and add the bay leaves. Cook for 15–20 minutes.

5 Reserve a few of the cooked beans and onions and beansprouts for garnish; stir the rest into the soup. Add the lemon wedges, reserved coconut cream, lemon juice and seasoning; stir well. Pour into soup bowls and serve, garnished with the reserved vegetables.

clear vegetable soup Energy 205kcal/851kJ; Protein 13.8g; Carbohydrate 8.6g, of which sugars 7.5g; Fat 13g, of which saturates 1.3g; Cholesterol 0mg; Calcium 579mg; Fibre 3.4g; Sodium 845mg.
bean & beansprout soup Energy 73kcal/304kJ; Protein 2.3g; Carbohydrate 5.7g, of which sugars 4.2g; Fat 4.8g, of which saturates 0.6g; Cholesterol 0mg; Calcium 40mg; Fibre 1.3g; Sodium 57mg.

Pumpkin & Coconut Soup

The natural sweetness of the pumpkin is heightened by the addition of a little sugar in this attractive soup, and this is balanced by the chillies, shrimp paste and dried shrimp. Coconut cream blurs the boundaries beautifully.

Serves 4–6

2 garlic cloves, crushed
4 shallots, finely chopped
2.5ml/½ tsp shrimp paste
1 lemon grass stalk, chopped
2 fresh green chillies, seeded
15ml/1 tbsp dried shrimp soaked for 10 minutes in warm water
600ml/1 pint/2½ cups chicken stock
450g/1lb pumpkin, cut into 2cm/¾in chunks
600ml/1 pint/2½ cups coconut cream
30ml/2 tbsp Thai fish sauce
5ml/1 tsp sugar
115g/4oz small cooked prawns (shrimp), peeled
salt and ground black pepper

To garnish

2 fresh red chillies, seeded and thinly sliced
10–12 fresh basil leaves

1 Put the garlic, shallots, shrimp paste, lemon grass, green chillies and salt to taste in a mortar. Drain the dried shrimp, discarding the soaking liquid, and add them, then use a pestle to grind the mixture into a paste. Alternatively, place all the ingredients in a food processor and process to a paste.

2 Bring the chicken stock to the boil in a large pan. Add the ground paste and stir well to dissolve.

3 Add the pumpkin chunks and bring to a simmer. Simmer for 10–15 minutes, or until the pumpkin is tender.

4 Stir in the coconut cream, then bring the soup back to simmering point. Do not let it boil. Add the fish sauce, sugar and ground black pepper to taste.

5 Add the prawns and cook for a further 2–3 minutes, until they are heated through. Serve in warm soup bowls, garnished with chillies and basil leaves.

Northern Thai Squash Soup with Banana Flower

As the title of the recipe suggests, this comes from northern Thailand. It is quite hearty, something of a cross between a soup and a stew. Butternut squash has a full flavour that works very well in this dish. The banana flower isn't essential, but it does add a unique and authentic flavour.

Serves 4

1 butternut squash, about 300g/11oz
1 litre/1¾ pints/4 cups vegetable stock
90g/3½oz/scant 1 cup green beans, cut into 2.5cm/1in pieces
45g/1¾oz dried banana flower (optional)
15ml/1 tbsp Thai fish sauce
225g/8oz raw prawns (shrimp)
small bunch fresh basil
cooked rice, to serve

For the chilli paste

115g/4oz shallots, sliced
10 drained bottled green peppercorns
1 small fresh green chilli, seeded and finely chopped
2.5ml/½ tsp shrimp paste

1 Peel the butternut squash and cut it in half. Scoop out the seeds with a teaspoon and discard, then cut the flesh into neat cubes. Set aside.

2 To make the chilli paste, pound the shallots, peppercorns, chilli and shrimp paste together using a mortar and pestle, or purée them in a spice blender.

3 Heat the stock gently in a large pan, then stir in the chilli paste. Add the squash, beans and banana flower, if using. Bring to the boil and cook for 15 minutes.

4 Add the fish sauce, prawns and basil. Bring to simmering point, then simmer for 3 minutes. Serve in warmed bowls, accompanied by rice.

pumpkin & coconut Energy 73kcal/310kJ; Protein 6.5g; Carbohydrate 10.4g, of which sugars 9.8g; Fat 0.9g, of which saturates 0.4g; Cholesterol 56mg; Calcium 102mg; Fibre 1.3g; Sodium 399mg.
squash soup Energy 64kcal/271kJ; Protein 11.3g; Carbohydrate 3.4g, of which sugars 2.8g; Fat 0.7g, of which saturates 0.2g; Cholesterol 110mg; Calcium 82mg; Fibre 1.7g; Sodium 199mg.

Cheat's Shark Fin Soup

Shark's fin soup is a delicacy. In this vegetarian version, short lengths of noodles mimic shark's fin needles.

Serves 4–6

4 dried Chinese mushrooms
25ml/1½ tbsp dried cloud ear (wood ear) mushrooms
115g/4oz cellophane noodles
30ml/2 tbsp vegetable oil
2 carrots, cut into fine strips
115g/4oz canned bamboo shoots, rinsed, drained and cut into strips
1 litre/1¾ pints/4 cups vegetable stock
15ml/1 tbsp soy sauce
15ml/1 tbsp arrowroot or potato flour
30ml/2 tbsp water
1 egg white, beaten (optional)
5ml/1 tsp sesame oil
salt and freshly ground black pepper
2 spring onions (scallions), finely chopped, to garnish
Chinese red vinegar, to serve (optional)

1 Soak the mushrooms and cloud ears separately in warm water for 20 minutes. Drain well. Discard the stems from the mushrooms and slice the caps thinly. Cut the cloud ears into fine strips, discarding any hard bits. Soak the noodles in hot water until soft. Drain and cut into short lengths. Set aside.

2 Heat the oil in a large pan. Add the mushrooms and stir-fry for 2 minutes. Add the cloud ears, stir-fry for 2 minutes, then stir in the carrots, bamboo shoots and noodles.

3 Add the stock to the pan. Bring to the boil, reduce the heat and simmer gently for 15–20 minutes. Season with salt, pepper and soy sauce.

4 Blend the arrowroot or potato flour with a little water. Pour into the soup, stirring all the time to prevent lumps from forming as the soup continues to simmer. Remove the pan from the heat. Stir in the egg white if using, so that it sets to form small threads in the hot soup. Stir in the sesame oil, then pour the soup into individual bowls. Sprinkle each portion with chopped spring onions and offer the Chinese red vinegar separately, if using.

Coconut & Seafood Soup

The long list of ingredients could mislead you into thinking that this soup is complicated and very time-consuming to prepare. In fact, it is extremely easy to put together and the flavours work beautifully.

Serves 4

600ml/1 pint/2½ cups fish stock
5 thin slices fresh galangal or fresh root ginger
2 lemon grass stalks, chopped
3 kaffir lime leaves, shredded
bunch garlic chives, about 25g/1oz
small bunch fresh coriander (cilantro), about 15g/½oz
15ml/1 tbsp vegetable oil
4 shallots, chopped
400ml/14fl oz can coconut milk
30–45ml/2–3 tbsp Thai fish sauce
45–60ml/3–4 tbsp Thai green curry paste
450g/1lb raw large prawns (shrimp), peeled and deveined
450g/1lb prepared squid, cleaned and cut into rings or strips
a little fresh lime juice (optional)
salt and ground black pepper
60ml/4 tbsp crisp fried shallot slices, to serve

1 Pour the fish stock into a large pan and add the slices of galangal or ginger, the lemon grass and half the shredded kaffir lime leaves.

2 Reserve a few garlic chives for the garnish, then chop the remainder. Add half the chopped garlic chives to the pan. Strip the coriander leaves from the stalks and set the leaves aside. Add the stalks to the pan. Bring to the boil, reduce the heat to low and cover the pan, then simmer gently for 20 minutes. Strain the stock into a bowl.

3 Rinse and dry the pan. Add the oil and shallots. Cook over a medium heat for 5–10 minutes, until the shallots are just beginning to brown.

4 Stir in the strained stock, coconut milk, the remaining kaffir lime leaves and 30ml/2 tbsp of the fish sauce. Heat gently until simmering and cook over a low heat for 5–10 minutes.

5 Stir in the curry paste and prawns, then cook for 3 minutes. Add the squid and cook for a further 2 minutes. Add the lime juice, if using, and season, adding more fish sauce to taste. Stir in the remaining chives and the reserved coriander leaves. Serve in bowls and sprinkle each portion with fried shallots and whole garlic chives.

Variations

- *Instead of squid, you could add 400g/14oz firm white fish, such as monkfish, cut into small pieces.*
- *You could also replace the squid with mussels. Steam 675g/1½lb live mussels in a tightly covered pan for 3–4 minutes, or until they have opened. Discard any that remain shut, then remove them from their shells and add to the soup.*

shark fin soup Energy 124kcal/518kJ; Protein 2.4g; Carbohydrate 18.9g, of which sugars 1.2g; Fat 4.4g, of which saturates 0.5g; Cholesterol 0mg; Calcium 11mg; Fibre 0.5g; Sodium 184mg.
coconut & seafood soup Energy 205kcal/871kJ; Protein 37.7g; Carbohydrate 7.5g, of which sugars 5.8g; Fat 3g, of which saturates 0.8g; Cholesterol 473mg; Calcium 144mg; Fibre 0.4g; Sodium 449mg.

Prawn & Pineapple Broth

This simple dish is often served as an appetite enhancer because of its hot and sour flavour. It is also popular as a tasty accompaniment to plain rice or noodles. In some restaurants, the broth is presented in a hollowed-out pineapple, which has been halved lengthways.

Serves 4

30ml/2 tbsp vegetable oil
15–30ml/1–2 tbsp tamarind paste
15ml/1 tbsp sugar
450g/1lb fresh prawns (shrimp), peeled and deveined
4 thick fresh pineapple slices, cored and cut into bitesize chunks
salt and ground black pepper
fresh coriander (cilantro) and mint leaves, to garnish
steamed rice or plain noodles, to serve (optional)

For the spice paste
4 shallots, chopped
4 red chillies, chopped
25g/1oz fresh root ginger, peeled and chopped
1 lemon grass stalk, trimmed and chopped
5ml/1 tsp shrimp paste

1 Make the spice paste. Using a mortar and pestle or a food processor, grind the shallots, chillies, ginger and lemon grass to a paste. Add the shrimp paste and mix well.

2 Heat the oil in a wok or heavy pan. Stir in the spice paste and fry until fragrant. Stir in the tamarind paste and the sugar, then pour in 1.2 litres/2 pints/5 cups water. Mix well and bring to the boil. Reduce the heat and simmer for 10 minutes. Season the broth with salt and pepper.

3 Add the prawns and pineapple to the broth and simmer for 4–5 minutes, or until the prawns are cooked. Using a slotted spoon, lift the prawns and pineapple out of the broth and divide them among four warmed bowls. Ladle over some of the broth and garnish with coriander and mint leaves. The remaining broth can be served separately as a drink, or spooned over steamed rice or plain noodles, if you want to transform this into a slightly more substantial dish.

Wonton, Pak Choi & Prawn Soup

A well-flavoured chicken stock is a must for this classic Chinese snack, which is popular on fast-food stalls in towns and cities throughout southern China.

Serves 4

200g/7oz minced (ground) pork
200g/7oz cooked, peeled prawns (shrimp), thawed if frozen
10ml/2 tsp rice wine or dry sherry
10ml/2 tsp light soy sauce
5ml/1 tsp sesame oil
24 thin wonton wrappers
1.2 litres/2 pints/5 cups chicken stock
12 tiger prawns (jumbo shrimp), shelled, with tails still on
350g/12oz pak choi (bok choy), coarsely shredded (about 6 cups)
salt and ground black pepper
4 spring onions (scallions), sliced and 1cm/½in piece fresh root ginger, finely shredded, to garnish

1 Put the pork, prawns, rice wine or sherry, soy sauce and sesame oil in a large bowl. Add plenty of seasoning and toss the ingredients until well mixed.

2 Put about 10ml/2 tsp of pork mixture in the centre of each wonton wrapper. Bring up the sides of the wrapper and pinch them together to seal the filling in a small bundle.

3 Bring a large pan of water to the boil. Add the wontons and cook for 3 minutes, then drain well and set aside.

4 Pour the stock into a large pan and bring to the boil. Season to taste. Add the tiger prawns and cook for 2–3 minutes, until just tender. Add the wontons and pak choi, then cook for a further 1–2 minutes. Ladle the soup into bowls and garnish with spring onions and ginger.

Cook's Tip
Use a classic 'spider' or large slotted spoon to lower the wontons into the hot oil.

prawn broth Energy 192kcal/808kJ; Protein 20.4g; Carbohydrate 14.2g, of which sugars 13.9g; Fat 6.4g, of which saturates 0.8g; Cholesterol 219mg; Calcium 111mg; Fibre 1.3g; Sodium 216mg.
wonton soup Energy 208kcal/874kJ; Protein 26.8g; Carbohydrate 11.8g, of which sugars 2.2g; Fat 6.2g, of which saturates 2g; Cholesterol 179mg; Calcium 234mg; Fibre 2.4g; Sodium 655mg.

Crab & Asparagus Soup

Generally, jars of asparagus preserved in brine are used for this recipe, or fresh asparagus that has been steamed until tender.

Serves 4

15ml/1 tbsp vegetable oil
2 shallots, finely chopped
2 garlic cloves, finely chopped
15ml/1 tbsp rice flour or cornflour (cornstarch)
225g/8oz/1⅓ cups cooked crab meat, chopped
450g/1lb preserved asparagus, finely chopped, or 450g/1lb fresh asparagus, trimmed and steamed
salt and ground black pepper
basil and coriander (cilantro) leaves, to garnish
fish sauce, to serve

For the stock

1 meaty chicken carcass
25g/1oz dried shrimp, soaked in water for 30 minutes, rinsed and drained
2 onions, peeled and quartered
2 garlic cloves, crushed
15ml/1 tbsp fish sauce
6 black peppercorns
sea salt

1 To make the stock, put the chicken carcass into a large pan. Add all the other stock ingredients, except the salt, and pour in 2 litres/3½ pints/8 cups water. Bring to the boil, boil for a few minutes, skim off any foam, then reduce the heat and simmer with the lid on for 1½–2 hours. Remove the lid and simmer for a further 30 minutes to reduce the stock.

2 Skim off any fat, season, then strain the stock and measure out 1.5 litres/2½ pints/6¾ cups.

3 Heat the oil in a deep pan or wok. Stir in the shallots and garlic, until they begin to colour. Remove from the heat, stir in the flour, and then pour in the stock. Put the pan back over the heat and bring to the boil, stirring constantly, until smooth.

4 Add the crab meat and asparagus, reduce the heat and leave to simmer for 15–20 minutes. Season to taste with salt and pepper, then ladle the soup into bowls, garnish with fresh basil and coriander leaves, and serve with a splash of fish sauce.

Chinese Crab & Corn Soup

The delightful combination of shellfish and corn makes this a universal favourite, but dressing fresh crab does increase the preparation time somewhat. Using frozen white crab meat will work just as well.

Serves 4

600ml/1 pint/2½ cups fish or chicken stock
2.5cm/1in piece fresh root ginger, peeled and very finely sliced
425g/15oz can creamed corn
150g/5oz cooked white crab meat
15ml/1 tbsp arrowroot or cornflour (cornstarch)
15ml/1 tbsp rice wine or dry sherry
15–30ml/1–2 tbsp light soy sauce
1 egg white
salt and ground white pepper
shredded spring onions (scallions), to garnish

1 Put the stock and ginger in a large pan and bring to the boil. Reduce the heat a little while you stir in the creamed corn, then bring the mixture back to the boil.

2 Switch off the heat and add the crab meat to the pan. Put the arrowroot or cornflour in a cup and stir in the rice wine or sherry to make a smooth paste; stir this into the soup. Cook over a low heat for about 3 minutes until the soup has thickened and is slightly glutinous in consistency. Add light soy sauce, salt and white pepper to taste.

3 In a bowl, whisk the egg white to a stiff foam. Gradually fold it into the soup. Ladle the soup into heated bowls, garnish each portion with spring onions and serve.

Cook's Tip
This soup is sometimes made with whole kernel corn, but creamed corn gives a better texture. If you can't find it in a can, use thawed frozen creamed corn instead; the result will be just as good.

crab & asparagus soup Energy 158kcal/652kJ; Protein 9.8g; Carbohydrate 7.6g, of which sugars 4g; Fat 9.9g, of which saturates 5.6g; Cholesterol 38mg; Calcium 87mg; Fibre 3.2g; Sodium 147mg.
crab & sweetcorn soup Energy 201kcal/852kJ; Protein 11.3g; Carbohydrate 33.8g, of which sugars 9.9g; Fat 3.2g, of which saturates 0.5g; Cholesterol 27mg; Calcium 17mg; Fibre 1.4g; Sodium 695mg.

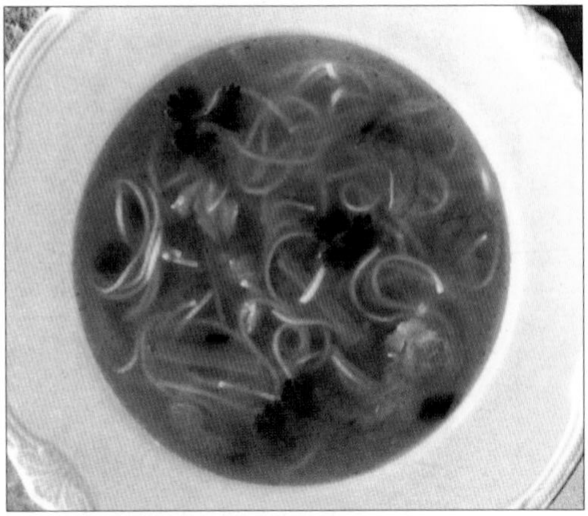

Crab & Egg Noodle Broth

This delicious broth is the ideal solution when you are hungry, time is short and you need a fast, nutritious and filling meal.

Serves 4

75g/3oz thin egg noodles
25g/1oz/2 tbsp unsalted butter
1 small bunch spring onions (scallions), chopped
1 celery stick, sliced
1 medium carrot, cut into batons
1.2 litres/2 pints/5 cups chicken stock
60ml/4 tbsp dry sherry
115g/4oz white crab meat, fresh or frozen
pinch of celery salt
pinch of cayenne pepper
10ml/2 tsp lemon juice
1 small bunch coriander (cilantro) or flat-leaf parsley, roughly chopped, to garnish

1 Bring a large pan of salted water to the boil. Toss in the egg noodles and cook according to the instructions on the packet. Cool under cold running water and leave immersed in water until required.

2 Heat the butter in another large pan, add the spring onions, celery and carrot, cover and cook the vegetables over a gentle heat for 3–4 minutes until soft. Take care not to brown them. Add the chicken stock and dry sherry, bring to the boil and simmer for a further 5 minutes.

3 Flake the crab meat between your fingers on to a plate and remove any stray pieces of shell.

4 Drain the noodles and add to the broth together with the crab meat. Season to taste with celery salt and cayenne pepper and stir in the lemon juice. Return to a simmer.

5 Ladle the broth into shallow soup plates, scatter with roughly chopped coriander or parsley and serve immediately.

Cook's Tip
Fresh and frozen crab meat have a better flavour than canned crab, which tends to taste rather bland.

Crab & Chilli Soup

Prepared fresh crab is perfect for creating an exotic soup in minutes.

Serves 4

45ml/3 tbsp olive oil
1 red onion, finely chopped
2 fresh red chillies, seeded and finely chopped
1 garlic clove, finely chopped
450g/1lb fresh white crab meat
30ml/2 tbsp chopped fresh parsley
30ml/2 tbsp chopped fresh coriander (cilantro)
juice of 2 lemons
1 lemon grass stalk
1 litre/1¾ pints/4 cups good fish or chicken stock
15ml/1 tbsp fish sauce
150g/5oz vermicelli or angel hair pasta, broken into 5–7.5cm/2–3in lengths
salt and ground black pepper

For the coriander relish

50g/2oz/1 cup fresh coriander (cilantro) leaves
1 fresh green chilli, seeded and chopped
15ml/1 tbsp sunflower oil
25ml/1½ tbsp lemon juice
2.5ml/½ tsp ground roasted cumin seeds

1 Heat the olive oil in a pan and cook the onion, red chillies and garlic. Cook until the onion is very soft. Transfer to a bowl. Stir in the fresh white crab meat, fresh parsley and coriander and lemon juice. Set aside.

2 Bruise the lemon grass with a pestle. Pour the stock and fish sauce into a pan. Add the lemon grass and bring to the boil, then add the pasta. Simmer, uncovered, for 3–4 minutes or according to the packet instructions, until just tender.

3 Meanwhile, make the relish. Place the fresh coriander, chilli, oil, lemon juice and cumin in a food processor or blender and process to form a coarse paste. Season to taste.

4 Remove and discard the lemon grass from the soup. Stir the chilli and crab mixture into the soup and season it well with salt and ground black pepper. Bring to the boil, reduce the heat and simmer for 2 minutes. Ladle the soup into four deep, warmed bowls and put a spoonful of the relish in the centre of each. Serve immediately.

crab & egg noodle Energy 172kcal/721kJ; Protein 8.2g; Carbohydrate 15.9g, of which sugars 2.7g; Fat 7.1g, of which saturates 3.9g; Cholesterol 41mg; Calcium 56mg; Fibre 1.4g; Sodium 247mg.
crab & chilli soup Energy 228kcal/951kJ; Protein 23.6g; Carbohydrate 5.4g, of which sugars 5g; Fat 12.6g, of which saturates 3.7g; Cholesterol 90mg; Calcium 199mg; Fibre 1.1g; Sodium 767mg.

Chicken Soup with Crab Cakes

This tasty noodle soup can be a meal in itself.

Serves 6

small bunch of coriander (cilantro), with roots on
1.2–1.4kg/2½–3lb chicken
8 garlic cloves, sliced
2 star anise
2 carrots, chopped
2 celery sticks, chopped
1 onion, chopped
30ml/2 tbsp soy sauce
150g/5oz egg noodles
30ml/2 tbsp vegetable oil
60ml/4 tbsp fish sauce
1.5ml/¼ tsp chilli powder
150g/5oz/2½ cups beansprouts
2 spring onions (scallions), sliced
salt and ground black pepper

For the crab cakes

5ml/1 tsp red curry paste
5ml/1 tsp cornflour (cornstarch)
5ml/1 tsp fish sauce
1 small egg yolk
15ml/1 tbsp chopped fresh coriander (cilantro)
175g/6oz white crab meat
50g/2oz/1 cup fresh white breadcrumbs
30ml/2 tbsp vegetable oil

1 Cut the roots off the coriander stems, wash and place in a heavy pan. Strip the stems and set the leaves aside. Add the chicken to the pan with half the garlic, the star anise, carrots, celery, onion and soy sauce. Add water to cover, bring to the boil, cover and simmer for 1 hour, or until the chicken is cooked.

2 Make the crab cakes by combining all the ingredients except the oil in a bowl and dividing into 12 small patties. Cook the noodles according to the packet instructions. Drain and set aside. Fry the remaining garlic until golden, then drain.

3 Lift the chicken out of the stock, pull off the skin, and tear the meat into large strips. Strain the stock and pour 1.2 litres/2 pints/5 cups into a large pan. Stir in the fish sauce, chilli powder and seasoning. Bring to simmering point.

4 Fry the crab cakes in hot oil for 2–3 minutes on each side. Divide the noodles, fried garlic, beansprouts, spring onions and chicken among soup bowls. Arrange two of the crab cakes on each, ladle in the chicken broth and garnish with the coriander.

Chicken & Crab Noodle Soup

The chicken makes a delicious stock for this light noodle soup.

Serves 6

2 chicken legs, skinned
1.75 litres/3 pints/7½ cups cold water
large bunch of spring onions (scallions)
2.5cm/1in piece fresh root ginger, sliced
5ml/1 tsp black peppercorns
2 garlic cloves, halved
75g/3oz rice noodles
115g/4oz fresh white crab meat
30ml/2 tbsp light soy sauce
salt and ground black pepper, to taste
coriander (cilantro) leaves, to garnish

For the omelettes

4 eggs
30ml/2 tbsp chopped fresh coriander (cilantro) leaves
15ml/1 tbsp extra virgin olive oil

1 Put the chicken and water in a pan. Bring to the boil, reduce the heat and cook gently for 20 minutes. Skim the surface occasionally. Slice half the spring onions and add to the pan with the ginger, peppercorns, garlic and salt to taste. Cover and simmer for 1½ hours.

2 Meanwhile, soak the noodles according to the packet instructions. Drain and refresh under cold water. Shred the remaining spring onions and set aside.

3 To make the omelettes, beat the eggs with the coriander and seasoning. Heat a little of the olive oil in a small frying pan and use the mixture to make three omelettes. Roll up the omelettes tightly one at a time and slice thinly.

4 Remove the chicken from the stock and leave to cool. Strain the stock into a clean pan. Remove and finely shred the chicken meat.

5 Bring the stock to the boil. Add the noodles, chicken, spring onions and crab meat, then simmer for 1–2 minutes. Stir in the soy sauce and season. Ladle the soup into bowls and top each with sliced omelette and coriander leaves.

chicken w. crab cakes Energy 250kcal/1049kJ; Protein 10.9g; Carbohydrate 28.8g, of which sugars 3.5g; Fat 10.9g, of which saturates 1.8g; Cholesterol 62mg; Calcium 74mg; Fibre 1.9g; Sodium 638mg.
chicken noodle soup Energy 159kcal/664kJ; Protein 13.5g; Carbohydrate 10.6g, of which sugars 0.4g; Fat 6.9g, of which saturates 1.7g; Cholesterol 157mg; Calcium 46mg; Fibre 0g; Sodium 526mg.

Chicken & Tiger Prawn Laksa

Laksa is a spicy noodle soup enriched with coconut milk.

Serves 6

6 dried red chillies, seeded
225g/8oz vermicelli, broken
15ml/1 tbsp shrimp paste
10 shallots, chopped
3 garlic cloves
1 lemon grass stalk, roughly chopped
25g/1oz/¼ cup macadamia nuts
grated rind and juice of 1 lime
60ml/4 tbsp groundnut (peanut) oil
2.5ml/1½ tsp ground turmeric
5ml/1 tsp ground coriander
1.5 litres/2½ pints/6 cups fish or chicken stock
450g/1lb raw tiger prawns (jumbo shrimps), shelled and deveined
450g/1lb skinless, boneless chicken breast portions, cut into long thin strips
2 x 400g/14oz cans coconut milk
115g/4oz/1 cup beansprouts
½ cucumber, cut into strips
small bunch of spring onions (scallions), shredded, plus extra to garnish
salt and ground black pepper
1 lime, cut into wedges, to serve

1 Soak the chillies in hot water for 45 minutes. Cook the vermicelli according to the packet instructions. Drain; set aside. Drain the chillies and put them in a food processor or blender with the shrimp paste, shallots, garlic, lemon grass, nuts, lime rind and juice. Process to form a thick paste.

2 Heat 45ml/3 tbsp of the oil in a large, heavy pan. Add the spice paste and cook for 1–2 minutes, stirring. Add the turmeric and coriander and cook for another 2 minutes. Stir in the stock; simmer for 25 minutes, then strain and set aside.

3 Heat the remaining oil in the clean pan and fry the prawns until pink. Remove and set aside. Add the chicken and fry for 4–5 minutes, until just cooked.

4 Pour in the fish or chicken stock and coconut milk. Reheat gently. Add the vermicelli and tiger prawns; and heat for 2 minutes. Stir in the beansprouts, cucumber strips and shredded spring onions, spoon into soup bowls, garnish with spring onions and serve with lime wedges.

Steamboat

This dish is named after the utensil in which it is cooked – a type of fondue with a funnel and a moat.

Serves 8

8 Chinese dried mushrooms, soaked in warm water
1.5 litres/2½ pints/6¼ cups well-flavoured chicken stock
10ml/2 tsp rice wine
10ml/2 tsp sesame oil
225g/8oz each lean pork and rump (round) steak, thinly sliced
1 skinless boneless chicken breast portion, thickly sliced
2 chicken livers, trimmed and sliced
225g/8oz raw prawns (shrimp), peeled
450g/1lb white fish fillets, skinned and cubed
200g/7oz fish balls (from Asian food stores)
115g/4oz fried tofu, each piece halved
leafy green vegetables, such as lettuce, Chinese leaves (Chinese cabbage), spinach leaves and watercress, cut into 15cm/6in lengths
225g/8oz Chinese rice vermicelli
8 eggs
½ bunch spring onions (scallions), chopped
salt and ground white pepper
soy sauce, chilli sauce, plum sauce and hot mustard, to serve

1 Drain the mushrooms, reserving the soaking liquid in a large pan. Cut off and discard the stems; slice the caps finely. Add the stock to the pan, with the rice wine and sesame oil. Bring to the boil, season, then reduce to a simmer.

2 Put the meat, seafood, fish balls, tofu, green vegetables and mushrooms in bowls on the table with the sauces. Soak the vermicelli in hot water for 5 minutes, drain and place in eight soup bowls. Crack an egg for each diner in a small bowl; place on a side table.

3 Add the spring onions to the stock, bring to the boil and fuel the steamboat. Pour the stock into the moat. Each guest cooks the foods of his choice in the hot stock, using chopsticks or fondue forks. When all the ingredients have been cooked, pour the stock into the bowls of noodles. Slide an egg into each bowl and stir so that the egg cooks and forms threads, then serve.

chicken laksa Energy 414kcal/1734kJ; Protein 36.4g; Carbohydrate 38.9g, of which sugars 8.8g; Fat 12.6g, of which saturates 1.9g; Cholesterol 199mg; Calcium 129mg; Fibre 1.1g; Sodium 352mg.
steamboat Energy 243kcal/1020kJ; Protein 35g; Carbohydrate 4.1g, of which sugars 0.8g; Fat 9.7g, of which saturates 2.6g; Cholesterol 299mg; Calcium 168mg; Fibre 0.4g; Sodium 304mg.

Monkfish Broth

Lemon grass, chillies and galangal are among the flavourings used in this fragrant soup.

Serves 2–3

1 litre/1¾ pints/4 cups fish or light chicken stock
4 lemon grass stalks
3 limes
2 small fresh hot red chillies, seeded and thinly sliced
2cm/¾in piece fresh galangal, peeled and thinly sliced
6 coriander (cilantro) stalks, with leaves
2 kaffir lime leaves, coarsely chopped (optional)
350g/12oz monkfish fillet, skinned and cut into 2.5cm/1in pieces
15ml/1 tbsp rice vinegar
45ml/3 tbsp fish sauce
30ml/2 tbsp chopped coriander (cilantro) leaves, to garnish

1 Pour the stock into a pan and bring it to the boil. Meanwhile, slice the bulb end of each lemon grass stalk diagonally into pieces about 3mm/⅛ in thick. Peel off four wide strips of lime rind with a potato peeler, taking care to avoid the white pith underneath which would make the soup bitter. Squeeze the limes and reserve the juice.

2 Add the sliced lemon grass, lime rind, chillies, galangal and coriander stalks to the stock, with the kaffir lime leaves, if using. Simmer for 1–2 minutes.

3 Add the monkfish, rice vinegar and fish sauce, with half the reserved lime juice. Simmer for about 3 minutes, until the fish is just cooked. Lift out and discard the coriander stalks, taste the broth and add more lime juice if necessary; the soup should taste quite sour. Sprinkle with the coriander leaves and serve.

Variations
Prawns (shrimp), scallops, squid, sole or flounder can be substituted for the monkfish. If you use kaffir lime leaves, you will need the juice of only 2 limes.

Red Monkfish Soup

This light and creamy coconut soup provides a base for a colourful fusion of red-curried monkfish and rice noodles.

Serves 4

175g/6oz flat rice noodles
30ml/2 tbsp vegetable oil
2 garlic cloves, chopped
15ml/1 tbsp red curry paste
450g/1lb monkfish tail, cut into bitesize pieces
300ml/½ pint/1¼ cups coconut cream
750ml/1¼ pints/3 cups hot chicken stock
45ml/3 tbsp fish sauce
15ml/1 tbsp palm sugar (jaggery)
60ml/4 tbsp roasted peanuts, roughly chopped
4 spring onions (scallions), shredded lengthways
50g/2oz/½ cup beansprouts
large handful of fresh Thai basil leaves
salt and ground black pepper
1 fresh red chilli, seeded and cut lengthways into slivers, to garnish

1 Soak the noodles in a bowl of boiling water for 10 minutes, or according to the packet instructions. Drain.

2 Heat the oil in a wok or pan over a high heat. Add the garlic and cook for 2 minutes. Stir in the curry paste and cook for 1 minute, until fragrant.

3 Add the bitesize pieces of monkfish and stir-fry over a high heat for 4–5 minutes, until just tender. Pour in the coconut cream and hot chicken stock.

4 Stir in the fish sauce and palm sugar, and bring just to the boil. Add the drained flat rice noodles and cook for 1–2 minutes, until they are tender.

5 Stir in half the peanuts, half the spring onions, half the beansprouts, the basil and seasoning. Ladle the soup into deep individual soup bowls and sprinkle over the remaining peanuts. Garnish with the remaining spring onions, beansprouts and the slivers of red chilli.

monkfish broth Energy 92kcal/394kJ; Protein 19.8g; Carbohydrate 1.8g, of which sugars 1.6g; Fat 0.8g, of which saturates 0.1g; Cholesterol 16mg; Calcium 50mg; Fibre 0.8g; Sodium 1096mg.
red monkfish soup Energy 379kcal/1589kJ; Protein 25.5g; Carbohydrate 41.2g, of which sugars 4.7g; Fat 12g, of which saturates 2g; Cholesterol 18mg; Calcium 49mg; Fibre 0.9g; Sodium 111mg.

Smoked Mackerel & Tomato Soup

All the ingredients for this unusual soup are cooked in a single pan, so it is not only quick and easy to prepare, but requires little clearing up afterwards. Smoked mackerel gives the soup a robust flavour, but it is tempered by the citrus tones provided by the lemon grass and tamarind.

Serves 4

200g/7oz smoked mackerel fillets
4 tomatoes
1 litre/1¾ pints/4 cups vegetable stock
1 lemon grass stalk, finely chopped
5cm/2in piece fresh galangal or root ginger, finely diced or sliced
4 shallots, finely chopped
2 garlic cloves, finely chopped
2.5ml/½ tsp dried chilli flakes
15ml/1 tbsp fish sauce
5ml/1 tsp palm sugar (jaggery) or light muscovado (brown) sugar
45ml/3 tbsp thick tamarind juice, made by mixing tamarind paste with warm water
small bunch fresh chives or spring onions (scallions), to garnish

1 Prepare the smoked mackerel fillets. Remove and discard the skin, if necessary, then chop the flesh into large pieces. Carefully remove any stray bones with your fingers or by using a pair of sterilized tweezers.

2 Cut the tomatoes in half, squeeze out and discard most of the seeds, then finely dice the flesh with a sharp knife. Place in bowls and set aside.

3 Pour the stock into a large pan and add the lemon grass, galangal or ginger, shallots and garlic. Bring to the boil, reduce the heat and simmer for 15 minutes.

4 Add the fish, tomatoes, chilli flakes, fish sauce, sugar and tamarind juice. Simmer for around 4–5 minutes, until the fish and tomatoes are heated through. Ladle into individual soup bowls, garnish with the chives or spring onions and serve.

Chinese Fish Ball Soup

This light Chinese soup can be found in coffee shops and at *tze char* stalls, where food is ordered from the menu and cooked on the spot. Often eaten as a snack or light lunch, the soup is garnished with spring onions and fresh chillies, and the Malays often add an extra drizzle of chilli sauce or chilli sambal.

Serves 4–6

For the fish balls
450g/1lb fresh fish fillets (such as haddock, cod, whiting or bream), boned and flaked
15–30ml/1–2 tbsp rice flour
salt and ground black pepper

For the soup
1.5 litres/2½ pints/6 cups fish or chicken stock
15–30ml/1–2 tbsp light soy sauce
4–6 mustard greens, chopped
90g/3½oz mung bean thread noodles, soaked in hot water until soft

For the garnish
2 spring onions (scallions), trimmed and finely sliced
1 fresh red or green chilli, seeded and finely sliced
fresh coriander (cilantro) leaves, finely chopped

1 To make the fish balls, grind the boned and flaked flesh to a paste, using a mortar and pestle or food processor. Season the paste with salt and pepper and stir in 60ml/4 tbsp water. Add enough rice flour to form a pliable paste. Take small portions of fish paste into your hands and squeeze them carefully to mould into balls.

2 Meanwhile, bring the stock to the boil in a deep pan and season to taste with soy sauce. Drop in the fish balls and simmer for 5 minutes. Add the shredded mustard greens and cook for 1 minute.

3 Divide the soaked mung noodles among four to six bowls. Using a slotted spoon, add the fish balls and cooked mustard greens to the noodles, then ladle over the hot stock. Garnish the soup with the finely sliced spring onions and chilli and sprinkle the chopped coriander over the top.

mackerel soup Energy 226kcal/940kJ; Protein 11.2g; Carbohydrate 10.2g, of which sugars 8.5g; Fat 15.9g, of which saturates 3.3g; Cholesterol 53mg; Calcium 39mg; Fibre 2.1g; Sodium 653mg.
Chinese fish ball soup Energy 127kcal/533kJ; Protein 14.9g; Carbohydrate 14.8g, of which sugars 0.5g; Fat 0.6g, of which saturates 0.1g; Cholesterol 35mg; Calcium 17mg; Fibre 0.2g; Sodium 408mg.

Chicken Mulligatawny Soup

This world-famous broth hails from the days of the British Raj. It is full of flavour and makes a substantial main-course soup.

Serves 4–6

900g/2lb boneless chicken portions, skinned
600ml/1 pint/2½ cups water
6 green cardamom pods
5cm/2in piece cinnamon stick
4–6 curry leaves
15ml/1 tbsp ground coriander
5ml/1 tsp ground cumin
2.5ml/½ tsp ground turmeric
3 garlic cloves, crushed
1 onion, finely chopped
115g/4oz creamed coconut or 120ml/4fl oz/½ cup coconut cream
juice of 2 lemons
deep-fried onions, to garnish

1 Place the chicken portions in a large pan with the water. Bring to the boil, then simmer for about 1 hour, or until the chicken is tender.

2 Skim the surface, then remove the chicken pieces with a slotted spoon and keep warm.

3 Reheat the stock in the pan. Add all the remaining ingredients, except the chicken and deep-fried onions. Simmer for 10–15 minutes, then strain and return the chicken to the soup. Reheat the soup and serve garnished with the deep-fried onions.

Variation

To make a delicious Chicken Mulligatawny Soup with Lentils, cook the chicken portions as step 1. Remove from the stock and keep warm. Now cook 175g/6oz/⅔ cup red lentils in the reserved stock for 30 minutes until tender. Add 115g/4oz diced potato and cook for a further 20 minutes. Add the remaining ingredients and cook as step 3. Cut the chicken into bitesize pieces and add to the strained soup. Serve garnished as before.

Spicy Chicken & Mushroom Soup

This creamy chicken soup has just enough spice to make it a great winter warmer, but not so much that it overwhelms the flavour of the mushrooms.

Serves 4

225g/8oz boneless chicken, skinned
75g/3oz/6 tbsp ghee or unsalted (sweet) butter
2.5ml/½ tsp crushed garlic
5ml/1 tsp garam masala
5ml/1 tsp crushed black peppercorns
5ml/1 tsp salt
1.5ml/¼ tsp grated nutmeg
1 medium leek, sliced
75g/3oz/1 cup mushrooms, sliced
50g/2oz/⅓ cup corn
300ml/½ pint/1¼ cups water
250ml/8fl oz/1 cup single (light) cream
15ml/1 tbsp chopped fresh coriander (cilantro)
5ml/1 tsp crushed dried red chillies (optional)

1 Cut the boneless chicken pieces into very fine strips. Melt the ghee or butter in a medium pan. Lower the heat slightly and add the garlic and garam masala. Lower the heat even further and add the black peppercorns, salt and nutmeg.

2 Finally, add the chicken pieces, sliced leek, mushrooms and corn, and cook, stirring constantly, for 5–7 minutes, or until the chicken is cooked through.

3 Remove from the heat and leave to cool slightly. Transfer three-quarters of the mixture into a food processor or blender. Add the water and process for about 1 minute.

4 Pour the resulting purée back into the pan and stir with the rest of the mixture. Bring to the boil over a medium heat. Lower the heat and stir in the cream.

5 Add the fresh coriander and taste for seasoning. Serve hot, garnished with the crushed red chillies, if you like.

chicken mulligatawny Energy 301kcal/1258kJ; Protein 37.8g; Carbohydrate 3.3g, of which sugars 1.9g; Fat 15.3g, of which saturates 11.9g; Cholesterol 105mg; Calcium 20mg; Fibre 0.1g; Sodium 97mg.
chicken & mushroom Energy 335kcal/1388kJ; Protein 17.1g; Carbohydrate 3.1g, of which sugars 2.7g; Fat 28.3g, of which saturates 17.6g; Cholesterol 114mg; Calcium 75mg; Fibre 1.4g; Sodium 310mg.

Chicken Broth of Prosperity

The origin of this dish is rather obscure. Like many dishes that grace the family table in China, especially during celebrations such as Chinese New Year, the ingredients are symbolic. Ham and quail's eggs suggest the wealth and prosperity alluded to in the title, while the chicken represents the legendary phoenix, a symbol of rebirth. This soup is very substantial, and so thick that it could be plated rather than served in bowls.

Serves 4

4 quail's eggs
750ml/1 1/4 pints/3 cups fresh chicken stock
2 chicken breast fillets
150g/5oz Chinese or Serrano ham, finely diced
30ml/2 tbsp sesame oil
30ml/2 tbsp light soy sauce
2.5ml/1/2 tsp ground black pepper
2 eggs, lightly beaten
30ml/2 tbsp cornflour (cornstarch) mixed to a paste with 60ml/4 tbsp cold water

1 Cook the quail's eggs in a pan of boiling water for 8 minutes. Drain, refresh under cold water and remove the shells. Set the eggs aside.

2 Pour the chicken stock into a large pan and bring to the boil. Add the chicken breast fillets, lower the heat slightly and simmer for 10 minutes or until cooked through. Using tongs, lift them out of the pan and leave to cool.

3 Add the ham to the pan of stock and simmer for 15 minutes. Meanwhile, cut the chicken into shreds.

4 Add the sesame oil, soy sauce and pepper to the ham and stock mixture. Simmer gently for 2 minutes, then add the shredded chicken and eggs, stirring constantly so that the eggs form strands. Simmer for 2 minutes.

5 Stir in the cornflour paste. Continue to stir until the soup thickens, then add the shelled quail's eggs and heat through for 1–2 minutes. Ladle into warm bowls and serve.

Chicken & Almond Soup

This soup makes an excellent appetizer and, served with naan bread, will also make a satisfying lunch or supper dish.

Serves 4

75g/3oz/6 tbsp ghee or unsalted butter
1 medium leek, chopped
2.5ml/1/2 tsp shredded fresh root ginger
75g/3oz/3/4 cup ground almonds
5ml/1 tsp salt
2.5ml/1/2 tsp crushed black peppercorns
1 fresh green chilli, chopped
1 medium carrot, sliced
50g/2oz/1/2 cup frozen peas
115g/4oz/3/4 cup chicken breast fillet, cubed and skinned
15ml/1 tbsp chopped fresh coriander (cilantro), plus extra to garnish
450ml/3/4 pint/scant 2 cups water
250ml/8fl oz/1 cup single (light) cream

1 Melt the ghee or butter in a large karahi, wok or deep pan, and sauté the leek with the ginger until softened.

2 Lower the heat and add the ground almonds, salt, crushed peppercorns, chopped chilli, sliced carrot, peas and cubed chicken to the pan.

3 Fry for about 10 minutes or until the chicken is completely cooked, stirring constantly. Add the chopped fresh coriander.

4 Remove the pan from the heat and leave to cool slightly. Transfer the mixture to a food processor or blender and process for about 1 1/2 minutes.

5 Pour in the water and blend the mixture for a further 30 seconds until smooth.

6 Pour the soup back into the pan and bring to the boil, stirring. Lower the heat and gradually stir in the cream. Cook gently for a further 2 minutes, stirring occasionally. Serve garnished with more coriander.

broth of prosperity Energy 254kcal/1065kJ; Protein 29.9g; Carbohydrate 7.9g, of which sugars 0.9g; Fat 11.8g, of which saturates 2.6g; Cholesterol 217mg; Calcium 31mg; Fibre 0g; Sodium 1086mg.
chicken & almond Energy 425kcal/1760kJ; Protein 14.6g; Carbohydrate 5.5g, of which sugars 3.5g; Fat 38.5g, of which saturates 18.4g; Cholesterol 94mg; Calcium 119mg; Fibre 3g; Sodium 153mg.

Thai-style Chicken Soup

A fragrant blend of coconut milk, lemon grass, ginger and lime makes a delicious soup, with just a hint of chilli.

Serves 4

5ml/1 tsp oil
1–2 fresh red chillies, seeded and chopped
2 garlic cloves, crushed
1 large leek, finely sliced
550ml/18fl oz/2¼ cups chicken stock
450ml/¾ pint/scant 2 cups coconut milk
450g/1lb skinless, boneless chicken thighs, cut into bitesize pieces
30ml/2 tbsp Thai fish sauce
1 lemon grass stalk, split
2.5cm/1in piece fresh root ginger, peeled and crushed
5ml/1 tsp sugar
4 kaffir lime leaves (optional)
75g/3oz/¾ cup frozen peas, thawed
3 tbsp chopped fresh coriander (cilantro)

1 Heat the oil in a large pan. Add the chillies and garlic and cook for about 2 minutes. Add the leek and cook for 2 minutes longer.

2 Stir in the stock and coconut milk and bring to a boil over medium-high heat.

3 Add the chicken, fish sauce, lemon grass, ginger, sugar and lime leaves, if using. Lower the heat and simmer, covered, for 15 minutes until the chicken is tender, stirring occasionally.

4 Add the peas and cook for 3 minutes longer. Remove the lemon grass and stir in the coriander just before serving.

Cook's Tip

Whenever you have a roast chicken it is worth using the carcass to make stock. Remove all the skin from the remains of the bird and put the carcass into a large pan. Add a roughly chopped onion, carrot and celery stick, and a bouquet garni. Cover with water and bring to the boil. Skim off the scum and then simmer the stock for 1 hour. Strain through muslin (cheesecloth). Skim off the fat when the stock is cold.

Chicken Wonton Soup with Prawns

This soup is a fabulous restaurant classic.

Serves 4

275g/10oz boneless chicken breast, skinned
200g/7oz prawn (shrimp) tails, raw or cooked
5ml/1 tsp finely chopped fresh root ginger
2 spring onions (scallions), finely chopped
1 egg
10ml/2 tsp oyster sauce (optional)
1 packet wonton wrappers
15ml/1 tbsp cornflour paste
900ml/1½ pints/3¾ cups chicken stock
¼ cucumber, peeled and diced
salt and ground black pepper
1 spring onion, roughly shredded, 4 sprigs fresh coriander and 1 tomato, skinned, seeded and diced, to garnish

1 Place the chicken breast, 150g/5oz of the prawn tails, the ginger and spring onions in a food processor and process for 2–3 minutes. Add the egg, oyster sauce and seasoning and process briefly. Set aside.

2 Place eight wonton wrappers at a time on a surface, moisten the edges with cornflour paste and place 2.5ml/½ tsp of the chicken and prawn mixture in the centre of each. Fold them in half and pinch to seal. Simmer in salted water for 4 minutes.

3 Bring the chicken stock to the boil, add the remaining prawn tails and the cucumber and simmer for 3–4 minutes. Add the filled wontons and simmer for 3–4 minutes to warm through. Garnish with the spring onion, coriander and diced tomato.

Cook's Tip

Skinned, seeded and diced tomatoes make an attractive garnish. To prepare tomatoes in this way, remove the stalk and then using a sharp knife make a cross on the base of the tomato. Place in a bowl and cover with boiling water. Leave for 30 seconds, then drain. Gently pull the loosened skin away. Halve the tomatoes, scoop out the seeds with a teaspoon and finely dice the flesh.

Thai chicken Energy 342kcal/1425kJ; Protein 25.7g; Carbohydrate 11.6g, of which sugars 2.4g; Fat 21.7g, of which saturates 13g; Cholesterol 65mg; Calcium 40mg; Fibre 1.4g; Sodium 111mg.
chicken wonton Energy 216kcal/913kJ; Protein 29.3g; Carbohydrate 19.6g, of which sugars 0.5g; Fat 2.8g, of which saturates 0.7g; Cholesterol 193mg; Calcium 87mg; Fibre 0.9g; Sodium 155mg.

Chicken Soup with Crispy Shallots

This Thai-inspired soup is topped with crisp shallots.

Serves 6

40g/1½oz/3 tbsp butter
1 onion, finely chopped
2 garlic cloves, chopped
2.5cm/1in piece fresh root ginger, finely chopped
10ml/2 tsp green curry paste
2.5ml/½ tsp turmeric
400ml/14fl oz can coconut milk
475ml/16fl oz/2 cups chicken stock
2 lime leaves, shredded
1 lemon grass stalk, finely chopped
8 skinless, boneless chicken thighs
350g/12oz spinach, chopped
10ml/2 tsp fish sauce
30ml/2 tbsp lime juice
30ml/2 tbsp vegetable oil
salt and ground black pepper
2 shallots, thinly sliced
handful of Thai basil leaves, to garnish

1 Melt the butter in a large, heavy pan. Add the onion, garlic and ginger, then cook for 4–5 minutes, until softened. Stir in the curry paste and turmeric, and cook for a further 2–3 minutes, stirring constantly.

2 Pour in two-thirds of the coconut milk; cook for 5 minutes. Add the stock, lime leaves, lemon grass and chicken. Heat until simmering; cook for 15 minutes or until the chicken is tender.

3 Remove the chicken thighs with a draining spoon and set them aside to cool. Add the spinach to the pan and cook for 3–4 minutes. Stir in the remaining coconut milk and seasoning, then process the soup in a food processor or blender until almost smooth. Return the soup to the rinsed-out pan. Cut the chicken thighs into bitesize pieces and stir these into the soup with the fish sauce and lime juice.

4 Reheat the soup gently until hot, but do not let it boil. Meanwhile, heat the oil in a frying pan and cook the shallots for 6–8 minutes, until crisp and golden, stirring occasionally. Drain on kitchen paper. Ladle the soup into bowls, then top with the basil leaves and fried shallots, and serve.

Chinese Chicken & Chilli Soup

Ginger and lemon grass add an aromatic note to this tasty, refreshing soup, which can be served as a light lunch or appetizer. The soft vermicelli rice noodles are the perfect foil to the crunch of the cooked vegetables, and soak up the flavoursome liquid of this soup wonderfully well.

Serves 4

150g/5oz skinless boneless chicken breasts, cut into strips
2.5cm/1in piece fresh root ginger, finely chopped
5cm/2in piece lemon grass stalk, finely chopped
1 fresh red chilli, seeded and thinly sliced
8 baby corn cobs, halved lengthways
1 large carrot, cut into thin sticks
1 litre/1¾ pints/4 cups hot chicken stock
4 spring onions (scallions), thinly sliced
12 small shiitake mushrooms, sliced
115g/4oz/1 cup vermicelli rice noodles
30ml/2 tbsp soy sauce
salt and ground black pepper

1 Place the chicken strips, chopped ginger, chopped lemon grass and sliced chilli in a Chinese sand pot. Add the halved baby corn and the carrot sticks. Pour over the hot chicken stock and cover the pot.

2 Place the Chinese sand pot in an unheated oven. Set the temperature to 200°C/400°F/Gas 6 and cook the soup for 30–40 minutes, or until the stock is simmering and the chicken and vegetables are tender.

3 Add the spring onions and mushrooms, cover and return the pot to the oven for 10 minutes. Meanwhile place the noodles in a large bowl and cover with boiling water – soak for the required time, following the packet instructions.

4 Drain the noodles and divide among four warmed serving bowls. Stir the soy sauce into the soup and season with salt and pepper. Divide the soup among the bowls and serve.

chicken soup Energy 198kcal/827kJ; Protein 16.5g; Carbohydrate 6.5g, of which sugars 5.5g; Fat 12g, of which saturates 4.6g; Cholesterol 84mg; Calcium 157mg; Fibre 2.3g; Sodium 266mg.
chicken & chilli soup Energy 165kcal/693kJ; Protein 13.3g; Carbohydrate 26g, of which sugars 3.1g; Fat 0.9g, of which saturates 0.2g; Cholesterol 26mg; Calcium 23mg; Fibre 1.4g; Sodium 852mg.

Chicken & Ginger Soup

This aromatic soup is rich with coconut milk and intensely flavoured with galangal, lemon grass and kaffir lime leaves.

Serves 4–6

4 lemon grass stalks, roots trimmed
2 x 400ml/14fl oz cans coconut milk
475ml/16fl oz/2 cups chicken stock
2.5cm/1in piece root ginger, peeled and thinly sliced
10 black peppercorns, crushed
10 kaffir lime leaves, torn
300g/11oz skinless boneless chicken breast portions, cut into thin strips
115g/4oz/1 cup button (white) mushrooms
50g/2oz/½ cup baby corn cobs, quartered lengthways
60ml/4 tbsp lime juice
45ml/3 tbsp fish sauce
chopped fresh red chillies, spring onions (scallions) and fresh coriander (cilantro) leaves, to garnish

1 Cut off the lower 5cm/2in from each lemon grass stalk and chop it finely. Bruise the remaining pieces of stalk. Bring the coconut milk and chicken stock to the boil in a large pan. Add all the lemon grass, the ginger, peppercorns and half the lime leaves, lower the heat and simmer gently for 10 minutes. Strain into a clean pan.

2 Return the soup to the heat, then add the chicken, mushrooms and corn. Simmer for 5–7 minutes or until the chicken is cooked.

3 Stir in the lime juice and fish sauce, then add the remaining lime leaves. Serve hot, garnished with chillies, spring onions and coriander.

Cook's Tip
Store root ginger in the freezer. It thaws rapidly or can be shaved or grated while frozen.

Chicken Rice Soup

Light and refreshing, this soup is the perfect choice for a hot day. In the great tradition of chicken soup recipes, it also acts as a wonderful pick-me-up when you are feeling low or a little tired.

Serves 4

2 lemon grass stalks, trimmed, cut into 3 pieces, and lightly bruised
15ml/1 tbsp fish sauce
90g/3½ oz/½ cup short grain rice, rinsed
ground black pepper
sea salt
chopped coriander (cilantro) and 1 fresh green or red chilli, seeded and cut into thin strips, to garnish
1 lime, cut in wedges, to serve

For the stock
1 small chicken, about 900g/2lb
1 onion, quartered
2 garlic cloves, crushed
25g/1oz fresh root ginger, sliced
2 lemon grass stalks, cut in half lengthways and bruised
2 dried red chillies
30ml/2 tbsp fish sauce

1 Put the chicken into a deep pan. Add all the other stock ingredients and pour in 2 litres/3½ pints/8 cups water. Bring to the boil for a few minutes, then reduce the heat and simmer gently with the lid on for 2 hours.

2 Skim off any fat from the stock, strain and reserve. Remove the skin from the chicken and shred the meat with your fingers, or chop roughly using a sharp knife. Set aside.

3 Pour the stock back into the deep pan and bring to the boil. Reduce the heat and stir in the lemon grass stalks and fish sauce. Stir in the rice and simmer, uncovered, for about 40 minutes. Add the shredded chicken and season with the black pepper and sea salt to taste.

4 Ladle the piping hot soup into warmed individual bowls, garnish with chopped coriander and the thin strips of chilli. Put the lime wedges into a separate bowl and serve for squeezing over the soup if desired.

chicken & ginger soup Energy 87kcal/371kJ; Protein 13.1g; Carbohydrate 6.8g, of which sugars 6.7g; Fat 1.1g, of which saturates 0.4g; Cholesterol 35mg; Calcium 42mg; Fibre 0.3g; Sodium 620mg.
chicken rice soup Energy 147kcal/615kJ; Protein 12.8g; Carbohydrate 19.8g, of which sugars 1.4g; Fat 1.7g, of which saturates 0.4g; Cholesterol 53mg; Calcium 37mg; Fibre 0.8g; Sodium 317mg.

Spicy Chicken Soup

This fragrant soup is particularly popular in Singapore. Originally from Java, various versions are served at soup and noodle stalls specializing in Indonesian and Malay food.

Serves 6

1 small chicken, about 900g/2lb
2 lemon grass stalks, bruised
25g/1oz fresh root ginger, peeled and sliced
2 fresh kaffir lime leaves
1 dried red chilli
30ml/2 tbsp vegetable oil
50g/2oz mung bean thread noodles, soaked until pliable
3 hard-boiled eggs, peeled and halved
115g/4oz/½ cup beansprouts
a small bunch of fresh coriander (cilantro), roughly chopped, to garnish
2 limes, quartered, chilli oil and soy sauce, to serve

For the rempah

8 shallots, chopped
8 garlic cloves, chopped
6 candlenuts or macadamia nuts
50g/2oz galangal, chopped
2 lemon grass stalks, chopped
4 fresh kaffir lime leaves
15ml/1 tbsp ground coriander
10ml/2 tsp ground turmeric
15ml/1 tbsp vegetable oil

1 Using a mortar and pestle or a food processor, grind all the rempah ingredients to a paste. Set aside.

2 Put the chicken, lemon grass, ginger, lime leaves and chilli into a deep pan and pour in enough water to just cover. Bring to the boil, then cover and simmer for about 1 hour, until the chicken is tender. Remove the chicken, take off and discard the skin and tear the meat into shreds. Strain the stock.

3 In a wok or heavy pan, heat the oil. Stir in the rempah and cook for 1–2 minutes, until fragrant. Pour in the stock and stir well. Season to taste with salt and pepper.

4 Divide the noodles among six bowls. Add the hard-boiled eggs, beansprouts and shredded chicken. Ladle the steaming broth into each bowl and garnish with coriander. Serve immediately with the lime wedges, chilli oil and soy sauce.

Corn & Chicken Soup

Using a combination of chicken, creamed corn and whole kernels gives this classic Chinese soup a lovely texture. It tastes delicious, is suitably warming on a cold day and, above all, is easy to make if you are in a hurry or have friends for lunch.

Serves 4–6

1 skinless chicken breast fillet, about 115g/4oz, cubed
10ml/2 tsp light soy sauce
15ml/1 tbsp Chinese rice wine
5ml/1 tsp cornflour (cornstarch)
60ml/4 tbsp cold water
5ml/1 tsp sesame oil
15ml/1 tbsp vegetable oil
5ml/1 tsp grated fresh root ginger
1 litre/1¾ pints/4 cups chicken stock
425g/15oz can creamed corn
225g/8oz can whole kernel corn
2 eggs, beaten
salt and ground black pepper
2–3 spring onions (scallions), green parts only, cut into tiny rounds, to garnish

1 Mince (grind) the chicken in a food processor, taking care not to overprocess. Transfer the chicken to a bowl and stir in the soy sauce, rice wine, cornflour, water, sesame oil and seasoning. Cover with clear film (plastic wrap) and leave for about 15 minutes so that the chicken absorbs the flavours.

2 Heat a wok over medium heat. Add the vegetable oil and swirl it around. Add the ginger and stir-fry for a few seconds. Pour in the stock with the creamed corn and corn kernels. Bring to just below boiling point.

3 Spoon about 90ml/6 tbsp of the hot liquid into the chicken mixture until it forms a smooth paste and stir. Return to the wok. Slowly bring to the boil, stirring constantly, then simmer for 2–3 minutes or until the chicken is cooked.

4 Pour the beaten eggs into the soup in a slow steady stream, using a fork or chopsticks to stir the top of the soup in a figure-of-eight pattern. The egg will set in lacy shreds. Serve immediately with the spring onions on top.

spicy chicken soup Energy 411kcal/1708kJ; Protein 30g; Carbohydrate 7.1g, of which sugars 0.8g; Fat 29.3g, of which saturates 7.6g; Cholesterol 215mg; Calcium 39mg; Fibre 0.7g; Sodium 148mg.
corn & chicken soup Energy 196kcal/831kJ; Protein 10g; Carbohydrate 29.9g, of which sugars 10.7g; Fat 4.7g, of which saturates 1g; Cholesterol 77mg; Calcium 17mg; Fibre 1.6g; Sodium 447mg.

Duck & Preserved Lime Soup

This richly flavoured soup originates in southern China. This recipe can be made with chicken stock and leftover duck meat from a roasted duck, or by roasting a duck and slicing off the breast portion and thigh meat for the soup.

Serves 4–6

1 lean duck, about 1.5kg/3lb 5oz
2 preserved limes
25g/1oz root ginger, thinly sliced
sea salt and ground black pepper

For the garnish

vegetable oil, for frying
25g/1oz fresh root ginger, thinly sliced into strips
2 garlic cloves, thinly sliced into strips
2 spring onions (scallions), finely sliced

1 Place the duck in a large pan with enough water to cover. Season with salt and pepper and bring the water to the boil. Reduce the heat, cover the pot, and simmer for 1½ hours.

2 Add the preserved limes and ginger. Continue to simmer for another hour, skimming off the fat from time to time, until the liquid has reduced a little and the duck is so tender that it almost falls off the bone.

3 Meanwhile heat some vegetable oil in a wok. Stir in the ginger and garlic strips and fry until gold and crispy. Drain them well on kitchen paper and set aside for garnishing.

4 Remove the duck from the broth and shred the meat into individual bowls. Check the broth for seasoning, then ladle it over the duck in the bowls. Sprinkle the spring onions with the fried ginger and garlic over the top and serve.

Cook's Tip
Preserved limes have a distinct bitter flavour. Look for them in Asian markets.

Duck & Nut Soup with Jujubes

This rich soup is delicious. Packed with nuts and sweetened with jujubes (dried Chinese red dates), it resembles neither a soup nor a stew, but something in between. Served on its own, or with rice and pickles, it is a meal in itself.

Serves 4

30–45ml/2–3 tbsp vegetable oil
4 duck legs, split into thighs and drumsticks
juice of 1 coconut
60ml/4 tbsp fish sauce
4 lemon grass stalks, bruised
12 chestnuts, peeled
90g/3½oz unsalted cashew nuts, roasted
90g/3½oz unsalted almonds, roasted
90g/3½oz unsalted peanuts, roasted
12 jujubes
sea salt and ground black pepper
1 bunch fresh basil leaves, to garnish

1 Heat the oil in a wok or heavy pan. Brown the duck legs in the oil and drain on kitchen paper.

2 Bring 2 litres/3½ pints/7¾ cups water to the boil. Reduce the heat and add the coconut juice, fish sauce, lemon grass and duck legs. Cover the pan and simmer over a gentle heat for 2–3 hours. Skim off any fat.

3 Add the nuts and jujubes and cook for 40 minutes, until the chestnuts are soft and the duck is very tender. Skim off any fat, season to taste and sprinkle with basil leaves to serve.

Variation
Replace the jujubes with dates if you cannot find them.

Cook's Tip
To extract the coconut juice, pierce the eyes on top and turn the coconut upside down over a bowl.

duck & lime soup Energy 124kcal/520kJ; Protein 19.8g; Carbohydrate 0.3g, of which sugars 0.3g; Fat 6.5g, of which saturates 1.3g; Cholesterol 110mg; Calcium 19mg; Fibre 0g; Sodium 110mg.
duck & nut soup Energy 604kcal/2512kJ; Protein 43.8g; Carbohydrate 8.9g, of which sugars 3.6g; Fat 44g, of which saturates 9.2g; Cholesterol 165mg; Calcium 49mg; Fibre 3.1g; Sodium 231mg.

Pork & Lotus Root Broth

In this clear broth, which is often served as an appetizer, the slices of fresh lotus root look like delicate flowers floating in water.

Serves 4–6

450g/1lb fresh lotus root, peeled and thinly sliced
ground black pepper
1 fresh red chilli, seeded and finely sliced, and 1 small bunch basil leaves, to garnish

For the stock

450g/1lb pork ribs
1 onion, quartered
2 carrots, cut into chunks
25g/1oz dried squid or dried shrimp, soaked in water for 30 minutes, rinsed and drained
15ml/1 tbsp fish sauce
15ml/1 tbsp soy sauce
6 black peppercorns
sea salt

1 To make the stock, put the pork ribs into a large pan and cover with 1.5 litres/2½ pints/6¼ cups water. Bring to the boil, then skim off the layer of fat on top of the water and add the other ingredients. Reduce the heat, cover, and simmer very gently for 2 hours.

2 Take off the lid and simmer for a further 30 minutes to reduce the stock. Strain the stock and shred the meat off the pork ribs. Discard the other stock ingredients and bones.

3 Pour the strained pork stock back into the pan and bring it to the boil. Reduce the heat and add the peeled and sliced lotus root. Partially cover the pan with a lid and simmer gently for 30–40 minutes, until the slices of lotus root are tender.

4 Stir in the shredded meat and season the broth with salt and pepper. Ladle the soup into bowls and garnish with the chilli and basil leaves.

Cook's Tip

The lotus, an edible water lily, has been grown in China for centuries and is prized for its delicate flavour.

Pork & Prawn Soup

The secret of this soup is its richly flavoured stock.

Serves 4

225g/8oz pork fillet (tenderloin)
225g/8oz rice vermicelli, soaked in lukewarm water for 20 minutes
20 prawns (shrimp), shelled and deveined
115g/4oz/½ cup beansprouts
2 spring onions (scallions), sliced
2 fresh red chillies, seeded and finely sliced
1 garlic clove, finely sliced
chopped basil and coriander (cilantro) leaves
1 lime, cut into quarters, and fish sauce, to serve

For the stock

25g/1oz dried squid
675g/1½lb pork ribs
1 onion, peeled and quartered
2 carrots, cut into chunks
15ml/1 tbsp fish sauce
15ml/1 tbsp soy sauce
6 black peppercorns
salt

1 To make the stock, soak the squid in water for 30 minutes, rinse and drain. Put the ribs in a large pan with 2.5 litres/4½ pints/10 cups water. Boil, skim, and add the dried squid and remaining stock ingredients. Cover, simmer for 1 hour, then skim, remove the lid and continue to simmer for a further 1½ hours.

2 Strain the stock into a deep pan and bring to the boil. Add the pork and simmer for 25 minutes. Lift out the pork and slice it thinly. Keep the stock simmering over a low heat.

3 Drain the soaked rice vermicelli and cook in boiling water for 5 minutes until tender. Drain and divide the vermicelli equally among four bowls.

4 Cook the prawns in the stock for 1 minute, lift them out and add to the bowls with the pork slices. Ladle over the hot stock and sprinkle with beansprouts, spring onions, chillies, garlic and herbs.

5 Serve each bowl of soup with a wedge of lime to squeeze over it and fish sauce to splash on top.

pork & lotus root broth Energy 181kcal/756kJ; Protein 23.8g; Carbohydrate 4g, of which sugars 3.1g; Fat 7.8g, of which saturates 2.7g; Cholesterol 74mg; Calcium 65mg; Fibre 1.4g; Sodium 269mg.
pork & prawn soup Energy 234kcal/981kJ; Protein 26.2g; Carbohydrate 24.8g, of which sugars 1.6g; Fat 3.3g, of which saturates 1g; Cholesterol 137mg; Calcium 84mg; Fibre 1.1g; Sodium 681mg.

Sweet & Sour Pork Soup

This very quick, sharp and tangy soup is perfect for an impromptu supper. It can also be made with shredded chicken breast.

Serves 6–8

900g/2lb pork fillet (tenderloin), trimmed
1 unripe papaya, halved, seeded, peeled and shredded
3 shallots, chopped
5ml/1 tsp crushed black peppercorns
5 garlic cloves, chopped
15ml/1 tbsp shrimp paste
30ml/2 tbsp vegetable oil
1.5 litres/2½ pints/6 cups chicken stock
2.5cm/1in piece fresh root ginger, grated
120ml/4fl oz/½ cup tamarind water
15ml/1 tbsp clear honey
juice of 1 lime
4 spring onions (scallions), sliced
salt and ground black pepper
2 small fresh red chillies, seeded and sliced, to garnish

1 Cut the trimmed pork fillet into very fine strips, 5cm/2in in length. Mix with the shredded papaya and set aside. Process the chopped shallots, crushed black peppercorns, chopped garlic and shrimp paste together in a food processor or blender to form a smooth paste.

2 Heat the vegetable oil in a heavy pan and fry the shallot paste for 1–2 minutes. Pour in the chicken stock and bring to the boil. Reduce the heat. Add the pork and papaya mixure, ginger and tamarind water to the pan. Simmer for 7–8 minutes, until the pork is tender.

3 Stir in the honey, lime juice, most of the chillies and spring onions. Season to taste. Ladle the soup into bowls and serve at once, garnished with the remaining chillies and spring onions.

Cook's Tip
Unripe papayas are often served in salads in Asia and are also cooked as a vegetable.

Tamarind Pork & Vegetable Soup

This Filipino soup can be made with any combination of meat or fish and vegetables, as long as it is sour. Tamarind or star fruit are the most common souring agents.

Serves

2 litres/3½ pints/8 cups pork or chicken stock, or a mixture of stock and water
15–30ml/1–2 tbsp tamarind paste
30ml/2 tbsp patis (Filipino fish sauce)
25g/1oz fresh root ginger, finely grated
1 medium yam or sweet potato, cut into bitesize chunks
8–10 snake (yard long) beans
225g/8oz kangkong (water spinach) or ordinary spinach, well rinsed
350g/12oz pork tenderloin, sliced widthways
2–3 spring onions (scallions), white parts only, finely sliced
salt and ground black pepper

1 In a wok or deep pan, bring the stock to the boil. Stir in the tamarind paste, patis and ginger, reduce the heat and simmer for about 20 minutes. Season the mixture with salt and lots of pepper.

2 Add the yam and snake beans to the pan and cook gently for 3–4 minutes, until the yam is tender. Stir in the spinach and the sliced pork and simmer gently for 2–3 minutes, until the pork is just cooked and turns opaque.

3 Ladle the soup into individual warmed bowls and sprinkle the sliced spring onions over the top. You will need chopsticks and a spoon to eat with.

Cook's Tip
Fresh tamarind pods, packaged tamarind pulp and pots of tamarind paste are all available in Middle Eastern, Indian, African and South-east Asian food shops.

sweet & sour pork Energy 229kcal/963kJ; Protein 32.8g; Carbohydrate 11.1g, of which sugars 10.9g; Fat 6.2g, of which saturates 2.1g; Cholesterol 95mg; Calcium 37mg; Fibre 2.3g; Sodium 111mg.
tamarind pork Energy 126kcal/532kJ; Protein 14g; Carbohydrate 12.3g, of which sugars 4.1g; Fat 2.7g, of which saturates 0.9g; Cholesterol 37mg; Calcium 31mg; Fibre 2g; Sodium 417mg.

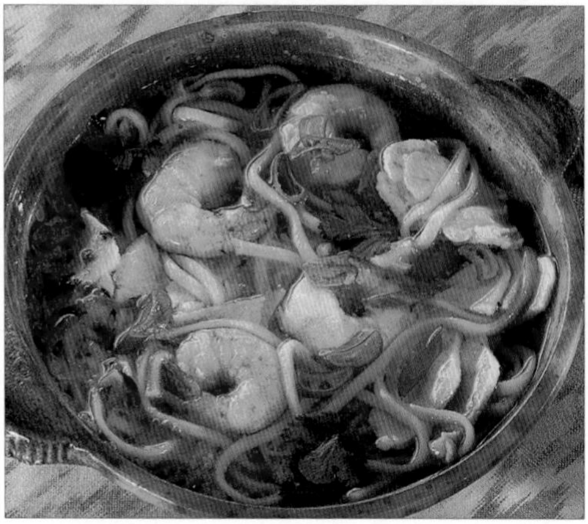

Pork & Noodle Broth with Prawns

This delicately flavoured Vietnamese soup is very quick and easy to make, but tastes really special.

Serves 4–6

350g/12oz pork chops or fillet (tenderloin)
225g/8oz raw prawn (shrimp) tails or cooked prawns
150g/5oz thin egg noodles
15ml/1 tbsp vegetable oil
10ml/2 tsp sesame oil
4 shallots or 1 medium onion, sliced
15ml/1 tbsp finely sliced fresh root ginger
1 garlic clove, crushed
5ml/1 tsp sugar
1.5 litres/2½ pints/6¼ cups chicken stock
2 kaffir lime leaves
45ml/3 tbsp fish sauce
juice of ½ lime
4 sprigs fresh coriander (cilantro) and 2 spring onions (scallions), green parts only, chopped, to garnish

1 If you are using pork chops, trim away any fat and the bones. Place the meat in the freezer for 30 minutes to firm, but not freeze, it. Slice the pork thinly and set aside. Peel and devein the prawns, if using raw prawn tails.

2 Bring a large pan of salted water to the boil and simmer the thin egg noodles according to the instructions on the packet. Drain and refresh the noodles under cold running water. Set aside until needed.

3 Heat the vegetable and sesame oils in a preheated wok, add the sliced shallots or onion and stir-fry for 3–4 minutes, until they are evenly browned. Remove the shallots or onion from the wok and set aside.

4 Add the ginger, garlic, sugar and chicken stock to the wok and bring to a simmer. Add the lime leaves, fish sauce and lime juice. Add the pork, then simmer for 15 minutes. Add the prawns and cooked noodles and simmer for 3–4 minutes to heat through. Serve in shallow bowls, garnished with coriander sprigs, the green parts of the spring onion and the browned shallots or onion.

Pork Bone Tea

This aromatic, peppery broth is a favourite at late-night hawker stalls.

Serves 4–6

500g/1¼lb meaty pork ribs, trimmed and cut into 5cm/2in lengths
225g/8oz pork loin
8 garlic cloves, unpeeled and bruised
2 cinnamon sticks
5 star anise
120ml/4fl oz/½ cup light soy sauce
50ml/2fl oz/¼ cup dark soy sauce
15ml/1 tbsp sugar
salt and ground black pepper
steamed rice, to serve

For the dipping sauce

120ml/4fl oz/½ cup light soy sauce
2 fresh red chillies, seeded and finely chopped

For the spice bag

6 cloves
15ml/1 tbsp dried orange peel
5ml/1 tsp black peppercorns
5ml/1 tsp coriander seeds
5ml/1 tsp fennel seeds

1 To make the dipping sauce, stir the soy sauce and chillies together in a small bowl and set aside. To make the spice bag, lay a piece of muslin (cheesecloth) flat and place all the spices in the centre. Gather up the edges and tie together.

2 Put the pork ribs and loin into a deep pan. Add the garlic, cinnamon sticks, star anise and spice bag. Pour in 2.5 litres/4½ pints/10 cups water and bring to the boil.

3 Skim off any fat from the surface of the liquid, then stir in the light and dark soy sauces and sugar. Reduce the heat and simmer, partially covered, for about 2 hours, until the pork is almost falling off the bones. Season to taste with salt and lots of black pepper.

4 Remove the pork loin from the broth and cut it into bitesize pieces. Divide the meat and ribs among four to six soup bowls and ladle the steaming broth over the top. Serve immediately with the soy and chilli sauce, as a dip for the pieces of pork, and steamed rice.

pork & noodle broth Energy 223kcal/936kJ; Protein 22.2g; Carbohydrate 18.1g, of which sugars 0.7g; Fat 7.3g, of which saturates 1.8g; Cholesterol 117mg; Calcium 41mg; Fibre 0.7g; Sodium 335mg.
pork bone tea Energy 49kcal/206kJ; Protein 8.1g; Carbohydrate 0.8g, of which sugars 0.8g; Fat 1.5g, of which saturates 0.5g; Cholesterol 24mg; Calcium 3mg; Fibre 0g; Sodium 145mg.

Pork & Sichuan Pickle Soup

Noodle soup can taste a bit bland, but not when Sichuan hot pickle is one of the ingredients. This tasty soup makes a great winter warmer.

Serves 4

1 litre/1¾ pints/4 cups chicken stock
350g/12oz egg noodles
15ml/1 tbsp dried shrimp, soaked in water
30ml/2 tbsp vegetable oil
225g/8oz lean pork, such as fillet (tenderloin), finely shredded
15ml/1 tbsp yellow bean paste
15ml/1 tbsp soy sauce
115g/4oz Sichuan hot pickle, rinsed, drained and shredded
pinch of sugar
salt and ground black pepper
2 spring onions (scallions), finely sliced, to garnish

1 Bring the stock to the boil in a large pan. Add the noodles and cook until almost tender. Drain the dried shrimp, rinse them under cold water, drain again and add to the stock. Lower the heat and simmer for a further 2 minutes. Keep hot.

2 Heat the oil in a frying pan or wok. Add the pork and stir-fry over a high heat for about 3 minutes.

3 Add the bean paste and soy sauce to the meat and stir-fry the mixture for 1 minute more. Add the hot pickle with a pinch of sugar. Stir-fry for another minute.

4 Divide the noodles and soup among individual serving bowls. Spoon the pork mixture on top, then sprinkle with the spring onions and serve immediately.

Cook's Tip

Sichuan hot pickle, also known as Szechuan (or Sichuan) preserved vegetables, is a pickle made from the stems of mustard cabbage, which are dried in the sun and then pickled in brine with chillies and spices.

Broth with Stuffed Cabbage Leaves

The Chinese have a tradition of cooking dumplings or stuffed vegetables in a clear broth.

Serves 4

10 Chinese leaves (Chinese cabbage) halved, main ribs removed
4 spring onions (scallions), green tops left whole, white part finely chopped
5–6 dried cloud ear (wood ear) mushrooms, soaked in hot water for 15 minutes
115g/4oz minced (ground) pork
115g/4oz prawns (shrimp), shelled, deveined and chopped
1 fresh chilli, seeded and chopped
30ml/2 tbsp fish sauce
15ml/1 tbsp soy sauce
4cm/1½in fresh root ginger, peeled and very finely sliced
chopped fresh coriander (cilantro), to garnish

For the stock

1 meaty chicken carcass
2 onions, peeled and quartered
4 garlic cloves, crushed
4cm/1½in fresh root ginger, chopped
30ml/2 tbsp fish sauce
30ml/2 tbsp soy sauce
6 black peppercorns
a few sprigs of fresh thyme
sea salt

1 To make the chicken stock, put the chicken carcass into a deep pan with all the other stock ingredients except the salt. Add 2 litres/3½ pints/8 cups of water. Bring to the boil. Skim, then cover and simmer for 1½–2 hours. Remove the lid and simmer for 30 minutes more. Skim, season, then strain. Measure 1.5 litres/2½ pints/6¼ cups into a clean pan.

2 Blanch the cabbage leaves in boiling water for 2 minutes, lift out and refresh under cold water. Blanch the spring onion tops and refresh. Tear each piece into 5 strips. Drain the cloud ears, squeeze dry, trim, chop and mix with the pork, prawns, spring onion whites, chilli, fish sauce and soy sauce. Divide the mixture among the cabbage leaves, fold in the bottom edges and sides, roll up and tie with the spring onion green.

3 Heat the stock, stir in the ginger and add the cabbage bundles. Cook very gently for 20 minutes. Garnish with coriander.

pork & sichuan pickle soup Energy 218kcal/911kJ; Protein 24.5g; Carbohydrate 7.8g, of which sugars 0.9g; Fat 9.7g, of which saturates 3g; Cholesterol 74mg; Calcium 90mg; Fibre 0.8g; Sodium 454mg.
broth w. cabbage Energy 80kcal/334kJ; Protein 12.7g; Carbohydrate 3.9g, of which sugars 3.7g; Fat 1.5g, of which saturates 0.5g; Cholesterol 74mg; Calcium 68mg; Fibre 1.4g; Sodium 891mg.

Pork Soup with Cloud Ears

One of China's most popular soups, this is famed for its clever balance of flavours. The 'hot' comes from the pepper, the 'sour' from the vinegar.

Serves 6

4–6 Chinese dried mushrooms
2–3 small pieces of cloud ear (wood ear) mushrooms
115g/4oz pork fillet (tenderloin), cut into fine strips
45ml/3 tbsp cornflour (cornstarch)
150ml/¼ pint/⅔ cup water
15–30ml/1–2 tbsp sunflower oil
1 small onion, finely chopped
1.5 litres/2½ pints/6 cups good quality beef or chicken stock
150g/5oz fresh firm tofu, diced
60ml/4 tbsp rice vinegar
15ml/1 tbsp light soy sauce
1 egg, beaten
5 ml/1 tsp sesame oil
salt and ground black pepper
2–3 spring onions (scallions), shredded, to garnish

1 Place the dried mushrooms in a bowl, with the pieces of cloud ear. Add sufficient warm water to cover and leave to soak for about 30 minutes.

2 Drain the mushrooms, reserving the soaking water. Cut off and discard the mushroom stems and slice the caps finely. Trim away any tough stems from the cloud ears, then chop them.

3 Lightly dust the strips of pork with some of the cornflour; mix the remaining cornflour to a paste with the water.

4 Heat the oil in a wok and fry the onion until soft. Increase the heat and fry the pork until it changes colour. Add the stock, mushrooms, soaking water and cloud ears. Bring to the boil, then simmer for 15 minutes. Stir in the cornflour paste to thicken. Add the tofu, vinegar, soy sauce, and salt and pepper.

5 Bring the soup to just below boiling point, then drizzle in the beaten egg so that it forms threads. Stir in the sesame oil and serve at once in deep, warmed soup bowls, garnished with spring onion shreds.

Pork Broth with Winter Melon

This soup uses two traditional South-east Asian ingredients – winter melon to absorb the flavours and tiger lilies to lift the broth with a floral scent. When choosing tiger lilies make sure they are light golden in colour. If you can't find winter melon, you could make the soup using another winter squash.

Serves 4

350g/12oz winter melon
25g/1oz light golden tiger lilies, soaked in hot water for 20 minutes
salt and ground black pepper
1 small bunch each coriander (cilantro) and mint, stalks removed, leaves chopped, to garnish

For the stock

25g/1oz dried shrimp, soaked in water for 15 minutes
500g/1¼lb pork ribs
1 onion, peeled and quartered
175g/6oz carrots, peeled and cut into chunks
15ml/1 tbsp fish sauce
15ml/1 tbsp soy sauce
4 black peppercorns

1 To make the stock, drain and rinse the dried shrimp. Put the pork ribs in a large pan and cover with 2 litres/3½ pints/8 cups water. Bring the water to the boil, skim off any fat, and add the dried shrimp and the remaining stock ingredients. Cover and simmer for 1½ hours, then skim again. Continue simmering, uncovered, for a further 30 minutes. Strain and check the seasoning. You should have about 1.5 litres/2½ pints/6¼ cups.

2 Halve the winter melon lengthways and remove the seeds and inner membrane. Finely slice the flesh into half-moons. Squeeze the soaked tiger lilies dry and tie them in a knot.

3 Bring the stock to the boil in a deep pan or wok. Reduce the heat and add the winter melon and tiger lilies. Simmer for 15–20 minutes, or until the melon is tender. Season to taste with salt and pepper, and serve in heated bowls, with the herbs on the top.

pork soup w. cloud ears Energy 109kcal/458kJ; Protein 7.8g; Carbohydrate 8.3g, of which sugars 1g; Fat 5.3g, of which saturates 1g; Cholesterol 44mg; Calcium 141mg; Fibre 0.4g; Sodium 210mg.
pork broth w. winter melon Energy 25kcal/103kJ; Protein 1.6g; Carbohydrate 2.6g, of which sugars 1.9g; Fat 0.9g, of which saturates 0.1g; Cholesterol 0mg; Calcium 55mg; Fibre 1.5g; Sodium 616mg.

Beef & Berry Soup

The fresh berries give this soup an unexpected kick and the tender beef makes a filling meal.

Serves 4

30ml/2 tbsp vegetable oil
450g/1lb tender beef steak
2 onions, finely sliced
25g/1oz/2 tbsp butter
1.2 litres/2 pints/5 cups good beef stock or bouillon
2.5ml/½ tsp salt
115g/4oz/1 cup fresh blueberries, blackberries or huckleberries, lightly mashed
about 15ml/1 tbsp honey

1 Heat the oil in a heavy pan until almost smoking. Add the steak and brown on both sides over medium-high heat. Remove the steak from the pan and set aside.

2 Turn the heat to low and add the sliced onions and butter to the pan. Stir well, scraping up the meat juices. Cook over low heat for 8–10 minutes until the onions are soft.

3 Add the beef stock or bouillon and salt, and bring to the boil, stirring well. Stir in the mashed berries and the honey, and simmer for 20 minutes.

4 Meanwhile, cut the steak into thin, bitesize slivers. Taste the soup and add more salt or honey if necessary. Add the steak to the pan. Simmer for 30 seconds, stirring all the time. Serve the soup piping hot.

Cook's Tip

To make beef stock, boil 450g/1lb beef bones in water for 10 minutes, then put them in a roasting pan with 900g/2lb shin of beef and 40g/1½oz butter. Brown in the oven for 40 minutes at 220°C/425°F/Gas 7, turning. Transfer to a pan and add a bouquet garni, a chopped leek, onion, celery stick and 2 carrots. Cover with cold water. Bring to the boil and remove any scum. Simmer for 4 hours. Strain through muslin (cheesecloth). Skim off the fat when the stock is cold.

Beef Noodle Soup

Nutritious and filling, this makes an intensely satisfying meal at any time of day.

Serves 6

500g/1¼lb dried noodles, soaked in water for 20 minutes
1 onion, halved and finely sliced
6–8 spring onions (scallions), cut into long pieces
2–3 fresh red chillies, seeded and finely sliced
115g/4oz/½ cup beansprouts
1 large bunch each fresh coriander (cilantro) and mint, stalks removed, leaves chopped, to garnish
2 limes, cut in wedges, and hoisin sauce and fish sauce, to serve

For the stock

1.5kg/3lb 5oz oxtail, trimmed of fat and cut into thick pieces
1kg/2¼lb beef shank or brisket
2 large onions
2 carrots
7.5cm/3in fresh root ginger, cut into chunks
6 cloves
2 cinnamon sticks
6 star anise
5ml/1 tsp black peppercorns
30ml/2 tbsp soy sauce
45–60ml/3–4 tbsp fish sauce
salt

1 To make the stock, put the oxtail into a large, deep pan and cover with water. Bring it to the boil and cook for 10 minutes. Drain the oxtail, rinsing off any scum, and return it to the clean pan with the other stock ingredients, apart from the fish sauce.

2 Cover with 3 litres/5¼ pints/12 cups water. Boil, then simmer for 2–3 hours with the lid on, and 1 hour without it. Skim, then strain 2 litres/3½ pints/8 cups stock into another pan.

3 Cut the cooked meat into thin pieces; discard the bones. Bring the stock to the boil, stir in the fish sauce, season to taste, and keep simmering until ready to use.

4 Cook the noodles in boiling water until tender, then drain and divide among six wide soup bowls. Top each serving with beef, onion, spring onions, chillies and beansprouts. Ladle the hot stock over the top, sprinkle with fresh herbs and serve with the lime wedges to squeeze over and the sauces to pass around.

beef & berry Energy 344kcal/1432kJ; Protein 26.8g; Carbohydrate 12g, of which sugars 10.3g; Fat 21.3g, of which saturates 8.2g; Cholesterol 79mg; Calcium 38mg; Fibre 2g; Sodium 113mg.
beef noodle soup Energy 180kcal/748kJ; Protein 10.8g; Carbohydrate 4.8g, of which sugars 4.1g; Fat 4.2g, of which saturates 1.6g; Cholesterol 24mg; Calcium 35mg; Fibre 1g; Sodium 219mg.

Spicy Aubergine Soup with Beef

A delicious, substantial soup form North Sumatra, this dish can be made with aubergines, green jackfruit or any of the squash family. For an authentic meal, serve the soup with a bowl of rice and a chilli sambal.

Serves 4

30ml/2 tbsp palm, groundnut (peanut) or corn oil
150g/5oz lean beef, cut into thin strips
500ml/17fl oz/2 cups coconut milk
10ml/2 tsp sugar
3–4 Thai aubergines (eggplants) or 1 large Mediterranean aubergine, cut into wedges
3–4 kaffir lime leaves
juice of 1 lime
salt

For the spice paste

4 shallots, chopped
4 fresh red Thai chillies, seeded and chopped
25g/1oz fresh root ginger, chopped
15g/½oz fresh turmeric, chopped, or 2.5ml/½ tsp ground turmeric
2 garlic cloves, chopped
5ml/1 tsp coriander seeds
2.5ml/½ tsp cumin seeds
2–3 candlenuts

To serve

cooked rice
1 lime, quartered (optional)
chilli sambal (optional)

1 Grind the spice paste ingredients to a coarse paste using a pestle and mortar or a food processor.

2 Heat the oil in a wok or heavy pan, stir in the spice paste and fry until fragrant. Add the beef, stirring, then add the coconut milk and sugar. Bring the liquid to the boil, then reduce the heat and simmer gently for 10 minutes..

3 Add the aubergine wedges and kaffir line leaves to the pan and cook gently for a further 5–10 minutes, until tender but not mushy. Stir in the lime juice and season with salt to taste.

4 Serve with rice, wedges of lime and chilli sambal, if you wish.

Chinese Leaf Soup with Meatballs

This wonderfully fragrant combination makes for a hearty, warming soup.

Serves 4

10 dried shiitake mushrooms
90g/3½oz bean thread noodles
675g/1½lb minced (ground) beef
10ml/2 tsp finely grated garlic
10ml/2 tsp finely grated fresh root ginger
1 fresh red chilli, seeded and chopped
6 spring onions (scallions), sliced
1 egg white
15ml/1 tbsp cornflour (cornstarch)
15ml/1 tbsp Chinese rice wine
30ml/2 tbsp sunflower oil
1.5 litres/2½ pints/6 cups beef or chicken stock
50ml/2fl oz/¼ cup light soy sauce
5ml/1 tsp sugar
150g/5oz enoki mushrooms, trimmed
200g/7oz Chinese leaves (Chinese cabbage) very thinly sliced
salt and ground black pepper

1 Place the dried mushrooms in a medium bowl and pour over 250ml/8fl oz/1 cup boiling water. Leave to soak for 30 minutes and then squeeze dry, reserving the liquid. Remove and discard the mushroom stems; thickly slice the caps and set aside.

2 Put the bean thread noodles in a large heatproof bowl and pour over boiling water to cover. Soak for 3–4 minutes, then drain, rinse and set aside.

3 Place the beef, garlic, ginger, chilli, spring onions, egg white, cornflour, rice wine and seasoning in a food processor. Process to combine well. Divide the mixture into 30 portions, then shape each one into a ball. Heat the stock.

4 Heat a wok and add the oil. Fry the meatballs, in batches, for 2–3 minutes on each side. Remove with a slotted spoon and drain on kitchen paper. Add the meatballs to the simmering beef stock with the soy sauce, sugar, shiitake mushrooms and reserved soaking liquid. Cook gently for 20–25 minutes.

5 Add the noodles, enoki mushrooms and cabbage and cook gently for 4–5 minutes. Serve in wide bowls.

spicy aubergine Energy 224kcal/938kJ; Protein 12.1g; Carbohydrate 14.6g, of which sugars 12.6g; Fat 13.6g, of which saturates 3.2g; Cholesterol 22mg; Calcium 79mg; Fibre 3g; Sodium 181mg.
Chinese leaf w. meatballs Energy 102kcal/424kJ; Protein 5.4g; Carbohydrate 5.8g, of which sugars 3g; Fat 6.5g, of which saturates 1.9g; Cholesterol 13mg; Calcium 39mg; Fibre 0.9g; Sodium 308mg.

Beef Broth with Water Spinach

Water spinach is a popular vegetable throughout Vietnam. When cooked, the stems remain crunchy while the leaves soften, lending a delightful contrast of texture to the dish. Served as an appetizer, this is a light soup with tender bites of beef and sour notes of lemon juice.

Serves 4–6

30ml/2 tbsp fish sauce
5ml/1 tsp sugar
175g/6oz beef fillet (tenderloin), finely sliced across the grain into 2.5cm/1in strips
1.2 litres/2 pints/5 cups beef or chicken stock
175g/6oz water spinach, trimmed, rinsed, leaves and stalks separated
juice of 1 lemon
ground black pepper
1 fresh red or green chilli, seeded and finely sliced, to garnish

1 In a bowl, stir the fish sauce with the sugar until it has dissolved. Toss in the beef strips and leave to marinate for 30 minutes. Pour the stock into a pan and bring it to the boil. Reduce the heat and add the water spinach. Stir in the lemon juice and season with pepper.

2 Place the meat strips in individual soup bowls and ladle the hot broth over the top. Garnish with the seeded and finely sliced chillies and serve.

Cook's Tip

It is important to marinate the beef strips so that they take on the flavourings. If you have time to prepare them in advance, they can be left to marinate overnight.

Variation

You can sprinkle coriander (cilantro) and mint or fried garlic and ginger over the top, if you prefer.

Paper-thin Sliced Beef Soup

This dish uses popular Japanese ingredients. The cooking is done at the table.

Serves 4

600g/1lb 6oz rump (round) steak
2 thin leeks, cut into thin strips
4 spring onions (scallions), quartered
8 shiitake mushroom caps
175g/6oz/2 cups oyster mushrooms, base part removed, torn into small pieces
½ head Chinese leaves (Chinese cabbage), cut into squares
300g/11oz shungiku, halved
275g/10oz firm tofu, halved and cut crossways in slices
10 x 6cm/4 x 2½in dashi-konbu, wiped with a damp cloth

For the lime sauce

1 lime
20ml/4 tsp mirin
60ml/4 tbsp rice vinegar
120ml/4fl oz/½ cup shoyu
4 x 6cm/1½ x 2½in dashi-konbu
5g/⅛oz kezuri-bushi

For the pink daikon

1 piece mooli (daikon), 6cm/2½in in length, peeled
1 dried chilli, seeded and sliced

1 To make the lime sauce, squeeze the lime and make up the juice to 120ml/4fl oz/½ cup with water. Pour into a bowl and add the mirin, rice vinegar, shoyu, dashi-konbu and kezuri-bushi. Cover and leave to stand overnight.

2 Make the pink mooli. Pierce the mooli in several places and insert the chilli strips. Leave for 20 minutes, then grate, squeeze out the liquid and divide among four small bowls.

3 Slice the meat thinly. Arrange meat, vegetables and tofu on platters. Fill a casserole three-quarters full of water and add the dashi-konbu. Boil, then transfer to a table burner.

4 Strain the citrus sauce and add 45ml/3 tbsp to each bowl of daikon. Remove the konbu from the stock. Add some tofu and vegetables to the pot.

5 Each guest cooks a slice of beef in the stock, then dips it in sauce. Tofu and vegetables are removed and dipped in the same way, and more are added to the pot.

broth w. water spinach Energy 61kcal/254kJ; Protein 7.4g; Carbohydrate 1.2g, of which sugars 1.1g; Fat 3g, of which saturates 1.1g; Cholesterol 17mg; Calcium 51mg; Fibre 0.6g; Sodium 60mg.
thin sliced beef soup Energy 290kcal/1216kJ; Protein 42.2g; Carbohydrate 8.3g, of which sugars 7.4g; Fat 9.9g, of which saturates 3.1g; Cholesterol 89mg; Calcium 425mg; Fibre 3.9g; Sodium 1000mg.

Tomato & Beef Soup

Another wholesome and much-loved classic, the tomatoes and spring onions give this light beef broth a superb flavour. It is quick and easy to make, and ideal as an appetizer or light lunch on a warm day. Use fresh rather than canned tomatoes to achieve the best flavour.

Serves 4

75g/3oz rump (round) steak
900ml/1½ pints/3¾ cups beef stock
30ml/2 tbsp tomato purée (paste)
6 tomatoes, halved, seeded and chopped
10ml/2 tsp caster (superfine) sugar
15ml/1 tbsp cornflour (cornstarch)
15ml/1 tbsp cold water
1 egg white
2.5ml/½ tsp sesame oil
salt and ground black pepper
2 spring onions (scallions), finely shredded

1 Cut the beef into thin strips and place in a pan. Pour over boiling water to cover. Cook for 2 minutes, then drain thoroughly and set aside.

2 Bring the stock to the boil in a clean pan. Stir in the tomato purée, then the tomatoes and sugar.

3 Add the beef strips, allow the stock to boil again, then lower the heat and simmer for 2 minutes.

4 Mix the cornflour to a paste with the water. Add the mixture to the soup, stirring constantly until it thickens slightly. Lightly beat the egg white in a cup.

5 Pour the egg white into the soup, stirring. When the egg white changes colour, season, stir and pour the soup into heated soup bowls.

6 Drizzle with sesame oil, sprinkle with spring onions and serve.

Beef & Ginger Soup

This fragrant soup is often eaten for breakfast.

Serves 4–6

1 onion
1.5kg/3–3½lb beef shank with bones
2.5cm/1in fresh root ginger
1 star anise
1 bay leaf
2 whole cloves
2.5ml/½ tsp fennel seeds
1 piece of cinnamon stick
3 litres/5 pints/12 cups water
fish sauce, to taste
juice of 1 lime
150g/5oz fillet (tenderloin) steak
450g/1lb fresh flat rice noodles
salt and ground black pepper

For the accompaniments

1 small red onion, sliced into rings
115g/4oz/½ cup beansprouts
2 fresh red chillies, seeded and sliced
2 spring onions (scallions), sliced
coriander (cilantro) leaves
lime wedges

1 Cut the onion in half. Grill (broil) under a high heat, cut side up, until the exposed sides are caramelized. Set aside.

2 Cut the meat into large chunks and then place in a large pan with the bones. Add the caramelized onion with the ginger, star anise, bay leaf, cloves, fennel seeds and cinnamon.

3 Add the water, bring to the boil, then simmer gently for 2–3 hours, skimming off the fat and scum occasionally.

4 Remove the meat from the stock and cut into small pieces, discarding the bones. Strain the stock and return to the pan together with the meat. Bring back to the boil and season with the fish sauce and lime juice.

5 Slice the fillet steak very thinly and then chill until required. Place the accompaniments in separate bowls.

6 Cook the noodles in boiling water until just tender. Drain and divide among soup bowls. Top with steak, pour the hot stock over and serve, offering the accompaniments separately so that each person may garnish their soup as they like.

tomato & beef soup Energy 79kcal/337kJ; Protein 6.2g; Carbohydrate 11.1g, of which sugars 7.6g; Fat 1.5g, of which saturates 0.5g; Cholesterol 11mg; Calcium 16mg; Fibre 1.5g; Sodium 58mg.
beef & ginger soup Energy 532kcal/2222kJ; Protein 36.7g; Carbohydrate 63.6g, of which sugars 1.6g; Fat 13.4g, of which saturates 5.4g; Cholesterol 82mg; Calcium 26mg; Fibre 0.6g; Sodium 102mg.

Beef & Aubergine Soup

A wonderful Khmer dish, this soup is sweet and spicy.

Serves 6

4 dried New Mexico chillies
15ml/1 tbsp vegetable oil
75ml/5 tbsp kroeung or Thai green curry paste
2–3 fresh red chillies
75ml/5 tbsp tamarind extract
15–30ml/1–2 tbsp fish sauce
30ml/2 tbsp palm sugar (jaggery)
12 Thai aubergines (eggplants), cut into bitesize chunks
1 bunch watercress, chopped
1 handful fresh curry leaves
sea salt and ground black pepper

For the stock

1kg/2¼lb beef shanks or brisket
2 large onions, quartered
2–3 carrots, cut into chunks
90g/3½oz fresh root ginger, sliced
2 cinnamon sticks
4 star anise
5ml/1 tsp black peppercorns
30ml/2 tbsp soy sauce
45–60ml/3–4 tbsp fish sauce

1 Mix all the stock ingredients, apart from the soy sauce and fish sauce, in a large pan. Cover with 3 litres/5 pints/12 cups water and bring to the boil. Simmer, covered, for 2–3 hours. Meanwhile, soak the dried chillies in water for 30 minutes. Split them open, remove the seeds and scoop out the pulp.

2 Add the sauces to the stock and simmer, uncovered, until it has reduced by about one third. Skim and strain into a bowl.

3 Tear the meat into thin strips and put half of it aside for the soup. Save the rest for another dish.

4 Heat the oil in a wok. Stir in the kroeung and chilli pulp with the whole chillies. Stir until the mixture sizzles. Add the tamarind extract, fish sauce, sugar and reserved stock. Stir well and bring to the boil.

5 Add the reserved beef, aubergines and watercress. Continue cooking for 20 minutes.

6 Dry-fry the curry leaves until they begin to crackle. Season the soup, stir in half the curry leaves and serve in heated bowls, with the remaining leaves on top.

Spicy Beef & Mushroom Soup

Ginger gives this satisfying soup a delightful tang.

Serves 4

10g/¼oz dried porcini mushrooms
6 spring onions (scallions)
115g/4oz carrots
350g/12oz lean rump (round) steak
about 30ml/2 tbsp oil
1 garlic clove, crushed
2.5cm/1in fresh root ginger, grated
1.2 litres/2 pints/5 cups beef stock
45ml/3 tbsp light soy sauce
60ml/4 tbsp sake or dry sherry
75g/3oz dried thin egg noodles
75g/3oz spinach, shredded
salt and ground black pepper

1 Break up the dried porcini, place them in a bowl and pour over 150ml/¼ pint/⅔ cup boiling water. Cover and leave the mushrooms to soak for 15 minutes.

2 Cut the spring onions and carrots into fine 5cm/2in-long strips. Trim any fat off the meat and slice into thin strips.

3 Heat the oil in a large pan and cook the beef in batches until browned. Remove and drain on kitchen paper. Add the garlic, ginger, spring onions and carrots to the pan and stir-fry for 3 minutes.

4 Add the beef stock, the mushrooms and their soaking liquid, the soy sauce, sherry and plenty of seasoning. Bring to the boil, reduce the heat and simmer, covered, for 10 minutes.

5 Break up the noodles slightly and add to the pan, with the spinach. Simmer gently for 5 minutes, or until the beef is tender. Adjust the seasoning before serving in warmed bowls.

Cook's Tip
Chilling the beef briefly in the freezer will make it much easier to slice into thin strips.

beef & aubergine Energy 303kcal/1276kJ; Protein 36.7g; Carbohydrate 16.5g, of which sugars 14.5g; Fat 10.6g, of which saturates 4.2g; Cholesterol 90mg; Calcium 35mg; Fibre 2.4g; Sodium 303mg.
spicy beef & mushroom Energy 315kcal/1316kJ; Protein 23.4g; Carbohydrate 17.4g, of which sugars 4g; Fat 15.5g, of which saturates 4.5g; Cholesterol 56mg; Calcium 57mg; Fibre 1.9g; Sodium 713mg.

Mongolian Firepot

This mode of cooking was introduced to China by 13th-century invaders. Guests cook the assembled ingredients at the table, dipping the meats in sauces.

Serves 6–8

900g/2lb boned leg of lamb
225g/8oz lamb's liver, trimmed
900ml/1½ pints/3¾ cups hot lamb stock
900ml/1½ pints/3¾ cups hot chicken stock
1cm/½in piece fresh root ginger, peeled and thinly sliced
45ml/3 tbsp rice wine
½ head Chinese leaves (Chinese cabbage), shredded
115g/4oz cellophane noodles
salt and ground black pepper

For the dipping sauce

50ml/2fl oz/¼ cup red wine vinegar
7.5ml/½ tbsp dark soy sauce
1cm/½in piece fresh root ginger, peeled and finely shredded
1 spring onion (scallion), shredded

To serve

tomato sauce, sweet chilli sauce, mustard oil and sesame oil
dry-fried coriander seeds, crushed

1 When buying the lamb, if possible ask your butcher to slice it thinly on a slicing machine. Place the liver in the freezer; slice it thinly too.

2 Mix both types of stock in a large pan. Add the ginger and rice wine, with salt and pepper to taste. Heat to simmering point; simmer for 15 minutes.

3 Arrange the meats and greens on platters. Soak the noodles, following the instructions on the packet.

4 Mix the dipping sauce ingredients in a small bowl. Place the other accompaniments in separate small dishes.

5 Fill the moat of the firepot with the simmering stock. Each guest cooks a portion of meat in the hot stock, then dips it in sauce and coats it in seeds.

6 When the meat has been eaten, add the vegetables and drained noodles. Cook for a minute or two, then serve as soup.

Sukiyaki

You will need a special cast-iron sukiyaki pan and burner or a similar table top cooker for this dish.

Serves 4

1kg/2¼lb beef topside (pot roast), thinly sliced
lard (shortening) or white cooking fat, for cooking
4 leeks, sliced diagonally into 1cm/½in pieces
8 shiitake mushrooms, stems removed
300g/11oz shirataki noodles, boiled for 2 minutes, drained and halved
2 pieces fried tofu, cubed
4 fresh eggs, to serve

For the sukiyaki stock

100ml/3½fl oz/scant ½ cup mirin (sweet rice wine)
45ml/3 tbsp sugar
105ml/7 tbsp soy sauce

For the seasoning mix

200ml/7fl oz/scant 1 cup dashi
100ml/3½fl oz/scant ½ cup sake
15ml/1 tbsp soy sauce

1 Make the sukiyaki stock. Mix the mirin, sugar and soy sauce in a pan, bring to the boil, then set aside. To make the seasoning mix, heat the dashi, sake and soy sauce in a pan. As soon as it boils, set aside.

2 Fan out the beef slices on a large serving plate. Put the lard for cooking on the same plate. Arrange all the remaining ingredients, except the eggs, on one or more large plates.

3 Stand the portable cooker on a suitably heavy mat. Melt the lard or white cooking fat, add three or four slices of beef and some leeks, then pour in the sukiyaki stock. Gradually add the remaining ingredients, except the eggs.

4 Place each egg in a ramekin and beat lightly. When the beef and vegetables are cooked, diners help themselves and dip the food in the raw egg before eating.

5 When the stock has thickened, stir in the seasoning mix and carry on cooking until all the ingredients have been eaten.

Mongolian firepot Energy 144kcal/606kJ; Protein 12.3g; Carbohydrate 12g, of which sugars 1.2g; Fat 5.1g, of which saturates 1.1g; Cholesterol 128mg; Calcium 193mg; Fibre 0.9g; Sodium 49mg.
sukiyaki Energy 868kcal/3633kJ; Protein 71.5g; Carbohydrate 51.7g, of which sugars 11.1g; Fat 43.2g, of which saturates 13.1g; Cholesterol 662mg; Calcium 605mg; Fibre 6.5g; Sodium 1695mg.

Rice Porridge

Originating in China, this dish has now spread through much of Asia and is loved for its comforting blandness. It is invariably served, though, with a few strongly flavoured accompaniments.

Serves 2

900ml/1 ½ pints/3¾ cups vegetable stock
200g/7oz/1¾ cups cooked rice
225g/8oz minced (ground) pork
15ml/1 tbsp fish sauce
2 heads pickled garlic, finely chopped
1 celery stick, finely diced
salt and ground black pepper

To garnish

30ml/2 tbsp groundnut (peanut) oil
4 garlic cloves, thinly sliced
4 small red shallots, finely sliced

1 Make the garnishes by heating the groundnut oil in a frying pan and cooking the garlic and shallots over a low heat until brown. Drain well on kitchen paper and reserve for the soup.

2 Pour the stock into a large pan. Bring to the boil and add the rice. Season the minced pork. Add it using a small teaspoon and tapping the spoon on the side of the pan so that the meat falls into the soup in small lumps.

3 Stir in the fish sauce and pickled garlic and simmer for about 10 minutes, until the pork is cooked. Stir in the celery.

4 Serve the rice porridge in individual warmed bowls. Sprinkle the prepared garlic and shallots on top and season with plenty of ground pepper.

Cook's Tip
Pickled garlic has a distinctive flavour and is available from Asian food stores.

Congee with Chinese Sausage

Congee – soft rice – is comfort food. Gentle on the stomach, it is frequently eaten for breakfast or served to convalescents. Throughout the East, people will frequently have just a cup of tea on rising; later they will settle down to a bowl of congee.

Serves 2–3

115g/4oz/generous ½ cup long-grain rice
25g/1oz/3 tbsp glutinous rice
1.2 litres/2 pints/5 cups water
about 2.5ml/½ tsp salt
5ml/1 tsp sesame oil
thin slice of fresh root ginger, peeled and bruised
2 Chinese sausages
1 egg, lightly beaten (optional)
2.5ml/½ tsp light soy sauce
roasted peanuts, chopped, and thin shreds of spring onion (scallion), to garnish

1 Wash both rices thoroughly. Drain and place in a large pan. Add the water, bring to the boil and immediately reduce to the lowest heat, using a heat diffuser if you have one.

2 Cook gently for 1¼–1½ hours, stirring from time to time. If the congee thickens too much, stir in a little boiling water. It should have the consistency of creamy pouring porridge.

3 About 15 minutes before serving, add salt to taste and the sesame oil, together with the piece of ginger.

4 Steam the Chinese sausages for about 10 minutes, then slice and stir into the congee. Cook for 5 minutes.

5 Just before serving, remove the ginger and stir in the lightly beaten egg, if using. Serve hot, garnished with the peanuts and spring onions and topped with a drizzle of soy sauce.

Variation
If you prefer, use roast duck instead of Chinese sausages. Congee is also popular with tea eggs.

rice porridge Energy 152kcal/636kJ; Protein 15.2g; Carbohydrate 17g, of which sugars 1.8g; Fat 2.5g, of which saturates 0.3g; Cholesterol 34mg; Calcium 12mg; Fibre 0g; Sodium 45mg.
congee w. Chinese sausage Energy 301kcal/1254kJ; Protein 7.2g; Carbohydrate 40.4g, of which sugars 0.8g; Fat 12g, of which saturates 4.2g; Cholesterol 16mg; Calcium 23mg; Fibre 0.2g; Sodium 610mg.

Onion Bhajias

A favourite snack in India, bhajias consist of a savoury vegetable mixture in a crisp and spicy batter. They can be served as an appetizer or as a side dish with curries.

Makes 20–25

2 large onions
225g/8oz/2 cups gram flour
2.5ml/½ tsp chilli powder
5ml/1 tsp ground turmeric
5ml/1 tsp baking powder
1.5ml/¼ tsp asafoetida
2.5ml/½ tsp each nigella, fennel, cumin and onion seeds, coarsely crushed
2 fresh green chillies, finely chopped
50g/2oz/2 cups fresh coriander (cilantro), chopped
vegetable oil, for deep-frying
salt

1 Using a sharp knife, slice the onions into thin rounds. Separate the slices and set them aside on a plate.

2 In a bowl mix together the flour, chilli powder, ground turmeric, baking powder and asafoetida. Add salt to taste. Sift the mixture into a large mixing bowl.

3 Add the coarsely crushed seeds, onion slices, green chillies and fresh coriander and toss together well.

4 Add enough cold water to make a paste, then stir in more water to make a thick batter that coats the onions and spices.

5 Heat enough oil in a karahi or wok for deep-frying. Drop spoonfuls of the mixture into the hot oil and fry the bhajias until they are golden brown. Leave enough space to turn the bhajias. Drain well and serve hot.

Variation
This versatile batter can be used with other vegetables, including okra, cauliflower and broccoli.

Vegetable Samosas

A selection of highly spiced vegetables in a pastry casing makes these samosas a delicious snack at any time of the day.

Makes 28

14 sheets of filo pastry, thawed and wrapped in a damp dish towel
oil, for brushing the pastries

For the filling
3 large potatoes, boiled and roughly mashed
75g/3oz/¾ cup frozen peas, thawed
50g/2oz/⅓ cup canned corn, drained
5ml/1 tsp ground coriander
5ml/1 tsp ground cumin
5ml/1 tsp dry mango powder (amchur)
1 small onion, finely chopped
2 fresh green chillies, finely chopped
30ml/2 tbsp coriander (cilantro) leaves, chopped
30ml/2 tbsp chopped fresh mint leaves
juice of 1 lemon
salt

1 Preheat the oven to 200°C/400°F/Gas 6. Cut each sheet of filo pastry in half lengthways and fold each piece in half lengthways to give 28 thin strips. Lightly brush with oil.

2 Toss all the filling ingredients together in a large mixing bowl until they are well blended. Adjust the seasoning with salt and lemon juice if necessary.

3 Using one strip of the pastry at a time, place 15ml/1 tbsp of the filling mixture at one end and fold the pastry diagonally over. Continue folding to form a triangle shape. Brush the samosas with oil. Bake for 10–15 minutes, until golden brown.

Cook's Tip
Work with one or two sheets of filo pastry at a time and keep the rest covered with a damp dish towel to prevent it drying out.

onion bhajias Energy 72kcal/301kJ; Protein 1.2g; Carbohydrate 8.8g, of which sugars 1.3g; Fat 3.8g, of which saturates 0.4g; Cholesterol 0mg; Calcium 23mg; Fibre 0.7g; Sodium 2mg.
vegetable samosas Energy 56kcal/235kJ; Protein 1.3g; Carbohydrate 10g, of which sugars 0.8g; Fat 1.4g, of which saturates 0.2g; Cholesterol 0mg; Calcium 16mg; Fibre 0.7g; Sodium 8mg.

Cauliflower Samosas

Throughout the East, these tasty snacks are sold by street vendors, and eaten at any time of day.

Makes about 20

1 packet 25cm/10in square spring roll wrappers, thawed if frozen
30ml/2 tbsp plain (all-purpose) flour, mixed to a paste with a little water
vegetable oil, for deep-frying
coriander (cilantro) leaves, to garnish

For the filling

25g/1oz/2 tbsp ghee or unsalted butter
1 small onion, finely chopped
1cm/½in piece fresh root ginger, chopped
1 garlic clove, crushed
2.5ml/½ tsp chilli powder
1 large potato, about 225g/8oz, cooked and finely diced
50g/2oz/½ cup cauliflower florets, lightly cooked and chopped into small pieces
50g/2oz/½ cup frozen peas, thawed
5–10ml/1–2 tsp garam masala
15ml/1 tbsp chopped fresh coriander (leaves and stems)
squeeze of lemon juice
salt

1 Heat the ghee or butter in a wok and fry the onion, ginger and garlic for 5 minutes until softened. Add the chilli powder, cook for 1 minute, then stir in the potato, cauliflower and peas. Sprinkle with garam masala and set aside to cool. Stir in the coriander, lemon juice and salt.

2 Cut the spring roll wrappers into three strips. Brush the edges with flour paste. Place a small spoonful of filling about 2cm/¾in in from the edge of one strip. Fold one corner over the filling to make a triangle and continue this folding until the entire strip has been used and a triangular pastry has been formed. Seal any open edges with more flour and water paste, adding more water if the paste is very thick.

3 Heat the oil for deep-frying to 190°C/375°F and fry the samosas until golden and crisp. Drain well on kitchen paper and serve hot garnished with coriander leaves and accompanied by cucumber, carrot and celery matchsticks, if you like.

Spicy Toasts

These crunchy toasts make an ideal snack or part of a brunch. They are especially delicious served with grilled tomatoes.

Makes 4

4 eggs
300ml/½ pint/1¼ cups milk
2 fresh green chillies, finely chopped
30ml/2 tbsp chopped fresh coriander (cilantro)
75g/3oz/¾ cup grated Cheddar or mozzarella cheese
2.5ml/½ tsp salt
1.5ml/¼ tsp ground black pepper
4 slices bread
corn oil, for frying

1 Break the eggs into a medium bowl and whisk together. Slowly add the milk and whisk again. Add the finely sliced chillies, chopped fresh coriander, Cheddar or mozzarella cheese, salt and pepper, and mix well.

2 Cut the bread slices in half diagonally, and soak them, one at a time, in the egg mixture.

3 Heat the oil in a medium frying pan and fry the bread slices over a medium heat, turning them once or twice, until they are golden brown.

4 Drain off any excess oil as you remove the toasts from the pan, and serve immediately.

Crisp-baked Coconut Chips

Coconut chips are a tasty nibble to serve with drinks and make an unusual alternative to nuts. The chips can be sliced ahead of time and frozen on open trays, then stored in freezer bags in batches until required.

Serves 8 as a snack

1 fresh coconut
salt

1 Preheat the oven to 160°C/325°F/Gas 3. First drain the coconut juice, either by piercing one of the coconut eyes with a sharp instrument or by breaking it carefully.

2 Lay the coconut on a board and hit the centre sharply with a hammer. The shell should break cleanly in two.

3 Having opened the coconut, use a broad-bladed knife to ease the flesh away from the hard outer shell. Taste a piece of the flesh just to make sure it is fresh. Peel away the brown skin with a vegetable peeler, if you like.

4 Slice the coconut flesh into wafer-thin shavings, using a food processor, mandoline or sharp knife. Sprinkle these evenly all over one or two baking sheets and sprinkle with salt. Bake for about 25–30 minutes or until crisp, turning them from time to time. Cool and serve. Any leftover chips can be stored in airtight containers.

cauliflower samosas Energy 105kcal/437kJ; Protein 1.4g; Carbohydrate 10.1g, of which sugars 0.6g; Fat 6.8g, of which saturates 1.3g; Cholesterol 3mg; Calcium 17mg; Fibre 0.6g; Sodium 12mg.
spicy toasts Energy 355kcal/1479kJ; Protein 16.6g; Carbohydrate 17.3g, of which sugars 4.4g; Fat 24.6g, of which saturates 7.7g; Cholesterol 213mg; Calcium 295mg; Fibre 0.4g; Sodium 383mg.
coconut chips Energy 83kcal/356kJ; Protein 1.1g; Carbohydrate 18.4g, of which sugars 18.4g; Fat 1.1g, of which saturates 0.8g; Cholesterol 0mg; Calcium 109mg; Fibre 0g; Sodium 413mg.

Roasted Coconut Cashew Nuts

Serve these hot and sweet cashew nuts in paper cones at parties. Not only do they look enticing and taste terrific, but the cones help to keep clothes and hands clean and can simply be recycled afterwards, saving on washing up.

Serves 6–8

15ml/1 tbsp groundnut (peanut) oil
30ml/2 tbsp clear honey
225g/8oz/2 cups cashew nuts
115g/4oz/1⅓ cups desiccated (dry unsweetened shredded) coconut
2 small fresh red chillies, seeded and finely chopped
salt and ground black pepper

1 Heat the oil in a wok or large frying pan and then stir in the honey. After a few seconds add the nuts and coconut, and stir-fry until both are golden brown.

2 Add the chillies, with salt and pepper to taste. Toss until all the ingredients are well mixed. Serve warm or cooled in paper cones or on saucers.

Crisp Fried Aubergine

The spicy gram flour coating on these slices is deliciously crisp, revealing the succulent aubergine beneath. Choose a firm aubergine with a glossy skin.

Serves 4

50g/2oz/½ cup gram flour
15ml/1 tbsp semolina or ground rice
2.5ml/½ tsp onion seeds
5ml/1 tsp cumin seeds
2.5ml/½ tsp fennel seeds or aniseeds
2.5–5ml/½–1 tsp hot chilli powder
2.5ml/½ tsp salt, or to taste
1 large aubergine (eggplant)
vegetable oil, for deep-frying

1 Sift the gram flour into a large mixing bowl and add the semolina or ground rice with the onion and cumin seeds, fennel or aniseeds, and the hot chilli powder and salt.

2 Halve the aubergine lengthways and cut each half into 5mm/¼in thick slices. Rinse them and shake off the excess water, but do not pat dry. With some of the water still clinging to the slices, add them to the spiced gram flour mixture. Toss them around until they are evenly coated with the flour. Use a spoon if necessary to ensure that all the flour is used.

3 Heat the oil in a karahi, wok or deep-fryer to a temperature of 190°C/375°F, or until a cube of bread dropped in the oil browns in about 45 seconds. If it floats immediately, the oil has reached the right temperature.

4 Fry the spice-coated aubergine slices in a single layer. Avoid overcrowding the pan as this will lower the oil temperature, resulting in a soggy texture. Fry until the aubergines are crisp and well browned. Drain on kitchen paper and serve with a chutney.

Green Curry Puffs

Shrimp paste and green curry sauce, used judiciously, give these puffs their distinctive, spicy, savoury flavour, and the addition of chilli steps up the heat.

Makes 24

24 small wonton wrappers, about 8cm/3¼in square, thawed if frozen
15ml/1 tbsp cornflour (cornstarch), mixed to a paste with 30ml/2 tbsp water
oil, for deep-frying

For the filling

1 small potato, about 115g/4oz, boiled and mashed
25g/1oz/¼ cup cooked petits pois (baby peas)
25g/1oz/¼ cup cooked corn
few sprigs fresh coriander (cilantro), chopped
1 small fresh red chilli, seeded and finely chopped
½ lemon grass stalk, finely chopped
15ml/1 tbsp soy sauce
5ml/1 tsp shrimp paste or Thai fish sauce
5ml/1 tsp Thai green curry paste

1 Combine the filling ingredients. Lay out one wonton wrapper and place a teaspoon of the filling in the centre. (Wonton wrappers dry out quickly, so keep them covered using clear film (plastic wrap) until you are ready to use them.)

2 Brush a little of the cornflour paste along two sides of the square. Fold the other two sides over to meet them, then press together to make a triangular pastry and seal in the filling. Make more pastries in the same way.

3 Heat the oil in a karahi, wok or deep-fryer to a temperature of 190°C/375°F, or until a cube of bread, dropped in the oil, browns in about 45 seconds.

4 Add the pastries to the oil, a few at a time, and fry them for about 5 minutes, until golden brown.

5 Remove the puffs from the fryer or wok and drain on kitchen paper. If you intend to serve the puffs hot, place them in a low oven to keep warm while cooking successive batches. The puffs also taste good cold.

coconut cashew nuts Energy 301kcal/1247kJ; Protein 7.2g; Carbohydrate 9.7g, of which sugars 5.5g; Fat 26.2g, of which saturates 11.1g; Cholesterol 0mg; Calcium 14mg; Fibre 3g; Sodium 95mg.
fried aubergine Energy 165kcal/689kJ; Protein 2.3g; Carbohydrate 14g, of which sugars 1.3g; Fat 11.5g, of which saturates 1.4g; Cholesterol 0mg; Calcium 9mg; Fibre 1.6g; Sodium 3mg.
green curry puffs Energy 32kcal/134kJ; Protein 1g; Carbohydrate 6.7g, of which sugars 0.4g; Fat 0.3g, of which saturates 0g; Cholesterol 1mg; Calcium 16mg; Fibre 0.4g; Sodium 58mg.

Potato Cakes with Stuffing

A few communities in India make these unusual potato cakes known as petis. They can be served as a starter or as a main meal with a fresh tomato salad.

Makes 8–10

15ml/1 tbsp vegetable oil
1 large onion, finely chopped
2 garlic cloves, finely crushed
5cm/2in piece fresh root ginger, finely crushed
5ml/1 tsp ground coriander
5ml/1 tsp ground cumin
2 fresh green chillies, finely chopped
30ml/2 tbsp each chopped fresh coriander (cilantro) and mint
225g/8oz lean minced (ground) beef or lamb
50g/2oz/⅓ cup frozen peas, thawed
juice of 1 lemon
900g/2lb potatoes, boiled and mashed
2 eggs, beaten
dry breadcrumbs, for coating
vegetable oil, for shallow-frying
salt
lemon wedges and salad leaves, to serve

1 Heat the oil and fry the onion, garlic, ginger, coriander, cumin, chillies and chopped herbs until the onion is translucent. Add the meat and peas and fry well until the meat is cooked, then season to taste with salt and lemon juice. The mixture should be very dry.

2 Divide the mashed potato into 8–10 portions, take one portion at a time and flatten into a pancake in the palm of your hand. Place a spoonful of the meat in the centre and gather the sides together to enclose the meat. Flatten it slightly to make a round.

3 Dip the cakes in beaten egg and then coat in breadcrumbs. Set aside to chill in the refrigerator for about 1 hour.

4 Heat the oil in a frying pan and shallow-fry the cakes until brown and crisp all over. Serve them hot with lemon wedges on a bed of salad leaves.

Spiced Potato Cakes with Chickpeas

Fragrant and spicy chickpeas go very well with these fiery potato cakes.

Makes 10–12

30ml/2 tbsp vegetable oil
30ml/2 tbsp ground coriander
30ml/2 tbsp ground cumin
2.5ml/½ tsp ground turmeric
2.5ml/½ tsp salt
2.5ml/½ tsp sugar
30ml/2 tbsp gram flour, mixed with a little water to make a paste
450g/1lb/3 cups cooked chickpeas, drained
2 fresh green chillies, chopped
5cm/2in piece fresh root ginger, crushed
75g/3oz/1½ cups fresh coriander (cilantro), chopped
2 firm tomatoes, chopped
fresh mint sprigs, to garnish

For the potato cakes

450g/1lb potatoes, boiled and mashed
4 fresh green chillies, finely chopped
50g/2oz/2 cups chopped fresh coriander (cilantro)
7.5ml/1½ tsp ground cumin
5ml/1 tsp dry mango powder (amchur)
vegetable oil, for frying
salt

1 Heat the oil in a karahi, wok or large pan. Add the coriander, cumin, turmeric, salt, sugar and gram flour paste and cook until the water has evaporated and the oil has separated.

2 Add the chickpeas to the spices in the pan, and stir in the chopped chillies, ginger, fresh coriander and tomatoes. Toss the ingredients well and simmer gently for about 5 minutes. Transfer to a serving dish and keep warm.

3 To make the potato cakes, place the mashed potato in a large bowl and add the green chillies, chopped fresh coriander, cumin, dry mango powder and salt. Mix together until all the ingredients are well blended.

4 Using your hands, shape the potato mixture into little cakes. Heat the oil in a shallow frying pan and fry the cakes on both sides until golden brown. Transfer to a serving dish, garnish with mint sprigs and serve with the spicy chickpeas.

potato cakes w. stuffing Energy 260kcal/1086kJ; Protein 10.6g; Carbohydrate 21.3g, of which sugars 3.4g; Fat 15.4g, of which saturates 3.6g; Cholesterol 88mg; Calcium 29mg; Fibre 1.9g; Sodium 62mg.
potato cakes w. chickpeas Energy 165kcal/690kJ; Protein 5.2g; Carbohydrate 17.5g, of which sugars 1.6g; Fat 8.9g, of which saturates 1.1g; Cholesterol 0mg; Calcium 69mg; Fibre 3g; Sodium 97mg.

Spring Rolls & Chilli Dipping Sauce

Miniature spring rolls make a delicious starter or unusual party finger-food.

Makes 20–24

25g/1oz rice vermicelli noodles
groundnut oil, for deep-frying
5ml/1 tsp grated fresh root ginger
2 spring onions (scallions), finely shredded
50g/2oz carrot, finely shredded
50g/2oz mangetouts (snow peas), shredded
25g/1oz young spinach leaves
50g/2oz fresh beansprouts
15ml/1 tbsp chopped fresh mint
15ml/1 tbsp chopped fresh coriander (cilantro)
30ml/2 tbsp fish sauce
20–24 spring roll wrappers, each 13cm/5in square
1 egg white, lightly beaten

For the dipping sauce

50g/2oz caster (superfine) sugar
50ml/2fl oz rice vinegar
30ml/2 tbsp water
2 fresh red chillies, seeded and finely chopped

1 Place the sugar, vinegar and water in a small pan. Heat gently, stirring until the sugar dissolves, then boil rapidly until it forms a light syrup. Stir in the chillies and leave to cool.

2 Soak the noodles according to the packet instructions, rinse and drain well. Cut the noodles into short lengths with scissors.

3 Heat 15ml/1 tbsp of the oil in a wok. Add the ginger and spring onions and stir-fry for 15 seconds. Add the carrot and mangetouts and stir-fry for 2–3 minutes. Toss in the spinach, beansprouts, mint, coriander, fish sauce and noodles and stir-fry for a further minute. Set aside to cool.

4 Soften the spring roll wrappers, following the directions on the packet. Arrange a wrapper in a diamond shape. Place a spoonful of filling just below the centre, then fold the bottom point over, fold in each side, then roll up tightly. Brush the end with beaten egg white to seal. Repeat until the filling is used up.

5 Half-fill a wok with oil and heat to 180°C/350°F. Deep-fry the spring rolls in batches for 3–4 minutes until golden and crisp. Drain on kitchen paper. Serve hot with the chilli dipping sauce.

Corn Fritters

These crunchy corn fritters are very easy to prepare and make a great appetizer for vegetarian guests.

Makes 12

3 corn cobs
1 garlic clove, crushed
small bunch fresh coriander (cilantro), chopped
1 small fresh red or green chilli, seeded and finely chopped
1 spring onion (scallion), chopped
15ml/1 tbsp soy sauce
75g/3oz/¾ cup rice flour or plain (all-purpose) flour
2 eggs, lightly beaten
60ml/4 tbsp water
oil, for shallow frying
salt and ground black pepper
sweet chilli sauce, to serve

1 Slice the kernels from the cobs into a large bowl. Add the garlic, chopped coriander, red or green chilli, spring onion, soy sauce, flour, beaten eggs and water; mix well and season.

2 Heat the oil in a large frying pan. Add spoonfuls of the corn mixture, gently spreading each one with the back of the spoon to make a roundish fritter. Cook for 1–2 minutes on each side. Drain and serve hot with sweet chilli sauce.

Crab & Water Chestnut Wontons

Serve these mouthwatering parcels as part of a dim sum selection – they are perfect for a buffet or as canapés with drinks.

Serves 4

50g/2oz/⅓ cup drained, canned water chestnuts
115g/4oz/generous ½ cup fresh white crab meat
12 wonton wrappers
salt and ground black pepper

1 Finely chop the water chestnuts, mix them with the crab meat and season. Fill the wonton wrappers, spring-roll fashion.

2 Prepare a steamer and cook the filled wontons for 5–8 minutes. Serve the wontons piping hot.

spring rolls & sauce Energy 105kcal/435kJ; Protein 0.9g; Carbohydrate 6.7g, of which sugars 2.6g; Fat 8.4g, of which saturates 0.9g; Cholesterol 0mg; Calcium 16mg; Fibre 0.3g; Sodium 5mg.
corn fritters Energy 49kcal/208kJ; Protein 2.3g; Carbohydrate 7.5g, of which sugars 0.6g; Fat 1.3g, of which saturates 0.3g; Cholesterol 32mg; Calcium 21mg; Fibre 0.6g; Sodium 102mg.
crab & water chestnut Energy 88kcal/374kJ; Protein 7g; Carbohydrate 14.7g, of which sugars 0.4g; Fat 0.5g, of which saturates 0.1g; Cholesterol 21mg; Calcium 66mg; Fibre 0.7g; Sodium 166mg.

Rice Cakes with Spicy Sauce

Rice cakes are a classic Thai appetizer. They are easy to make and can be kept in an airtight box for weeks.

Serves 4–6

175g/6oz/1 cup jasmine rice, thoroughly washed
350ml/12fl oz/1½ cups water
oil for frying and greasing

For the spicy dipping sauce

6–8 dried chillies, deseeded
2.5ml/½ tsp salt
2 shallots, chopped
2 garlic cloves, chopped
4 coriander (cilantro) roots
10 white peppercorns
250ml/8fl oz/1 cup coconut milk
5ml/1 tsp shrimp paste
115g/4oz minced (ground) pork
115g/4oz cherry tomatoes, chopped
15ml/1 tbsp fish sauce
15ml/1 tbsp palm sugar (jaggery)
30ml/2 tbsp tamarind juice
30 ml/2 tbsp coarsely chopped roasted peanuts
2 spring onions (scallions), finely chopped

1 Soak the chillies in warm water for 20 minutes. Drain and pound with salt in a mortar and pestle. Add the shallots, garlic, coriander roots and peppercorns and pound to a coarse paste.

2 Pour the coconut milk into a pan and boil until it begins to separate. Add the chilli paste. Cook for 2–3 minutes until it is fragrant. Stir in the shrimp paste. Cook for another minute.

3 Add the pork, stirring to break up any lumps. Cook for 5–10 minutes. Add the tomatoes, fish sauce, palm sugar and tamarind juice. Simmer until the sauce thickens. Stir in the peanuts and spring onions. Remove from the heat and leave to cool.

4 Put the rice in a pan, add the water and cover. Bring to the boil, reduce the heat and simmer gently for about 15 minutes. Turn out on to a lightly greased tray and press down with the back of a large spoon. Dry out overnight in a very low oven.

5 Break the dried rice into bitesize pieces. Heat the oil in a wok or deep-fat fryer. Deep-fry the rice cakes in batches for about 1 minute, until they puff up, taking care not to brown them. Drain and serve with the dipping sauce.

Chinese Garlic Mushrooms

High in protein and low in fat, marinated tofu makes an unusual stuffing for these baked mushroom caps.

Serves 4

8 large open mushrooms
3 spring onions (scallions), sliced
1 garlic clove, crushed
30ml/2 tbsp oyster sauce
275g/10oz packet marinated tofu, diced
200g/7oz can corn, drained
10ml/2 tsp sesame oil
salt and ground black pepper

1 Preheat the oven to 200°C/400°F/Gas 6. Finely chop the mushroom stalks and mix with the next three ingredients.

2 Stir in the diced marinated tofu and corn, season well, then spoon the filling into the mushroom caps.

3 Brush the edges of the mushrooms with the sesame oil. Place them in an ovenproof dish and bake for 12–15 minutes, until the mushrooms are just tender, then serve immediately.

Cook's Tip

The large open mushrooms used in this recipe are known as field (portabello) mushrooms and can be up to 10cm/4in in diameter. To prepare, simply wipe with kitchen paper or rinse briefly and dry before use – they don't need peeling.

rice cakes Energy 428kcal/1790kJ; Protein 28.9g; Carbohydrate 50.1g, of which sugars 9.7g; Fat 12.4g, of which saturates 2.7g; Cholesterol 111mg; Calcium 61mg; Fibre 1.6g; Sodium 1296mg.
garlic mushrooms Energy 86kcal/361kJ; Protein 7.9g; Carbohydrate 4g, of which sugars 3.2g; Fat 4.4g, of which saturates 0.6g; Cholesterol 0mg; Calcium 268mg; Fibre 2.2g; Sodium 701mg.

Fried Green Beans with Chilli

This dish is delicious and fast to make.

Serves 4

400g/14oz green beans
30ml/2 tbsp oil
2 garlic cloves, crushed
5ml/1 tsp sugar
30ml/2 tbsp chilli sauce, or amount to taste
100ml/3½fl oz/scant ½ cup water

1 Trim the beans and cut into 7.5cm/3in lengths. Boil a pan of water, blanch the beans for 2 minutes, then drain.

2 Heat the oil in a wok or heavy pan, add the garlic and fry until golden brown. Add the sugar and chilli sauce. Stir for 30 seconds, then add the beans. Stir rapidly for 2–3 minutes.

3 Add the water and bring quickly to the boil. Cook, stirring, until the beans are nearly dry. Serve hot with rice.

Hot & Sour Cabbage

This popular dish from Szechuan in western China can be served hot or cold.

Serves 6–8

450g/1lb pale green or white cabbage
45–60ml/3–4 tbsp vegetable oil
10–12 red Sichuan peppercorns
few whole dried red chillies
5ml/1 tsp salt
15ml/1 tbsp light brown sugar
15ml/1 tbsp light soy sauce
30ml/2 tbsp rice vinegar
few drops of sesame oil

1 Cut the cabbage leaves into 2.5 x 1cm/1 x ½in pieces.

2 Heat the oil in a wok until smoking, then add the peppercorns and chillies.

3 Add the cabbage to the wok and stir-fry for about 1–2 minutes. Add the salt and sugar, continue stirring for 1 minute more, then add the soy sauce, rice vinegar and sesame oil. Blend well and serve immediately.

Mini Phoenix Rolls

These filled omelette parcels are legendary.

Serves 4

2 large eggs, plus 1 egg white
75ml/5 tbsp cold water
5ml/1 tsp vegetable oil
175g/6oz lean pork, diced
75g/3oz/½ cup drained, canned water chestnuts
5cm/2in piece fresh root ginger, grated
4 dried Chinese mushrooms, soaked in hot water until soft
15ml/1 tbsp dry sherry
1.5ml/¼ tsp salt
large pinch of ground white pepper
30ml/2 tbsp rice vinegar
2.5ml/½ tsp sugar
fresh coriander (cilantro) or flat leaf parsley, to garnish

1 Lightly beat the 2 whole eggs with 45ml/3 tbsp of the water. Use the mixture to make 4 omelettes.

2 Mix the pork and water chestnuts in a food processor. Add 5ml/1 tsp of the ginger. Drain the mushrooms, chop the caps roughly and add these to the mixture. Process until smooth.

3 Scrape the pork paste into a bowl. Stir in the egg white, sherry, remaining water, salt and pepper. Mix thoroughly, cover the bowl and leave in a cool place for about 15 minutes.

4 Divide the pork mixture among the omelettes and roll them up. Steam over a high heat for 15 minutes.

5 Make a dipping sauce by mixing the remaining ginger with the rice vinegar and sugar in a small dish. Lift the rolls out of the steamer, then cut them diagonally in 1cm/½in slices. Arrange them on a plate, garnish with the coriander or flat leaf parsley leaves and serve with the sauce.

Cook's Tip

These rolls can be prepared a day in advance and steamed just before serving.

fried beans Energy 86kcal/356kJ; Protein 2g; Carbohydrate 6.4g, of which sugars 5.4g; Fat 6g, of which saturates 0.8g; Cholesterol 0mg; Calcium 38mg; Fibre 2.3g; Sodium 122mg.
hot & sour cabbage Energy 61kcal/253kJ; Protein 1g; Carbohydrate 4.9g, of which sugars 4.7g; Fat 4.2g, of which saturates 0.4g; Cholesterol 0mg; Calcium 29mg; Fibre 1.2g; Sodium 11mg.
mini pheonix rolls Energy 110kcal/460kJ; Protein 13.8g; Carbohydrate 0.8g, of which sugars 0.5g; Fat 5.4g, of which saturates 1.5g; Cholesterol 123mg; Calcium 22mg; Fibre 0.3g; Sodium 82mg.

Coriander Omelette Parcels

Stir-fried vegetables in black bean sauce make a great omelette filling.

Serves 4

130g/4½oz broccoli, cut into small florets
30ml/2 tbsp groundnut (peanut) oil
1cm/½in piece fresh root ginger, finely grated
1 large garlic clove, crushed
2 fresh red chillies, seeded and finely sliced
4 spring onions (scallions), sliced diagonally
175g/6oz/3 cups pak choi (bok choy), shredded
50g/2oz/2 cups fresh coriander (cilantro) leaves, plus extra to garnish
100g/4oz/½ cup beansprouts
45ml/3 tbsp black bean sauce
4 eggs
salt and ground black pepper

1 Blanch the broccoli in boiling salted water for 2 minutes, drain, then refresh under cold running water.

2 Meanwhile, heat 15ml/1 tbsp of the oil in a frying pan or wok. Add the ginger, garlic and half the chillies and stir-fry for 1 minute. Add the spring onions, broccoli and pak choi, and stir-fry for 2 minutes more.

3 Chop three-quarters of the coriander and add to the frying pan or wok. Add the beansprouts and stir-fry for 1 minute, then add the black bean sauce and heat through for 1 minute more. Remove the pan from the heat and keep warm.

4 Mix the eggs lightly with a fork and season well. Heat a little of the remaining oil in a small frying pan and add a quarter of the beaten egg. Swirl the egg until it covers the base of the pan, then scatter over a quarter of the reserved coriander leaves. Cook until set, then turn out on to a plate and keep warm while you make three more omelettes, adding more oil, when necessary.

5 Spoon the vegetable stir-fry on to the omelettes and roll up. Cut in half crossways and serve garnished with coriander leaves and the remaining chillies.

Rice Omelette Rolls

Rice omelettes make a great supper dish and are popular with children, who usually top them with a liberal helping of tomato ketchup.

Serves 4

1 skinless, boneless chicken thigh, about 115g/4oz, cubed
40ml/8 tsp butter
1 small onion, chopped
½ carrot, diced
2 shiitake mushrooms, stems removed and chopped
15ml/1 tbsp finely chopped fresh parsley
225g/8oz/2 cups cooked long grain white rice
30ml/2 tbsp tomato ketchup
6 eggs, lightly beaten
60ml/4 tbsp milk
5ml/1 tsp salt, plus extra to season
ground black pepper
tomato ketchup, to serve

1 Season the chicken with salt and pepper. Melt 10ml/2 tsp butter in a frying pan. Fry the onion for 1 minute, then add the chicken and fry until the cubes are cooked. Add the carrot and mushrooms, stir-fry over a medium heat until soft, then add the parsley. Set this mixture aside.

2 Wipe the frying pan, then add a further 10ml/2 tsp butter and stir in the rice. Mix in the fried ingredients, ketchup and pepper. Stir well, adding salt to taste, if necessary. Keep the mixture warm.

3 Beat the eggs with the milk in a bowl. Stir in the measured salt and add pepper to taste.

4 Melt 5ml/1 tsp of the remaining butter in an omelette pan. Pour in a quarter of the egg mixture and stir it briefly with a fork, then allow it to set for 1 minute. Top with a quarter of the rice mixture.

5 Fold the omelette over the rice and slide it to the edge of the pan to shape it into a curve. Slide it on to a warmed plate, cover with kitchen paper and press neatly into a rectangular shape. Keep hot while cooking three more omelettes from the remaining ingredients. Serve immediately, with tomato ketchup.

omelette parcels Energy 148kcal/614kJ; Protein 10.4g; Carbohydrate 6.2g, of which sugars 5.4g; Fat 9.3g, of which saturates 2.2g; Cholesterol 190mg; Calcium 152mg; Fibre 3g; Sodium 323mg.
rice omelette rolls Energy 322kcal/1347kJ; Protein 18.1g; Carbohydrate 22.8g, of which sugars 4.9g; Fat 18.5g, of which saturates 8.1g; Cholesterol 337mg; Calcium 80mg; Fibre 1.1g; Sodium 325mg.

Stuffed Omelettes

A chilli filling makes an interesting contrast to the delicate flavour of the egg.

Serves 4

30ml/2 tbsp groundnut (peanut) oil
2 garlic cloves, finely chopped
1 small onion, finely chopped
225g/8oz minced (ground) pork
30ml/2 tbsp fish sauce
5ml/1 tsp sugar
2 tomatoes, peeled and chopped
15ml/1 tbsp chopped fresh coriander (cilantro)
ground black pepper
fresh coriander (cilantro) sprigs and sliced fresh red chillies, to garnish

For the omelettes

5 eggs
15ml/1 tbsp fish sauce
30ml/2 tbsp groundnut (peanut) oil

1 Heat the oil in a wok and fry the garlic and onion for 3–4 minutes, until soft. Add the pork and cook for about 8 minutes, stirring frequently, until lightly browned.

2 Stir in the fish sauce, sugar and tomatoes, season to taste with pepper and simmer until slightly thickened. Mix in the fresh coriander. Remove from the heat and cover to keep warm while you make the omelettes.

3 Beat the eggs and fish sauce together lightly with a fork. Heat 15ml/1 tbsp of the oil in an omelette pan over a medium heat. When the oil is hot, but not smoking, add half the egg mixture and immediately tilt the pan to spread the egg into a thin, even layer. Cook over a medium heat until the omelette is just set and the underside is golden.

4 Spoon half the filling into the centre of the omelette. Fold into a neat square parcel by bringing the opposite sides of the omelette towards each other. Slide the parcel on to a serving dish, folded side down. Make another omelette parcel in the same way. Garnish with the coriander sprigs and chillies. Cut each omelette in half to serve.

Egg Foo Yung

Hearty and full of flavour, this can be cooked either as one large omelette or as individual omelettes. Either way, it is a clever way of using up leftover roast pork.

Serves 4

6 dried Chinese mushrooms soaked for 20 minutes in warm water
50g/2oz/¼ cup beansprouts
6 drained canned water chestnuts, finely chopped
50g/2oz baby spinach leaves, washed
45ml/3 tbsp vegetable oil
50g/2oz lean roast pork, cut into strips
3 eggs
2.5ml/½ tsp sugar
5ml/1 tsp rice wine or dry sherry
salt and ground black pepper
fresh coriander (cilantro) sprigs, to garnish

1 Drain the mushrooms. Cut off and discard the stems; slice the caps finely and mix with the beansprouts, water chestnuts and spinach leaves.

2 Heat 15ml/1 tbsp oil in a large heavy frying pan. Add the pork and vegetables and toss over the heat for 1 minute.

3 Beat the eggs in a bowl. Add the strips of roast pork and the vegetables and mix well.

4 Wipe the frying pan and heat the remaining oil. Pour in the egg mixture and tilt the pan so that it covers the base.

5 When the omelette has set on the underside, sprinkle the top with salt, pepper and sugar.

6 Invert a plate over the pan, turn both the pan and the plate over, and slide the omelette back into the pan to cook on the other side.

7 Cut the omelette into wedges, drizzle with rice wine or dry sherry and serve immediately, garnished with the sprigs of coriander.

stuffed omelettes Energy 305kcal/1267kJ; Protein 19.2g; Carbohydrate 4.8g, of which sugars 4.5g; Fat 23.6g, of which saturates 5.7g; Cholesterol 275mg; Calcium 48mg; Fibre 0.7g; Sodium 130mg.
egg foo yung Energy 153kcal/634kJ; Protein 8.1g; Carbohydrate 0.7g, of which sugars 0.5g; Fat 13.1g, of which saturates 2.3g; Cholesterol 151mg; Calcium 46mg; Fibre 0.5g; Sodium 80mg.

Hard-boiled Eggs in Red Sauce

A perennially popular snack, this spicy egg dish originally came from Indonesia. Served wrapped in a banana leaf, the Malays often eat it with plain steamed rice, sliced chillies, onion and coriander – ideal for a quick, tasty snack or light lunch.

Serves 4

vegetable oil, for deep-frying
8 eggs, hard-boiled and shelled
1 lemon grass stalk, trimmed, quartered and crushed
2 large tomatoes, skinned, seeded and chopped to a pulp
5–10ml/1–2 tsp sugar
30ml/2 tbsp dark soy sauce
juice of 1 lime
fresh coriander (cilantro) and mint leaves, coarsely chopped, to garnish

For the rempah

4–6 fresh red chillies, seeded and chopped
4 shallots, chopped
2 garlic cloves, chopped
2.5ml/½ tsp shrimp paste

1 Using a mortar and pestle or food processor, grind the ingredients for the rempah to form a smooth purée. Set aside.

2 Heat enough oil for deep-frying in a wok or heavy pan and deep-fry the whole boiled eggs until golden brown. Lift them out and drain.

3 Reserve 15ml/1 tbsp of the oil and discard the rest. Heat the oil in the wok or heavy pan and stir in the rempah until it becomes fragrant. Add the lemon grass, followed by the tomatoes and sugar. Cook for 2–3 minutes, until it forms a thick paste. Reduce the heat and stir in the soy sauce and lime juice.

4 Add 30ml/2 tbsp water to thin the sauce. Toss the eggs in it, making sure they are thoroughly coated, and serve hot, garnished with chopped coriander and mint leaves.

Variation
For a fusion twist, serve these with a cucumber raita.

Son-in-law Eggs

The fascinating name for this dish comes from a story about a prospective bridegroom who very much wanted to impress his future mother-in-law and devised a new recipe based on the only dish he knew how to make – boiled eggs.

Serves 4–6

30ml/2 tbsp vegetable oil
6 shallots, thinly sliced
6 garlic cloves, thinly sliced
6 fresh red chillies, sliced
oil, for deep-frying
6 hard-boiled eggs, shelled
salad leaves, to serve
sprigs of fresh coriander (cilantro), to garnish

For the sauce

75g/3oz/6 tbsp palm sugar (jaggery) or muscovado (brown) sugar
75ml/5 tbsp fish sauce
90ml/6 tbsp tamarind juice

1 To make the sauce, put the sugar, fish sauce and tamarind juice in a pan. Bring to the boil, stirring until the sugar dissolves, then lower the heat and simmer for 5 minutes. Taste and add more sugar, fish sauce or tamarind juice, if needed. Transfer the sauce to a bowl and set it aside.

2 Heat the vegetable oil in a frying pan and cook the shallots, garlic and chillies for 5 minutes. Transfer to a bowl.

3 Heat the oil in a deep-fryer or wok to 190°C/375°F or until a cube of bread, added to the oil, browns in about 45 seconds. Deep-fry the eggs in the hot oil for 3–5 minutes, until golden brown. Remove and drain well on kitchen paper. Cut the eggs in quarters and arrange them on a bed of leaves. Drizzle with the sauce and sprinkle over the shallot mixture. Garnish with coriander sprigs and serve immediately.

Cook's Tip
The level of heat varies, depending on which type of chillies are used and whether you include the seeds.

eggs in red sauce Energy 266kcal/1104kJ; Protein 15.6g; Carbohydrate 7.1g, of which sugars 6.7g; Fat 19.9g, of which saturates 4.2g; Cholesterol 387mg; Calcium 99mg; Fibre 1g; Sodium 739mg.
son-in-law eggs Energy 180kcal/752kJ; Protein 7.3g; Carbohydrate 18g, of which sugars 17.1g; Fat 9.4g, of which saturates 2g; Cholesterol 190mg; Calcium 50mg; Fibre 0.5g; Sodium 666mg.

Egg Rolls

The title of this recipe could lead to some confusion, especially in the United States, where egg rolls are the same as spring rolls. These egg rolls, however, are wedges of a rolled Thai-style flavoured omelette. They are frequently served as finger food at parties.

Serves 2

3 eggs, beaten
15ml/1 tbsp soy sauce
1 bunch garlic chives, thinly sliced
1–2 small fresh red or green chillies, seeded and finely chopped
small bunch fresh coriander (cilantro), chopped
pinch of sugar
salt and ground black pepper
15ml/1 tbsp groundnut (peanut) oil

For the dipping sauce
60ml/4 tbsp light soy sauce
fresh lime juice, to taste

1 Make the dipping sauce. Pour the soy sauce into a bowl. Add a generous squeeze of lime juice. Taste and add more lime juice if needed. Set the sauce aside.

2 Mix the eggs, soy sauce, chives, chillies and coriander. Add the sugar and season to taste. Heat the oil in a large frying pan, pour in the egg mixture and swirl the pan to cover the base and make an omelette.

3 Cook for 1–2 minutes, until the omelette is just firm and the underside is golden. Slide it out on to a plate and roll up as though it were a pancake. Leave to cool completely.

4 When the omelette is cool, slice it diagonally in 1cm/½in pieces. Arrange the slices on a serving platter and serve with the bowl of dipping sauce.

Cook's Tip
Wear gloves while preparing chillies or cut them up with a knife and fork. Wash your hands afterwards in warm, soapy water.

Rice Cakes with Coconut

These rice cakes take some time to prepare but are very easy to make.

Serves 4–6

150g/5oz/scant 1 cup jasmine rice
400ml/14fl oz/1⅔ cups boiling water

For the dip
1 garlic clove, coarsely chopped
small bunch fresh coriander (cilantro), coarsely chopped
90g/3½oz cooked prawns (shrimp), peeled and deveined
250ml/8fl oz/1 cup coconut milk
15ml/1 tbsp fish sauce
15ml/1 tbsp light soy sauce
15ml/1 tbsp tamarind juice, made by mixing tamarind pulp with warm water
5ml/1 tsp palm sugar (jaggery) or light muscovado (brown) sugar
30ml/2 tbsp roasted peanuts, coarsely chopped
1 fresh red chilli, seeded and chopped

1 Rinse the rice in a sieve (strainer) under running cold water until the water runs clear, then place the rice in a large, heavy pan and pour over the measured boiling water. Stir, bring back to the boil, then simmer, uncovered, for 15 minutes, by which time almost all the water should have been absorbed.

2 Reduce the heat to the lowest possible setting – use a heat diffuser if you have one. Cook the rice for a further 2 hours, by which time it should be crisp and stuck to the base of the pan. Continue to cook for a further 5–10 minutes, until the sides of the rice cake begin to come away from the edges of the pan.

3 Preheat the oven to 180°C/350°F/Gas 4. Remove the rice cake carefully and place it on a baking sheet. Bake the rice cake for 20 minutes, until it is crisp, then leave it to cool.

4 Meanwhile, make the dip. Place all the ingredients in a food processor and process to a smooth paste. Transfer to a wide serving bowl. Serve the rice cake with the dip. It can either be left whole for guests to break, cut into wedges or broken into pieces by the cook.

egg rolls Energy 305kcal/1269kJ; Protein 19.2g; Carbohydrate 4.9g, of which sugars 4.5g; Fat 23.6g, of which saturates 5.7g; Cholesterol 275mg; Calcium 48mg; Fibre 0.7g; Sodium 130mg.
rice cakes w. coconut Energy 152kcal/638kJ; Protein 6.2g; Carbohydrate 25.7g, of which sugars 5.3g; Fat 2.8g, of which saturates 0.5g; Cholesterol 29mg; Calcium 50mg; Fibre 0.7g; Sodium 255mg.

Rice Balls with Four Fillings

Japanese rice is ideal for making rice balls as it is easily moulded.

Serves 4
3 umeboshi, stoned (pitted)
45ml/3 tbsp sesame seeds, toasted
2.5ml/½ tsp mirin (sweet rice wine)
50g/2oz salmon fillet, skinned
50g/2oz smoked mackerel fillet
2 nori sheets, each cut into 8 strips
6 pitted black olives, chopped
fine salt
Japanese pickles, to serve

For the rice
450g/1lb/2¼ cups Japanese short grain rice, rinsed
550ml/18fl oz/2½ cups water

1 Put the rice in a heavy pan. Pour in the water and leave for 30 minutes. Cover tightly and bring to the boil, then simmer for 12 minutes. When you hear a crackling noise, remove from the heat and leave to stand, covered, for 15 minutes.

2 Toss the rice to aerate it. Leave to cool for 30 minutes.

3 Mash the umeboshi and mix to a paste with 15ml/1 tbsp of the sesame seeds and the mirin.

4 Break the salmon and mackerel into loose, chunky flakes.

5 Rinse a cup and shake off excess water. Scoop 30 ml/2 tbsp warm rice into the cup. Make a well in the centre and put in a quarter of the salmon. Cover with rice, pressing down well. Wet your hands and rub them with salt. Turn the rice in the cup out into one hand and squeeze to make a densely packed ball.

6 Wrap the rice ball with a nori strip. Make three more balls with salmon, four with mackerel and four with umeboshi paste.

7 Scoop about 45ml/3 tbsp rice into the cup. Mix in a quarter of the olives and mould into four balls. Coat with sesame seeds, but do not wrap with nori. Serve with pickles.

Dim Sum

A delicious Chinese snack, these tiny dumplings are popular in many specialist restaurants.

Serves 4
For the dough
150g/5oz/1¼ cups plain (all-purpose) flour
50ml/2fl oz/¼ cup boiling water
25ml/1½ tbsp cold water
7.5ml/1½ tsp vegetable oil

For the filling
75g/3oz minced (ground) pork
45ml/3 tbsp chopped canned bamboo shoots
7.5ml/1½ tsp light soy sauce, plus extra to serve
5ml/1 tsp dry sherry
5ml/1 tsp demerara (raw) sugar
2.5ml/½ tsp sesame oil
5ml/1 tsp cornflour (cornstarch)

To serve
mixed fresh lettuce leaves such as iceberg, frisée or Webbs
spring onion (scallion) curls
sliced red chilli
prawn (shrimp) crackers

1 To make the dough, sift the flour into a bowl. Stir in the boiling water, then the cold water together with the oil. Mix to form a ball and knead until smooth. Divide the mixture into 16 equal pieces and shape into rounds.

2 For the filling, mix together the pork, bamboo shoots, soy sauce, sherry, sugar and oil. Then stir in the cornflour.

3 Place a little of the filling in the centre of each dim sum round. Carefully pinch the edges of the dough together to form little 'purses'.

4 Line a steamer with a damp dish towel. Place the dim sum in the steamer and steam for 5–10 minutes. Serve immediately on a bed of lettuce with soy sauce, spring onion curls, sliced red chilli and prawn crackers.

Variation
As an alternative filling, substitute cooked, peeled prawns (shrimp) for the pork.

rice w. four fillings Energy 548kcal/2288kJ; Protein 15.4g; Carbohydrate 90.8g, of which sugars 1g; Fat 13g, of which saturates 2.1g; Cholesterol 19mg; Calcium 108mg; Fibre 1.3g; Sodium 243mg.
dim sum Energy 183kcal/773kJ; Protein 7.2g; Carbohydrate 31.5g, of which sugars 1.8g; Fat 3.8g, of which saturates 0.9g; Cholesterol 12mg; Calcium 55mg; Fibre 1.2g; Sodium 148mg.

Spiced Noodle Pancakes

The delicate rice noodles puff up in the hot oil to give a fabulous crunchy bite that melts in the mouth. For maximum enjoyment, serve the golden pancakes as soon as they are cooked and savour the subtle blend of spices and wonderfully crisp texture.

Serves 4

150g/5oz dried thin rice noodles
1 fresh red chilli, finely diced
10ml/2 tsp garlic salt
5ml/1 tsp ground ginger
¼ small red onion, very finely diced
5ml/1 tsp finely chopped lemon grass
5ml/1 tsp ground cumin
5ml/1 tsp ground coriander
large pinch of ground turmeric
salt
vegetable oil, for frying
sweet chilli sauce, for dipping

1 Roughly break up the noodles and place in a large bowl. Pour over enough boiling water to cover, and soak for 4–5 minutes. Drain and rinse under cold water. Dry on kitchen paper.

2 Transfer the noodles to a bowl and add the chilli, garlic salt, ground ginger, red onion, lemon grass, ground cumin, coriander and turmeric. Toss well to mix, and season with salt.

3 Heat 5–6cm/2–2½in oil in a wok. Working in batches, drop tablespoons of the noodle mixture into the oil. Flatten using the back of a skimmer and cook for 1–2 minutes on each side until crisp and golden. Lift out from the wok.

4 Drain the noodle pancakes on kitchen paper and carefully transfer to a plate or deep bowl. Serve immediately with the chilli sauce for dipping.

Cook's Tip
For deep-frying, choose very thin rice noodles. These can be cooked dry, but here are soaked and seasoned first.

Vegetable Tempura

These deep-fried fritters are based on kaki-age, a popular Japanese dish.

Serves 4

2 medium courgettes (zucchini)
½ medium aubergine (eggplant)
1 large carrot
½ small Spanish onion
vegetable oil, for deep-frying
salt and ground black pepper
sea salt flakes, lemon slices and Japanese soy sauce, to serve

For the batter

1 egg
120ml/4fl oz/½ cup iced water
115g/4oz/1 cup plain (all-purpose) flour

1 Using a vegetable peeler, pare strips of peel from the courgettes and aubergine to give a stripy effect. Cut the courgettes, aubergine and carrot into strips about 7.5–10cm/3–4in long and 3mm/⅛in wide and put them in a colander.

2 Sprinkle the vegetable strips with salt. Leave for about 30 minutes, then rinse thoroughly under cold running water. Drain.

3 Thinly slice the onion from top to base, discarding the plump pieces in the middle. Separate the layers so that there are lots of fine, long strips. Mix all the vegetables together and season to taste with salt and pepper.

4 Make the batter immediately before frying: mix the egg and iced water in a bowl, then sift in the flour. Mix very briefly with a fork or chopsticks – the batter should remain lumpy. Add the vegetables to the batter and mix to combine.

5 Half-fill a wok with oil and heat to 180°C/350°F or until a cube of day-old bread browns in 60 seconds. Scoop up one heaped tablespoon of the mixture at a time and carefully lower it into the oil to make a fritter. Deep-fry in batches for about 3 minutes until golden brown and crisp.

6 Drain the cooked fritters on kitchen paper, and serve at once, offering each diner sea salt flakes, lemon slices and a tiny bowl of Japanese soy sauce for dipping.

noodle pancakes Energy 248kcal/1031kJ; Protein 2.4g; Carbohydrate 32.7g, of which sugars 0.9g; Fat 11.5g, of which saturates 1.3g; Cholesterol 0mg; Calcium 32mg; Fibre 1.1g; Sodium 22mg.
vegetable tempura Energy 152kcal/633kJ; Protein 3.4g; Carbohydrate 14.9g, of which sugars 3.5g; Fat 9.2g, of which saturates 1.2g; Cholesterol 23mg; Calcium 45mg; Fibre 1.7g; Sodium 13mg.

Deep-fried Tofu Balls

There are many variations of these tasty tofu balls.

Makes 16

2 x 300g/11oz packets firm tofu
½ small carrot, diced
6 green beans, chopped
2 large (US extra large) eggs
30ml/2 tbsp sake
10ml/2 tsp mirin (sweet rice wine)
5ml/1 tsp salt
10ml/2 tsp soy sauce
pinch of caster (superfine) sugar
vegetable oil, for deep-frying

For the lime sauce
45ml/3 tbsp soy sauce
juice of ½ lime
5ml/1 tsp rice vinegar

To garnish
300g/11oz mooli (daikon), peeled
2 dried red chillies, halved and seeded
4 chives, finely chopped

1 Drain the tofu and wrap it in kitchen paper. Set a large plate with a weight on top and leave for 2 hours, or until it loses most of its liquid. Make the lime sauce by mixing all the ingredients in a bowl.

2 Cut the mooli for the garnish into 4cm/1½in thick slices. Make 3–4 holes in each slice with a skewer and insert chilli pieces into the holes. Leave for 15 minutes, then grate the mooli finely.

3 Boil the carrot and beans for 1 minute, then drain well.

4 In a food processor, process the tofu, eggs, sake, mirin, salt, soy sauce and sugar until smooth. Transfer to a bowl and mix in the carrot and beans. Oil your hands and shape the mixture into 16 little balls.

5 Deep-fry the tofu balls in oil until they are crisp and golden. Drain on kitchen paper.

6 Arrange the tofu balls on a serving plate and sprinkle with finely chopped chives. Put 30ml/2 tbsp grated mooli in each of four small bowls. Serve the balls with the lime sauce to be mixed with grated mooli by each guest.

Curried Sweet Potato Balls

These sweet potato balls, with roots in Chinese and South-east Asian cooking, are delicious dipped in a fiery red chilli sauce, fried black chilli sauce or hot peanut dipping sauce. Simple to make, they are ideal for serving as a nibble with a drink.

Serves 4

450g/1lb sweet potatoes or taro root, boiled or baked, and peeled
30ml/2 tbsp sugar
15ml/1 tbsp Indian curry powder or spice blend of your choice
25g/1oz fresh root ginger, peeled and grated
150g/5oz/1¼ cups glutinous rice flour or plain (all-purpose) flour
salt
sesame seeds or poppy seeds
vegetable oil, for deep-frying
dipping sauce, to serve

1 In a bowl, mash the cooked sweet potatoes or taro root. Beat in the sugar, curry powder and ginger. Add the rice flour (sift it if you are using plain flour) and salt, and work into a stiff dough – add more flour if necessary.

2 Pull off lumps of the dough and mould them into small balls – you should be able to make roughly 24 balls. Roll the balls on a bed of sesame seeds or poppy seeds until they are completely coated.

3 Heat enough oil for deep-frying in a wok. Fry the sweet potato balls in batches, until golden. Drain on kitchen paper. Serve the balls with wooden skewers to make it easier to dip them into a dipping sauce of your choice.

Variation
Also known as 'dasheen', taro root is a starchy tuber cultivated in many parts of Asia. If you opt to use it instead of the sweet potato in this recipe, you may need to add more sugar as it has a much nuttier taste when cooked.

deep-fried tofu balls Energy 40kcal/164kJ; Protein 3.9g; Carbohydrate 1.1g, of which sugars 0.9g; Fat 2.2g, of which saturates 0.4g; Cholesterol 24mg; Calcium 187mg; Fibre 0.3g; Sodium 380mg.
sweet potato balls Energy 354kcal/1495kJ; Protein 4.9g; Carbohydrate 61g, of which sugars 14.8g; Fat 11.8g, of which saturates 1.5g; Cholesterol 0mg; Calcium 84mg; Fibre 3.9g; Sodium 47mg.

Crunchy Summer Rolls

These delightful rice paper rolls filled with crunchy raw summer vegetables and fresh herbs are light and refreshing, either as a snack or an appetizer to a meal.

Serves 4

12 rice-paper roll wrappers
1 lettuce, leaves separated and ribs removed
2–3 carrots, cut into julienne strips
1 small cucumber, peeled, halved lengthways and seeded, and cut into julienne strips
3 spring onions (scallions), trimmed and cut into julienne strips
225g/8oz/1 cup beansprouts
1 bunch fresh mint leaves
1 bunch coriander (cilantro) leaves
dipping sauce, to serve

1 Pour some lukewarm water into a shallow dish. Soak the rice papers, two or three at a time, for about 5 minutes until they are pliable. Place the soaked papers on a clean dish towel and cover with a second dish towel to keep them moist.

2 Work with one paper at a time. Place a lettuce leaf towards the edge nearest to you, leaving about 2.5cm/1in to fold over. Place a mixture of the vegetables on top, followed by some mint and coriander leaves.

3 Fold the edge nearest to you over the filling, tuck in the sides, and roll tightly to the edge on the far side. Place the filled roll on a plate and cover with clear film (plastic wrap), so it doesn't dry out. Repeat with the remaining rice papers and vegetables. Serve with a dipping sauce of your choice. If you are making these summer rolls ahead of time, keep them in the refrigerator, under a damp dish towel, so that they remain moist.

Cook's Tip
Rice paper wrappers can be bought in Chinese and South-east Asian markets. You can also add pre-cooked shredded pork or prawn (shrimp) to summer rolls.

Rice Vermicelli & Salad Rolls

Here, a hearty noodle salad is wrapped in rice sheets.

Makes 8 rolls

50g/2oz rice vermicelli, soaked in warm water until soft
1 large carrot, shredded
15ml/1 tbsp sugar
15–30ml/1–2 tbsp fish sauce
8 x 20cm/8in rice-paper roll wrappers
8 large lettuce leaves
350g/12oz roast pork, sliced
115g/4oz/½ cup beansprouts
handful of mint leaves
8 cooked king prawns (jumbo shrimp), peeled, deveined and halved
½ cucumber, cut into fine strips
coriander (cilantro) leaves, to garnish

1 Drain the noodles. Cook in a pan of boiling water for about 2–3 minutes until tender. Drain, rinse under cold running water, drain well. Transfer to a bowl. Add the carrot and season with the sugar and fish sauce.

2 Assemble the rolls, one at a time. Dip a rice sheet in a bowl of warm water, then lay it flat on a surface. Place 1 lettuce leaf, 1–2 spoonfuls of the noodle mixture, a few slices of pork, some of the beansprouts and several mint leaves on the rice sheet.

3 Start rolling up the rice sheet into a cylinder. When half the sheet has been rolled up, fold both sides of the sheet towards the centre and lay two pieces of prawn along the crease.

4 Add a few of strips of cucumber and some of the coriander leaves. Continue to roll up the sheet to make a tight packet. Repeat with the remaining sheets. Garnish with the coriander.

Cook's Tip
For a spicy dip, combine some chopped garlic and chilli with 5ml/1tsp tomato purée (paste) and bring to the boil in 120ml/4fl oz/½ cup water. Stir in 15ml/1 tbsp peanut butter, 30ml/2 tbsp hoisin sauce, a pinch of sugar and the juice of a lime. Simmer for 3–4 minutes, add 50g/2oz ground peanuts, and cool.

crunchy summer rolls Energy 106kcal/445kJ; Protein 3.5g; Carbohydrate 21.2g, of which sugars 4.7g; Fat 0.7g, of which saturates 0.2g; Cholesterol 0mg; Calcium 44mg; Fibre 2.2g; Sodium 15mg.
rice vermicelli & salad Energy 202kcal/843kJ; Protein 15.4g; Carbohydrate 18.4g, of which sugars 2.7g; Fat 7.3g, of which saturates 1.6g; Cholesterol 52mg; Calcium 27mg; Fibre 1.1g; Sodium 66mg.

Tempeh Cakes with Dipping Sauce

These tasty little rissoles go very well with the light dipping sauce that accompanies them.

Makes 8

1 lemon grass stalk, outer leaves removed and inside finely chopped
2 garlic cloves, chopped
2 spring onions (scallions), finely chopped
2 shallots, finely chopped
2 fresh red chillies, seeded and finely chopped
2.5cm/1in piece fresh root ginger, finely chopped
60ml/4 tbsp chopped fresh coriander (cilantro), plus extra to garnish
250g/9oz/2¼ cups tempeh, thawed if frozen, sliced
15ml/1 tbsp fresh lime juice
5ml/1 tsp sugar
45ml/3 tbsp plain (all-purpose) flour
1 large (US extra large) egg, lightly beaten
salt and ground black pepper
vegetable oil, for frying

For the dipping sauce

45ml/3 tbsp mirin (sweet rice wine)
45ml/3 tbsp white wine vinegar
2 spring onions (scallions), thinly sliced
15ml/1 tbsp sugar
2 fresh red chillies, seeded and finely chopped
30ml/2 tbsp chopped fresh coriander (cilantro)
large pinch of salt

1 Make the dipping sauce. Mix together the mirin, vinegar, spring onions, sugar, chillies, coriander and salt in a small bowl. Cover with clear film (plastic wrap) and set aside.

2 Place the lemon grass, garlic, spring onions, shallots, chillies, ginger and coriander in a food processor or blender, then process to a coarse paste. Add the tempeh, lime juice and sugar and process until combined. Add the flour and egg, with salt and pepper to taste. Process to a coarse, sticky paste.

3 Scrape the paste into a bowl. Take one-eighth of the mixture at a time and form it into rounds with your hands.

4 Fry the tempeh cakes in a wok for 5–6 minutes, turning once, until golden. Drain, then serve with the sauce.

Fried Dried Anchovies with Peanuts

The Malays and Peranakans love fried dried anchovies. Generally, they are served as a snack with bread or as an accompaniment to coconut rice. The Malays also enjoy them with rice porridge, for breakfast.

Serves 4

4 dried red chillies, soaked in warm water until soft, seeded and chopped
4 shallots, chopped
2 garlic cloves, chopped
30ml/2 tbsp tamarind pulp, soaked in 150ml/¼ pint/⅔ cup water until soft
vegetable oil, for deep-frying
115g/4oz/1 cup peanuts
200g/7oz dried anchovies, heads removed, washed and drained
30ml/2 tbsp sugar
bread or rice, to serve

1 Using a mortar and pestle or food processor, grind the chillies, shallots and garlic to a coarse paste.

2 Squeeze the tamarind pulp to help soften it in the water and press it through a sieve (strainer). Measure out 120ml/4floz/½ cup of the tamarind water.

3 Heat enough oil for deep-frying in a wok. Lower the heat and deep-fry the peanuts in a wire basket, until they colour. Drain them well on kitchen paper. Add the anchovies to the oil and deep-fry until brown and crisp. Drain the anchovies on kitchen paper.

4 Pour out most of the oil from the wok, reserving 30ml/2 tbsp. Stir in the spice paste and fry. Add the sugar, anchovies and peanuts. Gradually stir in the tamarind water, so the mixture remains dry. Serve hot or cold with bread or rice.

Cook's Tip

Fresh chillies can be used instead of dried. Remove the skins by placing them under a hot grill (broiler) until the skins blacken and can be pulled off. Discard the seeds.

tempeh cakes w. sauce Energy 79kcal/332kJ; Protein 4.5g; Carbohydrate 9.1g, of which sugars 4.3g; Fat 2.3g, of which saturates 0.4g; Cholesterol 26mg; Calcium 192mg; Fibre 0.8g; Sodium 15mg.
anchovies w. peanuts Energy 338kcal/1400kJ; Protein 17g; Carbohydrate 4.8g, of which sugars 2.6g; Fat 28g, of which saturates 4.4g; Cholesterol 24mg; Calcium 134mg; Fibre 2g; Sodium 1475mg.

Goan Fish Cakes

Goan fish and shellfish are skilfully prepared with spices to make cakes of all shapes and sizes, whereas the rest of India makes fish kababs. Although haddock is used in this recipe, you can use other less expensive white fish, such as coley or whiting.

Makes 20

450g/1lb skinned haddock or cod
2 potatoes, peeled, boiled and coarsely mashed
4 spring onions (scallions), finely chopped
4 fresh green chillies, finely chopped
5cm/2in piece fresh root ginger, crushed
a few fresh coriander (cilantro) and mint sprigs, chopped
2 eggs
dry breadcrumbs, for coating
vegetable oil, for shallow-frying
salt and ground black pepper
lemon wedges and chilli sauce, to serve

1 Place the skinned fish in a lightly greased steamer and steam gently until cooked. Remove the steamer from the heat but leave the fish on the steaming tray until cool.

2 When the fish is cool, crumble it coarsely into a large bowl, using a fork. Mix in the mashed potatoes.

3 Add the spring onions, chillies, crushed ginger, chopped coriander and mint, and one of the eggs. Mix well and season to taste with salt and pepper.

4 Shape into cakes. Beat the remaining egg and dip the cakes in it, then coat with the breadcrumbs. Heat the oil and fry the cakes until brown on all sides. Serve as an appetizer or side dish, with the lemon wedges and chilli sauce.

Cook's Tip

For a quick version, used canned tuna in brine and omit step 1. Make sure the tuna is thoroughly drained before use.

Fish Cakes with Cucumber Relish

These wonderful small fish cakes are a popular appetizer in Thailand throughout South-east Asia.

Makes about 12

8 kaffir lime leaves
300g/11oz cod fillet, cut into chunks
30ml/2 tbsp red curry paste
1 egg
30ml/2 tbsp Thai fish sauce
5ml/1 tsp sugar
30ml/2 tbsp cornflour (cornstarch)
15ml/1 tbsp chopped fresh coriander (cilantro)
50g/2oz/½ cup green beans, thinly sliced
vegetable oil, for deep-frying

For the cucumber relish

60ml/4 tbsp coconut or rice vinegar
50g/2oz/¼ cup granulated (white) sugar
60ml/4 tbsp water
1 head pickled garlic
1cm/½in piece fresh root ginger, chopped
1 cucumber, cut into thin batons
4 shallots, thinly sliced

1 To make the cucumber relish, mix the coconut or rice vinegar, sugar and water in a pan. Heat gently, stirring constantly until the sugar has dissolved. Remove from the heat and leave to cool.

2 Place the garlic and ginger in a bowl. Add the cucumber and shallots. Mix in the vinegar and stir lightly. Cover and set aside.

3 Reserve two or three kaffir lime leaves for the garnish and thinly slice the remainder. Put the fish, curry paste and egg in a food processor and blend to a smooth paste. Transfer to a bowl and stir in the fish sauce, sugar, cornflour, sliced kaffir lime leaves, coriander and green beans. Shape the mixture into thick cakes.

4 Heat the oil in a deep-frying pan or wok to 190°C/375°F or until a cube of bread, added to the oil, browns in about 45 seconds. Fry the fish cakes, a few at a time, for 4–5 minutes, until cooked and evenly brown.

5 Lift out the fish cakes and drain them on kitchen paper. Keep each batch hot while frying successive batches. Garnish with the reserved kaffir lime leaves and serve with the cucumber relish.

Goan fish cakes Energy 80kcal/336kJ; Protein 5.5g; Carbohydrate 4.4g, of which sugars 0.3g; Fat 4.6g, of which saturates 0.6g; Cholesterol 27mg; Calcium 11mg; Fibre 0.2g; Sodium 43mg.
fish cakes w. relish Energy 54kcal/228kJ; Protein 5.4g; Carbohydrate 6.4g, of which sugars 5g; Fat 0.9g, of which saturates 0.2g; Cholesterol 27mg; Calcium 12mg; Fibre 0.2g; Sodium 22mg.

Chilli-seared Scallops on Pak Choi

Tender, succulent scallops are simply divine marinated in fresh chilli, fragrant mint and aromatic basil, then quickly seared in a piping hot wok and served on wilted greens.

Serves 4

20–24 king scallops or 24 queen scallops, cleaned
30ml/2 tbsp vegetable oil
finely grated rind and juice of 1 lemon
15ml/1 tbsp finely chopped fresh mint
15ml/1 tbsp finely chopped fresh basil
1 fresh red chilli, seeded and finely chopped
salt and ground black pepper
500g/1¼lb pak choi (bok choy)
extra chopped fresh mint and basil, to garnish (optional)

1 Place the scallops in a shallow, non-metallic bowl in a single layer. In a clean bowl, whisk together the vegetable oil, lemon rind and juice, chopped mint, basil and chilli and spoon over the scallops.

2 Season the scallops well with salt and black pepper, cover the bowl and set aside for 10 minutes to allow the flavours to blend.

3 Using a sharp knife, cut each head of pak choi lengthways into four equal-sized pieces.

4 Heat a frying pan or wok over a high heat. When the pan or wok is hot, drain the scallops (reserving the marinade) and add to the wok. Cook the scallops for 1 minute on each side, or until cooked to your liking.

5 Pour the marinade over the scallops and heat through briefly, then remove the wok from the heat and cover to keep warm.

6 Cook the pak choi for 2–3 minutes in a steamer over a pan of simmering water until the leaves are wilted.

7 Divide the greens among four warmed serving plates, then top with the reserved scallops and their juices. Add more chopped herbs as a garnish if you like, and serve immediately.

Spicy Fried Fish Cubes

Firm white fish cubes, coated in a spicy tomato mixture and deep-fried, make an excellent appetizer. They are messy for eating with the fingers, but taste so good that guests will waste no time in popping them into their mouths.

Serves 4–6

675g/1½lb cod fillet, or any other firm white fish
1 medium onion
15ml/1 tbsp lemon juice
5ml/1 tsp salt
5ml/1 tsp grated garlic
5ml/1 tsp crushed dried red chillies
7.5ml/1½ tsp garam masala
30ml/2 tbsp chopped fresh coriander (cilantro)
2 medium tomatoes
30ml/2 tbsp cornflour (cornstarch)
150ml/¼ pint/⅔ cup corn oil
apricot chutney, to serve

1 Skin the fish and remove any bones. Cut it into small cubes. Place in a bowl, cover and put in the refrigerator to chill.

2 Using a sharp knife, cut the onion into thin slices. Put in a bowl and add the lemon juice and salt.

3 Add the garlic, crushed dried red chillies, garam masala and fresh coriander. Mix well.

4 Peel the tomatoes by dropping them into boiling water for a few seconds. Remove with a slotted spoon and gently peel off the skins. Chop the tomatoes roughly and add to the onion mixture in the bowl.

5 Pour the contents of the bowl into a food processor or blender and process for about 30 seconds. Remove the fish from the refrigerator. Pour the contents of the food processor or blender over the fish and mix well.

6 Add the cornflour and mix again until the fish pieces are well coated with the onion mixture.

7 Heat the oil in a wok, karahi or deep pan. Lower the heat slightly and add the fish pieces, a few at a time. Turn them gently with a slotted spoon as they are liable to break easily. Cook for about 5 minutes until the fish is lightly browned.

8 Remove the fish pieces from the pan and drain on kitchen paper. Keep warm and continue frying the remaining fish. Serve with the apricot chutney.

Cook's Tip
Other suitable white fish includes haddock. You could even use smoked haddock (choose the natural-coloured undyed haddock for the best flavour). Monkfish is also suitable; it is a firm-fleshed fish that tastes similar to shellfish. Ask your fishmonger to remove the bone and fine membrane that covers the fish, or remove it yourself with a sharp knife. Whiting can also be used, but be careful to remove any bones.

scallops on pak choi Energy 199kcal/833kJ; Protein 26.7g; Carbohydrate 5.4g, of which sugars 1.9g; Fat 7.9g, of which saturates 1.2g; Cholesterol 47mg; Calcium 242mg; Fibre 2.6g; Sodium 355mg.
spicy fried fish cubes Energy 225kcal/936kJ; Protein 21.1g; Carbohydrate 4g, of which sugars 0.6g; Fat 14g, of which saturates 2g; Cholesterol 52mg; Calcium 18mg; Fibre 0.2g; Sodium 70mg.

Prawn & Vegetable Kebabs

This light and refreshing dish, with its delicate tang of coriander and lemon juice, looks great on a bed of lettuce leaves, and makes a perfect appetizer at a summer barbecue. To upgrade the recipe to a light lunch dish simply add some naan, and follow with a fresh mango sorbet.

Serves 4

30ml/2 tbsp chopped fresh coriander (cilantro)
5ml/1 tsp salt
2 fresh green chillies
45ml/3 tbsp lemon juice
30ml/2 tbsp oil
20 cooked king prawns (jumbo shrimp), peeled
1 medium courgette (zucchini), thickly sliced
1 medium onion, cut into 8 chunks
8 cherry tomatoes
8 baby corn cobs
mixed salad leaves, to serve

1 Place the chopped coriander, salt, green chillies, lemon juice and oil in a food processor or blender and process for a few seconds to form a paste.

2 Scrape the spice paste from the food processor and transfer it to a medium mixing bowl.

3 Devein the peeled prawns (see Cook's Tip below right), add to the spices and stir to coat well. Cover the bowl and set aside for the prawns to marinate for about 30 minutes.

4 Preheat the grill (broiler) to very hot. Arrange the vegetables and prawns alternately on four skewers.

5 Reduce the temperature of the grill to medium, and grill (broil) the prawn kebabs for 5–7 minutes until cooked and browned, turning once.

6 Serve the prawn and vegetable kebabs immediately on a bed of mixed salad leaves.

Glazed Garlic Prawns

It is best to peel the prawns for this dish as it helps them to absorb maximum flavour. Serve with salad as a first course or with rice and accompaniments for a more substantial meal.

Serves 4

15ml/1 tbsp oil
3 garlic cloves, roughly chopped
15–20 cooked king prawns (jumbo shrimp)
3 tomatoes, chopped
2.5ml/½ tsp salt
5ml/1 tsp crushed dried red chillies
5ml/1 tsp lemon juice
15ml/1 tbsp mango chutney
1 fresh green chilli, chopped
fresh coriander (cilantro) sprigs, to garnish

1 Heat the oil in a medium, heavy pan. Add the garlic and cook gently for a few minutes.

2 Set aside four whole prawns for the garnish. Peel the remainder and remove the black vein (see Cook's Tip below).

3 Lower the heat and add the chopped tomatoes to the pan with the salt, crushed red chillies, lemon juice, mango chutney and fresh green chilli. Stir gently to mix and cook for 2–3 minutes.

4 Add the peeled prawns, increase the heat and stir-fry until heated through. Transfer the prawns to a serving dish.

5 Serve garnished with fresh coriander sprigs. Add a whole cooked prawn, in the shell, to each portion.

Cook's Tip

Larger prawns have a black intestinal vein that runs down the back of the prawn. As this can affect the taste and appearance of the dish it is best to remove it. It is easily picked out using a skewer or the point of a knife.

prawn kebabs Energy 136kcal/566kJ; Protein 10.5g; Carbohydrate 3.4g, of which sugars 3g; Fat 9g, of which saturates 1.1g; Cholesterol 98mg; Calcium 83mg; Fibre 1.6g; Sodium 103mg.
glazed garlic prawns Energy 105kcal/440kJ; Protein 13.8g; Carbohydrate 4.9g, of which sugars 4.9g; Fat 3.4g, of which saturates 0.4g; Cholesterol 146mg; Calcium 66mg; Fibre 0.8g; Sodium 650mg.

Prawn & Sesame Toasts

These attractive little toast triangles are ideal for serving with pre-dinner drinks and are always a favourite hot snack at parties. They are surprisingly easy to prepare and you can cook them in just a few minutes.

Serves 4

225g/8oz peeled raw prawns (shrimp)
15ml/1 tbsp sherry
15ml/1 tbsp soy sauce
30ml/2 tbsp cornflour (cornstarch)
2 egg whites
4 slices white bread
115g/4oz/½ cup sesame seeds
oil, for deep-frying
sweet chilli sauce, to serve

1 Process the prawns, sherry, soy sauce and cornflour in a food processor.

2 In a grease-free bowl, whisk the egg whites until stiff. Fold them into the prawn and cornflour mixture.

3 Cut each slice of bread into four triangular quarters. Spread out the sesame seeds on a large plate. Spread the prawn paste over one side of each bread triangle, then press the coated sides into the sesame seeds so that they stick and cover the prawn paste.

4 Heat the oil in a karahi, wok or deep-fryer to a temperature of 190°C/375°F, or until a cube of bread dropped in the oil browns in about 45 seconds. Add the coated toasts, a few at a time, prawn side down, and deep-fry for 2–3 minutes, then turn and fry on the other side until golden.

5 Drain on kitchen paper and serve the toasts hot with sweet chilli sauce.

Cook's Tip

Make the prawn mixture and chill until ready to cook if you are making these toasts for a party.

Prawn & Spinach Pancakes

Serve these delicious filled pancakes hot. They can be eaten in the hand, but are rather messy, so do provide plenty of paper napkins if you choose the casual approach. Try to use red onions for this recipe if you can, although they are not essential.

Makes 4–6 pancakes

175g/6oz/1½ cups plain (all-purpose) flour
2.5ml/½ tsp salt
3 eggs
350ml/12fl oz/1½ cups semi-skimmed (low-fat) milk
15g/½oz/1 tbsp low-fat spread
1 tomato, quartered, fresh coriander (cilantro) sprigs and lemon wedges, to garnish

For the filling

30ml/2 tbsp oil
2 medium red onions, sliced
2.5ml/½ tsp crushed garlic
2.5cm/1in piece fresh root ginger, shredded
5ml/1 tsp chilli powder
5ml/1 tsp garam masala
5ml/1 tsp salt
2 tomatoes, sliced
225g/8oz frozen leaf spinach, thawed and drained
115g/4oz/1 cup frozen cooked peeled prawns (shrimp), thawed
30ml/2 tbsp chopped fresh coriander

1 To make the pancakes, sift the flour and salt together. Beat the eggs and add to the flour, beating constantly. Gradually stir in the milk. Leave the batter to stand for 1 hour.

2 Make the filling. Heat the oil in a deep frying pan and fry the sliced onions until golden.

3 Gradually add the crushed garlic, ginger, chilli powder, garam masala and salt, followed by the sliced tomatoes and spinach, stirring constantly.

4 Add the prawns and chopped coriander. Cook for a further 5–7 minutes or until any excess liquid has been absorbed. Keep warm.

5 Heat about 2.5ml/½ tsp of the low-fat spread in a 25cm/10in non-stick frying pan. Pour in about one-quarter of the pancake batter, tilting the pan so that the batter spreads well, coats the bottom of the pan and is evenly distributed.

6 When fine bubbles begin to appear on the surface, flip the pancake over using a spatula and cook for a further minute or so. Transfer to a plate and keep warm. Cook the remaining pancakes in the same way.

7 Fill the pancakes with the spinach and prawns. Serve warm, garnished with the tomato, coriander sprigs and lemon wedges.

Cook's Tip

To keep the pancakes warm while cooking the remainder, pile them on top of each other on a plate with a sheet of baking parchment between them to prevent them sticking. Place in a low oven.

prawn toasts Energy 207kcal/864kJ; Protein 8.6g; Carbohydrate 17.4g, of which sugars 1g; Fat 11.9g, of which saturates 1.5g; Cholesterol 57mg; Calcium 98mg; Fibre 1g; Sodium 427mg.
prawn pancakes Energy 268kcal/1127kJ; Protein 14g; Carbohydrate 33g, of which sugars 8.1g; Fat 10g, of which saturates 2.4g; Cholesterol 136mg; Calcium 229mg; Fibre 2.9g; Sodium 174mg.

Prawns with Pomegranate Seeds

This pretty dish makes an impressive appetizer, and is delicious served with a mixed salad. Exotic flavourings of garlic, ginger, pomegranate and coriander make the butterflied prawns extra special.

Serves 4
5ml/1 tsp crushed garlic
5ml/1 tsp grated fresh root ginger
5ml/1 tsp coarsely ground pomegranate seeds
5ml/1 tsp ground coriander
5ml/1 tsp salt
5ml/1 tsp chilli powder
30ml/2 tbsp tomato purée (paste)
60ml/4 tbsp water
45ml/3 tbsp chopped fresh coriander (cilantro)
30ml/2 tbsp corn oil
12 large cooked prawns (shrimp)
1 medium onion, sliced into rings

1 Put the garlic, ginger, pomegranate seeds, ground coriander, salt, chilli powder, tomato purée and water in a bowl. Stir in 30ml/2 tbsp of the chopped coriander. Add the oil and mix well.

2 Peel the prawns, rinse them gently and pat them dry on kitchen paper. Using a sharp knife, make a small slit at the back of each prawn and remove the black vein. Open out each prawn to make a butterfly shape.

3 Add the prawns to the spice mixture, making sure they are all well coated. Leave to marinate for about 2 hours.

4 Meanwhile, cut four squares of foil, about 20 x 20cm/8 x 8in. Preheat the oven to 230°C/450°F/Gas 8. When the prawns are ready, place three prawns and a few onion rings on to each square of foil, garnishing each with a little fresh coriander, and fold up into little packets.

5 Bake the prawns for 12–15 minutes. Put the foil packets on individual serving plates and open them up at the table so that the delicious fragrance from the prawns is sealed until the last minute.

Grilled Prawns

Prawns taste delicious when grilled, especially if they are first flavoured with spices.

Serves 4–6
18 large cooked prawns (shrimp)
60ml/4 tbsp lemon juice
5ml/1 tsp salt
5ml/1 tsp chilli powder
5ml/1 tsp crushed garlic
7.5ml/1½ tsp soft light brown sugar
45ml/3 tbsp corn oil, plus extra for basting
30ml/2 tbsp chopped fresh coriander (cilantro)
1 fresh green chilli, sliced
1 tomato, sliced
1 small onion, cut into rings
lemon wedges, to garnish

1 Peel the large cooked prawns and rinse them gently under cold running water. Pat dry. Make a slit at the back of each prawn and remove the black vein. Open each prawn out into a butterfly shape.

2 Mix the lemon juice with the salt, chilli powder, crushed garlic and light brown sugar in a bowl. Add the corn oil and chopped coriander, and mix well. Stir in the prawns and leave to marinate for 1 hour.

3 Preheat the grill (broiler) to the maximum setting. Place the green chilli, tomato slices and onion rings in a flameproof dish. Add the prawn mixture.

4 Grill (broil) for 10–15 minutes, basting several times with a brush dipped in oil. Serve immediately, garnished with the lemon wedges.

Cook's Tip
Although the recipe requires the prawns to be peeled, always buy prawns with their shells on and peel them yourself, as the flavour will be much better than that of prawns bought ready-peeled.

prawns w. pomegranate Energy 130kcal/544kJ; Protein 14.5g; Carbohydrate 3.3g, of which sugars 1.1g; Fat 6.8g, of which saturates 0.8g; Cholesterol 146mg; Calcium 73mg; Fibre 0.2g; Sodium 163mg.
grilled prawns Energy 141kcal/593kJ; Protein 13.4g; Carbohydrate 9g, of which sugars 8.7g; Fat 6g, of which saturates 0.7g; Cholesterol 146mg; Calcium 67mg; Fibre 0.2g; Sodium 143mg.

Quick-fried Prawns with Spices

These spicy prawns are stir-fried in moments to make a wonderful appetizer. This is fabulous finger food, so be sure to provide your guests with finger bowls.

Serves 4

450g/1lb large raw prawns (shrimp)
2.5cm/1in fresh root ginger, grated
2 garlic cloves, crushed
5ml/1 tsp hot chilli powder
5ml/1 tsp ground turmeric
10ml/2 tsp black mustard seeds
seeds from 4 green cardamom pods, crushed
50g/2oz/¼ cup ghee or butter
120ml/4fl oz/½ cup coconut milk
salt and ground black pepper
30–45ml/2–3 tbsp chopped fresh coriander (cilantro), to garnish
naan bread, to serve

1 Peel the prawns carefully, leaving the tails attached.

2 Using a small, sharp knife, make a slit along the back of each prawn and remove the dark vein. Rinse under cold running water, drain and pat dry.

3 Put the ginger, garlic, chilli powder, turmeric, mustard seeds and cardamom seeds in a bowl. Add the prawns and toss to coat completely in the spice mixture.

4 Heat a karahi or wok until hot. Add the ghee or butter and swirl it around until foaming.

5 Add the spiced prawns and stir-fry for 1–1½ minutes until they are just turning pink.

6 Stir in the coconut milk and simmer for 3–4 minutes until the prawns are just cooked through. Season to taste with salt and black pepper.

7 Sprinkle with the chopped fresh coriander and serve immediately, with naan bread.

Goan-style Mussels

Mussels make a marvellous appetizer. Serve them Goan-style, in a fragrant coconut sauce. They take only minutes to cook, and the wonderful aroma will stimulate even the most jaded appetite.

Serves 4

900g/2lb live mussels
115g/4oz creamed coconut (120ml/4fl oz/½ cup coconut cream)
450ml/¾ pint/scant 2 cups boiling water
45ml/3 tbsp oil
1 onion, finely chopped
3 garlic cloves, crushed
2.5cm/1in piece fresh root ginger, peeled and finely chopped
2.5ml/½ tsp ground turmeric
5ml/1 tsp ground cumin
5ml/1 tsp ground coriander
1.5ml/¼ tsp salt
chopped fresh coriander (cilantro), to garnish

1 Scrub the mussels under cold water and pull off any beards that remain attached to the shells. Discard any mussels that are open and which fail to snap shut when tapped.

2 Put the creamed coconut in a measuring jug or cup and pour in the boiling water. Stir with a wooden spoon until all the coconut has dissolved, then set aside until required. Heat the oil in a karahi, wok or heavy pan. Add the onion and fry for 5 minutes, stirring frequently.

3 Add the garlic and ginger and fry for 2 minutes. Stir in the turmeric, cumin, coriander and salt and fry for 2 minutes. Pour in the coconut liquid, stir well and bring to the boil. Reduce the heat and simmer for 5 minutes.

4 Add the mussels, cover the pan and cook over medium heat for 6–8 minutes, by which time all the mussels should have opened. Spoon the mussels on to a serving platter. If any of the mussels have failed to open, discard them immediately.

5 Pour the sauce over the mussels, garnish with the chopped fresh coriander, and serve.

quick-fried prawns Energy 388kcal/1618kJ; Protein 40.7g; Carbohydrate 5.1g, of which sugars 3.1g; Fat 22.9g, of which saturates 13.4g; Cholesterol 492mg; Calcium 248mg; Fibre 1.7g; Sodium 679mg.
Goan-style mussels Energy 339kcal/1405kJ; Protein 13.9g; Carbohydrate 5g, of which sugars 4.1g; Fat 29.5g, of which saturates 18.3g; Cholesterol 27mg; Calcium 149mg; Fibre 0.5g; Sodium 152mg.

Chilli Crabs

The essential ingredients of this delicious crab dish owe more to South-east Asian cuisine than India, and it is not surprising to discover that it comes from the eastern part of the country.

Serves 4

2 cooked crabs, about 675g/1½lb altogether
1cm/½in cube shrimp paste
2 garlic cloves
2 fresh red chillies, seeded, or 5ml/1 tsp chopped chilli from a jar
1cm/½in fresh root ginger, peeled and sliced
60ml/4 tbsp sunflower oil
300ml/½ pint/1¼ cups tomato ketchup
15ml/1 tbsp soft dark brown sugar
150ml/¼ pint/⅔ cup warm water
4 spring onions (scallions), chopped, to garnish
cucumber chunks and hot toast, to serve (optional)

1 Remove the large claws of one crab and turn it on to its back, with the head facing away from you. Use your thumbs to push the body up from the main shell. Discard the stomach sac and 'dead men's fingers', that is, lungs and any green matter. Leave the creamy brown meat in the shell, and cut the shell in half with a cleaver or strong knife. Cut the body section in half and crack the claws with a sharp blow from a hammer or cleaver. Avoid splintering the claws. Repeat with the other crab.

2 Grind the shrimp paste, garlic, chillies and ginger to a paste in a food processor or with a pestle and mortar.

3 Heat a karahi or wok and add the oil. Fry the spice paste, stirring constantly, without browning it, until fragrant. Stir in the tomato ketchup, sugar and water and mix the sauce well. When just boiling, add all the crab pieces and toss in the sauce until well coated and hot.

4 Serve the crab in a large bowl, sprinkled with the chopped spring onions. Place in the centre of the table for everyone to help themselves. Accompany this dish with cool cucumber chunks and hot toast for mopping up the sauce, if you like.

Spicy Crab with Coconut

This simple appetizer looks pretty and tastes absolutely delicious. Have all the ingredients ready and cook it just before calling your guests to the table. It needs no accompaniment other than some warmed plain naan bread.

Serves 4

40g/1½oz/½ cup desiccated (dry unsweetened shredded) coconut
2 garlic cloves
5cm/2in piece fresh root ginger, grated
2.5ml/½ tsp cumin seeds
1 small cinnamon stick
2.5ml/½ tsp ground turmeric
2 dried red chillies
15ml/1 tbsp coriander seeds
2.5ml/½ tsp poppy seeds
15ml/1 tbsp vegetable oil
1 medium onion, sliced
1 small green (bell) pepper, seeded and cut into strips
16 crab claws
fresh coriander (cilantro) sprigs, to garnish
150ml/¼ pint/⅔ cup natural (plain) low-fat yogurt, to serve

1 Put the desiccated coconut in a food processor and add the garlic, ginger, cumin seeds, cinnamon stick, turmeric, red chillies, coriander and poppy seeds. Process until well blended.

2 Heat the oil in a karahi, wok or heavy pan. Add the onion slices and fry over a medium heat for 2–3 minutes, until softened but not coloured.

3 Stir in the green pepper strips and toss over the heat for 1 minute. Using a slotted spoon, remove the vegetables from the pan and place them in a bowl.

4 Place the pan over a high heat. When it is hot, add the crab claws and stir-fry for 2 minutes. Return the vegetables to the pan with the coconut mixture. Toss over the heat until the mixture is fragrant and the crab claws and vegetables are coated in the spices. Serve on individual plates, garnished with the coriander. Offer the yogurt separately.

chilli crabs Energy 232kcal/971kJ; Protein 8.5g; Carbohydrate 21.8g, of which sugars 21g; Fat 12.9g, of which saturates 1.5g; Cholesterol 19mg; Calcium 28mg; Fibre 0.8g; Sodium 1347mg.
crab w. coconut Energy 186kcal/777kJ; Protein 19.5g; Carbohydrate 4.8g, of which sugars 3.8g; Fat 10.1g, of which saturates 5.8g; Cholesterol 72mg; Calcium 135mg; Fibre 2.6g; Sodium 556mg.

Crisp-fried Crab Claws

Crab claws are readily available from the freezer cabinet in many Asian stores and supermarkets. Thaw them thoroughly and dry on kitchen paper before coating them.

Serves 4

50g/2oz/⅓ cup rice flour
15ml/1 tbsp cornflour (cornstarch)
2.5ml/½ tsp sugar
1 egg
60ml/4 tbsp cold water
1 lemon grass stalk, root trimmed
2 garlic cloves, finely chopped
15ml/1 tbsp chopped fresh coriander (cilantro)
1–2 fresh red chillies, seeded and finely chopped
5ml/1 tsp Thai fish sauce
vegetable oil, for deep-frying
12 half-shelled crab claws, thawed if frozen
ground black pepper

For the chilli vinegar dip

45ml/3 tbsp sugar
120ml/4fl oz/½ cup water
120ml/4fl oz/½ cup red wine vinegar
15ml/1 tbsp Thai fish sauce
2–4 fresh red chillies, seeded and chopped

1 First make the chilli vinegar dip. Mix the sugar and water in a pan. Heat gently, stirring until the sugar has dissolved, then bring to the boil. Lower the heat and simmer for 5–7 minutes. Stir in the rest of the ingredients, pour into a serving bowl and set aside until ready to serve.

2 Combine the rice flour, cornflour and sugar together in a large mixing bowl. Beat the egg with the cold water, then stir the egg and water mixture into the flour mixture and beat well until it forms a light batter.

3 Cut off the lower 5cm/2in of the lemon grass stalk and chop it finely. Add the lemon grass to the batter, with the garlic, coriander, red chillies and fish sauce. Stir in pepper to taste.

4 Heat the oil in a deep-fryer or wok to 190°C/375°F or until a cube of bread browns in 45 seconds. Dip the crab claws into the batter, then fry, in batches, until golden. Serve with the dip.

Prawn Crackers

These are a popular addition to many Chinese and other Far Eastern meals and are often served before guests come to the table.

Serves 4–6

300ml/½ pint/1¼ cups vegetable oil
50g/2oz uncooked prawn crackers
table salt or a peanut dip to serve

1 Line a tray with kitchen paper. This will be used to blot the oil from the fried crackers.

2 Heat the oil in a large wok until it begins to smoke. Reduce the heat to maintain a steady temperature. Drop three or four prawn crackers into the oil.

3 After the crackers swell up, remove them from the oil with a slotted spoon. They will have cooked in seconds – do not leave them in the oil until they colour and become too crunchy. Transfer to the paper-lined tray to drain.

4 Repeat this process of cooking in batches, keeping an eye on the temperature of the fat – do not let it get so hot that it burns the crackers.

5 Serve sprinkled with salt or with a little pot of peanut dip.

Wonton Flowers with Sweet & Sour Sauce

These melt-in-the-mouth, crisp flowers make a delicious first course or snack – and take hardly any time at all to prepare.

Serves 4–6

16–20 wonton wrappers
vegetable oil, for deep-frying

For the sauce

15ml/1 tbsp vegetable oil
30ml/2 tbsp light brown sugar
45ml/3 tbsp rice vinegar
15ml/1 tbsp light soy sauce
15ml/1 tbsp tomato ketchup
45–60ml/3–4 tbsp stock or water
15ml/1 tbsp cornflour (cornstarch) mixed to a paste with a little water

1 Pinch the centre of each wonton wrapper and twist it around to form a floral shape.

2 Heat the oil in a wok and deep-fry the floral wontons for 1–2 minutes, until crisp. Remove and drain on kitchen paper.

3 To make the sauce, heat the oil in a wok or frying pan and add the sugar, vinegar, soy sauce, tomato ketchup and stock or water.

4 Stir in the cornflour paste to thicken the sauce. Continue stirring until smooth. Pour a little sauce over the wontons and serve immediately with the remaining sauce.

fried crab claws Energy 222kcal/926kJ; Protein 10.1g; Carbohydrate 16.9g, of which sugars 0g; Fat 12.8g, of which saturates 1.7g; Cholesterol 78mg; Calcium 62mg; Fibre 0.3g; Sodium 256mg.
prawn crackers Energy 143kcal/595kJ; Protein 0.1g; Carbohydrate 14.6g, of which sugars 0.6g; Fat 9.8g, of which saturates 0.9g; Cholesterol 0mg; Calcium 5mg; Fibre 0.3g; Sodium 192mg.
wonton flowers Energy 196kcal/817kJ; Protein 1.9g; Carbohydrate 19g, of which sugars 6.1g; Fat 13g, of which saturates 1.4g; Cholesterol 0mg; Calcium 27mg; Fibre 0.5g; Sodium 172mg.

Hot Chilli Prawns

These can be prepared up to eight hours in advance and are delicious either grilled or cooked on a barbecue.

Serves 4–6

I garlic clove, crushed
Icm/½in piece fresh root ginger, finely chopped
I small fresh red chilli, seeded and chopped
I0ml/2 tsp sugar
I5ml/I tbsp light soy sauce
I5ml/I tbsp vegetable oil
5ml/I tsp sesame oil
juice of I lime
675g/I½lb raw prawns (shrimp)
I75g/6oz cherry tomatoes
½ cucumber, cut into chunks
salt
I small bunch coriander (cilantro), roughly chopped, to garnish
lettuce leaves, to serve

I Pound the garlic, ginger, chilli and sugar to a paste in a mortar with a pestle.

2 Add the soy sauce, vegetable and sesame oils, lime juice and salt to taste. Place the prawns in a shallow dish and pour over the marinade. Set aside to marinate for up to 8 hours.

3 Soak some bamboo skewersfor about I hour.

4 Thread the marinated prawns, tomatoes and cucumber chunks alternately on to bamboo skewers

5 Cook under a preheated grill (broiler) or on a barbecue rack for 3–4 minutes. Transfer to a serving dish lined with a bed of lettuce and scatter over the coriander.

Variations

- *For a sweeter version replace the cucumber with small cubes of pineapple.*
- *Add chopped lemon grass to the marinade to get a really zesty, fresh flavour.*

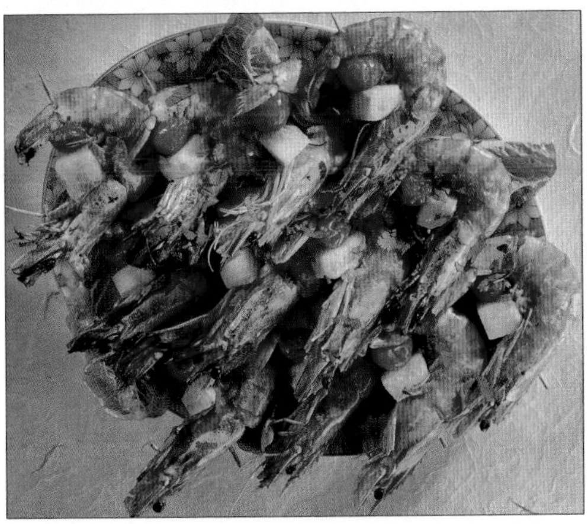

Stuffed Chillies

With less than 3 grams of total fat, this is a good choice for a healthy first course or for serving with drinks. It isn't too hot – unless you've chosen especially fiery chillies.

Serves 4

I0 fat fresh green chillies
II5g/4oz lean pork, chopped
75g/3oz raw tiger prawns (jumbo shrimp), peeled and deveined
I5g/½oz/½ cup fresh coriander (cilantro) leaves
5ml/I tsp cornflour (cornstarch)
I0ml/2 tsp sake or dry sherry
I0ml/2 tsp soy sauce
5ml/I tsp sesame oil
2.5ml/½ tsp salt
I5ml/I tbsp cold water
I fresh red and I fresh green chilli, seeded and sliced into rings, and cooked peas, to garnish

I Cut all the chillies in half lengthways, keeping the stalks intact. Scrape out and discard the seeds and set the chillies aside.

2 Mix the chopped pork, prawns and coriander leaves in a food processor. Process until smooth. Scrape into a bowl and mix in the cornflour, sake or sherry, soy sauce, sesame oil, salt and water. Cover the bowl and leave to marinate for I0 minutes.

3 Fill each half chilli with some of the meat mixture. Have ready a steamer or a heatproof plate and a pan with about 5cm/2in boiling water in the bottom.

4 Place the stuffed chillies in the steamer or on a plate, meat side up, and cover them with a lid or foil.

5 Steam for I5 minutes or until the meat filling is cooked. Serve immediately, garnished with the chilli rings and peas.

Cook's Tip
If you prefer a slightly hotter taste, leave the seeds in some of the chillies.

hot chilli prawns Energy I2Ikcal/5I0kJ; Protein 20.4g; Carbohydrate 3.Ig, of which sugars 2.9g; Fat 3.Ig, of which saturates 0.4g; Cholesterol 2I9mg; Calcium 95mg; Fibre 0.4g; Sodium 360mg.
stuffed chillies Energy 74kcal/309kJ; Protein 9.9g; Carbohydrate 3.Ig, of which sugars I.8g; Fat 2.2g, of which saturates 0.6g; Cholesterol 55mg; Calcium 27mg; Fibre 0.6g; Sodium 237mg.

Oyster Omelette

Often devoured as a late-night treat, oyster omelette is a favourite hawker stall snack in the streets of Singapore. Almost decadent in its rich use of oysters, this is a tasty and satisfying dish, inspired by the Chinese.

Serves 2

30ml/2 tbsp vegetable oil
2 garlic cloves, finely chopped
1 fresh red or green chilli, finely chopped
8 large fresh oysters, shelled and rinsed
15ml/1 tbsp light soy sauce
15ml/1 tbsp Chinese rice wine
4 eggs, lightly beaten with 30ml/2 tbsp milk
8 small fresh oysters, shelled and rinsed
chilli oil, for drizzling
salt and ground black pepper
fresh coriander (cilantro) leaves, finely chopped, to garnish

1 Heat the oil in a heavy frying pan. Stir in the garlic and chilli until they become fragrant.

2 Add the large oysters and cook for 1 minute, then stir in the soy sauce and rice wine. Season to taste with salt and black pepper.

3 Pour in the beaten egg mixture and, using a wooden spatula, pull it back from the edge of the pan until it begins to set.

4 Reduce the heat. Sprinkle the small oysters over the top of the egg and drizzle with chilli oil. Cover the pan and leave to steam for 5–10 minutes until firm.

5 Sprinkle the omelette with chopped coriander, cut it into wedges and serve it from the pan.

Variation
Clams can be used instead of oysters. Remove them from their shells and rinse them before adding them to the omelette.

Steamed Eggs with Shrimp Paste

Throughout China, and elsewhere in Asia, variations on this type of steamed omelette are cooked as a snack and may be eaten at any time of the day. As a finishing touch, cut the omelette into strips and splash it with chilli oil. Alternatively, serve it with a spicy dipping sauce.

Serves 2–4

5 eggs
115g/4oz small, fresh prawns (shrimp), shelled and deveined
a handful of beansprouts
2 spring onions (scallions), trimmed and finely sliced
10ml/2 tsp shrimp paste
1 bunch coriander (cilantro), chopped
15ml/1 tbsp vegetable oil
chilli oil, for drizzling
sea salt and ground black pepper
fresh coriander (cilantro) leaves, to garnish
dipping sauce, to serve

1 Beat the eggs in a bowl. Stir in the shelled and deveined prawns, beansprouts, trimmed and sliced spring onions, shrimp paste and chopped coriander. Season well.

2 Fill a pan one-third full with water and bring to the boil. Lightly oil a shallow, heatproof dish and place on top of the pan. Pour in the egg mixture and steam for 5–10 minutes, until the eggs are firm.

3 Cut the steamed omelette into strips and place these on a plate. Drizzle a little chilli oil over the strips and garnish with coriander leaves.

4 Serve the omelette strips with a dipping sauce, preferably one that is chilli-based or has a pungent flavour. Shrimp sauce or chilli sauce are good options.

Variation
If you prefer not to steam the omelette, fry it in a non-stick pan.

oyster omelette Energy 370kcal/1543kJ; Protein 32.2g; Carbohydrate 6.1g, of which sugars 1.3g; Fat 24.6g, of which saturates 4.9g; Cholesterol 481mg; Calcium 322mg; Fibre 0g; Sodium 1573mg.
eggs w. shrimp paste Energy 146kcal/606kJ; Protein 13.5g; Carbohydrate 0.9g, of which sugars 0.6g; Fat 10g, of which saturates 2.3g; Cholesterol 294mg; Calcium 64mg; Fibre 0.4g; Sodium 144mg.

Parchment-wrapped Prawns

These succulent pink prawns coated in a fragrant spice paste make the perfect dish for informal entertaining. Serve the prawns in their paper parcels and allow your guests to unwrap them at the table and enjoy the aroma of exotic spices as the parcel is opened, and the contents are revealed.

Serves 4

2 lemon grass stalks, very finely chopped
5ml/1 tsp very finely chopped galangal
4 garlic cloves, finely chopped
finely grated rind and juice of 1 lime
4 spring onions (scallions), chopped
10ml/2 tsp palm sugar (jaggery)
15ml/1 tbsp soy sauce
5ml/1 tsp fish sauce
5ml/1 tsp chilli oil
45ml/3 tbsp chopped fresh coriander (cilantro) leaves
30ml/2 tbsp chopped fresh Thai basil leaves
1kg/2¼lb raw tiger prawns (jumbo shrimp), heads and shells removed; tails left on
basil leaves and lime wedges, to garnish

1 Place the lemon grass, galangal, garlic, lime rind and juice and spring onions in a food processor or blender. Blend in short bursts until the mixture forms a coarse paste.

2 Transfer the paste to a large bowl and stir in the palm sugar, soy sauce, fish sauce, chilli oil and chopped herbs. Add the prawns to the paste and toss to coat evenly. Cover and marinate in the refrigerator for 30–60 minutes.

3 Cut out eight 20cm/8in squares of baking parchment. Place one-eighth of the prawn mixture in the centre of each parchment square, then fold over the edges and twist together to make a neat sealed parcel.

4 Place the parcels in a large bamboo steamer, cover and steam over a wok of simmering water for 10 minutes, or until the prawns are just cooked through. Serve immediately, garnished with basil leaves and lime wedges.

Grilled Prawns with Lemon Grass

In every market in Vietnam and Cambodia, there is bound to be someone cooking up citrus-scented snacks. The fragrant scent of lemon grass is hard to resist, but check what's cooking first, because the Vietnamese also like to cook frogs' legs and snails this way. The use of aromatic lemon grass for grilling, stir-frying or steaming shellfish is one of the classic features of Indo-Chinese cooking.

Serves 4

16 raw king prawns (jumbo shrimp), cleaned, with shells intact
120ml/4fl oz/½ cup fish sauce
30ml/2 tbsp sugar
15ml/1 tbsp vegetable or sesame oil
3 lemon grass stalks, trimmed and finely chopped

1 Using a small sharp knife, carefully slice open each king prawn shell along the back and pull out the black vein, using the point of the knife. Try to keep the rest of the shell intact. Place the deveined prawns in a shallow dish and set aside.

2 Put the fish sauce in a small bowl with the sugar, and beat together until the sugar has dissolved completely. Add the oil and lemon grass and mix well.

3 Pour the marinade over the prawns, using your fingers to rub it all over the prawns and inside the shells too. Cover the dish with clear film (plastic wrap) and chill for at least 4 hours.

4 Cook the prawns on a barbecue or under a conventional grill (broiler) for 2–3 minutes each side. Serve with little bowls of water for rinsing sticky fingers.

Cook's Tip

Big, juicy king prawns (jumbo shrimp) are best for this recipe, but smaller ones work equally well if king prawns are not available in your local shops.

wrapped prawns Energy 169kcal/713kJ; Protein 35.4g; Carbohydrate 2.4g, of which sugars 2.4g; Fat 2g, of which saturates 0.3g; Cholesterol 390mg; Calcium 163mg; Fibre 0.2g; Sodium 381mg.
prawns w. lemongrass Energy 97kcal/409kJ; Protein 9.2g; Carbohydrate 8.8g, of which sugars 8.7g; Fat 3.1g, of which saturates 0.4g; Cholesterol 98mg; Calcium 46mg; Fibre 0g; Sodium 897mg.

Grilled Stingray Wings with Chilli

Chargrilled stingray is a very popular street snack in Singapore. The grill stalls selling grilled chicken wings and satay often serve grilled stingray wings on a banana leaf with a generous dollop of chilli sambal. The cooked fish is eaten with fingers, or chopsticks, by tearing off pieces and dipping them in the sambal. If you can't find stingray wings, you could substitute a flat fish, such as plaice or flounder.

Serves 4

4 medium-sized stingray wings, about 200g/7oz, rinsed and patted dry
salt
4 banana leaves, about 30cm/12in square
2 fresh limes, halved

For the chilli sambal

6–8 fresh red chillies, seeded and chopped
4 garlic cloves, chopped
5ml/1 tsp shrimp paste
15ml/1 tbsp tomato purée (paste)
15ml/1 tbsp palm sugar (jaggery)
juice of 2 limes
30ml/2 tbsp vegetable or groundnut (peanut) oil

1 First make the chilli sambal. Using a mortar and pestle or food processor, grind the chillies with the garlic to form a paste. Beat in the shrimp paste, tomato purée and sugar. Add the lime juice and bind with the oil.

2 Prepare a charcoal grill. Rub each stingray wing with a little of the chilli sambal and place them on the rack. Cook for about 3–4 minutes on each side, until tender. Sprinkle with salt and serve on banana leaves with the remaining chilli sambal and the lime halves.

Cook's Tip

Banana leaves are available in Chinese and Asian markets, but you could use lettuce leaves instead.

Fish Cakes in Banana Leaves

The oily flesh of mackerel is ideal for these spicy cakes.

Serves 4–6

4 shallots, chopped
1 lemon grass stalk, trimmed and chopped
25g/1oz galangal, chopped
4 macadamia nuts, roasted
4 dried red chillies, soaked in warm water until soft, squeezed dry and seeded
5ml/1 tsp shrimp paste
5–10ml/1–2 tsp ground turmeric
250ml/8fl oz/1 cup coconut cream
15ml/1 tbsp dark soy sauce
10ml/2 tsp palm sugar (jaggery)
450g/1lb fresh mackerel, cleaned, skinned and flaked
4–6 kaffir lime leaves, finely shredded
2 eggs, lightly beaten
salt and ground black pepper
12 banana leaves, cut into pieces about 20cm/8in square
2 limes, quartered lengthways, and chilli or peanut sambal, to serve

1 Preheat the oven to 200°C/400°F/Gas 6. Using a food processor, grind the shallots, lemon grass, galangal, nuts and chillies to a paste. Blend in the shrimp paste, turmeric, coconut cream, soy sauce and sugar.

2 Put the flaked mackerel and lime leaves in a bowl. Pour in the spiced coconut cream and the beaten eggs. Season with salt and pepper. Mix to coat the fish.

3 Lay a square of banana leaf on a flat surface. Place 30ml/2 tbsp of the fish mixture just off centre and fold the sides of the leaf over the top, leaving room for expansion. Secure the package with a cocktail stick (toothpick) threaded through each end. Repeat with the rest of the mixture. Place on a baking sheet.

4 Bake the banana-wrapped fish cakes in the preheated oven for 30 minutes.

5 Serve in the banana leaves with the lime quarters for squeezing and the sambal for dipping.

stingray wings Energy 195kcal/823kJ; Protein 30.4g; Carbohydrate 4.5g, of which sugars 4.5g; Fat 6.3g, of which saturates 0.7g; Cholesterol 0mg; Calcium 83mg; Fibre 0.1g; Sodium 249mg.
fish cakes in leaves Energy 235kcal/977kJ; Protein 16.7g; Carbohydrate 6.2g, of which sugars 5.9g; Fat 16.1g, of which saturates 3.4g; Cholesterol 104mg; Calcium 44mg; Fibre 0.3g; Sodium 332mg.

Rolled Sardines with Plum Paste

This Japanese dish celebrates the harvest, when the sardine season peaks.

Serves 4

8 sardines, cleaned and filleted
5ml/1 tsp salt
4 umeboshi, about 30g/1¼oz total weight (choose the soft type)
5ml/1 tsp sake
5ml/1 tsp toasted sesame seeds
16 shiso leaves, cut in half lengthways
1 lime, thinly sliced, the centre hollowed out to make rings, to garnish

1 Carefully cut the sardine fillets in half lengthways and place them side by side in a large, shallow container. Sprinkle with salt.

2 Remove the stones (pits) from the umeboshi and put the fruit in a small mixing bowl with the sake and toasted sesame seeds. Mash to form a smooth paste.

3 Wipe the sardine fillets with kitchen paper. With a butter knife, spread some umeboshi paste thinly on to one of the sardine fillets, then press some shiso leaves on top. Roll up the sardine starting from the tail and pierce with a wooden cocktail stick (toothpick). Repeat to make 16 rolled sardines.

4 Preheat the grill (broiler) to high. Lay a sheet of foil on a baking tray and arrange the sardine rolls on this, spaced well apart. Grill (broil) for 4–6 minutes on each side, turning once.

5 Lay a few lime rings on four individual plates and arrange the rolled sardines alongside. Serve hot.

Cook's Tip
Sardines deteriorate very quickly and must be bought and eaten on the same day. Be careful when buying: the eyes and gills should not be too pink. If the fish 'melts' like cheese when grilled (broiled), throw it away.

Eel Wrapped in Bacon

Firm-fleshed and rich in flavour, eel is delicious grilled, braised, or stir-fried. These are best served with a dipping sauce, a crunchy salad, and jasmine rice.

Serves 4–6

2 lemon grass stalks, trimmed and chopped
25g/1oz fresh root ginger, peeled and chopped
2 garlic cloves, chopped
2 shallots, chopped
15ml/1 tbsp palm sugar (jaggery)
15ml/1 tbsp vegetable oil
30ml/2 tbsp fish sauce
1.2kg/2½lb fresh eel, skinned and cut into 2.5cm/1in pieces
12 slices streaky (fatty) bacon
ground black pepper
a small bunch of fresh coriander (cilantro) leaves, to garnish
chilli sambal for dipping

1 Using a mortar and pestle, pound the lemon grass, ginger, garlic and shallots with the sugar to form a paste. Add the oil and fish sauce, mix well and season with black pepper. Put the eel pieces in a dish and smear them thoroughly in this paste. Cover and place in the refrigerator for 2–3 hours to marinate.

2 Wrap each piece of marinated eel in a strip of bacon, including as much of the marinade as possible.

3 To cook the eel parcels, you can use a conventional grill (broiler), a well-oiled griddle pan, or a barbecue. If grilling over charcoal, you can skewer the eel parcels; otherwise, spread them over the grill or griddle pan. Cook the eel parcels until nice and crispy, roughly 2–3 minutes on each side. Serve with fresh coriander leaves and chilli sambal for dipping.

Cook's Tip
When buying fresh eel, it's worth asking the fishmonger to gut it, cut off the head, bone it, skin it and slice it for you – it makes life a lot easier!

sardines w. plum paste Energy 177kcal/740kJ; Protein 20.9g; Carbohydrate 0.7g, of which sugars 0.7g; Fat 9.9g, of which saturates 2.8g; Cholesterol 0mg; Calcium 94mg; Fibre 0.2g; Sodium 121mg.
eel in bacon Energy 460kcal/1911kJ; Protein 39.3g; Carbohydrate 0.8g, of which sugars 0.6g; Fat 33.3g, of which saturates 9.1g; Cholesterol 324mg; Calcium 43mg; Fibre 0.1g; Sodium 651mg.

Fried Prawn Balls

When the moon waxes in September, the Japanese celebrate the arrival of autumn by making an offering to the moon. The dishes offered, such as tiny rice dumplings, sweet chestnuts and these Shinjyo, should all be round in shape.

Makes about 14

150g/5oz raw prawns (shrimp), peeled
75ml/5 tbsp freshly made dashi (kombu and bonito stock) or instant dashi
1 large (US extra large) egg white, well beaten
30ml/2 tbsp sake
15ml/1 tbsp cornflour (cornstarch)
1.5ml/¼ tsp salt
vegetable oil, for deep-frying

To serve

25ml/1½ tbsp ground sea salt
2.5ml/½ tsp sansho
½ lemon, cut into 4 wedges

1 Mix the prawns, dashi stock, beaten egg white, sake, cornflour and salt in a food processor or blender, and process until smooth. Scrape from the mixture into a small mixing bowl.

2 In a wok or small pan, heat the vegetable oil to 175°C/347°F. Take two dessertspoons and wet them with a little vegetable oil. Scoop about 30ml/2 tbsp prawn-ball paste into the spoons and form a small ball. Carefully plunge the ball into the hot oil and deep-fry until lightly browned. Drain on a wire rack.

3 Repeat this process, one ball at a time, until all the prawn-ball paste is used.

4 Mix the salt and sansho on a small plate. Serve the fried prawn balls on a large serving platter or on four serving plates. Garnish with lemon wedges and serve hot with the sansho salt.

Cook's Tip

Sansho is a ground spice made from the dried pod of the prickly ash. Serve the sansho and salt in separate mounds, if you like.

Popiah

This tasty creation is a great do-it-yourself dish.

Serves 4–6

45ml/3 tbsp vegetable oil
225g/8oz firm tofu, rinsed, drained and diced
4 garlic cloves, finely chopped
4 rashers (strips) streaky (fatty) bacon, finely sliced
45ml/3 tbsp fermented soya beans, mashed
450g/1lb fresh prawns (shrimp), peeled and deveined
225g/8oz jicama (sweet turnip), peeled and shredded
450g/1lb bamboo shoots, rinsed and grated
15ml/1 tbsp dark soy sauce
10ml/2 tsp sugar
4–6 fresh red chillies, seeded and pounded
6–8 garlic cloves, crushed
kecap manis to taste
12 cos or romaine lettuce leaves
1 small cucumber, peeled, seeded and finely shredded
225g/8oz/1 cup beansprouts
2 Chinese sausages, fried and sliced
225g/8oz cooked prawns (shrimp), peeled
225g/8oz cooked crab meat
1 omelette, sliced into thin ribbons
fresh coriander (cilantro) leaves, roughly chopped
12 popiah wraps or Mexican corn tortillas

1 Heat the oil in a wok or heavy pan. Fry the tofu until golden brown. Remove from the oil and pat dry on kitchen paper.

2 Fry the garlic and bacon in the oil until they begin to colour. Stir in the fermented soya beans and fresh prawns. Add the jicama, bamboo shoots, soy sauce and sugar. Fry over a high heat to reduce the liquid. Toss in the fried tofu and cook the mixture gently until almost dry. Transfer to a serving dish.

3 Put the remaining ingredients in separate bowls on the table. Place the wraps on a serving plate. To serve, let each person smear the wrap with the chilli and garlic pastes, followed by the kecap manis, a lettuce leaf, a layer of cucumber and beansprouts, and a spoonful of the cooked filling. Add Chinese sausage, prawns and crab meat. Place a few strips of omelette on top with a sprinkling of coriander, then fold the edge of the wrap over the filling, tuck in the ends and roll it up.

fried prawn balls Energy 41kcal/170kJ; Protein 2.1g; Carbohydrate 1g, of which sugars 0g; Fat 3.2g, of which saturates 0.4g; Cholesterol 21mg; Calcium 9mg; Fibre 0g; Sodium 446mg.
popiah Energy 457kcal/1916kJ; Protein 32.3g; Carbohydrate 39.3g, of which sugars 5.8g; Fat 20.1g, of which saturates 4.9g; Cholesterol 213mg; Calcium 396mg; Fibre 4.5g; Sodium 989mg.

Crab Spring Rolls

Chilli and grated ginger add heat to these little treats.

Serves 4–6

15ml/1 tbsp groundnut (peanut) oil
5ml/1 tsp sesame oil
1 garlic clove, crushed
1 fresh red chilli, seeded and finely sliced
450g/1lb fresh stir-fry vegetables, such as beansprouts and shredded carrots, peppers and mangetouts (snow peas)
30ml/2 tbsp chopped coriander (cilantro)
2.5cm/1in piece of fresh root ginger, grated
15ml/1 tbsp rice wine or dry sherry
15ml/1 tbsp soy sauce
350g/12oz fresh dressed crab meat (brown and white meat)
12 spring roll wrappers
1 small egg, beaten
oil, for deep-frying
salt and ground black pepper
lime wedges and fresh coriander, to garnish
sweet-sour dipping sauce, to serve

1 Heat the groundnut and sesame oils in a clean, preheated wok. When hot, stir-fry the crushed garlic and chilli for 1 minute. Add the vegetables, coriander and ginger and stir-fry for 1 minute more. Drizzle over the rice wine or dry sherry and soy sauce. Allow the mixture to bubble up for 1 minute.

2 Using a slotted spoon, transfer the vegetables to a bowl. Set aside until cool, then stir in the crab meat and season with salt and pepper.

3 Soften the spring roll wrappers, following the directions on the packet. Place some of the filling on a wrapper, fold over the front edge and the sides and roll up neatly, sealing the edges with a little beaten egg. Repeat with the remaining wrappers and filling.

4 Heat the oil for deep-frying in the wok and fry the spring rolls in batches, turning several times, until brown and crisp. Remove with a slotted spoon, drain on kitchen paper and keep hot while frying the remainder. Garnish with lime wedges and coriander, and serve with a dipping sauce.

Crackling Rice Paper Fish Rolls

The wrappers hold their shape during cooking, yet dissolve in your mouth when eaten.

Makes 12

12 rice paper sheets, each about 20 x 10cm/8 x 4in
45ml/3 tbsp flour mixed to a paste with 45ml/3 tbsp water
vegetable oil, for deep-frying
fresh herbs, to garnish

For the filling

24 young asparagus spears, trimmed
225g/8oz raw prawns (shrimp), peeled and deveined
25ml/1½ tbsp olive oil
6 spring onions (scallions), finely chopped
1 garlic clove, crushed
2cm/¾in piece of fresh root ginger, grated
30ml/2 tbsp chopped fresh coriander (cilantro)
5ml/1 tsp five-spice powder
5ml/1 tsp finely grated lime or lemon rind
salt and ground black pepper

1 Make the filling. Bring a pan of lightly salted water to the boil; cook the asparagus for 3–4 minutes until tender. Drain, refresh under cold water and drain again. Cut the prawns into thirds.

2 Heat half of the oil in a small frying pan or wok and stir-fry the spring onions and garlic over a low heat for 2–3 minutes until soft. Transfer to a bowl and set aside.

3 Heat the remaining oil in the pan and stir-fry the prawns until they start to go pink. Add to the spring onion mixture with the remaining ingredients. Stir to mix.

4 To make each roll, brush a sheet of rice paper liberally with water and lay it on a clean surface. Place two asparagus spears and a spoonful of the prawn mixture just off centre.

5 Fold in the sides and roll up to make a fat cigar. Seal the ends with a little of the flour paste.

6 Heat the oil in a deep-fryer and fry the rolls in batches until pale golden. Drain well, garnish with herbs and serve.

crab spring rolls Energy 203kcal/844kJ; Protein 15g; Carbohydrate 13.9g, of which sugars 1.9g; Fat 9.3g, of which saturates 1.3g; Cholesterol 74mg; Calcium 94mg; Fibre 1.6g; Sodium 515mg.
crackling rice paper fish rolls Energy 105kcal/438kJ; Protein 5g; Carbohydrate 8.8g, of which sugars 0.7g; Fat 5.6g, of which saturates 0.7g; Cholesterol 37mg; Calcium 36mg; Fibre 0.8g; Sodium 38mg.

Fiery Tuna Spring Rolls

This modern take on the classic spring roll makes a substantial starter or lunchtime snack

Serves 4

1 large chunk of very fresh thick tuna steak
45ml/3 tbsp light soy sauce
30ml/2 tbsp wasabi
16 mangetouts (snow peas), trimmed
8 spring roll wrappers
sunflower oil, for deep-frying
soft noodles and stir-fried Asian greens, to serve
soy sauce and sweet chilli sauce, for dipping

1 Place the tuna on a board. Using a sharp knife cut it into eight slices, each measuring about 12 x 2.5cm/4½ x 1in.

2 Place the tuna steak in a large, non-metallic dish in a single layer. Mix together the light soy sauce and the wasabi and spoon evenly over the fish. Cover the fish and leave to marinate for 10–15 minutes.

3 Meanwhile, blanch the mangetouts in boiling water for about 1 minute, drain and refresh under cold water. Drain and pat dry with kitchen paper.

4 Place a spring roll wrapper on a clean work surface and place a piece of tuna on top, in the centre.

5 Top the tuna with two mangetouts and fold over the sides and roll up. Brush the edges of the wrappers to seal. Repeat with the remaining tuna, mangetouts and wrappers.

6 Fill a large wok one-third full with oil and heat to 180°C/350°F or until a cube of bread browns in 45 seconds. Working in batches, deep-fry the rolls for 1–2 minutes, until crisp and golden.

7 Drain the rolls on kitchen paper and serve immediately with soft noodles and Asian greens. Serve the spring rolls with side dishes of soy sauce and sweet chilli sauce for dipping.

Crispy Shanghai Spring Rolls

Crunchy on the outside, succulent in the centre, these are irresistible.

Makes 12

12 spring roll wrappers
30ml/2 tbsp plain (all-purpose) flour mixed to a paste with water
sunflower oil, for deep-frying

For the filling

6 Chinese dried mushrooms, soaked for 30 minutes in warm water
150g/5oz fresh firm tofu
30ml/2 tbsp sunflower oil
225g/8oz minced (ground) pork
225g/8oz peeled cooked prawns (shrimp), roughly chopped
2.5ml/½ tsp cornflour (cornstarch), mixed to a paste with 15ml/1 tbsp soy sauce
75g/3oz each shredded bamboo shoot or grated carrot, sliced water chestnuts and beansprouts
6 spring onions (scallions) or 1 young leek, finely chopped
a little sesame oil

1 Make the filling. Drain the mushrooms. Cut off and discard the stems and slice the caps finely. Slice the tofu.

2 Heat the oil in a wok and stir-fry the pork for 2–3 minutes or until the colour changes. Add the prawns, cornflour paste and bamboo shoot or carrot. Stir in the water chestnuts.

3 Increase the heat, add the beansprouts and spring onions or leek and toss for 1 minute. Stir in the mushrooms and tofu. Season, then stir in the sesame oil. Cool quickly on a platter.

4 Separate the spring roll wrappers. Place a wrapper on the work surface with one corner nearest you. Spoon some of the filling near the centre of the wrapper and fold the nearest corner over the filling.

5 Smear a little of the flour paste on the free sides, turn the sides to the middle and roll up. Repeat this procedure with the remaining wrappers and filling.

6 Deep-fry the spring rolls in batches until they are crisp and golden. Drain and serve at once, with a dip if you wish.

fiery tuna spring rolls Energy 171kcal/717kJ; Protein 14.1g; Carbohydrate 11.4g, of which sugars 1.7g; Fat 8g, of which saturates 1.3g; Cholesterol 14mg; Calcium 36mg; Fibre 0.8g; Sodium 825mg.
crispy Shanghai spring rolls Energy 38kcal/161kJ; Protein 1.1g; Carbohydrate 6.6g, of which sugars 0.6g; Fat 1g, of which saturates 0.1g; Cholesterol 0mg; Calcium 15mg; Fibre 0.5g; Sodium 88mg.

Lettuce Parcels

Known as sang choy in Hong Kong, this is a popular 'assemble-it-yourself' treat.

Serves 6

2 chicken breast fillets
4 Chinese dried mushrooms, soaked for 30 minutes in warm water to cover
30ml/2 tbsp vegetable oil
2 garlic cloves, crushed
6 drained canned water chestnuts, thinly sliced
30ml/2 tbsp light soy sauce
5ml/1 tsp Sichuan peppercorns, dry-fried and crushed
4 spring onions (scallions), finely chopped
5ml/1 tsp sesame oil
vegetable oil, for deep-frying
50g/2oz cellophane noodles
salt and ground black pepper
1 crisp lettuce and 60ml/4 tbsp hoisin sauce, to serve

1 Remove the skin from the chicken fillets, pat dry and set aside. Chop the chicken into thin strips. Drain the soaked mushrooms. Cut off and discard the mushroom stems; slice the caps finely and set aside.

2 Heat the oil in a wok or large frying pan. Add the garlic, then add the chicken. Stir-fry until the pieces are cooked through.

3 Add the sliced mushrooms, water chestnuts, soy sauce and peppercorns. Toss for 2–3 minutes, then season, if needed.

4 Stir in half of the spring onions, then the sesame oil. Remove from the heat and set aside.

5 Cut the chicken skin into strips, deep fry in hot oil until very crisp and drain on kitchen paper. Deep-fry the noodles until crisp. Drain on kitchen paper.

6 Crush the noodles and put in a serving dish. Top with the chicken skin, chicken mixture and the remaining spring onions. Arrange the lettuce leaves on a platter. Toss the chicken and noodles to mix. Invite guests to take a lettuce leaf, spread the inside with hoisin sauce and add a spoonful of filling, turning in the sides of the leaf and rolling it into a parcel before eating it.

Cabbage & Noodle Parcels

The noodles and mushrooms give an Oriental flavour to the cabbage rolls.

Serves 6

4 dried Chinese mushrooms, soaked in hot water until soft
50g/2oz cellophane noodles, soaked in hot water until soft
450g/1lb minced (ground) pork
2 garlic cloves, finely chopped
8 spring onions (scallions)
30ml/2 tbsp fish sauce
12 large outer green cabbage leaves

For the sauce

15ml/1 tbsp vegetable oil
1 small onion, finely chopped
2 garlic cloves, crushed
400g/14oz can chopped plum tomatoes
pinch of sugar
salt and ground black pepper

1 Drain the mushrooms, discard the stems and chop the caps. Put them in a bowl. Next, drain the noodles and cut them into short lengths. Add to the bowl with the pork and garlic. Chop two of the spring onions and add to the bowl. Season with the fish sauce and pepper.

2 Blanch the cabbage leaves a few at a time in a pan of boiling, lightly salted water for about 1 minute. Remove the leaves from the pan with a spoon and refresh under cold water. Drain the leaves and dry them well on kitchen paper. Blanch the remaining six spring onions in the same fashion. Drain well.

3 Fill one of the cabbage leaves with a generous spoonful of the pork and noodle filling. Roll up the leaf to enclose the filling, then tuck in the sides and continue rolling to make a tight parcel. Make more parcels in the same way.

4 Split each spring onion lengthways and use to tie the cabbage parcels together.

5 To make the sauce, fry the onion and garlic in the oil in a large pan until soft. Add the tomatoes, season with salt, pepper and a pinch of sugar, then bring to simmering point. Add the cabbage parcels. Cover and simmer for 20–25 minutes. Serve.

lettuce parcels Energy 237kcal/984kJ; Protein 15.3g; Carbohydrate 7.6g, of which sugars 1.1g; Fat 16.1g, of which saturates 2g; Cholesterol 41mg; Calcium 24mg; Fibre 0.6g; Sodium 41mg.
cabbage & noodle parcels Energy 159kcal/670kJ; Protein 18g; Carbohydrate 9.8g, of which sugars 3.4g; Fat 5.6g, of which saturates 1.4g; Cholesterol 47mg; Calcium 20mg; Fibre 1.3g; Sodium 238mg.

Five-spice Steamed Rolls

A great favourite at the hawker stalls in Singapore, these deep-fried steamed rolls are delicious with a dipping sauce.

Serves 4

225g/8oz minced (ground) pork
150g/5oz fresh prawns (shrimp), peeled and finely chopped
115g/4oz water chestnuts, finely chopped
15ml/1 tbsp light soy sauce
15ml/1 tbsp dark soy sauce
15ml/1 tbsp sour plum sauce
7.5ml/1½ tsp sesame oil
10ml/2 tsp Chinese five-spice powder
5ml/1 tsp glutinous rice flour or cornflour (cornstarch)
1 egg, lightly beaten
4 fresh tofu sheets or rice-paper roll wrappers, 18–20cm/7–8in square, soaked in warm water
vegetable oil, for deep-frying
chilli oil, for drizzling
soy sauce mixed with chopped chillies, to serve

1 Put the minced pork, chopped prawns and water chestnuts in a bowl. Add the soy sauces, sour plum sauce and sesame oil and mix well. Stir in the five-spice powder, glutinous rice flour or cornflour, and egg. Mix well.

2 Lay the tofu sheets on a flat surface and divide the minced pork mixture between them, placing spoonfuls towards the edge nearest you. Pull the nearest edge up over the filling, tuck in the sides and roll into a log, just like a spring roll. Moisten the last edge with a little water to seal the roll.

3 Fill a wok one-third of the way up with water and place a bamboo steamer into it. Heat the water and place the tofu rolls in the steamer. Cover and steam for 15 minutes. Remove the steamed rolls with tongs and place them on a clean dish towel.

4 Heat enough oil for deep-frying in a wok. Fry the steamed rolls in batches until crisp and golden. Drain them on kitchen paper and serve whole or sliced into portions. Drizzle with chilli oil and serve with a bowl of soy sauce mixed with chopped chillies for dipping.

Fresh Spring Rolls with Palm Heart

These rolls are often prepared for Filipino feasts.

Serves 3–4

1–2 carrots
6 spring onions (scallions)
400g/14oz can coconut palm heart, drained
225g/8oz tofu, rinsed
30–45ml/2–3 tbsp coconut or groundnut (peanut) oil
2 garlic cloves, finely chopped
12 fresh prawns (shrimp), shelled and deveined
30–45ml/2–3 tbsp light soy sauce
10ml/2 tsp sugar
salt and ground black pepper
coconut vinegar, to serve

For the spring roll wrappers

115g/4oz/1 cup plain (all-purpose) white flour
15ml/1 tbsp tapioca flour or cornflour (cornstarch)
pinch of salt
400ml/14fl oz/1⅔ cups water
corn oil, for frying

1 Sift the dry wrapper ingredients into a bowl. Pour in the water and whisk to a smooth batter. Set aside for 30 minutes.

2 Heat a non-stick pancake pan and wipe a little corn oil for frying all over the surface. Ladle a little of the batter into the pan, tilting it to spread the batter evenly over the base. Cook over a medium-low heat, on one side only, until the batter sets and begins to bubble up in the middle and loosens at the edges. Carefully transfer the wrapper to a plate. Repeat with the remaining batter to make 12 wrappers.

3 Cut the carrots into 5cm/2in long matchsticks and put aside. Cut off the green stems of the spring onions, halve lengthways and put aside. Cut the white stems into 5cm/2in lengths and then quarter each piece lengthways. Put aside. Blanch the palm hearts in a pan of boiling water for 2–3 minutes, refresh under cold running water, then cut into 5cm/2in strips. Put aside.

4 Cut the tofu into three rectangular pieces. Heat 15–30ml/1–2 tbsp oil in a wok or heavy frying pan, add the tofu pieces and fry until golden brown on both sides. Drain on kitchen paper, then cut each piece into thin strips and put aside.

5 Add the garlic to the wok and fry until fragrant. Add the carrots and stir-fry for 2–3 minutes. Add the white parts of the spring onions and the prawns and fry until they turn opaque. Add the palm hearts and tofu strips, followed by the soy sauce and sugar. Season the filling and tip on to a plate to cool.

6 Place a spring roll wrapper on a flat surface and position a lettuce leaf on it, making sure the frilly edge overlaps the wrapper on the side furthest away from you. Spoon some of the mixture into the middle of the leaf, making sure the strips of carrot, tofu and palm heart overlap the wrapper by the frilly edge of the lettuce. Fold the edge nearest to you over the filling and fold in the sides to form a bundle with the palm heart, carrot, tofu and frill of lettuce poking out of the top.

7 Using the reserved green spring onions, tie the bundle with a green ribbon and place it on a serving dish. Repeat with the remaining wrappers and filling to make 12 spring rolls. Serve with coconut vinegar for dipping.

five-spiced rolls Energy 278kcal/1157kJ; Protein 20.4g; Carbohydrate 10.8g, of which sugars 1.8g; Fat 17g, of which saturates 3.7g; Cholesterol 158mg; Calcium 61mg; Fibre 0.6g; Sodium 740mg.
fresh spring rolls Energy 307kcal/1289kJ; Protein 19.5g; Carbohydrate 32.8g, of which sugars 7g; Fat 11.7g, of which saturates 1.4g; Cholesterol 122mg; Calcium 433mg; Fibre 2.8g; Sodium 797mg.

Firecrackers

It's easy to see how these snacks got their name. They whizz round the wok like rockets, and when you take a bite, they explode with flavour.

Makes 16

16 large, raw king prawns (jumbo shrimp), heads and shells removed but tails left on
5ml/1 tsp red curry paste
15ml/1 tbsp fish sauce
16 small wonton wrappers, about 8cm/3¼in square, thawed if frozen
16 fine egg noodles, soaked in water until soft
oil, for deep-frying
1 lime, cut into wedges, to serve

1 Place the prawns on their sides and cut two slits through the underbelly of each, one about 1cm/½in from the head end and the other about 1cm/½in from the first cut, cutting across the prawn. This will prevent the prawns from curling when cooked.

2 Mix the curry paste with the fish sauce in a shallow dish. Add the prawns and turn them in the mixture until they are well coated. Cover and leave to marinate for 10 minutes.

3 Place a wonton wrapper on the work surface at an angle so that it forms a diamond shape, then fold the top corner over so that the point is in the centre. Place a prawn, slits down, on the wrapper, with the tail projecting from the folded end, then fold the bottom corner over the other end of the prawn.

4 Fold each side of the wrapper over in turn to make a tightly folded roll. Tie a noodle in a bow around the roll and set it aside. Repeat with the remaining prawns and wrappers.

5 Heat the oil in a wok to 190°C/375°F or until a cube of bread, added to the oil, browns in 40 seconds. Fry the prawns, a few at a time, for 5–8 minutes, until golden brown and cooked through. Drain well on kitchen paper and keep hot while you cook the remaining batches. Serve hot, with the lime.

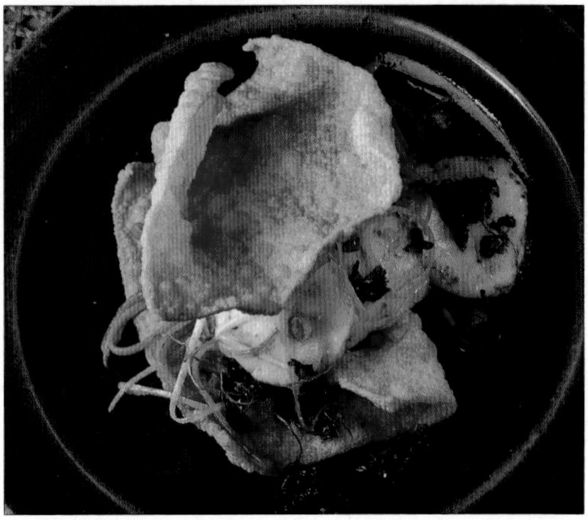

Seared Scallops with Wonton Crisps

Quick seared scallops with crisp vegetables in a lightly spiced sauce make a delightful starter.

Serves 4

16 medium scallops, halved
oil for deep-frying
8 wonton wrappers
45ml/3 tbsp olive oil
1 large carrot, cut into long thin strips
1 large leek, cut into long thin strips
juice of 1 lemon
juice of ½ orange
2 spring onions (scallions), sliced
30ml/2 tbsp, coriander (cilantro) leaves
salt and ground black pepper

For the relish

5ml/1 tsp Thai red curry paste
5ml/1 tsp grated fresh root ginger
1 garlic clove, finely chopped
15ml/1 tbsp soy sauce
15ml/1 tbsp olive oil

1 Combine the marinade ingredients in a bowl. Add the scallops, toss to coat and leave to marinate for 30 minutes.

2 Heat the oil in a large heavy pan or deep-fryer and deep-fry the wonton wrappers in small batches until crisp and golden. When the wrappers are ready, drain them on kitchen paper and set aside until required.

3 Heat half the olive oil in a large pan. Add the scallops and sear over a high heat for 1 minute or until golden, taking care not to overcook (they should feel firm to the touch but not rubbery). Using a slotted spoon, transfer the scallops to a plate.

4 Add the remaining olive oil to the pan. When hot, add the carrot and leek strips. Toss and turn the vegetables until they start to wilt and soften, but remain crisp. Season to taste with salt and pepper, stir in the lemon and orange juices and add a little more soy sauce if needed.

5 Return the scallops to the pan, mix lightly with the vegetables and heat for just long enough to warm through. Transfer to a bowl and add the spring onions and coriander. Sandwich a quarter of the mixture between two wonton crisps. Make three more 'sandwiches' in the same way and serve immediately.

firecrackers Energy 71kcal/298kJ; Protein 3.2g; Carbohydrate 7.1g, of which sugars 0.2g; Fat 3.5g, of which saturates 0.5g; Cholesterol 25mg; Calcium 20mg; Fibre 0.3g; Sodium 30mg.
seared scallops Energy 228kcal/955kJ; Protein 14.4g; Carbohydrate 15.3g, of which sugars 2.4g; Fat 12.6g, of which saturates 1.5g; Cholesterol 24mg; Calcium 74mg; Fibre 2.7g; Sodium 326mg.

Chilli Prawn Skewers

Choose very fresh prawns for this recipe, which makes a very attractive, light and spicy appetizer.

Serves 4

16 giant raw prawns (shrimp), shelled, tail section left intact
1 lime, cut into 8 wedges
60ml/4 tbsp sweet chilli sauce, for dipping

1 Soak eight bamboo skewers in water to stop them burning during cooking, then thread each with a prawn, a lime wedge, then another prawn. Brush the sweeet chilli sauce over.

2 Grill (broil) the skewers until the prawns are cooked. Serve immediately with more chilli sauce for dipping.

Tamarind Prawns

The flavour of tamarind is perfect with the prawns.

Serves 2–4

500g/1¼lb fresh, large prawns (shrimp)
45ml/3 tbsp tamarind pulp
30ml/2 tbsp kecap manis
15ml/1 tbsp sugar
ground black pepper
fresh coriander (cilantro) leaves and 2–4 fresh green chillies, seeded and quartered lengthways, to garnish

1 Devein the prawns. Remove the feelers and legs. Rinse well, pat dry and, using a sharp knife, make an incision along the curve of the tail.

2 Mix the tamarind pulp with 250ml/8fl oz/1 cup warm water. Soak until soft, squeezing it with your fingers to help soften it. Strain into a bowl and add the kecap manis, sugar and pepper. Pour over the prawns, cover and marinate for 1 hour.

3 Grill (broil) the prawns for 3 minutes on each side until cooked through, brushing frequently with the marinade. Serve immediately, garnished with coriander and chillies.

Shrimp Paste on Sugar Cane Sticks

To appreciate the full impact of this classic dish, eat it by itself.

Serves 4

50g/2oz pork fat
7.5ml/1½ tsp vegetable oil
1 onion, finely chopped
2 garlic cloves, crushed
1 egg
15ml/1 tbsp fish sauce
15ml/1 tbsp raw cane or soft dark brown sugar
15ml/1 tbsp cornflour (cornstarch)
350g/12oz raw prawns (shrimp), peeled and deveined
a piece of fresh sugar cane, about 20cm/8in long
salt and ground black pepper

1 Place the pork fat in a large pan of boiling water and boil for 2–3 minutes. Drain well and chop using a sharp knife. Set aside.

2 Heat the oil in a heavy pan and stir in the onion and garlic. Just as they begin to colour, remove from the heat and transfer them to a bowl. Beat in the egg, fish sauce and sugar, until the sugar has dissolved. Season with a little salt and plenty of black pepper, and then stir in the cornflour.

3 Add the pork fat and prawns to the mixture, and mix well. Grind in a mortar using a pestle.

4 Divide the paste into eight portions. Using a strong knife or cleaver, cut the sugar cane in half and then cut each half into quarters lengthways.

5 Take a piece of sugar cane in your hand and mould a portion of the paste around it, pressing it gently so the edges are sealed. Place the coated sticks on an oiled tray, while you make the remaining skewers in the same way.

6 For the best flavour, cook the shrimp paste skewers over a barbecue for 5–6 minutes, turning them frequently until they are nicely browned all over.

7 Alternatively, cook the skewers under a conventional grill (broiler). Serve immediately, while still hot.

chilli prawn skewers Energy 59kcal/247kJ; Protein 11.3g; Carbohydrate 2.6g, of which sugars 2.5g; Fat 0.4g, of which saturates 0.1g; Cholesterol 122mg; Calcium 61mg; Fibre 0.1g; Sodium 242mg.
tamarind prawns Energy 92kcal/387kJ; Protein 14.2g; Carbohydrate 6.1g, of which sugars 6g; Fat 1.3g, of which saturates 0.3g; Cholesterol 48mg; Calcium 121mg; Fibre 0.8g; Sodium 1627mg.
shrimp paste Energy 256kcal/1066kJ; Protein 17.5g; Carbohydrate 12g, of which sugars 4.8g; Fat 15.7g, of which saturates 5.7g; Cholesterol 239mg; Calcium 85mg; Fibre 0.2g; Sodium 192mg.

Scallops with Ginger Relish

Buy scallops in their shells to ensure their freshness; your fishmonger will open them for you if you find this difficult. The shells make excellent serving dishes.

Serves 4

8 king or queen scallops
4 whole star anise
30ml/2 tbsp vegetable oil
salt and ground white pepper
fresh coriander (cilantro) sprigs and whole star anise, to garnish

For the relish

½ cucumber, peeled
salt, for sprinkling
5cm/2in piece fresh root ginger, peeled and sliced into strips
10ml/2 tsp caster (superfine) sugar
45ml/3 tbsp rice wine vinegar
10ml/2 tsp syrup from a jar of preserved stem ginger
5ml/1 tsp sesame seeds, for sprinkling

1 To make the relish, halve the cucumber lengthways, remove the seeds, then slice the cucumber into a colander and sprinkle liberally with salt. Set aside to drain for 30 minutes.

2 To prepare the scallops, cut each into 2–3 slices and place the scallops with the corals in a bowl. Coarsely grind the star anise using a mortar and pestle and add it with the seasoning.

3 Cover the bowl and marinate the scallops in the refrigerator for about 1 hour.

4 Rinse the cucumber under cold water, then drain and pat dry with kitchen paper. Place in a bowl with the ginger, sugar, rice wine vinegar and syrup. Mix well, then cover with clear film (plastic wrap) and chill until the relish is needed.

5 Heat a wok and add the oil. When the oil is very hot, add the scallop slices and stir-fry them for 2–3 minutes. Place the cooked scallops on kitchen paper to drain off any excess oil.

6 Garnish the scallops with sprigs of coriander and whole star anise, and serve with the cucumber relish, sprinkled lightly with sesame seeds.

Shiitake & Scallop Bundles

A wok does double duty for making these delicate mushroom and seafood treats, first for steaming and then for deep-frying.

Serves 4

4 scallops
8 large fresh shiitake mushrooms
225g/8oz long yam, unpeeled
20ml/4 tsp miso
50g/2oz/1 cup fresh breadcrumbs
cornflour (cornstarch), for dusting
2 eggs, beaten
vegetable oil, for deep-frying
salt
4 lemon wedges, to serve

1 Slice the scallops in two horizontally, then sprinkle with salt. Remove the stalks from the shiitake and discard them. Cut shallow slits on the top of the shiitake to form a 'hash' symbol. Sprinkle with a little salt.

2 Heat a steamer and steam the long yam for 10–15 minutes, or until soft. Test with a skewer. Leave to cool, then remove the skin. Mash the flesh in a bowl, add the miso and mix well. Take the breadcrumbs into your hands and break them down finely. Mix half into the mashed long yam, keeping the rest on a small plate.

3 Fill the underneath of the shiitake caps with a scoop of mashed long yam. Smooth down with the flat edge of a knife and dust the mash with cornflour. Add a little mash to a slice of scallop and place on top.

4 Spread another 5ml/1 tsp mashed long yam on to the scallop and shape to completely cover. Make sure all the ingredients are clinging together. Repeat to make eight little mounds.

5 Place the beaten eggs in a shallow container. Dust the shiitake and scallop mounds with cornflour, then dip into the egg. Handle with care as the mash and scallop are quite soft. Coat well with the remaining breadcrumbs and deep-fry in hot oil until golden. Drain well on kitchen paper. Serve hot on individual plates with a wedge of lemon.

scallops w. ginger relish Energy 130kcal/542kJ; Protein 12.1g; Carbohydrate 4.9g, of which sugars 3.2g; Fat 7g, of which saturates 1g; Cholesterol 24mg; Calcium 31mg; Fibre 0.3g; Sodium 92mg.
shiitake bundles Energy 812kcal/3396kJ; Protein 45.8g; Carbohydrate 54g, of which sugars 12.6g; Fat 47.8g, of which saturates 7.5g; Cholesterol 428mg; Calcium 279mg; Fibre 7g; Sodium 741mg.

Crispy Salt & Pepper Squid

These delicious morsels of squid look stunning and are perfect served with drinks, or as an appetizer. The crisp, golden coating contrasts beautifully with the succulent squid inside. Serve them piping hot straight from the wok.

Serves 4

750g/1lb 10oz fresh squid, cleaned
juice of 4–5 lemons
15ml/1 tbsp ground black pepper
15ml/1 tbsp sea salt
10ml/2 tsp caster (superfine) sugar
115g/4oz/1 cup cornflour (cornstarch)
3 egg whites, lightly beaten
vegetable oil, for deep-frying
chilli sauce or sweet-and-sour sauce, for dipping
skewers or toothpicks, to serve

1 Cut the squid sac into large bitesize pieces and score a diamond pattern on each piece, using a sharp knife or a cleaver.

2 Trim the tentacles. Place in a large mixing bowl and pour over the lemon juice. Cover and marinate for 10–15 minutes. Drain well and pat dry.

3 In a separate bowl, mix together the pepper, salt, sugar and cornflour. Dip the squid pieces in the egg whites and then toss lightly in the seasoned flour, shaking off any excess.

4 Fill a wok one-third full of oil and heat to 180°C/350°F or until a cube of bread, dropped into the oil, browns in 40 seconds. Working in batches, deep-fry the squid for 1 minute. Drain the crispy pieces on kitchen paper and serve immediately, threaded on to skewers, with chilli or sweet-and-sour sauce for dipping.

Cook's Tip
Keep egg whites in a sealed plastic tub in the freezer, ready to thaw for use in dishes such as this.

Sweet & Sour Deep-fried Squid

This is an example of a dish where a Western influence comes into Asian food – with tomato ketchup and Worcestershire sauce used alongside more traditional ingredients.

Serves 4

900g/2lb fresh young, tender squid
vegetable oil, for deep-frying

For the marinade
60ml/4 tbsp light soy sauce
15ml/1 tbsp sugar

For the dipping sauce
30ml/2 tbsp tomato ketchup
15ml/1 tbsp Worcestershire sauce
15ml/1 tbsp light soy sauce
15ml/1 tbsp clear sesame oil
sugar or honey, to sweeten
chilli oil, to taste

1 First prepare the squid. Hold the body in one hand and pull off the head with the other. Sever the tentacles and discard the rest. Remove the backbone and clean the body sac inside and out. Pat dry using kitchen paper and cut into rings.

2 In a bowl, mix the soy sauce with the sugar until it dissolves. Toss in the squid rings and tentacles and marinate for 1 hour.

3 Meanwhile prepare the sauce. Mix together the tomato ketchup, Worcestershire sauce, soy sauce and oil. Sweeten with sugar or honey to taste and a little chilli oil to give the sauce a bit of bite. Set aside.

4 Heat enough vegetable oil for deep-frying in a wok or heavy pan. Thoroughly drain the squid of any marinade, pat with kitchen paper to avoid spitting, and fry until golden and crispy. Pat the crispy squid pieces dry on kitchen paper and serve immediately with the dipping sauce.

Cook's Tip
To avoid the spitting fat, lightly coat the squid in flour before deep-frying. Alternatively, fry in a deep-fat fryer with a lid or use a spatterproof cover on the wok or pan.

salt & pepper squid Energy 346kcal/1462kJ; Protein 31.2g; Carbohydrate 31.3g, of which sugars 2.6g; Fat 11.6g, of which saturates 1.8g; Cholesterol 422mg; Calcium 32mg; Fibre 0g; Sodium 1741mg.
sweet & sour squid Energy 315kcal/1320kJ; Protein 35.2g; Carbohydrate 4.5g, of which sugars 1.7g; Fat 17.6g, of which saturates 2.5g; Cholesterol 506mg; Calcium 39mg; Fibre 0g; Sodium 1361mg.

Dried Squid Satay

This dish from the Philippines is often made at the beach and served with iced fruit drinks or chilled serbesa (beer) to balance the saltiness. It is also good served with bread.

Serves
4–5 whole dried baby squid
30ml/2 tbsp light soy sauce
30ml/2 tbsp hoisin sauce
30ml/2 tbsp smooth peanut butter
juice of 1 kalamansi lime or ordinary lime
wooden or metal skewers
green mango or papaya salad, to serve
coriander (cilantro) sprigs, to serve

1 Rinse any floury residue off the squid and pat it dry with kitchen paper. Cut each squid into four or five narrow strips using scissors or a sharp knife.

2 Put the soy sauce, hoisin sauce, peanut butter and lime juice in a bowl and whisk well with a fork to form a thick, smooth marinade.

3 Toss the squid pieces in the peanut marinade, making sure they are well coated, and leave to marinate at room temperature for 30 minutes.

4 Meanwhile, prepare the barbecue or, if you are using the grill (broiler), preheat for 5 minutes before you start cooking.

5 If using wooden skewers, soak them in water for about 30 minutes to prevent them from charring when you start cooking. Thread the squid on to the damp skewers.

6 Place the satay on the barbecue or under the grill and cook for 2 minutes on each side, brushing occasionally with any remaining marinade.

7 Remove the squid from the grill and serve immediately, while it is piping hot. Garnish with fresh coriander sprigs if you wish, and eat with a fresh mango or papaya salad.

Crab & Tofu Dumplings

These little crab and ginger-flavoured dumplings are usually served as a side dish.

Serves 4–6
115g/4oz frozen white crab meat, thawed
115g/4oz tofu
1 egg yolk
30ml/2 tbsp rice flour or wheat flour
30ml/2 tbsp finely chopped spring onion (scallion), green part only
2cm/¾in fresh root ginger, grated
10ml/2 tsp light soy sauce
salt
vegetable oil, for deep-frying
50g/2oz mooli (daikon), very finely grated, to serve

For the dipping sauce
120ml/4fl oz/½ cup vegetable stock
15ml/1 tbsp sugar
45ml/3 tbsp dark soy sauce

1 Squeeze as much moisture out of the crab meat as you can. Press the tofu through a fine strainer with the back of a tablespoon. Combine the tofu and crab meat in a bowl.

2 Add the egg yolk, rice or wheat flour, spring onion, ginger and soy sauce and season to taste with salt. Mix thoroughly with a metal spoon to form a light paste.

3 To make the dipping sauce, combine the vegetable stock, sugar and soy sauce in a serving bowl.

4 Line a baking sheet with kitchen paper. Heat the vegetable oil in a wok or frying pan to 190°C/375°F. Meanwhile, shape the crab and tofu mixture into thumb-sized pieces. Fry the dumplings in batches of three at a time for 1–2 minutes. Drain them on the kitchen paper and serve immediately, accompanied by the dipping sauce and mooli.

Cook's Tip
Grate the mooli just before serving and press it in a sieve or strainer to remove excess liquid.

dried squid satay Energy 89kcal/374kJ; Protein 9.6g; Carbohydrate 2.2g, of which sugars 1.1g; Fat 4.7g, of which saturates 1.2g; Cholesterol 113mg; Calcium 11mg; Fibre 0.4g; Sodium 615mg.
crab & tofu dumplings Energy 74kcal/310kJ; Protein 6.3g; Carbohydrate 7.8g, of which sugars 3.6g; Fat 2g, of which saturates 0.4g; Cholesterol 47mg; Calcium 132mg; Fibre 0.3g; Sodium 762mg.

Asparagus with Crab Meat Sauce

The subtle flavour of fresh asparagus is enhanced by the equally delicate taste of the crab meat in this classic Chinese dish.

Serves 4

450g/1lb asparagus spears, trimmed
4 thin slices of peeled fresh root ginger
15ml/1 tbsp vegetable oil
2 garlic cloves, finely chopped
115g/4oz/⅔ cup fresh or thawed frozen white crab meat
5ml/1 tsp sake or dry sherry
150ml/¼ pint/⅔ cup semi-skimmed (low-fat) milk
15ml/1 tbsp cornflour (cornstarch)
45ml/3 tbsp cold water
salt and ground white pepper
1 spring onion (scallion), thinly shredded, to garnish

1 Bring a large pan of lightly salted water to the boil. Poach the trimmed asparagus for about 5 minutes until they are just crisp-tender. Drain the spears well and keep them hot in a shallow serving dish.

2 Bruise the slices of fresh, peeled root ginger with a rolling pin. Heat the oil in a non-stick frying pan or wok. Add the ginger and garlic for 1 minute and cook to release their flavour, then lift them out with a slotted spoon and discard them.

3 Add the crab meat to the flavoured oil and toss to mix. Drizzle over the sake or sherry, then pour in the milk. Cook, stirring often, for 2 minutes.

4 Meanwhile, put the cornflour in a small bowl with the water and mix to a smooth paste.

5 Add the cornflour paste to the pan, stirring constantly, then cook the mixture, continuing to stir, until it forms a thick and creamy sauce.

6 Season the sauce to taste with salt and pepper, spoon over the asparagus and garnish with shreds of spring onion. Serve immediately, while piping hot.

Singapore Chilli Crab

Perhaps Singapore's signature dish could be chilli crab. An all-time favourite at hawker stalls and coffee shops, steaming woks of crab deep-frying are a common sight. The crabs are placed in the middle of the table with a bowl for the discarded pieces of shell, and small bowls of water for cleaning your fingers. Crack the shells, then dip the meat into the cooking sauce. Mop up the spicy sauce with lots of crusty bread.

Serves 4

vegetable oil, for deep-frying
4 fresh crabs, about 250g/9oz each, cleaned
30ml/2 tbsp sesame oil
30–45ml/2–3 tbsp chilli sauce
45ml/3 tbsp tomato ketchup
15ml/1 tbsp soy sauce
15ml/1 tbsp sugar
250ml/8fl oz/1 cup chicken stock
2 eggs, beaten
salt and ground black pepper
finely sliced spring onions (scallions), and chopped coriander (cilantro) leaves, to garnish

For the spice paste
4 garlic cloves, chopped
25g/1oz fresh root ginger, chopped
4 fresh red chillies, seeded and chopped

1 Using a mortar and pestle or food processor, grind the ingredients for the spice paste and set aside.

2 Deep-fry the crabs in hot oil until the shells turn bright red. Remove from the oil and drain.

3 Heat the sesame oil in a wok and stir in the spice paste. Fry until fragrant and stir in the chilli sauce, ketchup, soy sauce and sugar. Toss in the fried crab and coat well.

4 Pour in the chicken stock, bring to the boil, then simmer for 5 minutes. Season.

5 Pour in the eggs, stirring gently, to let them set in the sauce. Serve immediately, garnished with spring onions and coriander.

asparagus w. crab Energy 121kcal/507kJ; Protein 10.4g; Carbohydrate 7.5g, of which sugars 3.9g; Fat 5.6g, of which saturates 1.1g; Cholesterol 23mg; Calcium 84mg; Fibre 1.9g; Sodium 126mg.
Singapore chilli crab Energy 276kcal/1144kJ; Protein 12.1g; Carbohydrate 8.6g, of which sugars 8.1g; Fat 21.7g, of which saturates 3.1g; Cholesterol 126mg; Calcium 23mg; Fibre 0.3g; Sodium 674mg

Cucumbers with Crab

These wonderful appetizers can be served whole or in slices and make a cool, refreshing start to a meal. The patis adds a very distinctive Filipino flavour to the dish.

Serves 8
4 whole cucumbers
1 small carrot
300g/10½oz crab meat
2 spring onions (scallions), white parts only, finely chopped
30ml/2 tbsp sesame oil
15ml/1 tbsp patis (Filipino fish sauce)
1 egg, lightly beaten
15g/1 tbsp cornflour (cornstarch)

1 Peel the cucumbers and cut each in half lengthways. Remove the seeds by running a spoon down the core. Discard the seeds and pulpy flesh to leave hollowed out 'boats' for the crab filling.

2 Dice the carrot finely and boil in a little water for 3 minutes, then drain.

3 Combine the crab meat with the spring onions, blanched carrot, sesame oil, patis, egg and cornflour. Mix well.

4 Stuff each cucumber half with the mixture, patting it in well.

5 Place the cucumber halves in steamer baskets and steam over simmering water for 8 minutes until just done. Do not overcook or the cucumber flesh will become mushy.

6 Remove from the steamer and serve hot, whole or sliced.

Cook's Tip
Courgettes (zucchini) also make good vegetable boats for this dish, and the crab meat can be substituted with prawns (shrimp) or minced pork.

Crab Cakes with Wasabi

There's more than a hint of heat in these crab cakes, thanks to wasabi, a powerful Japanese condiment, and root ginger. The dipping sauce doubles the dramatic impact.

Serves 6
4 spring onions (scallions)
450g/1lb fresh dressed crab meat (brown and white meat)
2.5cm/1in piece fresh root ginger, grated
30ml/2 tbsp chopped fresh coriander (cilantro)
30ml/2 tbsp mayonnaise
2.5–5ml/½–1 tsp wasabi paste
15ml/1 tbsp sesame oil
50–115g/2–4oz/1–2 cups fresh white breadcrumbs
30ml/2 tbsp vegetable oil, for frying
salt and ground black pepper

For the dipping sauce
5ml/1 tsp wasabi paste
90ml/6 tbsp soy sauce

1 Make the dipping sauce. Mix the wasabi and soy sauce in a small bowl. Set aside.

2 Chop the spring onions. Mix the crab meat, spring onions, ginger, coriander, mayonnaise, wasabi paste and sesame oil in a bowl. Season and stir in enough breadcrumbs to make a mixture that is firm enough to form patties. Chill the mixture for 30 minutes.

3 Form the crab mixture into 12 cakes. Heat the oil in a non-stick frying pan and fry the crab cakes for about 3–4 minutes on each side, until browned. Serve with the sauce.

Cook's Tips
- *Fresh crab meat will have the best flavour, but if it is not available, use frozen or canned crab meat.*
- *Wasabi is often described as horseradish mustard, although this Japanese paste is unrelated to either condiment. It is very hot, so use with caution.*

cucumbers w. crab Energy 109kcal/453kJ; Protein 10g; Carbohydrate 3.9g, of which sugars 2g; Fat 6g, of which saturates 0.9g; Cholesterol 55mg; Calcium 22mg; Fibre 0.7g; Sodium 332mg.
crab cakes w. wasabi Energy 190kcal/795kJ; Protein 16.2g; Carbohydrate 7.1g, of which sugars 0.6g; Fat 11g, of which saturates 1.4g; Cholesterol 55mg; Calcium 35mg; Fibre 0.3g; Sodium 388mg.

Thai Fish Cakes with Egg

These tangy little fish cakes, with a kick of Eastern spice, make a great appetizer.

Makes about 20

225g/8oz smoked haddock
225g/8oz fresh cod or haddock
1 small fresh red chilli, seeded and finely chopped
2 garlic cloves, chopped
1 lemon grass stalk, chopped
2 large spring onions (scallions), finely chopped
30ml/2 tbsp fish sauce
60ml/4 tbsp thick coconut milk
2 large eggs, lightly beaten
15ml/1 tbsp chopped fresh coriander (cilantro)
15ml/1 tbsp cornflour (cornstarch), plus more for moulding
oil, for frying
soy sauce, rice vinegar and/or fish sauce, for dipping

1 Remove the skin and any bones from the fish. Set the fresh fish aside and place the smoked fish in a bowl of cold water. Leave to soak for 10 minutes. Drain and dry well on kitchen paper. Chop all the fish roughly and place in a food processor.

2 Add the chilli, garlic, lemon grass, spring onions, fish sauce and coconut milk, and process until the fish is well blended with the spices. Add the eggs and coriander, and blend for a further few seconds. Scrape into a bowl, cover and chill for 1 hour.

3 To make the fish cakes, coat your hands with cornflour and shape large teaspoonfuls of fish mixture into neat balls, lightly coating each with the cornflour.

4 Heat 5–7.5cm/2–3in oil in a medium pan until it is hot enough to turn a crust of bread golden in about 1 minute. Fry the fish balls, 5–6 at a time, turning them carefully with a slotted spoon for 2–3 minutes, until they turn golden all over.

5 Remove the fish balls from the oil with a slotted spoon and drain on kitchen paper. Keep the cooked fish cakes warm in a low oven until you have finished frying them all.

6 Serve immediately with one or more of the dipping sauces.

Salmon & Ginger Fish Cakes

These light fish cakes are scented with the exotic flavours of sesame, lime and ginger. They make a tempting appetizer served simply with a wedge of lime for squeezing over, but are also perfect for a light lunch or supper, served with a crunchy, refreshing salad.

Makes 25

500g/1¼lb salmon fillet, skinned and boned
45ml/3 tbsp dried breadcrumbs
30ml/2 tbsp mayonnaise
30ml/2 tbsp sesame seeds
30ml/2 tbsp light soy sauce
finely grated rind of 2 limes
10ml/2 tsp finely grated fresh root ginger
4 spring onions (scallions), finely sliced
vegetable oil, for frying
salt and ground black pepper
spring onions (scallions), to garnish
lime wedges, to serve

1 Finely chop the salmon and place in a bowl. Add the breadcrumbs, mayonnaise, sesame seeds, soy sauce, lime rind, ginger and spring onions and use your fingers to mix well.

2 With wet hands, divide the mixture into 25 portions and shape each into a small round cake. Place the cakes on a baking sheet lined with baking parchment, cover and chill for at least two hours. They can be left overnight.

3 When you are ready to cook the fish cakes, heat about 5cm/2in vegetable oil in a wok and fry the fish cakes in batches, over a medium heat, for 2–3 minutes on each side.

4 Drain the fish cakes well on kitchen paper, season and serve warm or at room temperature, garnished with spring onion slivers and plenty of lime wedges for squeezing over.

Cook's Tip
When chopping the salmon, look out for stray bones and pick these out with tweezers.

thai fish cakes Energy 60kcal/250kJ; Protein 6.2g; Carbohydrate 0.9g, of which sugars 0.2g; Fat 3.5g, of which saturates 0.5g; Cholesterol 29mg; Calcium 15mg; Fibre 0.1g; Sodium 152mg.
salmon & ginger fish cakes Energy 83kcal/343kJ; Protein 4.6g; Carbohydrate 1.6g, of which sugars 0.2g; Fat 6.5g, of which saturates 0.9g; Cholesterol 11mg; Calcium 16mg; Fibre 0.2g; Sodium 117mg.

Ginger Chicken Wings

Many people regard chicken wings as the best part of the bird. Served this way, they are certainly delicious, and exactly the right size for an appetizer with drinks, or as a first course.

Serves 4

10–12 chicken wings, skinned
175ml/6fl oz/ ¾ cup natural (plain) low-fat yogurt
7.5ml/1 ½ tsp crushed fresh root ginger
5ml/1 tsp salt
5ml/1 tsp Tabasco sauce
15ml/1 tbsp tomato ketchup
5ml/1 tsp crushed garlic
15ml/1 tbsp lemon juice
15ml/1 tbsp fresh coriander (cilantro) leaves
15ml/1 tbsp oil
2 medium onions, sliced
15ml/1 tbsp shredded fresh root ginger

1 Place the chicken wings in a non-metallic bowl. Pour the yogurt into a separate bowl along with the ginger pulp, salt, Tabasco sauce, tomato ketchup, garlic pulp, lemon juice and half the fresh coriander leaves. Whisk together, then pour the mixture over the chicken wings and stir gently to coat the chicken completely.

2 Heat the oil in a wok or heavy frying pan and fry the onions until soft.

3 Add the chicken wings and cook over a medium heat, stirring occasionally, for 10–15 minutes.

4 Add the remaining coriander and the shredded ginger and serve hot.

Cook's Tip
You can substitute drumsticks or other chicken portions for the wings in this recipe, but remember to increase the cooking time.

Chicken in a Hot Red Sauce

In India, small chickens are used for this dish and it is served with unleavened bread. If you wish to serve it as an appetizer, use four poussins instead of chicken joints. Skin them first and make small gashes with a sharp knife to enable the spices to seep in.

Serves 4–6

20ml/4 tsp Kashmiri masala paste
60ml/4 tbsp tomato ketchup
5ml/1 tsp Worcestershire sauce
5ml/1 tsp five-spice powder
5ml/1 tsp sugar
8 chicken joints, skinned but not boned
45ml/3 tbsp vegetable oil
5cm/2in piece fresh root ginger, finely shredded
4 garlic cloves, finely crushed
juice of 1 lemon
a few fresh coriander (cilantro) leaves, finely chopped
salt

1 To make the marinade, mix together the Kashmiri masala, tomato ketchup, Worcestershire sauce, five-spice powder, salt and sugar. Leave to rest in a warm place until the sugar has completely dissolved.

2 Rub the chicken pieces with the marinade and leave to rest for at least a further 2 hours, or overnight if possible.

3 Heat the oil in a pan and fry half the ginger and all the garlic until golden. Add the chicken pieces, and fry until both sides are sealed. Cover and cook until the chicken is nearly tender and the sauce clings with the oil separating.

4 Sprinkle the chicken with the lemon juice, remaining ginger and the coriander leaves. Mix well, reheat and serve hot.

Cook's Tip
Masala is a term used in Indian cookery meaning a blend of spices. In this dish a hot and spicy Kashmiri masala paste is used. It's made from cinnamon, ginger, black pepper, cardamom, coriander and cumin.

ginger chicken wings Energy 272kcal/1143kJ; Protein 43.1g; Carbohydrate 6g, of which sugars 4.8g; Fat 8.6g, of which saturates 2g; Cholesterol 210mg; Calcium 51mg; Fibre 0.7g; Sodium 253mg.
chicken in red sauce Energy 257kcal/1075kJ; Protein 29.3g; Carbohydrate 5g, of which sugars 4.9g; Fat 13.4g, of which saturates 2.3g; Cholesterol 57mg; Calcium 17mg; Fibre 0.1g; Sodium 208mg.

Chicken Tikka

This extremely popular Indian first course is quick and easy to cook. The dish can also be served as a main course for four.

Serves 6

450g/1lb boneless chicken, skinned and cubed
5ml/1 tsp crushed fresh root ginger
5ml/1 tsp crushed garlic
5ml/1 tsp chilli powder
1.5ml/¼ tsp ground turmeric
5ml/1 tsp salt
150ml/¼ pint/⅔ cup natural (plain) low-fat yogurt
60ml/4 tbsp lemon juice
15ml/1 tbsp chopped fresh coriander (cilantro)
15ml/1 tbsp oil

For the garnish

mixed salad leaves
1 small onion, cut into rings
lime wedges
fresh coriander (cilantro)

1 In a medium bowl, mix together the chicken pieces, ginger, garlic, chilli powder, turmeric and salt.

2 Stir in the yogurt, lemon juice and fresh coriander and leave to marinate for at least 2 hours.

3 Place in a grill (broiler) pan or in a flameproof dish lined with foil and baste with the oil.

4 Preheat the grill to medium. Grill (broil) the chicken for 15–20 minutes until cooked, turning and basting several times. Serve on a bed of mixed salad leaves, garnished with onion rings, lime wedges and coriander.

Cook's Tip

To make the turning and basting of the chicken easier, thread the chicken pieces on to six soaked wooden skewers before placing under the grill (broiler).

Chicken Kofta Balti with Paneer

This rather unusual appetizer looks most elegant when served in small individual karahis.

Serves 6

For the koftas

450g/1lb boneless chicken, skinned and cubed
5ml/1 tsp crushed garlic
5ml/1 tsp shredded fresh root ginger
7.5ml/1½ tsp ground coriander
7.5ml/1½ tsp chilli powder
7.5ml/1½ tsp ground fenugreek
1.5ml/¼ tsp ground turmeric
5ml/1 tsp salt
30ml/2 tbsp chopped fresh coriander (cilantro)
2 fresh green chillies, chopped
600ml/1 pint/2½ cups water
corn oil, for frying

For the paneer mixture

1 medium onion, sliced
1 red (bell) pepper, seeded and cut into strips
1 green (bell) pepper, seeded and cut into strips
175g/6oz paneer, cubed
175g/6oz/1½ cups corn
fresh mint sprigs

1 Put all the kofta ingredients, apart from the oil, into a medium pan. Bring to the boil slowly over medium heat, and cook until all the liquid has evaporated. Remove from the heat and leave to cool slightly. Put the mixture into a food processor or blender and process for 2 minutes.

2 Transfer the mixture to a large mixing bowl. Taking a little of the mixture at a time, shape it into small balls, using your hands. You should be able to make about 12 koftas. Heat the corn oil in a karahi, wok or deep pan over a high heat. Reduce the heat slightly and drop the koftas carefully into the oil. Move them around gently to ensure that they cook evenly.

3 When the koftas are lightly browned, remove them from the oil with a slotted spoon and drain on kitchen paper. Set aside.

4 Heat the oil still remaining in the karahi, and flash-fry all the ingredients for the paneer mixture. This should take about 3 minutes over high heat. Divide the paneer mixture evenly between six individual karahis. Add two koftas to each serving, and garnish with mint sprigs.

chicken tikka Energy 415kcal/1730kJ; Protein 46g; Carbohydrate 2g, of which sugars 0.2g; Fat 24.8g, of which saturates 8.5g; Cholesterol 203mg; Calcium 21mg; Fibre 0.5g; Sodium 172mg.
kofta balti Energy 253kcal/1056kJ; Protein 24.7g; Carbohydrate 10.8g, of which sugars 6.7g; Fat 12.6g, of which saturates 2.2g; Cholesterol 57mg; Calcium 71mg; Fibre 1.8g; Sodium 471mg.

Pineapple Chicken Kebabs

This chicken dish has a delicate tang and the meat is very tender. The pineapple not only tenderizes the chicken but also gives it a slight sweetness.

Serves 6

225g/8oz can pineapple chunks
5ml/1 tsp ground cumin
5ml/1 tsp ground coriander
5ml/1 tsp chilli powder
2.5ml/½ tsp crushed garlic
5ml/1 tsp salt
30ml/2 tbsp natural (plain) low-fat yogurt
15ml/1 tbsp chopped fresh coriander (cilantro)
few drops of orange food colouring (optional)
275g/10oz boneless chicken, skinned and cubed
½ red (bell) pepper, seeded
½ yellow or green (bell) pepper, seeded
1 large onion
6 cherry tomatoes
15ml/1 tbsp oil
salad leaves, to serve

1 Drain the pineapple juice into a bowl. Reserve eight large chunks of pineapple and squeeze the juice from the remaining chunks into the bowl and set aside. You should have about 120ml/ 4fl oz/½ cup pineapple juice.

2 In a large bowl, mix together the spices, garlic, salt, yogurt, fresh coriander, food colouring and pineapple juice. You can omit the food colouring if you wish.

3 Add the chicken to the yogurt and spice mixture, cover and leave to marinate in a cool place for about 1–1½ hours.

4 Cut the peppers and onion into bitesize chunks.

5 Preheat the grill (broiler) to medium. Arrange the chicken pieces, vegetables and reserved pineapple chunks alternately on six metal skewers.

6 Brush the kebabs lightly with the oil, then place the skewers on a flameproof dish or in a grill pan, turning the chicken pieces and basting with the marinade regularly, for about 15 minutes until cooked through. Serve with salad leaves.

Chicken & Pasta Balti

This is not a traditional balti dish, as pasta is not eaten widely in India or Pakistan; however, it is included here as it is truly delicious! The crushed pomegranate seeds give this dish an unusual tangy flavour.

Serves 4–6

75g/3oz/¾ cup small pasta shells (the coloured ones look most attractive)
75ml/5 tbsp corn oil
4 curry leaves
4 whole dried red chillies
1 large onion, sliced
5ml/1 tsp garlic pulp
5ml/1 tsp chilli powder
5ml/1 tsp shredded fresh root ginger
5ml/1 tsp crushed pomegranate seeds
5ml/1 tsp salt
2 medium tomatoes, chopped
175g/6oz chicken, skinned, boned and cubed
225g/8oz/1½ cups canned chickpeas, drained
115g/4oz/1 cup corn
50g/2oz mangetouts (snow peas), diagonally sliced
15ml/1 tbsp chopped fresh coriander (cilantro)

1 Cook the pasta in boiling water, following the directions on the packet. Add 15ml/1 tbsp of the oil to the water to prevent the pasta from sticking together. When it is cooked, drain and set to one side in a sieve (strainer).

2 Heat the remaining oil in a deep round frying pan or a large karahi, and add the curry leaves, whole dried chillies and the onion. Fry for about 5 minutes.

3 Add the garlic, chilli powder, ginger, pomegranate seeds, salt and tomatoes. Stir-fry for about 3 minutes.

4 Next add the cubed chicken, chickpeas, corn and mangetouts to the onion mixture. Cook over a medium heat for about 5 minutes, stirring constantly.

5 Add the pasta and stir well. Cook for a further 7–10 minutes, until the chicken is cooked through.

6 Serve garnished with the fresh coriander, if you wish.

pineapple kebabs Energy 135kcal/565kJ; Protein 13.2g; Carbohydrate 13.6g, of which sugars 10.3g; Fat 3.5g, of which saturates 0.6g; Cholesterol 32mg; Calcium 31mg; Fibre 1.7g; Sodium 35mg.
chicken & pasta Energy 350kcal/1468kJ; Protein 20.6g; Carbohydrate 29.4g, of which sugars 5.9g; Fat 17.6g, of which saturates 2.7g; Cholesterol 36mg; Calcium 51mg; Fibre 4.2g; Sodium 157mg.

Scented Chicken Wraps

For sheer sophistication, these leaf-wrapped chicken bites take a lot of beating. They are surprisingly easy to make and can be deep-fried in minutes in the wok.

Serves 4

400g/14oz skinless chicken thighs, boned
45ml/3 tbsp soy sauce
30ml/2 tbsp finely grated garlic
15ml/1 tbsp cumin
15ml/1 tbsp ground coriander
15ml/1 tbsp golden caster (superfine) sugar
5ml/1 tsp finely grated fresh root ginger
1 fresh bird's eye chilli
30ml/2 tbsp oyster sauce
15ml/1 tbsp fish sauce
1 bunch of pandanus leaves, to wrap
vegetable oil, for deep-frying
sweet chilli sauce or chilli sambal, to serve

1 Using a cleaver or sharp knife, cut the chicken into bitesize pieces and place in a large mixing bowl.

2 Place the soy sauce, garlic, cumin, coriander, sugar, ginger, chilli, oyster sauce and fish sauce in a blender and process until smooth. Pour over the chicken, cover and leave to marinate in the refrigerator for 6-8 hours.

3 When ready to cook, drain the chicken from the marinade and wrap each piece in a pandanus leaf (you will need to cut the leaves to size) and secure with a cocktail stick (toothpick).

4 Fill a wok one-third full of oil and heat to 180°C/350°F or until a cube of bread, dropped into the oil, browns in 45 seconds. Carefully add the chicken parcels, three or four at a time, and deep-fry for 3–4 minutes, or until cooked through. Drain on kitchen paper and serve with the chilli sauce or sambal. (Do not eat the leaves!)

Cook's Tip
Pandanus leaves are usually available from Asian supermarkets.

Chicken & Vegetable Bundles

Leeks form the wrappers for these enchanting little vegetable bundles. They taste good on their own, but even better with the soy and sesame oil dip.

Serves 4

4 skinless, boneless chicken thighs
5ml/1 tsp cornflour (cornstarch)
10ml/2 tsp dry sherry
30ml/2 tbsp light soy sauce
2.5ml/½ tsp salt
large pinch of ground white pepper
4 fresh shiitake mushrooms
1 small carrot
1 small courgette (zucchini)
50g/2oz/½ cup sliced, drained, canned bamboo shoots
1 leek, trimmed
1.5ml/¼ tsp sesame oil

1 Remove any fat from the chicken thighs before cutting each thigh lengthways into eight strips. Place the strips in a bowl. Add the cornflour, sherry and half the soy sauce to the chicken in the bowl. Stir in the salt and pepper and mix well. Cover with clear film (plastic wrap) and leave in a cool place to marinate for 10 minutes.

2 Remove and discard the mushroom stems, then cut each mushroom cap in half (or in slices if very large). Cut the carrot and courgette into eight batons, each about 5cm/2in long, then mix the mushroom halves and bamboo shoots together.

3 Bring a small pan of water to the boil. Add the leek and blanch until soft. Drain thoroughly, then slit the leek down its length. Separate each layer to give eight long strips.

4 Divide the marinated chicken into eight portions. Do the same with the vegetables. Wrap each strip of leek around a portion of chicken and vegetables to make eight neat bundles. Prepare a steamer.

5 Steam the chicken and vegetable bundles over a high heat for 12–15 minutes or until the filling is cooked. Serve with a sauce made by mixing the remaining soy sauce with the sesame oil.

scented chicken wraps Energy 159kcal/669kJ; Protein 24.5g; Carbohydrate 6.8g, of which sugars 6.6g; Fat 3.9g, of which saturates 0.6g; Cholesterol 70mg; Calcium 10mg; Fibre 0.1g; Sodium 1055mg.
chicken bundles Energy 450kcal/1891kJ; Protein 46.9g; Carbohydrate 36.2g, of which sugars 16.4g; Fat 14g, of which saturates 2.3g; Cholesterol 105mg; Calcium 131mg; Fibre 10.8g; Sodium 901mg.

Drunken Chicken

As the chicken is marinated for several days, it is important to use a very fresh bird from a reputable supplier.

Serves 4–6

1 chicken, about 1.3kg/3lb
1cm/½in piece of fresh root ginger, peeled and thinly sliced
2 spring onions (scallions), trimmed
1.75 litres/3 pints/7½ cups water
15ml/1 tbsp salt
300ml/½ pint/1¼ cups dry sherry
spring onions (scallions), shredded, and fresh herbs, to garnish

1 Rinse and dry the chicken inside and out. Place the ginger and spring onions in the body cavity. Put the chicken in a large pan or flameproof casserole and just cover with water. Bring to the boil, skim and cook for 15 minutes.

2 Turn off the heat, cover the pan tightly and leave the chicken in the liquid for 3–4 hours, by which time it will be cooked.

3 Drain the chicken well. Pour 300ml/½ pint/1¼ cups of the stock into a jug (pitcher). Freeze the remaining stock.

4 Remove the skin from the chicken and joint it neatly. Divide each leg into a drumstick and thigh. Make two more portions from the wings and some of the breast. Finally cut away the remainder of the breast pieces (still on the bone) and divide each breast into two even portions.

5 Arrange the chicken portions in a shallow dish. Rub salt into the chicken and cover with clear film (plastic wrap). Leave in a cool place for several hours or overnight in the refrigerator.

6 Later, lift off any fat from the stock. Mix the sherry and stock and pour over the chicken. Cover again and marinate in the refrigerator for 2 or 3 days, turning occasionally.

7 To serve, cut the chicken in chunky pieces and arrange on a platter garnished with spring onion shreds and herbs.

Spicy Chicken Wings

Whole chickens or just the wings and drumsticks, marinated in spicy or tangy pastes and then grilled over charcoal or fried in a wok, are a common sight in the food stalls of Malaysia and Singapore. Spicy wings and drumsticks are very popular as a quick snack, and are often served on their own with a few sprigs of coriander and slices of chilli to munch on.

Serves 4

12 chicken wings
fresh coriander (cilantro) leaves, roughly chopped, and 2–3 fresh green chillies, seeded and quartered lengthways, to garnish

For the spice paste
4 shallots, chopped
4 garlic cloves, chopped
25g/1oz fresh root ginger, chopped
8 fresh red chillies, seeded and chopped
1 lemon grass stalk, trimmed and chopped
30ml/2 tbsp sesame oil
15ml/1 tbsp tomato purée (paste)
10ml/2 tsp sugar
juice of 2 limes
salt and ground black pepper

1 First make the spice paste. Using a mortar and pestle or food processor, grind the shallots, garlic, ginger, chillies and lemon grass to a paste. Bind with the oil and stir in the tomato purée, sugar and lime juice. Season with salt and pepper.

2 Rub the spice paste into the chicken wings, place in a bowl, cover and leave to marinate for 2 hours.

3 Heat a grill (broiler) or prepare the barbecue. Lift the wings out of the marinade and place them on a rack. Cook them for about 5 minutes each side until cooked through, brushing with marinade while they cook.

4 Serve the chicken hot, garnished with coriander and chillies, and provide napkins so that people can eat with their hands.

drunken chicken Energy 608kcal/2553kJ; Protein 35.4g; Carbohydrate 52.7g, of which sugars 29g; Fat 17.6g, of which saturates 1.9g; Cholesterol 82mg; Calcium 107mg; Fibre 3.7g; Sodium 97mg.
spicy chicken wings Energy 350kcal/1455kJ; Protein 30.7g; Carbohydrate 2.6g, of which sugars 2.6g; Fat 24.1g, of which saturates 5.9g; Cholesterol 134mg; Calcium 11mg; Fibre 0.1g; Sodium 99mg.

Chicken Teriyaki

A simple bowl of boiled rice is the ideal accompaniment to this subtle Japanese chicken dish.

Serves 4

450g/1lb boneless chicken breast portions, skinned
orange segments and mustard and cress (fine curled cress), to garnish

For the marinade

5ml/1 tsp sugar
15ml/1 tbsp sake
15 ml/1 tbsp dry sherry
30ml/2 tbsp dark soy sauce
grated rind of 1 orange

1 Place the chicken on a board and slice into long, thin strips using a cleaver or sharp knife.

2 Mix together the sugar, sake, dry sherry, soy sauce and grated orange rind in a bowl.

3 Place the chicken in a separate bowl, pour over the marinade and set aside to marinate for 15 minutes.

4 Add the chicken and the marinade to a preheated wok and stir-fry for 4–5 minutes, until the chicken is fully cooked. Serve garnished with orange segments and mustard and cress.

Cook's Tip

Chicken Teriyaki makes a good sandwich filling. Let it cool in the marinade so that it remains moist and succulent. Watercress goes well with the chicken, as would a little pickled ginger.

Variation

This Japanese classic has gained exceptional popularity in the United States, where it is served at food outlets nationwide. Some recipes add fresh ginger, and a tablespoon of honey or maple syrup instead of the sugar to sweeten the marinade.

Grilled Chicken Balls on Skewers

These little morsels make a great pre-dinner snack.

Serves 4

300g/11oz skinless chicken, minced (ground)
2 eggs
2.5ml/½ tsp salt
10ml/2 tsp plain (all-purpose) flour
10ml/2 tsp cornflour (cornstarch)
90ml/6 tbsp dried breadcrumbs
2.5cm/1in piece fresh root ginger, grated

For the yakitori sauce

60ml/4 tbsp sake
75ml/5 tbsp shoyu
15ml/1 tbsp mirin
15ml/1 tbsp sugar
2.5ml/½ tsp cornflour (cornstarch) blended with 5ml/1 tsp water

1 Soak eight bamboo skewers for about 30 minutes in water. Put all the ingredients for the chicken balls, except the ginger, in a food processor and process to blend well.

2 Shape the mixture into a small ball about half the size of a golf ball. Make a further 30–32 balls in the same way.

3 Squeeze the juice from the grated ginger into a small mixing bowl. Discard the pulp. Preheat the grill (broiler).

4 Add the ginger juice to a small pan of boiling water. Add the chicken balls, and boil for about 7 minutes, or until the colour of the meat changes and the balls float to the surface. Scoop the balls out using a slotted spoon and drain on kitchen paper.

5 In a small pan, mix all the ingredients for the yakitori sauce, except the cornflour paste. Bring to the boil, then simmer until the sauce has reduced slightly. Add the cornflour paste and stir until thickened. Transfer to a small bowl.

6 Drain the skewers and thread three or four balls on each. Grill (broil) for a few minutes, turning, until they brown. Brush with sauce and return to the heat. Repeat twice, then serve.

chicken teriyaki Energy 149kcal/630kJ; Protein 27.4g; Carbohydrate 3.8g, of which sugars 3.8g; Fat 1.3g, of which saturates 0.3g; Cholesterol 79mg; Calcium 21mg; Fibre 0.5g; Sodium 70mg.
chicken balls Energy 332kcal/1398kJ; Protein 30.4g; Carbohydrate 29g, of which sugars 7.4g; Fat 9.7g, of which saturates 2.6g; Cholesterol 339mg; Calcium 84mg; Fibre 0.6g; Sodium 325mg.

Duck Egg Nets

These attractive parcels are usually made using a conical dispenser, but a thin funnel also works well.

Makes about 12–15

4 coriander (cilantro) roots
2 garlic cloves
10 white peppercorns
pinch of salt
45ml/3 tbsp oil
1 small onion, finely chopped
115g/4oz minced (ground) pork
75g/3oz shelled prawns (shrimp), chopped
50g/2oz/½ cup roasted peanuts, ground
5ml/1 tsp palm sugar (jaggery)
fish sauce, to taste
6 duck eggs
coriander (cilantro) leaves
spring onion (scallion) tassels and sliced red chillies, to garnish

1 Using a mortar and pestle, grind the coriander roots, garlic, white peppercorns and salt into a paste.

2 Heat 30ml/2 tbsp of the oil, add the paste and fry until fragrant. Add the onion and cook until softened. Add the pork and prawns and continue to stir-fry until the meat is cooked.

3 Add the peanuts, palm sugar, salt and fish sauce, to taste. Stir the mixture and continue to cook until it becomes a little sticky. Remove from the heat. Transfer the mixture to a small bowl and set aside.

4 Beat the duck eggs in a bowl. Grease a non-stick frying pan with the remaining oil and heat. Using a small hole funnel or squeezy bottle, trail the eggs across the pan to make a net pattern, about 13cm/5in in diameter.

5 When the net is set, carefully remove it from the pan, and repeat until all the eggs have been used up.

6 To assemble, lay a few coriander leaves on each net and top with a spoonful of the filling. Turn in the edges to make neat square shapes. Repeat with the rest of the nets. Arrange on a serving dish, garnish and serve.

Stuffed Aubergines with Lamb

Lamb and aubergines go really well together. This dish uses different coloured peppers in the lightly spiced filling mixture.

Serves 4

2 medium aubergines (eggplants)
15ml/1 tbsp oil, plus extra for brushing
1 medium onion, sliced
5ml/1 tsp shredded fresh root ginger
5ml/1 tsp chilli powder
5ml/1 tsp crushed garlic
1.5ml/¼ tsp ground turmeric
5ml/1 tsp salt
5ml/1 tsp ground coriander
1 medium tomato, chopped
350g/12oz lean leg of lamb, minced (ground)
1 medium green (bell) pepper, seeded and roughly chopped
1 medium orange (bell) pepper, seeded and roughly chopped
30ml/2 tbsp chopped fresh coriander (cilantro)
plain rice, to serve

For the garnish

½ onion, sliced
2 cherry tomatoes, quartered
fresh coriander (cilantro)

1 Cut the aubergines in half lengthways, and scoop out and discard most of the flesh. Preheat the oven to 180°C/350°F/Gas 4. Place the aubergine shells cut side up in a lightly greased ovenproof dish.

2 In a medium heavy pan, heat the oil and fry the onion until golden brown. Gradually stir in the ginger, chilli powder, garlic, turmeric, salt and ground coriander. Add the chopped tomato, lower the heat and cook for about 5 minutes, stirring frequently.

3 Add the minced lamb and cook for 7–10 minutes more.

4 Add the chopped peppers and chopped fresh coriander to the lamb mixture and stir well.

5 Spoon the lamb mixture into the aubergine shells and brush the edge of the shells with a little oil. Bake in the oven for 1 hour or until cooked through and browned on top.

6 Serve with the garnish ingredients, on a bed of plain rice.

duck egg nets Energy 90kcal/376kJ; Protein 6.1g; Carbohydrate 1.1g, of which sugars 0.8g; Fat 6.9g, of which saturates 1.4g; Cholesterol 151mg; Calcium 23mg; Fibre 0.3g; Sodium 43mg.
aubergines w. lamb Energy 291kcal/1211kJ; Protein 19.5g; Carbohydrate 13.3g, of which sugars 11.7g; Fat 18.1g, of which saturates 6.5g; Cholesterol 67mg; Calcium 48mg; Fibre 4.6g; Sodium 563mg.

Koftas in a Spicy Sauce

Little meatballs are called koftas in Indian cooking and are usually served in a spicy curry sauce. This curry is popular in most Indian homes.

Serves 4

225g/8oz/1 cup lean minced (ground) lamb
10ml/2 tsp poppy seeds
1 medium onion, chopped
5ml/1 tsp shredded fresh root ginger
5ml/1 tsp crushed garlic
5ml/1 tsp salt
5ml/1 tsp chilli powder
7.5ml/1½ tsp ground coriander
30ml/2 tbsp fresh coriander (cilantro) leaves
1 small egg, beaten

For the sauce

75ml/2fl oz/½ cup natural (plain) low-fat yogurt
30ml/2 tbsp tomato purée (paste)
5ml/1 tsp chilli powder
5ml/1 tsp salt
5ml/1 tsp crushed garlic
5ml/1 tsp crushed fresh root ginger
5ml/1 tsp garam masala
10ml/2 tsp oil
1 cinnamon stick
400ml/14fl oz/1⅔ cups water

1 Place the lamb in a food processor and mince (grind) it further for about 1 minute. Scrape the meat into a bowl, sprinkle the poppy seeds on top and set aside.

2 Place the onion in the food processor with the next five ingredients and half the fresh coriander. Grind for about 30 seconds, then add it to the lamb. Add the egg and mix well. Leave to stand for about 1 hour.

3 To make the sauce, whisk together the yogurt, tomato purée, chilli powder, salt, crushed garlic, ginger and garam masala. Heat the oil with the cinnamon stick in a pan for about 1 minute, then pour in the sauce. Lower the heat and cook for another minute. Remove from the heat and set aside.

4 Roll small balls of the meat mixture using your hands. Return the sauce to the heat and stir in the water. Drop in the koftas one by one. Add the remaining coriander, cover with a lid and cook for 7–10 minutes, stirring occasionally. Serve hot.

Curried Lamb Samosas

Filo pastry is perfect for making samosas. Once you've mastered folding them, you'll be amazed at how quick they are to make. These lamb samosas have a simple filling that is tasty and quick to make – perfect for party fare.

Makes 12

25g/1oz/2 tbsp butter
225g/8oz/1 cup minced (ground) lamb
30ml/2 tbsp mild curry paste
12 sheets of filo pastry, thawed and wrapped in a damp dish towel
salt and ground black pepper

1 Heat a little of the butter in a large pan and add the lamb. Fry for 5–6 minutes, stirring occasionally until browned. Stir in the curry paste and cook for 1–2 minutes. Season and set aside. Preheat the oven to 200°C/400°F/Gas 6.

2 Melt the remaining butter in a pan. Cut the pastry sheets in half lengthways. Brush one strip of pastry with butter, then lay another strip on top and brush with more butter.

3 Place a spoonful of lamb in the corner of the strip and fold over to form a triangle at one end. Keep folding over in the same way to form a triangular shape.

4 Brush with butter and place on a baking sheet. Repeat using the remaining pastry and filling. Bake for 10–15 minutes until golden. Serve hot.

Variation

For Cashew Nut Samosas, mix together 225g/8oz cooked and mashed potato, 15ml/1 tbsp chopped cashew nuts, 5ml/1 tsp coconut milk powder, ½ chopped green chilli, 5ml/1 tsp mustard seeds, 5ml/1 tsp cumin seeds, 15ml/1 tbsp chopped fresh coriander (cilantro) and 5ml/1 tsp soft light brown sugar. Use to fill the samosas in place of the lamb filling. If you like, the mustard and cumin seeds can be dry-roasted first.

koftas in a spicy sauce Energy 96kcal/404kJ; Protein 5.2g; Carbohydrate 11.8g, of which sugars 1.2g; Fat 3.5g, of which saturates 1.4g; Cholesterol 18mg; Calcium 16mg; Fibre 1g; Sodium 29mg.
curried lamb samosas Energy 101kcal/423kJ; Protein 5g; Carbohydrate 10.4g, of which sugars 0.2g; Fat 4.6g, of which saturates 2.3g; Cholesterol 19mg; Calcium 37mg; Fibre 1g; Sodium 37mg.

Tandoori Masala Spring Lamb Chops

These spicy, lean and trimmed lamb chops are marinated for three hours and then cooked in the oven using very little oil. They make a tasty appetizer, served with a salad garnish, and would also serve three as a main course if served with rice.

Serves 6

6 small lean spring lamb chops
30ml/2 tbsp natural (plain) low-fat yogurt
15ml/1 tbsp tomato purée (paste)
10ml/2 tsp ground coriander
5ml/1 tsp crushed fresh root ginger
5ml/1 tsp crushed garlic
5ml/1 tsp chilli powder
a few drops of red food colouring (optional)
5ml/1 tsp salt
15ml/1 tbsp oil, plus extra for basting
45ml/3 tbsp lemon juice

For the salad garnish

lettuce leaves (optional)
lime wedges
1 small onion, sliced
fresh coriander (cilantro)

1 Rinse the chops and pat them dry. Trim off all excess fat with a small, sharp knife.

2 In a medium bowl, mix together the yogurt, tomato purée, ground coriander, ginger and garlic, chilli powder, food colouring (if using), salt, oil and lemon juice.

3 Rub this spice mixture over the lamb chops, and leave the chops to marinate in a cool place for at least 3 hours.

4 Preheat the oven to 240°C/475°F/Gas 9. Place the marinated chops in an ovenproof dish.

5 Using a brush, baste the chops with about 5ml/1 tsp oil and cook in the oven for 15 minutes. Lower the heat to 180°C/350°F/Gas 4 and cook for a further 10–15 minutes.

6 Check that the chops are cooked and serve immediately on a bed of lettuce leaves, if you like, garnished with lime wedges, sliced onion and fresh coriander.

Lamb Kebabs

First introduced by the Muslims, kebabs have now become a favourite Indian dish and are often sold at open stalls; the wonderful aroma of the spicy meat is guaranteed to stop passers-by in their tracks to buy one.

Serves 8

For the kebabs

900g/2lb lean minced (ground) lamb
1 large onion, roughly chopped
5cm/2in piece fresh root ginger, chopped
2 garlic cloves, crushed
1 fresh green chilli, finely chopped
5ml/1 tsp chilli powder
30ml/2 tbsp chopped fresh coriander (cilantro)
5ml/1 tsp garam masala
10ml/2 tsp ground coriander
5ml/1 tsp ground cumin
5ml/1 tsp salt
1 egg
15ml/1 tbsp natural (plain) low-fat yogurt
15ml/1 tbsp oil
mixed salad, to serve

For the raita

250ml/8fl oz/1 cup natural (plain) low-fat yogurt
½ cucumber, finely chopped
30ml/2 tbsp chopped fresh mint
1.5ml/¼ tsp salt

1 Put all the ingredients for the kebabs, except the yogurt and oil, into a food processor or blender and process until the mixture binds together. Spoon into a bowl, cover and leave to marinate for 1 hour.

2 To make the raita, mix together all the ingredients and chill for at least 15 minutes in a refrigerator.

3 Preheat the grill (broiler). Divide the lamb mixture into eight equal portions with lightly floured hands and mould into long sausage shapes. Thread on to skewers and chill.

4 Brush the kebabs lightly with the yogurt and oil and cook under a hot grill for 8–10 minutes, turning occasionally, until brown all over. Serve the kebabs on a bed of mixed salad, accompanied by the raita.

tandoori lamb chops Energy 233kcal/974kJ; Protein 29.2g; Carbohydrate 2.3g, of which sugars 0.2g; Fat 12.1g, of which saturates 5.1g; Cholesterol 100mg; Calcium 60mg; Fibre 0.4g; Sodium 79mg.
lamb kebabs Energy 257kcal/1070kJ; Protein 17.2g; Carbohydrate 5.1g, of which sugars 4.5g; Fat 18.8g, of which saturates 6g; Cholesterol 64mg; Calcium 33mg; Fibre 0.6g; Sodium 59mg.

Shammi Kebabs

These Indian treats are derived from the kebabs of the Middle East. They can be served either as appetizers or side dishes with a raita or chutney.

Serves 5–6

2 onions, finely chopped
250g/9oz lean lamb, boned and cubed
50g/2oz/¼ cup chana dhal or yellow split peas
5ml/1 tsp cumin seeds
5ml/1 tsp garam masala
4–6 fresh green chillies
5cm/2in piece fresh root ginger, grated
175ml/6fl oz/¾ cup water
juice of 1 lemon
a few fresh coriander (cilantro) and mint leaves, chopped, plus extra coriander sprigs to garnish
15ml/1 tbsp gram flour
2 eggs, beaten
vegetable oil, for shallow-frying
salt

1 Put the first seven ingredients and the water into a large pan with salt, and bring to the boil. Simmer, covered, until the meat and dhal are cooked. Remove the lid and continue to cook for a few more minutes, to reduce the excess liquid. Set the mixture aside to cool.

2 Transfer the cooled meat mixture to a food processor or blender and process well until the mixture becomes a rough, gritty paste.

3 Put the paste into a large mixing bowl and add the chopped coriander and mint leaves, lemon juice and gram flour. Knead well with your fingers for a good couple of minutes, to ensure that all ingredients are evenly distributed through the mixture, and any excess liquid has been thoroughly absorbed. When the colour appears even throughout, and the mixture has taken on a semi-solid, sticky rather than powdery consistency, the kebabs are ready for shaping into portions.

4 Divide the mixture into 10–12 equal portions and use your hands to roll each into a ball, then flatten slightly. Chill for 1 hour. Dip the kebabs in the beaten egg and shallow-fry each side until golden brown. Pat dry on kitchen paper.

Lamb Satay

These spicy lamb skewers are traditionally served with dainty diamond-shaped pieces of compressed rice.

Makes 25–30 skewers

1kg/2¼lb leg of lamb, boned
3 garlic cloves, crushed
15–30ml/1–2 tbsp chilli sambal or 5–10ml/1–2 tsp chilli powder
90ml/6 tbsp dark soy sauce
juice of 1 lemon
salt and ground black pepper
groundnut (peanut) or sunflower oil, for brushing

For the sauce

6 garlic cloves, crushed
15ml/1 tbsp chilli sambal or 2–3 fresh chillies, seeded and ground to a paste
90ml/6 tbsp dark soy sauce
25ml/1½ tbsp lemon juice
30ml/2 tbsp boiling water
thinly sliced onion and cucumber wedges, to serve

1 Cut the lamb into neat 1cm/½in cubes. Remove any pieces of gristle, but do not trim off any of the fat because this keeps the meat moist during cooking and enhances the flavour. Spread out the lamb cubes in a single layer in a shallow bowl.

2 Put the garlic, chilli sambal or chilli powder, soy sauce and lemon juice in a mortar. Add salt and pepper and grind to a paste. Alternatively, process the mixture using a food processor. Pour over the lamb and mix to coat. Cover and leave in a cool place for at least 1 hour.

3 Soak wooden or bamboo skewers in water to prevent them from scorching during cooking.

4 For the sauce, put the garlic into a bowl. Add the chilli sambal or fresh chillies, soy sauce, lemon juice and boiling water. Stir.

5 Preheat the grill (broiler). Thread the meat on to the skewers. and brush with oil and grill (broil), turning often. Brush the satay with a little of the sauce and serve hot, with the onion and cucumber wedges. Offer the sauce separately.

shammi kebabs Energy 246kcal/1025kJ; Protein 13.1g; Carbohydrate 8.6g, of which sugars 0.8g; Fat 18.1g, of which saturates 4.1g; Cholesterol 95mg; Calcium 29mg; Fibre 0.6g; Sodium 64mg.
lamb satay Energy 994kcal/4157kJ; Protein 104.1g; Carbohydrate 18.5g, of which sugars 9.4g; Fat 56.6g, of which saturates 26.1g; Cholesterol 380mg; Calcium 74mg; Fibre 3.7g; Sodium 2572mg.

Spicy Pork Spare Ribs

These make a great – if slightly messy – appetizer to an informal meal.

Serves 4

675–900g/1½–2lb meaty pork spare ribs
5ml/1 tsp Sichuan peppercorns
30ml/2 tbsp coarse sea salt
2.5ml/½ tsp Chinese five-spice powder
25ml/1½ tbsp cornflour (cornstarch)
groundnut (peanut) oil, for deep-frying
coriander (cilantro) sprigs, to garnish

For the marinade

30ml/2 tbsp light soy sauce
5ml/1 tsp caster (superfine) sugar
15ml/1 tbsp dry sherry
ground black pepper

1 Using a sharp, heavy cleaver, chop the spare ribs into pieces about 5cm/2in long. Place them in a shallow dish and set aside.

2 Heat a wok to medium heat. Add the Sichuan peppercorns and salt and dry-fry for about 3 minutes, stirring until the mixture colours slightly. Remove from the heat and stir in the five-spice powder. Cool, then grind to a fine powder.

3 Sprinkle 5ml/1 tsp of the spice powder over the spare ribs and rub in well with your hands. Add all the marinade ingredients and toss the ribs to coat thoroughly. Cover and leave in the refrigerator to marinate for about 2 hours.

4 Pour off any excess marinade from the spare ribs. Sprinkle the ribs with the cornflour and mix to coat evenly.

5 Deep-fry the spare ribs in batches for 3 minutes until golden. Remove and set aside. When all the batches have been cooked, reheat the oil and deep-fry the ribs for a second time for 1–2 minutes, until crisp and thoroughly cooked. Drain on kitchen paper. Transfer the ribs to a warm serving platter and sprinkle over 5–7.5ml/1–1½ tsp of the remaining spice powder.

6 Garnish with coriander sprigs and serve immediately.

Pork Satay with Pineapple Sauce

Children love these lightly spiced satay sticks.

Serves 4

500g/1¼lb pork fillet (tenderloin), cubed
salt and ground black pepper
fresh coriander (cilantro) leaves, roughly chopped, to garnish

For the marinade

4 shallots, chopped
4 garlic cloves, chopped
5ml/1 tsp ground coriander
5ml/1 tsp ground cumin
2.5ml/½ tsp ground turmeric
30ml/2 tbsp dark soy sauce
30ml/2 tbsp sesame oil

For the sauce

4 shallots, chopped
2 garlic cloves, chopped
4 dried red chillies, soaked in warm water until soft, seeded and chopped
1 lemon grass stalk, chopped
25g/1oz fresh root ginger, chopped
30ml/2 tbsp sesame oil
200ml/7fl oz/scant 1 cup coconut milk
10ml/2 tsp tamarind paste
10ml/2 tsp palm sugar (jaggery)
1 fresh pineapple, peeled, cored and cut into slices

1 To make the marinade, using a mortar and pestle, grind the shallots and garlic to a paste. Stir in the spices, soy sauce and oil. Rub the marinade into the meat. Cover and set aside for 2 hours at cool room temperature.

2 Meanwhile, prepare the sauce. Pound the shallots, garlic, chillies, lemon grass and ginger to form a paste. Heat the oil in a heavy pan and cook the paste for 2–3 minutes, then stir in the coconut milk, tamarind paste and sugar. Bring to the boil, then simmer for 5 minutes. Season and leave to cool.

3 Using a mortar and pestle, crush three pineapple slices; beat them into the sauce. Soak eight bamboo skewers in cold water. Prepare a barbecue. Drain the skewers and thread them with the marinated meat. Cook over the coals with the remaining slices of pineapple alongside. Char the pineapple slices and chop them into chunks. Barbecue the meat until just cooked, about 2–3 minutes each side, and serve immediately with the pineapple chunks and the sauce, garnished with coriander.

spicy pork spare ribs Energy 424kcal/1763kJ; Protein 32.2g; Carbohydrate 2.6g, of which sugars 1.3g; Fat 31.4g, of which saturates 9.8g; Cholesterol 111mg; Calcium 33mg; Fibre 0g; Sodium 345mg.
pork satay Energy 306kcal/1286kJ; Protein 28.4g; Carbohydrate 20.3g, of which sugars 19g; Fat 12.9g, of which saturates 2.9g; Cholesterol 79mg; Calcium 48mg; Fibre 2.3g; Sodium 98mg.

Steamed Pork Balls

Bitesize balls of steamed pork and mushrooms rolled in jasmine rice make a fabulous snack.

Serves 4

30ml/2 tbsp vegetable oil
200g/7oz/scant 3 cups finely chopped shiitake mushrooms
400g/14oz lean minced (ground) pork
4 spring onions (scallions), chopped
2 garlic cloves, crushed
15ml/1 tbsp fish sauce
15ml/1 tbsp soy sauce
15ml/1 tsp grated root ginger
60ml/4 tbsp finely chopped coriander (cilantro)
1 egg, lightly beaten
salt and ground black pepper
200g/7oz/1 cup cooked jasmine rice

For the dipping sauce

120ml/4fl oz/½ cup sweet chilli sauce
105ml/7 tbsp soy sauce
15ml/1 tbsp Chinese rice wine
5–10ml/1–2 tsp chilli oil

1 Heat the oil in a wok, then stir-fry the mushrooms for 2–3 minutes. Transfer to a food processor with the pork, spring onions, garlic, fish sauce, soy sauce, ginger, coriander and beaten egg. Season with salt and pepper and process for 30–40 seconds. Scrape the mixture into a bowl, cover and chill for 3–4 hours or overnight.

2 Place the jasmine rice in a bowl. With wet hands, divide the mushroom mixture into 20 portions and roll each one into a firm ball. Roll each ball in the rice, then arrange the balls, spaced apart, in two baking parchment-lined tiers of a bamboo steamer.

3 Cover the steamer and place over a wok of simmering water. Steam for 1 hour 15 minutes.

4 Meanwhile, combine all the dipping sauce ingredients in a small bowl and stir well.

5 When the pork balls are fully cooked, remove them from the steamer and serve them warm with the spicy dipping sauce.

Pork on Lemon Grass Sticks

This simple recipe makes a substantial snack, and the lemon grass sticks not only add a subtle flavour but also make a good talking point.

Serves 4

300g/11oz finely minced (ground) pork
4 garlic cloves, crushed
4 fresh coriander (cilantro) roots, finely chopped
2.5ml/½ tsp sugar
15ml/1 tbsp soy sauce or kecap manis
salt and ground black pepper
8 x 10cm/4in lengths of lemon grass stalk
sweet chilli sauce or chilli sambal, to serve

1 Place the minced pork, crushed garlic, chopped coriander root, sugar and soy sauce or kecap manis in a large bowl. Season with salt and pepper to taste and mix well.

2 Divide the pork mixture into eight portions and mould each one into a ball. It may help to dampen your hands before shaping the mixture to prevent it from sticking.

3 Stick a length of lemon grass halfway into each ball, then press the meat mixture around the lemon grass to make a shape like a chicken leg.

4 Cook the pork sticks under a hot grill (broiler) for 3–4 minutes on each side, until golden and cooked through.

5 Serve with the chilli sauce or sambal for dipping.

Variations

- *Slimmer versions of these pork sticks are perfect for parties. The mixture will be enough for 12 lemon grass sticks if you use it sparingly.*
- *Sweet and sour sauce can be used instead of sweet chilli sauce, or try a peach chutney for a fusion flavour.*

pork balls Energy 322kcal/1353kJ; Protein 25.8g; Carbohydrate 29.9g, of which sugars 14.3g; Fat 11.8g, of which saturates 2.7g; Cholesterol 111mg; Calcium 39mg; Fibre 0.8g; Sodium 893mg.
pork on lemon grass Energy 132kcal/552kJ; Protein 14.7g; Carbohydrate 2g, of which sugars 1.6g; Fat 7.3g, of which saturates 2.7g; Cholesterol 50mg; Calcium 10mg; Fibre 0.2g; Sodium 317mg.

Crispy Pork Balls

These crispy balls make a delicious party food.

Serves 4–6

4 slices of white bread, crusts removed
5ml/1 tsp olive oil
225g/8oz skinless, boneless pork meat, roughly chopped
50g/2oz/⅓ cup drained, canned water chestnuts
2 fresh red chillies, seeded and roughly chopped
1 egg white
10g/¼oz/¼ cup fresh coriander (cilantro) leaves
5ml/1 tsp cornflour (cornstarch)
2.5ml/½ tsp salt
1.5ml/¼ tsp ground white pepper
30ml/2 tbsp light soy sauce
5ml/1 tsp caster (superfine) sugar
30ml/2 tbsp rice vinegar
2.5ml/½ tsp chilli oil
shredded red chillies and fresh coriander (cilantro) sprigs

1 Preheat the oven to 120°C/250°F/Gas ½. Brush the bread slices with olive oil and cut them into 5mm/¼in cubes. Spread over a baking sheet and bake for 15 minutes until dry and crisp.

2 Meanwhile, mix together the pork meat, water chestnuts and chillies in a food processor. Process to a coarse paste.

3 Add the egg white, coriander, cornflour, salt, pepper and half the soy sauce. Process for 30 seconds. Scrape into a bowl, cover and set aside.

4 Remove the toasted bread cubes from the oven and set them aside. Raise the oven temperature to 200°C/400°F/Gas 6. Shape the pork mixture into 12 balls.

5 Crush the toasted bread cubes and coat the pork balls in the crumbs. Place on a baking sheet and bake for about 20 minutes or until the pork filling is cooked.

6 In a small bowl, mix the remaining soy sauce with the caster sugar, rice vinegar and chilli oil. Serve the sauce with the pork balls, garnished with shredded chillies and coriander sprigs.

Clear Rice Paper Rolls

Pretty as a picture, these transparent pork rollls allow the filling to be glimpsed through the wrap.

Serves 8

50g/2oz fine rice vermicelli
225g/8oz/1 cup beansprouts, rinsed and drained
8 crisp lettuce leaves, halved
fresh mint and coriander (cilantro) leaves
175g/6oz peeled cooked prawns (shrimp), thawed if frozen
225g/8oz tender cooked pork, sliced in strips
16 large rice-paper roll wrappers
black bean sauce, to serve

1 Soak the vermicelli in warm water until softened. Drain, then snip into short lengths. Heat a pan of boiling water for 1 minute, drain, rinse and drain again. Tip into a serving bowl. Put the beansprouts in a dish and arrange the lettuce and herb leaves on a platter. Put the prawns and pork in separate bowls.

2 Soften the rice papers in water as described on the packet, then place two on each plate. Each guest places a piece of lettuce on one end of a wrapper, tops it with noodles, beansprouts and herbs and adds some strips of pork.

3 Roll the wrapper one turn, place a few prawns on the open part, and complete the roll. Dip in black bean sauce. Prepare the second roll in the same way.

Variation
A simpler version of this recipe uses flavoured minced (ground) pork to fill these rice paper rolls. Begin by heating 15ml/1 tbsp oil in a frying pan, then fry 350g/12oz/1½ cups minced pork for 5–6 minutes, until browned all over. Season well, stir in 30ml/1 tbsp oyster sauce and leave to cool. Use the mixture to fill eight softened rice-paper wrappers, using the technique described in the recipe above. Serve with chilli dip.

crispy pork balls Energy 161kcal/676kJ; Protein 12.9g; Carbohydrate 15g, of which sugars 7.1g; Fat 5.9g, of which saturates 1.3g; Cholesterol 55mg; Calcium 19mg; Fibre 0.4g; Sodium 446mg.
clear rice paper rolls Energy 127kcal/534kJ; Protein 11.6g; Carbohydrate 16.5g, of which sugars 1g; Fat 1.5g, of which saturates 0.4g; Cholesterol 58mg; Calcium 36mg; Fibre 0.9g; Sodium 62mg.

Lion's Head Meat Balls

These larger-than-usual pork balls are first fried, then simmered in stock. They are often served with a fringe of greens such as pak choi to represent the lion's mane.

Serves 2–3

450g/1lb lean pork, minced (ground) finely with a little fat
4–6 drained canned water chestnuts, finely chopped
5ml/1 tsp finely chopped fresh root ginger
1 small onion, finely chopped
30ml/2 tbsp dark soy sauce
beaten egg, to bind
30ml/2 tbsp cornflour (cornstarch), seasoned with salt and ground black pepper
30ml/2 tbsp groundnut (peanut) oil
300ml/½ pint/1¼ cups chicken stock
2.5ml/½ tsp sugar
115g/4oz pak choi (bok choy), stalks trimmed and the leaves rinsed
salt and ground black pepper

1 Mix the pork, water chestnuts, ginger and onion with 15ml/1 tbsp of the soy sauce in a bowl. Add salt and pepper to taste, stir in enough beaten egg to bind, then form into eight or nine balls. Toss a little of the cornflour into the bowl and make a paste with the remaining cornflour and a little water.

2 Heat the oil in a large frying pan and brown the meat balls all over. Using a slotted spoon, transfer the meat balls to a wok or deep frying pan.

3 Add the stock, sugar and the remaining soy sauce to the oil that is left in the pan. Heat gently, stirring to incorporate the sediment on the bottom of the pan. Pour over the meat balls, cover and simmer for 20–25 minutes.

4 Increase the heat and add the pak choi. Continue to cook for 2–3 minutes or until the leaves are just wilted.

5 Lift out the greens and arrange on a serving platter. Top with the meat balls and keep hot. Stir the cornflour paste into the sauce. Bring to the boil, stirring, until it thickens. Pour over the meat balls and serve immediately.

Dry-cooked Pork Strips

This very simple dish is quick and light on a hot day. Pork, chicken, prawns and squid can all be cooked this way. With the lettuce and herbs, the pork strips make a very flavoursome snack, but you can also serve them with a dipping sauce.

Serves 2–4

15ml/1 tbsp groundnut (peanut) oil
30ml/2 tbsp fish sauce
30ml/2 tbsp soy sauce
5ml/1 tsp sugar
225g/8oz pork fillet (tenderloin), cut into thin, bitesize strips
8 lettuce leaves
shreds of spring onion (scallion)
chilli oil, for drizzling
fresh coriander (cilantro) leaves
a handful of fresh mint leaves

1 In a wok or heavy pan, heat the oil, fish sauce and soy sauce with the sugar. Add the pork and stir-fry over a medium heat, until all the liquid has evaporated. Cook the pork until it turns brown, almost caramelized, but not burnt.

2 For a light snack, serve the dry-cooked pork strips with a few salad leaves and add a few shreds of spring onion (scallion).

3 For wraps, drop a few strips on to large lettuce leaves, drizzle a little chilli oil over the top, add a few coriander and mint leaves, wrap them up and serve immediately. These make good finger food.

Cook's Tip
'Dry-cooking' usually refers to the large-scale reduction of the liquid content during cooking, rather than an absence of liquid.

Variation
Try serving the pork strips on basil leaves or flat leaf parsley, sprinkled with sliced red onion.

lion's head meat balls Energy 326kcal/1363kJ; Protein 35.2g; Carbohydrate 13.1g, of which sugars 3.3g; Fat 15g, of which saturates 3.4g; Cholesterol 139mg; Calcium 91mg; Fibre 1.1g; Sodium 893mg.
dry-cooked pork strips Energy 104kcal/435kJ; Protein 12.5g; Carbohydrate 2.1g, of which sugars 2g; Fat 5.1g, of which saturates 1.2g; Cholesterol 35mg; Calcium 13mg; Fibre 0.2g; Sodium 574mg.

Pork-stuffed Green Peppers

Small, thin-skinned peppers are best for this traditional Chinese dish.

Serves 4

225g/8oz minced (ground) pork
4–6 drained canned water chestnuts, finely chopped
2 spring onions (scallions), finely chopped
2.5ml/½ tsp finely chopped fresh root ginger
15ml/1 tbsp light soy sauce
15ml/1 tbsp Chinese rice wine or dry sherry
3–4 green (bell) peppers
15ml/1 tbsp cornflour (cornstarch)
oil for deep-frying

For the sauce

30ml/2 tbsp light soy sauce
5ml/1 tsp soft light brown sugar
1–2 fresh red chillies, finely chopped
75ml/5 tbsp ham stock or water

1 Mix the minced pork, chopped water chestnuts, spring onions and ginger. Add the soy sauce and wine or sherry and work them into the pork mixture so that they are evenly distributed.

2 Cut the peppers in half lengthways and remove the cores and seeds. If the peppers are large, halve them again to make quarters. Stuff the peppers with the pork mixture, pressing it down firmly. Sprinkle a little cornflour over the filled peppers.

3 Heat the oil for deep-frying in a wok, or use a deep-fryer. Using a large slotted spoon, carefully add the stuffed peppers, meat-side down, and fry them for 2–3 minutes. If you have cut the peppers into quarters, you will probably need to do this in batches. Lift out and drain on kitchen paper.

4 Let the oil cool slightly, then pour most of it into a separate container to discard or reuse in another recipe. Heat the oil remaining in the wok and add the peppers, this time placing them meat-side up. Add the sauce ingredients, shaking the wok so they do not stick to the bottom, and braise the peppers for 2–3 minutes. Lift them on to a serving dish, meat-side up, pour the sauce over and serve immediately.

Bacon-wrapped Beef on Skewers

In northern Vietnam, beef often features on the street menu. Grilled, stir-fried, or sitting majestically in a steaming bowl of pho, beef is used with pride. In Cambodia and southern Vietnam, snacks like this one would normally be made with pork or chicken.

Serves 4

225g/8oz beef fillet (tenderloin) or rump (round) steak, cut across the grain into 12 strips
12 thin strips of streaky (fatty) bacon
ground black pepper
chilli sambal, for dipping

For the marinade

15ml/1 tbsp groundnut (peanut) oil
30ml/2 tbsp fish sauce
30ml/2 tbsp soy sauce
4–6 garlic cloves, crushed
10ml/2 tsp sugar

1 To make the marinade, mix all the ingredients in a large bowl until the sugar dissolves. Season generously with black pepper. Add the beef strips, stir to coat them in the marinade, and set aside for about an hour.

2 Preheat a griddle pan over a high heat. Roll up each strip of beef and wrap it in a slice of bacon. Thread the rolls on to the skewers, so that you have three on each one.

3 Cook the bacon-wrapped rolls on the hot griddle for 4–5 minutes, turning once, until the bacon is golden and crispy. Serve immediately, with a bowl of chilli sambal for dipping.

Cook's Tip

These tasty skewers can also be cooked under a preheated grill (broiler), or over hot coals on the barbecue. Simply cook for 6–8 minutes, turning every couple of minutes so that the bacon is browned but not burned. Serve them as an appetizer ahead of the main course – they are light enough to whet the appetite without spoiling enjoyment of the rest of the meal.

pork-stuffed peppers Energy 198kcal/825kJ; Protein 12.5g; Carbohydrate 4.7g, of which sugars 4.3g; Fat 14.2g, of which saturates 3.1g; Cholesterol 37mg; Calcium 26mg; Fibre 2.3g; Sodium 942mg.
bacon-wrapped beef Energy 282kcal/1172kJ; Protein 21.7g; Carbohydrate 1.1g, of which sugars 1.1g; Fat 21.3g, of which saturates 7.1g; Cholesterol 69mg; Calcium 7mg; Fibre 0g; Sodium 745mg.

Bacon-rolled Enokitake

The Japanese name for this dish is obimaki enoki: an obi (belt or sash) is made from bacon and wrapped around enoki mushrooms before they are cooked. The strong, smoky flavour of the bacon complements the subtle flavour of the mushrooms.

Serves 4

450g/1lb fresh enoki mushrooms
6 rindless smoked streaky (fatty) bacon rashers (strips)
4 lemon wedges, to serve

1 Cut off the root part of each enokitake cluster 2cm/¾in from the end. Do not separate the stems. Cut the bacon rashers in half lengthways.

2 Divide the enokitake into 12 equal bunches. Take one bunch, then place the middle of the enokitake near the edge of one bacon rasher, with 2.5–4cm/1–1½in of enokitake protruding at each end.

3 Carefully roll up the bunch of enokitake in the bacon. Tuck any straying short stems into the bacon and slide the bacon slightly upwards at each roll to cover about 4cm/1½in of the enokitake. Secure the end of the bacon roll with a cocktail stick (toothpick). Repeat using the remaining enokitake and bacon to make 11 more rolls.

4 Preheat the grill (broiler) to a high temperature. Place the enokitake rolls on an oiled wire rack. Grill (broil) both sides until the bacon is crisp and the enokitake start to char. This takes about 10–13 minutes.

5 Place the enokitake rolls on a board. Using a fork and knife, chop each roll in half in the middle of the bacon belt.

6 Arrange the top part of the enokitake roll standing upright, the bottom part lying down next to it. Add a wedge of lemon to each portion and serve.

Beef Satay

The spicy peanut paste, satay, is a great favourite in South-east Asia and is used for grilling and stir-frying meats and seafood.

Serves 4–6

500g/1¼lb beef sirloin, cut in bitesize pieces
15ml/1 tbsp groundnut (peanut) oil
1 bunch rocket (arugula) leaves

For the satay
60ml/4 tbsp groundnut (peanut) or vegetable oil
5 garlic cloves, crushed
5 dried Serrano chillies, seeded and ground
10ml/2 tsp curry powder
50g/2oz/⅓ cup roasted peanuts, finely ground

1 To make the satay, heat the oil in a wok or heavy pan and stir in the garlic until it begins to colour. Add the chillies, curry powder and peanuts and stir over a gentle heat until the mixture begins to form a paste. Remove from the heat and leave the paste to cool.

2 Put the beef into a large bowl. Beat the groundnut oil into the satay and add the mixture to the pieces of beef. Mix well, so that the beef is evenly coated, and put aside to marinate for 30–40 minutes.

3 Soak four to six wooden skewers in water for 30 minutes to prevent them burning. Prepare a barbecue or preheat the grill (broiler). Thread the meat on to the skewers and cook for 2–3 minutes on each side. Serve with the rocket leaves for wrapping.

Cook's Tip

This is a great barbecue dish that works just as well with pork tenderloin, chicken breast, prawns or shrimp. Jars of satay paste are now available in many stores but they taste nothing like the homemade version, which you can pep up with as much garlic and chilli as you like. The beef is also delicious served with a salad, rice wrappers and a light dipping sauce.

bacon-rolled enokitake Energy 84kcal/348kJ; Protein 6g; Carbohydrate 0.5g, of which sugars 0.2g; Fat 6.5g, of which saturates 2.2g; Cholesterol 16mg; Calcium 8mg; Fibre 1.3g; Sodium 321mg.
beef satay Energy 289kcal/1199kJ; Protein 22.3g; Carbohydrate 2.5g, of which sugars 0.9g; Fat 21.1g, of which saturates 5g; Cholesterol 48mg; Calcium 52mg; Fibre 1.4g; Sodium 85mg.

Beef Fondue

The stock for this dish is flavoured with soy sauce, fish sauce and warm spices.

Serves 4–6

30ml/2 tbsp sesame oil
1 garlic clove, crushed
2 shallots, finely chopped
2.5cm/1in fresh root ginger, peeled and finely sliced
1 lemon grass stalk, cut into several pieces and bruised
30ml/2 tbsp sugar
250ml/8½fl oz/1 cup white rice vinegar
300ml/½ pint/1¼ cups beef stock
700g/1lb 10oz beef fillet (tenderloin), thinly sliced into rectangular strips
salt and ground black pepper
chopped or sliced salad vegetables, herbs and rice wrappers, to serve

For the dipping sauce

15ml/1 tbsp white rice vinegar
juice of 1 lime
5ml/1 tsp sugar
1 garlic clove, peeled and chopped
2 fresh red chillies, seeded and chopped
12 canned anchovy fillets, drained
2 slices of pineapple, cored and chopped

1 To make the dipping sauce, in a bowl, mix the vinegar and lime juice with the sugar, until the sugar dissolves. Using a mortar and pestle, pound the garlic, chillies and anchovy fillets to a paste, then add the pineapple and pound it to a pulp. Stir in the vinegar and lime juice mixture, and set aside.

2 When ready to eat, heat 15ml/1 tbsp of the sesame oil in a heavy pan, wok or fondue pot. Quickly stir-fry the garlic, shallots, ginger and lemon grass until fragrant and golden, then add the sugar, vinegar, beef stock and the remaining sesame oil. Bring to the boil, stirring, and season with salt and pepper.

3 Transfer the pan or fondue pot to a lighted burner at the table. Lay the beef strips on a large serving dish. Using chopsticks or fondue forks, each person cooks their own meat in the broth and dips it into the sauce. Serve with salad vegetables, chopped herbs and rice wrappers.

Chilli & Honey-cured Beef

Asian cooks will dry almost anything – dried beef is used here but fish, chillies, mushrooms, snake, mangoes and pigs' ears are also popular. Some dried goods are destined for stews, soups and medicinal purposes, whereas others are just for chewing on.

Serves 4

450g/1lb beef sirloin
2 lemon grass stalks, trimmed and chopped
2 garlic cloves, chopped
2 dried Serrano chillies, seeded and chopped
30–45ml/2–3 tbsp clear honey
15ml/1 tbsp fish sauce
30ml/2 tbsp soy sauce
rice wrappers, fresh herbs and dipping sauce, to serve (optional)

1 Trim the beef and cut it across the grain into thin, rectangular slices, then set aside.

2 Using a mortar and pestle, grind the chopped lemon grass, garlic and chillies to a paste. Stir in the honey, fish sauce and soy sauce. Put the beef into a bowl, add the paste and rub it into the meat.

3 Spread out the meat on a wire rack and place it in the refrigerator, uncovered, for 2 days, or until dry and hard.

4 Cook the dried beef on the barbecue or under a conventional grill (broiler) for about 3 minutes each side, and serve it with rice wrappers, fresh herbs and a dipping sauce.

Variation
This recipe also works well with venison. Cut the meat into thin strips and dry exactly as above. The resulting dish will give you a South-east Asian version of the famous biltong, a dish with Dutch roots created by South Africa's European pioneers. Biltong is often likened to beef jerky, but it is more likely to be made from game meats, including venison and ostrich.

beef fondue Energy 293kcal/1225kJ; Protein 28.9g; Carbohydrate 10.4g, of which sugars 10.1g; Fat 15.4g, of which saturates 5.1g; Cholesterol 72mg; Calcium 42mg; Fibre 0.5g; Sodium 333mg.
chilli & honey-cured beef Energy 158kcal/659kJ; Protein 17.3g; Carbohydrate 6.7g, of which sugars 6.6g; Fat 7g, of which saturates 2.9g; Cholesterol 43mg; Calcium 6mg; Fibre 0.1g; Sodium 405mg.

Prawns with Chayote in Turmeric Sauce

This delicious, attractively coloured dish contains the squash chayote, but courgette also works well.

Serves 4

1 or 2 chayotes or 2 or 3 courgettes (zucchini)
2 fresh red chillies, seeded
1 onion, quartered
5ml/1 tsp grated fresh root ginger
1 lemon grass stalk, lower 5cm/2in sliced, top bruised
2.5cm/1in fresh turmeric, peeled
200ml/7fl oz/scant 1 cup water
15ml/1 tbsp lemon juice
400ml/14fl oz can coconut milk
450g/1lb cooked, peeled prawns (shrimp)
salt
fresh red chilli shreds, to garnish
boiled rice, to serve

1 Peel the chayotes, remove the seeds and cut into strips. If using courgettes, cut into 5cm/2in strips.

2 Grind the fresh red chillies, onion, ginger, sliced lemon grass and the fresh turmeric to a paste in a food processor or with a mortar and pestle. Add the water to the paste mixture, with the lemon juice and salt to taste.

3 Pour into a pan. Add the top of the lemon grass stem. Bring to the boil and cook for 1–2 minutes. Add the chayote or courgette pieces and simmer for 2 minutes. Stir in the coconut milk. Taste and adjust the seasoning.

4 Stir in the prawns and cook gently for 2–3 minutes. Remove the lemon grass stalk. Garnish with shreds of chilli and serve with rice.

Cook's Tip
The chayote is a small, green pear-shaped squash, whose mild taste is rather like a cross between a cucumber and an apple.

Pineapple Curry with Prawns & Mussels

The delicate sweet-and-sour flavour of this curry comes from the pineapple, and although it seems an odd combination, it is rather delicious. Use the freshest shellfish that you can find.

Serves 4–6

600ml/1 pint/2½ cups coconut milk
30ml/2 tbsp curry paste
15ml/1 tbsp sugar
225g/8oz king prawns (jumbo shrimp), peeled and deveined
450g/1lb mussels, cleaned (see Cook's Tip)
175g/6oz fresh pineapple, finely crushed or chopped
2 bay leaves
2 fresh red chillies, chopped, and coriander (cilantro) leaves, to garnish

1 In a large pan, bring half the coconut milk to the boil and heat, stirring, until it separates.

2 Add the curry paste and cook until fragrant. Add the sugar and continue to cook for 1 minute.

3 Stir in the remainder of the coconut milk and bring back to the boil. Add the king prawns, mussels, chopped pineapple and bay leaves.

4 Reheat until boiling and then simmer for 3–5 minutes, until the prawns are cooked and the mussels have opened. Remove any mussels that have not opened and throw them away. Discard the bay leaves if you like. Serve the curry garnished with chopped red chillies and coriander leaves.

Cook's Tip
To clean mussels, scrub the shells with a stiff brush and rinse them under cold running water. Scrape off any barnacles and remove the 'beards' with a small knife. Rinse well.

prawns w. chayote Energy 131kcal/553kJ; Protein 22.1g; Carbohydrate 7.9g, of which sugars 7.5g; Fat 1.4g, of which saturates 0.4g; Cholesterol 219mg; Calcium 147mg; Fibre 1.1g; Sodium 325mg.
pineapple curry Energy 85kcal/358kJ; Protein 11.4g; Carbohydrate 7.4g, of which sugars 5.6g; Fat 1.4g, of which saturates 0.2g; Cholesterol 82mg; Calcium 90mg; Fibre 0.4g; Sodium 122mg.

Red Cooked Prawns on the Shell

This has become a staple dish in Chinese restaurants throughout South-east Asia. For aesthetic reasons, and to maximize the flavour, the prawns are not shelled, although you can remove the heads without compromising the flavour too much.

Serves 4

450g/1lb tiger prawns (jumbo shrimp)
30ml/2 tbsp vegetable oil
30ml/2 tbsp chopped root ginger
30ml/2 tbsp chopped garlic
1 large onion, sliced
30ml/2 tbsp tomato ketchup
30ml/2 tbsp oyster sauce
100ml/3½fl oz/scant ½ cup water
whole lettuce leaves, to serve

1 Clean the prawns and cut off 1cm/½in from the head end of each. Slice each prawn in half lengthways leaving the shells on.

2 Heat a wok. Dribble the vegetable oil around the rim so that it flows down to coat the surface. When the oil is hot, add the ginger and garlic. Stir-fry for 30 seconds.

3 Add the onion slices and stir-fry for 2 minutes. Toss the prawns into the wok and stir-fry over high heat for 2–3 minutes or until they have turned pink. Using a slotted spoon, transfer the prawns to a bowl.

4 Pour the tomato ketchup and oyster sauce into the wok, add the water and quickly bring to the boil, stirring all the time.

5 Arrange the lettuce leaves on a platter or on individual plates. Divide the prawns among them and spoon the sauce over. Serve immediately.

Cook's Tip
The prawns are eaten with the hands, so provide each guest a water bowl to rinse their fingers.

Prawns with Okra

This dish has a sweet taste with a strong chilli flavour. It should be cooked fast to prevent the okra from breaking up and releasing its distinctive, sticky juice.

Serves 4–6

60–90ml/4–6 tbsp oil
225g/8oz okra, washed, dried and left whole
4 cloves garlic, crushed
5cm/2in long piece fresh root ginger, crushed
4–6 fresh green chillies, cut diagonally
2.5ml/½ tsp ground turmeric
4–6 curry leaves
5ml/1 tsp cumin seeds
450g/1lb fresh king prawns (jumbo shrimp), peeled and deveined
10ml/2 tsp brown sugar
juice of 2 lemons
salt

1 Heat the oil in a frying pan and fry the okra over a fairly high heat until they are slightly crisp and browned on all sides. Remove from the oil and put to one side on a piece of kitchen paper.

2 In the same oil, gently fry the garlic, ginger, chillies, turmeric, curry leaves and cumin seeds for 2–3 minutes. Add the prawns and mix well. Cook until the prawns are tender.

3 Add the salt, sugar, lemon juice and fried okra. Increase the heat and quickly fry for a further 5 minutes, stirring gently to prevent the okra from breaking. Adjust the seasoning, if necessary. Serve hot.

Cook's Tip
Okra, sometimes known as 'lady's fingers', is a small, long seed pod that exudes a sticky liquid when the pod is cut. This liquid is useful for dishes that require a thick sauce, but for other dishes, such as this one, the pod must be left whole. Remove the stalk using a sharp knife but do not cut into the pod itself.

red cooked prawns Energy 154kcal/643kJ; Protein 11.3g; Carbohydrate 13.4g, of which sugars 10.6g; Fat 6.5g, of which saturates 0.9g; Cholesterol 35mg; Calcium 93mg; Fibre 1.8g; Sodium 934mg.
prawns w. okra Energy 143kcal/597kJ; Protein 14.5g; Carbohydrate 3.1g, of which sugars 2.4g; Fat 8.2g, of which saturates 1.1g; Cholesterol 146mg; Calcium 121mg; Fibre 1.6g; Sodium 146mg.

King Prawns with Onions & Fenugreek Leaves

An excellent partner for this mildly spiced prawn dish would be plain steamed basmati rice with vegetables.

Serves 4

3 medium onions
15ml/1 tbsp oil
6–8 curry leaves
1.5ml/¼ tsp onion seeds
1 fresh green chilli, seeded and diced
1 fresh red chilli, seeded and diced
12–16 frozen cooked king prawns (jumbo shrimp), thawed and peeled
5ml/1 tsp shredded fresh root ginger
5ml/1 tsp salt
15ml/1 tbsp fresh fenugreek leaves

1 Cut the onions into thin slices, using a sharp knife.

2 Heat the oil in a karahi, wok or heavy pan and gently fry the sliced onions with the curry leaves and onion seeds for about 3 minutes, stirring constantly to prevent the leaves from sticking.

3 Add the diced green and red chillies, followed by the prawns. Cook for about 5–7 minutes before adding the shredded root ginger and salt.

4 Finally, add the fenugreek leaves, cover and cook for a further 2–3 minutes before serving.

Cook's Tip
Small prawns (shrimp) will also work well in this recipe and are a less expensive option than king prawns. Buy unpeeled ones for the better flavour, but for a quicker meal use cooked, peeled prawns and just toss them in for long enough to warm them through. Allow 115g/4oz prawns per person.

Prawns with Green Vegetables

Mangetouts are superb crisply stir-fried with prawns in this fresh-tasting dish.

Serves 4–6

450g/1lb raw prawns (shrimp), peeled and deveined
½ egg white
15ml/1 tbsp cornflour (cornstarch), mixed to a paste with 10ml/2 tsp water
about 600ml/1 pint/2½ cups vegetable oil
175g/6oz mangetouts (snow peas), trimmed
5ml/1 tsp light brown sugar
15ml/1 tbsp finely chopped spring onion (scallion)
5ml/1 tsp finely chopped fresh root ginger
15ml/1 tbsp light soy sauce
15ml/1 tbsp Chinese rice wine or dry sherry
5ml/1 tsp chilli bean sauce
15ml/1 tbsp tomato purée (paste)
salt

1 Place the prawns in a bowl and mix with the egg white, cornflour paste and a pinch of salt. Heat 30–45ml/2–3 tbsp of the oil in a preheated wok and stir-fry the mangetouts for about 1 minute.

2 Add the sugar and a little salt and continue stirring for 1 more minute. Remove and place in the centre of a warmed serving platter.

3 Add the remaining oil to the wok and cook the prawns for 1 minute. Remove and drain.

4 Pour off all but about 15ml/1 tbsp of the oil. Add the spring onion and ginger to the wok.

5 Return the prawns to the wok and stir-fry for 1 minute, then add the soy sauce and rice wine or dry sherry. Blend the mixture thoroughly. Transfer half the prawns to one end of the serving platter.

6 Add the chilli bean sauce and tomato purée to the remaining prawns in the wok, blend well and place the 'red' prawns at the other end of the platter. Serve.

prawns and fenugreek Energy 150kcal/630kJ; Protein 22.8g; Carbohydrate 11.8g, of which sugars 7.2g; Fat 1.7g, of which saturates 0.2g; Cholesterol 219mg; Calcium 137mg; Fibre 1.8g; Sodium 221mg.
prawns w. vegetables Energy 228kcal/948kJ; Protein 14.5g; Carbohydrate 3.7g, of which sugars 1.9g; Fat 17.2g, of which saturates 2g; Cholesterol 146mg; Calcium 74mg; Fibre 0.7g; Sodium 148mg.

Stir-fried Chilli-garlic Prawns

Prawns have a particular affinity with garlic. To enhance the flavour of the garlic, fry it very gently without letting it brown completely. The spice-coated prawns make a mouthwatering appetizer or light lunch, when served with a salad, or they can be transformed into a main meal with the addition of warm naan bread.

Serves 4

16–20 peeled, cooked king prawns (jumbo shrimp)
1 fresh green chilli
15ml/1 tbsp vegetable oil
3 garlic cloves, roughly halved
3 tomatoes, chopped
2.5ml/½ tsp salt
5ml/1 tsp crushed dried red chillies
5ml/1 tsp lemon juice
mango chutney, to taste
fresh coriander (cilantro) sprigs and chopped spring onions (scallions), to garnish

1 Devein the prawns by making a shallow cut down the centre of the curved back of the prawn. Pull out the black vein with a cocktail stick (toothpick) or your fingers, then rinse the prawn thoroughly. Set aside.

2 Slice through the fresh green chilli and scrape out the seeds. Chop the chilli and set aside. Wash your hands thoroughly afterwards as the juice can sting open cuts or your eyes if you rub them.

3 In a wok, karahi or large pan, heat the vegetable oil over a low heat and fry the garlic halves gently until they are tinged with golden brown.

4 Add the chopped tomatoes, salt, crushed red chillies, lemon juice, mango chutney and the chopped fresh chilli. Stir the ingredients well.

5 Add the prawns to the pan, then increase the heat and stir-fry briskly, mixing the prawns with the other ingredients until they are thoroughly heated through. Transfer the prawns in the sauce to a warm serving dish and garnish with fresh coriander sprigs and chopped spring onions. Serve immediately.

Prawn & Mangetout Stir-fry

Nothing beats a stir-fry for a quick and tasty midweek meal, especially when it's spiced up with ginger, garlic and Tabasco. If you keep some prawns in the freezer most of this dish can be made with store cupboard ingredients.

Serves 4

15ml/1 tbsp oil
2 medium onions, diced
15ml/1 tbsp tomato purée (paste)
5ml/1 tsp Tabasco sauce
5ml/1 tsp lemon juice
5ml/1 tsp grated fresh root ginger
5ml/1 tsp crushed garlic
5ml/1 tsp chilli powder
5ml/1 tsp salt
15ml/1 tbsp chopped fresh coriander (cilantro)
175g/6oz/1½ cups frozen cooked peeled prawns (shrimp), thawed
12 mangetouts (snow peas), halved

1 Heat the oil in a karahi, wok or heavy pan and fry the onions until golden brown.

2 Mix the tomato purée with 30ml/2 tbsp water in a bowl. Stir in the Tabasco sauce, lemon juice, ginger and garlic, chilli powder and salt.

3 Lower the heat, pour the sauce over the onions and stir-fry for a few seconds until well mixed in.

4 Add the chopped coriander, prawns and mangetout halves to the pan and stir-fry for 5–7 minutes, or until the sauce is thick. Serve immediately on warmed plates.

Cook's Tip
Mangetouts, being small and almost flat, are perfect for stir-frying and are a popular ingredient in Asian cooking. They are particularly good stir-fried with prawns (shrimp) which need only minutes to heat through.

chilli-garlic prawns Energy 118kcal/495kJ; Protein 17.9g; Carbohydrate 3g, of which sugars 3g; Fat 3.9g, of which saturates 0.5g; Cholesterol 195mg; Calcium 83mg; Fibre 0.4g; Sodium 234mg.
prawn & mangetout Energy 125kcal/524kJ; Protein 17.6g; Carbohydrate 5.2g, of which sugars 3.6g; Fat 3.4g, of which saturates 0.4g; Cholesterol 171mg; Calcium 96mg; Fibre 1.3g; Sodium 436mg.

King Prawn Bhoona

The unusual and delicious flavour of this dish is achieved by grilling the marinated prawns to give them a chargrilled taste and then adding them to stir-fried onions and peppers.

Serves 4

45ml/3 tbsp natural (plain) low-fat yogurt
5ml/1 tsp paprika
5ml/1 tsp grated fresh root ginger
salt
12–16 cooked king prawns (jumbo shrimp), peeled and deveined
15ml/1 tbsp oil
3 medium onions, sliced
2.5ml/½ tsp fennel seeds, crushed
5cm/2in piece cinnamon stick
5ml/1 tsp crushed garlic
5ml/1 tsp chilli powder
1 medium yellow (bell) pepper, seeded and roughly chopped
1 medium red (bell) pepper, seeded and roughly chopped
15ml/1 tbsp fresh coriander (cilantro) leaves, to garnish

1 In a bowl, mix the yogurt, paprika, ginger and salt to taste. Pour this mixture over the prawns and leave to marinate for 30–45 minutes.

2 Heat the oil in a karahi, wok or heavy pan over medium heat and fry the sliced onions with the crushed fennel seeds and the piece of cinnamon stick.

3 Lower the heat and add the garlic and chilli powder. Stir over the heat until well mixed.

4 Add the peppers and stir-fry gently for 3–5 minutes.

5 Remove from the heat and transfer to a warm serving dish, discarding the cinnamon stick.

6 Preheat the grill (broiler) to medium. Put the prawns in a grill pan or flameproof dish and place under the heat to darken their tops and get a chargrilled flavour. Add to the onion mixture, garnish with the coriander and serve.

Prawns with Fenugreek & Seeds

Tender shellfish, crunchy vegetables and a thick curry sauce combine to produce a dish rich in flavour and texture.

Serves 4

30ml/2 tbsp oil
5ml/1 tsp mixed fenugreek, mustard and onion seeds
2 curry leaves
½ medium cauliflower, cut into small florets
8 baby carrots, halved lengthways
6 new potatoes, thickly sliced
50g/2oz/½ cup frozen peas
2 medium onions, sliced
30ml/2 tbsp tomato purée (paste)
2.5ml/½ tsp chilli powder
5ml/1 tsp ground coriander
5ml/1 tsp grated fresh root ginger
5ml/1 tsp crushed garlic
5ml/1 tsp salt
30ml/2 tbsp lemon juice
450g/1lb cooked peeled prawns (shrimp)
30ml/2 tbsp chopped fresh coriander (cilantro)
1 fresh red chilli, seeded and sliced
120ml/4fl oz/½ cup natural (plain) low-fat yogurt

1 Heat the oil in a karahi, wok or heavy pan. Lower the heat slightly and add the fenugreek, mustard and onion seeds and the curry leaves.

2 Increase the heat and add the cauliflower, carrots, potatoes and peas. Stir-fry quickly until browned, then remove the vegetables from the pan with a slotted spoon and drain on kitchen paper. Add the onions to the oil left in the pan and fry over a medium heat until golden brown.

3 While the onions are cooking, mix together the tomato purée, chilli powder, ground coriander, ginger, garlic, salt and lemon juice and pour the paste on to the onions.

4 Add the prawns and stir-fry over a low heat for about 5 minutes or until they are heated through.

5 Add the fried vegetables to the pan and mix together well. Add the fresh coriander and red chilli and pour in the yogurt. Warm through and serve.

king prawn bhoona Energy 175kcal/734kJ; Protein 22.6g; Carbohydrate 10.8g, of which sugars 7.9g; Fat 5g, of which saturates 0.8g; Cholesterol 220mg; Calcium 133mg; Fibre 1.9g; Sodium 230mg.
prawns w. seeds Energy 157kcal/664kJ; Protein 24.7g; Carbohydrate 10.4g, of which sugars 9.4g; Fat 2.2g, of which saturates 0.6g; Cholesterol 219mg; Calcium 169mg; Fibre 2.7g; Sodium 351mg.

Parsi Prawn Curry

This dish comes from the west coast of India, where fresh seafood is eaten in abundance. Fresh king prawns or tiger prawns are ideal.

Serves 4–6

60ml/4 tbsp vegetable oil
1 medium onion, finely sliced
6 garlic cloves, finely crushed
5ml/1 tsp chilli powder
7.5ml/1½ tsp ground turmeric
2 medium onions, finely chopped
60ml/4 tbsp tamarind juice
5ml/1 tsp mint sauce
15ml/1 tbsp demerara (raw) sugar
450g/1lb fresh king prawns (jumbo shrimp), peeled and deveined
75g/3oz/3 cups fresh coriander (cilantro), chopped
salt

1 Heat the oil in a frying pan and fry the sliced onion until golden brown. In a bowl, mix the garlic, chilli powder and turmeric with a little water to form a paste. Add to the browned onion and simmer for 3 minutes.

2 Add the chopped onions to the pan and fry until they become translucent, stirring frequently. Stir in the tamarind juice, mint sauce, sugar and salt, and gently simmer for a further 3 minutes.

3 Pat the prawns dry with kitchen paper. Add to the spice mixture with a small amount of water and stir-fry until the prawns turn a bright orange-pink colour.

4 When the prawns are cooked, add the fresh coriander and stir-fry over a high heat for a few minutes to thicken the sauce. Serve immediately, while piping hot.

Cook's Tip
Tamarind is usually sold in blocks of mashed pods or pulp or as a concentrated juice. It is used to sour the flavour of food.

Masala Prawns & Rice

Fragrant saffron rice and king prawns are combined with mushrooms, peas and spices for this delicious one-pot meal.

Serves 4–6

2 large onions, sliced and boiled
300ml/½ pint/1¼ cups natural (plain) low-fat yogurt
30ml/2 tbsp tomato purée (paste)
60ml/4 tbsp green masala paste
30ml/2 tbsp lemon juice
5ml/1 tsp black cumin seeds
5cm/2in piece cinnamon stick
4 green cardamom pods
1.5ml/¼ tsp salt
450g/1lb raw king prawns (jumbo shrimp), peeled and deveined
225g/8oz/3 cups button (white) mushrooms
225g/8oz/2 cups frozen peas, thawed
450g/1lb/generous 2⅓ cups basmati rice
300ml/½ pint/1¼ cups water
5ml/1 tsp saffron powder mixed with 90ml/6 tbsp milk
15ml/1 tbsp oil, plus extra for greasing

1 Mix the onions, yogurt, tomato purée, green masala paste, lemon juice, black cumin seeds, cinnamon stick and cardamom pods together in a large bowl and add salt to taste. Mix the prawns, mushrooms and peas into the marinade and leave to absorb the spices for at least 2 hours.

2 Wash the rice well, cover with boiling water and leave to soak for 5 minutes, then drain.

3 Grease the base of a heavy pan and add the prawns, vegetables and any marinade juice. Cover with the drained rice and smooth the surface gently until you have an even layer.

4 Pour the water all over the surface of the rice. Make random holes through the rice with the handle of a spoon and pour in the saffron milk.

5 Sprinkle the oil over the surface of the rice and place a circular piece of foil directly on top. Cover and steam gently over a low heat for 45–50 minutes until the rice is cooked. Gently toss the rice, prawns and vegetables together and serve hot.

Parsi prawn curry Energy 204kcal/852kJ; Protein 23.4g; Carbohydrate 8.8g, of which sugars 6.6g; Fat 8.6g, of which saturates 1g; Cholesterol 244mg; Calcium 145mg; Fibre 1.6g; Sodium 244mg.
masala prawns Energy 433kcal/1811kJ; Protein 24.6g; Carbohydrate 73.3g, of which sugars 6.1g; Fat 4.7g, of which saturates 0.7g; Cholesterol 147mg; Calcium 132mg; Fibre 3.3g; Sodium 168mg.

King Prawn Korma

This korma has a light, mild, creamy texture, and makes a good introduction to Indian cuisine for people who claim not to like spicy food.

Serves 4

12–16 cooked king prawns (jumbo shrimp), peeled and deveined
45ml/3 tbsp natural (plain) low-fat yogurt
45ml/3 tbsp low-fat fromage frais or ricotta cheese
5ml/1 tsp ground paprika
5ml/1 tsp garam masala
15ml/1 tbsp tomato purée (paste)
45ml/3 tbsp coconut milk
5ml/1 tsp chilli powder
150ml/¼ pint/⅔ cup water
15ml/1 tbsp oil
5ml/1 tsp crushed garlic
5ml/1 tsp grated fresh root ginger
½ cinnamon stick
2 green cardamom pods
salt
15ml/1 tbsp chopped fresh coriander (cilantro), to garnish

1 Rinse the prawns and drain them thoroughly to ensure that all excess liquid is removed.

2 Place the yogurt, fromage frais or ricotta, paprika, garam masala, tomato purée, coconut milk, chilli powder and water in a bowl. Stir the yogurt and coconut mixture together well and set aside.

3 Heat the oil in a karahi, wok or heavy pan, add the crushed garlic, ginger, cinnamon stick, cardamoms and salt to taste and fry over low heat.

4 Increase the heat and pour in the yogurt and coconut mixture. Bring to the boil, stirring occasionally.

5 Add the drained king prawns to the spices and continue to stir-fry until the prawns are thoroughly heated through and the sauce is quite thick.

6 Serve the korma in warmed bowls, garnished with the chopped fresh coriander.

Goan Prawn Curry

Cardamom, cloves and cinnamon are the essential flavourings for this dish.

Serves 4

15g/½oz/1 tbsp ghee or butter
2 garlic cloves, crushed
450g/1lb small raw prawns (shrimp), peeled and deveined
15ml/1 tbsp groundnut (peanut) oil
4 cardamom pods
4 cloves
5cm/2in piece cinnamon stick
15ml/1 tbsp mustard seeds
1 large onion, finely chopped
½–1 fresh red chilli, seeded and sliced
4 tomatoes, peeled, seeded and chopped
175ml/6fl oz/¾ cup fish stock or water
350ml/12fl oz/1½ cups coconut milk
45ml/3 tbsp Fragrant Spice Mix (see Cook's Tip)
10–20ml/2–4 tsp chilli powder
salt
turmeric-coloured basmati rice, to serve

1 Melt the ghee or butter in a wok, karahi or large pan, add the garlic and stir over a low heat for a few seconds. Add the prawns and stir-fry briskly to coat. Transfer to a plate. In the same pan, heat the oil and fry the cardamom, cloves and cinnamon for 2 minutes. Add the mustard seeds and fry for 1 minute. Add the onion and chilli and fry for 7–8 minutes or until softened and lightly browned.

2 Add the remaining ingredients except the prawns and bring to a slow simmer. Cook gently for 6–8 minutes and add the prawns. Simmer for 5–8 minutes until the prawns are cooked through. Serve the curry with basmati rice cooked with ground turmeric so that it is tinted a pale yellow colour, and lightly flavoured with the spice.

Cook's Tip

To make a Fragrant Spice Mix, dry-fry 25ml/1½ tbsp coriander seeds, 15ml/1 tbsp mixed peppercorns, 5ml/1 tsp cumin seeds, 1.5ml/¼ tsp fenugreek seeds and 1.5ml/¼ tsp fennel seeds until aromatic, then grind finely in a spice mill.

king prawn korma Energy 143kcal/601kJ; Protein 20.4g; Carbohydrate 5.4g, of which sugars 2.7g; Fat 4.8g, of which saturates 0.7g; Cholesterol 195mg; Calcium 168mg; Fibre 0.6g; Sodium 230mg.
Goan prawn curry Energy 171kcal/723kJ; Protein 21.9g; Carbohydrate 10g, of which sugars 7.4g; Fat 5.3g, of which saturates 2.5g; Cholesterol 227mg; Calcium 136mg; Fibre 1g; Sodium 344mg.

Cod & Prawn Green Coconut Curry

This quick curry involves very little preparation, and takes just minutes to cook, so it's ideal if friends spring a surprise visit. If you can't find green masala curry paste at your local grocer or supermarket, simply substitute another variety – the curry will taste just as good.

Serves 4
675g/1½lb cod fillets, skinned
90ml/6 tbsp green masala curry paste
175ml/6fl oz/¾ cup coconut milk
175g/6oz raw or cooked, peeled prawns (shrimp)
fresh coriander (cilantro), to garnish
basmati rice, to serve

1 Using a sharp knife, cut the skinned cod fillets into 4cm/1½in pieces.

2 Put the green masala curry paste and coconut milk in a frying pan. Heat to simmering and simmer gently for 5 minutes, stirring occasionally.

3 Add the cod pieces and prawns (if raw) to the cream mixture and cook gently for 5 minutes. If using ready-cooked prawns rather than raw shellfish, add them to the pan after this time has elapsed, and heat through.

4 Spoon into a serving dish, garnish the curry with fresh coriander and serve immediately with basmati rice.

Variation
Any firm white fish, such as monkfish, can be used instead of cod. Whole fish steaks can be cooked in the sauce, but allow an extra 5 minutes' cooking time and baste them with the sauce from time to time.

Rich Prawn Curry

A rich, flavoursome curry made with tiger prawns and a delicious blend of aromatic spices.

Serves 4
675g/1½lb tiger prawns (jumbo shrimp)
4 dried red chillies
25g/1oz/⅓ cup desiccated (dry unsweetened shredded) coconut
5ml/1 tsp black mustard seeds
1 large onion, chopped
30ml/2 tbsp oil
4 bay leaves
2.5cm/1in piece fresh root ginger, finely chopped
2 garlic cloves, crushed
15ml/1 tbsp ground coriander
5ml/1 tsp chilli powder
5ml/1 tsp salt
4 tomatoes, finely chopped
plain rice, to serve

1 Peel the prawns and discard the shells. Run a sharp knife along the centre back of each prawn to make a shallow cut and carefully remove the thin black intestinal vein. Set aside.

2 Put the dried red chillies, coconut, mustard seeds and onion in a large, heavy frying pan and dry-fry for 8–10 minutes or until the spices begin to brown. The onion should turn a deep golden brown but do not let it burn or it will taste bitter.

3 Pour the mixture into a food processor or blender and process to a coarse paste.

4 Heat the oil in the frying pan and fry the bay leaves for 1 minute. Add the chopped ginger and the garlic and fry for 2–3 minutes. Add the coriander, chilli powder, salt and the coconut paste and fry gently for 5 minutes.

5 Stir in the chopped tomatoes and about 175ml/6fl oz/¾ cup water and simmer gently for 5–6 minutes or until the sauce has thickened.

6 Add the prawns and cook for about 4–5 minutes or until they turn pink and the edges are curling slightly. Serve with plain boiled rice.

cod & prawn curry Energy 255kcal/1066kJ; Protein 38.9g; Carbohydrate 2.4g, of which sugars 2.3g; Fat 9.9g, of which saturates 1.5g; Cholesterol 163mg; Calcium 78mg; Fibre 0.4g; Sodium 235mg.
rich prawn curry Energy 219kcal/921kJ; Protein 32.3g; Carbohydrate 9.6g, of which sugars 6.3g; Fat 6.1g, of which saturates 3.7g; Cholesterol 329mg; Calcium 166mg; Fibre 2.6g; Sodium 335mg.

Prawns & Vegetables with Basmati Rice

This is an excellent combination of prawns and vegetables which is lightly flavoured with whole spices. Using frozen mixed vegetables speeds up the preparation time. Serve with a cool and refreshing raita.

Serves 4

300g/11oz/1½ cups basmati rice
15ml/1 tbsp oil
2 medium onions, sliced
3 green cardamom pods
2.5cm/1in cinnamon stick
4 black peppercorns
1 bay leaf
1.5ml/¼ tsp black cumin seeds
2.5cm/1in piece root ginger, grated
2 garlic cloves, roughly chopped
2 green chillies, seeded and chopped
30ml/2 tbsp chopped fresh coriander (cilantro)
30ml/2 tbsp lemon juice
115g/4oz/1 cup frozen vegetables (carrots, beans, corn and peas)
175–225g/6–8oz/1½–2 cups cooked peeled prawns (shrimp)
475ml/16fl oz/2 cups water

1 Wash the rice well in cold water and leave it to soak in plenty of water in a bowl for 30 minutes.

2 Heat the oil in a heavy pan and fry the sliced onions, cardamom pods, cinnamon stick, peppercorns, bay leaf, black cumin seeds, ginger, garlic and chillies for about 3 minutes, stirring constantly.

3 Add half the fresh coriander, the lemon juice, mixed vegetables and prawns. Stir for a further 3 minutes.

4 Drain the rice and add it to the pan. Gently stir in the water and bring to the boil. Lower the heat, add the remaining fresh coriander and cook, covered with a lid, for 15–20 minutes or until all the liquid has been absorbed and the rice is cooked. Allow to stand, still covered, for 5–7 minutes before serving.

Prawns with Mushroom Rice

Warm spices complement the flavour of mushrooms well in this tasty prawn dish.

Serves 4

150g/5oz/⅔ cup basmati rice
15ml/1 tbsp oil
1 medium onion, chopped
4 black peppercorns
2.5cm/1in cinnamon stick
1 bay leaf
1.5ml/¼ tsp cumin seeds
2 cardamom pods
5ml/1 tsp crushed garlic
5ml/1 tsp grated fresh root ginger
5ml/1 tsp garam masala
5ml/1 tsp chilli powder
7.5ml/1½ tsp salt
115g/4oz/1 cup cooked peeled prawns (shrimp)
115g/4oz/1½ cups mushrooms, cut into large pieces
30ml/2 tbsp chopped fresh coriander (cilantro)
120ml/4fl oz/½ cup natural (plain) low-fat yogurt
15ml/1 tbsp lemon juice
50g/2oz/½ cup frozen peas
250ml/8fl oz/1 cup water
1 fresh red chilli, seeded and sliced, to garnish

1 Wash the basmati rice well and leave to soak in cold water for 30 minutes.

2 Heat the oil in a heavy pan and add the chopped onion, peppercorns, cinnamon, bay leaf, cumin seeds, cardamom pods, garlic, ginger, garam masala, chilli powder and salt. Lower the heat and stir-fry for 2–3 minutes. Add the prawns to the spice mixture and cook for 2 minutes, then add the mushrooms.

3 Stir in the coriander and yogurt, followed by the lemon juice and peas, and cook for 2 more minutes.

4 Drain the rice and add it to the prawn mixture. Pour in the water, cover the pan and cook over a medium heat for about 15 minutes, checking once to make sure that the rice has not stuck to the base of the pan.

5 Remove the pan from the heat and leave to stand, still covered, for about 5 minutes. Transfer to a serving dish and serve garnished with the sliced red chilli.

prawns & vegetables Energy 409kcal/1708kJ; Protein 17.6g; Carbohydrate 73.6g, of which sugars 6.3g; Fat 5g, of which saturates 0.6g; Cholesterol 85mg; Calcium 93mg; Fibre 2.8g; Sodium 89mg.
prawns w. rice Energy 227kcal/951kJ; Protein 12.5g; Carbohydrate 40.3g, of which sugars 5.4g; Fat 2.1g, of which saturates 0.4g; Cholesterol 56mg; Calcium 117mg; Fibre 1.6g; Sodium 85mg.

Satay Prawns

This delicious dish is inspired by the classic Indonesian satay. The combination of mild peanuts, aromatic spices, sweet coconut milk and zesty lemon juice in the spicy dip is perfect and is guaranteed to have guests coming back for more.

Serves 4–6

450g/1lb raw king prawns (jumbo shrimp)
25ml/1½ tbsp vegetable oil

For the peanut sauce

25ml/1½ tbsp vegetable oil
15ml/1 tbsp chopped garlic
1 small onion, chopped
3–4 fresh red chillies, seeded and chopped
3 kaffir lime leaves, torn
1 lemon grass stalk, bruised and chopped
5ml/1 tsp medium curry paste
250ml/8fl oz/1 cup coconut milk
1cm/½in piece cinnamon stick
75g/3oz/⅓ cup crunchy peanut butter
45ml/3 tbsp tamarind juice, made by mixing tamarind paste with warm water
30ml/2 tbsp Thai fish sauce
30ml/2 tbsp palm sugar (jaggery) or light muscovado (brown) sugar
juice of ½ lemon

For the garnish

½ bunch fresh coriander (cilantro) leaves
4 fresh red chillies, finely sliced
spring onions (scallions), cut diagonally

1 Remove the heads from the prawns and peel the bodies, leaving the tail ends intact. Slit each prawn along the back with a small, sharp knife and remove the black intestinal vein. Rinse under cold running water, pat completely dry on kitchen paper and set the prawns aside.

2 To make the peanut sauce, heat half the oil in a wok or large, heavy frying pan. Add the garlic and onion and cook over a medium heat, stirring occasionally, for 3–4 minutes, until the mixture has softened but not browned.

3 Add the chillies, kaffir lime leaves, lemon grass and curry paste. Stir well and cook for a further 2–3 minutes, then stir in the coconut milk, cinnamon stick, peanut butter, tamarind juice, fish sauce, sugar and lemon juice. Cook, stirring constantly, until well blended.

4 Bring to the boil, then reduce the heat to low and simmer gently for 15–20 minutes, until the sauce thickens. Stir occasionally with a wooden spoon to prevent the sauce from sticking to the base of the wok or frying pan.

5 Thread the prawns on to skewers and brush with a little oil. Cook under a preheated grill (broiler) for 2 minutes on each side until they turn pink and are firm to the touch. Alternatively, pan-fry the prawns, then thread on to skewers.

6 Remove the cinnamon stick from the sauce and discard. Arrange the skewered prawns on a warmed platter, garnish with spring onions, coriander leaves and sliced red chillies, and serve with the sauce.

Prawn Salad with Curry Dressing

Curry spices add an unexpected twist to this salad. The warm flavours combine especially well with the sweet shellfish and grated apple. Curry paste is needed here rather than curry powder as there is no cooking, which is necessary to bring out the flavours of powdered spices.

Serves 4

1 ripe tomato, peeled
½ iceberg lettuce
1 small onion
1 small bunch fresh coriander (cilantro)
15ml/1 tbsp lemon juice
450g/1lb shelled cooked prawns (shrimp)
1 apple
8 whole cooked prawns, 8 lemon wedges and 4 fresh coriander sprigs, to garnish
salt

For the curry dressing

75ml/5 tbsp mayonnaise
5ml/1 tsp mild curry paste
15ml/1 tbsp tomato ketchup

1 Cut the tomato in half and squeeze each half gently to remove the seeds. Discard them, then cut each tomato half into large dice.

2 Shred the lettuce leaves finely and put in a large bowl. Finely chop the onion and coriander. Add to the bowl together with the tomato, moisten with lemon juice and season with salt.

3 To make the dressing, combine the mayonnaise, curry paste and tomato ketchup in a small bowl. Add 30ml/2 tbsp water to thin the dressing and season to taste with salt.

4 Combine the shelled prawns with the curry dressing and stir gently so that all the prawns are evenly coated with the dressing. Quarter and core the apple and coarsely grate the flesh into the prawn and dressing mixture.

5 Distribute the shredded lettuce mixture among four serving plates or bowls. Pile the prawn mixture in the centre of each and decorate each with two whole prawns, two lemon wedges and a sprig of coriander.

satay prawns Energy 219kcal/913kJ; Protein 16.6g; Carbohydrate 10.1g, of which sugars 9g; Fat 12.7g, of which saturates 2.4g; Cholesterol 146mg; Calcium 98mg; Fibre 1.2g; Sodium 414mg.
prawn salad Energy 259kcal/1078kJ; Protein 23.6g; Carbohydrate 6.4g, of which sugars 5.5g; Fat 15.6g, of which saturates 2.4g; Cholesterol 258mg; Calcium 154mg; Fibre 2.1g; Sodium 397mg.

Salt & Pepper Prawns

This is the simplest way of preparing prawns in their shells and Cantonese chefs have the technique down to a fine art. Chefs in Hong Kong are particularly skilled at using the flash stir-frying method where flames catch in the wok, but it is safer to simply stir-fry them over a high heat.

Serves 4

16 large tiger prawns (jumbo shrimp)
45ml/3 tbsp vegetable oil
15ml/1 tbsp chopped garlic
15ml/1 tbsp ground black pepper
10ml/2 tsp salt

1 Clean the prawns thoroughly and cut off 1cm/½in from the head end of each. Remove the whiskers.

2 If the prawns are particularly large, use a sharp knife to split each one in half down its length.

3 Heat a dry wok. Add the prawns to the hot pan and flash fry over high heat for 2 minutes or until they turn pink, shivering the wok to keep them on the move at all times. Tip the prawns into a bowl.

4 Add the oil to the wok and heat it. When it is very hot, add the garlic and fry for 1 minute, stirring constantly. Add the prawns, with the pepper and salt, and stir rapidly over high heat for 2–3 minutes.

5 Cover the wok with a lid and cook for 1 minute more, gently shaking the wok constantly to prevent any sticking or burning. Transfer the prawns to a warmed serving dish and serve immediately.

Cook's Tip
To appreciate the flavours at their best, this dish should always be served piping hot.

Stir-fried Prawns with Tamarind

The sour, tangy flavour that is characteristic of many Thai dishes comes from tamarind. Fresh tamarind pods can sometimes be bought, but preparing them for cooking is a laborious process. It is much easier to use a block of tamarind paste.

Serves 4–6

6 dried red chillies
30ml/2 tbsp vegetable oil
30ml/2 tbsp chopped onion
30ml/2 tbsp palm sugar (jaggery) or light muscovado (brown) sugar
30ml/2 tbsp chicken stock or water
15ml/1 tbsp Thai fish sauce
90ml/6 tbsp tamarind juice, made by mixing tamarind paste with warm water
450g/1lb raw prawns (shrimp), peeled
15ml/1 tbsp fried chopped garlic
30ml/2 tbsp fried sliced shallots
2 spring onions (scallions), chopped, to garnish

1 Heat a wok or large frying pan, but do not add any oil at this stage. Add the dried chillies and dry-fry them by pressing them against the surface of the wok or pan with a spatula, turning them occasionally. Do not let them burn. Set them aside to cool slightly.

2 Add the oil to the wok or pan and reheat. Add the chopped onion and cook over a medium heat, stirring occasionally, for 2–3 minutes, until softened and a light golden brown.

3 Add the sugar, chicken stock or water, fish sauce, dry-fried red chillies and the tamarind juice, stirring constantly until the sugar has dissolved. Bring to the boil, then lower the heat slightly.

4 Add the prawns, garlic and shallots. Toss over the heat for 3–4 minutes, until the prawns are cooked. Garnish with the spring onions and serve.

Cook's Tip
Peel a few of the prawns (shrimp) but leave their tails intact to use as a garnish, if you like.

salt & pepper prawns Energy 172kcal/717kJ; Protein 20.1g; Carbohydrate 2.7g, of which sugars 2.4g; Fat 9g, of which saturates 1.1g; Cholesterol 219mg; Calcium 97mg; Fibre 0.3g; Sodium 1197mg.
prawns w. tamarind Energy 100kcal/422kJ; Protein 13.6g; Carbohydrate 6.6g, of which sugars 6g; Fat 2.3g, of which saturates 0.3g; Cholesterol 146mg; Calcium 65mg; Fibre 0.3g; Sodium 321mg.

Prawn Fritters

Ukoy, or prawn fritters, are a delicious addition to a spread of dishes. Unusually, they are first shallow-fried, then deep-fried.

Serves 2–4

16 raw prawns (shrimp) in the shell
225g/8oz/2 cups plain (all-purpose) flour
5ml/1 tsp baking powder
2.5ml/½ tsp salt
1 egg, beaten
1 small sweet potato
1 garlic clove, crushed
115g/4oz/1½ cups beansprouts, soaked in cold water and well drained
vegetable oil, for shallow- and deep-frying
4 spring onions (scallions), chopped

For the dipping sauce

1 garlic clove, sliced
45ml/3 tbsp rice or wine vinegar
15–30ml/1–2 tbsp water
salt
6–8 small red chillies

1 To make the dipping sauce, mix the sliced garlic clove with the rice or wine vinegar in a bowl. Add the water, salt and red chillies. Divide the dipping sauce between two serving bowls.

2 Put the whole prawns in a pan with water to cover. Bring to the boil, then simmer for 4–5 minutes or until the prawns are pink and tender. Lift the prawns from the pan with a slotted spoon. Discard the heads and the body shell, but leave the tails on. Strain and reserve the cooking liquid. Allow to cool.

3 Sift the flour, baking powder and salt into a bowl. Add the beaten egg and about 300ml/½ pint/1¼ cups of the prawn stock to make a batter that has the consistency of double (heavy) cream.

4 Peel and grate the sweet potato using the large holes on a grater, and add it to the batter, then stir in the crushed garlic and the drained beansprouts.

5 Pour the oil for shallow-frying into a large frying pan. It should be about 5mm/¼in deep. Heat the oil in the frying pan. Taking a generous spoonful of the batter, drop it carefully into the frying pan so that it forms a fritter, about 7cm/3in across or the size of a large drop scone.

6 Make more fritters in the same way. As soon as the fritters have set, top each one with a single prawn and a few chopped spring onions. Continue to cook over a medium heat for 1 minute, then remove with a fish slice or metal spatula.

7 Heat the oil in a karahi, wok or deep-fryer to a temperature of 190°C/375°F, or until a cube of bread dropped in the oil browns in about 45 seconds. Deep-fry the prawn fritters in batches until they are crisp and golden brown. Drain the fritters on absorbent kitchen paper and then arrange them on a serving plate or platter. Offer a bowl of the sauce for dipping.

Spicy Prawns

These succulent and piquant shellfish beg to be eaten with the fingers, so provide finger bowls or hot cloths for your guests.

Serves 3–4

15–18 large raw prawns (shrimp), in the shell, about 450g/1lb
vegetable oil, for deep-frying
3 shallots or 1 small onion, very finely chopped
2 garlic cloves, crushed
1cm/½in piece fresh root ginger, peeled and very finely grated
1–2 fresh red chillies, seeded and finely sliced
2.5ml/½ tsp sugar, or to taste
3–4 spring onions (scallions), shredded, to garnish

For the fried salt

10ml/2 tsp salt
5ml/1 tsp Sichuan peppercorns

1 Make the fried salt by dry-frying the peppercorns and salt in a heavy frying pan over medium heat until the peppercorns begin to release their aroma. Cool the mixture, then tip into a mortar and crush with a pestle.

2 Carefully remove the heads and legs from the raw prawns and discard. Leave the body shells and the tails in place. Pat the prepared prawns dry with sheets of kitchen paper.

3 Heat the oil in a karahi, wok or deep-fryer to a temperature of 190°C/375°F, or until a cube of bread dropped in the oil browns in about 45 seconds. Fry the prawns for 1 minute, then lift them out and drain thoroughly on kitchen paper. Spoon 30ml/2 tbsp of the hot oil into a large frying pan, leaving the rest of the oil to one side to cool.

4 Heat the oil in the frying pan. Add the fried salt, with the shallots or onion, garlic, ginger, chillies and sugar. Toss the mixture together for 1 minute, then add the prawns and toss them over the heat for 1 minute more until they are coated and the shells are impregnated with the seasonings. Serve immediately, garnished with the spring onions.

prawn fritters Energy 711kcal/2996kJ; Protein 34g; Carbohydrate 101g, of which sugars 6.4g; Fat 21.9g, of which saturates 3.2g; Cholesterol 290mg; Calcium 282mg; Fibre 5.9g; Sodium 253mg.
spicy prawns Energy 122kcal/514kJ; Protein 20.1g; Carbohydrate 2.7g, of which sugars 2.4g; Fat 3.5g, of which saturates 0.5g; Cholesterol 219mg; Calcium 97mg; Fibre 0.3g; Sodium 1197mg.

Prawn Stew

Kangkong (or swamp cabbage) has delicate leaves and stems, which are delicious when lightly cooked. It is similar to spinach, which can be used instead in this bright stew of vegetables, prawns and strips of fish fillet. Serve with noodles or rice to make a substantial and tasty meal.

Serves 4–6

15ml/1 tbsp tamarind pulp
150ml/¼ pint/⅔ cup warm water
2 tomatoes
115g/4oz Chinese kangkong leaves or spinach
115g/4oz cooked large prawns (shrimp)
1.2 litres/2 pints/5 cups prepared fish or vegetable stock
½ mooli (daikon), peeled and finely diced
115g/4oz green beans, cut into 1cm/½in lengths
225g/8oz piece of cod or haddock fillet, skinned and cut into strips
Thai fish sauce, to taste
squeeze of lemon juice, to taste
salt and ground black pepper
boiled rice or noodles, to serve

1 Put the tamarind pulp in a bowl and pour over the warm water. Set aside while you peel and chop the tomatoes, discarding the seeds. Strip the spinach or kangkong leaves from the stems and tear into small pieces.

2 Remove the heads and shells from the prawns, leaving the tails intact.

3 Pour the prepared fish stock into a large pan and add the diced mooli. Cook the mooli for 5 minutes, then add the beans and continue to cook for 3–5 minutes more.

4 Add the fish strips, tomato and spinach. Strain in the tamarind juice and cook for 2 minutes. Stir in the prawns and cook for 1–2 minutes to heat. Season with salt and pepper and add a little fish sauce and lemon juice to taste. Transfer to individual serving bowls and serve immediately, with boiled rice or noodles.

Shellfish with Coconut Milk

Green curry paste, made with green chillies and plenty of fresh coriander, gives this seafood dish its unique flavour. It looks as good as it tastes.

Serves 4–6

450g/1lb mussels in their shells, cleaned
60ml/4 tbsp water
225g/8oz medium cuttlefish or squid
400ml/14fl oz/1⅔ cups coconut milk
300ml/½ pint/1¼ cups chicken or vegetable stock
350g/12oz monkfish, hoki or red snapper, skinned
150g/5oz raw or cooked prawn (shrimp) tails, peeled and deveined
75g/3oz green beans, trimmed and cooked
1 tomato, peeled, seeded and roughly chopped
torn basil leaves, to garnish
boiled rice, to serve

For the green curry paste
10ml/2 tsp coriander seeds
2.5ml/½ tsp cumin seeds
3 or 4 medium fresh green chillies, finely chopped
20ml/4 tsp sugar
10ml/2 tsp salt
2cm/¾in piece fresh root ginger, peeled and finely chopped
3 garlic cloves, crushed
1 medium onion, finely chopped
50g/2oz/2 cups fresh coriander (cilantro) leaves, finely chopped
2.5ml/½ tsp grated nutmeg
30ml/2 tbsp vegetable oil

1 Scrub the mussels in cold running water and pull off the 'beards'. Discard any that do not shut when sharply tapped. Put them in a pan with the water, cover and cook for 6–8 minutes. Discard any mussels that remain closed and remove three-quarters of the mussels from their shells. Set aside. Strain the cooking liquid and set aside.

2 To prepare the cuttlefish or squid, trim off the tentacles and discard the gut. Remove the cuttle shell or quill from inside the body and rub off the skin. Cut the body open and score in a criss-cross pattern with a sharp knife. Cut into strips and set aside.

3 To make the green curry paste, dry-fry the coriander and cumin seeds in a karahi or wok. Grind the chillies with the sugar and salt in a pestle with a mortar or in a food processor. Add the coriander and cumin seeds, ginger, garlic and onion and grind to a paste. Add the fresh coriander, nutmeg and oil and combine thoroughly.

4 Strain the coconut milk and pour the thin liquid into a karahi or wok with the stock and reserved cooking liquid from the mussels. Reserve the thick part of the coconut milk. Add 60–75ml/4–5 tbsp of the green curry paste to the wok and bring the mixture to the boil. Boil rapidly for a few minutes, until the liquid has reduced completely.

5 Add the thick part of the coconut milk. Stir well, then add the cuttlefish or squid and monkfish, hoki or red snapper. Simmer for 15–20 minutes. Then add the prawns, mussels, beans and tomato. Simmer for 2–3 minutes until heated through. Transfer to a warmed serving dish, garnish with torn basil leaves and serve immediately with boiled rice.

prawn stew Energy 62kcal/259kJ; Protein 11.5g; Carbohydrate 2.3g, of which sugars 2.1g; Fat 0.8g, of which saturates 0.2g; Cholesterol 55mg; Calcium 64mg; Fibre 1.3g; Sodium 91mg.
shellfish w. coconut Energy 192kcal/811kJ; Protein 25.3g; Carbohydrate 9.1g, of which sugars 5.8g; Fat 6.5g, of which saturates 1.1g; Cholesterol 150mg; Calcium 133mg; Fibre 1.5g; Sodium 231mg.

Seafood Nasi Goreng

This dish is similar to paella, with its delicious blend of succulent seafood and rice. Cook the rice the day before, if possible.

Serves 4–6

2 eggs
30ml/2 tbsp water
105ml/7 tbsp oil
2 fresh red chillies, halved and seeded
1cm/½in cube shrimp paste
2 garlic cloves, crushed
1 onion, roughly chopped
115g/4oz raw prawns (shrimp)
175–225g/6–8oz fresh mackerel fillets, skinned
225g/8oz fresh squid, cut into neat strips
675g/1½lb/6 cups cold cooked long grain rice, preferably basmati (about 350g/12oz/1¾ cups raw rice)
30ml/2 tbsp dark soy sauce
salt and ground black pepper
deep-fried onions, celery leaves and fresh coriander (cilantro) sprigs, to garnish

1 Put the eggs in a bowl and beat in the water, with salt and pepper to taste. Using a non-stick frying pan make two or three omelettes using as little oil as possible. Roll up each omelette and cut into strips when cold. Set aside. Shred one of the chillies and reserve it.

2 Put the shrimp paste in a food processor. Add the remaining chilli, the garlic and onion. Process to a fine paste. Heat the remaining oil in a wok and fry the paste, without browning, until it gives off a rich, spicy aroma. Add the mackerel and prawns and toss over the heat to seal in the juices, then cook for 2 minutes more, stirring constantly.

3 Add the squid and stir-fry for 2 minutes. Finally, stir in the cold rice, dark soy sauce and seasoning to taste. Reheat the rice fully, stirring all the time to keep the rice light and fluffy and prevent it from sticking to the base of the pan.

4 Spoon into individual dishes and arrange the omelette strips and reserved chilli on top. Garnish with the deep-fried onions, celery leaves and coriander sprigs.

Butterfly Prawns

A classic Cantonese restaurant dish, this takes its name from the way each prawn is slit and opened out so that it looks like a butterfly. The prawns are dipped in a very light batter, almost like tempura, and then quickly cooked in very hot oil until golden and beautifully crispy.

Serves 4

16 large prawns (shrimp)
30ml/2 tbsp plain (all-purpose) flour
15ml/1 tbsp self-raising (self-rising) flour
pinch of bicarbonate of soda (baking soda)
15ml/1 tbsp sesame oil
120ml/4fl oz/½ cup cold water
vegetable oil for deep-frying
sweet chilli dipping sauce, to serve

1 Clean the prawns and shell them, but leave the tails intact. Using a sharp knife, slit each prawn halfway through the back, then spread them flat so that they resemble butterflies.

2 Mix the plain flour and self-raising flour in a bowl. Add the bicarbonate of soda, then the sesame oil and cold water. Stir to make a smooth batter.

3 Heat the oil in a wok or deep-fryer to 190°C/375°F. Dip the prawns in turn in batter, gently shaking off the excess, and add to the hot oil. Repeat with more prawns, but do not overcrowd the wok or fryer.

4 After 2–3 minutes, when the prawns are golden brown, lift them out and drain on kitchen paper. Keep warm while cooking successive batches. Serve hot, with the sweet chilli dipping sauce.

Cook's Tip
Sweet chilli dipping sauce can be bought in all supermarkets and is a great store cupboard staple for anyone who enjoys Asian food.

nasi goreng Energy 463kcal/1929kJ; Protein 27.3g; Carbohydrate 49.4g, of which sugars 2.1g; Fat 17.1g, of which saturates 2.7g; Cholesterol 151mg; Calcium 49mg; Fibre 0.5g; Sodium 288mg.
butterfly prawns Energy 156kcal/653kJ; Protein 12.5g; Carbohydrate 7.3g, of which sugars 0.5g; Fat 8.8g, of which saturates 1.3g; Cholesterol 157mg; Calcium 64mg; Fibre 0.3g; Sodium 316mg.

Seared Prawn Salad

In this intensely flavoured salad, prawns and mango are partnered with a sweet-sour garlic dressing.

Serves 6

675g/1½lb medium raw prawns (shrimp), shelled and deveined, with tails on
finely shredded rind of 1 lime
½ fresh red chilli, seeded and finely chopped
30ml/2 tbsp olive oil, plus extra for brushing
1 ripe mango, cut into strips
2 carrots, cut into long thin shreds
10cm/4in piece cucumber, sliced
1 small red onion, halved and thinly sliced
a few sprigs of fresh coriander (cilantro)
a few sprigs of fresh mint
45ml/3 tbsp roasted peanuts, roughly chopped
salt and ground black pepper

For the dressing
1 large garlic clove, chopped
10–15ml/2–3 tsp sugar
juice of 2 limes
15–30ml/1–2 tbsp fish sauce
1 fresh red chilli, seeded
5–10ml/1–2 tsp light rice vinegar

1 Place the prawns in a bowl and add the lime rind and chilli. Season with salt and pepper and spoon the oil over them. Leave to marinate for 30–40 minutes.

2 For the dressing, pound the garlic with 10ml/2 tsp sugar until smooth. Work in the juice of 1½ limes and 15ml/1 tbsp of the fish sauce. Pour into a bowl and add half the chilli. Taste, then add more sugar, lime juice, fish sauce and vinegar as needed.

3 Toss the mango, carrots, cucumber and onion with half the dressing. Arrange the salad on individual plates or in bowls.

4 Heat a griddle pan until very hot. Brush with a little oil, then sear the prawns for 2–3 minutes on each side, until they turn pink. Arrange the prawns on the salads.

5 Sprinkle with the remaining dressing and scatter the herb sprigs, chilli and peanuts over the top. Serve immediately.

Prawns with Yellow Curry Paste

Fish and shellfish, such as prawns, and coconut milk, were made for each other. This is a very quick recipe if you buy the yellow curry paste ready-made. It keeps well in a screw-top jar in the refrigerator for up to four weeks.

Serves 4–6

600ml/1 pint/2½ cups coconut milk
30ml/2 tbsp yellow curry paste
15ml/1 tbsp fish sauce
2.5ml/½ tsp salt
5ml/1 tsp sugar
450g/1lb raw king prawns (jumbo shrimp), thawed if frozen, peeled and deveined
225g/8oz cherry tomatoes
juice of ½ lime
red (bell) peppers, seeded and cut into thin strips, and fresh coriander (cilantro) leaves, to garnish

1 Put half the coconut milk in a wok or large pan and bring to the boil. Add the yellow curry paste and stir until it disperses. Lower the heat and simmer gently for about 10 minutes.

2 Add the fish sauce, salt, sugar and remaining coconut milk to the sauce. Simmer for 5 minutes more.

3 Add the prawns and cherry tomatoes. Simmer gently for about 5 minutes until the prawns are pink and tender. Spoon into a serving dish, sprinkle with lime juice and garnish with strips of pepper and coriander.

Cook's Tips

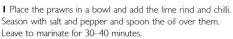

- *Unused coconut milk can be stored in the refrigerator for 1–2 days, or poured into a freezer container and frozen.*
- *If making your own coconut milk, instead of discarding the spent coconut, it can be reused to make a second batch of coconut milk. This will be of a poorer quality and should only be used to extend a good quality first quantity of milk.*
- *Leave newly made coconut milk to stand for 10 minutes. The coconut cream will float to the top – skim off with a spoon.*

seared prawn salad Energy 156kcal/656kJ; Protein 20.9g; Carbohydrate 8.9g, of which sugars 8.4g; Fat 4.3g, of which saturates 0.7g; Cholesterol 219mg; Calcium 102mg; Fibre 1.4g; Sodium 397mg.
prawns w. curry paste Energy 94kcal/397kJ; Protein 13.8g; Carbohydrate 7g, of which sugars 6.9g; Fat 1.4g, of which saturates 0.4g; Cholesterol 146mg; Calcium 92mg; Fibre 0.4g; Sodium 434mg.

Prawn & Cauliflower Curry

This is a basic fisherman's curry. Simple to make, it would traditionally be eaten from a communal bowl.

Serves 4

450g/1lb raw tiger prawns (jumbo shrimp), peeled, deveined and cleaned
juice of 1 lime
15ml/1 tbsp vegetable oil
1 red onion, roughly chopped
2 garlic cloves, roughly chopped
2 Thai chillies, seeded and chopped
1 cauliflower, broken into florets
5ml/1 tsp sugar
2 star anise, dry-fried and ground
10ml/2 tsp fenugreek, dry-fried and ground
450ml/¾ pint/2 cups coconut milk
1 bunch fresh coriander (cilantro), chopped, to garnish
salt and ground black pepper

1 In a bowl, toss the prawns in the lime juice and set aside. Heat a wok or heavy pan and add the oil. Stir in the onion, garlic and chillies. As they brown, add the cauliflower. Stir-fry for 2–3 minutes.

2 Toss in the sugar and spices. Add the coconut milk, stirring to make sure it is thoroughly combined. Reduce the heat and simmer for 10–15 minutes, or until the liquid has reduced and thickened a little. Add the prawns and lime juice and cook for 1–2 minutes, or until the prawns turn opaque. Season to taste, and sprinkle with coriander. Serve hot.

Cook's Tip
To devein prawns, make a shallow cut down the back of the prawn, lift out the thin, black vein, then rinse thoroughly under cold, running water.

Variation
Other popular combinations include prawns (shrimp) with butternut squash or pumpkin.

Mango & Prawn Curry

This sweet, spicy curry is simple to make, and the addition of mango and tamarind produces a very full, rich flavour. If you have enough time, make the sauce the day before to give the flavours time to develop even more. Serve small portions with plain steamed rice to temper the richness.

Serves 4

1 green mango
5ml/1 tsp hot chilli powder
15ml/1 tbsp paprika
2.5ml/½ tsp ground turmeric
4 garlic cloves, crushed
10ml/2 tsp finely grated fresh root ginger
30ml/2 tbsp ground coriander
10ml/2 tsp ground cumin
15ml/1 tbsp palm sugar (jaggery)
400g/14oz can coconut milk
10ml/2 tsp salt
15ml/1 tbsp tamarind paste
1kg/2¼lb large prawns (shrimp)
chopped coriander (cilantro), to garnish
steamed white rice, chopped tomato, cucumber and onion salad, to serve

1 Wash, stone (pit) and slice the mango and set aside. In a large bowl, combine the chilli powder, paprika, turmeric, garlic, ginger, ground coriander, ground cumin and palm sugar. Add 400ml/14fl oz/1⅔ cups cold water to the bowl and stir to combine the ingredients.

2 Pour the spice mixture into a wok, and place over a high heat and bring the mixture to the boil. Cover the wok with a lid, reduce the heat to low and simmer gently for 8–10 minutes.

3 Add the mango, coconut milk, salt and tamarind paste to the wok and stir to combine. Bring to a simmer and then add the whole prawns.

4 Cover the wok and cook gently for 10–12 minutes, or until the prawns have turned pink and are cooked.

5 Serve the curry garnished with chopped coriander, accompanied by steamed white rice and a tomato, cucumber and onion salad.

prawn & cauliflower Energy 157kcal/664kJ; Protein 24.7g; Carbohydrate 10.4g, of which sugars 9.4g; Fat 2.2g, of which saturates 0.6g; Cholesterol 219mg; Calcium 169mg; Fibre 2.7g; Sodium 351mg.
mango & prawn Energy 151kcal/648kJ; Protein 22.1g; Carbohydrate 14.1g, of which sugars 14g; Fat 1.1g, of which saturates 0.5g; Cholesterol 263mg; Calcium 143mg; Fibre 1g; Sodium 2102mg.

Stir-fried Prawns with Mangetouts

Mangetout means 'eat all' and you'll want to do just that when a recipe is as good as this one. The prawns remain beautifully succulent and the sauce is delicious.

Serves 4

300ml/½ pint/1¼ cups fish stock
350g/12oz raw tiger prawns (jumbo shrimp), peeled and deveined
15ml/1 tbsp vegetable oil
1 garlic clove, finely chopped
225g/8oz/2 cups mangetouts (snow peas)
1.5ml/¼ tsp salt
15ml/1 tbsp mirin (sweet rice wine) or dry sherry
15ml/1 tbsp oyster sauce
5ml/1 tsp cornflour (cornstarch)
5ml/1 tsp caster (superfine) sugar
15ml/1 tbsp cold water
1.5ml/¼ tsp sesame oil

1 Bring the fish stock to the boil in a frying pan. Add the prawns. Cook gently for 2 minutes until the prawns have turned pink, then lift them out on a slotted spoon and set aside.

2 Heat the vegetable oil in a non-stick frying pan or wok. When the oil is very hot, add the chopped garlic and cook for a few seconds, then add the mangetouts. Sprinkle with the salt. Stir-fry for 1 minute.

3 Add the prawns and mirin or sherry to the pan or wok. Toss the ingredients together over the heat for a few seconds, then add the oyster sauce and toss again.

4 Mix the cornflour and sugar to a paste with the water. Add to the pan and cook, stirring constantly, until the sauce thickens slightly. Drizzle with sesame oil.

Cook's Tip

Mirin is a sweet rice wine from Japan. It has quite a delicate flavour and is used for cooking. Rice wine for drinking is called sake. Both are available from Asian food stores. If you cannot locate mirin, dry sherry can be used instead.

Three Sea Flavours Stir-fry

This delectable seafood combination is a healthy choice and is also ideal for a special occasion meal. Fresh root ginger and spring onions enhance the flavour.

Serves 4

4 large scallops, with the corals
225g/8oz firm white fish fillet, such as monkfish or cod
115g/4oz raw tiger prawns (jumbo shrimp)
300ml/½ pint/1¼ cups fish stock
15ml/1 tbsp vegetable oil
2 garlic cloves, roughly chopped
5cm/2in piece fresh root ginger, thinly sliced
8 spring onions (scallions), cut into 4cm/1½in pieces
30ml/2 tbsp dry white wine
5ml/1 tsp cornflour (cornstarch)
15ml/1 tbsp cold water
salt and ground white pepper
noodles or rice, to serve

1 Separate the corals and slice each scallop in half horizontally. Cut the fish into chunks. Peel and devein the prawns.

2 Bring the fish stock to the boil in a pan. Add the prepared seafood, lower the heat and poach gently for 1–2 minutes until the fish, scallops and corals are just firm and the prawns have turned pink.

3 Remove the seafood, using a slotted spoon, and set aside. Reserve about 60ml/4 tbsp of the stock.

4 Heat the oil in a non-stick frying pan or wok over a high heat until very hot. Stir-fry the garlic, ginger and spring onions for a few seconds.

5 Add the seafood and wine. Stir-fry for 1 minute, then add the reserved stock and simmer for 2 minutes.

6 Mix the cornflour to form a smooth paste with the water. Add the mixture to the pan or wok and cook, stirring constantly just until the sauce thickens.

7 Season the stir-fry with salt and pepper to taste. Serve immediately, with noodles or rice.

prawns w. mangetouts Energy 125kcal/524kJ; Protein 17.6g; Carbohydrate 5.2g, of which sugars 3.6g; Fat 3.4g, of which saturates 0.4g; Cholesterol 171mg; Calcium 96mg; Fibre 1.3g; Sodium 436mg.
sea flavours stir-fry Energy 159Kcal/668kJ; Protein 26.2g; Carbohydrate 3.3g, of which sugars 0.6g; Fat 4.1g, of which saturates 0.6g; Cholesterol 103mg; Calcium 50mg; Fibre 0.3g; Sodium 172mg.

Gong Boa Prawns

This delicious sweet and sour sauce complements tiger prawns perfectly.

Serves 4

350g/12oz raw tiger prawns (jumbo shrimp)
½ cucumber, about 75g/3oz
300ml/½ pint/1¼ cups fish stock
15ml/1 tbsp vegetable oil
2.5ml/½ tsp crushed dried chillies
½ green (bell) pepper, seeded and cut into 2.5cm/1in strips
1 small carrot, thinly sliced
30ml/2 tbsp tomato ketchup
45ml/3 tbsp rice vinegar
15ml/1 tbsp sugar
150ml/¼ pint/⅔ cup vegetable stock
50g/2oz/½ cup drained canned pineapple chunks
10ml/2 tsp cornflour (cornstarch) mixed with 15ml/1 tbsp cold water
salt

1 Peel and devein the prawns. Rub them with 2.5ml/½ tsp salt; leave them for a few minutes, then wash and pat dry.

2 Using a narrow peeler or cannelle knife, pare strips of skin off the cucumber to give a stripy effect. Cut the cucumber in half lengthways and scoop out the seeds with a teaspoon. Cut the flesh into 5mm/¼in crescents.

3 Bring the fish stock to the boil in a pan. Add the prawns, lower the heat and poach the prawns for 2 minutes until they turn pink, then lift them out using a slotted spoon and set aside.

4 Heat the oil in a non-stick frying pan or wok over a high heat. Fry the chillies for a few seconds, then add the pepper strips and carrot slices and stir-fry for 1 minute more.

5 Stir the tomato ketchup, vinegar, sugar, stock and 1.5ml/¼ tsp salt into the pan and cook for 3 minutes more.

6 Add the prawns, cucumber and pineapple and cook for 2 minutes. Add the cornflour paste and cook, stirring constantly. Once the sauce thickens, serve the dish immediately, ideally with plain boiled or steamed rice.

Chilli & Coconut Prawns

Supply plenty of bread or rice when serving these superb prawns. The sauce is so tasty that diners will want to savour every last bite. Be warned, though, the chilli makes these fiery, even though tamarind has a taming influence.

Serves 4

8 shallots, chopped
4 garlic cloves, chopped
8–10 dried red chillies, soaked in warm water until soft, squeezed dry, seeded and chopped
5ml/1 tsp shrimp paste
30ml/2 tbsp vegetable or groundnut (peanut) oil
250ml/8fl oz/1 cup coconut cream
500g/1¼lb fresh prawns (shrimp), peeled and deveined
10ml/2 tsp tamarind paste
15ml/1 tbsp palm sugar (jaggery)
salt and ground black pepper
2 fresh red chillies, seeded and finely chopped, and fresh coriander (cilantro) leaves, to garnish
crusty bread or steamed rice and pickles, to serve

1 Using a mortar and pestle or food processor, grind the shallots, garlic and dried chillies to a coarse paste. Beat in the shrimp paste.

2 Heat the oil in a wok and stir in the paste until fragrant. Add the coconut cream and let it bubble up until it separates. Toss in the prawns, reduce the heat and simmer for 3 minutes.

3 Stir in the tamarind paste and the sugar and cook for a further 2 minutes until the sauce is very thick. Season with salt and pepper and scatter the chopped chillies and coriander over the top. Serve immediately with chunks of fresh, crusty bread to mop up the sauce, or with steamed rice and pickles.

Cook's Tip

Tamarind used to be an exotic ingredient, available only as pods which needed to be processed before use. Fortunately the paste is now a stocked supermarket item.

gong boa prawns Energy 147kcal/617kJ; Protein 16.3g; Carbohydrate 13.2g, of which sugars 10.7g; Fat 3.5g, of which saturates 0.5g; Cholesterol 171mg; Calcium 88mg; Fibre 1.1g; Sodium 296mg.
chilli & prawns Energy 211kcal/886kJ; Protein 23.6g; Carbohydrate 14.8g, of which sugars 13.1g; Fat 6.8g, of which saturates 1g; Cholesterol 244mg; Calcium 152mg; Fibre 1.1g; Sodium 351mg.

Prawns with Jasmine Rice

Strips of omelette are used to garnish this rice dish. Use your wok for frying the omelette – the sloping sides make it easy to spread the beaten egg thinly and then to slide it out.

Serves 4–6

45ml/3 tbsp vegetable oil
1 egg, beaten
1 onion, chopped
15ml/1 tbsp chopped garlic
15ml/1 tbsp shrimp paste
1kg/2¼lb/4 cups cooked jasmine rice
350g/12oz cooked shelled prawns (shrimp)
50g/2oz thawed frozen peas
oyster sauce, to taste
2 spring onions (scallions), chopped
15–20 Thai basil leaves, roughly snipped, plus a sprig, to garnish

1 Heat 15ml/1 tbsp of the oil in a wok or frying pan. Add the beaten egg and swirl it around to set in a thin pancake.

2 Cook the pancake (on one side only) over a gentle heat until golden. Slide the pancake on to a board, roll up and cut into thin strips. Set aside.

3 Heat the remaining oil in the wok or pan, add the onion and garlic and stir-fry for 2–3 minutes. Stir in the shrimp paste and mix well until thoroughly combined.

4 Add the rice, prawns and peas and toss and stir together, until everything is heated through.

5 Season with oyster sauce to taste, taking great care as the shrimp paste is salty. Mix in the spring onions and basil leaves. Transfer to a serving dish and top with the strips of egg pancake. Serve, garnished with a sprig of basil.

Cook's Tip
Leave a few prawns (shrimp) in their shells for an additional garnish, if you like.

Long Beans with Prawns

Popular in many Asian countries, long beans – like many other vegetables – are often stir-fried with garlic. This Cambodian recipe is livened up with prawns, as well as other flavourings, and works well either as a side dish or on its own with rice.

Serves 4

45ml/3 tbsp vegetable oil
2 garlic cloves, finely chopped
25g/1oz galangal or root ginger, finely shredded
450g/1lb fresh prawns (shrimp), shelled and deveined
1 onion, halved and finely sliced
450g/1lb long beans, trimmed and cut into 7.5cm/3in lengths
120ml/4fl oz/½ cup soy sauce

For the marinade
30ml/2 tbsp fish sauce
juice of 2 limes
10ml/2 tsp sugar
2 garlic cloves, crushed
1 lemon grass stalk, trimmed and finely sliced

1 To make the marinade, beat the fish sauce and lime juice in a bowl with the sugar until it has dissolved. Stir in the garlic and lemon grass. Add the prawns, cover, and chill for 1–2 hours.

2 Heat 30ml/2 tbsp of the oil in a wok or heavy pan. Stir in the chopped garlic and galangal or root ginger. Just as they begin to colour, toss in the marinated prawns. Stir-fry for a minute or until the prawns turn pink. Lift the prawns out on to a plate, reserving as much of the oil, garlic and galangal or root ginger as you can.

3 Add the remaining oil to the wok. Add the onion and stir-fry until slightly caramelized. Stir in the beans, then pour in the soy sauce. Cook for 2–3 minutes, until the beans are tender. Add the prawns and stir-fry until heated through. Serve immediately.

Cook's Tip
This recipe uses an unusually large quantity of soy sauce. If you feel it will be too salty for your taste, use less or choose a light variety.

prawns w. rice Energy 354kcal/1494kJ; Protein 17.8g; Carbohydrate 53.4g, of which sugars 0.9g; Fat 9.2g, of which saturates 1.5g; Cholesterol 158mg; Calcium 117mg; Fibre 0.8g; Sodium 233mg.
long beans w. prawns Energy 187kcal/782kJ; Protein 22.6g; Carbohydrate 9.3g, of which sugars 7.9g; Fat 6.9g, of which saturates 0.9g; Cholesterol 219mg; Calcium 156mg; Fibre 3.2g; Sodium 485mg.

Prawn Adobo in Coconut Milk

This recipe comes from the Bicol region of the Philippines, where coconut milk is a much-loved base for many dishes. The prawns are marinated first for extra flavour.

Serves 4

450g/1lb large raw peeled prawns (shrimp)
300ml/½ pint/1¼ cups coconut milk
4 garlic cloves, crushed
30ml/2 tbsp soy sauce
juice of 3 kalamansi limes

For the marinade

105ml/7 tbsp suka (Filipino coconut vinegar)
2.5ml/½ tsp ground black pepper
30ml/2 tbsp garlic purée (paste)
15ml/1 tbsp patis (Filipino fish sauce)

1 Blend the marinade ingredients in a shallow container, then marinate the prawns for a few hours or overnight in the refrigerator.

2 Remove the prawns and set aside. Pour the marinade into a heavy pan, add the coconut milk and stir well. Bring the mixture to the boil, then add the garlic, soy sauce and lime juice.

3 Simmer the sauce for 5 minutes, then lift the prawns out of the marinade and cook in the sauce for 5 minutes before serving hot with rice or bread.

Cook's Tips

- *In some regions, Filipino sour fruits called kamias are added, which give a lovely tartness. Kamias are related to star fruit (carambola), which can also be used.*
- *If you cannot find kalamansi limes, use ordinary limes instead.*

Mussels & Clams with Lemon Grass & Coconut Cream

Lemon grass has an incomparable aromatic flavour and is widely used with all kinds of seafood in Thailand as the flavours marry so perfectly.

Serves 6

1.8kg/4lb fresh mussels
450g/1lb baby clams
120ml/4fl oz/½ cup dry white wine
1 bunch spring onions (scallions), chopped
2 lemon grass stalks, chopped
6 kaffir lime leaves, chopped
10ml/2 tsp Thai green curry paste
200ml/7fl oz/scant 1 cup coconut cream
30ml/2 tbsp chopped fresh coriander (cilantro)
salt and ground black pepper
garlic chives, to garnish

1 Scrub the mussels' shells with a stiff brush and rinse under cold running water. Scrape off any barnacles and remove the 'beards' with a small knife. Rinse well. Scrub the clams. Discard any mussels or clams that are damaged or broken or which do not close immediately when tapped sharply.

2 Put the wine in a large pan with the spring onions, lemon grass and lime leaves. Stir in the curry paste. Simmer until the wine has almost evaporated.

3 Add the mussels and clams to the pan and increase the heat to high. Cover tightly and steam the shellfish for 5–6 minutes, until they open.

4 Using a slotted spoon, transfer the mussels and clams to a heated serving bowl, cover and keep hot. Discard any shellfish that remain closed. Strain the cooking liquid into a clean pan through a sieve (strainer) lined with muslin (cheesecloth) and simmer briefly to reduce to about 250ml/8fl oz/1 cup.

5 Stir the coconut cream and chopped coriander into the sauce and season to taste. Heat through. Pour the sauce over the shellfish, garnish with the garlic chives and serve.

prawn adobo Energy 121kcal/512kJ; Protein 21.5g; Carbohydrate 7g, of which sugars 4.7g; Fat 1g, of which saturates 0.3g; Cholesterol 219mg; Calcium 115mg; Fibre 0.6g; Sodium 1009mg.
mussels & clams Energy 267kcal/1119kJ; Protein 23.4g; Carbohydrate 2.2g, of which sugars 1.8g; Fat 16.8g, of which saturates 12.3g; Cholesterol 57mg; Calcium 254mg; Fibre 0.5g; Sodium 477mg.

Pan-steamed Mussels with Thai Herbs

Like so many Thai dishes, this is very easy to prepare. The lemon grass and kaffir lime leaves add a refreshing tang to the mussels.

Serves 4–6

1kg/2¼lb fresh mussels
2 lemon grass stalks, finely chopped
4 shallots, chopped
4 kaffir lime leaves, coarsely torn
2 fresh red chillies, sliced
15ml/1 tbsp Thai fish sauce
30ml/2 tbsp fresh lime juice
thinly sliced spring onions (scallions) and coriander (cilantro) leaves, to garnish

1 Scrub the mussels' shells with a stiff brush and rinse under cold running water. Scrape off any barnacles and remove the 'beards' with a small knife. Rinse well. Discard any mussels that are broken or which do not close when tapped sharply.

2 Place the mussels in a large, heavy pan and add the lemon grass, shallots, kaffir lime leaves, chillies, fish sauce and lime juice. Mix well. Cover the pan tightly and steam the mussels over a high heat, shaking the pan occasionally, for 5–7 minutes, until the shells have opened.

3 Using a slotted spoon, transfer the cooked mussels to a warmed serving dish or individual bowls. Discard any mussels that have failed to open.

4 Garnish the mussels with the thinly sliced spring onions and coriander leaves. Serve immediately.

Cook's Tip
Mussels are bought alive. They can sometimes be a little gritty, so it is worth putting them into a bucket of cold salted water as soon as you get home. Sprinkle a little oatmeal or flour over the water so that the mussels can feed on this and excrete the grit.

Spicy Squid

This aromatically spiced squid dish, cumi cumi smoor, is simple yet delicious. For speed, buy ready-cleaned squid.

Serves 3–4

675g/1½lb squid
45ml/3 tbsp groundnut (peanut) oil
1 onion, finely chopped
2 garlic cloves, crushed
1 beefsteak tomato, peeled and chopped
15ml/1 tbsp dark soy sauce
2.5ml/½ tsp grated nutmeg
6 cloves
150ml/¼ pint/⅔ cup water
juice of ½ lemon or lime
salt and ground black pepper
fresh coriander (cilantro) leaves and shredded spring onion (scallion), to garnish
boiled rice, to serve

1 Rinse and drain the squid, then slice lengthways along one side and open it out flat. Score the inside of the squid in a lattice pattern, using the blunt side of a sharp knife, then cut it crossways into long thin strips.

2 Heat a wok and add 15ml/1 tbsp of the oil. When hot, toss in the squid strips and stir-fry for 2–3 minutes, by which time the squid will have curled into attractive shapes or into firm rings. Lift out and set aside.

3 Wipe out the wok, add the remaining oil and heat it. Stir-fry the onion and garlic until soft and beginning to brown. Stir in the tomato, soy sauce, nutmeg, cloves, water and lemon or lime juice. Bring to the boil, lower the heat and add the squid with seasoning to taste.

4 Cook the mixture gently for a further 3–5 minutes, stirring from time to time to prevent sticking. Take care not to overcook the squid.

5 Divide boiled rice among three or four serving plates and spoon the spicy squid on top. Garnish with coriander leaves and shredded spring onions, and serve.

mussels w. Thai herbs Energy 48kcal/206kJ; Protein 8.9g; Carbohydrate 1.1g, of which sugars 0.8g; Fat 1g, of which saturates 0.2g; Cholesterol 20mg; Calcium 102mg; Fibre 0.2g; Sodium 283mg.
spicy squid Energy 223kcal/935kJ; Protein 26.4g; Carbohydrate 4.4g, of which sugars 2g; Fat 11.3g, of which saturates 1.7g; Cholesterol 380mg; Calcium 28mg; Fibre 0.6g; Sodium 190mg.

Curried Seafood with Coconut Milk

Fresh herbs and flavourings such as green chillies, kaffir lime leaves and lemon grass give this beautiful curry its green colour and fragrant flavour. The curry mixture is cooked for only a short while so that it retains its freshness.

Serves 4

225g/8oz small ready-prepared squid
225g/8oz raw tiger prawns (jumbo shrimp)
400ml/14fl oz/1⅔ cups coconut milk
2 kaffir lime leaves, finely shredded
30ml/2 tbsp Thai fish sauce
450g/1lb firm white fish fillets, skinned, boned and cut into chunks
2 fresh green chillies, seeded and finely chopped
30ml/2 tbsp torn fresh basil or coriander (cilantro) leaves
squeeze of fresh lime juice
cooked Thai jasmine rice, to serve

For the curry paste

6 spring onions (scallions), coarsely chopped
4 fresh coriander (cilantro) stems, coarsely chopped, plus 45ml/3 tbsp chopped fresh coriander
4 kaffir lime leaves, shredded
8 fresh green chillies, seeded and coarsely chopped
1 lemon grass stalk, coarsely chopped
2.5cm/1in piece fresh root ginger, peeled and coarsely chopped
45ml/3 tbsp chopped fresh basil
15ml/1 tbsp vegetable oil

1 To make the curry paste, put all the ingredients except the oil in a food processor and process to a paste. Alternatively, pound together in a mortar with a pestle. Stir in the oil.

2 Rinse the squid and pat dry with kitchen paper. Cut the bodies into rings and halve the tentacles, if necessary.

3 Heat a wok until hot, add the prawns and stir-fry, without any oil, for about 4 minutes, until they turn pink.

4 Remove the prawns from the wok and leave to cool slightly, then peel off the shells, leaving a few unshelled for the garnish. Make a shallow slit along the back of each one and remove the black intestinal vein.

5 Pour the coconut milk into the wok, then bring to the boil over a medium heat, stirring constantly. Add 30ml/2 tbsp of the curry paste, the shredded lime leaves and fish sauce and stir well to mix. Reduce the heat to low and simmer gently for about 10 minutes.

6 Add the squid, prawns and chunks of fish and cook for about 2 minutes, until the seafood is tender. Take care not to overcook the squid as it will become tough very quickly.

7 Just before serving, stir in the chillies and basil or coriander. Taste and adjust the flavour with a squeeze of lime juice. Garnish with prawns in their shells, and serve with jasmine rice.

Variation
You can use any firm-fleshed white fish for this curry, such as monkfish, cod, haddock or John Dory.

Stir-fried Squid with Ginger

The abundance of fish around the Gulf of Thailand sustains thriving markets for the restaurant and hotel trade, and every market naturally features stalls where delicious, freshly caught seafood is cooked and served. This recipe is popular among street traders. Squid needs the minimum of cooking and tastes great with garlic, lemon and ginger.

Serves 2

4 ready-prepared baby squid, total weight about 250g/9oz
15ml/1 tbsp vegetable oil
2 garlic cloves, finely chopped
30ml/2 tbsp soy sauce
2.5cm/1in piece fresh root ginger, peeled and finely chopped
juice of ½ lemon
5ml/1 tsp sugar
2 spring onions (scallions), chopped

1 Rinse the squid well and pat dry with kitchen paper. Cut the bodies into rings and halve the tentacles, if necessary.

2 Heat the oil in a wok or frying pan and cook the garlic until golden brown, but do not let it burn. Add the squid and stir-fry for 30 seconds over a high heat.

3 Add the soy sauce, ginger, lemon juice, sugar and spring onions. Stir-fry for a further 30 seconds, then serve.

Cook's Tips
- *Squid has an undeserved reputation for being rubbery in texture. This is always a result of overcooking it.*
- *Small squid generally have a sweeter flavour than those that are larger, and are usually more tender, too.*

Variation
This dish is often prepared with fresh galangal rather than ginger and works well with most kinds of seafood, including prawns (shrimp) and scallops.

curried seafood Energy 238kcal/1005kJ; Protein 40.6g; Carbohydrate 7g, of which sugars 6.2g; Fat 5.5g, of which saturates 0.9g; Cholesterol 288mg; Calcium 145mg; Fibre 1.4g; Sodium 622mg.
squid w. ginger Energy 169kcal/709kJ; Protein 20g; Carbohydrate 5.3g, of which sugars 3.6g; Fat 7.7g, of which saturates 1.2g; Cholesterol 281mg; Calcium 26mg; Fibre 0.2g; Sodium 1207mg.

Baked Stuffed Crab Shells

This French-inspired dish has been given an Asian twist with a combination of bean thread noodles and cloud ear mushrooms. It is time-consuming to cook the crabs yourself, so use freshly cooked crab meat from your fishmonger or supermarket. You will also need four small, empty crab shells. Cleaned shells can, in fact, be bought in some Asian markets, but many fishmongers will sell dressed crab within the shell so this does ease the preparation two-fold. As a last resort, four small individual ovenproof dishes will do.

Serves 4

25g/1oz dried bean thread (cellophane) noodles
6 dried cloud ear (wood ear) mushrooms
450g/1lb fresh crab meat
15ml/1 tbsp vegetable oil
10ml/2 tsp fish sauce
2 shallots, finely chopped
2 garlic cloves, finely chopped
2.5cm/1in fresh root ginger, peeled and grated
1 small bunch coriander (cilantro), stalks removed, leaves chopped
1 egg, beaten
25g/1oz/2 tbsp butter
salt and ground black pepper
fresh dill fronds, to garnish
chilli sauce, to serve

1 Preheat the oven to 180°C/350°F/Gas 4. Soak the bean thread noodles and cloud ear mushrooms separately in bowls of lukewarm water for 15 minutes. Squeeze dry and chop finely.

2 In a bowl, mix together the noodles and mushrooms with the crab meat. Add the oil, fish sauce, shallots, garlic, ginger and coriander. Season, then stir in the beaten egg.

3 Spoon the mixture into four small crab shells or use individual ovenproof dishes, packing it in tightly, and dot the top of each one with a little butter. Place the shells on a baking tray and cook for about 20 minutes, or until the filling in each shell is nicely browned.

4 Garnish with dill and serve immediately with a little chilli sauce to drizzle over the top.

Crab Meat in Vinegar

A refreshing summer tsumami (a Japanese dish that accompanies alcoholic drinks). For the dressing, use a Japanese or Greek cucumber, if possible – they are about one-third of the size of ordinary salad cucumbers and contain less water.

Serves 4

½ red (bell) pepper, seeded
pinch of salt
275g/10oz cooked white crab meat, or 2 x 165g/5½oz cans white crab meat, drained
about 300g/11oz Japanese, Greek or salad cucumber

For the vinegar mixture

15ml/1 tbsp rice vinegar
10ml/2 tsp caster (superfine) sugar
10ml/2 tsp awakuchi shoyu

1 Slice the red pepper into thin strips lengthways. Sprinkle with a little salt and leave for about 15 minutes. Rinse well and drain.

2 For the vinegar mixture, combine the rice vinegar, sugar and awakuchi shoyu in a small bowl.

3 Loosen the crab meat and mix it with the sliced red pepper in a mixing bowl. Divide among four small bowls.

4 If you use salad cucumber, scoop out the seeds. Finely grate the cucumber with a fine-toothed grater or use a food processor. Drain in a fine-meshed sieve (or strainer).

5 Mix the cucumber with the vinegar mixture, and pour a quarter on to the crab meat mixture in each bowl. Serve cold immediately, before the cucumber loses its colour.

Variation

The vinegar mixture is best made using awakuchi shoyu, but ordinary shoyu can be used instead. It will make a darker dressing, however.

stuffed crab shells Energy 215kcal/897kJ; Protein 23.3g; Carbohydrate 7.3g, of which sugars 1.9g; Fat 10.4g, of which saturates 4g; Cholesterol 132mg; Calcium 174mg; Fibre 1.1g; Sodium 718mg.
crab meat in vinegar Energy 82kcal/345kJ; Protein 13.3g; Carbohydrate 5.6g, of which sugars 5.4g; Fat 0.8g, of which saturates 0.1g; Cholesterol 50mg; Calcium 100mg; Fibre 0.9g; Sodium 560mg.

Crab with Spring Onions & Ginger

This recipe is far less complicated than it looks and will delight the eyes as much as the taste buds.

Serves 4

1 large or 2 medium crabs, about 675g/1½lb in total
30ml/2 tbsp Chinese rice wine or dry sherry
1 egg, lightly beaten
15ml/1 tbsp cornflour (cornstarch)
45–60ml/3–4 tbsp vegetable oil
15ml/1 tbsp finely chopped fresh root ginger
3–4 spring onions (scallions), cut into short lengths
30ml/2 tbsp soy sauce
5ml/1 tsp soft light brown sugar
about 75ml/5 tbsp stock
few drops of sesame oil

1 Cut the crab in half from the underbelly. Break off the claws and crack them with the back of a cleaver. Discard the legs and crack the shell, breaking it into several pieces. Discard the feathery gills and the sac. Put the pieces of crab in a bowl.

2 Mix together the rice wine or dry sherry, egg and cornflour and pour over the crab. Leave to marinate for 10–15 minutes.

3 Heat the oil in a preheated wok. Add the crab pieces, ginger and spring onions and stir-fry for about 2–3 minutes.

4 Add the soy sauce, sugar and stock and blend well. Bring to the boil, reduce the heat, cover and braise for 3–4 minutes. Transfer the crab to a serving dish, sprinkle with the sesame oil and serve.

Cook's Tip

For the very best flavour, buy a live crab and cook it yourself. However, if you prefer to buy a cooked crab, look for one that feels heavy for its size. This is an indication that it has fully grown into its shell and that there will be plenty of meat. Male crabs have larger claws, so will yield a greater proportion of white meat. However, females – identifiable by a broader, less-pointed tail flap – may contain coral, which many people regard as a delicacy.

Spiced Scallops in their Shells

Delicate, luxurious scallops are excellent steamed. When served with this spicy sauce, they make a delicious, yet simple, appetizer for four people or a light lunch for two. Each person spoons sauce on to the scallops before eating them.

Serves 2

8 scallops, shelled (ask the fishmonger to reserve the cupped side of 4 shells)
2 slices fresh root ginger, shredded
½ garlic clove, shredded
2 spring onions (scallions), green parts only, shredded
salt and ground black pepper

For the sauce

1 garlic clove, crushed
15ml/1 tbsp grated fresh root ginger
2 spring onions (scallions), white parts only, chopped
1–2 fresh green chillies, seeded and finely chopped
15ml/1 tbsp light soy sauce
15ml/1 tbsp dark soy sauce
10ml/2 tsp sesame oil

1 Remove the dark beard-like fringe and tough muscle from the scallops.

2 Place two scallops in each shell. Season lightly with salt and pepper, then scatter the ginger, garlic and spring onions on top. Place the shells in a bamboo steamer in a wok and steam for about 6 minutes, until the scallops look opaque. You may have to do this in batches, using a warm plate and dampened dish towel to keep the cooked scallops warm.

3 Meanwhile, make the sauce. Mix together the garlic, ginger, spring onions, chillies, soy sauces and sesame oil and pour into a small serving bowl.

4 Carefully remove each shell from the steamer, taking care not to spill the juices, and arrange them on a serving plate with the sauce bowl in the centre, or one shell to each individual plate with a small dish of sauce for each person. Serve immediately.

crab w. spring onions Energy 239kcal/997kJ; Protein 9.1g; Carbohydrate 18.1g, of which sugars 10.6g; Fat 14.1g, of which saturates 1.7g; Cholesterol 66mg; Calcium 26mg; Fibre 0g; Sodium 575mg.
scallops in their shells Energy 78kcal/331kJ; Protein 14.1g; Carbohydrate 3.7g, of which sugars 0.8g; Fat 1g, of which saturates 0.2g; Cholesterol 24mg; Calcium 33mg; Fibre 0.3g; Sodium 951mg.

Steamed Mussels in Coconut Milk

Mussels steamed in coconut milk and fresh aromatic herbs and spices make an ideal dish for informal entertaining. A wok makes short work of the cooking and the dish is great for a relaxed dinner with friends.

Serves 4

15ml/1 tbsp sunflower oil
6 garlic cloves, roughly chopped
15ml/1 tbsp finely chopped fresh root ginger
2 large fresh red chillies, seeded and finely sliced
6 spring onions (scallions), finely chopped
400ml/14fl oz/1⅔ cups coconut milk
45ml/3 tbsp light soy sauce
2 limes
5ml/1 tsp caster (superfine) sugar
1.6kg/3½lb mussels, scrubbed and beards removed
a large handful of chopped coriander (cilantro)
salt and ground black pepper

1 Heat the wok over a high heat and then add the oil. Stir in the garlic, ginger, chillies and spring onions and stir-fry for 30 seconds. Pour in the coconut milk, then add the soy sauce.

2 Grate the zest of the limes into the coconut milk mixture and add the sugar. Stir to mix and bring to the boil. Add the mussels. Return to the boil, cover and cook briskly for about 5–6 minutes, or until all the mussels have opened. Discard any mussels that remain closed.

3 Remove the wok from the heat and stir the chopped coriander into the mussel mixture. Season the mussels well with salt and pepper. Ladle into warmed bowls and serve.

Cook's Tip

For an informal supper with friends, take the wok straight to the table rather than serving in individual bowls. A wok makes a great serving dish, and there's something utterly irresistible about eating the mussels straight from it.

Clams with Miso & Mustard Sauce

Sweet and juicy, clams are excellent with this sweet-and-sour Japanese dressing.

Serves 4

900g/2lb carpet shell clams
15ml/1 tbsp sake
8 spring onions (scallions), green and white parts separated, then chopped in half
10g/¼oz dried wakame

For the dressing

60ml/4 tbsp shiro miso
20ml/4 tsp sugar
30ml/2 tbsp sake
15ml/1 tbsp rice vinegar
about 1.5ml/¼ tsp salt
7.5ml/1½ tsp English (hot) mustard

1 Wash the clams under running water. Discard any that remain open when tapped. Pour 1cm/½in water into a small pan. Add the clams and sake, cover, then bring to the boil. Cook for 5 minutes, then remove from the heat and leave to stand for 2 minutes.

2 Drain the clams, discarding any which have failed to open, and keep the liquid in a small bowl. When they have cooled slightly, remove the meat from most of the clam shells.

3 Cook the white part of the spring onions in a pan of boiling water for 2 minutes, then add the remaining green parts and cook for 2 minutes more. Drain well.

4 Mix the shiro miso, sugar, sake, rice vinegar and salt for the dressing in a small pan. Stir in 45ml/3 tbsp of the reserved clam liquid, and heat gently, stirring until the sugar has dissolved. Add the mustard, check the seasoning, and remove from the heat and leave to cool.

5 Soak the wakame in a bowl of water for about 10 minutes. Drain and squeeze out excess moisture.

6 Mix together the clams, onions, wakame and dressing in a bowl. Heap up in a large bowl or divide among four small bowls and serve cold.

steamed mussels Energy 165kcal/701kJ; Protein 22.1g; Carbohydrate 7.3g, of which sugars 7.2g; Fat 5.6g, of which saturates 1g; Cholesterol 48mg; Calcium 276mg; Fibre 0.2g; Sodium 1165mg.
clams w. miso Energy 114kcal/482kJ; Protein 12.8g; Carbohydrate 13.2g, of which sugars 11.6g; Fat 0.6g, of which saturates 0.2g; Cholesterol 50mg; Calcium 71mg; Fibre 0.3g; Sodium 1764mg.

Steamed Scallops with Ginger

It helps to have two woks when making this dish. Borrow an extra one from a friend, or use a large, heavy pan with a trivet for steaming the second plate of scallops. Take care not to overcook the tender seafood.

Serves 4

24 king scallops in their shells, cleaned
15ml/1 tbsp very finely shredded fresh root ginger
5ml/1 tsp very finely chopped garlic
1 large fresh red chilli, seeded and very finely chopped
15ml/1 tbsp light soy sauce
15ml/1 tbsp Chinese rice wine
a few drops of sesame oil
2–3 spring onions (scallions), very finely shredded
15ml/1 tbsp very finely chopped fresh chives
noodles or rice, to serve

1 Remove the scallops from their shells, then remove the membrane and hard white muscle from each one. Arrange the scallops on two plates. Rinse the shells, dry and set aside.

2 Fill two woks with 5cm/2in water and place a trivet in the base of each one. Bring to the boil.

3 Meanwhile, mix together the ginger, garlic, chilli, soy sauce, rice wine, sesame oil, spring onions and chives.

4 Spoon the flavourings over the scallops. Lower a plate into each of the woks. Turn the heat to low, cover and steam for 10–12 minutes.

5 Divide the scallops among four, or eight, of the reserved shells and serve immediately with noodles or rice.

Cook's Tip
Use the freshest scallops you can find. If you ask your fishmonger to shuck them, remember to ask for the shells.

Scallops & Tiger Prawns

Serve this light, delicate dish for lunch or supper accompanied by aromatic steamed rice or fine rice noodles and stir-fried pak choi or broccoli.

Serves 4

15ml/1 tbsp stir-fry oil or sunflower oil
500g/1¼lb raw tiger prawns (jumbo shrimp), peeled
1 star anise
225g/8oz scallops, halved horizontally if large
2.5cm/1in piece fresh root ginger, peeled and grated
2 garlic cloves, thinly sliced
1 red (bell) pepper, seeded and cut into thin strips
115g/4oz/1¾ cups shiitake or button (white) mushrooms, thinly sliced
juice of 1 lemon
5ml/1 tsp cornflour (cornstarch), mixed to a paste with 30ml/2 tbsp cold water
30ml/2 tbsp light soy sauce
salt and ground black pepper
chopped fresh chives, to garnish

1 Heat the oil in a wok until very hot. Put in the prawns and star anise and stir-fry over a high heat for 2 minutes.

2 Add the scallops, ginger and garlic and stir-fry for 1 minute more, by which time the prawns should have turned pink and the scallops opaque. Season with a little salt and plenty of pepper and then remove from the wok using a slotted spoon. Discard the star anise.

3 Add the red pepper and mushrooms to the wok and stir-fry for 1–2 minutes. Pour in the lemon juice, cornflour paste and soy sauce, bring to the boil and bubble this mixture for 1–2 minutes, stirring all the time, until the sauce is smooth and slightly thickened.

4 Stir the prawns and scallops into the sauce, cook for a few seconds until heated through, then season with salt and ground black pepper. Spoon on to individual plates and serve garnished with the chives.

scallops w. ginger Energy 392kcal/1621kJ; Protein 13.6g; Carbohydrate 4.5g, of which sugars 2.5g; Fat 34.1g, of which saturates 22.4g; Cholesterol 115mg; Calcium 63mg; Fibre 0.4g; Sodium 168mg.
scallops & tiger prawns Energy 212kcal/892kJ; Protein 36.3g; Carbohydrate 6.6g, of which sugars 3.3g; Fat 4.6g, of which saturates 0.8g; Cholesterol 270mg; Calcium 122mg; Fibre 1g; Sodium 877mg.

Spiced Scallops & Sugar Snap Peas

This is a great dish for special occasion entertaining.

Serves 4

45ml/3 tbsp oyster sauce
10ml/2 tsp soy sauce
5ml/1 tsp sesame oil
5ml/1 tsp golden caster (superfine) sugar
30ml/2 tbsp sunflower oil
2 fresh red chillies, finely sliced
4 garlic cloves, finely chopped
10ml/2 tsp finely chopped fresh root ginger
250g/9oz sugar snap peas, trimmed
500g/1¼lb king scallops, cleaned and halved, roes discarded
3 spring onions (scallions), finely shredded

For the noodle cakes
250g/9oz fresh thin egg noodles
10ml/2 tsp sesame oil
120ml/4fl oz/½ cup sunflower oil

1 Cook the noodles in boiling water until tender. Drain, toss with the sesame oil and 15ml/1 tbsp of the sunflower oil and spread out on a large baking sheet. Leave to dry in a warm place for 1 hour.

2 Heat 15ml/1 tbsp of the oil in a wok. Add a quarter of the noodle mixture, flatten it and shape it into a cake.

3 Cook the cake for about 5 minutes on each side until crisp and golden. Drain on kitchen paper and keep hot while you make the remaining three noodle cakes in the same way.

4 Mix the oyster sauce, soy sauce, sesame oil and sugar, stirring until the sugar has dissolved completely.

5 Heat a wok, add the sunflower oil, then stir-fry the chillies, garlic, ginger and sugar snaps for 1–2 minutes. Add the scallops and spring onions and stir-fry for 1 minute, then add the sauce mixture and cook for 1 minute.

6 Place a noodle cake on each plate, top with the scallop mixture and serve immediately.

Lemon Grass Snails

Although they are not shell fish, these snails cooked in their shells have a similar delicate quality.

Serves 4

24 fresh snails in their shells
225g/8oz lean minced (ground) pork, passed through the mincer (grinder) twice
3 lemon grass stalks, trimmed and finely chopped or ground (reserve the outer leaves)
2 spring onions (scallions), finely chopped
25g/1oz fresh root ginger, peeled and finely grated
1 fresh red chilli, seeded and finely chopped
10ml/2 tsp sesame or groundnut (peanut) oil
sea salt and ground black pepper
chilli sauce or other sauce, for dipping

1 Pull the snails out of their shells and place them in a colander. Rinse the snails thoroughly in plenty of cold water and pat dry with kitchen paper. Rinse the shells and leave to drain.

2 Chop the snails finely and put them in a bowl. Add the minced pork, lemon grass, spring onions, ginger, chilli and oil. Season with salt and pepper and mix well.

3 Select the best of the lemon grass leaves and tear each one into thin ribbons, roughly 7.5cm/3in long. Bend each ribbon in half and put it inside a snail shell, so that the ends are poking out. The idea is that each diner pulls the ends of the lemon grass ribbon to gently prize the steamed morsel out of its shell.

4 Using your fingers, stuff each shell with the snail and pork mixture, gently pushing it between the lemon grass ends to the back of the shell so that it fills the shell completely.

5 Fill a pan a third of the way up with water and bring it to the boil. Arrange the snail shells, open side up, in a steamer that fits the pan. Cover and steam for about 10 minutes, until the mixture is cooked. Serve hot with chilli sauce or another strong-flavoured dipping sauce of your choice.

spiced scallops Energy 689kcal/2888kJ; Protein 41.4g; Carbohydrate 59.9g, of which sugars 6.2g; Fat 33.3g, of which saturates 5.4g; Cholesterol 78mg; Calcium 73mg; Fibre 5g; Sodium 700mg.
lemon grass snails Energy 136kcal/573kJ; Protein 24.2g; Carbohydrate 0.2g, of which sugars 0.2g; Fat 4.3g, of which saturates 1.1g; Cholesterol 70mg; Calcium 9mg; Fibre 0.1g; Sodium 70mg.

Stuffed Squid with Shiitake Mushrooms

The smaller the squid, the sweeter the dish will taste. Be very careful not to overcook the flesh as it toughens very quickly.

Serves 4

8 small squid
50g/2oz cellophane noodles
30ml/2 tbsp groundnut (peanut) oil
2 spring onions (scallions), finely chopped
8 shiitake mushrooms, halved if large
250g/9oz minced (ground) pork
1 garlic clove, chopped
30ml/2 tbsp fish sauce
5ml/1 tsp caster (superfine) sugar
15ml/1 tbsp finely chopped fresh coriander (cilantro)
5ml/1 tsp lemon juice
salt and ground black pepper

1 Cut off the tentacles of the squid just below the eye. Remove the transparent 'quill' from inside the body and rub off the skin on the outside. Wash the squid thoroughly in cold water and set aside on a plate.

2 Bring a pan of water to the boil and add the noodles. Remove the pan from the heat and set the noodles aside to soak for 20 minutes.

3 Preheat the oven to 200°C/400°F/Gas 6. Heat 15ml/1 tbsp of the oil in a preheated wok and stir-fry the spring onions, shiitake mushrooms, pork and garlic for 4 minutes until the meat is golden and the spring onions and mushrooms have softened.

4 Drain the noodles and add to the wok, with the fish sauce, sugar, coriander, lemon juice and salt and pepper to taste.

5 Stuff the squid with the mixture and secure with cocktail sticks (toothpicks). Arrange the squid in an ovenproof dish, drizzle over the remaining oil and prick each squid twice. Bake in the preheated oven for 10 minutes. Serve hot.

Five-spice Squid

Squid is perfect for stir-frying as it should be cooked quickly. The spicy sauce makes the ideal accompaniment.

Serves 6

450g/1lb small squid, cleaned
45ml/3 tbsp oil
2.5cm/1in fresh root ginger, grated
1 garlic clove, crushed
8 spring onions (scallions), cut into 2.5cm/1in lengths
1 red (bell) pepper, seeded and cut into strips
1 fresh green chilli, seeded and thinly sliced
6 mushrooms, sliced
5ml/1 tsp Chinese five-spice powder
30ml/2 tbsp black bean sauce
30ml/2 tbsp soy sauce
5ml/1 tsp sugar
15ml/1 tbsp Chinese rice wine or dry sherry

1 Rinse the squid and pull away the outer skin. Dry on kitchen paper. Slit the squid open and score the inside into diamonds with a sharp knife. Cut the squid into strips.

2 Heat the oil in a preheated wok. Stir-fry the squid quickly. Remove the squid strips from the wok with a slotted spoon and set aside.

3 Add the ginger, garlic, spring onions, red pepper, chilli and mushrooms to the oil remaining in the wok and stir-fry for 2 minutes.

4 Return the squid to the wok and stir in the five-spice powder. Stir in the black bean sauce, soy sauce, sugar and rice wine or dry sherry. Bring to the boil and cook, stirring, for 1 minute. Serve immediately.

Variation
Use button (white) mushrooms for this recipe, or try a mixture of cultivated and wild mushrooms. Dried shiitake mushrooms would also be good but must be first soaked in water.

squid w. mushrooms Energy 356kcal/1486kJ; Protein 21.8g; Carbohydrate 15.2g, of which sugars 3.6g; Fat 23.6g, of which saturates 11.1g; Cholesterol 321mg; Calcium 55mg; Fibre 1.9g; Sodium 352mg.
five-spice squid Energy 134kcal/562kJ; Protein 15.1g; Carbohydrate 4.8g, of which sugars 3.5g; Fat 6.2g, of which saturates 0.9g; Cholesterol 203mg; Calcium 23mg; Fibre 0.9g; Sodium 956mg.

Squid with Broccoli

The slightly chewy squid contrasts beautifully with the crisp crunch of the broccoli to give this dish the perfect combination of textures so beloved by the Chinese.

Serves 4

300ml/½ pint/1¼ cups fish stock
350g/12oz prepared squid, cut into large pieces
225g/8oz broccoli
15ml/1 tbsp vegetable oil
2 garlic cloves, finely chopped
15ml/1 tbsp Chinese rice wine or dry sherry
10ml/2 tsp cornflour (cornstarch)
2.5ml/½ tsp caster (superfine) sugar
45ml/3 tbsp cold water
15ml/1 tbsp oyster sauce
2.5ml/½ tsp sesame oil
noodles, to serve

1 Bring the fish stock to the boil in a wok or pan. Add the squid pieces and cook for 2 minutes over medium heat until they are tender and have curled. Drain the squid pieces and set aside until required.

2 Trim the broccoli and cut it into small florets. Bring a pan of lightly salted water to the boil, add the broccoli and cook for 2 minutes until crisp-tender. Drain thoroughly.

3 Heat the vegetable oil in a wok or non-stick frying pan. When the oil is hot, add the garlic, stir-fry for a few seconds, then add the squid, broccoli and rice wine or sherry. Stir-fry the mixture over medium heat for about 2 minutes.

4 Mix the cornflour and sugar to a paste with the water. Stir the mixture into the wok or pan, with the oyster sauce. Cook, stirring, until the sauce thickens slightly. Just before serving, stir in the sesame oil. Serve with noodles.

Variation
Use pak choi (bok choy) instead of broccoli when it is available.

Squid in Hot Yellow Sauce

Simple fishermen's dishes such as this one are cooked in coastal regions throughout Asia. This one includes enough chillies to set your tongue on fire. To temper the heat, the dish is often served with rice or sago porridge, and finely shredded green mango tossed in lime juice.

Serves 4

500g/1¼lb fresh squid
juice of 2 limes
5ml/1 tsp salt
4 shallots, chopped
4 garlic cloves, chopped
25g/1oz galangal, chopped
25g/1oz fresh turmeric, chopped
6–8 fresh red chillies, seeded and chopped
30ml/2 tbsp vegetable oil
7.5ml/1½ tsp palm sugar (jaggery)
2 lemon grass stalks, crushed
4 lime leaves
400ml/14fl oz/1⅔ cups coconut milk
salt and ground black pepper
crusty bread or steamed rice, to serve

1 First prepare the squid. Hold the body sac in one hand and pull off the head with the other. Sever the tentacles just above the eyes, and discard the rest of the head and innards. With cold water, wash the body sac inside and out and remove the skin. Pat the squid dry, cut it into thick slices and put them in a bowl, along with the tentacles. Mix the lime juice with the salt and rub it into the squid. Set aside for 30 minutes.

2 Meanwhile, using a mortar and pestle or food processor, grind the shallots, garlic, galangal, turmeric and chillies to a coarse paste.

3 Heat the oil in a wok or heavy pan, and stir in the coarse paste. Cook the paste until fragrant, then stir in the palm sugar, lemon grass and lime leaves. Drain the squid of any juice and toss it around the wok, coating it in the flavourings.

4 Pour in the coconut milk and bring it to the boil. Reduce the heat and simmer for 5–10 minutes, until the squid is tender. Season and serve with crusty bread or steamed rice.

squid w. broccoli Energy 127kcal/536kJ; Protein 16g; Carbohydrate 4.4g, of which sugars 0.9g; Fat 4.8g, of which saturates 0.8g; Cholesterol 197mg; Calcium 44mg; Fibre 1.5g; Sodium 103mg.
squid in hot sauce Energy 185kcal/780kJ; Protein 19.8g; Carbohydrate 9.4g, of which sugars 7.6g; Fat 8g, of which saturates 1.4g; Cholesterol 281mg; Calcium 50mg; Fibre 0.2g; Sodium 739mg.

Mussels with Lemon Grass

Lemon grass and basil give this fragrant dish a subtle flavour. It makes a lovely light appetizer.

Serves 4

1.8–2kg/4–4½lb fresh mussels in their shells
2 lemon grass stalks
5cm/2in fresh root ginger, peeled
5–6 fresh basil sprigs
2 shallots, finely chopped
150ml/¼ pint/⅔ cup fish stock

1 Scrub the mussels under cold running water, scraping off any barnacles with a small, sharp knife. Pull or cut off the hairy 'beards'. Discard any mussels with damaged shells and any that remain open when they are sharply tapped.

2 Cut each lemon grass stalk in half and bruise with a rolling pin or a pestle. Cut the ginger into thin slices.

3 Pull the basil leaves off the stems and roughly chop half of them. Reserve the remainder.

4 Put the mussels, lemon grass, chopped basil, ginger, shallots and stock in a wok. Bring to the boil, cover and simmer for 5 minutes.

5 Discard the lemon grass and any mussels that remain closed, garnish with the reserved basil leaves and serve immediately.

Variations
- *Substitute half the total weight of mussels with clams. Clams take slightly longer to cook so add them to the wok with the other ingredients as in Step 4, and cook for 2 minutes before adding the mussels and simmering for a further 5 as directed.*
- *The liquor from the mussels combines with the fish stock to make a delicious sauce. Add a splash of white wine, if you like, but take care not to overwhelm the lemon grass flavour.*

Aromatic Mussels with Chilli

This dish is a version of the French classic, moules marinière, with the mussels being steamed open in a herb-infused stock with lemon grass and chilli instead of wine and parsley. The treatment also works with clams and snails.

Serves 4

600ml/1 pint/2½ cups chicken stock or beer, or a mixture of the two
1 fresh red chilli, seeded and chopped
2 shallots, finely chopped
3 lemon grass stalks, finely chopped
1 bunch ginger, coriander (cilantro) or basil leaves
1kg/2¼lb fresh mussels, cleaned and bearded
salt and ground black pepper

1 Pour the stock or beer into a deep pan. Add the chilli, shallots, lemon grass and most of the ginger, coriander or basil leaves, retaining a few leaves for the garnish. Bring to the boil. Cover and simmer for 10–15 minutes, then season to taste.

2 Check the mussels and discard any that are tightly closed or which fail to close when tapped on the work surface. Any mussels with damaged shells should also be discarded.

3 Add the remaining mussels to the stock. Stir well, cover and cook for 2 minutes, or until the mussels have opened. Discard any that remain closed. Ladle the mussels and cooking liquid into individual bowls.

Cook's Tips
- *Any mussels that will not close before cooking may be dead, and therefore rotten. Tightly-closed shells tend to signify the same – generally, these are the ones that will not open upon contact with the steam and should therefore also be discarded.*
- *Aromatic ginger leaves are hard to find outside Asia. If you can't find them, basil or coriander (cilantro) will work well.*

mussels w. lemon grass Energy 130kcal/551kJ; Protein 21.5g; Carbohydrate 3g, of which sugars 2.3g; Fat 2.3g, of which saturates 0.5g; Cholesterol 58mg; Calcium 230mg; Fibre 0.5g; Sodium 629mg.
mussels w. chilli Energy 75kcal/318kJ; Protein 13.6g; Carbohydrate 1.5g, of which sugars 1.1g; Fat 1.7g, of which saturates 0.3g; Cholesterol 30mg; Calcium 176mg; Fibre 0.8g; Sodium 162mg.

Fish with Mango Sauce

This salad is best served during the summer months, preferably out of doors. The dressing combines the flavour of rich mango with hot chilli, ginger and lime.

Serves 4

1 French loaf
4 redfish, black bream or porgy, about 275g/10oz each
15ml/1 tbsp vegetable oil
1 mango
1cm/½in piece fresh root ginger
1 fresh red chilli, seeded and finely chopped
30ml/2 tbsp lime juice
30ml/2 tbsp chopped fresh coriander (cilantro)
175g/6oz young spinach
150g/5oz pak choi (bok choy)
175g/6oz cherry tomatoes, halved

1 Preheat the oven to 180°C/350°F/Gas 4. Cut the French loaf into 20cm/8in lengths. Slice lengthways, then cut the bread into thick fingers.

2 Place the bread on a baking sheet and leave to dry in the oven for 15 minutes.

3 Preheat the grill (broiler) or light the barbecue and allow the embers to settle. Slash the fish deeply on both sides and moisten with oil. Cook the fish on the barbecue for 6 minutes, turning once.

4 Peel the mango and cut in half, discarding the stone (pit). Thinly slice one half and set aside. Place the other half in a food processor or blender.

5 Peel the ginger, grate finely, then add to the mango with the chilli, lime juice and fresh coriander. Process until smooth. Adjust to a pouring consistency with 30–45ml/2–3 tbsp water.

6 Wash the spinach and pak choi leaves and spin dry, then distribute them among four serving plates.

7 Place the fish on the leaves. Spoon on the mango dressing and finish with the reserved slices of mango and the tomato halves. Serve with the fingers of crisp French bread.

Braised Whole Fish in Chilli & Garlic Sauce

In India there are an increasing number of unusual dishes that borrow from other cultures. The vinegar in the sauce for this fish dish is typical of Goa, but the rice wine and bean sauce reveal a distinct Sichuan influence.

Serves 4–6

1 carp, bream, sea bass, trout, grouper or grey mullet, about 675g/1½lb, gutted
15ml/1 tbsp light soy sauce
15ml/1 tbsp rice wine or dry sherry
vegetable oil, for deep-frying

For the sauce
2 garlic cloves, finely chopped
2 or 3 spring onions (scallions), finely chopped, the white and green parts separated
5ml/1 tsp finely chopped fresh root ginger
30ml/2 tbsp chilli bean sauce
15ml/1 tbsp tomato purée (paste)
10ml/2 tsp soft light brown sugar
15ml/1 tbsp rice vinegar
120ml/4fl oz/½ cup chicken stock
15ml/1 tbsp cornflour (cornstarch), mixed to a paste with 10ml/2 tsp water
a few drops of sesame oil

1 Rinse and dry the fish well. Using a sharp knife, score both sides of the fish down to the bone with diagonal cuts about 2.5cm/1in apart. Rub both sides of the fish with the soy sauce and rice wine or sherry. Set aside for 10–15 minutes to marinate.

2 Heat sufficient oil for deep-frying in a wok. When it is hot, carefully add the fish and fry for 3–4 minutes on both sides, until golden brown.

3 To make the sauce, pour away all but about 15ml/1 tbsp of the oil. Push the fish to one side of the wok and add the garlic, the white part of the spring onions, the ginger, chilli bean sauce, tomato purée, sugar, vinegar and chicken stock. Bring to the boil and braise the fish in the sauce for 4–5 minutes, turning it over once. Add the green of the spring onions. Stir in the cornflour paste to thicken the sauce. Sprinkle over a little sesame oil and serve immediately.

fish w. mango Energy 457kcal/1937kJ; Protein 33.7g; Carbohydrate 64.1g, of which sugars 10.6g; Fat 9.1g, of which saturates 0.8g; Cholesterol 48mg; Calcium 317mg; Fibre 5.5g; Sodium 872mg.
braised whole fish Energy 261kcal/1088kJ; Protein 19.5g; Carbohydrate 8g, of which sugars 3.9g; Fat 17.1g, of which saturates 2.4g; Cholesterol 72mg; Calcium 59mg; Fibre 0.9g; Sodium 84mg.

Sweet & Sour Snapper

Comprising simply a whole deep-fried fish served with vegetables, this dish is distinguished by the sauce. This is based on Kao Liang wine vinegar, made from sorghum and millet grains.

Serves 4

4 dried Chinese black mushrooms
1 whole snapper or similar fish, about 800g/1¾lb, cleaned and scaled
15ml/1 tbsp salt
45ml/3 tbsp cornflour (cornstarch)
oil for deep- and shallow-frying
15ml/1 tbsp thinly sliced root ginger
15ml/1 tbsp crushed garlic
1 spring onion, cut into 2.5cm/1in lengths, plus extra, to garnish
30ml/2 tbsp thinly sliced bamboo shoots
½ red (bell) pepper, thinly sliced

For the sauce

60ml/4 tbsp Kao Liang wine vinegar
15ml/1 tbsp sugar
15ml/1 tbsp light soy sauce
10ml/2 tsp cornflour (cornstarch) mixed with 45ml/3 tbsp water
200ml/7fl oz/scant 1 cup water or stock

1 Soak the mushrooms in a bowl of boiling water for 20–30 minutes. Meanwhile, rinse the fish inside and out, then pat dry with kitchen paper. Make cuts diagonally across both sides of the fish. Rub with the salt, rinse again and pat dry. Dust the fish all over with the cornflour.

2 Heat the oil in a large wok. Carefully lower the fish into the oil and fry over medium heat for 7–8 minutes. Drain on kitchen paper. Place the fish on a serving platter and keep hot.

3 Drain the mushrooms and slice them thinly, discarding the stems. In a clean wok, heat 30ml/2 tbsp oil and stir-fry the ginger and garlic for 1 minute. Add the spring onions, bamboo shoots and pepper, with the sliced mushrooms. Stir-fry for 2 minutes more.

4 Mix all the sauce ingredients in a bowl. Add to the wok, bring to the boil and simmer for 1 minute, until the sauce thickens. Pour the sauce over the fish, garnish with spring onions and serve immediately.

Spicy Grilled Fish Fillets

The good thing about fish is that it can be grilled beautifully without sacrificing any flavour.

Serves 4

4 medium flat-fish fillets, such as plaice, sole or flounder, about 115g/4oz each
5ml/1 tsp crushed garlic
5ml/1 tsp garam masala
5ml/1 tsp chilli powder
1.5ml/¼ tsp ground turmeric
2.5ml/½ tsp salt
15ml/1 tbsp finely chopped fresh coriander (cilantro)
15ml/1 tbsp oil
30ml/2 tbsp lemon juice
tomato wedges, lime slices and grated carrot, to garnish

1 Line a flameproof dish or grill (broiler) pan with foil. Rinse the fish fillets, pat dry and put them in the foil-lined dish or pan.

2 In a bowl, mix the garlic, garam masala, chilli powder, turmeric, salt, coriander, oil and lemon juice.

3 Brush the fish fillets evenly all over with the spice mixture.

4 Preheat the grill to very hot, then lower the heat. Grill (broil) the fish for about 5 minutes, basting with the spice mixture, until it is cooked.

5 Serve immediately with a garnish of tomato wedges, lime slices and grated carrot.

Cook's Tip

Fish can easily be spoiled through over-cooking, so it is essential to grill (broil) it for just the right amount of time. No more than 5 minutes is usually sufficient to cook fillets of flat fish, such as plaice and sole. Test by lifting the flesh carefully with the tip of a knife. It should separate into flakes easily and should have lost that clear, milky appearance of raw fish. There is no need to turn flat fish over, as grilling on one side will be sufficient.

sweet & sour snapper Energy 332kcal/1389kJ; Protein 25.4g; Carbohydrate 14.2g, of which sugars 1.1g; Fat 19.8g, of which saturates 2.6g; Cholesterol 46mg; Calcium 61mg; Fibre 0.2g; Sodium 884mg.
spicy fish fillets Energy 314kcal/1312kJ; Protein 24.1g; Carbohydrate 18.2g, of which sugars 12.1g; Fat 16.6g, of which saturates 2g; Cholesterol 58mg; Calcium 30mg; Fibre 0.8g; Sodium 207mg.

Steamed Fish with Sour Plums

Shantou restaurants take great pride in steamed fish dishes like this one. The addition of sour plums is a particularly inspired touch, especially when salmon, pomfret or sea bass is used, as the tartness of the plums really cuts the rich oils in the fish and perfectly balances the dish.

Serves 4

1 whole fish, about 500g/1 ¼ lb, cleaned and scaled
4 canned sour plums
15ml/1 tbsp fish sauce
15ml/1 tbsp finely shredded root ginger
2 spring onions (scallions), finely shredded
3–4 rashers (strips) of streaky (fatty) bacon
fresh coriander (cilantro), to serve

1 Rinse the fish inside and out. Dry with kitchen paper. Cut deep slashes on either side of the fish, where the flesh is thickest. Put the fish on a plate that will fit into your steamer. If the fish is too large, cut it in half.

2 Drain the sour plums and put them in a bowl. Mash to a rough purée, using a potato masher or a spoon. Spread the purée over the fish.

3 Dribble the fish sauce over the fish and sprinkle with the ginger and spring onions. Lay the rashers of bacon on top.

4 Put the plate in the steamer. Steam the fish over rapidly boiling water for about 15 minutes or until it is cooked through. Transfer everything to a warm platter, garnish with the coriander and serve immediately.

Cook's Tip

If you do not have a steamer you can loosely wrap the fish and other ingredients in aluminium foil and place it in a moderate to hot oven on a baking tray. Check to see whether the fish is cooked through after 15 minutes. If not, reseal the foil and cook for a few more minutes.

Steamed Fish with Chilli Sauce

By leaving the fish whole and on the bone, maximum flavour is retained and the flesh remains beautifully moist and succulent.

Serves 4

1 large or 2 medium firm fish such as sea bass or grouper, scaled and cleaned
30ml/2 tbsp rice wine
3 fresh red chillies, seeded and thinly sliced
2 garlic cloves, finely chopped
2cm/¾in piece fresh root ginger, peeled and finely shredded
2 lemon grass stalks, crushed and finely chopped
2 spring onions (scallions), chopped
30ml/2 tbsp Thai fish sauce
juice of 1 lime
1 fresh banana leaf

For the chilli sauce

10 fresh red chillies, seeded and chopped
4 garlic cloves, chopped
60ml/4 tbsp Thai fish sauce
15ml/1 tbsp sugar
75ml/5 tbsp fresh lime juice

1 Thoroughly rinse the fish under cold running water. Pat it dry with kitchen paper. With a sharp knife, slash the skin of the fish a few times on both sides.

2 Mix together the rice wine, chillies, garlic, shredded ginger, lemon grass and spring onions in a non-metallic bowl. Add the fish sauce and lime juice and mix to a paste. Place the fish on the banana leaf and spread the spice paste evenly over it, rubbing it in well where the skin has been slashed.

3 Put a rack or a small upturned plate in the base of a wok. Pour in boiling water to a depth of 5cm/2in. Lift the banana leaf, together with the fish, and place it on the rack or plate. Cover with a lid and steam for 10–15 minutes, or until the fish is cooked.

4 Meanwhile, make the sauce. Place all the ingredients in a food processor and process until smooth. If the mixture seems to be too thick, add a little cold water. Scrape into a serving bowl.

5 Serve the fish hot, on the banana leaf if you like, with the sweet chilli sauce to spoon over the top.

fish w. sour plums Energy 188kcal/791kJ; Protein 20.4g; Carbohydrate 9.3g, of which sugars 9.2g; Fat 8g, of which saturates 2.4g; Cholesterol 45mg; Calcium 51mg; Fibre 1.7g; Sodium 658mg.
fish w. chilli sauce Energy 147kcal/619kJ; Protein 28.4g; Carbohydrate 5.5g, of which sugars 5.3g; Fat 1.3g, of which saturates 0.2g; Cholesterol 69mg; Calcium 56mg; Fibre 1g; Sodium 898mg.

Hot & Fragrant Trout

This wickedly hot spice paste could be used as a marinade for any fish or meat. It also makes a wonderful spicy dip for grilled meat.

Serves 4

2 large fresh green chillies, seeded and coarsely chopped
5 shallots, peeled
5 garlic cloves, peeled
30ml/2 tbsp fresh lime juice
30ml/2 tbsp Thai fish sauce
15ml/1 tbsp palm sugar (jaggery) or light muscovado (brown) sugar
4 kaffir lime leaves, rolled into cylinders and thinly sliced
2 trout or similar firm-fleshed fish, about 350g/12oz each, cleaned
fresh garlic chives, to garnish
boiled rice, to serve

1 Wrap the chillies, shallots and garlic in a foil package. Place under a hot grill (broiler) for 10 minutes, until softened.

2 When the package is cool enough to handle, tip the contents into a mortar or food processor and pound with a pestle or process to a paste.

3 Add the lime juice, fish sauce, sugar and lime leaves and mix well. With a teaspoon, stuff the mixture inside the fish. Smear a little on the skin too. Grill (broil) the fish for about 5 minutes on each side, until just cooked through. Lift the fish on to a platter, garnish with garlic chives and serve with rice.

Cook's Tip

Farmed rainbow trout is available all year. The better-flavoured wild brown trout, however, is rarely available and more expensive. Sea trout is also suitable for this dish; as it is a large fish, one will probably be sufficient for four people. For an economical dish, try mackerel. You can use one for each person or buy two larger fish; the larger fish will be easier to stuff.

Marinated Fried Fish with Ginger & Chilli

Fish and shellfish are a strong feature of the cuisine in the coastal region of southern India. Kerala, in the southernmost part of the country, produces some of the finest fish and shellfish dishes. These are flavoured with local spices, grown in the fabulous spice plantations that are the pride and joy of the state.

Serves 4–6

1 small onion, coarsely chopped
4 garlic cloves, crushed
5cm/2in piece fresh root ginger, chopped
5ml/1 tsp ground turmeric
10ml/2 tsp chilli powder
4 red mullet or snapper
vegetable oil, for shallow-frying
5ml/1 tsp cumin seeds
3 fresh green chillies, finely sliced
salt
lemon or lime wedges, to serve

1 In a food processor, grind the first five ingredients with salt to a smooth paste.

2 Make several slashes on both sides of the fish and rub them with the paste. Leave to rest for 1 hour. Excess fluid will be released as the salt dissolves, so lightly pat the fish dry with kitchen paper, without removing the paste.

3 Heat the vegetable oil and fry the cumin seeds and sliced chillies for 1 minute.

4 Add the fish, in batches if necessary, and fry on one side. When the first side is sealed, turn them over very gently to ensure they do not break. Fry until golden brown on both sides and fully cooked. Drain and serve hot, with lemon or lime wedges.

Variation

To enhance the flavour, add 15ml/1 tbsp chopped fresh coriander (cilantro) leaves to the spice paste in step 1.

hot & fragrant trout Energy 117kcal/490kJ; Protein 14.8g; Carbohydrate 7.9g, of which sugars 6.7g; Fat 3.1g, of which saturates 0.7g; Cholesterol 59mg; Calcium 36mg; Fibre 0.7g; Sodium 57mg.
fried fish w. ginger & chilli Energy 122kcal/509kJ; Protein 10.7g; Carbohydrate 1.3g, of which sugars 1.1g; Fat 8.3g, of which saturates 0.7g; Cholesterol 0mg; Calcium 42mg; Fibre 0.3g; Sodium 55mg.

Vinegar Fish

Fish cooked in a spicy mixture that includes chillies, ginger and vinegar is delicious. The method lends itself particularly well to strong-flavoured oily fish, such as the mackerel that are regularly caught off the coast of Goa.

Serves 2–3

2 or 3 mackerel, filleted
2 or 3 fresh red chillies, seeded
4 macadamia nuts or 8 almonds
1 red onion, quartered
2 garlic cloves, crushed
1cm/½in piece fresh root ginger, sliced
5ml/1 tsp ground turmeric
45ml/3 tbsp coconut oil or vegetable oil
45ml/3 tbsp wine vinegar
150ml/¼ pint/⅔ cup water
salt
deep-fried onions and finely chopped fresh chilli, to garnish
rice, to serve (optional)

1 Rinse the mackerel fillets in cold water and dry well on kitchen paper. Set aside.

2 Put the chillies, macadamia nuts or almonds, onion, garlic, ginger, turmeric and 15ml/1 tbsp of the oil in a food processor and process to form a paste. Alternatively, pound them together in a mortar with a pestle.

3 Heat the remaining oil in a karahi, wok or pan. Add the spice and nut paste to the pan and cook for 1–2 minutes without browning. Stir in the wine vinegar and water, and season with salt to taste. Bring the sauce to the boil, then lower the heat.

4 Add the mackerel fillets to the sauce and simmer for 6–8 minutes, or until the fish is tender and cooked.

5 Transfer the mackerel to a warm serving platter. Bring the spicy sauce to the boil and cook for 1 minute, or until it has reduced slightly.

6 Pour the sauce over the fish, garnish with the deep-fried onions and chopped chilli and serve with rice, if you like.

Stuffed Fish

Every community in India prepares stuffed fish but this version must be one of the most popular. The most widely used fish in India is the pomfret. Asian pomfret is available from Asian grocers or supermarkets, or sole works well instead.

Serves 4

2 large pomfrets (porgy), or Dover or lemon sole
10ml/2 tsp salt
juice of 1 lemon

For the masala

115g/4oz/1⅓ cups desiccated (dry unsweetened shredded) coconut
115g/4oz/4 cups fresh coriander (cilantro), including the tender stalks
8 fresh green chillies, or to taste
5ml/1 tsp cumin seeds
6 garlic cloves
10ml/2 tsp sugar
10ml/2 tsp lemon juice

1 Scale the fish and cut off the fins. Gut the fish and remove the heads, if you wish. Using a sharp knife, make two diagonal gashes on each side, then pat dry with kitchen paper.

2 Rub the fish inside and out with salt and lemon juice. Cover and leave to stand in a cool place for about 1 hour. Pat dry.

3 Grind all the ingredients for the masala together using a mortar and pestle or food processor. Stuff the fish with most of the masala mixture. Rub the rest into the gashes and all over the fish on both sides.

4 Place each fish on a separate piece of greased foil. Tightly wrap the foil over each fish. Place in a steamer and steam for 20 minutes, or bake in a preheated oven for 30 minutes at 200°C/400°F/Gas 6 or until cooked. Remove the fish from the foil and serve hot.

Cook's Tip
Try this fish steamed in banana leaves, as it is traditionally served.

vinegar fish Energy 624kcal/2589kJ; Protein 40.4g; Carbohydrate 1.4g, of which sugars 0.6g; Fat 50.8g, of which saturates 8.5g; Cholesterol 108mg; Calcium 65mg; Fibre 1.4g; Sodium 135mg.
stuffed fish Energy 287kcal/1194kJ; Protein 21.3g; Carbohydrate 5.4g, of which sugars 5.3g; Fat 20.2g, of which saturates 15.4g; Cholesterol 50mg; Calcium 103mg; Fibre 5.4g; Sodium 120mg.

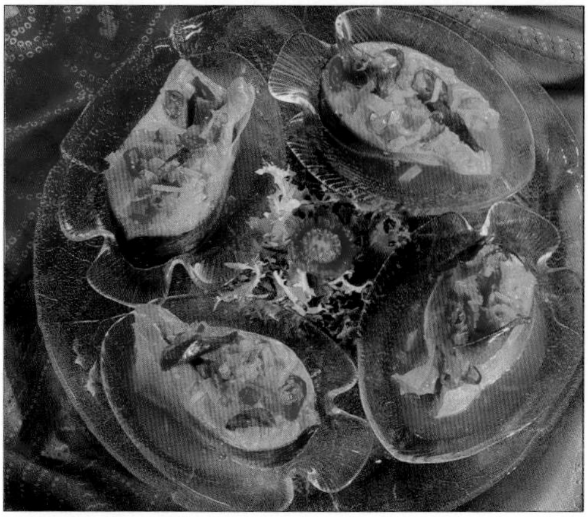

Pickled Fish Steaks

This dish is served cold, often as an appetizer. It also makes an ideal lunch when served with salad on a hot summer's day. Prepare it a day or two in advance, to allow the flavours to blend.

Serves 4–6

juice of 4 lemons
2.5cm/1in piece fresh root ginger, finely sliced
2 garlic cloves, crushed
2 fresh red chillies, finely chopped
3 fresh green chillies, finely chopped
4 thick, firm fish steaks
60ml/4 tbsp vegetable oil
4–6 curry leaves
1 onion, finely chopped
2.5ml/½ tsp ground turmeric
15ml/1 tbsp ground coriander
150ml/¼ pint/⅔ cup pickling vinegar
15ml/1 tbsp sugar
salt
salad leaves and fresh tomato, to garnish

1 In a bowl, mix the lemon juice with the ginger, garlic and chillies. Pat the fish dry and rub the mixture over all sides of the fish. Cover and marinate for 3–4 hours in the refrigerator.

2 Heat the oil in a frying pan and fry the curry leaves, onion, turmeric and coriander until the onion is translucent.

3 Place the fish steaks and their marinade in the frying pan and spoon the onion mixture over them. Cook for 5 minutes, then turn the fish over gently to avoid damaging the steaks.

4 Pour in the vinegar and add the sugar and salt. Bring to the boil, then lower the heat and simmer until the fish is cooked. Carefully transfer the steaks to a large platter or individual serving dishes and pour over the vinegar mixture. Cool, then chill for 24 hours before serving, garnished with the salad leaves and tomato.

Variation
Cod or haddock work particularly well for this dish but you could also try hake, swordfish or even firm and meaty tuna.

Fish & Vegetable Skewers

Threading firm fish cubes and colourful vegetables on skewers scores on several fronts. Not only does the food look good, but it is also easy to cook and serve.

Serves 4

275g/10oz firm white fish fillets, such as cod
45ml/3 tbsp lemon juice
5ml/1 tsp grated fresh root ginger
2 fresh green chillies, chopped
15ml/1 tbsp chopped fresh coriander (cilantro)
15ml/1 tbsp chopped fresh mint
5ml/1 tsp ground coriander
5ml/1 tsp salt
1 red (bell) pepper
1 green (bell) pepper
½ medium cauliflower
8–10 button (white) mushrooms
8 cherry tomatoes
15ml/1 tbsp oil
1 lime, quartered, to garnish (optional)
saffron rice, to serve

1 Cut the fish fillets into large and even-sized chunks suitable for threading on to skewers.

2 In a large bowl, stir together the lemon juice, ginger, chopped green chillies, fresh coriander, mint, ground coriander and salt. Add the fish chunks, cover and leave to marinate for about 30 minutes.

3 Cut the red and green peppers into large squares and divide the cauliflower into individual florets.

4 Preheat the grill (broiler) to hot. Arrange the peppers, cauliflower florets, button mushrooms and cherry tomatoes alternately with the fish pieces on four skewers.

5 Brush the kebabs with the oil and any remaining marinade. Transfer to a flameproof dish and grill (broil) for 7–10 minutes, turning occasionally, until the fish is cooked right through.

6 Garnish with lime quarters, if you like, and serve the kebabs on a bed of saffron rice.

pickled fish steaks Energy 97kcal/408kJ; Protein 12.5g; Carbohydrate 6.2g, of which sugars 5.4g; Fat 2.6g, of which saturates 0.5g; Cholesterol 57mg; Calcium 45mg; Fibre 1.1g; Sodium 84mg.
fish skewers Energy 160kcal/671kJ; Protein 18.7g; Carbohydrate 10.5g, of which sugars 9.6g; Fat 5g, of which saturates 0.8g; Cholesterol 32mg; Calcium 67mg; Fibre 4.7g; Sodium 63mg.

Green Fish Curry with Coconut

This dish combines all the delicious flavours of the East. A subtle blend of spices and a hint of coconut complement the flavour of the cod perfectly.

Serves 4

1.5ml/¼ tsp ground turmeric
30ml/2 tbsp lime juice
pinch of salt
4 cod fillets, skinned and cut into 5cm/2in chunks
1 onion, chopped
1 fresh green chilli, sliced
1 garlic clove, crushed
25g/1oz/¼ cup cashew nuts
2.5ml/½ tsp fennel seeds
30ml/2 tbsp desiccated (dry unsweetened shredded) coconut
30ml/2 tbsp oil
1.5ml/¼ tsp cumin seeds
1.5ml/¼ tsp ground coriander
1.5ml/¼ tsp ground cumin
1.5ml/¼ tsp salt
150ml/¼ pint/⅔ cup water
175ml/6fl oz/¾ cup natural (plain) low-fat yogurt
45ml/3 tbsp finely chopped fresh coriander (cilantro), plus extra to garnish
vegetable pilau rice, to serve

1 Mix together the turmeric, lime juice and salt, and rub over the fish. Cover and marinate for 15 minutes.

2 Meanwhile, grind the onion, chilli, garlic, cashew nuts, fennel seeds and coconut to a paste. Spoon the paste into a bowl and set aside.

3 Heat the oil in a large, heavy pan and fry the cumin seeds for 2 minutes or until they begin to splutter. Add the paste and fry for 5 minutes, then stir in the ground coriander, cumin, salt and water and cook for 2–3 minutes.

4 Stir in the yogurt and chopped fresh coriander. Simmer gently for 5 minutes. Gently stir in the fish pieces. Cover and cook gently for 10 minutes until the fish is tender. Garnish with more coriander. This curry is particularly good served with a vegetable pilau.

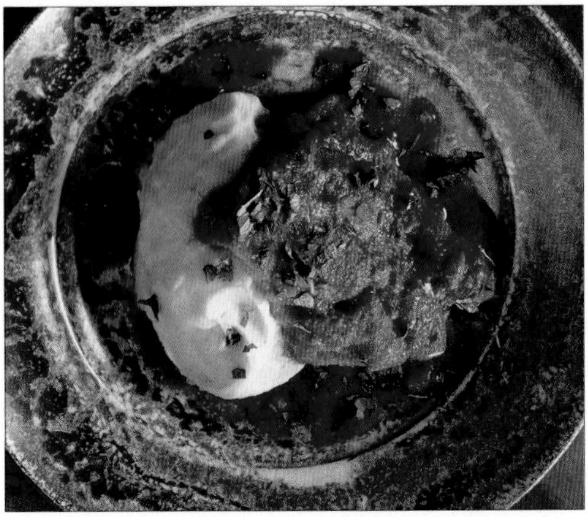

Cod in a Tomato Sauce

Dusting cod with spices before cooking gives it a delectable coating.

Serves 4

30ml/2 tbsp cornflour (cornstarch)
5ml/1 tsp salt
5ml/1 tsp garlic powder
5ml/1 tsp chilli powder
5ml/1 tsp ground ginger
5ml/1 tsp ground fennel seeds
5ml/1 tsp ground coriander
2 medium cod fillets, each cut into 2 pieces
15ml/1 tbsp oil
mashed potatoes, to serve

For the sauce
30ml/2 tbsp tomato purée (paste)
5ml/1 tsp garam masala
5ml/1 tsp chilli powder
5ml/1 tsp crushed garlic
5ml/1 tsp grated fresh root ginger
2.5ml/½ tsp salt
175ml/6fl oz/¾ cup water
15ml/1 tbsp oil
1 bay leaf
3 or 4 black peppercorns
1cm/½in piece cinnamon stick
15ml/1 tbsp chopped fresh coriander (cilantro)
15ml/1 tbsp chopped fresh mint

1 Mix together the cornflour, salt, garlic powder, chilli powder, ground ginger, ground fennel seeds and ground coriander. Use to coat the four cod pieces.

2 Preheat the grill (broiler) to very hot, then reduce the heat slightly and place the cod under the heat. After about 5 minutes spoon the oil over the cod. Turn the cod over and repeat the process. Cook for a further 5 minutes, check that the fish is cooked through and set aside.

3 Make the sauce by mixing together the tomato purée, garam masala, chilli powder, garlic, ginger, salt and water. Set aside.

4 Heat the oil in a karahi or wok and add the bay leaf, peppercorns and cinnamon. Pour the sauce into the pan and reduce the heat to low. Bring slowly to the boil, stirring occasionally, then simmer for about 5 minutes. Gently slide the pieces of fish into this mixture and cook for a further 2 minutes. Add the chopped fresh coriander and mint and serve the dish with mashed potatoes.

green fish curry Energy 608kcal/2527kJ; Protein 41g; Carbohydrate 13.3g, of which sugars 9.5g; Fat 43.8g, of which saturates 5.9g; Cholesterol 0mg; Calcium 168mg; Fibre 1.3g; Sodium 313mg.
cod in tomato sauce Energy 150kcal/635kJ; Protein 21.2g; Carbohydrate 8.5g, of which sugars 2.2g; Fat 3.8g, of which saturates 0.7g; Cholesterol 44mg; Calcium 34mg; Fibre 3.2g; Sodium 114mg.

Fish Fillets with a Chilli Sauce

For this recipe, the fish fillets are first marinated with fresh coriander and lemon juice, then cooked quickly before being served with a chilli sauce.

Serves 4

4 flat-fish fillets, such as plaice, sole or flounder, about 115g/4oz each
30ml/2 tbsp lemon juice
15ml/1 tbsp finely chopped fresh coriander (cilantro)
15ml/1 tbsp oil
lime wedges and a fresh coriander sprig, to garnish
saffron rice, to serve

For the sauce
5ml/1 tsp grated fresh root ginger
30ml/2 tbsp tomato purée (paste)
5ml/1 tsp sugar
5ml/1 tsp salt
15ml/1 tbsp chilli sauce
15ml/1 tbsp malt vinegar
300ml/½ pint/1¼ cups water

1 Rinse and pat dry the fish fillets and place in a medium bowl. Add the lemon juice, coriander and oil and rub into the fish. Leave to marinate for at least 1 hour.

2 Make the chilli sauce. Thoroughly mix the grated root ginger, tomato purée, sugar, salt and chilli sauce in a bowl. Stir in the vinegar and water.

3 Pour into a small pan and simmer gently over a low heat for about 6 minutes, stirring occasionally.

4 Meanwhile, preheat the grill (broiler) to medium. Lift the fish fillets out of the marinade and place them in a grill pan. Grill (broil) for about 5–7 minutes. When the fish is cooked, arrange it on a warmed serving dish.

5 The chilli sauce should now be fairly thick – about the consistency of a thick chicken soup. Spoon the sauce over the fish fillets, garnish with the lime wedges and coriander sprig and serve immediately with saffron rice.

Cod with a Spicy Mushroom Sauce

Grilling fish before adding it to a sauce helps to prevent it from breaking up during the cooking process.

Serves 4

4 cod fillets
15ml/1 tbsp lemon juice
15ml/1 tbsp oil
1 medium onion, chopped
1 bay leaf
4 black peppercorns, crushed
115g/4oz/1 cup mushrooms
175ml/6fl oz/¾ cup natural (plain) low-fat yogurt
5ml/1 tsp grated fresh root ginger
5ml/1 tsp crushed garlic
2.5ml/½ tsp garam masala
2.5ml/½ tsp chilli powder
5ml/1 tsp salt
15ml/1 tbsp fresh coriander (cilantro) leaves, to garnish
lightly cooked green beans, to serve

1 Preheat the grill (broiler). Remove the skin and any bones from the cod fillets. Sprinkle with lemon juice, then par-cook under the grill for 5 minutes on each side. Remove the fillets from the heat and set aside.

2 Heat the oil in a karahi or wok and fry the chopped onion with the bay leaf and peppercorns for 2–3 minutes. Lower the heat, add the whole mushrooms and stir-fry for a further 4–5 minutes.

3 In a bowl mix together the natural yogurt, crushed ginger and grated garlic, garam masala, chilli powder and salt. Pour this over the onions and stir-fry for 3 minutes.

4 Add the cod fillets to the sauce and cook for a further 2 minutes. Serve garnished with the fresh coriander and accompanied by lightly cooked green beans.

Cook's Tip
If you can find tiny button (white) mushrooms they look particularly attractive in this fish dish. Alternatively, choose from the many other pretty coloured varieties, such as ceps and oyster mushrooms.

fish fillets Energy 162kcal/684kJ; Protein 26.8g; Carbohydrate 3.8g, of which sugars 3.7g; Fat 4.5g, of which saturates 1g; Cholesterol 75mg; Calcium 37mg; Fibre 0.8g; Sodium 708mg.
cod w. spicy sauce Energy 202kcal/847kJ; Protein 31.7g; Carbohydrate 6.9g, of which sugars 3.4g; Fat 5.7g, of which saturates 0.9g; Cholesterol 70mg; Calcium 116mg; Fibre 0.3g; Sodium 131mg.

Fish Stew with Potatoes & Chilli

Cooking fish with vegetables is a tradition in eastern regions of India. This hearty dish with potatoes, peppers and tomatoes is perfect served with breads such as chapatis or parathas. You can try other combinations, such as green beans and spinach, but you do need a starchy vegetable in order to thicken the sauce.

Serves 4

30ml/2 tbsp vegetable oil
5ml/1 tsp cumin seeds
1 onion, chopped
1 red (bell) pepper, thinly sliced
1 garlic clove, crushed
2 fresh red chillies, finely chopped
2 bay leaves
2.5ml/½ tsp salt
5ml/1 tsp ground cumin
5ml/1 tsp ground coriander
5ml/1 tsp chilli powder
400g/14oz can chopped tomatoes
2 large potatoes, cut into 2.5cm/1in chunks
300ml/½ pint/1¼ cups fish stock
4 cod fillets
chapatis, to serve

1 Heat the oil in a karahi, wok or large pan over a medium heat and fry the cumin seeds for 30–40 seconds until they begin to splutter. Add the chopped onion, red pepper, garlic, chillies and bay leaves, and fry for 5–7 minutes more until the onions have softened and browned.

2 Add the salt, ground cumin, ground coriander and chilli powder to the onion and red pepper mixture. Cook for 1–2 minutes, stirring occasionally.

3 Stir in the tomatoes, potatoes and fish stock. Bring to the boil, then lower the heat and simmer for a further 10 minutes, or until the potatoes are almost tender.

4 Add the fish fillets, then cover the pan and leave to simmer for 5–6 minutes until the fish is just cooked. Serve the fish piping hot, with chapatis.

Fish in a Tomato & Onion Sauce

Fish is an essential element of the cuisine of eastern India. Bengal and Goa are both particularly well-known for their fish and shellfish dishes. In both regions, coconut is used extensively, and the difference in the taste lies in the spicing. This onion-rich dish is known as kalia in Bengal, and a firm-fleshed fish such as monkfish is essential, as it must withstand being cooked twice.

Serves 4

675g/1½lb firm-textured fish steaks, such as tuna or monkfish, skinned
30ml/2 tbsp lemon juice
5ml/1 tsp salt
5ml/1 tsp ground turmeric
vegetable oil, for shallow-frying
40g/1½oz/⅓ cup plain (all-purpose) flour
2.5ml/¼ tsp ground black pepper
60ml/4 tbsp vegetable oil
10ml/2 tsp sugar
1 large onion, finely chopped
15ml/1 tbsp grated fresh root ginger
15ml/1 tbsp crushed garlic
5ml/1 tsp ground coriander
2.5–5ml/½–1 tsp hot chilli powder
175g/6oz canned chopped tomatoes, including the juice
300ml/½ pint/1¼ cups warm water
30ml/2 tbsp chopped fresh coriander (cilantro) leaves, to garnish
plain boiled rice, to serve

1 Cut the fish into 7.5cm/3in pieces and put it in a large bowl. Add the lemon juice and sprinkle with half the salt and half the turmeric. Mix gently with your fingertips, then cover and set aside for 15 minutes.

2 Pour enough oil into a 23cm/9in frying pan to cover the base to a depth of 1cm/½in and heat over a medium setting. Mix the flour and pepper and dust the fish in the seasoned flour. Add to the oil in a single layer and fry until browned on both sides and a light crust has formed. Drain on kitchen paper.

3 In a karahi, wok or large pan, heat 60ml/4 tbsp oil. When the oil is hot, but not smoking, add the sugar and let it caramelize. As soon as the sugar is brown, add the finely chopped onion, ginger and garlic and fry for 7–8 minutes, until just beginning to colour. Stir regularly.

4 Add the ground coriander, chilli powder and the remaining turmeric. Stir-fry for about 30 seconds and add the tomatoes. Cook until the tomatoes are mushy and the oil separates from the spice paste, stirring regularly.

5 Pour the warm water and remaining salt into the pan, and bring to the boil. Carefully add the fried fish, reduce the heat to low and simmer, uncovered, for 5–6 minutes.

6 Transfer to a serving dish and garnish with the coriander leaves. Serve with plain boiled rice.

Cook's Tip

Choose fresh rather than frozen fish for the best flavour.

fish stew Energy 290kcal/1228kJ; Protein 31.2g; Carbohydrate 25.6g, of which sugars 8.1g; Fat 7.9g, of which saturates 1.2g; Cholesterol 24mg; Calcium 53mg; Fibre 2.9g; Sodium 57mg.
fish in sauce Energy 439kcal/1828kJ; Protein 34.8g; Carbohydrate 21.2g, of which sugars 8.9g; Fat 24.5g, of which saturates 2.9g; Cholesterol 78mg; Calcium 103mg; Fibre 3.3g; Sodium 116mg.

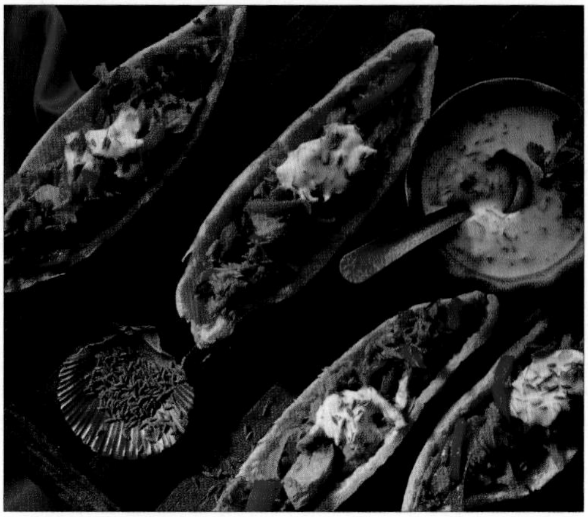

Tuna Curry

This is an easy dish to make when you want curry spice flavours but have little preparation time.

Serves 4

1 onion
1 red (bell) pepper
1 green (bell) pepper
30ml/2 tbsp oil
1.5ml/¼ tsp cumin seeds
2.5ml/½ tsp ground cumin
2.5ml/½ tsp ground coriander
2.5ml/½ tsp chilli powder
1.5ml/¼ tsp salt
2 garlic cloves, crushed
400g/14oz can tuna in brine, drained and flaked
1 fresh green chilli, finely chopped
2.5cm/1in piece fresh root ginger, grated
1.5ml/¼ tsp garam masala
5ml/1 tsp lemon juice
30ml/2 tbsp chopped fresh coriander (cilantro)
fresh coriander sprig, to garnish
pitta bread and cucumber raita, to serve

1 Thinly slice the onion and the red and green peppers, discarding the seeds from the peppers.

2 Heat the oil in a karahi, wok or heavy pan and stir-fry the cumin seeds for 2–3 minutes until they begin to spit and splutter.

3 Add the ground cumin, coriander, chilli powder and salt and cook for 2–3 minutes more. Then add the garlic, onion and peppers.

4 Fry the vegetables, stirring from time to time, for 5–7 minutes until the onion has browned. Stir in the tuna, chopped green chilli and grated ginger and cook for 5 minutes.

5 Add the garam masala, lemon juice and chopped fresh coriander and continue to cook the curry for a further 3–4 minutes.

6 Meanwhile, place the pitta breads on a grill (broiler) rack and grill (broil) until they just puff up. Split with a sharp knife. Serve the curry in the pitta breads with the cucumber raita, garnished with a coriander sprig.

Monkfish & Okra Curry

Okra, when cut into short lengths, releases a liquid that helps to thicken this tasty sauce surrounding tender morsels of monkfish.

Serves 4

450g/1lb monkfish
5ml/1 tsp ground turmeric
2.5ml/½ tsp chilli powder
2.5ml/½ tsp salt
5ml/1 tsp cumin seeds
2.5ml/½ tsp fennel seeds
2 dried red chillies
30ml/2 tbsp oil
1 onion, finely chopped
2 garlic cloves, crushed
4 tomatoes, peeled and finely chopped
150ml/¼ pint/⅔ cup water
225g/8oz okra, trimmed and cut into 2.5cm/1in lengths
5ml/1 tsp garam masala
plain rice, to serve

1 Remove the membrane and bones from the monkfish, cut into 2.5cm/1in cubes and place in a dish. Mix together the ground turmeric, chilli powder and 1.5ml/¼ tsp of the salt, and rub the mixture all over the fish. Cover and marinate for 15 minutes.

2 Put the cumin seeds, fennel seeds and chillies in a large, heavy pan and dry-roast the spice mixture for 3–4 minutes. Put the spices into a blender or use a mortar and pestle to grind to a coarse powder.

3 Heat 15ml/1 tbsp of the oil in the frying pan and fry the monkfish cubes for about 4–5 minutes. Remove with a slotted spoon and drain on kitchen paper.

4 Add the remaining oil to the pan and fry the onion and garlic for about 5 minutes. Add the roasted spice powder and the remaining salt and fry for 2–3 minutes. Stir in the tomatoes and water and simmer for 5 minutes.

5 Add the prepared okra and cook for about 5–7 minutes.

6 Return the fish to the pan together with the garam masala. Cover and simmer for 5–6 minutes or until the fish is tender. Serve immediately with plain rice.

tuna curry Energy 193kcal/813kJ; Protein 25.3g; Carbohydrate 8g, of which sugars 6.5g; Fat 7g, of which saturates 1g; Cholesterol 51mg; Calcium 48mg; Fibre 2.2g; Sodium 329mg.
monkfish & okra Energy 203kcal/851kJ; Protein 20.9g; Carbohydrate 7.7g, of which sugars 5.4g; Fat 10.2g, of which saturates 1.5g; Cholesterol 16mg; Calcium 119mg; Fibre 3.5g; Sodium 36mg.

Stir-fried Monkfish with Vegetables

Monkfish is fabulous stir-fried, as it holds its shape well during cooking. Here it is partnered with tomatoes and courgette in a mildly spiced sauce that complements the sweet flavour of the monkfish perfectly.

Serves 4

30ml/2 tbsp oil
2 medium onions, sliced
5ml/1 tsp crushed garlic
5ml/1 tsp ground cumin
5ml/1 tsp ground coriander
5ml/1 tsp chilli powder
900g/2lb monkfish, filleted and cut into cubes
30ml/2 tbsp fresh fenugreek leaves
2 tomatoes, seeded and sliced
1 courgette (zucchini), sliced
salt
15ml/1 tbsp lime juice

1 Heat the oil in a karahi, wok or heavy pan and fry the onions over a low heat until soft.

2 Meanwhile, mix together the garlic, cumin, coriander and chilli powder. Add this spice mixture to the onions and stir-fry for about 1 minute.

3 Add the fish and continue to stir-fry for 3–5 minutes until the fish is well cooked throughout.

4 Add the fenugreek, tomatoes and courgette, followed by salt to taste, and stir-fry for a further 2 minutes. Sprinkle with lime juice before serving.

Cook's Tip

Monkfish can be quite expensive, but is well worth using for this dish. As it has only one central bone, there are no fiddly bones to worry about. However, the dish would also work with cubed cod or uncooked, peeled prawns (shrimp). Watch the cooking times for both cod and prawns as overcooked cod will disintegrate and overcooked prawns will be tough. The prawns are cooked as soon as they turn pink.

Goan Fish Casserole

The cooking of Goa is a mixture of Portuguese and Indian; the addition of tamarind gives a slightly sour note to the spicy coconut sauce.

Serves 4

7.5ml/1½ tsp ground turmeric
5ml/1 tsp salt
450g/1lb monkfish fillet, cut into pieces
15ml/1 tbsp lemon juice
5ml/1 tsp cumin seeds
5ml/1 tsp coriander seeds
5ml/1 tsp black peppercorns
1 garlic clove, chopped
5cm/2in piece fresh root ginger, finely chopped
25g/1oz tamarind paste
150ml/¼ pint/⅔ cup hot water
30ml/2 tbsp vegetable oil
2 onions, halved and sliced lengthways
400ml/14fl oz/1⅔ cups coconut milk
4 mild fresh green chillies, seeded and cut into thin strips
16 large raw prawns (shrimp), peeled
30ml/2 tbsp chopped fresh coriander (cilantro) leaves, to garnish

1 Mix together the ground turmeric and salt in a small bowl. Place the monkfish in a shallow dish and sprinkle over the lemon juice, then rub the turmeric and salt mixture over the fish fillets to coat them completely. Cover and chill until you are ready to cook them.

2 Put the cumin seeds, coriander seeds and black peppercorns in a blender or small food processor and grind to a powder. Add the chopped garlic and ginger and process together for a few seconds more.

3 Preheat the oven to 200°C/400°F/Gas 6. Mix the tamarind paste with the hot water and set aside.

4 Heat the oil in a frying pan, add the onions and cook for 5–6 minutes, until softened and golden. Transfer the onions to a shallow earthenware dish.

5 Add the monkfish fillets to the oil remaining in the frying pan, and fry briefly over a high heat, turning them to seal on all sides. Remove the monkfish from the pan and place on top of the fried onions.

6 Add the ground spice mixture to the frying pan and cook over a medium heat, stirring constantly, for 1–2 minutes. Stir in the tamarind liquid, coconut milk and chilli strips and bring to the boil.

7 Pour the sauce into the earthenware dish to coat the fish completely.

8 Cover the dish and cook the fish casserole in the preheated oven for about 10 minutes.

9 Add the prawns, pushing them down so that they are completely immersed in the liquid, then cover the dish again and return it to the oven for 5 minutes, or until the prawns turn pink. Be careful not to overcook them or they will toughen. Check the seasoning and add more salt if necessary, then sprinkle with chopped coriander leaves and serve.

stir-fried monkfish Energy 266kcal/1122kJ; Protein 38.5g; Carbohydrate 12.1g, of which sugars 8g; Fat 7.6g, of which saturates 1.1g; Cholesterol 32mg; Calcium 68mg; Fibre 2.4g; Sodium 50mg.
Goan casserole Energy 220kcal/926kJ; Protein 28g; Carbohydrate 12.8g, of which sugars 10.5g; Fat 6.8g, of which saturates 1g; Cholesterol 113mg; Calcium 103mg; Fibre 1.4g; Sodium 720mg.

Mackerel in Tamarind

Coconut cream makes a heavenly sauce flavoured with ginger, chillies, coriander and turmeric in this delicious dish originating from Western India. Mackerel has a superbly rich flesh and yet it is a surprisingly inexpensive fish.

Serves 6–8

1kg/2¼ lb fresh mackerel fillets, skinned
30ml/2 tbsp tamarind pulp, soaked in 200ml/7fl oz/ scant 1 cup water
1 onion
1cm/½in piece fresh root ginger
2 garlic cloves
1 or 2 fresh red chillies, seeded, or 5ml/1 tsp chilli powder
5ml/1 tsp ground coriander
5ml/1 tsp ground turmeric
2.5ml/½ tsp ground fennel seeds
15ml/1 tbsp soft dark brown sugar
90–105ml/6–7 tbsp oil
200ml/7fl oz/scant 1 cup coconut cream
fresh chilli shreds, to garnish

1 Rinse the fish fillets in cold water and dry them well on kitchen paper. Put into a shallow dish and sprinkle with a little salt. Strain the tamarind and pour the juice over the fish fillets. Leave for 30 minutes.

2 Quarter the onion, peel and slice the ginger and peel the garlic. Grind the onion, ginger, garlic and chillies or chilli powder to a paste in a food processor or with a pestle and mortar. Add the ground coriander, turmeric, fennel seeds and sugar.

3 Heat half the oil in a frying pan. Drain the fish fillets and fry for 5 minutes, or until cooked. Set aside.

4 Wipe out the pan and heat the remaining oil. Fry the spice paste, stirring all the time, until it gives off a spicy aroma. Do not let it brown. Add the coconut cream and simmer gently for a few minutes. Add the fish fillets and gently heat through.

5 Taste for seasoning and serve sprinkled with shredded chilli.

Fish & Prawns in Herb Sauce

Bengalis are famous for their seafood dishes and like to use mustard oil in recipes because it imparts a unique taste, flavour and aroma. No feast in Bengal is complete without one of these celebrated fish dishes.

Serves 4–6

3 garlic cloves
5cm/2in piece fresh root ginger
1 large leek, roughly chopped
4 fresh green chillies
60ml/4 tbsp mustard oil or vegetable oil
15ml/1 tbsp ground coriander
2.5ml/½ tsp fennel seeds
15ml/1 tbsp crushed yellow mustard seeds, or 5ml/1 tsp mustard powder
175ml/6fl oz/¾ cup thick coconut milk
225g/8oz huss or monkfish fillets, cut into thick chunks
225g/8oz king prawns (jumbo shrimp), peeled and deveined, with tails intact
salt
115g/4oz/4 cups fresh coriander (cilantro), chopped
2 fresh green chillies, to garnish

1 In a food processor, grind the garlic, ginger, leek and chillies to a coarse paste. Add a little vegetable oil if the mixture is too dry and process the mixture again.

2 In a large frying pan, heat the mustard or vegetable oil with the paste until it is well blended. Keep the window open and take care not to overheat the mixture as any smoke from the mustard oil will sting the eyes.

3 Stir the ground coriander, fennel seeds, mustard and coconut milk into the pan. Gently bring the mixture to the boil and then lower the heat and simmer, uncovered, for about 5 minutes.

4 Add the fish chunks. Simmer for 2 minutes, then fold in the king prawns and cook until the prawns turn a vivid orange-pink colour. Season with salt, fold in the chopped fresh coriander and serve immediately, garnished with the fresh green chillies.

mackerel in tamarind Energy 578kcal/2420kJ; Protein 43.5g; Carbohydrate 35.2g, of which sugars 1.5g; Fat 30.2g, of which saturates 5.7g; Cholesterol 80mg; Calcium 48mg; Fibre 3.1g; Sodium 110mg.
fish & prawns Energy 148kcal/619kJ; Protein 14.1g; Carbohydrate 4g, of which sugars 2.5g; Fat 8.6g, of which saturates 1.1g; Cholesterol 78mg; Calcium 93mg; Fibre 1.6g; Sodium 118mg.

Braised Carp in Ginger Sauce

Braising fish in water and aromatics is a cooking method that is widely used in China. The recipe is very easy to make – the fish is simply braised in a tasty stock – but the combination of flavours is superb.

Serves 4

1 large carp, about 1kg/2¼lb, cleaned and scaled
400ml/14fl oz/1⅔ cups water
15ml/1 tbsp grated fresh root ginger
45ml/3 tbsp dark soy sauce
30ml/2 tbsp sesame oil
5ml/1 tsp sugar
pinch of salt and ground black pepper
4 cloves
15ml/1 tbsp cornflour (cornstarch) mixed with 30ml/2 tbsp water
spring onions, to garnish (optional)

1 Rinse the carp inside and out. Pat dry with kitchen paper. Make deep cuts diagonally across both sides of the fish. If the fish is too large for your wok, cut it into two pieces.

2 Pour the water into the wok and add the grated ginger, soy sauce, sesame oil, sugar, salt, pepper and cloves. Bring to the boil.

3 Carefully lower the fish into the liquid. Reduce the heat and braise the fish for 15 minutes or until it is cooked through. Lift the fish out and put it on a serving dish. Keep hot.

4 Stir the cornflour mixture into the liquid remaining in the wok. Bring to the boil and cook, stirring constantly, for 2 minutes or until the sauce thickens. Spoon the sauce over the fish and serve immediately.

Variation
If you cannot obtain carp, perch or sea bass make excellent substitutes in this and other carp recipes.

Salmon Marinated with Thai Spices

The raw fish is marinated for several days in a brine flavoured with Thai spices, which effectively 'cooks' it.

Serves 4–6

tail piece of 1 salmon, weighing about 675g/1½lb, cleaned, scaled and filleted
20ml/4 tsp coarse sea salt
20ml/4 tsp sugar
2.5cm/1in piece fresh root ginger, grated
2 lemon grass stalks, coarse outer leaves removed, thinly sliced
4 kaffir lime leaves, finely chopped or shredded
grated rind of 1 lime
1 fresh red chilli, seeded and finely chopped
5ml/1 tsp black peppercorns, coarsely crushed
30ml/2 tbsp chopped fresh coriander (cilantro)
fresh coriander sprigs and quartered kaffir limes, to garnish

For the dressing
150ml/¼ pint/⅔ cup mayonnaise
juice of ½ lime
10ml/2 tsp chopped fresh coriander (cilantro)

1 Remove any remaining bones from the salmon using a pair of tweezers. Put the coarse sea salt, sugar, ginger, lemon grass, lime leaves, lime rind, chopped chilli, crushed black peppercorns and chopped coriander in a bowl and mix together.

2 Spread one-quarter of the spice mixture in a shallow dish. Place one salmon fillet, skin down, on top. Spread two-thirds of the remaining mixture over the flesh, then place the remaining fillet on top, flesh side down. Sprinkle the rest of the spice mixture over the fish.

3 Cover with foil, then place a board on top. Add some weights, such as cans of fruit. Chill for 2–5 days, turning the fish daily in the spicy brine.

4 Make the dressing by mixing the mayonnaise, lime juice and chopped coriander in a bowl. Scrape the spices off the fish. Slice it as thinly as possible. Garnish with the coriander and kaffir lime leaves, and serve with the lime dressing.

carp in ginger sauce Energy 211kcal/883kJ; Protein 22.2g; Carbohydrate 5.4g, of which sugars 1.9g; Fat 11.4g, of which saturates 1.9g; Cholesterol 84mg; Calcium 62mg; Fibre 0g; Sodium 590mg.
salmon w. spices Energy 391kcal/1622kJ; Protein 23.3g; Carbohydrate 4.1g, of which sugars 4g; Fat 31.4g, of which saturates 5g; Cholesterol 75mg; Calcium 44mg; Fibre 0.4g; Sodium 166mg.

Fish Moolie

Choose a firm-textured fish for this dish so that the pieces stay intact during the brief cooking process.

Serves 4

500g/1¼lb monkfish or other firm-textured fish fillets, skinned and cut into 2.5cm/1in cubes
2.5ml/½ tsp salt
50g/2oz/⅔ cup desiccated (dry unsweetened shredded) coconut
6 shallots or small onions, roughly chopped
6 blanched almonds
2 or 3 garlic cloves, roughly chopped
2.5cm/1in piece fresh root ginger, peeled and sliced
2 lemon grass stalks, trimmed
10ml/2 tsp ground turmeric
45ml/3 tbsp vegetable oil
2 x 400ml/14fl oz cans coconut milk
1–3 fresh chillies, seeded and sliced
salt and ground black pepper
fresh chives, to garnish
boiled rice, to serve

1 Sprinkle the fish with the salt. Dry-fry the coconut in a wok or large frying pan over medium to low heat, turning all the time until it is crisp and golden. Transfer to a food processor and process to an oily paste. Scrape into a bowl and reserve.

2 Add the shallots or onions, almonds, garlic and ginger to the food processor. Cut off the lower 5cm/2in of the lemon grass stalks, chop them roughly and add to the processor bowl. Process the mixture to a paste. Add the turmeric to the mixture in the processor and process briefly to mix. Bruise the remaining lemon grass and set the stalks aside.

3 Heat the oil in a wok. Add the onion mixture and cook for a few minutes without browning. Stir in the coconut milk and bring to the boil, stirring constantly to prevent curdling. Add the cubes of fish, most of the sliced chilli and the bruised lemon grass stalks. Cook for 3–4 minutes. Stir in the coconut paste and cook for a further 2–3 minutes only. Do not overcook the fish. Taste and adjust the seasoning.

4 Remove the lemon grass. Transfer to a hot serving dish and sprinkle with the remaining slices of chilli. Garnish with chopped and whole chives and serve with boiled rice.

Escabeche

This dish of pickled fish and vegetables was brought to the Philippines by Spanish settlers in the late 1500s.

Serves 6

900g/2lb white fish fillets, such as sole or plaice
45–60ml/3–4 tbsp seasoned flour
vegetable oil, for shallow-frying

For the sauce

2.5cm/1in piece fresh root ginger, peeled and thinly sliced
2–3 garlic cloves, crushed
1 onion, cut into thin rings
30ml/2 tbsp vegetable oil
½ large green (bell) pepper, seeded and cut into small squares
½ large red (bell) pepper, seeded and cut into small squares
1 carrot, cut into matchsticks
25ml/1½ tbsp cornflour (cornstarch)
450ml/¾ pint/scant 2 cups water
45–60ml/3–4 tbsp herb or cider vinegar
15ml/1 tbsp soft light brown sugar
5–10ml/1–2 tsp Thai fish sauce
salt and ground black pepper
1 small chilli, seeded and sliced, and spring onions (scallions), finely shredded, to garnish
boiled rice, to serve

1 Wipe the fillets and pat them dry on kitchen paper, then dust them lightly with seasoned flour. Heat the oil in a frying pan and fry the fish in batches until golden and almost cooked. Transfer to an ovenproof dish and keep warm.

2 Make the sauce in a wok or large pan. Fry the ginger, garlic and onion in the oil for 5 minutes or until the onion is softened but not browned. Add the pepper squares and carrot strips and stir-fry for 1 minute.

3 Put the cornflour in a small bowl and add a little of the water to make a paste. Stir in the remaining water, the vinegar and the sugar. Pour the cornflour mixture over the vegetables in the wok and stir until the sauce boils and thickens a little. Season with fish sauce and salt and pepper if needed.

4 Add the fish to the sauce and reheat briefly without stirring. Transfer to a warmed serving platter and garnish with chilli and spring onions, if you like. Serve with boiled rice.

fish moolie Energy 319kcal/1335kJ; Protein 22.4g; Carbohydrate 16.7g, of which sugars 14.9g; Fat 18.6g, of which saturates 8.3g; Cholesterol 18mg; Calcium 96mg; Fibre 3g; Sodium 249mg.
escabeche Energy 414kcal/1721kJ; Protein 41.9g; Carbohydrate 1.3g, of which sugars 1g; Fat 26.7g, of which saturates 3.2g; Cholesterol 104mg; Calcium 30mg; Fibre 0.2g; Sodium 137mg.

Mixed Smoked Fish Kedgeree

An ideal breakfast dish on a cold weekend morning and a classic for brunch. Garnish with quartered hard-boiled eggs and season well.

Serves 6

450g/1lb mixed smoked fish and shellfish, such as smoked cod, smoked haddock and smoked mussels or oysters
300ml/½ pint/1¼ cups milk
175g/6oz/scant 1 cup long grain rice
1 slice of lemon
50g/2oz/4 tbsp butter
5ml/1 tsp medium-hot curry powder
2.5ml/½ tsp grated nutmeg
15ml/1 tbsp chopped fresh parsley
salt and ground black pepper
2 hard-boiled eggs, to garnish

1 Put the fish, but not the shellfish, in a large pan, add the milk and bring just to the boil. Lower the heat, cover and poach for 10 minutes, or until it flakes easily with the tip of a knife.

2 Remove the fish with a slotted spoon and set aside until cool enough to handle. Discard the milk. Remove the skin and any bones from the fish and flake the flesh. Mix with the smoked shellfish in a bowl and set aside.

3 Bring a pan of salted water to the boil, add the rice and slice of lemon and boil for 10 minutes, or according to the instructions on the packet, until just tender. Drain well and discard the lemon.

4 Melt the butter in a large frying pan and add the rice and fish. Shake the pan to mix all the ingredients together.

5 Stir in the curry powder, nutmeg, parsley and seasoning. Serve immediately, garnished with quartered eggs.

Cook's Tip
When flaking the fish, keep the pieces fairly large to give the dish a chunky consistency.

Kashmir Coconut Fish Curry

The combination of spices in this dish give an interesting depth of flavour to the creamy curry sauce.

Serves 4

30ml/2 tbsp vegetable oil
2 onions, sliced
1 green (bell) pepper, seeded and sliced
1 garlic clove, crushed
1 dried chilli, seeded and chopped
5ml/1 tsp ground coriander
5ml/1 tsp ground cumin
2.5ml/½ tsp ground turmeric
2.5ml/½ tsp hot chilli powder
2.5ml/½ tsp garam masala
15g/½oz/1 tbsp plain (all-purpose) flour
300ml/½ pint/1¼ cups coconut cream
675g/1½lb haddock fillet, skinned and chopped
4 tomatoes, peeled, seeded and chopped
15ml/1 tbsp lemon juice
30ml/2 tbsp ground almonds
30ml/2 tbsp double (heavy) cream
fresh coriander (cilantro) sprigs, to garnish
naan bread and rice, to serve

1 Heat the oil in a large pan over low heat. Add the onions, green pepper and garlic and cook, stirring occasionally, for 6–7 minutes, until the onions and pepper have softened but not coloured.

2 Stir in the dried chilli, ground coriander, cumin, turmeric, chilli powder, garam masala and flour and cook, stirring constantly, for 1 minute more.

3 Mix the coconut cream with 300ml/½ pint/1¼ cups boiling water and stir into the spicy vegetable mixture. Bring to the boil, cover with a tight-fitting lid and simmer gently for about 6 minutes.

4 Add the pieces of fish and the tomatoes, re-cover the pan and cook for 5–6 minutes, or until the fish has turned opaque and flakes easily with the tip of a knife. Uncover and gently stir in the lemon juice, ground almonds and double cream and heat through for a few minutes. Season well, garnish with coriander and serve with naan bread and rice.

kedgeree Energy 250kcal/1044kJ; Protein 17.7g; Carbohydrate 25.8g, of which sugars 2.5g; Fat 8.3g, of which saturates 5g; Cholesterol 55mg; Calcium 79mg; Fibre 0.1g; Sodium 950mg.
Kashmir fish curry Energy 496kcal/2068kJ; Protein 36.6g; Carbohydrate 18.9g, of which sugars 13.6g; Fat 31.1g, of which saturates 20.5g; Cholesterol 71mg; Calcium 75mg; Fibre 3.2g; Sodium 137mg.

Salmon with Shallots & Galangal

This is a thin, soupy curry with wonderfully strong flavours. Serve it in bowls with lots of sticky rice or bread to soak up the delicious juices.

Serves 4

450g/1lb salmon fillet
500ml/17fl oz/2¼ cups vegetable stock
4 shallots, finely chopped
2 garlic cloves, finely chopped
2.5cm/1in piece fresh galangal, finely chopped
tender bulbous portion of 1 lemon grass stalk, finely chopped
2.5ml/½ tsp dried chilli flakes
15ml/1 tbsp fish sauce
5ml/1 tsp palm sugar (jaggery) or light muscovado (brown) sugar
rice or fresh crusty bread, to serve

1 Wrap the salmon in clear film (plastic wrap) and place in the freezer for 30–40 minutes to firm up the flesh slightly.

2 Remove the fish from the freezer, unwrap it and remove the skin, then use a sharp knife to cut the fish into 2.5cm/1in cubes, removing any stray bones with your fingers or with tweezers as you do so.

3 Pour the stock into a large, heavy pan and bring it to the boil over a medium heat. Add the shallots, garlic, galangal, lemon grass, chilli flakes, fish sauce and sugar. Bring back to the boil, stir well, then reduce the heat and simmer gently for 15 minutes.

4 Add the cubes of salmon to the stock, bring back to the boil, then turn off the heat. Leave the curry to stand for 10–15 minutes until the fish is cooked through, then transfer to heated bowls and serve with plenty of rice or fresh crusty bread to mop up the juices.

Variation

Rosy pink salmon looks particularly pretty, but other types of fish would work equally well in this curry. Try cod, pollack, hoki or haddock. Monkfish is also suitable.

Salmon & Black-eyed Beans

This dish will keep for 4–5 days in a cool place.

Serves 4

150g/5oz salmon fillet, boned and skinned
400g/14oz can black-eyed beans (peas) in brine
50g/2oz fresh shiitake mushrooms, stalks removed
50g/2oz carrot, peeled
50g/2oz mooli (daikon), peeled
5g/⅛oz piece of dashi-konbu about 10cm/4in square
60ml/4 tbsp water
5ml/1 tsp caster (superfine) sugar
15ml/1 tbsp soy sauce
7.5ml/1½ tsp mirin (sweet rice wine)
salt
2.5cm/1in fresh root ginger, peeled

1 Slice the salmon into 1cm/½in thick pieces. Thoroughly salt the fillet and leave for 1 hour, then wash away the salt and cut it into 1cm/½in cubes. Par-boil in rapidly boiling water in a small pan for 30 seconds, then drain. Rinse under running water.

2 Slice the fresh ginger thinly lengthways, then stack the slices and cut into thin threads. Soak in cold water for 30 minutes, then drain well.

3 Drain the can of beans and tip the liquid into a medium pan. Set the beans and pan of liquid aside.

4 Chop all the vegetables into 1cm/½in cubes. Wipe the dried konbu with a damp dish towel or kitchen paper, then snip into shreds with scissors.

5 Add the salmon, vegetables and konbu to the bean liquid with the beans, water, sugar and 1.5ml/¼ tsp salt. Bring to the boil. Reduce the heat to low and cook for 6 minutes or until the carrot is cooked. Add the soy sauce and cook for about 4 minutes. Add the mirin, then remove the pan from the heat, mix well and check the seasoning. Leave for an hour. Serve garnished with the fresh sliced ginger.

salmon w. shallots Energy 220kcal/915kJ; Protein 23.8g; Carbohydrate 3g, of which sugars 2.6g; Fat 12.6g, of which saturates 2.2g; Cholesterol 56mg; Calcium 36mg; Fibre 0.2g; Sodium 320mg.
salmon & beans Energy 387kcal/1633kJ; Protein 33.7g; Carbohydrate 43.5g, of which sugars 5.6g; Fat 9.9g, of which saturates 1.9g; Cholesterol 38mg; Calcium 70mg; Fibre 8.2g; Sodium 588mg.

Sweet Soy Salmon

Teriyaki sauce forms the marinade for the salmon in this recipe. Served with soft-fried noodles, it makes a stunning dish, which people of all ages will enjoy.

Serves 4

350g/12oz salmon fillet
30ml/2 tbsp soy sauce
30ml/2 tbsp sake
60ml/4 tbsp mirin or sweet sherry
5ml/1 tsp soft light brown sugar
10ml/2 tsp grated fresh root ginger
3 garlic cloves, 1 crushed and 2 sliced into rounds
15ml/1 tbsp vegetable oil
225g/8oz dried egg noodles, cooked and drained
50g/2oz/1 cup alfalfa sprouts
10ml/2 tsp sesame seeds, lightly toasted

1 If you have time, chill the salmon briefly in the freezer to make it easier to slice. Using a sharp chopping knife, cut the salmon into thin slices. Place the slices of fish in a shallow dish.

2 In a measuring jug (pitcher), mix together the soy sauce, sake, mirin or sherry, sugar, ginger and crushed garlic. Pour the mixture over the salmon, cover and leave for 30 minutes in a cool place.

3 Preheat the grill (broiler). Drain the salmon, and scrape off and reserve the marinade. Place the salmon in a single layer on a baking sheet. Grill (broil) for 2–3 minutes without turning.

4 Meanwhile, heat a wok until hot, add the oil and swirl it around. Add the garlic rounds and cook until golden brown but not burnt.

5 Add the cooked noodles and reserved marinade to the wok and stir-fry for 3–4 minutes, until the marinade has reduced slightly to a syrupy glaze and coats the noodles.

6 Toss in the alfalfa sprouts, then remove immediately from the heat. Transfer to warmed serving plates and top with the salmon. Sprinkle with the toasted sesame seeds and serve.

Asian Seared Salmon

Salmon fillets only take a few minutes to cook, but make sure you allow enough time for the fish to soak up all the flavours of the marinade before you start to cook.

Serves 4

grated rind and juice of 1 lime
15ml/1 tbsp soy sauce
2 spring onions (scallions), sliced
1 fresh red chilli, seeded and finely chopped
2.5cm/1in piece fresh root ginger, peeled and grated
1 lemon grass stalk, finely chopped
4 salmon fillets, each about 175g/6oz
30ml/2 tbsp olive oil
salt and ground black pepper
45ml/3 tbsp fresh coriander (cilantro), to garnish
cooked egg noodles and stir-fried carrot, peppers and mangetouts (snow peas), to serve

1 Put the grated lime rind in a jug (pitcher) and pour in the lime juice. Add the soy sauce, spring onions, chilli, ginger and lemon grass. Season with pepper and stir well.

2 Place the salmon in a shallow non-metallic dish and pour the lime mixture over. Cover and marinate in the refrigerator for at least 30 minutes.

3 Brush a griddle pan with 15ml/1 tbsp of the olive oil and heat until hot. Remove the fish from the marinade, pat dry and add to the griddle pan. Cook the salmon fillets for 3 minutes on each side.

4 When the salmon fillets are almost cooked, pour the remaining marinade into a separate pan and heat it. Remove the salmon fillets from the griddle pan with tongs or a fish slice, taking care to keep them whole, and place them into the hot marinade. Simmer for 1–2 minutes.

5 Serve the salmon on a bed of freshly cooked egg noodles and stir-fried vegetables. Garnish with chopped coriander.

sweet soy salmon Energy 392kcal/1649kJ; Protein 19.3g; Carbohydrate 43.6g, of which sugars 4g; Fat 15.1g, of which saturates 2.9g; Cholesterol 45mg; Calcium 50mg; Fibre 2g; Sodium 664mg.
Asian salmon Energy 370kcal/1539kJ; Protein 35.8g; Carbohydrate 0.6g, of which sugars 0.5g; Fat 24.9g, of which saturates 4.1g; Cholesterol 88mg; Calcium 60mg; Fibre 0.6g; Sodium 350mg.

Salmon & Shimeji Parcels

In this Japanese recipe, the vegetables and salmon are wrapped and steamed with sake in their own moisture.

Serves 4
450g/1lb salmon fillet, skinned
30ml/2 tbsp sake or dry sherry
15ml/1 tbsp shoyu
about 250g/9oz/3 cups fresh shimeji mushrooms
8 fresh shiitake mushrooms
2.5cm/1in carrot
2 spring onions (scallions)
115g/4oz/1 cup mangetouts (snow peas)
salt

1 Cut the salmon into bitesize pieces. Marinate in the sake and shoyu for about 15 minutes, then drain and reserve the marinade. Preheat the oven to 190°C/375°F/Gas 5.

2 Clean the shimeji mushrooms and chop off the hard root. Remove and discard the stems from the shiitake. Carve a small white cross in the brown top of each shiitake cap.

3 Slice the carrot very thinly, then cut out 8 to 12 maple-leaf or flower shapes. Carefully slice the spring onions in half lengthways. Trim the mangetouts.

4 Cut four sheets of foil, each about 29 x 21cm/11½ x 8½in wide. Place the long side of one sheet facing towards you. Arrange the salmon and shimeji mushrooms in the centre, then place a spring onion diagonally across them. Put two shiitake on top, three to four mangetouts in a fan shape and then sprinkle with a few carrot leaves.

5 Sprinkle the marinade and a good pinch of salt over the top. Fold the two longer sides of the foil together, then fold the shorter sides to seal. Repeat to make four parcels.

6 Bake the parcels on a baking sheet for 15–20 minutes in the middle of the preheated oven. When the foil has expanded into a balloon, the dish is ready to serve.

Teriyaki Salmon en Papillote

The aromatic smell that wafts out of these fish parcels as you open them is deliciously tempting.

Serves 4
2 carrots
2 courgettes (zucchini)
6 spring onions (scallions)
2.5cm/1in piece fresh root ginger, peeled
1 lime
2 garlic cloves, thinly sliced
30ml/2 tbsp teriyaki marinade or fish sauce
5–10ml/1–2 tsp clear sesame oil
4 salmon fillets, about 200g/7oz each
ground black pepper
rice, to serve

1 Cut the carrots, courgettes and spring onions into matchsticks and set them aside. Cut the ginger into matchsticks and put these in a small bowl. Using a zester, pare the lime thinly. Add the pared rind to the ginger, with the garlic. Squeeze the lime juice.

2 Place the teriyaki marinade or fish sauce into a bowl and stir in the lime juice and sesame oil.

3 Preheat the oven to 220°C/425°F/Gas 7. Cut out four rounds of baking parchment, each with a diameter of 40cm/16in. Season the salmon with pepper. Lay a fillet at one side of each paper round, about 3cm/1¼ in off centre.

4 Sprinkle a quarter of the ginger mixture over each and pile a quarter of the vegetable matchsticks on top. Spoon a quarter of the teriyaki or fish sauce mixture over the top.

5 Fold the bare side of the baking parchment over the salmon and roll the edges of the parchment over to seal each parcel very tightly.

6 Place the salmon parcels on a baking sheet and cook in the oven for about 10–12 minutes, depending on the thickness of the fillets. Put the parcels on plates and serve with rice.

salmon & shimeji parcels Energy 231kcal/964kJ; Protein 25.2g; Carbohydrate 3.9g, of which sugars 3.3g; Fat 12.9g, of which saturates 2.2g; Cholesterol 56mg; Calcium 48mg; Fibre 2g; Sodium 328mg.
salmon en papillote Energy 321kcal/1337kJ; Protein 31.6g; Carbohydrate 5.3g, of which sugars 4.8g; Fat 16.6g, of which saturates 2.9g; Cholesterol 75mg; Calcium 46mg; Fibre 0.6g; Sodium 873mg.

Hoki Stir-fry

Any firm white fish, such as monkfish, hake or cod, can be used for this attractive stir-fry. You can vary the vegetables according to what is available, but try to include at least three different colours.

Serves 4–6

675g/1½ lb hoki fillet, skinned
pinch of five-spice powder
2 carrots
115g/4oz/1 cup small mangetouts (snow peas)
115g/4oz asparagus spears
4 spring onions (scallions)
45ml/3 tbsp groundnut (peanut) oil
2.5cm/1in piece fresh root ginger, peeled and cut into thin slivers
2 garlic cloves, finely chopped
300g/11oz/scant 1½ cups beansprouts
8–12 small baby corn cobs
15–30ml/1–2 tbsp light soy sauce
salt and ground black pepper

1 Cut the hoki into finger-size strips and season with salt, pepper and five-spice powder. Cut the carrots diagonally into slices as thin as the mangetouts.

2 Trim the mangetouts. Trim the asparagus spears and cut in half crossways. Trim the spring onions and cut them diagonally into 2cm/¾ in pieces, keeping the white and green parts separate. Set aside.

3 Heat a wok, then pour in the oil. As soon as it is hot, add the ginger and garlic. Stir-fry for 1 minute, then add the white parts of the spring onions and cook for 1 minute more.

4 Add the hoki strips and stir-fry for 2–3 minutes, until all the pieces of fish are opaque. Add the beansprouts and toss them around to coat them in the oil, then put in the carrots, mangetouts, asparagus and corn. Continue to stir-fry for 3–4 minutes, by which time the fish should be cooked, but all the vegetables will still be crunchy.

5 Add soy sauce to taste, toss everything quickly together, then stir in the green parts of the spring onions. Serve immediately.

Trout with Tamarind

Sometimes trout can taste rather bland, but this spicy sauce really gives it a zing.

Serves 4

4 trout, cleaned
6 spring onions (scallions), sliced
60ml/4 tbsp soy sauce
15ml/1 tbsp vegetable oil
30ml/2 tbsp chopped fresh coriander (cilantro) and strips of fresh red chilli, to garnish

For the sauce
50g/2oz tamarind pulp
105ml/7 tbsp boiling water
2 shallots, coarsely chopped
1 fresh red chilli, seeded and chopped
1cm/½in piece fresh root ginger, peeled and chopped
5ml/1 tsp soft light brown sugar
45ml/3 tbsp fish sauce

1 Slash the trout diagonally four or five times on each side. Place them in a shallow dish that is large enough to hold them all in a single layer.

2 Fill the cavity in each trout with spring onions and douse each fish with soy sauce. Carefully turn the fish over to coat both sides with the sauce. Sprinkle any remaining spring onions over the top.

3 To make the sauce, put the tamarind pulp in a small bowl and pour on the boiling water. Mash it well with a fork until it has softened.

4 Pour the tamarind mixture into a food processor or blender, and add the shallots, fresh chilli, ginger, sugar and fish sauce. Process to a coarse pulp. Scrape into a bowl.

5 Heat the oil in a large frying pan or wok and cook the trout, one at a time if necessary, for about 5 minutes on each side, until the skin is crisp and browned and the flesh cooked.

6 If cooking in batches, keep the cooked trout hot until all four fish have been fried. Serve the trout on warmed plates and spoon over some of the sauce. Sprinkle with the coriander and chilli and offer the remaining sauce separately.

hoki stir-fry Energy 183kcal/764kJ; Protein 22.4g; Carbohydrate 5g, of which sugars 3.8g; Fat 8.2g, of which saturates 1.1g; Cholesterol 0mg; Calcium 49mg; Fibre 2.3g; Sodium 295mg.
trout w. tamarind Energy 329kcal/1384kJ; Protein 47.9g; Carbohydrate 8.1g, of which sugars 6.3g; Fat 11.9g, of which saturates 2.5g; Cholesterol 192mg; Calcium 96mg; Fibre 1.2g; Sodium 978mg.

Trout with Black Rice

Pink trout fillets cooked with ginger make a stunning contrast to black rice.

Serves 2

2.5cm/1in piece fresh root ginger, peeled and grated
1 garlic clove, crushed
1 fresh red chilli, seeded and finely chopped
30ml/2 tbsp soy sauce
2 trout fillets, about 200g/7oz each
oil, for greasing

For the rice
15ml/1 tbsp sesame oil
50g/2oz/¾ cup fresh shiitake mushrooms, stems discarded, caps sliced
8 spring onions (scallions), finely chopped
150g/5oz/¾ cup black rice
4 slices fresh root ginger or galangal
900ml/1½ pints/3¾ cups boiling water or chicken stock

1 To make the rice, heat the sesame oil in a pan and fry the mushrooms with half the spring onions for 2–3 minutes.

2 Add the rice and sliced ginger to the pan and stir well. Cover with the boiling water or stock and bring to the boil. Reduce the heat, cover and simmer for 25–30 minutes or until the rice is tender. Drain well and cover to keep warm.

3 While the rice is cooking, preheat the oven to 200°C/400°F/Gas 6. In a small bowl mix together the grated ginger, garlic, chilli and soy sauce.

4 Place the fish, skin side up, in a lightly oiled shallow baking dish. Using a sharp knife, make several slits in the skin of the fish, then spread the ginger paste all over the fillets.

5 Cover the dish tightly with foil and cook in the oven for 20–25 minutes or until the trout fillets are cooked through.

6 Divide the rice between two warmed serving plates.

7 Remove the ginger. Lay the fish on top of the rice and sprinkle over the reserved spring onions, to garnish.

Marinated Sea Trout

Sea trout has a superb texture and a flavour like that of wild salmon. It is best served with strong but complementary flavours, such as chillies and lime, that cut the richness of its flesh.

Serves 6

6 sea trout cutlets, about 115g/4oz each, or wild or farmed salmon
2 garlic cloves, chopped
1 fresh long red chilli, seeded and chopped
45ml/3 tbsp chopped Thai basil
15ml/1 tbsp sugar or palm sugar (jaggery)
3 limes
400ml/14fl oz/1⅔ cups coconut milk
15ml/1 tbsp fish sauce

1 Place the sea trout cutlets side by side in a shallow dish. Using a pestle, pound the garlic and chilli in a large mortar to break both up roughly. Add 30ml/2 tbsp of the Thai basil with the sugar and continue to pound to a rough paste.

2 Grate the rind from 1 lime and squeeze the juice. Mix the rind and juice into the chilli paste, with the coconut milk. Pour the mixture over the cutlets. Cover and chill for about 1 hour. Cut the remaining limes into wedges.

3 Take the fish out of the refrigerator so that it can return to room temperature. Remove the cutlets from the marinade. Either cook on a barbecue, in an oiled hinged wire fish basket, or under a hot grill (broiler). Cook the fish for 4 minutes on each side, trying not to move them. They may stick to the grill rack if not seared first.

4 Strain the remaining marinade into a pan, reserving the contents of the sieve (strainer). Bring the marinade to the boil, then simmer gently for 5 minutes, stirring. Stir in the contents of the sieve and continue to simmer for 1 minute more. Add the fish sauce and the remaining Thai basil.

5 Lift each fish cutlet on to a plate, pour over the sauce and serve with the lime wedges.

trout w. black rice Energy 560kcal/2362kJ; Protein 45.6g; Carbohydrate 63.5g, of which sugars 3.3g; Fat 15.5g, of which saturates 1.4g; Cholesterol 0mg; Calcium 46mg; Fibre 2.3g; Sodium 1187mg.
marinated sea trout Energy 157kcal/662kJ; Protein 23.1g; Carbohydrate 5.9g, of which sugars 5.9g; Fat 4.7g, of which saturates 0.1g; Cholesterol 0mg; Calcium 46mg; Fibre 0.4g; Sodium 141mg.

Steamed Trout Fillets

This lovely dish can be prepared extremely quickly, and is suitable for any fish fillets. Serve it on a bed of noodles accompanied by ribbons of colourful vegetables such as carrots and peppers.

Serves 4

8 pink trout fillets of even thickness, about 115g/4oz each, skinned
50ml/2fl oz coconut cream
grated rind and juice of 2 limes
45ml/3 tbsp chopped fresh coriander (cilantro)
15ml/1 tbsp sunflower or groundnut (peanut) oil
2.5–5ml/½–1 tsp chilli oil
salt and ground black pepper
lime slices and coriander (cilantro) sprigs, to garnish

1 Cut four rectangles of baking parchment, about twice the size of the trout fillets. Place a fillet on each piece and season lightly with salt and pepper.

2 Mix together the coconut, lime rind and chopped coriander and spread a quarter of the mixture over each trout fillet. Sandwich another trout fillet on top.

3 Mix the lime juice with the oils, adjusting the quantity of chilli oil to your own taste, and drizzle the mixture over the trout 'sandwiches'.

4 Prepare a steamer. Fold up the edges of the paper and pleat them over the trout to make parcels, making sure they are well sealed. Place in the steamer insert and steam over the simmering water for about 10–15 minutes, depending on the thickness of the trout fillets. Serve immediately.

Cook's Tip

Chilli oil is widely available, but you can also make your own by adding 15ml/1 tbsp dried chilli flakes to 150ml/¼ pint/⅔ cup hot olive oil. Leave to cool, then bottle and store in a cool place.

Spicy Trout Parcels

Banana leaves make very good wrappers for fish cooked over coals. Sturdy enough to be handled without tearing, they seal in flavours and keep fish moist.

Serves 4

350g/12oz freshwater fish fillets, such as trout, cut into bitesize chunks
6 banana leaves
vegetable oil, for brushing
sticky rice, noodles or salad, to serve

For the marinade

2 shallots
5cm/2in turmeric root, peeled and grated
2 spring onions (scallions), finely sliced
2 garlic cloves, crushed
1–2 fresh green chillies, seeded and finely chopped
15ml/1 tbsp fish sauce
2.5ml/½ tsp raw cane sugar
salt and ground black pepper

1 To make the marinade, grate the shallots into a bowl, then combine with the other marinade ingredients. Season with salt and pepper. Toss the chunks of fish in the marinade, then cover and chill for 6 hours, or overnight.

2 Prepare a barbecue. Place one of the banana leaves on a flat surface and brush it with oil. Place the marinated fish on the banana leaf, spreading it out evenly, then fold over the sides to form an envelope. Place this envelope, fold side down, on top of another leaf and fold that one in the same manner. Repeat with the remaining leaves until they are all used up.

3 Secure the last layer of banana leaf with a piece of bendable wire. Place the banana leaf packet on the barbecue. Cook for about 20 minutes, turning it over from time to time to make sure it is cooked on both sides – the outer leaves will burn, but this is normal.

4 Carefully untie the wire (it will be hot) and unravel the packet. Check that the fish is cooked, and wrap and cook a little longer if it is not ready. Serve the trout unwrapped, with sticky rice, noodles or salad.

steamed trout fillets Energy 241kcal/1005kJ; Protein 25g; Carbohydrate 0.9g, of which sugars 0.9g; Fat 15.3g, of which saturates 7g; Cholesterol 0mg; Calcium 21mg; Fibre 0.2g; Sodium 75mg.
spicy trout parcels Energy 126kcal/528kJ; Protein 17.2g; Carbohydrate 0.7g, of which sugars 0.6g; Fat 6.1g, of which saturates 0.3g; Cholesterol 0mg; Calcium 12mg; Fibre 0.2g; Sodium 50mg.

Coconut Baked Snapper

Adding a couple of fresh red chillies to the marinade gives this dish a really spicy flavour. Serve the snapper with plain boiled rice.

Serves 4

1 snapper, about 1kg/2¼lb, scaled and cleaned
400ml/14fl oz/1⅔ cups coconut milk
105ml/7 tbsp dry white wine
juice of 1 lime
45ml/3 tbsp light soy sauce
1–2 fresh red chillies, seeded and finely sliced (optional)
60ml/4 tbsp chopped fresh parsley
45ml/3 tbsp chopped fresh coriander (cilantro)
salt and ground black pepper

1 Lay the snapper in an ovenproof shallow dish and season with a little salt and plenty of pepper.

2 Make the marinade. Mix together the coconut milk, wine, lime juice, soy sauce and chillies, if using. Stir in the herbs and pour over the fish. Cover with clear film (plastic wrap) and marinate in the refrigerator for about 4 hours, turning the fish over halfway through.

3 Preheat the oven to 190°C/375°F/Gas 5. Take the fish out of the marinade and wrap loosely in foil, spooning over the marinade before sealing the parcel.

4 Support the fish parcel in a roasting pan, put the pan in the oven and bake for 30–40 minutes, until the fish is cooked through and the flesh comes away easily from the bone.

Cook's Tips

• *Any type of snapper or trout can be used for this recipe. If you prefer, use one small fish per person, but be aware that small snapper can be very bony.*
• *Use light coconut milk for a less rich version of this dish. The flavour will be just as good.*

Red Snapper in Banana Leaves

Whole snappers infused with coconut cream, herbs and chilli make an impressive main course.

Serves 4

4 small red snapper, gutted and cleaned
4 large squares of banana leaf
50ml/2fl oz/¼ cup coconut cream
90ml/6 tbsp chopped coriander (cilantro)
90ml/6 tbsp chopped mint
juice of 3 limes
3 spring onions (scallions), finely sliced
4 kaffir lime leaves, finely shredded
2 fresh red chillies, seeded and finely sliced
4 lemon grass stalks, split lengthways
salt and ground black pepper
steamed rice and steamed Asian greens, to serve

1 Using a small sharp knife, score the fish diagonally on each side. Half fill a wok with water and bring to the boil.

2 Dip each square of banana leaf into the boiling water in the wok for 15–20 seconds so they become pliable. Lift out carefully, rinse under cold water and dry with kitchen paper.

3 Place the coconut cream, chopped herbs, lime juice, spring onions, lime leaves and chillies in a bowl and stir. Season well.

4 Lay the banana leaves flat, and place a fish and a split lemon grass stalk in the centre of each of them. Spread the herb mixture over each fish and fold over each banana leaf to form a neat parcel. Secure each parcel tightly with a bamboo skewer.

5 Place the parcels in a single layer in one or two tiers of a large bamboo steamer, then place over a wok of simmering water. Cover tightly and steam for 15–20 minutes, or until the fish is cooked through.

6 Remove the fish from the steamer and serve in their banana-leaf wrappings, with steamed rice and greens. Do not eat the banana leaves.

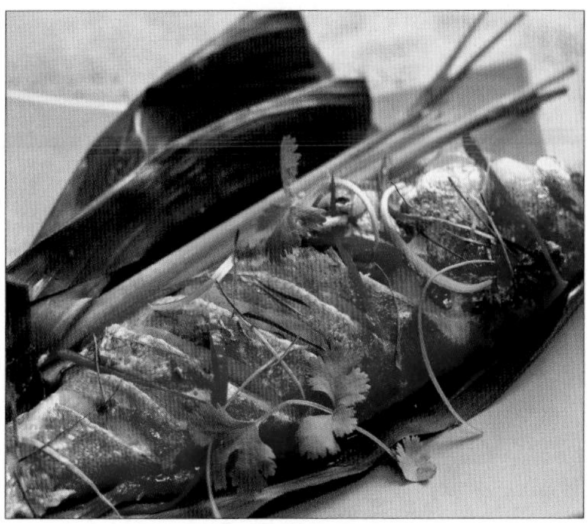

coconut baked snapper Energy 175kcal/738kJ; Protein 31.6g; Carbohydrate 1g, of which sugars 0.9g; Fat 4.2g, of which saturates 0.8g; Cholesterol 58mg; Calcium 92mg; Fibre 0.5g; Sodium 165mg.
red snapper Energy 185kcal/781kJ; Protein 39.4g; Carbohydrate 0.9g, of which sugars 0.8g; Fat 2.7g, of which saturates 0.6g; Cholesterol 74mg; Calcium 87mg; Fibre 0.1g; Sodium 168mg.

Steamed Sea Bass with Ginger

This is a delicious recipe for any whole white fish, such as sea bass or cod.

Serves 4

200ml/7fl oz/scant 1 cup coconut milk
10ml/2 tsp raw cane or muscovado (molasses) sugar
about 15ml/1 tbsp vegetable oil
2 garlic cloves, finely chopped
1 fresh red chilli, seeded and finely chopped
4cm/1½in fresh root ginger, peeled and grated
750g/1lb 10oz sea bass, gutted and skinned on one side
1 star anise, ground
1 bunch fresh basil, stalks removed
30ml/2 tbsp cashew nuts
sea salt and ground black pepper
rice and salad, to serve

1 Heat the coconut milk with the sugar in a small pan, stirring until the sugar dissolves, then remove from the heat. Heat the oil in a small frying pan and stir in the garlic, chilli and ginger. Cook until they begin to brown, then add the mixture to the coconut milk and mix well to combine.

2 Place the fish, skin side down, on a wide piece of foil and tuck up the sides to form a boat-shaped container. Using a sharp knife, cut several diagonal slashes into the flesh on the top and rub with the ground star anise. Season with salt and pepper, then spoon the coconut milk over to coat the fish.

3 Sprinkle half the basil leaves over the top of the fish and pull the foil packet almost closed. Lay the packet in a steamer. Cover the steamer, bring the water to the boil, reduce the heat and simmer for 20–25 minutes, or until just cooked.

4 Roast the cashew nuts in the frying pan, adding extra oil if necessary. Drain the nuts on kitchen paper, then grind them to crumbs. When the fish is cooked, lift it out of the foil and transfer it to a serving dish.

5 Spoon the cooking juices over, sprinkle with the cashew nut crumbs and garnish with the remaining basil leaves. Serve with rice and a salad.

Baked Sea Bass with Lemon Grass

Moist, tender sea bass is finely flavoured with a combination of aromatic ingredients in this simple claypot dish.

Serves 2–3

1 sea bass, about 675g/1½lb, cleaned and scaled
30ml/2 tbsp olive oil
2 lemon grass stalks, finely sliced
1 red onion, finely shredded
1 fresh red chilli, seeded and finely chopped
5cm/2in piece fresh root ginger, finely shredded
45ml/3 tbsp chopped fresh coriander (cilantro)
pared rind and juice of 2 limes
30ml/2 tbsp light soy sauce
salt and ground black pepper

1 Soak a fish clay pot in cold water for 20 minutes, then drain. Make four to five diagonal slashes on both sides of the fish. Repeat the slashes on one side in the opposite direction to give an attractive cross-hatched effect. Rub the sea bass inside and out with salt, pepper and 15ml/1 tbsp of the olive oil.

2 Mix the sliced lemon grass, red onion, chilli, ginger, coriander and lime rind in a bowl.

3 Place a little of the lemon grass and red onion mixture in the base of the clay pot, then lay the fish on top. Sprinkle the remaining mixture over the fish, then sprinkle over the lime juice, soy sauce and the remaining olive oil. Cover and place in an unheated oven.

4 Set the oven to 220°C/425°F/Gas 7 and cook the fish for 30–40 minutes, or until the flesh flakes easily when tested with a knife. Serve immediately.

Variation
This recipe will taste equally delicious with red or grey mullet, red snapper, salmon or tilapia. Depending on their weight, you may need to use two smaller fish rather than a single one.

sea bass w. ginger Energy 198kcal/830kJ; Protein 21.8g; Carbohydrate 6.9g, of which sugars 5.9g; Fat 9.5g, of which saturates 1.6g; Cholesterol 80mg; Calcium 177mg; Fibre 0.9g; Sodium 151mg.
sea bass w. lemon grass Energy 298kcal/1248kJ; Protein 43.7g; Carbohydrate 1.6g, of which sugars 1.1g; Fat 13g, of which saturates 1.9g; Cholesterol 180mg; Calcium 298mg; Fibre 0.3g; Sodium 156mg.

Fried Sea Bass with Leeks

Sea bass tastes sensational when cooked in this simple, sweet marinade.

Serves 4

1 sea bass, about 1.4–1.5kg/ 3–3½ lb, scaled and cleaned
8 spring onions (scallions)
60ml/4 tbsp teriyaki marinade
30ml/2 tbsp cornflour (cornstarch)
juice of 1 lemon
30ml/2 tbsp rice wine vinegar
5ml/1 tsp ground ginger
60ml/4 tbsp groundnut (peanut) oil
2 leeks, shredded
2.5cm/1in piece fresh root ginger, peeled and grated
105ml/7 tbsp fish stock
30ml/2 tbsp dry sherry
5ml/1 tsp caster (superfine) sugar
salt and ground black pepper

1 Make several diagonal slashes on either side of the sea bass, then season the fish inside and out with salt and ground black pepper. Trim the spring onions, cut them in half lengthways, then slice them diagonally into 2cm/¾in lengths. Put half of the spring onions in the cavity of the fish and reserve the rest.

2 In a shallow dish, mix together the teriyaki marinade, the cornflour, lemon juice, rice wine vinegar and ground ginger to make a smooth, runny paste. Turn the fish in the marinade to coat it thoroughly, working it into the slashes, then leave it to marinate for 20–30 minutes, turning it several times.

3 Heat a wok or frying pan that is large enough to hold the sea bass comfortably. Add the oil, then the leeks and grated ginger. Fry gently for about 5 minutes, until the leeks are tender. Remove the leeks and ginger and drain on kitchen paper.

4 Lift the sea bass out of the marinade and lower it into the hot oil. Fry over a medium heat for 2–3 minutes on each side. Stir the stock, sherry and sugar into the marinade. Season, and pour the mixture over the fish. Return the leeks, ginger and reserved spring onions to the wok. Cover and simmer for about 15 minutes, until the fish is cooked. Serve immediately.

Sea Bass with Chinese Chives

Chinese chives are widely available in oriental supermarkets but if you are unable to buy them, use half a large Spanish onion, finely sliced, instead, and common chives to garnish.

Serves 4

450g/1lb sea bass fillets
15ml/1 tbsp cornflour (cornstarch)
45ml/3 tbsp vegetable oil
175g/6oz Chinese chives
15ml/1 tbsp Chinese rice wine or dry sherry
5ml/1 tsp caster (superfine) sugar
salt and ground black pepper
Chinese chives with flowerheads, to garnish

1 Cut the fillets into large chunks and dust them lightly with cornflour, salt and pepper.

2 Heat 30ml/2 tbsp of the oil in a preheated wok. When the oil is hot, toss the chunks of fish in the wok briefly to seal, then set aside. The fish chunks will still be raw inside. Wipe out the wok with kitchen paper.

3 Cut the Chinese chives into 5cm/2in lengths and discard the flowers. Reheat the wok and add the remaining oil, then stir-fry the Chinese chives for 30 seconds.

4 Add the fish and rice wine or dry sherry, then bring to the boil and stir in the sugar. Cook, gently moving the fish pieces around in the wok to prevent sticking, until the fish is tender and just cooked through.

5 Serve hot, garnished with some flowering Chinese chives.

Variations

- *You could use halibut instead of sea bass for this recipe.*
- *Add two cloves of sliced garlic to the wok with the chopped chives for an even more fragrant dish.*

sea bass with leeks Energy 300kcal/1253kJ; Protein 31.1g; Carbohydrate 7.5g, of which sugars 6.7g; Fat 15.4g, of which saturates 2g; Cholesterol 120mg; Calcium 229mg; Fibre 2.6g; Sodium 271mg.
sea bass with chives Energy 180kcal/754kJ; Protein 23g; Carbohydrate 2.7g, of which sugars 1.7g; Fat 8.7g, of which saturates 1.1g; Cholesterol 90mg; Calcium 221mg; Fibre 0.9g; Sodium 140mg.

Fish with a Cashew Ginger Marinade

To capture the sweet, spicy flavour of this Indonesian favourite, marinated fish are wrapped in parcels before baking. When they are unwrapped at the table, their delicious aroma will make your mouth water.

Serves 4

1.2kg/2½lb sea bass or pomfret (porgy), scaled and cleaned
150g/5oz/1¼ cups raw cashew nuts
2 shallots or 1 small onion, finely chopped
1cm/½in fresh root ginger, finely chopped
1 garlic clove, crushed
1 small fresh red chilli, seeded and finely chopped
30ml/2 tbsp vegetable oil
15ml/1 tbsp shrimp paste
10ml/2 tsp sugar
30ml/2 tbsp tamarind sauce
30ml/2 tbsp tomato ketchup
juice of 2 limes
salt

1 Slash the whole fish three or four times on each side with a sharp knife. Set aside.

2 Grind the cashew nuts, shallots or onion, ginger, garlic and chilli to a fine paste in a mortar with a pestle or in a food processor. Add the vegetable oil, shrimp paste and sugar and season to taste with salt. Blend, then add the tamarind sauce, tomato ketchup and lime juice and blend again.

3 Cover both sides of the fish with the paste and set aside in the refrigerator for up to 8 hours to allow the flavours to mingle.

4 Wrap the fish in foil, securing the parcels carefully. Bake in a preheated oven at 180°C/350°F/Gas 4 for 30–35 minutes.

Cook's Tip

Also known as terasi in Indondesia and belacan or blachan in Malaysia, shrimp paste is made from salted and fermented shrimps and has an unpleasant smell which disappears during cooking. It adds an exotic aroma and flavour to Asian dishes.

Mackerel with Black Beans

Shiitake mushrooms, ginger and salted black beans are perfect partners for robustly flavoured mackerel fillets.

Serves 4

20 dried shiitake mushrooms
15ml/1 tbsp finely julienned fresh root ginger
3 star anise
8 x 115g/4oz mackerel fillets
45ml/3 tbsp dark soy sauce
15ml/1 tbsp Chinese rice wine
15ml/1 tbsp salted black beans
6 spring onions (scallions), finely shredded
30ml/2 tbsp sunflower oil
5ml/1 tsp sesame oil
4 garlic cloves, very thinly sliced
sliced cucumber and steamed basmati rice, to serve

1 Place the dried mushrooms in a large bowl and cover with boiling water. Soak for 20 minutes. Drain, reserving the soaking liquid, discard the stems and slice the caps thinly.

2 Place a trivet or a steamer rack in a large wok and pour in 5cm/2in of the mushroom liquid (top up with water if necessary). Add half the ginger and the star anise.

3 Divide the mackerel between two lightly oiled heatproof plates, skin side up. Cut three diagonal slits in each one. Insert the remaining ginger strips and sprinkle over the mushrooms. Bring the liquid to the boil and put one of the plates on the trivet.

4 Cover the wok, reduce the heat and steam for about 10–12 minutes, or until the mackerel is cooked. Repeat with the second plate of fish. Put all the fish on a platter and keep warm.

5 Ladle 105ml/7 tbsp of the steaming liquid from the wok into a pan with the soy sauce, wine and black beans. Place over a gentle heat and bring to a simmer. Spoon over the fish and sprinkle over the spring onions.

6 Heat the oils and stir-fry garlic for a few minutes until lightly golden. Pour over the fish and serve with sliced cucumber and steamed basmati rice.

fish with marinade Energy 452kcal/1886kJ; Protein 43.9g; Carbohydrate 10.4g, of which sugars 5g; Fat 26.3g, of which saturates 4.8g; Cholesterol 159mg; Calcium 290mg; Fibre 1.5g; Sodium 515mg.
mackerel w. beans Energy 693kcal/2872kJ; Protein 45.5g; Carbohydrate 1.9g, of which sugars 0.5g; Fat 55.9g, of which saturates 10.4g; Cholesterol 128mg; Calcium 35mg; Fibre 0.6g; Sodium 152mg.

Sour Carp Wraps

Carp is popular in China and South-east Asia. For a slightly simpler version of this dish, toss the cooked fish in the herbs and serve it with noodles or boiled rice and a salad.

Serves 4

500g/1¼lb carp fillets, each cut into 3 or 4 pieces
30ml/2 tbsp sesame oil or vegetable oil
10ml/2 tsp ground turmeric
1 small bunch each fresh coriander (cilantro) and basil, stalks removed
20 lettuce leaves or rice wrappers
fish sauce or other dipping sauce, to serve

For the marinade

30ml/2 tbsp tamarind paste
15ml/1 tbsp soy sauce
juice of 1 lime
1 fresh green or red chilli, finely chopped
2.5cm/1in galangal root, peeled and grated
a few sprigs of fresh coriander (cilantro) leaves, finely chopped

1 Prepare the marinade by mixing together all the marinade ingredients in a bowl. Toss the fish pieces into the mixture, cover with clear film (plastic wrap) and chill in the refrigerator for at least 6 hours, or overnight.

2 Lift the pieces of fish out of the marinade and lay them on a plate. Heat a wok or heavy pan, add the oil and stir in the turmeric. Working quickly, so that the turmeric doesn't burn, add the fish pieces, gently moving them around the wok for 2–3 minutes.

3 Add any remaining marinade to the pan and cook for a further 2–3 minutes, or until the pieces of fish are cooked.

4 To serve, divide the fish among four plates, sprinkle with the coriander and basil, and add some of the lettuce leaves or rice wrappers and a small bowl of dipping sauce to each serving. To eat, tear off a bitesize piece of fish, place it on a wrapper with a few herb leaves, fold it up into a roll, then dip it into the sauce.

Clay Pot Catfish

Wonderfully easy and tasty, this is a classic clay pot dish. Clay pots are regularly used for cooking and they enhance both the look and taste of this traditional favourite. However, you can use any heavy pot or pan. Serve with chunks of bread to mop up the caramelized, smoky sauce at the bottom of the pot.

Serves 4

30ml/2 tbsp sugar
15ml/1 tbsp sesame oil or vegetable oil
2 garlic cloves, crushed
45ml/3 tbsp fish sauce
350g/12oz catfish fillets, cut diagonally into 2 or 3 pieces
4 spring onions (scallions), cut into bitesize pieces
ground black pepper
chopped fresh coriander (cilantro), to garnish
fresh bread, to serve

1 Place the sugar in a clay pot or heavy pan, and add 15ml/1 tbsp water to wet it. Heat the sugar until it begins to turn golden brown, then add the oil and crushed garlic.

2 Stir the fish sauce into the caramel mixture and add 120ml/4fl oz/½ cup boiling water, then toss in the catfish pieces, making sure they are well coated with the sauce. Cover the pot, reduce the heat and simmer for about 5 minutes.

3 Remove the lid, season with pepper and gently stir in the spring onions. Simmer for 3–4 minutes to thicken the sauce.

4 Garnish with fresh coriander, and serve straight from the pot with chunks of fresh bread.

Cook's Tip
When using a traditional clay pot, always use a low to medium heat and heat the pot slowly, otherwise there is a risk of cracking it. They are designed to be used over a low flame, so if using an electric stove, use a heat diffuser.

sour carp wraps Energy 205kcal/856kJ; Protein 23.1g; Carbohydrate 1.6g, of which sugars 1.5g; Fat 11.9g, of which saturates 1.8g; Cholesterol 84mg; Calcium 102mg; Fibre 1.1g; Sodium 327mg.
clay pot catfish Energy 128kcal/537kJ; Protein 16.4g; Carbohydrate 8.3g, of which sugars 8.3g; Fat 3.4g, of which saturates 0.4g; Cholesterol 40mg; Calcium 18mg; Fibre 0.2g; Sodium 54mg.

Grey Mullet with Pork

This unusual combination of fish and meat makes a spectacular main dish.

Serves 4

1 grey mullet or snapper, about 900g/2lb, gutted and cleaned
50g/2oz lean pork
3 dried Chinese mushrooms, soaked in hot water until soft
2.5ml/½ tsp cornflour (cornstarch)
30ml/2 tbsp light soy sauce
15ml/1 tbsp vegetable oil
15ml/1 tbsp finely shredded fresh root ginger
15ml/1 tbsp shredded spring onion (scallion)
salt and ground black pepper
sliced spring onion (scallion), to garnish
rice, to serve

1 Make four diagonal cuts on either side of the fish and rub with a little salt; place the fish on a heatproof serving dish.

2 Cut the pork into thin strips. Place in a bowl. Drain the soaked mushrooms, remove and discard the stalks and slice the caps thinly. Add the mushrooms to the pork, with the cornflour and half the soy sauce. Stir in 5ml/1 tsp of the oil and a little black pepper. Arrange the pork mixture along the length of the fish. Sprinkle the ginger shreds over the top.

3 Cover the fish loosely with foil. Have ready a large pan or roasting pan, which is big enough to fit the heatproof dish inside it on a metal trivet. Pour in boiling water to a depth of 5cm/2in. Place the dish in the pan or roasting pan, cover and steam over a high heat for 15 minutes.

4 Test the fish by pressing the flesh gently. If it comes away from the bone with a slight resistance, the fish is cooked. Carefully pour away any excess liquid from the dish.

5 Heat the remaining oil in a small pan. When it is hot, fry the spring onion for a few seconds, then pour it over the fish, taking great care as it will splatter. Drizzle with the remaining soy sauce, garnish with sliced spring onion and serve with rice.

Skate Wings with Wasabi

Whole skate wings, dipped in a tempura batter and deep-fried until crisp and golden, look stunning.

Serves 4

4 x 250g/9oz skate wings
65g/2½oz/9 tbsp cornflour (cornstarch)
65g/2½oz/9 tbsp plain (all-purpose) flour
5ml/1 tsp salt
5ml/1 tsp Chinese five-spice powder
15ml/1 tbsp sesame seeds
200ml/7fl oz/scant 1 cup ice-cold soda water (club soda)
sunflower oil, for frying

For the mayonnaise

200ml/7fl oz/scant 1 cup mayonnaise
15ml/1 tbsp light soy sauce
finely grated rind and juice of 1 lime
5ml/1 tsp wasabi
15ml/1 tbsp finely chopped spring onion (scallion)

1 Using kitchen scissors, trim away the frill from the edges of the skate wings and discard. Set the fish aside.

2 In a large mixing bowl combine the cornflour, plain flour, salt, five-spice powder and sesame seeds. Gradually pour in the soda water and stir to mix. (It will be quite lumpy.)

3 Heat the oil for deep-frying. One at a time, dip the skate wings in the batter, then lower them carefully into the hot oil and deep-fry for 4–5 minutes, until the skate is fully cooked and crispy. Drain on kitchen paper. Set aside and keep warm.

4 Meanwhile, mix together all the mayonnaise ingredients and divide among four small bowls. Serve immediately with the skate wings.

Cook's Tip

Look for packets of tempura batter mix at health food shops and Asian markets. It doesn't take long to make your own batter, but sometimes seconds count.

grey mullet with pork Energy 228kcal/960kJ; Protein 34.7g; Carbohydrate 0.7g, of which sugars 0.6g; Fat 9.8g, of which saturates 2.3g; Cholesterol 62mg; Calcium 46mg; Fibre 0.1g; Sodium 647mg.
skate wings w. wasabi Energy 705kcal/2921kJ; Protein 31.9g; Carbohydrate 11.7g, of which sugars 1.2g; Fat 59.3g, of which saturates 11g; Cholesterol 38mg; Calcium 112mg; Fibre 0.5g; Sodium 792mg.

Grilled Swordfish Steaks

Crisp grilled asparagus with a shoyu and sake coating is an excellent accompaniment for marinated game fish.

Serves 4
4 x 175g/6oz swordfish steaks
2.5ml/½ tsp salt
300g/11oz shiro miso
45ml/3 tbsp sake

For the asparagus
25ml/1½ tbsp shoyu
25ml/1½ tbsp sake
8 asparagus spears, the hard ends discarded, each spear cut into three

1 Place the swordfish in a shallow container. Sprinkle with the salt on both sides and leave for 2 hours. Drain and wipe the fish with kitchen paper.

2 Mix the miso and sake, then spread half across the bottom of the cleaned container. Cover with a sheet of muslin (cheesecloth) the size of a dish towel, folded in half, then open the fold.

3 Place the swordfish steaks, side by side, on top, and cover with the muslin. Spread the rest of the miso mixture on the muslin. Make sure the muslin is touching the fish. Marinate for 2 days in the coolest part of the refrigerator.

4 Preheat the grill (broiler) to medium. Oil the wire rack and grill (broil) the fish slowly for about 8 minutes on each side, turning every 2 minutes. If the steaks are thin, check every time you turn the fish to see if they are ready.

5 Meanwhile, mix the shoyu and sake in a small bowl. Grill the asparagus for 2 minutes on each side, then dip into the shoyu and sake. Return to the grill for 2 minutes more on each side. Dip into the sauce again and set aside.

6 Serve the swordfish steaks hot on four individual serving plates that have been warmed in the oven. Garnish with the drained, grilled asparagus.

Spicy Pan-seared Tuna

This popular dish can be made with many types of thick-fleshed fish. Tuna is particularly suitable because it is delicious pan-seared and served a little rare.

Serves 4
1 small cucumber
10ml/2 tsp sesame oil
2 garlic cloves, crushed
4 tuna steaks

For the dressing
4cm/1½in fresh root ginger, peeled and roughly chopped
1 garlic clove, roughly chopped
2 fresh green chillies, seeded and roughly chopped
45ml/3 tbsp raw cane sugar
45ml/3 tbsp fish sauce
juice of 1 lime
60ml/4 tbsp water

1 To make the dressing, grind the ginger, garlic and chillies to a pulp with the sugar, using a mortar and pestle. Stir in the fish sauce, lime juice and water, and mix well. Leave the dressing to stand for 15 minutes.

2 Cut the cucumber in half lengthways and remove the seeds. Cut the flesh into long, thin strips. Toss the cucumber in the dressing and leave to soak for at least 15 minutes.

3 Wipe a heavy pan with the oil and rub the garlic around it. Heat the pan and add the tuna steaks. Sear for a few minutes on both sides, so that the outside is slightly charred but the inside is still rare. Lift the steaks on to a warm serving dish.

4 Using tongs or chopsticks, lift the cucumber strips out of the dressing and arrange them around the steaks. Drizzle the dressing over the tuna, and serve immediately.

Cook's Tip
Fresh root ginger is a wonderful ingredient. Thin slices can be added to boiling water to make a refreshing tea, and grated ginger makes a great addition to curries and stir-fries. Ginger freezes successfully and can be shaved or grated from frozen.

grilled swordfish Energy 240kcal/1009kJ; Protein 37g; Carbohydrate 2.8g, of which sugars 2.5g; Fat 8.2g, of which saturates 1.8g; Cholesterol 81mg; Calcium 18mg; Fibre 0.3g; Sodium 2269mg.
spicy pan-seared tuna Energy 176kcal/731kJ; Protein 12.3g; Carbohydrate 1.6g, of which sugars 1.6g; Fat 13.4g, of which saturates 2.2g; Cholesterol 14mg; Calcium 18mg; Fibre 0.3g; Sodium 25mg.

Sweet & Sour Fish

When fish such as red mullet or snapper is cooked in this way the skin becomes crisp, while the flesh stays moist and juicy.

Serves 4–6

1 large or 2 medium fish, such as snapper or mullet, heads removed
20ml/4 tsp cornflour (cornstarch)
120ml/4fl oz/½ cup vegetable oil
15ml/1 tbsp chopped garlic
15ml/1 tbsp chopped fresh root ginger
30ml/2 tbsp chopped shallots
225g/8oz cherry tomatoes
30ml/2 tbsp red wine vinegar
30ml/2 tbsp sugar
30ml/2 tbsp tomato ketchup
15ml/1 tbsp fish sauce
45ml/3 tbsp water
salt and ground black pepper
coriander (cilantro) leaves and shredded spring onions (scallions), to garnish

1 Rinse and dry the fish. Score the skin diagonally on both sides, then coat the fish lightly all over with 15ml/3 tsp of the cornflour. Shake off any excess.

2 Heat the oil in a wok or large frying pan. Add the fish and cook over a medium heat for 6–7 minutes. Turn the fish over and cook for 6–7 minutes more, until it is crisp and brown.

3 Remove the fish and place on a large platter. Pour off all but 30ml/2 tbsp of the oil from the wok or pan and reheat. Add the garlic, ginger and shallots and cook over a medium heat, stirring occasionally, for about 4 minutes, until golden.

4 Add the cherry tomatoes and cook until they burst open. Stir in the vinegar, sugar, tomato ketchup and fish sauce. Lower the heat and simmer gently for 1–2 minutes, then taste and adjust the seasoning.

5 In a cup, mix the remaining 5ml/1 tsp cornflour to a paste with the water. Stir into the sauce. Heat, stirring, until it thickens. Pour the sauce over the fish, garnish with coriander leaves and shredded spring onions and serve.

Chinese-spiced Fish Fillets

Coated with spicy breadcrumbs, this is the Chinese version of European fried fish.

Serves 4

65g/2½oz/generous ½ cup plain (all-purpose) flour
5ml/1 tsp Chinese five-spice powder
8 skinless fillets of fish, such as plaice or lemon sole, about 800g/1¾lb in total
1 egg, lightly beaten
40–50g/1½–2oz/scant 1 cup fine fresh breadcrumbs
groundnut (peanut) oil, for frying
25g/1oz/2 tbsp butter
4 spring onions (scallions), cut diagonally into thin slices
350g/12oz tomatoes, seeded and diced
30ml/2 tbsp soy sauce
salt and ground black pepper
red (bell) pepper strips and chives, to garnish

1 Sift the flour together with the Chinese five-spice powder and salt and pepper to taste on to a plate. Dip the fish fillets first in the seasoned flour, then in the beaten egg and finally in breadcrumbs.

2 Pour the groundnut oil into a large frying pan to a depth of 1cm/½in. Heat until it is very hot and starting to sizzle. Add the coated fillets, a few at a time, and fry for 2–3 minutes on each side, depending on their thickness, until just cooked and golden brown. Do not overcrowd the pan, or the temperature of the oil will drop and the fish will absorb too much of it and become greasy.

3 Drain the cooked fillets on kitchen paper, then transfer to serving plates and keep warm. Pour off all the oil from the frying pan, discarding it or reserving it for use in another dish, and wipe the pan out with kitchen paper.

4 Add the butter to the pan and cook the spring onions and tomatoes for 1 minute, then add the soy sauce.

5 Spoon the tomato mixture over the fish, garnish with red pepper strips and chives and serve.

sweet & sour fish Energy 233kcal/969kJ; Protein 21.9g; Carbohydrate 6.3g, of which sugars 3g; Fat 13.5g, of which saturates 1.6g; Cholesterol 54mg; Calcium 16mg; Fibre 0.5g; Sodium 335mg.
Chinese fish fillets Energy 433kcal/1820kJ; Protein 38.7g; Carbohydrate 24.1g, of which sugars 4.1g; Fat 21g, of which saturates 5.5g; Cholesterol 145mg; Calcium 145mg; Fibre 1.8g; Sodium 915mg.

Seafood Laksa

A laksa is a Malaysian stew of fish, poultry, meat or vegetables with noodles.

Serves 4–5

3 medium-hot fresh red chillies, seeded
4–5 garlic cloves
5ml/1 tsp mild paprika
10ml/2 tsp shrimp paste
25ml/1½ tbsp chopped fresh root ginger
250g/9oz small red shallots
25g/1oz fresh coriander (cilantro)
45ml/3 tbsp groundnut (peanut) oil
5ml/1 tsp fennel seeds, crushed
2 fennel bulbs, cut into thin wedges
600ml/1 pint/2½ cups fish stock
450ml/¾ pint/scant 2 cups coconut milk
juice of 1–2 limes
30–45ml/2–3 tbsp fish sauce
450g/1lb firm white fish fillet, cut into chunks
20 large raw prawns (shrimp), shelled and deveined
small bunch of basil
300g/11oz thin vermicelli rice noodles, cooked
2 spring onions (scallions), sliced

1 Process the chillies, garlic, paprika, shrimp paste, ginger and two shallots to a paste in a food processor. Set aside the coriander leaves. Add the stems to the paste with 15ml/1 tbsp oil and process again until fairly smooth.

2 Cook the remaining shallots, the fennel seeds and fennel wedges in the remaining oil in a large pan. When lightly browned, add 45ml/3 tbsp of the paste and stir-fry for about 2 minutes. Pour in the fish stock and simmer for 8–10 minutes.

3 Add the coconut milk, the juice of 1 lime and 30ml/2 tbsp of the fish sauce. Bring to a simmer and adjust the flavouring.

4 Add the chunks of fish. Cook for 2–3 minutes, then add the prawns and cook until they turn pink. Chop most of the basil and add to the pan with chopped coriander leaves.

5 Divide the noodles among four or five wide bowls, then ladle in the stew. Sprinkle with the sliced spring onions and whole basil leaves. Serve immediately.

Sizzling Chinese Steamed Fish

Steamed whole fish is very popular in China, and the wok is used as a steamer. In this recipe the fish is flavoured with garlic, ginger and spring onions cooked in sizzling hot oil.

Serves 4

4 rainbow trout, about 250g/9oz each
1.5ml/¼ tsp salt
2.5ml/½ tsp sugar
2 garlic cloves, finely chopped
15ml/1 tbsp finely diced fresh root ginger
5 spring onions (scallions), cut into 5cm/2in lengths and finely shredded
60ml/4 tbsp groundnut (peanut) oil
5ml/1 tsp sesame oil
45ml/3 tbsp light soy sauce
thread egg noodles and stir-fried vegetables, to serve

1 Make three diagonal slits on both sides of each fish and lay them on a heatproof plate. Place a small rack or trivet in a wok half-filled with water, cover and heat until just simmering.

2 Sprinkle the fish with the salt, sugar, garlic and ginger. Place the plate securely on the rack or trivet and cover. Steam gently for about 10–12 minutes, or until the flesh has turned pale pink and feels quite firm.

3 Turn off the heat, remove the lid and scatter the spring onions over the fish. Replace the lid.

4 Heat the groundnut and sesame oils in a small pan over a high heat until just smoking, then quickly pour a quarter over the spring onions on each of the fish – the shredded onions will sizzle and cook in the hot oil. Sprinkle the soy sauce over the top. Serve the fish and juices immediately with boiled noodles and stir-fried vegetables.

Cook's Tip

For the stir-fried vegetables, choose a variety of different colours and textures such as courgettes (zucchini) red, yellow, orange and green (bell) peppers, carrots and mushrooms.

seafood laksa Energy 524kcal/2199kJ; Protein 43.1g; Carbohydrate 65.1g, of which sugars 6.3g; Fat 10.1g, of which saturates 2g; Cholesterol 233mg; Calcium 162mg; Fibre 1.9g; Sodium 356mg.
Chinese steamed fish Energy 245kcal/1030kJ; Protein 36.9g; Carbohydrate 1.4g, of which sugars 1.3g; Fat 9.7g, of which saturates 2g; Cholesterol 149mg; Calcium 66mg; Fibre 0.3g; Sodium 790mg.

Classic Tandoori Chicken

This is probably the most famous of all the Indian dishes. Marinate the chicken well and cook in an extremely hot oven for a clay-oven-baked taste. If you want authentic charred spots on the chicken, place the dish under a hot grill for a few minutes after baking.

Serves 4–6

1.5kg/3lb oven-ready chicken
250ml/8fl oz/1 cup natural (plain) yogurt, beaten
60ml/4 tbsp tandoori masala paste
75g/3oz/6 tbsp ghee
salt
salad leaves, to serve
lemon twist and onion slices, to garnish

1 Using a sharp knife or scissors, remove the skin from the chicken and trim off any excess fat. Using a fork, beat the flesh at random.

2 Cut the chicken in half down the centre and through the breast. Cut each piece in half again. Make a few deep gashes diagonally into the flesh. Mix the yogurt with the masala paste and salt. Spread the chicken evenly with the yogurt mixture, spreading some into the gashes. Leave for at least 2 hours, but preferably overnight.

3 Preheat the oven to maximum heat. Place the chicken quarters on a wire rack in a deep baking tray. Spread the chicken with any excess marinade, but reserve a little for basting halfway through cooking time.

4 Melt the ghee and pour over the chicken to seal the surface. This helps to keep the centre moist during the roasting period. Cook in the preheated oven for 10 minutes, then remove, leaving the oven on.

5 Baste the chicken pieces with the remaining marinade. Return to the oven and switch off the heat. Leave the chicken in the oven for about 15–20 minutes without opening the door. Serve on a bed of salad leaves and garnish with the lemon twist and onion slices.

Spicy Tandoori Chicken

A delicious and popular Indian–Pakistani chicken dish which is traditionally cooked in a clay oven called a tandoor, this is extremely popular in the West and appears on the majority of restaurant menus.

Serves 4

4 chicken quarters, skinned
175ml/6fl oz/¾ cup natural (plain) low-fat yogurt
5ml/1 tsp garam masala
5ml/1 tsp grated fresh root ginger
5ml/1 tsp crushed garlic
7.5ml/1½ tsp chilli powder
1.5ml/¼ tsp ground turmeric
5ml/1 tsp ground coriander
15ml/1 tbsp lemon juice
5ml/1 tsp salt
few drops of red food colouring
15ml/1 tbsp oil
mixed salad leaves, to serve
lime wedges, to garnish

1 Rinse and pat dry the chicken quarters. Make two deep slits in the flesh of each piece, place in a dish and set aside.

2 Mix together the yogurt, garam masala, ginger, garlic, chilli powder, turmeric, coriander, lemon juice, salt, red food colouring and oil, and beat so that all the ingredients are well combined.

3 Cover the chicken quarters with the spice mixture, cover and leave to marinate for about 3 hours.

4 Preheat the oven to 240°C/475°F/Gas 9. Transfer the chicken pieces to an ovenproof dish.

5 Bake the chicken in the oven for 20–25 minutes or until the chicken is cooked right through and evenly browned on top.

6 Remove from the oven, arrange on salad leaves on a serving dish and garnish with lime wedges.

Cook's Tip
The traditional bright red colour is derived from food colouring. This is only optional and may be omitted if you prefer.

tandoori chicken Energy 610kcal/2530kJ; Protein 48.3g; Carbohydrate 3.8g, of which sugars 3.8g; Fat 44.6g, of which saturates 12.2g; Cholesterol 241mg; Calcium 114mg; Fibre 0g; Sodium 229mg.
spicy tandoori chicken Energy 340kcal/1425kJ; Protein 25.3g; Carbohydrate 44.6g, of which sugars 2.6g; Fat 6.6g, of which saturates 0.6g; Cholesterol 60mg; Calcium 31mg; Fibre 0.3g; Sodium 475mg.

Tandoori Chicken Kebabs

This dish originates from the plains of the Punjab at the foot of the Himalayas. Allow the chicken to marinate for about three hours to absorb the tandoori flavourings.

Serves 4

4 skinned chicken breast fillets, about 175g/6oz each
15ml/1 tbsp lemon juice
45ml/3 tbsp tandoori paste
45ml/3 tbsp natural (plain) low-fat yogurt
1 garlic clove, crushed
30ml/2 tbsp chopped fresh coriander (cilantro)
salt and ground black pepper
1 small onion, cut into wedges and separated into layers
a little oil, for brushing
fresh coriander sprigs, to garnish
pilau rice and naan bread, to serve

1 Chop the chicken breast fillets into 2.5cm/1in cubes, place in a mixing bowl and add the lemon juice, tandoori paste, yogurt, garlic, chopped coriander and seasoning. Cover and leave the chicken to marinate in the refrigerator for 2–3 hours.

2 Preheat the grill (broiler) to high. Thread alternate pieces of marinated chicken and onion on to four skewers.

3 Brush the onions with a little oil, place on a grill rack and cook under a high heat for 10–12 minutes, or until the chicken is thoroughly cooked, turning once midway through. Garnish the kebabs with fresh coriander sprigs and serve with pilau rice and naan bread.

Cook's Tip
Use chopped, boned and skinned chicken thighs, or turkey breasts, for a tasty and less expensive alternative.

Stuffed Roast Chicken

At one time this dish was cooked only in royal palaces and the ingredients varied according to individual chefs. The saffron and the rich stuffing make it a truly royal dish.

Serves 4–6

1 sachet saffron powder
2.5ml/½ tsp ground nutmeg
15ml/1 tbsp warm milk
1.3kg/3lb whole chicken
75g/3oz/6 tbsp ghee
75ml/5 tbsp hot water

For the stuffing
3 medium onions, finely chopped
2 fresh green chillies, chopped
50g/2oz/⅓ cup sultanas (golden raisins)
50g/2oz/½ cup ground almonds
50g/2oz dried apricots, soaked until soft
3 hard-boiled (hard-cooked) eggs, coarsely chopped
salt

For the masala
4 spring onions (scallions), chopped
2 cloves garlic, crushed
5ml/1 tsp five-spice powder
4–6 green cardamom pods
2.5ml/½ tsp ground turmeric
5ml/1 tsp ground black pepper
30ml/2 tbsp natural (plain) yogurt
50g/2oz/1 cup desiccated (dry unsweetened shredded) coconut, toasted

1 Mix together the saffron, nutmeg and milk. Use to brush the inside of the chicken and over the skin. Heat 50g/2oz/4 tbsp of the ghee in a large frying pan and fry the chicken on all sides to seal it. Remove and keep warm.

2 To make the stuffing, in the same ghee, fry the onions, chillies, and sultanas for 2–3 minutes. Allow to cool and add the ground almonds, apricots, chopped eggs and salt. Use to stuff the chicken.

3 Heat the remaining ghee in a large, heavy pan and gently fry all the masala ingredients except the coconut for 2–3 minutes. Add the water. Place the chicken on the bed of masala, cover the pan and cook until the chicken is tender. Remove the chicken from the pan. Cook the liquid to reduce excess fluids in the masala. When the mixture thickens, pour over the chicken. Sprinkle with toasted coconut and serve hot.

tandoori kebabs Energy 207kcal/871kJ; Protein 36.9g; Carbohydrate 3.2g, of which sugars 0.9g; Fat 5.2g, of which saturates 0.9g; Cholesterol 105mg; Calcium 59mg; Fibre 1.9g; Sodium 124mg.
stuffed chicken Energy 823kcal/3420kJ; Protein 55.7g; Carbohydrate 21.1g, of which sugars 19.1g; Fat 57.9g, of which saturates 19.7g; Cholesterol 383mg; Calcium 113mg; Fibre 4.9g; Sodium 252mg.

Jeera Chicken

An aromatic dish with a delicious, distinctive taste of cumin. Serve simply with a cooling cucumber raita.

Serves 4

45ml/3 tbsp cumin seeds
15ml/1 tbsp oil
2.5ml/½ tsp black peppercorns
4 green cardamom pods
2 fresh green chillies, finely chopped
2 garlic cloves, crushed
2.5cm/1in piece fresh root ginger, grated
5ml/1 tsp ground coriander
10ml/2 tsp ground cumin
2.5ml/½ tsp salt
8 chicken pieces, skinned
5ml/1 tsp garam masala
fresh coriander (cilantro) and chilli powder, to garnish
cucumber raita, to serve

1 Dry-roast 15ml/1 tbsp of the cumin seeds for 5 minutes and then set aside.

2 Heat the oil in a large, heavy pan or wok and fry the remaining cumin seeds, black peppercorns and cardamoms for about 2–3 minutes.

3 Add the chillies, garlic and ginger and fry for about 2 minutes.

4 Add the ground coriander, ground cumin and salt. Stir well, then cook for a further 2–3 minutes.

5 Add the chicken and stir to coat the pieces in the sauce. Cover with a lid and simmer for 20–25 minutes.

6 Add the garam masala and reserved toasted cumin seeds and cook for a further 5 minutes. Garnish with fresh coriander and chilli powder and serve with cucumber raita.

Cook's Tip
Dry-roast the cumin seeds in a small, heavy frying pan over a medium heat, stirring them until they turn a few shades darker and give off a wonderful roasted aroma.

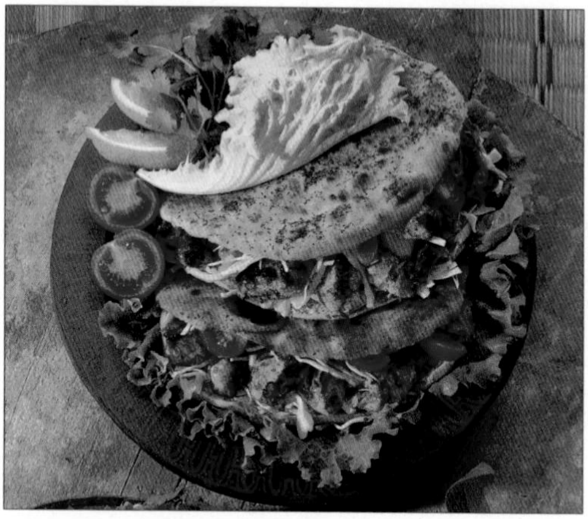

Chicken Naan Pockets

This easy dish is ideal for a light snack lunch or supper. If you do not have time to make your own naan breads, use the ready-baked naans available in most of today's supermarkets and Asian stores.

Serves 4

4 small naan, about 90g/3½oz each
45ml/3 tbsp natural (plain) low-fat yogurt
7.5ml/1½ tsp garam masala
5ml/1 tsp chilli powder
5ml/1 tsp salt
45ml/3 tbsp lemon juice
15ml/1 tbsp chopped fresh coriander (cilantro)
1 fresh green chilli, chopped
450g/1lb skinned boneless chicken, cubed
8 onion rings
2 tomatoes, quartered
½ white cabbage, shredded

For the garnish
mixed salad leaves
2 small tomatoes, halved
lemon wedges
fresh coriander (cilantro)

1 Cut into the middle of each naan to make a pocket, then set them aside.

2 Mix together the yogurt, garam masala, chilli powder, salt, lemon juice, fresh coriander and chopped green chilli.

3 Pour the marinade over the chicken, cover and leave to marinate for about 1 hour.

4 Preheat the grill (broiler) to very hot, then lower the heat to medium. Put the chicken pieces in a pan or flameproof dish lined with foil.

5 Grill (broil) for 15–20 minutes until tender and fully cooked, turning the chicken twice.

6 Remove from the heat and fill each naan with the chicken and then with the onion rings, tomatoes and cabbage. Serve garnished with mixed salad leaves, tomato halves, lemon wedges and coriander.

jeera chicken Energy 259kcal/1090kJ; Protein 49.1g; Carbohydrate 2.6g, of which sugars 0g; Fat 5.9g, of which saturates 1.1g; Cholesterol 140mg; Calcium 24mg; Fibre 0g; Sodium 123mg.
naan pockets Energy 410kcal/1733kJ; Protein 35.8g; Carbohydrate 51.3g, of which sugars 8.5g; Fat 8.2g, of which saturates 1.3g; Cholesterol 83mg; Calcium 227mg; Fibre 3.6g; Sodium 629mg.

Goan Chicken Curry

Coconut in all its forms is widely used to enrich Goan cuisine.

Serves 4

75g/3oz/1 cup desiccated (dry unsweetened shredded) coconut
30ml/2 tbsp vegetable oil
2.5ml/½ tsp cumin seeds
4 black peppercorns
15ml/1 tbsp fennel seeds
15ml/1 tbsp coriander seeds
2 onions, finely chopped
2.5ml/½ tsp salt
8 small chicken pieces, such as thighs and drumsticks, skinned
fresh coriander (cilantro) sprigs and lemon wedges, to garnish

1 Put the desiccated coconut in a bowl with 45ml/3 tbsp water. Leave to soak for 15 minutes.

2 Heat 15ml/1 tbsp of the oil in a karahi, wok or large pan and fry the cumin seeds, peppercorns, fennel and coriander seeds over a low heat for 3–4 minutes until they begin to splutter.

3 Add the finely chopped onions and fry for about 5 minutes without browning, stirring occasionally, until the onion has softened and turned opaque.

4 Stir in the coconut, along with the soaking water and salt, and continue to fry for a further 5 minutes, stirring occasionally to prevent the mixture from sticking to the pan.

5 Put the coconut mixture into a food processor or blender and process to form a coarse paste. Spoon into a bowl and set aside until required.

6 Heat the remaining oil and fry the chicken for 10 minutes. Add the coconut paste and cook over a low heat for 15–20 minutes, or until the coconut mixture is golden brown and the chicken is tender.

7 Transfer the curry to a warmed serving plate and garnish with sprigs of fresh coriander and lemon wedges. Mint and Coconut Chutney (see p447), rice or lentils make good accompaniments.

Chicken Dopiaza

Dopiaza translates literally as 'two onions' and describes this chicken dish in which two types of onion – large and small – are used at different stages.

Serves 4

30ml/2 tbsp oil
8 small onions, halved
2 bay leaves
8 green cardamom pods
4 cloves
3 dried red chillies
8 black peppercorns
2 medium onions, finely chopped
2 garlic cloves, crushed
2.5cm/1in piece fresh root ginger, finely chopped
5ml/1 tsp ground coriander
5ml/1 tsp ground cumin
2.5ml/½ tsp ground turmeric
5ml/1 tsp chilli powder
2.5ml/½ tsp salt
4 tomatoes, peeled and finely chopped
120ml/4fl oz/½ cup water
8 chicken pieces, such as thighs and drumsticks, skinned
plain rice, to serve

1 Heat half the oil in a wok or large heavy pan and fry the small onions for 10 minutes, or until golden brown. Remove and set aside.

2 Add the remaining oil and fry the bay leaves, cardamoms, cloves, chillies and peppercorns for 2 minutes. Add the medium onions, garlic and ginger and fry for 5 minutes. Stir in the ground spices, chilli powder and salt and cook for 2 minutes.

3 Add the tomatoes and water and simmer for 5 minutes until the sauce thickens. Add the chicken and cook for 15 minutes.

4 Add the reserved small onions, then cover and cook for a further 10 minutes, or until the chicken is cooked through. Spoon the mixture on to a serving dish or individual plates. Serve with plain boiled rice.

Cook's Tip
Soak the small onions in boiling water for 2–3 minutes to make them easier to peel.

Goan curry Energy 353kcal/1472kJ; Protein 33.3g; Carbohydrate 7.1g, of which sugars 5.4g; Fat 21.5g, of which saturates 11.9g; Cholesterol 158mg; Calcium 34mg; Fibre 3.6g; Sodium 143mg.
dopiaza Energy 331kcal/1391kJ; Protein 44.7g; Carbohydrate 9.8g, of which sugars 4.8g; Fat 13.1g, of which saturates 2.6g; Cholesterol 210mg; Calcium 51mg; Fibre 1.4g; Sodium 194mg.

Chicken Dhansak

Dhansak curries originally came from Iran with the Parsee community. The curries traditionally include lentils, which make the dish substantial and flavoursome.

Serves 4

75g/3oz/⅓ cup green lentils
475ml/16fl oz/2 cups chicken stock
15ml/1 tbsp oil
5ml/1 tsp cumin seeds
2 curry leaves
1 onion, finely chopped
2.5cm/1in piece fresh root ginger, chopped
1 fresh green chilli, finely chopped
5ml/1 tsp ground cumin
5ml/1 tsp ground coriander
1.5ml/¼ tsp salt
1.5ml/¼ tsp chilli powder
400g/14oz can chopped tomatoes
8 chicken pieces, skinned
90ml/6 tbsp chopped fresh coriander (cilantro)
5ml/1 tsp garam masala
boiled plain and yellow rice, to serve

1 Rinse the lentils under cold running water. Put into a pan with the stock. Bring to the boil, cover and simmer for about 15–20 minutes. Put the lentils and stock to one side.

2 Heat the oil in a large, heavy pan and fry the cumin seeds and curry leaves for 2 minutes. Add the onion, ginger and chilli and fry for about 5 minutes. Stir in the cumin, ground coriander, salt and chilli powder with 30ml/2 tbsp water.

3 Add the tomatoes and the chicken pieces to the spices. Cover and cook for 10–15 minutes.

4 Add the lentils and stock, half the chopped fresh coriander and the garam masala. Cook for a further 10 minutes or until the chicken is tender. Garnish with the remaining fresh coriander and serve with spiced plain and yellow rice.

Cook's Tip

Before cooking green lentils, always pick them over and remove any small sticks or stones that might be hidden.

Hot Chilli Chicken

Not for the faint-hearted, this fiery hot curry is made with a spicy chilli masala paste.

Serves 4

30ml/2 tbsp tomato purée (paste)
2 garlic cloves, roughly chopped
2 fresh green chillies, roughly chopped
5 dried red chillies
2.5ml/½ tsp salt
1.5ml/¼ tsp sugar
5ml/1 tsp chilli powder
2.5ml/½ tsp paprika
15ml/1 tbsp curry paste
15ml/1 tbsp oil
2.5ml/½ tsp cumin seeds
1 onion, finely chopped
2 bay leaves
5ml/1 tsp ground coriander
5ml/1 tsp ground cumin
1.5ml/¼ tsp ground turmeric
400g/14oz can chopped tomatoes
150ml/¼ pint/⅔ cup water
8 chicken thighs, skinned
5ml/1 tsp garam masala
sliced fresh green chillies, to garnish
chapatis and natural (plain) low-fat yogurt, to serve

1 Put the tomato purée, chopped garlic cloves, fresh green chillies and the dried red chillies into a food processor or blender.

2 Add the salt, sugar, chilli powder, paprika and curry paste. Process all the ingredients to a smooth paste, stopping once or twice to scrape down any of the mixture that has stuck to the sides of the bowl.

3 Heat the oil in a large, heavy pan and fry the cumin seeds for 2 minutes. Add the onion and bay leaves and fry for about 5 minutes.

4 Add the chilli paste and fry the mixture for 2–3 minutes. Add the ground coriander, cumin and turmeric and cook for 2 minutes. Add the tomatoes.

5 Pour in the water and stir to mix. Bring to the boil and simmer for 5 minutes until the sauce thickens. Add the chicken and garam masala. Cover and simmer for 25–30 minutes, until the chicken is tender. Garnish with sliced green chillies and serve with chapatis and natural low-fat yogurt.

chicken dhansak Energy 309kcal/1300kJ; Protein 43.2g; Carbohydrate 13.2g, of which sugars 3.2g; Fat 9.8g, of which saturates 1.5g; Cholesterol 110mg; Calcium 41mg; Fibre 2.3g; Sodium 106mg.
hot chilli chicken Energy 171kcal/715kJ; Protein 19.6g; Carbohydrate 4.6g, of which sugars 3.3g; Fat 8.4g, of which saturates 1.6g; Cholesterol 85mg; Calcium 81mg; Fibre 2.1g; Sodium 197mg.

Chicken in Cashew Nut Sauce

This strongly flavoured chicken dish has a deliciously thick and nutty sauce, and is best served with plain boiled rice.

Serves 4

2 medium onions
30ml/2 tbsp tomato purée (paste)
50g/2oz/½ cup cashew nuts
7.5ml/1½ tsp garam masala
5ml/1 tsp crushed garlic
5ml/1 tsp chilli powder
15ml/1 tbsp lemon juice
1.5ml/¼ tsp ground turmeric
5ml/1 tsp salt
15ml/1 tbsp natural (plain) low-fat yogurt
30ml/2 tbsp oil
30ml/2 tbsp chopped fresh coriander (cilantro)
15ml/1 tbsp sultanas (golden raisins)
450g/1lb boneless chicken, skinned and cubed
175g/6oz/2½ cups button (white) mushrooms
300ml/½ pint/1¼ cups water

1 Cut the onions into quarters, place in a food processor or blender and process for about 1 minute. Add the tomato purée, cashew nuts, garam masala, garlic, chilli powder, lemon juice, turmeric, salt and yogurt. Process the spiced onion mixture in the food processor for a further 1–1½ minutes.

2 In a heavy pan or karahi, heat the oil, lower the heat to medium and pour in the spice mixture from the food processor. Fry the mixture for 2 minutes, lowering the heat a little more if necessary.

3 When the spice mixture is lightly cooked, add half the chopped fresh coriander, the sultanas and the chicken cubes and continue to stir-fry for a further 1 minute.

4 Add the mushrooms, pour in the water and simmer. Cover the pan and cook over a low heat for about 10 minutes.

5 After this time, check that the chicken is cooked through and the sauce is thick. Cook for a little longer if necessary, then spoon into a serving bowl. Garnish with the remaining fresh coriander and serve.

Chicken Saag

A mildly spiced dish using a popular combination of spinach and chicken. This recipe is best made using fresh spinach.

Serves 4

225g/8oz fresh spinach leaves, washed but not dried
2.5cm/1in piece fresh root ginger, grated
2 garlic cloves, crushed
1 fresh green chilli, roughly chopped
200ml/7fl oz/scant 1 cup water
15ml/1 tbsp oil
2 bay leaves
1.5ml/¼ tsp black peppercorns
1 onion, finely chopped
4 tomatoes, peeled and finely chopped
10ml/2 tsp curry powder
5ml/1 tsp salt
5ml/1 tsp chilli powder
45ml/3 tbsp natural (plain) low-fat yogurt
8 chicken thighs, skinned
naan bread, to serve
natural (plain) low-fat yogurt and chilli powder, to garnish

1 Cook the wet spinach leaves, without extra water, in a tightly covered pan for 5 minutes. Put the cooked spinach, ginger, garlic and chilli with 50ml/2fl oz/¼ cup of the measured water into a food processor or blender and process to a thick purée. Set aside.

2 Heat the oil in a large, heavy pan, add the bay leaves and black peppercorns and fry for 2 minutes. Stir in the onion and fry for a further 6–8 minutes or until the onion has browned.

3 Add the tomatoes and simmer for about 5 minutes.

4 Stir in the curry powder, salt and chilli powder. Cook for 2 minutes over medium heat, stirring once or twice. Stir in the spinach purée and the remaining measured water, then simmer for 5 minutes. Add the yogurt, 15ml/1 tbsp at a time, and simmer for 5 minutes more.

5 Add the chicken thighs and stir to coat them in the sauce. Cover and cook for 25–30 minutes until the chicken is tender. Serve on naan bread, drizzle over some natural yogurt and dust with chilli powder.

chicken in sauce Energy 271kcal/1140kJ; Protein 40.4g; Carbohydrate 9.1g, of which sugars 5g; Fat 7.5g, of which saturates 1.6g; Cholesterol 108mg; Calcium 24mg; Fibre 1.2g; Sodium 605mg.
chicken saag Energy 238kcal/998kJ; Protein 34.7g; Carbohydrate 6.8g, of which sugars 5.6g; Fat 8.2g, of which saturates 1.8g; Cholesterol 158mg; Calcium 155mg; Fibre 3g; Sodium 735mg.

Chicken Tikka Masala

This is said to be the UK's favourite chicken dish. In this version, tender chicken pieces are cooked in a creamy, spicy tomato sauce and served on naan bread.

Serves 4

675g/1½lb skinned chicken breast portions
90ml/6 tbsp tikka paste
120ml/4fl oz/½ cup natural (plain) low-fat yogurt
15ml/1 tbsp oil
1 onion, chopped
1 garlic clove, crushed
1 fresh green chilli, seeded and chopped
2.5cm/1in piece fresh root ginger, grated
15ml/1 tbsp tomato purée (paste)
250ml/8fl oz/1 cup water
a little melted ghee or butter
15ml/1 tbsp lemon juice
fresh coriander (cilantro) sprigs, natural (plain) low-fat yogurt and toasted cumin seeds, to garnish
naan bread, to serve

1 Cut the chicken into 2.5cm/1in cubes. Mix 45ml/3 tbsp of the tikka paste and 60ml/4 tbsp of the yogurt in a bowl. Add the chicken and leave to marinate for 20 minutes.

2 Heat the oil in a heavy pan and fry the onion, garlic, chilli and ginger for 5 minutes. Add the remaining tikka paste and fry for 2 minutes. Stir in the tomato purée and water, bring to the boil and simmer for 15 minutes.

3 Meanwhile, thread the chicken pieces on to wooden kebab skewers. Preheat the grill (broiler).

4 Brush the chicken pieces with melted ghee or butter and cook under a medium heat for 15 minutes, turning occasionally.

5 Put the tikka sauce into a food processor or blender and process until smooth. Return to the pan.

6 Add the remaining yogurt and the lemon juice, remove the chicken from the skewers and add to the pan, then simmer for 5 minutes. Garnish with the fresh coriander, yogurt and toasted cumin seeds and serve on naan bread.

Chicken with Green Mango

Green, unripe mango is used for making various dishes on the Indian subcontinent, including pickles, chutneys and some meat, chicken and vegetable dishes. This is a fairly simple chicken dish to prepare and is good served with rice and dhal.

Serves 4

1 medium green mango
450g/1lb skinned boneless chicken, cubed
1.5ml/¼ tsp onion seeds
5ml/1 tsp grated fresh root ginger
2.5ml/½ tsp crushed garlic
5ml/1 tsp chilli powder
1.5ml/¼ tsp ground turmeric
5ml/1 tsp salt
5ml/1 tsp ground coriander
30ml/2 tbsp oil
2 medium onions, sliced
4 curry leaves
300ml/½ pint/1¼ cups water
2 medium tomatoes, quartered
2 fresh green chillies, chopped
30ml/2 tbsp chopped fresh coriander (cilantro)

1 To prepare the mango, peel off the skin and slice the flesh thickly. Discard the stone (pit) from the middle. Place the mango slices in a small bowl, cover and set aside.

2 Place the chicken cubes in a bowl and add the onion seeds, ginger, garlic, chilli powder, turmeric, salt and ground coriander. Mix to coat the chicken with the spices, then add half the mango slices.

3 In a medium, heavy pan, heat the oil and fry the sliced onions until golden brown. Add the curry leaves and stir lightly.

4 Gradually add the chicken pieces and mango to the onions in the pan, stirring all the time.

5 Pour in the water, lower the heat and cook for about 12–15 minutes, stirring occasionally, until the chicken is cooked through and the water has been absorbed.

6 Add the remaining mango slices, the quartered tomatoes, chopped green chillies and fresh coriander. Serve the curry hot.

chicken tikka Energy 261kcal/1101kJ; Protein 44.9g; Carbohydrate 10.2g, of which sugars 3.9g; Fat 4.8g, of which saturates 0.7g; Cholesterol 119mg; Calcium 240mg; Fibre 6.1g; Sodium 241mg.
chicken w. mango Energy 264kcal/1107kJ; Protein 26.6g; Carbohydrate 18.1g, of which sugars 13.1g; Fat 10.1g, of which saturates 1.8g; Cholesterol 118mg; Calcium 56mg; Fibre 3.1g; Sodium 114mg.

Chicken in Orange & Black Pepper Sauce

This low-fat version of a favourite Indian dish is very creamy and full of flavour.

Serves 4

225g/8oz low-fat fromage frais or ricotta cheese
50ml/2fl oz/¼ cup natural (plain) low-fat yogurt
120ml/4fl oz/½ cup orange juice
7.5ml/1½ tsp grated fresh root ginger
5ml/1 tsp crushed garlic
5ml/1 tsp ground black pepper
5ml/1 tsp salt
5ml/1 tsp ground coriander
1 small chicken, about 675g/1½lb, skinned and cut into 8 pieces
15ml/1 tbsp oil
1 bay leaf
1 large onion, chopped
15ml/1 tbsp fresh mint leaves
1 fresh green chilli, seeded and chopped

1 In a small mixing bowl, whisk the fromage frais or ricotta cheese with the yogurt, orange juice, ginger, garlic, pepper, salt and coriander.

2 Pour the fromage frais and orange mixture over the chicken, cover, and set aside for 3–4 hours.

3 Heat the oil with the bay leaf in a wok or heavy frying pan and fry the chopped onion for about 5 minutes or until just beginning to become soft.

4 Pour the chicken mixture into the pan with the onions and bay leaf and stir-fry for 3–5 minutes over a medium heat. Lower the heat, cover and cook for 7–10 minutes, adding a little water if the sauce is too thick. Add the fresh mint and chilli and serve.

Cook's Tip
If you prefer the spicy taste of curry leaves, you can use them instead of the bay leaf, but you will need to double the quantity.

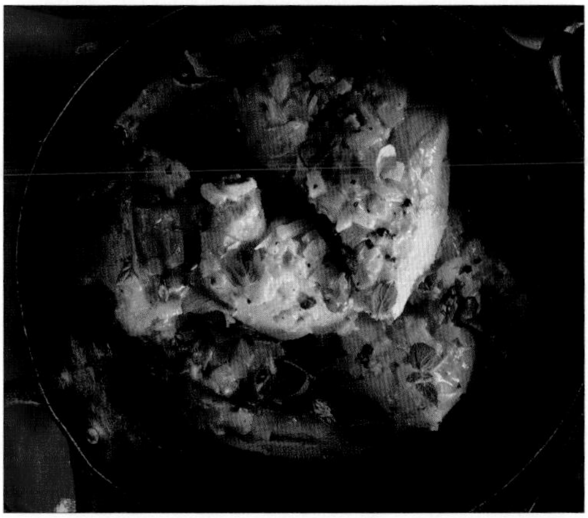

Spicy Masala Chicken

These tender chicken pieces have a sweet-and-sour taste. Serve cold with a salad and rice or hot with potatoes.

Serves 6

12 chicken thighs, skinned
90ml/6 tbsp lemon juice
5ml/1 tsp grated fresh root ginger
5ml/1 tsp crushed garlic
5ml/1 tsp crushed dried red chillies
5ml/1 tsp salt
5ml/1 tsp soft brown sugar
30ml/2 tbsp clear honey
30ml/2 tbsp chopped fresh coriander (cilantro)
1 fresh green chilli, finely chopped
30ml/2 tbsp vegetable oil
fresh coriander, to garnish
saffron rice and salad, to serve

1 Prick the chicken thighs with a fork, rinse them, pat dry with kitchen paper and set aside in a bowl.

2 In a large mixing bowl, mix together the lemon juice, grated ginger, garlic, crushed dried red chillies, salt, sugar and honey.

3 Transfer the chicken thighs to the spice mixture and coat well. Cover and set aside for about 45 minutes.

4 Preheat the grill (broiler) to medium. Add the fresh coriander and chopped chilli to the chicken thighs and place them in a flameproof dish.

5 Pour any remaining marinade over the chicken and brush with the oil.

6 Grill (broil) the chicken thighs for 15–20 minutes, turning and basting with the marinade occasionally, until cooked through and browned.

7 Serve cold, garnished with fresh coriander and accompanied by saffron rice and salad.

chicken in sauce Energy 268kcal/1129kJ; Protein 34.9g; Carbohydrate 14.8g, of which sugars 11.9g; Fat 8.3g, of which saturates 2.8g; Cholesterol 99mg; Calcium 96mg; Fibre 0.3g; Sodium 111mg.
spicy masala chicken Energy 165kcal/694kJ; Protein 18.9g; Carbohydrate 9.1g, of which sugars 9.1g; Fat 6.2g, of which saturates 1.2g; Cholesterol 95mg; Calcium 9mg; Fibre 0g; Sodium 409mg.

Chicken Korma

Although kormas are traditionally rich and high in fat, this recipe uses low-fat yogurt instead of cream, which gives the sauce a delicious creamy flavour while keeping down the fat content.

Serves 4

675g/1½lb skinned chicken breast portions
2 garlic cloves, crushed
2.5cm/1in piece fresh root ginger, roughly chopped
15ml/1 tbsp oil
3 green cardamom pods
1 onion, finely chopped
10ml/2 tsp ground cumin
1.5ml/¼ tsp salt
300ml/½ pint/1¼ cups natural (plain) low-fat yogurt
toasted flaked or sliced almonds (optional) and a fresh coriander (cilantro) sprig, to garnish
plain rice, to serve

1 Using a sharp knife, remove any visible fat from the chicken and cut the meat into 2.5cm/1in cubes.

2 Put the crushed garlic and ginger into a food processor or blender with 30ml/2 tbsp water and process to a smooth, creamy paste.

3 Heat the oil in a large, heavy pan and cook the chicken cubes for 8–10 minutes until browned on all sides. Remove the chicken cubes with a slotted spoon and set aside.

4 Add the cardamom pods and fry for 2 minutes. Add the finely chopped onion and fry for a further 5 minutes. Stir in the garlic and ginger paste, cumin and salt and cook, stirring, for a further 5 minutes. Add half the yogurt, stirring in a spoonful at a time, and cook over a low heat until it has all been absorbed.

5 Return the chicken to the pan. Cover and simmer over a low heat for 5–6 minutes or until the chicken is tender.

6 Add the remaining yogurt and simmer for a further 5 minutes. Garnish with toasted almonds and coriander and serve with rice.

Mild Chicken Curry with Lentils

In this low-fat dish, the mildly spiced sauce is thickened using low-fat lentils rather than the traditional onions fried in ghee. The resulting dish is delicious and filling as well as healthy.

Serves 4–6

75g/3oz/⅓ cup red lentils
30ml/2 tbsp mild curry powder
10ml/2 tsp ground coriander
5ml/1 tsp cumin seeds
475ml/16fl oz/2 cups vegetable stock
8 chicken thighs, skinned
225g/8oz fresh spinach, shredded, or frozen spinach, thawed and well drained
15ml/1 tbsp chopped fresh coriander (cilantro), plus extra to garnish
salt and ground black pepper
white or brown basmati rice and grilled (broiled) poppadums, to serve

1 Put the red lentils in a large, heavy pan and add the mild curry powder, ground coriander, cumin seeds and vegetable stock.

2 Bring the mixture to the boil, then lower the heat. Cover and simmer for 10 minutes, stirring often.

3 Add the chicken thighs and spinach. Replace the cover and simmer gently for a further 40 minutes, or until the chicken is cooked through.

4 Stir in the chopped coriander and season with salt and ground black pepper to taste. Serve garnished with fresh coriander sprigs and accompanied by white or brown basmati rice and poppadums.

Cook's Tip

Nourishing lentils are an excellent low-fat source of vitamins, protein and fibre. Yellow and red lentils, in particular, are very popular in Indian cooking, adding subtle colour and texture to dishes.

chicken korma Energy 274kcal/1160kJ; Protein 43.2g; Carbohydrate 14.4g, of which sugars 8.6g; Fat 5.4g, of which saturates 2.1g; Cholesterol 121mg; Calcium 53mg; Fibre 1.5g; Sodium 158mg.
mild chicken curry Energy 175kcal/739kJ; Protein 25.9g; Carbohydrate 9.6g, of which sugars 1.1g; Fat 4g, of which saturates 1g; Cholesterol 105mg; Calcium 103mg; Fibre 1.8g; Sodium 152mg.

Chicken Jalfrezi

A jalfrezi is a stir-fried curry which features onions, ginger and garlic in a rich pepper sauce.

Serves 4

675g/1½lb chicken breast portions
15ml/1 tbsp oil
5ml/1 tsp cumin seeds
1 onion, finely chopped
1 green (bell) pepper, seeded and finely chopped
1 red (bell) pepper, seeded and finely chopped
1 garlic clove, crushed
2cm/¾in piece fresh root ginger, finely chopped
15ml/1 tbsp curry paste
1.5ml/¼ tsp chilli powder
5ml/1 tsp ground coriander
5ml/1 tsp ground cumin
2.5ml/½ tsp salt
400g/14oz can chopped tomatoes
30ml/2 tbsp chopped fresh coriander (cilantro), plus extra to garnish
plain rice, to serve

1 Skin the chicken breast portions and remove any visible fat. Cut the meat into 2.5cm/1in cubes.

2 Heat the oil in a karahi, wok or heavy pan and fry the cumin seeds for 2 minutes until they splutter. Add the onion, peppers, garlic and ginger and fry for 6–8 minutes.

3 Add the curry paste and fry for about 2 minutes. Stir in the chilli powder, ground coriander, cumin and salt and add 15ml/1 tbsp water; fry for a further 2 minutes.

4 Add the chicken cubes and fry for about 5 minutes. Add the canned tomatoes and chopped fresh coriander. Cover the pan tightly with a lid and cook for about 15 minutes or until the chicken cubes are tender. Garnish with sprigs of fresh coriander and serve with rice.

Cook's Tip
Removing the skin and any visible fat from the chicken makes a healthier dish which is low in fat.

Karahi Chicken with Fresh Fenugreek

Fresh fenugreek is a flavour that many people are unfamiliar with and this recipe is a good introduction to this delicious herb. The chicken is boiled before being quickly stir-fried, to make sure that it is cooked all the way through.

Serves 4

115g/4oz boneless chicken thigh meat, skinned and cut into strips
115g/4oz chicken breast fillet, skinned and cut into strips
2.5ml/½ tsp crushed garlic
5ml/1 tsp chilli powder
2.5ml/½ tsp salt
10ml/2 tsp tomato purée (paste)
30ml/2 tbsp oil
1 bunch fresh fenugreek leaves
15ml/1 tbsp chopped fresh coriander (cilantro)
300ml/½ pint/1¼ cups water
pilau rice and wholemeal (whole-wheat) chapatis, to serve (optional)

1 Bring a pan of water to the boil, add the chicken strips and cook for about 5–7 minutes. Drain the chicken and set aside.

2 In a mixing bowl, combine the garlic, chilli powder and salt with the tomato purée.

3 Heat the oil in a large, heavy pan. Lower the heat and stir in the tomato purée and spice mixture.

4 Add the chicken pieces to the spices and stir-fry for 5–7 minutes, then lower the heat further.

5 Add the fenugreek leaves and chopped fresh coriander. Continue to stir-fry for 5–7 minutes until all the ingredients are well mixed.

6 Pour in the water, cover and cook for about 5 minutes, stirring several times, until the dish is simmering. Serve hot with pilau rice and warm wholemeal chapatis, if you like.

chicken jalfrezi Energy 254kcal/1067kJ; Protein 33.6g; Carbohydrate 15.1g, of which sugars 10.5g; Fat 7.1g, of which saturates 1.2g; Cholesterol 89mg; Calcium 49mg; Fibre 2.9g; Sodium 90mg.
karahi chicken Energy 127kcal/529kJ; Protein 13g; Carbohydrate 1.7g, of which sugars 0.7g; Fat 7.7g, of which saturates 1.2g; Cholesterol 60mg; Calcium 42mg; Fibre 0.9g; Sodium 64mg.

Karahi Chicken & Tomatoes with Mint

A traditional herb that goes deliciously well with spicy chicken is mint, which has cooling qualities to counter the heat of ginger and chillies. This mildly spiced recipe is perfect for children or those who like a piquant flavour without heat.

Serves 4

275g/10oz skinned chicken breast fillets, cut into strips
300ml/½ pint/1¼ cups water
30ml/2 tbsp oil
2 small bunches spring onions (scallions), roughly chopped
5ml/1 tsp shredded fresh root ginger
5ml/1 tsp crushed dried red chillies
30ml/2 tbsp lemon juice
15ml/1 tbsp chopped fresh coriander (cilantro)
15ml/1 tbsp chopped fresh mint
3 tomatoes, peeled, seeded and roughly chopped
5ml/1 tsp salt
fresh mint and coriander sprigs, to garnish

1 Put the strips of chicken breast and water into a pan, bring to the boil and lower the heat to medium. Cook for about 10 minutes, uncovered, or until the water has evaporated and the chicken is cooked. Remove the pan from the heat and set aside.

2 Heat the oil in a heavy pan and stir-fry the spring onions for 2 minutes until soft but not browned.

3 Add the cooked chicken strips and stir-fry for about 3 minutes over a medium heat.

4 Gradually add the shredded ginger, dried red chillies, lemon juice, chopped coriander and mint, tomatoes and salt and gently stir to blend all the flavours.

5 Transfer the spicy chicken mixture to a serving dish and garnish with a few sprigs of fresh mint and coriander before serving piping hot.

Red Hot Chicken Curry

This curry has a satisfyingly thick sauce, and uses sweet red and green peppers for extra colour and flavour.

Serves 4

2 medium onions
½ red (bell) pepper
½ green (bell) pepper
30ml/2 tbsp oil
1.5ml/¼ tsp fenugreek seeds
1.5ml/¼ tsp onion seeds
2.5ml/½ tsp crushed garlic
2.5ml/½ tsp grated fresh root ginger
5ml/1 tsp ground coriander
5ml/1 tsp chilli powder
5ml/1 tsp salt
400g/14oz can tomatoes
30ml/2 tbsp lemon juice
350g/12oz chicken, skinned and cubed
30ml/2 tbsp chopped fresh coriander (cilantro)
3 fresh green chillies, chopped
fresh coriander, to garnish

1 Using a sharp knife, dice the onions. Seed the peppers and cut them into chunks.

2 In a medium-sized heavy pan, heat the oil and fry the fenugreek and onion seeds until they turn a shade darker. Add the chopped onions, crushed garlic and fresh ginger. Fry for about 5 minutes until the onions turn golden brown. Reduce the heat to very low.

3 In a bowl, mix together the ground coriander, chilli powder, salt, canned tomatoes and lemon juice. Stir well.

4 Pour this mixture into the pan and increase the heat to medium. Stir-fry for about 3 minutes.

5 Add the chicken cubes and stir-fry for 5–7 minutes.

6 Add the chopped fresh coriander and green chillies, and the red and green pepper chunks.

7 Lower the heat, cover the pan and allow to simmer for about 10 minutes, until the chicken cubes are cooked.

8 Serve the curry hot, garnished with fresh coriander.

karahi chicken Energy 114kcal/482kJ; Protein 18.3g; Carbohydrate 4.1g, of which sugars 4g; Fat 2.9g, of which saturates 0.5g; Cholesterol 48mg; Calcium 48mg; Fibre 2g; Sodium 546mg.
red hot curry Energy 177kcal/747kJ; Protein 24.2g; Carbohydrate 15.8g, of which sugars 11.2g; Fat 2.5g, of which saturates 0.5g; Cholesterol 61mg; Calcium 51mg; Fibre 3.1g; Sodium 560mg.

Chicken with Spicy Onions

Chunky onion slices infused with toasted cumin seeds and shredded ginger add a delicious contrast to the flavour of the chicken.

Serves 4–6

1.3kg/3lb chicken, jointed and skinned
17.5ml/½ tsp turmeric
2.5ml/½ tsp chilli powder
60ml/4 tbsp oil
4 small onions, finely chopped
175g/6oz/6 cups fresh coriander (cilantro), coarsely chopped
5cm/2in piece fresh root ginger, finely shredded
2 fresh green chillies, finely chopped
10ml/2 tsp cumin seeds, dry-roasted
75ml/5 tbsp natural (plain) yogurt
75ml/5 tbsp double (heavy) cream
2.5ml/½ tsp cornflour (cornstarch)
salt

1 With a sharp knife, make a few slashes in the chicken joints and then rub the meat with the turmeric, chilli powder and salt to taste. Heat the oil in a large frying pan and fry the chicken pieces in batches until both sides are sealed. Remove to a plate and keep hot.

2 Reheat the oil remaining in the pan and add three-quarters of the chopped onions, most of the fresh coriander, half the ginger, the green chillies and the cumin seeds and fry until the onions are translucent.

3 Return the chicken to the pan with any juices and mix well. Cover and cook gently for 15 minutes.

4 Remove the pan from the heat and leave to cool a little. Mix the yogurt, cream and cornflour in a bowl and gradually fold into the chicken, mixing well.

5 Return the pan to the heat and cook gently until the chicken is tender. Just before serving, stir in the reserved chopped onion, coriander and ginger. Spoon into a serving bowl and serve hot.

Mughlai-style Chicken

In India, the cuisine of Andhra Pradesh is renowned for its pungency because the hottest variety of chilli is grown there. However, the region is also home to the subtle flavours of a style of cooking known as nizami. This recipe, with the heady aroma of saffron and the captivating flavour of a silky almond sauce, is a good example of a dish from the cooler end of the spectrum.

Serves 4–6

1 large onion
2 eggs
4 skinned chicken breast fillets
15–30ml/1–2 tbsp garam masala
90ml/6 tbsp ghee or vegetable oil
5cm/2in piece fresh root ginger, finely crushed
4 garlic cloves, finely crushed
4 cloves
4 green cardamom pods
5cm/2in piece cinnamon stick
2 bay leaves
15–20 saffron threads
150ml/¼ pint/⅔ cup natural (plain) yogurt, beaten with 5ml/1 tsp cornflour (cornstarch)
75ml/2½fl oz/⅓ cup double (heavy) cream
50g/2oz/½ cup ground almonds
salt and ground black pepper

1 Chop the onion finely. Break the eggs into a bowl, beat and season with salt and pepper.

2 Rub the chicken fillets with the garam masala, then brush with the beaten egg. In a karahi, wok, or large pan, heat the ghee or vegetable oil and fry the chicken until cooked through and browned on both sides. Remove from the pan and keep warm.

3 In the same pan, fry the chopped onion, ginger, garlic, cloves, cardamom pods, cinnamon and bay leaves. When the onion turns golden, remove the pan from the heat, allow the contents to cool a little and add the saffron and yogurt mixture. Stir well to prevent the yogurt from curdling.

4 Return the chicken to the pan, along with any juices, and gently cook until the chicken is tender. Adjust the seasoning. Just before serving, pour in the cream. Fold it in then repeat the process with the ground almonds. Serve when piping hot.

chicken with onions Energy 658kcal/2759kJ; Protein 94.2g; Carbohydrate 11.7g, of which sugars 8.3g; Fat 26.5g, of which saturates 8.8g; Cholesterol 288mg; Calcium 181mg; Fibre 3.6g; Sodium 263mg.
Mughlai-style chicken Energy 350kcal/1453kJ; Protein 25.8g; Carbohydrate 4.3g, of which sugars 3g; Fat 25.7g, of which saturates 6.8g; Cholesterol 139mg; Calcium 94mg; Fibre 0.8g; Sodium 99mg.

Chicken Curry with Sliced Apples

This mild yet tasty dish is pleasantly flavoured with a warming combination of spices and chilli. Yogurt and almonds make a creamy sauce, which is given an additional lift by the use of sliced apples.

Serves 4

10ml/2 tsp oil
2 medium onions, diced
1 bay leaf
2 cloves
2.5cm/1in piece cinnamon stick
4 black peppercorns
1 baby chicken, about 675g/1½lb, skinned and cut into 8 pieces
5ml/1 tsp garam masala
5ml/1 tsp grated fresh root ginger
5ml/1 tsp crushed garlic
5ml/1 tsp salt
5ml/1 tsp chilli powder
15ml/1 tbsp ground almonds
150ml/¼ pint/⅔ cup natural (plain) low-fat yogurt
2 green eating apples, peeled, cored and roughly sliced
15ml/1 tbsp chopped fresh coriander (cilantro)
15g/½oz flaked (sliced) almonds, lightly toasted, and fresh coriander leaves, to garnish

1 Heat the oil in a karahi, wok or heavy pan and fry the onions with the bay leaf, cloves, cinnamon and peppercorns for about 3–5 minutes until the onions are beginning to soften but have not yet begun to brown.

2 Add the chicken pieces to the onions and continue to stir-fry for at least another 3 minutes.

3 Lower the heat and add the garam masala, ginger, garlic, salt, chilli powder and ground almonds and cook, stirring constantly, for 2–3 minutes.

4 Pour in the yogurt and stir for a couple more minutes.

5 Add the apples and chopped coriander, cover and cook for about 10–15 minutes.

6 Check that the chicken is cooked through and serve immediately, garnished with the flaked almonds and whole coriander leaves.

Chicken & Potatoes with Rice

This dish, Murgh Biryani, is mainly prepared for important occasions in India, and is truly fit for royalty. Every cook in India has a subtle variation which is kept a closely guarded secret.

Serves 4–6

1.3kg/3lb skinned chicken breast portions, cut into large pieces
60ml/4 tbsp biryani masala paste
2 fresh green chillies, chopped
15ml/1 tbsp grated fresh root ginger
15ml/1 tbsp crushed garlic
50g/2oz/2 cups fresh coriander (cilantro), chopped
6–8 fresh mint leaves, chopped
150ml/¼ pint/⅔ cup natural (plain) yogurt, beaten
30ml/2 tbsp tomato purée (paste)
4 onions, finely sliced, deep-fried and crushed
450g/1lb/2¼ cups basmati rice, washed and drained
5ml/1 tsp black cumin seeds
5cm/2in piece cinnamon stick
4 green cardamom pods
2 black cardamom pods
vegetable oil, for shallow-frying
4 large potatoes, peeled and quartered
175ml/6fl oz/¾ cup milk, mixed with 90ml/6 tbsp water
1 sachet saffron powder, mixed with 90ml/6 tbsp milk
25g/1oz/2 tbsp ghee or unsalted butter
1 tomato, sliced
salt

For the garnish

ghee or unsalted (sweet) butter, for shallow-frying
50g/2oz/½ cup cashew nuts
50g/2oz/⅓ cup sultanas (golden raisins)

1 Mix the chicken pieces with the next nine ingredients and salt in a large bowl and marinate, covered, in a cool place for about 2 hours. Place in a large heavy pan and cook over a low heat for about 10 minutes. Set aside.

2 Boil a large pan of water and soak the rice with the cumin seeds, cinnamon stick and green and black cardamom pods for about 5 minutes. Drain well. If you prefer, some of the whole spices may be removed and discarded at this stage.

3 Heat the oil for shallow-frying and fry the quartered potatoes until they are evenly browned on all sides. Drain the potatoes and set them aside.

4 Place half the rice on top of the chicken in the pan in an even layer. Then make an even layer with the potatoes. Put the remaining rice on top of the potatoes and spread to make an even layer.

5 Sprinkle the water mixed with milk all over the rice. Make random holes through the rice with the handle of a spoon and pour into each a little saffron milk. Place a few knobs (pats) of ghee or butter on the surface, cover the pan and cook over a low heat for 35–45 minutes.

6 While the biryani is cooking, make the garnish. Heat a little ghee or butter and fry the cashew nuts and sultanas until they swell. Drain and set aside. When the biryani is ready, gently toss the rice, chicken and potatoes together, garnish with the nut mixture and serve hot.

curry w. apples Energy 349kcal/1450kJ; Protein 25g; Carbohydrate 14.2g, of which sugars 11.8g; Fat 21.8g, of which saturates 5.6g; Cholesterol 108mg; Calcium 140mg; Fibre 2.8g; Sodium 124mg.
chicken & potatoes Energy 988kcal/4142kJ; Protein 65g; Carbohydrate 105g, of which sugars 16.6g; Fat 34.8g, of which saturates 5.9g; Cholesterol 152mg; Calcium 212mg; Fibre 9.4g; Sodium 232mg.

Chicken Biryani

Biryanis originated in Persia and are traditionally made with a combination of meat and rice. They are often served at dinner parties and on festive occasions.

Serves 4

275g/10oz/1½ cups basmati rice
30ml/2 tbsp oil
1 onion, thinly sliced
2 garlic cloves, crushed
1 green chilli, finely chopped
2.5cm/1in piece fresh root ginger, finely chopped
675g/1½lb skinned chicken breast fillets, cut into 2.5cm/1in cubes
45ml/3 tbsp curry paste
1.5ml/¼ tsp salt
1.5ml/¼ tsp garam masala
3 tomatoes, cut into thin wedges
1.5ml/¼ tsp ground turmeric
2 bay leaves
4 green cardamom pods
4 cloves
1.5ml/¼ tsp saffron strands
Tomato and Fresh Chilli Chutney (see p447), to serve

1 Wash the rice in several changes of cold water. Put into a bowl, cover with water and leave to soak for 30 minutes.

2 Meanwhile, heat the oil in a large heavy frying pan and fry the onion for about 5–7 minutes until lightly browned. Add the garlic, chilli and ginger and fry for about 2 minutes. Add the chicken and fry for 5 minutes, stirring occasionally.

3 Add the curry paste, salt and garam masala and cook for 5 minutes. Stir in the tomato wedges and continue cooking for another 3–4 minutes, then remove from the heat and set aside.

4 Preheat the oven to 190°C/375°F/Gas 5. Bring a pan of water to the boil. Drain the rice and add it to the pan with the turmeric. Cook for about 10 minutes, or until the rice is almost tender. Drain the rice and toss together with the bay leaves, cardamoms, cloves and saffron.

5 Layer the rice and chicken in a shallow, ovenproof dish until all the mixture has been used, finishing off with a layer of rice. Cover and bake in the oven for 15–20 minutes or until the chicken is tender. Serve with Tomato and Fresh Chilli Chutney.

Chicken Pilau

Like biryanis, pilaus that include cooked meat and poultry make a convenient one-pot meal. A vegetable curry makes a good accompaniment, although for a simpler meal, such as supper, you could serve the pilau with a simple raita.

Serves 4

400g/14oz/2 cups basmati rice
75g/3oz/6 tbsp ghee or unsalted (sweet) butter
1 onion, sliced
1.5ml/¼ tsp mixed onion seeds and mustard seeds
3 curry leaves
5ml/1 tsp grated fresh root ginger
5ml/1 tsp crushed garlic
5ml/1 tsp ground coriander
5ml/1 tsp chilli powder
7.5ml/1½ tsp salt
2 tomatoes, sliced
1 potato, cubed
50g/2oz/½ cup frozen peas, thawed
175g/6oz skinned chicken breast fillets, cubed
60ml/4 tbsp chopped fresh coriander (cilantro)
2 fresh green chillies, chopped
750ml/1¼ pints/3 cups water

1 Wash the rice thoroughly under running water, then leave to soak for 30 minutes. Drain in a strainer or colander and set aside.

2 In a pan, melt the ghee or butter and fry the sliced onion until golden.

3 Add the onion and mustard seeds, the curry leaves, ginger, garlic, ground coriander, chilli powder and salt. Stir-fry for about 2 minutes over a low heat.

4 Add the sliced tomatoes, cubed potato, peas and chicken cubes and mix everything together well.

5 Add the rice and stir to combine with the other ingredients.

6 Add the coriander and chillies. Mix and stir-fry for 1 minute. Pour in the water, bring to the boil and then lower the heat. Cover tightly and cook for 20 minutes. Remove from the heat, leaving the lid in place, and leave the pilau to stand for 6–8 minutes. Serve hot.

chicken biryani Energy 562kcal/2354kJ; Protein 45.2g; Carbohydrate 70.3g, of which sugars 12.4g; Fat 11.2g, of which saturates 1.7g; Cholesterol 106mg; Calcium 128mg; Fibre 2.7g; Sodium 380mg.
chicken pilau Energy 649kcal/2713kJ; Protein 33.6g; Carbohydrate 87.3g, of which sugars 15.1g; Fat 18.3g, of which saturates 2.3g; Cholesterol 118mg; Calcium 73mg; Fibre 2.7g; Sodium 1105mg.

Chicken Biryani with Almonds

Biryani is a meal in itself and needs no accompaniment.

Serves 4

275g/10oz/1½ cups basmati rice
10 whole green cardamom pods
2.5ml/½ tsp salt
2 or 3 whole cloves
5cm/2in piece cinnamon stick
45ml/3 tbsp vegetable oil
3 onions, sliced
4 skinned chicken breast fillets, about 175g/6oz each, cubed
1.5ml/¼ tsp ground cloves
1.5ml/¼ tsp hot chilli powder
5ml/1 tsp ground cumin
5ml/1 tsp ground coriander
2.5ml/½ tsp ground black pepper
3 garlic cloves, chopped
5ml/1 tsp finely chopped fresh root ginger
juice of 1 lemon
4 tomatoes, sliced
30ml/2 tbsp chopped fresh coriander (cilantro)
150ml/¼ pint/⅔ cup natural (plain) yogurt, plus extra to serve
4–5 saffron threads, soaked in 10ml/2 tsp warm milk
150ml/¼ pint/⅔ cup water
toasted flaked (sliced) almonds and fresh coriander sprigs, to garnish

1 Wash the rice well and leave to soak in water for 30 minutes. Drain. Preheat the oven to 190°C/375°F/Gas 5. Remove the seeds from half the cardamom pods and grind them finely, using a mortar and pestle. Set aside the ground seeds.

2 Bring a pan of water to the boil. Add the rice with the salt, cardamoms, cloves and cinnamon stick. Boil for 2 minutes, then drain. Keep the rice hot in a covered pan.

3 Heat the oil in another pan, and fry the onions for 8 minutes, until browned. Add the chicken and the ground spices, including the ground cardamoms. Mix well, then add the garlic, ginger and lemon juice. Stir-fry for 5 minutes. Transfer to a casserole and arrange the tomatoes on top. Sprinkle on the coriander, spoon the yogurt on top and cover with the rice.

4 Drizzle the saffron milk over the rice and pour over the water. Cover, then bake in the oven for 1 hour. Transfer to a serving platter and discard the whole spices. Spoon over the yogurt, garnish with almonds and coriander and serve.

Curried Chicken & Rice

This simple but flavourful one-pot meal is the perfect choice for casual entertaining. The dish is delicately spiced and would be perfect accompanied by a salad or, if you have time, a curried vegetable side dish.

Serves 4

60ml/4 tbsp vegetable oil
4 garlic cloves, finely chopped
1 chicken, about 1.6kg/3–3½lb or chicken pieces, skin and bones removed and meat cut into bitesize pieces
5ml/1 tsp garam masala
450g/1lb/2⅓ cups jasmine rice, rinsed and drained
10ml/2 tsp salt
1 litre/1¾ pints/4 cups chicken stock
small bunch fresh coriander (cilantro), chopped, to garnish

1 Heat the oil in a wok or flameproof casserole that has a lid. Add the garlic and cook over low to medium heat until golden brown. Add the chicken, increase the heat and brown the pieces on all sides (see Cook's Tip).

2 Add the garam masala, stir well to coat the chicken all over in the spice, then tip in the drained rice. Add the salt and stir to mix.

3 Pour in the stock, stir well, then cover the wok or casserole and bring to the boil. Reduce the heat to low and simmer gently for 10 minutes, until the rice is cooked and tender.

4 Lift the wok or casserole off the heat, leaving the lid on, and leave for 10 minutes. Fluff up the rice grains with a fork and spoon on to a platter. Sprinkle with the coriander and serve immediately.

Cook's Tip
You will probably need to brown the chicken in batches, so don't be tempted to add too much at once.

chicken biryani Energy 600kcal/2518kJ; Protein 51.8g; Carbohydrate 72g, of which sugars 12.9g; Fat 11.9g, of which saturates 1.9g; Cholesterol 123mg; Calcium 138mg; Fibre 2.8g; Sodium 150mg.
curried chicken Energy 719kcal/3012kJ; Protein 56.7g; Carbohydrate 90.1g, of which sugars 0.3g; Fat 13.9g, of which saturates 1.9g; Cholesterol 140mg; Calcium 57mg; Fibre 0.6g; Sodium 1107mg.

Green Chicken Curry

Use fresh green chillies in this dish, if you like your curry hot. The mild aromatic flavour of the rice is a good foil for the spicy chicken.

Serves 3–4

4 spring onions (scallions), trimmed and coarsely chopped
1 or 2 fresh green chillies, seeded and coarsely chopped
2cm/¾in piece fresh root ginger, peeled
2 garlic cloves
5ml/1 tsp Thai fish sauce
large bunch fresh coriander (cilantro)
small handful of fresh parsley
30–45ml/2–3 tbsp water
30ml/2 tbsp sunflower oil
4 boneless chicken breast portions, skinned and diced
1 green (bell) pepper, seeded and thinly sliced
600ml/1 pint/2½ cups coconut milk
salt and ground black pepper
hot coconut rice, to serve

1 Put the spring onions, green chillies, ginger, garlic, fish sauce, coriander and parsley in a food processor or blender. Pour in 30ml/2 tbsp of the water and process to a smooth paste, adding a further 15ml/1 tbsp water if required.

2 Heat half the oil in a large frying pan. Cook the diced chicken until evenly browned. Transfer to a plate. Heat the remaining oil in the pan. Add the green pepper and stir-fry for 3–4 minutes, then add the chilli and ginger paste. Stir-fry for a further 3–4 minutes, until the mixture becomes fairly thick.

3 Return the chicken to the pan and add the coconut milk. Season with salt and pepper and bring to the boil, then reduce the heat, half-cover the pan and simmer for 8–10 minutes. When the chicken is cooked, transfer it, with the green pepper, to a plate. Boil the cooking liquid remaining in the pan for 10–12 minutes, until it is well reduced and fairly thick.

4 Return the chicken and pepper to the green curry sauce, stir well and cook gently for 2–3 minutes to heat through. Spoon the curry over the coconut rice, and serve immediately.

Fragrant Chicken Curry

This dish is perfect for a party as the chicken and sauce can be prepared in advance and combined and heated at the last minute.

Serves 4

45ml/3 tbsp oil
1 onion, coarsely chopped
2 garlic cloves, crushed
15ml/1 tbsp Thai red curry paste
1 litre/1¾ pints/4 cups coconut milk
2 lemon grass stalks, coarsely chopped
6 kaffir lime leaves, chopped
150ml/¼ pint/⅔ cup Greek (US strained plain) yogurt
30ml/2 tbsp apricot jam
1 cooked chicken, about 1.6kg/3–3½lb
30ml/2 tbsp chopped fresh coriander (cilantro)
salt and ground black pepper
kaffir lime leaves, shredded, toasted coconut and fresh coriander, to garnish
boiled rice, to serve

1 Heat the oil in a large pan. Add the onion and garlic and cook over a low heat for 5–10 minutes until soft. Stir in the red curry paste. Cook, stirring constantly, for 2–3 minutes.

2 Stir in the coconut milk, then add the lemon grass, lime leaves, yogurt and apricot jam. Stir well. Cover and simmer for 30 minutes.

3 Remove the pan from the heat and leave to cool slightly. Transfer the sauce to a food processor or blender and process to a smooth purée, then strain it back into the rinsed-out pan, pressing as much of the puréed mixture as possible through the sieve (strainer) with the back of a wooden spoon. Set aside while you prepare the chicken.

4 Remove the skin from the chicken, slice the meat off the bones and cut it into bitesize pieces. Add to the sauce.

5 Bring the sauce back to simmering point. Stir in the fresh coriander and season with salt and pepper. Garnish with extra lime leaves, shredded coconut and coriander. Serve with rice.

green curry Energy 359kcal/1515kJ; Protein 48.4g; Carbohydrate 13.8g, of which sugars 13.6g; Fat 12.8g, of which saturates 2.3g; Cholesterol 136mg; Calcium 131mg; Fibre 1.2g; Sodium 410mg.
fragrant curry Energy 760kcal/3162kJ; Protein 52.5g; Carbohydrate 16.4g, of which sugars 15.5g; Fat 54.6g, of which saturates 15.5g; Cholesterol 256mg; Calcium 187mg; Fibre 0.9g; Sodium 574mg.

Yellow Chicken Curry

The combination of slightly sweet coconut milk and fruit with savoury chicken and spices is at once a comforting, refreshing and exotic combination.

Serves 4
300ml/½ pint/1¼ cups chicken stock
30ml/2 tbsp thick tamarind juice, made by mixing tamarind paste with warm water
15ml/1 tbsp sugar
200ml/7fl oz/scant 1 cup coconut milk
1 green papaya, peeled, seeded and thinly sliced
250g/9oz boneless chicken breast portions, skinned and diced
juice of 1 lime
lime slices, to garnish

For the yellow curry paste
1 fresh red chilli, seeded and coarsely chopped
4 garlic cloves, coarsely chopped
3 shallots, coarsely chopped
2 lemon grass stalks, sliced
5cm/2in piece fresh turmeric, coarsely chopped, or 5ml/1 tsp ground
5ml/1 tsp shrimp paste
5ml/1 tsp salt

1 To make the yellow curry paste, put the red chilli, garlic, shallots, lemon grass and turmeric in a mortar or food processor. Add the shrimp paste and salt. Pound or process to a paste, adding a little water if necessary.

2 Pour the stock into a wok or medium pan and bring it to the boil. Stir in the curry paste. Bring back to the boil and add the tamarind juice, sugar and coconut milk. Add the papaya and chicken and cook over medium to high heat for about 15 minutes, stirring frequently, until the chicken is cooked.

3 Stir in the lime juice, transfer to a warm dish and serve immediately, garnished with lime slices.

Cook's Tip
Fresh turmeric is a vibrant orange colour. When preparing it, wear gloves to protect your hands from staining.

Coconut Chicken Curry

This mild coconut curry is flavoured with turmeric, coriander and cumin seeds and typical south-east Asian flavourings of fish sauce and shrimp paste.

Serves 4
60ml/4 tbsp vegetable oil
1 large garlic clove, crushed
1 chicken, about 1.5kg/3lb 5oz, chopped into 12 large pieces
400ml/14fl oz/1¾ cups coconut cream
250ml/8fl oz/1 cup chicken stock
30ml/2 tbsp Thai fish sauce
30ml/2 tbsp sugar
juice of 2 limes
1 bunch of spring onions (scallions), thinly sliced
2 small fresh red chillies, seeded and finely chopped, to garnish

For the curry paste
5ml/1 tsp dried chilli flakes
2.5ml/½ tsp salt
5cm/2in piece fresh turmeric, coarsely chopped, or 5ml/1 tsp ground
2.5ml/½ tsp coriander seeds
2.5ml/½ tsp cumin seeds
5ml/1 tsp dried shrimp paste

1 First make the curry paste. Put all the ingredients in a mortar, food processor or spice grinder and pound, process or grind to a smooth paste.

2 Heat the oil in a wok or frying pan and cook the garlic until golden. Add the chicken and cook until golden. Remove the chicken and set aside.

3 Reheat the oil in the wok and add the curry paste and then half the coconut cream. Cook for a few minutes until fragrant.

4 Return the chicken to the wok or pan, add the stock, mixing well, then add the remaining coconut cream, the fish sauce, sugar and lime juice. Stir well and bring to the boil, then lower the heat and simmer for 15 minutes.

5 Divide the curry between four warm serving bowls and sprinkle with the chopped fresh chillies and spring onions to garnish. Serve immediately.

yellow curry Energy 149kcal/633kJ; Protein 17.2g; Carbohydrate 18.9g, of which sugars 17.2g; Fat 1.1g, of which saturates 0.3g; Cholesterol 50mg; Calcium 70mg; Fibre 2.8g; Sodium 153mg.
coconut curry Energy 706kcal/2935kJ; Protein 48.1g; Carbohydrate 15.8g, of which sugars 15.6g; Fat 50.4g, of which saturates 12.8g; Cholesterol 240mg; Calcium 91mg; Fibre 1.5g; Sodium 305mg.

Red Chicken Curry with Bamboo Shoots

Bamboo shoots have a lovely crunchy texture, and it is quite acceptable to use canned ones instead of fresh. The unused curry paste will keep in the refrigerator for 3 months.

Serves 4–6

1 litre/1¾ pints/4 cups coconut milk
450g/1lb chicken breast fillet, skinned and cut into bitesize pieces
30ml/2 tbsp Thai fish sauce
15ml/1 tbsp sugar
225g/8oz drained canned bamboo shoots, rinsed and sliced
5 kaffir lime leaves, torn
salt and ground black pepper
chopped fresh red chillies and kaffir lime leaves, to garnish

For the red curry paste
5ml/1 tsp coriander seeds
2.5ml/½ tsp cumin seeds
12–15 fresh red chillies, seeded and roughly chopped
4 shallots, thinly sliced
2 garlic cloves, chopped
15ml/1 tbsp chopped galangal
2 lemon grass stalks, chopped
3 kaffir lime leaves, chopped
4 fresh coriander (cilantro) roots
10 black peppercorns
a good pinch of ground cinnamon
5ml/1 tsp ground turmeric
2.5ml/½ tsp shrimp paste
5ml/1 tsp salt
30ml/2 tbsp vegetable oil

1 To make the curry paste, dry-fry the coriander and cumin seeds for 1–2 minutes, then put in a mortar or food processor with the remaining ingredients except the oil and pound or process to a paste.

2 Add the oil, a little at a time, mixing or processing well after each addition. Transfer to a jar and keep in the refrigerator until ready to use.

3 Pour half the coconut milk into a large, heavy pan. Bring the milk to the boil, stirring constantly until it has separated.

4 Stir in 30ml/2 tbsp of the red curry paste and cook the mixture for 2–3 minutes, stirring constantly. Any remaining red curry paste can be stored for later use.

5 Add the chicken pieces, fish sauce and sugar to the pan. Stir well, then cook for 5–6 minutes until the chicken changes colour and is cooked through, stirring constantly to prevent the mixture from sticking to the bottom of the pan.

6 Add the remaining coconut milk to the chicken in the pan, then add the sliced bamboo shoots and torn kaffir lime leaves. Bring back to the boil over a medium heat, stirring constantly to prevent the mixture sticking, then taste and add salt and pepper if necessary.

7 To serve, spoon the curry into a warmed serving dish and garnish with chopped chillies and kaffir lime leaves.

Fragrant Grilled Chicken

If you have time, prepare the chicken in advance and leave it to marinate in the refrigerator for several hours – or even overnight.

Serves 4

450g/1lb chicken breast fillet, with skin
30ml/2 tbsp sesame oil
2 garlic cloves, crushed
2 coriander (cilantro) roots, finely chopped
2 small fresh red chillies, seeded and finely chopped
30ml/2 tbsp Thai fish sauce
5ml/1 tsp sugar
cooked rice, to serve
lime wedges, to garnish

For the sauce
90ml/6 tbsp rice vinegar
60ml/4 tbsp sugar
2.5ml/½ tsp salt
2 garlic cloves, crushed
1 small fresh red chilli, seeded and finely chopped
115g/4oz/4 cups fresh coriander (cilantro), finely chopped

1 Lay the chicken breast fillets between two sheets of clear film (plastic wrap), baking parchment or foil and beat with the side of a rolling pin or the flat side of a meat tenderizer until the meat is about half its original thickness. Place in a large, shallow dish or bowl.

2 Mix together the sesame oil, garlic, coriander roots, red chillies, fish sauce and sugar in a jug (pitcher), stirring until the sugar has dissolved. Pour the mixture over the chicken and turn to coat. Cover with clear film and set aside to marinate in a cool place for at least 20 minutes.

3 To make the sauce, heat the vinegar in a small pan, add the sugar and stir until dissolved. Add the salt and stir until the mixture begins to thicken. Add the remaining sauce ingredients, stir well, then spoon into a serving bowl.

4 Preheat the grill (broiler) and cook the chicken for 5 minutes. Turn over and baste with the marinade, then cook for 5 minutes more, or until cooked through and golden.

5 Serve with rice and the sauce, garnished with lime wedges.

red curry Energy 196kcal/827kJ; Protein 28.2g; Carbohydrate 11.2g, of which sugars 10.9g; Fat 4.5g, of which saturates 0.9g; Cholesterol 82mg; Calcium 76mg; Fibre 0.8g; Sodium 230mg.
fragrant chicken Energy 284kcal/1195kJ; Protein 36.8g; Carbohydrate 16.4g, of which sugars 16.3g; Fat 8.3g, of which saturates 1.5g; Cholesterol 106mg; Calcium 65mg; Fibre 1.3g; Sodium 71mg.

Barbecue Chicken with Lemon Grass

This is the perfect dish for a summer party, but you can also cook this tasty chicken in the oven if the weather proves disappointing.

Serves 4–6
1 chicken, about 1.6kg/3–3½lb, cut into 8–10 pieces
lime wedges and fresh red chillies, to garnish

For the marinade
2 lemon grass stalks, trimmed
2.5cm/1in piece fresh root ginger, peeled and thinly sliced
6 garlic cloves, coarsely chopped
4 shallots, coarsely chopped
½ bunch coriander (cilantro) roots, chopped
15ml/1 tbsp palm sugar (jaggery) or light muscovado (brown) sugar
120ml/4fl oz/½ cup coconut milk
30ml/2 tbsp Thai fish sauce
30ml/2 tbsp light soy sauce

1 To make the marinade, cut off the lower 5cm/2in of the lemon grass stalks and chop them coarsely. Put into a food processor with the ginger, garlic, shallots, coriander, sugar, coconut milk and sauces and process until smooth.

2 Place the chicken pieces in a dish, pour over the marinade and stir to mix well. Cover the dish and leave in a cool place to marinate for at least 4 hours, or preferably leave it in the refrigerator overnight.

3 Prepare the barbecue or preheat the oven to 200°C/400°F/Gas 6. Drain the chicken, reserving the marinade. If you are cooking in the oven, arrange the chicken pieces in a single layer on a rack set over a roasting pan.

4 Cook the chicken on the barbecue over moderately hot coals or on medium heat for a gas barbecue, or bake in the oven for 20–30 minutes. Turn the pieces and brush with the reserved marinade once or twice during cooking.

5 As soon as the chicken pieces are golden brown and cooked through, transfer them to a serving platter, garnish with the lime wedges and red chillies and serve immediately.

Lime Chicken with Sweet Potatoes

This chicken, delicately flavoured with garlic, turmeric and coriander, would traditionally be spit-roasted. However, it works very well as a conventional roast, and, cooked this way, it can be accompanied by the succulent addition of sweet potatoes flavoured with the delicious juices from the chicken.

Serves 4
4 garlic cloves, 2 finely chopped and 2 bruised but left whole
small bunch coriander (cilantro), with roots, coarsely chopped
10ml/2 tsp salt
5ml/1 tsp ground turmeric
5cm/2in piece fresh turmeric
1 roasting chicken, about 1.5kg/3¼lb
1 lime, cut in half
4 medium/large sweet potatoes, peeled and cut into thick wedges
300ml/½ pint/1¼ cups chicken or vegetable stock
30ml/2 tbsp soy sauce
salt and ground black pepper

1 Preheat the oven to 190°C/375°F/Gas 5. Calculate the cooking time for the chicken, allowing 20 minutes per 500g/1¼lb, plus 20 minutes.

2 Using a mortar and pestle or food processor, grind the chopped garlic, coriander, salt and turmeric to a paste.

3 Place the chicken in a roasting pan and smear it with the herb and spice paste. Squeeze the lime juice over and place the lime halves and garlic cloves in the cavity. Cover with foil and roast in the oven.

4 Meanwhile, bring a pan of water to the boil and parboil the sweet potatoes for 10–15 minutes, until just tender. Drain well and place them around the chicken in the roasting pan. Baste with the cooking juices and sprinkle with salt and pepper. Replace the foil and return the chicken to the oven.

5 About 20 minutes before the end of cooking, remove the foil and baste the chicken. Turn the sweet potatoes over.

6 At the end of the calculated roasting time, check that the chicken is cooked. Lift it out of the roasting pan, tilt it so that all the juices collected in the cavity drain into the pan, then place the bird on a carving board. Cover it with tented foil and leave it to rest before carving. Transfer the sweet potatoes to a serving dish and keep them hot in the oven while you make the gravy.

7 Pour away the oil from the roasting pan but keep the juices. Place the roasting pan on top of the stove and heat until the juices are bubbling. Pour in the stock. Bring the mixture to the boil, stirring constantly with a wooden spoon and scraping the base of the pan to incorporate the residue.

8 Stir in the soy sauce and check the seasoning before straining the gravy into a jug (pitcher). Serve it with the carved meat and the sweet potatoes.

barbecue chicken Energy 368kcal/1526kJ; Protein 30.6g; Carbohydrate 3.1g, of which sugars 3.1g; Fat 25.8g, of which saturates 7.5g; Cholesterol 160mg; Calcium 22mg; Fibre 0.1g; Sodium 135mg.
lime chicken Energy 620kcal/2581kJ; Protein 47g; Carbohydrate 21.3g, of which sugars 5.7g; Fat 38.9g, of which saturates 11.4g; Cholesterol 240mg; Calcium 43mg; Fibre 2.4g; Sodium 228mg.

Jade & Silver Chicken

The name of this dish stems from the use of broccoli and chicken, which symbolize jade and silver. Pretty, tasty and nutritious, it is a star item in most Chinese restaurants around the world. Traditionally, Chinese kinhua ham is used but this is rarely found outside China and any smoked or honey-cured ham can be used to good effect.

Serves 4

2 boneless chicken breast fillets, skin on
250ml/8fl oz/1 cup water
2 slices honey-cured or smoked ham
150g/5oz Chinese broccoli (kai lan) or tenderstem broccoli
15ml/1 tbsp cornflour (cornstarch)
½ chicken stock cube
30ml/2 tbsp Chinese wine
30ml/2 tbsp sesame oil
5ml/1 tsp ground black pepper

1 Put the chicken breasts in a pan and pour over the water. Bring to the boil, lower the heat and simmer for 10 minutes or until cooked through.

2 Lift out the chicken portions with tongs and put them on a board. Reserve the cooking liquid in the pan.

3 Slice the ham into 2.5cm/1in wide strips and cut the spears of broccoli into strips of similar length. Slice each piece of chicken in half lengthways and then in 2.5cm/1in strips.

4 Layer the broccoli, ham and chicken strips in a deep plate that will fit inside a wok or steamer. Steam the mixture over rapidly boiling water for 5 minutes.

5 Meanwhile, in a small bowl, mix the cornflour to a paste with a little of the water used for cooking the chicken. Crumble the chicken stock cube into the remaining water in the pan and add the cornflour paste Chinese wine, sesame oil and black pepper. Bring to the boil, stirring, until the sauce has the consistency of pouring cream.

6 Remove the steamed broccoli, ham and chicken from the steamer and pour the sauce over the top. Serve immediately.

Cashew Chicken

Although it is not native to South-east Asia, the cashew tree is highly prized in Thailand and the classic partnership of these slightly sweet nuts with chicken is immensely popular throughout the region.

Serves 4–6

450g/1lb boneless chicken breast portions
1 red (bell) pepper
2 garlic cloves, thinly sliced
4 dried red chillies, chopped
30ml/2 tbsp vegetable oil
30ml/2 tbsp oyster sauce
15ml/1 tbsp soy sauce
pinch of sugar
1 bunch spring onions (scallions), cut into 5cm/2in lengths
175g/6oz/1½ cups cashew nuts, roasted
coriander (cilantro) leaves, to garnish

1 Remove and discard the skin from the chicken breasts and trim off any excess fat. With a sharp knife, cut the chicken into bitesize pieces and set aside.

2 Halve the red pepper, scrape out the seeds and membranes and discard, then cut the flesh into 2cm/¾in dice.

3 Preheat a wok and then heat the oil. The best way to do this is to drizzle a 'necklace' of oil around the inner rim of the wok, so that it drops down to coat the entire inner surface. Make sure the coating is even by swirling the wok.

4 Add the garlic and dried chillies to the wok and stir-fry over a medium heat until golden. Do not let the garlic burn, otherwise it will taste bitter.

5 Add the chicken to the wok and stir-fry until it is cooked through, then add the red pepper. If the mixture is very dry, add a little water.

6 Stir in the oyster sauce, soy sauce and sugar. Add the spring onions and cashew nuts. Stir-fry for 1–2 minutes more, until heated through. Spoon into a warm dish and serve immediately, garnished with the coriander leaves.

jade & silver chicken Energy 182kcal/763kJ; Protein 22.9g; Carbohydrate 4.4g, of which sugars 0.9g; Fat 7.3g, of which saturates 1.3g; Cholesterol 63mg; Calcium 28mg; Fibre 1g; Sodium 261mg.
cashew chicken Energy 314kcal/1307kJ; Protein 24.7g; Carbohydrate 10.2g, of which sugars 6.2g; Fat 19.6g, of which saturates 3.7g; Cholesterol 53mg; Calcium 24mg; Fibre 1.7g; Sodium 268mg.

Chicken & Lemon Grass Curry

This truly delicious curry is exceptionally easy and takes less than 20 minutes to prepare and cook.

Serves 4

45ml/3 tbsp vegetable oil
2 garlic cloves, crushed
500g/1¼lb boneless chicken thighs, skinned and chopped into small pieces
45ml/3 tbsp Thai fish sauce
120ml/4fl oz/½ cup chicken stock
5ml/1 tsp sugar
1 lemon grass stalk, chopped into 4 pieces and lightly crushed
5 kaffir lime leaves, rolled into cylinders and thinly sliced across, plus extra to garnish
chopped roasted peanuts and chopped fresh coriander (cilantro), to garnish

For the curry paste

1 lemon grass stalk, coarsely chopped
2.5cm/1in piece fresh galangal, peeled and coarsely chopped
2 kaffir lime leaves, chopped
3 shallots, coarsely chopped
6 coriander roots, coarsely chopped
2 garlic cloves
2 fresh green chillies, seeded and coarsely chopped
5ml/1 tsp shrimp paste
5ml/1 tsp ground turmeric

1 To make the curry paste, place all the ingredients in a large mortar, or food processor, and pound with a pestle or process to a smooth paste.

2 Heat the vegetable oil in a wok or large frying pan, add the garlic and cook over a low heat, stirring frequently, until golden brown. Be careful not to let the garlic burn or it will taste bitter. Add the curry paste and stir-fry for about 30 seconds more.

3 Add the chicken pieces and stir until coated with the curry paste. Stir in the fish sauce and stock, with the sugar, and cook, stirring constantly, for 2 minutes more. Add the lemon grass and lime leaves, reduce the heat and simmer for 10 minutes. If the mixture begins to dry out, add a little more stock or water.

4 Remove the lemon grass, if you like. Spoon the curry into four dishes, garnish with the lime leaves, peanuts and fresh coriander and serve immediately.

Classic Balti Chicken

This recipe has a beautifully delicate flavour, and is probably the most popular of all balti dishes. Choose a young chicken as it will be more flavoursome.

Serves 4–6

1–1.3kg/2¼–3lb chicken
45ml/3 tbsp corn oil
3 medium onions, sliced
3 medium tomatoes, halved and sliced
2.5cm/1in cinnamon stick
2 large black cardamom pods
4 black peppercorns
2.5ml/½ tsp black cumin seeds
5ml/1 tsp grated fresh root ginger
5ml/1 tsp crushed garlic
5ml/1 tsp garam masala
5ml/1 tsp chilli powder
5ml/1 tsp salt
30ml/2 tbsp natural (plain) yogurt
60ml/4 tbsp lemon juice
30ml/2 tbsp chopped fresh coriander (cilantro)
2 fresh green chillies, chopped

1 Skin the chicken, then use a sharp knife to cut it into eight pieces. Wash and trim the chicken pieces, and set to one side.

2 Heat the oil in a large karahi, wok or deep pan. Add the onions and fry until they are golden brown. Add the tomatoes and stir well.

3 Add the piece of cinnamon stick, cardamoms, peppercorns, black cumin seeds, ginger, garlic, garam masala, chilli powder and salt. Lower the heat and stir-fry for 3–5 minutes.

4 Add the chicken pieces, two at a time, and stir-fry for at least 7 minutes or until the spice mixture has completely penetrated the chicken pieces and they are beginning to brown. Add the yogurt to the chicken and mix well.

5 Lower the heat and cover the pan with a piece of foil, making sure that the foil does not touch the food. Cook very gently for about 15 minutes, checking once to make sure the food is not catching on the bottom of the pan.

6 Finally, add the lemon juice, fresh coriander and green chillies. Serve immediately, straight from the pan.

chicken & lemon grass Energy 166kcal/694kJ; Protein 23.7g; Carbohydrate 5g, of which sugars 4.1g; Fat 5.8g, of which saturates 1.1g; Cholesterol 115mg; Calcium 105mg; Fibre 2.2g; Sodium 177mg.
balti chicken Energy 572kcal/2366kJ; Protein 27.1g; Carbohydrate 6.5g, of which sugars 3.8g; Fat 48.7g, of which saturates 22.8g; Cholesterol 180mg; Calcium 127mg; Fibre 1.8g; Sodium 187mg.

Khara Masala Balti Chicken

Whole spices (khara) are used in this recipe, giving it a wonderful, rich flavour. This is a dry dish so it is best served with plenty of creamy raita.

Serves 4

3 curry leaves
1.5ml/¼ tsp mustard seeds
1.5ml/¼ tsp fennel seeds
1.5ml/¼ tsp onion seeds
2.5ml/½ tsp crushed dried red chillies
2.5ml/½ tsp white cumin seeds
1.5ml/¼ tsp fenugreek seeds
2.5ml/½ tsp crushed pomegranate seeds
5ml/1 tsp salt
5ml/1 tsp shredded fresh root ginger
3 garlic cloves, sliced
60ml/4 tbsp corn oil
4 fresh green chillies, slit
1 large onion, sliced
1 medium tomato, sliced
675g/1½lb skinless, boneless chicken, cubed
15ml/1 tbsp chopped fresh coriander (cilantro)

1 Mix together the curry leaves, mustard seeds, fennel seeds, onion seeds, crushed red chillies, cumin seeds, fenugreek seeds, crushed pomegranate seeds and salt in a large bowl.

2 Add the shredded ginger and garlic cloves to the spice mixture in the bowl and stir well.

3 Heat the oil in a medium karahi, wok or deep pan. Add the spice mixture, then tip in the green chillies.

4 Spoon the sliced onion into the pan and fry over a medium heat for 5–7 minutes, stirring constantly to flavour the onion with the spices.

5 Finally add the tomato and chicken pieces, and cook over a medium heat for about 7 minutes. The chicken should be cooked through and the sauce reduced.

6 Stir everything together over the heat for a further 3–5 minutes. Serve from the pan, garnished with chopped fresh coriander.

Balti Chicken Pasanda

Yogurt and cream give this tasty dish its characteristic richness. Serve it with garlic and coriander naan to complement the almonds.

Serves 4

60ml/4 tbsp Greek (US strained plain) yogurt
2.5ml/½ tsp black cumin seeds
4 cardamom pods
6 whole black peppercorns
10ml/2 tsp garam masala
2.5cm/1in cinnamon stick
15ml/1 tbsp ground almonds
5ml/1 tsp crushed garlic
5ml/1 tsp grated fresh root ginger
5ml/1 tsp chilli powder
5ml/1 tsp salt
675g/1½lb skinless, boneless chicken, cubed
75ml/5 tbsp corn oil
2 medium onions, diced
3 fresh green chillies, chopped
30ml/2 tbsp chopped fresh coriander (cilantro), plus extra to garnish
120ml/4fl oz/½ cup single (light) cream

1 Mix the Greek yogurt, black cumin seeds, cardamom pods, whole black peppercorns, garam masala and cinnamon stick together in a medium mixing bowl. Add the ground almonds, garlic, ginger, chilli powder and salt and mix together well.

2 Add the cubed chicken pieces, stir to coat, and leave in the spice mixture to marinate for about 2 hours.

3 Heat the oil in a large karahi, wok or deep pan. Add the onions and fry for 2–3 minutes.

4 Tip in the chicken mixture and stir until it is well blended with the onions.

5 Cook for 12–15 minutes over a medium heat until the sauce thickens and the chicken is cooked through.

6 Add the chopped green chillies and fresh coriander to the chicken in the wok, and pour in the single cream. Bring to the boil, stirring constantly, and serve the dish garnished with more coriander, if you like.

khara masala Energy 299kcal/1254kJ; Protein 41.5g; Carbohydrate 3.4g, of which sugars 1.7g; Fat 13.5g, of which saturates 1.9g; Cholesterol 118mg; Calcium 28mg; Fibre 0.6g; Sodium 106mg.
chicken pasanda Energy 448kcal/1869kJ; Protein 45.6g; Carbohydrate 12.8g, of which sugars 6.9g; Fat 24.6g, of which saturates 6.7g; Cholesterol 135mg; Calcium 131mg; Fibre 2.2g; Sodium 132mg.

Balti Chicken Pieces with Cumin & Coriander

The potatoes are tossed in spices and cooked separately in the oven before being added to the chicken.

Serves 4
150ml/¼ pint/⅔ cup natural (plain) low-fat yogurt
25g/1oz/¼ cup ground almonds
7.5ml/1½ tsp ground coriander
2.5ml/½ tsp chilli powder
5ml/1 tsp garam masala
15ml/1 tbsp coconut milk
5ml/1 tsp crushed garlic
5ml/1 tsp grated fresh root ginger
30ml/2 tbsp chopped fresh coriander (cilantro)
1 fresh red chilli, seeded and chopped
225g/8oz skinned chicken breast fillets, cubed
15ml/1 tbsp oil
2 medium onions, sliced
3 green cardamom pods
2.5cm/1in cinnamon stick
2 cloves

For the potatoes
15ml/1 tbsp oil
8 baby potatoes, thickly sliced
1.5ml/¼ tsp cumin seeds
15ml/1 tbsp finely chopped fresh coriander (cilantro)

1 In a large bowl, mix together the first eight ingredients with half the fresh coriander and half the red chilli. Place the chicken pieces in the mixture, mix well, then cover and leave to marinate for about 2 hours.

2 Meanwhile, start to prepare the spicy potatoes. Heat the oil in a karahi, wok or heavy pan. Add the sliced potatoes, cumin seeds and fresh coriander and quickly stir-fry for 2–3 minutes.

3 Preheat the oven to 180°C/350°F/Gas 4. Spoon the potatoes into a baking dish, cover and bake for about 30 minutes or until they are cooked through.

4 Halfway through the potatoes' cooking time, heat the oil and fry the onions, cardamoms, cinnamon and cloves for 1½ minutes. Add the chicken mixture to the fried onions and stir-fry for 5–7 minutes. Lower the heat, cover and cook for 5–7 minutes. Top with the potatoes and garnish with coriander and red chilli.

Chicken & Tomato Balti

If you like tomatoes, you will love this chicken recipe. It makes a delicious semi-dry balti and is good served with a lentil dish and plain boiled rice.

Serves 4
60ml/4 tbsp corn oil
6 curry leaves
2.5ml/½ tsp mixed onion and mustard seeds
8 medium tomatoes, sliced
5ml/1 tsp ground coriander
5ml/1 tsp chilli powder
5ml/1 tsp salt
5ml/1 tsp ground cumin
5ml/1 tsp crushed garlic
675g/1½lb skinless, boneless chicken, cubed
150ml/¼ pint/⅔ cup water
15ml/1 tbsp sesame seeds, roasted
15ml/1 tbsp chopped fresh coriander (cilantro)

1 Heat the oil in a karahi, wok or deep round-bottomed frying pan. Add the curry leaves and mixed onion and mustard seeds.

2 Toss the seeds over the heat for 1–2 minutes so that they become fragrant. Do not let the seeds burn.

3 Lower the heat slightly and add the tomatoes.

4 While the tomatoes are gently cooking, mix together the ground coriander, chilli powder, salt, ground cumin and crushed garlic in a bowl.

5 Tip the spices on to the tomatoes in the wok or pan and stir well to mix thoroughly.

6 Add the chicken pieces and stir well. Stir-fry for about 5 minutes more.

7 Stir in the water and continue cooking, stirring occasionally, until the sauce thickens and the chicken is fully cooked and tender.

8 Sprinkle the roasted sesame seeds and chopped fresh coriander over the chicken and tomato balti. Serve immediately, from the pan.

balti chicken pieces Energy 269kcal/1126kJ; Protein 20.3g; Carbohydrate 22.9g, of which sugars 9.5g; Fat 11.6g, of which saturates 1.5g; Cholesterol 40mg; Calcium 136mg; Fibre 2.4g; Sodium 82mg.
chicken balti Energy 347kcal/1457kJ; Protein 43.4g; Carbohydrate 7.3g, of which sugars 4.7g; Fat 16.5g, of which saturates 2.4g; Cholesterol 118mg; Calcium 58mg; Fibre 1.8g; Sodium 118mg.

Balti Chicken in a Lentil Sauce

Traditionally, this dish is made with lamb, but it is equally delicious made with chicken breast.

Serves 4

30ml/2 tbsp chana dhal or yellow split peas
50g/2oz/¼ cup masoor dhal or red split peas
15ml/1 tbsp oil
2 medium onions, chopped
5ml/1 tsp crushed garlic
5ml/1 tsp grated fresh root ginger
2.5ml/½ tsp ground turmeric
7.5ml/1½ tsp chilli powder
5ml/1 tsp garam masala
2.5ml/½ tsp ground coriander
7.5ml/1½ tsp salt
175g/6oz skinned chicken breast fillets, cubed
45ml/3 tbsp fresh coriander (cilantro) leaves
1 or 2 fresh green chillies, seeded and chopped
30–45ml/2–3 tbsp lemon juice
300ml/½ pint/1¼ cups water
2 tomatoes, peeled and halved

For the tarka
5ml/1 tsp oil
2.5ml/½ tsp cumin seeds
2 garlic cloves
2 dried red chillies
4 curry leaves

1 Put the pulses in a pan with water and bring to the boil. Cook for 30–45 minutes until soft and mushy. Drain and set aside. Heat the oil in a karahi, wok or heavy frying pan and fry the onions until soft and golden brown. Stir in the garlic, ginger, turmeric, chilli powder, garam masala, ground coriander and salt.

2 Next, add the chicken pieces and fry for 5–7 minutes, stirring constantly over a medium heat to seal in the juices and lightly brown the meat.

3 Add half the fresh coriander, the green chillies, lemon juice and water and cook for 3–5 minutes. Stir in the cooked pulses, then add the tomatoes. Sprinkle over the remaining coriander leaves. Take the pan off the heat and set aside.

4 To make the tarka, heat the oil and add the cumin seeds, whole garlic cloves, dried red chillies and curry leaves. Heat for about 30 seconds, then pour over the top of the chicken and lentils. Serve the dish immediately.

Balti Chicken with Paneer & Peas

This is rather an unusual combination, but it really works well. Serve with plain boiled rice.

Serves 4

1 small chicken, about 675g/1½lb
30ml/2 tbsp tomato purée (paste)
45ml/3 tbsp natural (plain) low-fat yogurt
7.5ml/1½ tsp garam masala
5ml/1 tsp crushed garlic
5ml/1 tsp grated fresh root ginger
pinch of ground cardamom
15ml/1 tbsp chilli powder
1.5ml/¼ tsp ground turmeric
5ml/1 tsp salt
5ml/1 tsp sugar
10ml/2 tsp oil
2.5cm/1in cinnamon stick
2 black peppercorns
300ml/½ pint/1¼ cups water
115g/4oz paneer, cubed
30ml/2 tbsp fresh coriander (cilantro) leaves
2 fresh green chillies, seeded and chopped
50g/2oz/¼ cup low-fat fromage frais or ricotta cheese
75g/3oz/¾ cup frozen peas, thawed

1 Skin the chicken and cut it into six to eight equal pieces.

2 Mix the tomato purée, yogurt, garam masala, garlic, ginger, cardamom, chilli powder, turmeric, salt and sugar in a bowl.

3 Heat the oil with the whole spices in a karahi, wok or heavy pan, then pour the yogurt mixture into the oil. Lower the heat and cook gently for about 3 minutes, then pour in the water and bring to a simmer.

4 Add the chicken pieces to the pan. Stir-fry for 2 minutes, then cover the pan and cook over medium heat for about 10 minutes.

5 Add the paneer cubes to the pan, followed by half the coriander and half the green chillies. Mix well and cook for a further 5–7 minutes.

6 Stir in the fromage frais or ricotta and peas, heat through and serve with the reserved coriander and chillies.

chicken in a lentil sauce Energy 196kcal/823kJ; Protein 20.3g; Carbohydrate 9.8g, of which sugars 2.6g; Fat 8.7g, of which saturates 1.2g; Cholesterol 47mg; Calcium 41mg; Fibre 2.5g; Sodium 51mg.
chicken w. paneer Energy 313kcal/1303kJ; Protein 27.7g; Carbohydrate 7.3g, of which sugars 5.6g; Fat 19.3g, of which saturates 5.9g; Cholesterol 117mg; Calcium 87mg; Fibre 1.3g; Sodium 686mg.

Balti Chicken with Green & Red Chillies

Minced or ground chicken is seldom cooked in Indian homes. However, it works very well in this recipe.

Serves 4

275g/10oz skinned chicken breast fillet, cubed
2 plump fresh red chillies
3 plump fresh green chillies
30ml/2 tbsp oil
6 curry leaves
3 medium onions, sliced
7.5ml/1½ tsp crushed garlic
7.5ml/1½ tsp ground coriander
7.5ml/1½ tsp grated fresh root ginger
5ml/1 tsp chilli powder
5ml/1 tsp salt
15ml/1 tbsp lemon juice
30ml/2 tbsp chopped fresh coriander (cilantro)
chapatis and lemon wedges, to serve

1 Cook the chicken breast fillet in a pan of water for about 10 minutes until soft and cooked through. Remove with a slotted spoon and place in the bowl of a food processor fitted with a metal blade.

2 Roughly mince or grind the cooked chicken breast fillet.

3 Cut the chillies in half lengthways and remove the seeds for a milder flavour. Cut the flesh into strips and set aside.

4 Heat the oil in a karahi, wok or heavy pan and fry the curry leaves and onions until the onions are a soft golden brown. Lower the heat and stir in the garlic, ground coriander, ginger, chilli powder and salt.

5 Add the minced (ground) chicken to the onion and spices, and stir-fry for 3–5 minutes.

6 Add the lemon juice, the prepared chilli strips and most of the fresh coriander. Stir-fry for a further 3–5 minutes.

7 Serve, garnished with the remaining fresh coriander and accompanied by warm chapatis and lemon wedges.

Balti Chicken with Dhal & Leeks

This dish has rather an unusual combination of flavours. Slightly sour mango powder gives it a deliciously tangy flavour.

Serves 4–6

2 medium leeks
75g/3oz/⅓ cup chana dhal or yellow split peas
60ml/4 tbsp corn oil
6 large dried red chillies
4 curry leaves
5ml/1 tsp mustard seeds
10ml/2 tsp mango powder (amchur)
2 medium tomatoes, chopped
2.5ml/½ tsp chilli powder
5ml/1 tsp ground coriander
5ml/1 tsp salt
450g/1lb skinless, boneless chicken, cubed
15ml/1 tbsp chopped fresh coriander (cilantro), to garnish

1 Using a sharp knife, slice the leeks thinly into rounds. Separate the slices, rinse them in a colander under cold water to wash away any grit, then drain well.

2 Wash the chana dhal or split peas carefully and remove any grit or twigs.

3 Put the pulses into a pan with enough water to cover, and boil for about 10 minutes until they are soft but not mushy. Drain and set to one side in a bowl.

4 Heat the oil in a karahi, wok or deep pan. Lower the heat slightly and add the leeks, dried red chillies, curry leaves and mustard seeds. Stir-fry gently for a few minutes.

5 Add the mango powder, tomatoes, chilli powder, ground coriander, salt and chicken, and stir-fry for 7–10 minutes.

6 Mix in the cooked chana dhal or split peas and fry for a further 2 minutes, or until you are sure that the chicken is cooked right through.

7 Garnish with fresh coriander and serve immediately, from the pan.

balti chicken w. chillies Energy 139kcal/581kJ; Protein 18g; Carbohydrate 1.4g, of which sugars 0.5g; Fat 6.9g, of which saturates 0.9g; Cholesterol 48mg; Calcium 41mg; Fibre 0.6g; Sodium 48mg.
balti chicken w. dhal Energy 216kcal/906kJ; Protein 22.8g; Carbohydrate 11.4g, of which sugars 3.3g; Fat 9.1g, of which saturates 1.3g; Cholesterol 53mg; Calcium 34mg; Fibre 2.6g; Sodium 56mg.

Balti Chicken in Hara Masala Sauce

This chicken dish can be served as an accompaniment to any of the rice dishes in this book.

Serves 4

1 crisp green eating apple, peeled, cored and cut into small cubes
60ml/4 tbsp fresh coriander (cilantro) leaves
30ml/2 tbsp fresh mint leaves
120ml/4fl oz/½ cup natural (plain) low-fat yogurt
45ml/3 tbsp low-fat fromage frais or ricotta cheese
2 fresh green chillies, seeded and chopped
1 bunch spring onions (scallions), chopped
5ml/1 tsp salt
5ml/1 tsp sugar
5ml/1 tsp crushed garlic
5ml/1 tsp grated fresh root ginger
15ml/1 tbsp oil
225g/8oz skinned chicken breast fillets, cubed
25g/1oz/2 tbsp sultanas (golden raisins)

1 Place the apple, 45ml/3 tbsp of the fresh coriander, the mint, yogurt, fromage frais or ricotta, chillies, spring onions, salt, sugar, garlic and ginger in a food processor and pulse for about 1 minute.

2 Heat the oil in a karahi, wok or heavy pan, pour in the yogurt mixture and cook over a low heat for about 2 minutes.

3 Next, add the chicken pieces and blend everything together. Cook over a medium to low heat for 12–15 minutes or until the chicken is fully cooked.

4 Stir in the sultanas and the remaining 15ml/1 tbsp fresh coriander leaves and serve.

Cook's Tip
This dish makes an attractive centrepiece for a dinner party.

Balti Butter Chicken

Butter Chicken is one of the most popular balti chicken dishes, especially in the West. Cooked in butter, with aromatic spices, cream and almonds, this mild dish will be enjoyed by everyone. Serve with pilau rice.

Serves 4

150ml/¼ pint/⅔ cup natural (plain) yogurt
50g/2oz/½ cup ground almonds
7.5ml/1½ tsp chilli powder
1.5ml/¼ tsp crushed bay leaves
1.5ml/¼ tsp ground cloves
1.5ml/¼ tsp ground cinnamon
5ml/1 tsp garam masala
4 green cardamom pods
5ml/1 tsp grated fresh root ginger
5ml/1 tsp crushed garlic
400g/14oz/2 cups canned tomatoes
7.5ml/1¼ tsp salt
1kg/2¼lb skinless, boneless chicken, cubed
75g/3oz/6 tbsp butter
15ml/1 tbsp corn oil
2 medium onions, sliced
30ml/2 tbsp chopped fresh coriander (cilantro)
60ml/4 tbsp single (light) cream
coriander sprigs, to garnish

1 Put the yogurt in a bowl and add the ground almonds, chilli powder, crushed bay leaves, ground cloves, cinnamon, garam masala, cardamoms, ginger and garlic.

2 Chop the tomatoes and add them to the bowl with the salt. Mix thoroughly.

3 Put the chicken into a large mixing bowl and pour over the yogurt mixture. Set aside.

4 Melt together the butter and oil in a karahi, wok or deep pan. Add the onions and fry for about 3 minutes.

5 Add the chicken mixture and stir-fry for 7–10 minutes.

6 Sprinkle over about half of the coriander and mix well.

7 Pour over the single cream and stir in well. Heat through and serve, garnished with the remaining chopped fresh coriander and coriander sprigs.

chicken hara masala Energy 165kcal/693kJ; Protein 17.5g; Carbohydrate 11.8g, of which sugars 11.7g; Fat 5.7g, of which saturates 1.7g; Cholesterol 45mg; Calcium 106mg; Fibre 1.6g; Sodium 559mg.
balti butter chicken Energy 606kcal/2540kJ; Protein 84g; Carbohydrate 6.8g, of which sugars 3.4g; Fat 27.3g, of which saturates 3.8g; Cholesterol 239mg; Calcium 57mg; Fibre 1.3g; Sodium 214mg.

Balti Chicken in Thick Creamy Coconut Sauce

If you like the flavour of coconut, you will really love this aromatic curry.

Serves 4
15ml/1 tbsp ground almonds
15ml/1 tbsp desiccated (dry unsweetened shredded) coconut
75ml/2½fl oz/⅓ cup coconut milk
175g/6oz/⅔ cup low-fat fromage frais or ricotta cheese
7.5ml/1½ tsp ground coriander
5ml/1 tsp chilli powder
5ml/1 tsp crushed garlic
7.5ml/1½ tsp grated fresh root ginger
5ml/1 tsp salt
15ml/1 tbsp oil
225g/8oz skinned chicken fillet, cubed
3 green cardamom pods
1 bay leaf
1 dried red chilli, crushed
30ml/2 tbsp chopped fresh coriander (cilantro)

1 Using a heavy pan, dry-roast the ground almonds and desiccated coconut, stirring frequently, until they turn just a shade darker. Transfer the nut mixture to a mixing bowl.

2 Add the coconut milk, fromage frais or ricotta cheese, ground coriander, chilli powder, crushed garlic, ginger and salt to the mixing bowl.

3 Heat the oil in a karahi, wok or heavy pan and add the chicken cubes, cardamoms and bay leaf. Stir-fry for about 2 minutes to seal the chicken but not cook it.

4 Pour in the coconut milk mixture and blend everything together. Lower the heat, add the chilli and fresh coriander, cover and cook for 10–12 minutes, stirring occasionally. Uncover, then stir and cook for a further 2 minutes before serving, making sure the chicken is cooked.

Balti Chicken in Saffron Sauce

This is a beautifully aromatic chicken dish that is partly cooked in the oven.

Serves 4
50g/2oz/¼ cup butter
30ml/2 tbsp corn oil
1.2–1.3kg/2½–3lb chicken, skinned and cut into 8 pieces
1 medium onion, chopped
5ml/1 tsp crushed garlic
2.5ml/½ tsp crushed black peppercorns
2.5ml/½ tsp crushed cardamom pods
2.5ml/¼ tsp ground cinnamon
7.5ml/1½ tsp chilli powder
150ml/¼ pint/⅔ cup natural (plain) yogurt
50g/2oz/½ cup ground almonds
15ml/1 tbsp lemon juice
5ml/1 tsp salt
5ml/1 tsp saffron strands
150ml/¼ pint/⅔ cup water
150ml/¼ pint/⅔ cup single (light) cream
30ml/2 tbsp chopped fresh coriander (cilantro)

1 Preheat the oven to 180°C/350°F/Gas 4. Melt the butter with the oil in a karahi, wok or deep pan. Add the chicken pieces and fry until lightly browned, about 5 minutes. Remove the chicken using a slotted spoon, leaving behind the fat.

2 Add the onion to the same pan, and fry over a medium heat. Meanwhile, mix together the next 10 ingredients in a bowl. When the onions are lightly browned, pour the spice mixture into the pan and stir-fry for about 1 minute.

3 Add the chicken pieces, and continue to fry for a further 2 minutes, stirring constantly. Pour in the water and bring to a simmer. Transfer the contents of the pan to a casserole and cover with a lid, or, if using a karahi with heatproof handles, cover with foil. Transfer to the oven and cook for 30–35 minutes.

4 Once you are sure that the chicken is cooked right through, remove it from the oven. Transfer the mixture to a frying pan or place the karahi on the stove and stir in the cream.

5 Reheat gently for about 2 minutes. Garnish with fresh coriander and serve with a fruity pilau or plain boiled rice.

chicken in coconut sauce Energy 235kcal/982kJ; Protein 19.8g; Carbohydrate 5.5g, of which sugars 2.8g; Fat 15.2g, of which saturates 6.8g; Cholesterol 58mg; Calcium 39mg; Fibre 1g; Sodium 551mg.
chicken in saffron Energy 554kcal/2321kJ; Protein 75.6g; Carbohydrate 5.1g, of which sugars 4.7g; Fat 25.9g, of which saturates 12.2g; Cholesterol 255mg; Calcium 146mg; Fibre 0.8g; Sodium 792mg.

Balti Chicken with Vegetables

This is an excellent recipe for making a small amount of chicken go a long way. The carrots and courgettes add colour and boost the dish's nutritional value.

Serves 4–6

60ml/4 tbsp corn oil
2 medium onions, sliced
4 garlic cloves, thickly sliced
450g/1lb skinned chicken breast fillets, cut into strips
5ml/1 tsp salt
30ml/2 tbsp lime juice
3 fresh green chillies, chopped
2 medium carrots, cut into batons
2 medium potatoes, peeled and cut into 1cm/½in strips
1 medium courgette (zucchini), cut into batons
4 lime slices
15ml/1 tbsp chopped fresh coriander (cilantro)
2 fresh green chillies, cut into strips (optional)

1 Heat the oil in a large karahi, wok or deep pan. Lower the heat slightly and add the sliced onions. Fry until the onions are lightly browned and softened.

2 Add half the garlic slices and fry for a few seconds before adding the chicken strips and salt. Cook everything together, stirring, until all the moisture has evaporated and the chicken is lightly browned.

3 Add the lime juice, green chillies and all the vegetables to the pan. Increase the heat and add the rest of the garlic. Stir-fry for 7–10 minutes, or until the chicken is cooked through and the vegetables are just tender.

4 Transfer to a serving dish and garnish with the lime slices, fresh chopped coriander and green chilli strips, if you like. Serve the balti immediately.

Cook's Tip
Try other fresh vegetables in this dish, such as green beans, mangetouts (snow peas) and (bell) peppers.

Balti Chilli Chicken

Hot and spicy would be the best way of describing this mouthwatering balti dish. The smell of the fresh chillies while they are cooking is simply irresistible.

Serves 4–6

75ml/5 tbsp corn oil
8 large fresh green chillies, slit
2.5ml/½ tsp mixed onion seeds and cumin seeds
4 curry leaves
5ml/1 tsp grated fresh root ginger
5ml/1 tsp chilli powder
5ml/1 tsp ground coriander
5ml/1 tsp crushed garlic
5ml/1 tsp salt
2 medium onions, chopped
675g/1½lb skinned chicken fillets, cubed
15ml/1 tbsp lemon juice
15ml/1 tbsp roughly chopped fresh mint
15ml/1 tbsp roughly chopped fresh coriander (cilantro)
8–10 cherry tomatoes

1 Heat the oil in a karahi, wok or deep pan. Lower the heat slightly and add the slit green chillies. Fry until the skin starts to change colour.

2 Add the onion seeds and cumin seeds, curry leaves, ginger, chilli powder, ground coriander, garlic, salt and onions, and fry for a few seconds, stirring continuously.

3 Add the chicken pieces to the pan. Stir-fry over a medium heat for 7–10 minutes, or until the chicken is cooked right through. Do not overcook the chicken or it will become tough in texture.

4 Sprinkle on the lemon juice and add the roughly chopped fresh mint and coriander. Dot with the cherry tomatoes and serve from the pan.

Cook's Tip
Frying the whole spices before adding the chicken releases their lovely aromas.

chicken w. vegetables Energy 248kcal/1039kJ; Protein 21.2g; Carbohydrate 22.1g, of which sugars 10g; Fat 8.9g, of which saturates 1.2g; Cholesterol 53mg; Calcium 63mg; Fibre 3.7g; Sodium 70mg.
balti chilli chicken Energy 286kcal/1191kJ; Protein 19.1g; Carbohydrate 8.6g, of which sugars 7.6g; Fat 19.8g, of which saturates 7.4g; Cholesterol 87mg; Calcium 68mg; Fibre 2.3g; Sodium 562mg.

Balti Chicken in Tamarind Sauce

The tamarind in this recipe gives the dish a sweet and sour flavour.

Serves 4–6

60ml/4 tbsp tomato ketchup
15ml/1 tbsp tamarind paste
60ml/4 tbsp water
7.5ml/1½ tsp chilli powder
7.5ml/1½ tsp salt
15ml/1 tbsp granulated (white) sugar
7.5ml/1½ tsp grated fresh root ginger
7.5ml/1½ tsp crushed garlic
30ml/2 tbsp desiccated (dry unsweetened shredded) coconut
30ml/2 tbsp sesame seeds
5ml/1 tsp poppy seeds
5ml/1 tsp ground cumin
7.5ml/1½ tsp ground coriander
2 × 450g/1lb baby chickens, skinned and cut into 6–8 pieces each
75ml/5 tbsp corn oil
120ml/8 tbsp curry leaves
2.5ml/½ tsp onion seeds
3 large dried red chillies
2.5ml/½ tsp fenugreek seeds
10–12 cherry tomatoes
45ml/3 tbsp chopped fresh coriander (cilantro)
2 fresh green chillies, chopped

1 Put the tomato ketchup, tamarind paste and water into a large mixing bowl and use a fork to blend everything together. Add the chilli powder, salt, sugar, ginger, garlic, coconut, sesame and poppy seeds, cumin and coriander to the mixture. Stir to mix. Add the chicken pieces and stir until they are well coated with the spice mixture. Set aside.

2 Heat the oil in a karahi, wok or deep pan. Add the curry leaves, onion seeds, dried red chillies and fenugreek seeds and fry for about 1 minute.

3 Lower the heat to medium and add two or three chicken pieces at a time, with their sauce, mixing as you go. When all the pieces have been added to the pan, stir well, using a slotted spoon.

4 Simmer gently for about 12–15 minutes, or until the chicken is thoroughly cooked. Finally, add the tomatoes, fresh coriander and green chillies, and serve from the pan.

Balti Chicken Madras

This is a fairly hot chicken curry which is good served with either plain boiled rice, pilau rice or naan bread.

Serves 4

275g/10oz skinned chicken breast fillets
45ml/3 tbsp tomato purée (paste)
large pinch of ground fenugreek
1.5ml/¼ tsp ground fennel seeds
5ml/1 tsp grated fresh root ginger
7.5ml/1½ tsp ground coriander
5ml/1 tsp crushed garlic
5ml/1 tsp chilli powder
1.5ml/¼ tsp ground turmeric
30ml/2 tbsp lemon juice
5ml/1 tsp salt
300ml/½ pint/1¼ cups water
15ml/1 tbsp oil
2 medium onions, diced
2–4 curry leaves
2 fresh green chillies, seeded and chopped
15ml/1 tbsp fresh coriander (cilantro) leaves

1 Remove any visible fat from the chicken breasts and cut the meat into bitesize cubes.

2 Mix the tomato purée in a bowl with the fenugreek, fennel seeds, ginger, coriander, garlic, chilli powder, turmeric, lemon juice, salt and water.

3 Heat the oil in a karahi, wok or heavy pan and fry the diced onions together with the curry leaves until the onions are golden brown and softened.

4 Add the chicken pieces to the onions and stir over the heat for about 1 minute to seal the meat.

5 Next, pour in the prepared spice mixture and continue to stir the chicken for about 2 minutes.

6 Lower the heat and cook the spicy chicken for 8–10 minutes, stirring frequently to prevent the mixture from catching on the bottom of the pan.

7 Add the chopped chillies and fresh coriander leaves and serve the balti immediately.

chicken in tamarind Energy 286kcal/1191kJ; Protein 19.1g; Carbohydrate 8.6g, of which sugars 7.6g; Fat 19.8g, of which saturates 7.4g; Cholesterol 87mg; Calcium 68mg; Fibre 2.3g; Sodium 562mg.
chicken madras Energy 159kcal/667kJ; Protein 19.3g; Carbohydrate 11.5g, of which sugars 7.8g; Fat 4.4g, of which saturates 0.6g; Cholesterol 48mg; Calcium 65mg; Fibre 2.4g; Sodium 573mg.

Sweet & Sour Balti Chicken

This dish combines a sweet-and-sour flavour with a creamy texture. It is delicious served with pilau rice or naan bread.

Serves 4

45ml/3 tbsp tomato purée (paste)
30ml/2 tbsp Greek (US strained plain) yogurt
7.5ml/1½ tsp garam masala
5ml/1 tsp chilli powder
5ml/1 tsp crushed garlic
30ml/2 tbsp mango chutney
5ml/1 tsp salt
2.5ml/½ tsp sugar
60ml/4 tbsp corn oil
675g/1½lb skinned boneless chicken, cubed
150ml/¼ pint/⅔ cup water
2 fresh green chillies, chopped
30ml/2 tbsp chopped fresh coriander (cilantro)
30ml/2 tbsp single (light) cream

1 Mix the tomato purée, Greek yogurt, garam masala, chilli powder, crushed garlic, mango chutney, salt and sugar in a medium mixing bowl. Stir well.

2 Heat the oil in a karahi, wok or deep pan. Lower the heat slightly and pour in the spice mixture. Bring to the boil and cook for about 2 minutes, stirring occasionally.

3 Add the chicken pieces and stir until they are well coated.

4 Stir in the water to thin the sauce slightly. Continue cooking for 5–7 minutes, or until the chicken is fully cooked and tender.

5 Finally, add the fresh chillies, coriander and cream, cook for a further 2 minutes over a low heat, then serve.

Variation
If you like, you could lightly fry 1 sliced green (bell) pepper and 115g/4oz/1½ cups whole small button (white) mushrooms in 15ml/1 tbsp oil and add to the spice mixture with the chicken pieces in step 3.

Balti Chicken Vindaloo

This version of a popular dish from Goa is not as fiery as some, but will still suit those who like their curry to have a definite spicy impact.

Serves 4

1 large potato
150ml/¼ pint/⅔ cup malt vinegar
7.5ml/1½ tsp crushed coriander seeds
5ml/1 tsp crushed cumin seeds
7.5ml/1½ tsp chilli powder
1.5ml/¼ tsp ground turmeric
5ml/1 tsp crushed garlic
5ml/1 tsp grated fresh root ginger
5ml/1 tsp salt
7.5ml/1½ tsp paprika
15ml/1 tbsp tomato purée (paste)
large pinch of ground fenugreek
300ml/½ pint/1¼ cups water
225g/8oz skinned chicken breast fillets, cubed
15ml/1 tbsp oil
2 medium onions, sliced
4 curry leaves
2 fresh green chillies, chopped

1 Peel the potato, cut it into large, irregular shapes, place these in a bowl of water and set aside.

2 In a bowl, mix the vinegar, crushed coriander seeds, cumin, chilli powder, turmeric, garlic, ginger, salt, paprika, tomato purée, fenugreek and water.

3 Pour this spice mixture over the chicken, stir and set aside.

4 Heat the oil in a karahi, wok or heavy pan and quickly fry the onions with the curry leaves for 3–4 minutes without burning.

5 Lower the heat and add the chicken mixture to the pan with the spices. Continue to stir-fry for a further 2 minutes.

6 Drain the potato pieces and add to the pan. Cover with a lid and cook over a medium to low heat for 5–7 minutes, or until the sauce has thickened slightly and the chicken and potatoes are cooked through.

7 Stir in the chopped green chillies and serve.

sweet & sour chicken Energy 159kcal/667kJ; Protein 19.3g; Carbohydrate 11.5g, of which sugars 7.8g; Fat 4.4g, of which saturates 0.6g; Cholesterol 48mg; Calcium 65mg; Fibre 2.4g; Sodium 573mg.
balti vindaloo Energy 197kcal/831kJ; Protein 17.3g; Carbohydrate 23.1g, of which sugars 7.1g; Fat 4.8g, of which saturates 0.7g; Cholesterol 39mg; Calcium 47mg; Fibre 2.3g; Sodium 548mg.

Chicken with Lemon Sauce

Succulent chicken with a refreshing lemony sauce and just a hint of lime is a sure winner as a family meal that is quick and easy to prepare.

Serves 4

4 small skinless chicken breast fillets
5ml/1 tsp sesame oil
15ml/1 tbsp dry sherry
1 egg white, lightly beaten
30ml/2 tbsp cornflour (cornstarch)
15ml/1 tbsp vegetable oil
salt and ground white pepper
chopped coriander (cilantro) leaves and spring onions (scallions) and lemon wedges, to garnish

For the sauce

45ml/3 tbsp fresh lemon juice
30ml/2 tbsp sweetened lime juice
45ml/3 tbsp caster (superfine) sugar
10ml/2 tsp cornflour (cornstarch)
90ml/6 tbsp cold water

1 Arrange the chicken fillets in a single layer in a bowl. Mix the sesame oil with the sherry and add 2.5ml/½ tsp salt and 1.5ml/¼ tsp pepper. Pour over the chicken, cover and marinate for 15 minutes at room temperature.

2 Mix together the egg white and cornflour. Add the mixture to the chicken and turn the chicken with tongs until thoroughly coated.

3 Heat the vegetable oil in a non-stick frying pan or wok and fry the chicken fillets for about 15 minutes until they are golden brown on both sides.

4 Meanwhile, make the sauce. Combine the lemon juice, lime juice, sugar, cornflour and water in a small pan. Add 1.5ml/¼ tsp salt. Bring to the boil over a low heat, stirring constantly until the sauce is smooth and has thickened.

5 Cut the chicken into pieces and place on a warm serving plate. Pour the sauce over, garnish with the coriander leaves, spring onions and lemon wedges.

Chicken Rendang

This makes a marvellous dish for a buffet. Serve it with prawn crackers.

Serves 4

1 chicken, about 1.4kg/3lb
5ml/1 tsp sugar
75g/3oz/1 cup desiccated (dry unsweetened) coconut
4 small onions, chopped
2 garlic cloves, chopped
2.5cm/1in piece fresh root ginger, peeled and sliced
1–2 lemon grass stalks, root trimmed
2.5cm/1in piece fresh galangal, peeled and sliced
75ml/5 tbsp vegetable oil
10–15ml/2–3 tsp chilli powder
400ml/14fl oz can coconut milk
10ml/2 tsp salt
fresh chives and deep-fried anchovies, to garnish

1 Joint the chicken into eight pieces and remove the skin, sprinkle with the sugar and leave to stand for 1 hour. Meanwhile, dry-roast the coconut in a wok, turning all the time until it is crisp and golden. Tip into a food processor and process to an oily paste. Set aside.

2 Add the onions, garlic and ginger to the processor. Cut off the lower 5cm/2in of the lemon grass, chop and add to the processor with the galangal. Process to a fine paste.

3 Heat the oil in a wok or large pan and fry the onion mixture for a few minutes. Reduce the heat, stir in the chilli powder and cook for 2–3 minutes, stirring constantly. Spoon in 120ml/4fl oz/½ cup of the coconut milk and add salt to taste.

4 As soon as the mixture bubbles, add the chicken pieces, turning them until they are well coated with the spices. Pour in the coconut milk, stirring constantly to prevent curdling. Bruise the top of the lemon grass stalks and add to the wok or pan. Cover and cook for 45 minutes until the chicken is tender.

5 Just before serving, stir in the coconut paste. Bring to just below boiling point, then simmer for 5 minutes. Garnish with fresh chives and deep-fried anchovies and serve.

chicken with lemon Energy 235kcal/995kJ; Protein 30.9g; Carbohydrate 23.3g, of which sugars 14.1g; Fat 2.2g, of which saturates 0.5g; Cholesterol 88mg; Calcium 15mg; Fibre 0g; Sodium 97mg.
chicken rendang Energy 501kcal/2098kJ; Protein 55.4g; Carbohydrate 7.2g, of which sugars 7.2g; Fat 28.1g, of which saturates 12.5g; Cholesterol 158mg; Calcium 45mg; Fibre 2.6g; Sodium 1233mg.

Salt 'Baked' Chicken

This is a wonderful way of cooking chicken. All the delicious, succulent juices are sealed inside the salt crust – yet the flavour isn't too salty.

Serves 8

1.6kg/3½lb corn-fed chicken
1.5ml/¼ tsp fine sea salt
2.25kg/5lb coarse rock salt
15ml/1 tbsp vegetable oil
2.5cm/1in piece fresh root ginger, finely chopped
4 spring onions (scallions), cut into fine rings
boiled rice, garnished with shredded spring onions, to serve

1 Rinse the chicken. Pat it dry, both inside and out, with kitchen paper, then rub the inside with the sea salt. Place four pieces of damp kitchen paper on the bottom of a heavy deep pan or wok just large enough to hold the chicken.

2 Sprinkle a layer of rock salt over the kitchen paper, about 1cm/½in thick. Place the chicken on top of the layer of salt.

3 Pour the remaining salt over the chicken until it is completely covered. Dampen six more pieces of kitchen paper and place these around the rim of the pan or wok. Cover with a tight-fitting lid. Put the pan or wok over a high heat for 10 minutes or until it gives off a slightly smoky smell.

4 Immediately reduce the heat to medium and continue to cook the chicken for 30 minutes without lifting the lid. After 30 minutes, turn off the heat and leave for a further 10 minutes before carefully lifting the chicken out of the salt. Brush off any salt still clinging to the chicken and allow the bird to cool for 20 minutes before cutting it into serving-size pieces.

5 Heat the oil in a small pan until very hot. Add the ginger and spring onions and fry for a few seconds, then pour into a heatproof bowl and use as a dipping sauce for the chicken. Serve the chicken with rice, garnished with spring onions.

Spicy Fried Chicken

You cannot visit Malaysia or Singapore without trying the famous fried chicken. Indonesian in origin, ayam goreng puts Western fried chicken to shame. First the chicken is cooked in spices and flavourings to ensure a depth of taste, then it is simply deep-fried to form a crisp, golden skin.

Serves 4

2 shallots, chopped
4 garlic cloves, chopped
50g/2oz fresh root ginger or galangal, peeled and chopped
25g/1oz fresh turmeric, chopped
2 lemon grass stalks, chopped
6 whole chicken legs, separated into drumsticks and thighs
30ml/2 tbsp kecap manis
salt and ground black pepper
vegetable oil, for deep-frying

1 Using a mortar and pestle or food processor, grind the shallots, garlic, ginger or galangal, turmeric and lemon grass to a paste. Scrape into a bowl and set aside.

2 Place the chicken pieces in a heavy pan or flameproof pot and smear with the spice paste. Add the kecap manis and 150ml/¼ pint/⅔ cup water. Bring to the boil, reduce the heat and cook the chicken for about 25 minutes, turning it from time to time, until the liquid has evaporated. The chicken should be dry before deep-frying, but the spices should be sticking to it. Season with salt and pepper.

3 Heat enough oil for deep-frying in a wok. Fry the chicken pieces in batches until golden brown and crisp. Drain them on kitchen paper and serve hot with kecap manis.

Cook's Tip

Served with a sambal, or pickle, this makes a delicious snack, but for a main course, serve with yellow or fragrant coconut rice and a salad. If you cannot find kecap manis, use soy sauce sweetened with palm sugar (jaggery), which is sold in Chinese and Asian markets, or substitute the same quantity of dark soy sauce and 15ml/1 tbsp sugar.

salt 'baked' chicken Energy 133kcal/561kJ; Protein 30g; Carbohydrate 0g, of which sugars 0g; Fat 1.4g, of which saturates 0.4g; Cholesterol 88mg; Calcium 6mg; Fibre 0g; Sodium 75mg.
spicy fried chicken Energy 300kcal/1250kJ; Protein 31.9g; Carbohydrate 2.1g, of which sugars 0.9g; Fat 18.3g, of which saturates 2.9g; Cholesterol 158mg; Calcium 19mg; Fibre 0.2g; Sodium 136mg.

Caramelized Chicken Wings

These sticky, juicy chicken wings are irresistible.

Serves 2–4
75ml/5 tbsp sugar
60ml/4 tbsp water
30ml/2 tbsp vegetable oil
25g/1oz fresh root ginger, grated
12 chicken wings, split in two
chilli oil, for drizzling
mixed pickled vegetables, to serve

1 Heat the sugar and water in a heavy pan until it forms a golden syrup. Heat the oil in a wok and stir-fry the ginger until fragrant.

2 Add the chicken to the wok, brown them, then pour in the syrup and coat the chicken. Cover and cook for 30 minutes, until the chicken is tender. Drizzle chilli oil over and serve with pickles.

Barbecue Chicken

Perfect for a summer party.

Serves 4–6
1 chicken, cut into 8 pieces
lime wedges and fresh red chillies, to garnish

For the marinade
bulbs from 2 lemon grass stalks, chopped
2.5cm/1in piece fresh root ginger, peeled and thinly sliced
6 garlic cloves, coarsely chopped
4 shallots, coarsely chopped
½ bunch coriander (cilantro) roots, chopped
15ml/1 tbsp soft light brown sugar
120ml/4fl oz/½ cup coconut milk
30ml/2 tbsp fish sauce
30ml/2 tbsp light soy sauce

1 Make the marinade by processing all the ingredients in a food processor until smooth. Put the chicken pieces in a dish, pour over the marinade, cover and marinate for at least 4 hours.

2 Drain the chicken, reserving the marinade and cook over moderately hot coals for 20–30 minutes, turning and brushing with the marinade once or twice. Garnish and serve immediately.

Star Anise Chicken

The pungent flavour of star anise penetrates the chicken fillets and adds a wonderful aniseedy kick to the smoky flavour contributed by the barbecue. Serve the chicken with a refreshing salad.

Serves 4
4 skinless chicken breast fillets
2 whole star anise
30ml/2 tbsp soy sauce
30ml/2 tbsp vegetable oil
ground black pepper

1 Lay the skinless chicken breast fillets side by side in a shallow, non-metallic dish and add both pieces of star anise, keeping them whole.

2 Place the soy sauce in a small bowl. Add the oil and whisk together with a fork until the mixture emulsifies. Season to taste with black pepper to make a simple marinade.

3 Pour the marinade over the chicken and stir to coat each breast fillet all over. Cover the dish with clear film (plastic wrap) and chill in the refrigerator for up to 8 hours.

4 Prepare a barbecue. Cook the chicken fillets over medium hot coals for 8–10 minutes on each side, spooning over the marinade from time to time, until the chicken is cooked through. Transfer to a platter and serve immediately.

Variation
In wetter weather, this dish can be prepared indoors. Simply place the marinaded chicken fillets under a grill (broiler) and cook, turning once, for the same amount of time.

Cook's Tip
With its aroma of liquorice, star anise is the chief component in Chinese five-spice powder. In China, the points of the star are sometimes snapped off and sucked as a breath freshener.

chicken wings Energy 393kcal/1641kJ; Protein 30.5g; Carbohydrate 14.4g, of which sugars 14.4g; Fat 24.1g, of which saturates 6.3g; Cholesterol 134mg; Calcium 16mg; Fibre 0g; Sodium 91mg.
barbecue chicken Energy 374kcal/1553kJ; Protein 30.4g; Carbohydrate 6.1g, of which sugars 5.4g; Fat 25.4g, of which saturates 7.4g; Cholesterol 157mg; Calcium 28mg; Fibre 0.5g; Sodium 145mg.
star anise chicken Energy 210kcal/884kJ; Protein 36.1g; Carbohydrate 0.3g, of which sugars 0.3g; Fat 7.2g, of which saturates 1.2g; Cholesterol 105mg; Calcium 8mg; Fibre 0g; Sodium 357mg.

Crispy Five-spice Chicken

Tender strips of chicken fillet, with a delicately spiced rice flour coating, become deliciously crisp and golden when shallow-fried.

Serves 4

200g/7oz thin egg noodles
30ml/2 tbsp sunflower oil
2 garlic cloves, very thinly sliced
1 fresh red chilli, seeded and sliced
½ red (bell) pepper, seeded and very thinly sliced
300g/11oz carrots, peeled and cut into thin strips
300g/11oz Chinese broccoli or Chinese greens, roughly sliced
45ml/3 tbsp hoisin sauce
45ml/3 tbsp soy sauce
15ml/1 tbsp caster (superfine) sugar
4 skinless chicken breast fillets, cut into strips
2 egg whites, lightly beaten
115g/4oz/1 cup rice flour
15ml/1 tbsp Chinese five-spice powder
salt and ground black pepper
vegetable oil, for frying

1 Cook the noodles in boiling water for 2–4 minutes, or according to the packet instructions, drain and set aside.

2 Heat a wok, add the sunflower oil, and when it is hot add the garlic, chilli, red pepper, carrots and the broccoli or greens. Stir-fry over a high heat for 2–3 minutes.

3 Add the sauces and sugar to the wok and cook for a further 2–3 minutes. Add the drained noodles, toss to combine, then remove from the heat, cover and keep warm.

4 Dip the chicken strips into the egg white. Combine the rice flour and five-spice powder in a shallow dish and season with salt and ground black pepper. Add the chicken strips to the flour mixture and toss to coat.

5 Heat about 2.5cm/1in oil in a clean wok. When hot, shallow-fry the chicken for 3–4 minutes until crisp and golden.

6 To serve, divide the noodle mixture among warmed plates or bowls and top each serving with the chicken.

Bang Bang Chicken

Toasted sesame paste gives this dish an authentic flavour, although crunchy peanut butter can be used instead.

Serves 4

3 chicken breast fillets
1 garlic clove, crushed
2.5ml/½ tsp black peppercorns
1 small onion, halved
1 large cucumber, peeled, seeded and cut into thin strips
salt and ground black pepper

For the sauce

45ml/3 tbsp toasted sesame paste
15ml/1 tbsp light soy sauce
15ml/1 tbsp wine vinegar
2 spring onions (scallions), chopped
2 garlic cloves, crushed
5 × 1cm/2 × ½in piece fresh root ginger, peeled and cut into matchsticks
15ml/1 tbsp Sichuan peppercorns, dry-fried and crushed
5ml/1 tsp soft light brown sugar

For the chilli oil

60ml/4 tbsp groundnut (peanut) oil
5ml/1 tsp chilli powder

1 Place the chicken in a pan. Just cover with water, add the garlic, peppercorns and onion and bring to the boil. Skim the surface, season to taste, then cover. Cook for 25 minutes or until the chicken is just tender. Drain, reserving the stock.

2 Make the sauce by mixing the toasted sesame paste with 45ml/3 tbsp of the chicken stock, saving the rest for soup. Add the soy sauce, vinegar, spring onions, garlic, ginger and crushed peppercorns to the sesame mixture. Stir in sugar to taste.

3 Make the chilli oil by gently heating the oil and chilli powder together until foaming. Simmer for 2 minutes, cool, then strain off the red-coloured oil and discard the sediment.

4 Spread out the cucumber batons on a platter. Cut the chicken into pieces the same size as the batons and arrange on top. Pour over the sauce, drizzle on the chilli oil and serve.

five-spice chicken Energy 679kcal/2849kJ; Protein 43.9g; Carbohydrate 75.8g, of which sugars 17g; Fat 23.2g, of which saturates 3.7g; Cholesterol 103mg; Calcium 96mg; Fibre 6.3g; Sodium 1207mg.
bang bang chicken Energy 200kcal/838kJ; Protein 29.5g; Carbohydrate 2.8g, of which sugars 2.4g; Fat 7.9g, of which saturates 1.3g; Cholesterol 79mg; Calcium 89mg; Fibre 1.2g; Sodium 338mg.

Chicken with Hijiki Seaweed

The taste of hijiki – a type of seaweed – is somewhere between rice and vegetable. It goes well with meat or tofu products, especially when stir-fried in the wok first with a little oil.

Serves 2

90g/3½oz dried hijiki seaweed
150g/5oz chicken breast fillet
½ small carrot, about 5cm/2in
15ml/1 tbsp vegetable oil
100ml/3fl oz/scant ½ cup instant dashi powder plus 1.5ml/¼ tsp dashi-no-moto
30ml/2 tbsp sake
30ml/2 tbsp caster (superfine) sugar
45ml/3 tbsp shoyu
a pinch of cayenne pepper

1 Soak the hijiki in cold water for about 30 minutes. It will be ready to cook when it can be easily crushed between the fingers. Pour into a sieve (strainer) and wash under running water. Drain.

2 Peel the skin from the chicken and parboil the skin in rapidly boiling water for 1 minute, then drain. With a sharp knife, shave off all the yellow fat from the skin. Discard the clear membrane between the fat and the skin as well. Cut the skin into thin strips about 5mm/¼in wide and 2.5cm/1in long. Cut the meat into small, bitesize chunks.

3 Peel and chop the carrot into long, narrow matchsticks.

4 Heat the oil in a wok or frying pan and stir-fry the strips of chicken skin for 5 minutes, or until golden and curled up. Add the chicken meat and keep stirring until the colour changes.

5 Add the hijiki and carrot, then stir-fry for a further minute. Add the remaining ingredients. Lower the heat and toss over the heat for 5 minutes more.

6 Remove the wok from the heat and stand for 10 minutes. Season and serve in small individual bowls.

Stir-fried Chicken with Chillies

There are variations of this dish, using pork or seafood, throughout South-east Asia so, for a smooth and easy introduction to the cooking of the region, this typical, home-cooked stir-fry is a good place to start. Serve with a salad, rice wrappers and a dipping sauce.

Serves 4

15ml/1 tbsp sugar
30ml/2 tbsp sesame or groundnut (peanut) oil
2 garlic cloves, finely chopped
2–3 fresh green or red chillies, seeded and finely chopped
2 lemon grass stalks, finely sliced
1 onion, finely sliced
350g/12oz skinless chicken breast fillets, cut into bitesize strips
30ml/2 tbsp soy sauce
15ml/1 tbsp fish sauce
1 bunch fresh coriander (cilantro), stalks removed, leaves chopped
salt and ground black pepper
chilli sambal, to serve

1 Put the sugar into a pan with 5ml/1 tsp water. Heat gently until the sugar has dissolved and formed a caramel syrup. Set aside.

2 Heat a large wok or heavy pan and add the sesame or groundnut oil. Stir in the chopped garlic, chillies and lemon grass, and stir-fry until they become fragrant and golden. Add the onion and stir-fry for 1 minute, then add the chicken strips.

3 When the chicken is cooked through, add the soy sauce, fish sauce and caramel syrup. Stir to mix and heat through, then season with a little salt and pepper. Stir in the coriander and serve with chilli sambal.

Cook's Tip
When adding the oil to the hot wok, drizzle it around the inner rim like a necklace. The oil will run down to coat the entire surface of the wok. Swirl the wok several times to make sure the coating is even.

chicken with seaweed Energy 154kcal/644kJ; Protein 10g; Carbohydrate 10.4g, of which sugars 10.2g; Fat 8.4g, of which saturates 2g; Cholesterol 39mg; Calcium 76mg; Fibre 1.1g; Sodium 884mg.
stir-fried chicken w. chillies Energy 196kcal/819kJ; Protein 27.2g; Carbohydrate 0.4g, of which sugars 0.4g; Fat 9.5g, of which saturates 1.3g; Cholesterol 79mg; Calcium 7mg; Fibre 0g; Sodium 424mg.

Chicken with Mixed Vegetables

Far East Asian cooks are experts in making delicious dishes from a relatively small amount of meat and a lot of vegetables. Good news for anyone trying to eat less fat.

Serves 4

350g/12oz skinless chicken breast fillets
20ml/4 tsp vegetable oil
300ml/½ pint/1¼ cups chicken stock
75g/3oz/¾ cup drained, canned straw mushrooms
50g/2oz/½ cup sliced, drained, canned bamboo shoots
50g/2oz/⅓ cup drained, canned water chestnuts, sliced
1 small carrot, sliced
50g/2oz/½ cup mangetouts (snow peas)
15ml/1 tbsp dry sherry
15ml/1 tbsp oyster sauce
5ml/1 tsp caster (superfine) sugar
5ml/1 tsp cornflour (cornstarch)
15ml/1 tbsp cold water
salt and ground white pepper

1 Put the chicken in a shallow bowl. Add 5ml/1 tsp of the oil, 1.5ml/¼ tsp salt and a pinch of pepper. Cover and set aside for 10 minutes in a cool place.

2 Bring the stock to the boil in a pan. Add the chicken fillets and cook for 12 minutes, or until tender. Drain and slice, reserving 75ml/5 tbsp of the chicken stock.

3 Heat the remaining oil in a non-stick frying pan or wok, add all the vegetables and stir-fry for 2 minutes. Stir in the sherry, oyster sauce, caster sugar and reserved stock. Add the chicken to the pan and cook for 2 minutes more.

4 Mix the cornflour to a paste with the water. Add the mixture to the pan and cook, stirring, until the sauce thickens slightly. Season to taste with salt and pepper and serve immediately.

Cook's Tip
Water chestnuts give a dish great texture as they remain crunchy, no matter how long you cook them for.

Chicken with Young Ginger

Ginger plays a big role in Far East Asian cooking, particularly in the stir-fried dishes. Whenever possible, the juicier and more pungent young ginger is used. This is a simple and delicious way to cook chicken, pork or beef.

Serves 4

30ml/2 tbsp groundnut (peanut) oil
3 garlic cloves, finely sliced in strips
50g/2oz fresh young root ginger, finely sliced in strips
2 fresh red chillies, seeded and finely sliced in strips
4 chicken breast fillets or 4 boned chicken legs, skinned and cut into bitesize chunks
30ml/2 tbsp fish sauce
10ml/2 tsp sugar
1 small bunch coriander (cilantro) stalks removed, roughly chopped
ground black pepper
jasmine rice and crunchy salad or baguette, to serve

1 Heat a wok or heavy pan and add the oil. Add the garlic, ginger and chillies, and stir-fry until fragrant and golden. Add the chicken and toss it around the wok for 1–2 minutes.

2 Stir in the fish sauce and sugar, and stir-fry for a further 4–5 minutes until cooked. Season with pepper and add some of the fresh coriander.

3 Transfer the chicken to a serving dish and garnish with the remaining coriander. Serve hot with jasmine rice and a crunchy salad with fresh herbs, or with chunks of baguette.

Cook's Tip
Young ginger is generally available in Chinese and South-east Asian markets. It has smooth, thin skin, which clings to the flesh, whereas older ginger has thicker skin and is easier to peel. The flavour of young ginger has citric tones and the flesh is really juicy.

chicken with vegetables Energy 154kcal/646kJ; Protein 22.2g; Carbohydrate 4.9g, of which sugars 3.4g; Fat 4.3g, of which saturates 0.7g; Cholesterol 61mg; Calcium 17mg; Fibre 1g; Sodium 61mg.
chicken with ginger Energy 222kcal/935kJ; Protein 36.4g; Carbohydrate 3g, of which sugars 2.9g; Fat 7.3g, of which saturates 1.1g; Cholesterol 105mg; Calcium 32mg; Fibre 0.6g; Sodium 101mg.

Kung Po Chicken

This recipe, which hails from the Sichuan region of western China, has become one of the classic recipes in the Chinese repertoire. The combination of yellow salted beans and hoisin, spiked with chilli and softened with cashews, makes for a very tasty and spicy sauce.

Serves 3
1 egg white
10ml/2 tsp cornflour (cornstarch)
2.5ml/½ tsp salt
2–3 skinless chicken breast fillets, cut into neat pieces
30ml/2 tbsp yellow salted beans
15ml/1 tbsp hoisin sauce
5ml/1 tsp soft light brown sugar
15ml/1 tbsp dry sherry
15ml/1 tbsp wine vinegar
4 garlic cloves, crushed
150ml/¼ pint/⅔ cup chicken stock
45ml/3 tbsp sunflower oil
2–3 dried chillies, broken into small pieces
115g/4oz/1 cup roasted cashew nuts
fresh coriander (cilantro), to garnish

1 Lightly whisk the egg white in a dish, whisk in the cornflour and salt, then add the chicken and stir until coated.

2 In a separate bowl, mash the salted beans with a spoon. Stir in the hoisin sauce, brown sugar, dry sherry, vinegar, garlic and chicken stock.

3 Heat a wok, add the oil and then stir-fry the chicken, turning constantly, for about 2 minutes until tender. Either drain the chicken over a bowl to collect excess oil, or lift out each piece with a slotted spoon, leaving the oil in the wok.

4 Heat the reserved oil and fry the chilli pieces for 1 minute. Return the chicken to the wok and pour in the bean sauce mixture. Bring to the boil and stir in the cashew nuts. Spoon into a heated serving dish, garnish with coriander leaves and serve immediately.

Stir-fried Chicken with Basil

Thai basil has a unique, pungent flavour that is both spicy and sharp. Deep-frying the leaves adds another dimension to this quick and easy chicken dish.

Serves 4–6
45ml/3 tbsp vegetable oil
4 garlic cloves, thinly sliced
2–4 fresh red chillies, seeded and finely chopped
450g/1lb skinless chicken breast fillets, cut into bitesize pieces
45ml/3 tbsp fish sauce
10ml/2 tsp dark soy sauce
5ml/1 tsp sugar
10–12 fresh Thai basil leaves
2 fresh red chillies, seeded and finely chopped, and about 20 deep-fried Thai basil leaves, to garnish

1 Heat the oil in a wok or large, heavy frying pan. Add the garlic and chillies and stir-fry over a medium heat for about 1–2 minutes until the garlic is golden. Take care not to let the garlic burn, otherwise it will taste bitter.

2 Add the pieces of chicken to the wok or pan, in batches if necessary, and stir-fry until the chicken changes colour.

3 Stir in the fish sauce, soy sauce and sugar. Continue to stir-fry the mixture for 3–4 minutes, or until the chicken is fully cooked and golden brown.

4 Stir in the fresh Thai basil leaves. Spoon the mixture on to a warm platter, or into individual dishes. Garnish with the chopped chillies and deep-fried Thai basil and serve.

Cook's Tip
To deep-fry Thai basil leaves, heat groundnut (peanut) oil to 190°C/375°F. Add the leaves, which must be completely dry, and deep-fry them for about 30 seconds until they are crisp and translucent. Lift out the leaves and drain on kitchen paper.

kung po chicken Energy 490kcal/2040kJ; Protein 37.7g; Carbohydrate 12.4g, of which sugars 2.6g; Fat 31.9g, of which saturates 5.6g; Cholesterol 82mg; Calcium 24mg; Fibre 1.9g; Sodium 204mg.
stir-fried chicken w. basil Energy 135kcal/566kJ; Protein 18.3g; Carbohydrate 1.1g, of which sugars 1g; Fat 6.4g, of which saturates 1g; Cholesterol 53mg; Calcium 21mg; Fibre 0.4g; Sodium 167mg.

Lemon & Sesame Chicken

These delicate strips of chicken are at their best if you leave them to marinate overnight.

Serves 4

4 large chicken breast fillets, skinned and cut into strips
15ml/1 tbsp light soy sauce
15ml/1 tbsp Chinese rice wine
2 garlic cloves, crushed
10ml/2 tsp finely grated fresh root ginger
1 egg, lightly beaten
150g/5oz cornflour (cornstarch)
sunflower oil, for deep-frying
toasted sesame seeds, to sprinkle
rice or noodles, to serve

For the sauce
15ml/1 tbsp sunflower oil
2 spring onions (scallions), finely sliced
1 garlic clove, crushed
10ml/2 tsp cornflour (cornstarch)
90ml/6 tbsp chicken stock
10ml/2 tsp finely grated lemon rind
30ml/2 tbsp lemon juice
10ml/2 tsp sugar
2.5ml/½ tsp sesame oil
salt

1 Mix the chicken strips with the soy sauce, wine, garlic and ginger in a bowl. Toss together to combine, then cover and marinate in the refrigerator for 8–10 hours.

2 When ready to cook, add the beaten egg to the chicken and mix well, then drain off any excess liquid. Put the cornflour in a plastic bag, add the chicken pieces and shake to coat the strips.

3 Deep-fry the chicken in hot oil for 3–4 minutes for each batch. As each batch cooks, lift it out and drain on kitchen paper. Reheat the oil and deep-fry all the chicken in batches for a second time, for 2–3 minutes. Remove and drain well.

4 To make the sauce, add the oil to a hot wok and stir-fry the spring onions and garlic for 1–2 minutes. Add the remaining ingredients and cook for 2–3 minutes until thickened.

5 Return the chicken to the wok, toss lightly to coat with sauce, and sprinkle over the sesame seeds. Serve with rice or noodles.

Stir-fried Giblets with Garlic

Throughout China and the neighbouring countries, there is a keen appreciation of offal or variety meats. Giblets are popular and are used in various ways. Apart from being tossed into the stockpot, they are often stir-fried with garlic and ginger and served with rice. This dish, featuring fish sauce, is typical of Southern China.

Serves 2–4

30ml/2 tbsp groundnut (peanut) oil
2 shallots, halved and finely sliced
2 garlic cloves, finely chopped
1 fresh red chilli, seeded and finely sliced
25g/1oz fresh root ginger, peeled and shredded
225g/8oz chicken livers, trimmed and finely sliced
115g/4oz mixed giblets, finely sliced
15–30ml/1–2 tbsp fish sauce
1 small bunch coriander (cilantro), finely chopped
ground black pepper
steamed rice, to serve

1 Heat the oil in a wok or heavy pan. Stir in the shallots, garlic, chilli and ginger, and stir-fry until golden. Add the chicken livers and mixed giblets and stir-fry for a few minutes more, until browned on all sides.

2 Stir in the fish sauce, adjusting the quantity according to taste, and half the chopped coriander. Season with ground black pepper and garnish with the rest of the coriander. Serve hot, with steamed fragrant rice.

Variations
- *If you are not keen on giblets, simply increase the quantity of chicken livers to 275g/12oz.*
- *Alternatively, try this recipe with thinly-sliced lamb's liver.*
- *A red onion can be substituted for the shallots, and a red (bell) pepper used instead of chilli for a milder taste.*
- *Use Worcestershire sauce instead of fish sauce for a fusion version of this dish.*

lemon & sesame Energy 450kcal/1892kJ; Protein 38.2g; Carbohydrate 37.1g, of which sugars 2.5g; Fat 17.6g, of which saturates 2.6g; Cholesterol 157mg; Calcium 25mg; Fibre 0.1g; Sodium 397mg.
stir-fried giblets Energy 134kcal/556kJ; Protein 15.2g; Carbohydrate 1.5g, of which sugars 1.1g; Fat 7.4g, of which saturates 1.3g; Cholesterol 290mg; Calcium 12mg; Fibre 0.2g; Sodium 359mg.

Chinese Chicken with Cashew Nuts

The cashew nuts give this dish a delightful crunchy texture that contrasts well with the noodles.

Serves 4

4 skinless chicken breast fillets (about 175g/6oz each)
3 garlic cloves, crushed
60ml/4 tbsp soy sauce
30ml/2 tbsp cornflour (cornstarch)
225g/8oz/4 cups dried egg noodles
45ml/3 tbsp groundnut (peanut) or sunflower oil
15ml/1 tbsp sesame oil
115g/4oz/1 cup roasted cashew nuts
6 spring onions (scallions), cut into 5cm/2in pieces and halved lengthways
spring onion curls and a little chopped fresh red chilli, to garnish

1 Slice the chicken into strips, place in a bowl and stir in the garlic, soy sauce and cornflour. Cover with clear film (plastic wrap) and chill in the refrigerator for about 30 minutes.

2 Meanwhile, bring a pan of water to the boil and add the egg noodles. Turn off the heat and leave to stand for 5 minutes. Drain well and reserve.

3 Heat the oils in a large frying pan or wok. Add the chilled chicken and marinade juices and stir-fry over high heat for 3–4 minutes, or until golden brown.

4 Add the cashew nuts and spring onions to the pan or wok and stir-fry for a further 2–3 minutes.

5 Add the drained noodles and stir-fry for 2 minutes more. Toss the noodles well and serve immediately, garnished with the spring onion curls and chopped chilli.

Cook's Tip
For a milder garnish, seed the red chilli before chopping or finely dice some red (bell) pepper instead.

Chinese-style Chicken Salad

For a variation and to add more colour, add some cooked, peeled prawns to this lovely salad.

Serves 4

4 chicken breast fillets (about 175g/6oz each)
60ml/4 tbsp dark soy sauce
pinch of Chinese five-spice powder
squeeze of lemon juice
½ cucumber, peeled and cut into thin batons
5ml/1 tsp salt
45ml/3 tbsp sunflower oil
30ml/2 tbsp sesame oil
15ml/1 tbsp sesame seeds
30ml/2 tbsp Chinese rice wine or dry sherry
2 carrots, cut into thin batons
8 spring onions (scallions), shredded
75g/3oz/1 cup beansprouts

For the sauce
60ml/4 tbsp crunchy peanut butter
10ml/2 tsp lemon juice
10ml/2 tsp sesame oil
1.5ml/¼ tsp hot chilli powder
1 spring onion, finely chopped

1 Put the chicken into a pan and pour in water to cover. Add 15ml/1 tbsp of the soy sauce, the Chinese five-spice powder and lemon juice. Cover and bring to the boil, then lower the heat and simmer for 20 minutes. Drain the chicken and remove and discard the skin. Slice the flesh into thin strips.

2 Sprinkle the cucumber batons with salt, leave for 30 minutes, then rinse well and pat dry with kitchen paper.

3 Heat the oils in a small frying pan. Add the sesame seeds and cook for 30 seconds, then stir in the remaining soy sauce and the rice wine or sherry. Add the carrot batons and stir-fry for 2 minutes, then remove the pan from the heat.

4 Mix together the cucumber, spring onions, beansprouts, carrots, pan juices and chicken. Transfer to a shallow dish. Cover with clear film (plastic wrap) and chill in the refrigerator for 1 hour.

5 For the sauce, cream the first four ingredients together, then stir in the spring onion. Serve the chicken with the sauce.

chicken w. cashew Energy 717kcal/3007kJ; Protein 55.5g; Carbohydrate 54.3g, of which sugars 4.2g; Fat 32.3g, of which saturates 6.1g; Cholesterol 139mg; Calcium 44mg; Fibre 2.8g; Sodium 1363mg.
chicken salad Energy 452kcal/1886kJ; Protein 47g; Carbohydrate 4.1g, of which sugars 3g; Fat 27.2g, of which saturates 4.8g; Cholesterol 123mg; Calcium 53mg; Fibre 1.5g; Sodium 1720mg.

Sticky Ginger Chicken

For a fuller flavour, marinate the chicken drumsticks in the glaze for 30 minutes.

Serves 4

8 chicken drumsticks
30ml/2 tbsp lemon juice
25g/1oz/2 tbsp light muscovado (brown) sugar
5ml/1 tsp grated fresh root ginger
10ml/2 tsp soy sauce
ground black pepper

1 Slash the chicken drumsticks about three times through the thickest part of the flesh. Mix all the remaining ingredients in a bowl, then toss the drumsticks in the glaze.

2 Cook them under a hot grill (broiler) or on a barbecue, turning occasionally and brushing with the glaze, until golden and the juices run clear when the thickest part is pierced.

Chicken Opur

Opur is of Indonesian origin and a milder kind of curry. Traditionally, the spice blend is boiled rather being pre-fried in oil. It has a subtle taste of coconut milk with hints of tartness from the sour star fruit and tamarind concentrate.

Serves 4

4 chicken legs
500ml/16fl oz/2 cups coconut milk
2 lime leaves
2 stalks lemon grass
5ml/1 tsp salt
30ml/2 tbsp tamarind concentrate
5ml/1 tsp sugar
4 sour star fruit (carambola)
30ml/2 tbsp desiccated (dry unsweetened shredded) coconut

For the spice paste

2 red chillies, seeded and chopped
5 candlenuts
½ large onion, chopped
3 garlic cloves, chopped
30ml/2 tbsp ground coriander
5ml/1 tsp ground fennel
2 thin slices galangal
25g/1oz shrimp paste

1 Using a heavy knife or cleaver, separate each chicken leg into a thigh and a drumstick, and remove the skin if desired.

2 Put the coconut milk in a large pan, add the pieces of chicken and bring to the boil.

3 Using a mortar and pestle, grind the spice paste ingredients until fine and add to the pan with the lime leaves, bruised 5cm/2in root ends of the lemon grass stalks, salt, tamarind and sugar. Simmer for 20 minutes.

4 Slice each sour star fruit into two lengthways, remove the pith and add to the pan. Simmer for a further 10 minutes, until the chicken is cooked through.

5 While the chicken is cooking, dry-fry the desiccated coconut in another pan until it is light brown. When the chicken is cooked, sprinkle the coconut over the dish and serve immediately.

Orange Glazed Poussins

Succulent poussins coated in a spiced citrus glaze make a great alternative to a traditional roast.

Serves 4

4 poussins, 300–350g/11–12oz each
juice and finely grated rind of 2 oranges
2 garlic cloves, crushed
15ml/1 tbsp grated fresh root ginger
90ml/6 tbsp soy sauce
75ml/5 tbsp clear honey
2–3 star anise
30ml/2 tbsp Chinese rice wine
about 20 kaffir lime leaves
a large bunch of spring onions (scallions), shredded
60ml/4 tbsp butter
1 large orange, segmented, to garnish

1 Place the poussins in a deep, non-metallic dish. Combine the orange rind and juice, garlic, ginger, half the soy sauce, half the honey, star anise and rice wine, then coat the poussins with the mixture. Cover and marinate in the refrigerator for at least 6 hours.

2 Line a large, heatproof plate with the kaffir lime leaves and spring onions. Lift the poussins out of the marinade and place on the leaves. Reserve the marinade.

3 Place a trivet or steamer rack in the base of a large wok and pour in 5cm/2in water. Bring to the boil and carefully lower the plate of poussins on to the trivet. Cover, reduce the heat to low and steam for 45–60 minutes, or until the poussins are cooked through and tender. (Check the water level regularly and add more as needed.)

4 Remove the poussins from the wok and keep hot while you make the glaze. Wipe out the wok and pour in the reserved marinade, butter and the remaining soy sauce and honey. Bring to the boil, then reduce the heat and cook gently for 10–15 minutes, or until thick. Spoon the glaze over the poussins and serve immediately, garnished with the orange segments.

sticky ginger chicken Energy 234kcal/980kJ; Protein 29.2g; Carbohydrate 6.5g, of which sugars 6.5g; Fat 10.3g, of which saturates 2.7g; Cholesterol 155mg; Calcium 20mg; Fibre 0g; Sodium 145mg.
chicken opur Energy 292kcal/1225kJ; Protein 30.6g; Carbohydrate 13.9g, of which sugars 11.4g; Fat 13.2g, of which saturates 6.4g; Cholesterol 118mg; Calcium 136mg; Fibre 1.3g; Sodium 479mg
orange glazed poussins Energy 544kcal/2264kJ; Protein 36.2g; Carbohydrate 5.8g, of which sugars 5.8g; Fat 42.1g, of which saturates 14.5g; Cholesterol 215mg; Calcium 16mg; Fibre 0g; Sodium 207mg.

Thai Chicken Curry

This flavourful and fragrant, creamy curry is quite easy to make.

Serves 6

400ml/14oz can unsweetened coconut milk
6 skinless, chicken breast fillets, finely sliced
225g/8oz can bamboo shoots, drained and sliced
30ml/2 tbsp fish sauce
15ml/1 tbsp soft light brown sugar
cooked jasmine rice, to serve

For the green curry paste

4 fresh green chillies, seeded
1 lemon grass stalk, sliced
1 small onion, sliced
3 garlic cloves
1cm/½in piece galangal or fresh root ginger, peeled
grated rind of ½ lime
5ml/1 tsp coriander seeds
5ml/1 tsp cumin seeds
2.5ml/½ tsp fish sauce

To garnish

1 fresh red chilli, seeded and cut into fine strips
finely pared rind of ½ lime, finely shredded
fresh Thai purple basil or coriander (cilantro), chopped

1 First make the green curry paste: put all the ingredients in a food processor and process to a thick paste. Set aside.

2 Bring half the coconut milk to the boil in a large frying pan, then reduce the heat and simmer for about 5 minutes, or until reduced by half. Stir in the green curry paste and simmer for a further 5 minutes.

3 Add the finely sliced chicken breasts to the pan with the remaining coconut milk, bamboo shoots, fish sauce and sugar. Stir well to combine all the ingredients and bring the curry back to simmering point, then simmer gently for about 10 minutes, or until the chicken slices are cooked through. The mixture will look grainy or curdled during cooking; this is quite normal.

4 Spoon the curry and rice into warmed bowls, garnish with the chilli, lime rind, and basil or coriander, and serve.

Chicken & Tofu Curry

This very spicy curry has great textures and flavours.

Serves 4

30ml/2 tbsp groundnut (peanut) or soya oil
2 garlic cloves, crushed
2 onions, chopped
2.5cm/1in piece fresh root ginger, finely chopped
4 skinless chicken fillets, cut into bitesize pieces
15–30ml/1–2 tbsp Thai green or red curry paste
45ml/3 tbsp soy sauce
150g/5oz marinated deep-fried tofu
grated rind and juice of 1 lime
120ml/4fl oz/½ cup chicken stock
pinch of sugar
90g/3½oz watercress
20g/¾oz fresh coriander (cilantro), chopped
400ml/14fl oz/1⅔ cups coconut milk
30ml/2 tbsp peanuts, toasted and chopped, to garnish

1 Heat the oil in a non-stick wok or large frying pan, then stir-fry the garlic, onion and ginger for 4–5 minutes, until golden brown and softened. Add the chicken pieces and stir-fry for 2–3 minutes, until browned all over. Add the curry paste and stir to coat the chicken. Add the soy sauce, tofu, grated lime rind and juice, the stock and sugar, and stir-fry for 2 minutes.

2 Add the watercress and coriander, reserving a little for the garnish, and stir-fry for a further 2 minutes. Add the coconut milk and heat through gently, stirring occasionally, but do not allow to come to the boil.

3 Season to taste, then serve, garnished with the peanuts and reserved coriander.

Variation
Vary the vegetable accompaniments used to suit the season – mangetouts (snow peas), baby corn, courgettes (zucchini), carrots, broccoli florets and green beans all work well.

thai chicken curry Energy 236kcal/991kJ; Protein 33.8g; Carbohydrate 7.2g, of which sugars 5.9g; Fat 8.3g, of which saturates 1.6g; Cholesterol 165mg; Calcium 149mg; Fibre 3.1g; Sodium 253mg.
chicken & tofu Energy 444kcal/1851kJ; Protein 37.3g; Carbohydrate 14.6g, of which sugars 10g; Fat 26.7g, of which saturates 3.2g; Cholesterol 70mg; Calcium 699mg; Fibre 3.6g; Sodium 222mg.

Chicken & Sweet Potato Curry

Ho Chi Minh City is home to many stalls specializing in curries like this one. They all use Indian curry powder and coconut milk.

Serves 4

45ml/3 tbsp Indian curry powder
15ml/1 tbsp ground turmeric
500g/1¼lb skinless boneless chicken thighs or chicken breast fillets
25ml/1½ tbsp raw cane sugar
30ml/2 tbsp sesame oil
2 shallots, chopped
2 garlic cloves, chopped
4cm/1½in galangal, peeled and chopped
2 lemon grass stalks, chopped
10ml/2 tsp chilli paste or dried chilli flakes
2 medium sweet potatoes, peeled and cubed
45ml/3 tbsp chilli sambal
600ml/1 pint/2½ cups coconut milk
1 small bunch each fresh basil and coriander (cilantro), stalks removed
salt and ground black pepper

1 In a small bowl, mix together the curry powder and turmeric. Put the chicken in a bowl and coat with half of the spice. Set aside.

2 Heat the sugar in a small pan with 7.5ml/1½ tsp water, until the sugar dissolves and the syrup turns golden. Remove from the heat and set aside.

3 Heat a wok or heavy pan and add the oil. Stir-fry the shallots, garlic, galangal and lemon grass. Stir in the rest of the turmeric and curry powder with the chilli paste or flakes, followed by the chicken, and stir-fry for 2–3 minutes.

4 Add the sweet potatoes, then the chilli sambal, syrup, coconut milk and 150ml/¼ pint/⅔ cup water, mixing thoroughly to combine the flavours.

5 Bring to the boil, reduce the heat and cook for about 15 minutes until the chicken is cooked through. Season and stir in half the basil and coriander. Spoon into warmed bowls, garnish with the remaining herbs and serve immediately.

Chicken with Chinese Vegetables

The chicken can be replaced by almost any other meat or shellfish, such as pork, beef or prawns.

Serves 4

225–275g/8–10oz chicken, boned and skinned
5ml/1 tsp salt
½ egg white, lightly beaten
10ml/2 tsp cornflour (cornstarch) paste
60ml/4 tbsp vegetable oil
6–8 small dried shiitake mushrooms, soaked
115g/4oz sliced bamboo shoots, drained
115g/4oz mangetout (snow peas), trimmed
1 spring onion (scallion), cut into short sections
a few small pieces fresh root ginger, peeled
5ml/1 tsp soft light brown sugar
15ml/1 tbsp light soy sauce
15ml/1 tbsp Chinese rice wine or dry sherry
a few drops sesame oil

1 Cut the chicken into bitesize pieces. Place in a bowl and mix with a pinch of the salt, the egg white and the cornflour paste.

2 Heat the oil in a preheated wok, stir-fry the chicken over medium heat for about 30 seconds, then remove with a perforated spoon and keep warm.

3 Stir-fry the vegetables over high heat for about 1 minute. Add the salt, sugar and chicken. Blend, then add the soy sauce and wine or sherry. Stir a few more times. Sprinkle with the sesame oil and serve.

Cook's Tip
These popular oriental mushrooms are also known as Chinese black mushrooms and are available dried or fresh. Dried shiitake mushrooms have a strong, almost meaty flavour. To rehydrate, soak them in warm water for 20 minutes, stirring occasionally. Then strain (the liquid can be used in cooking) and use as fresh mushrooms. Fresh shiitake mushrooms have firm caps and a light brown meaty flesh with a distinctive flavour.

chicken & potato Energy 384kcal/1621kJ; Protein 29.5g; Carbohydrate 39.7g, of which sugars 20.7g; Fat 13.1g, of which saturates 2.5g; Cholesterol 131mg; Calcium 181mg; Fibre 5.8g; Sodium 373mg.
chicken w. vegetables Energy 317kcal/1329kJ; Protein 24.8g; Carbohydrate 46.2g, of which sugars 4.8g; Fat 3g, of which saturates 0.5g; Cholesterol 53mg; Calcium 65mg; Fibre 2.7g; Sodium 179mg.

Curry with Coconut & Chilli Relish

Fresh and roasted coconut gives this chicken curry its unique flavour.

Serves 4

15–30ml/1–2 tbsp tamarind pulp
1 fresh coconut, grated
30–45ml/2–3 tbsp vegetable oil
1–2 cinnamon sticks
12 chicken thighs, boned and cut into bitesize strips lengthways
600ml/1 pint/2½ cups coconut milk
15ml/1 tbsp brown sugar
1 fresh green and 1 red chilli, seeded and sliced
fresh coriander (cilantro) leaves, finely chopped (reserve a few leaves for garnishing)
2 limes
salt and ground black pepper
steamed rice, to serve

For the rempah spice paste

6–8 dried red chillies, soaked in warm water until soft, seeded and squeezed dry
6–8 shallots, chopped
4–6 garlic cloves, chopped
25g/1oz fresh root ginger, chopped
5ml/1 tsp shrimp paste
10ml/2 tsp ground turmeric
10ml/2 tsp five-spice powder

1 First make the rempah. Using a mortar and pestle or food processor, grind the chillies, shallots, garlic and ginger to a paste. Beat in the shrimp paste and stir in the dried spices.

2 Soak the tamarind pulp in 150ml/¼ pint/⅔ cup warm water until soft. Squeeze to extract the juice, then strain. In a heavy pan, roast half the grated coconut until brown, then grind it in a food processor until it resembles sugar grains.

3 Heat the oil in a heavy pan and stir in the rempah and cinnamon sticks until fragrant. Add the chicken, coconut milk, tamarind water and sugar. Cook gently for 10 minutes. Thicken by stirring in half the ground roasted coconut, and season.

4 Make a relish by mixing the remaining grated coconut with the chillies, coriander and juice of 1 lime. Cut the other lime into wedges. Spoon the curry into a serving dish and garnish with coriander. Serve with the rice, relish and lime wedges.

Jungle Curry of Guinea Fowl

A traditional wild food country curry, this dish can be made using any game, fish or chicken.

Serves 4

1 guinea fowl or similar game bird
15ml/1 tbsp vegetable oil
10ml/2 tsp green curry paste
15ml/1 tbsp fish sauce
2.5cm/1in piece fresh galangal, peeled and finely chopped
15ml/1 tbsp fresh green peppercorns
3 kaffir lime leaves, torn
15ml/1 tbsp whisky
300ml/½ pint/1¼ cups chicken stock
50g/2oz snake beans or yard-long beans, cut into 2.5cm/1in lengths (about ½ cup)
225g/8oz/3¼ cups chestnut mushrooms, sliced
1 piece drained, canned bamboo shoot, about 50g/2oz, shredded

1 Cut up the guinea fowl, remove and discard the skin, then take all the meat off the bones. Chop the meat into bitesize pieces and set aside on a plate.

2 Heat the oil in a wok or frying pan and add the curry paste. Stir-fry over a medium heat for 30 seconds, until the paste gives off its aroma. Add the fish sauce and the guinea fowl meat and stir-fry until the meat is browned all over. Add the galangal, peppercorns, lime leaves and whisky, then pour in the stock.

3 Bring to the boil. Add the vegetables, return to a simmer and cook gently for 2–3 minutes, until they are just cooked. Spoon into a dish, and serve.

Cook's Tip

Fresh green peppercorns are simply unripe berries. They are sold on the stem and look rather like miniature Brussels sprout stalks. Look for them at Thai supermarkets. If unavailable, substitute bottled green peppercorns, but rinse well and drain them before adding them to the curry.

curry w. coconut Energy 706kcal/2935kJ; Protein 48.1g; Carbohydrate 15.8g, of which sugars 15.6g; Fat 50.4g, of which saturates 12.8g; Cholesterol 240mg; Calcium 91mg; Fibre 1.5g; Sodium 305mg.
curry of guinea fowl Energy 321kcal/1345kJ; Protein 42.2g; Carbohydrate 1.1g, of which sugars 0.7g; Fat 15g, of which saturates 4.4g; Cholesterol 0mg; Calcium 72mg; Fibre 1.1g; Sodium 136mg.

Hot Sweet & Sour Duck Casserole

This tasty recipe can be made with any game bird, or even rabbit. It is a distinctively sweet, sour and hot dish best eaten with rice as an accompaniment.

Serves 4–6

1.3kg/3lb duck, jointed and skinned
4 bay leaves
10ml/2 tsp salt
75ml/5 tbsp vegetable oil
juice of 5 lemons
8 medium onions, finely chopped
4 or 5 garlic cloves, crushed
15ml/1 tbsp chilli powder
300ml/½ pint/1¼ cups pickling vinegar
5cm/2in piece fresh root ginger, shredded
115g/4oz/generous ½ cup sugar
15ml/1 tbsp garam masala

1 Place the prepared duck, bay leaves and salt in a large pan and cover with cold water. Bring to the boil, then simmer for 30–45 minutes, or until the duck is fully cooked. Remove the pieces of duck and keep warm. Reserve the liquid as a base for stock or soup.

2 In a large pan, heat the oil and lemon juice until it reaches smoking point. Add the onions, garlic and chilli powder and fry the onions until they are golden brown.

3 Add the vinegar, ginger and sugar and simmer until the sugar dissolves and the oil has separated from the mixture.

4 Return the duck to the pan and add the garam masala. Mix well, then reheat until the masala clings to the pieces of duck and the sauce is thick. Adjust the seasoning if necessary. If you prefer a thinner sauce, add a little of the reserved stock.

Cook's Tip
Be very careful when adding the onions and garlic to the oil and lemon juice mixture. Stand well back and use a spoon to scrape the onions into the pan, a few at a time. The hot mixture is likely to spit and splutter.

Duck Curry

Robust spices, coconut milk and chillies combined with orange make this a mouthwatering curry. The duck is best marinated for as long as possible.

Serves 4

4 duck breast portions, skinned and boned
30ml/2 tbsp five-spice powder
30ml/2 tbsp sesame oil
grated rind and juice of 1 orange
1 medium butternut squash, peeled and cubed
10ml/2 tsp Thai red curry paste
30ml/2 tbsp Thai fish sauce
15ml/1 tbsp palm sugar (jaggery) or light muscovado (brown) sugar
300ml/½ pint/1¼ cups coconut milk
2 fresh red chillies, seeded
4 kaffir lime leaves, torn
plain cooked noodles, to serve
small bunch coriander (cilantro), chopped, to garnish

1 Cut the duck meat into bitesize pieces and place in a bowl with the five-spice powder, sesame oil and grated orange rind and juice. Stir well to mix all the ingredients and coat the duck in the marinade.

2 Cover the bowl with clear film (plastic wrap) and set aside in a cool place to marinate for at least 15 minutes but preferably overnight.

3 Meanwhile, bring a pan of water to the boil. Add the butternut squash and cook for 10–15 minutes, until just tender. Drain well and set aside.

4 Pour the marinade from the duck into a wok and heat until boiling. Stir in the curry paste and cook for 2–3 minutes, until well blended and fragrant. Add the duck and cook for 3–4 minutes, stirring constantly, until browned on all sides.

5 Add the fish sauce and palm sugar and cook for 2 minutes more. Stir in the coconut milk until the mixture is smooth, then add the cooked squash, with the chillies and lime leaves.

6 Simmer gently, stirring frequently, for 5 minutes, then serve in a dish with the noodles, sprinkled with the coriander.

duck casserole Energy 328kcal/1374kJ; Protein 21.4g; Carbohydrate 30.6g, of which sugars 27.5g; Fat 15.9g, of which saturates 2.4g; Cholesterol 110mg; Calcium 56mg; Fibre 1.9g; Sodium 443mg.
duck curry Energy 306kcal/1282kJ; Protein 30.9g; Carbohydrate 10.9g, of which sugars 10.2g; Fat 15.8g, of which saturates 4.1g; Cholesterol 165mg; Calcium 86mg; Fibre 1.5g; Sodium 248mg.

Duck & Sesame Stir-fry

Wild duck is beautifully lean and full of flavour, and it is the best meat to use for this incredibly quick but tasty stir-fry. If you can't find any wild duck, use farmed duck but be sure to remove the skin and fat layer otherwise the meat will be too fatty for this recipe.

Serves 4

250g/9oz boneless wild duck meat
15ml/1 tbsp sesame oil
15ml/1 tbsp vegetable oil
4 garlic cloves, finely sliced
2.5ml/½ tsp dried chilli flakes
15ml/1 tbsp Thai fish sauce
15ml/1 tbsp light soy sauce
120ml/4fl oz/½ cup water
1 head broccoli, cut into small florets
coriander (cilantro) and 15ml/1 tbsp toasted sesame seeds, to garnish

1 Cut the duck meat into bitesize pieces. Heat the sesame and vegetable oils in a wok or large, heavy frying pan and stir-fry the sliced garlic over a medium heat until it is golden brown – do not let it burn.

2 Add the duck to the pan and stir-fry for a further 2 minutes, until the meat begins to brown.

3 Stir in the chilli flakes, fish sauce, soy sauce and water.

4 Add the broccoli and continue to stir-fry for about 2 minutes, until the duck is just cooked through.

5 Serve the stir-fry on warmed plates, garnished with coriander and sesame seeds.

Variations
- *Partridge, pheasant and pigeon are all suitable game birds for this recipe.*
- *Pak choi (bok choy) or Chinese flowering cabbage can be used instead of broccoli.*

Red Duck Curry

Slow simmering is the secret of this wonderful duck curry.

Serves 4

4 skinless duck breast fillets
400ml/14fl oz can coconut milk
200ml/7fl oz/scant 1 cup chicken stock
30ml/2 tbsp red curry paste
8 spring onions (scallions), finely sliced
10ml/2 tsp grated fresh root ginger
30ml/2 tbsp Chinese rice wine
15ml/1 tbsp fish sauce
15ml/1 tbsp soy sauce
2 lemon grass stalks, halved lengthways
3–4 kaffir lime leaves
300g/11oz pea aubergines (eggplants)
10ml/2 tsp sugar
salt and ground black pepper
10–12 fresh basil and mint leaves, to garnish
steamed jasmine rice, to serve

1 Using a sharp knife, cut the duck breast portions into neat bitesize pieces and set aside on a plate.

2 Place a wok over a low heat and add the coconut milk, stock, curry paste, spring onions, ginger, rice wine, fish and soy sauces, lemon grass and lime leaves. Stir well to mix, then bring to the boil over a medium heat.

3 Add the duck, aubergines and sugar to the wok and simmer for 25–30 minutes, stirring occasionally.

4 Remove the wok from the heat and leave to stand, covered, for about 15 minutes. Season to taste.

5 Ladle the duck curry into shallow bowls, garnish with fresh mint and basil leaves, and serve with steamed jasmine rice.

Cook's Tip
Tiny pea aubergines (eggplants) are sold in Asian stores. If you can't find them, use regular aubergines, cut into neat chunks.

duck stir-fry Energy 172kcal/718kJ; Protein 17.3g; Carbohydrate 2g, of which sugars 1.7g; Fat 10.6g, of which saturates 2.2g; Cholesterol 69mg; Calcium 71mg; Fibre 2.9g; Sodium 78mg.
red duck curry Energy 241kcal/1017kJ; Protein 31.1g; Carbohydrate 10.2g, of which sugars 10g; Fat 10.5g, of which saturates 2.3g; Cholesterol 165mg; Calcium 65mg; Fibre 1.8g; Sodium 546mg.

Duck with Pineapple

Duck and pineapple is a favourite combination, but the fruit must not be allowed to dominate as you will upset the delicate balance in sweet-sour flavour.

Serves 4

15ml/1 tbsp dry sherry
15ml/1 tbsp dark soy sauce
2 small skinless duck breast fillets
15ml/1 tbsp vegetable oil
2 garlic cloves, finely chopped
1 small onion, sliced
1 red (bell) pepper, seeded and cut into 2.5cm/1in squares
75g/3oz/½ cup drained, canned pineapple chunks
90ml/6 tbsp pineapple juice
15ml/1 tbsp rice vinegar
5ml/1 tsp cornflour (cornstarch)
15ml/1 tbsp cold water
5ml/1 tsp sesame oil
salt and ground white pepper
1 spring onion (scallion), shredded, to garnish

1 Mix together the sherry and soy sauce. Stir in 2.5ml/½ tsp salt and 1.5ml/¼ tsp white pepper. Put the duck fillets in a bowl and add the marinade. Cover with clear film (plastic wrap) and leave in a cool place for 1 hour.

2 Drain the marinated duck fillets and place them on a rack in a grill (broiler) pan, or on a preheated griddle pan. Cook using medium to high heat, for 10 minutes on each side. Leave the fillets to cool for 10 minutes, then cut the duck into bitesize pieces. It is fine if the meat is still pink inside.

3 Heat the vegetable oil in a non-stick frying pan or wok and stir-fry the garlic and onion for 1 minute. Add the red pepper, pineapple chunks, duck, pineapple juice and vinegar and toss over the heat for 2 minutes.

4 Mix the cornflour to a paste with the water. Add the mixture to the pan with 1.5ml/¼ tsp salt. Cook, stirring, until the sauce thickens. Stir in the sesame oil.

5 Spoon the duck and pineapple mixture into four warmed bowls, garnish with the spring onion shreds, and serve.

Duck with Pineapple & Ginger

Save time and effort by using the boneless duck breast fillets that are widely available.

Serves 2–3

2 duck breast fillets
4 spring onions (scallions), chopped
15ml/1 tbsp light soy sauce
225g/8oz can pineapple rings
75ml/5 tbsp water
4 pieces drained Chinese stem ginger in syrup, plus 45ml/3 tbsp syrup from the jar
30ml/2 tbsp cornflour (cornstarch) mixed to a paste with a little water
¼ each red and green (bell) pepper, seeded and cut into thin strips
salt and ground black pepper
cooked thin egg noodles, baby spinach and green beans, blanched, to serve

1 Strip the skin from the duck. Select a shallow bowl that will fit into your steamer and that will accommodate the duck fillets side by side. Spread out the spring onions in the bowl, arrange the duck on top and cover with baking parchment. Set the steamer over boiling water. Cook the duck for about 1 hour until tender. Remove the duck and leave to cool slightly.

2 Cut the duck fillets into thin slices. Place on a plate and moisten them with a little of the cooking juices from the steaming bowl. Strain the remaining juices into a small pan and set aside. Cover the duck slices and keep hot.

3 Drain the canned pineapple rings, reserving 75ml/5 tbsp of the juice. Add this to the reserved cooking juices in the pan, together with the measured water. Stir in the ginger syrup, then stir in the cornflour paste and cook, stirring until thickened. Season to taste.

4 Cut the pineapple and ginger into attractive shapes. Put the cooked noodles, baby spinach and green beans on a plate, add slices of duck and top with the pineapple, ginger and pepper strips. Pour over the sauce and serve.

duck w. pineapple Energy 682kcal/2861kJ; Protein 62.6g; Carbohydrate 40.3g, of which sugars 33.7g; Fat 34.4g, of which saturates 5.8g; Cholesterol 330mg; Calcium 83mg; Fibre 4g; Sodium 1419mg.
duck w. ginger Energy 253kcal/1071kJ; Protein 20.8g; Carbohydrate 33.1g, of which sugars 23.8g; Fat 6.8g, of which saturates 1.4g; Cholesterol 110mg; Calcium 31mg; Fibre 1.1g; Sodium 515mg.

Duck with Pineapple & Coriander

Marinating the duck really boosts the flavour, so remember to allow enough time for this.

Serves 4–6
1 small duck, skinned, trimmed and jointed
1 pineapple, skinned, cored and cut in half crossways
45ml/3 tbsp sesame or vegetable oil
4cm/1½in fresh root ginger, peeled and finely sliced
1 onion, sliced
salt and ground black pepper
1 bunch fresh coriander (cilantro), stalks removed, to garnish

For the marinade
3 shallots, grated
45ml/3 tbsp soy sauce
30ml/2 tbsp fish sauce
10ml/2 tsp five-spice powder
15ml/1 tbsp sugar
3 garlic cloves, crushed
1 bunch fresh basil, stalks removed, leaves finely chopped

1 To make the marinade, mix all the ingredients in a bowl and beat together until the sugar has dissolved. Place the duck joints in a wide dish and rub with the marinade. Cover and chill for 6 hours or overnight.

2 Take one of the pineapple halves and cut into 4–6 slices, and then again into half-moons, and set aside. Take the other pineapple half and chop it to a pulp. Using your hands, squeeze all the juice from the pulp into a bowl. Discard the pulp and reserve the juice.

3 Heat 30ml/2 tbsp of the oil in a wide pan. Stir in the ginger and the onion. When they begin to soften, add the duck to the pan and brown on both sides. Pour in the pineapple juice and any remaining marinade, then add water so that the duck is just covered. Bring to the boil, then simmer for about 25 minutes.

4 Meanwhile, heat the remaining oil in a heavy pan and sear the pineapple slices on both sides. Add to the duck, season to taste, and cook for a further 5 minutes, or until the duck is tender.

5 Arrange on a serving dish, garnish with coriander and serve.

Duck in Spicy Orange Sauce

Although this dish has something in common with duck à l'orange, the use of spices, lemon grass and chillies makes it quite different. Serve with steamed rice and a vegetable dish. This satisfying meal is bound to go down well with family and guests.

Serves 4
4 duck legs
4 garlic cloves, crushed
50g/2oz fresh root ginger, peeled and finely sliced
2 lemon grass stalks, trimmed, cut into 3 pieces and crushed
2 dried whole red chillies
15ml/1 tbsp palm sugar (jaggery)
5ml/1 tsp five-spice powder
30ml/2 tbsp chilli sambal
900ml/1½ pints/3¾ cups fresh orange juice
sea salt and ground black pepper
1 lime, cut into quarters, to serve

1 Place the duck legs, skin side down, in a large heavy pan or flameproof clay pot. Cook them on both sides over a medium heat for about 10 minutes, until browned and crispy. Transfer them to a plate and set aside.

2 Stir the garlic, ginger, lemon grass and chillies into the fat left in the pan, and cook until golden. Add the sugar, five-spice powder and chilli sambal, and mix well.

3 Stir in the orange juice and return the duck legs to the pan. Cover the pan and gently cook the duck for 1–2 hours, until the meat is tender and the sauce has reduced.

4 Skim any fat from the top of the sauce, then taste and adjust the flavouring if necessary. Serve in heated bowls, with lime wedges for squeezing over the duck.

Variation
You could substitute the duck with chicken thigh portions.

duck w. pineapple Energy 303kcal/1285kJ; Protein 18.9g; Carbohydrate 46g, of which sugars 15g; Fat 7.3g, of which saturates 0.9g; Cholesterol 73mg; Calcium 54mg; Fibre 3.8g; Sodium 95mg.
duck in orange sauce Energy 280kcal/1181kJ; Protein 30.8g; Carbohydrate 23.8g, of which sugars 23.8g; Fat 10g, of which saturates 2g; Cholesterol 165mg; Calcium 48mg; Fibre 0.4g; Sodium 195mg.

Braised Duck in Soy Sauce

Chinese cooks often braise duck, goose, chicken or pork in soy sauce and warm flavourings, such as star anise and cinnamon. Such dishes are commonly found at Malaysian Chinese hawker stalls and coffee shops, and there are many variations on the theme. Turmeric and lemon grass are sometimes added to the flavourings and, to achieve their desired fiery kick, chillies are always included.

Serves 4–6

1 duck (about 2kg/4½lb), washed and trimmed
15–30ml/1–2 tbsp Chinese five-spice powder
25g/1oz fresh turmeric, chopped
25g/1oz galangal, chopped
4 garlic cloves, chopped
30ml/2 tbsp sesame oil
12 shallots, peeled and left whole
2–3 lemon grass stalks, halved and lightly crushed
4 cinnamon sticks
8 star anise
12 cloves
600ml/1 pint/2½ cups light soy sauce
120ml/4fl oz/½ cup dark soy sauce
30–45ml/2–3 tbsp palm sugar (jaggery)
steamed jasmine rice and salad, to serve

1 Rub the duck, inside and out, with the five-spice powder and place in the refrigerator, uncovered, for 6–8 hours.

2 Using a mortar and pestle or food processor, grind the turmeric, galangal and garlic to a smooth paste. Heat the oil in a heavy pan and stir in the spice paste until it becomes fragrant. Stir in the shallots, lemon grass, cinnamon sticks, star anise and cloves. Pour in the soy sauces and stir in the sugar.

3 Place the duck in the pan, baste with the sauce, and add 550ml/18fl oz/2½ cups water. Bring to the boil, reduce the heat and cover the pan. Simmer gently for 4–6 hours, basting from time to time, until the duck is very tender. Garnish with the leftover spices, if you like, and serve with rice and salad.

Marmalade & Soy Roast Duck

Sweet-and-sour flavours, such as marmalade and soy sauce, complement the rich, fatty taste of duck beautifully. Serve these robustly flavoured duck breast fillets with simple accompaniments such as steamed sticky rice and stir-fried pak choi.

Serves 6

6 duck breast fillets
45ml/3 tbsp fine-cut marmalade
45ml/3 tbsp light soy sauce
salt and ground black pepper

1 Preheat the oven to 190°C/375°F/Gas 5. Place the duck breasts skin side up on a grill (broiler) rack and place in the sink. Pour boiling water all over the duck. This shrinks the skin and helps it crisp during cooking. Pat the duck dry with kitchen paper and transfer to a roasting pan.

2 Combine the marmalade and soy sauce, and brush over the duck. Season with a little salt and some black pepper and roast for 20–25 minutes, basting occasionally with the marmalade mixture in the pan.

3 Remove the duck breast fillets from the oven and leave to rest for 5 minutes. Slice the duck breast fillets and serve drizzled with any juices left in the pan.

Variations

- *Marmalade gives the duck a lovely citrus flavour but this recipe also works well if you substitute black cherry jam. Use a little plum sauce instead of the light soy sauce if you like, but not too much as the flavour of the cherries will be swamped.*
- *If the occasion calls for a little ceremony, roast a whole duck. You will need to prick the skin of the bird all over before roasting, so that the fat, which is trapped in a layer beneath the skin, will be released during cooking. This excess oily matter can then be drained off during cooking.*

duck in soy sauce Energy 119kcal/498kJ; Protein 10.2g; Carbohydrate 4.6g, of which sugars 3.4g; Fat 6.9g, of which saturates 1.5g; Cholesterol 50mg; Calcium 35mg; Fibre 1.1g; Sodium 412mg.
marmalade & soy duck Energy 160kcal/672kJ; Protein 19.9g; Carbohydrate 5.8g, of which sugars 5.8g; Fat 6.5g, of which saturates 2g; Cholesterol 110mg; Calcium 16mg; Fibre 0.1g; Sodium 645mg.

Stir-fried Crispy Duck

This stir-fry is delicious wrapped in steamed pancakes, with a little extra plum sauce.

Serves 2

350g/12oz duck breast fillets
30ml/2 tbsp plain (all-purpose) flour
60ml/4 tbsp oil
1 bunch spring onions (scallions), cut in strips, plus extra to garnish
275g/10oz/2½ cups finely shredded green cabbage
225g/8oz can water chestnuts, drained and sliced
50g/2oz/½ cup unsalted cashew nuts
cucumber, cut in strips
45ml/3 tbsp plum sauce
15ml/1 tbsp soy sauce
salt and ground black pepper

1 Remove any skin from the duck breast, then trim off a little of the fat. Thinly slice the meat. Season the flour with plenty of salt and pepper and use it to coat the pieces of duck all over.

2 Heat the oil in a wok and cook the duck slices in batches over a high heat until golden and crisp. Keep stirring to prevent the duck from sticking. As each batch cooks, remove the duck with a slotted spoon and drain on kitchen paper.

3 Add the spring onions to the wok and cook for 2 minutes, then stir in the cabbage and cook for 5 minutes, or until it has softened.

4 Return the duck to the pan with the water chestnuts, cashews and cucumber. Stir-fry for 2 minutes. Add the plum sauce and soy sauce, season with salt and black pepper to taste, then heat for 2 minutes. Serve in individual bowls, garnished with the sliced spring onions.

Cook's Tip
Water chestnuts are the perfect foil for the rich duck in this stir-fry, remaining crisp and crunchy after cooking.

Anita Wong's Duck

This is a famous Chinese dish that is perfect for a special occasion.

Serves 4–6

1 duck with giblets, about 2.25kg/5lb
60ml/4 tbsp vegetable oil
2 garlic cloves, chopped
2.5cm/1in piece fresh root ginger, peeled and thinly sliced
45ml/3 tbsp bean paste
30ml/2 tbsp light soy sauce
15ml/1 tbsp dark soy sauce
15ml/1 tbsp sugar
2.5ml/½ tsp five-spice powder
3 star anise points
450ml/¾ pint/scant 2 cups duck stock (see Cook's Tip)
salt
shredded spring onions (scallions), to garnish

1 Make the stock (see Cook's Tip), strain into a bowl and blot the surface with kitchen paper to remove excess fat. Measure 450ml/¾ pint/scant 2 cups into a jug (pitcher).

2 Heat the oil in a large pan. Fry the garlic without browning, then add the duck. Turn frequently until the outside is slightly brown. Transfer to a plate.

3 Add the ginger to the pan, then stir in the bean paste. Cook for 1 minute, then add both soy sauces, the sugar and the five-spice powder. Return the duck to the pan and fry until the outside is coated. Add the star anise and stock, and season to taste. Cover tightly; simmer gently for 2–2½ hours or until tender. Skim off the excess fat. Leave to cool completely.

4 Cut the duck into serving portions and pour over the sauce. Garnish with spring onion curls and serve cold.

Cook's Tip
To make the stock, put the duck giblets in a heavy pan with a small onion and a piece of bruised fresh root ginger. Cover with 600ml/1 pint/2½ cups water, bring to the boil and then simmer, covered, for 20 minutes.

stir-fried duck Energy 682kcal/2846kJ; Protein 36.9g; Carbohydrate 41.3g, of which sugars 26.3g; Fat 44.4g, of which saturates 7.5g; Cholesterol 151mg; Calcium 174mg; Fibre 5.8g; Sodium 844mg.
Anita Wong's duck Energy 233kcal/977kJ; Protein 22.7g; Carbohydrate 4.2g, of which sugars 1g; Fat 14.2g, of which saturates 3.1g; Cholesterol 113mg; Calcium 23mg; Fibre 1.3g; Sodium 652mg.

Fruity Duck Chop Suey

Skinning the duck reduces the fat, but this is still an indulgent recipe. If this worries you, use less duck and more noodles. Pineapple gives the dish a lovely fresh flavour.

Serves 4

250g/9oz fresh sesame noodles
2 skinless duck breast fillets
3 spring onions (scallions), cut into strips
2 celery sticks, cut into strips
1 fresh pineapple, peeled, cored and cut into strips
300g/11oz mixed vegetables, such as carrots, peppers, beansprouts and cabbage, shredded or cut into strips
90ml/6 tbsp plum sauce

1 Cook the noodles in a large pan of boiling water for 3 minutes. Drain. Slice the duck breast fillets into strips.

2 Meanwhile, heat a wok. Add the strips of duck and stir-fry for 2–3 minutes, Drain off all but 30ml/2 tbsp of the fat. Add the spring onions and celery to the wok and stir-fry for 2 minutes more.

3 Use a slotted spoon to remove the ingredients from the wok and set them aside in a bowl. Add the pineapple strips and mixed vegetables, and stir-fry for 2 minutes more.

4 Add the cooked noodles and plum sauce to the wok, then replace the duck, spring onion and celery mixture.

5 Stir-fry the duck mixture for about 2 minutes more, or until the noodles and vegetables are hot and the duck is cooked through. Serve immediately.

Cook's Tip
Fresh sesame noodles can be bought from large supermarkets – they are usually found in the chiller cabinets with fresh pasta.

Crispy & Aromatic Duck

This dish is often mistaken for Peking Duck. However, it uses a different cooking method. The result is still crispy, but the delightful aroma makes this dish special. Plum sauce may be used instead of duck sauce.

Serves 6–8

1.8–2.25kg/4–5¼lb oven-ready duckling
10ml/2 tsp salt
5–6 whole star anise
15ml/1 tbsp Sichuan peppercorns
5ml/1 tsp cloves
2–3 cinnamon sticks
3–4 spring onions (scallions)
3–4 slices fresh root ginger, unpeeled
75–90ml/5–6 tbsp Chinese rice wine or dry sherry
vegetable oil, for deep-frying

To serve
lettuce leaves
20–24 thin pancakes
120ml/4fl oz/½ cup duck sauce
6–8 spring onions, thinly shredded
½ cucumber, thinly shredded

1 Remove the wings from the duck. Split the body in half down the backbone. Thoroughly rub salt all over the two duck halves.

2 Place the duck in a dish with the star anise, peppercorns, cloves, cinnamon, spring onions, ginger and rice wine or dry sherry and set aside to marinate for at least 4–6 hours.

3 Place the duck with the marinade in a steamer positioned in a wok partly filled with boiling water and steam vigorously for 4 hours. Check the water level at intervals. Remove the duck from the liquid and leave to cool for at least 5–6 hours. It must be completely cold and dry or the skin will not get crispy.

4 Heat the oil in a wok until smoking, place the duck pieces in the oil, skin side down, and deep-fry for 5–6 minutes or until crisp and brown, turning just once at the very last moment.

5 Remove, drain, take the meat off the bone and place on a bed of lettuce leaves. To serve, wrap a portion of duck in each pancake with a little sauce, shredded spring onion and cucumber. Eat with your fingers.

fruity duck chop suey Energy 603kcal/2553kJ; Protein 36.3g; Carbohydrate 93g, of which sugars 28.1g; Fat 14.2g, of which saturates 1.7g; Cholesterol 138mg; Calcium 96mg; Fibre 6.9g; Sodium 167mg.
crispy & aromatic duck Energy 221kcal/921kJ; Protein 14.2g; Carbohydrate 12.5g, of which sugars 3.9g; Fat 12.7g, of which saturates 2.3g; Cholesterol 71mg; Calcium 17mg; Fibre 0.5g; Sodium 281mg.

Honey-glazed Quail with a Five-spice Marinade

Although the quail is a relatively small bird – 115–150g/4–5oz – it is surprisingly meaty. One bird is usually quite sufficient for one serving.

Serves 4
4 oven-ready quails
2 pieces star anise
10ml/2 tsp ground cinnamon
10ml/2 tsp fennel seeds
10ml/2 tsp ground Sichuan or Chinese pepper
pinch of ground cloves
1 small onion, finely chopped
1 garlic clove, crushed
60ml/4 tbsp clear honey
30ml/2 tbsp dark soy sauce
2 spring onions (scallions), roughly chopped, finely shredded rind of 1 mandarin orange or satsuma and radish and carrot 'flowers', to garnish
banana leaves, to serve

1 Remove the backbones from the quails by cutting down either side with a pair of kitchen scissors.

2 Flatten the birds with the palm of your hand and secure each one with two bamboo skewers.

3 Grind together the star anise, cinnamon, fennel seeds, pepper and cloves in a mortar with a pestle. Add the onion, garlic, honey and soy sauce and combine well.

4 Place the quails on a flat dish, cover with the spice mixture and put in the refrigerator to marinate for at least 8 hours, or overnight if possible.

5 Cook the quails under a preheated grill (broiler) or on a barbecue for 7–8 minutes on each side, basting from time to time with the marinade.

6 Arrange the marinated quails on a bed of banana leaves and garnish with the chopped spring onion, orange rind and radish and carrot 'flowers'.

Stir-fried Turkey with Mangetouts

Turkey is often a rather disappointing meat with a bland flavour. Here it is enlivened with a delicious marinade and combined with crunchy nuts to provide lovely contrasting textures.

Serves 4
30ml/2 tbsp sesame oil
90ml/6 tbsp lemon juice
1 garlic clove, crushed
1cm/½in fresh root ginger, grated (shredded)
5ml/1 tsp clear honey
450g/1lb turkey fillets, skinned and cut into strips
115g/4oz mangetouts (snow peas)
30ml/2 tbsp groundnut (peanut) oil
50g/2oz cashew nuts
6 spring onions (scallions), cut into strips
225g/8oz can water chestnuts, drained and thinly sliced
salt
saffron rice, to serve

1 Mix together the sesame oil, lemon juice, garlic, ginger and honey in a shallow, non-metallic dish. Add the turkey and mix well. Cover and leave to marinate for 3–4 hours.

2 Blanch the mangetouts in boiling salted water for 1 minute. Drain, refresh under cold running water and set aside.

3 Drain the marinade from the turkey strips and reserve the marinade until step 5.

4 Heat the groundnut oil in a preheated wok or large frying pan, add the cashew nuts and stir-fry for about 1–2 minutes, until golden brown. Remove the cashew nuts from the wok or frying pan, using a slotted spoon, and set aside.

5 Add the turkey to the wok or frying pan and stir-fry for 3–4 minutes, until golden brown. Add the spring onions, mangetouts, water chestnuts and reserved marinade.

6 Cook for a few minutes, until the turkey is tender and the sauce is bubbling and hot. Stir in the fried cashew nuts and serve with saffron rice.

glazed quail w. marinade Energy 159kcal/664kJ; Protein 13.2g; Carbohydrate 5.6g, of which sugars 5.6g; Fat 9.5g, of which saturates 2.6g; Cholesterol 68mg; Calcium 7mg; Fibre 0.1g; Sodium 404mg.
turkey w. mangetouts Energy 369kcal/1546kJ; Protein 43.6g; Carbohydrate 5.3g, of which sugars 3.4g; Fat 19.5g, of which saturates 3.8g; Cholesterol 83mg; Calcium 52mg; Fibre 1.9g; Sodium 173mg.

Peking Duck

As the Chinese discovered centuries ago, this is quite the best way to eat duck.

Serves 8

1 duck, about 2.25kg/5lb
45ml/3 tbsp clear honey
5ml/1 tsp salt
1 bunch spring onions (scallions), cut into strips
½ cucumber, seeded and cut into matchsticks
24–32 mandarin pancakes

For the dipping sauces

120ml/4fl oz/½ cup hoisin sauce
120ml/4fl oz/½ cup plum sauce

1 Place the duck on a trivet in the sink and scald with boiling water to firm up the skin. Drain thoroughly. Tie kitchen string (twine) firmly around the legs of the bird and hang it in a cool place, with a bowl underneath to catch the drips. Leave the duck overnight.

2 Next day, blend the honey, 30ml/2 tbsp water and salt and brush half the mixture over the duck skin. Hang up again for 2–3 hours. Repeat and leave to dry completely for a further 3–4 hours.

3 Preheat the oven to 230°C/450°F/Gas 8. Stand the duck on a rack in a roasting pan, place in the oven and reduce the temperature to 180°C/350°F/Gas 4. Roast for 1¾ hours without basting.

4 Check the skin is crisp; if not, increase the oven temperature to the maximum. Roast for 15 minutes more.

5 Pat the cucumber pieces dry on kitchen paper. Heat the pancakes by steaming them in a foil parcel for 5–10 minutes over boiling water. Pour the dipping sauces into small dishes to share between the guests.

6 Carve the duck into 4cm/1½in pieces. At the table, each guest smears a little sauce on a pancake, tops it with a small amount of crisp duck skin and meat and adds cucumber and spring onion strips, before rolling the pancake up and eating it.

Garlic-roasted Quails with Honey

This is a great Indo-Chinese favourite made with quails or other small poultry such as poussins. Crispy, tender and juicy, they are simple to prepare and delicious to eat. Once skewered, the quail can be roasted in the oven or cooked over a barbecue. Serve with fragrant steamed rice and keep the skewers in place as it will make them easier to dip.

Serves 4

150ml/¼ pint/⅔ cup mushroom soy sauce
45ml/3 tbsp honey
15ml/1 tbsp sugar
8 garlic cloves, crushed
15ml/1 tbsp black peppercorns, crushed
30ml/2 tbsp sesame oil
8 quails or poussins
hot chilli sauce, to serve

1 In a bowl, beat the mushroom soy sauce with the honey and sugar until the sugar has dissolved. Stir in the garlic, crushed peppercorns and sesame oil.

2 Open out and skewer the quails or poussins, put them in a dish and rub the marinade over them. Cover and chill for at least 4 hours.

3 Preheat the oven to 230°C/450°F/ Gas 8. Place the quails breast side down in a roasting pan or on a wire rack set over a baking tray, then put them in the oven for 10 minutes.

4 Take the quails or poussins out and turn them over so they are breast side up, baste well with the juices and return them to the oven for a further 15–20 minutes until cooked through. Serve immediately with chilli sauce for dipping or drizzling.

Cook's Tip

The quails can be roasted whole, or split down the backbone, opened out and secured with skewers. For the New Year, Tet, whole chickens are marinated in similar garlicky flavourings and cooked over charcoal or in the oven.

Peking duck Energy 174kcal/734kJ; Protein 16.9g; Carbohydrate 14.9g, of which sugars 4.7g; Fat 5.3g, of which saturates 1.7g; Cholesterol 85mg; Calcium 21mg; Fibre 0.7g; Sodium 334mg.
quails w. honey Energy 488kcal/2033kJ; Protein 41.6g; Carbohydrate 0g, of which sugars 0g; Fat 35.9g, of which saturates 9.1g; Cholesterol 218mg; Calcium 16mg; Fibre 0g; Sodium 150mg.

Spicy Lamb Tikka

One of the best ways of tenderizing meat is to marinate it in papaya, which must be unripe or it will lend its sweetness to what should be a savoury dish.

Serves 4

675g/1½lb lean lamb, cubed
1 unripe papaya
45ml/3 tbsp natural (plain) yogurt
5ml/1 tsp grated fresh root ginger
5ml/1 tsp chilli powder
5ml/1 tsp crushed garlic
1.5ml/¼ tsp turmeric
10ml/2 tsp ground coriander
5ml/1 tsp ground cumin
5ml/1 tsp salt
30ml/2 tbsp lemon juice
15ml/1 tbsp chopped fresh coriander (cilantro), plus extra to garnish
1.5ml/¼ tsp red food colouring
300ml/½ pint/1¼ cups corn oil
lemon wedges and onion rings, to garnish

1 Place the lamb in a large bowl. Peel the papaya, cut it in half and scoop out the seeds. Cut the flesh into cubes and place in a food processor or blender. Process in bursts until the papaya forms a purée, adding about 15ml/1 tbsp water if necessary.

2 Pour 30ml/2 tbsp of the papaya over the lamb and rub it in well with your fingers. Cover and set aside for at least 3 hours.

3 Meanwhile, mix the yogurt, ginger, chilli powder, garlic, turmeric, ground coriander, ground cumin, salt and lemon juice in a bowl. Add the fresh coriander, red food colouring and 30ml/2 tbsp of the oil and mix well. Pour the spicy yogurt mixture over the lamb and mix well.

4 Heat the remaining oil in a karahi, wok or deep pan. Lower the heat slightly and add the lamb cubes, a few at a time.

5 Deep-fry each batch for 5–7 minutes or until the lamb is thoroughly cooked and tender. Keep the cooked pieces warm while frying the remainder.

6 Transfer to a serving dish and garnish with lemon wedges, onion rings and fresh coriander. Serve with raita and freshly baked naan bread.

Indian Lamb Burgers

Serve this spicy Indian burger in a bun with chilli sauce and a salad of tomatoes, onion and lettuce, or unaccompanied as an unusual appetizer.

Serves 4–6

50g/2oz/⅓ cup chickpeas, soaked overnight in water
2 onions, finely chopped
250g/9oz lean lamb, cut into small cubes
5ml/1 tsp cumin seeds
5ml/1 tsp garam masala
4–6 fresh green chillies, roughly chopped
5cm/2in piece fresh ginger, crushed
175ml/6fl oz/¾ cup water
a few fresh coriander (cilantro) and mint leaves, chopped
juice of 1 lemon
15ml/1 tbsp gram flour
2 eggs, beaten
vegetable oil, for shallow-frying
½ lime
salt

1 Drain the chickpeas and cook them in a pan of boiling water for 1 hour. Drain again, return to the pan and add the onions, lamb, cumin seeds, garam masala, chillies, ginger and water, and salt to taste. Bring to the boil. Simmer, covered, until the meat and chickpeas are cooked.

2 Remove the lid and cook uncovered to reduce the excess liquid. Cool, and grind to a paste in a food processor.

3 Scrape the mixture into a mixing bowl and add the fresh coriander and mint, lemon juice and flour. Knead well. Divide into 10–12 portions and roll each into a ball, then flatten slightly. Chill for 1 hour.

4 Dip the burgers in the beaten egg and shallow-fry each side until golden brown. Serve hot, with the lime.

Variation
Chicken or lean pork would work well instead of the lamb in this recipe.

lamb tikka Energy 438kcal/1827kJ; Protein 34.4g; Carbohydrate 7.8g, of which sugars 7.7g; Fat 30.3g, of which saturates 10.4g; Cholesterol 128mg; Calcium 74mg; Fibre 2.3g; Sodium 162mg.
lamb burgers Energy 245kcal/1019kJ; Protein 14g; Carbohydrate 14.4g, of which sugars 4.9g; Fat 15.2g, of which saturates 3.7g; Cholesterol 95mg; Calcium 60mg; Fibre 2.1g; Sodium 67mg.

Lamb Meatballs in a Spicy Sauce

The word 'meatballs' conjures up something quite humdrum, but these spicy little patties, with their delectable sauce, are exciting and full of flavour.

Serves 6

For the meatballs

675g/1½lb lean minced (ground) lamb
1 fresh green chilli, roughly chopped
1 garlic clove, chopped
2.5cm/1in piece fresh root ginger, chopped
1.5ml/¼ tsp garam masala
1.5ml/¼ tsp salt
45ml/3 tbsp chopped fresh coriander (cilantro), plus extra to garnish
pilau rice, to serve

For the sauce

15ml/1 tbsp oil
1.5ml/¼ tsp mustard seeds
2.5ml/½ tsp cumin seeds
1 onion, chopped
1 garlic clove, chopped
2.5cm/1in piece fresh root ginger, finely chopped
5ml/1 tsp ground cumin
5ml/1 tsp ground coriander
2.5ml/½ tsp salt
2.5ml/½ tsp chilli powder
15ml/1 tbsp tomato purée (paste)
400g/14oz can chopped tomatoes

1 To make the meatballs, put all the ingredients into a food processor or blender and process until the mixture binds together. Shape the mixture into 18 balls. Cover and chill in the refrigerator for 10 minutes.

2 To make the sauce, heat the oil in a heavy pan and fry the mustard and cumin seeds until they splutter.

3 Add the onion, garlic and ginger and fry for 5 minutes. Stir in the remaining sauce ingredients and simmer for 5 minutes.

4 Add the meatballs to the spicy sauce. Bring to the boil, cover and simmer for 25–30 minutes, or until the meatballs are cooked through. Serve on a bed of pilau rice and garnish with chopped fresh coriander.

Lamb Chops Kashmiri-style

These chops are cooked in a unique way, being boiled in milk and then fried.

Serves 4

8–12 lamb chops, about 50–75g/2–3oz each
1 piece cinnamon bark
1 bay leaf
2.5ml/½ tsp fennel seeds
2.5ml/½ tsp black peppercorns
3 green cardamom pods
5ml/1 tsp salt
600ml/1 pint/2½ cups milk
150ml/¼ pint/⅔ cup evaporated milk
150ml/¼ pint/⅔ cup natural (plain) yogurt
30ml/2 tbsp plain (all-purpose) flour
5ml/1 tsp chilli powder
5ml/1 tsp grated fresh root ginger
2.5ml/½ tsp garam masala
2.5ml/½ tsp crushed garlic
pinch of salt
300ml/½ pint/1¼ cups corn oil
fresh mint sprigs and lime quarters, to garnish

1 Trim the lamb chops to remove any excess fat, and place them in a large pan. Add the cinnamon bark, bay leaf, fennel seeds, peppercorns, cardamoms and salt. Pour in the milk. Bring to the boil over a high heat.

2 Lower the heat and cook for 12–15 minutes, or until the milk has reduced to about half its original volume. At this stage, pour in the evaporated milk and lower the heat further. Simmer until the chops are cooked through and all the milk has evaporated.

3 While the chops are cooking, blend together the yogurt, flour, chilli powder, ginger, garam masala, crushed garlic and a pinch of salt in a mixing bowl.

4 Remove the chops from the pan and discard the whole spices. Add the chops to the spicy yogurt mixture.

5 Heat the oil in a deep pan, wok or medium karahi. Lower the heat slightly and add the chops. Fry until they are golden brown, turning them once or twice as they cook.

6 Transfer the chops to a serving dish, and garnish with mint sprigs and lime quarters. Serve immediately.

lamb meatballs Energy 248kcal/1037kJ; Protein 23.7g; Carbohydrate 3.9g, of which sugars 0.8g; Fat 15.7g, of which saturates 6.2g; Cholesterol 86mg; Calcium 43mg; Fibre 0.6g; Sodium 103mg.
lamb chops Energy 677kcal/2816kJ; Protein 38.5g; Carbohydrate 20.4g, of which sugars 13.8g; Fat 49.8g, of which saturates 20.9g; Cholesterol 142mg; Calcium 374mg; Fibre 0.2g; Sodium 224mg.

Lamb Korma with Mint

This superb dish of lamb cooked in a creamy sauce, flavoured with mint, coconut, chillies and a subtle blend of spices, is quick to cook because the lamb is sliced into thin strips.

Serves 4

2 fresh green chillies
120ml/4fl oz/½ cup natural (plain) low-fat yogurt
50ml/2fl oz/¼ cup coconut milk
15ml/1 tbsp ground almonds
5ml/1 tsp salt
5ml/1 tsp crushed garlic
5ml/1 tsp grated fresh root ginger
5ml/1 tsp garam masala
1.5ml/¼ tsp ground cardamom
large pinch of ground cinnamon
15ml/1 tbsp chopped fresh mint
15ml/1 tbsp oil
2 medium onions, diced
1 bay leaf
4 black peppercorns
225g/8oz lean lamb, cut into strips
150ml/¼ pint/⅔ cup water
fresh mint leaves, to garnish

1 Finely chop the chillies. Whisk the yogurt with the chillies, coconut milk, ground almonds, salt, garlic, ginger, garam masala, cardamom, cinnamon and mint.

2 Heat the oil in a karahi, wok or heavy pan and fry the onions with the bay leaf and peppercorns for about 5 minutes.

3 When the onions are soft and golden brown, add the lamb and stir-fry for about 2 minutes.

4 Pour in the yogurt and coconut mixture and the water, lower the heat, cover and cook for about 15 minutes or until the lamb is cooked through, stirring occasionally. Using two spoons, toss the mixture over the heat for a further 2 minutes. Serve garnished with fresh mint leaves.

Cook's Tip
Rice with peas and curry leaves goes very well with this korma.

Spiced Lamb with Tomatoes & Peppers

Select lean tender lamb from the leg for this lightly spiced curry with juicy peppers and wedges of onion. Serve warm naan bread to mop up the tomato-rich juices.

Serves 6

2.5cm/1in piece fresh root ginger
1.5kg/3¼lb lean boneless lamb, cubed
250ml/8fl oz/1 cup natural (plain) yogurt
30ml/2 tbsp sunflower oil
3 onions
2 red (bell) peppers, seeded and cut into chunks
3 garlic cloves, finely chopped
1 fresh red chilli, seeded and chopped
30ml/2 tbsp mild curry paste
2 × 400g/14oz cans chopped tomatoes
large pinch of saffron threads
800g/1¾lb plum tomatoes, halved, seeded and cut into chunks
salt and ground black pepper
chopped fresh coriander (cilantro), to garnish

1 Thinly peel the fresh root ginger, using a sharp knife or a vegetable peeler, then grate the peeled root finely. Set the grated ginger aside.

2 Mix the lamb with the yogurt in a bowl. Cover and chill for about 1 hour.

3 Heat the oil in a large pan. Drain the lamb and reserve the yogurt, then cook the lamb in batches until it is golden on all sides – this will take about 15 minutes in total. Remove the lamb from the pan using a slotted spoon and set aside.

4 Cut two of the onions into wedges (six from each onion) and add to the oil remaining in the pan. Fry the onions over a medium heat for 10 minutes, or until they soften and are beginning to colour.

5 Add the peppers and cook for 5 minutes. Use a slotted spoon to remove the vegetables from the pan and set aside.

6 Meanwhile, chop the remaining onion. Add it to the rest of the oil in the pan with the chopped garlic, chilli and grated ginger, and cook for 4–5 minutes, stirring frequently, until the onion has softened.

7 Stir in the curry paste and canned chopped tomatoes with the reserved yogurt. Return the lamb to the pan, season and stir well. Bring to the boil, then reduce the heat and simmer for 30 minutes.

8 Pound the saffron to a powder in a mortar, then stir in a little boiling water to dissolve the saffron. Add this liquid to the curry and stir well.

9 Return the onion and pepper mixture to the pan, then stir in the fresh tomatoes. Bring the curry back to simmering point and cook for 15 minutes. Garnish with chopped fresh coriander and serve hot.

lamb korma Energy 197kcal/823kJ; Protein 14.5g; Carbohydrate 13.6g, of which sugars 9.9g; Fat 10g, of which saturates 3.5g; Cholesterol 43mg; Calcium 101mg; Fibre 1.8g; Sodium 583mg.
spiced lamb Energy 559kcal/2343kJ; Protein 54.4g; Carbohydrate 20.5g, of which sugars 18.8g; Fat 29.6g, of which saturates 13.5g; Cholesterol 191mg; Calcium 139mg; Fibre 4.6g; Sodium 278mg.

Lamb with Spinach

Serve this Punjabi dish with plain boiled rice, naan bread or parathas.

Serves 4–6

5ml/1 tsp grated fresh root ginger
5ml/1 tsp crushed garlic
7.5ml/1½ tsp chilli powder
5ml/1 tsp salt
5ml/1 tsp garam masala
90ml/6 tbsp corn oil
2 medium onions, sliced
675g/1½lb lean lamb, cut into 5cm/2in cubes
600–900ml/1–1½ pints/2½–3¾ cups water
400g/14oz fresh spinach
1 large red (bell) pepper, seeded and chopped
3 fresh green chillies, chopped
45ml/3 tbsp chopped fresh coriander (cilantro)
15ml/1 tbsp lemon juice (optional)

1 Mix together the ginger, garlic, chilli powder, salt and garam masala in a bowl. Set to one side.

2 Heat the oil in a medium pan. Add the onions and fry for 10–12 minutes or until well browned. Add the cubed lamb to the sizzling onion slices and fry for about 2 minutes, stirring frequently. Add the spice mixture and stir thoroughly until the meat pieces are well coated.

3 Pour in the water and bring to the boil. As soon as it is boiling, cover the pan and lower the heat. Cook gently for 25–35 minutes without letting the contents of the pan burn. If there is still a lot of water in the pan when the meat has become tender, remove the lid and boil briskly to evaporate any excess.

4 Meanwhile, wash and chop the spinach roughly, then blanch it for about 1 minute in a pan of boiling water. Drain well. Add the spinach to the lamb as soon as the water has evaporated. Fry over a medium heat for 7–10 minutes, using a wooden spoon in a semi-circular motion.

5 Add the red pepper, green chillies and fresh coriander to the pan and stir over a medium heat for 2 minutes. Sprinkle over the lemon juice (if using) and serve immediately.

Spring Lamb Chops

Tender spring lamb has the best flavour. Here, quick-cooking chops are finely spiced to enhance the flavour without masking the sweetness of the lamb.

Serves 4

8 small lean spring lamb chops
1 large fresh red chilli, seeded
30ml/2 tbsp chopped fresh coriander (cilantro)
15ml/1 tbsp chopped fresh mint
5ml/1 tsp salt
5ml/1 tsp soft light brown sugar
5ml/1 tsp garam masala
5ml/1 tsp crushed garlic
5ml/1 tsp grated fresh root ginger
175ml/6fl oz/¾ cup low-fat natural (plain) yogurt
10ml/2 tsp oil
mixed salad, to serve

1 Trim any excess fat from each of the lamb chops. Place them in a large bowl.

2 Finely chop the chilli, then place in a bowl and mix with the chopped fresh coriander, mint, salt, brown sugar, garam masala, crushed garlic and ginger.

3 Pour the yogurt into the chilli mixture and, using a small whisk or a fork, mix together thoroughly.

4 Pour this mixture over the top of the chops and turn them with your fingers to make sure that they are completely covered. Cover and marinate overnight in the refrigerator.

5 Heat the oil in a karahi, wok or heavy pan and add the chops. Cook over a medium heat for about 20 minutes or until cooked right through, turning the chops from time to time. Alternatively, grill (broil) the chops, basting often with oil. Serve with the mixed salad.

Cook's Tip
You can freeze peeled fresh root ginger and grate it from frozen as you need it.

lamb w. spinach Energy 359kcal/1494kJ; Protein 28.7g; Carbohydrate 7.1g, of which sugars 4.7g; Fat 24.1g, of which saturates 7.6g; Cholesterol 95mg; Calcium 237mg; Fibre 4.8g; Sodium 780mg.
spring lamb chops Energy 310kcal/1285kJ; Protein 20.5g; Carbohydrate 5.1g, of which sugars 3.6g; Fat 23.3g, of which saturates 11.4g; Cholesterol 84mg; Calcium 70mg; Fibre 0.2g; Sodium 82mg.

Lamb with Courgettes

For this simple supper dish, lamb is cooked first with yogurt and then the sliced courgettes, which have already been browned, are added to the mixture.

Serves 4

15ml/1 tbsp oil
2 medium onions, chopped
225g/8oz lean lamb steaks, cut into strips
120ml/4fl oz/½ cup natural (plain) low-fat yogurt
5ml/1 tsp garam masala
5ml/1 tsp chilli powder
5ml/1 tsp crushed garlic
5ml/1 tsp grated fresh root ginger
2.5ml/½ tsp ground coriander
2 medium courgettes (zucchini), sliced
15ml/1 tbsp chopped fresh coriander (cilantro), to garnish

1 Heat the oil in a karahi, wok or heavy pan and fry the onions until golden brown (see Cook's Tip).

2 Add the lamb strips and stir-fry with the onions for 1 minute to seal the meat.

3 Put the yogurt, garam masala, chilli powder, garlic, ginger and ground coriander into a bowl. Whisk the mixture together.

4 Pour the yogurt mixture over the lamb and stir-fry for 2 minutes. Cover and cook over medium to low heat for 12–15 minutes.

5 Preheat the grill (broiler). Put the courgettes in a flameproof dish and brown lightly under the heat for about 3 minutes, turning once.

6 Check that the lamb is cooked through and the sauce is quite thick, then add the courgettes and serve garnished with the fresh coriander.

Cook's Tip
Stir the onions only occasionally so that their moisture will be retained.

Stir-fried Lamb with Baby Onions

The baby onions are stir-fried whole before being added to the lamb and pepper mixture in this recipe. Serve this dish with rice, lentils or naan bread.

Serves 4

15ml/1 tbsp oil
8 baby onions
225g/8oz boned lean lamb, cut into strips
5ml/1 tsp ground cumin
5ml/1 tsp ground coriander
15ml/1 tbsp tomato purée (paste)
5ml/1 tsp chilli powder
5ml/1 tsp salt
15ml/1 tbsp lemon juice
2.5ml/½ tsp onion seeds
4 curry leaves
300ml/½ pint/1¼ cups water
1 small red (bell) pepper, seeded and roughly sliced
1 small green (bell) pepper, seeded and roughly sliced
15ml/1 tbsp chopped fresh coriander (cilantro)
15ml/1 tbsp chopped fresh mint

1 Heat the oil in a karahi, wok or heavy pan and stir-fry the whole baby onions for about 3 minutes. Using a slotted spoon, remove the onions from the pan and set aside to drain. Set the pan aside, with the oil remaining in it.

2 Mix together the lamb strips, cumin, ground coriander, tomato purée, chilli powder, salt and lemon juice in a bowl until the lamb is well coated. Set aside.

3 Reheat the oil and briskly stir-fry the onion seeds and curry leaves for 2–3 minutes.

4 Add the lamb and spice mixture, and stir-fry for about 5 minutes, then pour in the measured water. Lower the heat and cook the lamb mixture gently for about 10 minutes, until the lamb is cooked through.

5 Add the peppers and half the fresh coriander and mint. Stir-fry for a further 2 minutes.

6 Finally, add the baby onions and the remaining chopped fresh coriander and mint, and serve immediately.

lamb w. courgettes Energy 198kcal/824kJ; Protein 15.8g; Carbohydrate 11.4g, of which sugars 8.3g; Fat 10.4g, of which saturates 3.7g; Cholesterol 43mg; Calcium 120mg; Fibre 1.7g; Sodium 84mg.
stir-fried lamb Energy 172kcal/717kJ; Protein 12.8g; Carbohydrate 8.5g, of which sugars 6.6g; Fat 9.9g, of which saturates 3.5g; Cholesterol 43mg; Calcium 24mg; Fibre 1.7g; Sodium 554mg.

Spiced Lamb with Chillies

This is a fairly hot stir-fry dish, although you can, of course, make it less so by either discarding the seeds from the chillies, or using just one of each colour.

Serves 4

225g/8oz lean lamb fillet
120ml/4fl oz/½ cup natural (plain) low-fat yogurt
1.5ml/¼ tsp ground cardamom
5ml/1 tsp grated fresh root ginger
5ml/1 tsp crushed garlic
5ml/1 tsp chilli powder
5ml/1 tsp garam masala
5ml/1 tsp salt
15ml/1 tbsp oil
2 medium onions, chopped
1 bay leaf
300ml/½ pint/1¼ cups water
2 fresh green chillies, sliced lengthways
2 fresh red chillies, sliced lengthways
30ml/2 tbsp fresh coriander (cilantro) leaves

1 Using a sharp knife, remove any excess fat from the lamb and cut the meat into even strips.

2 In a bowl, mix the yogurt, cardamom, ginger, garlic, chilli powder and garam masala. Stir in the salt. Add the lamb strips. Mix well in the spicy yogurt to coat evenly. Leave for about 1 hour to marinate.

3 Heat the oil in a karahi, wok or heavy pan and fry the onions for 3–5 minutes until golden.

4 Add the bay leaf, then add the lamb with the yogurt and spice mixture. Stir-fry for 2–3 minutes.

5 Pour the water over the spicy lamb mixture, cover and cook for 15–20 minutes over a low heat, checking and stirring occasionally. Once the water has evaporated, stir-fry the mixture for 1 minute longer.

6 Stir in the red and green chillies and the fresh coriander. Spoon into a serving dish and serve hot.

Khara Masala Lamb

This is a dish which involves a cooking technique called bhooning – stirring with a semi-circular motion.

Serves 4

15ml/1 tbsp oil
3 small onions, chopped
5ml/1 tsp shredded fresh root ginger
5ml/1 tsp sliced garlic
6 dried red chillies
3 cardamom pods
2 cinnamon sticks
6 black peppercorns
3 cloves
2.5ml/½ tsp salt
450g/1lb boned lean leg of lamb, cubed
600ml/1 pint/2½ cups water
2 fresh green chillies, sliced
30ml/2 tbsp chopped fresh coriander (cilantro)

1 Heat the oil in a large pan and add the onions. Lower the heat and fry the onions until they are lightly browned, stirring occasionally.

2 Add half the ginger and half the garlic, and stir well. Drop in half the red chillies, the cardamom pods, cinnamon, peppercorns, cloves and salt.

3 Add the lamb and fry over a medium heat. Stir constantly with a semi-circular movement, using a wooden spoon to scrape the bottom of the pan and prevent the meat from burning. Cook for about 5 minutes.

4 Stir in the water, cover with a lid and cook slowly over a medium to low heat for 35–40 minutes, or until the water has evaporated and the meat is tender, stirring from time to time to prevent the mixture from burning on the bottom of the pan.

5 Add the remaining ginger, garlic and dried red chillies, with the fresh green chillies and the chopped coriander. Continue to stir the mixture over the heat until some free oil is visible on the sides of the pan. Transfer the curry to a serving dish and serve immediately.

spiced lamb Energy 183kcal/764kJ; Protein 15.5g; Carbohydrate 14.1g, of which sugars 9.1g; Fat 7.8g, of which saturates 3.2g; Cholesterol 43mg; Calcium 102mg; Fibre 1.8g; Sodium 77mg.
khara masala lamb Energy 276kcal/1152kJ; Protein 24.3g; Carbohydrate 10.1g, of which sugars 7.2g; Fat 15.8g, of which saturates 6.2g; Cholesterol 86mg; Calcium 48mg; Fibre 1.8g; Sodium 102mg.

Spicy Lamb & Potato Stew

Indian spices transform a simple lamb and potato stew into a mouthwatering dish fit for princes.

Serves 6

675g/1½lb lean lamb fillet (tenderloin)
15ml/1 tbsp oil
1 onion, finely chopped
2 bay leaves
1 fresh green chilli, seeded and finely chopped
2 garlic cloves, finely chopped
10ml/2 tsp ground coriander
5ml/1 tsp ground cumin
2.5ml/½ tsp ground turmeric
2.5ml/½ tsp chilli powder
2.5ml/½ tsp salt
2 tomatoes, peeled and chopped
600ml/1 pint/2½ cups chicken stock
2 large potatoes, cut in large chunks
chopped fresh coriander (cilantro), to garnish

1 Remove any visible fat from the lamb and cut the meat into neat 2.5cm/1in cubes.

2 Heat the oil in a large, heavy pan and fry the onion, bay leaves, chilli and garlic for 5 minutes.

3 Add the cubed meat and cook for about 6–8 minutes until lightly browned.

4 Add the ground coriander, ground cumin, ground turmeric, chilli powder and salt and cook the spices for 3–4 minutes, stirring constantly to prevent the spices from sticking to the bottom of the pan.

5 Add the tomatoes and stock and simmer for 5 minutes. Bring to the boil, cover and simmer for 1 hour.

6 Add the bitesize chunks of potato to the simmering mixture, stir in, and cook for a further 30–40 minutes, or until the meat is tender and much of the excess juices have been absorbed, leaving a thick but minimal sauce. Garnish with chopped fresh coriander and serve piping hot.

Lamb Dhansak

This is time-consuming to make, but the excellent flavour is just reward.

Serves 4–6

90ml/6 tbsp vegetable oil
5 fresh green chillies, chopped
2.5cm/1in piece fresh root ginger, grated
3 garlic cloves, crushed, plus 1 garlic clove, sliced
2 bay leaves
5cm/2in piece cinnamon stick
900g/2lb lean lamb, cut into pieces
600ml/1 pint/2½ cups water
175g/6oz/¾ cup whole red lentils, washed and drained
50g/2oz/¼ cup each chana dhal or yellow split peas, husked moong dhal and split red lentils, washed and drained
2 potatoes, diced, soaked in water
1 aubergine (eggplant), chopped, soaked in water
4 onions, finely sliced, deep-fried and drained
50g/2oz fresh spinach, trimmed, washed and chopped
25g/1oz fresh or dried fenugreek leaves
2 carrots, sliced
115g/4oz fresh coriander (cilantro), chopped
50g/2oz fresh mint, chopped
30ml/2 tbsp dhansak masala
30ml/2 tbsp sambhar masala
5ml/1 tsp salt
10ml/2 tsp soft light brown sugar
60ml/4 tbsp tamarind juice

1 Heat 45ml/3 tbsp of the oil in a wok, karahi or large pan, and gently fry the fresh chillies, ginger, crushed garlic, bay leaves and cinnamon for 2 minutes. Add the lamb pieces and the measured water. Bring to the boil, then simmer, covered, until the lamb is half cooked.

2 Drain the meat stock into another pan and put the lamb aside. Add the whole red lentils, chana dhal or split peas, moong dhal and split red lentils to the stock and cook gently for 25–30 minutes at a low temperature until they are tender. Mash the lentils with the back of a spoon.

3 Drain the potatoes and aubergine and add to the lentils. Reserve a little of the deep-fried onions and stir the remainder into the pan, along with the spinach, fenugreek and carrot. Add some hot water to the pan if the mixture seems too thick. Cook until the vegetables are tender, then mash again with a spoon, keeping the vegetables a little coarse.

4 Heat 15ml/1 tbsp of the remaining oil in a large frying pan. Reserve a few coriander and mint leaves to use as a garnish, and gently fry the remaining leaves with the dhansak and sambhar masala, salt and sugar. Add the lamb pieces and fry gently for 5 minutes.

5 Add the lamb and spices to the lentil mixture and stir. Cover, reduce the heat to low and cook until the lamb is tender. The lentils will absorb liquid, so add more water if needed. Mix in the tamarind juice.

6 Heat the remaining vegetable oil in a small pan and fry the sliced garlic until golden brown. Sprinkle the fried garlic slices over the dhansak. Garnish with the remaining deep-fried onion and the reserved fresh coriander and mint leaves. Serve the dish hot, with Caramelized Basmati Rice (see p334), if you like.

spicy lamb Energy 284kcal/1192kJ; Protein 24g; Carbohydrate 14.1g, of which sugars 3.1g; Fat 15.1g, of which saturates 6.3g; Cholesterol 86mg; Calcium 23mg; Fibre 1.3g; Sodium 109mg.
lamb dhansak Energy 627kcal/2626kJ; Protein 43.6g; Carbohydrate 48.6g, of which sugars 12g; Fat 30.3g, of which saturates 9.4g; Cholesterol 114mg; Calcium 141mg; Fibre 6.5g; Sodium 177mg.

Lahore-style Lamb Curry

This hearty dish of braised lamb with chana dhal has a wonderfully aromatic flavour imparted by the winter spices.

Serves 4

60ml/4 tbsp vegetable oil
1 bay leaf
2 cloves
4 black peppercorns
1 onion, sliced
450g/1lb lean boneless lamb, cubed
1.5ml/¼ tsp ground turmeric
7.5ml/1½ tsp chilli powder
5ml/1 tsp crushed coriander seeds
2.5cm/1in piece cinnamon stick
5ml/1 tsp crushed garlic
7.5ml/1½ tsp salt
1.5 litres/2½ pints/6 cups water
50g/2oz/⅓ cup chana dhal (yellow split peas)
2 tomatoes, quartered
2 fresh green chillies, chopped
15ml/1 tbsp chopped fresh coriander (cilantro)

1 Heat the oil in a karahi, wok or large pan. Lower the heat slightly and add the bay leaf, cloves, peppercorns and onion. Fry for about 5 minutes, or until the onion is golden brown.

2 Add the cubed lamb, turmeric, chilli powder, coriander seeds, cinnamon stick, garlic and most of the salt, and stir-fry for about 5 minutes over a medium heat. Pour in 900ml/1½ pints/3¾ cups of the water and cover the pan with a lid or foil, making sure the foil does not come into contact with the food. Simmer for 35–40 minutes or until the lamb is tender.

3 Put the chana dhal into a large pan with the remaining measured water and a good pinch of salt and boil for 12–15 minutes, or until the water has almost evaporated and the dhal is soft enough to be mashed. If the mixture is too thick, add up to 150ml/¼ pint/⅔ cup water.

4 When the lamb is tender, remove the lid or foil and stir-fry the mixture using a wooden spoon, until some free oil begins to appear on the sides of the pan.

5 Add the cooked lentils to the lamb and mix together well. Stir in the tomatoes, chillies and chopped coriander and serve.

Glazed Lamb

Lemon and honey make a classic stir-fry combination in sweet dishes, and this lamb recipe shows how well they work together in savoury dishes, too. Serve with a fresh mixed salad to complete this delicious dish.

Serves 4

450g/1lb boneless lean lamb
15ml/1 tbsp grapeseed oil
175g/6oz mangetouts (snow peas), trimmed
3 spring onions (scallions), sliced
30ml/2 tbsp clear honey
juice of ½ lemon
30ml/2 tbsp chopped fresh coriander (cilantro)
15ml/1 tbsp sesame seeds
salt and ground black pepper

1 Using a cleaver, cut the lamb into thin strips.

2 Heat the wok, then add the oil. When the oil is hot, stir-fry the lamb until browned all over. Remove and keep warm.

3 Add the mangetouts and spring onions to the hot wok and stir-fry for 30 seconds.

4 Return the lamb to the wok and add the honey, lemon juice, chopped coriander and sesame seeds and season well. Stir thoroughly to mix. Bring to the boil, then allow to bubble vigorously for 1 minute until the lamb is completely coated in the honey mixture. Serve immediately.

Cook's Tip
Use a tender cut of lamb such as leg for this recipe.

Variation
This recipe would work just as well made with pork or chicken instead of lamb. You could substitute chopped fresh basil for the coriander if using chicken.

lamb curry Energy 331kcal/1379kJ; Protein 26.5g; Carbohydrate 9.7g, of which sugars 1.9g; Fat 20.6g, of which saturates 5.6g; Cholesterol 83mg; Calcium 40mg; Fibre 1.8g; Sodium 99mg.
glazed lamb Energy 223kcal/932kJ; Protein 19g; Carbohydrate 7.8g, of which sugars 7.4g; Fat 13.1g, of which saturates 4.9g; Cholesterol 67mg; Calcium 34mg; Fibre 1.2g; Sodium 78mg.

Creamy Lamb Korma

A heritage of the talented cooks who served the Mughal emperors, this is a rich and luxurious dish. Mild in flavour, it is ideal for serving when you are unsure about how hot your guests like their curries to be.

Serves 4–6

15ml/1 tbsp white sesame seeds
15ml/1 tbsp white poppy seeds
50g/2oz/½ cup blanched almonds
2 fresh green chillies, seeded
6 garlic cloves, sliced
5cm/2in piece fresh root ginger, sliced
1 onion, finely chopped
45ml/3 tbsp ghee or vegetable oil
6 green cardamom pods
5cm/2in piece cinnamon stick
4 cloves
900g/2lb lean lamb, boned and cubed
5ml/1 tsp ground cumin
5ml/1 tsp ground coriander
300ml/½ pint/1¼ cups double (heavy) cream mixed with 2.5ml/½ tsp cornflour (cornstarch)
salt
roasted sesame seeds, to garnish

1 Preheat a karahi, wok or large pan over a medium heat without any fat, and add the first seven ingredients. Stir until they begin to change colour. They should go just a shade darker.

2 Leave the mixture to cool, then grind to a fine paste using a mortar and pestle or in a food processor. Heat the ghee or oil in the pan over a low heat.

3 Fry the cardamoms, cinnamon and cloves until the cloves swell. Add the lamb, ground cumin and coriander and the prepared paste, and season with salt to taste. Increase the heat to medium and stir well. Reduce the heat to low, then cover the pan and cook until the lamb is almost done.

4 Remove from the heat, leave to cool a little and gradually fold in the cream, reserving 5ml/1 tsp to garnish.

5 When ready to serve, gently reheat the lamb, uncovered. Spoon into a dish and garnish with the sesame seeds and the reserved cream. This korma is very good served with pilau rice.

Lamb Curry with Cardamom Rice

This Indian-style lamb biryani, with the meat and rice cooked together in a clay pot, is a delicious meal in itself.

Serves 4

1 large onion, quartered
2 garlic cloves
1 fresh green chilli, halved and seeded
5cm/2in piece fresh root ginger
15ml/1 tbsp ghee
15ml/1 tbsp vegetable oil
675g/1½lb boned shoulder or leg of lamb, cut into chunks
15ml/1 tbsp ground coriander
10ml/2 tsp ground cumin
1 cinnamon stick, broken into 3 pieces
150ml/¼ pint/⅔ cup thick natural (plain) yogurt
150ml/¼ pint/⅔ cup water
75g/3oz/⅓ cup ready-to-eat dried apricots, cut into chunks
salt and ground black pepper

For the rice

250g/9oz/1⅓ cups basmati rice
6 cardamom pods, split open
25g/1oz/2 tbsp butter, cut into small pieces
45ml/3 tbsp toasted cashew nuts or flaked (sliced) almonds

For the garnish

1 onion, sliced and fried until golden
a few sprigs of fresh coriander (cilantro)

1 Soak a large clay pot or chicken brick in cold water for 20 minutes, then drain. Place the onion, garlic, chilli and ginger in a food processor or blender and process with 15ml/1 tbsp water to a smooth paste.

2 Heat the ghee and vegetable oil in a heavy frying pan. Fry the lamb chunks in batches over a high heat until golden brown. Remove from the pan using a slotted spoon and set aside. Scrape the onion paste into the remaining oil left in the frying pan, stir in the ground coriander and cumin, add the cinnamon stick pieces and fry for 1–2 minutes, stirring constantly with a wooden spoon.

3 Return the meat to the frying pan, then gradually add the yogurt, a spoonful at a time, stirring well between each addition with a wooden spoon. Season the meat well with plenty of salt and pepper and stir in the water.

4 Transfer the contents of the frying pan to the prepared clay pot, cover with the lid and place in an unheated oven. Set the oven to 180°C/350°F/Gas 4 and cook for 45 minutes.

5 Meanwhile, prepare the basmati rice. Place it in a bowl, cover with cold water and leave to soak for 20 minutes. Drain the rice and place it in a large pan of boiling salted water, bring back to the boil and cook for 10 minutes. Drain and stir in the split cardamom pods.

6 Remove the clay pot from the oven and stir in the chopped ready-to-eat apricots. Pile the cooked rice on top of the lamb and dot with the butter. Drizzle over 60ml/4 tbsp water, then sprinkle the cashew nuts or flaked almonds on top. Cover the pot, reduce the oven temperature to 150°C/300°F/Gas 2 and cook the meat and rice for 30 minutes. Remove the lid from the pot and fluff up the rice with a fork. Garnish with the fried onion and coriander, and serve.

creamy lamb korma Energy 149kcal/621kJ; Protein 9.6g; Carbohydrate 9.8g, of which sugars 7.5g; Fat 8.3g, of which saturates 2.6g; Cholesterol 29mg; Calcium 69mg; Fibre 1.4g; Sodium 61mg.
lamb curry Energy 769kcal/3208kJ; Protein 43.6g; Carbohydrate 67.6g, of which sugars 14.5g; Fat 36.2g, of which saturates 15g; Cholesterol 142mg; Calcium 134mg; Fibre 2.6g; Sodium 252mg.

Rogan Josh

This is one of the most popular lamb dishes to have originated in Kashmir. Traditionally, fatty meat on the bone is slow-cooked until most of the fat is separated from the meat. The fat that escapes from the meat is known as rogan, and josh refers to the red colour. This recipe, however, uses lean lamb.

Serves 4–6

45ml/3 tbsp lemon juice
250ml/8fl oz/1 cup natural (plain) yogurt
5ml/1 tsp salt
2 garlic cloves, crushed
2.5cm/1in piece fresh root ginger, finely grated
900g/2lb lean lamb fillet, cubed
60ml/4 tbsp vegetable oil
2.5ml/½ tsp cumin seeds
2 bay leaves
4 green cardamom pods
1 onion, finely chopped
10ml/2 tsp ground coriander
10ml/2 tsp ground cumin
5ml/1 tsp chilli powder
400g/14oz can chopped tomatoes
30ml/2 tbsp tomato purée (paste)
150ml/¼ pint/⅔ cup water
toasted cumin seeds and bay leaves, to garnish
plain boiled rice, to serve

1 In a large bowl, mix together the lemon juice, yogurt, salt, half the crushed garlic and the ginger. Add the lamb, cover and marinate in the refrigerator overnight.

2 Heat the oil in a karahi, wok or large pan and fry the cumin seeds for 2 minutes. Add the bay leaves and cardamom pods and fry for a further 2 minutes.

3 Add the onion and remaining garlic and fry for 5 minutes. Add the coriander, cumin and chilli powder. Fry for 2 minutes.

4 Add the marinated lamb to the pan and cook for a further 5 minutes, stirring occasionally to prevent the mixture from sticking to the base of the pan and starting to burn.

5 Stir in the tomatoes, tomato purée and water. Cover and simmer for 1–1½ hours. Garnish with toasted cumin seeds and bay leaves, and serve with the rice.

Curried Lamb & Lentils

This colourful curry is packed with protein and low in fat, so it makes a tasty yet healthy meal.

Serves 4

8 lean boned lamb leg steaks (about 500g/1¼lb total weight)
1 onion, chopped
2 carrots, diced
1 celery stick, chopped
15ml/1 tbsp hot curry paste
30ml/2 tbsp tomato purée (paste)
475ml/16fl oz/2 cups chicken or veal stock
175g/6oz/1 cup green lentils
salt and ground black pepper
fresh coriander (cilantro) leaves, to garnish
boiled rice, to serve

1 Cook the lamb steaks in a large, non-stick frying pan, without any added fat, for 2–3 minutes on each side, until browned.

2 Add the onion, carrots and celery and cook, stirring occasionally, for 2 minutes, then stir in the curry paste, tomato purée, stock and lentils.

3 Bring to the boil, lower the heat, cover with a tight-fitting lid and simmer gently for 30 minutes, until tender. Add some extra stock, if necessary.

4 Season to taste with salt and pepper. Spoon the curry on to warmed plates and serve immediately, garnished with coriander and accompanied by rice.

Cook's Tip

Lentils are one of the few pulses (legumes) that do not require prolonged soaking in cold water before cooking. However, just like dried beans and peas, they should not be seasoned with salt until after cooking or their skins will become unpleasantly tough. Both green and brown lentils keep their shape well, as do the rather more expensive small Puy lentils. Red and yellow lentils are not suitable for this recipe as they tend to disintegrate during cooking.

rogan josh Energy 557kcal/2335kJ; Protein 54.2g; Carbohydrate 20.4g, of which sugars 18.7g; Fat 29.5g, of which saturates 13.5g; Cholesterol 190mg; Calcium 139mg; Fibre 4.6g; Sodium 277mg.
curried lamb Energy 381kcal/1600kJ; Protein 35.5g; Carbohydrate 28.4g, of which sugars 4.3g; Fat 14.7g, of which saturates 6.6g; Cholesterol 95mg; Calcium 47mg; Fibre 3.2g; Sodium 144mg.

Minced Lamb with Curry Leaves & Chilli

The whole chillies pack quite a punch, but can be removed from the dish before serving.

Serves 4
10ml/2 tsp oil
2 medium onions, chopped
10 curry leaves
6 fresh green chillies
350g/12oz lean minced (ground) lamb
5ml/1 tsp crushed garlic
5ml/1 tsp grated fresh root ginger
5ml/1 tsp chilli powder
1.5ml/¼ tsp ground turmeric
5ml/1 tsp salt
2 tomatoes, peeled and quartered
15ml/1 tbsp chopped fresh coriander (cilantro)

1 Heat the oil in a karahi, wok or heavy pan and fry the onions with the curry leaves and three of the whole green chillies.

2 Put the lamb into a bowl. Mix with the crushed garlic, grated ginger and spices.

3 Add the minced lamb and salt to the onions and stir-fry for 7–10 minutes.

4 Add the tomatoes, coriander and remaining chillies and stir-fry for 2 minutes. Serve hot.

Cook's Tips
* *This aromatic curry also makes a terrific brunch if served with fried eggs.*
* *Curry leaves are available from Indian grocers and are best used fresh rather than dried as their flavour diminishes when dried. They will keep for several days in a plastic bag in the refrigerator. You can also freeze them.*

Lamb with Peas & Mint

A simple dish for a family meal, this is easy to prepare and very versatile. It is equally delicious whether served with plain boiled rice or chapatis. Another excellent use for the lamb mixture is for filling samosas.

Serves 4
15ml/1 tbsp oil
1 medium onion, chopped
2.5ml/½ tsp crushed garlic
2.5ml/½ tsp grated fresh root ginger
2.5ml/½ tsp chilli powder
1.5ml/¼ tsp ground turmeric
5ml/1 tsp ground coriander
5ml/1 tsp salt
2 medium tomatoes, sliced
275g/10oz lean leg of lamb, minced (ground)
1 large carrot, sliced or cut into batons
75g/3oz/½ cup petits pois (baby peas)
15ml/1 tbsp chopped fresh mint
15ml/1 tbsp chopped fresh coriander (cilantro)
1 fresh green chilli, chopped
fresh coriander, to garnish

1 In a deep, heavy frying pan, heat the oil and fry the chopped onion over a medium heat for 5 minutes until golden.

2 Meanwhile, in a small mixing bowl, mix the garlic, ginger, chilli powder, turmeric, ground coriander and salt. Stir well.

3 Add the sliced tomatoes and the spice mixture to the onions in the frying pan and fry for 2–3 minutes, stirring constantly.

4 Add the minced lamb to the mixture and stir-fry for about 7–10 minutes to seal.

5 Break up any lumps of meat which may form in the pan, using a potato masher if necessary.

6 Finally add the carrot, petits pois, chopped fresh mint and coriander and the chopped green chilli and mix well.

7 Cook, stirring, for 2–3 minutes until the carrot slices or batons and the petits pois are cooked, then serve immediately, garnished with fresh coriander sprigs.

minced lamb Energy 237kcal/987kJ; Protein 18.6g; Carbohydrate 10.3g, of which sugars 7.2g; Fat 13.8g, of which saturates 5.7g; Cholesterol 67mg; Calcium 48mg; Fibre 1.9g; Sodium 69mg.
lamb with peas & mint Energy 192kcal/802kJ; Protein 15.8g; Carbohydrate 7.6g, of which sugars 5.7g; Fat 11.2g, of which saturates 4.1g; Cholesterol 52mg; Calcium 49mg; Fibre 2.9g; Sodium 77mg.

Rezala

This delectable lamb recipe is a legacy of the Muslim Mughal era. It comes from Bengal where there is a tradition of Muslim cuisine.

Serves 4

1 large onion, roughly chopped
10ml/2 tsp grated fresh root ginger
10ml/2 tsp crushed garlic
4 or 5 cloves
2.5ml/½ tsp black peppercorns
6 green cardamom pods
5cm/2in piece cinnamon stick, halved
8 lamb rib chops
60ml/4 tbsp vegetable oil
1 large onion, finely sliced
175ml/6fl oz/¾ cup natural (plain) yogurt
50g/2oz/¼ cup butter
2.5ml/1 tsp salt
2.5ml/½ tsp ground cumin
2.5ml/½ tsp hot chilli powder
whole nutmeg
2.5ml/½ tsp granulated (white) sugar
15ml/1 tbsp lime juice
pinch of saffron, steeped in 15ml/1 tbsp hot water for 10–15 minutes
15ml/1 tbsp rose water
rose petals, to garnish
naan bread or boiled basmati rice, to serve (optional)

1 Process the onion in a blender or food processor. Add a little water if necessary to form a purée.

2 Put the purée in a glass bowl and add the grated ginger, crushed garlic, cloves, peppercorns, cardamom pods and cinnamon. Mix well.

3 Put the lamb chops in a large shallow glass dish and add the spice mixture. Mix thoroughly, cover the bowl and leave the lamb to marinate for 3–4 hours or overnight in the refrigerator. Bring back to room temperature before cooking.

4 In a karahi, wok or large pan, heat the oil over medium high heat and fry the sliced onion for 6–7 minutes, until golden brown. Remove the onion slices with a slotted spoon, squeezing out as much oil as possible on the side of the pan. Drain the onions on kitchen paper.

5 In the remaining oil, fry the marinated lamb chops for 4–5 minutes, stirring frequently. Reduce the heat to low, cover and cook for 5–7 minutes.

6 Meanwhile, mix the yogurt and butter together in a small pan and place over a low heat. Cook for 5–6 minutes, stirring constantly, then stir into the lamb chops along with the salt. Add the cumin and chilli powder and cover the pan. Cook for 45–50 minutes until the chops are tender.

7 Using a nutmeg grater, or the finest cutting surface on a large, stainless steel grater, grate about 2.5ml/½ tsp nutmeg.

8 Add the nutmeg and sugar to the pan containing the lamb, cook for 1–2 minutes and add the lime juice, saffron and rose water. Stir and mix well, simmer for 2–3 minutes and remove from the heat. Spoon into a dish and garnish with the fried onion and rose petals. Serve with naan bread or boiled basmati rice, if you like.

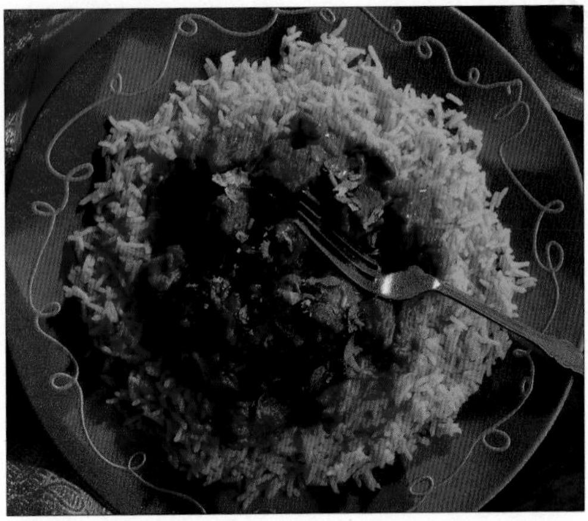

Lamb with Apricots

Dried apricots are a useful store cupboard ingredient and can really transform a curry or stew. Here they are combined with cinnamon, cardamom, cumin and coriander to make a delicious sauce with a hint of sweetness for lamb.

Serves 6

900g/2lb lean stewing lamb
15ml/1 tbsp oil
2.5cm/1in cinnamon stick
4 green cardamom pods
1 onion, chopped
15ml/1 tbsp curry paste
5ml/1 tsp ground cumin
5ml/1 tsp ground coriander
1.5ml/¼ tsp salt
175g/6oz/⅔ cup ready-to-eat dried apricots
350ml/12fl oz/1½ cups lamb stock
fresh coriander (cilantro), to garnish
saffron rice and mango chutney, to serve

1 Remove all the visible fat from the stewing lamb and cut into 2.5cm/1in cubes.

2 Heat the oil in a large, heavy pan and fry the cinnamon stick and cardamoms for 2 minutes. Add the onion and gently fry for about 6–8 minutes, stirring occasionally.

3 Add the curry paste and fry for 2 minutes. Stir in the ground cumin and coriander and the salt and stir-fry for a further 2–3 minutes.

4 Add the meat, apricots and the stock. Cover and cook for 1–1½ hours. Serve, garnished with fresh coriander, on saffron rice, with mango chutney in a separate bowl.

Cook's Tip
It is best to buy green cardamom pods from an Indian grocer or health food store, as the cardamoms sold in supermarkets are often bleached and do not have as full a flavour. Cardamom is a versatile spice in Indian cuisine, used in savoury and sweet dishes.

rezala Energy 545kcal/2263kJ; Protein 33.8g; Carbohydrate 15.5g, of which sugars 11g; Fat 39.3g, of which saturates 15.9g; Cholesterol 141mg; Calcium 134mg; Fibre 2g; Sodium 244mg.
lamb with apricots Energy 462kcal/1931kJ; Protein 28.5g; Carbohydrate 23.2g, of which sugars 17.6g; Fat 29.1g, of which saturates 7.8g; Cholesterol 86mg; Calcium 77mg; Fibre 5.8g; Sodium 114mg.

Mughlai-style Leg of Lamb

Legend has it that roasting a whole leg of lamb was first popularized by the Mongolian warrior Genghis Khan. Here the meat is permeated with spices.

Serves 4–6

4 large onions, chopped
4 garlic cloves
5cm/2in piece fresh root ginger, chopped
45ml/3 tbsp ground almonds
10ml/2 tsp ground cumin
10ml/2 tsp ground coriander
10ml/2 tsp ground turmeric
10ml/2 tsp garam masala
4–6 fresh green chillies
juice of 1 lemon
300ml/½ pint/1¼ cups natural (plain) yogurt, beaten
1.8kg/4lb leg of lamb
8–10 cloves
salt
15ml/1 tbsp flaked (sliced) almonds, to garnish
4 firm tomatoes, halved and grilled (broiled), to serve

1 Preheat the oven to 190°C/375°F/Gas 5. Place the onions, garlic, ginger, ground almonds, dry spices, chillies and lemon juice in a food processor or blender. Add salt to taste, and process to a smooth paste. Gradually add the yogurt and blend briefly to mix. Grease a large, deep roasting pan.

2 Remove most of the fat and skin from the lamb. Using a sharp knife, make deep pockets above the bone at each side of the thick end. Make deep diagonal gashes all down both sides of the meat.

3 Push the cloves firmly into the meat, spaced evenly on all sides.

4 Push some of the spice mixture into the pockets and gashes and spread the remainder evenly all over the meat. Place the meat on the roasting pan and loosely cover the whole pan with foil. Roast for 2–2½ hours, or until the meat is cooked, removing the foil for the last 10 minutes of cooking time.

5 Remove from the oven and leave to rest for about 10 minutes before carving. Garnish the roast with the almonds and serve with the tomatoes.

Kashmiri-style Lamb

This red-coloured, hot curry can be made milder by simply replacing the chilli powder with paprika and tomato purée.

Serves 4–6

60ml/4 tbsp vegetable oil
1.5ml/¼ tsp asafoetida
900g/2lb lean lamb, cubed
piece fresh root ginger, crushed
2 garlic cloves, crushed
60ml/4 tbsp rogan josh masala paste
5ml/1 tsp chilli powder, or 10ml/2 tsp sweet paprika plus 10ml/2 tsp tomato purée (paste)
8–10 strands saffron (optional), plus extra to garnish
salt
about 150ml/¼ pint/⅔ cup natural (plain) yogurt, beaten

1 Heat the oil in a pan and fry the asafoetida and lamb, stirring well to seal the meat. Reduce the heat, cover and cook for about 10 minutes.

2 Add the ginger, garlic, rogan josh masala paste, chilli powder or paprika and tomato purée (if you want a milder curry), and saffron. Mix well and add salt. If the meat is too dry, add a very small amount of boiling water. Cover the pan and cook on a low heat for a further 10 minutes.

3 Remove the pan from the heat and leave to cool a little. Add the yogurt 15ml/1 tbsp at a time, stirring constantly to avoid curdling. Return to a low heat and cook uncovered until thick. Garnish with a spoonful of yogurt and a few saffron strands.

Cook's Tip

Asafoetida is made from the sap of the roots and stem of a large plant similar to fennel in appearance. The sap dries into a resin, which is ground for culinary use. As it has a strong aroma it is used in only small amounts.

leg of lamb Energy 583kcal/2427kJ; Protein 50.7g; Carbohydrate 16.3g, of which sugars 9.4g; Fat 35.7g, of which saturates 11.6g; Cholesterol 175mg; Calcium 153mg; Fibre 1.4g; Sodium 181mg.
Kashmiri lamb Energy 547kcal/2280kJ; Protein 46g; Carbohydrate 2.8g, of which sugars 2.8g; Fat 39.3g, of which saturates 13.5g; Cholesterol 172mg; Calcium 89mg; Fibre 0g; Sodium 225mg.

Hot & Sour Lamb & Lentil Curry

This dish has a hot, sweet-and-sour flavour, through which should rise the slightly bitter flavour of fenugreek leaves.

Serves 4–6

90ml/6 tbsp vegetable oil
2 fresh red chillies, chopped
2 fresh green chillies, chopped
2.5cm/1in piece fresh root ginger, crushed
3 garlic cloves, crushed
2 bay leaves
5cm/2in piece cinnamon stick
900g/2lb lean lamb, cubed
600ml/1 pint/2½ cups water
350g/12oz/1½ cups mixed lentils (see Cook's Tip)
2 potatoes, cubed
1 aubergine (eggplant), cubed
2 courgettes (zucchini), cubed
4 onions, thinly sliced, deep-fried and drained
115g/4oz frozen spinach, thawed and drained
25g/1oz fenugreek leaves, fresh or dried
115g/4oz pumpkin, cubed
115g/4oz/4 cups fresh coriander (cilantro), chopped
50g/2oz/2 cups fresh mint, chopped, or 15ml/1 tbsp mint sauce
45ml/3 tbsp garam masala
10ml/2 tsp brown sugar
lemon juice, to taste
1 garlic clove, sliced
salt

1 Heat 45ml/3 tbsp of the oil in a pan, wok or karahi and fry the chillies, ginger and garlic for 2 minutes. Add the bay leaves, cinnamon, lamb and water. Bring to the boil, then reduce the heat and simmer until the lamb is half cooked.

2 Drain the water into another pan and put the lamb aside. Add the lentils to the water and cook until they are tender. Mash the lentils with the back of a spoon.

3 Add the cubes of potatoes and aubergine and stir into the mashed lentils, then add the courgette cubes and deep-fried onions. Stir in the spinach, fenugreek and pumpkin. Add some hot water if the mixture is too thick. Cook until the vegetables are tender, then mash again with a spoon, keeping the vegetables a little coarse.

4 Heat 15ml/1 tbsp of the oil in a frying pan, and gently fry the fresh coriander and mint (saving a little to garnish) with the masala, sugar and salt. Add the reserved lamb and fry gently for about 5 minutes.

5 Return the lamb and spices to the lentil and vegetable mixture and stir well. If the mixture seems dry, add more water. Heat gently until the lamb is fully cooked.

6 Add the lemon juice and mix well. Heat the remaining oil and fry the sliced clove of garlic until golden brown. Pour over the curry. Garnish with the remaining deep-fried onion slices and the reserved coriander and mint. Serve hot.

Cook's Tip
You might like to include bengal gram (a type of chickpea), moong dhal (small split yellow lentils) and masoor dhal (red split lentils). Cooking times will depend on the types chosen.

Hot Dry Meat Curry

This dish is nearly as hot as phaal (India's hottest curry) but the spices can still be distinguished above the fiery chilli.

Serves 4–6

30ml/2 tbsp vegetable oil
1 large onion, finely sliced
5cm/2in piece fresh root ginger, crushed
4 garlic cloves, crushed
6–8 curry leaves
45ml/3 tbsp extra-hot curry paste
15ml/1 tbsp chilli powder
5ml/1 tsp Indian five-spice powder
5ml/1 tsp ground turmeric
900g/2lb lean lamb, beef or pork, cubed
175ml/6fl oz/¾ cup thick coconut milk
salt
chopped tomato and coriander (cilantro) leaves, to garnish

1 Heat the oil in a large pan and fry the sliced onion, crushed ginger and garlic and the curry leaves until the onion is soft, stirring occasionally.

2 Stir in the curry paste, chilli, five-spice powder, turmeric and salt, and cook for a few moments, stirring frequently.

3 Add the meat and stir well over a medium heat to seal and evenly brown the meat pieces. Keep stirring until the oil separates. Cover and cook for about 20 minutes.

4 Add the coconut milk, mix well and simmer until the meat is cooked.

5 Towards the end of cooking, uncover the pan to reduce the excess liquid. Garnish and serve hot.

Cook's Tip
Indian five-spice powder contains aniseed, cumin, fenugreek, mustard and nigella. If you are unable to find it you can substitute garam masala or curry powder instead.

lamb & lentil curry Energy 419kcal/1762kJ; Protein 20.8g; Carbohydrate 56g, of which sugars 11.8g; Fat 14.2g, of which saturates 1.8g; Cholesterol 0mg; Calcium 189mg; Fibre 7.7g; Sodium 69mg.
hot dry meat curry Energy 558kcal/2323kJ; Protein 45g; Carbohydrate 6.9g, of which sugars 5.5g; Fat 39.2g, of which saturates 13.4g; Cholesterol 171mg; Calcium 46mg; Fibre 0.9g; Sodium 244mg.

Spicy Spring Lamb Roast

Coating a leg of lamb with a spicy, fruity rub gives it a wonderful flavour.

Serves 6

1.6kg/3–3½lb lean leg of spring lamb
5ml/1 tsp chilli powder
5ml/1 tsp crushed garlic
5ml/1 tsp ground coriander
5ml/1 tsp ground cumin
5ml/1 tsp salt
15ml/1 tbsp dried breadcrumbs
45ml/3 tbsp natural (plain) low-fat yogurt
30ml/2 tbsp lemon juice
30ml/2 tbsp sultanas (golden raisins)
15ml/1 tbsp oil

For the garnish

mixed salad leaves
fresh coriander (cilantro)
2 tomatoes, quartered
1 large carrot, shredded
lemon wedges

1 Preheat the oven to 180°C/350°F/Gas 4. Trim any excess fat from the lamb. Rinse the joint, pat it dry and set aside on a sheet of foil large enough to enclose it completely.

2 In a medium bowl, mix together the chilli powder, garlic, ground coriander, ground cumin and salt.

3 Mix together in a food processor the breadcrumbs, yogurt, lemon juice and sultanas.

4 Add the contents of the food processor to the spice mixture together with the oil and mix together well. Pour this on to the leg of lamb and rub all over the meat.

5 Enclose the meat in the foil and place in an ovenproof dish. Cook in the oven for about 1½ hours.

6 Remove the lamb from the oven, open the foil and, using the back of a spoon, spread the mixture evenly over the meat. Return the lamb, uncovered, to the oven for another 45 minutes or until it is cooked right through and tender.

7 Slice the meat and serve with the mixed salad leaves, fresh coriander, tomatoes, carrot and lemon wedges.

Lamb Pilau

A pilau is a rice dish containing whole spices, which can either be plain or combined with meat, chicken or vegetables.

Serves 4–6

30ml/2 tbsp corn oil
15ml/1 tbsp unsalted (sweet) butter or ghee
2 medium onions, sliced
5ml/1 tsp crushed garlic
5ml/1 tsp chilli powder
1.5ml/¼ tsp crushed fresh root ginger
1.5ml/¼ tsp ground turmeric
5ml/1 tsp garam masala
5ml/1 tsp salt
30ml/2 tbsp natural (plain) yogurt
2 medium tomatoes, sliced
450g/1lb lean minced (ground) lamb
30ml/2 tbsp chopped fresh coriander (cilantro)
2 medium fresh chillies, chopped
tomato slices

For the rice

450g/1lb/2¼ cups basmati rice
1.2 litres/2 pints/5 cups water
4 cloves
4 green cardamom pods
2.5ml/½ tsp black cumin seeds
6 black peppercorns
7.5ml/1½ tsp salt
15ml/1 tbsp chopped fresh coriander (cilantro)
2 fresh green chillies, chopped
15ml/1 tbsp lime juice
2.5ml/½ tsp saffron strands soaked in 30ml/2 tbsp milk (optional)

1 Wash the rice twice, drain and set aside in a sieve (strainer).

2 Heat the oil and ghee in a deep, round-bottomed frying pan or a large karahi. Add the onions and fry until golden brown.

3 Lower the heat to medium and add the garlic, chilli powder, ginger, turmeric, garam masala, salt, yogurt and tomatoes and stir-fry gently for about 1 minute.

4 Add the minced lamb and turn up the heat to high. Use a slotted spoon to fry the lamb, scraping the bottom of the pan to prevent it from burning.

5 Add the fresh coriander and chillies, and continue to stir, breaking up any lumps in the meat as you work. Once the lamb is throughly cooked, set it to one side.

6 Put the rinsed and drained rice into a large pan with the water, cloves, cardamom pods, cumin seeds, peppercorns and salt, and bring to the boil. When the rice has boiled for 2 minutes, drain off the water along with half the rice, leaving the rest in the pan.

7 Spread the cooked lamb over the rice in the pan and cover with the rice left in the strainer.

8 Add the fresh coriander, green chillies, lime juice and saffron in milk, if using.

9 Cover the pan with a tight-fitting lid and cook over a very low heat for 15–20 minutes.

10 Check that the rice is cooked through and mix gently with a slotted spoon before serving. Garnish with slices of tomato, if you like.

lamb roast Energy 478kcal/1987kJ; Protein 39.1g; Carbohydrate 3.5g, of which sugars 0.6g; Fat 34.4g, of which saturates 10.1g; Cholesterol 145mg; Calcium 37mg; Fibre 0g; Sodium 119mg.
lamb pilau Energy 609kcal/2543kJ; Protein 24.4g; Carbohydrate 79.6g, of which sugars 18.2g; Fat 21.5g, of which saturates 5.5g; Cholesterol 57mg; Calcium 70mg; Fibre 3.4g; Sodium 156mg.

Balti Bhoona Lamb

Bhooning is a very traditional way of stir-frying which simply involves semi-circular movements, scraping the bottom of the pan each time in the centre. Serve this dish of spring lamb with freshly made chapatis.

Serves 4

225–275g/8–10oz boneless lean spring lamb
3 medium onions
15ml/1 tbsp oil
15ml/1 tbsp tomato purée (paste)
5ml/1 tsp crushed garlic
7.5ml/1½ tsp finely grated fresh root ginger, plus 15ml/1 tbsp shredded
5ml/1 tsp salt
1.5ml/¼ tsp ground turmeric
600ml/1 pint/2½ cups water
15ml/1 tbsp lemon juice
15ml/1 tbsp chopped fresh coriander (cilantro)
15ml/1 tbsp chopped fresh mint
1 fresh red chilli, chopped

1 Using a sharp knife, remove any excess fat from the lamb and cut the meat into small cubes.

2 Dice the onions finely. Heat the oil in a karahi, wok or heavy pan and fry the onions until soft.

3 Meanwhile, mix together the tomato purée, garlic and ginger, salt and turmeric. Pour the spice mixture on to the onions in the pan and stir-fry for a few seconds.

4 Add the lamb and continue to stir-fry for about 2–3 minutes. Stir in the water, lower the heat, cover the pan and cook for 15–20 minutes, stirring occasionally.

5 When the water has almost evaporated, start bhooning over a medium heat, making sure that the sauce does not catch on the bottom of the pan. Continue for 5–7 minutes.

6 Pour in the lemon juice, followed by the shredded ginger, chopped fresh coriander, mint and red chilli. Stir to mix, then serve straight from the pan.

Balti Lamb with Potatoes & Fenugreek

The combination of lamb with fresh fenugreek works very well in this dish, which is delicious accompanied by plain boiled rice and mango chutney. Use only the fenugreek leaves, as the stalks can be rather bitter. This dish is traditionally served with rice.

Serves 4

450g/1lb lean minced (ground) lamb
5ml/1 tsp grated fresh root ginger
5ml/1 tsp crushed garlic
7.5ml/1½ tsp chilli powder
5ml/1 tsp salt
1.5ml/¼ tsp turmeric
45ml/3 tbsp corn oil
2 medium onions, sliced
2 medium potatoes, peeled, par-boiled and roughly diced
1 bunch fresh fenugreek, chopped
2 tomatoes, chopped
50g/2oz/½ cup frozen peas
30ml/2 tbsp chopped fresh coriander (cilantro)
3 fresh red chillies, seeded and sliced

1 Put the minced lamb, grated ginger, garlic, chilli powder, salt and turmeric into a large bowl, and mix together thoroughly. Set to one side.

2 Heat the oil in a karahi, wok or deep pan. Add the onion slices and fry for about 5 minutes until golden brown.

3 Add the minced lamb and fry over a medium heat for 5–7 minutes, stirring.

4 Stir in the potatoes, chopped fenugreek, tomatoes and peas and cook for a further 5–7 minutes, stirring constantly.

5 Just before serving, stir in the fresh coriander. Spoon into a large dish or on to individual plates and serve hot. Garnish with fresh red chillies.

balti bhoona lamb Energy 188kcal/785kJ; Protein 13.7g; Carbohydrate 12.1g, of which sugars 7.8g; Fat 10g, of which saturates 3.3g; Cholesterol 43mg; Calcium 69mg; Fibre 2.5g; Sodium 67mg.
balti lamb Energy 418kcal/1748kJ; Protein 27.3g; Carbohydrate 28.8g, of which sugars 9.2g; Fat 22.4g, of which saturates 7.1g; Cholesterol 86mg; Calcium 93mg; Fibre 4.5g; Sodium 123mg.

Balti Lamb in Yogurt

The lamb is marinated in spices, then cooked slowly in a hot yogurt sauce. The dish is served with dried apricots which have been lightly sautéed in ghee with cinnamon and cardamom.

Serves 4

15ml/1 tbsp tomato purée (paste)
175ml/6fl oz/¾ cup natural (plain) low-fat yogurt
5ml/1 tsp garam masala
1.5ml/¼ tsp cumin seeds
5ml/1 tsp salt
5ml/1 tsp crushed garlic
5ml/1 tsp grated fresh root ginger
5ml/1 tsp chilli powder
225g/8oz boneless lean spring lamb, cut into strips
15ml/1 tbsp oil
2 medium onions, finely sliced
25g/1oz/2 tbsp ghee or unsalted butter
2.5cm/1in cinnamon stick
2 green cardamom pods
5 dried apricots, quartered
15ml/1 tbsp fresh coriander (cilantro) leaves, to garnish

1 In a bowl, blend together the tomato purée, yogurt, garam masala, cumin seeds, salt, garlic, ginger and chilli powder. Add the lamb to the sauce and mix well. Cover and leave to marinate in a cool place for about 1 hour.

2 Heat 10ml/2 tsp of the oil in a wok or heavy frying pan and fry the onions over a medium heat until they are crisp and golden brown. Remove the onions using a slotted spoon, allow to cool and then grind down by processing briefly in a food processor or with a mortar and pestle. Reheat the oil remaining in the pan and return the onions to the wok.

3 Add the lamb and stir-fry for about 2 minutes. Cover with a lid, lower the heat and cook, stirring occasionally, for about 15 minutes or until the meat is cooked through. If required, add about 150ml/¼ pint/⅔ cup water during the cooking. Remove from the heat and set aside.

4 Heat the ghee or butter with the remaining 5ml/1 tsp of oil and drop in the cinnamon stick and cardamoms. Add the dried apricots and stir over a low heat for about 2 minutes. Pour this over the lamb. Serve garnished with the fresh coriander leaves.

Balti Lamb with Stuffed Vegetables

Aubergines and bright, mixed peppers are stuffed with an aromatic lamb filling and served on a bed of sautéed onions. The presentation is very attractive.

Serves 4–6

3 small aubergines (eggplants)
1 each red, green and yellow (bell) peppers

For the stuffing

45ml/3 tbsp corn oil
3 medium onions, sliced
5ml/1 tsp chilli powder
1.5ml/¼ tsp ground turmeric
5ml/1 tsp ground coriander
5ml/1 tsp ground cumin
5ml/1 tsp grated fresh root ginger
5ml/1 tsp crushed garlic
5ml/1 tsp salt
450g/1lb lean minced (ground) lamb
3 fresh green chillies, chopped
30ml/2 tbsp chopped fresh coriander (cilantro)

For the sautéed onions

45ml/3 tbsp corn oil
5ml/1 tsp mixed onion, mustard, fenugreek and white cumin seeds
4 dried red chillies
3 medium onions, roughly chopped
5ml/1 tsp salt
5ml/1 tsp chilli powder
2 medium tomatoes, sliced
2 fresh green chillies, chopped
30ml/2 tbsp chopped fresh coriander

1 Prepare the vegetables. Slit the aubergines lengthways up to the stalks; keep the stalks intact. Cut the tops off the peppers and remove the seeds.

2 Make the stuffing. Heat the oil in a medium pan. Add the onions and fry for about 3 minutes. Lower the heat and add the chilli powder, turmeric, ground coriander, ground cumin, ginger, garlic and salt, and stir-fry for about 1 minute. Add the lamb to the pan and increase the heat.

3 Stir-fry for 7–10 minutes or until the lamb is cooked, using a wooden spoon to scrape the bottom of the pan. Add the green chillies and fresh coriander towards the end. Remove from the heat, cover and set to one side.

4 Make the sautéed onions. Heat the oil in a karahi, wok or deep pan and add the mixed onion, mustard, fenugreek and white cumin seeds. Stir in the dried red chillies, and fry for about 1 minute. Add the onions and fry for about 2 minutes or until soft.

5 Add the salt, chilli powder, tomatoes, green chillies and fresh coriander. Cook for a further minute. Remove from the heat and set to one side.

6 The minced lamb should by now be cool enough to stuff the prepared aubergines and peppers. Fill the vegetables quite loosely with the meat mixture. As you stuff the vegetables, place them on top of the sautéed onions in the karahi. Cover with foil, making sure the foil doesn't touch the food, and cook over a low heat for about 15 minutes.

7 The dish is ready as soon as the aubergines and peppers are tender. Serve with a dish of plain boiled rice or a colourful pilau rice to complement the colours of the peppers.

lamb in yogurt Energy 222kcal/923kJ; Protein 15.2g; Carbohydrate 13.1g, of which sugars 9.5g; Fat 12.6g, of which saturates 6.5g; Cholesterol 57mg; Calcium 122mg; Fibre 1.5g; Sodium 136mg.
balti lamb Energy 336kcal/1398kJ; Protein 18.9g; Carbohydrate 18.9g, of which sugars 14.5g; Fat 21.2g, of which saturates 5.5g; Cholesterol 57mg; Calcium 75mg; Fibre 5.4g; Sodium 409mg.

Balti Lamb Tikka

This is a traditional tikka recipe, in which the lamb is marinated in yogurt and spices. The lamb is usually cut into cubes, but the cooking time can be halved by cutting it into strips.

Serves 4

450g/1lb lean boneless lamb, cut into strips
175ml/6fl oz/¾ cup natural (plain) yogurt
5ml/1 tsp ground cumin
5ml/1 tsp ground coriander
5ml/1 tsp chilli powder
5ml/1 tsp crushed garlic
5ml/1 tsp salt
5ml/1 tsp garam masala
30ml/2 tbsp chopped fresh coriander (cilantro)
30ml/2 tbsp lemon juice
30ml/2 tbsp corn oil
15ml/1 tbsp tomato purée (paste)
1 large green (bell) pepper, seeded and sliced
3 large fresh red chillies

1 Put the lamb strips, yogurt, ground cumin, ground coriander, chilli powder, garlic, salt, garam masala, fresh coriander and lemon juice into a large mixing bowl and stir thoroughly. Cover and marinate at cool room temperature for 1 hour.

2 Heat the oil in a karahi, wok or deep pan. Lower the heat slightly and stir in the tomato purée.

3 Add the lamb strips to the pan, a few at a time, leaving any excess marinade behind in the bowl.

4 Cook the lamb, stirring frequently, for 7–10 minutes or until it is well browned.

5 Finally, add the green pepper slices and the whole red chillies. Heat through, checking that the lamb is fully cooked, spoon into a serving dish and serve hot.

Cook's Tip
Coriander leaves can easily go soggy after washing, so dry them quickly on kitchen paper.

Balti Lamb Chops with Potatoes

These chops are marinated before being cooked in a deliciously spicy sauce.

Serves 6–8

8 lamb chops, about 50–75g/2–3oz each
30ml/2 tbsp olive oil
150ml/¼ pint/⅔ cup lemon juice
5ml/1 tsp salt
15ml/1 tbsp chopped fresh mint and coriander (cilantro)
150ml/¼ pint/⅔ cup corn oil
fresh mint sprigs and lime slices, to garnish

For the sauce
45ml/3 tbsp corn oil
8 medium tomatoes, roughly chopped
1 bay leaf
5ml/1 tsp garam masala
30ml/2 tbsp natural (plain) yogurt
5ml/1 tsp crushed garlic
5ml/1 tsp chilli powder
5ml/1 tsp salt
2.5ml/½ tsp black cumin seeds
3 black peppercorns
2 medium potatoes, peeled, roughly chopped and boiled

1 Put the chops into a large bowl. Mix together the olive oil, lemon juice, salt and fresh mint and coriander. Pour the oil mixture over the chops and rub it in well. Cover and leave to marinate for at least 3 hours in the refrigerator.

2 To make the sauce, heat the corn oil in a karahi, wok or deep pan. Lower the heat and add the chopped tomatoes. Stir-fry for about 2 minutes. Add the bay leaf, garam masala, yogurt, garlic, chilli powder, salt, black cumin seeds and black peppercorns, and stir-fry for a further 2–3 minutes. Lower the heat again and add the cooked potatoes, mixing everything together well. Remove from the heat and set to one side.

3 Heat 150ml/¼ pint/⅔ cup corn oil in a separate frying pan. Lower the heat slightly and fry the marinated chops until they are cooked through. This will take about 10–12 minutes. Remove and drain the cooked chops on kitchen paper.

4 Heat the sauce in the karahi, bringing it to the boil. Add the chops and lower the heat. Simmer for 5–7 minutes. Transfer to a warmed serving dish and garnish with the mint sprigs and lime slices.

balti lamb tikka Energy 290kcal/1209kJ; Protein 22.8g; Carbohydrate 5.1g, of which sugars 5.1g; Fat 20g, of which saturates 6.9g; Cholesterol 85mg; Calcium 49mg; Fibre 1.5g; Sodium 107mg.
balti lamb chops Energy 276kcal/1154kJ; Protein 16.5g; Carbohydrate 11.4g, of which sugars 3.5g; Fat 18.7g, of which saturates 5.2g; Cholesterol 57mg; Calcium 30mg; Fibre 1.7g; Sodium 80mg.

Warm Lamb & Noodle Salad

Here, thin slices of wok-fried lamb, fresh vegetables and rice noodles are tossed in an aromatic dressing.

Serves 4

30ml/2 tbsp red curry paste
60ml/4 tbsp sunflower oil
750g/1lb 11oz lamb neck (US shoulder or breast) fillets, thinly sliced
250g/9oz sugar snap peas
500g/1¼lb fresh rice noodles
1 red (bell) pepper, seeded and very thinly sliced
1 cucumber, sliced paper thin
6–7 spring onions (scallions), sliced diagonally
a large handful of fresh mint leaves

For the dressing

15ml/1 tbsp sunflower oil
juice of 2 limes
1 garlic clove, crushed
15ml/1 tbsp sugar
15ml/1 tbsp fish sauce
30ml/2 tbsp soy sauce

1 In a shallow dish, mix together the red curry paste and half the oil. Add the lamb slices and toss to coat. Cover and leave to marinate in the refrigerator for up to 24 hours.

2 Blanch the sugar snap peas in a pan of lightly salted boiling water for 1–2 minutes. Drain, refresh under cold water, drain again thoroughly and transfer to a large bowl.

3 Put the noodles in a separate bowl and pour over boiling water to cover. Leave to soak for 5–10 minutes, until tender, then drain well and separate into strands with your fingers.

4 Add the noodles to the sugar snap peas, then add the sliced red pepper, cucumber and spring onions. Toss lightly to mix.

5 Heat a wok over a high heat and add the remaining sunflower oil. Stir-fry the lamb, in two batches, for 3–4 minutes, or until cooked through, then add to the bowl of salad.

6 Place all the dressing ingredients in a jar, screw on the lid and shake well. Pour the dressing over the warm salad, sprinkle over the mint leaves and toss well to combine. Serve immediately.

Birthday Noodles with Hoisin Lamb

This sumptuous dish gets its name from the inclusion of boiled eggs in the recipe. Eggs symbolize continuity and fertility in China, so it is considered a fitting dish for birthday celebrations.

Serves 4

350g/12oz thick egg noodles
1kg/2¼ lb lean neck fillets of lamb
30ml/2 tbsp vegetable oil
115g/4oz fine green beans, trimmed and blanched
salt and ground black pepper
2 hard-boiled eggs, halved, and 2 spring onions (scallions), finely chopped, to garnish

For the marinade

2 garlic cloves, crushed
10ml/2 tsp grated fresh root ginger
30ml/2 tbsp soy sauce
30ml/2 tbsp rice wine
1–2 dried red chillies
30ml/2 tbsp vegetable oil

For the sauce

15ml/1 tbsp cornflour (cornstarch)
30ml/2 tbsp soy sauce
30ml/2 tbsp rice wine
grated rind and juice of ½ orange
15ml/1 tbsp hoisin sauce
15ml/1 tbsp wine vinegar
5ml/1 tsp soft light brown sugar

1 Bring a large pan of water to the boil and cook the noodles for 2 minutes. Drain, rinse and drain again. Set aside.

2 Cut the lamb into 5cm/2in thick medallions. Mix the ingredients for the marinade in a large shallow dish. Add the lamb and leave to marinate for at least 4 hours or overnight.

3 Heat the oil in a heavy pan. Fry the lamb for 5 minutes until browned. Add just enough water to cover. Bring to the boil, skim, then simmer for 40 minutes or until the meat is tender.

4 Make the sauce. Blend the cornflour with the remaining ingredients in a bowl. Stir into the lamb and mix well. Add the noodles and beans and simmer until cooked. Add salt and pepper to taste.

5 Divide among four large bowls, garnish with hard-boiled egg halves and spring onions and serve.

lamb & noodle salad Energy 820kcal/3418kJ; Protein 46g; Carbohydrate 76.4g, of which sugars 9.4g; Fat 36g, of which saturates 11.7g; Cholesterol 143mg; Calcium 55mg; Fibre 4.1g; Sodium 709mg.
birthday noodles Energy 605kcal/2545kJ; Protein 35.8g; Carbohydrate 62.8g, of which sugars 1.7g; Fat 25.3g, of which saturates 9g; Cholesterol 207mg; Calcium 48mg; Fibre 2.5g; Sodium 289mg.

Pork with Vegetables

This is a basic recipe for stir-frying any meat with any vegetables, according to seasonal availability.

Serves 4

225g/8oz pork fillet (tenderloin)
15ml/1 tbsp light soy sauce
5ml/1 tsp soft light brown sugar
5ml/1 tsp Chinese rice wine or dry sherry
10ml/2 tsp cornflour (cornstarch) mixed to a paste with a little water
115g/4oz/1⅔ cups mangetouts (snow peas)
115g/4oz button (white) mushrooms
1 carrot
1 spring onion (scallion)
60ml/4 tbsp vegetable oil
5ml/1 tsp salt
stock (optional)
few drops sesame oil

1 Cut the pork into thin slices. Marinate with about 5ml/1 tsp of the soy sauce, the sugar, rice wine or sherry and cornflour paste.

2 Trim the mangetouts. Thinly slice the mushrooms. Cut the carrot into pieces roughly the same size as the pork and cut the spring onion into short sections.

3 Heat the oil in a preheated wok or large, heavy pan, and stir-fry the pork for about 1 minute or until its colour changes. Remove with a slotted spoon and keep warm while you cook the vegetables.

4 Add the vegetables to the wok and stir-fry for about 2 minutes. Add the salt and the partly cooked pork, and a little stock or water if necessary. Continue cooking and stirring for about 1 minute, then add the remaining soy sauce and blend well. Sprinkle with the sesame oil and serve.

Cook's Tip

When preparing vegetables for stir-frying, cut them to even sizes so that they will take the same amount of time to cook.

Portuguese Pork

The Portuguese expanded their empire during the 15th century, establishing outposts in India and Malaysia. In these days, before refrigeration, spices were extremely valuable, and the Portuguese were keen to control the main trade routes both between Asia and Europe, and among different regions of Asia such as India, Indonesia, China and Japan. One major result of this Portuguese colonization was the influence of Portuguese cooking on Indian cuisine, as shown in this fiery pork curry recipe.

Serves 4–6

115g/4oz deep-fried onions, crushed
4 fresh red chillies
60ml/4 tbsp vindaloo curry paste
90ml/6 tbsp white wine vinegar
90ml/6 tbsp tomato purée (paste)
2.5ml/½ tsp fenugreek seeds
5ml/1 tsp ground turmeric
5ml/1 tsp crushed mustard seeds, or 2.5ml/½ tsp mustard powder
7.5ml/1½ tsp sugar
900g/2lb boneless pork spare ribs, cubed
250ml/8fl oz/1 cup water
salt
plain boiled rice, to serve

1 Place the crushed onions, chillies, curry paste, vinegar, tomato purée, fenugreek seeds, turmeric and mustard seeds or powder in a bowl, with sugar and salt to taste.

2 Add the pork cubes and mix well. Cover and marinate for 2 hours, then transfer to a large, heavy pan.

3 Stir in the water. Bring to the boil and simmer gently for 2 hours. Serve hot with the rice.

Cook's Tip

When preparing fresh chillies, it is a good idea to wear rubber gloves, especially if using the hotter varieties. Never touch your eyes, nose or mouth while handling them, and wash both the gloves and your hands with soap and warm water afterwards.

pork w. vegetables Energy 199kcal/826kJ; Protein 13.8g; Carbohydrate 5.7g, of which sugars 3g; Fat 13.6g, of which saturates 2.1g; Cholesterol 35mg; Calcium 26mg; Fibre 1.6g; Sodium 49mg.
Portuguese pork Energy 267kcal/1119kJ; Protein 34.6g; Carbohydrate 11.3g, of which sugars 7.3g; Fat 9.6g, of which saturates 2.5g; Cholesterol 95mg; Calcium 68mg; Fibre 2.2g; Sodium 166mg.

Chilli Pork with Curry Leaves

Curry leaves and chillies are two of the hallmark ingredients used in the southern states of India. This recipe is from the state of Andhra Pradesh, where the hottest chillies, known as guntur after the region where they are produced, are grown in abundance.

Serves 4–6

30ml/2 tbsp vegetable oil
1 large onion, finely sliced
5cm/2in piece fresh root ginger, grated
4 garlic cloves, crushed
12 curry leaves
45ml/3 tbsp extra-hot curry paste, or 60ml/4 tbsp hot curry powder
15ml/1 tbsp chilli powder
5ml/1 tsp five-spice powder
5ml/1 tsp ground turmeric
900g/2lb pork, cubed
175ml/6fl oz/¾ cup thick coconut milk
salt
red onion, finely sliced, to garnish
Indian bread and fruit raita, to serve

1 Heat the oil in a karahi, wok or large pan, and fry the onion, ginger, garlic and curry leaves until the onion is soft. Add the curry paste or powder, chilli and five-spice powder, turmeric and salt. Stir well.

2 Add the pork and stir well over a medium heat to seal and evenly brown the meat pieces. Keep stirring until the oil separates. Cover the pan and cook for about 20 minutes.

3 Stir in the coconut milk and simmer, covered, until the meat is cooked. Towards the end of cooking, uncover the pan to reduce the excess liquid. Garnish with onions and serve with any Indian bread, and with fruit raita, for a cooling effect.

Cook's Tip
For extra flavour, reserve half the curry leaves and add with the coconut milk in step 3.

Pork Balchao

This spicy stew is flavoured with vinegar and sugar, a combination that immediately identifies it as Goan.

Serves 4

60ml/4 tbsp vegetable oil
15ml/1 tbsp grated fresh root ginger
15ml/1 tbsp crushed garlic
2.5cm/1in piece cinnamon stick, broken up
2–4 dried red chillies, chopped or torn
4 cloves
10ml/2 tsp cumin seeds
10 black peppercorns
675g/1½lb cubed leg of pork, crackling and other visible fat removed
5ml/1 tsp ground turmeric
200ml/7fl oz/scant 1 cup warm water
25ml/1½ tbsp tomato purée (paste)
2.5ml/½ tsp chilli powder (optional)
1 large onion, finely sliced
5ml/1 tsp salt
5ml/1 tsp sugar
10ml/2 tbsp cider vinegar
fresh chillies, to garnish

1 Heat 30ml/2 tbsp of the oil in a karahi, wok or large pan, and add the ginger and garlic. Fry for 30 seconds.

2 Grind the cinnamon stick, dried chillies, cloves, cumin seeds and peppercorns to a fine powder, using a spice mill or coffee grinder reserved for spices. Add the spice mix to the pan and fry for a further 30 seconds, stirring.

3 Add the pork and turmeric and increase the heat slightly. Fry for 5–6 minutes or until the meat starts to release its juices, stirring regularly. Add the water, tomato purée and chilli powder, if using, and bring to the boil. Cover the pan and simmer gently for 35–40 minutes.

4 Heat the remaining oil and fry the sliced onion for 8–9 minutes until browned, stirring regularly. Add the fried onion to the pork along with the salt, sugar and cider vinegar. Stir, cover and simmer for 30–35 minutes or until the pork is tender. Remove from the heat and spoon into a serving dish. Garnish with fresh chillies and serve.

chilli pork Energy 283kcal/1182kJ; Protein 34.8g; Carbohydrate 11.1g, of which sugars 5.2g; Fat 11.5g, of which saturates 2.8g; Cholesterol 95mg; Calcium 58mg; Fibre 0.9g; Sodium 143mg.
pork balchao Energy 351kcal/1464kJ; Protein 38.5g; Carbohydrate 6.4g, of which sugars 1.7g; Fat 19.4g, of which saturates 3.9g; Cholesterol 106mg; Calcium 41mg; Fibre 0.4g; Sodium 629mg.

Curried Pork with Pickled Garlic

This very rich curry is best accompanied by lots of plain rice and perhaps a light vegetable dish. It could serve four if accompanied by a vegetable curry. Asian stores sell pickled garlic. It is well worth investing in a jar, as the taste is sweet and delicious.

Serves 2

130g/4½oz lean pork steaks
30ml/2 tbsp vegetable oil
1 garlic clove, crushed
15ml/1 tbsp Thai red curry paste
130ml/4½fl oz/generous ½ cup coconut cream
2.5cm/1in piece fresh root ginger, finely chopped
30ml/2 tbsp vegetable or chicken stock
30ml/2 tbsp Thai fish sauce
5ml/1 tsp sugar
2.5ml/½ tsp ground turmeric
10ml/2 tsp lemon juice
4 pickled garlic cloves, finely chopped
strips of lemon and lime rind, to garnish

1 Place the pork steaks in the freezer for 30–40 minutes, until firm, then, using a sharp knife, cut the meat into fine slivers, trimming off any excess fat.

2 Heat the oil in a wok or large, heavy frying pan and cook the garlic over low to medium heat until golden brown. Do not let it burn. Add the curry paste and stir it in well.

3 Add the coconut cream and stir until the liquid begins to reduce and thicken. Stir in the pork. Cook for 2 minutes more, until the pork is cooked through.

4 Add the ginger, stock, fish sauce, sugar and turmeric, stirring constantly, then add the lemon juice and pickled garlic. Spoon into bowls, garnish with strips of rind, and serve.

Cook's Tip
Thai red curry paste is a fiery curry paste made with hot red chillies, garlic, lemon grass, shrimp paste and turmeric.

Sweet & Sour Pork, Thai-style

It was the Chinese who originally created sweet and sour cooking, but the Thais also do it very well. This version has a fresher and cleaner flavour than the original. It makes a good one-dish meal when served over rice.

Serves 4

350g/12oz lean pork
30ml/2 tbsp vegetable oil
4 garlic cloves, thinly sliced
1 small red onion, sliced
30ml/2 tbsp Thai fish sauce
15ml/1 tbsp sugar
1 red (bell) pepper, seeded and diced
½ cucumber, seeded and sliced
2 plum tomatoes, cut into wedges
115g/4oz piece of fresh pineapple, cut into small chunks
2 spring onions (scallions), cut into short lengths
ground black pepper

For the garnish
coriander (cilantro) leaves
spring onions (scallions), shredded

1 Place the pork in the freezer for 30–40 minutes, until firm. Using a sharp knife, cut it into thin strips.

2 Heat the oil in a wok or large frying pan. Add the thinly sliced garlic. Cook over a medium heat until golden, then add the pork and stir-fry for 4–5 minutes. Add the red onion slices and toss to mix.

3 Add the fish sauce, sugar and ground black pepper to taste. Toss the mixture over the heat for 3–4 minutes more.

4 Stir in the diced red pepper, cucumber, tomatoes, pineapple and spring onions. Stir-fry for 3–4 minutes more, then spoon into a bowl. Garnish with the coriander and shredded spring onions, and serve.

Cook's Tip
Freezing the piece of pork slightly makes it much easier to carve extra-thin slices.

curried pork Energy 227kcal/947kJ; Protein 16.3g; Carbohydrate 9.8g, of which sugars 6.1g; Fat 14g, of which saturates 2.4g; Cholesterol 41mg; Calcium 30mg; Fibre 1g; Sodium 474mg.
sweet & sour pork Energy 168kcal/708kJ; Protein 20.3g; Carbohydrate 13.5g, of which sugars 12.9g; Fat 4g, of which saturates 1.3g; Cholesterol 55mg; Calcium 32mg; Fibre 2g; Sodium 604mg.

Lemon Grass Pork

Chillies and lemon grass flavour this simple stir-fry, while peanuts add an interesting contrast in texture. Look for jars of chopped lemon grass, which are handy when the fresh herb isn't available.

Serves 4

675g/1½lb boneless pork loin
2 lemon grass stalks, finely chopped
4 spring onions (scallions), thinly sliced
5ml/1 tsp salt
12 black peppercorns, coarsely crushed
30ml/2 tbsp groundnut (peanut) oil
2 garlic cloves, chopped
2 fresh red chillies, seeded and chopped
5ml/1 tsp soft light brown sugar
30ml/2 tbsp Thai fish sauce
25g/1oz/¼ cup roasted unsalted peanuts, chopped
ground black pepper
cooked rice noodles, to serve
coarsely torn coriander (cilantro) leaves, to garnish

1 Trim any excess fat from the pork. Cut the meat across into 5mm/¼in thick slices, then cut each slice into 5mm/¼in strips. Put the pork into a bowl with the lemon grass, spring onions, salt and crushed peppercorns; mix well. Cover with clear film (plastic wrap) and leave to marinate in a cool place for 30 minutes.

2 Preheat a wok, add the oil and swirl it around. Add the pork mixture and stir-fry over a medium heat for about 3 minutes, until browned all over.

3 Add the garlic and red chillies and stir-fry for a further 5–8 minutes over a medium heat, until the pork is cooked through and tender.

4 Add the sugar, fish sauce and chopped peanuts and toss to mix, then season to taste with black pepper. Serve immediately on a bed of rice noodles, garnished with the coarsely torn coriander leaves.

Pork & Pineapple Coconut Curry

The heat of this curry balances out the sweetness of the pineapple, and the coconut cream and spices make a smooth and fragrant dish. It takes very little time to cook, so is ideal for a quick supper before going out or for a midweek meal on a busy evening.

Serves 4

400ml/14fl oz can coconut milk
10ml/2 tsp Thai red curry paste
400g/14oz pork loin steaks, trimmed and thinly sliced
15ml/1 tbsp Thai fish sauce
5ml/1 tsp palm sugar (jaggery) or light muscovado (brown) sugar
15ml/1 tbsp tamarind juice, made by mixing tamarind paste with warm water
2 kaffir lime leaves, torn
½ medium pineapple, peeled and chopped
1 fresh red chilli, seeded and finely chopped

1 Pour the coconut milk into a bowl and let it settle, so that the cream rises to the surface. Scoop the cream into a measuring jug (cup). You should have about 250ml/8fl oz/1 cup. If necessary, add a little of the coconut milk.

2 Pour the measured coconut cream into a large pan and bring it to the boil.

3 Cook the coconut cream for about 10 minutes, until it separates, stirring frequently to prevent it from sticking to the base of the pan and scorching. Add the red curry paste and stir until well mixed. Cook, stirring occasionally, for about 4 minutes, until the paste is fragrant.

4 Add the sliced pork and stir in the fish sauce, sugar and tamarind juice. Cook, stirring constantly, for 1–2 minutes, until the sugar has dissolved and the pork is no longer pink.

5 Add the reserved coconut milk and the lime leaves. Bring to the boil, then stir in the pineapple. Reduce the heat and simmer gently for 3 minutes, or until the pork is fully cooked. Sprinkle over the chilli and serve.

lemon grass pork Energy 297kcal/1240kJ; Protein 37.9g; Carbohydrate 2.1g, of which sugars 1.7g; Fat 15.2g, of which saturates 3.6g; Cholesterol 106mg; Calcium 20mg; Fibre 0.6g; Sodium 119mg.
pork curry Energy 187kcal/790kJ; Protein 22.2g; Carbohydrate 15.3g, of which sugars 15.3g; Fat 4.5g, of which saturates 1.6g; Cholesterol 63mg; Calcium 55mg; Fibre 1.2g; Sodium 449mg.

Pork Belly with Five Spices

The Chinese influence on Thai cuisine stems from the early years of its history, when colonists from southern China settled in the country, bringing with them dishes like this, although Thai cooks have provided their own unique imprint. Lime and the whole of the coriander plant adds a full flavour to the spices used in this dish.

Serves 4

1 large bunch fresh coriander (cilantro) with roots
30ml/2 tbsp vegetable oil
1 garlic clove, crushed
30ml/2 tbsp five-spice powder
500g/1¼lb pork belly, cut into 2.5cm/1in pieces
400g/14oz can chopped tomatoes
150ml/¼ pint/⅔ cup hot water
30ml/2 tbsp dark soy sauce
45ml/3 tbsp Thai fish sauce
30ml/2 tbsp sugar
1 lime, halved

1 Cut off the coriander roots. Chop five of them finely and freeze the remainder for another occasion. Chop the coriander stalks and leaves and set them aside. Keep the roots separate.

2 Heat the oil in a large pan and cook the garlic until golden brown. Stirring constantly, add the chopped coriander roots and then the five-spice powder.

3 Add the pork and stir-fry until the meat is thoroughly coated in spices and has browned. Stir in the tomatoes and hot water. Bring to the boil, then stir in the soy sauce, fish sauce and sugar.

4 Reduce the heat, cover the pan and simmer for 30 minutes. Stir in the chopped coriander stalks and leaves, squeeze over the lime juice and serve.

Cook's Tip
Make sure that you buy Chinese five-spice powder, as the Indian variety is made up from quite different spices.

Pork in Preserved Beancurd

Cantonese chefs use two main types of preserved bean curd: the more common white variety known as fu yee in Cantonese, and a red one, known as lam yee. The latter not only has a more intense flavour, but it also gives the dish a very attractive bright red colour.

Serves 4

450g/1lb pork rib-eye steak streaked with a little fat
15ml/1 tbsp cornflour (cornstarch)
½ large onion
2 garlic cloves
30ml/2 tbsp oil
30ml/2 tbsp preserved red beancurd
5ml/1 tsp sugar
120ml/4 fl oz/½ cup water

1 With a sharp knife, cut the pork into thin medallions. Put the cornflour in a bowl or strong plastic bag, add the pork and toss lightly to coat.

2 Slice the onion and garlic finely. Heat the oil in a wok and fry the onion for 2 minutes. Add the garlic and fry for 1 minute.

3 Push the onion and garlic to the sides of the wok and add the pork slices to the centre. Stir-fry for 2–3 minutes, until the pork is well sealed. Bring the onion mixture back to the centre and mix it with the pork.

4 Add the preserved beancurd and mash well with your ladle or a fork. Continue to stir-fry the mixture until the pork is thoroughly coated in the beancurd mixture.

5 Add the sugar and water and bring to a brisk boil. When the sauce has reduced to about half the volume, the pork should be done. Serve hot with rice or noodles.

Cook's Tip
Stock up on specialist ingredients such as preserved red bean curd in specialist Asian supermarkets.

pork belly Energy 582kcal/2409kJ; Protein 20.6g; Carbohydrate 12.2g, of which sugars 12g; Fat 50.4g, of which saturates 17.1g; Cholesterol 90mg; Calcium 53mg; Fibre 1.8g; Sodium 818mg.
pork in beancurd Energy 215kcal/898kJ; Protein 24.9g; Carbohydrate 5.7g, of which sugars 1.9g; Fat 10.4g, of which saturates 2.3g; Cholesterol 71mg; Calcium 51mg; Fibre 0.2g; Sodium 82mg.

Stir-fried Pork with Dried Shrimp

You might expect the dried shrimp to give this dish a fishy flavour, but instead it simply imparts a delicious savoury taste.

Serves 4

250g/9oz pork fillet (tenderloin), sliced
30ml/2 tbsp vegetable oil
2 garlic cloves, finely chopped
45ml/3 tbsp dried shrimp
10ml/2 tsp dried shrimp paste or 5mm/¼in piece from block of shrimp paste
30ml/2 tbsp soy sauce
juice of 1 lime
15ml/1 tbsp palm sugar (jaggery) or light muscovado (brown) sugar
1 small fresh red or green chilli, seeded and finely chopped
4 pak choi (bok choy) or 450g/1lb spring greens (collards), shredded

1 Place the pork in the freezer for about 30 minutes, until firm. Using a sharp knife, cut it into thin slices.

2 Heat the oil in a wok or frying pan and cook the garlic until golden brown. Add the pork and stir-fry for about 4 minutes, until just cooked through.

3 Add the dried shrimp, then stir in the shrimp paste, with the soy sauce, lime juice and sugar.

4 Add the chilli and pak choi or spring greens and toss over the heat until the vegetables are just wilted. Transfer the stir-fried pork to warm individual bowls and serve immediately.

Cook's Tip

Pork fillet, or tenderloin, is the lean and tender muscle from the back loin of the pig. It is a prime cut of meat that is tender with little fat and is ideal for quick cooking such as here. It has a thin membrane that covers the meat, which needs to be removed before cooking.

Minced Pork Rolls in Beancurd Skin

This classic dish from Shantou is often cooked as a festive offering during Taoist festivals in China. Crinkly tofu skins are used as wrappers for the rich filling .

Serves 4

400g/14oz/1¾ cups minced (ground) pork
1 small carrot, thinly shredded
10ml/2 tsp light soy sauce
5ml/1 tsp ground black pepper
50g/2oz/⅓ cup finely chopped drained canned water chestnuts
8 spring onions (scallions), finely chopped
1 egg
25g/1oz/¼ cup cornflour (cornstarch)
1 package tofu skins
vegetable oil for deep-frying
sliced cucumber and chilli dipping sauce, to serve

1 Put the pork in a bowl and add the shredded carrot. Stir in the soy sauce, black pepper, water chestnuts and spring onions.

2 Lightly beat the egg in a small bowl and add it to the mixture. Stir to combine, then stir in the cornflour and mix well.

3 Bring a small pan of water to the boil. Pinch off a small lump of the pork mixture and boil for 2 minutes. Scoop it out, let it cool slightly, then taste and adjust the seasoning if necessary.

4 Keeping the remaining tofu sheets covered under a damp dish towel, place one sheet on a flat surface. Spread about 30ml/2 tbsp of the pork mixture along one edge. Roll over one and a half times, fold in the sides, then roll again to make a firm roll. Cut through the tofu to separate the roll from the sheet. Repeat until all the filling has been used.

5 Heat the oil in a wok or deep-fryer to 190°C/375°F. Add the rolls and fry for 3–4 minutes until golden brown and crisp. Drain on kitchen paper and leave to cool. Slice into diagonal pieces and serve with sliced cucumber and a chilli dip.

stir-fried pork Energy 200kcal/833kJ; Protein 23.1g; Carbohydrate 6.3g, of which sugars 6.2g; Fat 9.2g, of which saturates 1.7g; Cholesterol 96mg; Calcium 334mg; Fibre 2.4g; Sodium 1223mg.
pork rolls Energy 387kcal/1608kJ; Protein 23.8g; Carbohydrate 8.6g, of which sugars 2.4g; Fat 28.9g, of which saturates 6.1g; Cholesterol 114mg; Calcium 158mg; Fibre 0.9g; Sodium 361mg.

Spare Ribs in Black Bean Sauce

Spare ribs are popular in China. Recipes from the south tend to be less rich than those from the north, whose marinades contain considerably more wine. The best way to ensure the ribs are really succulent is to braise them, as deep-fried ribs tend to be dry.

Serves 4

500g/1¼lb pork spare ribs, cut into 5cm/2in lengths

For the marinade

30ml/2 tbsp light soy sauce
5ml/1 tsp sugar
30ml/2 tbsp black bean sauce
30ml/2 tbsp Chinese wine
30ml/2 tbsp oyster sauce
30ml/2 tbsp hoisin sauce
750ml/1¼ pints/3 cups water

1 Combine all the ingredients for the marinade in a large shallow dish. Add the ribs, making sure they are completely submerged. Cover and marinate for 30 minutes, turning the ribs once or twice.

2 Transfer the ribs, with the marinade, to a deep pan. Cover with a tight-fitting lid and bring to the boil. Cook over high heat for 15 minutes.

3 Lower the heat to medium and continue to cook the ribs for a further 40 minutes, until the pork is fully cooked and the sauce is very thick and glossy.

4 Pile the ribs on to a platter, pour the sauce over and serve. The best way to eat ribs is with the fingers, so be sure to have wipes handy, or offer finger bowls and napkins.

Cook's Tip

Ask your local butcher to chop the ribs into 5cm/2 in lengths if you do not have a suitable meat cleaver and chopping block at home. Rinse and pat them dry before marinating them.

Pork Fillet with Eggs & Mushrooms

Traditionally, this dish is served as a filling wrapped in thin pancakes, but it can also be served on its own with plain rice. The beauty of this dish is that once the ingredients are prepared, it takes moments to cook.

Serves 4

15g/½oz dried Chinese mushrooms
175–225g/6–8oz pork fillet (tenderloin)
225g/8oz Chinese leaves (Chinese cabbage)
115g/4oz bamboo shoots, drained
2 spring onions (scallions)
3 eggs
5ml/1 tsp salt
60ml/4 tbsp vegetable oil
15ml/1 tbsp light soy sauce
15ml/1 tbsp Chinese rice wine or dry sherry
few drops sesame oil

1 Rinse the mushrooms thoroughly in cold water and then soak in warm water for 25–30 minutes.

2 Rinse thoroughly again and discard the hard stalks, if any. Dry the mushrooms and thinly shred them.

3 Cut the pork fillet into matchstick-size shreds. Thinly shred the Chinese leaves, bamboo shoots and spring onions.

4 Beat the eggs with a pinch of salt. Heat a little oil in a wok, add the eggs and lightly scramble, but do not allow to become too dry. Remove from the wok.

5 Heat the remaining oil in the wok and stir-fry the pork for about 1 minute, or until the colour changes.

6 Add the vegetables to the wok and stir-fry for 1 minute. Add the remaining salt, the soy sauce and rice wine or sherry. Stir for 1 further minute before adding the scrambled eggs. Break up the scrambled eggs and blend well. Sprinkle with sesame oil and serve.

spare ribs Energy 722kcal/3012kJ; Protein 61.8g; Carbohydrate 2.6g, of which sugars 1g; Fat 51.9g, of which saturates 18.1g; Cholesterol 215mg; Calcium 59mg; Fibre 0.7g; Sodium 897mg.
pork fillet Energy 254kcal/1055kJ; Protein 18.6g; Carbohydrate 4.5g, of which sugars 3.9g; Fat 17.7g, of which saturates 3.3g; Cholesterol 178mg; Calcium 62mg; Fibre 1.7g; Sodium 365mg.

Aromatic Pork with Basil

The combination of moist, juicy pork and mushrooms, crisp green mangetouts and fragrant basil in this ginger- and garlic-infused stir-fry is absolutely delicious.

Serves 4
40g/1½oz cornflour (cornstarch)
500g/1¼lb pork fillet (tenderloin), thinly sliced
15ml/1 tbsp sunflower oil
10ml/2 tsp sesame oil
15ml/1 tbsp very finely shredded fresh root ginger
3 garlic cloves, thinly sliced
200g/7oz/scant 2 cups mangetouts (snow peas), halved
300g/11oz/generous 4 cups mixed mushrooms, sliced if large
120ml/4fl oz/½ cup Chinese cooking wine
45ml/3 tbsp soy sauce
a small handful of sweet basil leaves
salt and ground black pepper
steamed jasmine rice, to serve

1 Place the cornflour in a strong plastic bag. Season well and add the sliced pork. Shake the bag to coat the pork in flour and then remove the pork and shake off any excess flour. Set aside.

2 Preheat the wok over a high heat and add the oils. When very hot, stir in the ginger and garlic and cook for 30 seconds. Add the pork and cook over a high heat for about 5 minutes, stirring often, until sealed.

3 Add the mangetouts and mushrooms to the wok and stir-fry for 2–3 minutes. Add the Chinese cooking wine and soy sauce, stir-fry for 2–3 minutes and remove from the heat.

4 Just before serving, stir the sweet basil leaves into the pork. Serve with steamed jasmine rice.

Cook's Tip
For the mushroom medley, try to include fresh shiitake and oyster mushrooms as well as cultivated button (white) ones.

Ginger Pork with Black Bean Sauce

Preserved black beans provide a unique flavour in this dish. Look for them in specialist Chinese grocers.

Serves 4
350g/12oz pork fillet (tenderloin)
1 garlic clove, crushed
15ml/1 tbsp grated fresh root ginger
90ml/6 tbsp chicken stock
30ml/2 tbsp dry sherry
15ml/1 tbsp light soy sauce
5ml/1 tsp sugar
10ml/2 tsp cornflour (cornstarch)
45ml/3 tbsp groundnut (peanut) oil
2 yellow (bell) peppers, seeded and cut into strips
2 red (bell) peppers, seeded and cut into strips
1 bunch of spring onions (scallions), sliced diagonally
45ml/3 tbsp preserved black beans, coarsely chopped
fresh coriander (cilantro) sprigs, to garnish

1 Cut the pork into thin slices across the grain of the meat. Put the slices into a dish and mix them with the garlic and ginger. Cover with clear film (plastic wrap) and leave to marinate at room temperature for 15 minutes.

2 Blend together the stock, sherry, soy sauce, sugar and cornflour in a small bowl, then set the sauce mixture aside.

3 Heat the oil in a wok or large frying pan. Add the pork slices and stir-fry for 2–3 minutes. Add the yellow and red peppers and spring onions and stir-fry for a further 2 minutes.

4 Add the beans and sauce mixture and cook, stirring constantly, until thick. Serve immediately, garnished with the fresh coriander sprigs.

Cook's Tip
If you cannot find preserved black beans, use the same amount of black bean sauce instead.

aromatic pork Energy 298kcal/1248kJ; Protein 30.4g; Carbohydrate 14.6g, of which sugars 4.8g; Fat 9.8g, of which saturates 2.4g; Cholesterol 79mg; Calcium 41mg; Fibre 2g; Sodium 903mg.
ginger pork Energy 302kcal/1263kJ; Protein 23.8g; Carbohydrate 22.1g, of which sugars 13.4g; Fat 12.8g, of which saturates 3.1g; Cholesterol 55mg; Calcium 41mg; Fibre 4.1g; Sodium 341mg.

Pork Satay with Peanut Sauce

These delightful little satay sticks from Thailand make a good light meal or a drinks party snack.

Makes 8

½ small onion, chopped
2 garlic cloves, crushed
30ml/2 tbsp lemon juice
15ml/1 tbsp soy sauce
5ml/1 tsp ground coriander
2.5ml/½ tsp ground cumin
5ml/1 tsp ground turmeric
30ml/2 tbsp vegetable oil
450g/1lb pork fillet (tenderloin)
salt and ground black pepper
fresh coriander (cilantro) sprigs, to garnish
boiled rice, to serve

For the sauce

150ml/¼ pint/⅔ cup coconut cream
60ml/4 tbsp crunchy peanut butter
15ml/1 tbsp lemon juice
2.5ml/½ tsp ground cumin
2.5ml/½ tsp ground coriander
5ml/1 tsp soft brown sugar
15ml/1 tbsp soy sauce
1–2 dried red chillies, seeded and chopped
15ml/1 tbsp chopped fresh coriander

For the salad

½ small cucumber, peeled and diced
15ml/1 tbsp white wine vinegar
15ml/1 tbsp fresh coriander

1 Put the onion, garlic, lemon juice, soy sauce, ground coriander, cumin, turmeric and oil in a food processor and process until smooth. Cut the pork into strips, mix with the spice marinade in a bowl, cover with clear film (plastic wrap) and chill.

2 Preheat the grill (broiler). Thread two or three pork pieces on to each of eight soaked wooden skewers and grill (broil) for 2–3 minutes on each side, basting with the marinade.

3 To make the sauce, put all the ingredients into a pan, bring to the boil, stirring constantly, and simmer for 5 minutes.

4 Mix together all the salad ingredients. Arrange the satay sticks on a platter, garnish with coriander sprigs and season. Serve immediately with the sauce and boiled rice.

Stir-fried Pork with Ginger

Pork marries well with ginger, garlic and spring onions – three ingredients that are regarded as the essential basis of Chinese seasoning. This is a good Cantonese stand-by for those occasions when you fancy a simple meal. Be lavish with the ginger as it is the hallmark of this dish.

Serves 4

250g/9oz pork rib-eye steak
30ml/2 tbsp sesame oil
30ml/2 tbsp vegetable oil
15ml/1 tbsp sliced garlic
40g/1½oz fresh young root ginger, sliced into very fine strips
2 spring onions (scallions)
30ml/2 tbsp oyster sauce
5–10ml/1–2 tsp ground black pepper
30ml/2 tbsp Chinese rice wine
30ml/2 tbsp water

1 Using a sharp knife, cut the pork into thin strips. Place these on a board and tenderize them slightly, using a meat mallet or the blunt edge of a cleaver. Rub the strips with sesame oil and set them aside for 15 minutes.

2 Heat the vegetable oil in a wok. Add the sliced garlic and ginger and fry for 1 minute, until pale brown. Do not let the garlic burn or it will taste bitter.

3 Add the pork strips and spring onions. Stir-fry for 2 minutes, then add the oyster sauce and black pepper. Stir over the heat for 2 minutes until the seasonings have been thoroughly absorbed by the pork.

4 Pour in the wine and water. Continue to cook, stirring, for 2 minutes, until the liquid bubbles and the pork is fully cooked. Spoon into a heated bowl and serve.

Cook's Tip
You could substitute chunks of chicken or thinly sliced beef for the sliced pork steak used in this recipe. If using pork, always check that it has cooked through before serving.

pork satay Energy 189kcal/784kJ; Protein 14.5g; Carbohydrate 2.9g, of which sugars 2.2g; Fat 13.3g, of which saturates 5.8g; Cholesterol 35mg; Calcium 25mg; Fibre 0.9g; Sodium 70mg.
pork w. ginger Energy 179kcal/747kJ; Protein 25.3g; Carbohydrate 2.8g, of which sugars 2.1g; Fat 7.4g, of which saturates 1.9g; Cholesterol 71mg; Calcium 21mg; Fibre 0.7g; Sodium 614mg.

Sweet & Sour Pork Strips

This makes a marvellous warm salad.

Serves 4

30ml/2 tbsp dark soy sauce
15ml/1 tbsp clear honey
400g/14oz pork fillet (tenderloin)
6 shallots, thinly sliced lengthways
1 lemon grass stalk, thinly sliced
5 kaffir lime leaves, thinly sliced
5cm/2in piece fresh root ginger, peeled and finely sliced
½ red chilli, seeded and shredded
small bunch fresh coriander (cilantro), chopped

For the dressing

30ml/2 tbsp soft light brown sugar
30ml/2 tbsp fish sauce
juice of 2 limes
20ml/4 tsp thick tamarind juice, made by mixing tamarind paste with warm water

1 Preheat the grill (broiler). Mix the soy sauce and honey. Cut the pork lengthways into four strips. Place in a grill pan, coat with the honey mixture, then grill (broil) for about 10–15 minutes, turning and basting frequently, until the meat is cooked.

2 Slice the cooked pork across the grain, then shred. Place in a large bowl and add the remaining ingredients. Toss with the dressing, made by whisking all the ingredients together.

Chinese Spiced Pork Chops

Finger-licking pork chops are family favourites.

Serves 4

4 large pork chops
15ml/1 tbsp five-spice powder
30ml/2 tbsp soy sauce
30ml/2 tbsp garlic-infused oil

1 Arrange the pork chops in a dish. Sprinkle with the five-spice powder, then pour over the soy sauce and garlic-infused oil. Rub the mixture into the meat. Cover and chill for 2 hours.

2 Preheat the oven to 160°C/325°F/Gas 3. Uncover the dish and bake for 30–40 minutes, or until the pork is cooked through and tender. Serve immediately.

Pork Chops with Field Mushrooms

Barbecued pork chops are delicious with noodles.

Serves 4

4 pork chops
4 large field (portabello) mushrooms
45ml/3 tbsp vegetable oil
4 fresh red chillies, seeded and thinly sliced
45ml/3 tbsp fish sauce
90ml/6 tbsp fresh lime juice
4 shallots, chopped
5ml/1 tsp roasted ground rice
60ml/4 tbsp spring onions (scallions), shredded
coriander (cilantro), to garnish

For the marinade

2 garlic cloves, chopped
15ml/1 tbsp sugar
15ml/1 tbsp fish sauce
30ml/2 tbsp soy sauce
15ml/1 tbsp sesame oil
15ml/1 tbsp whisky or dry sherry
2 lemon grass stalks, finely chopped
2 spring onions (scallions), chopped

1 Make the marinade. Combine the garlic, sugar, sauces, oil and whisky or sherry in a large, shallow dish. Stir in the lemon grass and the chopped spring onions.

2 Add the pork chops, turning to coat them in the marinade. Cover and leave to marinate for 1–2 hours.

3 Lift the chops out of the marinade and place them on a barbecue grid over hot coals or on a grill (broiler) rack. Add the mushrooms and brush them with 15ml/1 tbsp of the oil. Cook the pork chops for 5–7 minutes on each side and the mushrooms for about 2 minutes. Brush both with the marinade while cooking.

4 Heat the remaining oil in a wok or small frying pan, then remove the pan from the heat and stir in the chillies, fish sauce, lime juice, shallots, ground rice and half the shredded spring onions. Put the pork chops and mushrooms on a large serving plate and spoon over the sauce. Garnish with the coriander leaves and remaining shredded spring onion.

sweet & sour pork Energy 194kcal/812kJ; Protein 19.4g; Carbohydrate 5.2g, of which sugars 0.5g; Fat 6.3g, of which saturates 1.6g; Cholesterol 55mg; Calcium 21mg; Fibre 0.2g; Sodium 64mg.
chinese spiced pork Energy 722kcal/2986kJ; Protein 32.6g; Carbohydrate 1.9g, of which sugars 0.6g; Fat 65g, of which saturates 22.5g; Cholesterol 144mg; Calcium 24mg; Fibre 0g; Sodium 647mg.
chops w. mushrooms Energy 342kcal/1423kJ; Protein 34g; Carbohydrate 1.7g, of which sugars 1.2g; Fat 22.1g, of which saturates 5.3g; Cholesterol 110mg; Calcium 21mg; Fibre 1.2g; Sodium 89mg.

Stir-fried Pork with Lychees

No extra oil is needed to cook this dish, as the pork produces enough tasty juices of its own.

Serves 4

450g/1lb fatty pork, such as belly pork, with the skin on or off
30ml/2 tbsp hoisin sauce
4 spring onions (scallions), sliced diagonally
175g/6oz lychees, peeled, stoned (pitted) and cut into slivers
salt and ground black pepper
fresh lychees and parsley sprigs, to garnish

1 Cut the pork into bitesize pieces and place in a dish. Pour the hoisin sauce over it and toss to coat. Cover with clear film (plastic wrap) and leave to marinate in a cool place for at least 30 minutes.

2 Heat a wok, then add the pork and stir-fry for 5 minutes, until crisp and golden. Add the spring onions and stir-fry for a further 2 minutes.

3 Sprinkle the lychee slivers over the pork, and season well with salt and pepper. Transfer to warmed plates, garnish with lychees and parsley sprigs and serve immediately.

Cook's Tip
Lychees have a very pretty pink skin which cracks easily when the fruit is pressed between finger and thumb, making them easy to peel. The fruit is a soft, fleshy berry and contains a long, shiny, brown seed. This is inedible and must be removed. The sweet flesh is pearly white and fragrant, similar in texture to a grape. When buying lychees, avoid any that are turning brown, as they will be over-ripe. Equally, avoid under-ripe lychees with green or beige skins. Look for fruit with as much red or pink in the skins as possible. Fresh lychees are delicate and should be used as soon after purchase as possible, but can be stored in the refrigerator for up to a week. If you cannot buy the fresh fruit, you could use drained canned lychees, but they do not have the same fragrance or flavour.

Stir Fried Pork & Vegetables

This delicious and colourful dish is a perfect example of the Chinese tradition of balancing and harmonizing colours, flavours and textures in food.

Serves 4

225g/8oz pork fillet (tenderloin), thinly sliced
15ml/1 tbsp light soy sauce
5ml/1 tsp light brown sugar
5ml/1 tsp Chinese rice wine or dry sherry
10ml/2 tsp cornflour (cornstarch) paste
115g/4oz firm tomatoes, skinned
175g/6oz courgettes (zucchini)
1 spring onion (scallion)
60ml/4 tbsp vegetable oil
5ml/1 tsp salt (optional)
stock or water, if necessary

1 Put the pork in a bowl with 5ml/1 tsp of the soy sauce, the sugar, rice wine or dry sherry and cornflour paste. Set aside to marinate.

2 Cut the tomatoes and courgettes into wedges. Slice the spring onion.

3 Heat the oil in a preheated wok and stir-fry the pork for 1 minute, or until it colours. Remove with a draining spoon, set aside and keep warm.

4 Add the tomatoes, courgettes and onions to the wok and stir-fry for 2 minutes.

5 Add the salt, if using, then the pork and a little stock or water, if the contents of the wok look dry, and stir-fry for 1 minute. Add the remaining soy sauce, mix well and serve.

Cook's Tip
The pork must be sliced thinly in order to cook quickly.

pork & lychees Energy 465kcal/1926kJ; Protein 17.9g; Carbohydrate 8.7g, of which sugars 8.6g; Fat 40.1g, of which saturates 14.8g; Cholesterol 81mg; Calcium 17mg; Fibre 0.5g; Sodium 206mg.
pork & vegetables Energy 199kcal/826kJ; Protein 13.8g; Carbohydrate 5.7g, of which sugars 3g; Fat 13.6g, of which saturates 2.1g; Cholesterol 35mg; Calcium 26mg; Fibre 1.6g; Sodium 49mg.

Braised Pork Belly with Greens

Pork belly becomes meltingly tender in this slow-braised dish flavoured with orange, cinnamon, star anise and ginger. The flavours meld and mellow during cooking to produce a rich, complex, rounded taste. Serve simply with rice and steamed greens.

Serves 4

800g/1¾lb pork belly, trimmed and cut into 12 pieces
400ml/14fl oz/1⅔ cups beef stock
75ml/5 tbsp soy sauce
grated rind and juice of 1 orange
15ml/1 tbsp finely shredded fresh root ginger
2 garlic cloves, sliced
15ml/1 tbsp hot chilli powder
15ml/1 tbsp muscovado (molasses) sugar
3 cinnamon sticks
3 cloves
10 black peppercorns
2–3 star anise
steamed greens and rice, to serve

1 Place the pork in a wok and pour over water to cover. Bring the water to the boil. Cover, reduce the heat and cook gently for 30 minutes.

2 Drain the pork and return to the wok with the stock, soy sauce, orange rind and juice, ginger, garlic, chilli powder, muscovado sugar, cinnamon sticks, cloves, peppercorns and star anise.

3 Pour over water to just cover the pork belly pieces and cook on a high heat until the mixture comes to a boil.

4 Cover the wok tightly with a lid, then reduce the heat to low and cook gently for 1½ hours, stirring occasionally to prevent the pork from sticking to the base of the wok.

5 Taste the sauce and season to taste. You are unlikely to need pepper, with peppercorns a prime ingredient, but may wish to add a little salt. Serve in warmed bowls.

Hot & Sour Pork

This tasty dish is cooked in the oven and uses less oil than a stir-fry. Trim any fat from the pork before cooking, for a healthy meal.

Serves 4

350g/12oz pork fillet (tenderloin)
5ml/1 tsp sunflower oil
2.5cm/1in piece fresh root ginger, grated
1 fresh red chilli, seeded and finely chopped
5ml/1 tsp Chinese five-spice powder
15ml/1 tbsp sherry vinegar
15ml/1 tbsp soy sauce
225g/8oz can pineapple chunks in natural juice
175ml/6fl oz/¾ cup chicken stock
20ml/4 tsp cornflour (cornstarch)
15ml/1 tbsp water
1 small green (bell) pepper, seeded and sliced
115g/4oz baby corn, halved
salt and ground black pepper
sprig of flat leaf parsley, to garnish
boiled rice, to serve

1 Preheat the oven to 160°C/325°F/Gas 3. Trim away any visible fat from the pork and cut into 1cm/½in-thick slices.

2 Brush the sunflower oil over the base of a flameproof casserole. Heat over a medium heat, then fry the pork for about 2 minutes on each side or until lightly browned.

3 Blend together the ginger, chilli, Chinese five-spice powder, sherry vinegar and soy sauce.

4 Drain the pineapple chunks, reserving the juice. Make the stock up to 300ml/½ pint/1¼ cups with the reserved juice, mix together with the spices and pour over the pork.

5 Slowly bring the stock to the boil. Blend the cornflour with the water and gradually stir into the pork. Add the green pepper and baby corn and season to taste.

6 Cover and cook in the oven for 30 minutes or until the pork is tender. Stir in the pineapple and cook for a further 5 minutes. Garnish with flat leaf parsley and serve with boiled rice.

pork belly w. greens Energy 543kcal/2260kJ; Protein 38.9g; Carbohydrate 6.6g, of which sugars 6.4g; Fat 40.4g, of which saturates 14.6g; Cholesterol 142mg; Calcium 19mg; Fibre 0g; Sodium 1475mg.
hot & sour pork Energy 195kcal/820kJ; Protein 21.3g; Carbohydrate 16.9g, of which sugars 9.9g; Fat 5.2g, of which saturates 1.5g; Cholesterol 55mg; Calcium 27mg; Fibre 1.4g; Sodium 610mg.

Sticky Pork Ribs

Many people assume pork ribs to be high in fat, but these fall well within acceptable limits. Take the time to marinate the meat as this allows all the flavours to permeate.

Serves 4

30ml/2 tbsp caster (superfine) sugar
2.5ml/½ tsp five-spice powder
45ml/3 tbsp hoisin sauce
30ml/2 tbsp yellow bean sauce
3 garlic cloves, finely chopped
15ml/1 tbsp cornflour (cornstarch)
2.5ml/½ tsp salt
16 meaty pork ribs
chives and sliced spring onion (scallion), to garnish
salad or rice, to serve

1 Combine the caster sugar, five-spice powder, hoisin sauce, bean sauce, garlic, cornflour and salt in a bowl. Mix well.

2 Place the pork ribs in an ovenproof dish and pour the marinade over. Mix thoroughly, cover with clear film (plastic wrap) and leave in a cool place for 1 hour.

3 Preheat the oven to 180°C/350°F/Gas 4. Unwrap the ovenproof dish, replace the plastic wrap with foil and bake the pork ribs for 40 minutes. Baste the ribs from time to time with the cooking juices.

4 Remove the foil, baste the ribs and continue to cook for 20 minutes until glossy and brown. Garnish with chives and sliced spring onion and serve with a salad or rice.

Cook's Tips

- *The ribs barbecue very well. Par-cook them in the oven for 40 minutes as described in step 3, then transfer them to the barbecue for 15 minutes to finish cooking. The sauce coating makes the ribs liable to burn, so watch them closely.*
- *Don't forget finger bowls when serving these. They are not called sticky ribs for nothing.*

Pork Chow Mein

A perfect, speedy meal, this family favourite is flavoured with sesame oil for an authentic oriental taste.

Serves 4

175g/6oz medium egg noodles
350g/12oz pork fillet (tenderloin)
30ml/2 tbsp sunflower oil
15ml/1 tbsp sesame oil
2 garlic cloves, crushed
8 spring onions (scallions), sliced
1 red (bell) pepper, seeded and roughly chopped
1 green (bell) pepper, seeded and roughly chopped
30ml/2 tbsp dark soy sauce
45ml/3 tbsp Chinese rice wine or dry sherry
175g/6oz beansprouts
45ml/3 tbsp chopped fresh flat leaf parsley
15ml/1 tbsp toasted sesame seeds

1 Soak the noodles according to the packet instructions. Drain well.

2 Thinly slice the pork fillet. Heat the sunflower oil in a preheated wok or large frying pan and cook the pork over a high heat until golden brown and cooked through.

3 Add the sesame oil to the wok or frying pan, with the garlic, spring onions and peppers. Cook over a high heat for 3–4 minutes, or until the vegetables are beginning to soften.

4 Reduce the heat slightly and stir in the noodles, with the soy sauce and rice wine or dry sherry. Stir-fry for 2 minutes.

5 Add the beansprouts and cook for a further 1–2 minutes. If the noodles begin to stick, add a splash of water. Stir in the parsley and serve sprinkled with the sesame seeds.

Cook's Tip

Flat leaf parsley, also known as Italian, French or continental parsley is similar in appearance to fresh coriander (cilantro). It has a stronger flavour than traditional curly parsley and a more exotic appearance for garnishing.

sticky pork ribs Energy 239kcal/1006kJ; Protein 32.4g; Carbohydrate 14.5g, of which sugars 10.9g; Fat 6g, of which saturates 2.1g; Cholesterol 95mg; Calcium 17mg; Fibre 0.1g; Sodium 291mg.
pork chow mein Energy 453kcal/1906kJ; Protein 30.8g; Carbohydrate 53.7g, of which sugars 11.3g; Fat 14.2g, of which saturates 3.4g; Cholesterol 75mg; Calcium 86mg; Fibre 5.6g; Sodium 896mg.

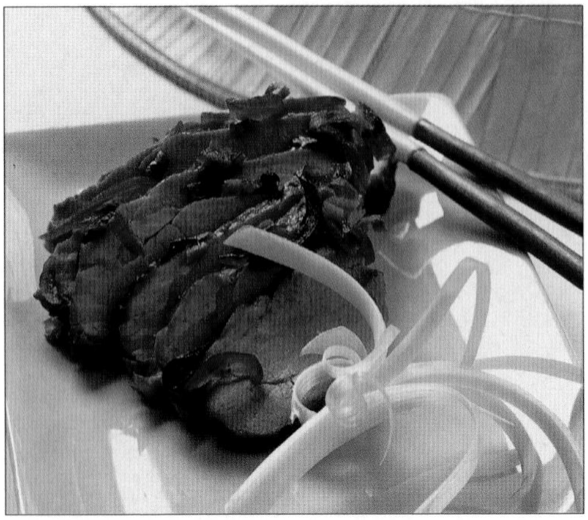

Cha Shao

This dish is often known as barbecue pork and is very popular in southern China. The marinade can be heated and served as a sauce.

Serves 6
900g/2lb pork fillet (tenderloin), trimmed
15ml/1 tbsp clear honey
45ml/3 tbsp rice wine
spring onion (scallion) curls, to garnish

For the marinade
150ml/¼ pint/⅔ cup dark soy sauce
90ml/6 tbsp rice wine
150ml/¼ pint/⅔ cup well-flavoured chicken stock
15ml/1 tbsp soft light brown sugar
1cm/½in piece fresh root ginger, peeled and finely sliced
40ml/2½ tbsp chopped onion

1 Mix all the marinade ingredients in a pan and bring to the boil, stirring. Simmer gently for 15 minutes. Leave to cool.

2 Put the pork fillets side by side in a shallow dish. Pour over 250ml/8fl oz/1 cup of the marinade, cover and chill for at least 8 hours, turning the meat over several times.

3 Preheat the oven to 200°C/400°F/Gas 6. Drain the pork fillets, reserving the marinade in the dish. Place the meat on a rack over a roasting pan and pour water into the pan to a depth of 1cm/½in. Place the pan in the oven and roast for 20 minutes.

4 Stir the honey and rice wine or sherry into the marinade. Remove the meat from the oven and place it into the marinade, turning to coat. Put back on the rack and roast for 20–30 minutes or until cooked. Serve hot or cold, in slices, garnished with spring onion curls.

Cook's Tip
You will have extra marinade when making this dish. Chill or freeze this and use to baste other grilled (broiled) dishes.

Roasted & Marinated Pork

Japanese cooks often use a soy sauce and citrus marinade to flavour meat, adding it before or after cooking. If possible, leave the meat to marinate overnight.

Serves 4
600g/1⅓lb pork fillet (tenderloin)
1 garlic clove, crushed
generous pinch of salt
4 spring onions (scallions), trimmed, white part only, shredded finely
10g/¼oz dried wakame seaweed, soaked in water for 20 minutes and drained
10cm/4in celery stick, trimmed and cut in thin shreds
1 carton mustard and cress (fine curled cress)

For the marinade
105ml/7 tbsp shoyu
45ml/3 tbsp sake
60ml/4 tbsp mirin (sweet rice wine)
1 lime, sliced into thin rings

1 Preheat the oven to 200°C/400°F/Gas 6. Rub the pork with crushed garlic and salt, and leave for 15 minutes. Meanwhile, mix the marinade ingredients in a container that is big enough to hold the pork. Set the marinade aside.

2 Roast the pork for 20 minutes, then turn the meat over and reduce the oven temperature to 180°C/350°F/Gas 4. Roast for a further 20 minutes, until the pork is cooked.

3 Add the hot pork to the marinade, cover and set aside for at least 2 hours.

4 Soak the shreds of spring onion and celery in iced water until curled. Drain well. Cut the drained wakame seaweed into narrow strips.

5 Lift the pork from the marinade, blot it with kitchen paper, then slice and arrange on a large platter. Surround with the vegetables and seaweed.

6 Strain the marinade into a gravy boat and serve with the pork and accompaniments.

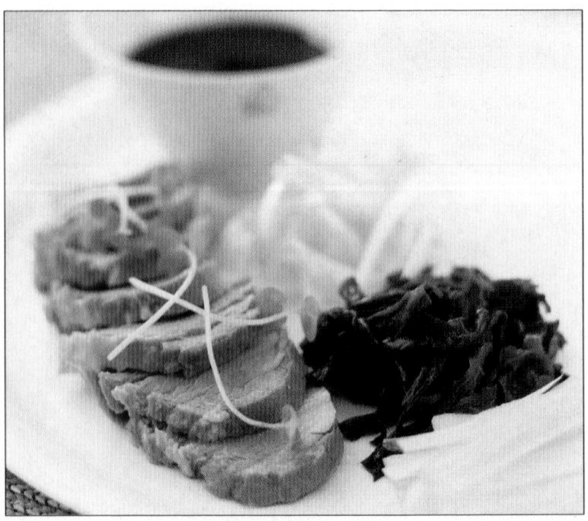

cha shao Energy 211kcal/886kJ; Protein 32.5g; Carbohydrate 4.8g, of which sugars 4.7g; Fat 6g, of which saturates 2.1g; Cholesterol 95mg; Calcium 14mg; Fibre 0g; Sodium 996mg.
roasted & marinated pork Energy 198kcal/830kJ; Protein 32.6g; Carbohydrate 0.9g, of which sugars 0.9g; Fat 6.2g, of which saturates 2.1g; Cholesterol 95mg; Calcium 24mg; Fibre 0.4g; Sodium 114mg.

Pork & Vegetable Stir-Fry

A quick and easy stir-fry of pork and a mixture of vegetables, this makes an excellent family lunch or supper dish.

Serves 4

225g/8oz can pineapple chunks
15ml/1 tbsp cornflour (cornstarch)
30ml/2 tbsp light soy sauce
15ml/1 tbsp Chinese rice wine or dry sherry
15ml/1 tbsp soft dark brown sugar
15ml/1 tbsp white wine vinegar
5ml/1 tsp Chinese five-spice powder
10ml/2 tsp olive oil
1 red onion, sliced
1 garlic clove, crushed
1 fresh red chilli, seeded and chopped
2.5cm/1in piece fresh root ginger
350g/12oz lean pork tenderloin, cut into thin strips
175g/6oz carrots
1 red (bell) pepper, seeded and sliced
175g/6oz mangetouts (snow peas), halved
115g/4oz beansprouts
200g/7oz can corn kernels
30ml/2 tbsp chopped fresh coriander (cilantro)
salt
15ml/1 tbsp toasted sesame seeds, to garnish

1 Drain the pineapple, reserving the juice. In a small bowl, blend the cornflour with the reserved pineapple juice. Add the soy sauce, rice wine or dry sherry, sugar, vinegar and five-spice powder, stir to mix and set aside.

2 Heat the oil in a preheated wok or large, non-stick frying pan. Add the onion, garlic, chilli and ginger and stir-fry for 30 seconds. Add the pork and stir-fry for 2–3 minutes.

3 Cut the carrots into matchstick strips. Add to the wok with the red pepper and stir-fry for 2–3 minutes. Add the mangetouts, beansprouts and corn and stir-fry the vegetables for 1–2 minutes.

4 Pour in the sauce mixture and the reserved pineapple and stir-fry until the sauce thickens. Reduce the heat and stir-fry for a further 1–2 minutes. Stir in the coriander and season to taste. Sprinkle with sesame seeds and serve immediately.

Black Pepper Pork

Thanks to the ginger and black pepper, this dish is beautifully warming. Fairly simple preparation, and mild spicing, make it a perfect, and healthy, alternative to the family takeaway on Friday night.

Serves 4–6

1 litre/1¾ pints/4 cups pork stock or water
45ml/3 tbsp fish sauce
30ml/2 tbsp soy sauce
15ml/1 tbsp sugar
4 garlic cloves, crushed
40g/1½oz fresh root ginger, peeled and finely shredded
15ml/1 tbsp ground black pepper
675g/1½lb pork shoulder or rump, cut into bitesize cubes
steamed jasmine rice, crunchy salad and pickles or stir-fried greens, such as water spinach or long beans, to serve

1 In a large heavy pan, bring the stock or water, fish sauce and soy sauce to the boil.

2 Reduce the heat and stir in the sugar, garlic, ginger, black pepper and pork. Cover the pan and simmer for about 1½ hours, until the pork is very tender and the liquid has reduced significantly.

3 Serve the pork with steamed jasmine rice, drizzling the braised juices over it, and accompany it with a fresh crunchy salad, pickles or stir-fried greens, such as stir-fried water spinach with fish sauce, or long beans.

Cook's Tip

If you have time, make this dish a day ahead so that all the flavours blend. Complete the dish to the end of Step 2, cool it quickly, cover and place in a refrigerator overnight. Next day, lift off any fat that has solidified on the surface, and reheat until piping hot. An electric wok is ideal for this.

pork & vegetable Energy 296kcal/1247kJ; Protein 24.9g; Carbohydrate 39.9g, of which sugars 24.5g; Fat 5.2g, of which saturates 1.5g; Cholesterol 55mg; Calcium 67mg; Fibre 4.4g; Sodium 645mg.
black pepper pork Energy 154kcal/647kJ; Protein 24.4g; Carbohydrate 4g, of which sugars 3.7g; Fat 4.5g, of which saturates 1.6g; Cholesterol 71mg; Calcium 13mg; Fibre 0.1g; Sodium 613mg.

Cinnamon Meat Loaf

Similar to the Vietnamese steamed pâtés, this type of meat loaf is usually served as a snack or light lunch, with a crusty baguette. Accompanied by tart pickles or a crunchy salad, and splashed with piquant sauce, it is light and very tasty.

Serves 4–6

30ml/2 tbsp fish sauce
25ml/1½ tbsp ground cinnamon
10ml/2 tsp sugar
5ml/1 tsp ground black pepper
15ml/1 tbsp potato starch
450g/1lb lean minced (ground) pork
25g/1oz pork fat, very finely chopped
4 shallots, very finely chopped
oil, for greasing
chilli oil or hot chilli sauce, for drizzling
red chilli strips, to garnish
bread or noodles, to serve

1 In a large bowl, mix together the fish sauce, ground cinnamon, sugar and black pepper. Beat in the potato starch.

2 Add the minced pork, the chopped pork fat and the shallots to the bowl and mix thoroughly. Cover and put in the refrigerator for 3–4 hours.

3 Preheat the oven to 180°C/350°F/Gas 4. Lightly oil a baking tin (pan) and spread the pork mixture in it – it should feel springy. This is due to the potato starch.

4 Cover with foil and bake in the oven for 35–40 minutes, removing the foil for the last 10 minutes.

5 Slice the meat loaf into strips. Drizzle the strips with chilli oil or hot chilli sauce, and serve them hot with bread or noodles.

Cook's Tip
Serve the meat loaf as a nibble with drinks by cutting it into bitesize squares or fingers.

Pork & Spring Onion Pancakes

Unusually, these pancakes are made from a batter based on mung beans.

Serves 4–6

225g/8oz/1¼ cups skinned, split mung beans
50g/2oz/⅓ cup glutinous rice
15ml/1 tbsp light soy sauce
15ml/1 tbsp roasted sesame seeds, crushed
2.5ml/½ tsp bicarbonate of soda
115g/4oz/½ cup beansprouts, blanched and dried
1 garlic clove, crushed
4 spring onions (scallions), chopped
115g/4oz cooked lean pork, shredded
30ml/2 tbsp sesame oil, plus extra for drizzling
salt and ground black pepper
fresh chives, to garnish
light soy sauce, to serve

1 Pick over the mung beans and put them in a bowl. Add the glutinous rice and pour in water to cover. Leave to soak for at least 8 hours.

2 Tip the beans and rice into a sieve (strainer), rinse under cold water, then drain. Put the mixture into a food processor and process to a batter with the consistency of thick cream.

3 Add the soy sauce, sesame seeds and bicarbonate of soda and process briefly to mix. When ready to cook, tip the batter into a bowl and add the beansprouts, garlic, spring onions and pork. Season to taste.

4 Heat about 10ml/2 tsp of the sesame oil in a large frying pan. Spoon in half the batter and spread it into a thick pancake.

5 Drizzle a little more sesame oil over the surface of the pancake, cover and cook over a medium heat until the underside is cooked. Invert the pancake on to a plate. Slide it back into the pan and cook on the other side for 3–4 minutes. Keep hot while cooking a second pancake. Cut the pancakes into wedges, garnish with chives, and serve with soy sauce.

cinnamon meat loaf Energy 158kcal/661kJ; Protein 16.8g; Carbohydrate 7.7g, of which sugars 4.5g; Fat 6.8g, of which saturates 1.5g; Cholesterol 47mg; Calcium 19mg; Fibre 0.8g; Sodium 54mg.
pork & spring onion pancakes Energy 90kcal/376kJ; Protein 6.7g; Carbohydrate 8.9g, of which sugars 1.6g; Fat 3.1g, of which saturates 0.6g; Cholesterol 12mg; Calcium 17mg; Fibre 1g; Sodium 195mg.

Madras Beef Curry

Although Madras is renowned for the best vegetarian food in India, meat-based recipes such as this beef curry are also extremely popular there.

Serves 4–6

60ml/4 tbsp vegetable oil
1 large onion, finely sliced
3 or 4 cloves
4 green cardamom pods
2 whole star anise
4 fresh green chillies, chopped
2 fresh or dried red chillies, chopped
45ml/3 tbsp Madras masala paste
5ml/1 tsp ground turmeric
450g/1lb lean beef, cubed
60ml/4 tbsp tamarind juice
sugar, to taste
salt
a few fresh coriander (cilantro) leaves, chopped, to garnish

1 Heat the oil in a karahi, wok or large pan over a medium heat and fry the onion slices for about 8 minutes until they turn golden brown.

2 Lower the heat, add all the spice ingredients, and fry for a further 2–3 minutes.

3 Add the cubed beef and mix well with the spices. Cover and cook over a low heat until the beef is tender and fully cooked. Cook uncovered on a higher heat for the last few minutes to reduce any excess liquid.

4 Fold in the tamarind juice, sugar and salt. Reheat the dish and garnish with the chopped coriander leaves. Pilau rice and a tomato and onion salad would make excellent accompaniments for this dish.

Cook's Tip
To tenderize the meat, add 60ml/4 tbsp white wine vinegar in step 2, along with the meat, and omit the tamarind juice.

Spicy Meat Loaf

This mixture is baked in the oven and provides a hearty meal on a cold winter day.

Serves 4–6

5 eggs
450g/1lb lean minced (ground) beef
30ml/2 tbsp grated fresh root ginger
30ml/2 tbsp crushed garlic
6 fresh green chillies, chopped
2 small onions, finely chopped
2.5ml/½ tsp ground turmeric
50g/2oz/2 cups fresh coriander (cilantro), chopped
175g/6oz potato, grated
salt
salad leaves, to serve
lemon twist, to garnish

1 Preheat the oven to 180°C/350°F/ Gas 4. Beat 2 eggs until fluffy and pour into a greased 900g/2lb loaf tin (pan).

2 Knead together the meat, ginger and garlic, 4 green chillies, 1 chopped onion, 1 beaten egg, the turmeric, fresh coriander, potato and salt.

3 Pack into the loaf tin and smooth the surface. Cook in the preheated oven for 45 minutes.

4 Meanwhile, beat the remaining eggs and fold in the remaining green chillies and onion. Remove the loaf tin from the oven and pour the mixture all over the meat.

5 Return to the oven and cook until the eggs have set. Serve the loaf hot on a bed of salad leaves, garnished with a twist of lemon.

Cook's Tip
It is always best to buy meat for mincing (grinding) by the piece if possible so that you can choose some with little fat and remove any remaining fat before you mince (grind) it.

beef curry Energy 359kcal/1493kJ; Protein 22.1g; Carbohydrate 26.9g, of which sugars 3.6g; Fat 18g, of which saturates 7.1g; Cholesterol 62mg; Calcium 20mg; Fibre 0.9g; Sodium 95mg.
spicy meat loaf Energy 272kcal/1133kJ; Protein 22.1g; Carbohydrate 7.3g, of which sugars 2g; Fat 17.6g, of which saturates 6.6g; Cholesterol 204mg; Calcium 73mg; Fibre 1.5g; Sodium 129mg.

Stewing Beef Curry

Madras curries originate from southern India and are aromatic, robust and pungent in flavour. This recipe uses stewing beef, but you can replace it with lean lamb if you prefer.

Serves 4

900g/2lb lean stewing beef
15ml/1 tbsp oil
1 large onion, finely chopped
4 cloves
4 green cardamom pods
2 green chillies, finely chopped
2.5cm/1in piece fresh root ginger, finely chopped
2 garlic cloves, crushed
2 dried red chillies
15ml/1 tbsp curry paste
10ml/2 tsp ground coriander
5ml/1 tsp ground cumin
2.5ml/½ tsp salt
150ml/¼ pint/⅔ cup beef stock
fresh coriander (cilantro), to garnish
boiled rice, to serve

1 Remove any visible fat from the beef and cut the meat into 2.5cm/1in cubes.

2 Heat the oil in a large, heavy frying pan and stir-fry the onion, cloves and cardamom pods for about 5 minutes. Add the fresh green chillies, ginger, garlic and dried red chillies and fry for a further 2 minutes.

3 Add the curry paste and fry for about 2 minutes. Add the cubed beef and fry for 5–8 minutes until all the meat pieces are lightly browned.

4 Add the coriander, cumin, salt and stock. Cover and simmer gently for 1–1½ hours or until the meat is tender. Serve with boiled rice and garnish with fresh coriander.

Cook's Tip
When whole cardamom pods are used as a flavouring, they are not meant to be eaten. In India, they are left on the side of the plate, along with any bones.

Beef Koftas with Coriander & Mint

Serve these tasty treats piping hot with naan bread, raita and a salad. Leftover koftas can be chopped coarsely and packed into pitta bread.

Makes 20–25

450g/1lb lean minced (ground) beef
30ml/2 tbsp grated fresh root ginger
30ml/2 tbsp crushed garlic
4 fresh green chillies, finely chopped
1 small onion, finely chopped
1 egg
2.5ml/½ tsp ground turmeric
5ml/1 tsp garam masala
50g/2oz/2 cups fresh coriander (cilantro), chopped
4–6 fresh mint leaves, chopped
175g/6oz potato
vegetable oil, for deep-frying
salt

1 Mix the minced meat, ginger, garlic, chillies, onion, egg, spices and herbs in a large bowl.

2 Grate the potato into the bowl, and season with salt to taste. Knead together to blend well and form a soft dough.

3 Shape the mixture into portions the size of golf balls. Place on a plate, cover and leave the koftas to rest for about 25 minutes.

4 In a karahi, wok or frying pan, heat the oil to medium-hot and fry the koftas in small batches until they are golden brown in colour. Drain well and serve hot.

Variation
This dish works equally well with lamb, but make sure it is lean. As always it is best to buy lean meat and mince (grind) it yourself if you are able to.

beef curry Energy 442kcal/1840kJ; Protein 52.2g; Carbohydrate 2.8g, of which sugars 0.1g; Fat 24.7g, of which saturates 9g; Cholesterol 131mg; Calcium 25mg; Fibre 0g; Sodium 147mg.
beef koftas Energy 80kcal/331kJ; Protein 4.1g; Carbohydrate 1.6g, of which sugars 0.1g; Fat 6.4g, of which saturates 1.7g; Cholesterol 18mg; Calcium 6mg; Fibre 0.1g; Sodium 18mg.

Beef Vindaloo

A fiery dish originally from Goa, a vindaloo is made using a unique blend of hot aromatic spices and vinegar to give it a distinctive flavour.

Serves 6

15ml/1 tbsp cumin seeds
4 dried red chillies
5ml/1 tsp black peppercorns
seeds from 5 green cardamom pods
5ml/1 tsp fenugreek seeds
5ml/1 tsp black mustard seeds
2.5ml/½ tsp salt
2.5ml/½ tsp demerara (raw) sugar
60ml/4 tbsp white wine vinegar
30ml/2 tbsp oil
1 large onion, finely chopped
900g/2lb lean stewing beef, cut into 2.5cm/1in cubes
2.5cm/1in piece fresh root ginger, finely chopped
1 garlic clove, crushed
10ml/2 tsp ground coriander
2.5ml/½ tsp ground turmeric
plain and saffron rice, to serve

1 Put the cumin seeds, chillies, peppercorns, cardamom seeds, fenugreek seeds and mustard seeds into a spice grinder (or a pestle and mortar) and grind to a fine powder.

2 Spoon into a bowl, add the salt, sugar and white wine vinegar and mix to a thin paste. Heat 15ml/1 tbsp of the oil in a large, heavy pan and fry the onion for 10 minutes.

3 Put the onions and the spice mixture into a food processor or blender and process to a coarse paste.

4 Heat the remaining oil in the frying pan and fry the meat cubes for about 10 minutes until lightly browned. Remove with a slotted spoon.

5 Add the ginger and garlic to the oil remaining in the pan and fry for 2 minutes. Stir in the ground coriander and turmeric and fry for a further 2 minutes.

6 Add the spice and onion paste and fry for about 5 minutes.

7 Return the beef cubes to the pan with 300ml/½ pint/1¼ cups water. Cover and simmer for about 1–1½ hours or until the meat is tender. Serve with plain and saffron rice.

Beef with Green Beans

Green beans cooked with beef is a variation on the traditional recipe which uses lamb. The sliced red pepper provides a contrast to the colour of the beans and chillies, and adds extra flavour.

Serves 4

275g/10oz fine green beans, cut into 2.5cm/1in pieces
15ml/1 tbsp oil
1 medium onion, sliced
5ml/1 tsp grated fresh root ginger
5ml/1 tsp crushed garlic
5ml/1 tsp chilli powder
6.5ml/1¼ tsp salt
1.5ml/¼ tsp ground turmeric
2 tomatoes, chopped
450g/1lb lean beef, cubed
475ml/16fl oz/2 cups water
1 red (bell) pepper, seeded and sliced
15ml/1 tbsp chopped fresh coriander (cilantro)
2 fresh green chillies, chopped
warm chapatis, to serve (optional)

1 Blanch the beans in boiling water for 3–4 minutes, then rinse under cold running water, drain and set aside.

2 Heat the oil in a large, heavy pan and gently fry the onion slices until golden brown.

3 In a bowl, mix the ginger, garlic, chilli powder, salt, turmeric and chopped tomatoes. Spoon the ginger and garlic mixture into the pan and stir-fry with the onion for 5–7 minutes.

4 Add the beef and stir-fry for a further 3 minutes. Pour in the water, bring to the boil and lower the heat. Half-cover the pan and cook for 1–1¼ hours until most of the water has evaporated and the meat is tender.

5 Add the green beans and mix everything together well.

6 Finally, add the red pepper, fresh coriander and green chillies. Cook the mixture, stirring, for a further 7–10 minutes, or until the beans are tender.

7 Spoon into a large bowl or individual plates. Serve the beef hot, with warm chapatis, if you like.

beef vindaloo Energy 352kcal/1469kJ; Protein 36.5g; Carbohydrate 9.5g, of which sugars 4.2g; Fat 19.2g, of which saturates 6.3g; Cholesterol 87mg; Calcium 44mg; Fibre 0.9g; Sodium 102mg.
beef w.beans Energy 309kcal/1289kJ; Protein 29.7g; Carbohydrate 15.1g, of which sugars 10g; Fat 15g, of which saturates 4.9g; Cholesterol 65mg; Calcium 70mg; Fibre 3.8g; Sodium 83mg.

Beef & Kidney with Spinach

Here, spinach is coarsely chopped and added towards the end of cooking, which retains the nutritional value of the spinach and gives the dish a lovely appearance.

Serves 4–6

5cm/2in piece fresh root ginger
30ml/2 tbsp vegetable oil
1 large onion, finely chopped
4 garlic cloves, crushed
60ml/4 tbsp mild curry paste, or 60ml/4 tbsp mild curry powder
1.5ml/¼ tsp ground turmeric
salt
900g/2lb steak and kidney, cubed
450g/1lb fresh spinach, trimmed, washed and chopped, or 450g/1lb frozen spinach, thawed and drained
60ml/4 tbsp tomato purée (paste)
2 large tomatoes, finely chopped

1 Using a sharp knife or vegetable peeler, remove the skin from the ginger. Grate it on the fine side of a metal grater.

2 Heat the oil in a frying pan, wok or karahi and fry the onion, ginger and garlic until the onion is soft and the ginger and garlic turn golden brown.

3 Lower the heat and add the curry paste or powder, turmeric and salt. Add the steak and kidney to the pan and mix well. Cover and cook, stirring frequently to prevent the mixture from sticking to the pan, for 20–30 minutes over a medium heat, until the meat is just tender.

4 Add the spinach and tomato purée and mix well. Cook uncovered until the spinach is softened and most of the liquid has evaporated.

5 Fold in the chopped tomatoes. Increase the heat, as the tomatoes will have a cooling effect on the other ingredients, and cook the mixture for a further 5 minutes, until they are soft.

6 Spoon into shallow bowls and serve piping hot with a simple accompaniment to offset the rich, gamey flavour of the dish, such as plain boiled basmati rice. Go easy on any side portions though, as this is a very rich and filling dish.

Beef Biryani

Biryani is one of the easiest and most relaxing ways of cooking when entertaining.

Serves 4

2 large onions
2 garlic cloves, chopped
2.5cm/1in piece fresh root ginger, peeled and roughly chopped
½–1 fresh green chilli, seeded and chopped
small bunch of fresh coriander (cilantro)
60ml/4 tbsp flaked (sliced) almonds
30–45ml/2–3 tbsp water
15ml/1 tbsp ghee or butter, plus 25g/1oz/2 tbsp butter for the rice
45ml/3 tbsp vegetable oil
30ml/2 tbsp sultanas (golden raisins)
500g/1¼lb braising or stewing steak, cubed
5ml/1 tsp ground coriander
15ml/1 tbsp ground cumin
2.5ml/½ tsp ground turmeric
2.5ml/½ tsp ground fenugreek
good pinch of ground cinnamon
175ml/6fl oz/¾ cup natural (plain) yogurt, whisked
275g/10oz/1½ cups basmati rice
about 1.2 litres/2 pints/5 cups hot chicken stock or water
salt and ground black pepper
2 hard-boiled eggs, quartered, to garnish
chapatis, to serve

1 Roughly chop one onion and place it in a food processor or blender. Add the garlic, ginger, chilli, fresh coriander and half the flaked almonds. Pour in the water and process to a smooth paste. Transfer the paste to a small bowl and set aside.

2 Finely slice the remaining onion into rings. Heat half the ghee or butter with half the oil in a heavy flameproof casserole and fry the onion for 10–15 minutes until a deep golden brown. Transfer to a plate. Fry the remaining almonds briefly until golden. Set aside. Quickly fry the sultanas until they swell. Transfer to the plate.

3 Heat the remaining ghee or butter in the casserole with a further 15ml/1 tbsp of the oil. Fry the meat, in batches, until browned. Transfer to a plate. Wipe the casserole clean with kitchen paper, heat the remaining oil and pour in the spice paste. Cook over a medium heat for 2–3 minutes, stirring, until the mixture begins to brown lightly. Stir in all the spices, season and cook for 1 minute more.

4 Lower the heat, then stir in the yogurt, a little at a time. Return the meat to the casserole. Stir to coat, cover tightly and simmer for 40–45 minutes until the meat is tender. Meanwhile, soak the rice in a bowl of cold water for 20 minutes.

5 Preheat the oven to 160°C/325°F/Gas 3. Drain the rice, place in a pan and add the hot chicken stock or water, with a little salt. Bring back to the boil, cover and cook for 5 minutes.

6 Drain the rice, and pile it on top of the meat. Using the handle of a spoon, make a hole through the rice and meat mixture, to the bottom of the pan. Place the fried onions, almonds and sultanas over the top and dot with butter.

7 Cover the casserole tightly with a double layer of foil and a lid. Cook in the oven for 30–40 minutes. Garnish and serve with chapatis.

beef & kidney Energy 536kcal/2230kJ; Protein 41.1g; Carbohydrate 8.3g, of which sugars 4.7g; Fat 37.8g, of which saturates 18.6g; Cholesterol 377mg; Calcium 209mg; Fibre 4.4g; Sodium 469mg.
beef biryani Energy 778kcal/3240kJ; Protein 40g; Carbohydrate 70.4g, of which sugars 13.4g; Fat 37.4g, of which saturates 11.8g; Cholesterol 94mg; Calcium 164mg; Fibre 2.3g; Sodium 183mg.

Citrus Beef Curry

This superbly aromatic curry is not exceptionally hot but it is full of flavour.

Serves 4

450g/1lb rump (round) steak
30ml/2 tbsp vegetable oil
30ml/2 tbsp medium curry paste
2 bay leaves
400ml/14fl oz/1⅔ cups coconut milk
300ml/½ pint/1¼ cups beef stock
30ml/2 tbsp lemon juice
grated rind and juice of ½ orange
15ml/1 tbsp sugar
115g/4oz baby (pearl) onions, peeled but left whole
225g/8oz new potatoes, halved
115g/4oz/1 cup unsalted roasted peanuts, roughly chopped
115g/4oz fine green beans, halved
1 red (bell) pepper, seeded and thinly sliced
unsalted roasted peanuts, to garnish (optional)

1 Trim any visible fat from the beef and cut the meat into 5cm/2in strips.

2 Heat the vegetable oil in a large, heavy pan, add the medium curry paste and cook over medium heat for 30 seconds, stirring constantly.

3 Add the beef and cook, stirring, for 2 minutes until it is beginning to brown and is thoroughly coated with the spices.

4 Stir in the bay leaves, coconut milk, stock, lemon juice, orange rind and juice, and sugar. Bring to the boil, stirring frequently.

5 Add the onions and potatoes, then bring back to the boil, reduce the heat and simmer, uncovered, for 5 minutes.

6 Stir in the peanuts, beans and pepper and simmer for a further 10 minutes, or until the beef and potatoes are tender. Serve in shallow bowls, with a spoon and fork, to enjoy all the rich and creamy juices. Sprinkle with extra unsalted roasted peanuts, if you like.

Chilli Beef with Basil

This is a dish for chilli lovers! It is very easy to prepare – all you need is a karahi or a wok.

Serves 2

about 90ml/6 tbsp vegetable oil
16–20 large fresh basil leaves
275g/10oz rump steak
30ml/2 tbsp Worcestershire sauce
5ml/1 tsp soft dark brown sugar
1 or 2 fresh red chillies, sliced into rings
3 garlic cloves, chopped
5ml/1 tsp chopped fresh root ginger
1 shallot, thinly sliced
30ml/2 tbsp finely chopped fresh basil leaves, plus extra to garnish
squeeze of lemon juice
salt and ground black pepper
rice, to serve

1 Heat the oil in a karahi or wok. Add the whole basil leaves and fry for about 1 minute until crisp and golden. Drain on kitchen paper. Remove the pan from the heat and pour off all but 30ml/2 tbsp of the oil.

2 Cut the steak across the grain into thin strips. Mix the Worcestershire sauce and sugar in a bowl. Add the beef, mix well, then cover and leave to marinate for about 30 minutes.

3 Reheat the oil until hot, add the chilli, garlic, ginger and shallot and stir-fry for 30 seconds. Add the beef and chopped basil, then stir-fry for about 3 minutes. Flavour with lemon juice, and add salt and pepper to taste.

4 Transfer the chilli beef to a warmed serving plate, sprinkle over the basil leaves to garnish and serve immediately with rice.

Cook's Tip

Although Worcestershire sauce is often thought of as archetypally English, it is actually based on an Indian recipe. Ingredients include molasses, anchovies and tamarind extract.

citrus beef curry Energy 476kcal/1990kJ; Protein 33.8g; Carbohydrate 27.5g, of which sugars 16.3g; Fat 26.4g, of which saturates 6.6g; Cholesterol 69mg; Calcium 77mg; Fibre 4.1g; Sodium 169mg.
chilli beef w. basil Energy 494kcal/2049kJ; Protein 31.1g; Carbohydrate 5.7g, of which sugars 4.9g; Fat 38.7g, of which saturates 6.2g; Cholesterol 81mg; Calcium 17mg; Fibre 0.4g; Sodium 1152mg.

Spicy Meatballs

Serve these spicy little meat patties, called pergedel djawa, with egg noodles and chilli sauce.

Serves 4–6

1cm/½in cube shrimp paste
1 large onion, roughly chopped
1 or 2 fresh red chillies, seeded and chopped
2 garlic cloves, crushed
15ml/1 tbsp coriander seeds
5ml/1 tsp cumin seeds
450g/1lb lean minced (ground) beef
10ml/2 tsp dark soy sauce
5ml/1 tsp soft dark brown sugar
juice of 1½ lemons
a little beaten egg
vegetable oil, for shallow-frying
salt and ground black pepper
chilli sambal, to serve
1 green and 2 red chillies, to garnish

1 Wrap the shrimp paste in a piece of foil and warm in a frying pan for 5 minutes, turning a few times. Unwrap and put in a food processor.

2 Add the onion, chillies and garlic to the food processor and process until finely chopped. Set aside. Dry-fry the coriander and cumin seeds in a hot frying pan for 1 minute, to release the aroma. Pour the seeds into a mortar and grind with a pestle.

3 Put the meat in a large bowl. Stir in the onion mixture. Add the ground spices, soy sauce, brown sugar, lemon juice and beaten egg. Season to taste.

4 Shape the meat mixture into small, even-size balls, and chill these for 5–10 minutes to firm them up.

5 Heat the oil in a wok or large frying pan and fry the meat balls for 4–5 minutes, turning often, until cooked through and browned. You may have to do this in batches.

6 Drain the meatballs on kitchen paper, and then pile them on to a warm serving platter or into a large serving bowl. Finely slice the green chilli and one of the red chillies and sprinkle over the meatballs. Garnish with the remaining red chilli, if you like.

Green Beef Curry with Aubergines

This is a very quick curry so be sure to use good-quality meat. Sirloin is recommended, but tender rump (round) steak could be used instead.

Serves 4–6

15ml/1 tbsp vegetable oil
45ml/3 tbsp Thai green curry paste (see Cook's Tip)
600ml/1 pint/2½ cups coconut milk
450g/1lb beef sirloin, trimmed and cut into thin strips
4 kaffir lime leaves, torn
15–30ml/1–2 tbsp Thai fish sauce
5ml/1 tsp palm sugar (jaggery) or light muscovado (brown) sugar
150g/5oz small Thai aubergines (eggplants), halved
a small handful of fresh Thai basil
2 fresh green chillies, shredded, to garnish

1 Heat the oil in a large, heavy pan or wok. Add the curry paste and cook for 1–2 minutes, until it is fragrant. Stir in half the coconut milk, a little at a time. Cook, stirring frequently, for about 5–6 minutes, until an oily sheen appears on the surface of the liquid.

2 Add the beef to the pan with the lime leaves, Thai fish sauce, sugar and aubergines. Cook for 2–3 minutes, then stir in the remaining coconut milk. Bring back to a simmer and cook until the meat and aubergines are tender. Stir in the basil just before serving. Garnish with the shredded green chillies.

Cook's Tip

To make the Thai green curry paste, put 15 fresh green chillies, 2 chopped lemon grass stalks, 3 sliced shallots, 2 garlic cloves, 15ml/1 tbsp chopped galangal, 4 chopped kaffir lime leaves, 2.5ml/½ tsp grated kaffir lime rind, 5ml/1 tsp chopped coriander root, 6 black peppercorns, 5ml/1 tsp each roasted coriander and cumin seeds, 15ml/1 tbsp sugar, 5ml/1 tsp salt and 5ml/1 tsp shrimp paste into a food processor and process until smooth. Gradually add 30ml/2 tbsp vegetable oil, processing after each addition.

spicy meatballs Energy 213kcal/881kJ; Protein 13.2g; Carbohydrate 3.4g, of which sugars 2.6g; Fat 16.3g, of which saturates 5.1g; Cholesterol 41mg; Calcium 23mg; Fibre 0.5g; Sodium 180mg.
green beef curry Energy 264kcal/1107kJ; Protein 26.3g; Carbohydrate 9.2g, of which sugars 9.2g; Fat 13.8g, of which saturates 4.9g; Cholesterol 65mg; Calcium 54mg; Fibre 0.8g; Sodium 238mg.

Mussaman Curry

This dish is traditionally based on beef, but chicken, lamb or tofu can be used instead.

Serves 4–6
675g/1½lb stewing steak
600ml/1 pint/2½ cups coconut milk
250ml/8fl oz/1 cup coconut cream
45ml/3 tbsp Mussaman curry paste
30ml/2 tbsp Thai fish sauce
15ml/1 tbsp palm sugar or light muscovado (brown) sugar
60ml/4 tbsp tamarind juice, made by soaking tamarind paste in warm water
6 green cardamom pods
1 cinnamon stick
1 large potato, about 225g/8oz, cut into even chunks
1 onion, cut into wedges
50g/2oz/½ cup roasted peanuts

1 Trim off any excess fat from the stewing steak, then, using a sharp knife, cut it into 2.5cm/1in chunks.

2 Pour the coconut milk into a large, heavy pan and bring to the boil over a medium heat. Add the chunks of beef, reduce the heat to low, partially cover the pan and simmer gently for about 40 minutes, or until tender.

3 Pour the coconut cream into a separate pan. Cook over a medium heat, stirring constantly, for about 5 minutes, or until it separates. Stir in the Mussaman curry paste and cook rapidly for 2–3 minutes, until fragrant and thoroughly blended.

4 Add the coconut cream and curry paste mixture to the pan with the beef and stir until thoroughly blended. Simmer for a further 4–5 minutes, stirring occasionally.

5 Stir the fish sauce, sugar, tamarind juice, cardamom pods, cinnamon stick, potato chunks and onion wedges into the beef curry. Continue to simmer for a further 15–20 minutes, or until the potato is cooked and tender. Add the roasted peanuts to the pan and mix well to combine. Cook for about 5 minutes more, then transfer to warmed individual serving bowls and serve immediately.

Thick Beef Curry in Sweet Peanut Sauce

This curry is rich and thicker than most other Thai curries. Serve it with boiled jasmine rice and salted eggs.

Serves 4–6
600ml/1 pint/2½ cups coconut milk
45ml/3 tbsp Thai red curry paste
45ml/3 tbsp Thai fish sauce
30ml/2 tbsp palm sugar (jaggery) or light muscovado (brown) sugar
2 lemon grass stalks, bruised
450g/1lb rump (round) steak, cut into thin strips
75g/3oz/¾ cup roasted peanuts, ground
2 fresh red chillies, sliced
5 kaffir lime leaves, torn
salt and ground black pepper
2 salted duck's eggs, cut in wedges, and 10–15 Thai basil leaves, to garnish

1 Pour half the coconut milk into a large, heavy pan. Place over a medium heat and bring to the boil, stirring constantly until the milk separates.

2 Stir in the red curry paste and cook for 2–3 minutes until the mixture is fragrant and thoroughly blended. Add the fish sauce, sugar and bruised lemon grass stalks. Mix well.

3 Continue to cook until the colour deepens. Gradually add the remaining coconut milk, stirring constantly. Bring back to the boil.

4 Add the beef and peanuts. Cook, stirring constantly, for 8–10 minutes, or until most of the liquid has evaporated. Add the chillies and lime leaves. Season to taste and serve, garnished with wedges of salted eggs and Thai basil leaves.

Cook's Tip
You can use a ready-made Thai curry paste for this recipe if you do not have time to make your own. There is a wide range available in most Asian stores and large supermarkets.

Mussaman curry Energy 626kcal/2610kJ; Protein 44.6g; Carbohydrate 24.8g, of which sugars 15.4g; Fat 39.3g, of which saturates 22.7g; Cholesterol 98mg; Calcium 74mg; Fibre 1.6g; Sodium 288mg.
thick beef curry Energy 243kcal/1019kJ; Protein 20.6g; Carbohydrate 11.7g, of which sugars 10.9g; Fat 13g, of which saturates 4.1g; Cholesterol 44mg; Calcium 43mg; Fibre 0.8g; Sodium 159mg.

Stir-fried Beef in Oyster Sauce

Mouthwatering tender rump steak is cooked here in a delicious combination with shiitake, oyster and straw mushrooms flavoured with garlic, ginger and chilli.

Serves 4–6

450g/1lb rump (round) steak
30ml/2 tbsp soy sauce
15ml/1 tbsp cornflour (cornstarch)
45ml/3 tbsp vegetable oil
15ml/1 tbsp chopped garlic
15ml/1 tbsp chopped fresh root ginger
225g/8oz/3¼ cups mixed mushrooms, such as shiitake, oyster and straw
30ml/2 tbsp oyster sauce
5ml/1 tsp sugar
4 spring onions (scallions), cut into short lengths
ground black pepper
2 fresh red chillies, seeded and cut into strips, to garnish

1 Place the steak in the freezer for 30–40 minutes, until firm, then, using a sharp knife, slice it on the diagonal into thin strips.

2 Mix together the soy sauce and cornflour in a large bowl. Add the steak, turning to coat well, cover with clear film (plastic wrap) and leave to marinate at room temperature for 1–2 hours.

3 Heat half the oil in a wok or large, heavy frying pan. Add the garlic and ginger and cook for 1–2 minutes, until fragrant. Drain the steak, add it to the wok or pan and stir well to separate the strips. Cook, stirring frequently, for a further 1–2 minutes, until the steak is browned all over and tender. Remove from the wok or pan and set aside.

4 Heat the remaining oil in the wok or pan. Add the mushrooms and stir-fry over a medium heat until golden brown.

5 Return the steak to the wok and mix it with the mushrooms. Spoon in the oyster sauce and sugar, mix well, then add ground black pepper to taste. Toss over the heat until all the ingredients are thoroughly combined. Stir in the spring onions. Pour the mixture on to a serving platter, garnish with the strips of red chilli and serve.

Dry Steak Curry with Cashews

Dry curries work very well as part of a spread of dishes, including dishes with lots of sauce, rice dishes and noodles. This dish would traditionally be made with buffalo meat, but stewing steak works well.

Serves 4–6

2tbsp/30ml peanut oil
900g/2lb stewing steak, cubed
400g/14oz can coconut milk
300ml/½ pint/1¼ cups beef stock
60ml/4 tbsp cashew nuts, finely crushed
juice of 2 limes
1 stick of lemon grass, lightly crushed
1 bay leaf
coriander (cilantro) leaves and fresh red chilli slices, to garnish

For the red curry paste
30ml/2 tbsp coriander seeds
5ml/1 tsp cumin seeds
seeds from 6 green cardamom pods
2.5ml/½ tsp grated or ground nutmeg
1.5ml/¼ tsp ground cloves
2.5ml/½ tsp ground cinnamon
20ml/4 tsp paprika
pared rind of 1 mandarin orange, finely chopped
4 or 5 small fresh red chillies, seeded and finely chopped
25ml/1½ tbsp sugar
2.5ml/½ tsp salt
1 piece lemon grass, about 10cm/4in long, shredded
3 garlic cloves, crushed
2cm/¾in piece fresh galangal, peeled and finely chopped
4 red shallots, finely chopped
1 piece shrimp paste, 2cm/¾in square
50g/2oz coriander (cilantro) root or stem, chopped
juice of ½ lime
30ml/2 tbsp vegetable oil

1 Heat the oil in a large wok and add the beef, browning it on all sides to seal in the juices. You may need to do this in batches. Put the seared meat to one side and discard the oil, wiping out the wok with kitchen paper.

2 Using a seive (strainer), add the coconut milk to the wok, pushing the thicker milk through with a wooden spoon. Add the steak. Pour in the beef stock, mix it with the coconut milk using a wooden spoon, and bring to the boil. Reduce the heat, cover the pan and simmer gently for 50 minutes.

3 Meanwhile, make the curry paste. Dry-fry all the seeds for 1–2 minutes. Transfer to a bowl and add the nutmeg, cloves, cinnamon, paprika and orange rind. Pound the chillies with the sugar and salt. Add the spice mixture, lemon grass, garlic, galangal, shallots and shrimp paste and pound to a paste. Work in the coriander, lime juice and oil.

4 Strain the beef, reserving the creamy sauce. Stir-fry a cupful of this liquid with 45ml/3 tbsp of the curry paste. Boil rapidly until all the liquid has evaporated. Stir in half of the rest of the beef cooking liquid, the crushed cashew nuts and the beef. Simmer, uncovered, for 15–20 minutes. The curry should be fairly dry.

5 Just before serving, squeeze and stir in the lime juice. Serve in warmed bowls, garnished with the coriander leaves and sliced red chillies.

stir-fried beef Energy 160kcal/670kJ; Protein 17.6g; Carbohydrate 2.9g, of which sugars 2.7g; Fat 8.8g, of which saturates 2g; Cholesterol 44mg; Calcium 10mg; Fibre 0.6g; Sodium 485mg.
dry steak curry Energy 296kcal/1238kJ; Protein 35.2g; Carbohydrate 4.9g, of which sugars 4.5g; Fat 15.2g, of which saturates 4.8g; Cholesterol 103mg; Calcium 66mg; Fibre 0.7g; Sodium 262mg.

Tangerine Peel Beef

The tangerine, like the orange, is a fruit with auspicious meaning. The Cantonese name for tangerine, kum, sounds like the word for gold, which symbolizes prosperity. It is a particularly popular flavouring in Cantonese and Sichuan cooking.

Serves 4

350g/12oz sirloin or rump steak
5ml/1 tsp bicarbonate of soda (baking soda)
10g/1/4oz dried tangerine peel
15ml/1 tbsp vegetable oil
2 garlic cloves, crushed
30ml/2 tbsp sesame oil
5ml/1 tsp sugar
8 spring onions (scallions), cut in 5cm/2in pieces
30ml/2 tbsp water

1 Slice the steak into thin strips. Put the bicarbonate of soda into a shallow dish, moisten it with a little water, then add the beef strips. Using clean hands, rub the bicarbonate of soda into the meat. Cover and set aside for 10 minutes.

2 Meanwhile, soak the tangerine peel in a bowl of water. When it is soft, drain it and slice it into thin strips.

3 Heat the oil in a wok and fry the garlic for 40 seconds, until light brown. Do not let it burn. Add the beef. Stir-fry over high heat for 1 minute, then stir in the tangerine peel.

4 Add the sesame oil, sugar, spring onions and water. Stir-fry for 2 minutes or until the beef is cooked the way you like it.

5 Spoon into a dish or individual bowls and serve immediately.

Variation
Thin strips of orange, lemon or lime peel can be used instead of tangerine. When paring the fruit, take care to remove only the coloured skin and not the bitter pith underneath. Dry the peel by placing it on sheets of kitchen paper and leaving it in a warm room overnight.

Spicy Shredded Beef

The beef in this recipe is cut into very fine strips. Freezing the beef briefly before preparation makes this easy.

Serves 2

25g/8oz rump or fillet of beef
15ml/1 tbsp each light and dark soy sauce
15ml/1 tbsp rice wine or medium-dry sherry
5ml/1 tsp soft dark brown sugar or golden sugar
90ml/6 tbsp vegetable oil
1 large onion, thinly sliced
2.5cm/1in piece fresh root ginger, peeled and grated
1 or 2 carrots, cut into matchsticks
2 or 3 fresh or dried chillies, halved, seeded (optional) and chopped
salt and ground black pepper
fresh chives, to garnish

1 Place the beef in the freezer for 30–40 minutes to firm up. With a sharp knife, slice the beef very thinly, then cut each slice into fine strips or shreds.

2 Mix together the light and dark soy sauces with the rice wine or medium-dry sherry and sugar in a bowl. Add the strips of beef and stir well to ensure they are evenly coated with the marinade.

3 Heat a wok and add half the oil. When it is hot, stir-fry the onion and ginger for 3–4 minutes, then transfer to a plate. Add the carrot, stir-fry for 3–4 minutes until slightly softened, then transfer to a plate and keep warm.

4 Heat the remaining oil in the wok, then quickly add the beef, with the marinade, followed by the chillies. Cook over high heat for 2 minutes, stirring all the time.

5 Return the fried onion and ginger to the wok and stir-fry for 1 minute more. Season with salt and pepper to taste, cover and cook for 30 seconds. Spoon the meat into two warmed bowls and add the strips of carrots. Garnish with fresh chives and serve immediately.

tangerine peel beef Energy 242kcal/1005kJ; Protein 20.3g; Carbohydrate 3.1g, of which sugars 3.1g; Fat 16.5g, of which saturates 4.5g; Cholesterol 51mg; Calcium 17mg; Fibre 0.4g; Sodium 65mg.
shredded beef Energy 532kcal/2207kJ; Protein 27.3g; Carbohydrate 19.3g, of which sugars 15.4g; Fat 38.1g, of which saturates 5.8g; Cholesterol 66mg; Calcium 59mg; Fibre 3.3g; Sodium 1154mg.

Beef Rendang

This spicy dish is usually served with the meat quite dry; if you prefer more sauce, add more water.

Serves 6–8

2 onions or 5 or 6 shallots, chopped
4 garlic cloves, chopped
2.5cm/1in piece fresh galangal, peeled and sliced, or 15ml/1 tbsp galangal paste
2.5cm/1in piece fresh root ginger, peeled and sliced
4–6 fresh red chillies, seeded and roughly chopped
lower part only of 1 lemon grass stalk, sliced
2.5cm/1in piece fresh turmeric, peeled and sliced, or 5ml/1 tsp ground turmeric
1kg/2¼lb prime beef in one piece
5ml/1 tsp coriander seeds, dry-fried
5ml/1 tsp cumin seeds, dry-fried
2 kaffir lime leaves, torn into pieces
2 × 400ml/14fl oz cans coconut milk
300ml/½ pint/1¼ cups water
30ml/2 tbsp dark soy sauce
5ml/1 tsp tamarind pulp, soaked in 60ml/4 tbsp warm water
8–10 small new potatoes, scrubbed
salt and ground black pepper
deep-fried onions, sliced fresh red chillies and spring onions (scallions), to garnish

1 Put the onions or shallots in a food processor. Add the garlic, galangal, ginger, chillies, sliced lemon grass and turmeric. Process to a fine paste or grind in a mortar, using a pestle.

2 Cut the meat into cubes using a large sharp knife, then place the cubes in a bowl. Grind the dry-fried coriander and cumin seeds, then add to the meat with the onion, chilli paste and kaffir lime leaves; stir well. Cover and leave in a cool place to marinate.

3 Pour the coconut milk and water into a wok, then stir in the spiced meat and the soy sauce. Strain the tamarind water and add to the wok. Stir over medium heat until the liquid boils, then simmer gently, half-covered, for 1½ hours. Add the potatoes and simmer for 20–25 minutes, or until meat and potatoes are tender. Add water if liked. Season and serve, garnished with deep-fried onions, chillies and spring onions.

Balti Beef

There's no marinating involved with this simple recipe, which can be prepared and cooked in under an hour.

Serves 4

1 red (bell) pepper
1 green (bell) pepper
15ml/1 tbsp oil
5ml/1 tsp cumin seeds
2.5ml/½ tsp fennel seeds
1 onion, cut into thick wedges
1 garlic clove, crushed
2.5cm/1in piece fresh root ginger, finely chopped
1 fresh red chilli, finely chopped
15ml/1 tbsp curry paste
2.5ml/½ tsp salt
675g/1½lb lean rump (round) or fillet steak (beef tenderloin), cut into thick strips
naan bread, to serve

1 Cut the red and green peppers into 2.5cm/1in chunks.

2 Heat the oil in a karahi, wok or frying pan and fry the cumin and fennel seeds for 2 minutes or until they begin to splutter. Add the onion, garlic, ginger and chilli and fry for a further 5 minutes.

3 Stir in the curry paste and salt and fry for a further 3–4 minutes.

4 Add the peppers and toss over the heat for about 5 minutes. Stir in the beef strips and continue to fry for 10–12 minutes or until the meat is tender. Serve from the pan, with warm naan bread.

Variations

- *This recipe would also work well with chicken breast fillet.*
- *You could add mangetouts (snow peas), trimmed and left whole, to the dish for added crunch. As they need only the minimum amount of cooking, add them for the last 5 minutes of cooking only.*

beef rendang Energy 289kcal/1210kJ; Protein 30.2g; Carbohydrate 15.4g, of which sugars 8.6g; Fat 12.2g, of which saturates 5g; Cholesterol 73mg; Calcium 63mg; Fibre 1.4g; Sodium 465mg.
balti beef Energy 374kcal/1556kJ; Protein 39.7g; Carbohydrate 7.8g, of which sugars 6.2g; Fat 20.5g, of which saturates 7g; Cholesterol 98mg; Calcium 43mg; Fibre 2.5g; Sodium 129mg.

Cantonese Beefsteak

This is a typical Hong Kong restaurant dish, which echoes Western-style steak but which is cooked by the traditional Cantonese stir-fried method. The unusual ingredient here is Worcestershire sauce, very likely a British colonial touch. This imparts a subtle vinegar and pepper flavour to the dish.

Serves 4

600g/1lb 6oz sirloin or rump steak
15ml/1 tbsp cornflour (cornstarch)
30ml/2 tbsp Chinese Mui Kwai Lo wine or sweet sherry
15ml/1 tbsp Worcestershire sauce
30ml/2 tbsp oyster sauce
45ml/3 tbsp vegetable oil
15ml/1 tbsp grated root ginger
2.5ml/½ tsp sugar
lettuce leaves, to serve

1 Slice the sirloin or rump steak thinly into medallions. Put the cornflour in a bowl or strong plastic bag. Add the steak and toss to coat.

2 In a small bowl, mix the wine or sherry, Worcestershire sauce and oyster sauce. Stir, then set aside.

3 Heat the oil in a wok or frying pan. Add the grated ginger and fry for 30 seconds. Add the beef. Stir-fry over high heat for 1 minute, then pour in the wine and sauce mixture. Stir-fry for 1 minute more, then sprinkle over the sugar.

4 Continue to stir for 2 minutes more for medium-rare, or 3 minutes for well-done beef. Serve on a bed of lettuce leaves.

Variations

- *The sauce in this recipe makes a delicious marinade for beef. Skewer the sliced steak, dust with cornflour and soak the skewers in a blend of the sauce ingredients before grilling (broiling) or cooking on the barbecue.*
- *Use demerara (raw) sugar instead of regular white sugar to impart extra depth of colour and flavour.*

Seared Garlic Beef

Flavoured with lots of garlic, the tender chunks of beef are wrapped in lettuce leaves and dipped in a piquant lime sauce. Beef is well suited to searing, and this can be done in a pan, but can also be chargrilled if you prefer.

Serves 4

350g/12oz beef fillet (tenderloin) or sirloin, cut into bitesize chunks
15ml/1 tbsp sugar
juice of 3 limes
2 garlic cloves, crushed
7.5ml/1½ tsp ground black pepper
30ml/2 tbsp unsalted roasted peanuts, finely chopped
12 lettuce leaves

For the marinade

15ml/1 tbsp groundnut (peanut) oil
45ml/3 tbsp mushroom soy sauce
10ml/2 tsp soy sauce
15ml/1 tbsp sugar
2 garlic cloves, crushed
7.5ml/1½ tsp ground black pepper

1 To make the marinade, beat together the oil, the two soy sauces and the sugar in a bowl, until the sugar has dissolved. Add the garlic and pepper and mix well. Add the beef and coat in the marinade. Leave for 1–2 hours.

2 In a small bowl, stir the sugar into the lime juice, until it has dissolved. Add the garlic and black pepper and beat well. Stir in the peanuts and put aside.

3 Heat a wok or heavy pan and sear the meat on all sides.

4 Serve immediately with lettuce leaves for wrapping and the lime sauce for dipping.

Variation

This delicious dish can also be made with quail or even ostrich. The marinade ensures that the meat remains juicy. If using poultry, ensure it is fully cooked and not simply seared.

Cantonese beefsteak Energy 365kcal/1518kJ; Protein 34.2g; Carbohydrate 5g, of which sugars 1.5g; Fat 22.2g, of which saturates 6.7g; Cholesterol 87mg; Calcium 17mg; Fibre 0g; Sodium 322mg.
seared garlic beef Energy 237kcal/986kJ; Protein 21.9g; Carbohydrate 5.2g, of which sugars 4.7g; Fat 14.3g, of which saturates 4.3g; Cholesterol 51mg; Calcium 12mg; Fibre 0.5g; Sodium 324mg.

Sizzling Steak

If you order this in a restaurant, it will probably be brought to the table sizzling on an individual hot metal platter set on a thick wooden board. This is a simpler version, which can easily be made at home.

Serves 2

2 rump (round) or sirloin steaks, total weight about 450g/1lb
15–30ml/1–2 tbsp vegetable oil
shredded spring onion (scallion), to garnish

For the marinade and sauce

15ml/1 tbsp brandy
15ml/1 tbsp rich brown sauce
30ml/2 tbsp sunflower oil
a few drops of sesame oil
2 garlic cloves, halved or crushed
150ml/¼ pint/⅔ cup beef stock
30ml/2 tbsp tomato ketchup
15ml/1 tbsp oyster sauce
15ml/1 tbsp Worcestershire sauce
salt and sugar

1 Put the steaks side by side in a bowl. Mix the brandy, brown sauce, sunflower oil, sesame oil and garlic and pour this marinade over the steaks. Cover and leave for 1 hour, turning once. Drain the meat well, reserving the marinade.

2 Heat the oil in a heavy, ridged frying pan and fry the steaks for 3–5 minutes on each side, depending on how well done you like them. Transfer to a plate and keep warm.

3 Pour the marinade into the frying pan. Stir in the beef stock, ketchup, oyster sauce and Worcestershire sauce, with salt and sugar to taste. Bring to the boil, boil rapidly to reduce by half, then taste again and adjust the seasoning if necessary.

4 Serve each steak on a very hot plate, pouring the sauce over each portion just before serving. Garnish with the spring onion.

Cook's Tip
If you don't have a ridged frying pan, simply use a large, heavy frying pan instead.

Seared Beef Rolls

Marinated in a mixture of vinegar, sake and shoyu, seared beef is a popular Japanese speciality.

Serves 4

500g/1¼lb chunk of beef thigh (a long, thin chunk looks better than a thick, round chunk)
generous pinch of salt
10ml/2 tsp vegetable oil
½ cucumber, cut into matchsticks
½ lemon, thinly sliced

For the marinade

200ml/7fl oz/scant 1 cup rice vinegar
70ml/4½ tbsp sake
135ml/4½fl oz/scant ⅔ cup shoyu
15ml/1 tbsp caster (superfine) sugar
1 garlic clove, thinly sliced
1 small onion, thinly sliced
sansho

1 Mix the marinade ingredients in a small pan and warm through until the sugar has dissolved. Remove from the heat and leave to cool.

2 Generously sprinkle the beef with the salt and rub well into the meat. Leave for 2–3 minutes, then rub the oil in evenly with your fingers. Fill a bowl with cold water.

3 Heat a griddle. When it is very hot, sear the beef, turning frequently until about 5mm/¼in of its depth is cooked. Immediately plunge the beef into the bowl of cold water for a few seconds to stop it from cooking further.

4 Drain and dry the meat with kitchen paper, and lay it in a shallow dish. Pour the marinade over, cover and place in the refrigerator for 1 day.

5 Drain the beef, reserving the marinade, and slice it thinly. Top each slice with a little onion and garlic from the marinade, and add some cucumber matchsticks and a sprinkling of sansho, to taste. Roll up and secure with a cocktail stick (toothpick).

6 Serve the seared beef rolls with the lemon slices and the strained marinade, for dipping.

sizzling steak Energy 469kcal/1956kJ; Protein 53.1g; Carbohydrate 4.1g, of which sugars 3.8g; Fat 26.7g, of which saturates 7.4g; Cholesterol 115mg; Calcium 20mg; Fibre 0.1g; Sodium 409mg.
seared beef rolls Energy 258kcal/1079kJ; Protein 28.7g; Carbohydrate 9.8g, of which sugars 9.8g; Fat 11.7g, of which saturates 4.8g; Cholesterol 73mg; Calcium 20mg; Fibre 0.3g; Sodium 82mg.

Chargrilled Beef & Shrimp Sauce

For these kebabs, thin strips of beef are marinated, chargrilled and served with shrimp sauce – a tasty combination. A teaspoon of shrimp paste is sometimes added to the marinade, but you may find the pungency of the accompanying shrimp sauce is sufficient.

Serves 4

450g/1lb beef rump (round), or fillet (tenderloin), cut across the grain into thin strips
lettuce leaves
1 small bunch fresh coriander (cilantro), to garnish
Vietnamese shrimp sauce, for dipping

For the marinade

2 lemon grass stalks, trimmed and chopped
2 shallots, chopped
2 garlic cloves, peeled and chopped
1 fresh red chilli, seeded and chopped
10ml/2 tsp sugar
30ml/2 tbsp fish sauce
15ml/1 tbsp soy sauce
15ml/1 tbsp groundnut (peanut) oil

1 For the marinade, pound the lemon grass, shallots, garlic and chilli with the sugar using a mortar and pestle, until it forms a paste. Beat in the fish sauce, soy sauce and groundnut oil. Toss the beef in the marinade, cover, and marinate for 1–2 hours to let the flavours develop.

2 Soak bamboo or wooden skewers in water for 20 minutes so they don't burn over the charcoal.

3 Prepare a barbecue, or preheat a conventional grill (broiler). Drain the skewers, thread them with the beef and place them over the coals. Cook for not much more than a minute on each side.

4 Wrap the beef in the lettuce leaves, garnish with the fresh coriander and serve with the pungent Vietnamese shrimp sauce for dipping.

Chilli Beef & Butternut

Stir-fried beef and sweet, orange-fleshed squash flavoured with warm spices, oyster sauce and fresh herbs makes a robust main course when served with rice or egg noodles. The addition of chilli and fresh root ginger gives the dish a wonderful vigorous bite.

Serves 4

30ml/2 tbsp sunflower oil
2 onions, cut into thick slices
500g/1¼lb butternut squash, peeled, seeded and cut into thin strips
675g/1½lb fillet steak (beef tenderloin)
60ml/4 tbsp soy sauce
90g/3½oz/½ cup golden caster (superfine) sugar
1 fresh bird's eye chilli or a milder red chilli, seeded and chopped
15ml/1 tbsp finely shredded fresh root ginger
30ml/2 tbsp fish sauce
5ml/1 tsp ground star anise
5ml/1 tsp five-spice powder
15ml/1 tbsp oyster sauce
4 spring onions (scallions), shredded
a small handful of sweet basil leaves
a small handful of mint leaves

1 Heat a wok over a medium to high heat and add the oil. When hot, stir in the onions and squash. Stir-fry for 2–3 minutes, then reduce the heat, cover and cook gently for 5–6 minutes, or until the vegetables are just tender.

2 Place the beef between two sheets of clear film (plastic wrap) and beat, with a mallet or rolling pin, until thin. Using a sharp knife, cut into thin strips.

3 In a separate wok, mix the soy sauce, sugar, chilli, ginger, fish sauce, star anise, five-spice powder and oyster sauce. Cook for 3–4 minutes, stirring frequently.

4 Add the beef to the soy sauce mixture in the wok and cook over a high heat for 3–4 minutes. Remove from the heat. Add the onion and squash slices to the beef and toss well with the spring onions and herbs. Serve immediately.

beef & shrimp sauce Energy 229kcal/952kJ; Protein 25.8g; Carbohydrate 1.5g, of which sugars 1.1g; Fat 13.3g, of which saturates 4.6g; Cholesterol 65mg; Calcium 10mg; Fibre 0.2g; Sodium 340mg.
chilli beef Energy 500kcal/2093kJ; Protein 41.3g; Carbohydrate 36.9g, of which sugars 33.8g; Fat 21.7g, of which saturates 7.2g; Cholesterol 98mg; Calcium 91mg; Fibre 2.9g; Sodium 1243mg.

Beef with Black Bean Sauce

The black bean sauce gives this low-fat dish a lovely rich flavour. The beef is first simmered in stock and then stir-fried with garlic, ginger, chilli and green pepper.

Serves 4

350g/12oz rump (round) steak, trimmed and thinly sliced
15ml/1 tbsp vegetable oil
300ml/½ pint/1¼ cups beef stock
2 garlic cloves, finely chopped
5ml/1 tsp grated fresh root ginger
1 fresh red chilli, seeded and finely chopped
15ml/1 tbsp black bean sauce
1 green (bell) pepper, seeded and cut into 2.5cm/1in squares
15ml/1 tbsp dry sherry
5ml/1 tsp cornflour (cornstarch)
5ml/1 tsp caster (superfine) sugar
45ml/3 tbsp cold water
salt
rice noodles, to serve

1 Place the sliced steak in a bowl. Add 5ml/1 tsp of the oil and stir to coat.

2 Bring the stock to the boil in a large pan. Add the sliced steak and cook for 2 minutes, stirring constantly to prevent the slices from sticking together. Lift out the beef and set aside.

3 Heat the remaining oil in a wok. Stir-fry the garlic, ginger and chilli with the black bean sauce for a few seconds.

4 Add the pepper and a little water. Cook for about 2 minutes more, then stir in the sherry. Add the beef slices to the pan and spoon the sauce over to coat them.

5 Mix the cornflour and sugar to a paste with the water. Pour the mixture into the pan. Cook, stirring, until the sauce has thickened. Season and serve the dish immediately, with boiled rice or rice noodles.

Cook's Tip
For extra colour, use half each of a green and red (bell) pepper.

Sukiyaki-style Beef

This dish incorporates all the traditional Japanese elements – meat, vegetables, noodles and tofu.

Serves 4

450g/1lb thick rump (round) steak
200g/7oz/3½ cups Japanese rice noodles
15ml/1 tbsp shredded suet
200g/7oz firm tofu, cut into dice
8 shiitake mushrooms, trimmed
2 leeks, sliced into 2.5cm/1in lengths
90g/3½ oz/scant 1 cup baby spinach, to serve

For the stock

15g/½oz/1 tbsp caster (superfine) sugar
90ml/6 tbsp rice wine
45ml/3 tbsp dark soy sauce
120ml/4fl oz/½ cup water

1 If there is time, chill the steak in the freezer for 30 minutes to make it easier to slice thinly. Cut the steak into thin, even slices with a very sharp knife.

2 Blanch the rice noodles in a large pan of boiling water for 2 minutes, then drain well.

3 Mix together all the ingredients for the stock in a bowl, stirring until the sugar has dissolved. Set aside.

4 Heat a wok, then add the suet. When the suet has melted, add the steak and stir-fry for 2–3 minutes, until it is cooked but still pink in colour.

5 Pour the stock over the beef and add the tofu, mushrooms and leeks. Cook, stirring occasionally, for 4 minutes, until the leeks are tender. Divide the different ingredients equally among individual plates, spoon the stock over them and serve immediately with a few baby spinach leaves each.

Cook's Tip
Add a touch of authenticity and serve this complete meal with chopsticks and a porcelain spoon to collect the stock juices.

beef w. black bean Energy 219kcal/912kJ; Protein 19.5g; Carbohydrate 8.4g, of which sugars 5.8g; Fat 12g, of which saturates 3.1g; Cholesterol 33mg; Calcium 69mg; Fibre 4.5g; Sodium 907mg.
Sukiyaki beef Energy 489kcal/2044kJ; Protein 34.7g; Carbohydrate 49g, of which sugars 6.9g; Fat 16.7g, of which saturates 6.5g; Cholesterol 68mg; Calcium 328mg; Fibre 2.4g; Sodium 916mg.

Beef with Tomatoes

This colourful and fresh-tasting mixture is the perfect way of serving sun-ripened tomatoes from the garden or farmers' market.

Serves 4

350g/12oz lean rump (round) steak, trimmed of fat
15ml/1 tbsp vegetable oil
300ml/½ pint/1¼ cups beef stock
1 garlic clove, finely chopped
1 small onion, sliced into rings
5 tomatoes, quartered
15ml/1 tbsp tomato purée (paste)
5ml/1 tsp caster (superfine) sugar
15ml/1 tbsp dry sherry
salt and ground white pepper
noodles, to serve

1 Slice the rump steak thinly. Place the steak slices in a bowl, add 5ml/1 tsp of the vegetable oil and stir to coat.

2 Bring the stock to the boil in a large pan. Add the beef and cook for 2 minutes, stirring constantly. Lift out the beef and set it aside on a plate.

3 Heat the remaining oil in a non-stick frying pan or wok until very hot. Stir-fry the garlic and onion for a few seconds.

4 Add the beef to the pan or wok, then tip in the tomatoes. Stir-fry for 1 minute more over high heat.

5 Mix the tomato purée, sugar, sherry and 15ml/1 tbsp cold water in a cup or small bowl. Stir into the beef and tomato mixture in the pan or wok, add salt and pepper to taste and mix thoroughly. Cook for 1 minute until the sauce is hot. Serve in heated bowls, with noodles.

Variation
Add 5–10ml/1–2 tsp soy sauce to the tomato purée (paste). You will not need to add any extra salt.

Stir-fried Beef & Mushrooms

Garlic and salted black beans is a classic Cantonese seasoning for beef.

Serves 4

30ml/2 tbsp soy sauce
30ml/2 tbsp Chinese rice wine
10ml/2 tsp cornflour (cornstarch)
10ml/2 tsp sesame oil
450g/1lb beef fillet (tenderloin), trimmed of fat
12 dried shiitake mushrooms
25ml/1½ tbsp salted black beans
5ml/1 tsp sugar
45ml/3 tbsp groundnut (peanut) oil
4 garlic cloves, thinly sliced
2.5cm/1in piece fresh root ginger, cut into fine strips
200g/7oz open cap mushrooms, sliced
1 bunch spring onions (scallions), sliced diagonally
1 fresh red chilli, seeded and finely shredded
salt and ground black pepper

1 In a large bowl, mix half the soy sauce, half the rice wine, half the cornflour and all the sesame oil with 15ml/1 tbsp cold water until smooth. Add a good pinch of salt and pepper. Slice the beef very thinly and add to the cornflour mixture. Rub the mixture into the beef. Set aside for 30 minutes.

2 Pour boiling water over the dried mushrooms and soak for 25 minutes. Drain, reserving 45ml/3 tbsp of the soaking water. Remove and discard the hard stalks and cut the caps in half. Mash the black beans with the sugar in a small bowl. Stir the remaining cornflour, soy sauce and rice wine together in another bowl.

3 Heat the oil in a wok and stir-fry the beef for 30–45 seconds, until just brown. Transfer it to a plate, then stir-fry the garlic, ginger, dried and fresh mushrooms for 2 minutes. Add half the spring onions with the mashed black beans and stir-fry for another 1–2 minutes.

4 Stir the beef back into the mixture in the wok, then add the reserved shiitake soaking water. Add the cornflour mixture and simmer, stirring, until the sauce thickens. Sprinkle the chilli and reserved spring onions over the beef and serve.

beef w. tomatoes Energy 172kcal/723kJ; Protein 20.5g; Carbohydrate 6.7g, of which sugars 6.4g; Fat 6.8g, of which saturates 1.9g; Cholesterol 52mg; Calcium 18mg; Fibre 1.6g; Sodium 74mg.
beef & mushrooms Energy 208kcal/873kJ; Protein 25.9g; Carbohydrate 4.7g, of which sugars 1.5g; Fat 8.8g, of which saturates 3.5g; Cholesterol 69mg; Calcium 20mg; Fibre 1.1g; Sodium 590mg.

Sichuan Beef with Tofu

China's western province is famous for its spicy cuisine, full of strong flavours. Sichuan peppercorns, which feature in this meat dish, are not, in fact, peppercorns, but the dried berries of a type of ash tree. But, they do have a very peppery flavour.

Serves 4

200g/7oz/1 cup fragrant jasmine or basmati rice
30ml/2 tbsp groundnut (peanut) or soya oil
4 garlic cloves, finely chopped
600g/1lb 6oz beef rump (round) steak or fillet (tenderloin), cut into thin strips
500g/1¼lb firm tofu, drained and diced
1 head broccoli, coarsely chopped
90ml/6 tbsp soy sauce
pinch of sugar
juice of 1 lime
ground Sichuan peppercorns
sweet chilli sauce or another dipping sauce, to serve

1 Cook the rice in a large pan of salted boiling water until tender, following the instructions on the packet, then put it into a bowl and keep it hot.

2 Heat the oil in a large non-stick wok or frying pan, then add the garlic and stir-fry for a few seconds, until golden. Increase the heat to high, add the strips of steak and stir-fry for 1–2 minutes to seal.

3 Add the tofu cubes and broccoli and stir-fry for a few seconds. Stir in the soy sauce, sugar, lime juice and ground Sichuan peppercorns, then stir-fry for about 2 minutes. Transfer to warm serving plates or bowls and serve immediately with the rice and chilli sauce or other sauce.

Cook's Tip
Tofu, also known as beancurd, is a form of vegetable protein based on soya beans. There are two basic types: soft or silken tofu, which has a very light texture, and firm tofu, which is the type used in the recipe above.

Stir-fried Beef with Sesame Sauce

Similar to stir-fried beef with satay, the spicy peanut sauce, this recipe has a deliciously rich, spicy and nutty flavour.

Serves 4

450g/1lb beef sirloin or fillet (tenderloin), cut into thin strips
15ml/1 tbsp groundnut (peanut) or sesame oil
2 garlic cloves, finely chopped
2 fresh red chillies, seeded and finely chopped
7.5ml/1½ tsp sugar
30ml/2 tbsp sesame paste
30–45ml/2–3 tbsp beef stock or water
sea salt and ground black pepper
red chilli strips, to garnish
1 lemon, cut into quarters, to serve

For the marinade
15ml/1 tbsp groundnut (peanut) oil
30ml/2 tbsp fish sauce
30ml/2 tbsp soy sauce

1 In a bowl, mix together the ingredients for the marinade. Toss in the beef, making sure it is well coated. Leave to marinate for 30 minutes.

2 Heat the groundnut or sesame oil in a wok. Add the garlic and chillies and cook until golden and fragrant. Stir in the sugar. Add the beef, tossing it around the wok to sear it.

3 Stir in the sesame paste and enough stock or water to thin it down. Cook for 1–2 minutes, making sure the beef is coated with the sauce.

4 Season the sauce with salt and pepper. Spoon into warmed bowls, garnish with chilli strips and serve with lemon wedges.

Variation
Chicken breast fillet or pork fillet can be used instead of beef, but extend the cooking time to ensure that the poultry or pork is fully coated. Serve chicken or pork with orange wedges instead of lemon.

Sichuan beef Energy 646kcal/2694kJ; Protein 55g; Carbohydrate 46.9g, of which sugars 4.1g; Fat 26.2g, of which saturates 7.6g; Cholesterol 87mg; Calcium 731mg; Fibre 3.8g; Sodium 1714mg.
beef w. sesame sauce Energy 269kcal/1119kJ; Protein 26.2g; Carbohydrate 0g, of which sugars 0g; Fat 18.2g, of which saturates 5.2g; Cholesterol 65mg; Calcium 31mg; Fibre 0.3g; Sodium 73mg.

Peking Beef & Pepper Stir-fry

Once the steak has marinated, this colourful dish can be prepared in just a few minutes.

Serves 4

350g/12oz rump (round) or sirloin steak, sliced into strips
30ml/2 tbsp soy sauce
30ml/2 tbsp medium sherry
15ml/1 tbsp cornflour (cornstarch)
5ml/1 tsp brown sugar
15ml/1 tbsp sunflower oil
15ml/1 tbsp sesame oil
1 garlic clove, finely chopped
15ml/1 tbsp grated fresh root ginger
1 red (bell) pepper, seeded and sliced
1 yellow (bell) pepper, seeded and sliced
115g/4oz/1 cup sugar snap peas
4 spring onions (scallions), cut into 5cm/2in pieces
30ml/2 tbsp oyster sauce
hot noodles, to serve

1 Mix together the steak strips, soy sauce, sherry, cornflour and brown sugar in a bowl. Cover with clear film (plastic wrap) and leave in a cool place to marinate for 30 minutes.

2 Heat a wok or large frying pan and add the sunflower and sesame oils. When the oils are hot, add the garlic and ginger and stir-fry for about 30 seconds.

3 Add the red and yellow peppers, sugar snap peas and spring onions and stir-fry over high heat for 3 minutes.

4 Add the steak with the marinade juices to the wok or frying pan and stir-fry for a further 3–4 minutes.

5 Finally, pour in the oyster sauce and 60ml/4 tbsp water and cook, stirring constantly, until the sauce has thickened slightly. Serve immediately with hot noodles.

Cook's Tip
Although it is made from oysters, plus other ingredients, oyster sauce will not impart a fishy flavour to the meat.

Simmered Beef Slices & Vegetables

This one-pot dish is a family favourite in Japan. It is a good example of how a small amount of meat can be stretched with vegetables to make a tasty and nutritious low-fat meal.

Serves 4

250g/9oz lean fillet (beef tenderloin) or rump (round) steak, trimmed of fat and very thinly sliced
1 large onion
15ml/1 tbsp vegetable oil
450g/1lb small potatoes, halved then soaked in water
1 carrot, cut into 5mm/¼in rounds
45ml/3 tbsp frozen peas, thawed and blanched for 1 minute

For the seasonings
30ml/2 tbsp caster (superfine) sugar
75ml/5 tbsp shoyu
15ml/1 tbsp mirin (sweet rice wine)
15ml/1 tbsp sake or dry sherry

1 Cut the thinly sliced beef slices into 2cm/¾in wide strips, and slice the onion lengthways into 5mm/¼n pieces.

2 Heat the vegetable oil in a pan and lightly fry the beef and onion slices. When the colour of the meat changes, drain the potatoes and add to the pan.

3 Once the potatoes are coated with the oil in the pan, add the carrot. Pour in just enough water to cover, then bring to the boil, skimming a few times.

4 Boil vigorously for 2 minutes, then rearrange the ingredients so that the potatoes are underneath the beef and vegetables.

5 Reduce the heat to medium-low and add all the seasonings. Simmer for 20 minutes, partially covered, or until most of the liquid has evaporated.

6 Check if the potatoes are cooked. Add the peas and cook to heat through, then remove the pan from the heat. Serve the beef and vegetables immediately in four small serving bowls.

beef & pepper stir-fry Energy 225kcal/940kJ; Protein 22.7g; Carbohydrate 11.9g, of which sugars 8.9g; Fat 9.9g, of which saturates 2.4g; Cholesterol 52mg; Calcium 23mg; Fibre 3g; Sodium 713mg.
beef slices & veg. Energy 276kcal/1160kJ; Protein 17.8g; Carbohydrate 31.5g, of which sugars 13.2g; Fat 9.2g, of which saturates 2.9g; Cholesterol 36mg; Calcium 28mg; Fibre 2.3g; Sodium 1394mg.

Braised Beef in Peanut Sauce

This slow-cooked stew was originally Spanish. It retains much of its original charm, but has acquired a uniquely oriental flavour. Rice and peanuts are used to thicken the juices, yielding a rich, glossy sauce.

Serves 4–6

900g/2lb braising steak
30ml/2 tbsp vegetable oil
15ml/1 tbsp annatto seeds
2 medium onions, chopped
2 garlic cloves, crushed
275g/10oz celeriac or swede (rutabaga), roughly chopped
475ml/16fl oz/2 cups beef stock
375g/12oz new potatoes, peeled and cut into large dice
15ml/1 tbsp fish sauce
30ml/2 tbsp tamarind sauce
10ml/2 tsp sugar
1 bay leaf
1 fresh thyme sprig
45ml/3 tbsp long grain rice
30ml/2 tbsp peanut butter
15ml/1 tbsp white wine vinegar
salt and ground black pepper

1 Cut the beef into 2.5cm/1in cubes and set aside. Heat the oil in a flameproof casserole, add the annatto seeds and stir until the oil is dark red in colour. Remove the seeds with a slotted spoon and discard.

2 Add the onions, garlic and celeriac or swede to the casserole and fry for 3–5 minutes, until softened but not coloured. Add the beef and fry until lightly and evenly browned. Add the stock, potatoes, fish sauce, tamarind sauce, sugar, bay leaf and thyme. Bring to a simmer, cover and cook for 2 hours.

3 Meanwhile, soak the rice in cold water for 30 minutes. Drain the rice and grind with the peanut butter in a mortar with a pestle or in a food processor.

4 When the beef is tender, add 60ml/4 tbsp of the cooking liquid to the rice and nut mixture. Blend until smooth, then stir into the casserole. Simmer gently, uncovered, for about 15–20 minutes, until thickened. Stir in the wine vinegar, and spoon into warmed bowls. Serve.

Beef Stew with Star Anise

This stew is prized as a breakfast dish, and on chilly mornings people often queue up for a bowl of it on their way to work. Traditionally, it has an orange hue from the oil in which annatto seeds have been fried, but here the colour comes from turmeric.

Serves 4–6

500g/1¼lb lean beef, cut into bitesize cubes
15ml/1 tbsp ground turmeric
30ml/2 tbsp sesame or vegetable oil
3 shallots, chopped
3 garlic cloves, chopped
2 fresh red chillies, seeded and chopped
2 lemon grass stalks, cut into several pieces and bruised
15ml/1 tbsp curry powder
4 star anise, roasted and ground to a powder
700ml/scant 1¼ pints hot beef or chicken stock, or boiling water
45ml/3 tbsp fish sauce
30ml/2 tbsp soy sauce
15ml/1 tbsp raw cane sugar
1 bunch fresh basil, stalks removed
salt and ground black pepper
1 onion, halved and finely sliced, and chopped fresh coriander (cilantro) leaves, to garnish
steamed fragrant rice, or chunks of baguette, to serve

1 Toss the beef in the ground turmeric and set aside. Heat a wok or heavy pan and add the oil. Stir in the shallots, garlic, chillies and lemon grass, and cook until they become fragrant.

2 Add the curry powder, all but 10ml/2 tsp of the roasted star anise, and the beef. Brown the beef, then pour in the stock or water, fish sauce, soy sauce and sugar. Stir and bring to the boil.

3 Reduce the heat and cook gently for about 40 minutes, or until the meat is tender and the liquid has reduced.

4 Season to taste with salt and pepper, stir in the reserved roasted star anise, and add the basil. Transfer the stew to a serving dish and garnish with the sliced onion and coriander. Serve with steamed rice, or chunks of baguette.

beef in peanut sauce Energy 365kcal/1529kJ; Protein 30.8g; Carbohydrate 17.5g, of which sugars 16.4g; Fat 19.6g, of which saturates 6.2g; Cholesterol 65mg; Calcium 64mg; Fibre 1.2g; Sodium 238mg.
beef w. star anise Energy 147kcal/615kJ; Protein 18.2g; Carbohydrate 2.7g, of which sugars 1.6g; Fat 7.1g, of which saturates 2.9g; Cholesterol 44mg; Calcium 10mg; Fibre 0.5g; Sodium 405mg.

Beef Stir-fry with Crisp Parsnips

Wonderful crisp shreds of parsnip add extra crunchiness to this unusual stir-fry – a great supper dish to share with friends.

Serves 4
350g/12oz parsnips
450g/1lb rump (round) steak
450g/1lb trimmed leeks
2 red (bell) peppers, seeded
350g/12oz courgettes (zucchini)
90ml/6 tbsp vegetable oil
2 garlic cloves, crushed
45ml/3 tbsp hoisin sauce
salt and ground black pepper

1 Peel the parsnips and cut in half lengthways. Place the flat surface on a chopping board and cut them into thin strips. Finely shred each piece. Rinse in cold water and drain thoroughly. Dry the parsnips on kitchen paper to absorb any excess water, if necessary.

2 Cut the steak into thin strips. Split the leeks in half lengthways and thickly slice at an angle.

3 Roughly chop the peppers and thinly slice the courgettes.

4 Heat the oil in a preheated wok or large frying pan. Fry the parsnips until crisp and golden. You may need to do this in batches, adding a little more oil if necessary. Remove with a slotted spoon and drain on kitchen paper.

5 Stir-fry the steak in the wok or frying pan until golden and cooked through. You may need to do this in batches, adding more oil if necessary. Remove and drain on kitchen paper.

6 Stir-fry the garlic, leeks, peppers and courgettes for about 10 minutes, or until golden brown and beginning to soften but still retaining a little bite. Season the mixture well.

7 Return the meat to the pan with the hoisin sauce. Stir-fry for 2–3 minutes, or until piping hot. Adjust the seasoning and serve with the crisp parsnips piled on top.

Beef with Charred Aubergines

To obtain the unique, smoky flavour that is integral to this dish, aubergines are charred over a flame, or charcoal grill, then skinned, chopped to a pulp and added to a minced meat mixture. Although popular in parts of South-east Asia, the method is more associated with the cooking of India, the Middle East, and North Africa.

Serves 4
2 aubergines (eggplants)
15ml/1 tbsp vegetable or groundnut (peanut) oil
2 shallots, finely chopped
4 garlic cloves, peeled and finely chopped
1 fresh red chilli, finely chopped
350g/12oz minced (ground) beef
30ml/2 tbsp fish sauce
sea salt and ground black pepper
crusty bread or rice and salad, to serve

1 Place the aubergines directly over an open flame if you have a gas hob, or under a hot grill (broiler). Turn them over from time to time, until the skin is charred all over. Put the aubergines into a plastic bag to sweat for a few minutes.

2 Hold each aubergine by its stalk under running cold water, while you peel off the skin. Squeeze out the excess water and chop the aubergines roughly on a board.

3 Heat the oil in a large, heavy pan. Stir in the shallots, garlic and chilli and fry until golden. Add the minced beef and stir-fry for about 5 minutes.

4 Stir in the fish sauce and the aubergines and cook gently, stirring frequently, for about 20 minutes, until the meat is tender.

5 Season with salt and pepper and serve with crusty bread or rice and a salad.

Variation
This dish can also be made with beef or pork – either way it is delicious served with chunks of fresh, crusty bread.

beef w. parsnips Energy 481kcal/2002kJ; Protein 31.6g; Carbohydrate 24.1g, of which sugars 16.9g; Fat 29.2g, of which saturates 6.5g; Cholesterol 65mg; Calcium 100mg; Fibre 8.8g; Sodium 214mg.
beef w. aubergines Energy 251kcal/1050kJ; Protein 27.2g; Carbohydrate 7.2g, of which sugars 6.2g; Fat 12.8g, of which saturates 2.9g; Cholesterol 75mg; Calcium 29mg; Fibre 3g; Sodium 87mg.

Sesame Steak

Toasted sesame seeds bring their distinctive smoky aroma to the scrumptious marinade in this recipe.

Serves 4

450g/1lb rump steak
30ml/2 tbsp sesame seeds
15ml/1 tbsp sesame oil
30ml/2 tbsp vegetable oil
115g/4oz small mushrooms, quartered
1 large green pepper, seeded and cut into strips
4 spring onions, chopped diagonally
boiled rice, to serve

For the marinade

10ml/2 tsp cornflour (cornstarch)
30ml/2 tbsp Chinese rice wine or dry sherry
15ml/1 tbsp lemon juice
15ml/1 tbsp soy sauce
few drops of Tabasco sauce
2.5cm/1in fresh root ginger, grated
1 garlic clove, crushed

1 Trim the steak and cut into thin strips about 1 × 5cm/½ × 2in.

2 Make the marinade. In a bowl, blend the cornflour with the rice wine or dry sherry, then stir in the lemon juice, soy sauce, Tabasco sauce, ginger and garlic. Stir in the steak strips, cover and leave in a cool place for 3–4 hours.

3 Place the sesame seeds in a wok or large frying pan and dry-fry over a moderate heat, shaking the pan, until the seeds are golden. Set aside.

4 Heat the sesame and vegetable oils in the wok or frying pan. Drain the steak, reserving the marinade, and stir-fry a few pieces at a time until browned. Remove with a slotted spoon.

5 Add the mushrooms and green pepper and stir-fry for 2–3 minutes. Add the spring onions and cook for 1 minute more.

6 Return the steak to the wok or frying pan, together with the reserved marinade, and stir over a moderate heat for a further 2 minutes until the ingredients are evenly coated with glaze. Sprinkle over the sesame seeds and serve immediately with boiled rice.

Beef & Vegetable Table Top Broth

In Japanese, this dish is called shabu shabu, which refers to the swishing sound made as wafer-thin slices of beef, tofu and vegetables cook in a special broth.

Serves 4–6

450g/1lb sirloin steak, trimmed
1.75 litres/3 pints/7½ cups water
½ sachet instant dashi powder or ½ vegetable stock cube
150g/5oz carrots
6 spring onions (scallions), sliced
150g/5oz Chinese leaves (Chinese cabbage), roughly chopped
225g/8oz mooli (daikon), shredded
115g/4oz canned bamboo shoots, drained and sliced
175g/6oz tofu, cut into large dice
10 shiitake mushrooms, fresh or dried
salt
275g/10oz udon noodles, cooked, to serve

For the sesame dipping sauce

50g/2oz sesame seeds or 30ml/2 tbsp tahini paste
120ml/4fl oz/½ cup instant dashi stock or vegetable stock
60ml/4 tbsp dark soy sauce
10ml/2 tsp sugar
30ml/2 tbsp sake (optional)
10ml/2 tsp wasabi powder (optional)

For the ponzu dipping sauce

45ml/3 tbsp lemon juice
15ml/1 tbsp rice vinegar or white wine vinegar
45ml/3 tbsp dark soy sauce
15ml/1 tbsp tamari sauce
15ml/1 tbsp mirin or 5ml/1 tsp sugar
1.5ml/¼ tsp instant dashi powder or ¼ vegetable stock cube

1 Place the beef in the freezer for 30 minutes. Slice it very thinly using a sharp knife. Arrange it on a serving plate, cover and set aside. Bring the water to the boil in a Japanese donabe, a fondue pot or any other covered flameproof casserole with an unglazed outside. Stir in the dashi powder or stock cube, cover and simmer for 8–10 minutes. Transfer to a heat source (its own stand or a hot plate) to simmer at the table.

2 Bring a pan of salted water to the boil. Cut grooves along the length of the carrots, then slice thinly. Blanch the carrots, spring onions, Chinese leaves and mooli, separately, for 2–3 minutes each, and drain. Arrange on serving dishes, together with the bamboo shoots and tofu. If using dried mushrooms, put them in a bowl, cover with hot water and soak for 3–4 minutes, then drain. Slice the shiitake mushrooms.

3 To make the sesame sauce, dry-fry the sesame seeds, if using, in a heavy pan over medium heat. Grind with a mortar and pestle. Mix the ground sesame seeds or tahini paste, stock, soy sauce, sugar, sake and wasabi powder, if using. Pour into a dish.

4 To make the ponzu dipping sauce, put all the ingredients in a screw-top jar and shake vigorously. Pour into a shallow dish.

5 To serve, arrange the plates of vegetables and dishes of sauce around the broth and provide your guests with chopsticks and individual bowls so that they can help themselves to what they want, cook it in the broth and then serve themselves. Towards the end of the meal, each guest can take a portion of noodles and ladle a little stock over them before eating.

sesame steak Energy 354kcal/1472kJ; Protein 28.1g; Carbohydrate 5.8g, of which sugars 3.3g; Fat 23.4g, of which saturates 6g; Cholesterol 65mg; Calcium 65mg; Fibre 1.7g; Sodium 257mg.
table top broth Energy 251kcal/1056kJ; Protein 18.1g; Carbohydrate 27.8g, of which sugars 5g; Fat 8.2g, of which saturates 1.5g; Cholesterol 30mg; Calcium 163mg; Fibre 2.3g; Sodium 833mg.

Dry Beef & Peanut Butter Curry

Although this is called a dry curry, the method of cooking keeps the beef succulent.

Serves 4–6

400g/14oz can coconut milk
900g/2lb stewing beef, finely chopped
300ml/½ pint/1¼ cups beef stock
30–40ml/2–3 tbsp red curry paste
30ml/2 tbsp crunchy peanut butter
juice of 2 limes
lime slices, shredded coriander (cilantro) and fresh red chilli slices, to garnish

1 Strain the coconut milk into a bowl, retaining the thicker coconut milk in the strainer or sieve.

2 Pour the thin coconut milk from the bowl into a large, heavy pan, then scrape in half the residue from the sieve. Reserve the remaining thick coconut milk. Add the chopped beef. Pour in the beef stock and bring to the boil. Reduce the heat, cover the pan and simmer gently for 50 minutes.

3 Strain the beef, reserving the cooking liquid, and place a cupful of liquid in a wok. Stir in 30–45ml/2–3 tbsp of the curry paste, according to taste. Boil rapidly until all the liquid has evaporated. Stir in the reserved thick coconut milk, the peanut butter and the beef. Simmer, uncovered, for 15–20 minutes, adding a little more cooking liquid if the mixture starts to stick to the pan, but keep the curry dry.

4 Just before serving, stir in the lime juice. Serve in warmed bowls, garnished with the lime slices, shredded coriander and sliced red chillies.

Variation
The curry is equally delicious made with lean leg or shoulder of lamb, or with pork fillet (tenderloin).

Malaysian Sizzling Steak

This Malaysian method of sizzling richly marinated meat on a cast iron griddle can be applied with equal success to sliced chicken or pork.

Serves 4–6

1 garlic clove, crushed
2.5cm/1in piece fresh root ginger, finely chopped
10ml/2 tsp black peppercorns
15ml/1 tbsp sugar
30ml/2 tbsp tamarind sauce
45ml/3 tbsp dark soy sauce
15ml/1 tbsp oyster sauce
4 slices rump (round) steak, each about 200g/7oz
vegetable oil, for brushing

For the dipping sauce
75ml/5 tbsp beef stock
30ml/2 tbsp tomato ketchup
5ml/1 tsp chilli sauce
juice of 1 lime

1 Pound together the garlic, ginger, peppercorns, sugar and tamarind sauce in a mortar with a pestle. Mix in the soy sauce and oyster sauce, then spoon over the steaks. Set aside in the refrigerator to marinate for up to 8 hours.

2 Heat a cast iron griddle plate over a high heat until very hot. Scrape the marinade from the meat and reserve. Brush the meat with oil and cook for 2 minutes on each side for rare and 3–4 minutes on each side for medium, depending on thickness.

3 Meanwhile, make the sauce. Pour the marinade into a pan and add the stock, tomato ketchup, chilli sauce and lime juice. Set over a low heat and simmer to heat through. Serve the steak and hand the dipping sauce separately.

Cook's Tip
Probably the most popular spice in the world, peppercorns are the berries of a tropical climbing shrub, Piper nigrum. *The berries ripen when they turn from green to red. Black pepper is obtained from berries that are just turning red – they are picked and dried in the sun where they turn wrinkled and black to produce the peppercorns that are widely used in cooking.*

beef & peanut butter Energy 296kcal/1238kJ; Protein 35.2g; Carbohydrate 4.9g, of which sugars 4.5g; Fat 15.2g, of which saturates 4.8g; Cholesterol 103mg; Calcium 66mg; Fibre 0.7g; Sodium 262mg.
Malaysian sizzling steak Energy 313kcal/1304kJ; Protein 35.4g; Carbohydrate 2.7g, of which sugars 2.5g; Fat 17.8g, of which saturates 4.9g; Cholesterol 77mg; Calcium 13mg; Fibre 0.1g; Sodium 273mg.

Oxtail in Hot Tangy Sauce

Considered a delicacy in some parts of South-east Asia, oxtail and the tails of water buffalo are generally cooked for special feasts. In Malaysia and Singapore, oxtail is cooked in European-style stews by the Eurasians and Hainanese but the Malays and Indonesians prefer to cook it slowly in a hot, tangy sauce.

Serves 4–6

8 shallots, chopped
8 garlic cloves, chopped
4–6 fresh red chillies, seeded and chopped
25g/1oz fresh galangal, chopped
30ml/2 tbsp rice flour or plain (all-purpose) flour
15ml/1 tbsp ground turmeric
8–12 oxtail joints, cut roughly the same size and trimmed of fat
45ml/3 tbsp vegetable oil
400g/14oz can plum tomatoes, drained
2 lemon grass stalks, halved and bruised
a handful of fresh kaffir lime leaves
225g/8oz tamarind pulp, soaked in 600ml/1 pint/2½ cups water, squeezed and strained
30–45ml/2–3 tbsp sugar
salt and ground black pepper

1 Using a mortar and pestle or food processor, grind the shallots, garlic, chillies and galangal to a coarse paste. Mix the flour with the ground turmeric and spread it on a flat surface. Roll the oxtail in the flour and set aside.

2 Heat the oil in a heavy pan or earthenware pot. Stir in the spice paste and cook until fragrant and golden. Add the oxtail joints and brown on all sides. Add the tomatoes, lemon grass stalks, lime leaves and tamarind juice. Add enough water to cover the oxtail, and bring it to the boil. Skim off any fat from the surface. Reduce the heat, put the lid on the pan and simmer the oxtail for 2 hours.

3 Stir in the sugar, season and continue to cook, uncovered, for a further 30–40 minutes, until the meat is very tender. Serve the stew hot, straight from the pan.

Venison with Lentils & Tomatoes

Venison curries well and tastes good in this simple dish. Serve it with pilau rice, naan bread or bhaturas.

Serves 4

60ml/4 tbsp corn oil
1 bay leaf
2 cloves
4 black peppercorns
1 medium onion, sliced
450g/1lb diced venison
2.5ml/½ tsp ground turmeric
7.5ml/1½ tsp chilli powder
5ml/1 tsp garam masala
5ml/1 tsp crushed coriander seeds
2.5cm/1in cinnamon stick
5ml/1 tsp crushed garlic
5ml/1 tsp grated fresh root ginger
7.5ml/1½ tsp salt
1.5 litres/2½ pints/6 cups water
50g/2oz/⅓ cup split red lentils
2 medium tomatoes, quartered
2 fresh green chillies, chopped
15ml/1 tbsp chopped fresh coriander (cilantro)

1 Heat the oil in a karahi, wok or deep pan. Lower the heat slightly and add the bay leaf, cloves, peppercorns and onion slices. Fry for about 5 minutes, or until the onions are golden brown, stirring occasionally. Add the diced venison, turmeric, chilli powder, garam masala, coriander seeds, cinnamon stick, garlic, ginger and most of the salt, and stir-fry for about 5 minutes over a medium heat.

2 Pour in 900ml/1½ pints/3½ cups of the water and cover the pan with a lid. Simmer over a low heat for about 35–40 minutes, or until the water has evaporated and the meat is tender.

3 Put the lentils into a pan with the remaining 600ml/1 pint/2½ cups water and boil for about 12–15 minutes, or until the water has almost evaporated and the lentils are soft enough to mash. If the lentils are too thick, add up to 150ml/¼ pint/⅔ cup more water to loosen the mixture.

4 When the meat is tender, stir-fry the mixture using a wooden spoon, until some free oil begins to appear on the sides of the pan. Add the cooked lentils to the venison and mix together well. Add the tomatoes, chillies and fresh coriander and serve.

oxtail in sauce Energy 386kcal/1611kJ; Protein 34.5g; Carbohydrate 11.3g, of which sugars 6.6g; Fat 22.6g, of which saturates 7.7g; Cholesterol 125mg; Calcium 31mg; Fibre 1.2g; Sodium 191mg.
venison w. lentils Energy 294kcal/1235kJ; Protein 30g; Carbohydrate 12.7g, of which sugars 3g; Fat 15g, of which saturates 2.7g; Cholesterol 56mg; Calcium 58mg; Fibre 2g; Sodium 78mg.

Parsnip, Aubergine & Cashew Biryani

Full of the flavours of India, this hearty supper dish is great for those chilly winter evenings.

Serves 4–6

1 small aubergine (eggplant), sliced
275g/10oz basmati rice
3 parsnips
3 onions
2 garlic cloves
2.5cm/1in piece fresh root ginger, peeled
about 60ml/4 tbsp vegetable oil
175g/6oz/1½ cups unsalted cashew nuts
40g/1½oz/3 tbsp sultanas (golden raisins)
1 red (bell) pepper, seeded and sliced
5ml/1 tsp ground cumin
5ml/1 tsp ground coriander
2.5ml/½ tsp chilli powder
120ml/4fl oz/½ cup natural (plain) yogurt
300ml/½ pint/1¼ cups vegetable stock
25g/1oz/2 tbsp butter
salt and ground black pepper
2 hard-boiled eggs, quartered, and sprigs of fresh coriander (cilantro), to garnish

1 Sprinkle the aubergine with salt and leave for 30 minutes. Rinse, pat dry and cut into bitesize pieces. Soak the rice in a bowl of cold water for 40 minutes. Peel and core the parsnips. Cut into 1cm/½in pieces. Process 1 onion, the garlic and ginger in a food processor. Add 30–45ml/2–3 tbsp water and process to a paste.

2 Finely slice the remaining onions. Heat 45ml/3 tbsp of the oil in a large flameproof casserole and fry the onions gently for 10–15 minutes until they are soft and deep golden brown. Remove and drain. Add 40g/1½oz of the cashew nuts to the pan and stir-fry for 2 minutes, checking that they do not burn. Add the sultanas and fry until they swell. Remove and drain on kitchen paper. Add the aubergine and pepper to the pan and stir-fry for 4–5 minutes. Drain on kitchen paper. Fry the parsnips for 4–5 minutes. Stir in the remaining cashew nuts and fry for 1 minute. Set aside.

3 Add the remaining 15ml/1 tbsp of oil to the pan. Add the onion paste. Cook, stirring, over moderate heat for 4–5 minutes, until the mixture turns golden. Stir in the cumin, coriander and chilli powder. Cook, stirring, for 1 minute, then reduce the heat and add the yogurt.

4 Bring the mixture slowly to the boil and stir in the stock, parsnips, aubergine and peppers. Season with salt and pepper, cover and simmer for 30–40 minutes, until the parsnips are tender, and then transfer to an ovenproof casserole.

5 Preheat the oven to 150°C/300°F/Gas 2. Drain the rice and add to 300ml/½ pint/1¼ cups salted boiling water. Cook gently for 5–6 minutes, until the rice is tender but slightly undercooked.

6 Drain the rice and pile it in a mound on top of the parsnips. Make a hole from the top to the base using the handle of a wooden spoon. Sprinkle the reserved fried onions, cashew nuts and sultanas over the rice and dot with butter. Cover with a double layer of foil, then secure in place with a lid. Cook in the oven for 35–40 minutes. Serve garnished with eggs and coriander.

Aubergine Curry

A simple and delicious way of cooking aubergines which retains their full flavour.

Serves 4

2 large aubergines (eggplants)
115g/4oz/1½ cups button (white) mushrooms
15ml/1 tbsp oil
2.5ml/½ tsp black mustard seeds
1 bunch spring onions (scallions), finely chopped
2 garlic cloves, crushed
1 fresh red chilli, finely chopped
2.5ml/½ tsp chilli powder
5ml/1 tsp ground cumin
5ml/1 tsp ground coriander
1.5ml/¼ tsp ground turmeric
5ml/1 tsp salt
400g/14oz can chopped tomatoes
15ml/1 tbsp chopped fresh coriander (cilantro), plus a sprig to garnish

1 Preheat the oven to 200°C/400°F/Gas 6. Wrap each aubergine in foil and bake for 1 hour or until soft. Unwrap and leave to cool.

2 Cut the button mushrooms in half, or in quarters if large, and set aside.

3 While the aubergines are baking, heat the oil in a heavy pan and fry the mustard seeds for 2 minutes until they begin to splutter.

4 Add the spring onions, mushrooms, garlic and chilli and fry for 5 minutes. Stir in the chilli powder, cumin, ground coriander, turmeric and salt and fry for 3–4 minutes.

5 Add the tomatoes and simmer for 5 minutes.

6 Cut each of the cooked aubergines in half lengthways and scoop out the soft flesh into a mixing bowl. Mash the flesh roughly with a fork.

7 Add the mashed aubergines and chopped fresh coriander to the pan. Bring to the boil and simmer for 5 minutes or until the sauce thickens. Serve garnished with a fresh coriander sprig.

parsnip biryani Energy 824kcal/3430kJ; Protein 19.7g; Carbohydrate 96.4g, of which sugars 26.4g; Fat 40.7g, of which saturates 9.4g; Cholesterol 14mg; Calcium 166mg; Fibre 9.1g; Sodium 207mg.
aubergine curry Energy 87kcal/363kJ; Protein 3.6g; Carbohydrate 8.4g, of which sugars 5.5g; Fat 4.7g, of which saturates 0.7g; Cholesterol 0mg; Calcium 57mg; Fibre 4g; Sodium 19mg.

Aubergine & Pepper Tempura with Sweet Chilli Dip

These crunchy vegetables in a beautifully light batter are quick and easy to make and taste very good with the piquant dip.

Serves 4

2 aubergines (eggplants)
2 red (bell) peppers
vegetable oil, for deep-frying

For the tempura batter

250g/9oz/2¼ cups plain (all-purpose) flour
2 egg yolks
500ml/17fl oz/2¼ cups iced water
5ml/1 tsp salt

For the dip

150ml/¼ pint/⅔ cup water
10ml/2 tsp sugar
1 fresh red chilli, seeded and finely chopped
1 garlic clove, crushed
juice of ½ lime
5ml/1 tsp rice vinegar
35ml/2½ tbsp Thai fish sauce
½ small carrot, finely grated

1 Slice the aubergines into thin batons. Halve and seed the peppers and slice them thinly. Mix together all the dip ingredients in a bowl and stir until the sugar has dissolved. Cover with clear film (plastic wrap) and set aside.

2 Set aside 30ml/2 tbsp of the flour for the tempura. Put the egg yolks in a bowl and beat in the iced water. Add the rest of the flour with the salt and stir briefly together – the mixture should be lumpy and not properly mixed. If it is too thick, add a little more iced water. Use the batter immediately. Heat the oil in a karahi, wok or deep-fryer to a temperature of 190°C/375°F, or until a cube of bread dropped in the oil browns in about 45 seconds.

3 Dust a few aubergine batons and pepper slices with the reserved flour, then dip into the batter and drop into the hot oil, taking care as the oil will froth up. Make two or three more fritters. Cook for 3–4 minutes, until golden and crisp all over, then lift out with a slotted spoon. Drain on kitchen paper. Repeat with the remaining vegetables. Serve with the dip.

Aubergine & Sweet Potato Stew with Coconut Milk

Aubergines and sweet potatoes go well together and the coconut milk adds a mellow note.

Serves 6

400g/14oz baby aubergines (eggplants) or 2 standard aubergines
60ml/4 tbsp groundnut (peanut) oil
225g/8oz Thai red shallots or other small shallots or pickling onions
5ml/1 tsp fennel seeds, lightly crushed
4 or 5 garlic cloves, thinly sliced
25ml/1½ tbsp finely chopped fresh root ginger
475ml/16fl oz/2 cups vegetable stock
2 lemon grass stalks, outer layers discarded, finely chopped or minced (ground)
15g/½oz fresh coriander (cilantro), stalks and leaves chopped separately
3 kaffir lime leaves, lightly bruised
2 or 3 small fresh red chillies
45–60ml/3–4 tbsp Thai green curry paste
675g/1½lb sweet potatoes, peeled and cut into thick chunks
400ml/14fl oz/1⅔ cups coconut milk
2.5–5ml/½–1 tsp palm sugar (jaggery) or light muscovado (brown) sugar
250g/9oz/3½ cups mushrooms, thickly sliced
juice of 1 lime, to taste
salt and ground black pepper
boiled rice and 18 fresh Thai basil or ordinary basil leaves, to serve

1 Trim the aubergines. Slice baby aubergines in half lengthways. Cut standard aubergines into chunks.

2 Heat half the oil in a wide pan or deep, lidded frying pan. Add the aubergines and cook uncovered over medium heat, stirring occasionally, until lightly browned on all sides. Remove from the pan and set aside.

3 Slice four or five of the shallots. Cook the whole shallots in the oil remaining in the pan, adding a little more oil if necessary, until lightly browned. Set aside with the aubergines. Add the remaining oil to the pan and cook the sliced shallots, fennel seeds, garlic and ginger over a low heat for 5 minutes.

4 Pour in the vegetable stock, then add the lemon grass, chopped coriander stalks and any roots, lime leaves and whole chillies. Cover and simmer over a low heat for 5 minutes.

5 Stir in 30ml/2 tbsp of the curry paste and the sweet potatoes. Simmer gently for about 10 minutes, then return the aubergines and browned shallots to the pan and cook for a further 5 minutes.

6 Stir in the coconut milk and the sugar. Season to taste with salt and pepper, then stir in the mushrooms and simmer gently for 5 minutes, or until all the vegetables are cooked and tender. Stir in more curry paste and lime juice to taste, followed by the chopped coriander leaves. Adjust the seasoning, if necessary, and ladle the vegetables into warmed bowls. Sprinkle basil leaves over the stew and serve with rice.

tempura w. dip Energy 410kcal/1722kJ; Protein 9.1g; Carbohydrate 56.4g, of which sugars 8.3g; Fat 18.1g, of which saturates 2.7g; Cholesterol 101mg; Calcium 116mg; Fibre 5.4g; Sodium 12mg.
aubergine & sweet potato Energy 147kcal/627kJ; Protein 3.2g; Carbohydrate 29.1g, of which sugars 11.3g; Fat 3g, of which saturates 0.6g; Cholesterol 0mg; Calcium 72mg; Fibre 4.9g; Sodium 125mg.

Stuffed Aubergines in Seasoned Tamarind Juice

This spicy aubergine dish will add a refreshing tang to any meal.

Serves 4

12 baby aubergines (eggplants)
30ml/2 tbsp vegetable oil
1 small onion, chopped
10ml/2 tsp grated fresh root ginger
10ml/2 tsp crushed garlic
5ml/1 tsp coriander seeds
5ml/1 tsp cumin seeds
10ml/2 tsp white poppy seeds
10ml/2 tsp sesame seeds
10ml/2 tsp desiccated (dry unsweetened shredded) coconut
15ml/1 tbsp dry-roasted skinned peanuts
2.5–5ml/½–1 tsp chilli powder
5ml/1 tsp salt
6–8 curry leaves
1 or 2 dried red chillies, chopped
2.5ml/½ tsp concentrated tamarind paste

1 Make three deep slits lengthways on each aubergine, without cutting through, then soak in salted water for 20 minutes. Drain and dry on kitchen paper.

2 Heat half the oil in a pan and sauté the onion for 3–4 minutes. Add the ginger and garlic and cook for 30 seconds. Add the coriander and cumin seeds and sauté for 30 seconds, then add the poppy seeds, sesame seeds and coconut. Sauté for 1 minute, stirring constantly. Leave to cool slightly, then grind the spices in a food processor, adding 105ml/7 tbsp warm water. The mixture should form a thick, slightly coarse paste.

3 Mix the peanuts, chilli powder and salt into the paste. Stuff the aubergine slits with the spice and reserve any remaining paste.

4 Heat the remaining oil in a karahi, wok or large pan over a medium heat and add the curry leaves and chillies. Let the chillies blacken, then add the aubergines and the tamarind blended with 105ml/7 tbsp hot water. Add any remaining spice paste and stir to mix. Cover the pan and simmer gently for 15–20 minutes or until the aubergines are tender. Serve with chapatis and a meat or poultry dish, if you like.

Herb & Chilli Aubergines

Plump and juicy aubergines taste sensational steamed until tender and then tossed in a fragrant mint and coriander dressing with crunchy water chestnuts.

Serves 4

500g/1¼lb firm baby aubergines (eggplants)
30ml/2 tbsp vegetable oil
6 garlic cloves, very finely chopped
15ml/1 tbsp fresh root ginger, very finely chopped
8 spring onions (scallions), cut diagonally into 2.5cm/1in lengths
2 fresh red chillies, seeded and thinly sliced
45ml/3 tbsp light soy sauce
15ml/1 tbsp Chinese rice wine
15ml/1 tbsp golden caster (superfine) sugar
a large handful of mint leaves
30–45ml/2–3 tbsp roughly chopped coriander (cilantro) leaves
8 drained canned water chestnuts
50g/2oz/½ cup roasted peanuts, roughly chopped
steamed egg noodles or rice, to serve

1 Cut the aubergines in half lengthways and place them on a heatproof plate. Fit a steamer rack in a wok and add 5cm/2in of water. Bring the water to the boil, lower the plate on to the rack and reduce the heat to low.

2 Cover the plate and steam the aubergines for 25–30 minutes, until they are cooked through. Remove the plate from on top of the steamer and set the aubergines aside to cool.

3 Heat the oil in a clean, dry wok and place over a medium heat. When hot, add the garlic, ginger, spring onions and chillies and stir-fry for 2–3 minutes. Remove from the heat and stir in the soy sauce, rice wine and sugar.

4 Add the mint leaves, chopped coriander, water chestnuts and peanuts to the cooled aubergine and toss.

5 Pour the garlic-ginger mixture evenly over the vegetables, toss gently and serve with steamed egg noodles or rice.

stuffed aubergines Energy 141kcal/585kJ; Protein 2.1g; Carbohydrate 5.1g, of which sugars 3.5g; Fat 12g, of which saturates 1.7g; Cholesterol 0mg; Calcium 43mg; Fibre 3.3g; Sodium 14mg.
chilli aubergines Energy 177kcal/739kJ; Protein 6.2g; Carbohydrate 12.1g, of which sugars 9g; Fat 12g, of which saturates 1.9g; Cholesterol 0mg; Calcium 46mg; Fibre 4.4g; Sodium 823mg.

Mushroom Curry

This is a delicious way of cooking mushrooms. It goes well with meat dishes, but is also great served on its own.

Serves 4

30ml/2 tbsp oil
2.5ml/½ tsp cumin seeds
1.5ml/¼ tsp black peppercorns
4 green cardamom pods
1.5ml/¼ tsp ground turmeric
1 onion, finely chopped
5ml/1 tsp ground cumin
5ml/1 tsp ground coriander
2.5ml/½ tsp garam masala
1 fresh green chilli, finely chopped
2 garlic cloves, crushed
2.5cm/1in piece fresh root ginger, grated
400g/14oz can chopped tomatoes
1.5ml/¼ tsp salt
450g/1lb/6 cups button (white) mushrooms, halved
chopped fresh coriander (cilantro), to garnish

1 Heat the oil in a large, heavy pan and fry the cumin seeds, peppercorns, cardamom pods and turmeric for 2–3 minutes.

2 Add the onion and fry for about 5 minutes until golden. Stir in the cumin, ground coriander and garam masala and fry for a further 2 minutes.

3 Add the chilli, garlic and ginger and fry for 2–3 minutes, stirring all the time to prevent the spices from sticking to the pan. Add the tomatoes and salt. Bring to the boil and simmer for 5 minutes.

4 Add the mushrooms. Cover and simmer over a low heat for 10 minutes. Garnish with chopped coriander before serving.

Cook's Tip
The distinctive flavour of mushrooms goes well with this mixture of spices. If you don't want to use button (white) mushrooms, you can substitute any other mushrooms. Dried mushrooms can be added, if you like. Their intense flavour holds its own against the taste of the curry spices. Soak dried mushrooms before using, and add them to the recipe with the tomatoes.

Cauliflower & Coconut Milk Curry

A delicious vegetable stew which combines rich coconut milk with spices and is perfect as a vegetarian main course or as part of a buffet.

Serves 4

1 cauliflower
2 medium tomatoes
1 onion, chopped
2 garlic cloves, crushed
1 fresh green chilli, seeded
2.5ml/½ tsp ground turmeric
30ml/2 tbsp sunflower oil
400ml/14fl oz/1⅔ cups coconut milk
250ml/8fl oz/1 cup water
5ml/1 tsp sugar
5ml/1 tsp tamarind pulp, soaked in 45ml/3 tbsp warm water
salt

1 Trim the stalk from the cauliflower and divide into tiny florets. Peel the tomatoes, if you like, then chop them into 1–2.5cm/½–1in pieces.

2 Grind the chopped onion, garlic, green chilli and ground turmeric to a paste in a food processor.

3 Heat the oil in a karahi, wok or large frying pan and fry the spice paste to bring out the aromatic flavours, without allowing it to brown.

4 Add the cauliflower florets and toss well to coat in the spices. Stir in the coconut milk, water, sugar and salt to taste. Simmer for 5 minutes. Strain the tamarind and reserve the juice.

5 Add the tamarind juice and chopped tomatoes to the pan, then cook for 2–3 minutes only. Taste and adjust the seasoning if necessary, then serve.

Cook's Tip
Always be careful when preparing chillies as they can burn sensitive skin. Wear plastic gloves or wash hands thoroughly after preparation.

mushroom curry Energy 110kcal/459kJ; Protein 4.2g; Carbohydrate 7.1g, of which sugars 3.3g; Fat 7.7g, of which saturates 1.1g; Cholesterol 0mg; Calcium 32mg; Fibre 2.2g; Sodium 18mg.
cauliflower curry Energy 119kcal/495kJ; Protein 3.6g; Carbohydrate 11.5g, of which sugars 5.5g; Fat 6.7g, of which saturates 1.1g; Cholesterol 97mg; Calcium 111mg; Fibre 2.3g; Sodium 13mg.

Mushroom & Okra Curry

The sliced okra not only flavours this unusual curry, but thickens it, too.

Serves 4

4 garlic cloves, roughly chopped
2.5cm/1in piece fresh root ginger, roughly chopped
1 or 2 fresh red chillies, seeded and chopped
175ml/6fl oz/¾ cup cold water
15ml/1 tbsp sunflower oil
5ml/1 tsp coriander seeds
5ml/1 tsp cumin seeds
5ml/1 tsp ground cumin
seeds from 2 green cardamom pods, ground
pinch of ground turmeric
400g/14oz can chopped tomatoes
450g/1lb/6 cups mushrooms, quartered if large
225g/8oz okra, trimmed and sliced
30ml/2 tbsp chopped fresh coriander (cilantro)
basmati rice, to serve

For the mango relish
1 large ripe mango, about 500g/1¼lb
1 small garlic clove, crushed
1 small onion, finely chopped
10ml/2 tsp grated fresh root ginger
1 fresh red chilli, seeded and finely chopped
a pinch each of salt and sugar

1 To make the mango relish, peel the mango, cut the flesh off the stone and chop it finely. Put it in a bowl. Mash with a fork and mix in the garlic, onion, ginger, chilli, salt and sugar. Set aside.

2 Put the garlic, ginger, chillies and 45ml/3 tbsp of the water in a blender or food processor and blend to a smooth paste.

3 Heat the oil in a large pan. Add the coriander and cumin seeds, and the ground cumin, ground cardamom and turmeric, and cook for 1 minute, until aromatic. Scrape in the garlic paste, then add the tomatoes, mushrooms and okra. Pour in the remaining water. Stir to mix well, and bring to the boil. Reduce the heat, cover and simmer the curry for 5 minutes.

4 Remove the lid, increase the heat slightly and cook for 5–10 minutes more, until the okra is tender. Stir in the fresh coriander and serve with the rice and the mango relish.

Mushrooms, Peas & Tofu

Tofu has become an extremely popular vegetarian protein and has a particularly delicious texture when fried, as in this substantial recipe.

Serves 4–6

75ml/6 tbsp ghee or vegetable oil
225g/8oz firm tofu, cubed
1 onion, finely chopped
a few fresh mint leaves, chopped
50g/2oz/2 cups fresh coriander (cilantro), chopped
3 fresh green chillies, chopped
3 garlic cloves, roughly chopped
2.5cm/1in piece fresh root ginger, sliced
5ml/1 tsp ground turmeric
5ml/1 tsp garam masala
salt
225g/8oz/3 cups tiny button (white) mushrooms
225g/8oz/2 cups frozen peas, thawed and drained
175ml/6fl oz/¾ cup natural (plain) yogurt, mixed with 5ml/1 tsp cornflour (cornstarch)
fresh mint sprig, to garnish

1 Heat the ghee or vegetable oil in a frying pan and fry the tofu cubes until they are golden brown on all sides. Remove and drain on kitchen paper.

2 Grind the onion, mint, coriander, chillies, garlic and ginger in a mortar and pestle or food processor to a fairly smooth paste. Remove and mix in the turmeric, garam masala and salt.

3 Remove the excess ghee or oil from the pan, leaving about 15ml/1 tbsp. Heat and fry the paste until the raw onion smell disappears and the oil separates.

4 Add the mushrooms, peas and tofu. Mix together well. Cool the mixture and gradually fold in the yogurt. Simmer for about 10 minutes. Garnish with a sprig of mint and serve hot.

mushroom & okra Energy 152kcal/645kJ; Protein 5.9g; Carbohydrate 24.2g, of which sugars 22.7g; Fat 4.4g, of which saturates 0.7g; Cholesterol 0mg; Calcium 143mg; Fibre 8g; Sodium 55mg.
mushroom & tofu Energy 294kcal/1217kJ; Protein 14.4g; Carbohydrate 14g, of which sugars 7.3g; Fat 20.3g, of which saturates 3.7g; Cholesterol 10mg; Calcium 174mg; Fibre 3.5g; Sodium 210mg.

Okra with Green Mango & Lentils

If you like okra, you'll love this spicy tangy dish. Serve with rice for a main course.

Serves 4

115g/4oz/½ cup toor dhal or yellow split peas
450g/1lb okra
15ml/1 tbsp oil
2.5ml/½ tsp onion seeds
2 onions, sliced
2.5ml/½ tsp ground fenugreek
1.5ml/¼ tsp ground turmeric
5ml/1 tsp ground coriander
7.5ml/1½ tsp chilli powder
5ml/1 tsp grated fresh root ginger
5ml/1 tsp crushed garlic
1 green mango, peeled and sliced
7.5ml/1½ tsp salt
2 red chillies, seeded and sliced
30ml/2 tbsp chopped fresh coriander (cilantro)
1 tomato, sliced

1 Wash the toor dhal thoroughly to remove any grit and place in a large pan with enough cold water to cover. Bring to the boil and cook for 30–45 minutes until soft but not mushy.

2 Trim the okra and cut the pods into 1cm/½in pieces.

3 Heat the oil in a karahi, wok or heavy pan and fry the onion seeds until they begin to pop. Add the onions and fry until golden brown. Lower the heat and stir in the ground fenugreek, turmeric and coriander, and the chilli powder, ginger and garlic.

4 Add the mango slices and the okra pieces. Stir well and then add the salt, red chillies and fresh coriander. Stir-fry together for 3–4 minutes or until the okra is well cooked and tender.

5 Finally, add the cooked dhal and sliced tomato, and cook for a further 3 minutes. Serve hot.

Cook's Tip
When buying okra, always choose small, bright-green ones with no brown patches. If cooking whole, trim off the conical cap, taking care not to pierce through to the seed pod where there are tiny edible seeds and a sticky juice.

Corn & Pea Curry

Tender corn cooked in a spicy tomato sauce makes a flavoursome curry. It is perfect served with chapatis.

Serves 4

6 frozen corn cobs, thawed
15ml/1 tbsp oil
2.5ml/½ tsp cumin seeds
1 onion, finely chopped
2 garlic cloves, crushed
1 fresh green chilli, finely chopped
15ml/1 tbsp curry paste
5ml/1 tsp ground coriander
5ml/1 tsp ground cumin
1.5ml/¼ tsp ground turmeric
2.5ml/½ tsp salt
2.5ml/½ tsp sugar
400g/14oz can chopped tomatoes
15ml/1 tbsp tomato purée (paste)
150ml/¼ pint/⅔ cup water
115g/4oz/1 cup frozen peas, thawed
30ml/2 tbsp chopped fresh coriander (cilantro)
chapatis, to serve (optional)

1 Using a sharp knife, cut each piece of corn in half crossways to make 12 equal pieces in total.

2 Bring a large pan of water to the boil and cook the corn cob pieces for 10–12 minutes. Drain well.

3 Heat the oil in a large, heavy pan and fry the cumin seeds for 2 minutes or until they begin to splutter. Add the onion, garlic and chilli and fry for about 5–6 minutes until the onion is golden.

4 Add the curry paste and fry for 2 minutes. Stir in the remaining spices, the salt and sugar, and fry for a further 2–3 minutes, adding some water if the mixture is too dry.

5 Add the chopped tomatoes and tomato purée together with the water and simmer for 5 minutes or until the sauce thickens. Add the peas and cook for a further 5 minutes.

6 Stir in the pieces of corn and the fresh coriander and cook for 6–8 minutes more, until the corn and peas are tender. Serve with chapatis for mopping up the rich sauce, if you like.

okra w. lentils Energy 253kcal/1063kJ; Protein 11.3g; Carbohydrate 31.6g, of which sugars 13.7g; Fat 10.1g, of which saturates 1.4g; Cholesterol 0mg; Calcium 220mg; Fibre 8.2g; Sodium 25mg.
corn & pea curry Energy 260kcal/1090kJ; Protein 8.6g; Carbohydrate 29.8g, of which sugars 7.1g; Fat 12.9g, of which saturates 1.7g; Cholesterol 0mg; Calcium 68mg; Fibre 5.6g; Sodium 46mg.

Sweet Pumpkin & Peanut Curry

A hearty, soothing curry that is perfect for autumn or winter evenings. Its cheerful colour alone will brighten you up – and it tastes terrific.

Serves 4

30ml/2 tbsp vegetable oil
4 garlic cloves, crushed
4 shallots, finely chopped
30ml/2 tbsp yellow curry paste
600ml/1 pint/2½ cups vegetable stock
2 kaffir lime leaves, torn
15ml/1 tbsp chopped fresh galangal
450g/1lb pumpkin, peeled, seeded and diced
225g/8oz sweet potatoes, diced
90g/3½oz/scant 1 cup peanuts, roasted and chopped
300ml/½ pint/1¼ cups coconut milk
90g/3½oz/1½ cups chestnut mushrooms, sliced
15ml/1 tbsp soy sauce
30ml/2 tbsp Thai fish sauce
50g/2oz/⅓ cup pumpkin seeds, toasted, and fresh green chilli flowers, to garnish

1 Heat the oil in a large pan. Add the garlic and shallots and cook over a medium heat, stirring occasionally, for 10 minutes, until softened and golden. Do not let them burn.

2 Add the yellow curry paste and stir-fry over a medium heat for 30 seconds, until fragrant, then add the stock, lime leaves, galangal, pumpkin and sweet potatoes. Bring to the boil, stirring frequently, then reduce the heat to low and simmer gently for 15 minutes.

3 Add the peanuts, coconut milk and mushrooms. Stir in the soy sauce and fish sauce and simmer for 5 minutes more. Spoon into warmed individual serving bowls, garnish with the pumpkin seeds and chillies and serve.

Cook's Tip
The well-drained vegetables from any of these curries would make a very tasty filling for a pastry or pie. This may not be an Eastern tradition, but it is a good example of fusion food.

Stuffed Onions, Potatoes & Courgettes

The vegetarian filling of these vegetables is tomato-red, mildly-spiced and accented with the tart taste of lemon. They are delicious cold and are good served as an appetizer as well as a main course.

Serves 4

4 potatoes, peeled
4 onions, skinned
4 courgettes (zucchini), halved widthways
2–4 garlic cloves, chopped
45–60ml/3–4 tbsp olive oil
45–60ml/3–4 tbsp tomato purée (paste)
1.5ml/¼ tsp curry powder
large pinch of ground allspice
seeds of 2–3 cardamom pods
juice of ½ lemon
30–45ml/2–3 tbsp chopped fresh parsley
90–120ml/6–8 tbsp vegetable stock
salt and ground black pepper
salad, to serve (optional)

1 Bring a large pan of salted water to the boil. Starting with the potatoes, then the onions and finally the courgettes, add to the boiling water and cook until they become almost tender but not cooked through. Allow about 10 minutes for the potatoes, 8 minutes for the onions and 4–6 minutes for the courgettes. Remove the vegetables from the pan and leave to cool.

2 When the vegetables are cool enough to handle, hollow them out. Preheat the oven to 190°C/375°F/Gas 5.

3 Finely chop the cut-out vegetable flesh and put in a bowl. Add the garlic, half the olive oil, the tomato purée, ras al hanout or curry powder, allspice, cardamom seeds, lemon juice, parsley, salt and pepper and mix well together. Use the stuffing mixture to fill the hollowed vegetables.

4 Arrange the stuffed vegetables in a baking tin (pan) and drizzle with the stock and the remaining oil. Roast for 35–40 minutes, or until golden brown. Serve warm with a salad, if you like.

pumpkin & peanut Energy 306kcal/1279kJ; Protein 9.6g; Carbohydrate 24.5g, of which sugars 11.4g; Fat 19.6g, of which saturates 3.3g; Cholesterol 0mg; Calcium 160mg; Fibre 6.4g; Sodium 409mg.
stuffed vegetables Energy 201kcal/842kJ; Protein 5.5g; Carbohydrate 30.3g, of which sugars 5g; Fat 6, of which saturates 1.2g; Cholesterol 0mg; Calcium 72mg; Fibre 4.4g; Sodium 28mg.

Curried Stuffed Peppers

Hot, spicy and delicious, these fabulous peppers are a colourful addition to any meal.

Serves 4–6

15ml/1 tbsp sesame seeds
15ml/1 tbsp white poppy seeds
5ml/1 tsp coriander seeds
60ml/4 tbsp desiccated (dry unsweetened shredded) coconut
½ onion, sliced
2.5cm/1in piece fresh root ginger, sliced
4 garlic cloves, sliced
handful of fresh coriander (cilantro)
6 fresh green chillies
60ml/4 tbsp vegetable oil
2 potatoes, boiled and coarsely mashed
salt
2 each green, red and yellow (bell) peppers
30ml/2 tbsp sesame oil
5ml/1 tsp cumin seeds
60ml/4 tbsp tamarind juice

1 In a frying pan, dry-fry the sesame, poppy and coriander seeds, then add the coconut and continue to roast until the coconut turns golden brown. Add the onion, ginger, garlic, coriander, and two of the chillies, and roast for a further 5 minutes. Cool, and grind to a paste using a mortar and pestle or food processor. Set aside.

2 Heat 30ml/2 tbsp of the oil in a frying pan and fry the ground paste for 4–5 minutes. Add the potatoes and salt, and stir well until the spices have blended evenly into the potatoes.

3 Trim the bases of the peppers so that they stand, then slice off the tops and reserve. Remove the seeds and any white pith. Fill the peppers with equal amounts of the potato mixture and replace the tops.

4 Slit the remaining chillies and remove the seeds, if you like. Heat the sesame oil and remaining vegetable oil in a frying pan and fry the cumin seeds and the slit green chillies. When the chillies turn white, add the tamarind juice and bring to the boil. Place the peppers over the mixture, cover the pan and cook until the peppers are just tender. Serve immediately.

Stuffed Sweet Peppers

This is an unusual recipe where the stuffed peppers are steamed rather than baked, but the result is beautifully light and tender. The filling incorporates typical Thai ingredients such as red curry paste and fish sauce. Kaffir lime leaves also add a delicate citrus flavour.

Serves 4

3 garlic cloves
2 coriander (cilantro) roots
400g/14oz/3 cups mushrooms, quartered
5ml/1 tsp Thai red curry paste
1 egg, lightly beaten
15ml/1 tbsp Thai fish sauce
15ml/1 tbsp light soy sauce
2.5ml/½ tsp sugar
3 kaffir lime leaves, finely chopped
4 yellow (bell) peppers, halved lengthways and seeded

1 Finely chop the garlic cloves and coriander roots. In a mortar or spice grinder pound or blend the garlic with the coriander roots. Scrape into a bowl.

2 Put the mushrooms in a food processor and pulse briefly until they are finely chopped.

3 Add to the garlic mixture, then stir in the Thai red curry paste, beaten egg and Thai fish sauce. Add the soy sauce, sugar and lime leaves.

4 Place the pepper halves in a single layer in a steamer basket. Spoon the mixture loosely into the pepper halves. Do not pack the mixture down tightly or the filling will dry out too much.

5 Bring the water in the steamer to the boil, then lower the heat to a simmer. Steam the peppers for 15 minutes, or until the flesh is tender. Serve hot.

Variation
Use red or orange (bell) peppers rather than yellow, if you prefer, or a combination of the two.

curried peppers Energy 257kcal/1065kJ; Protein 3.3g; Carbohydrate 18.6g, of which sugars 8.2g; Fat 19.3g, of which saturates 7.1g; Cholesterol 0mg; Calcium 34mg; Fibre 4g; Sodium 15mg.
stuffed sweet peppers Energy 95kcal/399kJ; Protein 5.6g; Carbohydrate 12.8g, of which sugars 12g; Fat 2.8g, of which saturates 0.7g; Cholesterol 48mg; Calcium 53mg; Fibre 4.5g; Sodium 301mg.

Spinach & Potato Curry

Spinach, potatoes and traditional Indian spices are the main ingredients in this simple but authentic curry.

Serves 4

450g/1lb spinach
15ml/1 tbsp oil
5ml/1 tsp black mustard seeds
1 onion, thinly sliced
2 garlic cloves, crushed
2.5cm/1in piece fresh root ginger, finely chopped
675g/1½lb potatoes, cut into 2.5cm/1in chunks
5ml/1 tsp chilli powder
5ml/1 tsp salt
120ml/4fl oz/½ cup water

1 Wash and trim the spinach, then blanch it in a pan of boiling water for about 3–4 minutes.

2 Drain the spinach thoroughly and set aside. When it is cool enough to handle, use your hands to squeeze out any remaining liquid (see Cook's Tips) and set aside.

3 Heat the oil in a large, heavy pan and fry the mustard seeds for 2 minutes or until they splutter.

4 Add the sliced onion, garlic cloves and chopped ginger to the mustard seeds and fry for 5 minutes, stirring.

5 Add the potato chunks, chilli powder, salt and water, and cook for a further 8 minutes.

6 Add the drained spinach. Cover the pan with a lid and simmer for 10–15 minutes or until the potatoes are tender. Serve hot.

Cook's Tips

- *To make certain that the spinach is completely dry, put it in a clean dish towel, roll up tightly and squeeze gently to remove any excess liquid.*
- *Use a waxy variety of potato for this dish so that the pieces do not break up during cooking.*

Spicy Potato & Tomato Curry

Diced potatoes are cooked gently in a fresh tomato sauce, which is flavoured with curry leaves, green chillies and ginger.

Serves 4

2 medium potatoes
15ml/1 tbsp oil
2 medium onions, finely chopped
4 curry leaves
1.5ml/¼ tsp onion seeds
1 fresh green chilli, seeded and chopped
4 tomatoes, sliced
5ml/1 tsp grated fresh root ginger
5ml/1 tsp crushed garlic
5ml/1 tsp chilli powder
5ml/1 tsp ground coriander
1.5ml/¼ tsp salt
5ml/1 tsp lemon juice
15ml/1 tbsp chopped fresh coriander (cilantro)
3 hard-boiled eggs, to garnish

1 Peel the potatoes and cut them into small cubes.

2 Heat the oil in a karahi, wok or heavy pan and stir-fry the onions, curry leaves, onion seeds and green chilli for about 40 seconds.

3 Add the tomatoes and cook for about 2 minutes over a low heat.

4 Add the ginger and garlic, chilli powder, ground coriander and salt to taste. Continue to stir-fry for 1–2 minutes, then add the potatoes and cook over a low heat for 5–7 minutes until the potatoes are tender.

5 Add the lemon juice and fresh coriander and stir to mix together.

6 Shell the hard-boiled eggs, cut into quarters, and add as a garnish to the finished dish.

Cook's Tip

Use vine-ripened tomatoes, if possible, for the best flavour. Locally grown tomatoes in season are also more likely to have a fuller flavour than those bought out of season.

spinach & potato Energy 180kcal/758kJ; Protein 6.4g; Carbohydrate 30.6g, of which sugars 4.7g; Fat 4.4g, of which saturates 0.6g; Cholesterol 0mg; Calcium 208mg; Fibre 4.3g; Sodium 668mg.
potato & tomato Energy 161kcal/676kJ; Protein 4.4g; Carbohydrate 27.8g, of which sugars 8.6g; Fat 4.5g, of which saturates 0.7g; Cholesterol 0mg; Calcium 45mg; Fibre 3.1g; Sodium 25mg.

Courgette Curry with Tomatoes

Thickly sliced courgettes are combined with authentic Indian spices for a tasty vegetable curry.

Serves 4

675g/1½lb courgettes (zucchini)
30ml/2 tbsp oil
2.5ml/½ tsp cumin seeds
2.5ml/½ tsp mustard seeds
1 onion, thinly sliced
2 garlic cloves, crushed
1.5ml/¼ tsp ground turmeric
1.5ml/¼ tsp chilli powder
5ml/1 tsp ground coriander
5ml/1 tsp ground cumin
2.5ml/½ tsp salt
15ml/1 tbsp tomato purée (paste)
400g/14oz can chopped tomatoes
150ml/¼ pint/⅔ cup water
15ml/1 tbsp chopped fresh coriander (cilantro)
5ml/1 tsp garam masala
rice or naan bread, to serve

1 Trim the ends from the courgettes and then cut them evenly into 1cm/½in thick slices.

2 Heat the oil in a large, heavy pan and fry the cumin and the mustard seeds for 2 minutes until they begin to splutter.

3 Add the sliced onion and crushed garlic to the seeds in the pan, and fry for about 5–6 minutes.

4 Add the turmeric, chilli powder, ground coriander, cumin and salt, and fry for 2–3 minutes.

5 Add the sliced courgettes all at once, and cook for 5 minutes, stirring so that they do not burn.

6 Mix together the tomato purée and chopped tomatoes and add to the pan with the water. Cover and simmer for 10 minutes until the sauce thickens.

7 Stir in the fresh coriander and garam masala, then cook for 5 minutes or until the courgettes are tender. Serve the curry with rice or naan bread.

Potatoes with Spicy Cottage Cheese

This makes an excellent low-fat lunch for any day of the week.

Serves 4

4 medium baking potatoes
225g/8oz/1 cup low-fat cottage cheese
10ml/2 tsp tomato purée (paste)
2.5ml/½ tsp ground cumin
2.5ml/½ tsp ground coriander
2.5ml/½ tsp chilli powder
2.5ml/½ tsp salt
15ml/1 tbsp oil
2.5ml/½ tsp mixed onion and mustard seeds
3 curry leaves
30ml/2 tbsp water

For the garnish

mixed salad leaves
fresh coriander (cilantro) sprigs
lemon wedges
2 tomatoes, quartered

1 Preheat the oven to 180°C/350°F/Gas 4. Wash each potato and pat dry. Make a slit in the middle of each potato. Prick the potatoes a few times with a fork or skewer, then wrap them individually in foil. Bake in the oven directly on the shelf for about 1 hour, or until soft. Put the cottage cheese into a heatproof dish and set aside.

2 In a separate bowl, mix the tomato purée, ground cumin, ground coriander, chilli powder and salt.

3 Heat the oil in a small pan for about 1 minute. Add the mixed onion and mustard seeds and the curry leaves. When the curry leaves turn a shade darker, pour the tomato purée mixture into the pan and turn the heat immediately to low. Add the water and mix well. Cook for a further minute, then pour the spicy tomato mixture on to the cottage cheese and stir together well.

4 Check that the baked potatoes are cooked right through, by inserting a knife or skewer into the middle of the flesh. If it is soft, unwrap the potatoes from the foil and divide the cottage cheese equally between them.

5 Garnish the filled potatoes with mixed salad leaves, coriander sprigs, lemon wedges and tomato quarters and serve hot.

courgette curry Energy 133kcal/552kJ; Protein 5.8g; Carbohydrate 10.5g, of which sugars 6.8g; Fat 8g, of which saturates 1.1g; Cholesterol 0mg; Calcium 94mg; Fibre 3.3g; Sodium 27mg.
potatoes w. cheese Energy 196kcal/827kJ; Protein 11.2g; Carbohydrate 28.6g, of which sugars 3.8g; Fat 5g, of which saturates 1.2g; Cholesterol 3mg; Calcium 94mg; Fibre 1.5g; Sodium 188mg.

Spicy Root Vegetable Gratin

Subtly spiced, this rich gratin is a substantial lunch or supper dish.

Serves 4

2 large potatoes, total weight about 450g/1lb
2 sweet potatoes, total weight about 275g/10oz
175g/6oz celeriac
15ml/1 tbsp unsalted (sweet) butter
5ml/1 tsp curry powder
5ml/1 tsp ground turmeric
2.5ml/½ tsp ground coriander
5ml/1 tsp mild chilli powder
3 shallots, chopped
150ml/¼ pint/⅔ cup single (light) cream
150ml/¼ pint/⅔ cup milk
salt and ground black pepper
chopped fresh flat leaf parsley, to garnish

1 Peel the potatoes, sweet potatoes and celeriac and cut into thin, even slices using a sharp knife or the slicing attachment on a food processor. Immediately place the vegetables in a bowl of cold water to prevent them from discolouring.

2 Preheat the oven to 180°C/350°F/Gas 4. Heat half the butter in a heavy pan, add the curry powder, ground turmeric and coriander and half the chilli powder. Cook for 2 minutes, then leave to cool slightly. Drain the vegetables, then pat them dry with kitchen paper. Place in a bowl, add the spice mixture and the shallots, and mix well.

3 Arrange the vegetables in a shallow baking dish, seasoning well with salt and pepper between the layers. Mix the cream and milk together, pour the mixture over the vegetables, then sprinkle the remaining chilli powder on top.

4 Cover the dish with baking parchment and bake for 45 minutes. Remove the baking parchment, dot the vegetables with the remaining butter and bake for a further 50 minutes, or until the top is golden brown. Serve the gratin garnished with chopped parsley.

Stuffed Baby Vegetables

The combination of potatoes and aubergines is popular in Indian cooking.

Serves 4

12 small potatoes
8 baby aubergines (eggplants)

For the stuffing

15ml/1 tbsp sesame seeds
30ml/2 tbsp ground coriander
30ml/2 tbsp ground cumin
2.5ml/½ tsp salt
1.5ml/¼ tsp chilli powder
2.5ml/½ tsp ground turmeric
10ml/2 tsp granulated sugar
1.5ml/¼ tsp garam masala
15ml/1 tbsp gram flour
2 garlic cloves, crushed
15ml/1 tbsp lemon juice
30ml/2 tbsp chopped fresh coriander (cilantro)

For the sauce

15ml/1 tbsp oil
2.5ml/½ tsp black mustard seeds
400g/14oz can chopped tomatoes
30ml/2 tbsp chopped fresh coriander
150ml/¼ pint/⅔ cup water

1 Preheat the oven to 200°C/400°F/Gas 6. Make deep slits in the potatoes and aubergines to hold the stuffing, ensuring that you do not cut right through.

2 Mix all the ingredients for the stuffing together on a plate.

3 Carefully spoon the spicy stuffing mixture into each of the slits in the potatoes and aubergines.

4 Arrange the stuffed potatoes and aubergines in a greased ovenproof dish, filling side up.

5 For the sauce, heat the oil in a heavy pan and fry the mustard seeds for 2 minutes until they begin to splutter, then add the canned tomatoes, chopped coriander and any leftover stuffing. Stir in the water. Bring to the boil and simmer for 5 minutes until the sauce thickens.

6 Pour the sauce over the potatoes and aubergines. Cover and bake in the oven for 25–30 minutes until the potatoes and aubergines are soft.

vegetable gratin Energy 268kcal/1129kJ; Protein 5.8g; Carbohydrate 37.7g, of which sugars 9.8g; Fat 11.6g, of which saturates 7.1g; Cholesterol 31mg; Calcium 127mg; Fibre 3.6g; Sodium 117mg.
stuffed vegetables Energy 222kcal/938kJ; Protein 6.5g; Carbohydrate 35.3g, of which sugars 6.6g; Fat 7.3g, of which saturates 1.2g; Cholesterol 0mg; Calcium 72mg; Fibre 4.4g; Sodium 31mg.

Mixed Vegetable Curry

You can use any combination of vegetables that are in season for this basic recipe.

Serves 4

15ml/1 tbsp oil
2.5ml/½ tsp black mustard seeds
2.5ml/½ tsp cumin seeds
1 onion, thinly sliced
2 curry leaves
1 fresh green chilli, finely chopped
2.5cm/1in piece fresh root ginger, finely chopped
30ml/2 tbsp curry paste
1 small cauliflower, broken into florets
1 large carrot, thickly sliced
115g/4oz green beans, cut into 2.5cm/1in lengths
1.5ml/¼ tsp ground turmeric
1.5ml/¼ tsp chilli powder
2.5ml/½ tsp salt
2 tomatoes, finely chopped
50g/2oz/½ cup frozen peas, thawed
150ml/¼ pint/⅔ cup vegetable stock
fresh curry leaves, to garnish

1 Heat the oil in a large, heavy pan and fry the mustard seeds and cumin seeds for 2 minutes until they begin to splutter. If they are very lively, put a lid on the pan.

2 Add the onion and the curry leaves and fry for 5 minutes.

3 Add the chopped chilli and fresh ginger and fry for 2 minutes. Stir in the curry paste, mix well and fry for 3–4 minutes.

4 Add the cauliflower florets, sliced carrot and beans, and cook for 4–5 minutes. Add the turmeric, chilli powder, salt and tomatoes and cook for 2–3 minutes.

5 Finally add the thawed peas and cook for a further 2–3 minutes. Pour in the stock. Cover and simmer over a low heat for 10–15 minutes until all the vegetables are tender. Serve garnished with curry leaves.

Variation
To turn this dish into a non-vegetarian main course, add some prawns (shrimp) or cubes of cooked chicken with the stock.

Vegetable Korma

Here the aim is to produce a subtle, aromatic curry rather than an assault on the senses.

Serves 4

50g/2oz/¼ cup butter
2 onions, sliced
2 garlic cloves, crushed
2.5cm/1in piece fresh root ginger, grated
5ml/1 tsp ground cumin
15ml/1 tbsp ground coriander
6 cardamom pods
5cm/2in piece of cinnamon stick
5ml/1 tsp ground turmeric
1 fresh red chilli, seeded and finely chopped
1 potato, peeled and cut into 2.5cm/1in cubes
1 small aubergine (eggplant), chopped
115g/4oz/1½ cups mushrooms, thickly sliced
175ml/6fl oz/¾ cup water
115g/4oz green beans, cut into 2.5cm/1in lengths
60ml/4 tbsp natural (plain) yogurt
150ml/¼ pint/⅔ cup double (heavy) cream
5ml/1 tsp garam masala
salt and ground black pepper
fresh coriander (cilantro) sprigs, to garnish
boiled rice and poppadums, to serve

1 Melt the butter in a heavy pan. Add the onions and cook for 5 minutes until soft. Add the garlic and ginger and cook for 2 minutes, then stir in the cumin, coriander, cardamom pods, cinnamon stick, turmeric and finely chopped chilli. Cook, stirring constantly, for 30 seconds.

2 Add the potato cubes, aubergine and mushrooms and the water. Cover the pan, bring to the boil, then lower the heat and simmer for 15 minutes.

3 Add the beans and cook, uncovered, for 5 minutes. With a slotted spoon, remove the vegetables to a warmed serving dish and keep hot.

4 Allow the cooking liquid to bubble up until it has reduced a little. Season with salt and pepper to taste, then stir in the yogurt, double cream and garam masala. Pour the sauce over the vegetables and garnish with fresh coriander. Serve with boiled rice and poppadums.

vegetable curry Energy 128kcal/532kJ; Protein 7.2g; Carbohydrate 13.5g, of which sugars 7.7g; Fat 5.5g, of which saturates 0.9g; Cholesterol 0mg; Calcium 66mg; Fibre 4.3g; Sodium 24mg.
korma Energy 381kcal/1577kJ; Protein 5.1g; Carbohydrate 20.9g, of which sugars 9.9g; Fat 31.4g, of which saturates 19.3g; Cholesterol 78mg; Calcium 95mg; Fibre 3.9g; Sodium 108mg.

Mixed Thai Vegetables in Coconut Milk

A most delicious way of cooking vegetables. If you don't like highly spiced food, use fewer red chilli peppers.

Serves 4–6

450g/1lb mixed vegetables, such as aubergines (eggplants), baby corn, carrots, snake beans and patty pan squash
8 red chillies, seeded
2 lemon grass stalks, chopped
4 kaffir lime leaves, torn
30ml/2 tbsp vegetable oil
250ml/8fl oz/1 cup coconut milk
30ml/2 tbsp fish sauce
salt
15–20 Thai basil leaves, to garnish

1 Cut the vegetables into similar-size shapes using a sharp knife.

2 Put the red chillies, lemon grass and kaffir lime leaves in a mortar and grind together with a pestle.

3 Heat the oil in a wok or large, deep frying pan. Add the chilli mixture and fry for 2–3 minutes.

4 Stir in the coconut milk and bring to the boil. Add the vegetables and cook for about 5 minutes or until they are tender. Season with the fish sauce and salt, and garnish with basil leaves.

Variation
For Broccoli and Courgettes in Coconut, steam or lightly boil 350g/12oz broccoli florets and 350g/12oz thickly sliced courgettes (zucchini). Stir-fry 15ml/1 tbsp black mustard seeds and 6 curry leaves for 1 minute and then add 225g/8oz sliced onion and 2 chopped fresh green chillies. Cook for 10 minutes until softened. Add 250ml/8fl oz/1 cup coconut milk and salt. Add a pinch of saffron threads and 30ml/2 tbsp fresh coriander (cilantro). Serve.

Mixed Vegetables in Coconut Sauce

A vegetable dish is an essential part of an Indian meal, even for a simple occasion, where one or two vegetable dishes may be served with a lentil dhal, a raita, and bread or boiled rice. There are many ways to make a vegetable curry, but this recipe, in which the vegetables are simmered in coconut milk, is typical of South India.

Serves 4

225g/8oz potatoes, cut into 5cm/2in cubes
115g/4oz green beans
150g/5oz carrots, scraped and cut into 5cm/2in cubes
500ml/17fl oz/2¼ cups hot water
1 small aubergine (eggplant), about 225g/8oz, quartered lengthways
75g/3oz coconut milk powder
5ml/1 tsp salt
30ml/2 tbsp vegetable oil
6–8 fresh or 8–10 dried curry leaves
1 or 2 dried red chillies, chopped into small pieces
5ml/1 tsp ground cumin
5ml/1 tsp ground coriander
2.5ml/½ tsp ground turmeric
Indian bread, to serve

1 Put the cubed potatoes, green beans and carrots in a large pan, add 300ml/½ pint/1¼ cups of the hot water and bring to the boil. Reduce the heat a little, cover the pan and continue to cook for 5 minutes.

2 Cut the aubergine quarters into 5cm/2in pieces. Rinse. Add to the pan.

3 Blend the coconut milk powder with the remaining hot water and add to the vegetables, with the salt. Bring to a slow simmer, cover and cook for 6–7 minutes.

4 In a small pan heat the oil over a medium heat and add the curry leaves and the dried red chillies. Immediately follow with the ground cumin, coriander and turmeric. Stir-fry the spices together for 15–20 seconds and pour the entire contents of the pan over the vegetables. Stir to distribute the spices evenly and remove the pan from the heat. Serve the mixed vegetables with any Indian bread.

mixed Thai vegetables Energy 59kcal/242kJ; Protein 1.7g; Carbohydrate 3.6g, of which sugars 3.5g; Fat 4.2g, of which saturates 0.6g; Cholesterol 0mg; Calcium 48mg; Fibre 1.1g; Sodium 49mg.
vegetables in coconut Energy 80kcal/335kJ; Protein 1.2g; Carbohydrate 5.6g, of which sugars 5.3g; Fat 6.1g, of which saturates 0.9g; Cholesterol 0mg; Calcium 29mg; Fibre 2.3g; Sodium 71mg.

Spiced Vegetables with Coconut

This spicy and substantial stir-fry could be served as an appetizer, or as a vegetarian main course for two. Eat it with spoons and forks, and provide hunks of Granary bread for mopping up the delicious coconut milk.

Serves 2–4

1 red chilli
2 large carrots
6 celery sticks
1 fennel bulb
30ml/2 tbsp grapeseed oil
2.5cm/1in fresh root ginger, grated
1 garlic clove, crushed
3 spring onions (scallions), sliced
400ml/14fl oz can coconut milk
15ml/1 tbsp chopped fresh coriander (cilantro)
salt and ground black pepper
fresh coriander sprigs, to garnish

1 Halve, seed and finely chop the chilli. If necessary, wear rubber gloves to protect your hands.

2 Thinly slice the carrots and the celery sticks on the diagonal. Trim the fennel bulb and slice roughly, using a sharp knife.

3 Heat the wok, then add the oil. When the oil is hot, add the chilli, fennel, carrots, celery, ginger, garlic and spring onions and stir-fry for 2 minutes.

4 Stir in the coconut milk with a large spoon and bring the mixture to the boil.

5 Stir in the coriander, and salt and pepper, and serve garnished with coriander sprigs.

Cook's Tip

When buying fennel, look for well-rounded bulbs; flatter ones are immature and will not have developed their full aniseed-like flavour. The bulbs should be white with overlapping ridged layers. Avoid any that look damaged or bruised. The fennel should be dry, but not desiccated.

Sweet & Sour Vegetables with Paneer

The cheese used in this recipe is Indian paneer, which can be bought at some Asian stores; tofu can be used in its place.

Serves 4

1 green (bell) pepper, seeded and cut into squares
1 yellow (bell) pepper, seeded and cut into squares
8 cherry tomatoes
8 cauliflower florets
8 pineapple chunks
8 cubes paneer
plain, boiled rice, to serve

For the seasoned oil

15ml/1 tbsp oil
30ml/2 tbsp lemon juice
5ml/1 tsp salt
5ml/1 tsp crushed black peppercorns
15ml/1 tbsp clear honey
30ml/2 tbsp chilli sauce

1 Preheat the grill (broiler) to hot. Thread the pepper squares, cherry tomatoes, cauliflower florets, pineapple chunks and paneer cubes on to four skewers, alternating the ingredients. Place the skewers on a flameproof dish or in a grill pan.

2 In a small bowl, combine all the ingredients for the seasoned oil. If too thick, add 15ml/1 tbsp water.

3 Brush the vegetables with the seasoned oil. Grill (broil) for about 10 minutes until the vegetables begin to darken slightly, turning the skewers regularly to cook evenly. Serve on a bed of plain boiled rice.

Cook's Tip

Metal skewers are ideal for this recipe. Some of the traditional Indian ones are very pretty, and will enhance the colour of the dish. Wooden or bamboo skewers can be used instead, but remember to soak them in water for at least 30 minutes before threading them with the vegetables and paneer, or the exposed tips may burn under the heat.

spiced vegetables Energy 59kcal/248kJ; Protein 2.2g; Carbohydrate 11.3g, of which sugars 10.9g; Fat 0.9g, of which saturates 0.3g; Cholesterol 0mg; Calcium 105mg; Fibre 4.8g; Sodium 175mg.
sweet & sour vegetables Energy 137kcal/576kJ; Protein 6g; Carbohydrate 18.7g, of which sugars 18.2g; Fat 4.7g, of which saturates 1.1g; Cholesterol 3mg; Calcium 58mg; Fibre 3.9g; Sodium 75mg.

Spiced Vegetable Curry with Yogurt

This is a very delicately spiced vegetable dish that is particularly appetizing when served with plain yogurt. It is also a good accompaniment to a main course of heavily spiced curries.

Serves 4–6

350g/12oz mixed vegetables, such as beans, peas, potatoes, cauliflower, carrots, cabbage, mangetouts (snow peas) and mushrooms
30ml/2 tbsp vegetable oil
5ml/1 tsp cumin seeds, freshly roasted
2.5ml/½ tsp mustard seeds
2.5ml/½ tsp onion seeds
5ml/1 tsp ground turmeric
2 garlic cloves, crushed
6–8 curry leaves
1 dried red chilli
salt
5ml/1 tsp granulated (white) sugar
150ml/¼ pint/⅔ cup natural (plain) yogurt mixed with 5ml/1 tsp cornflour (cornstarch)

1 Prepare all the vegetables you have chosen: string the beans; thaw the peas, if frozen; peel and cube the potatoes; cut the cauliflower into florets; dice the carrots; shred the cabbage; trim the mangetouts; wipe the mushrooms and leave whole.

2 Heat a large pan with enough water to cook all the vegetables and bring to the boil. First add the potatoes and carrots and cook until nearly tender, then add all the other vegetables and cook until crisp-tender. All the vegetables should be crunchy except the potatoes. Drain.

3 Heat the oil in a frying pan and fry the cumin, mustard and onion seeds, the turmeric, garlic, curry leaves and dried chilli gently until the garlic is golden brown and the chilli nearly burnt. Reduce the heat.

4 Fold in the drained vegetables, add the sugar and salt and gradually add the yogurt and cornflour mixture. Heat until piping hot, and serve immediately.

Vegetable Kashmiri

This is a wonderful vegetable curry, in which fresh mixed vegetables are cooked in a spicy aromatic yogurt sauce. The spicing is quite gentle, so it will appeal to most palates.

Serves 4

10ml/2 tsp cumin seeds
8 black peppercorns
seeds from 2 green cardamom pods
5cm/2in piece cinnamon stick
2.5ml/½ tsp grated nutmeg
30ml/2 tbsp oil
1 fresh green chilli, chopped
2.5cm/1in piece fresh root ginger, grated
5ml/1 tsp chilli powder
2.5ml/½ tsp salt
2 large potatoes, cut into 2.5cm/1in chunks
225g/8oz cauliflower, broken into florets
225g/8oz okra, trimmed and thickly sliced
150ml/¼ pint/⅔ cup natural (plain) low-fat yogurt
150ml/¼ pint/⅔ cup vegetable stock
toasted flaked (sliced) almonds and fresh coriander (cilantro) sprigs, to garnish

1 Grind the cumin seeds and peppercorns, cardamom seeds, cinnamon stick and nutmeg to a fine powder using a spice blender or a pestle and mortar.

2 Heat the oil in a large, heavy pan and fry the chilli and ginger for 2 minutes, stirring all the time.

3 Add the chilli powder, salt and ground spice mixture, and fry for about 2–3 minutes, stirring constantly to prevent the spices from sticking to the bottom of the pan.

4 Stir in the potatoes, cover and cook for 10 minutes over a low heat, stirring from time to time.

5 Add the cauliflower and okra and cook for 5 minutes.

6 Add the yogurt and stock. Bring to the boil, then reduce the heat. Cover and simmer for 20 minutes, or until all the vegetables are tender. Garnish with the toasted almonds and the coriander sprigs.

spiced vegetable curry Energy 81kcal/337kJ; Protein 2g; Carbohydrate 9g, of which sugars 7.1g; Fat 4.4g, of which saturates 0.7g; Cholesterol 0mg; Calcium 67mg; Fibre 1.4g; Sodium 37mg.
vegetable Kashmiri Energy 149kcal/630kJ; Protein 8.3g; Carbohydrate 24.9g, of which sugars 6.9g; Fat 2.7g, of which saturates 0.7g; Cholesterol 1mg; Calcium 193mg; Fibre 4.3g; Sodium 54mg.

Vegetable Biryani

This is a good-tempered dish made from everyday ingredients, and thus indispensable for the cook catering for an unexpected vegetarian guest.

Serves 4–6

175g/6oz/scant 1 cup long grain rice, rinsed
2 whole cloves
seeds from 2 cardamom pods
450ml/¾ pint/scant 2 cups vegetable stock
2 garlic cloves
1 small onion, roughly chopped
5ml/1 tsp cumin seeds
5ml/1 tsp ground coriander
2.5ml/½ tsp ground turmeric
2.5ml/½ tsp chilli powder
1 large potato, cut into 2.5cm/1in cubes
2 carrots, sliced
½ cauliflower, broken into florets
50g/2oz green beans, cut into 2.5cm/1in lengths
30ml/2 tbsp chopped fresh coriander (cilantro), plus extra to garnish
30ml/2 tbsp lime juice
salt and ground black pepper

1 Put the rice, cloves and cardamom seeds into a large, heavy pan. Pour over the stock and bring to the boil. Reduce the heat, cover the pan and simmer for 20 minutes or until all the stock has been absorbed.

2 Meanwhile, put the garlic cloves, onion, cumin seeds, ground coriander, turmeric, chilli powder and seasoning into a blender or food processor together with 30ml/2 tbsp water. Blend to a smooth paste. Scrape the paste into a large flameproof casserole.

3 Preheat the oven to 180°C/350°F/Gas 4. Cook the spicy paste in the casserole over a low heat for 2 minutes, stirring occasionally. Add the potato cubes, carrots, cauliflower, beans and 90ml/6 tbsp water. Cover and cook over a low heat for 12 minutes, stirring occasionally. Add the chopped fresh coriander.

4 Remove the cloves from the rice. Spoon the rice over the vegetables. Sprinkle with the lime juice. Cover and cook in the oven for 25 minutes or until the vegetables are tender. Fluff up the rice with a fork before serving, garnished with coriander.

Broad Bean & Cauliflower Curry

This is a hot and spicy vegetable curry, tasty when served with cooked rice (especially a brown basmati variety), a few poppadums and cucumber raita.

Serves 4

2 garlic cloves, chopped
2.5cm/1in piece fresh root ginger
1 fresh green chilli, seeded and chopped
30ml/2 tbsp oil
1 onion, sliced
1 large potato, chopped
15ml/1 tbsp curry powder, mild or hot
1 cauliflower, cut into small florets
600ml/1 pint/2½ cups vegetable stock
275g/10oz can broad (fava) beans
juice of ½ lemon (optional)
salt and ground black pepper
fresh coriander (cilantro) sprig, to garnish
plain rice, to serve

1 Blend the chopped garlic, ginger, chopped chilli and 15ml/1 tbsp of the oil in a food processor or blender until the mixture forms a smooth paste.

2 In a large, heavy pan, fry the sliced onion and chopped potato in the remaining oil for 5 minutes, then stir in the spice paste and curry powder. Cook for another minute.

3 Add the cauliflower florets to the onion and potato and stir well until they are thoroughly combined with the spicy mixture, then pour in the stock and bring to the boil over medium to high heat.

4 Season well, cover and simmer for 10 minutes. Add the beans with the liquid from the can and cook, uncovered, for a further 10 minutes.

5 Check the seasoning and adjust if necessary. Add a good squeeze of lemon juice, if you like, and serve hot, garnished with coriander and accompanied by plain boiled rice.

vegetable biryani Energy 260kcal/1089kJ; Protein 5.7g; Carbohydrate 50.4g, of which sugars 11.3g; Fat 4.1g, of which saturates 0.6g; Cholesterol 0mg; Calcium 49mg; Fibre 3g; Sodium 27mg.
broad bean curry Energy 210kcal/883kJ; Protein 11.3g; Carbohydrate 26.2g, of which sugars 5.3g; Fat 7.4g, of which saturates 1g; Cholesterol 0mg; Calcium 85mg; Fibre 8.1g; Sodium 35mg.

Stir-fried Seeds & Vegetables

The contrast between the crunchy seeds and vegetables and the rich, savoury sauce is what makes this dish so delicious. Serve with rice.

Serves 4

30ml/2 tbsp vegetable oil
30ml/2 tbsp sesame seeds
30ml/2 tbsp sunflower seeds
30ml/2 tbsp pumpkin seeds
2 garlic cloves, finely chopped
2.5cm/1in piece fresh root ginger, peeled and finely chopped
2 large carrots, cut into batons
2 large courgettes (zucchini), cut into batons
90g/3½oz/1½ cups oyster mushrooms, torn in pieces
165g/5½oz watercress or spinach leaves, coarsely chopped
small bunch fresh mint or coriander (cilantro), leaves and stems chopped
60ml/4 tbsp black bean sauce
30ml/2 tbsp light soy sauce
15ml/1 tbsp palm sugar (jaggery) or muscovado (brown) sugar
30ml/2 tbsp rice vinegar

1 Heat the oil in a wok or large frying pan. Add the seeds. Toss over a medium heat for 1 minute, then add the garlic and ginger, and stir-fry until the ginger is aromatic and the garlic is golden. Do not let the garlic burn or it will taste bitter.

2 Add the carrot and courgette batons and the torn mushrooms to the wok or pan and stir-fry over a medium heat for a further 5 minutes, or until all the vegetables are crisp-tender and are golden at the edges.

3 Add the watercress or spinach with the fresh herbs. Toss over the heat for 1 minute, then stir in the black bean sauce, soy sauce, sugar and vinegar. Stir-fry for 1–2 minutes, until combined and hot. Serve immediately.

Cook's Tip
Oyster mushrooms have acquired their name because of their texture, rather than flavour, which is quite superb. They are delicate, so it is usually better to tear them into pieces along the lines of the gills, rather than slice them with a knife.

Vegetable Forest Curry

This is a thin, soupy curry with lots of fresh green vegetables and robust flavours. In the forested regions of Thailand, where it originated, it would be made using edible wild leaves and roots. Serve it with rice or noodles for a simple lunch or supper.

Serves 2

600ml/1 pint/2½ cups water
5ml/1 tsp Thai red curry paste
5cm/2in piece fresh galangal or fresh root ginger
90g/3½oz/scant 1 cup green beans
2 kaffir lime leaves, torn
8 baby corn cobs, halved widthways
2 heads Chinese broccoli, chopped
90g/3½oz/1 cup beansprouts
15ml/1 tbsp drained bottled green peppercorns, crushed
10ml/2 tsp granulated sugar
5ml/1 tsp salt

1 Heat the water in a large pan. Add the red curry paste and stir until it has dissolved completely. Bring to the boil.

2 Meanwhile, using a sharp knife, peel and finely chop the fresh galangal or root ginger.

3 Add the galangal or ginger, green beans, lime leaves, baby corn, broccoli and beansprouts to the pan. Stir in the crushed peppercorns, sugar and salt. Bring back to the boil, then reduce the heat to low and simmer for 2 minutes. Serve immediately.

Cook's Tip
Galangal is a tuber (a kind of root), which looks similar to ginger. There are several different types: some are more peppery in flavour whereas others taste slightly of cardamoms. Galangal is used mostly in Thai and Indonesian cuisine. If you are not able to find fresh galangal you can substitute ginger in most recipes.

seeds & vegetables Energy 205kcal/849kJ; Protein 6.9g; Carbohydrate 9.7g, of which sugars 7.7g; Fat 15.6g, of which saturates 2g; Cholesterol 0mg; Calcium 159mg; Fibre 3.4g; Sodium 294mg.
forest curry Energy 154kcal/643kJ; Protein 14.9g; Carbohydrate 14.1g, of which sugars 11.8g; Fat 4.5g, of which saturates 0.8g; Cholesterol 0mg; Calcium 173mg; Fibre 9.1g; Sodium 678mg..

Savoury Fried Rice

This is typical Thai street food, eaten at all times of the day. The recipe can be adapted to use whatever vegetables you have available, and you could also add meat or shellfish.

Serves 2

30ml/2 tbsp vegetable oil
2 garlic cloves, finely chopped
1 small fresh red chilli, seeded and finely chopped
50g/2oz/½ cup cashew nuts, toasted
50g/2oz/⅔ cup desiccated (dry unsweetened shredded) coconut, toasted
2.5ml/½ tsp palm sugar (jaggery) or light muscovado (brown) sugar
30ml/2 tbsp light soy sauce
15ml/1 tbsp rice vinegar
1 egg
115g/4oz/1 cup green beans, sliced
½ spring cabbage or 115g/4oz spring greens (collards) or pak choi (bok choy), shredded
90g/3½oz/1 cup jasmine rice, cooked
lime wedges, to serve

1 Heat the oil in a wok or large, heavy frying pan. Add the garlic and cook over a medium to high heat until golden. Do not let it burn or it will taste bitter.

2 Add the red chilli, cashew nuts and toasted coconut to the wok or pan and stir-fry briefly, taking care to prevent the coconut from scorching. Stir in the sugar, soy sauce and rice vinegar. Toss over the heat for 1–2 minutes.

3 Push the stir-fry to one side of the wok or pan and break the egg into the empty side. When the egg is almost set stir it into the garlic and chilli mixture with a wooden spatula or spoon.

4 Add the green beans, spring cabbage or greens, and cooked rice. Stir over the heat until the greens have just wilted, then spoon into a dish to serve.

5 Serve hot, offering lime wedges separately, for squeezing over.

Curry with Lemon Grass Rice

Firm new potatoes, baby corn, broccoli, pepper and spinach make a fabulous combination cooked in a hot spicy curry. Fragrant jasmine rice, subtly flavoured with lemon grass and cardamom, is the perfect accompaniment.

Serves 4

10ml/2 tsp vegetable oil
400ml/14fl oz/1⅔ cups coconut milk
300ml/½ pint/1¼ cups vegetable stock
225g/8oz new potatoes, halved or quartered, if large
8 baby corn cobs
5ml/1 tsp golden caster (superfine) sugar
185g/6½oz/1¼ cups broccoli florets
1 red (bell) pepper, seeded and sliced lengthways
115g/4oz spinach, tough stalks removed, leaves shredded
30ml/2 tbsp chopped fresh coriander (cilantro)
salt and ground black pepper

For the spice paste

1 fresh red chilli, seeded and chopped
3 fresh green chillies, seeded and chopped
1 lemon grass stalk, outer leaves removed and lower 5cm/2in finely chopped
2 shallots, chopped
finely grated rind of 1 lime
2 garlic cloves, chopped
5ml/1 tsp ground coriander
2.5ml/½ tsp ground cumin
1cm/½in piece fresh galangal, finely chopped, or 2.5ml/½ tsp dried galangal (optional)
30ml/2 tbsp chopped fresh coriander (cilantro)
15ml/1 tbsp chopped fresh coriander roots and stems (optional)

For the rice

225g/8oz/1¼ cups jasmine rice, rinsed
6 cardamom pods, bruised
1 lemon grass stalk, outer leaves removed, cut into 3 pieces
475ml/16fl oz/2 cups water

1 Make the spice paste. Place all the ingredients in a food processor and process to a coarse paste. Heat the oil in a large, heavy pan. Add the paste and stir-fry over a medium heat for 1–2 minutes, until fragrant. Pour in the coconut milk and stock and bring to the boil. Reduce the heat, add the potatoes and simmer gently for about 15 minutes, until almost tender.

2 Meanwhile, put the rice into a large pan with the cardamoms and lemon grass. Pour in the water. Bring to the boil, reduce the heat, cover, and cook for 10–15 minutes, until the water has been absorbed and the rice is tender and slightly sticky.

3 Season to taste with salt, stir well, then replace the lid and leave to stand for 10 minutes.

4 Add the baby corn to the potatoes, season with salt and pepper to taste, then cook for 2 minutes. Stir in the sugar, broccoli and red pepper, and cook for 2 minutes more, or until the vegetables are tender.

5 Stir the shredded spinach and half the fresh coriander into the vegetable mixture. Cook for 2 minutes, then spoon the curry into a warmed serving dish.

6 Remove and discard the cardamom pods and lemon grass from the rice and fluff up the grains with a fork. Garnish with the remaining fresh coriander and serve with the rice.

savoury rice Energy 571kcal/2368kJ; Protein 16.1g; Carbohydrate 30.5g, of which sugars 8.7g; Fat 43.7g, of which saturates 18.2g; Cholesterol 95mg; Calcium 187mg; Fibre 8.5g; Sodium 1197mg.
curry w. rice Energy 347kcal/1455kJ; Protein 10.8g; Carbohydrate 68.9g, of which sugars 14g; Fat 3.4g, of which saturates 0.6g; Cholesterol 0mg; Calcium 138mg; Fibre 4.5g; Sodium 734mg.

Spicy Chickpea & Aubergine Stew

Aubergines and chickpeas go particularly well with the warm spices in this substantial dish.

Serves 4
3 garlic cloves
2 large onions
3 large aubergines (eggplants)
200g/7oz/1 cup chickpeas, soaked overnight
60ml/4 tbsp olive oil
2.5ml/½ tsp ground cumin
2.5ml/½ tsp ground cinnamon
2.5ml/½ tsp ground coriander
3 x 400g/14oz cans chopped tomatoes
salt and ground black pepper
boiled rice, to serve

For the garnish
30ml/2 tbsp olive oil
1 onion, sliced
1 garlic clove, sliced
sprigs of fresh coriander (cilantro)

1 Chop the garlic and onions and set aside. Cut the aubergines into bitesize cubes.

2 Place the aubergine cubes in a colander and sprinkle them with salt. Sit the colander in a bowl and leave for 30 minutes, to allow the bitter juices to escape. Rinse the aubergines with cold water and dry on kitchen paper.

3 Drain the chickpeas and put in a pan with enough water to cover. Bring to the boil and simmer for 1–1½ hours, or until tender. Drain.

4 Heat the oil in a large pan. Add the garlic and onions, and cook until soft. Add the spices and cook, stirring, for a few seconds. Add the aubergines and stir. Cook for 5 minutes.

5 Add the tomatoes and chickpeas and season with salt and pepper. Cover and simmer for 20 minutes.

6 To make the garnish, heat the oil in a frying pan and, when very hot, add the sliced onion and garlic. Fry until golden and crisp. Serve the stew with rice, topped with the onion and garlic and garnished with coriander.

Masala Chana

Chickpeas are used and cooked in a variety of ways all over the Indian subcontinent. Tamarind adds a sharp, tangy flavour.

Serves 4
225g/8oz/1¼ cups dried chickpeas, soaked overnight and drained
50g/2oz tamarind stick
120ml/4fl oz/½ cup boiling water
30ml/2 tbsp oil
2.5ml/½ tsp cumin seeds
1 onion, finely chopped
2 garlic cloves, crushed
2.5cm/1in piece fresh root ginger, grated
1 fresh green chilli, finely chopped
5ml/1 tsp ground cumin
5ml/1 tsp ground coriander
1.5ml/¼ tsp ground turmeric
2.5ml/½ tsp salt
225g/8oz tomatoes, peeled and finely chopped
2.5ml/½ tsp garam masala
chopped fresh chillies and chopped onion, to garnish

1 Place the chickpeas in a large pan with double the volume of cold water. Bring to the boil and boil vigorously for 10 minutes.

2 Skim off any scum that has risen to the surface of the liquid, using a slotted spoon. Lower the heat, cover the pan and simmer for 1–1½ hours or until the chickpeas are soft.

3 Meanwhile, break up the tamarind and soak in the boiling water for about 15 minutes. Rub the tamarind through a sieve (strainer) into a bowl, discarding any stones and fibre.

4 Heat the oil in a large, heavy pan and fry the cumin seeds for 2 minutes until they splutter. Add the onion, garlic, ginger and chilli, and fry for 5 minutes.

5 Stir in the cumin and coriander, with the turmeric and salt and fry for 3–4 minutes. Add the chopped tomatoes. Bring to the boil and then simmer for 5 minutes.

6 Drain the chickpeas and add to the tomato mixture together with the garam masala and tamarind pulp. Cover and simmer gently for about 15 minutes. Garnish with the chopped chillies and onion before serving.

chickpea stew Energy 201kcal/843kJ; Protein 7.1g; Carbohydrate 22.3g, of which sugars 10.4g; Fat 10g, of which saturates 1.4g; Cholesterol 0mg; Calcium 57mg; Fibre 5.9g; Sodium 175mg.
masala chana Energy 255kcal/1074kJ; Protein 13.1g; Carbohydrate 32.2g, of which sugars 4.1g; Fat 9.2g, of which saturates 1.1g; Cholesterol 0mg; Calcium 105mg; Fibre 6.8g; Sodium 284mg.

Black-eyed Bean & Potato Curry

Nutty-flavoured black-eyed beans make a nutritious supper dish, especially when mixed with potatoes. This hot and spicy combination will be ideal for an autumn or winter evening.

Serves 4–6

2 potatoes
225g/8oz/1¼ cups black-eyed beans (peas), soaked overnight and drained
1.5ml/¼ tsp bicarbonate of soda (baking soda)
5ml/1 tsp five-spice powder
1.5ml/¼ tsp asafoetida
2 onions, finely chopped
2.5cm/1in piece fresh root ginger, crushed
a few fresh mint leaves
450ml/¾ pint/scant 2 cups water
60ml/4 tbsp vegetable oil
2.5ml/½ tsp each ground cumin, ground coriander, ground turmeric and chilli powder
4 fresh green chillies, chopped
75ml/5 tbsp tamarind juice
115g/4oz/4 cups fresh coriander (cilantro), chopped
2 firm tomatoes, chopped
salt

1 Cut the potatoes into cubes and boil in lightly salted water until tender.

2 Place the drained black-eyed beans in a heavy pan and add the bicarbonate of soda, five-spice powder, asafoetida, chopped onions, crushed root ginger, mint leaves and the measured water. Bring to the boil and simmer for an hour or until the beans are soft. Drain off any excess water and reserve.

3 Heat the oil in a frying pan. Gently fry the ground cumin and coriander, the turmeric and chilli powder with the green chillies and tamarind juice, until they are well blended.

4 Pour the spice mixture over the black-eyed beans and mix well.

5 Add the potatoes, fresh coriander, tomatoes and salt. Mix well, and, if necessary, thin with a little reserved water. Reheat and serve.

Boiled Egg Curry

This dish can be served on its own, with a biryani or pilau, and it also makes a good accompaniment to fried whole fish.

Serves 3–6

10ml/2 tsp white poppy seeds
10ml/2 tsp white sesame seeds
10ml/2 tsp whole coriander seeds
30ml/2 tbsp desiccated (dry unsweetened shredded) coconut
350ml/½fl oz/1½ cups tomato juice
10ml/2 tsp gram flour
5ml/1 tsp crushed fresh root ginger
5ml/1 tsp chilli powder
1.5ml/¼ tsp asafoetida
salt
5ml/1 tsp sugar
6 hard-boiled eggs, halved
30ml/2 tbsp sesame oil
5ml/1 tsp cumin seeds
4 dried red chillies
6–8 curry leaves
4 garlic cloves, finely sliced

1 Heat a frying pan and dry-fry the poppy, sesame and coriander seeds for 3–4 minutes. Add the desiccated coconut and dry-fry until it browns.

2 Cool and grind the ingredients together using a pestle and mortar or a food processor.

3 Take a little of the tomato juice and mix with the gram flour to a smooth paste. Add the ginger, chilli powder, asafoetida, salt and sugar and the ground spices. Add the remaining tomato juice, place in a pan and simmer gently for 10 minutes.

4 Add the hard-boiled eggs and cover with the sauce. Heat the oil in a frying pan and fry the remaining ingredients until the chillies turn dark brown. Pour the spices and oil over the egg curry, fold the ingredients together and reheat. Serve hot.

Cook's Tip

Gram flour, or besan, is made from ground chickpeas. It is less starchy than wheat flour and is used extensively in Indian cooking. For a recipe like this that uses a very tiny amount as a thickener, plain (all-purpose) flour can be substituted.

bean & potato curry Energy 266kcal/1118kJ; Protein 11.8g; Carbohydrate 36.8g, of which sugars 8.5g; Fat 9g, of which saturates 1.1g; Cholesterol 0mg; Calcium 110mg; Fibre 8.8g; Sodium 28mg.
boiled egg curry Energy 229kcal/953kJ; Protein 10.7g; Carbohydrate 4.6g, of which sugars 3.7g; Fat 19g, of which saturates 6.7g; Cholesterol 254mg; Calcium 81mg; Fibre 1.7g; Sodium 276mg.

Eggs on Chipsticks

This is an unusual and delicious way of combining eggs with potato sticks, and is known as *sali pur eeda* in the Parsee language. The potato sticks are fried with chillies, turmeric and coriander. Eggs are then broken over the top and cooked until just set. It makes an unusual light lunch or supper dish and is incredibly quick to prepare and cook.

Serves 4–6

225g/8oz salted chipsticks
2 fresh green chillies, finely chopped
a few coriander (cilantro) sprigs, chopped
1.5ml/¼ tsp ground turmeric
60ml/4 tbsp vegetable oil
75ml/5 tbsp water
6 eggs
3 spring onions (scallions), finely chopped
salt and ground black pepper

1 In a large bowl, mix the salted chipsticks with the chopped chillies, coriander and turmeric.

2 Heat 30ml/2 tbsp of the oil in a heavy frying pan. Add the chipstick mixture and water. Cook until the chipsticks turn soft, and then crisp.

3 Place a dinner plate over the frying pan, and hold in place as you turn the pan over and carefully transfer the chipstick 'pancake' on to the plate. Heat the remaining oil in the pan and slide the 'pancake' back into the frying pan to brown the other side. Do this very gently, so that no chipsticks break off.

4 Gently break the eggs over the top, cover the frying pan and leave the eggs to set over a low heat. Season well and sprinkle with spring onions. Cook until the base is crisp. Serve hot for breakfast in the Parsee style, or with chapatis and a salad for lunch or supper.

Cook's Tip
As the chipsticks cook, the starch they contain will cause them to stick together. To encourage this, use a spoon to press them down.

Spicy Omelette

Another popular contribution by the Parsees, this irresistible omelette of potato, peas and corn is known to them as poro. Parsee cuisine offers some unique flavours, which appeal to both Eastern and Western palates.

Serves 4–6

30ml/2 tbsp vegetable oil
1 onion, finely chopped
2.5ml/½ tsp ground cumin
1 garlic clove, crushed
1 or 2 fresh green chillies, finely chopped
a few coriander (cilantro) sprigs, chopped, plus extra, to garnish
1 firm tomato, chopped
1 small potato, cubed and boiled
25g/1oz/¼ cup cooked peas
25g/1oz/¼ cup cooked corn, or drained canned corn
2 eggs, beaten
25g/1oz/¼ cup grated Cheddar or Monterey Jack cheese
salt and ground black pepper

1 Heat the oil in a karahi, wok or omelette pan, and add the onion, cumin, garlic, chillies, coriander, tomato, potato, peas and corn. Mix well.

2 Cook over a medium heat, stirring, for 5 minutes, until the potato and tomato are almost tender. Season well.

3 Preheat the grill (broiler) to high. Increase the heat under the pan and pour in the beaten eggs. Reduce the heat, cover and cook until the bottom layer is brown. Turn the omelette over and sprinkle with the grated cheese. Place under the hot grill, cooking until the egg sets and the cheese has melted.

4 Garnish the omelette with sprigs of coriander and serve with salad for a light lunch. If you prefer, serve it for breakfast, in the typical Parsee style.

Variation
You can use different vegetables. Try thickly sliced button (white) mushrooms, which can be added in step 1.

eggs on chipsticks Energy 276kcal/1153kJ; Protein 8.7g; Carbohydrate 20.4g, of which sugars 0.6g; Fat 18.5g, of which saturates 6.8g; Cholesterol 190mg; Calcium 58mg; Fibre 2.5g; Sodium 373mg.
spicy omelette Energy 93kcal/388kJ; Protein 4g; Carbohydrate 3.7g, of which sugars 1.2g; Fat 7.1g, of which saturates 1.9g; Cholesterol 67mg; Calcium 46mg; Fibre 0.6g; Sodium 104mg.

Scrambled Eggs with Chilli

This is a lovely way to liven up scrambled eggs. Prepare all the ingredients ahead so that the vegetables can be cooked quickly and retain crunch and colour.

Serves 4

30ml/2 tbsp sunflower oil
1 onion, finely sliced
225g/8oz Chinese leaves (Chinese cabbage), finely sliced or cut in diamonds
200g/7oz can corn
1 small fresh red chilli, seeded and finely sliced
30ml/2 tbsp water
2 eggs, beaten
salt and ground black pepper
deep-fried onions, to garnish

1 Heat a karahi, wok or deep pan. Add the oil and, when it is hot, fry the onion until soft but not browned.

2 Add the Chinese leaves and toss the mixture over the heat until well mixed.

3 Add the corn, chilli and water. Cover with a lid and cook for 2 minutes.

4 Remove the lid and stir in the beaten eggs and seasoning. Stir constantly until the eggs are creamy and just set. Serve on warmed plates, sprinkled with crisp deep-fried onions.

Variations

- *Chinese leaves give this dish a delicate flavour, which complements the corn and eggs well, but you could substitute other vegetables for a different flavour and appearance. Instead of Chinese leaves, you could try finely shredded spring greens (collards) or white cabbage. A mandolin is a useful implement for finely shredding vegetables such as these.*
- *Red, green or yellow (bell) peppers could also be used in place of the Chinese leaves and give the dish a bright appearance.*

Purée of Lentils with Baked Eggs

This unusual dish of brown lentils spiced with coriander and mint makes an excellent supper. For a nutty flavour you could add a 400g/14oz can of unsweetened chestnut purée to the lentil mixture.

Serves 4

450g/1lb/2 cups washed brown lentils
3 leeks, thinly sliced
10ml/2 tsp coriander seeds, crushed
15ml/1 tbsp chopped fresh coriander (cilantro)
30ml/2 tbsp chopped fresh mint
15ml/1 tbsp red wine vinegar
1 litre/1¾ pints/4 cups vegetable stock
4 eggs
salt and ground black pepper
generous handful of fresh parsley, chopped, to garnish

1 Put the lentils in a deep pan. Add the leeks, coriander seeds, fresh coriander, mint, vinegar and stock. Bring to the boil, then lower the heat and simmer for 30–40 minutes, until the lentils are cooked and have absorbed all the liquid.

2 Preheat the oven to 180°C/350°F/Gas 4.

3 Season the lentils with salt and pepper, and mix well. Spread out in four lightly greased baking dishes.

4 Using the back of a spoon, make a hollow in the lentil mixture in each dish. Break an egg into each hollow. Cover the dishes with foil and bake for 15–20 minutes, or until the egg whites are set and the yolks are still soft. Sprinkle with plenty of parsley and serve at once.

Cook's Tip

If you prefer, the lentil mixture can be put into a large dish. Make four indentations in the mixture to hold the eggs.

eggs w. chilli Energy 168kcal/702kJ; Protein 5.6g; Carbohydrate 17.3g, of which sugars 8.4g; Fat 9g, of which saturates 1.5g; Cholesterol 95mg; Calcium 48mg; Fibre 2.1g; Sodium 175mg.
purée of lentils Energy 470kcal/1990kJ; Protein 35.9g; Carbohydrate 68.4g, of which sugars 6g; Fat 7.9g, of which saturates 1.9g; Cholesterol 190mg; Calcium 148mg; Fibre 8.8g; Sodium 116mg.

Balti Potatoes with Aubergines

Using baby potatoes adds to the attractiveness of this dish. Choose the smaller variety of aubergines, too, as they are tastier than the large ones, which contain a lot of water and little flavour. You can buy small aubergines from specialist grocers.

Serves 4

10–12 baby potatoes
6 small aubergines (eggplants)
1 medium red (bell) pepper
15ml/1 tbsp oil
2 medium onions, sliced
4–6 curry leaves
2.5ml/½ tsp onion seeds
5ml/1 tsp crushed coriander seeds
2.5ml/½ tsp cumin seeds
5ml/1 tsp grated fresh root ginger
5ml/1 tsp crushed garlic
5ml/1 tsp crushed dried red chillies
15ml/1 tbsp chopped fresh fenugreek leaves
5ml/1 tsp chopped fresh coriander (cilantro)
15ml/1 tbsp natural (plain) low-fat yogurt
fresh coriander leaves, to garnish

1 Cook the unpeeled potatoes in a pan of boiling water until they are just soft, but still whole.

2 Cut the aubergines into quarters if very small, or eighths if using larger aubergines.

3 Cut the pepper in half, remove the seeds and ribs, then slice the flesh into thin even strips.

4 Heat the oil in a karahi, wok or heavy pan and fry the sliced onions, curry leaves, onion seeds, crushed coriander seeds and cumin seeds until the onion slices are a soft golden brown, stirring constantly.

5 Add the ginger, garlic, crushed chillies and fenugreek, followed by the aubergines and potatoes. Stir everything together and cover the pan with a lid. Lower the heat and cook the vegetables for 5–7 minutes.

6 Remove the lid, add the fresh coriander followed by the yogurt and stir well. Serve garnished with coriander leaves.

Balti Stir-fried Vegetables with Cashew Nuts

This quick and versatile stir-fry will accommodate most other combinations of vegetables – you do not have to use the selection suggested here.

Serves 4

2 medium carrots
1 medium red (bell) pepper, seeded
1 medium green (bell) pepper, seeded
2 courgettes (zucchini)
115g/4oz green beans
1 medium bunch spring onions (scallions)
15ml/1 tbsp vegetable oil
4–6 curry leaves
2.5ml/½ tsp cumin seeds
4 dried red chillies
10–12 cashew nuts
5ml/1 tsp salt
30ml/2 tbsp lemon juice
fresh mint leaves, to garnish

1 Prepare the vegetables: cut the carrots, peppers and courgettes into matchsticks, halve the beans and chop the spring onions. Set aside.

2 Heat the oil in a karahi, wok or heavy pan and fry the curry leaves, cumin seeds and dried red chillies for about 1 minute.

3 Add the vegetables and nuts, and stir them around gently. Add the salt and lemon juice. Continue to stir and cook for about 3–5 minutes.

4 Transfer the vegetables to a serving dish, garnish with fresh mint leaves and serve immediately.

Variation
Small florets of broccoli or cauliflower are delicious cooked in a stir-fry so that they retain their crunch. You could use them in place of the courgettes (zucchini). Or you could use mushrooms, mangetouts (snow peas) and beansprouts.

balti potatoes Energy 94kcal/396kJ; Protein 3.6g; Carbohydrate 17.3g, of which sugars 3.4g; Fat 1.8g, of which saturates 0.3g; Cholesterol 0mg; Calcium 55mg; Fibre 2.9g; Sodium 19mg.
balti vegetables Energy 105kcal/436kJ; Protein 4.2g; Carbohydrate 11.2g, of which sugars 10.1g; Fat 5.1g, of which saturates 0.9g; Cholesterol 0mg; Calcium 56mg; Fibre 3.9g; Sodium 510mg.

Karahi Potatoes with Whole Spices

The potato is transformed into something quite exotic when it is cooked like this.

Serves 4

15ml/1 tbsp vegetable oil
5ml/1 tsp cumin seeds
3 curry leaves
5ml/1 tsp crushed dried red chillies
2.5ml/½ tsp mixed onion, mustard and fenugreek seeds
2.5ml/½ tsp fennel seeds
3 garlic cloves, sliced
2.5cm/1in piece fresh root ginger, grated
2 onions, sliced
6 new potatoes, thinly sliced
15ml/1 tbsp chopped fresh coriander (cilantro)
1 fresh red chilli, seeded and sliced
1 fresh green chilli, seeded and sliced

1 Heat the oil in a karahi, wok or heavy pan. Lower the heat slightly and add the cumin seeds, curry leaves, dried red chillies, mixed onion, mustard and fenugreek seeds, fennel seeds, garlic slices and ginger. Fry for 1 minute.

2 Add the onions and fry for a further 5 minutes, or until the onions are golden brown.

3 Add the potatoes, fresh coriander and sliced fresh red and green chillies and mix well. Cover the pan tightly with a lid or foil; if using foil, make sure that it does not touch the food. Cook over a very low heat for about 7 minutes or until the potatoes are tender.

4 Remove the pan from the heat, and take off the lid or foil cover. Serve hot.

Cook's Tip

Choose a waxy variety of new potato for this fairly hot vegetable dish; if you use a very soft potato, it will not be possible to cut it into thin slices without it breaking up. Suitable varieties are often labelled 'salad potatoes' when sold at supermarkets. Leave the skin on for a tastier result.

Balti Mushrooms in a Creamy Garlic Sauce

This is a simple and delicious Balti recipe which could be accompanied by bread or one of the rice side dishes from this book.

Serves 4

350g/12oz/4½ cups button (white) mushrooms
15ml/1 tbsp vegetable oil
1 bay leaf
3 garlic cloves, roughly chopped
2 green chillies, seeded and chopped
225g/8oz/1 cup low-fat fromage frais or ricotta cheese
15ml/1 tbsp chopped fresh mint
15ml/1 tbsp chopped fresh coriander (cilantro)
5ml/1 tsp salt
fresh mint and coriander leaves, to garnish

1 Cut the button mushrooms in half, or in quarters if large, and set aside.

2 Heat the oil in a karahi, wok or heavy pan, then add the bay leaf, chopped garlic and chillies, and quickly stir-fry for about 1 minute.

3 Add the mushrooms. Stir-fry for another 2 minutes.

4 Remove from the heat and stir in the fromage frais or ricotta cheese, followed by the mint, coriander and salt. Return to the heat and stir-fry for 2–3 minutes, then transfer to a warmed serving dish and garnish with mint and coriander leaves.

Cook's Tip

Balti curries have their origins in Baltistan, the area that is now North Pakistan. They are traditionally aromatic but not heavily flavoured with chilli, and bread is usually used to scoop up the food. However, rice also goes well with all the dishes.

karahi potatoes Energy 129kcal/539kJ; Protein 3.7g; Carbohydrate 20.7g, of which sugars 5.3g; Fat 4.2g, of which saturates 0.6g; Cholesterol 0mg; Calcium 41mg; Fibre 1.8g; Sodium 14mg.
balti mushrooms Energy 153kcal/633kJ; Protein 5.4g; Carbohydrate 3.1g, of which sugars 2.8g; Fat 13.3g, of which saturates 4.4g; Cholesterol 5mg; Calcium 90mg; Fibre 1.5g; Sodium 28mg.

Balti Dhal with Spring Onions & Tomatoes

This rich-tasting dish is made using toor dhal, a shiny, yellow split lentil which resembles chana dhal. Fresh fenugreek leaves are perfect with pulses and impart a stunning aroma.

Serves 4

115g/4oz/½ cup toor dhal or yellow split peas
30ml/2 tbsp vegetable oil
1.5ml/¼ tsp onion seeds
1 medium bunch spring onions (scallions), roughly chopped
5ml/1 tsp crushed garlic
1.5ml/¼ tsp ground turmeric
7.5ml/1½ tsp grated fresh root ginger
5ml/1 tsp chilli powder
30ml/2 tbsp fresh fenugreek leaves
5ml/1 tsp salt
150ml/¼ pint/⅔ cup water
6–8 cherry tomatoes
30ml/2 tbsp fresh coriander (cilantro) leaves
½ green (bell) pepper, seeded and sliced
15ml/1 tbsp lemon juice
shredded spring onion tops and fresh coriander leaves, to garnish

1 Cook the dhal in a pan of boiling water for 40–45 minutes until soft and mushy. Drain and set aside.

2 Heat the oil with the onion seeds in a karahi, wok or heavy pan for a few seconds until hot.

3 Add the drained dhal to the pan and stir-fry with the onion seeds for about 3 minutes.

4 Add the spring onions followed by the garlic, turmeric, ginger, chilli powder, fenugreek leaves and salt, and continue to stir-fry for 5–7 minutes.

5 Pour in just enough of the water to loosen the mixture.

6 Add the whole cherry tomatoes, coriander leaves, green pepper and lemon juice. Stir well and serve garnished with shredded spring onion tops and coriander leaves.

Balti Corn with Cauliflower & Mint

This quick and tasty vegetable dish can be made with frozen corn, so it is an excellent store-cupboard standby. If you do not have any cauliflower, substitute broccoli or another vegetable such as slices of courgette.

Serves 4

3 small onions
1 fresh red chilli
15ml/1 tbsp vegetable oil
4 curry leaves
1.5ml/¼ tsp onion seeds
175g/6oz/1 cup frozen corn
½ small cauliflower, separated into florets
3–7 mint leaves

1 Using a sharp knife dice the onions finely. Slit the chilli, scrape out the seeds and then slice the flesh thinly.

2 Heat the oil in a karahi, wok or heavy pan and stir-fry the curry leaves and onion seeds for about 30 seconds.

3 Add the diced onions to the pan and fry them for 5–8 minutes until golden brown.

4 Add the chilli, frozen corn and cauliflower florets and stir-fry for 5–8 minutes more.

5 Toss with the mint leaves and serve immediately.

Cook's Tips

- *It is best to eat this dish immediately after it has been cooked, as the flavour tends to spoil if it is kept warm.*
- *Whole mint leaves can be frozen in the summer when they are plentiful for use during the winter. They are then added while frozen to dishes such as this where they are mixed in with other ingredients. Frozen herbs are not suitable for garnishes, however.*

balti dhal Energy 196kcal/823kJ; Protein 9.7g; Carbohydrate 24g, of which sugars 4.7g; Fat 7.7g, of which saturates 1g; Cholesterol 0mg; Calcium 72mg; Fibre 3.2g; Sodium 23mg.
balti corn Energy 130kcal/545kJ; Protein 5.7g; Carbohydrate 18g, of which sugars 9.1g; Fat 4.4g, of which saturates 0.6g; Cholesterol 0mg; Calcium 57mg; Fibre 3.6g; Sodium 133mg.

Balti Dhal with Green & Red Chillies

The white urad dhal which is used in this recipe should ideally be soaked overnight as this makes it easier to cook. Serve with freshly made chapatis.

Serves 4

115g/4oz/½ cup urad dhal
10ml/2 tsp butter
10ml/2 tsp vegetable oil
1 bay leaf
2 onions, sliced
1 cinnamon stick
2.5cm/1in piece fresh root ginger, grated
2 garlic cloves
2 green chillies, seeded and sliced lengthways
2 red chillies, seeded and sliced lengthways
15ml/1 tbsp chopped fresh mint

1 Soak the dhal overnight in enough cold water to cover. Boil in water until the individual grains are soft enough to break into two. Set aside.

2 Heat the butter with the oil in a wok or heavy frying pan over a medium heat. Fry the bay leaf with the onions and the cinnamon.

3 Add the grated ginger, whole garlic cloves and half the green and red chillies.

4 Drain almost all the water from the lentils. Add the lentils to the wok or frying pan, then add the remaining green and red chillies and finally the chopped fresh mint. Heat through briefly and serve while piping hot.

Cook's Tip
If you like your curries milder, replace some of the chillies with some finely chopped green or red (bell) peppers.

Tofu & Crunchy Vegetables

Tofu is best if marinated lightly before it is cooked.

Serves 4

2 x 225g/8oz packets smoked tofu, diced
45ml/3 tbsp soy sauce
30ml/2 tbsp dry sherry or vermouth
15ml/1 tbsp sesame oil
45ml/3 tbsp groundnut (peanut) or sunflower oil
2 leeks, thinly sliced
2 carrots, cut into batons
1 large courgette (zucchini), thinly sliced
115g/4oz baby corn, halved
115g/4oz button (white) or shiitake mushrooms, sliced
15ml/1 tbsp sesame seeds
cooked noodles dressed with sesame oil, to serve (optional)

1 Place the tofu in a shallow dish. Mix together the soy sauce, sherry or vermouth and sesame oil and pour over the tofu. Cover with clear film (plastic wrap) and leave to marinate in a cool place for at least 30 minutes. Drain the tofu cubes and reserve the marinade.

2 Heat a wok or large, heavy frying pan and add the groundnut oil. When the oil is hot, add the tofu cubes and stir-fry until browned all over. Remove the tofu from the pan.

3 Add the leeks, carrots, courgette and baby corn to the pan and stir-fry for about 2 minutes. Add the mushrooms and cook for 1 minute more.

4 Return the tofu to the pan and pour in the reserved marinade. Heat, stirring gently, until bubbling, then sprinkle with the sesame seeds. Serve immediately with hot cooked noodles dressed with a little sesame oil, if you like.

Cook's Tip
The actual cooking of this dish takes just a few minutes, so have all the ingredients prepared before you start.

balti dhal w. chillies Energy 148kcal/620kJ; Protein 7.6g; Carbohydrate 16.6g, of which sugars 1.1g; Fat 6.1g, of which saturates 0.7g; Cholesterol 0mg; Calcium 44mg; Fibre 2g; Sodium 15mg.
tofu & vegetables Energy 251kcal/1040kJ; Protein 12.6g; Carbohydrate 7.2g, of which sugars 5.8g; Fat 18.3g, of which saturates 2.4g; Cholesterol 0mg; Calcium 578mg; Fibre 3.8g; Sodium 877mg.

Beans with Mochi Rice Cake

Aduki beans are commonly used in traditional Asian desserts. This sweet soupy stew is perfect in the winter, and makes a filling yet light meal in itself.

Serves 4
130g/4½oz/⅔ cup dried aduki beans
pinch of baking powder
130g/4½ oz/scant ¾ cup caster (superfine) sugar
1.5ml/¼ tsp salt
4 mochi rice cakes

1 Rinse the aduki beans and soak them overnight in 1 litre.1¾ pints/4 cups water.

2 Pour the beans and the soaking water into a large heavy pan, then bring to the boil. Reduce the heat to medium-low and add the baking powder. Cover the pan and cook for about 30 minutes.

3 Add a further 1 litre/1¾ pints/4 cups water, and bring back to the boil. Reduce the heat to low, and cook for a further 30 minutes.

4 To test that the beans are ready, pick out and press one bean between the fingers. It should crush without any resistance. If it is still hard, cook for another 15–20 minutes, then test again.

5 Divide the sugar into two equal heaps. Add one heap to the pan containing the beans and stir gently. Cook for about 3 minutes, then add the rest and wait for another 3 minutes.

6 Add the salt and cook for another 3 minutes. The stew is now ready to eat. Reduce the heat and keep warm.

7 Cut the mochi in half. Grill (broil) under a moderate heat unitl light golden brown and puffy. Turn several times to ensure an even colouring.

8 Put two pieces of mochi into each bowl and pour the soupy stew around them. Serve hot.

Red-cooked Tofu with Chinese Mushrooms

Red-cooked is a term used for Chinese dishes cooked with dark soy sauce.

Serves 2–4
6 dried Chinese mushrooms
225g/8oz firm tofu
45ml/3 tbsp dark soy sauce
30ml/2 tbsp Chinese rice wine or medium-dry sherry
10ml/2 tsp soft dark brown sugar
1 garlic clove, crushed
15ml/1 tbsp grated fresh root ginger
2.5ml/ ½ tsp Chinese five-spice powder
pinch of ground roasted Szechuan peppercorns
5ml/1 tsp cornflour (cornstarch)
30ml/2 tbsp groundnut (peanut) oil
5–6 spring onions (scallions), sliced into short lengths
small fresh basil leaves, to garnish
cooked rice noodles, to serve

1 Soak the dried Chinese mushrooms in warm water for 20–30 minutes, until soft.

2 Cut the tofu into 2.5cm/1in cubes and place in a shallow dish. Combine the soy sauce, rice wine or sherry, sugar, garlic, ginger, five-spice powder and Szechuan pepper. Pour this over the tofu, toss lightly and marinate for 10 minutes. Drain and stir in the cornflour into the marinade.

3 Drain the mushrooms, reserving 90ml/6 tbsp of the soaking liquid. Strain this into the cornflour mixture, mix well and set aside. Squeeze out any excess liquid from the mushrooms, remove the tough stalks and slice the caps.

4 Heat the oil in a wok and stir-fry the tofu for 2–3 minutes, until golden. Remove it with a slotted spoon and set aside.

5 Add the mushrooms and the white parts of the spring onions to the wok and stir-fry for 2 minutes. Pour in the cornflour mixture and stir for 1 minute, until the mixture thickens. Return the tofu to the wok with the green parts of the spring onions. Simmer for 1–2 minutes. Serve with basil leaves and noodles.

beans w. rice cake Energy 295kcal/1240kJ; Protein 10g; Carbohydrate 58.2g, of which sugars 6.7g; Fat 2.7g, of which saturates 0.4g; Cholesterol 0mg; Calcium 66mg; Fibre 4.6g; Sodium 79mg.
red-cooked tofu Energy 150kcal/624kJ; Protein 7.1g; Carbohydrate 10.1g, of which sugars 5.3g; Fat 9.6g, of which saturates 1.2g; Cholesterol 0mg; Calcium 319mg; Fibre 0.2g; Sodium 809mg.

Fried Garlic Tofu

A simple and inexpensive recipe that can be quickly and easily prepared to make a tasty and nutritious midweek family supper. In summer, serve with mixed salad leaves or steamed greens and minted new potatoes and, in winter, serve with baked potatoes.

Serves 4

500g/1¼lb firm tofu
50g/2oz/¼ cup butter
2 garlic cloves, thinly sliced
200g/7oz enoki or other mushrooms
45ml/3 tbsp soy sauce
30ml/2 tbsp sake or lemon juice

1 Wrap the tofu in kitchen paper, place a weighted plate on top and leave for up to 1 hour to drain off excess water.

2 Slice the tofu to make 16 slices using a sharp knife.

3 Melt one-third of the butter in a frying pan. Add the garlic and cook over a medium heat, stirring, until golden, but do not allow it to burn. Remove the garlic from the pan.

4 Melt half the remaining butter in the pan, add the mushrooms and cook for 3–4 minutes, until golden, then remove the mushrooms from the pan.

5 Place the tofu in the pan with the remaining butter and cook over a medium heat. Turn over and cook the other side until golden and the tofu is warmed through.

6 Return the garlic to the pan, add the soy sauce and sake or lemon juice and simmer for 1 minute. Transfer to warm serving plates and serve immediately with the mushrooms.

Cook's Tip
Enoki mushrooms are slender and extremely delicate, with long thin stems and tiny white caps. They have a sweet, almost fruity flavour.

Stir-fried Crispy Tofu

The asparagus grown in the part of Asia where this recipe originated tends to have slender stalks. Look for it in Thai markets or substitute the thin asparagus popularly known as sprue.

Serves 2

250g/9oz fried tofu cubes
30ml/2 tbsp groundnut (peanut) oil
15ml/1 tbsp green curry paste
30ml/2 tbsp light soy sauce
2 kaffir lime leaves, rolled into cylinders and thinly sliced
30ml/2 tbsp sugar
150ml/¼ pint/⅔ cup vegetable stock
250g/9oz Asian asparagus, trimmed and sliced into 5cm/2in lengths
30ml/2 tbsp roasted peanuts, finely chopped

1 Preheat the grill (broiler) to medium. Place the tofu cubes in a grill pan and cook for 2–3 minutes, then turn them over and continue to cook until they are crisp and golden brown all over. Watch them carefully; they must not be allowed to burn.

2 Heat the oil in a wok or heavy frying pan. Add the green curry paste and cook over a medium heat, stirring constantly, for 1–2 minutes, until it gives off its aroma.

3 Stir the soy sauce, lime leaves, sugar and vegetable stock into the wok or pan and mix well. Bring to the boil, then reduce the heat to low so that the mixture is just simmering.

4 Add the asparagus and simmer gently for 5 minutes. Meanwhile, chop each piece of tofu into four, then add to the pan with the peanuts.

5 Toss to coat all the ingredients in the sauce, then spoon into a warmed dish and serve immediately.

Variation
Substitute slim carrot sticks or broccoli florets for the asparagus.

fried garlic tofu Energy 196kcal/810kJ; Protein 11.5g; Carbohydrate 2.1g, of which sugars 1.4g; Fat 15.8g, of which saturates 7.2g; Cholesterol 27mg; Calcium 645mg; Fibre 0.6g; Sodium 884mg.
crispy tofu Energy 287kcal/1195kJ; Protein 14.3g; Carbohydrate 20.3g, of which sugars 19.5g; Fat 17g, of which saturates 2.1g; Cholesterol 0mg; Calcium 682mg; Fibre 2.1g; Sodium 1075mg.

Thai Vegetable Curry with Lemon Grass Rice

Fragrant jasmine rice, subtly flavoured with lemongrass and cardamom, is the perfect accompaniment to this richly spiced vegetable curry. Don't be put off by the long list of ingredients, this curry is very simple to make.

Serves 4

10ml/2 tsp vegetable oil
400ml/14fl oz/1⅔ cups coconut milk
300ml/½ pint/1¼ cups vegetable stock
225g/8oz new potatoes, halved or quartered, if large
130g/4½oz baby corn cobs
5ml/1 tsp golden caster (superfine) sugar
185g/6½oz broccoli florets
1 red (bell) pepper, seeded and sliced lengthways
115g/4oz spinach, tough stalks removed and shredded
30ml/2 tbsp chopped fresh coriander (cilantro)
salt and ground black pepper

For the spice paste
1 red chilli, seeded and chopped
3 green chillies, seeded and chopped
1 lemongrass stalk, outer leaves removed and lower 5cm/2in finely chopped
2 shallots, chopped
finely grated rind of 1 lime
2 garlic cloves, chopped
5ml/1 tsp ground coriander
2.5ml/½ tsp ground cumin
1cm/½in fresh galangal, finely chopped or 2.5ml/½ tsp dried (optional)
30ml/2 tbsp chopped fresh coriander (cilantro)
15ml/1 tbsp chopped fresh coriander (cilantro) roots and stems (optional)

For the rice
225g/8oz/generous 1 cup jasmine rice, rinsed
1 lemon grass stalk, outer leaves removed and cut into 3 pieces
6 cardamom pods, bruised

1 Make the spice paste. Place all the ingredients in a food processor or blender and blend to a coarse paste.

2 Heat the oil in a large heavy pan and fry the spice paste for 1–2 minutes, stirring constantly. Add the coconut milk and stock, and bring to the boil.

3 Reduce the heat, add the potatoes and simmer for about 15 minutes. Add the baby corn and seasoning, then cook for 2 minutes. Stir in the sugar, broccoli and red pepper, and cook for 2 minutes more until the vegetables are tender. Stir in the shredded spinach and half the fresh coriander. Cook for 2 minutes.

4 Meanwhile, prepare the rice. Tip the rinsed rice into a large pan and add the lemon grass and cardamom pods. Pour over 475ml/16fl oz/2 cups water.

5 Bring to the boil, then reduce the heat, cover, and cook for 10–15 minutes until the water is absorbed and the rice is tender and slightly sticky. Season with salt, leave to stand for 10 minutes, then fluff up the rice with a fork.

6 Remove the spices and serve the rice with the curry, sprinkled with the remaining fresh coriander.

Spiced Tofu Stir-fry

Any cooked vegetable could be added to this tasty stir-fry but it is always a good idea to try to achieve a contrast in colours and textures to make the dish more interesting.

Serves 4

10ml/2 tsp ground cumin
15ml/1 tbsp paprika
5ml/1 tsp ground ginger
good pinch of cayenne pepper
15ml/1 tbsp caster (superfine) sugar
275g/10oz firm tofu
60ml/4 tbsp olive oil
2 garlic cloves, crushed
1 bunch of spring onions (scallions), sliced
1 red (bell) pepper, seeded and sliced
1 yellow (bell) pepper, seeded and sliced
225g/8oz/generous 3 cups brown cap (cremini) mushrooms, halved or quartered
1 large courgette (zucchini), sliced
115g/4oz fine green beans, halved
50g/2oz/⅔ cup pine nuts
15ml/1 tbsp lime juice
15ml/1 tbsp maple syrup
salt and ground black pepper

1 Mix together the ground cumin, paprika, ginger, cayenne and sugar in a bowl and season with plenty of salt and pepper.

2 Cut the tofu into cubes with a sharp knife and gently toss the cubes in the spice mixture to coat.

3 Heat half the olive oil in a wok or large, heavy frying pan. Add the tofu cubes and cook over a high heat for 3–4 minutes, turning carefully from time to time. Remove with a slotted spoon and set aside. Wipe out the wok or pan.

4 Add the remaining oil to the wok or pan and stir-fry the garlic and spring onions for 3 minutes. Add the remaining vegetables and stir-fry over a medium heat for 6 minutes, or until they are beginning to soften and turn golden. Season well.

5 Return the tofu cubes to the wok or frying pan and add the pine nuts, lime juice and maple syrup. Heat through gently, stirring, then transfer to warm serving bowls and serve.

Thai vegetable curry Energy 300kcal/1256kJ; Protein 3.2g; Carbohydrate 35.1g, of which sugars 14.3g; Fat 3g, of which saturates 0.8g; Cholesterol 0mg; Calcium 72mg; Fibre 5.9g; Sodium 123mg.
spiced tofu stir-fry Energy 294kcal/1218kJ; Protein 10.3g; Carbohydrate 11.4g, of which sugars 10.4g; Fat 23.4g, of which saturates 2.4g; Cholesterol 0mg; Calcium 383mg; Fibre 3.3g; Sodium 11mg.

Tofu with Lemon Grass & Basil

In parts of Asia, aromatic pepper leaves are used as the herb element in this dish but, because these can be difficult to track down, you can use basil leaves instead. For the best results, leave the tofu to marinate for the full hour. This very tasty dish is a wonderful way to cook tofu.

Serves 3–4

3 lemon grass stalks, finely chopped
45ml/3 tbsp soy sauce
2 fresh red Serrano chillies, seeded and finely chopped
2 garlic cloves, crushed
5ml/1 tsp ground turmeric
10ml/2 tsp sugar
300g/11oz tofu, rinsed, drained, patted dry and cut into bitesize cubes
30ml/2 tbsp groundnut (peanut) oil
45ml/3 tbsp roasted peanuts, chopped
1 bunch fresh basil, stalks removed
salt

1 In a bowl, mix together the lemon grass, soy sauce, chillies, garlic, turmeric and sugar until the sugar has dissolved. Add a little salt to taste and add the tofu, making sure it is well coated. Leave to marinate for 1 hour.

2 Heat a wok or heavy pan. Pour in the oil, add the marinated tofu, and cook, stirring frequently, until it is golden brown on all sides. Add the peanuts and most of the basil leaves and stir-fry quickly so that the basil becomes aromatic without wilting.

3 Divide the tofu among individual serving dishes, sprinkle the remaining basil leaves over the top and serve hot or at room temperature.

Variation
Lime, coriander (cilantro) or curry leaves would work well in this simple stir-fry.

Crisp-fried Tofu in Tomato Sauce

This is a light, tasty tofu-based dish. Soy sauce is used here, but Thai fish sauce can be substituted for those who eat fish. You can use a combination of vegetable and peanut oils if you want a milder nutty taste.

Serves 4

vegetable or groundnut (peanut) oil, for deep-frying
450g/1lb firm tofu, rinsed and cut into bitesize cubes
4 shallots, finely sliced
1 fresh red chilli, seeded and chopped
25g/1oz fresh root ginger, peeled and finely chopped
4 garlic cloves, finely chopped
6 large ripe tomatoes, peeled, seeded and finely chopped
15–30ml/1–2 tbsp light soy sauce
10ml/2 tsp sugar
mint leaves and strips of fresh red chilli, to garnish
ground black pepper

1 Heat enough oil for deep-frying in a wok or heavy pan. Fry the tofu, in batches, until crisp and golden. Remove with a slotted spoon and drain on kitchen paper.

2 Reserve 30ml/2 tbsp oil in the wok. Add the shallots, chilli, ginger and garlic and stir-fry until fragrant. Stir in the tomatoes, soy sauce and sugar. Reduce the heat and simmer the mixture for 10–15 minutes until it resembles a sauce. Stir in 105ml/7 tbsp water and bring to the boil.

3 Season with a little pepper and return the tofu to the pan. Mix well and simmer gently for 2–3 minutes to heat through. Spoon into heated bowls, garnish with mint leaves and chilli strips and serve immediately.

Cook's Tip
This recipe is delicious as a side dish or as a main dish with noodles or rice. It is nutritious too, thanks to the tofu, which is an excellent vegetable protein, free from cholesterol.

tofu w. lemon grass Energy 115kcal/480kJ; Protein 7.4g; Carbohydrate 4.5g, of which sugars 3.9g; Fat 7.6g, of which saturates 1g; Cholesterol 0mg; Calcium 388mg; Fibre 0.2g; Sodium 804mg.
tofu in tomato sauce Energy 234kcal/974kJ; Protein 11g; Carbohydrate 11.1g, of which sugars 10.1g; Fat 16.5g, of which saturates 2g; Cholesterol 0mg; Calcium 619mg; Fibre 2.7g; Sodium 25mg.

Snake Beans with Tofu

Another name for snake beans is yard-long beans. This is something of an exaggeration but they do grow to lengths of 35cm/14in and more. Look for them in Asian stores and markets, but if you can't find any, substitute other green beans, such as French beans or runner beans. Mangetouts (snow peas) or sugar snaps also work well in this dish.

Serves 4

500g/1 ¼lb snake beans, thinly sliced
200g/7oz silken tofu, cut into cubes
2 shallots, thinly sliced
200ml/7fl oz/scant 1 cup coconut milk
115g/4oz/1 cup roasted peanuts, chopped
juice of 1 lime
10ml/2 tsp palm sugar (jaggery) or light muscovado (brown) sugar
60ml/4 tbsp soy sauce
5ml/1 tsp dried chilli flakes

1 Bring a pan of lightly salted water to the boil. Add the beans and blanch them for 30 seconds.

2 Drain the beans immediately, then refresh under cold water and drain again, shaking well to remove as much water as possible. Place in a serving bowl and set aside.

3 Put the tofu and shallots in a pan with the coconut milk. Heat gently, stirring, until the tofu begins to crumble.

4 Add the peanuts, lime juice, sugar, soy sauce and chilli flakes. Heat, stirring, until the sugar has dissolved.

5 Pour the sauce over the beans, toss to combine and serve immediately.

Variations
The sauce also works very well with broad (fava) beans. Alternatively, stir in sliced yellow or red (bell) pepper.

Peanut & Tofu Cutlets

These delicious patties make a filling and satisfying midweek meal served with lightly steamed green vegetables or a crisp salad, and a tangy salsa or ketchup.

Serves 4

90g/3½oz/½ cup brown rice
15ml/1 tbsp vegetable oil
1 onion, finely chopped
1 garlic clove, crushed
200g/7oz/1¾ cups peanuts
small bunch of fresh coriander (cilantro), chopped
250g/9oz firm tofu, drained and crumbled
30ml/2 tbsp soy sauce
30ml/2 tbsp olive oil

1 Cook the rice according to the instructions on the packet until tender, then drain. Heat the vegetable oil in a large, heavy frying pan and cook the onion and garlic over a low heat, stirring occasionally until softened and golden.

2 Meanwhile, spread out the peanuts on a baking sheet and toast under the grill (broiler) for a few minutes, until browned. Place the peanuts, onion, garlic, rice, coriander, tofu and soy sauce in a blender or food processor and process until the mixture comes together in a thick paste.

3 Divide the paste into eight equal-size mounds and form each mound into a cutlet shape or square.

4 Heat the olive oil in a large, heavy frying pan. Add the cutlets, in two batches if necessary, and cook for 5–10 minutes on each side, until golden and heated through. Remove from the pan and drain well. Serve immediately.

Variations
The herbs and nuts can be varied. Try:
- *Walnuts with rosemary or sage*
- *Cashew nuts with coriander (cilantro) or parsley*
- *Hazelnuts with parsley, thyme or sage.*

snake beans w. tofu Energy 167kcal/697kJ; Protein 9.9g; Carbohydrate 12.9g, of which sugars 9.3g; Fat 10g, of which saturates 1g; Cholesterol 7mg; Calcium 327mg; Fibre 3.4g; Sodium 191mg.
peanut & tofu cutlets Energy 495kcal/2059kJ; Protein 20.2g; Carbohydrate 27.1g, of which sugars 5.3g; Fat 34.7g, of which saturates 5.9g; Cholesterol 0mg; Calcium 381mg; Fibre 4.4g; Sodium 543mg.

Tofu with Four Mushrooms

Four different kinds of mushrooms combine beautifully with tofu in this sophisticated and flavoursome recipe.

Serves 4

350g/12oz firm tofu
2.5ml/½ tsp sesame oil
10ml/2 tsp light soy sauce
15ml/1 tbsp vegetable oil
2 garlic cloves, finely chopped
2.5ml/½ tsp grated fresh root ginger
115g/4oz/scant 2 cups fresh shiitake mushrooms, stalks removed
175g/6oz/scant 2 cups fresh oyster mushrooms
115g/4oz/scant 2 cups canned straw mushrooms, drained
115g/4oz/scant 2 cups button (white) mushrooms, halved
15ml/1 tbsp dry sherry
15ml/1 tbsp dark soy sauce
90ml/6 tbsp vegetable stock
5ml/1 tsp cornflour (cornstarch)
15ml/1 tbsp cold water
ground white pepper
salt
2 shredded spring onions (scallions), to garnish

1 Put the tofu in a dish. Sprinkle with the sesame oil, light soy sauce and a large pinch of pepper. Marinate for 10 minutes, then drain and cut into 2.5 x 1cm/1 x ½in pieces.

2 Heat the vegetable oil in a large non-stick frying pan or wok. Add the garlic and ginger and stir-fry for a few seconds. Add all the mushrooms and stir-fry for a further 2 minutes.

3 Stir in the dry sherry, dark soy sauce and stock. Season to taste. Lower the heat and simmer gently for 4 minutes.

4 Place the cornflour in a bowl with the water. Mix to make a smooth paste. Stir the cornflour mixture into the pan or wok and cook, stirring constantly to prevent lumps, until thickened.

5 Carefully add the pieces of tofu, toss gently to coat thoroughly in the sauce and simmer for 2 minutes.

6 Transfer to a warmed serving dish, sprinkle with the shredded spring onions and serve immediately.

Simmered Tofu with Vegetables

Quick and easy, this is perfect for a family supper.

Serves 4

4 dried shiitake mushrooms
450g/1lb mooli (daikon)
350g/12oz firm tofu
115g/4oz/¾ cup green beans,
5ml/1 tsp long grain rice
115g/4oz carrots, sliced
300g/11oz baby potatoes, unpeeled
750ml/1¼ pints/3 cups vegetable stock
30ml/2 tbsp sugar
75ml/5 tbsp shoyu
45ml/3 tbsp sake
15ml/1 tbsp mirin

1 Put the dried shiitake mushrooms in a bowl. Add 250ml/8fl oz/1 cup water and soak for 2 hours. Drain, discarding the liquid. Remove and discard the stems.

2 Peel the mooli and slice it into 1cm/½in discs. Put the slices in cold water to prevent them from discolouring.

3 Drain and rinse the tofu, then pat dry with kitchen paper. Cut the tofu into pieces of about 2.5 x 5cm/1 x 2in.

4 Bring a pan of water to the boil. Blanch the beans for 2 minutes. Drain, cool under running water and drain again.

5 Put the mooli slices in the clean pan. Pour in water to cover and add the rice. Bring to the boil, then reduce the heat and simmer for 15 minutes. Drain off the liquid and the rice.

6 Add the drained mushrooms, carrots and potatoes to the mooli in the pan. Pour in the vegetable stock, bring to the boil, skim, then add the sugar, shoyu and sake. Shake the pan gently to mix the ingredients thoroughly.

7 Cover with a circle of baking parchment and a tight-fitting lid and simmer for 30 minutes or until the sauce has reduced by half. Add the tofu and green beans. Warm through for 2 minutes, then add the mirin. Taste the sauce and add more shoyu if required. Serve immediately in warmed bowls.

tofu w. four mushrooms Energy 118kcal/491kJ; Protein 9.3g; Carbohydrate 2.9g, of which sugars 1.1g; Fat 7.4g, of which saturates 0.9g; Cholesterol 0mg; Calcium 456mg; Fibre 1.2g; Sodium 455mg.
tofu w. vegetables Energy 142kcal/597kJ; Protein 4.2g; Carbohydrate 27.6g, of which sugars 15.1g; Fat 0.9g, of which saturates 0.3g; Cholesterol 0mg; Calcium 92mg; Fibre 3.3g; Sodium 1406mg.

Tofu with Peppers & Pine Nuts

Variations on stuffed peppers appear the world over, but this is a good alternative to the more usual meat- or rice-based recipes. The use of garlic or herb olive oil enhances the flavour, while the pine nuts create a crunchy topping that contrasts nicely with the filling.

Serves 4

4 red (bell) peppers
1 orange (bell) pepper, seeded and coarsely chopped
1 yellow (bell) pepper, seeded and coarsely chopped
60ml/4 tbsp garlic or herb olive oil
250g/9oz firm tofu
50g/2oz/½ cup pine nuts

1 Preheat the oven to 220°C/425°F/Gas 7. Cut the red peppers in half, leaving the stalks intact, and discard the seeds. Place the red pepper halves on a baking sheet and fill with the chopped orange and yellow peppers. Drizzle with half the garlic or herb olive oil and bake for 25 minutes, until the edges of the peppers are beginning to char.

2 Meanwhile, unpack the tofu blocks and discard the liquid, then wrap the tofu in layers of kitchen paper. Put a large plate on top as a weight and leave for 30 minutes to allow the excess liquid to be absorbed by the paper.

3 Cut the tofu into small, even cubes using a sharp knife.

4 Remove the peppers from the oven, but leave the oven on. Tuck the tofu cubes in among the chopped orange and yellow peppers. Sprinkle evenly with the pine nuts and drizzle with the remaining oil. Bake for a further 15 minutes, or until well browned. Serve warm or at room temperature.

Cook's Tip
Once you have opened a packet of tofu, any that is unused should be rinsed and put in a bowl with fresh water to cover. Change the water every day and use the tofu within 5 days.

Tofu & Broccoli with Fried Shallots

This meltingly tender tofu flavoured with spices and served with broccoli makes a perfect lunch. To give the recipe that little bit extra, deep-fry some crispy shallots to serve on the side, if you like.

Serves 4

500g/1¼lb block of firm tofu, drained
45ml/3 tbsp kecap manis
30ml/2 tbsp sweet chilli sauce
45ml/3 tbsp soy sauce
5ml/1 tsp sesame oil
5ml/1 tsp finely grated fresh root ginger
400g/14oz tenderstem broccoli, halved lengthways
45ml/3 tbsp roughly chopped coriander (cilantro), and 30ml/2 tbsp toasted sesame seeds, to garnish
steamed rice or noodles, to serve

1 Cut the tofu into four triangular pieces by slicing the block in half widthways, then diagonally. Place in a heatproof dish.

2 In a small bowl, combine the kecap manis, chilli sauce, soy sauce, sesame oil and ginger, then pour over the tofu. Leave the tofu to marinate for at least 30 minutes, turning occasionally.

3 Place the broccoli on a heatproof plate and place on a trivet or steamer rack in a wok. Cover and steam for 4–5 minutes, until just tender. Remove and keep warm.

4 Place the dish of tofu on the trivet or steamer rack in the wok, cover and steam for 4–5 minutes.

5 Divide the broccoli among four warmed serving plates and top each one with a triangle of tofu.

6 Spoon the remaining juices over the tofu and broccoli, then sprinkle with the coriander and toasted sesame seeds.

7 Serve immediately with steamed rice or noodles.

tofu w. peppers Energy 311kcal/1287kJ; Protein 9.3g; Carbohydrate 17g, of which sugars 15.9g; Fat 23.2g, of which saturates 2.7g; Cholesterol 0mg; Calcium 340mg; Fibre 4.2g; Sodium 13mg.
tofu & broccoli Energy 202kcal/840kJ; Protein 16.5g; Carbohydrate 6.9g, of which sugars 5.6g; Fat 12.1g, of which saturates 1.7g; Cholesterol 0mg; Calcium 750mg; Fibre 3.5g; Sodium 938mg.

Shiitake Mushroom Namul

In this tempting namul dish the distinctive taste of sesame oil emphasizes the well-rounded, meaty taste of the shiitake mushrooms. The mushrooms are quickly sautéed to soften them as well as to accentuate their characteristic rich and earthy flavours.

Serves 2

12 dried shiitake mushrooms, soaked in warm water for about 30 minutes until softened
10ml/2 tsp sesame seeds
2 garlic cloves, crushed
30ml/2 tbsp vegetable oil
½ spring onion (scallion), finely chopped
10ml/2 tsp sesame oil
salt

1 When the soaked shiitake mushrooms have reconstituted and become soft, drain and slice them, discarding the stems, and then place them in a bowl. Add the sesame seeds, crushed garlic and a pinch of salt, and blend the ingredients together.

2 Coat a frying pan or wok with the vegetable oil and place over high heat. Add the seasoned mushroom slices and quickly stir-fry them, so that they soften slightly but do not lose their firmness.

3 Remove from the heat and stir in the spring onion and sesame oil. Transfer to a shallow dish and serve.

Cook's Tip
It is important to drain the shiitake mushrooms thoroughly to ensure that their dark colour does not overwhelm the dish. Try squeezing the mushrooms gently to remove all the liquid, and then pat dry with kitchen paper.

Variation
Fresh chestnut mushrooms may be used instead of shiitake.

Vegetable Stew with Roasted Tomato & Garlic Sauce

This lightly spiced stew makes a perfect match for rice, enriched with a little butter or olive oil. Add some chopped fresh coriander and a handful each of raisins and toasted pine nuts to the rice to make it extra special.

Serves 6

45ml/3 tbsp olive oil
250g/9oz shallots
1 large onion, chopped
2 garlic cloves, chopped
5ml/1 tsp cumin seeds
5ml/1 tsp ground coriander seeds
5ml/1 tsp paprika
5cm/2in piece cinnamon stick
2 fresh bay leaves
300–450ml/½–¾ pint/1¼–scant 2 cups good vegetable stock
good pinch of saffron threads
450g/1lb carrots, thickly sliced
2 green (bell) peppers, seeded and thickly sliced
115g/4oz ready-to-eat dried apricots, halved if large
5–7.5ml/1–1½ tsp ground toasted cumin seeds
450g/1lb squash, peeled, seeded and cut into chunks
pinch of sugar, to taste
25g/1oz/2 tbsp butter (optional)
salt and ground black pepper
45ml/3 tbsp fresh coriander (cilantro) leaves, to garnish

For the roasted tomato and garlic sauce

1kg/2¼lb tomatoes, halved
5ml/1 tsp sugar
45ml/3 tbsp olive oil
1–2 fresh red chillies, seeded and chopped
2–3 garlic cloves, chopped
5ml/1 tsp fresh thyme leaves

1 Preheat the oven to 180°C/350°F/Gas 4. For the sauce, place the tomatoes, cut sides uppermost, in a roasting pan. Season well with salt and pepper and sprinkle the sugar over the top, then drizzle with the olive oil. Roast for 30 minutes.

2 Sprinkle the chillies, garlic and thyme over the tomatoes, stir to mix and roast for another 30–45 minutes, until the tomatoes are collapsed but still a little juicy. Cool, then process in a food processor to make a thick sauce. Sieve to remove the seeds.

3 Heat 30ml/2 tbsp of the oil in a large pan or deep frying pan and cook the shallots until browned all over. Remove from the pan and set aside. Add the chopped onion to the pan and cook over a low heat for 5–7 minutes, until softened. Stir in the garlic and cumin seeds and cook for a further 3–4 minutes.

4 Add the ground coriander seeds, paprika, cinnamon stick and bay leaves. Cook, stirring constantly, for another 2 minutes, then mix in the vegetable stock, saffron, carrots and green peppers. Season well, cover and simmer gently for 10 minutes.

5 Stir in the apricots, 5ml/1 tsp of the ground toasted cumin, the browned shallots and the squash. Stir in the tomato sauce.

6 Cover the pan and cook for a further 5 minutes. Uncover and continue to cook, stirring occasionally, for 10–15 minutes.

7 Adjust the seasoning, adding a little more cumin and a pinch of sugar to taste. Remove and discard the cinnamon stick. Stir in the butter, if using, and serve sprinkled with coriander leaves.

shiitake namul Energy 167kcal/689kJ; Protein 2.2g; Carbohydrate 1.1g, of which sugars 0.2g; Fat 17.2g, of which saturates 2.2g; Cholesterol 0mg; Calcium 38mg; Fibre 1.2g; Sodium 4mg.
vegetable stew Energy 133kcal/552kJ; Protein 5.7g; Carbohydrate 10.5g, of which sugars 7.1g; Fat 8g, of which saturates 0g; Cholesterol 0mg; Calcium 94mg; Fibre 4.3g; Sodium 32mg.

Crisp Deep-fried Vegetables

Stir-fried, steamed or deep-fried vegetables served with a dipping sauce are common fare throughout Asia, and often appear among the delightful 'no-name' dishes popular with tourists in Thailand.

Serves 4–6

6 eggs
1 long aubergine (eggplant), peeled, halved lengthways and sliced into half moons
1 long sweet potato, peeled and sliced into rounds
1 small butternut squash, peeled, seeded, halved lengthways and cut into half moons
salt and ground black pepper
vegetable oil, for deep-frying
chilli sambal or hot chilli sauce for dipping

1 Beat the eggs in a wide bowl. Season with salt and pepper. Toss the vegetables in the egg to coat thoroughly.

2 Heat enough oil for deep-frying in a large wok. Cook the vegetables in small batches, making sure there is plenty of egg coating each piece.

3 When they turn golden, lift them out of the oil with a slotted spoon and drain on kitchen paper.

4 Keep the vegetables hot while successive batches are being fried. Serve warm with chilli sambal, hot chilli sauce or a dipping sauce of your choice.

Mushrooms with Loofah Squash

Loofah squash – also known as ridged gourd – is easy to work with and is available in most Asian markets. It resembles a long courgette, usually lighter in colour and with ridges from one end to the other.

Serves 4

750g/1lb 10oz loofah squash, peeled
30ml/2 tbsp groundnut (peanut) or sesame oil
2 shallots, halved and sliced
2 garlic cloves, finely chopped
115g/4oz/1½ cups button (white) mushrooms, quartered
15ml/1 tbsp mushroom sauce
10ml/2 tsp soy sauce
4 spring onions (scallions), cut into 2cm/¾in pieces
fresh coriander (cilantro) leaves and thin strips of spring onion (scallion), to garnish

1 Using a sharp knife, cut the loofah squash diagonally into 2cm/¾in-thick pieces and set aside.

2 Heat the oil in a large wok or heavy pan. Stir in the halved shallots and garlic, stir-fry until they begin to colour and turn golden, then add the mushrooms.

3 Add the mushroom and soy sauces, and the squash. Reduce the heat, cover and cook gently for a few minutes until the squash is tender. Just before serving, stir in the spring onion pieces and allow to warm through. Spoon into warmed serving bowls and garnish with the coriander and spring onion strips.

Mushrooms with Garlic Chilli Sauce

Succulent spiced mushrooms taste great when cooked over coals.

Serves 4

12 large field (portabello), chestnut or oyster mushrooms
4 garlic cloves, roughly chopped
6 coriander (cilantro) roots, roughly chopped
15ml/1 tbsp sugar
30ml/2 tbsp light soy sauce
ground black pepper

For the dipping sauce
15ml/1 tbsp sugar
90ml/6 tbsp rice vinegar
5ml/1 tsp salt
1 garlic clove, crushed
1 small fresh red chilli, seeded and finely chopped

1 If using wooden skewers, soak eight of them in cold water for at least 30 minutes to prevent them from burning when exposed to direct heat.

2 Make the dipping sauce by heating the sugar, rice vinegar and salt in a small pan, stirring occasionally until the sugar and salt have dissolved.

3 Add the garlic and chilli to the mixture, pour into a serving dish and keep warm.

4 In a mortar pound or blend the garlic and coriander roots. Scrape the mixture into a bowl and mix with the sugar, soy sauce and a little pepper.

5 Trim and wipe the mushrooms and cut them in half. Thread three mushroom halves on to each skewer. Lay the filled skewers side by side in a shallow dish.

6 Brush the soy sauce mixture over the mushrooms and leave to marinate for 15 minutes.

7 Cook on a barbecue or under a hot grill (broiler) for 2–3 minutes on each side. Serve with the dipping sauce.

deep-fried vegetables Energy 280kcal/1164kJ; Protein 8.3g; Carbohydrate 11.9g, of which sugars 5.7g; Fat 22.7g, of which saturates 3.7g; Cholesterol 190mg; Calcium 90mg; Fibre 3.5g; Sodium 84mg.
mushrooms w. squash Energy 89kcal/371kJ; Protein 2.3g; Carbohydrate 6.7g, of which sugars 5.2g; Fat 6.1g, of which saturates 0.9g; Cholesterol 0mg; Calcium 65mg; Fibre 2.6g; Sodium 221mg.
mushrooms w. chilli sauce Energy 51kcal/215kJ; Protein 2.5g; Carbohydrate 9.7g, of which sugars 8.7g; Fat 0.5g, of which saturates 0.1g; Cholesterol 0mg; Calcium 12mg; Fibre 1.3g; Sodium 1031mg.

Stir-fried Water Spinach

In Malaysia, this dish is a favourite with roadside vendors. Water spinach is an excellent source of Vitamin A, which helps to promote healthy bones, skin, hair and also aids vision. Serve this aromatic dish as part of a vegetarian meal, or as a side dish to accompany main meat or fish courses.

Serves 3–4

30ml/2 tbsp groundnut (peanut) oil
2 garlic cloves, finely chopped
2 fresh red or green chillies, seeded and finely chopped
500g/1¼lb water spinach
45ml/3 tbsp chilli sauce
salt and ground black pepper

1 Heat a wok or large pan and add the oil. Stir in the garlic and chillies and stir-fry for 1 minute, then add the water spinach and toss around the pan.

2 Once the water spinach leaves begin to wilt, add the chilli sauce, making sure it coats the spinach. Season to taste with salt and pepper and serve immediately.

Variations

- *Although water spinach is traditionally favoured in this recipe, you could substitute any type of green, leafy vegetable, particularly ordinary spinach. Tougher vegetables, such as cabbage or spring greens (collards), may need to be blanched in boiling water prior to stir-frying with the other ingredients. Thoroughly wash the leaves, then immerse in boiling water for about 15 seconds until softened slightly.*
- *Some non-leafy vegetables also work well as the principal component. Cauliflower and, when in season, asparagus, can be stir-fried in the same way. With the cauliflower, simply cut off the heads, divide into florets and add directly to the pan with the garlic and chillies. The asparagus will require blanching. Trim off the woody bases and stand the heads in a small jug (pitcher) of boiling water for 3–4 minutes. Slice and add to the garlic and chillies in the pan.*

Okra & Coconut Stir-fry

Stir-fried okra spiced with mustard, cumin and red chillies and sprinkled with freshly grated coconut makes a great combination. It is the perfect way to enjoy these succulent pods, with the sweetness of the coconut complementing the warm spices.

Serves 4

600g/1lb 6oz okra
60ml/4 tbsp sunflower oil
1 onion, finely chopped
15ml/1 tbsp mustard seeds
15ml/1 tbsp cumin seeds
2–3 dried red chillies
10–12 curry leaves
2.5ml/½ tsp ground turmeric
90g/3½oz freshly grated coconut
salt and ground black pepper
poppadums, rice or naan bread, to serve

1 With a sharp knife, cut each of the okra pods diagonally into 1cm/½in lengths. Set aside. Heat a wok and add the sunflower oil.

2 When the oil is hot, add the chopped onion and stir-fry over a medium heat for about 5 minutes until softened.

3 Add the mustard seeds, cumin seeds, chillies and curry leaves to the onions and stir-fry over a high heat for about 2 minutes.

4 Add the okra and turmeric to the wok and continue to stir-fry over a high heat for 3–4 minutes.

5 Remove the wok from the heat, sprinkle the coconut over the fried vegetables and season well with salt and ground black pepper. Serve the dish immediately on warmed plates with poppadums, steamed rice or naan bread.

Cook's Tip

Fresh okra is widely available from many supermarkets and Asian stores. Choose fresh, firm, green specimens and avoid any pods that are limp or turning brown.

stir-fried water spinach Energy 92kcal/379kJ; Protein 3.8g; Carbohydrate 4.6g, of which sugars 4g; Fat 6.5g, of which saturates 0.8g; Cholesterol 0mg; Calcium 214mg; Fibre 2.8g; Sodium 297mg.
okra & coconut stir-fry Energy 191kcal/790kJ; Protein 5.1g; Carbohydrate 6.2g, of which sugars 5.1g; Fat 16.5g, of which saturates 5.1g; Cholesterol 0mg; Calcium 249mg; Fibre 7.1g; Sodium 15mg.

Glazed Pumpkin

Pumpkins, butternut squash and winter melons can all be cooked in this way. For non-vegetarians, you could use fish sauce instead of the soy sauce.

Serves 4

200ml/7fl oz/scant 1 cup coconut milk
15ml/1 tbsp soy sauce
30ml/2 tbsp palm sugar (jaggery) or light muscovado (brown) sugar
30ml/2 tbsp groundnut (peanut) oil
4 garlic cloves, finely chopped
25g/1oz fresh root ginger, peeled and finely shredded
675g/1½lb pumpkin flesh, cubed
ground black pepper
a handful of curry or basil leaves, to garnish
fried onion rings, to garnish
chilli oil, for drizzling
plain or coconut rice, to serve

1 In a bowl, beat the coconut milk and the soy sauce with the sugar, until it has dissolved. Set aside.

2 Heat the oil in a wok or heavy pan and stir in the garlic and ginger. Stir-fry until they begin to colour, then stir in the pumpkin cubes, mixing well.

3 Stir in the coconut milk and bring to the boil. Reduce the heat, cover and simmer for about 20 minutes, until the pumpkin is tender and the sauce has reduced. Season with pepper and garnish with curry or basil leaves and fried onion rings. Serve hot with plain or coconut rice, drizzled with a little chilli oil.

Cook's Tip

For a quick coconut rice, rinse 350g/12oz/1¾ cups Thai fragrant rice and put in a pan with 400ml/14 fl oz/1¾ cups coconut milk, 2.5ml/½ tsp ground coriander, a cinnamon stick, a bruised lemon grass stalk and a bay leaf. Add salt to taste. Bring to the boil, cover and simmer for 8–10 minutes, or until the liquid has been absorbed. Fork through lightly, remove the solid spices and serve.

Buddhist Vegetarian Noodles

During Buddhist festivals in China, this dish takes centre stage as temple chefs cook huge cauldrons of it to serve to devotees, free of charge. It is a simple dish, redolent with flavour and with a beautifully crunchy texture.

Serves 4

10 dried Chinese black mushrooms
4 pieces sweet dried tofu wafers
300g/11oz rice vermicelli
45ml/3 tbsp vegetable oil
30ml/2 tbsp crushed garlic
1 large onion, thinly sliced
100g/3¾oz/½ cup beansprouts
115g/4oz drained canned bamboo shoots, sliced into thin strips
115g/4oz Chinese long beans or green beans, sliced into thin strips
30ml/2 tbsp hoisin sauce
30ml/2 tbsp oyster sauce
30ml/2 tbsp dark soy sauce
45ml/3 tbsp sesame oil
400ml/14fl oz/1⅔ cups water

1 Soak the dried mushrooms in a bowl of boiling water for 20–30 minutes until soft. Meanwhile soak the beancurd wafers and rice vermicelli until soft, following the directions on the packets.

2 Drain the mushrooms thoroughly, then cut off and discard the stems and slice the caps into thin strips. Drain the tofu wafers and slice them thinly. Drain the noodles and set them aside.

3 Heat the oil in a wok and fry the garlic for 40 seconds, until light brown. Add the onion and stir-fry for 2 minutes, then add the beansprouts, bamboo shoots, beans and mushrooms. Stir-fry for 1 minute, then stir in the hoisin sauce, oyster sauce, soy sauce and sesame oil.

4 Add the tofu wafers to the wok and stir-fry for 2 minutes more. Add the noodles and pour in the water. Toss over the heat for about 4 minutes, until all the ingredients are cooked and the mixture is well blended. Spoon into a bowl and serve.

glazed pumpkin Energy 114kcal/477kJ; Protein 1.5g; Carbohydrate 14.3g, of which sugars 13.4g; Fat 6g, of which saturates 0.9g; Cholesterol 0mg; Calcium 68mg; Fibre 1.7g; Sodium 323mg.
vegetarian noodles Energy 509kcal/2116kJ; Protein 12.7g; Carbohydrate 73g, of which sugars 9.9g; Fat 18.6g, of which saturates 2.2g; Cholesterol 0mg; Calcium 200mg; Fibre 3.3g; Sodium 726mg.

Corn & Cashew Nut Curry

This is a substantial curry, thanks largely to the potatoes and corn kernels, which makes it a great winter dish. It is deliciously aromatic, but, as the spices are added in relatively small amounts, the resulting flavour is fairly mild.

Serves 4

30ml/2 tbsp vegetable oil
4 shallots, chopped
90g/3½oz/scant 1 cup cashew nuts
5ml/1 tsp red curry paste
400g/14oz potatoes, peeled and cut into chunks
1 lemon grass stalk, finely chopped
200g/7oz can chopped tomatoes
600ml/1 pint/2½ cups boiling water
200g/7oz/generous 1 cup drained canned whole kernel corn
4 celery sticks, sliced
2 kaffir lime leaves, central rib removed, rolled into cylinders and thinly sliced
15ml/1 tbsp tomato ketchup
15ml/1 tbsp light soy sauce
5ml/1 tsp palm sugar (jaggery) or light muscovado (brown) sugar
4 spring onions (scallions), thinly sliced
small bunch fresh basil, chopped

1 Heat the oil in a wok. Add the shallots and stir-fry over a medium heat for 2–3 minutes, until softened. Add the cashew nuts and stir-fry for a few minutes until they are golden.

2 Stir in the red curry paste. Stir-fry for 1 minute, then add the potatoes, lemon grass, tomatoes and boiling water.

3 Bring back to the boil, then reduce the heat to low, cover and simmer gently for 15–20 minutes, or until the potatoes are tender when tested with the tip of a knife.

4 Stir the corn, celery, lime leaves, ketchup, soy sauce and sugar into the wok. Simmer for a further 5 minutes, until heated through, then spoon into warmed serving bowls.

5 Sprinkle with the sliced spring onions and basil and serve.

Jungle Curry

This fiery, flavoursome vegetarian curry is almost dominated by the chilli. Its many variations make it a favourite with Buddhist monks who value the way it adds variety to their vegetarian diet. Often sold from countryside stalls, jungle curry can be served with plain rice or noodles, or chunks of crusty bread. It can be eaten for breakfast or enjoyed as a pick-me-up at any time of day.

Serves 4

30ml/2 tbsp vegetable oil
2 onions, roughly chopped
2 lemon grass stalks, roughly chopped and bruised
4 fresh green chillies, seeded and finely sliced
4cm/1½in galangal or fresh root ginger, peeled and chopped
3 carrots, peeled, halved lengthways and sliced
115g/4oz snake beans
grated rind of 1 lime
15ml/1 tbsp rice vinegar
15ml/1 tbsp soy sauce or 10ml/2 tsp soy sauce and 5ml/1 tsp vegetarian fish sauce
5ml/1 tsp black peppercorns, crushed
15ml/1 tbsp sugar
10ml/2 tsp ground turmeric
115g/4oz canned bamboo shoots
75g/3oz spinach, roughly chopped
150ml/¼ pint/⅔ cup coconut milk
chopped fresh coriander (cilantro) and mint leaves, to garnish

1 Heat a wok or heavy pan and add the oil. Once hot, stir in the onions, lemon grass, chillies and galangal or ginger. Add the carrots and beans with the lime rind and stir-fry for 1–2 minutes.

2 Stir in the rice vinegar, soy sauce and vegetarian fish sauce, if using. Add the crushed peppercorns, sugar and turmeric, then stir in the bamboo shoots and the chopped spinach.

3 Stir in the coconut milk and simmer for about 10 minutes, until the vegetables are tender. Garnish with coriander and mint.

corn & cashew nut Energy 298kcal/1245kJ; Protein 8.8g; Carbohydrate 27.6g, of which sugars 8.9g; Fat 17.7g, of which saturates 3.1g; Cholesterol 0mg; Calcium 33mg; Fibre 3.5g; Sodium 981mg.
jungle curry Energy 119kcal/496kJ; Protein 3.8g; Carbohydrate 18.6g, of which sugars 15.3g; Fat 3.8g, of which saturates 0.5g; Cholesterol 0mg; Calcium 125mg; Fibre 4.3g; Sodium 60mg.

Yellow Vegetable Curry

This hot and spicy curry made with coconut milk has a creamy richness that contrasts wonderfully with the heat of chilli and the bite of lightly cooked vegetables.

Serves 4

30ml/2 tbsp sunflower oil
30–45ml/2–3 tbsp yellow curry paste (see Cook's Tip)
200ml/7fl oz/scant 1 cup coconut cream
300ml/½ pint/1¼ cups coconut milk
150ml/¼ pint/⅔ cup vegetable stock
200g/7oz snake beans, cut into 2cm/¾in lengths
200g/7oz baby corn
4 baby courgettes (zucchini), sliced
1 small aubergine (eggplant), cubed or sliced
10ml/2 tsp palm sugar (jaggery) or light muscovado (brown) sugar
fresh coriander (cilantro) leaves, to garnish
noodles or rice, to serve

1 Heat a large wok over a medium heat and add the oil. When hot, add the curry paste and stir-fry for 1–2 minutes. Add the coconut cream and cook gently for 8–10 minutes, or until the mixture starts to separate.

2 Add the coconut milk, stock and vegetables and cook gently for 8–10 minutes, until the vegetables are just tender. Stir in the sugar, garnish with coriander leaves and serve with freshly cooked noodles or rice.

Cook's Tip

To make the curry paste, mix 10ml/2 tsp each hot chilli powder, ground coriander and ground cumin in a sturdy food processor, preferably one with an attachment for processing smaller quantities. Add 5ml/1 tsp ground turmeric, 15ml/1 tbsp chopped fresh galangal, 10ml/2 tsp crushed garlic, 30ml/2 tbsp finely chopped lemon grass, 4 finely chopped red shallots and 5ml/1 tsp chopped lime rind. Add 30ml/2 tbsp cold water and blend to a smooth paste. Add a little more water if necessary.

Silver Threads of Longevity

The 'silver threads' of the recipe title are cellophane noodles. In China these symbolize longevity and are often served at birthdays and other special occasions. Also known as glass noodles, transparent vermicelli or translucent noodles, they are made from green mung beans and are widely used in both hot and cold dishes. Here they are teamed with lily buds, which contribute a mild, sweet taste and crunchy texture.

Serves 4

50g/2oz dried lily buds
150g/5oz cellophane noodles
100g/3¾oz/½ cup beansprouts
45ml/3 tbsp vegetable oil
30ml/2 tbsp crushed garlic
30ml/2 tbsp oyster sauce
30ml/2 tbsp light soy sauce
45ml/3 tbsp sesame oil
200ml/7fl oz/scant 1 cup water
chopped fresh coriander (cilantro), to garnish

1 Soak the lily buds in a bowl of warm water for 30 minutes or until soft. Meanwhile, soak the cellophane noodles in a separate bowl of warm water for 15 minutes.

2 Drain the lily buds, rinse them under cold water and drain again. Snip off the hard ends.

3 Drain the noodles. Using a pair of scissors or a sharp knife, chop the strands into shorter lengths for easier handling.

4 Heat the oil in a wok and fry the garlic for 40 seconds. Do not let the garlic burn. Add the beansprouts. Stir-fry vigorously for 1 minute. Add the lily buds and the noodles and toss over the heat for 2 minutes.

5 Add the oyster sauce, soy sauce and sesame oil. Pour in the water. Continue to toss over the heat until the liquid is hot and the noodles and lily buds are coated in the mixture.

6 Spoon into a heated serving dish and garnish with the chopped coriander. Serve immediately.

yellow vegetable curry Energy 126kcal/528kJ; Protein 4.7g; Carbohydrate 12.7g, of which sugars 11.9g; Fat 6.7g, of which saturates 1.1g; Cholesterol 5mg; Calcium 90mg; Fibre 2.5g; Sodium 752mg.
silver threads Energy 307kcal/1274kJ; Protein 3.3g; Carbohydrate 34.8g, of which sugars 3.4g; Fat 16.7g, of which saturates 2.2g; Cholesterol 0mg; Calcium 15mg; Fibre 0.6g; Sodium 663mg.

Sprouting Beans & Pak Choi

Stir-frying is a great way to cook vegetables as they retain their colour, texture and most of their nutrients.

Serves 4

45ml/3 tbsp groundnut (peanut) oil
3 spring onions (scallions), sliced
2 garlic cloves, cut into slivers
2.5cm/1in piece fresh root ginger, cut into slivers
1 carrot, cut into thick batons
150g/5oz/scant 1 cup sprouting beans (lentils, mung beans, chickpeas)
200g/7oz pak choi (bok choy), shredded
50g/2oz/½ cup unsalted cashew nuts or halved almonds
salt and ground black pepper

For the sauce

45ml/3 tbsp light soy sauce
30ml/2 tbsp dry sherry
15ml/1 tbsp sesame oil
150ml/¼ pint/⅔ cup cold water
5ml/1 tsp cornflour (cornstarch)
5ml/1 tsp clear honey

1 Heat a large wok and add the oil. When the oil is hot, add the spring onions, garlic, ginger and carrot and stir-fry over a medium heat for 2 minutes.

2 Add the sprouting beans and stir-fry for a further 2 minutes. Add the pak choi and cashew nuts or almonds and stir-fry until the leaves are just wilting.

3 Mix all the sauce ingredients together in a jug (pitcher) and pour into the wok, stirring constantly.

4 When all the vegetables are coated in a thin glossy sauce, season with salt and pepper. Serve immediately.

Variation

You can use a variety of other Chinese greens besides pak choi (bok choy). Try Chinese leaves (Chinese cabbage), Chinese flowering cabbage, Chinese spinach, also known as callaloo, or Chinese water spinach.

Potato Curry with Yogurt

Variations of this simple Indian curry are popular in Singapore, where fusion dishes like this one cater for a community that includes people from all over Asia, as well as from Europe and the Americas.

Serves 4

6 garlic cloves, chopped
25g/1oz fresh root ginger, peeled and chopped
30ml/2 tbsp ghee, or 15ml/1 tbsp oil and 15g/½oz/1 tbsp butter
6 shallots, halved lengthways and sliced along the grain
2 fresh green chillies, seeded and finely sliced
10ml/2 tsp sugar
a handful of fresh or dried curry leaves
2 cinnamon sticks
5–10ml/1–2 tsp ground turmeric
15ml/1 tbsp garam masala
500g/1¼lb waxy potatoes, cut into bitesize pieces
2 tomatoes, peeled, seeded and quartered
250ml/8fl oz/1 cup Greek (US strained plain) yogurt
salt and ground black pepper
5ml/1 tsp red chilli powder, and fresh coriander (cilantro) and mint leaves, finely chopped, to garnish
1 lemon, quartered, to serve

1 Using a mortar and pestle or a food processor, grind the garlic and ginger to a coarse paste. Heat the ghee in a heavy pan and stir in the shallots and chillies, until fragrant. Add the garlic and ginger paste with the sugar, and stir until the mixture begins to colour. Stir in the curry leaves, cinnamon sticks, turmeric and garam masala, and toss in the potatoes, making sure they are coated in the spice mixture.

2 Pour in just enough cold water to cover the potatoes. Bring to the boil, then reduce the heat and simmer until the potatoes are just cooked – they should still have a bite to them.

3 Season with salt and pepper to taste. Gently toss in the tomatoes to heat them through. Fold in the yogurt so that it is streaky. Transfer to a warmed serving dish.

4 Sprinkle with the chilli powder, coriander and mint. Serve immediately, with lemon to squeeze over.

beans & pak choi Energy 230kcal/954kJ; Protein 5g; Carbohydrate 11.3g, of which sugars 7.6g; Fat 17.7g, of which saturates 3.3g; Cholesterol 0mg; Calcium 46mg; Fibre 2.4g; Sodium 848mg.
potato curry w. yogurt Energy 231kcal/967kJ; Protein 6.7g; Carbohydrate 26.2g, of which sugars 7.4g; Fat 12.4g, of which saturates 4.1g; Cholesterol 0mg; Calcium 110mg; Fibre 2g; Sodium 63mg.

Cauliflower & Potato Curry

Potatoes and cauliflower make a wonderful combination for a curry, and a substantial side dish. Here they are combined with the mild flavours of cumin, coriander and turmeric with just enough chilli to give the dish that little extra punch.

Serves 4

450g/1lb potatoes, cut into 2.5cm/1in chunks
30ml/2 tbsp vegetable oil
5ml/1 tsp cumin seeds
1 fresh green chilli, finely chopped
450g/1lb cauliflower, broken into florets
5ml/1 tsp ground coriander
5ml/1 tsp ground cumin
1.5ml/¼ tsp chilli powder
2.5ml/½ tsp ground turmeric
2.5ml/½ tsp salt
chopped fresh coriander (cilantro), to garnish
tomato and onion salad and pickle, to serve

1 Par-cook the potatoes in a large pan of boiling water for about 10 minutes. Drain well and set aside.

2 Heat the oil in a large, heavy pan. Add the cumin seeds and fry them for 2 minutes until they begin to splutter. Add the chilli and fry for a further 1 minute.

3 Add the cauliflower florets and fry, stirring, for 5 minutes.

4 Add the potatoes and the ground spices and salt and cook for a further 7–10 minutes, or until both the vegetables are tender. Garnish with fresh coriander and serve with tomato and onion salad and pickle.

Variation
Use sweet potatoes instead of ordinary potatoes for a curry with a sweeter flavour.

Mixed Stir-fry with Peanut Sauce

Wherever you go in Asia, stir-fried vegetables will be on the menu.

Serves 4–6

6 dried shiitake mushrooms, soaked in lukewarm water for 20 minutes
20 tiger lily buds, soaked in lukewarm water for 20 minutes
60ml/4 tbsp sesame oil
225g/8oz tofu, sliced
1 large onion, finely sliced
1 large carrot, finely sliced
300g/11oz pak choi (bok choy), leaves separated from stems
225g/8oz can bamboo shoots, drained and rinsed
50ml/2fl oz/¼ cup soy sauce
10ml/2 tsp sugar

For the peanut sauce
15ml/1 tbsp sesame oil
2 garlic cloves, finely chopped
2 fresh red chillies, seeded and finely chopped
90g/3½oz/scant 1 cup unsalted roasted peanuts, finely chopped
150ml/5fl oz/⅔ cup coconut milk
30ml/2 tbsp hoisin sauce
15ml/1 tbsp soy sauce
15ml/1 tbsp sugar

1 To make the sauce, heat the oil in a wok and stir-fry the garlic and chillies until they begin to colour, then add almost all of the peanuts. Stir-fry for 2–3 minutes, then add the remaining ingredients. Boil, then simmer until thickened. Keep warm.

2 Drain the mushrooms and lily buds and squeeze out any excess water. Cut the mushroom caps into strips and discard the stalks. Trim off the hard ends of the lily buds and tie a knot in the centre of each one.

3 Heat 30ml/2 tbsp of the oil in a wok and brown the tofu on both sides. Drain and cut it into strips.

4 Heat the remaining oil in the wok and stir-fry the onion, carrot and pak choi stems for 2 minutes. Add the mushrooms, lily buds, tofu and bamboo shoots and stir-fry for 1 minute more. Toss in the pak choi leaves, soy sauce and sugar. Stir-fry until heated through. Garnish with the remaining peanuts and serve with the peanut sauce.

cauliflower & potato Energy 177kcal/744kJ; Protein 6.5g; Carbohydrate 22.8g, of which sugars 4.3g; Fat 7.3g, of which saturates 1.1g; Cholesterol 0mg; Calcium 37mg; Fibre 3.2g; Sodium 24mg.
stir-fry w. peanut sauce Energy 157kcal/656kJ; Protein 5.5g; Carbohydrate 13g, of which sugars 11.4g; Fat 9.6g, of which saturates 2.1g; Cholesterol 0mg; Calcium 110mg; Fibre 5.5g; Sodium 65mg.

Mixed Vegetables Monk-style

Chinese monks eat neither meat nor fish, so 'Monk-style' dishes are always fine for vegetarians.

Serves 4

50g/2oz dried tofu sticks
10g/¼oz dried cloud ear (wood ear) mushrooms
8 dried shiitake mushrooms
15ml/1 tbsp vegetable oil
115g/4oz fresh lotus root, peeled and sliced
75g/3oz/¾ cup drained, canned straw mushrooms
115g/4oz/1 cup baby corn cobs, cut in half
30ml/2 tbsp light soy sauce
15ml/1 tbsp sake or dry sherry
10ml/2 tsp sugar
150ml/¼ pint/⅔ cup vegetable stock
75g/3oz/¾ cup mangetouts (snow peas)
5ml/1 tsp cornflour (cornstarch)
15ml/1 tbsp cold water
salt

1 Put the tofu sticks in a bowl. Cover them with hot water and leave to soak for 1 hour. The cloud ear and dried shiitake mushrooms should be soaked in separate bowls of hot water for 20 minutes.

2 Drain the cloud ears, trim off and discard the hard base from each and cut the rest into bitesize pieces. Drain the shiitake mushrooms, discard the stems and slice the caps.

3 Drain the tofu sticks. Cut them into 5cm/2in long pieces, discarding any hard pieces.

4 Heat the oil in a wok and stir-fry the cloud ears, shiitake mushrooms and lotus root for about 30 seconds. Add the tofu, straw mushrooms, baby corn cobs, soy sauce, sherry, sugar and stock. Boil, then simmer, covered, for 20 minutes.

5 Trim the mangetouts and cut them in half. Add to the vegetable mixture, with salt to taste, and cook, uncovered, for 2 minutes more. Mix the cornflour to a paste with the water and add to the wok. Cook, stirring, until the sauce thickens. Serve immediately.

Spicy Vegetables in Coconut Milk

This makes a robust main vegetarian dish, and the sauce enriches plain rice beautifully. The classic vegetables to use are aubergine, cabbage, cauliflower and long beans. The spice blend is exceptionally fragrant with a mix of eight ingredients.

Serves 4

200g/7oz cauliflower
1 purple aubergine or 2 brinjals
5 snake beans
200g/7oz cabbage
30ml/2 tbsp oil
450ml/16fl oz/scant 2 cups coconut milk
2.5ml/½ tsp salt
2.5ml/½ tsp sugar

For the spice paste

4 dried chillies, soaked in warm water until soft
5 shallots, chopped
3 garlic cloves, chopped
4 candlenuts
5g/⅛oz fresh turmeric, peeled
3 thin slices fresh galangal
2 lemon grass stalks, 5cm/2in of root end chopped

1 Slice the cauliflower, aubergine or brinjals, snake beans and cabbage into bitesize pieces. Wash and drain.

2 Grind the spice paste ingredients to a fine paste using a pestle and mortar. Heat the oil in a heavy pan and stir-fry the paste for 4 minutes until the oil separates.

3 Add the coconut milk, salt and sugar. Bring to the boil and add the vegetables. Cook for 15 minutes until all the vegetables are soft. Serve hot.

Cook's Tips

- *Galangal is very like ginger but has its own distinct aroma, so if you can find it in your local Asian market, do use it in this recipe. If you cannot, use ginger instead.*
- *Always bash your lemon grass with the back of a heavy knife to bruise and soften it before you chop it and add it to your spice blends. This helps to release the aroma.*

spicy vegetables Energy 487kcal/2032kJ; Protein 16.9g; Carbohydrate 72.7g, of which sugars 0.8g; Fat 14g, of which saturates 2.5g; Cholesterol 112mg; Calcium 46mg; Fibre 1.1g; Sodium 547mg.
vegetables monk-style Energy 95kcal/399kJ; Protein 3.3g; Carbohydrate 12g, of which sugars 4.6g; Fat 3.6g, of which saturates 0.4g; Cholesterol 0mg; Calcium 91mg; Fibre 1.4g; Sodium 885mg.

Galangal Vegetables & Rice

The galangal and lemon grass give this mixed vegetable dish a wonderful flavour. It has a delicious, savoury sauce and the vegetables retain their crunch, making the dish as delicious and nutritious as it is colourful. It is also has a mild flavour that children will enjoy.

Serves 2–4

115g/4oz/generous ½ cup brown basmati rice, rinsed and drained
350ml/12fl oz/1½ cups vegetable stock
2.5cm/1in piece fresh root galangal, peeled
2 garlic cloves, crushed
30ml/1 tbsp groundnut (peanut) oil
115g/4oz/1½ cups button (white) mushrooms
15ml/1 tbsp vegetable oil
1 large onion, sliced
175g/6oz carrots, cut into matchsticks
225g/8oz courgettes, cut into matchsticks
175–225g/6–8oz/about 1½ cups broccoli, broken into florets
15ml/1 tbsp light soy sauce
15ml/1 tbsp rice vinegar

1 Put the rice in a pan and pour in the vegetable stock. Slowly bring to the boil, then cover with a tight-fitting lid and simmer over a low heat for 20–25 minutes, until the rice is tender and the water has been absorbed, Drain, and keep the rice hot.

2 Crush the galangal and garlic together in a mortar and pestle to make a paste. Heat oil to a wok, then

3 Slice the mushrooms, including the stems. Heat the groundnut oil in a wok and stir in the galangal paste.

4 When the ginger and garlic aromas are released, add the carrots and stir-fry for 2–3 minutes, then add the broccoli and onions and stir-fry for 2 minutes.

5 Add the mushrooms and courgettes and stir-fry for 2–3 minutes more, by which time all the vegetables should be tender but should still retain a bit of 'bite'.

6 Add the cooked rice to the vegetables in the wok, and toss briefly over the heat to mix and heat through. Toss in the soy sauce and rice vinegar, ensuring that the flavourings are evenly dispersed Spoon into warmed individual bowls or plates and serve immediately.

Variation

If you want to give this dish even more taste and colour, infuse a few strands of saffron in a little freshly boiled water and add this vibrant orange-yellow solution to the stock when you boil the rice. It will dye the rice yellow and give the meal a really delicious extra dimension of flavour.

Coconut Noodles & Vegetables

When everyday vegetables are livened up with Thai spices and flavours, the result is a delectable dish that everyone will enjoy.

Serves 4–6

30ml/2 tbsp sunflower oil
1 lemon grass stalk, finely chopped
15ml/1 tbsp red curry paste
1 onion, thickly sliced
3 courgettes (zucchini), thickly sliced
115g/4oz Savoy cabbage, thickly sliced
2 carrots, thickly sliced
150g/5oz broccoli, stem thickly sliced and florets separated
2 x 400ml/14fl oz cans coconut milk
475ml/16fl oz/2 cups vegetable stock
150g/5oz dried egg noodles
30ml/2 tbsp soy sauce
60ml/4 tbsp chopped fresh coriander (cilantro)

For the garnish

2 lemon grass stalks, split
1 bunch fresh coriander (cilantro)
8–10 small fresh red chillies

1 Heat the oil in a wok. Add the lemon grass and red curry paste and stir-fry for 2–3 seconds. Add the onion and cook over a medium heat, stirring occasionally, until softened.

2 Add the courgettes, cabbage, carrots and slices of broccoli stem. Toss the vegetables with the onion mixture. Cook over a low heat, stirring occasionally, for a further 5 minutes.

3 Increase the heat, stir in the coconut milk and vegetable stock and bring to the boil.

4 Add the broccoli florets and the noodles, lower the heat and simmer gently for 20 minutes.

5 To make the garnish, gather the coriander into a small bouquet and lay it on a platter. Tuck the lemon grass halves into the coriander bouquet and add the chillies to resemble flowers.

6 Stir the soy sauce and chopped coriander into the noodle mixture. Spoon on to the platter, taking care not to disturb the herb bouquet, and serve immediately.

vegetables & rice Energy 430kcal/1788kJ; Protein 12.5g; Carbohydrate 58.2g, of which sugars 11.2g; Fat 16.2g, of which saturates 2.2g; Cholesterol 0mg; Calcium 127mg; Fibre 6.5g; Sodium 569mg.
coconut noodles & veg. Energy 192kcal/808kJ; Protein 5.6g; Carbohydrate 29.4g, of which sugars 11.5g; Fat 6.6g, of which saturates 1.4g; Cholesterol 8mg; Calcium 83mg; Fibre 2.4g; Sodium 554mg.

Tung Tong

Popularly called 'gold bags', these crisp pastry purses have a coriander-flavoured filling based on water chestnuts and corn. They are the perfect vegetarian snack and look very impressive.

Makes 18

18 spring roll wrappers, about 8cm/3¼in square, thawed if frozen
oil, for deep-frying
plum sauce, to serve

For the filling
4 baby corn cobs
130g/4½oz can water chestnuts, drained and chopped
1 shallot, coarsely chopped
1 egg, separated
30ml/2 tbsp cornflour (cornstarch)
60ml/4 tbsp water
small bunch fresh coriander (cilantro), chopped
salt and ground black pepper

1 Make the filling. Place the baby corn, water chestnuts, shallot and egg yolk in a food processor or blender. Process to a coarse paste. Place the egg white in a cup and whisk it lightly with a fork.

2 Put the cornflour in a small pan and stir in the water until smooth. Add the corn mixture and chopped coriander and season with salt and pepper to taste. Cook over a low heat, stirring constantly, until thickened.

3 Leave the filling to cool slightly, then place 5ml/1 tsp in the centre of a spring roll wrapper. Brush the edges with the beaten egg white, then gather up the points and press them firmly together to make a pouch or bag.

4 Repeat with the remaining wrappers and filling, keeping the finished bags and the wrappers covered until needed so they do not dry out.

5 Heat the oil in a deep-fryer or wok until a cube of bread, added to the oil, browns in about 45 seconds. Fry the bags, in batches, for about 5 minutes, until golden brown. Drain on kitchen paper and serve hot, with the plum sauce.

Radish Cake

Closely related to yam cake, this recipe makes innovative use of the large white radish that is also known as mooli or daikon. As a vegetable, white radish is fairly bland, although it is useful for making soup stock. Process it to a paste and mix it with rice flour, however, and it is magically transformed.

Serves 6–8

50g/2oz dried shrimp
1kg/2¼lb white radish (mooli)
300g/11oz/2 cups rice flour
115g/4oz/1 cup tapioca flour or 115g/4oz/1 cup cornflour (cornstarch)
750ml/1¼ pints/3 cups water
5ml/1 tsp salt
30ml/2 tbsp vegetable oil
30ml/2 tbsp light soy sauce
30ml/2 tbsp sesame oil
2.5ml/½ tsp ground black pepper
dipping sauce, optional, to serve

1 Put the dried shrimp in a bowl and pour over water to cover. Soak for 1 hour, until soft.

2 Meanwhile, peel the radish and chop it roughly. Process it in batches in a blender or food processor to a soft white purée. Scrape into a strainer and press down with a spoon to extract as much liquid as possible. Tip the radish purée into a bowl and stir in the rice flour and the tapioca or cornflour. Add the water and salt. Mix well.

3 Drain the soaked shrimp and chop them roughly. Spoon the radish purée into a non-stick pan and cook over low heat, stirring frequently, for 5 minutes.

4 Heat the vegetable oil in a frying pan or wok. Add the chopped shrimp and fry for 2 minutes, then add the radish purée. Stir well, then add the soy sauce, sesame oil and black pepper. Mix thoroughly to combine.

5 Press the mixture into a lightly oiled steaming tray. Steam over a pan of rapidly boiling water for 20 minutes. Set aside. When cold, slice into bitesize pieces and serve plain or with a dipping sauce of your choice.

tung tong Energy 55kcal/229kJ; Protein 1.2g; Carbohydrate 6.3g, of which sugars 0.4g; Fat 2.9g, of which saturates 0.4g; Cholesterol 12mg; Calcium 19mg; Fibre 0.5g; Sodium 42mg.
radish cake Energy 263kcal/1099kJ; Protein 7g; Carbohydrate 44.2g, of which sugars 2.7g; Fat 6.3g, of which saturates 0.9g; Cholesterol 32mg; Calcium 111mg; Fibre 1.9g; Sodium 560mg.

Plain Boiled Rice

Basmati rice is always a good choice. It is easy to cook and produces an excellent finished result. It is slimmer than other long grain rice and has a delicate flavour. Although slightly more expensive, it is well worth buying as it is the perfect rice for accompanying curries.

Serves 4–6

350g/12oz/1¾ cups basmati rice
150ml/1 tbsp ghee, unsalted butter or olive oil
450ml/¾ pint/scant 2 cups water
salt

1 Rinse the basmati rice well in cold water until most of the starch is removed and the water runs clear.

2 Heat the ghee, butter or oil in a pan and sauté the drained rice thoroughly for about 2–3 minutes.

3 Add the water and salt and bring to the boil. Reduce the heat to low, cover and cook gently for 10–15 minutes. To serve, fluff the grains gently with a fork.

Cook's Tips

- *Always test the rice after it has cooked for about 10 minutes; it should be just cooked.*
- *As a guide, 75g/3oz/scant ½ cup raw rice will give you an ample helping for one person.*

Variation

To make a fragrantly spiced version, sauté 4–6 green cardamom pods, 4 cloves, 5cm/2in piece cinnamon stick, 2.5ml/½ tsp black cumin seeds and 2 bay leaves. Add 350g/12oz/1¾ cups drained basmati rice and proceed as for plain boiled rice. For an even more luxurious rice, add 6–8 strands of saffron and sauté with the spices.

Indian Pilau Rice

This traditional spiced rice is the perfect accompaniment for meat, fish or vegetarian dishes.

Serves 4

225g/8oz/1¼ cups basmati rice
15ml/1 tbsp vegetable oil
1 small onion, finely chopped
1 garlic clove, crushed
5ml/1 tsp fennel seeds
15ml/1 tbsp sesame seeds
2.5ml/½ tsp ground turmeric
5ml/1 tsp ground cumin
1.5ml/¼ tsp salt
2 whole cloves
4 cardamom pods, lightly crushed
5 black peppercorns
450ml/¾ pint/scant 2 cups chicken or vegetable stock
fresh coriander (cilantro), to garnish

1 Wash the rice well and leave to soak in water for 30 minutes. Heat the oil in a heavy pan, add the onion and garlic and fry gently for 5–6 minutes until softened.

2 Stir in the fennel and sesame seeds, the turmeric, cumin, salt, cloves, cardamom pods and peppercorns and fry for about a minute. Drain the rice well, add to the pan and stir-fry for a further 3 minutes.

3 Pour on the stock. Bring to the boil, then cover. Reduce the heat to very low and simmer gently for 20 minutes, without removing the lid, until all the liquid has been absorbed.

4 Remove from the heat and leave to stand for 2–3 minutes. Fluff up the rice with a fork, transfer to a warmed serving dish and garnish with coriander.

Cook's Tip

In South India, where large quantities of rice are eaten, people prefer a rice which will absorb the spicy flavours of seasonings. In this recipe, basmati rice is cooked in the traditional way to seal in all the flavour.

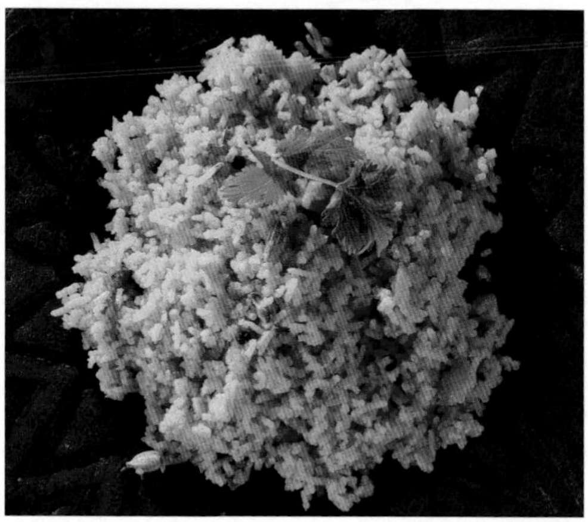

plain boiled rice Energy 342kcal/1430kJ; Protein 6.5g; Carbohydrate 69.9g, of which sugars 0g; Fat 3.5g, of which saturates 2g; Cholesterol 8mg; Calcium 17mg; Fibre 0g; Sodium 23mg.
Indian pilau rice Energy 302kcal/1258kJ; Protein 5.8g; Carbohydrate 46.4g, of which sugars 1g; Fat 10.1g, of which saturates 1.1g; Cholesterol 0mg; Calcium 49mg; Fibre 0.8g; Sodium 2mg.

Colourful Pilau Rice

This lightly spiced rice makes an extremely attractive accompaniment to many Balti dishes, and is easily made.

Serves 4–6

450g/1lb/2⅓ cups basmati rice
75g/3oz/6 tbsp unsalted butter
4 cloves
4 green cardamom pods
1 bay leaf
5ml/1 tsp salt
1 litre/1¾ pints/4 cups water
a few drops each of yellow, green and red food colouring

1 Wash the basmati rice twice, drain well and set aside in a sieve (strainer).

2 Melt the butter in a medium pan, and add the cloves, cardamoms, bay leaf and salt. Lower the heat and add the rice. Fry for about 1 minute, stirring constantly.

3 Add the water to the rice and spices and bring to the boil. As soon as it has boiled, cover the pan and reduce the heat. Cook for 10–15 minutes. Taste a grain of rice after 10 minutes; it should be slightly al dente (soft but with a bite in the centre).

4 Just before you are ready to serve the rice, pour a few drops of each colouring at different sides of the pan. Leave to stand for 5 minutes so that the colours can 'bleed' into the rice. Mix gently with a fork and serve.

Variation

For Almond Pilau, fry 1.5ml/¼ tsp cumin seeds with the cloves and cardamoms at step 2. When the rice has almost cooked, drain it and gently stir in a pinch of saffron threads and 15ml/1 tbsp ground almonds. Leave the rice to stand for a few minutes before serving. Omit the food colouring.

Fruity Pilau

Sultanas and almonds make this a flavoursome rice to serve alongside rich curries.

Serves 4–6

450g/1lb/2⅓ cups basmati rice
75g/3oz/6 tbsp unsalted butter
15ml/1 tbsp corn oil
1 bay leaf
6 black peppercorns
4 green cardamom pods
5ml/1 tsp salt
75g/3oz/½ cup sultanas (golden raisins)
50g/2oz/½ cup flaked (sliced) almonds
1 litre/1¾ pints/4 cups water

1 Wash the basmati rice twice, drain well and set aside in a sieve (strainer).

2 Heat the butter and oil in a medium pan. Lower the heat and add the bay leaf, peppercorns and cardamoms. Stir-fry for about 30 seconds.

3 Add the rice, salt, sultanas and flaked almonds. Stir-fry for about 1 minute, then pour in the water. Bring to the boil, then cover with a tightly fitting lid and lower the heat. Cook for 10–15 minutes. Taste a grain of rice after 10 minutes; it should be slightly al dente (soft but with a bite in the centre).

4 Turn off the heat and leave the rice to stand, still covered, for about 5 minutes. The rice will continue cooking gently during this time. Serve.

Variation

For Mushroom Pilau, boil the rice without any of the flavourings for 15 minutes and then drain. Stir-fry 10ml/2 tsp cumin seeds, 1.5ml/½ tsp fennel seeds and 1 star anise for 30 seconds. Add half a chopped onion and 75g/3oz/1 cup sliced mushrooms, and cook over a medium to high heat for 5 minutes. Add to the rice and transfer to a casserole. Heat in the oven at 190°C/375°F/Gas 5 for 30 minutes.

pilau rice Energy 362kcal/1509kJ; Protein 5.6g; Carbohydrate 59.9g, of which sugars 0.1g; Fat 10.7g, of which saturates 6.5g; Cholesterol 27mg; Calcium 17mg; Fibre 0g; Sodium 403mg.
fruity pilau Energy 464kcal/1934kJ; Protein 7.7g; Carbohydrate 69.2g, of which sugars 9.1g; Fat 17.2g, of which saturates 7.1g; Cholesterol 27mg; Calcium 45mg; Fibre 0.9g; Sodium 79mg.

Nut Pilau

Versions of this rice dish are cooked throughout Asia, always with the best-quality long grain rice. In India, basmati rice is the natural choice. In this particular interpretation of the recipe, walnuts and cashew nuts are added. Serve the pilau with a raita or yogurt.

Serves 4

15ml/1 tbsp vegetable oil
1 onion, chopped
1 garlic clove, crushed
1 large carrot, coarsely grated
225g/8oz/generous 1 cup basmati rice, soaked for 20–30 minutes
5ml/1 tsp cumin seeds
10ml/2 tsp ground coriander
10ml/2 tsp black mustard seeds
4 green cardamom pods
450ml/ ¾ pint/scant 2 cups vegetable stock
1 bay leaf
75g/3oz/ ¾ cup mixed unsalted walnuts and cashew nuts
salt and ground black pepper
fresh coriander (cilantro) sprigs, to garnish

1 Heat the oil in a karahi, wok or large pan. Fry the onion, garlic and carrot for 3–4 minutes. Drain the rice and add to the pan with the spices. Cook for 2 minutes, stirring to coat the grains in oil.

2 Pour in the stock, stirring. Add the bay leaf and season well.

3 Bring to the boil, lower the heat, cover and simmer very gently for 10–12 minutes without stirring.

4 Remove the pan from the heat without lifting the lid. Leave to stand for 5 minutes, then check the rice. If it is cooked, there will be small steam holes on the surface of the rice. Discard the bay leaf and the cardamom pods.

5 Stir in the walnuts and cashew nuts and check the seasoning. Spoon on to a warmed platter, garnish with the fresh coriander and serve.

Sultana & Cashew Pilau

The secret of a perfect pilau is to wash the rice thoroughly, then soak it briefly. This softens and moistens the grains, enabling the rice to absorb moisture during cooking, which results in fluffier rice.

Serves 4

600ml/1 pint/2½ cups hot chicken or vegetable stock
generous pinch of saffron threads
50g/2oz/¼ cup butter
1 onion, chopped
1 garlic clove, crushed
2.5cm/1in piece cinnamon stick
6 green cardamom pods
1 bay leaf
250g/9oz/1⅓ cups basmati rice, soaked in water for 20–30 minutes
50g/2oz/⅓ cup sultanas (golden raisins)
15ml/1 tbsp vegetable oil
50g/2oz/½ cup cashew nuts
naan bread and tomato and onion salad, to serve

1 Pour the hot chicken stock into a jug (pitcher). Stir in the saffron threads and set aside.

2 Heat the butter in a pan and fry the onion and garlic for 5 minutes. Stir in the cinnamon stick, cardamoms and bay leaf and cook for 2 minutes.

3 Drain the rice and add to the pan, then cook, stirring, for 2 minutes more. Pour in the saffron stock and add the sultanas. Bring to the boil, stir, then lower the heat, cover and cook gently for 10 minutes or until the rice is tender and all the liquid has been absorbed.

4 Meanwhile, heat the oil in a wok, karahi or large pan and fry the cashew nuts until browned. Drain on kitchen paper, then sprinkle the cashew nuts over the rice. Serve with naan bread and tomato and onion salad.

Cook's Tip
Saffron powder can be used instead of saffron threads, if you prefer. Dissolve it in the hot stock.

nut pilau Energy 376kcal/1562kJ; Protein 7.5g; Carbohydrate 50g, of which sugars 4g; Fat 16g, of which saturates 1.4g; Cholesterol 0mg; Calcium 42mg; Fibre 1.6g; Sodium 7mg.
sultana pilau Energy 457kcal/1905kJ; Protein 7.8g; Carbohydrate 62g, of which sugars 10.2g; Fat 19.8g, of which saturates 8.1g; Cholesterol 27mg; Calcium 30mg; Fibre 0.8g; Sodium 115mg.

Herby Rice Pilau

A quick and easy recipe to make, this simple pilau is delicious to eat. Serve with a main course meat, poultry or vegetarian curry accompanied by a selection of fresh seasonal vegetables such as broccoli florets, baby corn, asparagus and carrots.

Serves 4

1 onion
1 garlic clove
225g/8oz/generous 1 cup mixed brown basmati and wild rice
15ml/1 tbsp olive oil
5ml/1 tsp ground cumin
5ml/1 tsp ground turmeric
50g/2oz/⅓ cup sultanas (golden raisins)
750ml/1¼ pints/3 cups vegetable stock
30–45ml/2–3 tbsp chopped fresh mixed herbs
salt and ground black pepper
sprigs of fresh herbs and 25g/1oz/¼ cup pistachio nuts, chopped, to garnish

1 Chop the onion and crush the garlic clove.

2 Wash the rice under cold running water until the water runs clear, then drain well.

3 Heat the oil in a large pan, add the onion and garlic, and cook gently for 5 minutes, stirring occasionally.

4 Add the ground cumin and turmeric and drained rice and cook gently for 1 minute, stirring. Stir in the sultanas and vegetable stock, bring to the boil, cover and simmer gently for 20–25 minutes, stirring occasionally.

5 Stir in the chopped mixed herbs and season with salt and pepper to taste.

6 Spoon the pilau into a warmed serving dish and garnish with fresh herb sprigs and a sprinkling of chopped pistachio nuts. Serve immediately.

Tomato & Spinach Pilau

A tasty and nourishing dish for vegetarians and meat-eaters alike.

Serves 4

225g/8oz/generous 1 cup brown basmati rice
30ml/2 tbsp vegetable oil
15ml/1 tbsp ghee or unsalted butter
1 onion, chopped
2 garlic cloves, crushed
3 tomatoes, peeled and chopped
10ml/2 tsp dhana jeera powder, or 5ml/1 tsp ground coriander and 5ml/1 tsp ground cumin
2 carrots, coarsely grated
900ml/1½ pints/3¾ cups vegetable stock
275g/10oz young spinach leaves
50g/2oz/½ cup unsalted cashew nuts
salt and ground black pepper
naan bread, to serve

1 Wash the basmati rice. Place it in a bowl, cover with cold water and leave to soak for 20 minutes. Drain the rice and place it in a large pan of boiling salted water, bring back to the boil and cook for 10 minutes.

2 Heat the oil and ghee or butter in a karahi, wok or large pan, and fry the onion and garlic for 4–5 minutes until soft. Add the tomatoes and cook for 3–4 minutes, stirring, until the mixture thickens. Drain the rice, add it to the pan and cook for a further 1–2 minutes, stirring, until the grains of rice are coated.

3 Stir in the dhana jeera powder or coriander and cumin, then add the carrots. Season with salt and pepper. Pour in the stock and stir well to mix.

4 Bring to the boil, then cover tightly and simmer over a very gentle heat for 20–25 minutes, until the rice is tender.

5 Lay the spinach on the surface of the rice, cover again, and cook for a further 2–3 minutes, until the spinach has wilted. Fold the spinach into the rest of the rice.

6 Dry-fry the cashew nuts until lightly browned and sprinkle over the rice mixture. Serve with naan bread.

herby rice pilau Energy 246kcal/1032kJ; Protein 5.1g; Carbohydrate 55.1g, of which sugars 9.8g; Fat 0.5g, of which saturates 0g; Cholesterol 0mg; Calcium 48mg; Fibre 1.1g; Sodium 7mg.
tomato pilau Energy 384kcal/1598kJ; Protein 9.9g; Carbohydrate 55.9g, of which sugars 7.8g; Fat 13.4g, of which saturates 2.1g; Cholesterol 0mg; Calcium 156mg; Fibre 3.8g; Sodium 151mg.

Fragrant Meat Pilau

This rice dish acquires its delicious taste not only from the spices but the richly flavoured meat stock.

Serves 4–6

450g/1lb/2⅓ cups basmati rice
900g/2lb boned chicken pieces, or lean lamb, cubed
600ml/1 pint/2½ cups water
4 green cardamom pods
2 black cardamom pods
10 black peppercorns
4 cloves
1 medium onion, sliced
8–10 saffron strands
2 garlic cloves, crushed
5cm/2in piece fresh root ginger
5cm/2in piece cinnamon stick
salt
175g/6oz/1 cup sultanas (golden raisins) and sautéed blanched almonds, to garnish

1 Wash the rice under cold running water until the water runs clear. Drain the rice well and set aside.

2 In a large pan, cook the cubed chicken or lamb in the measured water with the cardamom pods, peppercorns, cloves, onion and salt, until the meat is cooked.

3 Remove the meat with a slotted spoon and keep warm. Strain the stock if you wish, and return to the pan.

4 Add the rice, saffron, garlic, ginger and cinnamon to the stock and bring to the boil.

5 Quickly add the meat and stir well. Bring back to the boil, reduce the heat and cover. Simmer, covered, for about 10–15 minutes.

6 Remove the pan from the heat and leave to stand for 5 minutes. Garnish with sultanas and sautéed blanched almonds and serve.

Tricolour Pilau

Most Indian restaurants in the West serve this popular vegetable pilau, which has three different vegetables. The effect is easily achieved with frozen peas and corn, but for entertaining or a special occasion dinner, you may prefer to use fresh produce.

Serves 4–6

225g/8oz/generous 1 cup basmati rice
30ml/2 tbsp vegetable oil
2.5ml/½ tsp cumin seeds
2 dried bay leaves
4 green cardamom pods
4 cloves
1 onion, finely chopped
1 carrot, finely diced
50g/2oz/½ cup frozen peas, thawed
50g/2oz/⅓ cup frozen corn, thawed
25g/1oz/¼ cup cashew nuts, lightly fried
475ml/16fl oz/2 cups water
1.5ml/¼ tsp ground cumin
salt

1 Wash the rice, then soak it in cold water for 20 minutes.

2 Heat the oil in a karahi, wok, or large pan over a medium heat, and fry the cumin seeds for 2 minutes. Add the bay leaves, cardamoms and cloves, and fry gently for 2 minutes more, stirring the spices from time to time.

3 Add the onion and fry until lightly browned. Stir in the diced carrot and cook, stirring, for 3–4 minutes.

4 Drain the soaked basmati rice and add to the contents of the pan. Stir well to mix. Add the peas, corn and fried cashew nuts.

5 Add the measured water and the ground cumin, and stir in salt to taste. Bring to the boil, cover and simmer for 10–15 minutes over a low heat until all the water is absorbed.

6 Leave to stand, covered, for 10 minutes. Fluff up the rice with a fork, transfer to a warmed dish and serve.

meat pilau Energy 436kcal/1830kJ; Protein 41.9g; Carbohydrate 60.7g, of which sugars 0g; Fat 2.4g, of which saturates 0.5g; Cholesterol 105mg; Calcium 26mg; Fibre 0g; Sodium 91mg.
tricolour pilau Energy 221kcal/922kJ; Protein 4.9g; Carbohydrate 35.5g, of which sugars 1.8g; Fat 6.5g, of which saturates 0.9g; Cholesterol 0mg; Calcium 18mg; Fibre 0.8g; Sodium 36mg.

Pea & Mushroom Pilau

Tiny white mushrooms and petits pois, or baby peas, look great in this delectable rice dish.

Serves 6

450g/1lb/2¼ cups basmati rice
15ml/1 tbsp vegetable oil
2.5ml/½ tsp cumin seeds
2 black cardamom pods
2 cinnamon sticks
3 garlic cloves, sliced
5ml/1 tsp salt
1 medium tomato, sliced
50g/2oz/⅔ cup button (white) mushrooms
75g/3oz/¾ cup petits pois (baby peas)
750ml/1¼ pints/3 cups water

1 Wash the rice well and leave it to soak in water for 30 minutes.

2 In a medium, heavy pan, heat the oil and add the cumin seeds, cardamom, cinnamon sticks, garlic and salt.

3 Add the tomato and mushrooms and stir-fry for 2–3 minutes.

4 Tip the rice into a colander and drain it thoroughly. Add it to the pan with the petits pois. Stir gently, making sure that you do not break up the grains of rice.

5 Add the water and bring to the boil. Lower the heat, cover and continue to cook for 10–15 minutes. Just before serving, remove the lid from the pan and fluff up the rice with a fork. Spoon into a dish and serve immediately.

Cook's Tip

Petits pois are small green peas, picked when very young. The tender, sweet peas inside the immature pods are ideal for this delicately flavoured rice dish. However, if you can't find petits pois, garden peas can be used instead.

Rice with Seeds & Spices

Toasted sunflower and sesame seeds impart a rich, nutty flavour to rice spiced with turmeric, cardamom and coriander, for this delicious change from plain boiled rice, and a colourful accompaniment to serve with spicy curries. Basmati rice gives the best texture and flavour, but you can use ordinary long grain rice instead, if you prefer.

Serves 4

5ml/1 tsp sunflower oil
2.5ml/½ tsp ground turmeric
6 cardamom pods, lightly crushed
5ml/1 tsp coriander seeds, lightly crushed
1 garlic clove, crushed
200g/7oz/1 cup basmati rice, washed, soaked for 30 minutes, and drained
400ml/14fl oz/1⅔ cups vegetable stock
115g/4oz/½ cup natural (plain) yogurt
15ml/1 tbsp toasted sunflower seeds
15ml/1 tbsp toasted sesame seeds
salt and ground black pepper
coriander (cilantro) leaves, to garnish

1 Heat the oil in a non-stick frying pan and fry the turmeric, cardamom pods, coriander seeds and garlic for about 1 minute, stirring constantly.

2 Add the rice and stock, bring to the boil, then cover and simmer for 10–15 minutes, or until just tender.

3 Stir in the yogurt and the toasted sunflower and sesame seeds. Season with salt and pepper and serve hot, garnished with coriander leaves.

Cook's Tip

Seeds are particularly rich in minerals, so they are a good addition to all kinds of dishes. Light toasting will improve their fine flavour.

pea & mushroom Energy 304kcal/1272kJ; Protein 6.9g; Carbohydrate 62.2g, of which sugars 0.3g; Fat 2.8g, of which saturates 0.3g; Cholesterol 0mg; Calcium 22mg; Fibre 0.7g; Sodium 1mg.
rice with seeds Energy 241kcal/1007kJ; Protein 5.7g; Carbohydrate 42g, of which sugars 0.1g; Fat 5.5g, of which saturates 0.7g; Cholesterol 0mg; Calcium 46mg; Fibre 0.5g; Sodium 2mg.

Saffron Rice

The saffron crocus is a perennial bulb that flowers for only two weeks of the year, and each stigma has to be removed by hand and dried with care. Consequently, saffron is said to be worth its weight in gold. Kashmir in the northern region of India is a major producer, so it isn't surprising that the subcontinent has some wonderful recipes for this beautifully fragrant spice.

Serves 6

450g/1lb/2⅓ cups basmati rice
750ml/1¼ pints/3 cups water
3 green cardamom pods
2 cloves
5ml/1 tsp salt
45ml/3 tbsp semi-skimmed (low-fat) milk
2.5ml/½ tsp saffron threads, crushed

1 Wash the rice, put it in a bowl and pour over water to cover. Leave to soak for 20 minutes.

2 Drain the basmati rice and put it in a large pan with the measured water. Add the cardamoms, cloves and salt. Stir, then bring to the boil. Lower the heat, cover the pan tightly, and simmer for 5 minutes.

3 Meanwhile, place the milk in a small pan. Add the saffron threads and heat through gently.

4 Pour the saffron milk over the rice and stir. Cover again and continue cooking over a low heat for 5–6 minutes.

5 Remove the pan from the heat without lifting the lid. Leave the rice to stand for about 5 minutes, then fork through just before serving.

Cook's Tip
Washing and soaking the rice before cooking makes it fluffier.

Glutinous Rice in a Lotus Leaf

For maximum impact, serve this piping hot and open it at the table, so that guests can enjoy the aroma.

Serves 4

400g/14oz/2 cups glutinous rice
4 dried Chinese black mushrooms
15ml/1 tbsp salt
1 large lotus leaf, about 50cm/20in in diameter
30ml/2 tbsp vegetable oil
2 garlic cloves, crushed
200g/7oz skinless, boneless chicken, diced
1 Chinese sausage, finely sliced
8 drained canned Chinese chestnuts
30ml/2 tbsp light soy sauce
15ml/1 tbsp dark soy sauce
30ml/2 tbsp oyster sauce
30ml/2 tbsp sesame oil
30ml/2 tbsp chopped spring onions (scallions)
5ml/1 tsp ground black pepper
chilli sauce, to serve

1 Rinse the glutinous rice under running water until the water runs clear, then soak it in a bowl of water for 2 hours. Soak the mushrooms in a separate bowl of boiling water for 30 minutes.

2 Drain the rice, tip it into a bowl and stir in the salt. Line a large steamer with clean muslin (cheesecloth) and spoon in the rice. Cover and steam over a wok of boiling water for 15 minutes. Remove and set aside.

3 Soak the lotus leaf in warm water for 15 minutes. Drain the mushrooms, discard the stems, then chop the caps finely.

4 Heat the oil in a wok and fry the garlic for 40 seconds. Add the chicken and sausage. Stir-fry for 2 minutes, then add the mushrooms, chestnuts, soy sauces, oyster sauce, sesame oil, spring onions and black pepper. Stir-fry for 2 minutes.

5 Sprinkle over 15ml/1 tbsp water, add the rice and cook for 2–3 minutes more. Drain the lotus leaf. Lay it on a flat surface and pile the fried ingredients in the centre. Gather up the sides of the leaf and fold into a large bundle. Tuck the sides in firmly.

6 Place the lotus parcel seam side down, on a plate inside the steamer. Steam for 10 minutes. Serve with chilli sauce.

saffron rice Energy 269kcal/1125kJ; Protein 5.2g; Carbohydrate 55.1g, of which sugars 0.7g; Fat 2.8g, of which saturates 1.5g; Cholesterol 6mg; Calcium 16mg; Fibre 0.2g; Sodium 399mg.
glutinous rice Energy 596kcal/2488kJ; Protein 23.6g; Carbohydrate 79.5g, of which sugars 2.7g; Fat 19.3g, of which saturates 3.9g; Cholesterol 44mg; Calcium 45mg; Fibre 0.9g; Sodium 979mg.

Basmati Rice with Vegetables

Serve this delectable dish with roast chicken, lamb cutlets or pan-fried fish. Add the vegetables near the end of cooking so that they retain their crispness and colour.

Serves 4

1 onion
2 garlic cloves
350g/12oz/1¾ cups basmati rice
45ml/3 tbsp vegetable oil
750ml/1¼ pints/3 cups water or vegetable stock
115g/4oz/⅔ cup fresh or drained canned corn
1 red or green (bell) pepper, seeded and chopped
1 large carrot, grated
fresh chervil sprigs, to garnish

1 Chop the onion and crush the garlic cloves.

2 Wash the rice in a sieve (strainer), and then soak in cold water for 20 minutes. Drain very thoroughly.

3 Heat the oil in a large pan and fry the onion for a few minutes over a medium heat until it starts to soften.

4 Add the rice to the pan and fry for about 10 minutes, stirring constantly to prevent the rice from sticking to the base of the pan. Stir in the crushed garlic.

5 Pour in the water or stock and stir into the rice well. Bring to the boil, then lower the heat. Cover the pan and simmer for 10 minutes.

6 Sprinkle the corn over the rice, spread the chopped pepper on top and sprinkle over the grated carrot.

7 Cover tightly and simmer over a low heat until the rice is tender, then mix with a fork.

8 Pile the vegetables and rice on to a serving plate and garnish with chervil sprigs.

Caramelized Basmati Rice

This dish is the traditional accompaniment to a dhansak curry. Sugar is caramelized in hot oil before the rice is added, along with whole spices.

Serves 4

225g/8oz/generous 1 cup basmati rice
45ml/3 tbsp vegetable oil
20ml/4 tsp sugar
4 or 5 green cardamom pods, bruised
2.5cm/1in piece cinnamon stick
4 cloves
1 bay leaf, crumpled
2.5ml/½ tsp salt
475ml/16fl oz/2 cups hot water

1 Wash the rice, put it in a bowl and pour over water to cover. Leave to soak for 20 minutes.

2 Drain the rice in a colander, shaking it a little as you do so. Run the washed grains through your fingers to check that there is no excess water trapped between them. Set aside.

3 In a large pan, heat the vegetable oil over a medium heat. When the oil is hot, sprinkle the sugar over the surface and wait until it has caramelized. Do not stir.

4 Reduce the heat to low and add the spices and bay leaf. Allow to sizzle for 15–20 seconds, then add the rice and salt. Fry gently, stirring, for 2–3 minutes.

5 Pour in the water and bring to the boil. Let it boil steadily for 2 minutes, then reduce the heat to very low. Cover the pan and cook for 8 minutes.

6 Remove the rice from the heat and leave to stand for 6–8 minutes. Fluff up the rice with a fork and serve.

Cook's Tip
Watch the sugar carefully so that it does not burn.

rice w. vegetables Energy 449kcal/1877kJ; Protein 8.1g; Carbohydrate 83g, of which sugars 7.7g; Fat 9.3g, of which saturates 1.1g; Cholesterol 0mg; Calcium 30mg; Fibre 1.8g; Sodium 85mg.
caramelized rice Energy 306kcal/1276kJ; Protein 4.2g; Carbohydrate 52.7g, of which sugars 7.9g; Fat 8.5g, of which saturates 1g; Cholesterol 0mg; Calcium 15mg; Fibre 0g; Sodium 246mg.

Basmati Rice with Potato

Rice is eaten at all meals in Indian and Pakistani homes. There are several ways of cooking rice, and mostly whole spices are used. Always choose a good-quality basmati rice.

Serves 4

300g/11oz/1½ cups basmati rice
15ml/1 tbsp vegetable oil
1 small cinnamon stick
1 bay leaf
1.5ml/¼ tsp black cumin seeds
3 green cardamom pods
1 medium onion, sliced
5ml/1 tsp grated fresh root ginger
5ml/1 tsp crushed garlic
1.5ml/¼ tsp ground turmeric
7.5ml/1½ tsp salt
1 large potato, roughly diced
475ml/16fl oz/2 cups water
15ml/1 tbsp chopped fresh coriander (cilantro)

1 Wash the rice well and leave it to soak in water for 20 minutes. Heat the oil in a heavy pan, add the cinnamon, bay leaf, black cumin seeds, cardamoms and onion and stir-fry for about 2 minutes.

2 Add the ginger, garlic, turmeric, salt and potato, and stir-fry for 1 minute.

3 Drain the rice thoroughly. Add it to the potato and spices in the pan and stir to mix.

4 Pour in the water, followed by the coriander. Bring to the boil, cover the pan, reduce the heat and simmer for 10–15 minutes. Remove from the heat and leave to stand, still covered, for 5–10 minutes before serving.

Cook's Tip
It is important to observe the standing time of this dish before serving. Use a slotted spoon to serve the rice and potato mixture and handle it gently to avoid breaking the delicate grains of rice.

Basmati Rice & Peas with Curry Leaves

This is a very simple rice dish, but it is full of flavour and can make a useful quick main course.

Serves 4

300g/11oz/1½ cups basmati rice
15ml/1 tbsp vegetable oil
6–8 curry leaves
1.5ml/¼ tsp mustard seeds
1.5ml/¼ tsp onion seeds
30ml/2 tbsp fresh fenugreek leaves
5ml/1 tsp crushed garlic
5ml/1 tsp grated fresh root ginger
5ml/1 tsp salt
115g/4oz/1 cup frozen peas
475ml/16fl oz/2 cups water

1 Wash the rice well and leave it to soak in a bowl of water for 30 minutes.

2 Heat the oil in a heavy pan and add the curry leaves, mustard seeds, onion seeds, fenugreek leaves, garlic, ginger and salt and stir-fry for 2–3 minutes.

3 Drain the rice, add it to the pan and stir gently.

4 Add the frozen peas and water and bring to the boil. Lower the heat, cover with a lid and cook for 10–15 minutes. Remove from the heat and leave to stand, still covered, for 10 minutes.

5 When ready to serve, fluff up the rice with a fork. Spoon the mixture on to serving plates and serve immediately.

Cook's Tip
Fenugreek is an important spice in Indian cuisine. It has a strong distinctive curry aroma while cooking and imparts a rich flavour to dishes. The leaves are available fresh and dried from Indian markets and stores, and are used sparingly in dishes, as the flavour is intense.

rice w. potato Energy 354kcal/1482kJ; Protein 7.1g; Carbohydrate 70.4g, of which sugars 1.5g; Fat 4.8g, of which saturates 0.6g; Cholesterol 0mg; Calcium 28mg; Fibre 0.7g; Sodium 744mg.
rice & peas Energy 329kcal/1373kJ; Protein 8.1g; Carbohydrate 64.4g, of which sugars 0.7g; Fat 4.1g, of which saturates 0.5g; Cholesterol 0mg; Calcium 27mg; Fibre 1.4g; Sodium 493mg.

Red Fried Rice

This vibrant rice dish owes its appeal as much to the bright colours of its ingredients – red onion, red pepper and cherry tomatoes – as it does to their flavours.

Serves 2

130g/4½oz/¾ cup basmati rice
30ml/2 tbsp groundnut (peanut) oil
1 small red onion, chopped
1 red (bell) pepper, seeded and chopped
225g/8oz cherry tomatoes, halved
2 eggs, beaten
salt and ground black pepper

1 Wash the rice several times under cold running water. Drain well.

2 Cook the rice in boiling water for 10–12 minutes. Drain well and allow to cool completely.

3 Meanwhile, heat the oil in a wok until very hot. Add the onion and red pepper and stir-fry for 2–3 minutes.

4 Add the cherry tomatoes and continue stir-frying for 2 minutes more.

5 Pour in the beaten eggs all at once. Cook for 30 seconds without stirring, then stir to break up the egg as it sets.

6 Add the cold, cooked rice to the wok and toss it over the heat with the vegetables and egg mixture for 3 minutes. Season with salt and pepper, and serve immediately.

Variation
To add even more colour to this bright dish, you could replace the red (bell) pepper with an orange or green variety.

Tomato Biryani

Although generally served as an accompaniment to meat, poultry or fish dishes, this tasty rice dish can also be eaten as a complete meal on its own.

Serves 4

400g/14oz/2 cups basmati rice
15ml/1 tbsp vegetable oil
2.5ml/½ tsp onion seeds
1 medium onion, sliced
2 medium tomatoes, sliced
1 orange or yellow (bell) pepper, seeded and sliced
5ml/1 tsp grated fresh root ginger
5ml/1 tsp crushed garlic
5ml/1 tsp chilli powder
30ml/2 tbsp chopped fresh coriander (cilantro)
1 medium potato, diced
7.5ml/1½ tsp salt
50g/2oz/½ cup frozen peas
750ml/1¼ pints/3 cups water

1 Wash the rice well and leave it to soak in water for 30 minutes. Heat the oil in a heavy pan and fry the onion seeds for about 30 seconds. Add the sliced onion and fry for 5 minutes, stirring occasionally to prevent the slices from sticking to the pan.

2 Add the sliced tomatoes and pepper, ginger, garlic and chilli powder. Stir-fry for 2 minutes.

3 Add the fresh coriander, potato, salt and peas and stir-fry over a medium heat for a further 5 minutes.

4 Transfer the rice to a colander and drain it thoroughly. Add it to the spiced tomato and potato mixture and stir-fry for 1–2 minutes.

5 Pour in the water and bring to the boil, then lower the heat to medium. Cover and cook the rice for 12–15 minutes. Leave to stand for 5 minutes and then serve.

Cook's Tip
Plain rice can look a bit dull; it is greatly enhanced by adding colourful ingredients such as tomatoes, (bell) peppers and peas.

red fried rice Energy 437kcal/1821kJ; Protein 12.6g; Carbohydrate 57.4g, of which sugars 10.5g; Fat 17.6g, of which saturates 3.1g; Cholesterol 190mg; Calcium 62mg; Fibre 3g; Sodium 85mg.
tomato biryani Energy 475kcal/1990kJ; Protein 11.5g; Carbohydrate 102.9g, of which sugars 9g; Fat 1.9g, of which saturates 0.3g; Cholesterol 0mg; Calcium 47mg; Fibre 3.5g; Sodium 18mg.

Festive Rice

This pretty dish is traditionally shaped into a cone and surrounded by a variety of accompaniments before being served.

Serves 8

450g/1lb/2⅓ cups jasmine rice
60ml/4 tbsp vegetable oil
2 garlic cloves, crushed
2 onions, thinly sliced
2.5ml/½ tsp ground turmeric
750ml/1¼ pints/3 cups water
400ml/14fl oz can coconut milk
1 or 2 lemon grass stalks, bruised

For the accompaniments

omelette strips
2 fresh red chillies, seeded and shredded
cucumber chunks
tomato wedges
deep-fried onions
prawn (shrimp) crackers

1 Put the jasmine rice in a large strainer and rinse it thoroughly under cold water. Drain well.

2 Heat the oil in a large, heavy pan. Stir-fry the onion, garlic and turmeric over a low heat for 2–3 minutes, until the onions have softened. Add the rice and stir well to coat in oil.

3 Pour in the water and coconut milk and add the lemon grass. Bring to the boil, stirring. Cover the pan and cook gently for 12 minutes, or until all the liquid has been absorbed by the rice.

4 Remove the pan from the heat and lift the lid. Cover with a clean dish towel, replace the lid and leave to stand in a warm place for 15 minutes. Remove the lemon grass, mound the rice mixture in a cone on a serving platter and garnish with the accompaniments, then serve.

Cook's Tip

Lemon grass is the stalk of a perennial grass, and is widely available in supermarkets. It can also be grown in a pot indoors.

Jungle Rice

Originally, this dish of indigenous edible plants was cooked by people living on the fringes of Indonesian jungles. Today, it is likely to be prepared with garden vegetables. The main flavour comes from the shrimp paste and chillies.

Serves 4

350g/12oz/1¾ cups jasmine rice
1 whole mackerel or snapper
30ml/2 tbsp vegetable oil
4 eggs
4 shallots, sliced
4 garlic cloves, sliced
2 fresh green chillies, sliced
2 green beans, finely diced
2 lime leaves, finely shredded
small sprig fresh sweet basil, chopped
6 fresh mint leaves, shredded
5ml/1 tsp salt
sliced cucumber, to serve (optional)

For the sambal

50g/2oz terasi shrimp paste, toasted
5 fresh red chillies, finely chopped
juice of 2 limes

1 Grind all the sambal ingredients with a mortar and pestle until smooth, and set aside.

2 Put the jasmine rice in a sieve (strainer), rinse under cold water until the water runs clear, then put it in a pan and cover with water up to 4cm/½in above the rice. Cook over a medium heat for 12–15 minutes until tender.

3 Clean the mackerel or snapper, pat dry with kitchen paper, then grill (broil) for about 7 minutes on each side until cooked through. Carefully debone the fish and flake the flesh into a bowl.

4 Heat the oil and fry the eggs, then remove to a plate.

5 While the rice is still warm, mix in the prepared vegetables, fish, lime leaves, herbs and salt, and mix in the shrimp paste sambal to taste. Spoon on to warmed serving plates, top each with a fried egg, and serve with sliced cucumber, if using.

festive rice Energy 303kcal/1263kJ; Protein 6.4g; Carbohydrate 49.5g, of which sugars 4.2g; Fat 8.6g, of which saturates 2g; Cholesterol 53mg; Calcium 41mg; Fibre 0.5g; Sodium 212mg.
jungle rice Energy 487kcal/2032kJ; Protein 16.9g; Carbohydrate 72.7g, of which sugars 0.8g; Fat 14g, of which saturates 2.5g; Cholesterol 112mg; Calcium 46mg; Fibre 1.1g; Sodium 547mg.

Coconut Rice

This rich dish is usually served with a tangy papaya salad to balance the sweetness of the coconut milk and sugar. It is one of those comforting treats that everyone enjoys.

Serves 4–6
250ml/8fl oz/1 cup water
475ml/16fl oz/2 cups coconut milk
2.5ml/½ tsp salt
30ml/2 tbsp sugar
450g/1lb/2⅔ cups jasmine rice

1 Place the measured water, coconut milk, salt and sugar in a heavy pan. Wash the jasmine rice in several changes of cold water until it runs clear.

2 Add the rice to the pan, cover tightly with a lid and bring to the boil over a medium heat.

3 Reduce the heat to low and simmer gently, without lifting the lid unnecessarily, for 15–20 minutes, until the rice is tender and cooked through. Test it by biting a grain; it should be slightly al dente (soft but with a bite in the centre).

4 Turn off the heat and leave the rice to rest in the pan, still covered with the lid, for a further 5–10 minutes.

5 Gently fluff up the rice with a fork before transferring it to a warmed dish and serving.

Cook's Tip
Jasmine rice, or Thai fragrant rice, is an aromatic long grain rice with a subtle flavour. It is slightly sticky when cooked.

Variation
For a special occasion, serve in a halved papaya and garnish with thin shreds of fresh coconut. Use a vegetable peeler to pare the coconut finely, as you would when making curls of Parmesan cheese.

Rice with Lime & Lemon Grass

It is unusual to find brown rice given the Thai treatment, but the nutty flavour of the grains is enhanced by the fragrance of limes and lemon grass in this delicious dish.

Serves 4
2 limes
1 lemon grass stalk
225g/8oz/generous 1 cup brown long grain rice
15ml/1 tbsp olive oil
1 onion, chopped
2.5cm/1in piece fresh root ginger, finely chopped
7.5ml/1½ tsp coriander seeds
7.5ml/1½ tsp cumin seeds
750ml/1¼ pints/3 cups vegetable stock
60ml/4 tbsp chopped fresh coriander (cilantro)
spring onion (scallion) green and toasted coconut strips, to garnish
lime wedges, to serve

1 Pare the limes, using a cannelle knife (zester) or fine grater, taking care to avoid cutting the bitter pith. Set the rind aside.

2 Finely chop the lower portion of the lemon grass stalk and set it aside.

3 Rinse the rice in plenty of cold water until the water runs clear. Tip it into a sieve (strainer) and drain thoroughly.

4 Heat the oil in a large pan. Add the onion, ginger, coriander and cumin seeds, lemon grass and lime rind and cook over a low heat for 2–3 minutes.

5 Add the rice to the pan and cook, stirring constantly, for 1 minute, then pour in the stock and bring to the boil. Reduce the heat to very low and cover the pan. Cook gently for 30 minutes, then check the rice. If it is still crunchy, cover the pan and cook for 3–5 minutes more. Remove from the heat.

6 Stir in the fresh coriander, fluff up the rice grains with a fork, cover the pan and leave to stand for 10 minutes. Transfer to a warmed dish, garnish with spring onion and toasted coconut strips, and serve with lime wedges.

coconut rice Energy 255kcal/1068kJ; Protein 4.7g; Carbohydrate 48.9g, of which sugars 5.2g; Fat 4.3g, of which saturates 3.5g; Cholesterol 0mg; Calcium 40mg; Fibre 0.8g; Sodium 109mg.
rice w. lime Energy 235kcal/996kJ; Protein 4.3g; Carbohydrate 47.3g, of which sugars 1.9g; Fat 4.5g, of which saturates 0.8g; Cholesterol 0mg; Calcium 35mg; Fibre 1.9g; Sodium 6mg.

Steamed Rice

Rice is such a staple food in China, that 'have you had rice?' is a synonym for 'have you eaten?' Stick to the amounts given in this recipe for perfect results.

Serves 4

225g/8oz/generous 1 cup long grain rice, rinsed and drained
a pinch of salt

1 Put the rice into a heavy pan or clay pot. Add 600ml/1 pint/2½ cups water to cover the rice by 2.5cm/1in. Add the salt, and then bring the water to the boil. Reduce the heat, cover the pan and cook gently for about 20 minutes, or until all the water has been absorbed.

2 Remove the pan from the heat and leave to steam, covered, for a further 5–10 minutes. Fluff up with a fork, and serve.

Fragrant Coconut Rice

Originally from India and Thailand, coconut rice is popular throughout Asia. Rich and nourishing, it is often served with a tangy fruit and vegetable salad, and complements some of the spicier curries from the continent. The pandanus provides the fragrance.

Serves 4

1 litre/1¾ pints/4 cups coconut milk
450g/1lb/2¼ cups short grain rice, washed and drained
1 pandanus (screwpine) leaf, tied in a loose knot
salt

1 Heat the coconut milk in a heavy pan and stir in the rice with a little salt.

2 Add the pandanus leaf and bring the liquid to the boil. Simmer until the liquid has been absorbed.

3 Turn off the heat and cover with a clean dish towel and the lid. Steam for a further 15–20 minutes. Fluff it up and serve.

Steamed Sticky Rice

Sticky rice requires a long soak in water before being cooked in a bamboo steamer. It is used for savoury and sweet dishes, especially rice cakes, and is available in Chinese and Asian stores, as well as some supermarkets.

Serves 4

350g/12oz/1¾ cups sticky rice

1 Put the rice into a large bowl and fill the bowl with cold water. Leave the rice to soak for at least 6 hours.

2 Drain the rice, rinse thoroughly, and drain again.

3 Fill a wok or heavy pan one-third full with water. Place a bamboo steamer, with the lid on, over the wok or pan and bring the water to the boil.

4 Uncover the steamer and place a dampened piece of muslin (cheesecloth) over the rack. Tip the rice into the middle and spread it out. Fold the muslin over the rice, cover and steam for 25 minutes until the rice is tender but firm.

Cook's Tip

The volume of rice grains doubles when cooked, which is a useful point to remember when planning to cook sticky rice for a meal. The grains clump together when cooked, making this type of rice ideal for moulding. It is fairly bulky, so is often served with a dipping sauce.

Variation

Sticky rice can be enjoyed as a sweet, filling snack with sugar and coconut milk.

steamed rice Energy 202kcal/845kJ; Protein 4.2g; Carbohydrate 44.9g, of which sugars 0g; Fat 0.3g, of which saturates 0g; Cholesterol 0mg; Calcium 11mg; Fibre 0g; Sodium 0mg.
fragrant coconut rice Energy 459kcal/1927kJ; Protein 9.1g; Carbohydrate 102g, of which sugars 12.3g; Fat 1.3g, of which saturates 0.5g; Cholesterol 0mg; Calcium 94mg; Fibre 0g; Sodium 275mg.
steamed sticky rice Energy 314kcal/1314kJ; Protein 6.5g; Carbohydrate 69.8g, of which sugars 0g; Fat 0.5g, of which saturates 0g; Cholesterol 0mg; Calcium 17mg; Fibre 0g; Sodium 0mg.

Chicken & Basil Coconut Rice

For this dish, the rice is partially boiled before being simmered with coconut so that it fully absorbs the additional flavours.

Serves 4

350g/12oz/1¾ cups jasmine rice, rinsed
30ml/2 tbsp groundnut (peanut) oil
1 large onion, finely sliced into rings
1 garlic clove, crushed
1 fresh red chilli, seeded and finely sliced
1 fresh green chilli, seeded and finely sliced
generous handful of basil leaves
3 skinless chicken breast fillets, about 350g/12oz, finely sliced
5mm/¼in piece of lemon grass, pounded or finely chopped
600ml/1 pint/2½ cups coconut cream
salt and ground black pepper

1 Bring a pan of lightly salted water to the boil. Add the rice to the pan and boil for about 6 minutes, until partially cooked. Drain and set aside.

2 Heat the oil in a frying pan and fry the onion rings for 5–10 minutes until golden and crisp. Lift out, drain on kitchen paper and set aside.

3 Fry the garlic and chillies in the same oil for 2–3 minutes, then add the basil leaves and fry briefly until they begin to wilt.

4 Remove a few basil leaves and set them aside for the garnish, then add the chicken slices to the pan with the lemon grass and fry for 2–3 minutes until golden.

5 Add the rice and stir-fry for a few minutes to coat the grains, then pour in the coconut cream. Cook for 4–5 minutes or until the rice is tender, adding a little water if necessary. Adjust the seasoning.

6 Pile the rice into a warmed serving dish, or individual plates, sprinkle with the fried onion rings and some torn basil leaves, and serve immediately.

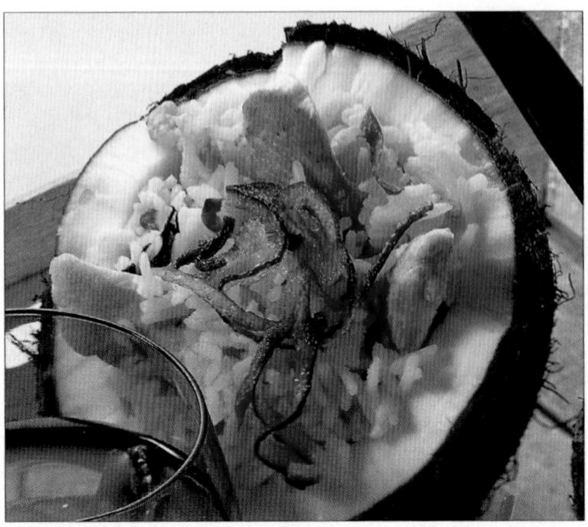

Rice with Vegetables & Mushrooms

A Cantonese staple, this originally called for ten different greens to be cooked with the rice. The tradition doesn't have to be followed to the letter for it to taste scrumptious, but it is a good idea to use several vegetables, plus a little meat for extra flavour.

Serves 4

4 dried Chinese black mushrooms
150ml/¼ pint/⅔ cup boiling water
30ml/2 tbsp vegetable oil
2 garlic cloves, chopped
150g/5oz lean pork, finely sliced
150g/5oz pak choi (bok choy), finely sliced
30ml/2 tbsp peas, thawed if frozen
30ml/2 tbsp light soy sauce
5ml/1 tsp ground black pepper
5ml/1 tsp cornflour (cornstarch) mixed to a paste with 15ml/1 tbsp cold water
800g/1¾lb/7 cups cooked rice

1 Put the mushrooms in a heatproof bowl and pour over the boiling water. Leave to soak for 20–30 minutes, until soft. Using a slotted spoon, transfer the mushrooms to a board. Cut off and discard the stems. Chop the caps finely. Strain the soaking liquid into a measuring jug (cup) and set aside.

2 Heat the oil in a wok, add the garlic and fry over medium heat for 40 seconds, until light brown. Do not let it burn or it will become bitter. Add the pork and fry for 2 minutes.

3 Add the pak choi, peas and mushrooms. Stir to mix, then add the soy sauce, black pepper and the mushroom soaking liquid. Cook, stirring frequently, for 4 minutes.

4 Add the cornflour paste and stir until the mixture thickens slightly. Finally stir in the cooked rice. As soon as it is piping hot, spoon the mixture into a heated bowl and serve.

Variation
Use any combination of green vegetables for this dish.

chicken & basil rice Energy 492kcal/2064kJ; Protein 28.8g; Carbohydrate 83.1g, of which sugars 11.6g; Fat 4.8g, of which saturates 0.9g; Cholesterol 61mg; Calcium 83mg; Fibre 1.1g; Sodium 220mg.
rice w. vegetables Energy 199kcal/834kJ; Protein 4.6g; Carbohydrate 43.4g, of which sugars 6.6g; Fat 0.7g, of which saturates 0.1g; Cholesterol 0mg; Calcium 23mg; Fibre 1.6g; Sodium 232mg.

Fried Rice with Mushrooms

A tasty rice and mushroom dish that is very low in saturated fat, yet sufficiently filling to be almost a meal in itself.

Serves 4
225g/8oz/1 1/4 cups long grain rice
15ml/1 tbsp vegetable oil
1 egg, lightly beaten
2 garlic cloves, crushed
175g/6oz/2 1/4 cups button (white) mushrooms or mixed wild and cultivated mushrooms, sliced
15ml/1 tbsp light soy sauce
1.5ml/1/4 tsp salt
2.5ml/1/2 tsp sesame oil
cucumber matchsticks, to garnish

1 Rinse the rice until the water runs clear, then drain well. Place in a pan. Measure the depth of the rice against your index finger, then cover with cold water to the same depth.

2 Bring the water to the boil. Stir the rice, boil for a few minutes, then cover the pan. Lower the heat to a simmer and cook for 5–8 minutes until all of the water has been absorbed.

3 Remove the pan from the heat and, without lifting the lid, leave for another 10 minutes before forking up the rice.

4 Heat 5ml/1 tsp of the vegetable oil in a non-stick frying pan or wok. Add the egg and cook, stirring with a chopstick or wooden spoon, until scrambled. Immediately remove the egg and set aside in a bowl.

5 Add the remaining vegetable oil to the pan or wok. When it is hot, stir-fry the garlic for a few seconds, then add the mushrooms and stir-fry for 2 minutes, adding a little water, if needed, to prevent burning. Stir in the cooked rice and cook for 4 minutes more.

6 Add the scrambled egg, soy sauce, salt and sesame oil. Mix together and cook for 1 minute to heat through. Serve the rice immediately, garnished with cucumber matchsticks.

Stir-fried Rice with Vegetables

The ginger gives this rice dish a wonderful flavour. Serve it as a vegetarian main course or as an unusual vegetable accompaniment.

Serves 2–4
115g/4oz/generous 1/2 cup brown basmati rice, rinsed and drained
350ml/12fl oz/1 1/2 cups vegetable stock
2.5cm/1in piece of fresh root ginger, finely sliced
1 garlic clove, halved
5cm/2in piece of pared lemon rind
115g/4oz/1 1/2 cups shiitake mushrooms
15ml/1 tbsp groundnut (peanut) oil
15ml/1 tbsp ghee or butter
175g/6oz baby carrots, trimmed
225g/8oz baby courgettes (zucchini), halved
175–225g/6–8oz/about 1 1/2 cups broccoli, broken into florets
6 spring onions (scallions), sliced
15ml/1 tbsp light soy sauce
10ml/2 tsp toasted sesame oil

1 Put the rice in a pan and pour in the stock. Add the ginger, garlic and lemon rind. Slowly bring to the boil, then cover and cook very gently for 20–25 minutes until the rice is tender. Remove the pan from the heat. Discard the flavourings and keep the pan covered with a clean dish towel and the lid so that the rice stays warm.

2 Slice the mushrooms, discarding the stems. Heat the oil and ghee or butter in a wok and stir-fry the carrots for 4–5 minutes until partially tender.

3 Add the mushrooms and courgettes, stir-fry for 2–3 minutes, then add the broccoli and spring onions and cook for a further 3 minutes, by which time all the vegetables should be tender but should still retain a bit of 'bite'.

4 Add the cooked rice to the vegetables, and toss briefly over the heat to mix and heat through. Toss with the soy sauce and sesame oil. Spoon into a large warmed dish or into individual bowls and serve immediately.

rice w. mushrooms Energy 245kcal/1023kJ; Protein 6.6g; Carbohydrate 45.4g, of which sugars 0.4g; Fat 3.8g, of which saturates 0.7g; Cholesterol 48mg; Calcium 21mg; Fibre 0.5g; Sodium 287mg.
stir-fried rice Energy 430kcal/1788kJ; Protein 12.5g; Carbohydrate 58.2g, of which sugars 11.2g; Fat 16.2g, of which saturates 2.2g; Cholesterol 0mg; Calcium 127mg; Fibre 6.5g; Sodium 569mg.

Special Fried Rice

More colourful and elaborate than other fried rice dishes, special fried rice is a meal in itself.

Serves 4

50g/2oz/⅓ cup cooked peeled prawns (shrimp)
3 eggs
5ml/1 tsp salt
2 spring onions (scallions), finely chopped
60ml/4 tbsp vegetable oil
115g/4oz lean pork, finely diced
15ml/1 tbsp light soy sauce
15ml/1 tbsp Chinese rice wine
450g/1lb/6 cups cooked rice
115g/4oz green peas

1 Pat the prawns dry with kitchen paper. Put the eggs in a bowl with a pinch of the salt and a few pieces of spring onion. Whisk lightly.

2 Heat half the oil in a wok, add the pork and stir-fry until golden. Add the prawns and cook for 1 minute, then add the soy sauce and rice wine. Spoon the pork and prawn mixture into a bowl and keep hot.

3 Heat the remaining oil in the wok and lightly scramble the eggs. Add the rice and stir well with chopsticks.

4 Add the remaining salt and spring onions, the stir-fried prawns, pork and peas. Toss well over the heat to combine and serve either hot or cold.

Variation
If you don't have any Chinese rice wine, substitute dry sherry.

Cook's Tip
The weight of rice increases about two and a half times after cooking. When a recipe calls for cooked rice, use just under half the weight in uncooked rice.

Fragrant Harbour Fried Rice

This tasty rice dish celebrates the Chinese name for Hong Kong, which is Fragrant Harbour.

Serves 4

about 90ml/6 tbsp vegetable oil
2 eggs, beaten
8 shallots, sliced
115g/4oz peeled cooked prawns (shrimp)
3 garlic cloves, crushed
115g/4oz cooked pork, cut into thin strips
4 dried shiitake mushrooms, soaked, stems removed and sliced
115g/4oz Chinese sausage, cooked and sliced at an angle
225g/8oz/generous 1 cup long grain rice, cooked, cooled quickly and chilled
30ml/2 tbsp light soy sauce
115g/4oz/1 cup frozen peas, thawed
2 spring onions (scallions), shredded
salt and ground black pepper
coriander (cilantro) leaves, to garnish

1 Heat about 15ml/1 tbsp of the oil in a frying pan, add the eggs and make an omelette. Slide the omelette out, roll it up and cut into strips. Set aside.

2 Heat a wok, add 15ml/1 tbsp of the remaining oil and stir-fry the shallots until crisp and golden. Remove and set aside. Add the prawns and garlic to the wok, with a little more oil if needed, fry for 1 minute, then remove.

3 Heat 15ml/1 tbsp more oil in the wok and stir-fry the pork and mushrooms for 2 minutes; add the cooked Chinese sausage slices and heat for a further 2 minutes. Lift the ingredients out of the wok and keep warm.

4 Reheat the wok with the remaining oil and stir-fry the rice until it glistens. Stir in the soy sauce, salt and pepper, plus half the cooked ingredients. Add the peas and half the spring onions and toss over the heat until the peas are cooked. Pile the fried rice on a heated platter, top with the remaining cooked ingredients and garnish with the coriander leaves.

special fried rice Energy 343kcal/1434kJ; Protein 20.2g; Carbohydrate 40.5g, of which sugars 4.2g; Fat 11.2g, of which saturates 1.6g; Cholesterol 124mg; Calcium 91mg; Fibre 2.4g; Sodium 632mg.
fragrant harbour rice Energy 450kcal/1872kJ; Protein 14.5g; Carbohydrate 51g, of which sugars 4.4g; Fat 20.9g, of which saturates 3.1g; Cholesterol 113mg; Calcium 48mg; Fibre 1.1g; Sodium 58mg.

Pineapple Rice

This way of presenting rice not only looks spectacular, it also tastes so good that it can easily be served solo.

Serves 4

75g/3oz/¾ cup unsalted peanuts
1 large pineapple
45ml/3 tbsp groundnut (peanut) or sunflower oil
1 onion, chopped
1 garlic clove, crushed
2 chicken breast fillets, about 225g/8oz, cut into strips
225g/8oz/generous 1 cup jasmine rice, rinsed
600ml/1 pint/2½ cups chicken stock
1 lemon grass stalk, bruised
2 thick slices of ham, cut into julienne strips
1 fresh red chilli, seeded and very finely sliced
salt

1 Dry-fry the peanuts in a non-stick frying pan until golden. When cool, grind one-sixth of them in a coffee or herb mill and chop the remainder.

2 Cut a lengthways slice of pineapple, slicing through the leaves, then cut out the flesh to leave a neat shell. Chop 115g/4oz of the pineapple into cubes. Put the remainder aside for use in another dish.

3 Heat the oil in a large pan and fry the onion and garlic for 3–4 minutes until soft. Add the chicken strips and stir-fry over a medium heat for a few minutes until evenly brown.

4 Add the rice to the pan. Toss with the chicken mixture for a few minutes, then pour in the stock, with the lemon grass and a little salt. Bring to just below boiling point, then lower the heat, cover the pan and simmer gently for 10–12 minutes until both the rice and the chicken pieces are tender.

5 Stir the chopped peanuts, the pineapple cubes and the strips of ham into the rice, then spoon the mixture into the pineapple shell. Sprinkle the ground peanuts and the sliced chilli over the top and serve.

Seafood Fried Rice

This is one of those dishes that is found throughout China, although the ingredients will vary depending on the location. This simple version allows the flavour of the seafood to take centre stage. For festive occasions, luxury ingredients such as lobster and scallops are often added.

Serves 4

30ml/2 tbsp vegetable oil
2 garlic cloves, crushed
2 eggs, lightly beaten
100g/3¾oz raw or cooked prawns (shrimps), peeled
800g/1¾lb/7 cups cold cooked rice
30ml/2 tbsp light soy sauce
2.5ml/½ tsp ground black pepper
2 spring onions (scallions), chopped
spring onion curls (see Cook's Tip) to serve

1 Heat the oil in a wok and fry the garlic until golden brown. Do not let it burn or it will become bitter. Push the garlic aside to leave a clear space in the centre of the wok. Add the eggs and cook until they set to form an omelette.

2 Cut the omelette up roughly in the wok, and push it aside. Add the prawns and rice and stir rapidly for 5 minutes or until the shrimps are cooked and the rice is piping hot.

3 Sprinkle over the soy sauce. Add the black pepper and chopped spring onions. Toss to mix, then spoon into a bowl and serve garnished with the spring onion curls.

Cook's Tip

Spring onion (scallion) curls make a dramatic garnish. Trim four spring onions, removing the roots and bulbs. Using a sharp knife, finely shred the spring onions to within 2.5cm/1in of the root end. Place the shredded spring onions in a bowl of iced water and chill for at least 30 minutes or until the shredded ends have curled. Drain on kitchen paper.

pineapple rice Energy 563kcal/2356kJ; Protein 28.9g; Carbohydrate 66.2g, of which sugars 19.8g; Fat 20.5g, of which saturates 2.8g; Cholesterol 56mg; Calcium 62mg; Fibre 3.5g; Sodium 189mg.
seafood fried rice Energy 386kcal/1629kJ; Protein 13.1g; Carbohydrate 62.6g, of which sugars 0.7g; Fat 11.1g, of which saturates 2.1g; Cholesterol 144mg; Calcium 73mg; Fibre 0.3g; Sodium 619mg.

Chinese Jewelled Rice

Another fried rice medley, this time with crab meat and water chestnuts, providing contrasting textures and flavours.

Serves 4

350g/12oz/1¾ cups long grain rice
45ml/3 tbsp vegetable oil
1 onion, roughly chopped
4 dried black Chinese mushrooms, soaked for 10 minutes in warm water to cover
115g/4oz cooked ham, diced
175g/6oz drained canned white crab meat
75g/3oz/½ cup drained canned water chestnuts
115g/4oz/1 cup peas, thawed if frozen
30ml/2 tbsp oyster sauce
5ml/1 tsp sugar
salt

1 Rinse the rice in cold water, drain well, then add to a pan of lightly salted boiling water. Cook for 10–12 minutes. Drain, refresh under cold water, drain again and cool quickly.

2 Heat half the oil in a wok. When very hot, stir-fry the rice for 3 minutes. Transfer the cooked rice to a bowl and set aside.

3 Heat the remaining oil in the wok and cook the onion until softened but not coloured. Drain the mushrooms, cut off and discard the stems, then chop the caps.

4 Add the chopped mushrooms to the wok, with all the remaining ingredients except the rice. Stir-fry for 2 minutes, then add the rice and stir-fry for about 3 minutes more. Spoon into heated bowls and serve.

Cook's Tip
Always preheat a wok before stir-frying. When you add the oil, drizzle it in a 'necklace' just below the rim of the hot wok. As the oil runs down, it will coat the inner surface evenly as it heats through.

Jewelled Rice with Fried Eggs

This vibrant, colourful stir-fry makes a tasty light meal, or can be served as an accompaniment to simply grilled meat or fish.

Serves 4

2 fresh corn on the cob
60ml/4 tbsp sunflower oil
2 garlic cloves, finely chopped
4 red Asian shallots, thinly sliced
1 small fresh red chilli, finely sliced
90g/3½oz carrots, cut into thin matchsticks
90g/3½oz fine green beans, cut into 2cm/¾in lengths
1 red (bell) pepper, seeded and cut into 1cm/½in dice
90g/3½oz/1¼ cups baby button (white) mushrooms
500g/1¼lb/5 cups cooked long grain rice, completely cooled
45ml/3 tbsp light soy sauce
10ml/2 tsp green curry paste
4 eggs
crisp green salad leaves and lime wedges, to serve

1 First shuck the corn cobs. Remove all the papery leaves, and the silky threads, then with a sharp knife cut at the base of the kernels right down the length of the cob.

2 Heat 30ml/2 tbsp of the sunflower oil in a wok over a high heat. When hot, add the garlic, shallots and chilli. Stir-fry for about 2 minutes.

3 Add the carrots, green beans, shucked corn kernels, red pepper and mushrooms to the wok and stir-fry for 3–4 minutes. Add the cooked, cooled rice and stir-fry for a further 4–5 minutes.

4 Mix together the light soy sauce and curry paste and add to the wok. Toss to mix well and stir-fry for 2–3 minutes.

5 Meanwhile, fry the eggs one at a time in the remaining oil in a frying pan. As each egg is cooked, remove it from the pan and place on a plate. Keep the cooked eggs hot.

6 Ladle the rice into four bowls or plates and top each portion with a fried egg. Serve with crisp green salad leaves and wedges of lime to squeeze over.

chinese jewelled rice Energy 474kcal/1979kJ; Protein 22.5g; Carbohydrate 77.5g, of which sugars 4.3g; Fat 7.8g, of which saturates 1.1g; Cholesterol 48mg; Calcium 86mg; Fibre 1.9g; Sodium 710mg.
jewelled rice w. eggs Energy 392kcal/1648kJ; Protein 13.6g; Carbohydrate 51.4g, of which sugars 8.2g; Fat 16.1g, of which saturates 3.6g; Cholesterol 261mg; Calcium 79mg; Fibre 2.2g; Sodium 968mg.

Chicken & Egg on Rice

The age-old question of which came first, the chicken or the egg, is addressed in this Japanese dish. It is traditionally cooked in a lidded ceramic bowl called a *doni-buri*.

Serves 4

250g/9oz skinless, boneless chicken thighs
4 fresh mitsuba or parsley sprigs, trimmed
300ml/½ pint/1¼ cups water and 25ml/1½ tbsp instant dashi powder
30ml/2 tbsp caster (superfine) sugar
60ml/4 tbsp mirin
60ml/4 tbsp shoyu
2 small onions, sliced thinly lengthways
4 large (US extra large) eggs, beaten
275g/10oz/scant 1½ cups Japanese short grain rice cooked with 375ml/13fl oz/scant 1⅔ cups water
shichimi togarashi, to serve (optional)

1 Cut the chicken thighs into 2cm/¾in square bitesize chunks. Chop the roots of the fresh mitsuba or parsley into 2.5cm/1in lengths. Set aside.

2 Pour the dashi stock, sugar, mirin and shoyu into a frying pan with a lid and bring to the boil. Add the onion slices to the pan and lay the chicken pieces on top. Cook over a high heat for 5 minutes, shaking the pan frequently.

3 When the chicken is cooked, sprinkle with the mitsuba or parsley, and pour the beaten eggs over to cover the chicken. Cover and wait for 30 seconds. Do not stir.

4 Remove from the heat and leave to stand for 1 minute. The egg should be just cooked but still soft, rather than set. Do not leave it so that the egg becomes a firm omelette.

5 Scoop the warm rice on to four individual serving plates, then pour the soft eggs and chicken mixture on to the rice.

6 Serve immediately while warm, with a little shichimi togarashi if you want a spicy taste.

Garlic & Ginger Rice

Throughout China and South-east Asia, when rice is served on the side, it is usually steamed and plain, or fragrant with the flavours of ginger and herbs. The combination of garlic and ginger is popular in both countries and complements almost any vegetable, fish or meat dish.

Serves 4–6

15ml/1 tbsp vegetable or groundnut (peanut) oil
2–3 garlic cloves, finely chopped
25g/1oz fresh root ginger, finely chopped
225g/8oz/generous 1 cup long grain rice, rinsed in several bowls of water and drained
900ml/1½ pints/3¾ cups chicken stock
a bunch of fresh coriander (cilantro) leaves, finely chopped
a bunch of fresh basil and mint (optional), finely chopped

1 Heat the oil in a clay pot or heavy pan. Stir in the garlic and ginger and fry until golden. Stir in the rice and allow it to absorb the flavours for 1–2 minutes.

2 Pour in the stock and stir to make sure the rice doesn't stick. Bring the stock to the boil, then reduce the heat. Sprinkle the coriander over the surface of the stock with the finely chopped basil and mint, if using. Cover the pan, and leave to cook gently for 20–25 minutes, until the rice has absorbed all the liquid.

3 Turn off the heat and gently fluff up the rice to mix in the herbs. Cover and leave to stand for 10 minutes before serving.

Cook's Tip
Use home-made chicken stock if possible. It has a superior flavour to stock made using cubes and you can control the level of salt. Whenever you have a chicken carcass – after a roast chicken dinner, for instance – make and freeze the stock.

chicken & egg on rice Energy 417Kcal/1743kJ; Protein 25.2g; Carbohydrate 56.9g, of which sugars 1.9g; Fat 7.8g, of which saturates 2.1g; Cholesterol 256mg; Calcium 70mg; Fibre 0.2g; Sodium 935mg.
garlic & ginger rice Energy 165kcal/658kJ; Protein 3.9g; Carbohydrate 31.7g, of which sugars 0.5g; Fat 2.3g, of which saturates 0.2g; Cholesterol 0mg; Calcium 40mg; Fibre 1.1g; Sodium 8mg.

Fried Rice with Chicken

This substantial and tasty supper dish is based on jasmine rice cooked in coconut milk. Diced chicken, red pepper and corn kernels add colour and extra flavour.

Serves 4

475ml/16fl oz/2 cups water
50g/2oz/½ cup coconut milk powder
350g/12oz/1¾ cups jasmine rice, rinsed
30ml/2 tbsp groundnut (peanut) oil
2 garlic cloves, chopped
1 small onion, finely chopped
2.5cm/1in piece fresh root ginger, peeled and grated
225g/8oz skinned chicken breast fillets, cut into 1cm/½in pieces
1 red (bell) pepper, seeded and sliced
115g/4oz/1 cup drained canned whole kernel corn
5ml/1 tsp chilli oil
5ml/1 tsp hot curry powder
2 eggs, beaten
salt
spring onion (scallion) shreds, to garnish

1 Pour the water into a pan and whisk in the coconut milk powder. Add the rice and bring to the boil. Reduce the heat, cover and cook for 12 minutes, or until the rice is tender and the liquid has been absorbed.

2 Spread the rice on a baking sheet and cool down as quickly as possible.

3 Heat the oil in a wok, add the garlic, onion and ginger and stir-fry over a medium heat for 2 minutes.

4 Push the onion mixture to the sides of the wok, add the chicken to the centre and stir-fry for 2 minutes. Add the rice and toss well. Stir-fry over a high heat for about 3 minutes more, until the chicken is cooked through.

5 Stir in the sliced red pepper, corn, chilli oil and curry powder, with salt to taste. Toss over the heat for 1 minute. Stir in the beaten eggs and cook for 1 minute more. Garnish with the spring onion shreds and serve.

Fragrant Rice with Chicken & Mint

Serve this refreshing dish simply drizzled with fish sauce, or as part of a celebratory meal.

Serves 4

350g/12oz/1¾ cups long grain rice, rinsed and drained
2–3 shallots, halved and finely sliced
1 bunch of fresh mint, stalks removed, leaves finely shredded
2 spring onions (scallions), finely sliced, to garnish
chilli sambal, to serve

For the stock

2 meaty chicken legs
1 onion, peeled and quartered
4cm/1½in fresh root ginger, peeled and coarsely chopped
15ml/1 tbsp fish sauce
3 black peppercorns
1 bunch of fresh mint
sea salt

1 To make the stock, put the chicken legs into a deep pan. Add all the other ingredients, except the salt, and pour in 1 litre/1¾ pints/4 cups water. Bring the water to the boil, skim, then cover and simmer for 1 hour.

2 Remove the lid, increase the heat and cook for a further 30 minutes to reduce the stock. Skim, strain and season with salt. Measure 750ml/1¼ pints/3 cups stock. Remove the chicken meat from the bone and shred.

3 Put the rice in a heavy pan and stir in the stock, which should be roughly 2.5cm/1in above the rice; if not, top it up. Bring the liquid to the boil, cover the pan and cook for about 25 minutes, or until all the water has been absorbed.

4 Remove the pan from the heat and fork in the shredded chicken, shallots and most of the mint. Cover the pan again and leave the flavours to mingle for 10 minutes.

5 Tip the rice into bowls, or on to a serving dish, garnish with the remaining mint and the spring onions, and serve with chilli sambal.

fried rice w. chicken Energy 489kcal/2044kJ; Protein 16.3g; Carbohydrate 82.9g, of which sugars 7.5g; Fat 10.1g, of which saturates 1.7g; Cholesterol 95mg; Calcium 50mg; Fibre 1.4g; Sodium 249mg.
fragrant rice Energy 426kcal/1784kJ; Protein 25.6g; Carbohydrate 72.9g, of which sugars 1.8g; Fat 3.1g, of which saturates 0.7g; Cholesterol 92mg; Calcium 53mg; Fibre 0.5g; Sodium 82mg.

Stir-fried Rice with Sausage

This traditional stir-fried rice recipe includes Chinese pork sausage, but can also be made with strips of pork. Prepared this way, the dish can be eaten as a snack, or as part of a meal with grilled and roasted meats accompanied by a vegetable dish or salad.

Serves 4

25g/1oz dried cloud ear (wood ear) mushrooms, soaked in water for 20 minutes
15ml/1 tbsp vegetable or sesame oil
1 onion, sliced
2 fresh green or red chillies, seeded and finely chopped
2 Chinese sausages (15cm/6in long), each sliced into 10 pieces
175g/6oz prawns (shrimp), shelled and deveined
30ml/2 tbsp fish sauce, plus extra for drizzling
10ml/2 tsp five-spice powder
1 bunch of fresh coriander (cilantro), stalks removed, leaves finely chopped
450g/1lb/4 cups cold steamed rice
ground black pepper

1 Drain the soaked cloud ear mushrooms, put them on a board and cut them into strips, discarding any very tough bits.

2 Heat a wok or heavy pan and add the oil. Add the onion and chillies. Fry until they begin to colour, then stir in the mushrooms.

3 Add the sausage slices, moving them around the wok or pan until they begin to brown. Add the prawns and move them around until they turn opaque. Stir in the fish sauce, the five-spice powder and 30ml/2 tbsp of the coriander.

4 Season the sausage and prawn mix well with pepper, then quickly stir in the rice, making sure it doesn't stick to the pan. As soon as the rice is heated through, sprinkle with the remainder of the chopped coriander and serve with fish sauce on the side, to drizzle over.

Fried Rice with Pork

This is great for using up last night's leftover rice, but for safety's sake, it must have been cooled quickly and kept in the refrigerator, then fried until heated all the way through.

Serves 4–6

45ml/3 tbsp vegetable oil
1 onion, chopped
15ml/1 tbsp chopped garlic
115g/4oz tender pork, cut into small cubes
2 eggs, beaten
500g/2¼lb/5 cups cooked rice
30ml/2 tbsp fish sauce
15ml/1 tbsp dark soy sauce
2.5ml/½ tsp caster (superfine) sugar

To serve
4 spring onions (scallions), finely sliced
2 fresh red chillies, sliced
1 lime, cut into wedges

1 Heat the oil in a wok or large frying pan. Add the onion and garlic and cook for about 2 minutes until softened.

2 Add the pork to the softened onion and garlic. Stir-fry until the pork changes colour and is fully cooked.

3 Tip in the beaten eggs and stir-fry over the heat until scrambled into small lumps.

4 Add the rice and continue to stir and toss, to coat it with the oil and prevent it from sticking.

5 Add the fish sauce, soy sauce and sugar and mix well. Continue to fry until the rice is hot. Spoon into warmed bowls and serve, with sliced spring onions, chillies and lime wedges.

Cook's Tips
- *Rice should be completely cold before frying otherwise it will not become properly browned.*
- *If you like, you can drizzle sweet, sour or hot chilli dipping sauce over the rice when serving.*

rice w. sausage Energy 388kcal/1632kJ; Protein 16.3g; Carbohydrate 45.8g, of which sugars 1.9g; Fat 16.8g, of which saturates 5.8g; Cholesterol 105mg; Calcium 91mg; Fibre 0.7g; Sodium 491mg.
fried rice w. pork Energy 229kcal/965kJ; Protein 7.5g; Carbohydrate 36.2g, of which sugars 1.5g; Fat 7g, of which saturates 1.3g; Cholesterol 55mg; Calcium 34mg; Fibre 0.4g; Sodium 147mg.

Fried Rice with Beef

One of the joys of cooking Chinese food is the ease and speed with which a really good meal can be prepared. This delectable beef and rice stir-fry can be on the table in 15 minutes.

Serves 4

200g/7oz beef steak, chilled
15ml/1 tbsp vegetable oil
2 garlic cloves, finely chopped
1 egg
250g/9oz/2¼ cups cooked jasmine rice
½ medium head broccoli, coarsely chopped
30ml/2 tbsp dark soy sauce
15ml/1 tbsp light soy sauce
5ml/1 tsp light muscovado (brown) sugar
15ml/1 tbsp fish sauce
ground black pepper
chilli sauce, to serve

1 Trim the steak and cut into very thin strips with a sharp knife.

2 Heat the oil in a wok or frying pan and cook the garlic over a low to medium heat until golden. Do not let it burn. Increase the heat to high, add the steak and stir-fry for 2 minutes.

3 Move the pieces of beef to the edges of the wok or pan and break the egg into the centre. When the egg starts to set, break it up with chopsticks and then stir-fry it with the meat.

4 Add the rice and toss all the contents of the wok together, scraping up any residue on the base, then add the broccoli, soy sauces, sugar and fish sauce and stir-fry for 2 minutes more. Season to taste with pepper, spoon into heated bowls and serve immediately with chilli sauce.

Cook's Tip

Soy sauce is made from fermented soya beans. The first extraction is sold as light soy sauce and has a delicate, 'beany' fragrance. Dark soy sauce is more intensely flavoured and has been allowed to mature for longer. The darker kind is also traditionally used to intensify the colour of a dish.

Five Ingredients Rice

The Japanese love rice so much they invented many ways to enjoy it. Here, chicken and vegetables are cooked with short grain rice, making a healthy light lunch.

Serves 4

275g/10oz/1¼ cups Japanese short grain rice
90g/3½oz carrot, peeled
2.5ml/½ tsp lemon juice
90g/3½oz canned bamboo shoots, drained
225g/8oz/3 cups oyster mushrooms
8 fresh parsley sprigs
350ml/12fl oz/1½ cups water and 7.5ml/1½ tsp instant dashi powder
150g/5oz skinless chicken breast fillet, cut into 2cm/¾in chunks
30ml/2 tbsp shoyu
30ml/2 tbsp sake
25ml/1½ tbsp mirin (sweet rice wine)
pinch of salt

1 Put the rice in a large bowl and wash under cold water until the water remains clear. Drain and set aside for 30 minutes.

2 Using a sharp knife, cut the carrot into 5mm/¼in rounds, then cut the discs into flowers. Slice the canned bamboo shoots into thin matchsticks.

3 Tear the oyster mushrooms into thin strips. Chop the parsley. Put it in a sieve (strainer) and pour over hot water from the kettle to wilt the leaves. Allow to drain and then set aside.

4 Heat the dashi stock in a large pan and add the carrots and bamboo shoots. Bring to the boil and add the chicken. Remove any scum that forms on the surface, then add the shoyu, sake, mirin and salt.

5 Add the rice and mushrooms and cover with a tight-fitting lid. Bring back to the boil, wait 5 minutes, then reduce the heat and simmer for 10 minutes. Remove from the heat without lifting the lid and leave to stand for 15 minutes. Add the wilted parsley and serve.

fried rice w. beef Energy 385kcal/1606kJ; Protein 20.7g; Carbohydrate 52.7g, of which sugars 2.5g; Fat 9.8g, of which saturates 2.8g; Cholesterol 81mg; Calcium 59mg; Fibre 1.6g; Sodium 590mg.
five ingredients rice Energy 331kcal/1386kJ; Protein 16.2g; Carbohydrate 61.1g, of which sugars 5.5g; Fat 1.2g, of which saturates 0.2g; Cholesterol 26mg; Calcium 32mg; Fibre 1.5g; Sodium 567mg.

Red Rice and Aduki Beans

This is a savoury version of a popular Japanese sweetmeat.

Serves 4

65g/2½oz/⅓ cup dried aduki beans
5ml/1 tsp salt
300g/11oz/1½ cups glutinous rice, washed and drained
50g/2oz/¼ cup Japanese short grain rice, washed and drained
45ml/3 tbsp roasted sesame seeds mixed with 5ml/1 tsp sea salt

1 Put the aduki beans in a heavy pan and pour in 450ml/¾ pint/scant 2 cups water. Bring to the boil, then simmer, covered, for 20–30 minutes, or until the beans look swollen but are still firm. Drain, reserving the liquid in a large bowl. Add the salt. Return the beans to the pan.

2 Bring another 450ml/¾ pint/scant 2 cups water to the boil. Add to the beans and return to the boil, then simmer for 30 minutes, until the beans' skins start to crack. Drain and add the liquid to the bowl of salted liquid you saved earlier. Cover the beans and leave to cool.

3 Add the rice to the bean liquid. Leave to soak for 4–5 hours. Drain the rice and reserve the liquid. Mix the rice and beans.

4 Bring a steamer of water to the boil. Turn off the heat. Place a tall glass in the centre of the steaming compartment. Pour the rice and beans into the steamer and gently pull the glass out. The hole in the middle will allow even distribution of the steam. Steam on high for 10 minutes.

5 Using your fingers, sprinkle the rice mixture with the reserved liquid from the bowl. Cover again and repeat the process twice more at 10 minute intervals, then leave to steam for 15 minutes more. Remove from the heat. Leave to stand for 10 minutes, then spoon into a large bowl or banana leaf, sprinkle with the sesame seed mixture and serve.

Sticky Rice Parcels

It is a pleasure to cut these parcels open and discover the delicious filling inside.

Serves 4

450g/1lb/2⅔ cups glutinous rice
20ml/4 tsp vegetable oil
15ml/1 tbsp dark soy sauce
1.5ml/¼ tsp five-spice powder
15ml/1 tbsp dry sherry
4 skinless, boneless chicken thighs, each cut into 4 pieces
8 dried shiitake mushrooms, soaked, stems removed and caps diced
25g/1oz dried shrimps, soaked and drained
50g/2oz/½ cup canned bamboo shoots, drained and sliced
300ml/½ pint/1¼ cups chicken stock
10ml/2 tsp cornflour (cornstarch), mixed with 15ml/1 tbsp cold water
4 lotus leaves, soaked in warm water until soft
salt and ground white pepper

1 Rinse the rice in a colander until the water runs clear, then soak in a bowl of water for 2 hours. Drain the rice and tip it into a bowl. Stir in 5ml/1 tsp of the oil and 2.5ml/½ tsp salt.

2 Line a large steamer with muslin (cheesecloth). Add the soaked rice, cover and steam for 45 minutes, stirring occasionally. Leave to cool.

3 Mix the soy sauce, five-spice powder and sherry in a bowl, stir in the chicken pieces, cover and marinate for 20 minutes.

4 Heat the remaining oil in a wok, stir-fry the chicken for 2 minutes, then add the mushrooms, shrimps, bamboo shoots and stock. Mix well, bring to the boil, then simmer for 10 minutes. Add the cornflour paste and cook, stirring, until the sauce has thickened. Season to taste.

5 Spread one-eighth of the rice to a round in the centre of each lotus leaf. Divide the chicken mixture among the leaves, putting it on top of the rice, and then top with more rice. Fold the leaves around the filling to make four neat parcels. Steam, seam side down, for 30 minutes over a high heat. Serve.

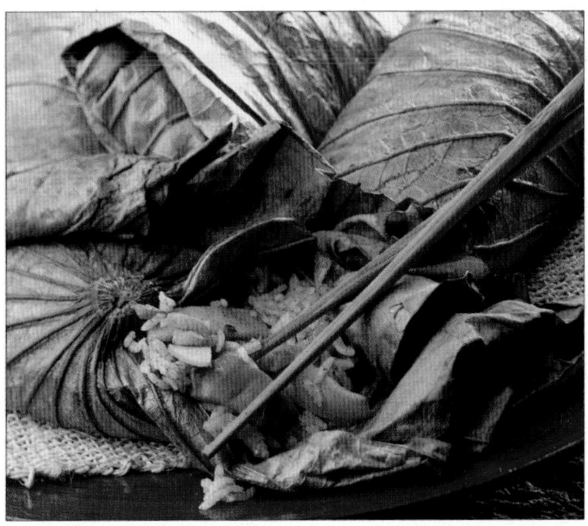

red rice Energy 432kcal/1807kJ; Protein 12.4g; Carbohydrate 78.7g, of which sugars 0.5g; Fat 7.2g, of which saturates 1g; Cholesterol 0mg; Calcium 105mg; Fibre 2.2g; Sodium 496mg.
sticky rice parcels Energy 565kcal/2369kJ; Protein 37.3g; Carbohydrate 87.1g, of which sugars 0.3g; Fat 6.1g, of which saturates 0.7g; Cholesterol 102mg; Calcium 101mg; Fibre 0.2g; Sodium 336mg.

Rice Cakes with Dipping Sauce

Easy to make, these rice cakes will keep almost indefinitely in an airtight container. Start making them at least a day before you plan to serve them, so the rice can dry out overnight.

Serves 4–6
175g/6oz/1 cup Thai jasmine rice
oil, for deep-frying and greasing
dipping sauce, for serving

1 Preheat the oven to the lowest setting. Grease a baking sheet. Wash the rice in several changes of water. Put it in a pan, add 350ml/12fl oz/1½ cups water and cover tightly. Bring to the boil, reduce the heat and simmer gently for about 15 minutes.

2 Remove the lid and fluff up the rice. Spoon it on to the baking sheet and press it down with the back of a spoon. Leave in the oven to dry out overnight.

3 Break the rice into bitesize pieces. Heat the oil in a wok or deep-fryer to 190°C/375°F or until a cube of bread, added to the oil, browns in 40 seconds. Deep-fry the rice cakes, in batches, for about 1 minute, until they puff up but are not browned. Remove and drain well. Serve with the dipping sauce.

Cook's Tip
For a spicy meat-based dipping sauce to serve with the rice cakes, soak 6 dried red chillies in warm water, drain, then grind to a paste with 2 chopped shallots, 2.5ml/½ tsp salt, 2 chopped garlic cloves, 4 chopped coriander (cilantro) roots and 10 white peppercorns. Heat 250ml/8fl oz/1 cup coconut milk. When it starts to separate, stir in the chilli paste and cook for 3 minutes. Add 15ml/1 tbsp shrimp paste and 115g/4oz minced (ground) pork. Cook, stirring, for 10 minutes, then stir in 4 chopped cherry tomatoes, 15ml/1 tbsp each fish sauce and brown sugar, 30ml/2 tbsp each tamarind juice and chopped roasted peanuts, and 2 chopped spring onions (scallions). Cook until thick, then pour into a bowl and cool.

Sticky Rice Cakes Filled with Pork

These rice cakes are substantial enough to serve for supper, with a salad and dipping sauce.

Makes 2 cakes
15ml/1 tbsp vegetable oil
2 garlic cloves, chopped
225g/8oz lean pork, cut into bitesize chunks
30ml/2 tbsp fish sauce
2.5ml/½ tsp sugar
10ml/2 tsp ground black pepper
115g/4oz lotus seeds, soaked for 6 hours and drained
2 lotus or banana leaves, trimmed and cut into 25cm/10in squares
500g/1¼lb/5 cups cooked sticky rice
salt

1 Heat the oil in a heavy pan. Stir in the garlic, until it begins to colour, then add the pork, fish sauce, sugar and pepper. Cover and cook over a low heat for about 45 minutes, or until the pork is tender. Leave to cool, then shred the pork.

2 Meanwhile, cook the lotus seeds in boiling water for about 10 minutes. When soft, drain, pat dry and leave to cool.

3 Place a quarter of the cooked sticky rice in the middle of each lotus or banana leaf. Place half the shredded pork and half the lotus seeds on the rice.

4 Drizzle some of the cooking juices from the pork over the top. Place another quarter of the rice on top, moulding and patting it with your fingers to make sure the pork and lotus seeds are enclosed like a cake. Fold the leaf edge nearest to you over the rice, tuck in the sides, and fold the whole packet over to form a tight, square bundle. Tie it with string. Repeat with the second leaf and the remaining ingredients.

5 Fill a wok one-third full of water. Place a double-tiered bamboo steamer, with its lid on, on top. Bring the water to the boil, lift the bamboo lid and place a rice cake on the rack in each tier. Cover and steam for about 45 minutes. Carefully open up the parcels and serve.

rice cakes Energy 180kcal/750kJ; Protein 2.3g; Carbohydrate 25.7g, of which sugars 2.3g; Fat 7.5g, of which saturates 0.9g; Cholesterol 0mg; Calcium 7mg; Fibre 0.1g; Sodium 136mg.
sticky rice cakes w. pork Energy 555kcal/2343kJ; Protein 32.3g; Carbohydrate 80.9g, of which sugars 2.6g; Fat 13.6g, of which saturates 3g; Cholesterol 71mg; Calcium 65mg; Fibre 1.1g; Sodium 84mg.

Chinese Clay Pot Rice with Chicken

This Cantonese dish is a great family one-pot meal. It can also be found on Chinese stalls and in some coffee shops. The traditional clay pot ensures that the ingredients remain moist, while allowing the flavours to mingle, but any earthenware pot such as a Spanish or Portuguese one will do. This recipe also works well with prawns or strips of pork fillet.

Serves 4

500g/1¼lb chicken breast fillets, cut into thin strips
5 dried shiitake mushrooms, soaked in hot water for 30 minutes, until soft
1 Chinese sausage, sliced
750ml/1¼pints/3 cups chicken stock
225g/8oz/generous 1 cup long grain rice, washed and drained
fresh coriander (cilantro) leaves, finely chopped, to garnish

For the marinade

30ml/2 tbsp sesame oil
45ml/3 tbsp oyster sauce
30ml/2 tbsp soy sauce
25g/1oz fresh root ginger, finely grated
2 spring onions (scallions), trimmed and finely sliced
1 fresh red chilli, seeded and finely sliced
5ml/1 tsp sugar

1 In a bowl, mix together the ingredients for the marinade. Toss in the chicken, making sure it is well coated. Set aside.

2 Drain the shiitake mushrooms and squeeze out excess water. Remove any hard stems and halve the caps. Add the mushroom caps and the Chinese sausage to the chicken.

3 Bring the stock to the boil in a clay pot or heavy pan. Stir in the rice and bring it back to the boil. Reduce the heat, cover the pot, and simmer on a low heat for 15–20 minutes, until almost all the liquid has been absorbed.

4 Spread the marinated mixture over the top of the rice and cover the pot. Leave to steam for about 10–15 minutes, until all the liquid is absorbed and the chicken is cooked. Garnish with coriander and serve.

Nasi Goreng

One of the most popular and best-known dishes from Indonesia, this is a marvellous way to use up left-over rice and meats.

Serves 4–6

350g/12oz/1¾ cups basmati rice (dry weight), cooked and cooled
2 eggs
30ml/2 tbsp water
105ml/7 tbsp sunflower oil
10ml/2 tsp shrimp paste
2–3 fresh red chillies, shredded
2 garlic cloves, crushed
1 onion, sliced
225g/8oz fillet (tenderloin) of pork or beef, cut into strips
115g/4oz cooked, peeled prawns (shrimp)
225g/8oz cooked chicken, chopped
30ml/2 tbsp dark soy sauce
salt and ground black pepper
deep-fried onions, to garnish

1 Separate the grains of the cooked rice with a fork. Cover and set aside. Beat the eggs with the water and seasoning.

2 Heat 15ml/1 tbsp of the oil in a frying pan or wok, pour in about half the egg mixture and cook until set, without stirring. Roll up the omelette, slide it on to a plate, cut into strips and set aside. Make another omelette in the same way.

3 Put the shrimp paste and half the shredded chillies into a food processor. Add the garlic and onion. Process to a paste.

4 Heat the remaining oil in a wok. Fry the paste, without browning, until it gives off a spicy aroma.

5 Add the strips of pork or beef and toss the meat over the heat, to seal in the juices. Cook the meat in the wok for about 2 minutes, stirring constantly.

6 Add the prawns, cook for 2 minutes, then add the chicken, rice, and soy sauce, with salt and pepper to taste, stirring until heated through. Serve in individual bowls, garnished with omelette strips, shredded chilli and deep-fried onions.

clay pot rice Energy 371kcal/1560kJ; Protein 36.2g; Carbohydrate 46.8g, of which sugars 1g; Fat 4g, of which saturates 1.2g; Cholesterol 93mg; Calcium 54mg; Fibre 0.7g; Sodium 721mg.
nasi goreng Energy 463kcal/1929kJ; Protein 27.3g; Carbohydrate 49.4g, of which sugars 2.1g; Fat 17.1g, of which saturates 2.7g; Cholesterol 151mg; Calcium 49mg; Fibre 0.5g; Sodium 288mg.

Shiitake Fried Rice

Shiitake mushrooms have a strong, earthy aroma and flavour. This is an easy recipe, and is almost a meal in itself.

Serves 4

2 eggs
15ml/1 tbsp water
45ml/3 tbsp vegetable oil
350g/12oz shiitake mushrooms
8 spring onions (scallions), sliced diagonally
1 garlic clove, crushed
½ green (bell) pepper, seeded and chopped
25g/1oz/2 tbsp butter
175–225g/6–8oz/about 1 cup long grain rice (raw weight), cooked and cooled
15ml/1 tbsp medium-dry sherry
30ml/2 tbsp dark soy sauce
15ml/1 tbsp chopped fresh coriander (cilantro)
salt

1 Beat the eggs with the water and season with a little salt. Heat 15ml/1 tbsp of the oil in a preheated wok or large frying pan, pour in the eggs and cook to make a large omelette. Lift the sides of the omelette and tilt the wok so that the uncooked egg can run underneath and be cooked. Roll up the omelette and slice thinly.

2 Remove and discard the mushroom stalks, if they are tough. Slice the caps thinly, halving them if they are large.

3 Heat 15ml/1 tbsp of the remaining oil in the wok and stir-fry the spring onions and garlic for 3–4 minutes until softened but not brown. Transfer them to a plate with a slotted spoon.

4 Add the green pepper and stir-fry for about 2–3 minutes, then add the butter and the remaining oil. As the butter begins to sizzle, add the mushrooms and stir-fry over a moderate heat for 3–4 minutes until both vegetables are soft.

5 Loosen the rice grains as much as possible. Pour the sherry over the mushrooms and then stir in the rice. Heat the rice over a medium heat, stirring to prevent it sticking. If the rice seems very dry, add a little more oil. Stir in the cooked spring onions, garlic and omelette slices, the soy sauce and chopped coriander. Cook for a few minutes until hot and serve.

Chinese Leaves & Black Rice

The slightly nutty, chewy black glutinous rice contrasts beautifully with the Chinese leaves in this tasty stir-fry, which looks very dramatic. It is a good dish for dieters as it is low in saturated fat.

Serves 4

225g/8oz/1⅓ cups black glutinous rice or brown rice
900ml/1½ pints/3¾ cups vegetable stock
15ml/1 tbsp vegetable oil
225g/8oz Chinese leaves (Chinese cabbage), cut into 1cm/½in strips
4 spring onions (scallions), thinly sliced
salt and ground white pepper
2.5ml/½ tsp sesame oil

1 Rinse the rice until the water runs clear, then drain and tip into a pan. Add the stock and bring to the boil. Lower the heat, cover the pan and cook gently for 30 minutes.

2 Remove the pan from the heat and leave it to stand for 15 minutes without lifting the lid.

3 Heat the vegetable oil in a non-stick frying pan or wok. Stir-fry the Chinese leaves over a medium heat for 2 minutes, adding a little water to prevent them from burning.

4 Drain the rice, stir it into the pan and cook for 4 minutes, using two spatulas or spoons to toss it with the Chinese leaves over the heat.

5 Add the spring onions, with salt and white pepper to taste. Drizzle over the sesame oil. Cook for 1 minute more, stirring constantly. Serve immediately.

Variation
This works well with any type of cabbage. It's particularly good with thinly-sliced Brussels sprouts, and you can add some chopped Chinese or purple-sprouting broccoli for good measure.

shiitake fried rice Energy 245kcal/1023kJ; Protein 6.6g; Carbohydrate 45.4g, of which sugars 0.4g; Fat 3.8g, of which saturates 0.7g; Cholesterol 48mg; Calcium 21mg; Fibre 0.5g; Sodium 287mg.
Chinese leaves & black rice Energy 243kcal/1029kJ; Protein 4.8g; Carbohydrate 48.9g, of which sugars 3.8g; Fat 4.5g, of which saturates 0.7g; Cholesterol 0mg; Calcium 37mg; Fibre 2.4g; Sodium 6mg.

Fresh Rice Noodles

Dried rice noodles are generally available in Asian supermarkets, but fresh ones are quite different and not that difficult to make. The freshly made noodle sheets can be served as a snack, with sugar or honey, or dipped into a savoury sauce.

Serves 4
225g/8oz/2 cups rice flour
600ml/1 pint/2½ cups water
a pinch of salt
15ml/1 tbsp vegetable oil, plus extra for brushing
slivers of fresh red chilli and fresh ginger, and coriander (cilantro) leaves, to garnish (optional)

1 Place the flour in a bowl and stir in some of the water to form a paste. Pour in the rest of the water, beating it to make a lump-free batter. Add the salt and oil and leave to stand for 15 minutes.

2 Meanwhile, fill a wide pan with water. Cut a piece of smooth cotton cloth a little larger than the diameter of the pan. Stretch it over the top of the pan, pulling the edges tautly down over the sides, then wind a piece of string around the edge, to secure.

3 Using a sharp knife, make three small slits, about 2.5cm/1in from the edge of the cloth, at regular intervals. Boil the water.

4 Stir the batter and ladle 30–45ml/2–3 tbsp on to the cloth, swirling it to form a 13–15cm/5–6in wide circle. Cover with a domed lid, such as a wok lid, and steam for 1 minute, or until the noodle sheet is translucent.

5 Carefully insert a spatula or knife under the noodle sheet and prise it off the cloth. (If it doesn't peel off easily, you may need to steam it a little longer.) Transfer the noodle sheet to a lightly oiled baking tray, brush lightly with oil, and cook the remaining batter in the same way.

6 Garnish with slivers of fresh chillies and ginger, and coriander leaves, if you like, and serve.

Soft Fried Noodles

This is a great dish for times when you are feeling a little peckish and fancy something simple but satisfying. Drain the cooked noodles and ladle them into the wok a few at a time, swirling them with the onions, so they don't all clump together on contact with the hot oil.

Serves 4–6
30ml/2 tbsp vegetable oil
30ml/2 tbsp finely chopped spring onions (scallions)
350g/12oz dried egg noodles, cooked and drained
soy sauce, to taste
salt and ground black pepper

1 Heat the oil in a wok and fry the spring onions for about 30 seconds. Add the noodles and separate the strands. Fry the noodles until they are heated through, lightly browned and crisp on the outside, but still soft inside. Season with soy sauce, salt and pepper. Serve immediately.

Plain Noodles with Four Flavours

A wonderfully simple way of serving noodles, this dish allows each individual diner to season their own, sprinkling over the four flavours as they like. Flavourings are always put out in little bowls whenever noodles are served.

Serves 4
4 small fresh red or green chillies
60ml/4 tbsp fish sauce
60ml/4 tbsp rice vinegar
sugar
mild or hot chilli powder
350g/12oz fresh or dried noodles

1 Finely chop the chillies, and mix half of them with the fish sauce in a small bowl. Mix the remaining chillies with the rice vinegar in another small bowl. Put the sugar and chilli powder in separate small bowls.

2 Cook the noodles until tender, following the instructions on the packet. Drain well, tip into a large bowl, and serve with the four flavours handed separately.

fresh rice noodles Energy 217kcal/908kJ; Protein 6.4g; Carbohydrate 46.1g, of which sugars 1.5g; Fat 0.6g, of which saturates 0.1g; Cholesterol 0mg; Calcium 51mg; Fibre 1.3g; Sodium 11mg.
soft fried noodles Energy 262kcal/1107kJ; Protein 7.2g; Carbohydrate 42g, of which sugars 1.3g; Fat 8.5g, of which saturates 1.8g; Cholesterol 18mg; Calcium 18mg; Fibre 1.8g; Sodium 105mg.
noodles w. four flavours Energy 321kcal/1341kJ; Protein 4.5g; Carbohydrate 72.4g, of which sugars 1g; Fat 0.2g, of which saturates 0g; Cholesterol 0mg; Calcium 12mg; Fibre 0.2g; Sodium 278mg.

Egg Fried Noodles

Yellow bean sauce gives these noodles a lovely savoury flavour.

Serves 4–6

350g/12oz medium-thick egg noodles
60ml/4 tbsp vegetable oil
4 spring onions (scallions), cut into 1cm/½in rounds
juice of 1 lime
15ml/1 tbsp soy sauce
2 garlic cloves, finely chopped
175g/6oz skinless, boneless chicken breast, sliced
175g/6oz raw prawns (shrimp), peeled and deveined
175g/6oz squid, cleaned and cut into rings
15ml/1 tbsp yellow bean sauce
15ml/1 tbsp fish sauce
15ml/1 tbsp soft light brown sugar
2 eggs
coriander (cilantro) leaves, to garnish

1 Cook the noodles in a pan of boiling water until just tender, then drain well and set aside.

2 Heat half the oil in a wok or large frying pan. Add the spring onions, stir-fry for 2 minutes, then add the noodles, lime juice and soy sauce and stir-fry for 2–3 minutes. Transfer the mixture to a bowl and keep warm.

3 Heat the remaining oil in the wok or pan. Add the garlic, chicken, prawns and squid. Stir-fry over a high heat until cooked. Stir in the yellow bean sauce, fish sauce and sugar, then break the eggs into the mixture, stirring gently until they set.

4 Add the noodles, toss lightly to mix, and heat through. Serve garnished with coriander leaves.

Cook's Tip
Be careful not to overcook the prawns (shrimp). If they turn pink before the chicken and squid are cooked, remove them from the wok or pan.

Fried Noodles with Ginger

Here is a simple noodle dish that is low in saturated fat and would go well with most Oriental dishes. It can also be served alone for two or three people.

Serves 4

handful of fresh coriander (cilantro)
225g/8oz dried egg noodles
10ml/2 tsp sesame oil
15ml/1 tbsp groundnut (peanut) or vegetable oil
5cm/2in piece fresh root ginger, cut into fine shreds
6–8 spring onions (scallions), cut into shreds
30ml/2 tbsp light soy sauce
salt and ground black pepper

1 Strip the leaves from the coriander stalks. Pile the leaves on to a chopping board and coarsely chop them using a cleaver or large, sharp knife.

2 Bring a large pan of lightly salted water to the boil and cook the noodles according to the instructions on the packet.

3 Drain the noodles, rinse under cold water, drain again and tip into a bowl. Add the sesame oil and toss to coat.

4 Heat a wok until hot, add the groundnut or vegetable oil and swirl it around. Add the ginger and stir-fry for a few seconds, then add the spring onions and noodles. Stir-fry for 3–4 minutes, until the noodles are hot.

5 Drizzle over the soy sauce, then sprinkle the chopped coriander on top of the noodles.

6 Add salt and ground black pepper to taste. Toss and serve in heated bowls.

Variation
If you don't like the flavour of coriander (cilantro), use flat leaf parsley or even some chopped rocket (arugula).

egg fried noodles Energy 410kcal/1728kJ; Protein 26.2g; Carbohydrate 45.6g, of which sugars 4.2g; Fat 15g, of which saturates 3g; Cholesterol 224mg; Calcium 60mg; Fibre 2g; Sodium 422mg.
fried noodles w. ginger Energy 253kcal/1067kJ; Protein 7.4g; Carbohydrate 41.6g, of which sugars 2.2g; Fat 7.5g, of which saturates 1.6g; Cholesterol 17mg; Calcium 25mg; Fibre 1.9g; Sodium 637mg.

Spicy Fried Noodles

This is a wonderfully versatile dish as you can adapt it to include your favourite ingredients.

Serves 4

225g/8oz egg thread noodles
60ml/4 tbsp vegetable oil
2 garlic cloves, finely chopped
175g/6oz pork fillet (tenderloin), sliced into thin strips
1 skinless, boneless chicken breast portion (about 175g/6oz), sliced into thin strips
115g/4oz/1 cup cooked peeled prawns (shelled shrimp), rinsed if canned
45ml/3 tbsp fresh lemon juice
45ml/3 tbsp fish sauce
30ml/2 tbsp soft light brown sugar
2 eggs, beaten
½ fresh red chilli, seeded and finely chopped
50g/2oz/¼ cup beansprouts
60ml/4 tbsp roasted peanuts, chopped
3 spring onions (scallions), cut into 5cm/2in lengths and shredded
45ml/3 tbsp chopped fresh coriander (cilantro)

1 Bring a large pan of water to the boil. Add the noodles, remove the pan from the heat and leave for 5 minutes.

2 Heat 45ml/3 tbsp of the oil in a wok and cook the garlic for 30 seconds. Add the pork and chicken and stir-fry until lightly browned, then add the prawns; stir-fry for 2 minutes. Stir in the lemon juice, then add the fish sauce and sugar.

3 Drain the noodles and add to the wok or pan with the remaining 15ml/1 tbsp oil. Toss all the ingredients together, then pour the beaten eggs over the noodles. Stir-fry until almost set, then add the chilli and beansprouts.

4 Divide the roasted peanuts, spring onions and coriander leaves into two equal portions, add one portion to the pan and stir-fry for about 2 minutes.

5 Tip the noodles on to a serving platter. Sprinkle on the remaining peanuts, spring onions and chopped coriander; serve.

Chinese Stir-fried Noodles

This Chinese dish of stir-fried rice noodles and seafood is one of the most popular items on the hawker stalls. Breakfast, lunch, supper, mid-morning, mid-afternoon or late evening, there's always a bowl of these noodles to be had. Variations include red snapper, clams and pork.

Serves 3–4

45ml/3 tbsp vegetable oil
2 garlic cloves, finely chopped
2 fresh red chillies, seeded and finely sliced
1 Chinese sausage, finely sliced
12 fresh prawns (shrimp), peeled
2 small squid, trimmed, cleaned, skinned and sliced
500g/1¼lb cooked rice noodles
30ml/2 tbsp light soy sauce
45ml/3 tbsp kecap manis
2–3 mustard green leaves, chopped
a handful of beansprouts
2 eggs, lightly beaten
ground black pepper
fresh coriander (cilantro) leaves, to garnish

1 Heat a wok and add the oil. Stir in the garlic and chillies and fry until fragrant. Add the Chinese sausage, followed by the prawns and squid, tossing them to mix thoroughly. Stir-fry for 3–4 minutes, until the prawns and squid are cooked.

2 Toss in the noodles and mix well. Add the soy sauce and kecap manis, and toss in the mustard leaves and beansprouts. Stir-fry for 1–2 minutes, until the leaves begin to wilt.

3 Quickly stir in the eggs for a few seconds until set. Season with black pepper, and spoon into heated bowls. Garnish with coriander and serve immediately.

Variations

- *You can replace kecap manis with the same quantity of dark soy sauce mixed with a little sugar.*
- *If you are unable to locate Chinese sausage (available from Asian stores), substitute pepperoni or use thinly sliced pork fillet.*

spicy fried noodles Energy 597kcal/2504kJ; Protein 39.3g; Carbohydrate 50.8g, of which sugars 10.3g; Fat 27.8g, of which saturates 5.5g; Cholesterol 226mg; Calcium 76mg; Fibre 2.9g; Sodium 250mg.
stir-fried noodles Energy 618kcal/2582kJ; Protein 24.8g; Carbohydrate 100g, of which sugars 1.1g; Fat 12.9g, of which saturates 2.1g; Cholesterol 217mg; Calcium 96mg; Fibre 0.5g; Sodium 716mg.

Noodles with Yellow Bean Sauce

Served solo, steamed leeks, courgettes and peas might be bland, but with a punchy bean sauce and a touch of chilli, they take on a whole new character.

Serves 4

150g/5oz thin egg noodles
200g/7oz baby leeks, sliced lengthways
200g/7oz baby courgettes (zucchini), halved lengthways
200g/7oz sugar snap peas, trimmed
200g/7oz/1¾ cups fresh or frozen peas
15ml/1 tbsp vegetable oil
5 garlic cloves, sliced
45ml/3 tbsp yellow bean sauce
45ml/3 tbsp sweet chilli sauce
30ml/2 tbsp sweet soy sauce
50g/2oz/½ cup cashew nuts, to garnish

1 Cook the noodles according to the packet instructions, drain and set aside.

2 Line a large bamboo steamer with some perforated baking parchment and add the leeks, courgettes, sugar snaps and peas. Cover and stand over a wok of simmering water.

3 Steam the vegetables for about 5 minutes, then remove and set aside. Drain and dry the wok.

4 Heat the vegetable oil in the wok and stir-fry the sliced garlic for 1–2 minutes.

5 In a separate bowl, mix together the yellow bean, sweet chilli and soy sauces, then pour into the wok. Stir to mix with the garlic, then add the steamed vegetables and the noodles and toss together to combine.

6 Cook the vegetables and noodles for 2–3 minutes, stirring frequently, until heated through.

7 Divide the vegetable noodles among four warmed serving bowls and sprinkle over the cashew nuts to garnish.

Egg Noodles with Asparagus

This dish is simplicity itself with a wonderful contrast of textures and flavours. Use young asparagus, which is beautifully tender and cooks in minutes. If you have a large wok, you can easily double the quantities of noodles and vegetables to serve four. Don't double the soy sauce, though – just add enough to taste.

Serves 2

115g/4oz dried egg noodles
15ml/1 tbsp vegetable oil
1 small onion, chopped
2.5/1in piece fresh root ginger, grated
2 garlic cloves, crushed
175g/6oz young asparagus spears, trimmed
115g/4oz/½ cup beansprouts
4 spring onions (scallions), sliced
45ml/3 tbsp light soy sauce
salt and ground black pepper

1 Bring a large pan of salted water to the boil. Add the noodles and cook until just tender or al dente. Drain, rinse under cold running water, drain again and set aside.

2 Heat a wok and add the vegetable oil. When it is very hot, stir-fry the onion, ginger and garlic for 2–3 minutes, making sure that you move them around to prevent them from burning.

3 Add the asparagus and stir-fry for a further 2–3 minutes, then add the noodles and beansprouts and toss over fairly high heat for 2 minutes, until the noodles are hot.

4 Stir in the spring onions and soy sauce and mix well to combine. Season to taste, adding salt sparingly as the sauce will add quite a salty flavour.

5 Stir-fry for 1 minute more before serving in individual bowls.

Variation

For a contrast in textures, stir-fry half the asparagus spears and cook the rest under a hot grill (broiler) or on a hot griddle pan until lightly charred.

noodles w. yellow bean Energy 296kcal/1241kJ; Protein 14.2g; Carbohydrate 44.9g, of which sugars 7.4g; Fat 7.8g, of which saturates 1.6g; Cholesterol 11mg; Calcium 61mg; Fibre 8.2g; Sodium 209mg.
noodles w. asparagus Energy 339kcal/1427kJ; Protein 12.6g; Carbohydrate 50.1g, of which sugars 7.9g; Fat 11.2g, of which saturates 2.2g; Cholesterol 17mg; Calcium 71mg; Fibre 4.8g; Sodium 1712mg.

Sesame Noodles with Spring Onions

This simple but very tasty warm salad can be prepared and cooked in just a few minutes.

Serves 4

2 garlic cloves, roughly chopped
30ml/2 tbsp Chinese sesame paste
15ml/1 tbsp dark sesame oil
30ml/2 tbsp soy sauce
30ml/2 tbsp rice wine
15ml/1 tbsp honey
pinch of five-spice powder
350g/12oz soba or buckwheat noodles
4 spring onions (scallions), finely sliced diagonally
salt and ground black pepper
50g/2oz beansprouts, 7.5cm/3in piece of cucumber, cut into matchsticks, and toasted sesame seeds, to garnish

1 Process the garlic, sesame paste, oil, soy sauce, rice wine, honey and five-spice powder with a pinch each of salt and pepper in a blender or food processor until smooth.

2 Cook the noodles in a pan of boiling water until just tender, following the directions on the packet.

3 Drain the noodles thoroughly and tip them into a bowl.

4 Toss the hot noodles with the dressing and the spring onions. Top with the beansprouts, cucumber and sesame seeds and serve in individual bowls.

Cook's Tips

- *If you can't find Chinese sesame paste, then use either tahini paste or smooth peanut butter instead.*
- *Five-spice powder is a fantastic ingredient for perking up dishes and adding a good depth of flavour. The five different spices – Sichuan pepper, cinnamon, cloves, fennel seeds and star anise – complement each other. The aniseed flavour of star anise predominates.*

Sesame Noodle Salad

Toasted sesame oil adds a nutty flavour to this warm Asian-style salad.

Serves 4

250g/9oz medium egg noodles
200g/7oz/1¾ cup sugar snap peas or mangetouts (snow peas)
2 tomatoes
3 spring onions (scallions)
2 carrots, cut into julienne strips
30ml/2 tbsp chopped fresh coriander (cilantro)
15ml/1 tbsp sesame seeds
fresh coriander (cilantro), to garnish

For the dressing

10ml/2 tsp light soy sauce
15ml/1 tbsp toasted sesame oil
15ml/1 tbsp sunflower oil
4cm/1½in piece fresh root ginger, finely grated
1 garlic clove, crushed

1 Bring a large pan of lightly salted water to the boil. Add the egg noodles, and bring back to the boil. Cook for 2 minutes.

2 Slice the sugar snap peas or mangetouts diagonally, add to the pan and cook for a further 2 minutes. Drain and rinse under cold running water.

3 Meanwhile, make the dressing. Whisk together the soy sauce, sesame and sunflower oils, grated fresh root ginger and crushed garlic in a small bowl.

4 Cut the tomatoes in half and scoop out the seeds with a teaspoon, then chop roughly. Using a sharp knife, cut the spring onions into fine shreds.

5 Tip the noodles and the peas or mangetouts into a large bowl and add the carrots, tomatoes and coriander.

6 Pour the dressing over the top of the noodle mixture, and toss with your hands to combine. Place in a large serving bowl or platter, or on individual salad plates.

7 Sprinkle with sesame seeds, coriander and spring onions.

noodles w. spring onions Energy 410kcal/1735kJ; Protein 12.4g; Carbohydrate 71g, of which sugars 6.2g; Fat 10g, of which saturates 0.7g; Cholesterol 0mg; Calcium 80mg; Fibre 3.5g; Sodium 539mg.
sesame noodle salad Energy 386kcal/1622kJ; Protein 10.9g; Carbohydrate 52.9g, of which sugars 8.6g; Fat 16g, of which saturates 3g; Cholesterol 19mg; Calcium 85mg; Fibre 5.1g; Sodium 310mg.

Rice Noodles with Fresh Herbs

Raid the kitchen garden (or your favourite stall at the farmers' market) for the best combination of fresh herbs to make this stunning yet very simple salad. Sharp flavourings – lime juice and fish sauce – provide the dressing, and the textures of crisp vegetables and soft chillies contrast beautifully with the rice vermicelli.

Serves 4

½ small cucumber
225g/8oz dried rice vermicelli
4–6 lettuce leaves, shredded
115g/4oz/½ cup beansprouts
1 bunch mixed herbs, such as basil, coriander (cilantro), mint and oregano, stalks removed, leaves shredded
juice of ½ lime
fish sauce, to drizzle

1 Peel the cucumber and cut it in half lengthways. Remove and discard the seeds using a teaspoon, then cut the flesh into matchsticks.

2 Add the rice sticks to a pan of boiling water, loosening them gently, and cook for 3–4 minutes, or until just tender – they should retain a bit of bite or firmness in the centre. Drain, rinse under cold water, and drain again.

3 In a bowl, toss the shredded lettuce, beansprouts, cucumber and herbs together.

4 Add the noodles and lime juice and toss together to mix.

5 Drizzle with a little fish sauce for seasoning, and serve the noodles immediately, either alone or with a stir-fried seafood or chicken dish to make a complete meal.

Cook's Tip

If possible, really go to town on the herb selection, using different varieties of mint, ginger leaves, oregano and thyme to provide the leafy bedding for this dish and give it a really distinctive, fragrant flavour.

Sweet & Hot Vegetable Noodles

This noodle dish has the colour of fire, but only the mildest suggestion of heat. Ginger and plum sauce give it its fruity flavour, while lime adds a delicious tang.

Serves 4

130g/4½oz dried rice noodles
30ml/2 tbsp groundnut (peanut) oil
2.5cm/1in piece fresh root ginger, sliced into thin batons
1 garlic clove, crushed
130g/4½oz canned bamboo shoots, drained, sliced into thin batons
2 medium carrots, sliced into batons
130g/4½oz/generous ⅔ cup beansprouts
1 small white cabbage, shredded
30ml/2 tbsp fish sauce
30ml/2 tbsp soy sauce
30ml/2 tbsp plum sauce
10ml/2 tsp sesame oil
15ml/1 tbsp palm sugar (jaggery) or light muscovado (brown) sugar
juice of ½ lime
90g/3½oz mooli (daikon), sliced into thin batons
small bunch fresh coriander (cilantro), chopped
60ml/4 tbsp sesame seeds, toasted

1 Cook the noodles in a large pan of boiling water, following the instructions on the packet. Meanwhile, heat the oil in a wok or large frying pan and stir-fry the ginger and garlic for about 3 minutes over a medium heat, until golden.

2 Drain the noodles and set them aside. Add the bamboo shoots to the wok, increase the heat to high and stir-fry for 5 minutes.

3 Add the carrots, beansprouts and cabbage and stir-fry for a further 5 minutes, until they are beginning to char on the edges.

4 Stir in the sauces, sesame oil, sugar and lime juice. Add the mooli and coriander and toss to mix.

5 Spoon into a bowl, sprinkle with the sesame seeds and serve.

rice noodles w. herbs Energy 217kcal/908kJ; Protein 6.4g; Carbohydrate 46.1g, of which sugars 1.5g; Fat 0.6g, of which saturates 0.1g; Cholesterol 0mg; Calcium 51mg; Fibre 1.3g; Sodium 11mg.
sweet & hot noodles Energy 368kcal/1530kJ; Protein 8.8g; Carbohydrate 45.8g, of which sugars 17.6g; Fat 16.5g, of which saturates 2.3g; Cholesterol 0mg; Calcium 200mg; Fibre 6.2g; Sodium 650mg.

Crispy Noodles with Vegetables

Deep-frying noodles gives them a lovely, crunchy texture. They taste great in this colourful stir-fry.

Serves 3–4

115g/4oz dried vermicelli rice noodles or cellophane noodles
groundnut (peanut) oil, for deep-frying
115g/4oz snake beans or green beans, cut into short lengths
2.5cm/1in piece fresh root ginger, cut into shreds
1 fresh red chilli, sliced
115g/4oz/1½ cups fresh shiitake or button (white) mushrooms, thickly sliced
2 large carrots, cut into thin strips
2 courgettes (zucchini), cut into thin strips
a few Chinese cabbage leaves, coarsely shredded
75g/3oz/¾ cup beansprouts
4 spring onions (scallions), shredded
30ml/2 tbsp light soy sauce
30ml/2 tbsp Chinese rice wine
5ml/1 tsp sugar
30ml/2 tbsp roughly torn fresh coriander (cilantro) leaves

1 Break the noodles into 7.5cm/3in lengths. Half-fill a wok with oil and heat it to 180°C/350°F. Deep-fry the raw noodles, in batches, for 1–2 minutes until puffed and crispy. Drain on kitchen paper. Carefully pour off all but 30ml/2 tbsp of the oil.

2 Reheat the oil in the wok. When hot, add the beans and stir-fry for 2–3 minutes. Add the ginger, chilli, mushrooms, carrots and courgettes and stir-fry for 1–2 minutes.

3 Add the Chinese cabbage, beansprouts and spring onions. Toss over the heat for 1 minute, then add the soy sauce, rice wine and sugar. Cook, stirring, for about 30 seconds.

4 Add the noodles and coriander and toss to mix, without crushing the noodles. Serve at once, piled on a plate.

Cook's Tip
If a milder flavour is preferred, carefully remove the seeds and pith from the chilli.

Five-flavour Noodles

Cabbage is one of the best vegetables for stir-frying, and tastes good with ginger and garlic in this simple dish. The seaweed adds a delicious finishing touch.

Serves 4

300g/11oz dried thin egg noodles
200g/7oz pork fillet (tenderloin), trimmed and thinly sliced
25ml/1½ tbsp vegetable oil
10g/¼oz fresh root ginger, grated
1 garlic clove, crushed
200g/7oz/1¾ cups green cabbage, roughly chopped
115g/4oz/2 cups beansprouts
1 green (bell) pepper, seeded and cut into fine strips
1 red (bell) pepper, seeded and cut into fine strips
salt and ground black pepper
20ml/4 tsp ao-nori seaweed, to garnish (optional)

For the seasoning

60ml/4 tbsp Worcestershire sauce
15ml/1 tbsp light soy sauce
15ml/1 tbsp oyster sauce
15ml/1 tbsp sugar
white pepper, to taste

1 Cook the egg noodles according to the packet instructions and drain.

2 Using a sharp knife, carefully cut the pork fillet into 3–4cm/1¼–1½in strips and season with plenty of salt and pepper. Heat 7.5ml/1½ tsp of the oil in a large frying pan or wok and stir-fry the pork until just cooked, then transfer to a dish.

3 Wipe the pan or wok with kitchen paper, and heat the remaining oil. When the oil is hot, add the ginger, garlic and cabbage and stir-fry for 1 minute.

4 Add the beansprouts and stir until softened, then add the green and red peppers and cook for 1 minute, stirring over a medium heat. Return the strips of cooked pork fillet to the pan or wok and toss lightly to mix.

5 Add the drained cooked egg noodles. Stir in all the seasoning ingredients. Stir-fry for 2–3 minutes, until heated through. Serve in heated bowls and sprinkle each portion with ao-nori seaweed, if you like.

crispy noodles Energy 204kcal/854kJ; Protein 24.6g; Carbohydrate 39.9g, of which sugars 4.3g; Fat 3.9g, of which saturates 0.8g; Cholesterol 76mg; Calcium 38mg; Fibre 1.2g; Sodium 206mg.
five-flavour noodles Energy 425Kcal/1799kJ; Protein 28.2g; Carbohydrate 62.6g, of which sugars 9.4g; Fat 8.6g, of which saturates 2.6g; Cholesterol 67mg; Calcium 82mg; Fibre 4.4g; Sodium 844mg.

Stir-fried Noodles with Beansprouts

Beansprouts are highly nutritious and make a valuable contribution to this low-fat dish, which combines egg noodles with peppers and soy sauce.

Serves 4

175g/6oz dried egg noodles
15ml/1 tbsp vegetable oil
1 garlic clove, finely chopped
1 small onion, halved and sliced
225g/8oz/1 cup beansprouts
1 small red (bell) pepper, seeded and cut into strips
1 small green (bell) pepper, seeded and cut into strips
30ml/2 tbsp light soy sauce
salt and ground white pepper

1 Bring a pan of water to the boil. Cook the noodles for 4 minutes until just tender, or according to the instructions on the packet. Drain, refresh under cold water and drain again.

2 Heat the oil in a non-stick frying pan or wok. When the oil is very hot, add the garlic, stir briefly, then add the onion slices. Cook, stirring, for 1 minute, then add the beansprouts and peppers. Stir-fry for 2–3 minutes.

3 Stir in the cooked noodles and toss over the heat, using two spatulas or wooden spoons, for 2–3 minutes or until the ingredients are well mixed and have heated through.

4 Add the soy sauce, then season to taste with salt and ground white pepper. Stir thoroughly before serving the noodle mixture in heated bowls.

Cook's Tip

Store beansprouts in the refrigerator and use within a day of purchase, as they tend to lose their crispness and become slimy and unpleasant quite quickly. The most commonly used beansprouts are sprouted mung beans, but many different beans can be sprouted – try sprouting your own.

Thai Noodles with Chinese Chives

This recipe requires a little time for preparation, but the cooking time is very fast.

Serves 4

350g/12oz dried rice noodles
1cm/½in piece fresh root ginger, peeled and grated
30ml/2 tbsp light soy sauce
45ml/3 tbsp vegetable oil
225g/8oz Quorn (mycoprotein), cut into small cubes
2 garlic cloves, crushed
1 large onion, cut into thin wedges
115g/4oz fried tofu, thinly sliced
1 fresh green chilli, seeded and thinly sliced
175g/6oz/¾ cup beansprouts
2 large bunches garlic chives, total weight about 115g/4oz, cut into 5cm/2in lengths
50g/2oz/½ cup roasted peanuts, ground
30ml/2 tbsp dark soy sauce
30ml/2 tbsp chopped fresh coriander (cilantro), and 1 lemon, cut into wedges, to garnish

1 Place the noodles in a bowl, cover with warm water and leave to soak for 30 minutes. Drain and set aside.

2 Mix the ginger, light soy sauce and 15ml/1 tbsp of the oil in a bowl. Add the Quorn, then set aside for 10 minutes. Drain, reserving the marinade.

3 Heat 15ml/1 tbsp of the remaining oil in a frying pan and cook the garlic for a few seconds. Add the Quorn and stir-fry for 3–4 minutes. Using a slotted spoon, transfer to a plate.

4 Heat the remaining oil in the pan and stir-fry the onion for 3–4 minutes, until softened and tinged with brown. Add the tofu and chilli, stir-fry briefly and then add the noodles. Stir-fry over a medium heat for 4–5 minutes.

5 Stir in the beansprouts, garlic chives and most of the ground peanuts, reserving a little for the garnish. Stir well, then add the Quorn, the dark soy sauce and the reserved marinade.

6 When hot, spoon on to serving plates and garnish with the remaining ground peanuts, the coriander and lemon.

noodles w. beansprouts Energy 244kcal/1030kJ; Protein 8g; Carbohydrate 39.9g, of which sugars 7.8g; Fat 7g, of which saturates 1.5g; Cholesterol 13mg; Calcium 34mg; Fibre 3.5g; Sodium 352mg.
noodles w. chinese chives Energy 444kcal/1857kJ; Protein 16g; Carbohydrate 77.6g, of which sugars 4.3g; Fat 6.5g, of which saturates 0.9g; Cholesterol 0mg; Calcium 230mg; Fibre 5g; Sodium 1227mg.

Crispy Fried Rice Vermicelli

This crisp tangle of fried rice vermicelli is tossed in a piquant sauce.

Serves 4–6

vegetable oil, for deep and shallow frying
175g/6oz rice vermicelli
15ml/1 tbsp chopped garlic
4–6 small dried red chillies
30ml/2 tbsp chopped shallots
15ml/1 tbsp dried shrimps, rinsed
115g/4oz minced (ground) pork
115g/4oz raw peeled prawns (shrimp), chopped
30ml/2 tbsp brown bean sauce
30ml/2 tbsp rice vinegar
45ml/3 tbsp fish sauce
75g/3oz soft light brown sugar
30ml/2 tbsp lime juice
115g/4oz/½ cup beansprouts

For the garnish

2 spring onions (scallions), shredded
30ml/2 tbsp fresh coriander (cilantro) leaves
2-egg omelette, rolled and sliced
2 fresh red chillies, seeded and cut into thin strips

1 Heat oil for deep-frying. Break the vermicelli into 7.5cm/3in lengths and deep-fry in handfuls until they puff up. Lift out with a slotted spoon and drain on kitchen paper.

2 Heat 30ml/2 tbsp oil in a wok and fry the garlic, chillies, shallots and dried shrimps for about 1 minute. Add the pork and stir-fry for 3–4 minutes, until no longer pink. Add the prawns and fry for 2 minutes. Spoon into a bowl and set aside.

3 Add the brown bean sauce, vinegar, fish sauce and sugar to the wok. Bring to a gentle boil, stir to dissolve the sugar and cook until thick and syrupy.

4 Add the lime juice and adjust the seasoning. The sauce should be sweet, sour and salty. Add the pork and prawn mixture with the beansprouts and stir them into the sauce.

5 Add the fried rice noodles to the wok and toss gently to coat them in the sauce. Serve in warmed bowls, garnished with the spring onions, coriander leaves, omelette strips and chillies.

Toasted Noodles with Vegetables

Slightly crisp noodle cakes topped with vegetables make a superb dish.

Serves 4

15ml/1 tbsp vegetable oil
175g/6oz dried egg vermicelli, cooked and drained
2 garlic cloves, finely chopped
115g/4oz/1 cup baby corn cobs, halved lengthways
115g/4oz/1½ cups fresh shiitake mushrooms, halved
3 celery sticks, sliced
1 carrot, diagonally sliced
115g/4oz/½ cup mangetouts (snow peas)
75g/3oz/¾ cup sliced, drained, canned bamboo shoots
15ml/1 tbsp cornflour (cornstarch) mixed with 15ml/1 tbsp water
15ml/1 tbsp dark soy sauce
5ml/1 tsp sugar
300ml/½ pint/1¼ cups vegetable stock
salt and ground white pepper
spring onion (scallion) curls, to garnish

1 Heat 2.5ml/½ tsp of the oil in a non-stick frying pan or wok. When it starts to smoke, spread half the noodles over the base. Fry for 2–3 minutes until lightly toasted. Carefully turn the noodles over (they stick together like a cake), fry the other side, then slide on to a heated serving plate. Keep hot.

2 Repeat with the remaining noodles to make two cakes.

3 Heat the remaining oil in the clean pan, then fry the garlic for a few seconds. Add the corn cobs and the mushrooms and stir-fry for 3 minutes. Add the remaining vegetables and stir-fry for 2 minutes or until the vegetables are crisp-tender.

4 Add the cornflour paste, soy sauce, sugar and stock. Cook, stirring, until the sauce thickens. Season, divide between the noodle cakes, garnish with spring onion curls and serve.

Variation
Sliced fennel tastes good in this stir-fry, either as an addition or instead of the sliced bamboo shoots.

fried rice vermicelli Energy 204kcal/854kJ; Protein 10.6g; Carbohydrate 33.9g, of which sugars 4.3g; Fat 2.9g, of which saturates 0.6g; Cholesterol 76mg; Calcium 38mg; Fibre 1.2g; Sodium 206mg.
toasted noodles w. veg. Energy 230kcal/964kJ; Protein 7.9g; Carbohydrate 44.6g, of which sugars 5.4g; Fat 2.4g, of which saturates 0.3g; Cholesterol 0mg; Calcium 52mg; Fibre 2.8g; Sodium 623mg.

Prawn Noodle Salad

Light and refreshing, this salad has all the tangy flavour of the sea.

Serves 4

115g/4oz cellophane noodles, soaked in hot water until soft
16 cooked peeled prawns (shrimp)
1 small green (bell) pepper, seeded and cut into strips
½ cucumber, cut into strips
1 tomato, cut into strips
2 shallots, finely sliced
salt and ground black pepper
coriander (cilantro) leaves, to garnish

For the dressing

15ml/1 tbsp rice vinegar
30ml/2 tbsp fish sauce
30ml/2 tbsp fresh lime juice
pinch of salt
2.5ml/½ tsp fresh root ginger, grated
1 lemon grass stalk, finely chopped
1 fresh red chilli, seeded and finely sliced
30ml/2 tbsp mint, roughly chopped
few sprigs tarragon, roughly chopped
15ml/1 tbsp chopped chives

1 Make the dressing by combining all the ingredients in a small bowl or jug (pitcher); whisk well.

2 Drain the noodles, then plunge them in a pan of boiling water for 1 minute. Drain, rinse under cold running water and drain again well.

3 In a large bowl, combine the noodles with the pepper, cucumber, tomato and shallots. Lightly season with salt and pepper, then toss with the dressing.

4 Spoon the noodles on to individual plates, arranging the prawns on top. Garnish each serving with coriander leaves and serve immediately.

Variation
Instead of prawns, try squid, scallops, mussels or crab.

Stir-fried Prawns with Noodles

One of the most appealing aspects of Asian food is its appearance. Ingredients are carefully chosen so that each dish, even a simple stir-fry like this one, is balanced in terms of colour, texture and flavour.

Serves 4

130g/4½oz rice noodles
30ml/2 tbsp groundnut (peanut) oil
1 large garlic clove, crushed
150g/5oz large prawns (shrimp), peeled and deveined
15g/½oz dried shrimp
1 piece mooli (daikon), about 75g/3oz, grated
15ml/1 tbsp fish sauce
30ml/2 tbsp soy sauce
30ml/2 tbsp light muscovado (brown) sugar
30ml/2 tbsp lime juice
90g/3½oz/⅓ cup beansprouts
40g/1½oz/⅓ cup peanuts, chopped
15ml/1 tbsp sesame oil
chopped coriander (cilantro), 5ml/1 tsp dried chilli flakes and 2 shallots, finely chopped, to garnish

1 Soak the noodles in a bowl of boiling water for 5 minutes, or according to the packet instructions. Heat the oil in a wok or large frying pan. Add the garlic, and stir-fry over a medium heat for 2–3 minutes, until golden brown.

2 Add the prawns, dried shrimp and grated mooli and stir-fry for a further 2 minutes. Stir in the fish sauce, soy sauce, sugar and lime juice.

3 Drain the noodles thoroughly, then snip them into smaller lengths with scissors. Add to the wok or pan with the beansprouts, peanuts and sesame oil. Toss to mix, then stir-fry for 2 minutes. Serve immediately, garnished with the coriander, chilli flakes and shallots.

Cook's Tip
Some cooks salt the mooli and leave it to drain, then rinse and dry before use.

prawn noodle salad Energy 156kcal/653kJ; Protein 7.4g; Carbohydrate 29.4g, of which sugars 5.4g; Fat 0.7g, of which saturates 0.1g; Cholesterol 49mg; Calcium 68mg; Fibre 2.1g; Sodium 417mg.
prawns w. noodles Energy 397kcal/1675kJ; Protein 21.3g; Carbohydrate 56.5g, of which sugars 3.2g; Fat 11.1g, of which saturates 2.4g; Cholesterol 89mg; Calcium 72mg; Fibre 3.3g; Sodium 567mg.

Singapore Noodles

Dried Chinese mushrooms add an intense flavour to this lightly curried dish.

Serves 4
20g/¾oz dried shiitake mushrooms
225g/8oz fine egg noodles
10ml/2 tsp sesame oil
45ml/3 tbsp groundnut (peanut) oil
2 garlic cloves, crushed
1 small onion, chopped
1 fresh green chilli, seeded and thinly sliced
10ml/2 tsp curry powder
115g/4oz green beans, halved
115g/4oz Chinese leaves (Chinese cabbage), thinly shredded
4 spring onions (scallions), sliced
30ml/2 tbsp soy sauce
115g/4oz cooked prawns (shrimp), peeled and deveined
salt

1 Soak the mushrooms for 30 minutes. Drain, reserving 30ml/2 tbsp of the water. Discard the stems and slice the caps.

2 Bring a pan of lightly salted water to the boil and cook the noodles according to the directions on the packet. Drain, tip into a bowl and toss with the sesame oil.

3 Heat the groundnut oil in a preheated wok and stir-fry the garlic, onion and chilli for 3 minutes. Stir in the curry powder and cook for 1 minute. Add the mushrooms, green beans, Chinese leaves and spring onions. Stir-fry for 3–4 minutes until the vegetables are tender, but still crisp.

4 Add the noodles, soy sauce, reserved mushroom soaking water and prawns. Toss over the heat for 2–3 minutes until the noodles and prawns are heated through.

Variation
Ring the changes with the vegetables used in this dish. Try mangetouts (snow peas), broccoli, sweet peppers or baby corn cobs. The prawns (shrimp) can be omitted.

Stir-fried Noodles in Seafood Sauce

Recent discoveries along the Yellow River suggest that the Chinese were enjoying noodles made from millet some 4000 years ago! With all the different grains that are now cultivated, they have clearly never looked back.

Serves 4
225g/8oz Chinese egg noodles
8 spring onions (scallions), trimmed
8 asparagus spears, plus extra steamed asparagus spears, to serve
5cm/2in piece fresh root ginger, peeled
30ml/2 tbsp vegetable oil
3 garlic cloves, chopped
60ml/4 tbsp oyster sauce
450g/1lb cooked crab meat (all white, or two-thirds white and one-third brown)
30ml/2 tbsp rice vinegar
15–30ml/1–2 tbsp light soy sauce

1 Put the noodles in a large pan, cover with lightly salted boiling water, cover and leave for 3–4 minutes, or for the time suggested on the packet. Drain, tip into a bowl and set aside.

2 Cut off the green spring onion tops and slice them thinly. Set aside. Cut the white parts into 2cm/¾in lengths and quarter them lengthways. Cut the asparagus spears on the diagonal into 2cm/¾in pieces, and slice the ginger into very fine matchsticks.

3 Heat the oil in a frying pan or wok until very hot, then add the ginger, garlic and white spring onion batons. Stir-fry over a high heat for 1 minute.

4 Add the oyster sauce, crab meat, soy sauce and rice vinegar to taste. Stir-fry for about 2 minutes, until the crab and sauce are hot. Add the noodles and toss until heated through.

5 At the last moment, toss in the spring onion tops and serve with a few extra asparagus spears.

Singapore noodles Energy 314kcal/1316kJ; Protein 19.2g; Carbohydrate 50.3g, of which sugars 5.9g; Fat 4g, of which saturates 0.6g; Cholesterol 70mg; Calcium 74mg; Fibre 1.6g; Sodium 81mg.
noodles in sauce Energy 385kcal/1622kJ; Protein 28.5g; Carbohydrate 45.9g, of which sugars 6.4g; Fat 10.9g, of which saturates 2.2g; Cholesterol 98mg; Calcium 167mg; Fibre 2.4g; Sodium 1233mg.

Noodles with Crab & Mushrooms

This is a dish of contrasting flavours, textures and colours, and requires some skill and dexterity from the cook. While one hand gently turns the noodles in the pan, the other takes chunks of fresh crab meat and drops them into the steaming wok. Here the crab meat is cooked separately to make it easier.

Serves 4

25g/1oz dried cloud ear (wood ear) mushrooms, soaked in warm water for 20 minutes
115g/4oz dried cellophane noodles, soaked in warm water for 20 minutes
30ml/2 tbsp vegetable or sesame oil
3 shallots, halved and thinly sliced
2 garlic cloves, crushed
2 fresh green or red chillies, seeded and sliced
1 carrot, peeled and cut into thin diagonal rounds
5ml/1 tsp sugar
45ml/3 tbsp oyster sauce
15ml/1 tbsp soy sauce
225g/8oz fresh, raw crab meat, cut into bitesize chunks
ground black pepper
fresh coriander (cilantro) leaves, to garnish

1 Remove the centres from the soaked cloud ear mushrooms and cut the mushrooms in half. Drain the soaked noodles and cut them into 30cm/12in pieces and put aside.

2 Heat a wok and add 15ml/1 tbsp of the oil. Stir in the shallots, garlic and chillies, and cook until fragrant. Add the carrot and cook for 1 minute, then add the mushrooms and cook for 1 minute more. Stir in the sugar with the oyster and soy sauces, followed by the noodles. Pour in 400ml/14fl oz/1⅔ cups water or chicken stock, cover the wok and cook for about 5 minutes, or until the noodles are soft and have absorbed most of the sauce.

3 Meanwhile, heat the remaining oil in a heavy pan. Add the crab meat and cook until it is nicely pink and tender. Season well with black pepper. Arrange the noodles and crab meat on a serving dish and garnish with coriander.

Buckwheat Noodles with Salmon

Young pea sprouts are only available for a short time. You can substitute watercress, mustard cress, young leeks or your favourite green vegetable or herb in this dish.

Serves 4

225g/8oz buckwheat or soba noodles
15ml/1 tbsp oyster sauce
juice of ½ lemon
30ml/2 tbsp olive oil, preferably light oil
115g/4oz smoked salmon, cut into fine strips
115g/4oz young pea sprouts
2 ripe tomatoes, peeled, seeded and cut into strips
15ml/1 tbsp chopped fresh chives
salt and ground black pepper

1 Cook the buckwheat or soba noodles in a large pan of salted boiling water, following the directions on the packet. Drain, then rinse under cold running water and drain well.

2 Tip the noodles into a large bowl. Add the oyster sauce and lemon juice and season with pepper to taste. Moisten with the olive oil and toss to coat the strands.

3 Add the smoked salmon, pea sprouts, tomatoes and chives. Mix well and serve at once, either straight from the bowl or on individual salad plates.

Cook's Tips

- *A light olive oil is recommended for this salad so that the delicate flavour of the pea sprouts is not overwhelmed. An alternative would be to use another light, flavourless oil, such as sunflower or safflower oil.*
- *Buckwheat noodles are pale in colour and pliable. They are often eaten with a thick, gravy-like sauce in China. They come in different shapes depending on how the dough is rolled. You might encounter round and long noodles, flat noodles, or thin noodle sheets where the dough has been pared with a knife.*

noodles w. crab Energy 252kcal/1051kJ; Protein 12.9g; Carbohydrate 35.7g, of which sugars 10.3g; Fat 6.3g, of which saturates 0.7g; Cholesterol 41mg; Calcium 97mg; Fibre 1.6g; Sodium 770mg.
noodles w. salmon Energy 343kcal/1443kJ; Protein 16.3g; Carbohydrate 47.9g, of which sugars 3.8g; Fat 10.9g, of which saturates 1.2g; Cholesterol 10mg; Calcium 29mg; Fibre 3.5g; Sodium 814mg.

Noodles with Prawns & Ham

This recipe combines prawns with ham and chicken, which may seem unconventional until you remember that the Spanish do something very similar in their paella.

Serves 4–6

30ml/2 tbsp vegetable oil
2 garlic cloves, sliced
5ml/1 tsp fresh root ginger, peeled and chopped
2 fresh red chillies, seeded and chopped
75g/3oz lean ham, thinly sliced
1 skinless chicken breast fillet, thinly sliced
16 uncooked tiger prawns (jumbo shrimp), peeled, tails left intact and deveined
115g/4oz green beans, trimmed
225g/8oz/1 cup beansprouts
50g/2oz Chinese chives
450g/1lb egg noodles, cooked in boiling water until tender, then drained
30ml/2 tbsp dark soy sauce
15ml/1 tbsp oyster sauce
salt and ground black pepper
5ml/1 tsp sesame oil
2 spring onions (scallions), cut into strips, and fresh coriander (cilantro) leaves, to garnish

1 Heat 15ml/1 tbsp of the oil in a wok or large frying pan. When the oil is hot, stir-fry the garlic, ginger and chillies for 2 minutes, until aromatic.

2 Add the prepared ham, chicken, prawns and green beans to the wok or frying pan.

3 Stir-fry the mixture for about 2 minutes over a high heat or until the chicken and prawns are thoroughly cooked. Transfer to a bowl and set aside.

4 Heat the remaining oil in the wok or frying pan. When the oil is hot, add the beansprouts and Chinese chives. Stir-fry for 1–2 minutes.

5 Add the noodles and toss to mix. Season with soy sauce, oyster sauce, salt and pepper. Drizzle with sesame oil and serve immediately in individual bowls, garnished with spring onions and coriander.

Curried Noodles with Chicken

Chicken or pork can be used in this tasty dish. It is so quick and easy to prepare and cooks in next to no time, making it the perfect snack for busy people.

Serves 2

30ml/2 tbsp vegetable oil
10ml/2 tsp magic paste
1 lemon grass stalk, finely chopped
5ml/1 tsp red curry paste
90g/3½oz skinless chicken breast fillets or pork fillet (tenderloin), sliced into thin strips
30ml/2 tbsp light soy sauce
400ml/14fl oz/1⅔ cups coconut milk
2 kaffir lime leaves, rolled into cylinders and thinly sliced
250g/9oz dried medium egg noodles
90g/3½oz Chinese leaves (Chinese cabbage), shredded
90g/3½oz spinach or watercress, shredded
juice of 1 lime
small bunch fresh coriander (cilantro) or flat leaf parsley, chopped

1 Heat the oil in a wok or large, heavy frying pan. Add the magic paste and lemon grass and stir-fry over a low to medium heat for 4–5 seconds, until they give off their aroma.

2 Stir in the curry paste, then add the strips of chicken or pork to the wok or pan. Stir-fry over a medium to high heat for 2 minutes, until the chicken or pork is coated in the paste and seared on all sides.

3 Add the soy sauce, coconut milk and sliced lime leaves. Bring the coconut milk to a simmer, then add the noodles. Simmer gently for about 4 minutes, tossing the mixture occasionally to make sure that the noodles cook evenly and do not clump together.

4 Add the Chinese leaves and the shredded spinach or watercress. Stir well. Add the lime juice. Spoon into a serving bowl or two individual bowls, sprinkle with the chopped fresh coriander or parsley, and serve.

noodles w. prawns Energy 302kcal/1277kJ; Protein 25.9g; Carbohydrate 35.5g, of which sugars 2.6g; Fat 7.3g, of which saturates 1.7g; Cholesterol 122mg; Calcium 56mg; Fibre 2.4g; Sodium 1031mg.
noodles w. chicken Energy 702kcal/2965kJ; Protein 28.7g; Carbohydrate 101.6g, of which sugars 14.2g; Fat 23g, of which saturates 4.9g; Cholesterol 69mg; Calcium 187mg; Fibre 4.7g; Sodium 1564mg.

Sesame Duck & Noodle Salad

This salad is complete in itself and makes a lovely summer lunch.

Serves 4

2 skinless duck breast fillets
1 tbsp vegetable oil
150g/5oz sugar snap peas
2 carrots, cut into 7.5cm/3in batons
225g/8oz medium egg noodles
6 spring onions (scallions), sliced
salt
30ml/2 tbsp coriander (cilantro) leaves, to garnish

For the marinade

15ml/1 tbsp sesame oil
5ml/1 tsp ground coriander
5ml/1 tsp five-spice powder

For the dressing

15ml/1 tbsp garlic vinegar or white wine vinegar
5ml/1 tsp soft light brown sugar
5ml/1 tsp soy sauce
15ml/1 tbsp toasted sesame seeds
45ml/3 tbsp sunflower oil
30ml/2 tbsp sesame oil
ground black pepper

1 Slice the duck breast fillets thinly across and put them in a shallow dish. Mix the ingredients for the marinade, pour over the duck and coat thoroughly. Cover and leave to marinate in a cool place for 30 minutes.

2 Heat the oil in a frying pan, add the slices of duck breast and stir-fry for 3–4 minutes until cooked. Set aside.

3 Bring a pan of lightly salted water to the boil. Place the sugar snap peas and carrots in a steamer that will fit on top of the pan. When the water boils, add the noodles. Place the steamer on top and steam the vegetables, while cooking the noodles for the time suggested on the packet.

4 Set the steamed vegetables aside. Drain the noodles, refresh them under cold running water and drain again. Place them in a serving bowl.

5 Make the dressing by whisking all the ingredients in a bowl. Pour over the noodles and mix well. Add the sugar snap peas, carrots, spring onions and duck slices and toss to mix. Garnish with the coriander leaves and serve.

Shredded Duck & Noodle Salad

This piquant marinated duck salad makes a mouthwatering first course or a delicious light meal. If you like, toss the salad in a quick and easy dressing made by whisking together soy sauce, mirin, sugar, garlic and chilli oil.

Serves 4

4 skinless duck breast fillets, sliced
30ml/2 tbsp Chinese rice wine
10ml/2 tsp finely grated fresh root ginger
60ml/4 tbsp soy sauce
15ml/1 tbsp sesame oil
15ml/1 tbsp clear honey
10ml/2 tsp five-spice powder
toasted sesame seeds, to garnish

For the noodles

150g/5oz cellophane noodles, cooked
large handful of fresh mint and coriander (cilantro) leaves
1 red (bell) pepper, seeded and finely sliced
4 spring onions (scallions), finely shredded and sliced
50g/2oz mixed salad leaves

1 Place the duck breast slices in a non-metallic bowl. Mix together the rice wine, ginger, soy sauce, sesame oil, clear honey and five-spice powder. Toss to coat, cover and marinate in the refrigerator for 3–4 hours.

2 Heat the oil in a frying pan, add the slices of duck breast and stir-fry for 3–4 minutes until cooked. Set aside.

3 Double over a large sheet of heavy foil. Place the foil on a heatproof plate. Place the duck breast slices on it and spoon the marinade over. Fold the foil to enclose the duck and juices and scrunch the edges to seal. Steam on a rack over simmering water for 50–60 minutes, then leave to rest for 15 minutes.

4 Mix the noodles, herbs, red pepper, spring onions and salad leaves in a bowl. Remove the skin from the duck and shred the flesh. Divide the noodle salad among four plates and top with the duck. Sprinkle with the sesame seeds and serve immediately.

sesame duck Energy 550kcal/2301kJ; Protein 25.3g; Carbohydrate 47g, of which sugars 4.2g; Fat 31.6g, of which saturates 5.2g; Cholesterol 99mg; Calcium 70mg; Fibre 4.5g; Sodium 192mg.
shredded duck Energy 398kcal/1671kJ; Protein 32.8g; Carbohydrate 41.7g, of which sugars 10.8g; Fat 11.6g, of which saturates 2.2g; Cholesterol 165mg; Calcium 40mg; Fibre 1g; Sodium 1688mg.

Lamb & Ginger Noodle Stir-fry

Fresh root ginger adds a bright tang to this lamb and noodle dish, giving it a simultaneously hot and yet refreshing taste.

Serves 4

45ml/3 tbsp sesame oil
3 spring onions (scallions), sliced
2 garlic cloves, crushed
2.5cm/1in piece fresh root ginger, peeled and finely sliced
1 fresh red chilli, seeded and finely sliced
1 red (bell) pepper, seeded and sliced
450g/1lb lean boneless lamb, cut into fine strips
115g/4oz/1½ cups fresh shiitake mushrooms, sliced
2 carrots, cut into matchstick strips
300g/11oz fresh Chinese egg noodles
300g/11oz pak choi (bok choy), shredded
soy sauce, to serve

1 Heat half the oil in a wok. Stir-fry the spring onions and garlic for about 5 minutes, or until golden. Add the ginger, chilli and red pepper and fry for 5 minutes more, until the chilli and pepper start to soften. Remove the vegetables and set aside.

2 Add the remaining oil and stir-fry the lamb in batches until golden. Add the mushrooms and carrots and stir-fry for 2–3 minutes.

3 Remove the lamb mixture from the wok and set aside with the red pepper mixture. Add the noodles and pak choi to the wok and stir-fry for 5 minutes.

4 Finally, replace all the cooked ingredients in the wok and stir-fry for a couple more minutes. Serve in heated bowls, with soy sauce on the side to sprinkle over.

Cook's Tip
If fresh egg noodles are not available, use the dried type. Cook them according to the packet instructions, drain and rinse under cold water, then drain well.

Wheat Noodles with Stir-fried Pork

Dried wheat noodles, sold in straight bundles like sticks, are versatile and robust. They keep well, so are handy items to have in the storecupboard, ready for quick and easy recipes like this one.

Serves 4

225g/8oz pork loin, cut into thin strips
225g/8oz dried wheat noodles, soaked in lukewarm water for 20 minutes
15ml/1 tbsp groundnut (peanut) oil
2 garlic cloves, finely chopped
2–3 spring onions (scallions), trimmed and chopped
45ml/3 tbsp kroeung or magic paste
15ml/1 tbsp fish sauce
30ml/2 tbsp unsalted roasted peanuts, finely chopped
chilli oil, for drizzling

For the marinade

30ml/2 tbsp fish sauce
30ml/2 tbsp soy sauce
15ml/1 tbsp groundnut (peanut) oil
10ml/2 tsp sugar

1 In a bowl, combine the ingredients for the marinade, stirring constantly until all the sugar dissolves. Toss in the strips of pork, making sure that they are well coated in the marinade. Put aside for 30 minutes.

2 Drain the wheat noodles. Bring a large pan of water to the boil. Drop in the noodles, untangling them with chopsticks, if necessary. Cook for 4–5 minutes, until tender.

3 Drain the noodles thoroughly, then divide them among individual serving bowls. Keep the noodles warm.

4 Meanwhile, heat a wok. Pour in the oil and stir-fry the garlic and spring onions, until fragrant. Add the pork, tossing it around the wok for 2 minutes. Stir in the kroeung or magic paste and fish sauce for 2 minutes – add a splash of water if the wok gets too dry – and tip the pork on top of the noodles.

5 Sprinkle the peanuts over the top and drizzle with chilli oil. Serve immediately.

lamb & ginger Energy 820kcal/3418kJ; Protein 46g; Carbohydrate 76.4g, of which sugars 9.4g; Fat 36g, of which saturates 11.7g; Cholesterol 143mg; Calcium 55mg; Fibre 4.1g; Sodium 709mg.
noodles w. pork Energy 340kcal/1435kJ; Protein 19.6g; Carbohydrate 46g, of which sugars 4.4g; Fat 9.9g, of which saturates 1.4g; Cholesterol 35mg; Calcium 23mg; Fibre 1.9g; Sodium 41mg.

Cellophane Noodles with Pork

Simple, speedy and very satisfying, this is an excellent way of using mung bean noodles. It scores high on presentation too, thanks to the contrast between the translucent, thread-like noodles and the vibrant colour of the vegetables.

Serves 2

200g/7oz cellophane noodles
30ml/2 tbsp vegetable oil
15ml/1 tbsp magic paste
200g/7oz minced (ground) pork
1 fresh green or red chilli, seeded and finely chopped
300g/11oz/scant 1½ cups beansprouts
bunch spring onions (scallions), finely chopped
30ml/2 tbsp soy sauce
30ml/2 tbsp fish sauce
30ml/2 tbsp sweet chilli sauce
15ml/1 tbsp soft light brown sugar
30ml/2 tbsp rice vinegar
30ml/2 tbsp roasted peanuts, chopped, and a small bunch fresh coriander (cilantro), chopped, to garnish

1 Place the noodles in a large bowl, cover with boiling water and soak for 10 minutes. Drain the noodles and set aside until ready to use.

2 Heat the oil in a wok or large, heavy frying pan. Add the magic paste and stir-fry for 2–3 seconds, then add the pork. Stir-fry the meat, breaking it up with a wooden spatula, for 2–3 minutes, until browned all over.

3 Add the chopped chilli to the meat and stir-fry for 3–4 seconds, then add the beansprouts and chopped spring onions, stir-frying for a few seconds after each addition.

4 Snip the noodles into 5cm/2in lengths and add to the wok or pan, with the soy sauce, fish sauce, sweet chilli sauce, sugar and rice vinegar.

5 Toss the ingredients together over the heat until the noodles have warmed through. Pile on to a platter or into a large bowl. Sprinkle the peanuts and coriander over the top and serve.

Rice Rolls Stuffed with Pork

Steamed rice sheets are very tasty when filled with pork, rolled up, drizzled in herb oil, and then dipped in a hot chilli sauce. Generally, they are eaten as a snack, or served as an appetizer.

Serves 6

25g/1oz dried cloud ear (wood ear) mushrooms, soaked in warm water for 30 minutes
350g/12oz minced (ground) pork
30nl/2 tbsp fish sauce
10ml/2 tsp sugar
15ml/1 tbsp vegetable or groundnut (peanut) oil
2 garlic cloves, finely chopped
2 shallots, finely chopped
2 spring onions (scallions), trimmed and finely chopped
24 fresh rice sheets, 7.5cm/3in square
ground black pepper
herb oil, for drizzling
hot chilli sauce, for dipping

1 Drain the mushrooms and squeeze out any excess water. Cut off and discard the hard stems. Finely chop the rest of the mushrooms and put them in a bowl. Add the minced pork, fish sauce and sugar and mix well.

2 Heat the oil in a wok or heavy pan. Add the garlic, shallots and spring onions. Stir-fry until golden, then add the pork mixture and stir-fry for 5–6 minutes, until the pork is cooked. Season with pepper.

3 Place the rice sheets on a flat surface. Spoon a tablespoon of the pork mixture on to the middle of each sheet. Fold one side over the filling, tuck in the sides, and roll to enclose the filling, so that it resembles a short spring roll.

4 Place the filled rice rolls on a serving plate, drizzle with herb oil, and serve with chilli sauce.

Cook's Tip

To make life easy, prepared, fresh rice sheets are available in Asian markets and grocery stores.

noodles w. pork Energy 593kcal/2504kJ; Protein 47.8g; Carbohydrate 72.1g, of which sugars 4.7g; Fat 14.6g, of which saturates 2.8g; Cholesterol 106mg; Calcium 53mg; Fibre 3.2g; Sodium 1461mg.
rice rolls stuffed w. pork Energy 160kcal/670kJ; Protein 13.8g; Carbohydrate 16g, of which sugars 2.4g; Fat 4.4g, of which saturates 1.1g; Cholesterol 37mg; Calcium 13mg; Fibre 0.6g; Sodium 43mg.

Crispy Noodles with Beef

Rice vermicelli is deep-fried before being added to this multi-textured dish.

Serves 4

450g/1lb rump (round) steak
teriyaki sauce, for brushing
175g/6oz rice vermicelli
groundnut (peanut) oil, for deep-frying and stir-frying
8 spring onions (scallions), diagonally sliced
2 garlic cloves, crushed
4–5 carrots, cut into julienne strips
1–2 fresh red chillies, seeded and finely sliced
2 small courgettes (zucchini), diagonally sliced
5ml/1 tsp grated fresh root ginger
60ml/4 tbsp rice vinegar
90ml/6 tbsp light soy sauce
about 475ml/16fl oz/2 cups spicy stock

1 Beat the steak to about 2.5cm/1in thick. Place in a shallow dish, brush with teriyaki sauce and marinate for 2–4 hours.

2 Separate the rice vermicelli into manageable loops. Pour oil into a large wok to a depth of about 5cm/2in, and heat until a strand of vermicelli cooks as soon as it is lowered into the oil.

3 Carefully add a loop of vermicelli to the oil. Almost immediately, turn to cook on the other side, then remove and drain on kitchen paper. Repeat with the remaining loops. Transfer the cooked noodles to a bowl and keep them warm.

4 Clean out the wok and heat 15ml/1 tbsp groundnut oil. Fry the steak for about 30 seconds on each side, then remove and cut into thick slices.

5 Add a little extra oil to the wok, and stir-fry the spring onions, garlic and carrots for 5–6 minutes. Add the chillies, courgettes and ginger and stir-fry for 1–2 minutes.

6 Stir in the rice vinegar, soy sauce and stock. Cook for 4 minutes until the sauce has thickened slightly. Return the steak to the wok and cook for a further 1–2 minutes. Spoon the steak, vegetables and sauce over the noodles and toss lightly.

Chap Chae

A Korean stir-fry of beef, mixed vegetables and noodles.

Serves 4

225g/8oz rump (round) steak
marinade (see Cook's Tip)
115g/4oz cellophane noodles, soaked for 20 minutes in hot water to cover, then drained
4 dried shiitake mushrooms, soaked, stems removed, caps sliced
vegetable oil, for frying
2 eggs, separated
1 carrot, cut into matchsticks
1 onion, sliced
2 courgettes (zucchini), cut into strips
½ red (bell) pepper, cut into strips
4 button mushrooms, sliced
75g/3oz/⅓ cup beansprouts
15ml/1 tbsp light soy sauce
salt and ground black pepper
sliced spring onions (scallions) and sesame seeds, to garnish

1 Put the steak in the freezer until it is firm enough to cut into 5cm/2in strips, and mix with the marinade in a shallow dish. Cook the noodles in boiling water for 5 minutes. Drain and snip into short lengths.

2 For the garnish, first fry the beaten egg yolks and then the whites in oil in a small frying pan. When set, remove, cut into diamond shapes and set aside.

3 Heat the oil in a wok. Drain the beef and stir-fry it until it changes colour. Add the vegetables; cook until crisp and tender.

4 Add the noodles and season with soy sauce, salt and pepper. Cook for 1 minute. Spoon into a serving dish and garnish with egg diamonds, spring onions and sesame seeds.

Cook's Tip

To make the marinade, blend together 15ml/1 tbsp sugar, 30ml/2 tbsp light soy sauce, 45ml/3 tbsp sesame oil, 4 finely chopped spring onions (scallions), 1 crushed garlic clove and 10ml/2 tsp crushed toasted sesame seeds.

crispy noodles w. beef Energy 410kcal/1712kJ; Protein 30.7g; Carbohydrate 41.4g, of which sugars 6.6g; Fat 13.5g, of which saturates 3g; Cholesterol 66mg; Calcium 49mg; Fibre 1.9g; Sodium 1687mg.
chap chae Energy 321kcal/1337kJ; Protein 19.6g; Carbohydrate 28.5g, of which sugars 4.2g; Fat 14g, of which saturates 3.7g; Cholesterol 128mg; Calcium 52mg; Fibre 1.6g; Sodium 348mg.

Chow Mein

This is a hugely popular way of dealing with leftovers.

Serves 2–3

225g/8oz lean beef steak
225g/8oz can bamboo shoots, drained
1 leek, trimmed
25g/1oz dried shiitake mushrooms, soaked until soft
150g/5oz Chinese leaves (Chinese cabbage)
450g/1lb cooked egg noodles, drained
90ml/6 tbsp vegetable oil
30ml/2 tbsp dark soy sauce
15ml/1 tbsp cornflour (cornstarch)
15ml/1 tbsp dry sherry
5ml/1 tsp sesame oil
5ml/1 tsp caster (superfine) sugar
salt and ground black pepper

1 Slice the beef, bamboo shoots and leek into matchsticks. Drain the mushrooms, reserving 90ml/6 tbsp of the soaking water. Cut off and discard the stems, then slice the caps. Chop the Chinese leaves and sprinkle with salt. Pat the noodles dry.

2 Heat a third of the oil in a large frying pan and sauté the noodles. After turning them over once, use a wooden spatula to press against the bottom of the pan until they form a flat, even cake. Cook for about 4 minutes or until crisp at the bottom. Turn over, cook for 3 minutes more, then slide on to a heated plate and keep warm.

3 Heat 30ml/2 tbsp of the remaining oil in a wok. Add the leek and meat strips and stir-fry for 10–15 seconds. Sprinkle over half the soy sauce and then add the bamboo shoots and mushrooms. Toss for 1 minute, then push to one side.

4 Heat the remaining oil in the centre of the wok and sauté the Chinese leaves for 1 minute. Mix with the meat and vegetables and toss together for 30 seconds.

5 Mix the cornflour with the reserved mushroom water. Stir into the wok with the sherry, sesame oil, sugar and remaining soy sauce. Cook for 15 seconds to thicken, then serve with the noodle cake.

Special Chow Mein

A more elaborate chow mein, this shows how extra ingredients can be incorporated. Chinese sausages are available from most Chinese supermarkets.

Serves 4–6

450g/1lb egg noodles
45ml/3 tbsp vegetable oil
2 garlic cloves, sliced
5ml/1 tsp chopped fresh root ginger
2 fresh red chillies, seeded and chopped
2 Chinese sausages, total weight about 75g/3oz, rinsed and sliced (optional)
1 skinless, boneless chicken breast portion, thinly sliced
16 uncooked tiger prawns (jumbo shrimp), peeled, tails left intact, and deveined
115g/4oz/scant 1 cup green beans
225g/8oz/1 cup beansprouts
small bunch garlic chives
30ml/2 tbsp soy sauce
15ml/1 tbsp oyster sauce
15ml/1 tbsp sesame oil
salt and ground black pepper
2 shredded spring onions (scallions) and fresh coriander (cilantro) leaves, to garnish

1 Cook the noodles in a large pan of boiling water, according to the instructions on the packet. Drain well.

2 Heat 15ml/1 tbsp of the oil in a wok and stir-fry the garlic, ginger and chillies for 2 minutes. Add the sausage slices, if using, with the chicken, prawns and beans. Stir-fry over a high heat for 2 minutes, or until the chicken and prawns are cooked. Transfer the mixture to a bowl and set aside.

3 Heat the rest of the oil in the wok. Add the beansprouts and garlic chives and stir-fry for 1–2 minutes. Add the drained noodles and toss over the heat to mix. Season with the soy sauce, oyster sauce and salt and pepper to taste.

4 Return the prawn mixture to the wok. Mix well with the noodles and toss until heated through.

5 Stir in the sesame oil. Spoon into a warmed bowl and serve, garnished with the spring onions and coriander leaves.

chow mein Energy 604kcal/2541kJ; Protein 41.1g; Carbohydrate 71.5g, of which sugars 15.1g; Fat 18.9g, of which saturates 4.5g; Cholesterol 100mg; Calcium 115mg; Fibre 7.4g; Sodium 1194mg.
special chow mein Energy 359kcal/1516kJ; Protein 19.6g; Carbohydrate 47.6g, of which sugars 2.9g; Fat 11.4g, of which saturates 2.3g; Cholesterol 106mg; Calcium 53mg; Fibre 2.3g; Sodium 1102mg.

Fried Noodles with Beef & Satay

If you relish chillies and peanuts, this delicious dish makes the perfect choice, but remember – it's fiery.

Serves 4

25ml/1½ tbsp vegetable oil
300g/11oz beef sirloin, cut against the grain into thin slices
225g/8oz dried rice sticks (vermicelli), soaked in warm water for 20 minutes
225g/8oz/1 cup beansprouts
5–10ml/1–2 tsp fish sauce
1 small bunch each of fresh basil and mint, stalks removed, leaves shredded, to garnish
pickles, to serve

For the satay

4 dried Serrano chillies, seeded
60ml/4 tbsp groundnut (peanut) oil
4–5 garlic cloves, crushed
5–10ml/1–2 tsp curry powder
40g/1½oz/⅓ cup roasted peanuts, finely ground

1 To make the satay, grind the Serrano chillies in a mortar with a pestle. Heat the groundnut oil in a heavy pan or wok and stir in the garlic until it begins to colour. Add the chillies, curry powder and peanuts and stir over a low heat, until the mixture forms a paste. Remove the pan from the heat and leave the mixture to cool.

2 Heat a wok or heavy pan, and pour in 15ml/1 tbsp of the oil. Add the sliced beef and cook for 1–2 minutes, and stir in 7.5ml/1½ tsp of the spicy peanut satay paste. Tip the beef on to a clean plate and set aside. Drain the rice sticks.

3 Add the remaining oil to the wok and add the rice sticks and 15ml/1 tbsp satay. Toss the noodles until coated and cook for 4–5 minutes. Toss in the beef for 1 minute, then add the beansprouts with the fish sauce. Tip the noodles on to a serving dish and sprinkle with the basil and mint. Serve with pickles.

Variation

Prawns (shrimp), pork or chicken can be used instead of beef, and the fresh herbs can be varied accordingly.

Bamie Goreng

This fried noodle dish is wonderfully accommodating. You can add other vegetables, such as mushrooms, tiny pieces of chayote, broccoli, leeks or beansprouts. Use whatever is to hand, balancing textures, colours and flavours.

Serves 6–8

450g/1lb dried egg noodles
2 eggs
25g/1oz/2 tbsp butter
90ml/6 tbsp vegetable oil
1 chicken breast fillet, sliced
115g/4oz pork fillet (tenderloin), sliced
115g/4oz calf's liver, sliced (optional)
2 garlic cloves, crushed
115g/4oz peeled cooked prawns (shrimp)
115g/4oz pak choi (bok choy)
2 celery sticks, finely sliced
4 spring onions (scallions), shredded
about 60ml/4 tbsp chicken stock
dark soy sauce and light soy sauce
salt and ground black pepper
deep-fried onions and shredded spring onions (scallions), to garnish

1 Cook the noodles in a pan of lightly salted water for about 3–4 minutes. Drain, rinse and drain again. Set aside.

2 Put the eggs in a bowl, beat and season to taste. Heat the butter with 5ml/1 tsp oil in a small pan, add the eggs and stir over a low heat until scrambled but still moist. Set aside.

3 Heat the remaining oil in a wok and fry the chicken, pork and liver, if using, with the garlic for 2–3 minutes, until the meat is cooked through. Add the prawns, pak choi, sliced celery and shredded spring onions and toss to mix.

4 Add the noodles and toss over the heat until the prawns and noodles are heated through and the greens are lightly cooked. Add enough stock to moisten, and season with dark and light soy sauce to taste. Add the scrambled eggs and toss to mix. Spoon the bamie goreng on to a serving platter and serve, garnished with deep-fried onions and shredded spring onions.

beef & satay Energy 536kcal/2244kJ; Protein 24.4g; Carbohydrate 50.5g, of which sugars 2.1g; Fat 24.8g, of which saturates 5.7g; Cholesterol 44mg; Calcium 52mg; Fibre 2.3g; Sodium 253mg.
bamie goreng Energy 478kcal/2010kJ; Protein 16.8g; Carbohydrate 64.2g, of which sugars 5.1g; Fat 18.9g, of which saturates 3.2g; Cholesterol 86mg; Calcium 323mg; Fibre 2.9g; Sodium 466mg.

Tarka Dhal

Probably the most popular Indian lentil dish found today, Tarka Dhal is found on most Indian and Pakistani restaurant menus.

Serves 4

115g/4oz/½ cup masoor dhal (red split lentils)
50g/2oz/¼ cup mung dhal or yellow split peas
600ml/1 pint/2½ cups water
5ml/1 tsp grated fresh root ginger
5ml/1 tsp crushed garlic
1.5ml/¼ tsp ground turmeric
2 fresh green chillies, chopped
7.5ml/1½ tsp salt

For the tarka
30ml/2 tbsp oil
1 onion, sliced
1.5ml/¼ tsp mixed mustard and onion seeds
4 dried red chillies
1 tomato, sliced

For the garnish
15ml/1 tbsp chopped fresh coriander (cilantro)
1 or 2 fresh green chillies, seeded and sliced
15ml/1 tbsp chopped fresh mint

1 Boil all the masoor dhal and mung dhal or yellow split peas in the water with the ginger and garlic, turmeric and chopped green chillies for 15–20 minutes, or until soft.

2 Pound the mixture with a rolling pin or mash with a fork until it has the consistency of a creamy chicken soup.

3 If the lentil mixture looks too dry, add a little more water. Season with the salt. To prepare the tarka, heat the oil in a heavy pan and fry the onion with the mustard and onion seeds, dried red chillies and tomato for 2 minutes.

4 Spoon the mashed lentils into a serving dish and pour the tarka over. Garnish with fresh coriander, green chillies and mint, and serve immediately.

Cook's Tip
Use 1 or 2 red chillies if you want a milder tarka for the dhal.

Lentils Seasoned with Fried Spices

A simple supper dish for family or friends using traditional Indian lentils and peas.

Serves 4–6

115g/4oz/½ cup red gram (pigeon peas)
50g/2oz/¼ cup Bengal gram
4 fresh green chillies
5ml/1 tsp ground turmeric
1 large onion, sliced
400g/14oz can chopped tomatoes
60ml/4 tbsp vegetable oil
2.5ml/½ tsp mustard seeds
2.5ml/½ tsp cumin seeds
1 garlic clove, crushed
6 curry leaves
2 dried red chillies
salt
deep-fried onions and fresh coriander (cilantro), to garnish

1 Place the red gram and Bengal gram in a heavy pan and pour in 350ml/12fl oz/1½ cups water. Add the chillies, turmeric and onion slices and bring to the boil. Simmer, covered, until the lentils are soft and the water has evaporated.

2 Mash the lentils with the back of a spoon. When nearly smooth, add the tomatoes and salt to taste, and mix well. If necessary, thin with a little hot water.

3 Heat the oil in a frying pan. Fry the remaining ingredients until the garlic browns. Pour the oil and spices over the lentils and cover. After 5 minutes, mix well, garnish, and serve.

Cook's Tips
• *Red gram, or pigeon peas, are the fruit of a small shrub but are used as a vegetable. They form a staple food in India as well as Africa and the Caribbean, and you will find them in Asian and Caribbean stores and markets.*
• *Bengal gram, or channa, is a small variety of chickpea, which is commonly used in Indian cuisine.*

tarka dhal Energy 213kcal/897kJ; Protein 11.3g; Carbohydrate 28.2g, of which sugars 2.7g; Fat 7.1g, of which saturates 0.9g; Cholesterol 0mg; Calcium 42mg; Fibre 2.5g; Sodium 18mg.
lentils with spices Energy 213kcal/893kJ; Protein 9.1g; Carbohydrate 25.7g, of which sugars 6.5g; Fat 9.1g, of which saturates 1.1g; Cholesterol 0mg; Calcium 50mg; Fibre 3g; Sodium 21mg.

Green Lentils & Rice

Also known as continental lentils, green lentils retain their shape and colour when cooked. They are an important source of protein and add a robust flavour to dishes such as this. Chillies, ginger, cardamoms and cinnamon make this a lively main-course rice, excellent served with a vegetable curry or a simple salad.

Serves 4–6

350g/12oz/1¾ cups patna rice
175g/6oz/¾ cup green lentils
50g/2oz/¼ cup ghee
1 onion, finely chopped
2 garlic cloves, crushed
2.5cm/1in piece fresh root ginger, shredded
4 fresh green chillies, chopped
4 cloves
2.5cm/1in piece cinnamon stick
4 green cardamom pods
5ml/1 tsp ground turmeric
600ml/1 pint/2½ cups water
salt

1 Wash the rice and lentils, then soak them in a bowl of cold water for 20 minutes.

2 Gently heat the ghee in a large, heavy pan with a tight-fitting lid and fry the onion, garlic, ginger, chillies, cloves, cinnamon, cardamoms, turmeric and salt to taste until the onion is soft and translucent.

3 Drain the rice and lentils and add them to the spices in the pan. Sauté for 2–3 minutes. Add the water and bring the mixture to the boil.

4 Reduce the heat, cover and cook for about 20–25 minutes, or until all the water has been absorbed.

5 Take the pan off the heat and leave to rest with the lid on for 5 minutes.

6 Just before serving, gently toss the rice and lentils with a flat spatula, taking care not to break the delicate grains.

Courgettes with Split Lentils & Tomatoes

The nutty flavour of lentils goes particularly well with courgettes and tomatoes, perked up with a selection of aromatic spices. Serve with rice or bread for a filling and tasty supper.

Serves 4–6

225g/8oz courgettes (zucchini)
1 large onion, finely sliced
2 garlic cloves, crushed
2 fresh green chillies, chopped
175g/6oz/⅔ cup mung dhal or yellow split peas
2.5ml/½ tsp ground turmeric
60ml/4 tbsp vegetable oil
2.5ml/½ tsp mustard seeds
2.5ml/½ tsp cumin seeds
1.5ml/¼ tsp asafoetida
a few fresh coriander (cilantro) and mint leaves, chopped
6–8 curry leaves
2.5ml/½ tsp sugar
200g/7oz can chopped tomatoes
60ml/4 tbsp lemon juice
salt

1 Cut the courgettes into wedges. Finely slice the onion and crush the garlic. Chop the green chilles.

2 In a pan, simmer the mung dhal or split peas and turmeric in 300ml/½ pint/1¼ cups water, until cooked but not mushy. Drain the cooked dhal, retaining the cooking liquid, and set aside while you cook the vegetables.

3 Heat the oil in a frying pan and add the courgette wedges, sliced onion, crushed garlic and chopped chillies. Add the mustard and cumin seeds, asafoetida, fresh coriander and mint, and stir in the curry leaves and sugar. Fry the ingredients together, stirring occasionally, and then add the chopped tomatoes. Mix well and add salt to taste.

4 Cover and cook until the courgettes are nearly tender but still crunchy.

5 Fold in the drained dhal and the lemon juice. If the dish is too dry, add some of the reserved cooking water. Reheat thoroughly and serve immediately.

green lentils & rice Energy 376kcal/1574kJ; Protein 11.8g; Carbohydrate 61.6g, of which sugars 1g; Fat 9.2g, of which saturates 4g; Cholesterol 0mg; Calcium 37mg; Fibre 2.7g; Sodium 5mg.
courgettes w. lentils Energy 210kcal/880kJ; Protein 9.5g; Carbohydrate 25.7g, of which sugars 7.1g; Fat 8.5g, of which saturates 1g; Cholesterol 0mg; Calcium 55mg; Fibre 3.3g; Sodium 18mg.

Creamy Black Lentils

Black lentils, or urad dhal, are available whole, split, and skinned and split.

Serves 4–6

175g/6oz/¾ cup black lentils, soaked
50g/2oz/¼ cup red split lentils
120ml/4fl oz/½ cup double (heavy) cream, plus extra to serve
120ml/4fl oz/½ cup natural (plain) yogurt
5ml/1 tsp cornflour (cornstarch)
40g/1½oz/3 tbsp ghee or vegetable oil
1 onion, finely chopped
5cm/2in piece fresh root ginger, crushed
4 fresh green chillies, chopped
1 tomato, chopped
2.5ml/½ tsp chilli powder
2.5ml/½ tsp ground turmeric
2.5ml/½ tsp ground cumin
2 garlic cloves, sliced
salt
coriander (cilantro) sprigs and sliced fresh red chilli, to garnish

1 Drain the black lentils and place in a large pan with the red lentils. Cover with water and bring to the boil. Reduce the heat, cover the pan and simmer until tender. Mash with a spoon, and leave to cool.

2 In a bowl, mix together the cream, yogurt and cornflour, and stir into the lentils in the pan.

3 Heat 15g/½oz/1 tbsp of the ghee or oil in a karahi, wok or large pan, and fry the onion, ginger, half the green chillies and the tomato until the onion is soft.

4 Add the ground spices and salt, and fry for a further 2 minutes. Stir into the lentil mixture and mix well. Reheat, transfer to a warmed serving dish and keep warm.

5 Heat the remaining ghee or oil in a frying pan over a low heat and fry the garlic slices and remaining chillies until the garlic slices are golden brown.

6 Pour over the lentils, and fold in the garlic and chilli just before serving. Garnish and serve with extra cream so that diners can add more as they eat, if they wish.

Lentils Seasoned with Garlic Oil

This dish is popular in southern India, where there are numerous variations. A single vegetable can be added to the lentils, or a combination of two or more. It is traditionally served with steamed rice dumplings or stuffed rice pancakes. The garlic-flavoured lentils are also extremely satisfying with plain boiled rice.

Serves 4–6

120ml/4fl oz/½ cup vegetable oil
2.5ml/½ tsp mustard seeds
2.5ml/½ tsp cumin seeds
2 dried red chillies
1.5ml/¼ tsp asafoetida
6–8 curry leaves
2 garlic cloves, crushed, plus 2 sliced
30ml/2 tbsp desiccated (dry unsweetened shredded) coconut
225g/8oz/1 cup red lentils, washed and drained
10ml/2 tsp sambhar masala or other curry powder
2.5ml/½ tsp ground turmeric
450ml/¾ pint/scant 2 cups water
450g/1lb mixed vegetables, such as okra, courgettes (zucchini), aubergine (eggplant), cauliflower, shallots and (bell) peppers, chopped
60ml/4 tbsp tamarind juice
4 firm tomatoes, quartered
a few coriander (cilantro) leaves, chopped

1 Heat half the oil in a karahi, wok or large pan, and stir-fry the next seven ingredients until the coconut begins to brown.

2 Stir in the prepared red lentils with the masala and turmeric. Stir-fry for 2–3 minutes and add the water. Bring to the boil and reduce the heat to low.

3 Cover the pan and leave to simmer for 25–30 minutes, or until the lentils are mushy. Add the chopped mixed vegetables, tamarind juice and tomato quarters. Cook until the vegetables are just tender.

4 Heat the remaining oil in a small pan over a low heat, and fry the garlic slices until golden. Stir in the fresh coriander leaves, then pour over the lentils and vegetables. Mix together at the table before serving.

black lentils Energy 309kcal/1289kJ; Protein 11g; Carbohydrate 26.2g, of which sugars 3.8g; Fat 18.6g, of which saturates 10.1g; Cholesterol 28mg; Calcium 77mg; Fibre 2.2g; Sodium 38mg.
lentils w. garlic oil Energy 321kcal/1340kJ; Protein 12g; Carbohydrate 27.2g, of which sugars 4.6g; Fat 19.1g, of which saturates 4.7g; Cholesterol 0mg; Calcium 56mg; Fibre 3.9g; Sodium 24mg.

Lentils & Rice

Here, lentils are cooked with whole and ground spices, potato, rice and onion to produce a tasty and nutritious meal.

Serves 4

150g/5oz/¾ cup tuvar dhal or red split lentils
115g/4oz/½ cup basmati rice
1 large potato
1 large onion
30ml/2 tbsp vegetable oil
4 whole cloves
1.5ml/¼ tsp cumin seeds
1.5ml/¼ tsp ground turmeric
10ml/2 tsp salt
300ml/½ pint/1¼ cups water

1 Wash the tuvar dhal or red split lentils and rice in several changes of cold water. Put into a bowl and cover with water. Leave to soak for 15 minutes, then transfer to a sieve (strainer) and drain well.

2 Peel the potato, then cut it into 2.5cm/1in chunks. Using a sharp knife, thinly slice the onion and set aside.

3 Heat the oil in a heavy pan and fry the cloves and cumin seeds for 2 minutes until the seeds are beginning to splutter.

4 Add the onion and potato chunks and fry for 5 minutes. Add the lentils, rice, turmeric and salt and continue to fry for a further 3 minutes.

5 Add the water. Bring to the boil, cover and simmer gently for 15–20 minutes until all the water has been absorbed and the potato chunks are tender. Leave to stand, covered, for about 10 minutes before serving.

Cook's Tip
Red split lentils are widely available in most supermarkets. Before cooking they are salmon-coloured and they turn a pale, dull yellow during cooking. They have a mild, pleasant, nutty flavour. Soaking them in water speeds up the cooking process but isn't strictly necessary.

Spinach Dhal

Many different types of dhal are eaten in India and each region has its own speciality. This is a delicious, lightly spiced dish with a mild nutty flavour from the yellow lentils, which combine well with the spinach.

Serves 4

175g/6oz/1 cup chana dhal or yellow split peas
175ml/6fl oz/¾ cup water
15ml/1 tbsp vegetable oil
1.5ml/¼ tsp black mustard seeds
1 onion, thinly sliced
2 garlic cloves, crushed
2.5cm/1in piece fresh root ginger, grated
1 fresh red chilli, finely chopped
275g/10oz frozen spinach, thawed
1.5ml/¼ tsp chilli powder
2.5ml/½ tsp ground coriander
2.5ml/½ tsp garam masala
2.5ml/½ tsp salt

1 Wash the chana dhal or split peas in several changes of cold water. Put into a bowl and cover with plenty of water. Leave to soak for 30 minutes.

2 Drain the dhal or split peas and put them in a large pan with the water. Bring to the boil, cover and simmer for 20–25 minutes, or until they are soft.

3 Meanwhile, heat the oil in a large, heavy pan and fry the mustard seeds for 2 minutes until they begin to splutter.

4 Add the onion, garlic, ginger and chilli and fry for 5–6 minutes until softened but not coloured.

5 Add the spinach and cook for 10 minutes or until the spinach is dry and the liquid has evaporated. Stir in the remaining spices and salt, and cook for 2–3 minutes.

6 Drain the dhal or split peas, add them to the spinach mixture and cook for about 5 minutes. Transfer to a warmed serving dish and serve immediately.

lentils & rice Energy 263kcal/1111kJ; Protein 12.1g; Carbohydrate 53.3g, of which sugars 2.4g; Fat 0.8g, of which saturates 0.1g; Cholesterol 0mg; Calcium 32mg; Fibre 2.6g; Sodium 1002mg.
spinach dhal Energy 226kcal/949kJ; Protein 13.3g; Carbohydrate 28.7g, of which sugars 2.9g; Fat 7.3g, of which saturates 0.9g; Cholesterol 0mg; Calcium 152mg; Fibre 3.8g; Sodium 114mg.

South Indian Lentils & Vegetables

Lentils are perfect for easy, inexpensive meals. Choose a selection of your favourite vegetables, such as potato, cauliflower, carrots and beans, for this tasty dish.

Serves 4–6

60ml/4 tbsp vegetable oil
2.5ml/½ tsp mustard seeds
2.5ml/½ tsp cumin seeds
2 dried red chillies
1.5ml/¼ tsp asafoetida
6–8 curry leaves
2 garlic cloves, crushed
30ml/2 tbsp desiccated (dry unsweetened shredded) coconut
225g/8oz/1 cup masoor dhal or red split lentils
10ml/2 tsp sambhar masala or garam masala
2.5ml/½ tsp ground turmeric
450g/1lb mixed vegetables, in bitesize pieces
60ml/4 tbsp tamarind juice
4 firm tomatoes, quartered
60ml/4 tbsp vegetable oil
2 garlic cloves, finely sliced
handful fresh coriander (cilantro), chopped

1 Heat the oil in a heavy pan. Fry the mustard seeds, cumin seeds, dried red chillies, asafoetida, curry leaves, crushed garlic and desiccated coconut until the coconut browns.

2 Mix in the masoor dhal or red split lentils, sambhar masala and ground turmeric. Stir in 450ml/¾ pint/scant 2 cups water.

3 Simmer the mixture until the lentils are mushy. Add the mixed vegetables, tamarind juice and tomatoes. Cook until the vegetables are just tender.

4 In the oil, fry the garlic slices and fresh coriander. Pour over the lentils and vegetables. Mix at the table before serving.

Variation
Courgettes (zucchini), aubergines (eggplants), (bell) peppers, mangetouts (snow peas) and broccoli would also taste wonderful in this curry.

Rice Layered with Bengal Gram

This rice and lentil dish is served with a gourd curry, or palida, which is prominently flavoured with fenugreek and soured with dried mangosteen.

Serves 4–6

175g/6oz/⅔ cup Bengal gram or lentils of your choice
600ml/1 pint/2½ cups water
2.5ml/½ tsp ground turmeric
50g/2oz deep-fried onions, crushed
45ml/3 tbsp green masala paste
a few fresh mint and coriander (cilantro) leaves, chopped
350g/12oz/1¾ cups basmati rice, cooked
30ml/2 tbsp ghee
salt

For the curry
60ml/4 tbsp vegetable oil
1.5ml/¼ tsp fenugreek seeds
15g/½oz dried fenugreek leaves
2 garlic cloves, crushed
5ml/1 tsp ground coriander
5ml/1 tsp cumin seeds
5ml/1 tsp chilli powder
60ml/4 tbsp gram flour mixed with 60ml/4 tbsp water
450g/1lb bottle gourd, peeled, pith and seeds removed and cut into bitesize pieces, or marrow (large zucchini) or firm courgettes (zucchini) prepared in the same way
175ml/6fl oz/¾ cup tomato juice
6 dried mangosteen (kokum), or juice of 3 lemons
salt

1 For the rice, boil the Bengal gram in the water with the turmeric until the grains are soft. Drain and reserve the water for the curry. Toss the Bengal gram gently with the deep-fried onions, green masala paste, mint and coriander. Add salt to taste.

2 Grease a heavy pan and place a layer of rice in the bottom. Add the Bengal gram mixture and another layer of the remaining rice. Place small knobs (pats) of ghee on top, sprinkle with a little water and heat gently until steam rises from the mixture.

3 To make the curry, heat the oil in a pan and fry the fenugreek seeds and leaves and the garlic until the garlic turns golden brown. Mix the ground coriander, cumin seeds and chilli powder to a paste with a little water. Add to the pan and simmer until all the water has evaporated. Add the gram-flour paste, gourd and the tomato juice. Add the mangosteen or lemon juice and salt. Cook until the gourd is soft. Serve hot.

lentils & vegetables Energy 313kcal/1306kJ; Protein 11.4g; Carbohydrate 25.5g, of which sugars 4.1g; Fat 19.1g, of which saturates 4.7g; Cholesterol 0mg; Calcium 49mg; Fibre 3.7g; Sodium 21mg.
rice w. Bengal gram Energy 326kcal/1367kJ; Protein 11.3g; Carbohydrate 39.6g, of which sugars 2.9g; Fat 14.8g, of which saturates 3.7g; Cholesterol 0mg; Calcium 62mg; Fibre 2.3g; Sodium 82mg.

Lentil Dhal with Roasted Garlic & Whole Spices

This aromatic lentil dhal makes a sustaining and comforting meal when served with rice or Indian breads and any dry-spiced dish, particularly a cauliflower or potato dish. The spicy garnish offers a contrast in texture and flavour.

Serves 4–6

40g/1½oz/3 tbsp butter or ghee
1 onion, chopped
2 fresh green chillies, seeded and chopped
15ml/1 tbsp chopped fresh root ginger
225g/8oz/1 cup yellow or red lentils
900ml/1½ pints/3¾ cups water
45ml/3 tbsp roasted garlic purée
5ml/1 tsp ground cumin
5ml/1 tsp ground coriander
200g/7oz tomatoes, peeled and diced
a little lemon juice
salt and ground black pepper
30–45ml/2–3 tbsp coriander (cilantro) sprigs, to garnish

For the spicy garnish

30ml/2 tbsp groundnut (peanut) oil
4 or 5 shallots, sliced
2 garlic cloves, thinly sliced
15g/½oz/1 tbsp butter or ghee
5ml/1 tsp cumin seeds
5ml/1 tsp mustard seeds
3 or 4 small dried red chillies
8–10 fresh curry leaves

1 First begin the spicy garnish. Heat the oil in a large, heavy pan. Add the shallots and fry them over a medium heat, stirring occasionally, until they are crisp and browned. Add the garlic and cook, stirring, for a moment or two until the garlic colours slightly. Use a slotted spoon to remove the mixture from the pan and set it aside in a bowl.

2 For the dhal, melt the butter or ghee in the pan and cook the onion, chillies and ginger for 10 minutes, until golden. Stir in the lentils and water, then bring to the boil, reduce the heat and part-cover the pan. Simmer, stirring occasionally, for 50–60 minutes, until similar to a very thick soup.

3 Stir in the roasted garlic purée, ground cumin and coriander, then season with salt and pepper to taste. Cook for a further 10–15 minutes, uncovered, stirring frequently. Stir in the tomatoes and then adjust the seasoning, adding a little lemon juice to taste if necessary.

4 Finish the spicy garnish. Melt the butter or ghee in a frying pan. Add the cumin and mustard seeds and fry until the mustard seeds pop. Stir in the chillies, curry leaves and the shallot mixture, then immediately swirl the mixture into the cooked dhal. Garnish with coriander and serve.

Cook's Tip

Ghee is a type of clarified butter that has had all the milk solids removed by heating. Because the milk solids have been removed, ghee has a high smoking point and can therefore be cooked at higher temperatures than ordinary butter.

Masoor Dhal with Spiced Prawns

This richly spiced dhal, topped with succulent prawns, makes a very satisfying supper.

Serves 4

30ml/2 tbsp vegetable oil
1 large onion, finely chopped
3 cloves garlic, chopped
2.5cm/1in piece fresh root ginger, peeled and finely chopped
10ml/2 tsp cumin seeds
10ml/2 tsp ground coriander
5ml/1 tsp hot chilli powder
5ml/1 tsp ground turmeric
7 curry leaves
1 carrot, chopped
6 fine green beans, cut into thirds
150g/5oz/1¾ cups split red lentils, rinsed
850ml/1½ pints/3½ cups vegetable stock
salt and ground black pepper

For the prawns

5ml/1 tsp ground cumin
5ml/1 tsp ground coriander
5ml/1 tsp hot chilli powder
30ml/2 tbsp groundnut (peanut) oil
20 raw tiger prawns (shrimp), peeled and tail left on, sliced down the back and deveined
chopped fresh coriander (cilantro), to garnish

1 First prepare the prawns. Mix together the cumin, coriander, chilli powder and oil in a bowl. Pat the prawns dry using kitchen paper and add to the spices. Season with salt, and stir well until the prawns are coated. Set aside to marinate.

2 Heat the oil in a large, heavy pan and fry the onion for 8 minutes until softened and beginning to turn golden. Add the garlic, ginger and spices and cook for 1 minute.

3 Stir in the curry leaves, carrot, beans and lentils. Cook, stirring continuously, for 1 minute then add the stock. Bring to the boil then simmer, half-covered, for 20–25 minutes, stirring occasionally, until the lentils are very tender. Season to taste.

4 Heat a large wok. Add the prawns and their spices and stir-fry for a few minutes until they are pink and just cooked.

5 Divide the dhal among four bowls, top with the prawns and garnish with the coriander.

lentil dhal Energy 262kcal/1095kJ; Protein 10.3g; Carbohydrate 26.9g, of which sugars 4.6g; Fat 13.3g, of which saturates 6.2g; Cholesterol 23mg; Calcium 36mg; Fibre 3.1g; Sodium 84mg.
masoor dhal w. prawns Energy 298kcal/1250kJ; Protein 19.3g; Carbohydrate 28.6g, of which sugars 5.4g; Fat 12.7g, of which saturates 1.5g; Cholesterol 98mg; Calcium 120mg; Fibre 4.7g; Sodium 143mg.

Cucumber Curry

Served hot, this unusual curry is good with fish dishes, and it can also be served cold with cooked meats.

Serves 4–6

120ml/4fl oz/½ cup water and 115g/4oz creamed coconut, or 175ml/6fl oz/¾ cup coconut cream
2.5ml/½ tsp ground turmeric
5ml/1 tsp sugar
1 large cucumber, cut into small pieces
1 large red (bell) pepper, cut into small pieces
50g/2oz/½ cup salted peanuts, crushed
60ml/4 tbsp vegetable oil
2 dried red chillies
5ml/1 tsp cumin seeds
5ml/1 tsp mustard seeds
4–6 curry leaves
4 garlic cloves, crushed
salt
a few whole salted peanuts, to garnish

1 Place the water and creamed coconut, or coconut cream (without water), in a heavy pan with the turmeric, sugar and salt. Bring to the boil, then simmer until the mixture becomes a smooth, thick sauce.

2 Add the cucumber, red pepper and crushed peanuts and simmer for about 5 minutes. Remove from the heat.

3 Heat the oil in a karahi, wok or frying pan. Fry the chillies and cumin with the mustard seeds until they start to pop.

4 Reduce the heat, add the curry leaves and garlic and fry for 2 minutes. Pour over the cucumber mixture and stir well until heated through. Transfer to a warmed serving dish, garnish with whole peanuts and serve.

Cook's Tip
The mustard seeds used extensively in Indian cooking are black and not yellow (which are ground and used to prepare English mustard). They are always fried to release their sweet aroma and flavour.

Spicy Cabbage

Another spicy twist on a Western favourite. This nutritious side dish is a great way to jazz up the flavour of cabbage for those not usually keen on the vegetable. Note the colourful variations.

Serves 4

225g/8oz/2½ cups cabbage
1 small onion
2 medium carrots
50g/2oz/¼ cup ghee or butter
2.5ml/½ tsp white cumin seeds
3–8 dried red chillies, to taste
2.5ml/½ tsp salt
30ml/2 tbsp lemon juice

1 Use a mandolin, if you have one, to shred the cabbage finely. Alternatively, use a sharp knife to slice through the layers of the cabbage.

2 Slice the onion and grate the carrots coarsely.

3 Melt the ghee or butter in a medium pan and fry the cumin seeds and dried chillies for about 30 seconds.

4 Add the onion and fry for about 2 minutes.

5 Add the cabbage and carrots and stir-fry for a further 5 minutes or until the cabbage is soft.

6 Finally, stir in the salt and lemon juice and serve immediately.

Variation
You will get a different appearance as well as flavour if you use different kinds of cabbage for this recipe. White cabbage has a delicate taste, whereas Savoy cabbage and spring greens (collards) have a fuller flavour. You could also try red cabbage and use a red onion as well for a colourful alternative.

cucumber curry Energy 273kcal/1127kJ; Protein 4.6g; Carbohydrate 6.3g, of which sugars 4.1g; Fat 25.8g, of which saturates 13.1g; Cholesterol 0mg; Calcium 28mg; Fibre 1.3g; Sodium 44mg.
spicy cabbage Energy 148kcal/611kJ; Protein 1.2g; Carbohydrate 7.5g, of which sugars 6.8g; Fat 12.7g, of which saturates 5.9g; Cholesterol 0mg; Calcium 42mg; Fibre 2.5g; Sodium 16mg.

Karahi Shredded Cabbage with Mangetouts & Corn

This is one of the best ways to cook cabbage, stir-fried with butter and crushed spices. This side dish makes a wonderful accompaniment to many meat, poultry or fish curries.

Serves 4

15ml/1 tbsp corn oil
50g/2oz/¼ cup ghee or butter
2.5ml/½ tsp crushed coriander seeds
2.5ml/½ tsp white cumin seeds
6 dried red chillies
1 small Savoy cabbage, shredded
12 mangetouts (snow peas)
3 fresh red chillies, seeded and sliced
12 baby corn cobs
salt
25g/1oz/¼ cup flaked (sliced) almonds, toasted, and 15ml/1 tbsp chopped fresh coriander (cilantro), to garnish

1 Heat the oil and ghee or butter in a large frying pan, karahi or wok and add the crushed coriander seeds, white cumin seeds and dried red chillies.

2 Add the shredded cabbage and mangetouts, and stir-fry for about 5 minutes.

3 Add the sliced fresh red chillies, baby corn and salt, and fry for a further 3 minutes.

4 Garnish with the toasted almonds and fresh coriander and serve hot.

Cook's Tip
This dish is strongly spiced with red chillies, both fresh and dried, but the recipe also works well with fewer chillies if you prefer a milder flavour. If you have large dried red chillies in your store cupboard (pantry) you might want to reduce the quantity to just one.

Curried Cauliflower

In this dish mild-tasting cauliflower is wonderfully enhanced by a creamy, spicy sauce.

Serves 4–6

15ml/1 tbsp gram flour
120ml/4fl oz/½ cup water
5ml/1 tsp chilli powder
15ml/1 tbsp ground coriander
5ml/1 tsp ground cumin
5ml/1 tsp mustard powder
5ml/1 tsp ground turmeric
60ml/4 tbsp vegetable oil
6–8 curry leaves
5ml/1 tsp cumin seeds
1 cauliflower, broken into florets
175ml/6fl oz/¾ cup thick coconut milk
juice of 2 lemons
salt
lime wedges, to serve

1 Put the gram flour in a small bowl and stir in enough of the water to make a smooth paste.

2 Add the chilli, coriander, ground cumin, mustard, turmeric and salt. Add the remaining water and keep mixing to blend all the ingredients well.

3 Heat the oil in a frying pan, and add the curry leaves and cumin seeds. Add the spice paste and simmer for about 5 minutes, stirring frequently. If the sauce becomes too thick, add a little hot water.

4 Add the cauliflower florets and the coconut milk. Bring the mixture to the boil and then reduce the heat. Cover with a lid and cook until the cauliflower is tender but still retains a bit of a crunch. (If you like your cauliflower more tender, cook for a little longer.)

5 Add the lemon juice, mix well and serve the curry hot with the wedges of lime to squeeze over.

Variation
This sauce also goes well with broccoli. For a pretty presentation use whole miniature vegetables.

karahi cabbage Energy 235kcal/978kJ; Protein 4.4g; Carbohydrate 21.9g, of which sugars 9.8g; Fat 15.1g, of which saturates 7.1g; Cholesterol 27mg; Calcium 71mg; Fibre 2.8g; Sodium 221mg.
curried cauilflower Energy 122kcal/504kJ; Protein 3.7g; Carbohydrate 7.4g, of which sugars 3.3g; Fat 8.8g, of which saturates 1.2g; Cholesterol 0mg; Calcium 34mg; Fibre 1.4g; Sodium 41mg.

Spiced Aubergine

Chunks of aubergine are coated in a rich sauce and sprinkled with sesame seeds to make an unusual side dish that is quick to cook. This straightforward yet versatile vegetarian dish can be served hot, warm or cold, as the occasion demands.

Serves 4–6

2 aubergines (eggplants), total weight about 600g/1lb 6oz, cut into large chunks
15ml/1 tbsp salt
5ml/1 tsp chilli powder, or to taste
75ml/5 tbsp sunflower oil
15ml/1 tbsp rice wine or medium-dry sherry
100ml/3½fl oz/scant ½ cup water
75ml/5 tbsp chilli bean sauce (see Cook's Tip)
salt and ground black pepper
a few toasted sesame seeds, to garnish

1 Place the aubergine chunks on a plate, sprinkle them with the salt and leave to stand for 15–20 minutes. Rinse well, drain and dry thoroughly on kitchen paper. Toss the aubergine chunks in the chilli powder.

2 Heat a wok and add the oil. When the oil is hot, add the aubergine chunks, with the rice wine or sherry. Stir constantly until the aubergine chunks start to turn a little brown. Stir in the water, cover the wok and steam for 2–3 minutes. Add the chilli bean sauce and cook for 2 minutes. Season to taste, then spoon on to a serving dish, sprinkle with sesame seeds and serve.

Cook's Tip
If you can't get hold of chilli bean sauce, use 15–30ml/1–2 tbsp chilli paste mixed with 2 crushed garlic cloves, 15ml/1 tbsp each dark soy sauce and rice vinegar, and 10ml/2 tsp light soy sauce.

Carrot & Cauliflower Stir-fry

Slicing the carrots into thin batons helps them cook quickly. This dish has a crunchy texture and uses only a few whole spices.

Serves 4

2 large carrots
1 small cauliflower
15ml/1 tbsp vegetable oil
1 bay leaf
2 cloves
1 small cinnamon stick
2 cardamom pods
3 black peppercorns
5ml/1 tsp salt
50g/2oz/½ cup frozen peas, thawed
10ml/2 tsp lemon juice
15ml/1 tbsp chopped fresh coriander (cilantro), plus fresh leaves to garnish

1 Cut the carrots into thin batons about 2.5cm/1in long. Separate the cauliflower into small florets.

2 Heat the oil in a karahi, wok or heavy pan and add the bay leaf, cloves, cinnamon stick, cardamom pods and peppercorns. Quickly stir-fry over a medium heat for 30–35 seconds, then add the salt.

3 Add the carrot batons and cauliflower florets and continue to stir-fry for 3–5 minutes.

4 Add the peas, lemon juice and chopped coriander and cook for a further 4–5 minutes. Serve garnished with the whole coriander leaves.

Variation
Substitute broccoli or sliced courgette (zucchini) for the cauliflower, if you like.

Cook's Tip
As both carrots and cauliflower can be eaten raw, they need only minimal cooking or they will lose their crunchy texture.

spiced aubergine Energy 193kcal/798kJ; Protein 1.7g; Carbohydrate 8.7g, of which sugars 8.2g; Fat 17.1g, of which saturates 2.1g; Cholesterol 0mg; Calcium 18mg; Fibre 3.2g; Sodium 309mg.
carrot & cauliflower Energy 98kcal/405kJ; Protein 5.3g; Carbohydrate 9.7g, of which sugars 6.5g; Fat 4.5g, of which saturates 0.7g; Cholesterol 0mg; Calcium 43mg; Fibre 3.6g; Sodium 514mg.

Mooli, Beetroot & Carrot Stir-fry

This is a dazzlingly colourful dish with a crunchy texture and fragrant taste. It is low in saturated fat and cholesterol-free and would be ideal for a summer lunch.

Serves 4

25g/1oz/⅓ cup pine nuts
115g/4oz mooli (daikon), peeled
115g/4oz raw beetroot (beets), peeled
115g/4oz carrots, peeled
15ml/1 tbsp vegetable oil
1 orange
30ml/2 tbsp chopped fresh coriander (cilantro)
salt and ground black pepper

1 Heat a non-stick wok or frying pan. Add the pine nuts and toss over a medium heat until golden brown. Remove the nuts and spread them on a plate. Set aside.

2 Using a sharp knife, cut the mooli, beetroot and carrots into long, thin strips of a fairly uniform size. Keep them separate on a chopping board.

3 Reheat the wok or frying pan, then add the oil. When the oil is hot, add each vegetable separately and stir-fry for 2–3 minutes over a medium to high heat, removing each when it is tender but retains some bite. As each vegetable is cooked, reserve it on a warmed dish.

4 Cut the orange in half. Squeeze the juice, using a citrus juicer or a reamer, and pour the juice into a bowl.

5 Reheat the wok or frying pan, then pour in the orange juice and simmer for 2 minutes.

6 Arrange the vegetables on a warmed platter, sprinkle over the coriander and season with salt and pepper.

7 Drizzle the reduced orange juice over the top of the stir-fried vegetables, sprinkle the top with the pine nuts, and serve.

Spicy Potatoes & Cauliflower

This dish makes a substantial accompaniment to any meat or fish curry or dhal, perfect with Indian breads or rice and a raita such as cucumber and yogurt.

Serves 2

225g/8oz potatoes
75ml/5 tbsp groundnut (peanut) oil
5ml/1 tsp ground cumin
5ml/1 tsp ground coriander
1.5ml/¼ tsp ground turmeric
1.5ml/¼ tsp cayenne pepper
1 fresh green chilli, seeded and finely chopped
1 medium cauliflower, broken into small florets
5ml/1 tsp cumin seeds
2 garlic cloves, cut into shreds
15–30ml/1–2 tbsp fresh coriander (cilantro), finely chopped
salt

1 Cook the potatoes in their skins in boiling salted water for about 20 minutes, until just tender. Drain and leave to cool. When cool enough to handle, peel and cut into 2.5cm/1in cubes.

2 Heat 45ml/3 tbsp of the oil in a frying pan or wok. When hot, add the ground cumin, coriander, turmeric, cayenne pepper and chilli. Let the spices sizzle for a few seconds.

3 Add the cauliflower and about 60ml/4 tbsp water. Cook over medium heat, stirring constantly, for 6–8 minutes. Add the potatoes and stir-fry for 2–3 minutes. Season with salt, then remove from the heat.

4 Heat the remaining oil in a small frying pan. When hot, add the cumin seeds and garlic, and cook until lightly browned. Pour the mixture over the vegetables. Sprinkle with the chopped coriander and serve at once.

Cook's Tip
Divide the cauliflower into small florets so that it will cook evenly and quickly.

mooli, beetroot & carrot Energy 103kcal/427kJ; Protein 2.1g; Carbohydrate 7.8g, of which sugars 7.5g; Fat 7.2g, of which saturates 0.7g; Cholesterol 0mg; Calcium 33mg; Fibre 2.1g; Sodium 31mg.
spicy potatoes Energy 409kcal/1698kJ; Protein 10.3g; Carbohydrate 26.6g, of which sugars 6.7g; Fat 29.7g, of which saturates 3.8g; Cholesterol 0mg; Calcium 52mg; Fibre 5.4g; Sodium 31mg.

Potatoes in Tomato Sauce

This delicious curry makes an excellent accompaniment to almost any other savoury dish, but goes particularly well with Balti dishes. Served with rice, it makes a great vegetarian main course.

Serves 4

10ml/2 tsp vegetable oil
1.5ml/¼ tsp onion seeds
4 curry leaves
2 medium onions, diced
400g/14oz can tomatoes
5ml/1 tsp ground cumin
7.5ml/1½ tsp ground coriander
5ml/1 tsp chilli powder
5ml/1 tsp grated fresh root ginger
5ml/1 tsp crushed garlic
1.5ml/¼ tsp ground turmeric
5ml/1 tsp salt
15ml/1 tbsp lemon juice
15ml/1 tbsp chopped fresh coriander (cilantro)
2 medium potatoes, diced

1 Heat the oil in a karahi, wok or heavy pan and add the onion seeds, curry leaves and diced onions. Fry over a medium heat for a few minutes, stirring occasionally and being careful not to burn the onions.

2 Meanwhile, place the canned tomatoes in a bowl and add the ground cumin and coriander, chilli powder, ginger, garlic, turmeric, salt, lemon juice and fresh coriander. Mix the ingredients together until well blended.

3 Pour this mixture into the pan and stir for about 1 minute to mix thoroughly with the onions.

4 Finally, add the diced potatoes, cover the pan and cook gently for 7–10 minutes over low heat. Check that the potatoes are properly cooked through, then serve.

Variations
This curry is also delicious if you add a few cauliflower or broccoli florets with the potatoes, or if you substitute diced parsnips for the potatoes. To emphasize the tomato flavour, stir in 15ml/1 tbsp tomato purée (paste).

Potatoes in Red Sauce

This is a lightly spiced dish, perfect for children or those who like mild curries.

Serves 4–6

450g/1lb small new potatoes
7.5ml/1½ tsp coriander seeds
7.5ml/1½ tsp cumin seeds
4 garlic cloves
90ml/6 tbsp vegetable oil
45ml/3 tbsp thick tamarind juice (see Cook's Tip)
60ml/4 tbsp tomato purée (paste)
4 curry leaves
5ml/1 tsp sugar
salt
coriander (cilantro) sprig, to garnish

1 Boil the potatoes until they are fully cooked but still retain their shape. To test, insert a thin sharp knife into the centre of the potatoes. They should be just tender. Drain the potatoes and set aside.

2 Grind the coriander seeds with the cumin seeds and garlic to a coarse paste using a mortar and pestle or food processor.

3 Heat the oil in a karahi, wok or frying pan. Fry the paste, tamarind juice, tomato purée, curry leaves, salt and sugar until the oil separates.

4 Add the potatoes and stir to coat them in the spicy tomato mixture. Reduce the heat, cover the pan and simmer for about 5 minutes. Garnish and serve.

Cook's Tip
You can buy tamarind concentrate or break off a piece of tamarind slab equivalent to 15ml/1 tbsp. Soak in 150ml/¼ pint/⅔ cup hot water for 10 minutes. Mash the tamarind into a paste and pass it through a sieve (strainer). The fine pulp and juice will go through, leaving behind the fibrous husk. Strain the juice. Tamarind pods have a long shelf life and they require soaking to release their juice.

potatoes in tomato sauce Energy 158kcal/667kJ; Protein 4.7g; Carbohydrate 29.7g, of which sugars 10g; Fat 3.3g, of which saturates 0.5g; Cholesterol 0mg; Calcium 52mg; Fibre 3.4g; Sodium 517mg.
potatoes in red sauce Energy 231kcal/962kJ; Protein 1.9g; Carbohydrate 19.2g, of which sugars 2.5g; Fat 16.8g, of which saturates 2.1g; Cholesterol 0mg; Calcium 7mg; Fibre 1.1g; Sodium 13mg.

Bombay Potatoes

This authentic dish belongs to the Gujarati, a totally vegetarian sect and the largest population group in the city of Mumbai.

Serves 4–6

2 onions
2 fresh green chillies
large bunch fresh coriander (cilantro)
450g/1lb new potatoes
5ml/1 tsp ground turmeric
60ml/4 tbsp vegetable oil
2 dried red chillies
6–8 curry leaves
1.5ml/¼ tsp Asafoetida
2.5ml/½ tsp each cumin, mustard, onion, fennel and nigella seeds
lemon juice, to taste
salt

1 Chop the onions and chillies finely, and coarsely chop the coriander.

2 Scrub the potatoes under cold running water and cut them into small pieces.

3 Boil the potatoes in water with a little salt and 2.5ml/½ tsp of the turmeric for 10–15 minutes, or until tender. Drain the potatoes well, then mash them and set aside.

4 Heat the oil in a frying pan and fry the dried chillies and curry leaves until the chillies are nearly burnt.

5 Add the chopped onions, green chillies, fresh coriander and remaining turmeric to the pan, with the asafoetida, cumin, mustard, onion, fennel and nigella seeds. Cook, stirring occasionally, until the onions are soft.

6 Fold in the potatoes and add a few drops of water. Cook over a low heat for about 10 minutes, stirring well to ensure the spices are evenly mixed.

7 Add lemon juice to taste, and serve immediately.

Spinach, Potatoes & Red Chillies

India is blessed with at least 18 varieties of spinach. If you have access to an Indian or Chinese grocer, look out for some of the more unusual varieties.

Serves 4–6

225g/8oz potatoes
60ml/4 tbsp vegetable oil
2.5cm/1in piece fresh root ginger, crushed
4 garlic cloves, crushed
1 onion, chopped
2 fresh green chillies, chopped
2 dried red chillies, chopped
5ml/1 tsp cumin seeds
225g/8oz fresh spinach, trimmed, washed and chopped, or 225g/8oz frozen spinach, thawed and drained
salt
2 firm tomatoes, roughly chopped, to garnish

1 Wash the potatoes and cut into quarters. If using small new potatoes, leave them whole. Heat the oil in a frying pan and fry the potatoes until brown on all sides. Remove and put aside.

2 Remove the excess oil, leaving about 15ml/1 tbsp in the pan. Fry the ginger, garlic, onion, green chillies, dried red chillies and cumin seeds until the onion is golden brown.

3 Add the potatoes and salt, and stir well. Cover the pan and cook over a medium heat, stirring occasionally, until the potatoes are tender when pierced with a sharp knife.

4 Add the spinach and stir well. Using two wooden spoons or spatulas, toss the mixture over the heat until the spinach is tender and all the excess fluid has evaporated.

5 Spoon into a heated serving dish or on to individual plates and garnish with the chopped tomatoes. Serve hot.

Variation
This recipe also tastes very good if you substitute sweet potatoes for ordinary potatoes. Slice them just before cooking, or they may discolour.

Bombay potatoes Energy 143kcal/595kJ; Protein 2.1g; Carbohydrate 17.4g, of which sugars 4.7g; Fat 7.7g, of which saturates 0.9g; Cholesterol 0mg; Calcium 21mg; Fibre 1.7g; Sodium 10mg.
spinach & potatoes Energy 135kcal/560kJ; Protein 3g; Carbohydrate 13.5g, of which sugars 5.9g; Fat 8g, of which saturates 1g; Cholesterol 0mg; Calcium 86mg; Fibre 2.6g; Sodium 62mg.

Fiery Spiced Potatoes

The quantity of red chillies used here may be too fiery for some palates. For a milder version, seed the chillies, use fewer, or replace them with a roughly chopped sweet red pepper instead.

Serves 4

12–14 baby new potatoes, peeled and halved
15ml/1 tbsp vegetable oil
2.5ml/½ tsp crushed dried red chillies
2.5ml/½ tsp cumin seeds
2.5ml/½ tsp fennel seeds
2.5ml/½ tsp crushed coriander seeds
1 medium onion, sliced
3 or 4 fresh red chillies, chopped
15ml/1 tbsp chopped fresh coriander (cilantro)
salt

1 Boil the potatoes in a pan of salted water until just cooked but still firm. Remove from the heat and drain off the water.

2 In a karahi, wok or deep pan, heat the oil quickly over high heat, then turn down the heat to medium. Add the crushed chillies, cumin, fennel and coriander seeds and a little salt and quickly stir-fry for about 30–40 seconds.

3 Add the onion and fry gently until golden brown. Then add the new potatoes, fresh red chillies and fresh coriander.

4 Cover and cook for 5–7 minutes over a very low heat. Serve hot.

Cook's Tip
Baby new potatoes have a wonderful flavour and texture, which are absolutely perfect for this dish. If you want to try older potatoes, choose ones that retain their shape well and cut them into large chunks. Watch them carefully so that they do not overcook and fall apart.

Spiced Potatoes & Carrots Parisienne

Ready-prepared 'Parisienne' vegetables are available in some supermarkets. These are simply root vegetables that have been peeled and cut into perfectly spherical shapes. This dish looks very fresh and appetizing and is delicious. If you can't locate 'Parisienne' vegetables, you can simply dice the potatoes and carrots yourself, or cut them into batons.

Serves 4

175g/6oz carrots Parisienne
175g/6oz potatoes Parisienne
115g/4oz green beans, sliced
75g/3oz/6 tbsp butter
15ml/1 tbsp vegetable oil
1.5ml/¼ tsp onion seeds
1.5ml/¼ tsp fenugreek seeds
4 dried red chillies
2.5ml/½ tsp mustard seeds
6 curry leaves
1 medium onion, sliced
5ml/1 tsp salt
4 garlic cloves, sliced
4 fresh red chillies
15ml/1 tbsp chopped fresh coriander (cilantro)
15ml/1 tbsp chopped fresh mint, plus 1 mint sprig to garnish

1 Drop the carrots, potatoes and green beans into a pan of boiling water, and cook for about 7 minutes, or until they are just tender but not overcooked. Drain in a colander, then refresh under cold water to arrest the cooking process. Drain again and set to one side.

2 Heat the butter and oil in a deep frying pan or a large karahi and add the onion seeds, fenugreek seeds, dried red chillies, mustard seeds and curry leaves. When these have sizzled for a few seconds, add the onion and fry for 3–5 minutes, stirring the mixture occasionally.

3 Add the salt, garlic and fresh chillies, followed by the cooked vegetables, and stir gently for about 5 minutes, over a medium heat.

4 Add the fresh coriander and mint, and serve hot, garnished with a sprig of mint.

fiery spiced potatoes Energy 97kcal/408kJ; Protein 2.2g; Carbohydrate 15g, of which sugars 1.8g; Fat 3.7g, of which saturates 0.5g; Cholesterol 0mg; Calcium 17mg; Fibre 1g; Sodium 11mg.
potatoes & carrots Energy 252kcal/1044kJ; Protein 3.5g; Carbohydrate 16.1g, of which sugars 5.7g; Fat 19.9g, of which saturates 10.4g; Cholesterol 40mg; Calcium 72mg; Fibre 3g; Sodium 628mg.

Masala Mashed Potatoes

This delightfully simple variation on the popular Western side dish can be used as an accompaniment to just about any main course dish, not just Indian food. There are easily obtainable alternatives to mango powder if you cannot get hold of it (see Cook's Tip).

Serves 4

3 medium potatoes
15ml/1 tbsp chopped fresh mint and coriander (cilantro), mixed
5ml/1 tsp mango powder (amchur)
5ml/1 tsp salt
5ml/1 tsp crushed black peppercorns
1 fresh red chilli, chopped
1 fresh green chilli, chopped
50g/2oz/¼ cup butter

1 Boil the potatoes until soft, drain, and then mash them using a masher or potato ricer.

2 Stir the remaining ingredients together in a small bowl.

3 Stir the spice mixture into the mashed potatoes. Mix together thoroughly with a fork and serve warm as an accompaniment to your main dish.

Cook's Tip

Mango powder, also known as amchur, is the unripe green fruit of the mango tree ground to a powder. The sour mangoes are sliced and dried in the sun, turning a light brown, before they are ground. Mango powder adds a fruity sharpness and a slightly resinous bouquet to a dish. It is widely used with vegetables and is usually added towards the end of the cooking time. If mango powder is unavailable, the nearest substitute is lemon or lime juice, in double or treble quantity.

Potatoes in Yogurt Sauce

It is nice to use tiny new potatoes with the skins on for this recipe. The yogurt adds a tangy flavour to this fairly spicy dish, which is delicious served with plain or wholemeal chapatis.

Serves 4

small bunch fresh coriander (cilantro)
12 new potatoes, halved
275g/10oz/1¼ cups natural (plain) low-fat yogurt
300ml/½ pint/1¼ cups water
1.5ml/¼ tsp ground turmeric
5ml/1 tsp chilli powder
5ml/1 tsp ground coriander
2.5ml/½ tsp ground cumin
5ml/1 tsp soft brown sugar
1.5ml/¼ tsp salt
15ml/1 tbsp vegetable oil
5ml/1 tsp cumin seeds
2 green chillies, sliced

1 Cut off the roots and any thick stalks from the coriander and chop the leaves finely. Set aside.

2 Boil the potatoes in salted water with their skins on until they are just tender, then drain and set aside.

3 Mix together the yogurt, water, turmeric, chilli powder, ground coriander, ground cumin, sugar and salt in a bowl. Set aside.

4 Heat the oil in a medium, heavy pan and stir in the cumin seeds. Fry for 1 minute.

5 Reduce the heat, stir in the spicy yogurt mixture and cook for about 3 minutes over medium heat.

6 Add the chopped fresh coriander, green chillies and cooked potatoes. Blend everything together and cook for a further 5–7 minutes, stirring from time to time. Serve hot.

Cook's Tip

If new potatoes are unavailable, use 450g/1lb ordinary waxy potatoes instead. Peel them and cut into large chunks, then cook as described above.

masala potatoes Energy 219kcal/919kJ; Protein 3.1g; Carbohydrate 28.9g, of which sugars 3g; Fat 10.9g, of which saturates 6.7g; Cholesterol 27mg; Calcium 13mg; Fibre 1.8g; Sodium 600mg.
potatoes in yogurt Energy 161kcal/677kJ; Protein 5.9g; Carbohydrate 24.7g, of which sugars 7g; Fat 5.1g, of which saturates 1g; Cholesterol 1mg; Calcium 154mg; Fibre 1.1g; Sodium 73mg.

Potatoes in Chilli Tamarind Sauce

In this favourite potato dish from the state of Karnataka, the combination of chilli and tamarind awakens the taste buds immediately. This version adapts the traditional recipe slightly, to reduce the customary pungency and enhance the fiery appearance of this delicious combination.

Serves 4–6

450g/1lb small new potatoes, washed and dried
25g/1oz whole dried red chillies, preferably Kashmiri
7.5ml/1½ tsp cumin seeds
4 garlic cloves, chopped
90ml/6 tbsp vegetable oil
60ml/4 tbsp thick tamarind juice
30ml/2 tbsp tomato purée (paste)
4 curry leaves
5ml/1 tsp sugar
1.5ml/¼ tsp asafoetida
salt
coriander (cilantro) sprigs and lemon wedges, to garnish

1 Boil the new potatoes until they are just tender, ensuring they do not break. Drain and cool the potatoes in iced water to prevent them from cooking further.

2 Soak the chillies for 5 minutes in warm water. Drain and grind with the cumin seeds and garlic to a coarse paste, either using a mortar and pestle or in a food processor.

3 Heat the oil and fry the paste, tamarind juice, tomato purée, curry leaves, sugar, asafoetida and salt until the oil can be seen to have separated from the spice paste.

4 Add the potatoes and stir to coat. Reduce the heat, cover and simmer for 5 minutes. Transfer to a warmed serving dish, or individual bowls, garnish with coriander sprigs and lemon wedges, and serve.

Variation

Chunks of large potatoes can be used as an alternative to new potatoes. Alternatively, try this dish with sweet potatoes. The spicy sweet-and-sour taste works very well in this variation.

Potatoes with Roasted Poppy Seeds

Poppy seeds are used in Indian cooking as thickening agents, and to lend a nutty taste to sauces.

Serves 4

45ml/3 tbsp white poppy seeds
45ml/3 tbsp vegetable oil
675g/1½lb potatoes, peeled and cut into 1cm/½in cubes
2.5ml/½ tsp black mustard seeds
2.5ml/½ tsp onion seeds
2.5ml/½ tsp cumin seeds
2.5ml/½ tsp fennel seeds
1 or 2 dried red chillies, chopped or broken into small pieces
2.5ml/½ tsp ground turmeric
2.5ml/½ tsp salt
150ml/¼ pint/⅔ cup warm water
fresh coriander (cilantro) sprigs, to garnish
pooris and natural (plain) yogurt, to serve

1 Preheat a karahi, wok or large pan over a medium heat. When the pan is hot, reduce the heat slightly and add the poppy seeds. Stir them around in the pan until they are just a shade darker. Remove from the pan and leave to cool.

2 In the pan, heat the vegetable oil over a medium heat and fry the cubes of potato until they are light brown. Remove them with a slotted spoon and drain on kitchen paper.

3 To the same oil, add the mustard seeds. As soon as they begin to pop, add the onion, cumin and fennel seeds and the chillies. Let the chillies blacken, but remove them from the pan before they burn.

4 Stir in the turmeric and follow quickly with the fried potatoes and salt. Stir well and add the warm water. Cover the pan with the lid and reduce the heat to low. Cook for 8–10 minutes, or until the potatoes are tender.

5 Grind the cooled poppy seeds in a mortar and pestle or spice grinder. Stir the ground seeds into the potatoes. A thick paste should form and cling to the potatoes. If there is too much liquid, continue to stir over a medium heat until you have the right consistency. Transfer to a serving dish. Garnish with coriander and serve with pooris and natural yogurt.

potatoes in chilli sauce Energy 178kcal/741kJ; Protein 2.5g; Carbohydrate 16g, of which sugars 2.6g; Fat 12.1g, of which saturates 1.5g; Cholesterol 0mg; Calcium 19mg; Fibre 0.9g; Sodium 23mg.
potatoes w. poppy seeds Energy 289kcal/1207kJ; Protein 6.4g; Carbohydrate 30.8g, of which sugars 2.3g; Fat 16.6g, of which saturates 2.3g; Cholesterol 0mg; Calcium 104mg; Fibre 2.6g; Sodium 24mg.

Spiced Coconut Mushrooms

Here is an unusual and delicious way to cook mushrooms. They can be served with almost any Indian meal as well as with traditional Western grilled or roasted meats and poultry.

Serves 4

30ml/2 tbsp groundnut (peanut) oil
2 garlic cloves, finely chopped
2 fresh red chillies, seeded and sliced into rings
3 shallots, finely chopped
225g/8oz/3 cups brown cap (cremini) mushrooms, thickly sliced
150ml/¼ pint/⅔ cup coconut milk
30ml/2 tbsp chopped fresh coriander (cilantro)
salt and ground black pepper

1 Heat a karahi, wok or frying pan until hot, add the oil and swirl it around. Add the garlic and chillies, then stir-fry for a few seconds.

2 Add the shallots and stir-fry them for 2–3 minutes until softened. Add the mushrooms and stir-fry for 3 minutes.

3 Pour in the coconut milk and bring to the boil. Boil rapidly over a high heat until the liquid has reduced by about half and coats the mushrooms. Season to taste with salt and pepper.

4 Sprinkle over the chopped coriander and toss the mushrooms gently to mix. Serve immediately.

Variations

- *Use chopped fresh chives instead of chopped fresh coriander (cilantro), if you wish.*
- *White (button) mushrooms or field (portabello) mushrooms would also work well instead of brown cap (cremini) mushrooms.*
- *Sprinkle some chopped toasted cashew nuts over the mushrooms before serving, if you like.*

Spinach with Mushrooms

A tasty vegetable that is often overlooked, spinach is highly nutritious. Cooked in this way it tastes wonderful. Serve with chapatis.

Serves 4

450g/1lb spinach, thawed if frozen
30ml/2 tbsp vegetable oil
2 medium onions, diced
6–8 curry leaves
1.5ml/¼ tsp onion seeds
5ml/1 tsp crushed garlic
5ml/1 tsp grated fresh root ginger
5ml/1 tsp chilli powder
5ml/1 tsp salt
7.5ml/1½ tsp ground coriander
1 large red (bell) pepper, seeded and sliced
115g/4oz/1½ cups mushrooms, roughly chopped
225g/8oz/1 cup low-fat fromage frais or ricotta cheese
30ml/2 tbsp fresh coriander (cilantro) leaves

1 If using fresh spinach, blanch it briefly in boiling water and drain thoroughly. If using frozen spinach, drain well. Set aside.

2 Heat the oil in a karahi, wok or heavy pan and fry the onions with the curry leaves and the onion seeds for 1–2 minutes. Add the garlic, ginger, chilli powder, salt and ground coriander. Stir-fry for a further 2–3 minutes.

3 Add half the red pepper slices and all the mushrooms and continue to stir-fry for 2–3 minutes.

4 Add the spinach and stir-fry for 4–6 minutes, then add the fromage frais or ricotta and half the fresh coriander, followed by the remaining red pepper slices. Stir-fry for a further 2–3 minutes before serving, garnished with the remaining coriander.

Cook's Tip

Whether you use fresh or frozen spinach, make sure it is well drained, otherwise the stir-fried mixture will be too wet when you add the fromage frais or ricotta. Tip the spinach into a colander, and press it against the sides of the colander with a wooden spoon to extract as much liquid as possible.

coconut mushrooms Energy 76kcal/313kJ; Protein 2g; Carbohydrate 3.4g, of which sugars 3g; Fat 6.1g, of which saturates 0.8g; Cholesterol 0mg; Calcium 26mg; Fibre 0.8g; Sodium 46mg.
spinach Energy 225kcal/933kJ; Protein 10.8g; Carbohydrate 10g, of which sugars 6.2g; Fat 16.2g, of which saturates 6.1g; Cholesterol 24mg; Calcium 215mg; Fibre 3.4g; Sodium 164mg.

Courgettes with Mushrooms in a Yogurt Sauce

The slightly tart flavour of yogurt makes a creamy sauce which is delicious with cooked mushrooms and courgettes.

Serves 4

15ml/1 tbsp vegetable oil
1 medium onion, roughly chopped
5ml/1 tsp ground coriander
5ml/1 tsp ground cumin
5ml/1 tsp salt
2.5ml/½ tsp chilli powder
225g/8oz/3 cups mushrooms, sliced
2 courgettes (zucchini), sliced
45ml/3 tbsp natural (plain) low-fat yogurt
15ml/1 tbsp chopped fresh coriander (cilantro)

1 Heat the oil in a heavy pan and fry the onion until golden brown. Lower the heat to medium, add the ground coriander, cumin, salt and chilli powder and stir together well.

2 Once the onion and the spices are well blended, add the mushrooms and courgettes, and stir-fry gently for about 5 minutes until soft. If the mixture is too dry, add just a little water to loosen.

3 Add the yogurt and mix it well into the vegetables.

4 Sprinkle with chopped fresh coriander and serve immediately.

Cook's Tip
Yogurt has a great affinity with stir-fried vegetables and this lovely combination of yogurt, sliced courgettes (zucchini) and mushrooms would make a tasty accompaniment to serve with poultry or lamb dishes. If you prefer, you could use aubergines (eggplants) or (bell) peppers instead.

Stuffed Okra

A delicious accompaniment to any dish, this can also be served with thick, creamy yogurt, which gives an excellent contrast in flavour.

Serves 4–6

225g/8oz large okra
15ml/1 tbsp mango powder (amchur)
2.5ml/½ tsp ground ginger
2.5ml/½ tsp ground cumin
2.5ml/½ tsp chilli powder (optional)
2.5ml/½ tsp turmeric
a few drops of vegetable oil
30ml/2 tbsp cornflour (cornstarch), placed in a plastic bag
vegetable oil, for frying
salt

1 Wash the okra and dry on kitchen paper. Carefully trim off the tops without making a hole. Using a sharp knife, make a slit lengthways in the centre of each okra but do not cut all the way through.

2 In a bowl, mix the mango powder, ginger, cumin, chilli if using, turmeric and salt with a few drops of oil. Leave the mixture to rest for 1–2 hours.

3 Using your fingers, part the slit of each okra carefully and fill each with as much of the spice filling as possible.

4 Put all the okra into the plastic bag with the cornflour and shake the bag carefully to coat the okra evenly.

5 Fill a frying pan with enough oil to sit 2.5cm/1in deep, heat it and fry the okra in small batches for about 5–8 minutes, or until they are brown and slightly crisp. Serve hot.

Cook's Tip
Dusting the okra in cornflour before frying helps to ensure that none of the sticky liquid escapes and keeps the pods perfectly crisp.

courgettes with mushrooms Energy 90kcal/374kJ; Protein 5g; Carbohydrate 7.5g, of which sugars 3.4g; Fat 4.9g, of which saturates 0.7g; Cholesterol 0mg; Calcium 69mg; Fibre 1.7g; Sodium 16mg.
stuffed okra Energy 176kcal/734kJ; Protein 1.7g; Carbohydrate 15.5g, of which sugars 1.4g; Fat 12.4g, of which saturates 1.6g; Cholesterol 0mg; Calcium 92mg; Fibre 2.3g; Sodium 12mg.

Okra in Yogurt

This tangy vegetable dish can be served as an accompaniment, but it also makes an excellent vegetarian meal if served with tarka dhal and warm, freshly made chapatis.

Serves 4

450g/1lb okra
15ml/1 tbsp vegetable oil
2.5ml/½ tsp onion seeds
3 medium fresh green chillies, chopped
1 medium onion, sliced
1.5ml/¼ tsp ground turmeric
2.5ml/½ tsp salt
15ml/1 tbsp natural (plain) low-fat yogurt
2 medium tomatoes, sliced
15ml/1 tbsp chopped fresh coriander (cilantro)
chapatis, to serve

1 Wash and trim the okra, cut into 1cm/½in pieces and place in a bowl. Set aside.

2 Heat the oil in a medium, heavy pan, add the onion seeds, green chillies and onion, and fry for about 5 minutes until the onion has turned golden brown.

3 Reduce the heat. Add the ground turmeric and salt to the pan and fry for about 1 minute.

4 Next, add the prepared okra, turn the heat to medium-high and quickly stir-fry the okra until they are lightly golden.

5 Stir in the yogurt, tomatoes and chopped coriander. Cook for a further 2 minutes.

6 Transfer the okra to a serving dish and serve immediately with freshly made chapatis.

Cook's Tip
It is always wise to wear plastic or rubber gloves when preparing chillies as they contain a strong irritant that will sting open cuts or eyes if it comes into contact with them.

Masala Okra

In this popular vegetable dish the okra pods are stir-fried with a dry masala mixture to make a tasty accompaniment to a curry with lots of sauce.

Serves 4

450g/1lb okra
2.5ml/½ tsp ground turmeric
5ml/1 tsp chilli powder
15ml/1 tbsp ground cumin
15ml/1 tbsp ground coriander
1.5ml/¼ tsp salt
1.5ml/¼ tsp sugar
15ml/1 tbsp lemon juice
30ml/2 tbsp chopped fresh coriander (cilantro)
15ml/1 tbsp vegetable oil
2.5ml/½ tsp cumin seeds
2.5ml/½ tsp black mustard seeds
chopped fresh tomatoes, to garnish
poppadums, to serve

1 Wash, dry and trim the stalks away from the top of the okra, being careful not to pierce the pod itself, otherwise the sticky juices will be released and will affect the final dish. Set the okra aside. In a bowl, mix together the turmeric, chilli powder, cumin, ground coriander, salt, sugar, lemon juice and fresh coriander.

2 Heat the oil in a large, heavy pan. Add the cumin seeds and mustard seeds, and fry for about 2 minutes or until they start to splutter.

3 Scrape in the spice mixture and continue to fry for 2 minutes.

4 Add the okra, cover and cook over a low heat for 10 minutes, or until tender. Garnish with chopped fresh tomatoes and serve with poppadums.

Cook's Tip
When buying okra, choose firm, brightly coloured pods that are less than 10cm/4in long; larger ones can be stringy.

okra in yogurt Energy 79kcal/328kJ; Protein 4g; Carbohydrate 6.8g, of which sugars 5.5g; Fat 4.2g, of which saturates 0.8g; Cholesterol 0mg; Calcium 196mg; Fibre 5.2g; Sodium 18mg.
masala okra Energy 211kcal/873kJ; Protein 5g; Carbohydrate 6.3g, of which sugars 5.2g; Fat 18.7g, of which saturates 7.1g; Cholesterol 0mg; Calcium 246mg; Fibre 7.6g; Sodium 15mg.

Stir-fried Paneer with Mushrooms & Peas

Indian cheese, known as paneer, is a very versatile ingredient. It is used in both sweet and savoury dishes. Indian housewives generally make this cheese at home, although in recent years it has become available commercially.

Serves 4–6

90ml/6 tbsp ghee or vegetable oil
225g/8oz paneer, cubed
1 onion, finely chopped
a few fresh mint leaves, chopped, plus extra sprigs to garnish
50g/2oz/1 cup chopped fresh coriander (cilantro)
3 fresh green chillies, chopped
3 garlic cloves
2.5cm/1in piece fresh root ginger, sliced
5ml/1 tsp ground turmeric
5ml/1 tsp chilli powder (optional)
5ml/1 tsp garam masala
225g/8oz/3 cups tiny button (white) mushrooms, washed
225g/8oz/2 cups frozen peas, thawed
175ml/6fl oz/¾ cup natural (plain) yogurt or coconut cream
salt

1 Heat the ghee or oil in a karahi, wok or large pan, and fry the paneer cubes until they are golden brown on all sides. Remove and drain on kitchen paper.

2 Grind the onion, mint, coriander, chillies, garlic and ginger with a mortar and pestle or in a food processor to a fairly smooth paste. Transfer to a bowl and mix in the turmeric, chilli powder, if using, and garam masala, with salt to taste.

3 Remove the excess ghee or oil from the pan, leaving about 15ml/1 tbsp. Heat and fry the paste over a medium heat for 8–10 minutes, or until the raw onion smell disappears and the oil separates. Add the mushrooms, peas and paneer and mix well. Cool the mixture slightly and fold in the yogurt. Simmer for about 10 minutes, until the vegetables are tender. Garnish with fresh mint and serve.

Corn on the Cob in a Rich Onion Sauce

Corn is grown extensively in the Punjab region, where it is used in many delicacies. Corn bread, makki ki roti, along with spiced mustard greens, sarson ka saag, is a combination that is hard to beat and it is what the Punjabis thrive on. Here, corn is cooked in a thick, rich onion sauce, in another classic Punjabi dish. It is excellent served with naan bread.

Serves 4

4 corn on the cob, thawed if frozen
vegetable oil, for frying
1 large onion, finely chopped
2 garlic cloves, crushed
5cm/2in piece fresh root ginger, crushed
2.5ml/½ tsp ground turmeric
2.5ml/½ tsp onion seeds
2.5ml/½ tsp cumin seeds
2.5ml/½ tsp chilli powder
6–8 curry leaves
2.5ml/½ tsp sugar
200ml/7fl oz/scant 1 cup natural (plain) yogurt
chilli powder, to taste

1 Cut each corn cob in half, using a heavy knife or cleaver to make clean cuts and avoid damaging the kernels.

2 Heat the oil in a karahi, wok or large pan and fry the corn until golden brown. Remove the corn and set aside. Remove any excess oil, leaving about 30ml/2 tbsp in the pan.

3 Grind the onion, garlic and ginger to a paste using a mortar and pestle or in a food processor. Transfer the paste to a bowl and mix in the spices, curry leaves and sugar.

4 Heat the oil and fry the onion paste mixture over a low heat for 8–10 minutes until all the spices have blended well and the oil separates from the sauce.

5 Cool the onion paste mixture and fold in the yogurt. Mix to a smooth sauce. Add the corn and mix well, so that all the pieces are covered with the sauce. Reheat gently for about 10 minutes. Serve hot.

stir-fried paneer Energy 154kcal/643kJ; Protein 10.4g; Carbohydrate 13g, of which sugars 4.9g; Fat 7.2g, of which saturates 1.7g; Cholesterol 6mg; Calcium 139mg; Fibre 2.6g; Sodium 133mg.
corn on the cob Energy 155kcal/649kJ; Protein 4.5g; Carbohydrate 31.9g, of which sugars 20.4g; Fat 3.4g, of which saturates 1.6g; Cholesterol 2mg; Calcium 93mg; Fibre 4.1g; Sodium 790mg.

Peppers Filled with Vegetables

Nigella, or kalonji, has a mild, slightly nutty flavour and is best toasted for a few seconds in a dry frying pan before being used in a recipe. This helps to bring out its flavour.

Serves 6

6 large evenly shaped red or yellow (bell) peppers
500g/1 ¼lb waxy potatoes
1 small onion, chopped
4 or 5 garlic cloves, chopped
5cm/2in piece fresh root ginger, chopped
1 or 2 fresh green chillies, seeded and chopped
105ml/7 tbsp water
90–105ml/6–7 tbsp vegetable oil
1 aubergine (eggplant), diced
10ml/2 tsp cumin seeds
5ml/1 tsp nigella seeds
2.5ml/ ½ tsp ground turmeric
5ml/1 tsp ground coriander
5ml/1 tsp ground toasted cumin seeds
cayenne pepper
about 30ml/2 tbsp lemon juice
salt and ground black pepper
30ml/2 tbsp chopped fresh coriander (cilantro), to garnish

1 Cut the tops off the peppers, then remove and discard the seeds. Cut a thin slice off the base of any wobbly peppers so that they stand upright. Bring a large pan of lightly salted water to the boil. Add the peppers and cook for 5–6 minutes. Drain and leave them upside down in a colander.

2 Cook the potatoes in lightly salted, boiling water for 10–12 minutes until just tender. Drain, cool and peel, then cut into 1cm/ ½in dice.

3 Put the onion, garlic, ginger and green chillies in a food processor or blender with 60ml/4 tbsp of the water and process to a purée.

4 Heat 45ml/3 tbsp of the vegetable oil in a large, deep frying pan and cook the aubergine, stirring occasionally, until it is evenly browned. Remove the aubergine from the pan using a slotted spoon and set aside. Add another 30ml/2 tbsp of the vegetable oil to the pan, add the potatoes and cook until lightly browned. Remove the potatoes from the pan and set aside.

5 If necessary, add another 15ml/1 tbsp sunflower oil to the pan, then add the cumin and nigella seeds. Fry briefly until the seeds darken, then add the turmeric, coriander and ground cumin. Cook for 15 seconds. Stir in the onion and garlic purée and fry, scraping the pan with a spatula, until the mixture begins to brown.

6 Return the potatoes and aubergine to the pan, season with salt, pepper and one or two pinches of cayenne. Add the remaining water and 15ml/1 tbsp lemon juice and then cook, stirring, until the liquid evaporates. Preheat the oven to 190°C/375°F/Gas 5.

7 Fill the peppers with the spiced vegetable mixture and place on a lightly greased baking tray. Brush the peppers with a little oil and bake for 30–35 minutes until they are browned. Leave to cool a little, then sprinkle with a little more lemon juice. Garnish with the coriander and serve.

Asparagus with Galangal & Chilli

This is an excitingly different way of cooking asparagus. The crunchy texture is retained and the flavour is complemented by the addition of galangal and fresh red chilli.

Serves 4

350g/12oz asparagus
30ml/2 tbsp vegetable oil
1 garlic clove, crushed
15ml/1 tbsp sesame seeds, toasted
2.5cm/1in piece fresh galangal, finely shredded
1 fresh red chilli, seeded and finely chopped
15ml/1 tbsp Thai fish sauce
15ml/1 tbsp light soy sauce
45ml/3 tbsp water
5ml/1 tsp palm sugar (jaggery) or light muscovado (brown) sugar

1 Snap the asparagus stalks. They will break naturally at the junction between the woody base and the more tender portion of the stalk when you bend the stems. Discard the woody parts of the stems.

2 Heat the oil in a wok and stir-fry the garlic, sesame seeds and shredded galangal for 3–4 minutes, until the garlic is just beginning to turn golden.

3 Add the asparagus stalks and chilli, toss to mix, then add the fish sauce, soy sauce, water and sugar.

4 Using two spoons, toss the mixture over the heat for a further 2 minutes, or until the asparagus just begins to soften and the liquid is reduced by half.

5 Carefully transfer the asparagus and sauce to a warmed serving platter and serve immediately.

Variation
Try this with broccoli or pak choi (bok choy). The sauce also works very well with green beans.

peppers w. vegetables Energy 234kcal/976kJ; Protein 4.2g; Carbohydrate 28.1g, of which sugars 14.8g; Fat 12.4g, of which saturates 2.4g; Cholesterol 0mg; Calcium 45mg; Fibre 5.5g; Sodium 21mg.
asparagus w. chilli Energy 108kcal/447kJ; Protein 3.8g; Carbohydrate 4.3g, of which sugars 3.3g; Fat 8.5g, of which saturates 1.1g; Cholesterol 0mg; Calcium 55mg; Fibre 1.8g; Sodium 537mg.

Stewed Chickpeas

In this recipe, chickpeas and spices combine to make a fiery and delicious tomato and aubergine dish to add interest to any plain meat or rice dish.

Serves 6–8

about 60ml/4 tbsp olive oil
1 large aubergine (eggplant) cut into bitesize chunks
2 onions, thinly sliced
3–5 garlic cloves, chopped
1–2 green (bell) peppers, thinly sliced or chopped
1–2 fresh hot chillies, chopped
4 fresh or canned tomatoes, diced
30–45ml/2–3 tbsp tomato purée (paste), if using fresh tomatoes
5ml/1 tsp ground turmeric
pinch of curry powder or ras al hanout
cayenne pepper, to taste
400g/14oz can chickpeas, drained and rinsed
juice of ½–1 lemon
30–45ml/2–3 tbsp chopped fresh coriander (cilantro) leaves
salt

1 Heat half the oil in a frying pan, add the aubergine chunks and fry until brown, adding more oil if necessary. When cooked, transfer the aubergine to a strainer, standing over a bowl, and leave to drain.

2 Heat the remaining oil in the pan, add the onions, garlic, peppers and chillies and fry until softened. Add the diced tomatoes, tomato purée, if using, spices and salt, and cook, stirring, until the mixture is of a sauce consistency. Add a little water if necessary.

3 Add the chickpeas to the sauce and cook for about 5 minutes, then add the aubergine, stir to mix and cook for 5–10 minutes until the flavours are well combined. Add lemon juice to taste, then add the coriander leaves. Chill before serving.

Cook's Tip
It is important to strain and rinse canned chickpeas thoroughly, as the canning liquid has a rather overpowering aroma and flavour that will unbalance the dish.

Sweet Cinnamon Carrots

A honey and cinnamon coating makes these glazed carrots extra special.

Serves 4

450g/1lb carrots, peeled and cut into batons
25g/1oz/2 tbsp butter
2.5ml/½ tsp ground cinnamon
15ml/1 tbsp clear honey
15ml/1 tbsp chopped fresh coriander (cilantro)
salt and ground black pepper
sprig of fresh coriander, to garnish

1 Steam or boil the carrots for 5 minutes until crisply tender. Drain well and return to the pan.

2 Add the butter to the pan to melt and add the cinnamon and honey. Season to taste with salt and pepper.

3 Add the chopped fresh coriander and toss well to coat the carrots with the flavoured butter. Serve garnished with a sprig of fresh coriander.

Sweet & Sour Onions

Cooked in this way, sweet baby onions make an unusual, yet tasty side dish.

Serves 6

450g/1lb baby onions, peeled
50ml/2fl oz/¼ cup wine vinegar
45ml/3 tbsp olive oil
40g/1½oz/⅓ cup caster (superfine) sugar
45ml/3 tbsp tomato purée (paste)
1 bay leaf
2 parsley sprigs
65g/2½oz/½ cup raisins
salt and ground black pepper

1 Put all the ingredients in a pan with 300ml/½ pint/1¼ cups water. Bring to the boil and simmer gently, uncovered, for 45 minutes or until the onions are tender and most of the liquid has evaporated.

2 Remove the bay leaf and parsley, check the seasoning and transfer to a serving dish. Serve at room temperature.

chickpea stew Energy 79kcal/331kJ; Protein 2.9g; Carbohydrate 9.4g, of which sugars 5.3g; Fat 3.7g, of which saturates 1.1g; Cholesterol 0mg; Calcium 62mg; Fibre 3.7g; Sodium 88mg.
cinnamon carrots Energy 97kcal/402kJ; Protein 0.7g; Carbohydrate 11.8g, of which sugars 11.2g; Fat 5.5g, of which saturates 3.4g; Cholesterol 13mg; Calcium 30mg; Fibre 2.7g; Sodium 67mg.
sweet & sour onions Energy 150kcal/628kJ; Protein 1.9g; Carbohydrate 24.1g, of which sugars 21.6g; Fat 5.8g, of which saturates 0.8g; Cholesterol 0mg; Calcium 38mg; Fibre 2g; Sodium 28mg.

Dried Fruit and Nut Halek

Versions of this unusual dish are often associated with Hassidic Jewish fare. It is fragrant with rose water and the sweet flavours of dried fruits and nuts, and goes very well with spicy curry dishes.

Serves about 10

60ml/4 tbsp blanched almonds
60ml/4 tbsp unsalted pistachio nuts
60ml/4 tbsp walnuts
15–30ml/1–2 tbsp hazelnuts
30ml/2 tbsp unsalted shelled pumpkin seeds
90ml/6 tbsp raisins, chopped
90ml/6 tbsp pitted prunes, diced
90ml/6 tbsp dried apricots, diced
60ml/4 tbsp dried cherries
sugar or honey, to taste
juice of ½ lemon
30ml/2 tbsp rose water
seeds from 4–5 cardamom pods
pinch of ground cloves
pinch of freshly grated nutmeg
1.5ml/¼ tsp ground cinnamon
fruit juice of choice, if necessary

1 Roughly chop the almonds, pistachio nuts, walnuts, hazelnuts and pumpkin seeds and put in a bowl.

2 Add the chopped raisins, prunes, apricots and cherries to the nuts and seeds and toss to combine. Stir in sugar or honey to taste and mix well until thoroughly combined.

3 Add the lemon juice, rose water, cardamom seeds, cloves, nutmeg and cinnamon to the fruit and nut mixture and mix until thoroughly combined.

4 If the dish is too thick, add a little fruit juice to thin the mixture. Pour into a serving bowl, cover and chill in the refrigerator until ready to serve.

Variation
Use any combination of unsalted nuts and dried fruits to make this dish. For a really succulent version that goes well with dry curries and biryanis, soak the dried fruits in orange juice before adding them to the recipe.

Spicy Bitter Gourds

Bitter gourds are widely used in India, often combined with other vegetables in a curry. They are also known as karelas and resemble small cucumbers with a warty skin. Gourds that are about 10cm/4in long are usually slightly less bitter than the tiny ones.

Serves 4

675g/1½lb bitter gourds
15ml/1 tbsp vegetable oil
2.5ml/½ tsp cumin seeds
6 spring onions (scallions), finely chopped
5 tomatoes, finely chopped
2.5cm/1in piece fresh root ginger, finely chopped
2 garlic cloves, crushed
2 fresh green chillies, finely chopped
2.5ml/½ tsp chilli powder
5ml/1 tsp ground coriander
5ml/1 tsp ground cumin
45ml/3 tbsp soft dark brown sugar
15ml/1 tbsp gram flour
fresh coriander (cilantro) sprigs, to garnish
salt

1 Bring a large pan of lightly salted water to the boil. Peel the bitter gourds and halve them. Discard the seeds. Cut into 2cm/¾in pieces, then cook in the boiling water for about 10–15 minutes or until just tender. Drain well.

2 Heat the oil in a large, heavy pan and fry the cumin seeds for 2 minutes until they begin to splutter.

3 Add the spring onions and fry for 3–4 minutes. Add the tomatoes, ginger, garlic and chillies, and cook the mixture, stirring occasionally, for a further 5 minutes.

4 Add 2.5ml/½ tsp salt, the remaining spices and sugar to the pan and cook for a further 2–3 minutes. Add the bitter gourds to the pan and mix well.

5 Sprinkle over the gram flour. Stir well, cover and simmer over a low heat for 5–8 minutes or until all the gram flour has been absorbed into the sauce. Stir well, then serve garnished with fresh coriander sprigs.

halek Energy 350kcal/1479kJ; Protein 29.8g; Carbohydrate 705.3g, of which sugars 699.3g; Fat 81.4g, of which saturates 6.4g; Cholesterol 0mg; Calcium 603mg; Fibre 40.7g; Sodium 189mg.
spicy bitter gourds Energy 304kcal/1268kJ; Protein 8.9g; Carbohydrate 27g, of which sugars 19.6g; Fat 18.6g, of which saturates 2.8g; Cholesterol 0mg; Calcium 89mg; Fibre 3.8g; Sodium 19mg.

Green Beans with Corn

Frozen green beans are useful for this dish, as they are quick to cook. It makes an excellent vegetable accompaniment.

Serves 4

15ml/1 tbsp vegetable oil
1.5ml/¼ tsp mustard seeds
1 medium red onion, diced
50g/2oz/⅓ cup frozen corn
50g/2oz/¼ cup canned red kidney beans, drained
175g/6oz frozen green beans
1 fresh red chilli, seeded and diced
1 garlic clove, chopped
2.5cm/1in piece fresh root ginger, finely chopped
15ml/1 tbsp chopped fresh coriander (cilantro)
5ml/1 tsp salt
1 medium tomato, seeded and diced, to garnish

1 Heat the oil in a karahi, wok or heavy pan for about 30 seconds, then add the mustard seeds and onion. Stir-fry for 2–3 minutes.

2 Add the corn, red kidney beans and green beans. Stir-fry for 3–5 minutes.

3 Add the red chilli, chopped garlic and ginger, coriander and salt, and stir-fry for 2–3 minutes.

4 Remove the pan from the heat. Transfer the vegetables to a serving dish and garnish with the diced tomato.

Cook's Tip

This is a good stand-by dish as it uses frozen and canned ingredients. To make sure you have always got a chilli available for making this dish, or others like it, you can freeze whole fresh chillies, washed but not blanched.

Vegetables & Beans with Curry Leaves

Bright, shiny green curry leaves look like small bay leaves, although they are not as tough. A popular seasoning ingredient in Indian cooking, curry leaves add a spicy flavour to dishes such as this dry vegetable and bean curry.

Serves 4

3 fresh green chillies
1 medium carrot
50g/2oz green beans
1 medium red (bell) pepper
15ml/1 tbsp vegetable oil
6 curry leaves
3 garlic cloves, sliced
3 dried red chillies
1.5ml/¼ tsp onion seeds
1.5ml/¼ tsp fenugreek seeds
115g/4oz/½ cup drained canned red kidney beans
5ml/1 tsp salt
30ml/2 tbsp lemon juice

1 Cut the chillies in half lengthways. Remove the membranes and seeds and chop the flesh.

2 Cut the carrot into strips and slice the green beans diagonally. Remove the seeds and stalk from the pepper and cut the flesh into strips.

3 Heat the oil in a karahi, wok or deep heavy pan. Add the curry leaves, sliced garlic cloves, dried chillies, and onion and fenugreek seeds.

4 When these ingredients turn a shade darker, add the chillies, kidney beans, carrot strips, green beans and pepper strips, stirring constantly.

5 Stir in the salt and the lemon juice. Lower the heat, cover and cook for about 5 minutes.

6 Transfer the hot curry to a serving dish and serve immediately.

green beans w. corn Energy 79kcal/331kJ; Protein 2.9g; Carbohydrate 9.3g, of which sugars 3.7g; Fat 3.7g, of which saturates 0.5g; Cholesterol 0mg; Calcium 58mg; Fibre 2.7g; Sodium 88mg.
vegetables & beans Energy 86kcal/358kJ; Protein 3.3g; Carbohydrate 10.6g, of which sugars 4.9g; Fat 3.7g, of which saturates 0.5g; Cholesterol 0mg; Calcium 38mg; Fibre 3.1g; Sodium 118mg.

Kidney Bean Curry

This is a popular Punjabi-style dish using red kidney beans. You can replace the dried beans with a 400g/14oz can if you prefer. Other pulses also work well in this dish.

Serves 4

225g/8oz/scant 1 cup dried red kidney beans
30ml/2 tbsp oil
2.5ml/½ tsp cumin seeds
1 onion, thinly sliced
1 fresh green chilli, finely chopped
2 garlic cloves, crushed
2.5cm/1in piece fresh root ginger, grated
30ml/2 tbsp curry paste
5ml/1 tsp ground cumin
5ml/1 tsp ground coriander
2.5ml/½ tsp chilli powder
2.5ml/½ tsp salt
400g/14oz can chopped tomatoes
30ml/2 tbsp chopped fresh coriander (cilantro)

1 Leave the kidney beans to soak overnight in a bowl of cold water.

2 Drain the beans and put in a large pan with double the volume of water. Boil vigorously for 10 minutes. Skim off any scum. Cover and cook for 1–1½ hours or until the beans are soft. If you want to reduce the cooking time, cook the beans in a pressure cooker for 20–25 minutes.

3 Meanwhile, heat the oil in a large, heavy frying pan and fry the cumin seeds for 2 minutes until they begin to splutter. Add the onion, chilli, garlic and ginger, and fry for 5 minutes.

4 Stir in the curry paste, cumin, ground coriander, chilli powder and salt, and stir-fry for a further 5 minutes.

5 Add the tomatoes and simmer for 5 minutes. Drain the beans and stir them in with the fresh coriander, reserving a little of the herb for the garnish. Cover and cook for 15 minutes, adding a little water if necessary. Serve garnished with the reserved fresh coriander.

Mung Beans with Potatoes

Small mung beans are one of the quicker-cooking pulses. They do not require soaking and are easy and convenient to use. In this recipe they are cooked with potatoes and Indian spices to give a tasty and nutritious dish.

Serves 4

175g/6oz/1 cup mung beans
750ml/1¼ pints/3 cups water
225g/8oz potatoes, cut into 2cm/¾in chunks
30ml/2 tbsp oil
2.5ml/½ tsp cumin seeds
1 fresh green chilli, finely chopped
1 garlic clove, crushed
2.5cm/1in piece fresh root ginger, finely chopped
1.5ml/¼ tsp ground turmeric
2.5ml/½ tsp chilli powder
5ml/1 tsp salt
5ml/1 tsp sugar
4 curry leaves
5 tomatoes, peeled and finely chopped
15ml/1 tbsp tomato purée (paste)
curry leaves, to garnish
boiled rice, to serve

1 Wash the beans. Pour the water into a pan, add the beans and bring to the boil. Boil for 15 minutes, then reduce the heat, cover the pan and simmer until soft, about 30 minutes cooking time. Drain.

2 In a separate pan, par-boil the potatoes in boiling water for 10 minutes, then drain well.

3 Heat the oil in a heavy pan and fry the cumin seeds until they splutter. Add the chilli, garlic and ginger, and fry for 3–4 minutes.

4 Add the turmeric, chilli powder, salt and sugar, and cook for 2 minutes, stirring to prevent the mixture from sticking to the pan.

5 Add the four curry leaves, chopped tomatoes and tomato purée, and simmer for about 5 minutes until the sauce thickens. Mix the tomato sauce and the potatoes with the mung beans and heat through. Garnish with the extra curry leaves and serve immediately.

kidney bean curry Energy 156kcal/653kJ; Protein 6.4g; Carbohydrate 17g, of which sugars 5.4g; Fat 7.6g, of which saturates 1g; Cholesterol 0mg; Calcium 90mg; Fibre 5.1g; Sodium 236mg.
mung beans Energy 265kcal/1118kJ; Protein 13.8g; Carbohydrate 37.4g, of which sugars 5.7g; Fat 7.9g, of which saturates 1.1g; Cholesterol 0mg; Calcium 58mg; Fibre 5.8g; Sodium 34mg.

Masala Beans with Fenugreek

The term masala refers to the blending of several spices to achieve a distinctive taste, with different spice-combinations being used to complement specific ingredients. Households will traditionally create their own blends, and many are unique.

Serves 4

1 onion
5ml/1 tsp ground cumin
5ml/1 tsp ground coriander
5ml/1 tsp sesame seeds
5ml/1 tsp chilli powder
2.5ml/½ tsp crushed garlic
1.5ml/¼ tsp ground turmeric
5ml/1 tsp salt
30ml/2 tbsp vegetable oil
1 tomato, quartered
225g/8oz/1½ cups green beans, blanched
1 bunch fresh fenugreek leaves, stems discarded
60ml/4 tbsp chopped fresh coriander (cilantro)
15ml/1 tbsp lemon juice

1 Roughly chop the onion. Mix together the cumin and coriander, sesame seeds, chilli powder, garlic, turmeric and salt.

2 Put the chopped onion and spice mixture into a food processor or blender, and process for 30–45 seconds until you have a rough paste.

3 In a karahi, wok or large pan, heat the oil over a medium heat and fry the spice paste for about 5 minutes, stirring the mixture occasionally.

4 Add the tomato quarters, blanched green beans, fresh fenugreek and chopped coriander.

5 Stir-fry the contents of the pan for about 5 minutes, then sprinkle in the lemon juice and serve.

Variation
Instead of fresh fenugreek, you can also use 15ml/1 tbsp dried fenugreek for this recipe. Dried fenugreek is readily available from Indian stores and markets.

Green Beans Tempura

This dish is distinguished by the green beans, which are coated in a light tempura batter. This cooking technique is thought to have been taken to Japan by Portuguese sailors in the early days of exploration. It is now a widely embraced method of cooking vegetables throughout Asia.

Serves 4

400g/14oz green beans
100g/3¾oz/scant 1 cup plain (all-purpose) flour
1 egg
vegetable oil, for deep-frying
salt

1 Trim the beans and blanch them in a large pan of boiling water for 1 minute. Drain and refresh in iced water, then drain again well.

2 Sift the flour into a bowl and stir in enough cold water to make a medium paste. Add the egg and beat well, then season with salt.

3 Heat the oil in a large pan or deep-fryer to 170°C/340°F or until a cube of day-old bread browns in 40 seconds. Dip the beans in the batter to coat, add to the hot oil and deep-fry until crisp and golden brown. Drain on kitchen paper and serve immediately.

Variation
You can prepare other vegetables in exactly the same way. Try mushrooms, baby corn cobs, red (bell) pepper strips or carrots cut into thin batons.

Cook's Tip
A deep wok is ideal for deep frying but be careful and have a damp cloth or lid on standby in case it starts to flame.

masala beans Energy 70kcal/289kJ; Protein 1.6g; Carbohydrate 2.7g, of which sugars 2.1g; Fat 6g, of which saturates 0.7g; Cholesterol 0mg; Calcium 47mg; Fibre 2g; Sodium 6mg.
green beans tempura Energy 227kcal/945kJ; Protein 5.8g; Carbohydrate 22.6g, of which sugars 2.7g; Fat 13.2g, of which saturates 1.8g; Cholesterol 48mg; Calcium 78mg; Fibre 3g; Sodium 18mg.

Tofu Stir-fry

The use of tofu in this recipe creates a pleasant creamy texture, which contrasts delightfully with the crunchy stir-fried vegetables. Make sure you buy firm tofu which is easy to cut neatly.

Serves 2–4

115g/4oz hard white cabbage
2 green chillies
225g/8oz firm tofu
45ml/3 tbsp vegetable oil
2 garlic cloves, crushed
3 spring onions (scallions), chopped
175g/6oz green beans, topped and tailed
175g/6oz baby corn, halved
115g/4oz beansprouts
45ml/3 tbsp smooth peanut butter
25ml/1½ tbsp dark soy sauce
300ml/½ pint/1¼ cups coconut milk

1 Shred the white cabbage. Carefully remove the seeds from the chillies and chop them finely. Wear rubber gloves to protect your hands, if necessary.

2 Cut the tofu into strips.

3 Heat a wok, then add 30ml/2 tbsp of the oil. When the oil is hot, add the tofu, stir-fry for 3 minutes, then remove it and set it aside. Wipe out the wok with kitchen paper.

4 Add the remaining oil. When it is hot, add the garlic, spring onions and chillies and stir-fry for 1 minute. Add the green beans, corn and beansprouts and stir-fry for a further 2 minutes.

5 Add the peanut butter and soy sauce to the wok. Stir well to coat the vegetables. Add the tofu to the vegetables in the wok.

6 Pour the coconut milk over the vegetables, simmer for 3 minutes and serve hot.

Madras Sambal

There are many variations of this popular dish but it is regularly cooked in one form or another in almost every south Indian home. You can use any combination of vegetables that are in season.

Serves 4

225g/8oz/1 cup tuvar dhal or red split lentils
600ml/1 pint/2½ cups water
2.5ml/½ tsp ground turmeric
2 large potatoes, cut into 2.5cm/1in chunks
30ml/2 tbsp vegetable oil
2.5ml/½ tsp black mustard seeds
1.5ml/¼ tsp fenugreek seeds
4 curry leaves
1 onion, thinly sliced
115g/4oz green beans, cut into 2.5cm/1in lengths
5ml/1 tsp salt
2.5ml/½ tsp chilli powder
15ml/1 tbsp lemon juice
toasted coconut, to garnish
Fresh Coriander Relish, to serve (see p444)

1 Wash the tuvar dhal or lentils in several changes of water. Place in a heavy pan with the measured water and the turmeric. Bring to the boil, then reduce the heat, cover the pan and simmer for 30–35 minutes until the lentils are soft.

2 Par-cook the potatoes in a large pan of boiling water for 10 minutes. Drain well and set aside.

3 Heat the oil in a large frying pan and fry the mustard and fenugreek seeds and the curry leaves for 2–3 minutes until the seeds begin to splutter. Add the sliced onion and the green beans and stir-fry for 7–8 minutes. Add the par-boiled potatoes and cook for a further 2 minutes.

4 Drain the lentils. Stir them into the potato mixture with the salt, chilli powder and lemon juice. Simmer for 2 minutes or until heated through. Garnish with toasted coconut and serve with freshly made coriander relish.

tofu stir-fry Energy 242kcal/1004kJ; Protein 11g; Carbohydrate 11.2g, of which sugars 8.9g; Fat 17.3g, of which saturates 2.9g; Cholesterol 0mg; Calcium 356mg; Fibre 3.4g; Sodium 1072mg.
madras sambal Energy 401kcal/1687kJ; Protein 16.7g; Carbohydrate 50.8g, of which sugars 5.1g; Fat 16g, of which saturates 8.9g; Cholesterol 0mg; Calcium 52mg; Fibre 6.7g; Sodium 36mg.

Sambal Nanas

Side dishes are known as sambals in Indonesia and Malaysia, and can be paste-like mixtures used as flavourings or finely chopped or sliced cold vegetables or fruits. Here sweet pineapple and cucumber are dressed with a savoury sauce.

Serves 8–10

1 small or ½ large fresh ripe pineapple
½ cucumber, halved lengthways
50g/2oz dried shrimps
1 large fresh red chilli, seeded
1cm/½in cube shrimp paste, prepared (see Cook's Tip)
juice of 1 large lemon or lime
soft light brown sugar, to taste (optional)
salt

1 Cut off both ends of the pineapple. Stand it upright on a board, then slice off the skin from top to bottom, cutting out the spines. Remove the central core. Cut the pineapple into thin slices and set aside.

2 Trim the ends from the cucumber and slice thinly. Sprinkle with salt and set aside. Place the dried shrimps in a food processor and chop fairly finely. Add the chilli, prepared shrimp paste and lemon or lime juice and process again to a paste.

3 Rinse the cucumber, drain and dry on kitchen paper. Mix with the pineapple and chill. Just before serving, spoon in the spice mixture with sugar to taste. Mix well and serve.

Cook's Tip

The pungent shrimp paste, also called blachan, is popular in many South-east Asian countries, and is available in Asian supermarkets. Because it can taste a bit raw in a sambal, dry-fry it before use by wrapping in foil and heating in a frying pan over a low heat for 5 minutes, turning from time to time. If the shrimp paste is to be fried with other spices, this preliminary cooking can be left out.

Balti Baby Vegetables

There is a wide and wonderful selection of baby vegetables available in supermarkets these days, and this simple recipe does full justice to their delicate flavour and attractive appearance. Serve as part of a main meal or even as a light appetizer.

Serves 4–6

10 new potatoes, halved
12–14 baby carrots
12–14 baby courgettes (zucchini)
30ml/2 tbsp corn oil
15 baby onions
30ml/2 tbsp chilli sauce
5ml/1 tsp crushed garlic
5ml/1 tsp grated fresh root ginger
5ml/1 tsp salt
400g/14oz/scant 3 cups drained canned chickpeas
10 cherry tomatoes
5ml/1 tsp crushed dried red chillies
30ml/2 tbsp sesame seeds

1 Bring a medium pan of salted water to the boil and add the new potatoes and baby carrots. Cook for 12–15 minutes, then add the courgettes, and boil for a further 5 minutes or until all the vegetables are just tender. Take care not to overcook the vegetables, as they will be given a brief additional cooking time later.

2 Drain the vegetables well and put them in a bowl. Set aside.

3 Heat the oil in a karahi, wok or deep pan and add the baby onions. Fry until the onions turn golden brown. Lower the heat and add the chilli sauce, garlic, ginger and salt, taking care not to burn the mixture.

4 Stir in the chickpeas and stir-fry over a medium heat until the moisture has evaporated.

5 Add the cooked vegetables and cherry tomatoes, and stir over the heat with a slotted spoon for about 2 minutes.

6 Sprinkle the crushed red chillies and sesame seeds evenly over the vegetable mixture and serve.

sambal nanas Energy 48kcal/203kJ; Protein 3.2g; Carbohydrate 8.6g, of which sugars 8.5g; Fat 0.3g, of which saturates 0g; Cholesterol 25mg; Calcium 77mg; Fibre 1.1g; Sodium 219mg.
balti baby vegetables Energy 221kcal/929kJ; Protein 9g; Carbohydrate 32.5g, of which sugars 11g; Fat 7.1g, of which saturates 0.9g; Cholesterol 0mg; Calcium 90mg; Fibre 6.5g; Sodium 174mg.

Vegetables with Almonds

Yogurt gives this dish a tangy flavour and also makes it creamy.

Serves 4

30ml/2 tbsp vegetable oil
2 medium onions, sliced
5cm/2in piece fresh root ginger, shredded
5ml/1 tsp crushed black peppercorns
1 bay leaf
1.5ml/¼ tsp ground turmeric
5ml/1 tsp ground coriander
5ml/1 tsp salt
2.5ml/½ tsp garam masala
175g/6oz/2½ cups mushrooms, thickly sliced
1 medium courgette (zucchini), thickly sliced
50g/2oz green beans, cut into 2.5cm/1in lengths
15ml/1 tbsp roughly chopped fresh mint
150ml/¼ pint/⅔ cup water
30ml/2 tbsp natural (plain) low-fat yogurt
25g/1oz/¼ cup flaked (sliced) almonds

1 Heat the oil in a heavy pan, and fry the onions, ginger, peppercorns and bay leaf for 3–5 minutes.

2 Lower the heat and stir in the turmeric, coriander, salt and garam masala. Gradually add the sliced mushrooms, courgette, green beans and mint. Stir gently to coat the vegetables, being careful not to break them up.

3 Pour in the water and bring to a simmer, then lower the heat and cook until the water has evaporated.

4 Beat the yogurt lightly with a fork, then pour it on to the vegetables in the pan and mix together well until the vegetables are coated.

5 Cook the vegetables for a further 2–3 minutes, stirring occasionally, until they are just tender. Spoon into a large serving dish or on to individual plates. Serve immediately, garnished with the flaked almonds.

Spring Vegetable Stir-fry

A colourful, dazzling medley of fresh and sweet young vegetables.

Serves 4

15ml/1 tbsp groundnut (peanut) oil
1 garlic clove, sliced
2.5cm/1in piece fresh root ginger, finely chopped
115g/4oz baby carrots
115g/4oz patty pan squash
115g/4oz baby corn
115g/4oz green beans, trimmed
115g/4oz sugar snap peas, trimmed
115g/4oz young asparagus, cut into 7.5cm/3in pieces
8 spring onions (scallions), trimmed and cut into 5cm/2in pieces
115g/4oz cherry tomatoes

For the dressing

juice of 2 limes
15ml/1 tbsp clear honey
15ml/1 tbsp soy sauce
5ml/1 tsp sesame oil

1 Heat the groundnut oil in a wok or large frying pan.

2 Add the garlic and root ginger, and stir-fry over high heat for 1 minute.

3 Add the carrots, patty pan squash, baby corn and beans, and stir-fry for another 3–4 minutes.

4 Add the sugar snap peas, asparagus, spring onions and cherry tomatoes and stir-fry for a further 1–2 minutes.

5 Mix the dressing ingredients together and add to the pan.

6 Stir well and then cover the pan. Cook for 2–3 minutes more, until the vegetables are just tender but still crisp.

Cook's Tip
Stir-fries take very little time to cook, so prepare this dish at the last minute.

vegetables w. almonds Energy 182kcal/754kJ; Protein 6.7g; Carbohydrate 14.7g, of which sugars 7.7g; Fat 11.4g, of which saturates 1.3g; Cholesterol 0mg; Calcium 97mg; Fibre 3.1g; Sodium 17mg.
vegetable stir-fry Energy 134kcal/554kJ; Protein 7.8g; Carbohydrate 9.4g, of which sugars 8.6g; Fat 7.4g, of which saturates 1.1g; Cholesterol 0mg; Calcium 195mg; Fibre 6.2g; Sodium 566mg.

Stuffed Bananas

Bananas are cooked with spices in many different ways in southern India. Some recipes contain large quantities of chillies, but the taste is skilfully mellowed by adding coconut milk and tamarind juice. Green bananas are available from Indian stores, or you can use plantains or unripe eating bananas that are firm to the touch.

Serves 4

1 bunch fresh coriander (cilantro)
4 green bananas or 2 plantains
30ml/2 tbsp ground coriander
15ml/1 tbsp ground cumin
5ml/1 tsp chilli powder
2.5ml/½ tsp salt
1.5ml/¼ tsp ground turmeric
5ml/1 tsp sugar
15ml/1 tbsp gram flour
90ml/6 tbsp vegetable oil
1.5ml/¼ tsp cumin seeds
1.5ml/¼ tsp black mustard seeds

1 Set aside two or three coriander sprigs for the garnish. If necessary, remove the roots and any thick stems from the remaining coriander, then chop the leaves finely.

2 Trim the bananas or plantains and cut each crossways into three equal pieces, leaving the skin on. Make a lengthwise slit along each piece of banana, without cutting all the way through the flesh.

3 On a plate mix together the ground coriander, cumin, chilli powder, salt, turmeric, sugar, gram flour, chopped fresh coriander and 15ml/1 tbsp of the oil. Combine well to form a paste.

4 Carefully stuff each piece of banana with the spice mixture, taking care not to break the bananas in half.

5 Heat the remaining oil in a wok, karahi or large pan, and fry the cumin and mustard seeds for 2 minutes or until they begin to splutter. Add the bananas and toss gently in the oil.

6 Cover and simmer over a low heat for 15 minutes, stirring from time to time, until the bananas are soft but not mushy. Garnish with the fresh coriander sprigs, and serve immediately.

Steamed Vegetables with Spicy Dip

In Thailand, steamed vegetables are often partnered with raw ones to create the contrasting textures that are such a feature of the national cuisine. Fortunately, it is also an extremely healthy way to serve them.

Serves 4

1 head broccoli, divided into florets
130g/4½oz/1 cup green beans, trimmed
130g/4½oz asparagus, trimmed
½ head cauliflower, divided into florets
8 baby corn cobs
130g/4½oz mangetouts (snow peas) or sugar snap peas
salt

For the dip

1 fresh green chilli, seeded
4 garlic cloves, peeled
4 shallots, peeled
2 tomatoes, halved
5 pea aubergines (baby eggplants)
30ml/2 tbsp lemon juice
30ml/2 tbsp soy sauce
2.5ml/½ tsp salt
5ml/1 tsp sugar

1 Place the broccoli, green beans, asparagus and cauliflower in a steamer and steam over boiling water for about 4 minutes, until just tender but still with a 'bite'. Transfer to a bowl and add the baby corn and mangetouts or sugar snap peas. Season to taste with a little salt. Toss to mix, then set aside.

2 To make the dip, preheat the grill (broiler). Wrap the chilli, garlic cloves, shallots, tomatoes and aubergines in a foil package. Grill (broil) for 10 minutes, until the vegetables have softened, turning the package over once or twice.

3 Unwrap the foil and place its contents in a mortar or food processor. Add the lemon juice, soy sauce, salt and sugar. Pound with a pestle or process to a fairly liquid paste.

4 Scrape the spicy dip into a serving bowl or four individual bowls. Serve immediately, surrounded by the steamed and raw vegetables.

stuffed bananas Energy 256kcal/1067kJ; Protein 1.6g; Carbohydrate 26.1g, of which sugars 21g; Fat 16.8g, of which saturates 2g; Cholesterol 0mg; Calcium 11mg; Fibre 1.2g; Sodium 1mg.
steamed vegetables Energy 108kcal/454kJ; Protein 11.5g; Carbohydrate 10.7g, of which sugars 9.2g; Fat 2.3g, of which saturates 0.5g; Cholesterol 0mg; Calcium 119mg; Fibre 7.6g; Sodium 590mg.

Stir-fried Pineapple with Ginger

This dish makes an interesting accompaniment to grilled meat or strongly flavoured fish such as tuna or swordfish. If the idea seems strange, think of it as resembling a fresh mango chutney, but with pineapple as the principal ingredient.

Serves 4

1 pineapple
15ml/1 tbsp vegetable oil
2 garlic cloves, finely chopped
2 shallots, finely chopped
5cm/2in piece fresh root ginger, peeled and finely shredded
30ml/2 tbsp light soy sauce
juice of ½ lime
1 large fresh red chilli, seeded and finely shredded

1 Trim and peel the pineapple. Cut out the core and dice the flesh into small pieces.

2 Heat the oil in a wok or frying pan. Stir-fry the garlic and shallots over a medium heat for 2–3 minutes, until golden. Do not let the garlic burn or the dish will taste bitter.

3 Add the pineapple. Stir-fry for about 2 minutes, or until the pineapple cubes start to turn golden on the edges.

4 Add the ginger, soy sauce, lime juice and shredded chilli.

5 Toss the mixture together until well mixed. Cook over a low heat for a further 2 minutes. Serve the pineapple as an accompaniment.

Variation

This also tastes excellent if peaches or nectarines are substituted for the diced pineapple. Use three or four, depending on their size.

Chilli & Mustard-flavoured Pineapple

Pineapple is cooked with coconut milk and a blend of spices in this dish, which could be served with any meat, fish or vegetable curry. The chilli adds heat, and the mustard seeds lend a rich, nutty flavour that complements the sharpness of the pineapple, while the coconut milk provides a creamy sweetness.

Serves 4

1 pineapple
50ml/2fl oz/¼ cup water
150ml/¼ pint/⅔ cup coconut milk
2.5ml/½ tsp ground turmeric
2.5ml/½ tsp crushed dried chillies
5ml/1 tsp salt
10ml/2 tsp sugar
15ml/1 tbsp groundnut (peanut) oil
2.5ml/½ tsp mustard seeds
2.5ml/½ tsp cumin seeds
1 small onion, finely chopped
1 or 2 dried red chillies, broken
6–8 fresh curry leaves

1 Using a sharp knife, halve the pineapple lengthways, then cut each half lengthways into two, so that you end up with four boat-shaped wedges. Peel them and remove the eyes and the central core. Cut into bitesize pieces.

2 Put the pineapple in a karahi, wok or large pan and add the measured water, with the coconut milk, turmeric and crushed chillies. Bring to a slow simmer over low heat, and cook, covered, for 10–12 minutes, or until the pineapple is soft but not mushy. Add the salt and sugar, and cook, uncovered, until the sauce thickens.

3 Heat the oil in a second pan, and add the mustard seeds. As soon as they begin to pop, add the cumin seeds and the onion. Fry for 6–7 minutes, stirring regularly, until the onion is soft.

4 Add the chillies and curry leaves. Fry for 1–2 minutes more, then pour the mixture over the pineapple. Stir well, then remove from the heat. Serve hot or at room temperature.

pineapple w. ginger Energy 115kcal/490kJ; Protein 1.2g; Carbohydrate 22g, of which sugars 21.6g; Fat 3.2g, of which saturates 0.3g; Cholesterol 0mg; Calcium 41mg; Fibre 2.6g; Sodium 539mg.
chilli pineapple Energy 138kcal/584kJ; Protein 1.5g; Carbohydrate 26.7g, of which sugars 25.5g; Fat 3.6g, of which saturates 0.5g; Cholesterol 0mg; Calcium 57mg; Fibre 2.6g; Sodium 47mg.

Stir-fried Chinese Leaves

This simple way of cooking Chinese leaves preserves their delicate flavour and is very quick to prepare.

Serves 4

675g/1½lb Chinese leaves (Chinese cabbage)
15ml/1 tbsp vegetable oil
2 garlic cloves, finely chopped
2.5 ml/1in piece of fresh root ginger, finely chopped
2.5ml/½ tsp salt
15ml/1 tbsp oyster sauce
4 spring onions (scallions), cut into 2.5cm/1in lengths

1 Stack the Chinese leaves together and cut them into 2.5cm/1in slices.

2 Heat the oil in a wok or large deep pan. Stir-fry the garlic and ginger for 1 minute.

3 Add the Chinese leaves to the wok or pan and stir-fry for 2 minutes. Sprinkle the salt over and drizzle with the oyster sauce. Toss the leaves over the heat for 2 minutes more.

4 Stir in the spring onions. Toss the mixture well, transfer it to a heated serving plate and serve.

Variation
Use the same treatment for shredded cabbage and leeks. If you want to cut down on preparation time, you can often find this combination of vegetables, ready-prepared, in bags at the supermarket.

Cook's Tip
For guests who are vegetarian, substitute 15 ml/1 tbsp light soy sauce and 5ml/1 tsp of caster (superfine) sugar for the oyster sauce. This rule can be applied to many dishes.

Stir-fried Beansprouts

This fresh and crunchy vegetable, which is synonymous with Chinese restaurants, tastes even better when stir-fried at home.

Serves 4

15ml/1 tbsp vegetable oil
1 garlic clove, finely chopped
5ml/1 tsp grated fresh root ginger
1 small carrot, cut into matchsticks
50g/2oz/½ cup canned bamboo shoots, drained and cut into matchsticks
450g/1lb/2 cups beansprouts
2.5ml/½ tsp salt
large pinch of ground white pepper
15ml/1 tbsp Chinese rice wine or dry sherry
15ml/1 tbsp light soy sauce
2.5ml/½ tsp sesame oil

1 Heat the vegetable oil in a non-stick frying pan or wok. Add the chopped garlic and grated ginger and stir-fry for a few minutes, over a high heat.

2 Add the carrot and bamboo shoot matchsticks to the pan or wok and stir-fry for a few minutes.

3 Add the beansprouts to the pan or wok with the salt and pepper. Drizzle over the rice wine or sherry and toss the beansprouts over the heat for 3 minutes until hot.

4 Sprinkle over the soy sauce and sesame oil, toss to mix thoroughly, then spoon into a bowl and serve immediately.

Variation
Add a handful of flaked (sliced) almond, toasted until golden.

Cook's Tip
Beansprouts keep best when stored in the refrigerator or other cool place in a bowl of cold water, but you must remember to change the water daily.

stir-fried Chinese leaves Energy 77kcal/321kJ; Protein 2.6g; Carbohydrate 9.8g, of which sugars 9.6g; Fat 3.2g, of which saturates 0.3g; Cholesterol 0mg; Calcium 87mg; Fibre 3.7g; Sodium 74mg.
stir-fried beansprouts Energy 76kcal/318kJ; Protein 3.9g; Carbohydrate 6.9g, of which sugars 4.5g; Fat 3.4g, of which saturates 0.5g; Cholesterol 0mg; Calcium 31mg; Fibre 2.3g; Sodium 278mg.

Spinach with Spicy Chickpeas

This richly flavoured dish makes an excellent accompaniment to a dry curry, or with a rice-based stir-fry. It is particularly good served drizzled with a little plain yogurt – the sharp, creamy flavour complements the complex spices perfectly.

Serves 4

200g/7oz dried chickpeas
30ml/2 tbsp sunflower oil
2 onions, halved and thinly sliced
10ml/2 tsp ground coriander
10ml/2 tsp ground cumin
5ml/1 tsp hot chilli powder
2.5ml/½ tsp ground turmeric
15ml/1 tbsp medium curry powder
400g/14oz can chopped tomatoes
5ml/1 tsp caster (superfine) sugar
salt and ground black pepper
30ml/2 tbsp chopped mint leaves
115g/4oz baby leaf spinach

1 Soak the chickpeas in cold water overnight. Drain, rinse and place in a large pan. Cover with water and bring to the boil. Reduce the heat and simmer for 45 minutes to 1¼ hours, or until just tender. Drain and set aside.

2 Heat the oil in a wok, add the onions and cook over a low heat for 15 minutes, until lightly golden.

3 Add the ground coriander and cumin, chilli powder, turmeric and curry powder to the onions in the wok and stir-fry for 1–2 minutes.

4 Add the tomatoes, sugar and 105ml/7 tbsp water to the wok and bring to the boil. Cover, reduce the heat and simmer gently for 15 minutes, stirring occasionally.

5 Add the chickpeas to the wok, season well and cook gently for 8–10 minutes. Stir in the chopped mint.

6 Divide the spinach leaves between shallow bowls, top with the chickpea mixture and serve immediately.

Chinese Leaves in Coconut Milk

The idea of cooking Chinese leaves in coconut milk comes from Melaka and Johor, where the culinary culture is influenced by the Chinese, Malay and Peranakans. With good agricultural ground, there is an abundance of vegetables which, in this part of Malaysia, are often cooked in coconut milk. For this dish, you could use green beans, curly kale, or any type of cabbage, all of which are delicious served with steamed, braised or grilled fish dishes.

Serves 4

4 shallots, chopped
2 garlic cloves, chopped
1 lemon grass stalk, trimmed and chopped
25g/1oz fresh root ginger, peeled and chopped
2 red chillies, seeded and chopped
5ml/1 tsp shrimp paste
5ml/1 tsp turmeric powder
5ml/1 tsp palm sugar (jaggery)
15ml/1 tbsp sesame or groundnut (peanut) oil
400ml/14fl oz/1⅔ cups coconut milk
450g/1lb Chinese leaves (Chinese cabbage) or kale, cut into thick ribbons, or pak choi (bok choy), separated into leaves, or a mixture of the two
salt and ground black pepper

1 Using a mortar and pestle or food processor, grind the shallots, garlic, lemon grass, ginger and chillies to a paste. Scrape into a bowl and add the shrimp paste, turmeric and sugar. Beat well to combine the ingredients.

2 Heat the oil in a wok or heavy pan, and stir in the spice paste. Cook until fragrant and beginning to colour.

3 Pour in the coconut milk, mix well, and let it bubble it up to thicken.

4 Drop in the Chinese leaves or other greens, coating them in the coconut milk, and cook for a minute or two until wilted. Season with salt and pepper to taste, spoon into a warmed serving dish and serve immediately.

spinach w. chickpeas Energy 267kcal/1122kJ; Protein 13.3g; Carbohydrate 35.5g, of which sugars 10.2g; Fat 9g, of which saturates 1.1g; Cholesterol 0mg; Calcium 170mg; Fibre 8.2g; Sodium 83mg.
cabbage & coconut milk Energy 112kcal/469kJ; Protein 2.1g; Carbohydrate 13g, of which sugars 12.6g; Fat 6.1g, of which saturates 1g; Cholesterol 0mg; Calcium 89mg; Fibre 2.6g; Sodium 119mg.

Water Spinach with Nuoc Cham

Nuoc cham is a Vietnamese chilli, garlic and fish sauce.

Serves 3–4

30ml/2 tbsp groundnut (peanut) oil
2 garlic cloves, finely chopped
2 red or green Thai chillies, seeded and finely chopped
500g/1¼lb fresh water spinach
45ml/3tbsp nuoc cham
salt and ground black pepper

1 Heat the oil in a wok and stir in the garlic and chillies. Stir-fry for 1 minute, then add the spinach and toss around in the wok.

2 Once the leaves have wilted a little, add the nuoc cham and ensure all the leaves are coated. Season to taste and serve.

Chinese Vegetable Stir-fry

This is a typical vegetable dish popular all over China.

Serves 4

45ml/3 tbsp sunflower oil
15ml/1 tbsp sesame oil
1 garlic clove, chopped
225g/8oz broccoli florets, cut into small pieces
115g/4oz sugar snap peas
1 head Chinese leaves (Chinese cabbage), about 450g/1lb, or Savoy cabbage, sliced
4 spring onions (scallions), finely chopped
30ml/2 tbsp soy sauce
30ml/2 tbsp Chinese rice wine or dry sherry
30–45ml/2–3 tbsp water
15ml/1 tbsp sesame seeds, lightly toasted

1 Heat the oils in a preheated wok; add the garlic and stir-fry for 30 seconds. Add the broccoli florets and stir-fry for 3 minutes. Add the sugar snap peas and cook for 2 minutes.

2 Toss in the Chinese leaves or cabbage and the spring onions and stir-fry for a further 2 minutes. Pour on the soy sauce, rice wine or dry sherry and water and stir-fry for a further 4 minutes, or until the vegetables are just tender. Sprinkle with the toasted sesame seeds and serve hot.

Chinese Crispy Seaweed

In northern China, a special kind of seaweed is used for this dish, but spring greens make a very successful alternative. Serve as part of a Chinese spread.

Serves 4

225g/8oz spring greens (collards)
groundnut (peanut) or sunflower oil, for deep-frying
1.5ml/¼ tsp salt
10ml/2 tsp soft light brown sugar
30ml/2 tbsp toasted, flaked (sliced) almonds

1 Cut out and discard any tough stalks from the spring greens. Place about six leaves on top of each other, then roll them up into a tight roll.

2 Using a sharp knife, slice across into thin shreds. Lay on a tray and leave to dry for about 2 hours.

3 Heat about 5–7.5cm/2–3in of oil in a wok or pan to 190°C/375°F. Carefully place a handful of the leaves into the oil – it will bubble and spit for the first 10 seconds and then die down. Deep-fry for about 45 seconds, or until a slightly darker green: do not let the leaves burn.

4 Remove with a slotted spoon, drain on kitchen paper and transfer to a serving dish. Keep warm in the oven while frying the remainder.

5 When you have fried all the shredded leaves, sprinkle with the salt and sugar and toss lightly. Garnish with the toasted almonds and serve immediately.

Cook's Tips

- *Make sure that your deep-frying pan is deep enough to allow the oil to bubble up during cooking. The pan should be less than half full.*
- *Test the oil is hot enough by dropping in a cube of day-old bread. It should start to sizzle and turn golden immediately.*

water spinach Energy 120kcal/500kJ; Protein 3g; Carbohydrate 5g, of which sugars 3g; Fat 10g, of which saturates 2g; Cholesterol 0mg; Calcium 36mg; Fibre 3.3g; Sodium 200mg.
Chinese vegetable stir-fry Energy 161kcal/668kJ; Protein 6.5g; Carbohydrate 10.9g, of which sugars 8g; Fat 9.5g, of which saturates 1.2g; Cholesterol 0mg; Calcium 98mg; Fibre 5.3g; Sodium 548mg.
crispy seaweed Energy 171kcal/707kJ; Protein 3.3g; Carbohydrate 4.4g, of which sugars 3.9g; Fat 15.7g, of which saturates 1.7g; Cholesterol 0mg; Calcium 137mg; Fibre 2.5g; Sodium 13mg.

Asian-style Courgette Fritters

This is an excellent cultural fusion: a twist on Japanese tempura, using Indian spices and gram flour in the batter. Also known as besan, gram flour is more commonly used in Indian cooking and gives a wonderfully crisp texture, while the courgette baton inside becomes meltingly tender. If you're feeling adventurous, vary the vegetable content by dipping some thinly sliced squash or pumpkin batons with the courgettes. This is an ideal treat for kids.

Serves 4

90g/3½oz/¾ cup gram flour
5ml/1 tsp baking powder
2.5ml/½ tsp ground turmeric
10ml/2 tsp ground coriander
5ml/1 tsp ground cumin
5ml/1 tsp chilli powder
250ml/8fl oz/1 cup beer
600g/1lb 6oz courgettes (zucchini), cut into batons
sunflower oil, for deep-frying
salt

1 Sift the gram flour, baking powder, turmeric, coriander, cumin and chilli powder into a large bowl. Stir lightly to mix through.

2 Season the mixture with salt and make a hollow in the centre. Pour in a little of the beer, and gradually mix in the surrounding dry ingredients. Add more beer, continuing to mix gently, to make a thick batter. Be careful not to overmix.

3 Fill a large wok one-third full with sunflower oil and heat to 180°C/350°F, or until a cube of bread, dropped into the oil, browns in 45 seconds.

4 Working in batches, dip the courgette batons in the spiced batter and then deep-fry for 1–2 minutes, or until crisp and golden. Lift out of the wok using a slotted spoon. Drain on kitchen paper and keep warm while frying the remaining batches.

5 Serve the courgette fritters on heated plates, or on banana leaves if these are available.

Morning Glory with Fried Shallots

This recipe isn't a novel way of using the pretty creeper that twines along your fence, but rather relates to its Asian cousin. This leafy annual vine requires a good deal of moisture to grow and favours boggy ground, hence the synonym 'swamp cabbage'. It is widely cultivated in China and South-east Asia.

Serves 4

2 bunches morning glory, total weight about 250g/9oz, trimmed and coarsely chopped into 2.5cm/1in lengths
30ml/2 tbsp vegetable oil
4 shallots, thinly sliced
6 large garlic cloves, thinly sliced
sea salt
1.5ml/¼ tsp dried chilli flakes

1 Place the morning glory in a steamer and steam over a pan of boiling water for 30 seconds, until just wilted. If necessary, cook it in batches. Place the leaves in a bowl or spread them out on a large serving plate.

2 Heat the oil in a wok and stir-fry the shallots and garlic over a medium to high heat until golden. Spoon the mixture over the morning glory, sprinkle with a little sea salt and the chilli flakes and serve immediately.

Cook's Tip

Other names for morning glory include water spinach, water convolvulus and swamp cabbage. It is a green leafy vegetable with long jointed stems and arrow-shaped leaves. The stems remain crunchy while the leaves wilt like spinach when cooked. It is a staple stir-fry ingredient of many South-east Asian cultures, and works best when prepared simply, as here.

Variation

Use spinach instead of morning glory, or substitute young spring greens (collards), sprouting broccoli or Swiss chard. The texture may be tougher, so blanch leaves before using, if necessary.

Asian-style fritters Energy 241kcal/999kJ; Protein 7.3g; Carbohydrate 15.3g, of which sugars 4.6g; Fat 15.6g, of which saturates 1.9g; Cholesterol 0mg; Calcium 83mg; Fibre 3.8g; Sodium 15mg.
morning glory w. shallots Energy 58kcal/240kJ; Protein 2.9g; Carbohydrate 4.2g, of which sugars 2g; Fat 3.4g, of which saturates 0.4g; Cholesterol 0mg; Calcium 112mg; Fibre 2g; Sodium 89mg.

Broccoli with Soy Sauce

A wonderfully simple dish that you will want to make again and again. The broccoli cooks in next to no time, so don't start cooking until you are almost ready to eat.

Serves 4

450g/1lb broccoli
15ml/1 tbsp vegetable oil
2 garlic cloves, crushed
30ml/2 tbsp light soy sauce
salt
fried garlic slices, to garnish

1 Cut the thick stems from the broccoli; cut off any particularly woody bits, then cut the stems lengthways into thin slices. Separate the head of the broccoli into large florets.

2 Bring a pan of lightly salted water to the boil. Add the broccoli and cook for 3–4 minutes until tender but still crisp.

3 Tip the broccoli into a colander, drain thoroughly and arrange in a heated serving dish.

4 Heat the oil in a small pan. Fry the garlic for 2 minutes to release the flavour, then remove it with a slotted spoon.

5 Pour the oil over the broccoli, taking care as it will splatter. Drizzle the soy sauce over the broccoli, sprinkle over the fried garlic and serve immediately.

Cook's Tip
Fried garlic slices make a good garnish but take care that the oil used does not get too hot; if the garlic burns, it will taste unpleasantly bitter.

Variation
Most leafy vegetables taste delicious prepared this way. Try blanched cos or romaine lettuce and you may be surprised at how crisp and clean the taste is.

Broccoli with Sesame Seeds

This simple treatment is ideal for broccoli and other brassicas, including Brussels sprouts. Adding a sprinkling of toasted sesame seeds to give extra crunch is an inspired touch, and there are a number of other easy ways to vary the recipe according to taste.

Serves 2

225g/8oz purple-sprouting broccoli
15ml/1 tbsp vegetable oil
15ml/1 tbsp soy sauce
15ml/1 tbsp toasted sesame seeds
salt and ground black pepper

1 Using a sharp knife, cut off and discard any thick stems from the broccoli and cut the broccoli into long, thin florets. Stems that are young and tender can be sliced into rounds.

2 Mix the soy sauce with the sesame seeds, then season with salt and ground black pepper.

3 Heat the vegetable oil in a wok or large frying pan and add the broccoli. Stir-fry for 3–4 minutes, or until tender, adding a splash of water if the pan becomes too dry.

4 Add the sesame seed and soy sauce mix to the broccoli, toss to combine and ensure that all the broccoli is coated, then serve immediately.

Variations
- *Sprouting broccoli has been used for this recipe, but when it is not available an ordinary variety of broccoli, such as calabrese, will also work very well.*
- *An even better choice would be Chinese broccoli, which is often available in Asian markets under the name gailan.*
- *Try this recipe with some pickled ginger. The flavour goes spectacularly well with broccoli or calabrese, and the resulting pale pink colour contrasts beautifully with the dark green. Pickled ginger is a little less potent than its fresh counterpart.*

broccoli w. soy sauce Energy 65kcal/271kJ; Protein 5.2g; Carbohydrate 2.7g, of which sugars 2.2g; Fat 3.8g, of which saturates 0.6g; Cholesterol 0mg; Calcium 64mg; Fibre 2.9g; Sodium 543mg.
broccoli w. sesame Energy 270kcal/1115kJ; Protein 13.1g; Carbohydrate 5.4g, of which sugars 4.6g; Fat 21.7g, of which saturates 3.3g; Cholesterol 0mg; Calcium 229mg; Fibre 7.1g; Sodium 1089mg.

Sautéed Green Beans

The smoky flavour of the dried shrimps used in this recipe adds an extra dimension to green beans cooked in this way.

Serves 4

450g/1lb green beans
15ml/1 tbsp vegetable oil
3 garlic cloves, finely chopped
5 spring onions (scallions), cut into 2.5cm/1in lengths
25g/1oz dried shrimps, soaked in warm water and drained
15ml/1 tbsp light soy sauce
salt

1 Trim the green beans. Cut each green bean in half.

2 Bring a pan of lightly salted water to the boil and cook the beans for 3–4 minutes until tender but still crisp. Drain, refresh under cold water and drain again.

3 Heat the oil in a non-stick frying pan or wok until very hot. Stir-fry the garlic and spring onions for 30 seconds, then add the shrimps. Mix lightly.

4 Add the green beans and soy sauce. Toss the mixture over the heat until the beans are hot. Serve immediately.

Variation
For more colour and a contrast in texture, stir-fry sliced red, yellow or orange (bell) peppers in the wok and cook for a few minutes until just tender but still crunchy. Add the garlic and spring onions (scallions) and proceed as above.

Cook's Tip
Don't be tempted to use too many dried shrimps. Their flavour is very strong and could overwhelm the more delicate taste of the green beans.

Green Beans with Ginger

This is a simple and delicious way of enlivening green beans. The dish can be served hot or cold and, accompanied by an omelette and some crusty bread, makes a perfect light lunch or supper.

Serves 4

450g/1lb/3 cups green beans
15ml/1 tbsp olive oil
5ml/1 tsp sesame oil
2 garlic cloves, crushed
2.5cm/1in piece fresh root ginger, finely chopped
30ml/2 tbsp dark soy sauce

1 Top the beans, but leave the tails on. Steam the beans over a pan of boiling salted water, or in an electric steamer, for 4 minutes, or until just tender.

2 Meanwhile, heat the olive oil and sesame oil in a heavy pan. Add the crushed garlic and sauté for 2 minutes, stirring constantly to prevent the garlic from burning.

3 Stir in the ginger and soy sauce and cook, stirring constantly, for a further 2–3 minutes until the liquid has reduced, then pour this mixture over the warm beans.

4 Leave for a few minutes to allow all the flavours to mingle, then toss the beans several times before serving.

Variations
This recipe also works well with mangetouts (snow peas) or sugar snap peas. Or try using shelled broad (fava) beans or fresh peas, in season.

Cook's Tip
Sesame oil has a delicious, nutty taste and is valued more for its flavour than as a cooking medium. It burns easily, so if you do use it for frying, mix it with other more durable oils such as the olive oil used in this recipe.

sautéed green beans Energy 62kcal/254kJ; Protein 2.4g; Carbohydrate 4.2g, of which sugars 3.1g; Fat 4.1g, of which saturates 0.6g; Cholesterol 0mg; Calcium 42mg; Fibre 2.5g; Sodium 534mg.
green beans w. ginger Energy 64kcal/265kJ; Protein 2.6g; Carbohydrate 4.6g, of which sugars 3.2g; Fat 4.1g, of which saturates 0.6g; Cholesterol 0mg; Calcium 42mg; Fibre 2.6g; Sodium 534mg.

Dry-cooked Green Beans

A particular style of Sichuan cooking is to 'dry cook', which basically means that no stock or water is involved. The slim green beans available all the year round from supermarkets are ideal for use in this quick and tasty recipe, but, as with all of these versatile vegetable dishes, there are worthy substitutes.

Serves 6
175ml/6fl oz/¾ cup sunflower oil
450/1lb fresh green beans, topped, tailed and cut in half
5 x 1cm/2 x ½in piece fresh root ginger, peeled and cut into matchsticks
5ml/1 tsp sugar
10ml/2 tsp light soy sauce
salt and ground black pepper

1 Heat the oil in a wok. When the oil is just beginning to smoke, add the beans and stir-fry them for 1–2 minutes until just tender.

2 Lift out the green beans on to a plate lined with kitchen paper. Using a ladle, carefully remove all but 30ml/2 tbsp oil from the wok. The excess oil will play no further part in this recipe, so should be allowed to cool completely before being strained and bottled for future use.

3 Reheat the remaining oil in the wok, add the ginger and stir-fry for a minute or two to flavour the oil.

4 Return the green beans to the wok, stir in the sugar, soy sauce and salt and pepper, and toss together quickly to ensure the beans are well coated.

5 Tip the beans into a heated bowl and serve immediately.

Variation
Fresh green beans are available for most of the year now, but this simple recipe works just as well with other more seasonal vegetables such as baby asparagus spears or okra.

Carrots in Sweet Vinegar

This fascinating side dish is a Japanese invention, whereby carrot strips are made tender and sweet thanks to several hours' marinating in rice vinegar, shoyu and mirin. They make an excellent accompaniment for and contrast to rich dishes such as fried aubergine with miso sauce.

Serves 4
2 large carrots, peeled
5ml/1 tsp salt
30ml/2 tbsp sesame seeds

For the marinade
75ml/5 tbsp rice vinegar
30ml/2 tbsp shoyu
45ml/3 tbsp mirin (sweet rice wine)

1 Cut the carrots into thin matchsticks, 5cm/2in long.

2 Put the carrots and salt into a mixing bowl, and mix well with your hands. After 25 minutes, rinse the wilted carrot in cold water, then drain.

3 In another bowl, mix together the marinade ingredients. Add the carrots, and leave to marinate for 3 hours.

4 Put a wok on a high heat, add the sesame seeds and toss constantly until the seeds start to pop. Remove from the heat and cool.

5 Chop the sesame seeds with a large, sharp knife on a large chopping board. Place the carrots in a bowl, sprinkle with the sesame seeds and serve cold.

Cook's Tip
This marinade is called san bai zu, and is one of the basic sauces in Japanese cooking. Shoyu is an essential ingredient and you should use the pale awakuchi soy sauce if available. Dilute the marinade with 15ml/1 tbsp second dashi stock, then add sesame seeds and a few dashes of sesame oil for a very tasty and healthy salad dressing.

dry-cooked beans Energy 223kcal/917kJ; Protein 1.4g; Carbohydrate 3.1g, of which sugars 2.4g; Fat 22.9g, of which saturates 2.8g; Cholesterol 0mg; Calcium 27mg; Fibre 1.7g; Sodium 0mg.
carrots in sweet vinegar Energy 110kcal/461kJ; Protein 2g; Carbohydrate 16.4g, of which sugars 16g; Fat 4.5g, of which saturates 0.7g; Cholesterol 0mg; Calcium 70mg; Fibre 1.8g; Sodium 1040mg.

Aubergines with Sesame Sauce

Steaming is a wonderful way of cooking aubergines as it avoids the problem of their tendency to soak up oil.

Serves 4

2 large aubergines (eggplants)
400ml/14fl oz/1⅔ cups second dashi stock made using water and instant dashi powder
25ml/1½ tbsp sugar
15ml/1 tbsp shoyu
15ml/1 tbsp sesame seeds, ground
15ml/1 tbsp sake
15ml/1 tbsp cornflour (cornstarch)
salt

For the vegetables

130g/4½oz shimeji mushrooms
115g/4oz/¾ cup fine green beans
100ml/3fl oz/scant ½ cup second dashi stock
25ml/1½ tbsp sugar
15ml/1 tbsp sake
1.5ml/¼ tsp salt
dash of shoyu

1 Peel the aubergines and cut them in quarters lengthways. Prick all over then soak in salted water for 30 minutes. Drain and steam in a covered bamboo basket for 20 minutes.

2 Mix the stock, sugar, shoyu and 1.5ml/¼ tsp salt in a large pan. Add the aubergines, cover and simmer for a further 15 minutes. Mix a few tablespoonfuls of stock from the pan with the ground sesame seeds. Add this mixture to the pan and stir well to combine.

3 Mix the sake and the cornflour, add to the pan with the aubergines and stock and stir over the heat until the sauce becomes quite thick. Remove the pan from the heat.

4 Prepare the vegetables. Cut off the hard base part of the mushrooms and separate the large block into smaller chunks. Trim the beans and cut them in half.

5 Mix the remaining ingredients with the beans and mushrooms in a pan and cook for 7 minutes until just tender. Serve the aubergines and their sauce in individual bowls with the vegetables on the top.

Braised Aubergine & Courgettes

Black bean sauce is the key to this simple, spicy and sensational accompaniment.

Serves 4

1 large aubergine (eggplant), halved and sliced
2 small courgettes (zucchini)
2 fresh red chillies
2 garlic cloves
15ml/1 tbsp vegetable oil
1 small onion, diced
15ml/1 tbsp black bean sauce
15ml/1 tbsp dark soy sauce
45ml/3 tbsp cold water
salt

1 Layer all the slices of aubergine in a colander, sprinkling each layer with salt. Leave the aubergine in the sink to stand for about 20 minutes. Cut the courgettes into wedges.

2 Remove the stalks from the chillies, cut them in half lengthways and scrape out and discard the pith and seeds. Chop the chillies finely.

3 Cut the garlic cloves in half. Place them cut side down and chop them finely by slicing first in one direction and then in the other.

4 Rinse the aubergine slices under cold running water to remove the salt. Drain and dry thoroughly on kitchen paper.

5 Heat the oil in a wok or non-stick frying pan. Quickly stir-fry the garlic, chillies and onion with the black bean sauce.

6 Add the aubergine and stir-fry for 2 minutes, sprinkling over a little water to prevent them from burning. Stir in the courgettes, soy sauce and water. Cook, stirring often, for 5 minutes. Spoon into a heated dish and serve.

Variation
For a fiery result, retain the chilli seeds and add to the mixture.

aubergines w. sesame sauce Energy 79kcal/333kJ; Protein 2.9g; Carbohydrate 10.2g, of which sugars 9.6g; Fat 2.9g, of which saturates 0.5g; Cholesterol 0mg; Calcium 52mg; Fibre 3.3g; Sodium 272mg.
braised aubergine Energy 66kcal/276kJ; Protein 3g; Carbohydrate 6.1g, of which sugars 4.2g; Fat 3.5g, of which saturates 0.5g; Cholesterol 0mg; Calcium 34mg; Fibre 2.9g; Sodium 270mg.

Charred Aubergine with Chillies

One of the wonderful things about aubergines is that they can be placed in the flames of a fire, or over hot charcoal, or directly over a gas flame of a stove, and still taste great.

Serves 4

2 aubergines (eggplants)
30ml/2 tbsp groundnut (peanut) or vegetable oil
2 spring onions (scallions), finely sliced
2 red Serrano chillies, seeded and finely sliced
15ml/1 tbsp fish sauce
25g/1oz/½ cup fresh basil leaves
salt
15ml/1 tbsp roasted peanuts, crushed, to garnish
hot chilli sauce, to serve

1 Place the aubergines over a barbecue or under a hot grill (broiler), or directly over a gas flame, and, turning them, cook until charred all over and soft when pressed. Put them into a plastic bag to sweat for 1 minute.

2 Holding the aubergines by the stalks, carefully peel off the skin under cold running water. Squeeze the excess water from the peeled flesh, remove the stalk and pull the flesh apart in long strips. Place these strips in a serving dish.

3 Heat the oil in a small pan and quickly stir in the spring onions. Remove the pan from the heat and stir in the chillies, fish sauce, basil leaves and a little salt to taste. Pour this dressing over the aubergines, toss gently and scatter the crushed peanuts over the top.

4 Serve at room temperature and, for those who like a little extra fire, splash on some hot chilli sauce.

Cook's Tip
If you cook the aubergines over a barbecue, the flesh is even easier to remove. Slit the blackened skins and scoop out the flesh, then pull the flesh apart into strips and continue as above.

Seven-spice Aubergines

Seven-spice powder is the key ingredient that gives these aubergines a lovely warm flavour. The coating is deliciously crunchy.

Serves 4

2 egg whites
90ml/6 tbsp cornflour (cornstarch)
5ml/1 tsp salt
15ml/1 tbsp Thai or Chinese seven-spice powder
15ml/1 tbsp mild chilli powder
500g/1¼lb aubergines (eggplants), thinly sliced
sunflower oil, for deep-frying
fresh mint leaves, to garnish
hot chilli sauce, to serve

1 Put the egg whites in a large grease-free bowl and beat with an electric whisk until light and foamy, but not dry.

2 Combine the cornflour, salt, seven-spice powder and chilli powder and spread evenly on to a large plate.

3 Fill a wok one-third full of oil and heat to 180°C/350°F or until a cube of day-old bread, dropped into the oil, browns in 40 seconds.

4 Dip the aubergine slices in the egg white and then into the spiced flour mixture to coat. Deep-fry in batches for 3–4 minutes, or until crisp and golden. Drain on kitchen paper and transfer to a platter to keep hot.

5 Serve the aubergine garnished with mint leaves and with hot chilli sauce on the side for dipping.

Cook's Tip
Seven-spice powder is a commercial blend of spices, usually comprising coriander, cumin, cinnamon, star anise, chilli, cloves and lemon peel.

aubergine w. chillies Energy 100kcal/419kJ; Protein 2.1g; Carbohydrate 9.4g, of which sugars 8.8g; Fat 6.4g, of which saturates 0.9g; Cholesterol 0mg; Calcium 42mg; Fibre 3.7g; Sodium 15mg.
seven-spice aubergines Energy 203kcal/850kJ; Protein 2.7g; Carbohydrate 23.5g, of which sugars 2.5g; Fat 11.7g, of which saturates 1.4g; Cholesterol 0mg; Calcium 17mg; Fibre 2.5g; Sodium 45mg.

Chinese Potatoes with Chilli Beans

East meets West in this American-style dish with a Chinese flavour – the sauce is particularly tasty.

Serves 4

4 medium firm or waxy potatoes, cut into thick chunks
30ml/2 tbsp sunflower or groundnut (peanut) oil
3 spring onions (scallions), sliced
1 large fresh chilli, seeded and sliced
2 garlic cloves, crushed
400g/14oz can red kidney beans, drained
30ml/2 tbsp soy sauce
15ml/1 tbsp sesame oil
salt and ground black pepper
15ml/1 tbsp sesame seeds, to garnish
chopped fresh coriander (cilantro) or parsley, to garnish

1 Cook the potatoes in a large pan of boiling water for 20–30 minutes or until they are just tender. Take care not to overcook. Drain, return to the clean pan and cover to keep warm.

2 Heat the oil in a large frying pan or wok over a medium to high heat. Add the spring onions and chilli and stir-fry for about 1 minute, then add the garlic and stir-fry for a few seconds.

3 Add the potatoes, stirring well, then the beans and finally the soy sauce and sesame oil.

4 Season to taste and continue to cook the vegetables until they are well heated through. Shake the pan occasionally, but do not stir or you risk breaking up the potatotes.

5 Spoon the mixture on to a heated platter, sprinkle with the sesame seeds and the coriander or parsley and serve hot.

Cook's Tip
When returning the cooked potatoes to the clean pan in step 1, cover them with a few sheets of kitchen paper before replacing the pan lid. This will stop them turning soggy.

New Potatoes in Dashi Stock

As the stock evaporates in this delicious dish, the onion becomes meltingly soft and caramelized, making a wonderful sauce that coats the potatoes.

Serves 4

15ml/1 tbsp vegetable oil
15ml/1 tbsp toasted sesame oil
1 small onion, thinly sliced
1kg/2¼lb baby new potatoes, unpeeled
200ml/7fl oz/scant 1 cup water with 5ml/1 tsp instant dashi powder
45ml/3 tbsp shoyu, dark soy sauce or kecap manis

1 Heat the vegetable and sesame oils in a wok or large pan. Add the onion slices and stir-fry for 30 seconds, then add the potatoes. Stir constantly, until all the potatoes are well coated in sesame oil, and have begun to sizzle.

2 Pour on the dashi stock and shoyu, dark soy sauce or kecap manis and reduce the heat to the lowest setting. Cover the wok or pan and cook for 15 minutes, using a slotted spoon to turn the potatoes every 5 minutes so that they cook evenly.

3 Uncover the wok or pan, increase the heat and cook for a further 5 minutes to reduce the liquid. If there is already very little liquid remaining, remove the wok or pan from the heat, cover and leave to stand for 5 minutes. Check that the potatoes are cooked, then remove from the heat.

4 Transfer the potatoes and onions to a deep serving bowl. Pour the sauce over the top and serve immediately.

Cook's Tip
Toasted sesame oil is recommended because of its distinctive aroma, but mixing it with vegetable oil not only moderates the flavour, it also lessens the likelihood of the oil burning when heated in the pan.

potatoes w. chilli beans Energy 272kcal/1141kJ; Protein 9.7g; Carbohydrate 34.8g, of which sugars 5.7g; Fat 11.4g, of which saturates 1.6g; Cholesterol 0mg; Calcium 107mg; Fibre 7.6g; Sodium 936mg.
potatoes in dashi stock Energy 210kcal/890kJ; Protein 4.8g; Carbohydrate 42.4g, of which sugars 4.9g; Fat 3.5g, of which saturates 0.7g; Cholesterol 0mg; Calcium 21mg; Fibre 2.7g; Sodium 829mg.

Slow-cooked Shiitake with Shoyu

Shiitake mushrooms cooked slowly are so rich and filling, that some people call them 'vegetarian steak'. This is a useful side dish which also makes a flavoursome addition to other dishes.

Serves 4

20 dried shiitake mushrooms
30ml/2 tbsp vegetable oil
30ml/2 tbsp shoyu
5ml/1 tsp toasted sesame oil

1 Start soaking the dried shiitake the day before. Put them in a large bowl almost full of water. Cover the shiitake with a plate or lid to stop them floating to the surface of the water. Leave to soak overnight.

2 Remove the shiitake from the soaking water and gently squeeze out the water with your fingers.

3 Measure 120ml/4fl oz/½ cup of the liquid in the bowl, and set aside.

4 Heat the oil in a wok or a large frying pan. Stir-fry the shiitake over a high heat for 5 minutes, stirring constantly.

5 Reduce the heat to the lowest setting, then stir in the reserved soaking liquid and the shoyu.

6 Cook the mushrooms until there is almost no moisture left, stirring frequently. Sprinkle with the toasted sesame oil and remove from the heat.

7 Leave to cool, then slice and arrange the shiitake on a large serving plate.

Variation

Cut the slow-cooked shiitake into thin strips. Mix with 600g/1⅓lb/5¼ cups cooked brown rice and 15ml/1 tbsp finely chopped chives. Sprinkle with toasted sesame seeds.

Fragrant Mushrooms in Lettuce Leaf Saucers

This quick and easy vegetable dish looks great served on lettuce leaves, and it means the mushrooms can be scooped up and eaten with the fingers. It's a lovely treat for children.

Serves 2

30ml/2 tbsp vegetable oil
2 garlic cloves, finely chopped
2 baby cos or romaine lettuces, or Little Gem (Bibb) lettuces
1 lemon grass stalk, chopped
2 kaffir lime leaves, rolled in cylinders and thinly sliced
200g/7oz/3 cups oyster or brown cap (cremini) mushrooms, or a mixture of the two, sliced
1 small fresh red chilli, seeded and finely chopped
juice of ½ lemon
30ml/2 tbsp light soy sauce
5ml/1 tsp palm sugar (jaggery) or light muscovado (brown) sugar
small bunch fresh mint, leaves removed from the stalks

1 Heat the oil in a wok or frying pan. Add the garlic and cook over a medium heat, stirring occasionally, until golden. Do not let it burn or it will taste bitter.

2 Meanwhile, separate the individual lettuce leaves. Rinse them well, dry in a salad spinner or blot with kitchen paper, and set aside.

3 Increase the heat under the wok or pan and add the chopped lemon grass, sliced lime leaves and sliced mushrooms. Stir-fry for about 2 minutes.

4 Add the chilli, lemon juice, soy sauce and sugar to the wok or pan. Toss the mixture over the heat to combine the ingredients together, then stir-fry for a further 2 minutes.

5 Arrange the lettuce leaves on one large or two individual salad plates. Spoon a small amount of the mushroom mixture on to each leaf, top with a mint leaf and serve.

slow cooked shiitake w. shoyu Energy 16kcal/69kJ; Protein 2g; Carbohydrate 1g, of which sugars 0.8g; Fat 0.5g, of which saturates 0.1g; Cholesterol 0mg; Calcium 7mg; Fibre 1.1g; Sodium 539mg.
mushrooms in lettuce saucers Energy 145kcal/600kJ; Protein 3.6g; Carbohydrate 5.5g, of which sugars 4g; Fat 12.2g, of which saturates 1.5g; Cholesterol 0mg; Calcium 87mg; Fibre 2g; Sodium 12mg.

Mushroom & Choi Sum Stir-fry

Use the mushrooms recommended for this dish – wild oyster and shiitake mushrooms have particularly distinctive, delicate flavours that work well when stir-fried.

Serves 4

4 dried black Chinese mushrooms
150ml/¼ pint/⅔ cup hot water
450g/1lb pak choi (bok choy) or choi sum
50g/2oz/¾ cup oyster mushrooms, preferably wild
50g/2oz/¾ cup fresh shiitake mushrooms
15ml/1 tbsp vegetable oil
1 garlic clove, crushed
30ml/2 tbsp oyster sauce

1 Soak the dried Chinese mushrooms in the hot water for 15 minutes to soften.

2 Tear the pak choi or choi sum into bitesize pieces with your fingers. Place in a bowl and set aside.

3 If any of the oyster or shiitake mushrooms are particularly large, use a sharp knife to halve them.

4 Drain the Chinese mushrooms and cut off the stems. Heat a wok, then add the oil. When the oil is hot, stir-fry the garlic until it has softened but not coloured.

5 Add the greens to the wok and stir-fry for 1 minute. Toss in the oyster and shiitake mushrooms with the Chinese mushroom caps, and stir-fry for 1 minute.

6 Add the oyster sauce, toss well and serve immediately.

Cook's Tip
Pak choi, also called bok choy, and its cousin, choi sum, are both attractive members of the cabbage family, with long, smooth white stems and dark green leaves. Choi sum is also known as flowering cabbage and is distinguished by its yellow flowers.

Fried Vegetables with Chilli Sauce

A wok makes the ideal pan for frying slices of aubergine, butternut squash and courgette because they become beautifully tender and succulent. The beaten egg in this recipe gives a satisfyingly substantial coating.

Serves 4

3 large (US extra large) eggs
1 aubergine (eggplant), halved lengthways and cut into long, thin slices
½ small butternut squash, peeled, seeded and cut into long, thin slices
2 courgettes (zucchini), trimmed and cut into long, thin slices
105ml/7 tbsp vegetable or sunflower oil
salt and ground black pepper
sweet chilli sauce, or a dip of your own choice, to serve (see below for suggestion)

1 Beat the eggs in a large bowl. Season the egg mixture with salt and pepper. Add the slices of aubergine, butternut squash and courgette. Toss the vegetable slices until they are coated all over in the egg.

2 Have a warmed dish ready lined with kitchen paper. Heat the oil in a wok. When it is hot, add the vegetables, one strip at a time, making sure that each strip has plenty of egg clinging to it.

3 Do not cook more than eight strips of vegetable at a time or the oil will cool down too much.

4 As each strip turns golden and is cooked, lift it out, using a wire basket or slotted spoon, and transfer to the plate. Keep hot while cooking the remaining vegetables. Serve with the sweet chilli sauce as a dip.

Variation
Instead of sweet chilli sauce, try a simple mix of mango chutney and chilli dip. The spicy fruity flavour goes particularly well with the butternut squash.

mushroom & choi sum Energy 57kcal/237kJ; Protein 3.7g; Carbohydrate 2.1g, of which sugars 1.8g; Fat 3.8g, of which saturates 0.5g; Cholesterol 0mg; Calcium 193mg; Fibre 2.7g; Sodium 159mg.
vegetables w. chilli sauce Energy 113kcal/468kJ; Protein 5.2g; Carbohydrate 3.6g, of which sugars 3.1g; Fat 8.8g, of which saturates 1.6g; Cholesterol 95mg; Calcium 56mg; Fibre 2g; Sodium 36mg.

Onion, Mango & Peanut Chaat

Chaats are spiced relishes of vegetables and nuts, delicious with many savoury Indian dishes.

Serves 4

90g/3½oz/scant 1 cup unsalted peanuts
15ml/1 tbsp groundnut (peanut) oil
1 onion, chopped
½ cucumber, seeded and diced
1 mango, peeled, stoned (pitted) and diced
1 fresh green chilli, seeded and chopped
30ml/2 tbsp chopped fresh coriander (cilantro)
15ml/1 tbsp chopped fresh mint
about 15ml/1 tbsp lime juice
pinch of light muscovado (brown) sugar

For the chaat masala

10ml/2 tsp ground toasted cumin seeds
2.5ml/½ tsp cayenne pepper
5ml/1 tsp mango powder (amchur)
2.5ml/½ tsp garam masala
a pinch of ground asafoetida
salt and ground black pepper

1 To make the chaat masala, grind all the spices together, then season with 2.5ml/½ tsp each salt and pepper.

2 Fry the peanuts in the oil until lightly browned, then drain on kitchen paper until cool.

3 Mix the onion, cucumber, mango, chilli, fresh coriander and mint in a bowl. Sprinkle in 5ml/1 tsp of the chaat masala. Stir in the peanuts and then add lime juice and/or sugar to taste. Set the mixture aside for 20–30 minutes for the flavours to mature.

4 Spoon the mixture into a serving bowl, sprinkle another 5ml/1 tsp of the chaat masala over and serve.

Cook's Tip

Any remaining chaat masala will keep in a sealed jar for 4–6 weeks.

Roasties with Peanut Sauce

Whether a side dish or a main course, these roasted vegetables served with a dipping sauce are a real treat.

Serves 4

1 long, slender aubergine (eggplant), partially peeled and cut into long strips
2 courgettes (zucchini), partially peeled and cut into long strips
1 thick, long sweet potato, cut into long strips
2 leeks, trimmed, halved widthways and lengthways
2 garlic cloves, chopped
25g/1oz fresh root ginger, peeled and chopped
60ml/4 tbsp vegetable or groundnut (peanut) oil
salt
30ml/3 tbsp roasted peanuts, ground, to garnish
fresh crusty bread, to serve

For the sauce

4 garlic cloves, chopped
2–3 fresh red chillies, seeded and chopped
5ml/1 tsp shrimp paste
115g/4oz/1 cup roasted peanuts, crushed
15ml/1 tbsp dark soy sauce
juice of 1 lime
5ml/1 tsp Chinese rice vinegar
10ml/2 tsp clear honey
salt and ground black pepper

1 Preheat the oven to 200°C/400°F/Gas 6. Arrange the vegetables in a shallow oven dish. Using a food processor, grind the garlic and ginger to a paste, and smear it over the vegetables. Sprinkle with a little salt and pour over the oil. Roast for about 45 minutes, until the vegetables are tender and slightly browned – toss them in the oil halfway through cooking.

2 Meanwhile, make the sauce. Using a food processor, grind the garlic and chillies to a paste. Beat in the shrimp paste and peanuts. Stir in the soy sauce, lime juice, vinegar and honey, and blend with a little water so that the sauce is the consistency of pouring cream. Season with salt and pepper and adjust the sweet and sour balance to taste.

3 Arrange the roasted vegetables on a plate. Drizzle the sauce over them, or serve it separately in a bowl. Sprinkle the ground peanuts over the top and serve warm with fresh crusty bread.

onion & peanut chaat Energy 204kcal/848kJ; Protein 8g; Carbohydrate 12g, of which sugars 7.9g; Fat 14.2g, of which saturates 2.6g; Cholesterol 0mg; Calcium 45mg; Fibre 2.7g; Sodium 6mg.
roasties Energy 361kcal/1502kJ; Protein 11.9g; Carbohydrate 22.7g, of which sugars 11.1g; Fat 25.4g, of which saturates 4.1g; Cholesterol 0mg; Calcium 76mg; Fibre 6.9g; Sodium 292mg.

Sweet & Sour Vegetables with Tofu

Big, bold and beautiful, this is a hearty stir-fry that will satisfy the hungriest guests.

Serves 4

4 shallots
3 garlic cloves
30ml/2 tbsp groundnut (peanut) oil
250g/9oz Chinese leaves (Chinese cabbage), shredded
8 baby corn cobs, sliced diagonally
2 red (bell) peppers, seeded and thinly sliced
200g/7oz/1¾ cups mangetouts (snow peas), trimmed and sliced
250g/9oz firm tofu, rinsed, drained and cut in 1cm/½in cubes
60ml/4 tbsp vegetable stock
30ml/2 tbsp light soy sauce
15ml/1 tbsp sugar
30ml/2 tbsp rice vinegar
2.5ml/½ tsp dried chilli flakes
small bunch of fresh coriander (cilantro), chopped

1 Slice the shallots thinly using a sharp knife. Finely chop the garlic cloves.

2 Heat the oil in a wok or large frying pan and cook the shallots and garlic for 2–3 minutes over a medium heat, until golden. Do not let the garlic burn or it will taste bitter.

3 Add the shredded Chinese leaves, toss over the heat for 30 seconds, then add the sliced baby corn cobs and repeat the process.

4 Add the red peppers, mangetouts and tofu in the same way as the leaves and baby corn, each time adding a single ingredient and tossing it over the heat for about 30 seconds before adding the next ingredient.

5 Pour in the stock and soy sauce. Mix together the sugar and vinegar in a small bowl, stirring until the sugar has dissolved, then add to the wok or pan.

6 Tip the mixture into a warmed bowl, sprinkle over the chilli flakes and coriander, toss to mix well and serve.

Spring Vegetable Stir-fry

Fast, fresh and packed with healthy vegetables, this stir-fry is delicious served with marinated tofu and rice or noodles. This recipe contains very little saturated fat, so scores highly with slimmers, but has sufficient bulk to ward off hunger. Ideal as a quick supper on the go.

Serves 4

2 spring onions (scallions)
175g/6oz spring greens (collard)
15ml/1 tbsp vegetable oil
5ml/1 tsp toasted sesame oil
1 garlic clove, chopped
2.5cm/1in piece fresh root ginger, finely chopped
225g/8oz baby carrots
350g/12oz broccoli florets
175g/6oz asparagus tips
30ml/2 tbsp light soy sauce
15ml/1 tbsp apple juice
15ml/1 tbsp sesame seeds, toasted

1 Trim the spring onions and cut them diagonally into thin slices, using a sharp knife.

2 Wash the spring greens and drain in a colander, then blot with kitchen paper and shred finely.

3 Heat a frying pan or wok over a high heat. Add the vegetable oil and the sesame oil, and reduce the heat. Add the garlic and sauté for 2 minutes. Do not let the garlic burn or it will gain a bitter taste.

4 Add the chopped ginger, carrots, broccoli and asparagus tips to the pan and stir-fry for 4 minutes.

5 Add the spring onions and spring greens and stir-fry for a further 2 minutes.

6 Add the soy sauce and apple juice and cook for 1–2 minutes until the vegetables are tender. If they appear too dry, simply add a little water to soften them up.

7 Tip the mixture into a warmed serving dish or four individual bowls, sprinkle the sesame seeds on top and serve.

sweet & sour vegetables Energy 144kcal/604kJ; Protein 5.2g; Carbohydrate 23.7g, of which sugars 18.2g; Fat 3.7g, of which saturates 0.5g; Cholesterol 0mg; Calcium 73mg; Fibre 4.7g; Sodium 611mg.
spring vegetable stir-fry Energy 134kcal/554kJ; Protein 7.8g; Carbohydrate 9.4g, of which sugars 8.6g; Fat 7.4g, of which saturates 1.1g; Cholesterol 0mg; Calcium 195mg; Fibre 6.2g; Sodium 566mg.

Yogurt Salad

If this salad looks and tastes familiar, it isn't surprising. It is very similar to coleslaw, except that yogurt is used instead of mayonnaise, and cashew nuts are added.

Serves 4

115g/4oz cabbage
350ml/12fl oz/1½ cups natural (plain) low-fat yogurt
10ml/2 tsp clear honey
2 medium carrots, thickly sliced
2 spring onions (scallions), roughly chopped
50g/2oz/⅓ cup sultanas (golden raisins)
50g/2oz/½ cup cashew nuts (optional)
16 white grapes, halved
2.5ml/½ tsp salt
5ml/1 tsp chopped fresh mint

1 Use a mandolin, if you have one, to shred the cabbage finely. Alternatively, use a sharp knife to slice through the layers of the cabbage.

2 Using a fork, beat the yogurt in a bowl with the honey.

3 In a separate bowl, which will be suitable for serving the salad, mix together the carrots, spring onions, cabbage, sultanas, cashew nuts (if you are using them), grapes, salt and the chopped fresh mint.

4 Pour the sweetened yogurt mixture over the salad, mix well and serve.

Variation

For Squash and Yogurt Salad, mix together 2.5ml/½ tsp dry mustard, 2.5ml/½ tsp ground cumin, 2.5ml/½ tsp salt, 5ml/1 tsp grated fresh root ginger and 150ml/¼ pint/⅔ cup natural yogurt. Chop half a green (bell) pepper and add to the spicy yogurt. Peel 250g/9oz butternut squash, then slice it and boil or steam until tender. Add to the yogurt mixture and stir well.

Nutty Salad

The smooth creamy dressing is perfect with the crunchy nuts.

Serves 4

150g/5oz can red kidney beans
1 medium onion, cut into 12 rings
1 medium green courgette (zucchini), sliced
1 medium yellow courgette (zucchini), sliced
50g/2oz/⅔ cup pasta shells, cooked
50g/2oz/½ cup cashew nuts
25g/1oz/¼ cup peanuts
fresh coriander (cilantro) and lime wedges, to garnish

For the dressing

115g/4oz/½ cup low-fat fromage frais or ricotta cheese
30ml/2 tbsp natural (plain) low-fat yogurt
1 fresh green chilli, chopped
15ml/1 tbsp chopped fresh coriander (cilantro)
2.5ml/½ tsp crushed dried red chillies
15ml/1 tbsp lemon juice
salt and ground black pepper

1 Drain the kidney beans. Arrange them with the onion rings, courgette slices and pasta in a salad dish and sprinkle the cashew nuts and peanuts over the top.

2 In a separate bowl, mix together the fromage frais or ricotta cheese, yogurt, green chilli, fresh coriander and salt and pepper to taste. Beat well using a fork until all the ingredients are thoroughly combined. You may find it easier to add the coriander leaves a few at a time and mix in, to allow their flavour to permeate the mixture and ensure the resulting dressing is smooth in texture.

3 Sprinkle the crushed red chillies and lemon juice over the dressing. Garnish the salad with fresh coriander and lime wedges, and serve with the dressing.

Cook's Tip

Make the dressing just before serving the salad, so that the flavour of the coriander will be at its most intense.

yogurt salad Energy 189kcal/792kJ; Protein 6.9g; Carbohydrate 20.5g, of which sugars 19.5g; Fat 9.6g, of which saturates 1.2g; Cholesterol 1mg; Calcium 184mg; Fibre 1g; Sodium 74mg.
nutty salad Energy 236kcal/980kJ; Protein 9.2g; Carbohydrate 15.1g, of which sugars 6.1g; Fat 15.8g, of which saturates 4.3g; Cholesterol 3mg; Calcium 102mg; Fibre 3.5g; Sodium 167mg.

Spinach & Mushroom Salad

This salad is especially good served with glazed garlic prawns (shrimp) or any other seafood curry.

Serves 4
10 baby corn cobs
115g/4oz/3 cups mushrooms
2 medium tomatoes
20 small spinach leaves
8–10 onion rings
salt and ground black pepper
fresh coriander (cilantro) sprigs and lime slices, to garnish (optional)

1 Halve the baby corn cobs and slice the mushrooms and tomatoes.

2 Arrange all the salad ingredients in a large serving bowl. Season with salt and pepper and garnish with fresh coriander and lime slices, if you like.

Tofu & Cucumber Salad

This is a nutritious and refreshing salad with a hot, sweet and sour dressing. It is ideal for a buffet.

Serves 4–6
1 small cucumber
vegetable oil, for frying
115g/4oz firm tofu
115g/4oz beansprouts, trimmed and rinsed
salt
celery leaves, to garnish

For the dressing
1 small onion, grated
2 garlic cloves, crushed
2.5ml/½ tsp chilli powder
30–45ml/2–3 tbsp dark soy sauce
15–30ml/1–2 tbsp rice vinegar
10ml/2 tsp soft dark brown sugar
salt

1 Trim the ends from the cucumber and then cut it into neat cubes.

2 Sprinkle the trimmed cucumber with salt and set aside while you prepare the remaining ingredients.

3 Heat a little oil in a pan and fry the tofu on both sides until golden brown. Drain well on absorbent kitchen paper and cut into cubes.

4 Prepare the dressing by blending together the onion, garlic and chilli powder. Stir in the soy sauce, vinegar, sugar and salt to taste, or shake in a closed, screw-topped jar.

5 Just before serving, rinse the cucumber under cold running water. Drain and dry thoroughly.

6 Toss the cucumber, tofu and beansprouts together in a serving bowl and pour over the dressing. Garnish with the celery leaves and serve immediately.

Baby Vegetable Salad with a Chilli Dressing

Warm salads make a pleasant change, and the flavours of the dressing are enhanced. Take the opportunity in spring to use the new season's baby vegetables for this mouthwatering combination, which makes an excellent accompaniment to spicy meals or to grilled meat or fish.

Serves 6
10 baby potatoes, halved
15 baby carrots
10 baby courgettes (zucchini)
115g/4oz/1½ cups button (white) mushrooms

For the dressing
45ml/3 tbsp lemon juice
25ml/1½ tbsp vegetable oil
15ml/1 tbsp chopped fresh coriander (cilantro)
5ml/1 tsp salt
2 fresh green chillies, finely sliced

1 Boil the potatoes, carrots and courgettes in water until tender. Drain them and place in a serving dish with the mushrooms.

2 Make the dressing in a separate bowl. Mix together the lemon juice, oil, fresh coriander, salt and chillies.

3 Toss the vegetables thoroughly in the chilli dressing and serve immediately.

Variation
For a mild version of this dish replace the green chillies with finely chopped green (bell) pepper.

Cook's Tip
As well as looking extremely attractive, the tiny baby vegetables give this salad a lovely flavour. Other baby vegetables, such as leeks, baby corn or cauliflower florets, can be used just as well.

spinach & mushroom Energy 21kcal/89kJ; Protein 2g; Carbohydrate 2.4g, of which sugars 2.2g; Fat 0.5g, of which saturates 0.1g; Cholesterol 0mg; Calcium 29mg; Fibre 1.5g; Sodium 309mg.
tofu & cucumber Energy 52kcal/215kJ; Protein 2.6g; Carbohydrate 4.3g, of which sugars 3.6g; Fat 2.8g, of which saturates 0.3g; Cholesterol 0mg; Calcium 109mg; Fibre 0.5g; Sodium 537mg.
baby vegetable salad Energy 89kcal/372kJ; Protein 2.2g; Carbohydrate 12.8g, of which sugars 5g; Fat 3.6g, of which saturates 0.5g; Cholesterol 0mg; Calcium 30mg; Fibre 2.3g; Sodium 20mg.

Mango, Tomato & Red Onion Salad

This salad makes a delicious appetizer. The under-ripe mango blends well with the tomato.

Serves 4

1 firm under-ripe mango
2 large tomatoes or 1 beefsteak tomato, sliced
½ red onion, sliced thinly into rings
½ cucumber, peeled and thinly sliced
chopped chives, to garnish

For the dressing

30ml/2 tbsp vegetable oil
15ml/1 tbsp lemon juice
1 garlic clove, crushed
2.5ml/½ tsp hot pepper sauce
salt and ground black pepper

1 Using a sharp knife or peeler, remove the skin from the mango, then cut the flesh into bitesize pieces.

2 Arrange the mango, tomatoes, onion and cucumber on a large serving plate.

3 Make the dressing. Blend the oil, lemon juice, garlic, pepper sauce and seasoning in a blender or food processor, or shake vigorously in a small screw-top jar.

4 Spoon the dressing over the salad. Garnish with the chopped chives and serve.

Cook's Tip

When cutting a mango, first peel the skin off with a sharp knife or peeler. Next, cut the fleshy cheeks from each side. Trim carefully around the fruit, following the curvature of the stone (pit), to remove all the flesh. You will end up with the stone, two cheeks and two thinner strips of fruit, which can then be sliced.

Peppery Bean Salad

This pretty salad uses canned beans for speed and convenience.

Serves 4–6

425g/15oz can red kidney beans
425g/15oz can black-eyed beans (peas)
425g/15oz can chickpeas
¼ red (bell) pepper
¼ green (bell) pepper
6 radishes
15ml/1 tbsp chopped spring onion (scallion), plus extra to garnish

For the dressing

5ml/1 tsp ground cumin
15ml/1 tbsp tomato ketchup
30ml/2 tbsp olive oil
15ml/1 tbsp white wine vinegar
1 garlic clove, crushed
2.5ml/½ tsp hot pepper sauce
salt

1 Drain the red kidney beans, black-eyed beans and chickpeas, and rinse under cold running water. Shake off the excess water and tip them into a large bowl.

2 Core, seed and chop the red and green peppers. Trim the radishes and slice thinly. Add the peppers, radishes and spring onion to the bowl.

3 To make the dressing, mix together the cumin, tomato ketchup, oil, white wine vinegar and crushed garlic in a small bowl. Add a little salt, if necessary, and hot pepper sauce to taste, and stir again thoroughly to combine.

4 Pour the dressing over the salad and mix. Cover the salad and chill for at least 1 hour before serving, garnished with the sliced spring onion.

Cook's Tip

Look out for cans of mixed beans at the supermarket. These contain a colourful medley and would be perfect for this salad.

mango & red onion salad Energy 89kcal/369kJ; Protein 1.1g; Carbohydrate 8.6g, of which sugars 7.9g; Fat 5.8g, of which saturates 0.8g; Cholesterol 0mg; Calcium 17mg; Fibre 1.9g; Sodium 7mg.
peppery bean salad Energy 243kcal/1025kJ; Protein 14.1g; Carbohydrate 37.6g, of which sugars 9.1g; Fat 5g, of which saturates 0.8g; Cholesterol 0mg; Calcium 146mg; Fibre 12.8g; Sodium 823mg.

Sweet Potato & Carrot Salad

This warm salad has a piquant flavour. As a main course, it will serve two.

Serves 4
1 medium sweet potato
2 carrots, cut into thick diagonal slices
3 medium tomatoes
8–10 iceberg lettuce leaves
75g/3oz/½ cup drained canned chickpeas

For the dressing
15ml/1 tbsp clear honey
90ml/6 tbsp natural (plain) low-fat yogurt
2.5ml/½ tsp salt
5ml/1 tsp coarsely ground black pepper

For the garnish
15ml/1 tbsp walnuts
15ml/1 tbsp sultanas (golden raisins)
1 small onion, cut into rings

1 Peel and dice the sweet potato. Cook in boiling water until soft but not mushy. Remove from the heat, cover the pan and set aside.

2 Cook the carrots in a pan of boiling water for just a few minutes, making sure that they remain crunchy.

3 Drain the water from the sweet potatoes and carrots and mix them together in a bowl.

4 Slice the tops off the tomatoes, then scoop out and discard the seeds. Roughly chop the flesh.

5 Line a serving bowl with the lettuce leaves. Add the carrots, chickpeas and tomatoes to the potatoes and carrots. Mix lightly, then spoon the mixture into the lettuce-lined bowl.

6 Put all the dressing ingredients in a screw-top jar and shake well to combine, or put them into a bowl and beat using a whisk or fork until well incorporated.

7 Garnish the salad with the walnuts, sultanas and onion rings. Pour the dressing over the salad or serve it in a separate bowl.

Spicy Potato Salad

This tasty salad is quick to prepare, and makes a satisfying accompaniment to grilled or barbecued meat or fish.

Serves 6
900g/2lb potatoes
2 red (bell) peppers
2 celery sticks
1 shallot
2 or 3 spring onions (scallions)
1 fresh green chilli
1 garlic clove, crushed
10ml/2 tsp finely chopped fresh chives
10ml/2 tsp finely chopped fresh basil
15ml/1 tbsp finely chopped fresh parsley
30ml/2 tbsp single (light) cream
45ml/3 tbsp mayonnaise
5ml/1 tsp prepared mild mustard
7.5ml/1½ tsp sugar
salt
chopped fresh chives, to garnish

1 Peel the potatoes and cut into chunks. Boil in salted water for 10–12 minutes, until tender. Drain and cool, then place in a large mixing bowl.

2 Halve the peppers, cut away and discard the core and seeds and cut the flesh into small pieces. Finely chop the celery, shallot and spring onions and slice the chilli very thinly, discarding the seeds. Add the vegetables to the potatoes together with the garlic and herbs.

3 Mix the cream, mayonnaise, mustard and sugar in a small bowl, stirring until the mixture is well combined.

4 Pour the dressing over the salad and stir gently to coat evenly. Serve, garnished with the chopped chives.

Cook's Tip
New potatoes would also work deliciously well in this recipe. Scrub them lightly to remove any earth, leaving the skins on, and, unless they are very small, halve them. Cook them until just tender; test them with a knife.

sweet potato & carrot Energy 153kcal/648kJ; Protein 4.7g; Carbohydrate 26.7g, of which sugars 15.4g; Fat 3.9g, of which saturates 0.6g; Cholesterol 0mg; Calcium 88mg; Fibre 3.9g; Sodium 95mg.
spicy potato salad Energy 178kcal/748kJ; Protein 3.9g; Carbohydrate 31.4g, of which sugars 8.7g; Fat 4.9g, of which saturates 1g; Cholesterol 5mg; Calcium 48mg; Fibre 3.3g; Sodium 118mg.

Fennel Coleslaw with Sultanas & Caraway Seeds

A variation on traditional coleslaw in which the aniseed flavour of fennel plays a major role.

Serves 4
175g/6oz fennel
2 spring onions (scallions)
175g/6oz carrots
175g/6oz white cabbage
115g/4oz celery
50g/2oz/⅓ cup sultanas (golden raisins)
2.5ml/½ tsp caraway seeds
15ml/1 tbsp chopped fresh parsley
45ml/3 tbsp extra virgin olive oil
5ml/1 tsp lemon juice
shreds of spring onion (scallion), to garnish

1 Using a sharp knife, cut the fennel and spring onions into thin slices.

2 Cut the carrots into fine strips. Use a mandolin, if you have one, to slice the cabbage and celery finely. Alternatively, use a sharp knife.

3 Place in a bowl with the fennel and spring onions. Add the sultanas and caraway seeds, and toss lightly to mix.

4 Stir in the chopped parsley, olive oil and lemon juice, and mix all the ingredients very thoroughly. Cover and chill for 3 hours to allow the flavours to mingle. Serve garnished with shreds of spring onion.

Cook's Tip
The carrot can be coarsely grated, if you prefer.

Variation
Use sour cream instead of olive oil for a creamier dressing.

Carrot & Orange Salad

A fruit and a vegetable that could have been made for each other form the basis of this fresh-tasting salad.

Serves 4
450g/1lb carrots
2 large oranges
15ml/1 tbsp olive oil
30ml/2 tbsp lemon juice
pinch of sugar (optional)
30ml/2 tbsp chopped pistachio nuts or toasted pine nuts
salt and ground black pepper

1 Peel the carrots and grate them into a large bowl.

2 Using a sharp knife, cut a thin slice of peel and pith from each end of the oranges. Place cut side down on a plate and cut off the peel and pith in strips. Remove any remaining pith. Cut out each segment leaving the pithy membrane behind. Squeeze the remaining juice from the membrane into a bowl.

3 Mix together the olive oil, lemon juice and orange juice from the bowl. Season with a little salt and pepper to taste, and sugar, if you like.

4 Toss the orange segments together with the carrots and pour the dressing over.

5 Sprinkle the salad with the pistachio nuts or pine nuts before serving.

Variation
Sliced eating apple would also work well in this recipe.

Cook's Tip
Be careful to remove all the pith from the orange segments so that you can easily cut just the segment away from the membrane.

fennel coleslaw Energy 145kcal/604kJ; Protein 1.9g; Carbohydrate 15.6g, of which sugars 15.3g; Fat 8.7g, of which saturates 1.2g; Cholesterol 0mg; Calcium 70mg; Fibre 3.8g; Sodium 46mg.
carrot & orange Energy 101kcal/424kJ; Protein 1.8g; Carbohydrate 17.4g, of which sugars 16.8g; Fat 3.2g, of which saturates 0.5g; Cholesterol 0mg; Calcium 75mg; Fibre 4.4g; Sodium 33mg.

Rice Salad

The sky's the limit with this recipe. Use whatever fruit, vegetables and even leftover meat that you might have, mix with cooked rice, and pour over the fragrant dressing.

Serves 4–6

350g/12oz/3 cups cooked rice
1 Asian pear, cored and diced
50g/2oz dried shrimp, chopped
1 avocado, peeled, stoned (pitted) and diced
½ medium cucumber, finely diced
2 lemon grass stalks, finely chopped
30ml/2 tbsp sweet chilli sauce
1 fresh green or red chilli, seeded and finely sliced
115g/4oz/1 cup flaked (sliced) almonds, toasted
small bunch fresh coriander (cilantro), chopped
fresh Thai sweet basil leaves, to garnish

For the dressing

300ml/½ pint/1¼ cups water
10ml/2 tsp shrimp paste
15ml/1 tbsp palm sugar (jaggery) or light muscovado (brown) sugar
2 kaffir lime leaves, torn into small pieces
½ lemon grass stalk, sliced

1 To make the dressing, put the measured water in a small pan with the shrimp paste, palm sugar or light muscovado sugar, kaffir lime leaves and sliced lemon grass.

2 Heat gently, stirring constantly, until the sugar dissolves, then bring to boiling point and simmer for 5 minutes. Strain into a bowl and set aside until cold.

3 Put the cooked rice in a large salad bowl and fluff up the grains with a fork. Add the cored and diced Asian pear, dried shrimp, diced avocado, cucumber, lemon grass and sweet chilli sauce. Mix well.

4 Add the sliced chilli, flaked almonds and chopped coriander to the bowl and toss well. Garnish the salad with Thai basil leaves and serve with the bowl of dressing to spoon over the top of individual portions.

Marigold Salad with Curried Eggs

This dish draws mild Indian spices into a British salad. The dressing has a mild, creamy curry flavour and looks lovely poured over semi-soft boiled eggs strewn with golden and orange marigold petals.

Serves 4

4 medium eggs
5ml/1tsp mild curry powder or paste
75ml/5 tbsp mayonnaise
60ml/4 tbsp single (light) cream
15ml/1 tbsp chopped parsley
1 bag of mixed salad leaves with light and dark red lettuce
1 pot marigold head, using the petals only

1 Boil the eggs by placing them in a pan of boiling water for four minutes. Plunge them in cold water and allow to cool. Shell them carefully and cut into quarters.

2 Stir together the curry powder or paste, mayonnaise and cream in a mixing bowl.

3 Place the chopped parsley and mixed salad leaves in individual bowls, scatter with the eggs and then pour over the curried cream sauce.

4 Add a generous scattering of marigold petals. Serve as a salad with baked ham and thick wholemeal (whole-wheat) bread.

Cook's Tip

Plunging boiled eggs into cold water straight after their cooking time eliminates the dark circle around the yolk that forms if they are left to cool naturally.

Variation

For a spicy picnic lunch, serve the salad alongside rice salad, onion bhajis and samosas.

rice salad Energy 398kcal/1664kJ; Protein 16.2g; Carbohydrate 34.9g, of which sugars 6.7g; Fat 22.4g, of which saturates 2.6g; Cholesterol 63mg; Calcium 249mg; Fibre 4.1g; Sodium 550mg.
marigold salad Energy 493kcal/2034kJ; Protein 7.9g; Carbohydrate 1.3g, of which sugars 1.2g; Fat 51g, of which saturates 7.1g; Cholesterol 241mg; Calcium 100mg; Fibre 1.7g; Sodium 137mg.

Raw Vegetable Yam

In this context, the word 'yam' does not refer to the starchy vegetable that resembles sweet potato, but rather to a unique style of Thai cooking. Yam dishes are salads made with raw or lightly cooked vegetables, dressed with a special spicy sauce.

Serves 4

50g/2oz watercress or baby spinach, chopped
½ cucumber, finely diced
2 celery sticks, finely diced
2 carrots, finely diced
1 red (bell) pepper, seeded and finely diced
2 tomatoes, seeded and finely diced
small bunch fresh mint, chopped
90g/3½oz cellophane noodles

For the yam

2 small fresh red chillies, seeded and finely chopped
60ml/4 tbsp light soy sauce
45ml/3 tbsp lemon juice
5ml/1 tsp palm sugar (jaggery) or light muscovado (brown) sugar
60ml/4 tbsp water
1 head pickled garlic, finely chopped, plus 15ml/1 tbsp vinegar from the jar
50g/2oz/scant ½ cup peanuts, roasted and chopped
90g/3½oz fried tofu, finely chopped
15ml/1 tbsp sesame seeds, toasted

1 Place the watercress or spinach, cucumber, celery, carrots, red pepper and tomatoes in a bowl. Add the chopped mint and toss together.

2 Soak the noodles in boiling water for 3 minutes, or according to the packet instructions, then drain well and snip with scissors into shorter lengths. Add them to the vegetables.

3 To make the yam, put the chopped chillies in a pan and add the soy sauce, lemon juice, sugar and water. Place over a medium heat and stir until the sugar has dissolved. Add the chopped garlic, with the pickling vinegar from the jar, then mix in the chopped nuts, tofu and toasted sesame seeds.

4 Pour the yam over the vegetables and noodles, toss together until well mixed, and serve immediately.

Mushroom Yam

The food of southern Thailand is notoriously hot, and the Muslim community have introduced richer curry flavours reminiscent of Indian food.

Serves 4

90g/3½oz Chinese leaves (Chinese cabbage), shredded
90g/3½oz/generous 1 cup beansprouts
90g/3½oz/scant 1 cup green beans, trimmed
90g/3½oz broccoli, preferably the purple sprouting variety, divided into florets
15ml/1 tbsp sesame seeds, toasted

For the yam

60ml/4 tbsp coconut cream
5ml/1 tsp Thai red curry paste
90g/3½oz/1¼ cups oyster mushrooms or field (portabello) mushrooms, sliced
60ml/4 tbsp coconut milk
5ml/1 tsp ground turmeric
5ml/1 tsp thick tamarind juice, made by mixing tamarind paste with warm water
juice of ½ lemon
60ml/4 tbsp light soy sauce
5ml/1 tsp palm sugar (jaggery) or light muscovado (brown) sugar

1 Steam the shredded Chinese leaves, beansprouts, green beans and broccoli separately or blanch them in boiling water for 1 minute per batch. Drain, place in a serving bowl and leave to cool.

2 To make the yam, pour the coconut cream into a wok or frying pan and heat gently for 2–3 minutes, until it separates. Stir in the red curry paste. Cook over a low heat for 30 seconds, until the mixture is fragrant. Increase the heat to high and add the mushrooms to the wok or pan. Cook for a further 2–3 minutes.

3 Pour in the coconut milk and add the ground turmeric, tamarind juice, lemon juice, soy sauce and sugar to the wok or pan. Mix thoroughly.

4 Pour the mixture over the prepared vegetables and toss well to combine. Sprinkle with the toasted sesame seeds and serve.

vegetable yam Energy 276kcal/1152kJ; Protein 12.1g; Carbohydrate 28.8g, of which sugars 9g; Fat 12.4g, of which saturates 1.5g; Cholesterol 0mg; Calcium 415mg; Fibre 3.1g; Sodium 1101mg.
mushroom yam Energy 109kcal/451kJ; Protein 4g; Carbohydrate 5.6g, of which sugars 4.8g; Fat 8g, of which saturates 4.9g; Cholesterol 0mg; Calcium 69mg; Fibre 2.4g; Sodium 25mg.

Fruit & Vegetable Salad

This Thai fruit salad is traditionally presented with the main course and serves as a cooler to counteract the heat of the chillies that will inevitably be present in the other dishes. It is a typically harmonious balance of flavours.

Serves 4–6

1 small pineapple
1 small mango, peeled and sliced
1 green apple, cored and sliced
6 rambutans or lychees, peeled and stoned (pitted)
115g/4oz/1 cup green beans, trimmed and halved
1 red onion, sliced
1 small cucumber, cut into short sticks
115g/4oz/1½ cups beansprouts
2 spring onions (scallions), sliced
1 ripe tomato, quartered
225g/8oz cos, romaine or iceberg lettuce leaves
salt

For the coconut dipping sauce

30ml/2 tbsp coconut cream
30ml/2 tbsp sugar
75ml/5 tbsp boiling water
1.5ml/¼ tsp chilli sauce
15ml/1 tbsp Thai fish sauce
juice of 1 lime

1 To make the coconut dipping sauce, spoon the coconut cream, sugar and boiling water into a screw-top jar. Add the chilli and fish sauces and lime juice, close tightly and shake to mix thoroughly.

2 Trim both ends of the pineapple with a serrated knife, then cut away the outer skin. Remove the central core with an apple corer. Alternatively, quarter the pineapple lengthways and remove the portion of core from each wedge with a knife. Chop the pineapple and set aside with the other fruits.

3 Bring a small pan of lightly salted water to the boil over a medium heat. Add the green beans and cook for 3–4 minutes, until just tender but still retaining some 'bite'. Drain, refresh under cold running water, drain well again and set aside.

4 To serve, arrange all the fruits and vegetables in small heaps on a platter or in a shallow bowl. Pour the coconut sauce into a small serving bowl and serve separately as a dip.

Warm Vegetable Salad with Peanut Sauce

Based on the Indonesian dish gado-gado, this salad is topped with hard-boiled egg and substantial enough to serve as a main course.

Serves 2–4

8 new potatoes
225g/8oz broccoli, cut into small florets
200g/7oz/1½ cups green beans
2 carrots, cut into thin ribbons with a vegetable peeler
1 red pepper, seeded and cut into strips
50g/2oz/½ cup sprouted beans
sprigs of watercress, to garnish

For the peanut sauce

15ml/1 tbsp sunflower oil
1 bird's eye chilli, seeded and sliced
1 garlic clove, crushed
5ml/1 tsp ground coriander
5ml/1 tsp ground cumin
60ml/4 tbsp crunchy peanut butter
75ml/5 tbsp water
15ml/1 tbsp dark soy sauce
1cm/½in piece fresh root ginger, finely grated
5ml/1 tsp soft dark brown sugar
15ml/1 tbsp lime juice
60ml/4 tbsp coconut milk

1 First make the peanut sauce. Heat the oil in a pan, add the chilli and garlic, and cook for 1 minute or until softened. Add the spices and cook for 1 minute. Stir in the peanut butter and water, then cook for 2 minutes, stirring constantly.

2 Add the soy sauce, ginger, sugar, lime juice and coconut milk, then stir over a low heat for 3 minutes. Set aside in a bowl.

3 Bring a pan of lightly salted water to the boil, add the potatoes and cook for 10–15 minutes, until tender. Drain, then halve or thickly slice the potatoes, depending on their size.

4 Meanwhile, steam the broccoli and green beans for 4–5 minutes until just tender Add the carrots 2 minutes before the end of the cooking time.

5 Arrange the vegetables on a platter. Garnish with watercress and serve with the peanut sauce.

fruit & vegetable salad Energy 151kcal/645kJ; Protein 3.4g; Carbohydrate 34.3g, of which sugars 33g; Fat 1.1g, of which saturates 0.2g; Cholesterol 0mg; Calcium 78mg; Fibre 4.8g; Sodium 35mg.
warm vegetable salad Energy 490Kcal/2043kJ; Protein 18.9g; Carbohydrate 28.5g, of which sugars 21g; Fat 34.3g, of which saturates 8.6g; Cholesterol 116mg; Calcium 80mg; Fibre 6.2g; Sodium 493mg.

Bamboo Shoot Salad

This hot, sharp-flavoured salad originated in north-eastern Thailand. Use canned whole bamboo shoots, if you can find them – they have more flavour than sliced ones.

Serves 4

400g/14oz canned bamboo shoots, cut in large pieces
25g/1oz/about 3 tbsp glutinous rice
30ml/2 tbsp chopped shallots
15ml/1 tbsp chopped garlic
45ml/3 tbsp chopped spring onions (scallions)
30ml/2 tbsp Thai fish sauce
30ml/2 tbsp fresh lime juice
5ml/1 tsp sugar
2.5ml/½ tsp dried chilli flakes
20–25 small fresh mint leaves
15ml/1 tbsp toasted sesame seeds

1 Rinse the bamboo shoots under cold running water, then drain them and pat them thoroughly dry with kitchen paper. Set them aside.

2 Dry-roast the rice in a frying pan until it is golden brown. Leave to cool slightly, then tip into a mortar and grind to fine crumbs with a pestle.

3 Transfer the rice to a bowl and add the shallots, garlic, spring onions, fish sauce, lime juice, sugar, chillies and half the mint leaves. Mix well.

4 Add the bamboo shoots to the bowl and toss to mix. Serve sprinkled with the toasted sesame seeds and the remaining mint leaves.

Cook's Tip
Glutinous rice is an especially sticky rice when boiled, which makes it easy to eat using chopsticks. In this recipe, however, it is toasted and ground.

Curried Red Cabbage Slaw

This recipe takes a well-known Middle-eastern dish and gives it a spicy Indian twist – a delicious way to use red cabbage when it is in season and add vibrant colour to a meal. It may be served hot or cold.

Serves 4–6

½ red cabbage
1 red (bell) pepper
½ red onion
60ml/4 tbsp red, white wine vinegar or cider vinegar
60ml/4 tbsp sugar, or to taste
120ml/4fl oz/½ cup Greek (US strained plain) yogurt or natural (plain) yogurt
120ml/4fl oz/½ cup mayonnaise, preferably home-made
1.5ml/¼ tsp curry powder
2–3 handfuls of raisins
salt and ground black pepper

1 Slice the cabbage finely. Dice the peppers and onion. Put the cabbage, peppers and red onions in a bowl and toss to combine the vegetables well.

2 In a small pan, heat the vinegar and sugar over a low to moderate heat until the sugar has dissolved, then pour over the vegetables. Leave to cool slightly.

3 Combine the yogurt and mayonnaise, then mix into the cabbage mixture. Season to taste with curry powder, salt and ground black pepper, then mix in the raisins.

4 Refrigerate for at least 2 hours before serving. Just before serving, drain off any excess liquid and briefly stir the slaw again over a low heat, or serve it chilled.

Variation
If you prefer, ready-made mayonnaise can be used.

bamboo shoot salad Energy 72kcal/305kJ; Protein 3.9g; Carbohydrate 13g, of which sugars 6.2g; Fat 0.7g, of which saturates 0.1g; Cholesterol 0mg; Calcium 31mg; Fibre 1.9g; Sodium 185mg.
cabbage slaw Energy 286kcal/1194kJ; Protein 3.5g; Carbohydrate 31.6g, of which sugars 31g; Fat 17g, of which saturates 2.6g; Cholesterol 17mg; Calcium 108mg; Fibre 3.1g; Sodium 134mg.

Green Papaya Salad

This salad appears in many guises in South-east Asia. As green papaya is not always easy to get hold of, finely grated carrots, cucumber or even crisp green apple can be used instead. Alternatively, use very thinly sliced white cabbage.

Serves 4

1 green papaya
4 garlic cloves, coarsely chopped
15ml/1 tbsp chopped shallots
3 or 4 fresh red chillies, seeded and sliced
2.5ml/½ tsp salt
2 or 3 snake beans or 6 green beans, cut into 2cm/¾in lengths
2 tomatoes, cut into thin wedges
45ml/3 tbsp Thai fish sauce
15ml/1 tbsp caster (superfine) sugar
juice of 1 lime
30ml/2 tbsp crushed roasted peanuts
sliced fresh red chillies, to garnish

1 Cut the papaya in half lengthways. Scrape out the seeds with a spoon and discard. Using a swivel vegetable peeler or a small sharp knife, remove the peel from the papaya. Shred the flesh finely in a food processor or using a grater.

2 Put the garlic, shallots, red chillies and salt in a large mortar and grind to a paste with a pestle. Add the shredded papaya, a small amount at a time, pounding with the pestle until it becomes slightly limp and soft.

3 Add the sliced snake or green beans and wedges of tomato to the mortar and crush them lightly with the pestle until they are incorporated.

4 Season the mixture with the fish sauce, sugar and lime juice. Transfer the salad to a serving dish and sprinkle with the crushed roasted peanuts.

5 Garnish with the sliced red chillies and serve the salad immediately.

Sweet & Sour Salad

Acar bening makes a perfect accompaniment to spicy dishes and curries, with its sharp, clean taste and bright colours.

Serves 8

1 small cucumber
1 small, ripe pineapple or 425g/15oz can pineapple rings
1 onion, thinly sliced
1 green (bell) pepper, seeded and thinly sliced
3 firm tomatoes, chopped
30ml/2 tbsp golden granulated sugar
45–60ml/3–4 tbsp white wine vinegar
120ml/4fl oz/½ cup water
salt
seeds of 1 or 2 pomegranates, to garnish

1 Halve the cucumber lengthways, remove the seeds, slice and spread on a plate with the onion. Sprinkle with salt. After 10 minutes, rinse and dry.

2 If using a fresh pineapple, peel and core it, removing all the eyes, then cut it into bitesize pieces. If using canned pineapple, drain the rings and cut them into small wedges. Place the pineapple in a bowl with the cucumber, onion, green pepper and tomatoes.

3 Heat the sugar, vinegar and measured water in a pan, stirring until the sugar has dissolved. Remove the pan from the heat and leave to cool. When cold, add a little salt to taste and pour over the fruit and vegetables. Cover and chill until required. Serve in small bowls, garnished with pomegranate seeds.

Variation
To make an Indonesian-style cucumber salad, salt a cucumber as described in the recipe. Make half the dressing and pour it over the cucumber. Add a few chopped spring onions (scallions). Cover and chill. Serve the salad sprinkled with toasted sesame seeds.

papaya salad Energy 109kcal/461kJ; Protein 3.4g; Carbohydrate 16.5g, of which sugars 15.9g; Fat 3.8g, of which saturates 0.7g; Cholesterol 0mg; Calcium 40mg; Fibre 3.5g; Sodium 811mg.
sweet & sour salad Energy 38kcal/161kJ; Protein 0.9g; Carbohydrate 8.4g, of which sugars 8.1g; Fat 0.3g, of which saturates 0.1g; Cholesterol 0mg; Calcium 18mg; Fibre 1.5g; Sodium 6mg.

Fruit & Raw Vegetable Gado Gado

A banana leaf can be used instead of the mixed salad leaves to line the platter for a special occasion.

Serves 6

½ cucumber
2 pears (not too ripe) or 175g/6oz wedge of yam bean
1 or 2 eating apples
juice of ½ lemon
mixed salad leaves
6 small tomatoes, cut into wedges
3 slices fresh pineapple, cored and cut into wedges
3 eggs, hard-boiled, shelled and sliced or quartered
175g/6oz egg noodles, cooked, cooled and chopped
deep-fried onions, to garnish

For the peanut sauce

2–4 fresh red chillies, seeded and ground, or 15ml/1 tbsp chilli sambal
300ml/½ pint/1¼ cups coconut milk
350g/12oz/1¼ cups crunchy peanut butter
15ml/1 tbsp dark soy sauce or soft dark brown sugar
5ml/1 tsp tamarind pulp, soaked in 45ml/3 tbsp warm water
coarsely crushed peanuts
salt

1 To make the peanut sauce, put the ground chillies or chilli sambal in a pan. Pour in the coconut milk, then stir in the peanut butter. Heat gently, stirring, until well blended.

2 Simmer gently until the sauce thickens, then stir in the soy sauce or sugar. Strain in the tamarind juice, add salt to taste, and stir well. Spoon into a bowl and sprinkle with a few coarsely crushed peanuts.

3 To make the salad, core the cucumber and peel the pears or wedge of yam bean. Cut them into matchsticks. Finely shred the apple(s) and sprinkle them with the lemon juice. Spread a bed of mixed leaves on a flat platter, then pile the fruit and vegetables on top.

4 Add the sliced or quartered hard-boiled eggs and chopped noodles. Garnish with the deep-fried onions. Serve immediately, with the peanut sauce.

Scented Fish Salad

For a tropical taste of the Far East, try this delicious fish salad scented with coconut, fruit and warm Thai spices.

Serves 4

350g/12oz fillet of red mullet, sea bream or snapper
1 cos or romaine lettuce
1 papaya or mango, peeled and sliced
1 pitaya, peeled and sliced
1 large ripe tomato, cut into wedges
½ cucumber, peeled and cut into batons
3 spring onions (scallions), sliced
salt

For the marinade

5ml/1 tsp coriander seeds
5ml/1 tsp fennel seeds
2.5ml/½ tsp cumin seeds
5ml/1 tsp caster (superfine) sugar
2.5ml/½ tsp hot chilli sauce
30ml/2 tbsp garlic oil

For the dressing

15ml/1 tbsp coconut cream
45ml/3 tbsp boiling water
60ml/4 tbsp groundnut (peanut) oil
finely grated rind and juice of 1 lime
1 fresh red chilli, seeded and finely chopped
5ml/1 tsp sugar
45ml/3 tbsp chopped fresh coriander (cilantro)

1 Cut the fish into even strips, removing any stray bones. Place it on a plate.

2 To make the marinade, put the coriander, fennel and cumin seeds in a mortar. Add the sugar and crush with a pestle. Stir in the chilli sauce, garlic oil, and salt to taste and mix to a paste. Spread the paste over the fish, cover and leave to marinate in a cool place for at least 20 minutes.

3 To make the dressing, place the coconut cream and salt in a screw-top jar. Stir in the water. Add the oil, lime rind and juice, chilli, sugar and coriander. Shake well.

4 Place the salad ingredients in a bowl and add the dressing.

5 Heat a large non-stick frying-pan, add the fish and cook for 5 minutes, turning once. Add the cooked fish to the salad, toss lightly and serve immediately.

gado gado Energy 577kcal/2411kJ; Protein 21.2g; Carbohydrate 46.3g, of which sugars 21g; Fat 35.5g, of which saturates 8.4g; Cholesterol 95mg; Calcium 88mg; Fibre 6.8g; Sodium 482mg.
fish salad Energy 339kcal/1410kJ; Protein 18.2g; Carbohydrate 15.7g, of which sugars 15.6g; Fat 23g, of which saturates 5.2g; Cholesterol 0mg; Calcium 119mg; Fibre 3.9g; Sodium 94mg.

Aubergine Salad with Shrimp & Egg

An appetizing and unusual salad that you will find yourself making over and over again. Roasting the aubergines really brings out their flavour.

Serves 4–6
2 aubergines (eggplants)
15ml/1 tbsp vegetable oil
30ml/2 tbsp dried shrimp, soaked in warm water for 10 minutes
15ml/1 tbsp coarsely chopped garlic
1 hard-boiled egg, chopped
4 shallots, thinly sliced into rings
fresh coriander (cilantro) leaves and 2 fresh red chillies, seeded and sliced, to garnish

For the dressing
30ml/2 tbsp fresh lime juice
5ml/1 tsp palm sugar (jaggery) or light muscovado (brown) sugar
30ml/2 tbsp Thai fish sauce

1 Preheat the grill (broiler) to medium or preheat the oven to 180°C/350°F/Gas 4. Prick the aubergines several times with a skewer, then arrange on a baking sheet. Cook them under the grill for 30–40 minutes, or until they are charred and tender. Alternatively, roast them by placing them directly on the shelf of the oven for about 1 hour, turning them at least twice. Remove the aubergines and set aside until they are cool enough to handle.

2 Meanwhile, make the dressing. Put the lime juice, palm or muscovado sugar and fish sauce into a small bowl. Whisk well with a fork or balloon whisk. Cover with clear film (plastic wrap) and set aside until required. When the aubergines are cool enough to handle, peel off the skin and cut the flesh into medium slices.

3 Heat the oil in a small frying pan. Drain the dried shrimp thoroughly and add them to the pan with the garlic. Cook over a medium heat for about 3 minutes, until golden. Remove from the pan and set aside.

4 Arrange the aubergine slices on a serving dish. Top with the hard-boiled egg, shallots and dried shrimp mixture. Drizzle over the dressing and garnish with the coriander and red chillies.

Seafood Salad with Fragrant Herbs

This is a spectacular salad. The luscious combination of prawns, scallops and squid makes it the ideal choice for a special celebration.

Serves 4–6
350g/12oz squid
250ml/8fl oz/1 cup fish stock or water
12 raw king prawns (jumbo shrimp), peeled and deveined, with tails intact
12 scallops
50g/2oz cellophane noodles, soaked in warm water for 30 minutes
½ cucumber, cut into thin batons
1 lemon grass stalk, finely chopped
2 kaffir lime leaves, finely shredded
2 shallots, thinly sliced
30ml/2 tbsp chopped spring onions (scallions)
30ml/2 tbsp fresh coriander (cilantro) leaves
12–15 fresh mint leaves, coarsely torn
4 fresh red chillies, seeded and cut into slivers
juice of 1 or 2 limes
30ml/2 tbsp Thai fish sauce
fresh coriander sprigs, to garnish

1 Wash the squid. Pull away the head and tentacles. Remove the ink sac and discard. Pull out all the innards and long transparent 'pen', and discard with the thin body skin. Keep the two small side fins. Slice across the head just under the eyes, severing the tentacles. Discard the rest of the head. Squeeze the tentacles at the head end to push out the round beak and discard. Rinse the pouch and tentacles. Slice into rings.

2 Pour the fish stock or water into a medium pan, set over a high heat and bring to the boil. Cook each type of seafood separately in the stock for 3–4 minutes. Remove with a slotted spoon and set aside to cool.

3 Drain the noodles. Using scissors, cut them into short lengths, about 5cm/2in long. Place them in a serving bowl and add the cucumber, lemon grass, kaffir lime leaves, shallots, spring onions, coriander, mint and chillies.

4 Pour over the lime juice and fish sauce. Mix well, then add the seafood. Toss lightly. Garnish with the fresh coriander and serve.

aubergine salad Energy 91kcal/380kJ; Protein 7.3g; Carbohydrate 4.8g, of which sugars 4.5g; Fat 4.9g, of which saturates 0.9g; Cholesterol 85mg; Calcium 116mg; Fibre 3.2g; Sodium 347mg.
seafood salad Energy 137kcal/578kJ; Protein 20g; Carbohydrate 10.2g, of which sugars 1.2g; Fat 1.8g, of which saturates 0.4g; Cholesterol 171mg; Calcium 61mg; Fibre 0.9g; Sodium 154mg.

Tangy Chicken Salad

This fresh and lively dish typifies the character of Thai cuisine. It is ideal for a light lunch on a hot and lazy summer's day.

Serves 4–6

4 skinned chicken breast fillets
2 garlic cloves, crushed
30ml/2 tbsp soy sauce
30ml/2 tbsp vegetable oil
120ml/4fl oz/½ cup coconut cream
30ml/2 tbsp Thai fish sauce
juice of 1 lime
30ml/2 tbsp palm sugar (jaggery) or light muscovado (brown) sugar
115g/4oz/½ cup water chestnuts, sliced
50g/2oz/½ cup cashew nuts, roasted and coarsely chopped
4 shallots, thinly sliced
4 kaffir lime leaves, thinly sliced
1 lemon grass stalk, thinly sliced
5ml/1 tsp chopped fresh galangal
1 large fresh red chilli, seeded and finely chopped
2 spring onions (scallions), thinly sliced
10–12 fresh mint leaves, torn
1 lettuce, separated into leaves, to serve
2 fresh red chillies, seeded and sliced, to garnish

1 Place the chicken in a large dish. Rub with the garlic, soy sauce and 15ml/1 tbsp of the oil. Cover and leave to marinate for 1–2 hours.

2 Heat the remaining oil in a wok or frying pan and stir-fry the chicken for 3–4 minutes on each side, or until cooked. Remove and set aside to cool.

3 In a pan, heat the coconut cream, fish sauce, lime juice and sugar. Stir until the sugar has dissolved; set aside.

4 Tear the cooked chicken into strips and put it in a bowl. Add the sliced water chestnuts, roasted and chopped cashew nuts, shallots, kaffir lime leaves, lemon grass, galangal, red chilli, spring onions and mint leaves.

5 Pour the coconut dressing over the mixture and toss well. Serve the chicken on a bed of lettuce leaves and garnish with sliced red chillies.

Pomelo Salad

Peanuts, prawns, crab and pomelo make an unusual as well as refreshing and palate-cleansing salad to serve with a selection of other South-east Asian dishes.

Serves 4–6

30ml/2 tbsp vegetable oil
4 shallots, finely sliced
2 garlic cloves, finely sliced
1 large pomelo
15ml/1 tbsp roasted peanuts
115g/4oz cooked peeled prawns (shrimp)
115g/4oz cooked crab meat
10–12 small fresh mint leaves

For the dressing

30ml/2 tbsp Thai fish sauce
15ml/1 tbsp palm sugar (jaggery) or light muscovado (brown) sugar
30ml/2 tbsp fresh lime juice

For the garnish

2 spring onions (scallions), sliced
2 fresh red chillies, seeded and thinly sliced
fresh coriander (cilantro) leaves
shredded fresh coconut (optional)

1 To make the dressing, mix the fish sauce, sugar and lime juice in a bowl. Whisk well, then cover with clear film (plastic wrap) and set aside.

2 Heat the oil in a small frying pan, add the shallots and garlic, and cook over a medium heat until they are golden. Remove from the pan and set aside.

3 Peel the pomelo and break the flesh into small pieces, taking care to remove any membranes.

4 Grind the peanuts coarsely and put them in a salad bowl. Add the pomelo flesh, prawns, crab meat, mint leaves and the shallot mixture. Pour over the dressing, toss lightly and sprinkle with the spring onions, chillies and coriander leaves. Add the shredded coconut, if using. Serve immediately.

Cook's Tip

The pomelo is a large citrus fruit with pinkish-yellow flesh and a sharp taste.

chicken salad Energy 349kcal/1453kJ; Protein 24.3g; Carbohydrate 11.5g, of which sugars 9.8g; Fat 23.2g, of which saturates 12.3g; Cholesterol 43mg; Calcium 49mg; Fibre 1.7g; Sodium 200mg.
pomelo salad Energy 92kcal/383kJ; Protein 7.7g; Carbohydrate 3.8g, of which sugars 3.4g; Fat 5.2g, of which saturates 0.7g; Cholesterol 51mg; Calcium 45mg; Fibre 0.4g; Sodium 143mg.

Beef & Mushroom Salad

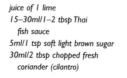

All the ingredients for this traditional Thai dish – known as yam nua yang – are widely available in larger supermarkets.

Serves 4

675g/1½lb fillet or rump (round) steak
30ml/2 tbsp olive oil
2 small mild red chillies, seeded and sliced
225g/8oz/3¼ cups fresh shiitake mushrooms, stems removed and caps sliced

For the dressing

3 spring onions (scallions), finely chopped
2 garlic cloves, finely chopped
juice of 1 lime
15–30ml/1–2 tbsp Thai fish sauce
5ml/1 tsp soft light brown sugar
30ml/2 tbsp chopped fresh coriander (cilantro)

To serve

1 cos or romaine lettuce, torn into strips
175g/6oz cherry tomatoes, halved
5cm/2in piece cucumber, peeled, halved and thinly sliced
45ml/3 tbsp toasted sesame seeds

1 Preheat the grill (broiler) to medium, then cook the steak for 2–4 minutes on each side, depending on how well done you like it. (In Thailand, the beef is traditionally served quite rare.) Leave to cool for at least 15 minutes. Slice the meat as thinly as possible and place the slices in a bowl.

2 Heat the olive oil in a small frying pan. Add the seeded and sliced red chillies and the sliced shiitake mushroom caps. Cook for 5 minutes, stirring occasionally. Turn off the heat and add the steak slices to the pan. Stir well to coat the beef slices in the chilli and mushroom mixture.

3 To make the dressing, mix all the ingredients in a bowl, then pour it over the meat mixture and toss gently. Arrange the lettuce, tomatoes and cucumber on a serving plate. Spoon the steak mixture in the centre and sprinkle the sesame seeds over. Serve immediately.

Coronation Potatoes

The connection between this recipe and traditional Indian cooking is tenuous, but coronation dressing is so popular that it would have been odd to omit it.

Serves 6

450g/1lb new potatoes
45ml/3 tbsp ready-made French dressing
3 spring onions (scallions), chopped
6 eggs, hard-boiled and halved
frilly lettuce leaves
¼ cucumber, cut into thin strips
6 large radishes, sliced
salad cress (optional)
salt and ground black pepper

For the coronation dressing

30ml/2 tbsp olive oil
1 small onion, chopped
15ml/1 tbsp mild curry powder or korma spice mix
10ml/2 tsp tomato purée (paste)
30ml/2 tbsp lemon juice
30ml/2 tbsp sherry
300ml/½ pint/1¼ cups mayonnaise
150ml/¼ pint/⅔ cup natural (plain) yogurt

1 Boil the potatoes in salted water until tender. Drain them, transfer to a large bowl and toss in the French dressing while they are still warm.

2 Stir in the spring onions and the salt and pepper, and leave to cool thoroughly.

3 Meanwhile, make the coronation dressing. Heat the olive oil in a frying pan. Fry the onion for 3 minutes, until soft. Stir in the curry powder or spice mix and fry for a further 1 minute. Remove from the heat and mix in all the other dressing ingredients.

4 Stir the dressing into the potatoes, add the eggs, then chill.

5 Line a serving platter with lettuce leaves and pile the salad in the centre. Sprinkle over the cucumber and radishes with the cress, if using.

beef & mushroom Energy 441kcal/1834kJ; Protein 42.3g; Carbohydrate 3.9g, of which sugars 3.8g; Fat 28.5g, of which saturates 8.3g; Cholesterol 98mg; Calcium 110mg; Fibre 2.6g; Sodium 119mg.
coronation potatoes Energy 590kcal/2443kJ; Protein 10.6g; Carbohydrate 18.1g, of which sugars 5.7g; Fat 51.9g, of which saturates 8.9g; Cholesterol 228mg; Calcium 114mg; Fibre 1.6g; Sodium 403mg.

Cucumber & Shallot Salad

In Malaysia and Singapore, this light, refreshing salad is served with Indian food almost as often as the cooling mint-flavoured cucumber raita. The Malays also enjoy this salad with many of their spicy fish and grilled meat dishes. It can be made ahead of time and keeps well in the refrigerator. Serve it as a salad, or a relish.

Serves 4

1 cucumber, peeled, halved lengthways and seeded
4 shallots, halved lengthways and sliced finely along the grain
1–2 fresh green chillies, seeded and sliced finely lengthways
60ml/4 tbsp coconut milk
5–10ml/1–2 tsp cumin seeds, dry-roasted and ground to a powder
salt
1 lime, quartered, to serve

1 Slice the cucumber halves finely into half moon shapes and sprinkle with salt to draw out the juices. Set aside for about 15 minutes. Rinse well in cold, fresh water and drain off any excess water.

2 Put the cucumber, shallots and chillies in a bowl. Pour in the coconut milk and toss well. Sprinkle most of the roasted cumin seeds over the top.

3 Just before serving, toss the salad again, season with salt, and sprinkle over the rest of the roasted cumin. Transfer to individual side dishes or a salad bowl and serve with lime wedges to squeeze over the salad.

Cook's Tip
You can buy Thai red shallots at Asian markets and food stores.

Variation
Use mild red onions instead of shallots and add some fresh pineapple, chopped into small pieces. Omit the chillies.

Sweet & Sour Cucumber Salad

This salad is a great addition to a summer barbecue or the salad table, and is a delightful accompaniment to any meat, poultry and seafood dishes. The best cucumbers to use here are the short, fat Asian ones.

Serves 4–6

2 cucumbers
30ml/2 tbsp sugar
100ml/3½fl oz/½ cup rice vinegar
juice of half a lime
2 green Thai chillies, seeded and finely sliced
2 shallots, halved and finely sliced
1 small bunch each fresh coriander (cilantro) and mint, stalks removed, leaves finely chopped
salt
fresh coriander leaves and an edible flower (optional), to garnish

1 Use a vegetable peeler to remove strips of the cucumber peel. Halve the cucumbers lengthways and cut into slices. Place the slices on a plate and sprinkle with a little salt. Leave them to stand for 15 minutes. Put the cucumber slices in a colander, rinse off the salt under cold running water, drain and pat dry with kitchen paper.

2 In a bowl, mix the sugar with the vinegar until it has dissolved, then stir in the lime juice and a little salt to taste.

3 Add the chillies, shallots, herbs and cucumber to the dressing and leave to stand for 15–20 minutes. Transfer to a serving dish and garnish with coriander leaves and a flower, if you like.

Cook's Tips
- *There are a number of edible flowers you could use to decorate this salad. Try nasturtiums, borage, chives or colourful English marigold (pot marigold) petals.*
- *If you can only find an English salad cucumber, opt for a single, medium-sized one.*

cucumber & shallot salad Energy 17kcal/68kJ; Protein 0.7g; Carbohydrate 3.3g, of which sugars 2.7g; Fat 0.1g, of which saturates 0g; Cholesterol 0mg; Calcium 19mg; Fibre 0.7g; Sodium 15mg.
sweet & sour cucumber Energy 60kcal/250kJ; Protein 1.3g; Carbohydrate 13.8g, of which sugars 12.2g; Fat 0.3g, of which saturates 0g; Cholesterol 0mg; Calcium 42mg; Fibre 1.5g; Sodium 6mg.

Cucumber Jewel Salad

With its clean taste and bright, jewel-like colours, this Malaysian salad makes a perfect accompaniment to a variety of spicy dishes and curries. Pomegranate seeds, though not traditional, make a beautiful garnish.

Serves 8

1 small cucumber
1 onion, thinly sliced
1 small, ripe pineapple or 425g/15oz can pineapple rings
1 green (bell) pepper, seeded and thinly sliced
3 firm tomatoes, chopped
30ml/2 tbsp sugar
45–60ml/3–4 tbsp white wine vinegar
120ml/4fl oz/½ cup water
salt
seeds of 1–2 pomegranates, to garnish

1 Halve the cucumber lengthways, remove the seeds, slice and spread on a plate with the onion. Sprinkle with salt. After about 10 minutes, rinse off the salt thoroughly and pat dry.

2 If using a fresh pineapple, peel and core it, removing all the eyes, then cut it into bitesize pieces. If using canned pineapple, drain the rings and cut them into small wedges. Place the pineapple in a bowl with the cucumber, onion, green pepper and tomatoes.

3 Heat the sugar, vinegar and water in a pan, stirring until the sugar has dissolved. Remove the pan from the heat and leave to cool. When cold, add a little salt to taste and pour over the fruit and vegetables. Cover and chill until required. Serve in small bowls, garnished with pomegranate seeds.

Variation
To make this Indonesian-style, salt a salad cucumber as described in the recipe. Make half the dressing and pour it over the cucumber. Add a few chopped spring onions (scallions). Cover and chill. Serve scattered with toasted sesame seeds.

Mixed Salad with Lettuce Wraps

Traditionally, an Asian-style table salad is served to accompany spring rolls and pork or shrimp balls, where pieces of the salad might be wrapped around a meaty morsel. When served on its own, as here, the vegetables and fruit in this dish are usually folded into little packets using lettuce leaves or rice wrappers, and then dipped in a sauce, or added bit by bit to bowls of rice or noodles. The salad itself can vary from a bowl of fresh, leafy herbs to a more substanital combination of beansprouts, water chestnuts, mangoes, bananas, star fruit, peanuts and rice noodles.

Serves 4–6

1 crunchy lettuce, leaves separated
½ cucumber, peeled and thinly sliced
2 carrots, finely sliced
200g/7oz/1 cup beansprouts
2 unripe star fruit, finely sliced
2 green bananas, finely sliced
1 firm papaya, cut in half, seeds removed, peeled and finely sliced
leaves from 1 bunch fresh mint and leaves from 1 bunch fresh basil
juice of 1 lime
dipping sauce, to serve

1 Arrange the salad ingredients attractively on a large plate, with the lettuce leaves placed on one side so that they can be used as wrappers.

2 Squeeze the lime juice over the sliced fruits, particularly the bananas to help them retain their colour, and place the salad in the middle of the table. Serve with a dipping sauce.

Cook's Tip
As this salad is meant to be eaten in the hand, supply guests with some napkins, plus finger bowls filled with warm water. Add some lime and lemon slices to the water so that everyone can freshen up afterwards.

cucumber jewel salad Energy 53kcal/224kJ; Protein 0.9g; Carbohydrate 12.3g, of which sugars 12.1g; Fat 0.3g, of which saturates 0.1g; Cholesterol 0mg; Calcium 20mg; Fibre 1.5g; Sodium 6mg.
salad w. lettuce wraps Energy 107kcal/453kJ; Protein 3.1g; Carbohydrate 23g, of which sugars 20.6g; Fat 0.9g, of which saturates 0.2g; Cholesterol 0mg; Calcium 72mg; Fibre 3.8g; Sodium 14mg.

Soya Beansprout Salad

High in protein and vitamins, soya beansprouts are highly nutritious as well as being delicious, and are favoured in Cambodia. Unlike mung beansprouts, they are slightly poisonous when raw and need to be parboiled before use, though this only takes a minute. This salad is often eaten with noodles and rice.

Serves 4

450g/1lb/2 cups fresh soya beansprouts
2 spring onions (scallions), finely sliced
1 small bunch fresh coriander (cilantro), stalks removed, to garnish

For the dressing

15ml/1 tbsp sesame oil
30ml/2 tbsp fish sauce
15ml/1 tbsp white rice vinegar
10ml/2 tsp palm sugar (jaggery) or soft dark brown sugar
1 red chilli, seeded and finely sliced
15g/½oz fresh young root ginger, finely shredded

1 First make the dressing. In a bowl, beat the oil, fish sauce and rice vinegar with the sugar, until it dissolves. Stir in the chilli and ginger and leave to stand for 30 minutes to allow the flavours to develop.

2 Bring a large pan of salted water to the boil. Drop in the beansprouts and blanch for 1 minute only. Tip into a colander, drain, then refresh under running cold water until cool. Drain again and put them into a clean dish towel. Shake out the excess water.

3 Put the beansprouts into a bowl and add the spring onions. Pour over the dressing and toss well. Garnish with coriander leaves and serve.

Variation
Any other edible sprouted bean or pea can be used instead of the beansprouts.

Gado Gado

This Indonesian salad packs a punch, combining lightly steamed vegetables and hard-boiled eggs with a richly flavoured peanut and soy sauce dressing.

Serves 6

225g/8oz new potatoes, halved
2 carrots, cut into sticks
115g/4oz green beans
½ small cauliflower, broken into florets
¼ firm white cabbage, shredded
200g/7oz/¾ cup bean or lentil sprouts
4 eggs, hard-boiled and quartered
bunch of watercress or rocket (arugula)

For the sauce

90ml/6 tbsp crunchy peanut butter
1 garlic clove, crushed
30ml/2 tbsp dark soy sauce
15ml/1 tbsp dry sherry or Chinese rice wine
10ml/2 tsp caster (superfine) sugar
15ml/1 tbsp fresh lemon juice
5ml/1 tsp anchovy extract
300ml/½ pint/1¼ cups water

1 Place the halved potatoes in a metal colander or steamer and set over a pan of gently boiling water. Cover the pan or steamer with a lid and cook the potatoes for 10 minutes.

2 Add the rest of the vegetables to the steamer and steam for a further 10 minutes until tender. Leave to cool.

3 Arrange the vegetables on a plate with the eggs and cress or rocket.

4 Beat together all the sauce ingredients in a large mixing bowl until smooth. Drizzle a little over the salad then pour the rest into a small bowl and serve separately.

Variation
There are a whole range of nut butters, such as hazelnut, almond and cashew, available. Alternatively, make your own peanut butter by blending 225g/8oz peanuts with 120ml/4fl oz/½ cup groundnut (peanut) oil in a food processor.

soya beansprout salad Energy 95kcal/396kJ; Protein 4.5g; Carbohydrate 8.4g, of which sugars 5.6g; Fat 5.6g, of which saturates 0.5g; Cholesterol 3mg; Calcium 54mg; Fibre 2.4g; Sodium 79mg.
gado gado Energy 235kcal/979kJ; Protein 12.7g; Carbohydrate 18.3g, of which sugars 10.6g; Fat 12.5g, of which saturates 3.2g; Cholesterol 127mg; Calcium 91mg; Fibre 4.8g; Sodium 494mg.

Mixed Seaweed Salad

Seaweed is a nutritious, alkaline food which is rich in fibre. Its unusual flavours are a great complement to fish and tofu dishes. This salad is extremely low in fat.

Serves 4

5g/⅛oz each dried wakame, dried arame and dried hijiki seaweeds
about 130g/4½oz fresh enoki mushrooms
15ml/1 tbsp rice vinegar
6.5ml/1¼ tsp salt
2 spring onions (scallions)
a few ice cubes
½ cucumber, cut lengthways
250g/9oz mixed salad leaves

For the dressing
60ml/4 tbsp rice vinegar
7.5ml/1½ tsp toasted sesame oil
15ml/1 tbsp shoyu
15ml/1 tbsp water with a pinch of instant dashi powder
2.5cm/1in piece fresh root ginger, finely grated

1 Soak the dried wakame seaweed for 10 minutes in one bowl of water and, in a separate bowl of water, soak the dried arame and hijiki seaweeds together for 30 minutes.

2 Trim the hard end of the enoki mushroom stalks, then cut the bunch in half and separate the stems.

3 Cook the wakame and enoki mushrooms in boiling water for 2 minutes, then add the arame and hijiki for a few seconds. Immediately remove from the heat.

4 Drain in a sieve (strainer) and sprinkle over the vinegar and salt while still warm. Chill until needed.

5 Slice the spring onions into long, thin, strips, then soak in a bowl of cold water with a few ice cubes added to make them curl up. Drain. Slice the cucumber into thin, half-moon shapes.

6 Mix the dressing ingredients in a bowl. Arrange the mixed salad leaves in a large bowl with the cucumber on top, then add the seaweed and mushroom mixture. Decorate the salad with spring onion curls and serve with the dressing.

Hijiki & Radish Salad

Hijiki is a mild-tasting seaweed and combined with radishes, cucumber and beansprouts, it makes a refreshing salad to accompany a rich main dish.

Serves 4

15g/½oz/½ cup hijiki seaweed
250g/9oz/1¼ cups radishes, sliced into very thin rounds
1 small cucumber, finely sliced
75g/3oz/⅔ cup beansprouts

For the dressing
15ml/1 tbsp sunflower oil
15ml/1 tbsp toasted sesame oil
30ml/2 tbsp rice vinegar or 15ml/1 tbsp wine vinegar
15ml/1 tbsp mirin (sweet rice wine)
5ml/1 tsp light soy sauce

1 Soak the hijiki in a bowl of cold water for 10–15 minutes until it is rehydrated, then drain, rinse under cold running water and drain again. It should almost triple in volume.

2 Place the hijiki in a pan of water. Bring the water to the boil, then reduce the heat and simmer the hijiki for about 30 minutes or until tender.

3 Meanwhile, make the dressing. Whisk the oils with the vinegar and mirin in a bowl until combined, add the soy sauce, and whisk again to mix well.

4 Drain the cooked hijiki in a sieve (strainer) and arrange it in a shallow bowl or platter or on individual salad plates with the prepared radishes, cucumber and beansprouts. Pour over the dressing and toss lightly to combine.

Cook's Tip
Hijiki is a type of seaweed that is popular in Japan. It resembles wakame and is generally sold dried and finely shredded. It is available in airtight packages in many supermarkets and Asian stores. It keeps very well in the store cupboard (pantry).

mixed seaweed salad Energy 26kcal/107kJ; Protein 1.5g; Carbohydrate 2.1g, of which sugars 2g; Fat 1.3g, of which saturates 0.2g; Cholesterol 0mg; Calcium 28mg; Fibre 1.2g; Sodium 272mg.
hijiki & radish salad Energy 70kcal/289kJ; Protein 1.2g; Carbohydrate 2.5g, of which sugars 2.1g; Fat 5.7g, of which saturates 0.8g; Cholesterol 0mg; Calcium 21mg; Fibre 1g; Sodium 98mg.

Noodle, Tofu & Beansprout Salad

Bean thread noodles look like spun glass on this stunning salad, which owes its goodness to fresh beansprouts, diced tomato and cucumber in a sweet-sour dressing.

Serves 4

25g/1oz cellophane noodles
500g/1¼lb mixed sprouted beans and pulses (aduki, chickpea, mung, lentil)
4 spring onions (scallions), finely shredded
115g/4oz firm tofu, diced
1 ripe plum tomato, seeded and diced
½ cucumber, peeled, seeded and diced
60ml/4 tbsp chopped fresh coriander (cilantro)
45ml/3 tbsp chopped fresh mint
60ml/4 tbsp rice vinegar
10ml/2 tsp caster (superfine) sugar
10ml/2 tsp sesame oil
5ml/1 tsp chilli oil
salt and ground black pepper

1 Place the cellophane noodles in a bowl and pour over enough boiling water to cover. Cover and leave to soak for 12–15 minutes.

2 Drain the noodles and then refresh them under cold, running water and drain again. Using a pair of scissors, cut the noodles into roughly 7.5cm/3in lengths and transfer to a bowl.

3 Fill a wok one-third full of boiling water and place over high heat. Add the sprouted beans and pulses and blanch the mixture for 1 minute. Drain, transfer to the noodle bowl and add the spring onions, tofu, tomato, cucumber and herbs.

4 Combine the rice vinegar, sugar, sesame oil and chilli oil and toss into the noodle mixture. Transfer to a serving dish and chill for 30 minutes before serving.

Cook's Tip
If you leave the salad to stand for half an hour to an hour, the flavours will improve as they develop and fuse together.

Fried Tofu Salad with Tangy Sauce

The sweet-sour sauce makes this traditional street snack the perfect foil to grilled meats and stir-fried noodles. If you cannot find kecap manis, simply use dark soy sauce with a little more tomato ketchup to achieve the same balance of flavour.

Serves 4

vegetable oil, for deep-frying
450g/1lb firm rectangular tofu, rinsed, patted dry and cut into blocks
1 small cucumber, partially peeled in strips, seeded and shredded
2 spring onions (scallions), trimmed, halved and shredded
2 handfuls of fresh beansprouts, rinsed and drained
fresh coriander (cilantro) leaves, to garnish

For the sauce

30ml/2 tbsp tamarind pulp, soaked in water until soft
15ml/1 tbsp sesame or groundnut (peanut) oil
4 shallots, finely chopped
4 garlic cloves, finely chopped
2 fresh red chillies, seeded
2.5ml/½ tsp shrimp paste
115g/4oz/1 cup roasted peanuts, crushed
30–45ml/2–3 tbsp kecap manis
15ml/1 tbsp tomato ketchup

1 First make the sauce. Squeeze the tamarind pulp to soften it in the water, and then strain through a sieve (strainer). Measure out 120ml/4fl oz/½ cup tamarind pulp.

2 Heat the sesame or groundnut oil in a wok or heavy pan, and stir in the shallots, garlic and chillies, until fragrant. Stir in the shrimp paste and the peanuts, until they emit a nutty aroma. Add the kecap manis, tomato ketchup and tamarind pulp and blend to form a thick sauce. Set aside and leave to cool.

3 Deep-fry the blocks of tofu in oil until golden brown all over. Pat dry on kitchen paper and cut each block into slices. Arrange the fried tofu slices on a plate with the cucumber, spring onions and beansprouts. Drizzle a little of the sauce over the top and serve the remainder separately in a bowl, garnished with the fresh coriander leaves.

noodle salad Energy 126kcal/528kJ; Protein 7.2g; Carbohydrate 14.8g, of which sugars 7.2g; Fat 4.4g, of which saturates 0.6g; Cholesterol 0mg; Calcium 209mg; Fibre 3.1g; Sodium 17mg.
tofu salad Energy 423kcal/1749kJ; Protein 17.9g; Carbohydrate 7.8g, of which sugars 4.5g; Fat 35.8g, of which saturates 5.3g; Cholesterol 0mg; Calcium 607mg; Fibre 2.8g; Sodium 296mg.

Fried Egg Salad

Chillies and eggs may seem unlikely partners, but actually work very well together. The peppery flavour of the watercress makes it the perfect foundation for this tasty and unusual salad.

Serves 2

15ml/1 tbsp groundnut (peanut) oil
1 garlic clove, thinly sliced
4 eggs
2 shallots, thinly sliced
2 small fresh red chillies, seeded and thinly sliced
½ small cucumber, finely diced
1cm/½in piece fresh root ginger, peeled and grated
juice of 2 limes
30ml/2 tbsp soy sauce
5ml/1 tsp caster (superfine) sugar
small bunch coriander (cilantro)
1 bunch watercress, coarsely chopped

1 Heat the oil in a frying pan. Add the garlic and cook over a low heat until it starts to turn golden. Crack in the eggs. Break the yolks with a wooden spatula, then fry until the eggs are almost firm. Remove from the pan and set aside.

2 Mix the shallots, chillies, cucumber and ginger in a bowl. In a separate bowl, whisk the lime juice with the soy sauce and sugar. Pour this dressing over the vegetables and toss lightly.

3 Set aside a few coriander sprigs for the garnish. Chop the rest and add them to the salad. Toss it again.

4 Reserve a few watercress sprigs and arrange the remainder on two serving plates. Cut the fried eggs into slices and divide them between the watercress mounds. Spoon the shallot mixture over them and serve, garnished with the reserved coriander and watercress.

Variation
Chinese sausages, which taste a bit like pepperoni, would make a good addition to the salad if thinly sliced.

Mooli, Broad Beans & Salmon Roe

This unusual combination of muted colours, flavours and textures makes it ideal company for a refreshing glass of cold sake.

Serves 4

200g/7oz mooli (daikon), peeled
1 nori sheet
1kg/2¼lb broad (fava) beans in their pods, shelled
1.5ml/¼ tsp wasabi paste from tube or 2.5ml/½ tsp wasabi powder mixed with 1.5ml/¼ tsp water
20ml/4 tsp shoyu
60ml/4 tbsp ikura (salmon roe)
salt

1 Grate the mooli finely with a mooli grater, or use a food processor to chop it into fine shreds. Place the mooli in a sieve (strainer) and let the juices drain. Meanwhile, tear the nori with your hands into flakes about 1cm/½in square.

2 In a small pan, cook the broad beans in plenty of rapidly boiling salted water for about 4 minutes. Drain and immediately cool under running water. Remove the skins.

3 Mix the wasabi paste with the shoyu in a small mixing bowl. Add the nori flakes, toasted if you wish, and skinned beans, and mix well.

4 Divide the beans among four individual small bowls, heap on the grated mooli, then spoon the ikura on top. Serve cold. Diners can mix everything together before eating.

Cook's Tips
• The bright inner green part of broad (fava) beans makes a delicious snack when cooked. Simply boil shelled, unskinned beans in very salty water then drain. To eat, snap off the top part of the skin and squeeze the contents into your mouth.
• Toast the nori sheet before tearing into small pieces. Do this by waving the edges over a medium gas flame a few times.

fried egg salad Energy 235kcal/977kJ; Protein 14.8g; Carbohydrate 6.4g, of which sugars 5.6g; Fat 17.2g, of which saturates 3.9g; Cholesterol 381mg; Calcium 154mg; Fibre 1.2g; Sodium 1234mg.
mooli, broad beans Energy 79kcal/335kJ; Protein 7.4g; Carbohydrate 11.6g, of which sugars 2.5g; Fat 0.6g, of which saturates 0.1g; Cholesterol 0mg; Calcium 59mg; Fibre 6.1g; Sodium 369mg.

Aubergine Salad

Roasting aubergines really brings out their flavour.

Serves 4–6

2 aubergines (eggplants)
15ml/1 tbsp vegetable oil
30ml/2 tbsp dried shrimp, soaked in warm water for 10 minutes
15ml/1 tbsp coarsely chopped garlic
1 hard-boiled egg, chopped
4 shallots, thinly sliced into rings
fresh coriander (cilantro) leaves and 2 fresh red chillies, seeded and sliced, to garnish

For the dressing

30ml/2 tbsp fresh lime juice
5ml/1 tsp soft light brown sugar
30ml/2 tbsp fish sauce

1 Preheat the grill (broiler) to medium. Prick the aubergines several times with a skewer, then arrange on a baking sheet. Cook them under the grill for 30–40 minutes, or until they are charred and tender. Remove and set aside until they are cool enough to handle.

2 Meanwhile, make the dressing. Put the lime juice, sugar and fish sauce into a small bowl. Whisk well with a fork or balloon whisk. Cover with clear film (plastic wrap) and set aside.

3 When the aubergines are cool enough to handle, peel off the skin and cut the flesh into medium slices.

4 Heat the oil in a small frying pan. Drain the dried shrimp thoroughly and add them to the pan with the garlic. Cook over a medium heat for about 3 minutes, until golden. Remove from the pan and set aside.

5 Arrange the aubergine slices on a serving dish. Top with the hard-boiled egg, shallots and dried shrimp mixture. Drizzle over the dressing and garnish with the coriander and red chillies.

Variation
For a special occasion, use salted duck's or quail's eggs instead.

Mixed Salad with Coconut

Tender young vegetables, dry roasted coconut and dried prawns make a salad that is a feast of flavours and textures. In towns close to the Thai-Malaysian border, where influences from both cuisines are at work, this salad is known as kerabu, and often served with some of the spicier dishes of the region.

Serves 4

115g/4oz fresh coconut, grated
30ml/2 tbsp dried prawns (shrimp), soaked in warm water until soft
225g/8oz/1 cup beansprouts, rinsed and drained
1 small cucumber, peeled, seeded and cut into julienne strips
2–3 spring onions (scallions), trimmed, cut into 2.5cm/1in pieces and halved lengthways
a handful of young, tender mangetouts (snow peas), halved diagonally
a handful of green beans, halved lengthways
a handful of fresh chives, chopped into 2.5cm/1in pieces
a handful of fresh mint leaves, finely chopped
2–3 fresh red chillies, seeded and sliced finely lengthways
juice of 2 limes
10ml/2 tsp sugar
salt and ground black pepper

1 Dry-roast the coconut in a heavy pan until it is lightly browned and emits a nutty aroma. Using a mortar and pestle or a food processor, grind the roasted coconut to a coarse powder. Transfer the powder to a bowl and set aside.

2 Drain the soaked dried prawns, add them to the mortar or food processor and grind them coarsely, too.

3 Put the vegetables, herbs and chillies into a bowl. Mix the lime juice with the sugar and pour it over the salad. Season with salt and pepper.

4 Add the ground coconut and dried prawns to the salad, and toss well until thoroughly mixed.

5 To serve, divide the salad among four individual salad plates, mounding it up in the centre.

aubergine salad Energy 61kcal/254kJ; Protein 4.8g; Carbohydrate 3.6g, of which sugars 2.8g; Fat 3.2g, of which saturates 0.6g; Cholesterol 57mg; Calcium 75mg; Fibre 1.6g; Sodium 408mg.
mixed salad w. coconut Energy 141kcal/585kJ; Protein 4.5g; Carbohydrate 6.4g, of which sugars 5.1g; Fat 11g, of which saturates 9.1g; Cholesterol 8mg; Calcium 54mg; Fibre 4.6g; Sodium 86mg.

Lotus Stem Salad

You may be lucky enough to find fresh lotus stems in an Asian market, or, as here, you can use the ones preserved in brine.

Serves 4

½ cucumber
225g/8oz jar preserved lotus stems, drained and cut into 5cm/2in strips
2 shallots, finely sliced
25g/1oz/½ cup fresh basil leaves, shredded
salt
fresh coriander (cilantro) leaves, to garnish

For the dressing

juice of 1 lime
30ml/2 tbsp fish sauce
1 fresh red chilli, seeded and chopped
1 garlic clove, crushed
15ml/1 tbsp sugar

1 To make the dressing, mix together the dressing ingredients in a bowl, whisk well and set aside.

2 Peel the cucumber and cut it into 5cm/2in batons. Soak the batons in cold salted water for 20 minutes. Put the lotus stems into a bowl of water. Using a pair of chopsticks, stir the water so that the loose fibres of the stems wrap around the sticks.

3 Drain the stems and put them in a clean bowl. Drain the cucumber batons and add to the bowl, then add the shallots, shredded basil leaves and the prepared dressing. Toss to mix and then leave the salad to marinate for 20 minutes before serving. Garnish with fresh coriander leaves.

Variation

If you cannot find the lotus stems, lotus roots make a good substitute and are readily available in Asian markets. When buying fresh, choose roots that feel heavy for their size, as this is an indication that they are full of liquid. They should be peeled and soaked in water with a little lemon juice before being added to the salad, to retain their pale colour.

Green Mango Salad

This simple salad has a refreshingly tangy, sweet flavour and a lovely texture, and is delicious served with steamed or stir-fried prawns, and with barbecued or seared beef.

Serves 4

450g/1lb green mangoes
grated rind and juice of 2 limes
30ml/2 tbsp sugar
30ml/2 tbsp fish sauce
2 fresh green chillies, seeded and finely sliced
1 small bunch fresh coriander (cilantro), stalks removed, finely chopped
salt

1 Peel, halve and stone (pit) the green mangoes, and slice them into thin strips.

2 In a bowl, mix together the lime rind and juice, sugar and fish sauce. Add the mango strips with the chillies and about three quarters of the coriander. Add salt to taste and leave to stand for 20 minutes to allow the flavours to mingle.

3 Serve on individual salad plates, garnished with the remaining chopped coriander.

Variation

Top the salad with crayfish tails. You can usually buy these preserved in brine, in a 320g/11½oz can. Simply drain and arrange on the salad as you wish.

Cook's Tip

Although the sweet and juicy orange and yellow mangoes and papayas are devoured in vast quantities when ripe, they are also popular for cooking when green. Their rather different, tart flavour and crunchy texture make them ideal for salads and stews. Green mangoes have a dark green skin and can be found at many Chinese and Asian markets.

lotus stem salad Energy 40kcal/168kJ; Protein 1.4g; Carbohydrate 8.3g, of which sugars 7.5g; Fat 0.3g, of which saturates 0g; Cholesterol 0mg; Calcium 55mg; Fibre 1.7g; Sodium 573mg.
green mango salad Energy 69kcal/293kJ; Protein 1.2g; Carbohydrate 16.2g, of which sugars 15.8g; Fat 0.4g, of which saturates 0.1g; Cholesterol 0mg; Calcium 39mg; Fibre 3.6g; Sodium 7mg.

Pickled Ginger

The Chinese love cooking with ginger. Warming, good for the heart, and believed to aid digestion, it finds its way into salads, soups, stir-fries and puddings. Pickled ginger is an immensely useful condiment, easy to prepare and often served with noodles and rice.

Serves 4–6

225g/8oz fresh young ginger, peeled
10ml/2 tsp salt
200ml/7fl oz/1 cup white rice vinegar
50g/2oz/¼ cup sugar

1 Place the ginger in a bowl and sprinkle with salt. Cover and place in the refrigerator for 24 hours.

2 Drain off any excess liquid and pat the ginger dry with a clean dish towel.

3 Slice each knob of ginger very finely along the grain, like thin rose petals, and place them in a clean bowl or a sterilized jar suitable for storing.

4 In a small bowl beat the vinegar and 50ml/2fl oz/¼ cup water with the sugar, until it has dissolved. Pour the pickling liquid over the ginger and cover or seal. Store in the refrigerator or a cool place for about a week.

Cook's Tips

- *Juicy and tender with a pinkish-yellow skin, young ginger is less fibrous than the mature rhizome. When pickled in vinegar, the flesh turns pale pink.*
- *Aside from its obvious application in Chinese cookery, pickled ginger is also served with sushi. It can also enliven less exotic dishes such as a pear and walnut salad, a few slices of cold roast duck, or even something as simple as a ham sandwich. It is valued for the way in which it cuts through oily flavours, so this pickle also tastes good with smoked mackerel.*

Pickled Vegetables

Popular pickles include the trio of cucumber, mooli and carrot – green, white and orange in colour. These tend to be served as snacks for nibbling, or as part of a table salad. They are also used as accompaniments to grilled meats and shellfish.

Serves 4–6

300ml/½ pint/1¼ cups white rice vinegar
90g/3½oz/scant ½ cup sugar
450g/1lb carrots, cut into 5cm/2in matchsticks
450g/1lb mooli (daikon), halved lengthways, and cut into thin crescents
600g/1lb 6oz cucumbers, partially peeled in strips and cut into 5cm/2in matchsticks
15ml/1 tbsp salt

1 Put the vinegar and sugar in a large bowl and whisk with a fork or balloon whisk until all the sugar has dissolved.

2 Add the carrots and mooli to the vinegar mixture and toss well to coat. Cover the bowl with clear film (plastic wrap) and place in the refrigerator for 24 hours.

3 Spread out the cucumber strips on several plates and sprinkle with the salt. Leave for 30 minutes, then tip into a colander, rinse under cold water and drain well.

4 Add the cucumber slices to the carrot and mooli and toss well in the pickling liquid. Cover and refrigerate as before.

5 Lift the vegetables out of the pickling liquid to serve immediately, or spoon them into a jar. Seal with clear film and a tight-fitting lid and store in the refrigerator.

Cook's Tip

To sterilize pickling jars, place them in a deep pan and pour in enough hot water to cover them. Allow the water to boil for ten minutes, then remove the jars, drain and allow to air-dry.

pickled ginger Energy 36kcal/151kJ; Protein 0.2g; Carbohydrate 9.1g, of which sugars 9.1g; Fat 0.1g, of which saturates 0g; Cholesterol 0mg; Calcium 20mg; Fibre 0.4g; Sodium 678mg.
pickled vegetables Energy 104kcal/438kJ; Protein 1.8g; Carbohydrate 24.5g, of which sugars 24.1g; Fat 0.5g, of which saturates 0.2g; Cholesterol 0mg; Calcium 59mg; Fibre 3.1g; Sodium 1013mg.

Vietnamese Shrimp Sauce

Popular as a condiment for roasted and grilled meats, this sauce is also added to soups, broths and noodles. As it includes the fiercely pungent fermemted shrimp paste mam tom, this sauce is powerful and should be used in moderation.

Makes 200ml/7fl oz/ scant 1 cup

3 garlic cloves, chopped
1 fresh red chilli, seeded and chopped
1 small bunch fresh coriander (cilantro), stalks removed
30ml/2 tbsp sugar
juice of 3 limes
30ml/2 tbsp mam tom (Vietnamese shrimp sauce)
30ml/2 tbsp nuoc mam (Vietnamese fish sauce)

1 Using a mortar and pestle, pound the garlic, chilli, coriander and sugar to a paste.

2 Add the lime juice, man tom and nuoc mam. Mix well and serve with grilled meats.

Fried Black Chilli Sauce

Thai in origin, this spicy, salty sauce adds a unique flavour to many soups, such as the sour fish soup enjoyed throughout Cambodia and Vietnam. It is also used as a dip for grilled and roasted meats.

Makes 200ml/7fl oz/ scant 1 cup

50g/2oz dried shrimp, soaked in water for 20 minutes
12 dried red chillies, soaked in water for 20 minutes
120ml/4fl oz/½ cup vegetable oil
8 garlic cloves, finely chopped
4 shallots or 1 onion, chopped
30ml/2 tbsp Thai shrimp paste
30ml/2 tbsp palm sugar (jaggery)

1 Drain the shrimp and, using a mortar and pestle, pound them to a paste.

2 Drain the chillies, discard the stalks and seeds and chop finely.

3 Heat the oil in a wok and stir-fry the garlic and shallots or onion until fragrant. Add the pounded shrimp, chillies, Thai shrimp paste and palm sugar. Stir-fry until the chillies are dark in colour.

4 Remove from the heat and pour into a serving bowl or individual dipping bowls. Serve hot or cold.

Cook's Tip
Nuoc mam is a fish sauce made by layering anchovies and salt in wooden boxes and pressing them to gradually extract the pungent liquid. This is an age-old tradition all over South-east Asia, and variations of this condiment appear in many recipes.

Kimchi

This Korean speciality is now enjoyed all over Asia, thanks to the immigrants who couldn't live without the favourite food of the home country. In the past, large stone pots were filled with this pickled cabbage, and buried in the ground for the winter.

Serves 4–6

675g/1½lb Chinese leaves (Chinese cabbage), shredded
1 large or 2 medium yam beans, total weight about 675g/1½lb or 2 hard pears, peeled and thinly sliced
60ml/4 tbsp salt
200ml/7fl oz/scant 1 cup water
4 spring onions (scallions), chopped
4 garlic cloves, crushed
2.5cm/1in piece fresh root ginger, peeled and finely chopped
10–15ml/2–3 tsp chilli powder

1 Place the Chinese leaves and yam beans or pears in a bowl and sprinkle evenly with salt. Mix well, then press the vegetable mixture down into the bowl.

2 Pour the water over the vegetables, if necessary putting a plate over them so that they remain submerged, then cover the bowl and leave overnight in a cool place.

3 The following day, drain off the brine from the vegetables and set it aside. Mix the brined vegetables with the spring onions, garlic, ginger and chilli powder. Pack the mixture into a 900g/2lb jar or two smaller ones. Pour over the reserved brine.

4 Cover with clear film (plastic wrap) and place on a sunny windowsill or in a warm place for 2–3 days.

Cook's Tip
Today, it is recommended that the mixture is stored in the refrigerator after its initial spell in the sunshine. It will keep for several weeks in a tightly lidded jar.

shrimp paste Energy 362kcal/1521kJ; Protein 13g; Carbohydrate 47g, of which sugars 39g; Fat 15g, of which saturates 2.7g; Cholesterol 0mg; Calcium 149mg; Fibre 6.8g; Sodium 23mg.
chilli sauce Energy 1059kcal/4389kJ; Protein 30g; Carbohydrate 43g, of which sugars 40g; Fat 86g, of which saturates 10g; Cholesterol 253mg; Calcium 653mg; Fibre 2g; Sodium 2171mg.
kimchi Energy 45kcal/190kJ; Protein 2.3g; Carbohydrate 8.5g, of which sugars 8g; Fat 0.4g, of which saturates 0g; Cholesterol 0mg; Calcium 76mg; Fibre 3.2g; Sodium 240mg.

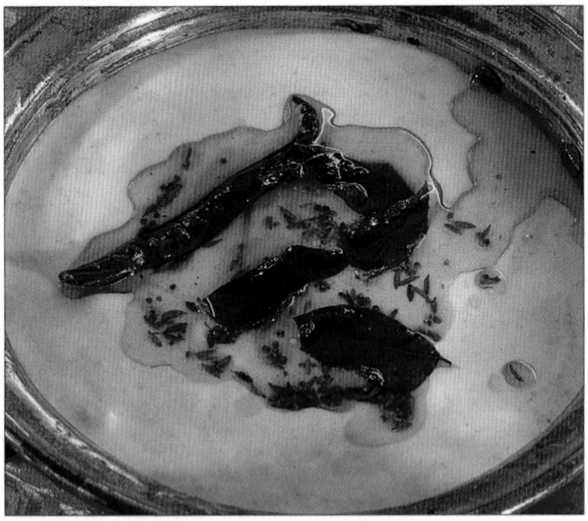

Spiced Yogurt

Yogurt is always a welcome accompaniment to hot curries. Here, it is topped with a hot spice mixture to provide a contrast in both taste and temperature.

Makes 450ml/¾ pint/ scant 2 cups

450ml/¾ pint/scant 2 cups natural (plain) yogurt
2.5ml/½ tsp freshly ground fennel seeds
2.5ml/½ tsp sugar
60ml/4 tbsp vegetable oil
1 dried red chilli
1.5ml/¼ tsp mustard seeds
1.5ml/¼ tsp cumin seeds
4–6 curry leaves
a pinch each of asafoetida and ground turmeric
salt

1 In a heatproof serving dish, mix together the yogurt, fennel seeds, salt and sugar. Cover and chill until you are nearly ready to serve.

2 Heat the oil in a frying pan and fry the dried chilli, mustard and cumin seeds, curry leaves, asafoetida and turmeric.

3 When the chilli turns dark, pour the oil and spices over the yogurt. Fold the yogurt together with the spices at the table just before serving.

Variation
Asafoetida is quite bitter. Leave it out, if you prefer.

Cook's Tip
You must keep asafoetida in an airtight container because its sulphurous odour will affect other foods and spices. It is most commonly available as a powder or granules, and is also sold in lumps that need to be crushed before using. It is a very powerful spice and should therefore be used in minute quantities. Even in its ground state, asafoetida lasts well over a year if stored properly, away from light and air.

Grape & Walnut Raita

Refreshing raitas are served to cool the effect of hot curries. Cucumber and mint raita is the best known combination. Here is an unusual fruit and nut version, which is particularly good with beef curries.

Serves 4

350ml/12fl oz/1½ cups natural (plain) yogurt
75g/3oz seedless grapes
50g/2oz/½ cup shelled walnuts
2 firm bananas
5ml/1 tsp sugar
5ml/1 tsp freshly ground cumin seeds
salt
1.5ml/¼ tsp freshly roasted cumin seeds, chilli powder or paprika, to garnish

1 Place the yogurt in a chilled bowl and add the grapes and walnuts.

2 Slice the bananas directly into the bowl and fold in gently before they turn brown.

3 Add the sugar, salt and ground cumin, and gently mix together.

4 Chill, and just before serving, sprinkle on the cumin seeds, chilli powder or paprika.

Variations
- *Instead of grapes, try kiwi fruit, peaches or nectarines.*
- *Almonds or hazelnuts can be used instead of or as well as the walnuts.*
- *For Coconut and Raisin Raita, coarsely grate half a fresh coconut by hand or using a food processor. Mix in a bowl with 225g/8oz natural (plain) yogurt and 2.5ml/½ tsp sugar. Stir in 25g/1oz chopped fresh coriander (cilantro) or mint, and add salt to taste. Transfer to a serving bowl.*

spiced yogurt Energy 441kcal/1842kJ; Protein 25.2g; Carbohydrate 41.6g, of which sugars 36.4g; Fat 21.5g, of which saturates 4.3g; Cholesterol 6mg; Calcium 884mg; Fibre 0g; Sodium 379mg.
grape & walnut raita Energy 202kcal/847kJ; Protein 7.2g; Carbohydrate 23.2g, of which sugars 21.5g; Fat 9.8g, of which saturates 1.2g; Cholesterol 1mg; Calcium 186mg; Fibre 1.1g; Sodium 75mg.

Sweet & Sour Raita

This raita teams honey with mint sauce, chilli and fresh coriander to make a soothing mixture with underlying warmth. It goes well with biryanis.

Serves 4

475ml/16fl oz/2 cups natural (plain) low-fat yogurt
5ml/1 tsp salt
5ml/1 tsp sugar
30ml/2 tbsp clear honey
7.5ml/1½ tsp mint sauce
30ml/2 tbsp roughly chopped fresh coriander (cilantro)
1 fresh green chilli, seeded and finely chopped
1 medium onion, diced
50ml/2fl oz/¼ cup water

1 Pour the yogurt into a bowl and whisk it well. Add the salt, sugar, honey and mint sauce.

2 Taste to check the sweetness and add more honey, if desired.

3 Reserve a little chopped coriander for the garnish and add the rest to the yogurt mixture, with the chilli, onion and water.

4 Whisk once again and pour into a serving bowl. Garnish with the reserved coriander and place in the refrigerator until ready to serve.

Variation

For Spinach Raita, finely chop 225g/8oz cooked spinach. Add to 450ml/¾ pint/scant 2 cups natural (plain) yogurt and mix in 2 chopped green chillies, 1.5ml/¼ tsp sugar, and salt and pepper to taste.

Cook's Tip

A 5–10cm/2–4in piece of peeled, seeded and grated cucumber can also be added to raita. Drain the cucumber in a colander, pressing it against the sides to extract excess liquid, which would dilute the raita.

Sweet & Sour Tomato & Onion Relish

This delicious relish can be served with any savoury meal. Choose vine-ripened tomatoes, if you can, as they have a superior flavour.

Serves 4

2 medium firm tomatoes
1 medium onion
1 fresh green chilli
15ml/1 tbsp fresh mint leaves
15ml/1 tbsp fresh coriander (cilantro) leaves
2.5ml/½ tsp Tabasco sauce
15ml/1 tbsp clear honey
2.5ml/½ tsp salt
30ml/2 tbsp lime juice
15ml/1 tbsp natural (plain) low-fat yogurt

1 Place the tomatoes in hot water for a few seconds. Lift each tomato out in turn, using a slotted spoon. The skins should have split, making it easy to remove them. Peel off carefully.

2 Cut the tomatoes in half, and squeeze out the seeds. Chop the flesh roughly. Set them aside while you prepare the other ingredients.

3 Using a sharp knife, roughly chop the onion, green chilli, mint and fresh coriander.

4 Place the herb mixture in a food processor with the Tabasco sauce, honey, salt and lime juice. Add the tomatoes to this and grind everything together for a few seconds.

5 Pour into a small serving bowl. Stir in the yogurt just before you serve the relish.

Cook's Tip

This relish will keep for up to 1 week in the refrigerator: prepare up to the end of step 4 but do not add the yogurt until just before you want to serve it.

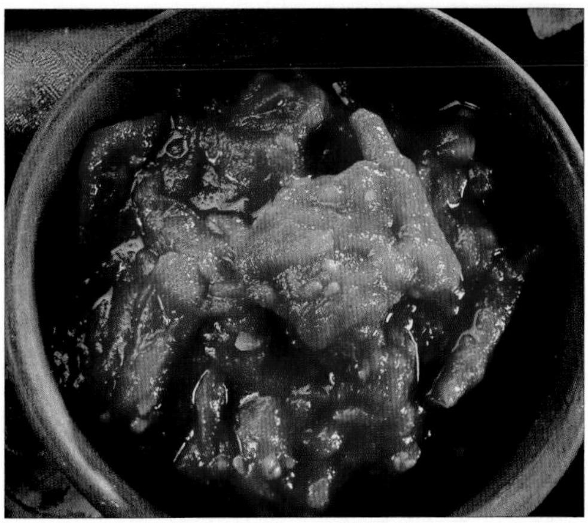

sweet & sour raita Energy 98kcal/413kJ; Protein 6.7g; Carbohydrate 16.2g, of which sugars 15.8g; Fat 1.4g, of which saturates 0.6g; Cholesterol 2mg; Calcium 255mg; Fibre 0.8g; Sodium 595mg.
tomato & onion relish Energy 29kcal/123kJ; Protein 1g; Carbohydrate 5.8g, of which sugars 5.4g; Fat 0.4g, of which saturates 0.1g; Cholesterol 0mg; Calcium 39mg; Fibre 1.2g; Sodium 257mg.

Fresh Coriander Relish

Delicious as an accompaniment to kebabs, samosas and bhajias, this relish can also be used as a spread for cucumber or tomato sandwiches.

Makes about 450g/1lb/ 2 cups

30ml/2 tbsp vegetable oil
1 dried red chilli
1.5ml/¼ tsp each cumin, fennel and onion seeds
1.5ml/¼ tsp asafoetida
4 curry leaves
115g/4oz/1⅓ cups desiccated (dry unsweetened shredded) coconut
10ml/2 tsp sugar
3 fresh green chillies, chopped
175–225g/6–8oz fresh coriander (cilantro), chopped
60ml/4 tbsp mint sauce
juice of 3 lemons
salt

1 Heat the oil in a frying pan and add the dried chilli, the cumin, fennel and onion seeds, the asafoetida, curry leaves, desiccated coconut, sugar and salt. Fry, stirring often, until the coconut turns golden brown. Tip into a bowl and leave to cool.

2 Grind the spice mixture with the green chillies, fresh coriander and mint sauce. Moisten with lemon juice. Scrape into a bowl and chill before serving.

Cook's Tip
This may seem like a lot of coriander, but it is compacted when ground with the spices.

Variation
For Coriander (cilantro) and Walnut Relish, put 90ml/6 tbsp fresh coriander leaves, 2 garlic cloves, 50g/2oz chopped onion and 60ml/4 tbsp sugar into a food processor and grind until thick. Add 50g/2oz/½ cup chopped walnuts and mix well. Add salt and ground black pepper to taste.

Tomato Relish

This is a simple relish that can be served with most meals. It provides a contrast to hot curries, with its crunchy texture and refreshing ingredients.

Serves 4–6

2 small fresh green chillies
2 limes
2.5ml/½ tsp sugar, or to taste
2 onions, finely chopped
4 firm tomatoes, finely chopped
½ cucumber, finely chopped
a few fresh coriander (cilantro) leaves, chopped
salt and ground black pepper
a few fresh mint leaves, to garnish

1 Using a sharp knife, cut both chillies in half. Scrape out the seeds, then chop the chillies finely and set aside.

2 Squeeze the limes. Pour the juice into a glass bowl and add the sugar, with salt and pepper to taste. Set the bowl aside until the sugar and salt have dissolved, stirring the mixture occasionall to aid this process.

3 Add the chopped chillies to the bowl, with the chopped onions, tomatoes, cucumber and fresh coriander leaves. Mix the vegetables well.

4 Cover the bowl with clear film (plastic wrap) and place in the refrigerator for at least 3 hours, so that the flavours blend. Just before serving, taste the relish and add more salt, pepper or sugar if needed. Garnish with mint and serve.

Cook's Tip
For a milder flavour, use just one chilli, or dispense with the chilli altogether and substitute a green (bell) pepper.

coriander relish Energy 1121kcal/4640kJ; Protein 17.2g; Carbohydrate 42.7g, of which sugars 36.5g; Fat 98.5g, of which saturates 64.3g; Cholesterol 0mg; Calcium 631mg; Fibre 28.3g; Sodium 534mg.
tomato relish Energy 20kcal/82kJ; Protein 1g; Carbohydrate 3.6g, of which sugars 3.1g; Fat 0.2g, of which saturates 0g; Cholesterol 0mg; Calcium 16mg; Fibre 0.8g; Sodium 5mg.

Fried Sesame Seed Chutney

This versatile chutney doubles as a dip, and also a sandwich filling with thin slices of cucumber.

Serves 4

175g/6oz/¾ cup sesame seeds
5ml/1 tsp salt
120–150ml/4–5fl oz/½–⅔ cup water
2 fresh green chillies, seeded and diced
60ml/4 tbsp chopped fresh coriander (cilantro)
15ml/1 tbsp chopped fresh mint
15ml/1 tbsp tamarind paste
30ml/2 tbsp granulated (white) sugar
5ml/1 tsp vegetable oil
1.5ml/¼ tsp onion seeds
4 curry leaves
onion rings, sliced chillies and fresh coriander leaves, to garnish

1 Dry-roast the sesame seeds by putting them into a pan without adding any oil. Cook over medium to high heat, tossing them occasionally so that they brown evenly all over. Watch them carefully as they will burn if left. Leave the seeds to cool and then grind them in a coffee grinder until they become a grainy powder.

2 Transfer the sesame powder to a bowl. Add the salt, water, diced chillies, coriander, mint, tamarind paste and sugar, and use a fork to mix everything together.

3 Taste and adjust the seasoning, if necessary; the mixture should have a sweet and sour flavour. Add a little more tamarind paste if it needs to be more sour, or sugar to sweeten, if required.

4 Heat the oil in a heavy pan and fry the onion seeds and curry leaves together.

5 Tip the ground sesame seeds into the pan and stir-fry for about 45 seconds. Transfer the chutney to a serving dish and leave to cool completely.

6 Garnish with onion rings, sliced green and red chillies and fresh coriander leaves and serve with your chosen curry.

Apricot Chutney

Chutneys can add zest to most meals, and in India you will usually find a selection of different kinds served in tiny bowls for people to choose from. Dried apricots are readily available from supermarkets and health food shops.

Makes about 450g/1lb/2 cups

450g/1lb/2 cups dried apricots, finely diced
5ml/1 tsp garam masala
275g/10oz/1¼ cups soft light brown sugar
450ml/¾ pint/scant 2 cups malt vinegar
5ml/1 tsp grated fresh root ginger
5ml/1 tsp salt
75g/3oz/½ cup sultanas (golden raisins)
450ml/¾ pint/scant 2 cups water

1 Put the dried apricots and garam masala into a medium pan and add the light brown sugar, malt vinegar, ginger, salt, sultanas and water. Mix thoroughly with a spoon.

2 Bring to the boil, then reduce the heat and simmer for 30–35 minutes, stirring occasionally.

3 When the chutney has thickened to a fairly stiff consistency, spoon it into 2–3 clean jam jars and leave to cool. This chutney should be stored in the refrigerator.

Variation

For Orchard Fruit Chutney, put 675g/1½lb peeled, cored and chopped cooking apples into a large pan with 115g/4oz/¼ cup each dried peaches and apricots and 50g/2oz/scant ½ cup raisins. Chop 5 garlic cloves and grate a 5cm/2in piece of fresh root ginger and add them to the pan. Add 350g/12oz soft light brown sugar, 400ml/14fl oz/1⅔ cups malt vinegar, 10ml/2 tsp salt and 5ml/1 tsp cayenne pepper. Bring the mixture to the boil and simmer for 30 minutes, stirring frequently.

sesame seed chutney Energy 303kcal/1256kJ; Protein 8.5g; Carbohydrate 8.6g, of which sugars 8.4g; Fat 26.3g, of which saturates 3.7g; Cholesterol 0mg; Calcium 327mg; Fibre 4.2g; Sodium 506mg.
apricot chutney Energy 2015kcal/8594kJ; Protein 22.1g; Carbohydrate 505.4g, of which sugars 503.7g; Fat 3.6g, of which saturates 0.1g; Cholesterol 0mg; Calcium 532mg; Fibre 29.9g; Sodium 2060mg.

Fresh Tomato & Onion Chutney

Chutneys are served with most meat dishes in Indian cuisine. This one is lightly spiced and perfect to accompany a heavily spiced meal.

Serves 4
8 tomatoes
1 medium onion, chopped
45ml/3 tbsp light muscovado (brown) sugar
5ml/1 tsp garam masala
5ml/1 tsp ground ginger
175ml/6fl oz/¾ cup malt vinegar
5ml/1 tsp salt
15ml/1 tbsp clear honey
natural (plain) yogurt, sliced green chilli and fresh mint leaves, to garnish

1 Cut the tomatoes into quarters.

2 Place them with the onion in a heavy pan, and add the sugar, garam masala, ginger, vinegar, salt and honey.

3 Half-cover the pan with a lid and cook over a low heat for about 20 minutes.

4 Mash the tomatoes with a fork to break them up, then continue to cook them on a slightly higher heat until the chutney thickens.

5 Spoon the chutney into a bowl and leave to cool, then cover and place in the refrigerator until needed.

6 Serve chilled, garnished with yogurt, sliced chilli and mint leaves.

Cook's Tips
- *This chutney will keep for about 2 weeks in a covered container in the refrigerator. Add the garnish when ready to serve.*
- *Malt vinegar is generally used for chutneys that require a rich flavour as it has a fuller flavour than white wine vinegar.*
- *The sugar and vinegar give the chutney its flavour as well as its keeping qualities.*

Tomato Chutney with Cinnamon & Nigella

This delicious relish is especially suited to lentil dishes. If kept in a covered bowl in the refrigerator, it will keep for a week.

Makes 450–500g/1–1¼lb/ 2–2¼ cups
90ml/6 tbsp vegetable oil
5cm/2in piece cinnamon stick
4 cloves
5ml/1 tsp freshly roasted cumin seeds
5ml/1 tsp nigella seeds
4 bay leaves
5ml/1 tsp mustard seeds, crushed
4 garlic cloves
800g/1¾lb canned, chopped tomatoes
5cm/2in piece fresh root ginger, crushed
5ml/1 tsp chilli powder
5ml/1 tsp ground turmeric
60ml/4 tbsp soft light brown sugar

1 Pour the oil into a frying pan, karahi or wok and place over a medium heat. When the oil is hot, fry the cinnamon, cloves, cumin and nigella seeds, bay leaves and mustard seeds for about 5 minutes.

2 Crush the garlic cloves and add them to the spice mixture. Fry until golden. Meanwhile, drain the tomatoes, reserving the juices.

3 Add the ginger, chilli powder, turmeric, sugar and the reserved tomato juices. Simmer until reduced to a thick consistency, add the tomatoes and cook for 15–20 minutes. Cool and serve.

Cook's Tip
Nigella seeds, or kalonji, are frequently used in Indian cooking. They are small black oval-shaped seeds that have a strong, slightly peppery taste a little like oregano. They are most often seen sprinkled over naan breads. They add depth to the flavour of this chutney but can be omitted if you are unable to find them.

tomato & onion chutney Energy 102kcal/434kJ; Protein 2g; Carbohydrate 22.9g, of which sugars 21.7g; Fat 1g, of which saturates 0.3g; Cholesterol 0mg; Calcium 29mg; Fibre 2.2g; Sodium 21mg.
tomato chutney Energy 1038kcal/4334kJ; Protein 9.6g; Carbohydrate 96.2g, of which sugars 87.5g; Fat 71.6g, of which saturates 9g; Cholesterol 0mg; Calcium 133mg; Fibre 8g; Sodium 84mg.

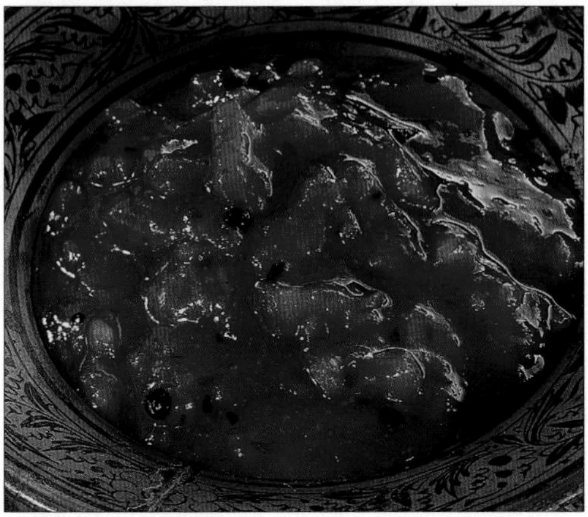

Mango Chutney

Chutneys are usually served as an accompaniment to curry but this one is particularly nice served in a cheese sandwich or as a dip with poppadums.

Makes 450g/1lb/2 cups
450g/1lb green (unripe) mangoes
60ml/4 tbsp malt vinegar
2.5ml/½ tsp crushed dried chillies
6 cloves
6 peppercorns
5ml/1 tsp roasted cumin seeds
2.5ml/½ tsp onion seeds
salt
175g/6oz/scant 1 cup sugar
5cm/2in piece fresh root ginger, thinly sliced
2 garlic cloves, crushed
thin rind of 1 orange or lemon (optional)

1 Use a sharp knife to cut two thick slices from either side of the large flat stone (pit) of each mango. Make criss-cross cuts in the flesh on each slice and then turn inside out. The cubes of flesh will stand proud of the skin. Cut these off close to the skin. Cut the remaining flesh from around the stone.

2 Pour the vinegar into a pan, and add the chillies, cloves, peppercorns, cumin and onion seeds, salt and sugar. Place over a low heat and simmer to infuse (steep) the spices in the vinegar – about 15 minutes.

3 Add the mangoes, ginger, garlic and peel, if using. Simmer until the mango is mushy and most of the vinegar has evaporated. When cool, pour into sterilized bottles. Cover and leave for a few days before serving.

Cook's Tip
Fresh root ginger freezes very well, which can be handy if you find it difficult to get fresh ginger locally. It can be sliced or grated straight from the freezer and will thaw on contact with hot food.

Mint & Coconut Chutney

Makes about 350ml/12fl oz/1½ cups
50g/2oz fresh mint leaves
90ml/6 tbsp desiccated (dry unsweetened shredded) coconut
15ml/1 tbsp sesame seeds
1.5ml/¼ tsp salt
175ml/6fl oz/¾ cup natural (plain) yogurt

1 Finely chop the fresh mint leaves, using a sharp knife.

2 Put the mint with the desiccated coconut, sesame seeds, salt and yogurt into a food processor or blender and process until smooth. Transfer the chutney to a sterilized jar, cover and chill until needed.

Tomato & Fresh Chilli Chutney

Makes about 475ml/16fl oz/2 cups
1 red (bell) pepper
4 tomatoes, chopped
2 fresh green chillies, chopped
1 garlic clove, crushed
1.5ml/¼ tsp salt
2.5ml/½ tsp sugar
5ml/1 tsp chilli powder
45ml/3 tbsp tomato purée (paste)
15ml/1 tbsp chopped fresh coriander (cilantro)

1 Halve the red pepper and remove the core and seeds. Roughly chop the red pepper halves.

2 Process the pepper with the tomatoes, chillies, garlic, salt, sugar, chilli powder, tomato purée and coriander with 30ml/2 tbsp water in a food processor until smooth. Transfer to a sterilized jar, cover and chill until needed.

Cook's Tip
This chutney can be stored in the refrigerator for up to 5 days.

mango chutney Energy 1401kcal/5997kJ; Protein 8.7g; Carbohydrate 360.7g, of which sugars 356.6g; Fat 2.2g, of which saturates 0.9g; Cholesterol 0mg; Calcium 238mg; Fibre 27.8g; Sodium 1019mg.
mint chutney Energy 753kcal/3117kJ; Protein 18.6g; Carbohydrate 21.7g, of which sugars 18.9g; Fat 66.6g, of which saturates 50.2g; Cholesterol 2mg; Calcium 559mg; Fibre 13.5g; Sodium 181mg.
tomato chutney Energy 187kcal/794kJ; Protein 9.7g; Carbohydrate 33.2g, of which sugars 30g; Fat 2.5g, of which saturates 0.5g; Cholesterol 0mg; Calcium 175mg; Fibre 7.5g; Sodium 157mg.

Fresh Coconut Chutney with Onion & Chilli

Serve a bowl of this tasty fresh chutney as an accompaniment for any Indian-style main course.

Serves 4–6

200g/7oz fresh coconut, grated
3 or 4 fresh green chillies, seeded and chopped
20g/¾oz fresh coriander (cilantro), chopped, plus 2 or 3 sprigs to garnish
30ml/2 tbsp chopped fresh mint
30–45ml/2–3 tbsp lime juice
about 2.5ml/½ tsp salt
about 2.5ml/½ tsp caster (superfine) sugar
15–30ml/1–2 tbsp coconut milk (optional)
30ml/2 tbsp groundnut (peanut) oil
5ml/1 tsp nigella seeds
1 small onion, very finely chopped

1 Place the coconut, chillies, coriander and mint in a food processor. Add 30ml/2 tbsp of the lime juice, then process until thoroughly chopped.

2 Scrape the mixture into a bowl and add more lime juice to taste. Add salt and sugar to taste. If the mixture is dry, stir in 15–30ml/1–2 tbsp coconut milk.

3 Heat the oil in a small pan and fry the nigella seeds until they begin to pop, then reduce the heat and add the onion. Fry, stirring frequently, for 4–5 minutes, until the onion is soft.

4 Stir the onion mixture into the coconut mixture and leave to cool. Garnish with coriander before serving.

Cook's Tip
Nigella seeds, sometimes called black onion seeds or black cumin, can be found in Asian grocery stores, usually sold under the name kalonji.

Hot Thai Pickled Shallots

Pickling Thai shallots in this way demands some patience, while the vinegar and spices work their magic, but the results are definitely worth the wait. Thinly sliced, the shallots are often used as a condiment with South-east Asian meals.

Makes 2–3 jars

5–6 small red or green bird's eye chillies
500g/1¼lb Thai pink shallots, peeled
2 large garlic cloves, peeled, halved and green shoots removed

For the vinegar
40g/1½oz/3 tbsp sugar
10ml/2 tsp salt
5cm/2in piece fresh root ginger, peeled and sliced
15ml/1 tbsp coriander seeds
2 lemon grass stalks, cut in half lengthways
4 kaffir lime leaves or pared strips of lime rind
600ml/1 pint/2½ cups cider vinegar
15ml/1 tbsp chopped fresh coriander (cilantro)

1 The chillies can be left whole or halved and seeded. The pickle will be hotter if you leave the seeds in. If leaving the chillies whole, prick them several times with a cocktail stick (toothpick). Bring a large pan of water to the boil. Add the chillies, shallots and garlic. Blanch for 1–2 minutes, then drain. Rinse all the vegetables under cold water, then drain again.

2 Prepare the vinegar. Put the sugar, salt, ginger, coriander seeds, lemon grass and lime leaves or lime rind in a pan, pour in the vinegar and bring to the boil. Reduce the heat to low and simmer for 3–4 minutes. Leave to cool.

3 Remove and discard the ginger, then bring the vinegar back to the boil. Add the fresh coriander, garlic and chillies and cook for 1 minute.

4 Pack the shallots into warmed, sterilized jars, distributing the lemon grass, lime leaves, chillies and garlic among them. Pour over the hot vinegar. Cool, then seal and store in a cool, dark place for 2 months before eating.

coconut chutney Energy 145kcal/597kJ; Protein 1.6g; Carbohydrate 2.8g, of which sugars 2.5g; Fat 14.3g, of which saturates 9.4g; Cholesterol 0mg; Calcium 40mg; Fibre 3.3g; Sodium 11mg.
Thai pickled shallots Energy 127kcal/536kJ; Protein 2.3g; Carbohydrate 30.4g, of which sugars 26.5g; Fat 0.4g, of which saturates 0g; Cholesterol 0mg; Calcium 52mg; Fibre 2.7g; Sodium 7mg.

Red Onion, Garlic & Lemon Relish

This powerful relish is flavoured with spices and punchy preserved lemons. It reached India by way of Spain, being introduced by Jewish refugees forced to leave that country in the 15th century.

Serves 6

45ml/3 tbsp olive oil
3 large red onions, sliced
2 heads of garlic, separated into cloves and peeled
10ml/2 tsp coriander seeds, crushed but not finely ground
10ml/2 tsp light muscovado (brown) sugar, plus a little extra
pinch of saffron threads
5cm/2in piece cinnamon stick
2 or 3 small whole dried red chillies (optional)
2 fresh bay leaves
30–45ml/2–3 tbsp sherry vinegar
juice of ½ small orange
30ml/2 tbsp chopped preserved lemon
salt and ground black pepper

1 Heat the oil in a heavy pan. Add the onions and stir, then cover and reduce the heat to the lowest setting. Cook for 10–15 minutes, stirring occasionally, until the onions are soft and pale gold in colour.

2 Add the whole peeled garlic cloves and the crushed coriander seeds. Cover and cook for 5–8 minutes until the garlic is soft.

3 Add a pinch of salt, lots of pepper and the sugar. Stir, then cook, uncovered, for 5 minutes. Soak the saffron in about 45ml/3 tbsp warm water for 5 minutes, then add it to the onions, with the soaking water. Add the cinnamon stick, dried chillies, if using, and bay leaves. Stir in 30ml/2 tbsp of the sherry vinegar and the orange juice.

4 Cook over a low heat, uncovered, until the onions are very soft and most of the liquid has evaporated. Stir in the preserved lemon and cook gently for a further 5 minutes. Taste and adjust the seasoning, adding more salt, sugar and/or vinegar to taste. Serve warm or at room temperature. The relish tastes best if it is left to stand for 24 hours.

Thai Red Curry Sauce

Serve this with mini spring rolls or spicy Indonesian crackers, or toss it into freshly cooked rice noodles for a delicious main-meal accompaniment.

Serves 4

200ml/7fl oz/scant 1 cup coconut cream
10–15ml/2–3 tsp Thai red curry paste
4 spring onions, plus extra, to garnish
30ml/2 tbsp chopped fresh coriander
1 red chilli, seeded and thinly sliced into rings
5ml/1 tsp soy sauce
juice of 1 lime
sugar, to taste
25g/1oz/¼ cup dry-roasted peanuts
salt and pepper

1 Pour the coconut cream into a small bowl and stir in the curry paste.

2 Trim and finely slice the spring onions diagonally. Stir into the coconut cream with the coriander and chilli.

3 Stir in the soy sauce, lime juice, sugar, salt and pepper to taste. Pour the sauce into a small serving bowl

4 Finely chop the dry-roasted peanuts and sprinkle them over the sauce. Serve immediately. Garnish with spring onions sliced lengthways.

Cook's Tip
The dip may be prepared in advance up to the end of step 3. Sprinkle the peanuts over just before serving.

Variation
- *Use half a teaspoonful of ready-chopped chilli instead of the frech chilli for a quick and extra-fiery dip.*
- *Use salted roasted cashew nuts in place of the peanuts.*

red onion relish Energy 79kcal/326kJ; Protein 1.3g; Carbohydrate 10.4g, of which sugars 8.1g; Fat 3.9g, of which saturates 0.5g; Cholesterol 0mg; Calcium 27mg; Fibre 1.4g; Sodium 4mg.
Thai red curry sauce Energy 416kcal/1792kJ; Protein 36.2g; Carbohydrate 5.2g, of which sugars 4.8g; Fat 27.9g, of which saturates 4.4g; Cholesterol 88mg; Calcium 75mg; Fibre 1.1g; Sodium 132mg.

Green Chilli Pickle

Southern India is the source of some of the hottest curries and pickles. You might imagine that eating them would be a case of going for the burn, but they actually cool the body.

Makes 450–550g/1–1¼lb/2–2½ cups

50g/2oz/4 tbsp yellow mustard seeds, crushed
50g/2oz/4 tbsp freshly ground cumin seeds
25g/1oz/¼ cup ground turmeric
50g/2oz garlic cloves, crushed, plus 20 small garlic cloves, peeled but left whole
150ml/¼ pint/⅔ cup white vinegar
75g/3oz/6 tbsp sugar
10ml/2 tsp salt
150ml/¼ pint/⅔ cup mustard oil
450g/1lb small fresh green chillies

1 Mix the mustard and cumin seeds, the turmeric, crushed garlic, vinegar, sugar and salt together in a sterilized glass bowl.

2 Cover with a cloth and leave to rest for 24 hours. This enables the spices to infuse and the sugar and salt to melt.

3 Heat the mustard oil in a frying pan and gently fry the spice mixture for about 5 minutes. (Keep a window open while cooking with mustard oil as it is pungent and the smoke may irritate the eyes.)

4 Add the whole, peeled garlic cloves and fry for a further 5 minutes.

5 Halve each fresh green chilli, washing your hands carefully afterwards. Add the chillies and cook gently until tender but still green in colour. This will take about 30 minutes over low heat.

6 Cool thoroughly, then pour into sterilized jars, ensuring that the oil is evenly distributed if you are using more than one jar. Leave to rest for a week before serving.

Hot Lime Pickle

A good lime pickle is not only delicious served with any meal, but it also increases the appetite and aids digestion.

Makes 450g/1lb/2 cups

25 limes
225g/8oz/1 cup salt
50g/2oz/½ cup fenugreek powder
50g/2oz/½ cup mustard powder
150g/5oz/½ cup chilli powder
15g/½oz/2 tbsp ground turmeric
600ml/1 pint/2½ cups mustard oil
5ml/1 tsp asafoetida
30ml/2 tbsp yellow mustard seeds, crushed

1 Cut each lime into 8 pieces and remove the seeds, if you like. Put the limes in a large sterilized jar or glass bowl.

2 Add the salt and toss with the limes. Cover and leave in a warm place for 1–2 weeks, until they become soft and dull brown in colour.

3 Mix together the fenugreek powder, mustard powder, chilli powder and turmeric, and add to the limes. Cover and leave to rest in a warm place for a further 2 or 3 days.

4 Heat the mustard oil in a frying pan and fry the asafoetida and mustard seeds. When the oil reaches smoking point, pour it over the limes.

5 Mix well, cover with a clean cloth and leave in a warm place for about 1 week before serving or bottling.

Bombay Duck Pickle

Boil (or bombil) is the name of a fish that is found off the west coast of India during the monsoon season. How this fish acquired the name Bombay duck in the Western world is unknown. Bombay duck can be served hot or cold, and is usually eaten with Indian breads and vegetable dishes.

Serves 4–6

6–8 pieces boil (Bombay duck)
60ml/4 tbsp vegetable oil
2 fresh red chillies, chopped
15ml/1 tbsp sugar
450g/1lb cherry tomatoes, halved
115g/4oz deep-fried onions
red onion rings, to garnish (optional)

1 Soak the fish in water for 5 minutes and then pat it dry using kitchen paper.

2 Heat the oil in a frying pan and fry the fish pieces for about 30–45 seconds on both sides until crisp. Be careful not to burn them or they will taste bitter. Drain well. Transfer the drained fish pieces to a plate and leave to cool, and then break them into small pieces.

3 Cook the remaining ingredients until the tomatoes become pulpy and the onions are blended into a sauce. Fold in the Bombay duck and mix well. Leave to cool, then garnish and serve, or ladle into a hot sterilized jar, cover and leave to cool.

green chilli pickle Energy 1953kcal/8134kJ; Protein 51.5g; Carbohydrate 176.9g, of which sugars 95.2g; Fat 123.3g, of which saturates 14.7g; Cholesterol 0mg; Calcium 488mg; Fibre 8.2g; Sodium 96mg.
lime pickle Energy 4698kcal/19386kJ; Protein 57g; Carbohydrate 151.3g, of which sugars 64g; Fat 438.1g, of which saturates 53.4g; Cholesterol 0mg; Calcium 2172mg; Fibre 0g; Sodium 88610mg.
Bombay duck pickle Energy 156kcal/652kJ; Protein 11.8g; Carbohydrate 5g, of which sugars 4.3g; Fat 10g, of which saturates 1.9g; Cholesterol 22mg; Calcium 22mg; Fibre 1.4g; Sodium 141mg.

Sweet & Sour Pineapple

This may sound like a Chinese recipe, but it is a traditional Bengali dish known as tok. The predominant flavour is ginger, and the pieces of golden pineapple, dotted with plump, juicy raisins, have plenty of visual appeal with taste to match. It is equally delicious if made with mangoes instead of the pineapple.

Serves 4

800g/1¾lb canned pineapple rings or chunks in natural juice
15ml/1 tbsp vegetable oil
2.5ml/½ tsp black mustard seeds
2.5ml/½ tsp cumin seeds
2.5ml/½ tsp onion seeds
10ml/2 tsp grated fresh root ginger
5ml/1 tsp crushed dried chillies
50g/2oz/⅓ cup seedless raisins
115g/4oz/½ cup sugar
7.5ml/1½ tsp salt

1 Drain the pineapple in a colander and reserve the juice. Chop the pineapple rings or chunks finely (you should have approximately 500g/1¼lb).

2 Heat the vegetable oil in a karahi, wok or large pan over a medium heat and immediately add the mustard seeds. As soon as they pop, add the cumin seeds, then the onion seeds. Add the ginger and chillies, and stir-fry the spices briskly for 30 seconds until they release their flavours.

3 Add the pineapple, raisins, sugar and salt. Add 300ml/½ pint/1¼ cups of the juice (made up with cold water if necessary) and stir into the pineapple mixture.

4 Bring the mixture to the boil, reduce the heat to medium and cook, uncovered, for 20–25 minutes.

Cucumber Sangchae

The refreshing, succulent taste of this simple salad makes a perfect accompaniment for a main meal on a hot summer's night. Small pickling cucumbers are the best for this dish; they are not as watery as the larger specimens and they do not require peeling.

Serves 2

400g/14oz pickling or salad cucumber
30ml/2 tbsp salt

For the dressing

2 spring onions (scallions), finely chopped
2 garlic cloves, crushed
5ml/1 tsp cider vinegar
5ml/1 tsp salt
3ml/½ tsp Korean chilli powder
10ml/2 tsp toasted sesame seeds
10ml/2 tsp sesame oil
5ml/1 tsp gochujang chilli paste
10ml/2 tsp sugar

1 Cut the cucumber lengthways into thin slices and put into a colander. Sprinkle with the salt, mix well and leave for 30 minutes.

2 Place the cucumber slices in a damp dish towel and gently squeeze out as much of the water as possible.

3 Place the spring onions in a large bowl. Add the crushed garlic, vinegar, salt and chilli powder, and stir to combine. Sprinkle in the sesame seeds and mix in the sesame oil, chilli paste and sugar.

4 Blend the cucumber with the dressing. Chill before serving.

Variations

- *Add very finely sliced red (bell) pepper for additional colour and sweetness.*
- *A few chopped fresh mint leaves make an interesting addition to the sangchae.*

pineapple Energy 215kcal/915kJ; Protein 1.2g; Carbohydrate 55.7g, of which sugars 55.6g; Fat 0.1g, of which saturates 0g; Cholesterol 0mg; Calcium 38mg; Fibre 1.4g; Sodium 5mg.
cucumber sangchae Energy 105kcal/432kJ; Protein 3.3g; Carbohydrate 9.2g, of which sugars 7.4g; Fat 6.2g, of which saturates 0.9g; Cholesterol 0mg; Calcium 78mg; Fibre 2.2g; Sodium 1973mg.

Kashmir Chutney

In the true tradition of Asian cookery, this is a typical family recipe passed down through the generations. It is wonderful with curries and all kinds of grilled meat.

Makes approx. 2.75kg/6lb
1kg/2¼lb green apples
15g/½oz garlic cloves
1 litre/1¾ pints/4 cups malt vinegar
450g/1lb dates
115g/4oz preserved ginger
450g/1lb seeded raisins
450g/1lb brown sugar
½ tsp cayenne pepper
25g/1oz salt

1 Quarter the apples, remove the cores and chop coarsely.

2 Peel and chop the garlic.

3 Place the apple and garlic in a pan with enough vinegar to cover and boil until soft. Chop the dates and ginger and add them to the cooked apple and garlic together with all the other ingredients. Boil gently for 45 minutes.

4 Spoon the mixture into sterilized jars and seal immediately.

Cook's Tip
- *To oven-sterilize jars and bottles for chutneys and preserves, check them first for cracks or damage, then wash them thoroughly in hot, soapy water. Rinse well and drain. Next, stand the jars, slightly apart, on a baking sheet lined with kitchen paper. Rest any lids on top. Place in a cold oven, then heat to 110°C/225°F/Gas ¼ and bake for 30 minutes. Leave to cool slightly before filling them with chutney or preserves.*
- *To sterlize using the boiling water method, place the washed containers in a deep pan, open-end up. Pour hot (not boiling) water into the pan to cover the containers. Bring the water to the boil for 10 minutes before draining the jars.*

Coconut & Peanut Relish with Hot Chilli & Garlic Dipping Sauce

This pair of flavoursome accompaniments can be served with many Indonesian dishes.

Makes 120ml/4fl oz/½ cup of each
For the coconut and peanut relish
115g/4oz fresh coconut, grated, or desiccated (dry unsweetened shredded) coconut
175g/6oz/1 cup salted peanuts
5mm/¼in cube shrimp paste
1 small onion, quartered
2–3 garlic cloves, crushed
45ml/3 tbsp vegetable oil
2.5ml/½ tsp tamarind pulp, soaked in 30ml/2 tbsp warm water
5ml/1 tsp coriander seeds, roasted and ground
2.5ml/½ tsp cumin seeds, roasted and ground
5ml/1 tsp soft dark brown sugar

For the hot chilli and garlic dipping sauce
1 garlic clove
2 fresh Thai red chillies, seeded and roughly chopped
10ml/2 tsp sugar
5ml/1 tsp tamarind juice
60ml/4 tbsp soy sauce
juice of ½ lime

1 Dry-fry the coconut in a wok over a medium heat, stirring the coconut constantly until crisp and golden in colour. Allow to cool and add half to the peanuts in a bowl. Toss together to mix.

2 Pound the shrimp paste, onion and garlic to a paste with a mortar and pestle. Fry the paste in hot oil, without browning.

3 Strain the tamarind and reserve the juice. Add the coriander, cumin, tamarind juice and brown sugar to the fried paste in the pan. Cook for 3 minutes, stirring. Stir in the remaining coconut and leave to cool. When cold, mix with the peanut and coconut mixture. Leave to stand for 30 minutes before serving.

4 To make the dipping sauce, pound the garlic, chillies and sugar to a paste with a mortar and pestle. Add the tamarind juice, soy sauce and lime juice, and mix together. Leave the dipping sauce to stand for 30 minutes before serving.

Kashmir Energy 3920kcal/16737kJ; Protein 22.6g; Carbohydrate 1014.4g, of which sugars 1012.2g; Fat 3.3g, of which saturates 0g; Cholesterol 0mg; Calcium 599mg; Fibre 33.7g; Sodium 12139mg.
coconut & peanut relish Energy 309kcal/1284kJ; Protein 14g; Carbohydrate 10.9g, of which sugars 7.5g; Fat 23.6g, of which saturates 4.2g; Cholesterol 19mg; Calcium 77mg; Fibre 3g; Sodium 431mg.

Chilli & Shrimp Paste

There is a saying in Indonesia: 'If your eyes do not water, the food is not good.' This should give you some idea of the fieriness of this paste, which is served with everything.

Serves 4
15ml/1 tbsp palm, groundnut (peanut) or vegetable oil
2 shallots, finely chopped
3 garlic cloves, finely chopped
4 spring onions (scallions), finely chopped
8 red Thai chillies, seeded and finely chopped
10–15ml/2–3 tsp shrimp paste

1 Heat the oil in a small wok or heavy pan. Stir in the shallots, garlic, spring onions and chillies and fry until fragrant and beginning to colour.

2 Add the shrimp paste and continue to fry for about 5 minutes, until dark and blended. Remove from the heat and leave to cool.

3 Spoon the spice paste into a jar, cover and store in the refrigerator for up to 1 week.

Kalamansi Sauce

This popular Filipino dipping sauce can be served with anything but is particularly good with fish and rice dishes.

Serves 4
2 kalamansi limes
60ml/4 tbsp patis (fish sauce)

1 Squeeze the juice from the limes and put in a small bowl. Add the patis and beat together until thoroughly blended.

2 Spoon the sauce into a jar, cover and store in the refrigerator for 1–2 days.

Chilli, Garlic & Ginger Sauce

Regarded as the holy trinity of herbs in South-east Asia, chillies, garlic and ginger have an extraordinary affinity when they are combined in the correct proportions.

Makes about 300ml/½ pint/ 1¼ cups
10 fresh red chillies
10 cloves garlic
50g/2oz fresh root ginger
200ml/7fl oz/scant 1 cup rice vinegar
2.5ml/½ tsp salt
30ml/2 tbsp vegetable oil
2 spring onions (scallions)

1 Wash the chillies and pat them dry. It is important that you do not introduce moisture into the sauce as it will encourage bacterial growth and the sauce will not keep well. Do not remove the seeds of the chillies in this case as the sauce is intended to give sweet, sharp fire to dishes. Chop roughly.

2 Peel the garlic and wipe dry with kitchen paper: do not wash it. Chop the flesh roughly.

3 With a sharp paring knife, peel or scrape off the thin outer skin of the ginger. If the roots you are using have any green stems attached, do not discard these. Roughly chop the ginger.

4 Place all three ingredients in a mortar and pestle or food processor and process until fine, but not of purée consistency. To facilitate the grinding, add a spoonful or two of the vinegar.

5 Turn the mixture into a bowl and combine with the remaining vinegar and the salt. Heat the oil in a small pan or wok and add to the sauce. Finely chop the spring onions and mix them in well. Keep the sauce in a jar with a screw-top lid until required.

Cook's Tip/Variation
Stir a little of this piquant sauce into yogurt for a great dip.

chilli & shrimp paste Energy 46kcal/191kJ; Protein 2.6g; Carbohydrate 2.2g, of which sugars 1.3g; Fat 3g, of which saturates 0.4g; Cholesterol 13mg; Calcium 44mg; Fibre 0.5g; Sodium 111mg.
kalamansi sauce Energy 8kcal/33kJ; Protein 0.5g; Carbohydrate 1.5g, of which sugars 1.4g; Fat 0g, of which saturates 0g; Cholesterol 0mg; Calcium 4mg; Fibre 0g; Sodium 1068mg.
chilli sauce Energy 339Kcal/1405kJ; Protein 13.9g; Carbohydrate 18.1g, of which sugars 3.5g; Fat 23.9g, of which saturates 2.7g; Cholesterol 0mg; Calcium 100mg; Fibre 4.6g; Sodium 1070mg.

Tamarind & Lime Sauce

This popular hot and sour dipping sauce is usually prepared for freshly grilled fish or steamed shellfish.

Serves 4

2 kalamansi limes
30ml/2 tbsp tamarind paste
2 spring onions (scallions), white parts only, finely chopped
2 red chillies, seeded and finely chopped

1 Squeeze the juice from the limes and put in a small bowl. Add the tamarind paste and mix together. Add a little water to thin the mixture until it is of dipping consistency. Stir in the spring onions and chillies.

2 Spoon the sauce into a jar, cover and store in the refrigerator for up to 1 week.

Lime & Chilli Dip

If you cannot find kalamansi limes for this dip, use regular limes and make sure that you grate the rind very finely to avoid a bitter taste. Lime leaves are available from Asian stores.

Serves 4

6 kalamansi limes
4 red chillies
2 garlic cloves
2 spring onions (scallions)
2 kaffir lime leaves
5ml/1 tsp sugar
15ml/1 tbsp fish sauce
30ml/2 tbsp water

1 Finely grate the rind of one lime into a bowl. Squeeze the juice from all the limes into the bowl and, with a spoon, scoop out the flesh. Discard the seeds.

2 Finely chop the chillies, garlic and spring onions. Shred the lime leaves finely. Mix these ingredients into the lime juice and add the sugar, fish sauce and water. Stir everything together and serve in small dipping bowls.

Ginger & Garlic Salt

This is a classic dip for Cantonese fried chicken and is quick and easy to prepare.

Serves 4

50g/2oz fresh root ginger, peeled
4 garlic cloves
30ml/2 tbsp vegetable oil
15ml/1 tbsp sesame oil
2.5ml/½ tsp sugar
5ml/1 tsp salt
2.5ml/½ tsp freshly ground black pepper
1 spring onion (scallion)

1 Grate the ginger and finely chop the garlic. Blend in a small bowl and mix in the oils, sugar, salt and pepper. Microwave for 1 minute.

2 Chop the spring onion very finely and stir it into the sauce. Leave the sauce to cool and store it in a jar with a screw top, in the refrigerator, if you are not using it immediately.

Coconut Vinegar Sauce

This spicy dipping sauce is perfect with many different foods, such as steamed shellfish, spring rolls and fried chicken.

Serves 4

60ml/4 tbsp coconut vinegar
3 red chillies, seeded and finely chopped
4 spring onions (scallions), white parts only, finely chopped
4 garlic cloves, finely chopped

1 Spoon the vinegar into a small bowl. Add the chillies, spring onions and garlic and mix well together.

2 Spoon the sauce into a jar, cover and store in the refrigerator for up to 1 week.

3 Taste and adjust the proportions if necessary, adding more water or lime juice as needed. Serve the dip with fish and chicken dishes or salads

lime & chilli dip Energy 22kcal/95kJ; Protein 1.5g; Carbohydrate 3.5g, of which sugars 3.3g; Fat 0.4g, of which saturates 0.1g; Cholesterol 0mg; Calcium 46mg; Fibre 1.4g; Sodium 275mg.
tamarind & lime sauce Energy 6kcal/23kJ; Protein 0.6g; Carbohydrate 0.6g, of which sugars 0.6g; Fat 0.1g, of which saturates 0g; Cholesterol 0mg; Calcium 10mg; Fibre 0.2g; Sodium 6mg.
ginger & garlic salt Energy 110kcal/452kJ; Protein 0.7g; Carbohydrate 2g, of which sugars 0.9g; Fat 11.1g, of which saturates 1.3g; Cholesterol 0mg; Calcium 7mg; Fibre 0.5g; Sodium 499mg.
coconut vinegar sauce Energy 21kcal/85kJ; Protein 1.8g; Carbohydrate 2.2g, of which sugars 0.7g; Fat 0.3g, of which saturates 0g; Cholesterol 0mg; Calcium 14mg; Fibre 0.6g; Sodium 4mg.

Indonesian Peanut Sauce

Also known as bumbu satay, this is a very popular dipping sauce for fried and grilled meats and steamed vegetables. Sambal kacang is closely related to the peanut sauces of Malaysia, Vietnam and Thailand, and is always available at street stalls. To make an authentic Indonesian peanut sauce, the peanuts must be very finely ground, which can be done in a blender.

Serves 4

15–30ml/1–2 tbsp groundnut (peanut) or vegetable oil
1 shallot, finely chopped
2 garlic cloves, finely chopped
150g/5oz/¾ cup plus 30ml/2 tbsp unsalted peanuts, finely ground
15ml/1 tbsp shrimp paste
15ml/1 tbsp palm sugar (jaggery)
15ml/1 tbsp tamarind paste
15ml/1 tbsp kecap manis (Indonesian sweet soy sauce)
5ml/1 tsp chilli powder
300ml/½ pint/1¼ cups water

1 Heat the oil in a heavy pan, stir in the shallot and garlic and fry until golden brown.

2 Add the ground peanuts, shrimp paste and sugar and continue to fry for 3–4 minutes, until the peanuts begin to colour and release some of their oil.

3 Stir in the tamarind paste, kecap manis and chilli powder. Add the water. Bring the liquid to the boil and then reduce to a gentle simmer for 15–20 minutes, until the sauce has reduced and thickened. Small deposits of oil may appear on the surface of the mixture.

4 Remove the pan from the heat and leave the sauce to cool for at least 30 minutes.

5 Pour the mixture into an electric blender or food processor and blend to form a smooth sauce.

6 Spoon the sauce into a jar, cover and store in the refrigerator for up to 1 week.

Satay Sauce

There are many versions of this tasty peanut sauce. This one is very speedy and it tastes delicious drizzled over chicken kebabs. For parties, spear chunks of chicken with cocktail sticks (toothpicks) and arrange around a bowl of warm satay sauce.

Serves 4

200ml/7fl oz/scant 1 cup coconut cream
60ml/4 tbsp crunchy peanut butter
5ml/1 tsp Worcestershire sauce
few drops of Tabasco sauce
fresh coconut, to garnish (optional)

1 Pour the coconut cream into a small pan and heat it gently over a low heat for about 2 minutes.

2 Add the peanut butter to the coconut cream and stir vigorously using a hand whisk or fork until the mixture is thoroughly blended.

3 Continue to heat the coconut and peanut mixture, but do not allow to boil.

4 Add the Worcestershire sauce and stir well.

5 Add a few drops of Tabasco sauce to taste – be cautious, as you may prefer this sauce to be mild and sweet rather than fiery. Pour into a serving bowl and keep it warm with a piece of foil lightly sealed over the top.

6 Use a vegetable peeler to carefully shave thin strips from a piece of fresh coconut, if using.

7 When ready to serve, stir the sauce and scatter the coconut over it. Serve it warm with grilled meat, fish or vegetables.

Cook's Tip
This is a good sauce to make ahead. Reheat it when required.

peanut sauce Energy 309kcal/1284kJ; Protein 14g; Carbohydrate 10.9g, of which sugars 7.5g; Fat 23.6g, of which saturates 4.2g; Cholesterol 19mg; Calcium 77mg; Fibre 3g; Sodium 431mg.
satay sauce Energy 385kcal/1588kJ; Protein 6g; Carbohydrate 5.2g, of which sugars 4.3g; Fat 37.9g, of which saturates 27.9g; Cholesterol 0mg; Calcium 18mg; Fibre 0.8g; Sodium 81mg.

Sambal Belacan

In Malaysia this condiment is ubiquitous, and gives a punch of heat to rice, curries and stir-fries. It is an acquired taste, but once you are used to the fiery flavour it is quite addictive.

Serves 4

15ml/1 tbsp shrimp paste
4 fresh red chillies, seeded (reserve the seeds)
2 kaffir lime leaves, spines removed, and chopped
2.5ml/½ tsp sugar
1.5ml/¼ tsp salt
juice of 1 lime
lime wedges, to serve

1 In a small, heavy pan, dry-roast the shrimp paste until it is aromatic and crumbly. Using a mortar and pestle or food processor, grind the roasted shrimp paste with the chillies to form a paste. Grind in half the chilli seeds and the lime leaves.

2 Add the sugar and salt, and stir in the rest of the chilli seeds. Moisten with the lime juice. Spoon the sambal into little dishes and serve with wedges of lime to squeeze over it.

Hot Tomato Sambal

This is a popular sambal that goes well with most kinds of meat and poultry.

Makes 120ml/4fl oz/½ cup

3 ripe tomatoes
2.5ml/½ tsp salt
5ml/1 tsp chilli sauce
60ml/4 tbsp fish sauce or soy sauce
15ml/1 tbsp chopped fresh coriander

1 Use a sharp knife to cut a little cross in the skin at the base of each tomato. Place the tomatoes in a bowl and cover with boiling water for 30 seconds to loosen their skins.

2 When they are cool enough to handle, remove the skins from the tomatoes and halve and deseed them. Chop the remaining flesh finely.

3 Place the chopped tomatoes in a bowl and mix with the salt, chilli sauce, fish sauce or soy sauce and coriander. Transfer to a serving bowl or to small dipping bowls and serve.

Hot Chilli & Garlic Dipping Sauce

Sambals are placed on the table as a condiment and are used mainly for dipping meat and fish in Indonesia. They are quite strong and should be used sparingly.

Makes 120ml/4fl oz/½ cup

1 garlic clove, crushed
2 small fresh red chillies, seeded and finely chopped
10ml/2 tsp sugar
5ml/1 tsp tamarind sauce
60ml/4 tbsp soy sauce
juice of ½ lime

1 Pound the garlic, chillies and sugar until smooth in a mortar with a pestle. Alternatively, grind them together in a blender.

2 Add the tamarind sauce, soy sauce and lime juice. Stir well.

Sambal Serondeng

This is a superb Indonesian dressing for curries and always makes an appearance on festive tables. It has been enthusiastically adopted into the cuisine of Malaysia, where fiery food is also much loved.

Serves 6–8

2 lemon grass stalks
50g/2oz tempeh (fermented soya bean cake)
30ml/2 tbsp vegetable or groundnut (peanut) oil
5 shallots, finely sliced
4 garlic cloves, finely sliced
3 fresh red chillies, seeded and finely sliced
175g/6oz fresh coconut, grated, or 100g/3½oz desiccated (dry unsweetened shredded) coconut
2.5ml/½ tsp salt
2.5ml/½ tsp sugar

1 Trim the lemon grass stalks and slice the 7.5cm/3in at the root end into very thin rounds.

2 Cut the tempeh into small dice, and fry it in the oil in a wok or heavy pan until light brown. Crush it coarsely.

3 Heat another wok without oil and dry-fry the lemon grass, shallots, garlic and chillies until just sizzled. Add the coconut, and stir-fry until all the ingredients are golden brown in colour.

4 Add the crushed tempeh, salt and sugar and fry, stirring, until well mixed. Remove from the heat and leave to cool before storing in an airtight container. Keep the serondeng in the refrigerator and eat within a week.

sambal belacan Energy 16kcal/67kJ; Protein 2.5g; Carbohydrate 1g, of which sugars 1g; Fat 0.3g, of which saturates 0g; Cholesterol 19mg; Calcium 70mg; Fibre 0.6g; Sodium 314mg.
hot chilli & garlic sauce Energy 86kcal/362kJ; Protein 4.2g; Carbohydrate 17.3g, of which sugars 14.7g; Fat 0.4g, of which saturates 0g; Cholesterol 0mg; Calcium 32mg; Fibre 0.6g; Sodium 3565mg.
hot tomato sambal Energy 82kcal/349kJ; Protein 4.4g; Carbohydrate 14.6g, of which sugars 14g; Fat 1.1g, of which saturates 0.3g; Cholesterol 0mg; Calcium 61mg; Fibre 3.8g; Sodium 5286mg.
sambal serondeng Energy 109kcal/450kJ; Protein 1.5g; Carbohydrate 1.5g, of which sugars 1.3g; Fat 10.8g, of which saturates 7g; Cholesterol 0mg; Calcium 40mg; Fibre 1.9g; Sodium 7mg.

Sambal Goreng

Traditional additions to this sauce are fine strips of calf's liver, chicken livers, green beans or hard-boiled eggs. A westernized version is shown here.

Makes 900ml/1½ pints/ 3¾ cups

2.5cm/1in cube shrimp paste
2 onions, quartered
2 garlic cloves, crushed
2.5cm/1in fresh lengkuas, peeled and sliced
2 fresh red chillies, seeded and sliced
1.5ml/¼ tsp salt
30ml/2 tbsp vegetable oil
45ml/3 tbsp tomato purée (paste)
600ml/1 pint/2½ cups stock or water
additional ingredients of your choice (see variations)
60ml/4 tbsp tamarind juice
pinch sugar
45ml/3 tbsp coconut milk or coconut cream

1 Grind the shrimp paste, with the onions and garlic, to a paste in a food processor or with a pestle and mortar. Add the lengkuas and salt. Process or pound the mixture to a fine paste.

2 Fry the paste in hot oil for 1–2 minutes, without browning, until the mixture gives off a rich aroma.

3 Add the tomato purée and the stock or water and cook for about 10 minutes. Add 350g/12oz cooked chicken pieces and 50g/2oz cooked and sliced green beans, or one of the combinations of ingredients below, to half the quantity of the sauce. Cook in the sauce for 3–4 minutes, then stir in the tamarind juice, sugar and coconut milk or cream just before serving.

Variations

- *Tomato Sambal Goreng – Add 450g/1lb of skinned, seeded and coarsely chopped tomatoes, before the stock.*
- *Prawn Sambal Goreng – Add 350g/12oz cooked, peeled prawns (shrimp) and 1 (bell) pepper, seeded and chopped.*
- *Egg Sambal Goreng – Add 3 or 4 hard-boiled eggs, shelled and chopped, and 2 tomatoes, skinned, seeded and chopped.*

Mixed Vegetable Pickle

If you can obtain fresh turmeric, it makes such a difference to the colour and appearance of Acar Campur. You can use almost any vegetable, bearing in mind that you need a balance of textures, flavours and vibrant colours.

Makes 2–3 x 300g/11oz jars

1 fresh red chilli, seeded and sliced
1 onion, quartered
2 garlic cloves, crushed
1cm/½ in cube shrimp paste
4 macadamia nuts or 8 almonds
2.5cm/1in fresh turmeric, peeled and sliced, or 5ml/1 tsp ground turmeric
50ml/2fl oz/¼ cup sunflower oil
475ml/16fl oz/2 cups white vinegar
250ml/8fl oz/1 cup water
25–50g/1–2oz sugar
3 carrots
225g/8oz green beans
1 small cauliflower
1 cucumber
225g/8oz white cabbage
115g/4oz dry-roasted peanuts, roughly crushed
salt

1 Blend the chilli, onion, garlic, shrimp paste, nuts and turmeric in a food processor or pound in a mortar with a pestle.

2 Heat the oil and stir-fry the paste to release the aroma. Add the vinegar, water, and sugar and salt to taste. Bring to the boil. Simmer for 10 minutes.

3 Cut the carrots into flower shapes. Cut the green beans into short, neat lengths. Separate the cauliflower into neat, bitesize florets. Peel and seed the cucumber and cut the flesh in neat, bitesize pieces. Cut the cabbage in neat, bitesize pieces.

4 Blanch each vegetable separately, in a large pan of boiling water, for 1 minute. Transfer to a colander and rinse with cold water, to halt the cooking. Drain well.

5 Add the vegetables to the sauce. Slowly bring to the boil and allow to cook for 5–10 minutes. Do not overcook – the vegetables should still be crunchy.

6 Add the peanuts and cool. Spoon into clean jars with lids.

sambal goreng Energy 418kcal/1736kJ; Protein 8.2g; Carbohydrate 47.5g, of which sugars 35.9g; Fat 23.2g, of which saturates 2.4g; Cholesterol 0mg; Calcium 160mg; Fibre 8.3g; Sodium 173mg.
vegetable pickle Energy 517kcal/2141kJ; Protein 12.7g; Carbohydrate 28.4g, of which sugars 25.6g; Fat 39.7g, of which saturates 5.8g; Cholesterol 0mg; Calcium 202mg; Fibre 11.9g; Sodium 73mg.

Sweet & Sour Ginger Sambal

This hot sambal is delicious with fish, chicken or pork.

Makes 90ml/6 tbsp
4–5 small fresh red chillies, seeded and chopped
2 shallots, chopped
2 garlic cloves
2cm/¾ in fresh root ginger
30ml/2 tbsp sugar
1.5ml/¼ tsp salt
45ml/3 tbsp rice vinegar or white wine vinegar

1 Pound together the chillies and shallots or onion in a mortar with a pestle. Alternatively, grind them in a food processor.

2 Add the garlic, ginger, sugar and salt and continue to pound or grind until smooth. Stir in the vinegar and mix well.

Cook's Tip
This sambal will keep in the refrigerator for up to a week.

Hoisin Dip

This dip is great with spring rolls or prawn crackers.

Serves 4
4 spring onions (scallions)
4cm/1½in fresh root ginger
2 fresh red chillies
2 garlic cloves
60ml/4 tbsp hoisin sauce
120ml/4fl oz/½ cup passata (bottled strained tomatoes)
5ml/1 tsp sesame oil (optional)

1 Trim off and discard the green ends of the spring onions. Slice the white parts very thinly.

2 Peel and finely chop the fresh root ginger. Halve and seed the chillies. Slice finely. Finely chop the garlic.

3 Stir together the hoisin sauce, passata, spring onions, ginger, chillies, garlic and sesame oil, if using. Serve within 1 hour.

Cucumber Sambal

This sauce has a piquant flavour but does not have the heat of chillies found in other sambals.

Makes 150ml/¼ pint/⅔ cup
1 garlic clove, crushed
5ml/1 tsp fennel seeds
10ml/2 tsp sugar
2.5ml/½ tsp salt
2 shallots or 1 small onion, finely sliced
120ml/4fl oz/½ cup rice vinegar or white wine vinegar
¼ cucumber, finely diced

1 Pound together the garlic, fennel seeds, sugar and salt in a mortar with a pestle. Alternatively, grind them together in a food processor.

2 Stir in the shallots or onion, vinegar and cucumber and set aside for at least 6 hours to allow the flavours to combine.

3 Serve chilled within a day of making.

Vietnamese Dipping Sauce

Serve this dip in a small bowl as an accompaniment to spring rolls or meat or fish dishes.

Makes 150ml/¼ pint/⅔ cup
1–2 small fresh red chillies, seeded and finely chopped
1 garlic clove, crushed
15ml/1 tbsp roasted peanuts
60ml/4 tbsp coconut milk
30ml/2 tbsp fish sauce
juice of 1 lime
10ml/2 tsp sugar
5ml/1 tsp chopped fresh coriander (cilantro)

1 Pound the chilli with the garlic in a mortar with a pestle.

2 Add the peanuts and pound until crushed. Add the coconut milk, fish sauce, lime juice, sugar and coriander. Mix well and leave for several hours for the flavours to develop.

ginger sambal Energy 150kcal/636kJ; Protein 2.3g; Carbohydrate 36.4g, of which sugars 35.1g; Fat 0.4g, of which saturates 0g; Cholesterol 0mg; Calcium 46mg; Fibre 0.8g; Sodium 557mg.
hoisin dip Energy 29kcal/123kJ; Protein 1.3g; Carbohydrate 6g, of which sugars 5.4g; Fat 0.2g, of which saturates 0g; Cholesterol 0mg; Calcium 13mg; Fibre 0.6g; Sodium 315mg.
cucumber sambal Energy 71kcal/298kJ; Protein 1.5g; Carbohydrate 16.7g, of which sugars 15.2g; Fat 0.2g, of which saturates 0g; Cholesterol 0mg; Calcium 39mg; Fibre 1.4g; Sodium 988mg.
Vietnamese sauce Energy 160kcal/672kJ; Protein 6.4g; Carbohydrate 18.1g, of which sugars 16.9g; Fat 7.4g, of which saturates 1.4g; Cholesterol 0mg; Calcium 52mg; Fibre 0.9g; Sodium 2206mg.

Sour Mango Sambal

This Malaysian favourite is known as sambal asam, sour sambal, and is made with green mango or papaya. It is served in small quantities as a relish to accompany fried fish and shellfish, spicy grilled foods and fiery curries, but it can also be served on its own as a refreshing snack.

Serves 4

5ml/1 tsp shrimp paste
4 fresh red chillies, seeded
7.5ml/1½ tsp salt
5ml/1 tsp sugar
1 green mango, peeled and shredded
juice of ½ lime

1 In a small, heavy pan, dry-roast the shrimp paste over a low heat until it is aromatic and crumbly. Alternatively, wrap the block of paste in foil and, using a heatproof toasting fork, hold it over a flame for about 20 seconds. Set aside.

2 Using a mortar and pestle or food processor, grind the chillies with the salt to form a paste.

3 Add the shrimp paste and sugar to the mortar or food processor and pound it into the spicy paste until you get a smooth, uniform blend. Transfer this to a small mixing bowl..

4 Toss the shredded mango into the paste and moisten with the lime juice. Mix well, until the pieces of fruit have an even coating of flavourings, and serve.

Cook's Tip

Mangoes are widely available, but for this recipe you need an unripe fruit, in which the flesh is just starting to turn yellow. A ripe mango is too soft and sweet. Similarly, if you want to try making the sambal with papaya, opt for an unripe fruit. You may find a better selection of fruits and vegetables for Asian recipes in a specialist Asian food store than in your regular local supermarket.

Vegetable Sambal

There are numerous versions of acar, a pickle created in Singapore. Penang acar, acar Kunin and acar awak all consist of a medley of vegetables that can be served as a relish or side dish. You can experiment with different vegetables.

Serves 6–10

450g/1lb carrots, peeled and cut into matchsticks
450g/1lb daikon (mooli or white radish), peeled and cut into matchsticks
2 small cucumbers, halved lengthways, seeded and cut into matchsticks
6 dried red chillies, soaked in warm water to soften, squeezed dry and seeded
6 garlic cloves, chopped
50g/2oz fresh root ginger, peeled and chopped
50g/2oz fresh turmeric, chopped
30ml/2 tbsp vegetable or groundnut (peanut) oil
6 shallots, sliced
2 lemon grass stalks, halved and bruised
45–60ml/3–4 tbsp rice vinegar or white wine vinegar
30ml/2 tbsp sugar
45ml/3 tbsp roasted peanuts
30ml/2 tbsp roasted sesame seeds
salt

1 Put the vegetables into a bowl, sprinkle with salt and set aside for about 15 minutes. Rinse the vegetables, drain and pat dry.

2 Using a mortar and pestle or a food processor, grind the chillies, garlic, ginger and turmeric together until they form a smooth paste.

3 Heat the oil in a wok. Stir in the shallots and lemon grass and fry until golden. Stir in the spice paste and fry until fragrant. Add the vegetables, tossing them around the wok to coat them.

4 Add the vinegar and sugar and continue to cook the vegetables until they are tender, with just a little bite to them.

5 Season to taste with salt and put the vegetables into a large serving bowl. Leave the mixture to cool, then toss in the peanuts and sesame seeds. The pickle can be stored in a non-metallic container in the refrigerator, or a cool place, for 3–4 days.

sour mango sambal Energy 34Kcal/143kJ; Protein 1.7g; Carbohydrate 6.5g, of which sugars 6.4g; Fat 0.3g, of which saturates 0.1g; Cholesterol 6mg; Calcium 28mg; Fibre 1g; Sodium 794mg.
vegetable sambal Energy 96Kcal/398kJ; Protein 2.3g; Carbohydrate 9.6g, of which sugars 8.8g; Fat 5.6g, of which saturates 0.9g; Cholesterol 0mg; Calcium 52mg; Fibre 2.3g; Sodium 18mg.

Naan

Probably the most popular bread enjoyed with an Indian curry is naan, which was introduced from Persia. In Persian, the word 'naan' means bread. Traditionally, naan is not rolled, but patted and stretched until the teardrop shape is achieved. You can, of course, roll it out to a circle, then gently pull the lower end, which will give you the traditional shape.

Makes 3
225g/8oz/2 cups unbleached strong white bread flour
2.5ml/½ tsp salt
15g/½oz fresh yeast
60ml/4 tbsp lukewarm milk
15ml/1 tbsp vegetable oil
30ml/2 tbsp natural (plain) yogurt
1 egg, beaten
30–45ml/2–3 tbsp melted ghee or butter, for brushing

1 Sift the flour and salt together into a large bowl. In a smaller bowl, cream the yeast with the milk. Set aside for 15 minutes. Add the yeast and milk mixture, vegetable oil, yogurt and egg to the flour. Combine the mixture using your hands until it forms a soft dough. Add a little lukewarm water if the dough is too dry.

2 Turn the dough out on to a lightly floured surface and knead for about 10 minutes, or until it feels smooth. Return the dough to the bowl, cover and leave in a warm place for about 1 hour, or until it has doubled in size. Preheat the oven to its highest setting – it should not be any lower than 230°C/450°F/Gas 8.

3 Turn out the dough back on to the floured surface and knead for a further 2 minutes. Divide into three equal pieces, shape into balls and roll out into teardrop shapes 25cm/10in long, 13cm/5in wide and 5mm–8mm/¼–⅓in thick.

4 Preheat the grill (broiler) to its highest setting. Meanwhile, place the naan on preheated baking sheets and bake for 3–4 minutes, or until puffed up. Remove from the oven and place under the hot grill for a few seconds until the tops brown slightly. Brush with ghee or butter and serve warm.

Garlic & Coriander Naan

Traditionally cooked in a very hot clay oven known as a tandoor, naan are usually eaten with dry meat or vegetable dishes.

Makes 3
275g/10oz/2½ cups unbleached strong white bread flour
5ml/1 tsp salt
5ml/1 tsp dried yeast
60ml/4 tbsp natural (plain) yogurt
15ml/1 tbsp melted butter or ghee, plus 30–45ml/2–3 tbsp for brushing
1 garlic clove, finely chopped
5ml/1 tsp black onion seeds
15ml/1 tbsp chopped fresh coriander (cilantro)
10ml/2 tsp clear honey

1 Sift the flour and salt together into a large bowl. In a smaller bowl, cream the yeast with the yogurt. Set aside for 15 minutes. Add the yeast mixture to the flour with 15ml/1 tbsp melted butter or ghee, and add the chopped garlic, black onion seeds, chopped coriander and honey, mixing to a soft dough.

2 Tip out the dough on to a lightly floured surface and knead for about 10 minutes until smooth and elastic. Place in a lightly oiled bowl, cover with lightly oiled clear film (plastic wrap) and leave to rise in a warm place for 45 minutes, or until the dough has doubled in bulk.

3 Preheat the oven to 230°C/450°F/Gas 8. Place three heavy baking sheets in the oven to heat. Turn the dough out on to a lightly floured surface and knock back (punch down). Divide into three equal pieces and shape each into a ball.

4 Cover two of the balls of dough with oiled clear film and roll out the third into a teardrop shape about 25cm/10in long, 13cm/5in wide and about 5mm–8mm/¼–⅓in thick. Preheat the grill (broiler) to its highest setting. Place the single naan on the hot baking sheets and bake for 3–4 minutes, or until puffy.

5 Remove the naan from the oven and place under the hot grill for a few seconds or until browned slightly. Wrap in a dish towel to keep warm while you roll out and cook the remaining naan. Brush with melted butter or ghee and serve warm.

naan Energy 316kcal/1336kJ; Protein 9.4g; Carbohydrate 58.6g, of which sugars 1.5g; Fat 6.5g, of which saturates 1.1g; Cholesterol 63mg; Calcium 123mg; Fibre 2.3g; Sodium 357mg.
garlic & coriander naan Energy 374kcal/1585kJ; Protein 10.4g; Carbohydrate 74.2g, of which sugars 2.9g; Fat 6.1g, of which saturates 3g; Cholesterol 11mg; Calcium 176mg; Fibre 2.8g; Sodium 706mg.

Spiced Naan

Another excellent recipe for naan bread, this time with fennel seeds, onion seeds and cumin seeds.

Makes 6

450g/1lb/4 cups strong white bread flour
5ml/1 tsp baking powder
2.5ml/½ tsp salt
1 sachet easy-blend (rapid-rise) dried yeast
5ml/1 tsp caster (superfine) sugar
5ml/1 tsp fennel seeds
10ml/2 tsp onion seeds
5ml/1 tsp cumin seeds
150ml/¼ pint/⅔ cup hand-hot milk
30ml/2 tbsp vegetable oil, plus extra for brushing
150ml/¼ pint/⅔ cup natural (plain) yogurt
1 egg, beaten

1 Sift the flour, baking powder and salt into a mixing bowl. Stir in the yeast, sugar, fennel seeds, onion seeds and cumin seeds. Make a well in the centre. Stir the hand-hot milk into the flour mixture, then add the oil, yogurt and beaten egg. Mix to form a ball of dough.

2 Tip the dough out on to a lightly floured surface and knead it for 10 minutes until smooth. Return to the clean, lightly oiled bowl and roll the dough to coat it with oil. Cover the bowl with clear film (plastic wrap) and set aside in a warm place until the dough has doubled in bulk.

3 Put six heavy baking sheets in the oven and preheat the oven to 240°C/475°F/Gas 9. Also preheat the grill (broiler). Knead the dough again lightly and divide it into six pieces. Keep five pieces covered while working with the sixth. Quickly roll the piece of dough out to a teardrop shape, brush lightly with oil and slap the naan on to a hot baking sheet. Repeat with the remaining dough.

4 Bake the naan in the oven for 3 minutes until puffed up, then place the baking sheets under the grill for about 30 seconds or until the naan are lightly browned. Serve hot or warm as an accompaniment to an Indian curry.

Chapatis

A chapati is an unleavened bread made from chapati flour, a ground wholemeal flour known as atta, which is finer than the Western equivalent. If you cannot find it, use an equal quantity of a mix of standard wholemeal flour and plain flour. Chapatis are the everyday bread of the Indian home, and great with curry.

Makes 8–10

225g/8oz/2 cups chapati flour or wholemeal (whole-wheat) flour
2.5ml/½ tsp salt
175ml/6fl oz/¾ cup water

1 Sift the flour and salt into a mixing bowl. Make a well in the centre and gradually stir in the water, mixing well with your fingers.

2 Form a supple dough and knead for 7–10 minutes. Cover with clear film (plastic wrap) and leave to one side for 15–20 minutes to rest.

3 Divide the dough into 8–10 equal portions. Roll out each piece to a circle on a well-floured surface.

4 Place a tava (chapati griddle) or heavy frying pan over a high heat. When steam rises from it, lower the heat to medium and add the first chapati to the pan.

5 When the chapati begins to bubble, turn it over. Press down with a clean dish towel or a flat spoon and turn once again.

6 Remove the cooked chapati from the pan and keep warm in a piece of foil lined with kitchen paper while you cook the other chapatis.

7 Repeat the process until all the breads are cooked. Serve hot.

spiced naan Energy 311kcal/1318kJ; Protein 11g; Carbohydrate 63.8g, of which sugars 4.9g; Fat 3.2g, of which saturates 0.9g; Cholesterol 34mg; Calcium 197mg; Fibre 2.3g; Sodium 211mg.
chapatis Energy 99kcal/421kJ; Protein 3.7g; Carbohydrate 19.9g, of which sugars 0.5g; Fat 1.1g, of which saturates 0.2g; Cholesterol 0mg; Calcium 38mg; Fibre 1.9g; Sodium 165mg.

Red Lentil Pancakes

This is a type of dosa, which is essentially a pancake from southern India, but used in a similar fashion to north Indian bread.

Makes 6

150g/5oz/¾ cup long grain rice
50g/2oz/¼ cup red lentils
250ml/8fl oz/1 cup warm water
5ml/1 tsp salt
2.5ml/½ tsp ground turmeric
2.5ml/½ tsp ground black pepper
30ml/2 tbsp chopped fresh coriander (cilantro)
vegetable oil, for frying and drizzling

1 Place the rice and lentils in a large bowl, cover with the warm water, cover and soak for at least 8 hours or overnight.

2 Drain off the water and reserve. Place the rice and lentils in a food processor and blend until smooth. Blend in the reserved water. Scrape into a bowl, cover with clear film (plastic wrap) and leave in a warm place to ferment for about 24 hours.

3 Stir in the salt, turmeric, pepper and coriander. Heat a heavy frying pan over a medium heat for a few minutes until hot. Smear with oil and add about 30–45ml/2–3 tbsp batter.

4 Using the rounded base of a soup spoon, gently spread the batter out, using a circular motion, to make a pancake that is about 15cm/6in in diameter.

5 Cook in the pan for 1½–2 minutes, or until set. Drizzle a little oil over the pancake and around the edges. Turn over and cook for about 1 minute, or until golden brown. Keep the cooked pancakes warm in a low oven or on a plate over simmering water while cooking the remaining pancakes. Serve warm.

Variation
Add 60ml/4 tbsp grated coconut to the batter just before cooking for a richer flavour.

Parathas

Making a paratha is similar to making flaky pastry. The difference lies in the handling of the dough; this can be handled freely, unlike that for a flaky pastry.

Makes 12–15

350g/12oz/3 cups chapati flour or a mixture of wholemeal (whole-wheat) flour and plain (all-purpose) flour, plus 50g/2oz/½ cup for dusting
50g/2oz/½ cup plain (all-purpose) flour
5ml/1 tsp salt
40g/1½oz/3 tbsp ghee or unsalted butter, melted
water, to mix

1 Sift the flours and salt into a bowl. Make a well in the centre and add 10ml/2 tsp of the melted ghee or butter. Fold it into the flour to make a crumbly texture.

2 Gradually add water to make a soft, pliable dough. Knead until smooth. Cover and leave to rest for 30 minutes.

3 Divide the dough into 12–15 equal portions and keep covered. Take one portion at a time and roll out on a lightly floured surface to about 10cm/4in in diameter.

4 Brush the dough with a little of the melted ghee or butter and sprinkle with flour.

5 Make a straight cut from the centre to the edge of the dough, then lift a cut edge and roll the dough into a cone shape. Lift it and flatten it again into a ball.

6 Roll the dough out again on a lightly floured surface until it is 18cm/7in wide.

7 Heat a griddle and cook one paratha at a time, placing a little of the remaining ghee or butter along the edges. Cook on each side until golden brown. Serve hot.

red lentil pancakes Energy 117kcal/492kJ; Protein 3.9g; Carbohydrate 24.7g, of which sugars 0.3g; Fat 0.3g, of which saturates 0g; Cholesterol 0mg; Calcium 14mg; Fibre 0.5g; Sodium 331mg.
parathas Energy 108kcal/456kJ; Protein 2.3g; Carbohydrate 19.2g, of which sugars 0.4g; Fat 43g, of which saturates 24g; Cholesterol 64mg; Calcium 35mg; Fibre 0.8g; Sodium 132mg.

Missi Rotis

This is a speciality from the Punjab. Gram flour, also known as besan, is used instead of the usual chapati flour. In the Punjab, missi rotis are very popular with a glass of lassi, a refreshing yogurt drink.

Makes 4

115g/4oz/1 cup gram flour
115g/4oz/1 cup wholemeal (whole-wheat) flour
1 fresh green chilli, seeded and chopped
½ onion, finely chopped
15ml/1 tbsp chopped fresh coriander (cilantro)
2.5ml/½ tsp ground turmeric
2.5ml/½ tsp salt
15ml/1 tbsp vegetable oil
120–150ml/4–5fl oz/½–⅔ cup lukewarm water
30–45ml/2–3 tbsp melted unsalted ghee or butter

1 Mix the two types of flour, the chilli, onion, coriander, turmeric and salt together in a large bowl. Stir in the oil.

2 Mix in sufficient lukewarm water to make a pliable soft dough. Tip out the dough on to a lightly floured surface and knead until smooth.

3 Place the dough in a lightly oiled bowl, cover with lightly oiled clear film (plastic wrap) and leave to rest for 30 minutes.

4 Place the dough on a lightly floured surface. Divide into four equal pieces and shape into balls in the palms of your hands. Roll out each ball into a thick round about 15–18cm/6–7in in diameter.

5 Heat a griddle or heavy frying pan over a medium heat for a few minutes until hot.

6 Brush both sides of one roti with a little melted ghee or butter. Add it to the griddle or frying pan and cook for about 2 minutes, turning after 1 minute. Brush the cooked roti lightly with melted ghee or butter again, slide it on to a plate and keep warm in a low oven while cooking the remaining rotis in the same way. Serve the rotis warm.

Tandoori Rotis

Roti means bread and is a common food eaten in central and northern India. Tandoori roti is traditionally baked in a tandoor, or clay oven, but it can also be made successfully in an electric or gas oven at the highest setting.

Makes 6

350g/12oz/3 cups chapati flour or wholemeal (whole-wheat) flour
5ml/1 tsp salt
250ml/8fl oz/1 cup water
30–45ml/2–3 tbsp melted ghee or unsalted butter

1 Sift the flour and salt into a large mixing bowl. Add the water and mix to a soft, pliable dough.

2 Knead on a lightly floured surface for 3–4 minutes until smooth. Place the dough in a lightly oiled bowl, cover with lightly oiled clear film (plastic wrap) and leave to rest for about 1 hour.

3 Tip out the dough on to a lightly floured surface. Divide the dough into six pieces and shape each into a ball. Press out into a larger round with the palm of your hand, cover with lightly oiled clear film and leave to rest for about 10 minutes.

4 Meanwhile, preheat the oven to 230°C/450°F/Gas 8. Place three baking sheets in the oven to heat. Roll the rotis into 15cm/6in rounds, place two on each baking sheet and bake for 8–10 minutes. Brush with melted ghee or butter and serve warm.

Cook's Tip
Chapati flour, known as atta, is a fine wholemeal (whole-wheat) flour used in Indian breads.

missi rotis Energy 125kcal/523kJ; Protein 4.5g; Carbohydrate 18g, of which sugars 1g; Fat 45g, of which saturates 24g; Cholesterol 64mg; Calcium 423mg; Fibre 1.5g; Sodium 18mg.
tandoori rotis Energy 244kcal/1030kJ; Protein 5.5g; Carbohydrate 45.3g, of which sugars 0.9g; Fat 5.8g, of which saturates 2.5g; Cholesterol 0mg; Calcium 82mg; Fibre 1.8g; Sodium 329mg.

Bhaturas

These leavened and deep-fried breads are from the Punjab, where the local people enjoy them with a bowl of spicy chickpea curry. The combination has become a classic over the years and is known as choley bhature. Bhaturas must be eaten hot and cannot be reheated.

Makes 10

15g/½oz fresh yeast
5ml/1 tsp sugar
120ml/4fl oz/½ cup lukewarm water
200g/7oz/1¾ cups strong white bread flour
50g/2oz/⅓ cup semolina
2.5ml/½ tsp salt
15g/½oz/1 tbsp ghee or butter
30ml/2 tbsp natural (plain) yogurt
vegetable oil, for frying

1 Mix the yeast with the sugar and water in a jug (pitcher).

2 Sift the flour into a large bowl and stir in the semolina and salt. Rub in the ghee or butter.

3 Add the yeast mixture and yogurt, and mix to a dough. Turn out on to a lightly floured surface and knead for 10 minutes, or until smooth and elastic.

4 Place the dough in an oiled bowl, cover with oiled clear film (plastic wrap) and leave to rise in a warm place for about 1 hour, or until doubled in bulk.

5 Turn the dough out on to a lightly floured surface and knock back (punch down). Divide into ten equal pieces and shape each into a ball. Flatten into discs with the palm of your hand. Roll out on a lightly floured surface into 13cm/5in rounds.

6 Pour oil to a depth of 1cm/½in into a deep frying pan. Heat, and slide one bhatura into the oil. Fry for about 1 minute, turning over after 30 seconds.

7 Drain the bhatura well on kitchen paper. Keep each bhatura warm in a low oven while frying the remaining bhaturas. Serve immediately, while hot.

Pooris

These delicious little deep-fried breads, shaped into discs, make it temptingly easy to over-indulge. In most areas, they are made of wholemeal flour, but in the east and north-east of India, they are made from plain refined flour, and are known as loochis.

Makes 12

115g/4oz/1 cup unbleached plain (all-purpose) flour
115g/4oz/1 cup wholemeal (whole-wheat) flour
2.5ml/½ tsp salt
2.5ml/½ tsp chilli powder (optional)
30ml/2 tbsp vegetable oil, plus extra for frying
100–120ml/3½–4fl oz/7–8 tbsp water

1 Sift the flours, salt and chilli powder, if using, into a large mixing bowl. Add the vegetable oil then add sufficient water to mix to a dough.

2 Tip the dough out on to a lightly floured surface and knead for 8–10 minutes until smooth.

3 Place in an oiled bowl and cover with oiled clear film (plastic wrap). Leave for 30 minutes.

4 Place the dough on the floured surface. Divide into 12 pieces. Keeping the rest of the dough covered, roll one piece into a 13cm/5in round. Repeat with the remaining dough. Stack the pooris, layered between clear film, to keep them moist.

5 Pour vegetable oil to a depth of 2.5cm/1in in a deep frying pan and heat it to 180°C/350°F. Using a metal spatula, lift one poori and slide it into the oil; it will sink but then return to the surface and begin to sizzle. Gently press the poori into the oil. It will puff up. Turn the poori over after a few seconds and allow it to cook for a further 20–30 seconds.

6 Remove the poori from the pan and pat dry with kitchen paper. Place the cooked poori on a large baking tray and keep warm in a low oven while you cook the remaining pooris. Serve warm.

bhaturas Energy 140kcal/590kJ; Protein 2.6g; Carbohydrate 19.6g, of which sugars 0.5g; Fat 6.3g, of which saturates 1.3g; Cholesterol 0mg; Calcium 35mg; Fibre 0.7g; Sodium 102mg.
pooris Energy 120kcal/501kJ; Protein 2.1g; Carbohydrate 13.5g, of which sugars 0.3g; Fat 6.7g, of which saturates 0.8g; Cholesterol 0mg; Calcium 17mg; Fibre 1.2g; Sodium 164mg.

Ensaimadas

These sweet bread rolls are a popular snack in the Philippines and come with various fillings.

Makes 10–12

30ml/2 tbsp caster (superfine) sugar, plus extra for sprinkling
150ml/¼ pint/⅔ cup warm water
15ml/1 tbsp active dried yeast
450g/1lb/4 cups strong white bread flour
5ml/1 tsp salt
115g/4oz/½ cup butter, softened, plus 30ml/2 tbsp melted butter for brushing
4 egg yolks
90–120ml/6–8 tbsp warm milk
115g/4oz/1 cup grated Cheddar cheese (or similar well-flavoured hard cheese)

1 Dissolve 5ml/1 tsp of the sugar in the warm water, then sprinkle in the dried yeast. Stir, then set aside for 10 minutes or until frothy. Sift the flour and salt into a large bowl.

2 Cream the softened butter with the remaining sugar in a large bowl. When it is fluffy, beat in the egg yolks and a little of the sifted flour. Gradually stir in the remaining flour with the yeast mixture and enough milk to form a soft but not sticky dough. Transfer to an oiled plastic bag. Close the bag loosely, leaving plenty of room for the dough to rise. Leave in a warm place for about 1 hour, until the dough doubles in bulk.

3 On a lightly floured surface, knock back (punch down) the dough, then roll it out into a large rectangle. Brush the surface with half the melted butter, sprinkle with the cheese, then roll up from a long side like a Swiss (jelly) roll. Knead the dough thoroughly, then divide into 10–12 pieces.

4 Roll each piece of dough into a thin rope, 38cm/15in long. On greased baking sheets, coil each rope into a loose spiral. Leave to rise for about 45 minutes or until doubled in size. Preheat the oven to 220°C/425°F/Gas 7. Bake the ensaimadas for 15–20 minutes, until golden. Remove from the oven, then brush with the remaining melted butter and sprinkle with caster sugar. Serve warm.

Sugar Bread Rolls

These delicious sweet rolls make an unusual end to a meal.

Makes 10

350g/12oz/3 cups strong white bread flour
5ml/1 tsp salt
15ml/1 tbsp caster (superfine) sugar
5ml/1 tsp dried yeast
150ml/¼ pint/⅔ cup hand-hot water
3 egg yolks
50g/2oz/¼ cup unsalted butter, softened, plus 25g/1oz/2 tbsp extra
75g/3oz Cheddar or Monterey Jack cheese, grated
50g/2oz/¼ cup sugar

1 Sift the flour, salt and caster sugar into a food processor fitted with a dough blade or the bowl of an electric mixer fitted with a dough hook. Make a well in the centre. Dissolve the yeast in the hand-hot water and pour into the well. Add the egg yolks and leave for a few minutes until bubbles appear on the surface of the liquid.

2 Mix the ingredients for 30–45 seconds to form a firm dough. Add the softened butter and knead for 2–3 minutes in a food processor, or for 4–5 minutes with an electric mixer, until smooth. Transfer the dough to a floured bowl, cover and leave in a warm place to rise until doubled in bulk.

3 Transfer the dough to a lightly floured surface and divide it into ten pieces. Spread the grated cheese over the surface. Roll each of the dough pieces into a 13cm/5in length, incorporating the cheese as you do so. Coil into snail shapes and place on a lightly greased high-sided baking tray measuring 30 x 20cm/12 x 8in.

4 Cover the rolls with clear film (plastic wrap) and leave in a warm place for 45 minutes or until doubled in bulk.

5 Preheat the oven to 190°C/375°F/Gas 5 and then bake the rolls for 20–25 minutes, until golden. Melt the remaining butter, brush it over the rolls, sprinkle with the sugar and allow to cool. Separate the rolls before serving.

ensaimadas Energy 327kcal/1371kJ; Protein 8.7g; Carbohydrate 38.6g, of which sugars 4.3g; Fat 16.1g, of which saturates 9.3g; Cholesterol 117mg; Calcium 172mg; Fibre 1.4g; Sodium 162mg.
sugar bread rolls Energy 195kcal/822kJ; Protein 6.1g; Carbohydrate 34g, of which sugars 7.3g; Fat 4.6g, of which saturates 2.2g; Cholesterol 68mg; Calcium 115mg; Fibre 1.1g; Sodium 255mg.

Pears in Spiced Wine

Familiar Indian spices, infused in a red wine syrup, give pears a lovely warm flavour. The colour is beautiful, too.

Serves 4

1 bottle full-bodied red wine
1 cinnamon stick
4 cloves
2.5ml/½ tsp freshly grated nutmeg
2.5ml/½ tsp ground ginger
8 peppercorns
175g/6oz/scant 1 cup caster (superfine) sugar
thinly pared rind of ½ orange
thinly pared rind of ½ lemon
8 firm ripe pears

1 Pour the wine into a heavy pan into which the pears will fit snugly when standing upright.

2 Stir the cinnamon stick, cloves, nutmeg, ginger, peppercorns, caster sugar and citrus rinds into the wine.

3 Peel the pears, leaving the stalks intact, and stand them in the pan. The wine should only just cover the pears.

4 Bring the liquid to the boil, lower the heat, cover and simmer very gently for 30 minutes, or until the pears are tender. Using a slotted spoon, transfer the pears to a bowl.

5 Boil the poaching liquid until it has reduced by half and is thick and syrupy.

6 Strain the syrup over and around the pears and serve the dessert hot or cold.

Cook's Tip
Serve the pears with a mascarpone cream, made by combining equal quantities of mascarpone cheese and double (heavy) cream, and adding a little vanilla extract for flavour. They also taste good with yogurt or ice cream.

Melon & Strawberry Salad

A beautiful and colourful fruit salad, this is suitable to serve as a refreshing appetizer or to round off a rich and spicy meal. Don't be tempted to chill the salad; it tastes best at room temperature.

Serves 4

1 Galia or Ogen melon
1 honeydew melon or other melon of your choice (see Cook's Tip)
½ watermelon
225g/8oz/2 cups strawberries
15ml/1 tbsp lemon juice
15ml/1 tbsp clear honey
15ml/1 tbsp chopped fresh mint

1 Prepare the melons by cutting them in half and discarding the seeds by scraping them out with a spoon.

2 Use a melon baller to scoop out the flesh into balls or a knife to cut it into cubes. Place these in a fruit bowl.

3 Rinse and take the stems off the strawberries, twisting them so that they remove the hull at the same time. If the hull remains inside, use a fine, sharp knife to cut it out. Cut the berries in half and add them to the bowl.

4 Mix together the lemon juice and honey and add 15ml/1 tbsp water to make this easier to pour over the fruit. Mix into the fruit gently.

5 Sprinkle the chopped mint over the top of the fruit and serve.

Cook's Tip
Use whichever melons are available: replace Galia or Ogen with cantaloupe melon, or replace watermelon with Charentais, for example. Try to choose three melons with a variation in colour for an attractive effect.

pears in spiced wine Energy 378kcal/1595kJ; Protein 1g; Carbohydrate 65.7g, of which sugars 65.7g; Fat 0.2g, of which saturates 0g; Cholesterol 0mg; Calcium 53mg; Fibre 3.9g; Sodium 22mg.
melon & strawberry Energy 204kcal/867kJ; Protein 3.9g; Carbohydrate 47.5g, of which sugars 47.5g; Fat 1.2g, of which saturates 0.3g; Cholesterol 0mg; Calcium 66mg; Fibre 2.9g; Sodium 128mg.

Citrus Fruit Salad

This is a very appetizing and refreshing salad, with a typically Indian combination of citrus fruits seasoned with salt and pepper. You could use all fresh fruits, if you prefer.

Serves 6

2 navel oranges
1 honeydew melon
½ watermelon
1 fresh mango
115g/4oz seedless green and black grapes
225g/8oz canned mandarin segments, drained
225g/8oz canned grapefruit segments, drained
juice of 1 lemon
2.5ml/½ tsp sugar
1.5ml/¼ tsp freshly ground cumin seeds
salt and ground black pepper

1 Using a sharp knife, cut a thin slice of peel and pith from each end of an orange. Place cut side down on a plate and cut off the peel and pith in strips. Remove any remaining pith. Cut out each segment leaving the membrane behind. Squeeze the remaining juice from the membrane. Repeat with the other orange.

2 Cut the honeydew melon in half and scrape out the seeds using a spoon. Remove the seeds from the watermelon in the same way. Use a melon baller to scoop out the flesh into balls or a knife to cut it into cubes.

3 Using a sharp knife, take two thick slices from either side of the large flat stone (pit) of the mango without peeling the fruit. Make a lattice slices into the flesh and then turn the skin inside out. The cubes of flesh will stand proud of the skin and can be easily cut off.

4 Place all the fruit in a large serving bowl and add the lemon juice. Toss gently to prevent damaging the fruit.

5 Mix together the remaining ingredients and sprinkle over the fruit. Gently toss, chill thoroughly and serve.

Spiced Fruit Salad

Exotic fruits are becoming commonplace in supermarkets these days and it is fun to experiment with the different varieties. Look out in particular for physalis, star fruit, papaya and passion fruit.

Serves 4–6

75g/3oz/6 tbsp sugar
300ml/½ pint/1¼ cups water
30ml/2 tbsp syrup from a jar of preserved stem ginger
2 pieces star anise
2.5cm/1in cinnamon stick
1 clove
juice of ½ lemon
2 fresh mint sprigs
1 mango
2 bananas, sliced
8 fresh or drained canned lychees
225g/8oz/2 cups strawberries, hulled and halved
2 pieces preserved stem ginger, cut into sticks
1 medium pineapple

1 Put the sugar, water, ginger syrup, star anise, cinnamon, clove, lemon juice and mint into a pan. Bring to the boil, then simmer for 3 minutes. Strain into a bowl and set aside to cool.

2 Remove the top and bottom from the mango and cut off the outer skin. Stand the mango on one end and remove the flesh in two pieces either side of the flat stone (pit). Slice evenly.

3 Add the mango slices to the syrup with the bananas, lychees, strawberries and stem ginger. Mix in well, making sure the fruits are well coated in the sugary liquid.

4 Cut the pineapple in half by slicing down the centre, using a very sharp knife. Loosen the flesh with a smaller, serrated knife, and remove the flesh by cutting around the rim and scooping it out. The pineapple halves will resemble two boat shapes. Do not discard the pineapple flesh, but cut it into chunks and add to the fruity syrup.

5 Spoon some of the fruit salad into the pineapple halves and serve on a large dish. There will be sufficient fruit salad in the bowl to refill the pineapple halves at least once.

citrus fruit salad Energy 167kcal/710kJ; Protein 3.2g; Carbohydrate 39.5g, of which sugars 39.4g; Fat 0.8g, of which saturates 0.2g; Cholesterol 0mg; Calcium 72mg; Fibre 3.1g; Sodium 66mg.
spiced fruit salad Energy 110kcal/468kJ; Protein 1.3g; Carbohydrate 27.1g, of which sugars 26.2g; Fat 0.3g, of which saturates 0.1g; Cholesterol 0mg; Calcium 25mg; Fibre 2.4g; Sodium 18mg.

Zingy Papaya, Lime & Ginger Salad

This refreshing, fruity salad makes a lovely light breakfast, as well as a great dessert. Choose really ripe, fragrant papayas for the best flavour. Mangoes also work well.

Serves 2
2 large ripe papayas
juice of 1 fresh lime
2 pieces preserved stem ginger, finely sliced

1 Cut the papaya in half lengthways and scoop out the seeds, using a teaspoon. Using a sharp knife, cut the flesh into thin slices and arrange on a platter.

2 Squeeze the lime juice over the papaya and sprinkle with the sliced stem ginger. Serve immediately.

Fruit with Granadilla Dressing

Granadillas or passion fruit make a delectable dressing for an exotic fruit salad. Granadilla flesh has a slight scent of lime.

Serves 6
1 mango
1 papaya
2 kiwi fruit
coconut ice cream, to serve

For the dressing
2 granadillas or 3 passion fruit
thinly pared juice and rind of 1 lime
5ml/1 tsp hazelnut oil
15ml/1 tbsp clear honey

1 Peel the mango and cut it into chunks. Peel and halve the papaya, scoop out the seeds, chop the flesh and add it to the bowl. Peel and slice the kiwi fruit. Mix all the fruit in a serving bowl.

2 Make the dressing. Halve the granadillas or passion fruit and scoop the seeds into a sieve (strainer) over a small bowl. Press to extract all the juices. Whisk in the remaining ingredients and pour over the fruit. Chill, then seve with the ice cream.

Warm Fruits in Coconut Milk

This dish of sweet vegetables cooked with bananas in coconut milk is a favourite among many rural Malays and Indonesians. Served as a sweet snack, or for breakfast, it is both nourishing and warming.

Serves 4–6
900ml/1½ pints/3¾ cups coconut milk
2 small pumpkin, seeded and cut into bitesize cubes
2 sweet potatoes, cut into bitesize pieces
1 pandan (screwpine) leaf
150g/5oz/¾ cup palm sugar (jaggery)
2.5ml/½ tsp salt
3 bananas, cut into thick diagonal slices

1 Bring the coconut milk to the boil in a heavy pan. Stir in the pumpkin, sweet potatoes and pandan leaf.

2 Continue to boil for 1 minute, then reduce the heat and simmer for about 15 minutes, until the pumpkin and sweet potato are tender but retain their shape well.

3 Using a slotted spoon, lift the pumpkin and sweet potato pieces out of the coconut milk and put them on a plate.

4 Add the sugar and salt to the coconut milk and stir until the sugar has dissolved. Bring the sweetened coconut milk to the boil, then reduce the heat and simmer for 5 minutes.

5 Add the bananas to the sweetened coconut milk and simmer for 4 minutes.

6 Put the pumpkin and sweet potato back into the pan and gently mix all the ingredients together. Remove the pandan leaf and serve warm.

papaya, lime & ginger Energy 118kcal/503kJ; Protein 1.7g; Carbohydrate 28.9g, of which sugars 28.9g; Fat 0.3g, of which saturates 0g; Cholesterol 0mg; Calcium 76mg; Fibre 7.2g; Sodium 17mg.
fruit w. granadilla Energy 66kcal/278kJ; Protein 1g; Carbohydrate 14.6g, of which sugars 14.5g; Fat 0.8g, of which saturates 0.1g; Cholesterol 0mg; Calcium 26mg; Fibre 2.9g; Sodium 7mg.
warm fruits Energy 89Kcal/380kJ; Protein 2g; Carbohydrate 20.8g, of which sugars 20.8g; Fat 0.4g, of which saturates 0.2g; Cholesterol 0mg; Calcium 50mg; Fibre 0.3g; Sodium 159mg.

Chinese Fruit Salad

For an unusual fruit salad with an oriental flavour, try this mixture of fruits in a tangy lime and lychee syrup, topped with a light sprinkling of toasted sesame seeds.

Serves 4

115g/4oz/½ cup caster (superfine) sugar
300ml/½ pint/1¼ cups water
thinly pared rind and juice of 1 lime
400g/14oz can lychees in syrup
1 ripe mango, peeled, stoned (pitted) and sliced
1 eating apple, cored and sliced
2 bananas, chopped
1 star fruit (carambola), sliced (optional)
5ml/1 tsp sesame seeds

1 To make the syrup, place the sugar in a pan with the water and the lime rind. Heat gently until the sugar dissolves, then increase the heat and boil gently for about 7–8 minutes. Remove from the heat and set aside to cool.

2 Drain the lychees and reserve the juice. Pour the juice into the cooled lime syrup with the lime juice. Mix well.

3 Place all the prepared fruit in a bowl and pour over the lime and lychee syrup. Chill for about 1 hour.

4 Heat a heavy pan or wok over a medium heat and dry-fry the sesame seeds until they are golden brown.

5 Just before serving, sprinkle the fruit salad with sesame seeds.

Cook's Tip

To prepare a mango, cut through the fruit lengthways, about 1cm/½in either side of the centre. Then, using a sharp knife, cut the flesh from the central piece away from the stone (pit). Make even criss-cross cuts in the flesh of both side pieces. Hold one side piece in both hands, bend it almost inside out and remove the cubes of flesh with a spoon. Repeat with the other side piece.

Blush Fruit in Rose Pouchong

This delightfully fragrant and quick-to-prepare Asian dessert couples the subtle flavours of apples and raspberries with an infusion of rose-scented tea.

Serves 4

5ml/1 tsp rose pouchong tea
5ml/1 tsp rose water (optional)
50g/2oz/¼ cup sugar
5ml/1 tsp lemon juice
5 eating apples
175g/6oz/1½ cups fresh raspberries

1 Warm a large teapot. Add the rose pouchong tea and 900ml/1½ pints/3¾ cups of boiling water together with the rose water, if using. Allow to stand and infuse for 4 minutes.

2 Spoon the sugar and the lemon juice into a stainless-steel pan. Pour the tea through a small sieve (strainer) into the pan, and stir to dissolve the sugar.

3 Peel the apples, then cut into quarters and core. Add the apples to the pan of syrup. Return the pan to the heat and bring the syrup to simmering point. Cook the apples for about 5 minutes, until just tender.

4 Transfer the apples and syrup to a large metal tray and leave to cool to room temperature.

5 Pour the cooled apples and syrup into a bowl, add the raspberries and mix to combine. Spoon into individual dishes or bowls and serve immediately.

Variation

A fruit tea such as rosehip and hibiscus could be used instead of the rose pouchong, or try cranberry and raspberry to highlight the flavour of the berries.

Chinese fruit salad Energy 264kcal/1123kJ; Protein 1.7g; Carbohydrate 66.1g, of which sugars 64.9g; Fat 1g, of which saturates 0.2g; Cholesterol 0mg; Calcium 36mg; Fibre 2.4g; Sodium 6mg.
blush fruit Energy 95kcal/409kJ; Protein 1g; Carbohydrate 24g, of which sugars 24g; Fat 0.2g, of which saturates 0.1g; Cholesterol 0mg; Calcium 22mg; Fibre 2.7g; Sodium 4mg.

Jellied Mango Puddings

Light and sophisticated, these jellied mango puddings make delightful desserts. Served with a selection of tropical fruits, they add a refreshing touch to the end of a spicy meal.

Serves 4

750ml/1 ¼ pints/3 cups coconut milk
150g/5oz/¾ cup sugar
15ml/1 tbsp powdered gelatine
1 egg yolk
1 large, ripe mango, stoned (pitted) and puréed
4 slices ripe jackfruit or pineapple, quartered
1 banana, cut into diagonal slices
1 kiwi fruit, sliced
4 lychees, peeled
2 passion fruit, split open, to decorate

1 In a heavy pan, heat the coconut milk with the sugar, stirring all the time, until it has dissolved.

2 Add the gelatine and keep stirring until it has dissolved. Remove from the heat.

3 Put the egg yolk in a bowl and beat together with the mango purée. Add the mixture to the coconut milk and stir until smooth. Spoon the mixture into individual, lightly oiled moulds and leave to cool. Chill for 2–3 hours until set.

4 To serve, arrange the fruit on individual plates, leaving enough room for the jellies. Dip the base of each mould briefly into hot water, and then invert the puddings on to the plates. Lift off the moulds and decorate with passion fruit pulp.

Variation
The tangy fruitiness of mango is particularly delicious in these jellied puddings, and this is the version you are most likely to encounter in its homelands of Malaysia and Singapore. However, papaya, banana, durian or avocado work well also.

Sweet Aduki Bean Paste Jellies

These jellies look like blocks of ice in which semi-precious jewels have been set.

Serves 12

200g/7oz can aduki beans
40g/1 ½oz/3 tbsp caster (superfine) sugar

For the agar-agar jelly
2 x 5g/⅛oz sachets powdered agar-agar
900ml/1 ½ pints/3¾ cups water
100g/3¾oz/½ cup caster (superfine) sugar
rind of ¼ orange in one piece

1 Drain the beans and heat them in a pan. When steam begins to rise, reduce the heat and stir in the sugar, one-third at a time, until dissolved. Remove the pan from the heat.

2 To make the jelly, dissolve one agar-agar sachet in half the water in a pan. Add 3 tablespoons of the sugar and the orange rind. Bring to the boil and cook for 2 minutes, stirring constantly. Remove the orange rind and pour half the liquid into a 16 x 10cm/6 x 4in shallow dish. Leave at room temperature to set.

3 Mix the bean paste with the agar-agar liquid in the pan. Move the pan on to a wet dish towel and stir for 8 minutes. Pour into an 18 x 7.5 x 2cm/7 x 3 x ¾in container and leave to set for 1 hour at room temperature, followed by another hour in the refrigerator. Turn upside down on to a chopping board covered with kitchen paper, leave for 1 minute, then cut into 12 cubes.

4 Line 12 ramekins with clear film (plastic wrap). Cut the jelly block into 12 squares and put one in each ramekin. Place a bean paste cube on top of each one.

5 Using the remaining water and agar-agar, make up another batch of jelly as in Step 2. Stir in the remaining sugar. Boil for 2 minutes, then place the pan on a wet dish towel and stir for 5 minutes. When the mixture starts to thicken, pour it over the cubes in the ramekins. Twist the clear film at the top to seal tightly. Leave to set in the refrigerator for at least 1 hour, then remove the jellies from the ramekins and serve.

jellied mango puddings Energy 305kcal/1300kJ; Protein 2.9g; Carbohydrate 72.6g, of which sugars 72g; Fat 2.4g, of which saturates 0.8g; Cholesterol 50mg; Calcium 109mg; Fibre 3g; Sodium 216mg.
sweet aduki bean paste jellies Energy 94kcal/401kJ; Protein 4.1g; Carbohydrate 20.5g, of which sugars 12.4g; Fat 0.1g, of which saturates 0g; Cholesterol 0mg; Calcium 20mg; Fibre 1.9g; Sodium 2mg.

Mango & Coconut Stir-fry

Choose a ripe mango for this recipe. If you buy one that is a little under-ripe, leave it in a warm place for a day or two before using.

Serves 4

¼ coconut
1 large, ripe mango
juice and finely grated rind of 2 limes
15ml/1 tbsp sunflower oil
15g/½oz/1 tbsp butter
30ml/2 tbsp clear honey
crème fraîche or ice cream, to serve

1 Prepare the coconut. Drain the milk and remove the flesh. Cut with a vegetable peeler so that it forms flakes.

2 Peel the mango. Cut the stone (pit) out of the middle of the fruit. Cut each half of the mango into slices. Place the mango slices in a bowl and pour over the lime juice and rind. Set aside.

3 Meanwhile, heat a karahi or wok, then add 10ml/2 tsp of the oil. When the oil is hot, add the butter. Once the butter has melted, stir in the coconut flakes and stir-fry for 1–2 minutes until the coconut is golden brown. Remove and drain on kitchen paper. Wipe out the pan. Strain the mango slices, reserving the juice.

4 Heat the pan again and add the remaining oil. When the oil is hot, add the mango and stir-fry for 1–2 minutes, then add the juice and leave to bubble and reduce for 1 minute.

5 Stir in the honey. When it has dissolved, spoon the mango and its juices into a large serving bowl or individual dishes. Sprinkle on the stir-fried coconut flakes and serve with crème fraîche or ice cream.

Variation
Nectarine or peach slices can be used instead of the mango.

Stewed Pumpkin in Coconut Cream

Fruit stewed in coconut milk is a popular dessert in Thailand. Pumpkins, bananas and melons can all be prepared in this simple but tasty way.

Serves 4–6

1kg/2¼lb kabocha pumpkin
750ml/1¼ pints/3 cups coconut milk
175g/6oz/scant 1 cup sugar
pinch of salt
4–6 fresh mint sprigs, to decorate

1 Cut the pumpkin in half using a large, sharp knife, then cut into manageable segments. Cut the rind away and discard it. Scoop out the seed cluster with a spoon and reserve – if you wish you can toast them and use for decoration (see Tip).

2 Using a sharp knife, cut the pumpkin flesh into pieces that are about 5cm/2in long and 2cm/¾in thick.

3 Pour the coconut milk into a pan. Add the sugar and salt, and bring to the boil.

4 Add the pumpkin and simmer for about 10–15 minutes, or until it is tender.

5 Serve warm, in individual dishes. If you wish, decorate each serving with a mint sprig and toasted pumpkin seeds (see Cook's Tip).

Cook's Tip
To make the decoration, wash the reserved pumpkin seeds to remove any fibres, then pat them dry on kitchen paper. Roast them in a dry frying pan without any oil, or spread them out on a baking sheet and grill (broil) until golden brown, tossing them frequently to prevent them from burning. Watch them carefully as they will burn if left. These seeds can be prepared in advance and used cold to decorate the stewed pumpkin.

mango & coconut Energy 301kcal/1243kJ; Protein 2.4g; Carbohydrate 7.7g, of which sugars 7.6g; Fat 29.2g, of which saturates 22.4g; Cholesterol 8mg; Calcium 14mg; Fibre 6.1g; Sodium 34mg.
stewed pumpkin Energy 164kcal/701kJ; Protein 1.7g; Carbohydrate 40.3g, of which sugars 39.4g; Fat 0.7g, of which saturates 0.4g; Cholesterol 0mg; Calcium 100mg; Fibre 1.7g; Sodium 139mg.

Mangoes with Sticky Rice

Sticky rice is just as good in desserts as in savoury dishes, and mangoes, with their delicate fragrance and velvety flesh, complement it especially well. You need to start preparing this dish the day before you intend to serve it.

Serves 4

175ml/6fl oz/¾ cup thick coconut milk
115g/4oz/⅔ cup white glutinous rice
45ml/3 tbsp sugar
pinch of salt
2 ripe mangoes
strips of pared lime rind, to decorate

1 Pour the coconut milk into a bowl and leave to stand until the cream rises to the top.

2 Rinse the glutinous rice thoroughly in several changes of cold water until it runs clear, then leave to soak overnight in a bowl of fresh cold water.

3 Drain the rice well and spread it out evenly in a steamer lined with muslin (cheesecloth). Cover and steam over a double boiler or a pan of simmering water for about 20 minutes, or until the rice is tender.

4 Reserve 45ml/3 tbsp of the cream from the top of the coconut milk. Pour the remainder into a pan and add the sugar and salt. Heat, stirring constantly, until the sugar has dissolved, then bring to the boil. Remove the pan from the heat, pour the coconut milk into a bowl and leave to cool.

5 Tip the cooked rice into a bowl and pour over the cooled coconut milk mixture. Stir well, then leave the rice mixture to stand for 10–15 minutes.

6 Meanwhile, peel the mangoes, cut the flesh away from the central stones (pits) and cut into slices.

7 Spoon the rice on to individual serving plates. Arrange the mango slices on one side, then drizzle with the reserved coconut cream. Decorate with strips of lime rind and serve.

Papayas in Jasmine Flower Syrup

The fragrant flower syrup can be prepared in advance, using fresh jasmine flowers from a houseplant or the garden. It tastes fabulous with papayas, but it is also good with all sorts of desserts. Try it with ice cream or spooned over warm pancakes.

Serves 2

105ml/7 tbsp water
45ml/3 tbsp palm sugar (jaggery) or light muscovado (brown) sugar
20–30 jasmine flowers, plus a few extra to decorate (optional)
2 ripe papayas
juice of 1 lime

1 Place the water and sugar in a small pan. Heat gently, stirring occasionally, until the sugar has dissolved, then simmer, without stirring, over a low heat for 4 minutes.

2 Pour into a bowl, leave to cool slightly, then add the jasmine flowers. Leave to infuse (steep) for at least 20 minutes.

3 Peel the papayas and slice in half lengthways. Scoop out and discard the seeds. Place the papayas on serving plates and squeeze over the lime.

4 Strain the syrup into a clean bowl, discarding the flowers. Spoon the syrup over the papayas. If you like, decorate with a few fresh jasmine flowers.

Variation

Slices of mango would work well in this recipe in place of papayas.

Cook's Tip

Although scented white jasmine flowers are perfectly safe to eat, it is important to be sure that they have not been sprayed with pesticides or other harmful chemicals. Washing them may not remove all the residue.

mangoes w. rice Energy 200kcal/846kJ; Protein 3.1g; Carbohydrate 46g, of which sugars 24.3g; Fat 0.8g, of which saturates 0.2g; Cholesterol 0mg; Calcium 32mg; Fibre 2g; Sodium 51mg.
papayas in syrup Energy 197kcal/837kJ; Protein 1.6g; Carbohydrate 49.9g, of which sugars 49.9g; Fat 0.3g, of which saturates 0g; Cholesterol 0mg; Calcium 81mg; Fibre 6.6g; Sodium 17mg.

Toffee Apples

A wickedly sweet way to end a meal, this dessert of crisp pieces of apple with a crunchy coating evokes memories of childhood.

Serves 4

4 firm eating apples
115g/4oz/1 cup plain (all-purpose) flour
about 120ml/4fl oz/½ cup water
1 egg, beaten
vegetable oil, for deep-frying, plus 30ml/2 tbsp for the toffee
115g/4oz/½ cup sugar

1 Peel and core each apple and cut into eight pieces. Dust each piece of apple with a little of the flour.

2 Sift the remaining flour into a mixing bowl, then slowly add the cold water and stir well to make a smooth batter.

3 Add the beaten egg and blend well.

4 Heat the oil in a karahi, wok or deep-fryer to a temperature of 190°C/375°F, or until a cube of bread dropped in the oil browns in about 45 seconds. Dip the apple pieces in the batter and deep-fry, in batches, for about 3 minutes or until golden. Remove and drain on kitchen paper. Drain off the oil from the pan.

5 Heat the remaining oil in the pan, add the sugar and stir constantly until the sugar has caramelized. Quickly add the apple pieces and blend well so that each piece of apple is thoroughly coated with the toffee.

6 Dip the apple pieces in cold water to harden before serving.

Variation
Try this recipe with bananas or pineapple pieces for a delicious change.

Sesame Fried Fruits

For this deep-fried dessert you can use any firm fruit that is in season. Pineapple and apples are fantastic, but the batter also works well with banana. Serve them as soon as they are fried so that they retain their crispness.

Serves 4

115g/4oz/1 cup plain (all-purpose) flour
2.5ml/½ tsp bicarbonate of soda (baking soda)
30ml/2 tbsp sugar
1 egg
90ml/6 tbsp water
15ml/1 tbsp sesame seeds or 30ml/2 tbsp desiccated (dry unsweetened shredded) coconut
2 apples
½ fresh pineappe, cubed
vegetable oil, for deep-frying
salt
fresh mint sprigs and lychees, to decorate
30ml/2 tbsp clear honey, to serve

1 Sift the flour, bicarbonate of soda and a pinch of salt into a bowl. Stir in the sugar.

2 Whisk in the egg and just enough water to make a thin batter. Then whisk in the sesame seeds or the desiccated coconut.

3 Peel the apples. Cut them into quarters and remove the core and pips. Halve these pieces. Don't do this until you are ready to cook them, because once peeled, they will quickly discolour.

4 Heat the oil in a karahi, wok or deep-fryer to a temperature of 190°C/375°F, or until a cube of bread dropped in the oil browns in about 45 seconds. Dip the fruit pieces in the batter, then gently drop a few pieces at a time into the hot oil. Fry until golden brown.

5 Remove the fruits from the oil and drain on kitchen paper.

6 Decorate with mint sprigs and lychees and serve immediately with clear honey.

toffee apples Energy 457kcal/1940kJ; Protein 3.4g; Carbohydrate 97.3g, of which sugars 61.6g; Fat 8.8g, of which saturates 1.1g; Cholesterol 0mg; Calcium 73mg; Fibre 2.5g; Sodium 14mg.
sesame fruits Energy 389kcal/1632kJ; Protein 6.2g; Carbohydrate 53.9g, of which sugars 29.7g; Fat 18g, of which saturates 2.5g; Cholesterol 48mg; Calcium 80mg; Fibre 2.3g; Sodium 21mg.

Coconut Fried Bananas

These deliciously sweet treats are a favourite with children and adults alike. In Thailand, you will find them on sale from portable roadside stalls and markets at almost every hour of the day and night.

Serves 4

115g/4oz/1 cup plain (all-purpose) flour
2.5ml/½ tsp bicarbonate of soda (baking soda)
pinch of salt
30ml/2 tbsp sugar
1 egg, beaten
90ml/6 tbsp water
30ml/2 tbsp desiccated (dry unsweetened shredded) coconut
4 firm bananas
vegetable oil, for deep-frying
fresh mint sprigs, to decorate
30ml/2 tbsp clear honey, to serve (optional)

1 Sift the flour, bicarbonate of soda and salt into a large bowl. Stir in the sugar and the egg, and whisk in just enough of the water to make quite a thin batter.

2 Whisk the dessicated coconut into the batter so that it is evenly distributed.

3 Peel the bananas. Carefully cut each one in half lengthways, then in half crossways to make 16 pieces of about the same size. Don't do this until you are ready to cook them because, once peeled, bananas will quickly discolour.

4 Heat the oil in a karahi, wok or deep-fryer to a temperature of 190°C/375°F or until a cube of bread, dropped in the oil, browns in about 45 seconds. Dip the banana pieces in the batter, then gently drop a few into the oil.

5 Deep-fry until golden brown, then lift out and drain well on kitchen paper.

6 Cook the remaining banana pieces in the same way. Serve immediately with honey, if using, and wrap them in banana leaves for a really striking presentation.

Deep-fried Bananas

Fry these bananas at the last minute, so that the outer crust of batter is crisp in texture and the banana is soft and warm inside.

Serves 8

115g/4oz/1 cup self-raising (self-rising) flour
40g/1½oz/⅓ cup rice flour
2.5ml/½ tsp salt
200ml/7fl oz/scant 1 cup water
finely grated lime rind
8 small bananas
vegetable oil, for deep-frying
caster (superfine) sugar and 1 lime, cut into wedges, to serve

1 Sift the self-raising flour, the rice flour and the salt together into a bowl. Add just enough of the water to make a smooth, coating batter. Mix well, then stir in the lime rind.

2 Heat the oil in a karahi, wok or deep-fryer to a temperature of 190°C/375°F, or until a cube of bread dropped in the oil browns in about 45 seconds.

3 Peel the bananas and dip them into the batter two or three times.

4 Deep-fry the battered bananas in batches in the hot oil until crisp and golden.

5 Drain and serve hot, dredged with sugar. Offer the lime wedges to squeeze over the bananas.

Variation
For Banana Fritters using evaporated (unsweetened condensed) milk, sift 115g/4oz/1 cup plain (all-purpose) flour and a pinch of salt into a bowl. Make a well in the centre and add 1 beaten egg. Blend the egg and the flour together, and as the mixture becomes thick, stir in a 175g/6oz can evaporated milk to make a smooth batter. Heat oil for deep-frying to 190°C/375°F and split 4 bananas in half lengthways. Dip them in the batter and deep-fry until golden. Roll in caster (superfine) sugar and serve.

coconut bananas Energy 412kcal/1725kJ; Protein 6.2g; Carbohydrate 53.4g, of which sugars 29.2g; Fat 20.7g, of which saturates 2.8g; Cholesterol 48mg; Calcium 83mg; Fibre 2.3g; Sodium 21mg.
deep-fried bananas Energy 377kcal/1571kJ; Protein 5g; Carbohydrate 39.6g, of which sugars 22.7g; Fat 22.5g, of which saturates 9.9g; Cholesterol 63mg; Calcium 26mg; Fibre 3.2g; Sodium 30mg.

Fried Pineapple

A very simple and quick dessert – fresh pineapple fried in butter, brown sugar and lime juice, and sprinkled with toasted coconut. The slightly sharp taste of the fruit makes this a very refreshing treat at the end of a rich meal.

Serves 4
1 pineapple
40g/1½oz/3 tbsp butter
15ml/1 tbsp desiccated (dry unsweetened shredded) coconut
60ml/4 tbsp soft light brown sugar
60ml/4 tbsp fresh lime juice
lime slices, to decorate
thick and creamy natural (plain) yogurt, to serve

1 Using a sharp knife, cut the top off the pineapple and peel off the skin, taking care to remove the eyes.

2 Cut the pineapple in half and remove and discard the woody core. Cut the flesh lengthways into 1cm/½in wedges.

3 Heat the butter in a large, heavy frying pan or wok. When it has melted, add the pineapple wedges and cook over a medium heat for 1–2 minutes on each side, or until they have turned pale golden in colour.

4 Meanwhile, dry-fry the desiccated coconut in a small frying pan until lightly browned. Remove the pan from the heat and set aside.

5 Sprinkle the soft light brown sugar into the pan with the pineapple, add the lime juice and cook, stirring constantly, until the sugar has dissolved.

6 Divide the pineapple wedges among four bowls, sprinkle with the coconut, decorate with the lime slices and serve with the yogurt.

Honeyed Apples

These scrumptious treats are best prepared for a select number as they require the cook's complete attention. The honey coating crispens when the fritters are dipped in iced water.

Serves 4–5
4 crisp eating apples
juice of ½ lemon
25g/1oz/¼ cup cornflour (cornstarch)
sunflower oil, for deep-frying
toasted sesame seeds, for sprinkling

For the fritter batter
115g/4oz/1 cup plain (all-purpose) flour
generous pinch of salt
120–150ml/4–5fl oz/½–⅔ cup water
30ml/2 tbsp sunflower oil
2 egg whites

For the sauce
250ml/8fl oz/1 cup clear honey
120ml/4fl oz/½ cup sunflower oil
5ml/1 tsp white wine vinegar

1 Peel, core and cut the apples into eighths, brush each piece lightly with lemon juice, then dust with cornflour.

2 To make the sauce, heat the honey and oil in a pan, stirring constantly until blended. Remove from the heat and stir in the white wine vinegar.

3 To make the batter, sift the flour and salt into a bowl, then stir in the water and oil. Whisk the egg whites until stiff peaks form and then fold them into the batter.

4 Heat the oil in a karahi, wok or deep-fryer to a temperature of 190°C/375°F, or until a cube of bread dropped in the oil browns in about 45 seconds. Spear each piece of apple in turn on a skewer, dip in the batter and fry in the hot oil until golden. Drain on kitchen paper. Place the fritters in a dish and pour the sauce over.

5 Transfer the fritters to a lightly oiled serving dish, and sprinkle with the toasted sesame seeds. Serve the honeyed fritters at once, offering bowls of iced water for dipping to crispen the honey coating.

fried pineapple Energy 238kcal/1004kJ; Protein 1.2g; Carbohydrate 36.2g, of which sugars 36.2g; Fat 11g, of which saturates 7.2g; Cholesterol 21mg; Calcium 47mg; Fibre 2.9g; Sodium 67mg.
honeyed apples Energy 564kcal/2361kJ; Protein 3.8g; Carbohydrate 67.8g, of which sugars 45.7g; Fat 32.8g, of which saturates 3.9g; Cholesterol 0mg; Calcium 39mg; Fibre 2g; Sodium 35mg.

Fruits in Lemon Grass Syrup

This exotic and refreshing fruit salad can be made with any combination of tropical fruits, so don't feel you have to stick to those suggested here. Just go for a balance of colour, flavour and texture.

Serves 6

1 firm papaya
1 small pineapple
2 small star fruit, sliced into stars
12 fresh lychees, peeled and stoned (pitted), or 14oz/400g can lychees
2 firm yellow or green bananas, peeled and cut diagonally into slices
mint leaves, to decorate

For the syrup

115g/4oz/generous ½ cup caster (superfine) sugar
2 lemon grass stalks, bruised and halved lengthways

1 To make the syrup, put 225ml/7½ fl oz/1 cup water into a heavy pan with the sugar and lemon grass stalks. Bring to the boil, stirring constantly until the sugar has dissolved, then reduce the heat and simmer for 15 minutes. Leave to cool.

2 Peel and halve the papaya, remove the seeds and slice the flesh crossways. Peel the pineapple and slice it into rounds. Remove the core and cut each round in half. (Keep the core and slice it for a stir-fry.)

3 Put all the fruit into a bowl. Pour the syrup, including the lemon grass stalks, over the top and toss to combine. Cover and chill for 6 hours, or overnight. Before serving in dessert bowls, remove the lemon grass stalks and decorate each portion with mint leaves.

Variation
You can flavour the syrup with ginger rather than lemon grass, if you prefer. Either use fresh or preserved stem ginger, cut into thick slices, and add to the pan with the water and sugar.

Grilled Fruit with Lime Cheese

Grilled fruits make a fine finale to an al fresco party, whether they are cooked over hot coals or under a hot grill. The lemon grass skewers give the fruit a subtle lemon tang.

Serves 4

4 long fresh lemon grass stalks
1 mango, peeled, stoned (pitted) and sliced
1 papaya, peeled, seeded and diced
1 star fruit, cut into slices and halved
8 fresh bay leaves
nutmeg
60ml/4 tbsp maple syrup
50g/2oz/⅓ cup demerara (raw) sugar

For the lime cheese

150g/5oz/⅔ cup curd cheese or low-fat soft cheese
120ml/4fl oz/½ cup double (heavy) cream
grated rind and juice of ½ lime
30ml/2 tbsp icing (confectioners') sugar

1 Prepare the barbecue or preheat the grill (broiler). Cut the top of each lemon grass stalk into a point with a sharp knife. Discard the outer leaves, then use the back of the knife to bruise the length of each stalk to release the oils. Thread each stalk, skewer-style, with the fruit pieces and bay leaves.

2 Support a piece of foil on a baking sheet and roll up the edges to make a rim. Grease the foil, lay the kebabs on top and grate a little nutmeg over each. Drizzle the maple syrup over, dust liberally with the sugar and grill (broil) for 5 minutes.

3 Make the lime cheese by combining the cheese, cream, grated lime rind, juice and icing sugar in a bowl. Serve immediately with the lightly charred fruit kebabs.

Cook's Tip
Only fresh lemon grass will work as skewers for this recipe. The preserved kind is a useful store-cupboard (pantry) item for making curries, but too soft to use with skewers.

fruit w. lime cheese Energy 360kcal/1508kJ; Protein 7.1g; Carbohydrate 43.4g, of which sugars 43.3g; Fat 19.3g, of which saturates 12g; Cholesterol 50mg; Calcium 98mg; Fibre 3.7g; Sodium 219mg.
fruits in lemon grass syrup Energy 174kcal/742kJ; Protein 1.3g; Carbohydrate 44.2g, of which sugars 43.4g; Fat 0.3g, of which saturates 0g; Cholesterol 0mg; Calcium 38mg; Fibre 2.7g; Sodium 6mg.

Clementines in Spiced Syrup

The unusual fruit of a small evergreen tree, harvested just before ripening, star anise is a useful spice. Not only does it add a delicate flavour, but it also makes an attractive decoration, especially with citrus fruits.

Serves 6

350ml/12fl oz/1½ cups sweet dessert wine
75g/3oz/6 tbsp caster (superfine) sugar
6 star anise
1 cinnamon stick
1 vanilla pod (bean)
1 strip of thinly pared lime rind
30ml/2 tbsp Cointreau or another orange liqueur (see Variations)
12 clementines

1 Put the wine, sugar, star anise and cinnamon in a large pan. Split the vanilla pod open with a sharp knife and add it to the pan with the lime rind.

2 Bring to the boil, lower the heat and simmer for 10 minutes, stirring frequently to ensure that all the sugar is dissolved.

3 Pour the spiced vanilla syrup into a bowl and set aside to cool. When it is completely cold, stir in the Cointreau.

4 Peel the clementines. Leave some clementines whole and cut the rest in half. Arrange them in a shallow dish. Pour over the spicy syrup and chill overnight.

5 Serve chilled, spooning the clementines into a glass serving bowl, or six individual dessert dishes.

Variations

- *Tangerines or oranges can be used instead of clementines, if you prefer.*
- *As an alternative to the Cointreau, you can use Grand Marnier or Mandarine Napoléon. The latter is made by blending a distillate of fresh tangerine peel with cognac.*

Pineapple with Papaya Sauce

Pineapple cooked this way takes on a superb flavour and is sensational when served with the sweet papaya sauce. This sauce can also be served with savoury dishes, particularly grilled chicken and game birds as well as pork and lamb.

Serves 6

1 sweet pineapple
melted butter, for greasing and brushing
2 pieces drained preserved stem ginger in syrup, cut into fine matchsticks, plus 30ml/2 tbsp stem ginger syrup from the jar
30ml/2 tbsp demerara (raw) sugar
pinch of ground cinnamon
fresh mint sprigs, to decorate

For the sauce

1 ripe papaya, peeled and seeded
175ml/6fl oz/¾ cup apple juice

1 Peel the pineapple and take spiral slices off the outside to remove the eyes. Cut it crossways into six slices, each 2.5cm/1in thick. Line a baking sheet with a sheet of foil, rolling up the sides to make a rim. Grease the foil with melted butter. Preheat the grill (broiler).

2 Arrange the pineapple slices on the lined baking sheet. Brush with butter, then top with the ginger matchsticks, sugar and cinnamon. Drizzle over the stem ginger syrup. Grill (broil) for 5–7 minutes or until the slices are golden and lightly charred on the surface.

3 Meanwhile, make the sauce. Cut a few slices from the papaya and set aside, then purée the rest with the apple juice in a blender or food processor.

4 Press the purée through a sieve (strainer) placed over a bowl, then stir in any juices from cooking the pineapple.

5 Serve the pineapple slices with a little sauce drizzled around each plate. Decorate with the reserved papaya slices and the mint sprigs.

clementines in syrup Energy 4027kcal/17183kJ; Protein 16.2g; Carbohydrate 1053.6g, of which sugars 1053.6g; Fat 1.3g, of which saturates 0g; Cholesterol 0mg; Calcium 880mg; Fibre 15.6g; Sodium 106mg.
pineapple w. papaya sauce Energy 97kcal/415kJ; Protein 0.7g; Carbohydrate 24.7g, of which sugars 24.7g; Fat 0.2g, of which saturates 0g; Cholesterol 0mg; Calcium 33mg; Fibre 2.3g; Sodium 19mg.

Toffee Plums with Coconut Rice

Red, juicy plums seared in a wok with sugar acquire a rich caramel coating.

Serves 4

6 or 8 firm, ripe plums
90g/3½oz/½ cup caster (superfine) sugar

For the rice

115g/4oz sticky glutinous rice
150ml/¼ pint/⅔ cup coconut cream
45ml/3 tbsp caster (superfine) sugar
a pinch of salt

1 First prepare the rice. Rinse it in several changes of water, then leave to soak overnight in a bowl of cold water.

2 Line a large bamboo steamer that will fit in your wok with muslin (cheesecloth). Drain the rice and transfer to the steamer.

3 Cover the rice and steam over simmering water for 25–30 minutes, until the rice is tender. (Check the water level and add more if necessary.) Transfer the steamed rice to a wide bowl and set aside.

4 Combine the coconut cream with the sugar and salt and pour into a clean wok. Heat gently and bring to the boil, then remove from the heat and pour over the rice. Stir to mix well.

5 Using a sharp knife, cut the plums in half and remove their stones (pits). Sprinkle the sugar over the cut sides.

6 Heat a non-stick wok over a medium-high flame. Working in batches, place the plums in the wok, cut side down, and cook for 1–2 minutes, or until the sugar caramelizes. You may need to wipe out the wok with kitchen paper in between batches.

7 Mould the rice into rounds and place on warmed plates, then spoon over the caramelized plums. Alternatively, simply spoon the rice into four warmed bowls and top with the plums.

8 Drizzle any syrup remaining in the wok over and around the fruit.

Papaya Baked with Ginger

Ginger is responsible for enhancing the flavour of papaya in this recipe, which takes no more than ten minutes to prepare. Take care not to overcook the papaya or its flesh will become very watery.

Serves 4

2 ripe papayas
2 pieces preserved stem ginger in syrup, drained, plus 15ml/1 tbsp syrup from the jar
8 amaretti or other dessert biscuits (cookies), coarsely crushed
45ml/3 tbsp raisins
shredded, finely pared rind and juice of 1 lime
25g/1oz/¼ cup pistachio nuts, chopped
15ml/1 tbsp light muscovado (brown) sugar
60ml/4 tbsp double (heavy) cream, plus extra to serve

1 Preheat the oven to 200°C/400°F/Gas 6. Cut the papayas in half and scoop out their seeds.

2 Place the halves in a baking dish and set aside. Cut the stem ginger into fine matchsticks.

3 Make the filling. Combine the crushed amaretti, stem ginger matchsticks and raisins in a bowl.

4 Stir in the lime rind and juice and two-thirds of the nuts, then add the sugar and cream. Mix well.

5 Fill the papaya halves and drizzle with the ginger syrup. Sprinkle with the remaining nuts. Bake for about 25 minutes or until tender.

6 Serve each papaya half with a generous helping of cream.

Variation
For a slightly different serving suggestion, try Greek (US strained plain) yogurt and almonds instead of cream and pistachios.

toffee plums w. rice Energy 271kcal/1148kJ; Protein 2.8g; Carbohydrate 66.3g, of which sugars 43.4g; Fat 0.4g, of which saturates 0.2g; Cholesterol 0mg; Calcium 52mg; Fibre 0.8g; Sodium 86mg.
papaya w. ginger Energy 292kcal/1228kJ; Protein 3.6g; Carbohydrate 44.6g, of which sugars 35.7g; Fat 12.3g, of which saturates 5.7g; Cholesterol 17mg; Calcium 84mg; Fibre 4.2g; Sodium 127mg.

Pumpkin Purée in Banana Leaves

This is a traditional pudding that can be made with small, sweet pumpkins, butternut squash or sweet cassava. If opting for the traditional pumpkin, find a lighter-coloured one as it is likely have a softer texture. This is a very moreish dessert, or snack, which can be eaten hot or cold.

Serves 6

1 small pumpkin, about 1.3kg/3lb, peeled, seeded and cubed
250ml/8fl oz/1 cup coconut milk
45ml/3 tbsp palm sugar (jaggery)
15ml/1 tbsp tapioca starch
12 banana leaves, cut into 15cm/6in squares
salt

1 Bring a pan of salted water to the boil. Add the pumpkin flesh and cook for 15 minutes, or until tender. Drain and mash with a fork or purée in a blender.

2 In a pan, heat the coconut milk with the sugar and a pinch of salt. Blend the tapioca starch with 15ml/1 tbsp water and 15ml/1 tbsp of the hot coconut milk. Add it to the coconut milk and beat well.

3 Beat the mashed pumpkin into the coconut milk or, if using a blender, add the coconut milk to the pumpkin and purée them together thoroughly.

4 Spoon equal amounts of the pumpkin purée into the centre of each banana leaf square. Fold in the sides and thread a cocktail stick (toothpick) through the open ends to enclose the purée completely.

5 Fill the bottom third of a wok with water. Place a bamboo steamer on top. Place as many stuffed banana leaves as you can into the steamer, folded side up – you may have to cook them in batches. Cover the steamer and steam the parcels for 15 minutes. Open them and serve hot or cold, with long-handled teaspoons to eat with.

Pumpkin with Coconut Custard

Sweet and fragrant, this dessert is sheer indulgence. The hot coconut sauce is the perfect topping.

Serves 4–8

1 small pumpkin, about 1.3kg/3lb, halved, seeded and fibres removed
400ml/14fl oz/1⅔ cups coconut milk
3 large (US extra large) eggs
45ml/3 tbsp palm sugar (jaggery), plus a little extra for sprinkling
salt

For the sauce

250ml/8fl oz/1 cup coconut cream
30ml/2 tbsp palm sugar (jaggery)

1 Preheat the oven to 180°C/350°F/Gas 4. Place the pumpkin halves, skin side down, in a baking dish.

2 In a large bowl, whisk the coconut milk with a pinch of salt, the eggs and sugar, until the mixture is thick and smooth. Pour the custard into each pumpkin half and sprinkle a little extra sugar over the top of the custard and the rim of the pumpkin.

3 Bake in the oven for 35–40 minutes. The pumpkin should feel tender when a skewer is inserted in it, and the custard should feel firm when lightly touched. If you like, you can brown the top further under the grill (broiler).

4 Just before serving, heat the coconut cream in a pan with a pinch of salt and the sugar. Scoop out servings of pumpkin flesh with the custard and place it in bowls. Pour a little sweetened coconut cream over the top to serve.

Variation

Baked mangoes or butternut squash are the obvious substitutes for pumpkin, but – surprisingly – baked avocados also combine wonderfully well with sweet ingredients and are a really luxurious treat when in season. If using avocados, you may need to adjust the quantity of custard, and the cooking time.

pumpkin purée Energy 76kcal/323kJ; Protein 1.7g; Carbohydrate 17g, of which sugars 13.6g; Fat 0.6g, of which saturates 0.3g; Cholesterol 0mg; Calcium 79mg; Fibre 2.2g; Sodium 46mg.
pumpkin w. custard Energy 217kcal/906kJ; Protein 4.5g; Carbohydrate 16.3g, of which sugars 15.7g; Fat 15.4g, of which saturates 11.9g; Cholesterol 71mg; Calcium 71mg; Fibre 1.3g; Sodium 87mg.

Kheer

Both Muslim and Hindu communities in India prepare kheer, which is traditionally served in mosques and temples.

Serves 4–6

15g/½oz/1 tbsp ghee
5cm/2in piece cinnamon stick
175g/6oz/¾ cup soft light (or dark) brown sugar
115g/4oz/1 cup coarsely ground rice
1.2 litres/2 pints/5 cups full cream (whole) milk
5ml/1 tsp ground cardamom
50g/2oz/⅓ cup sultanas (golden raisins)
25g/1oz/¼ cup flaked (sliced) almonds
2.5ml/½ tsp freshly grated nutmeg, to serve

1 In a heavy pan, melt the ghee and fry the cinnamon stick and soft brown sugar. Watch carefully while frying and when the sugar begins to caramelize reduce the heat immediately, or remove the pan from the heat, as sugar can burn very quickly.

2 Return the pan to the heat and add the rice and half the milk. Bring to the boil, stirring constantly to avoid the milk boiling over. Reduce the heat and simmer until the rice is cooked, stirring regularly.

3 Stir in the remaining milk, with the ground cardamom, sultanas and almonds. Leave to simmer until the mixture thickens, stirring constantly to prevent the kheer from sticking to the base of the pan, about 1½ hours.

4 When the mixture is thick and creamy, spoon it into a serving dish or individual dishes. Serve the kheer hot or cold, sprinkled with the freshly grated nutmeg. Decorate with tinfoil, if you like.

Cook's Tip
Kheer is traditionally cooked twice: once until the rice grains disintegrate and then with the spices and flavourings. This recipe uses ground rice and so it will take less time to cook.

Sweet Fried Loops

These irresistible fritters are delicious served with hot chocolate or coffee.

Makes about 24

450ml/15fl oz/scant 2 cups water
15ml/1 tbsp olive oil
15ml/1 tbsp caster (superfine) sugar, plus extra for dredging
2.5ml/½ tsp salt
150g/5oz/1¼ cups plain (all-purpose) flour
1 large (US extra large) egg
sunflower oil, for deep-frying

1 Mix the water, oil, sugar and salt in a large pan and bring to the boil. Remove from the heat, and then sift in the flour. Beat well with a wooden spoon until smooth.

2 Beat in the egg to make a smooth, glossy mixture with a piping consistency. Spoon into a piping (pastry) bag fitted with a large star nozzle.

3 Heat the oil in a karahi, wok or deep-fryer to a temperature of 190°C/375°F, or until a cube of bread dropped in the oil browns in about 45 seconds. Pipe loops of the mixture, two at a time, into the hot oil. Cook the loops for 3–4 minutes until they are golden.

4 Lift out the loops with a wire skimmer or slotted spoon and drain them on kitchen paper. Dredge them with caster sugar and serve warm.

Variation
Add 2.5ml/½ tsp cinnamon to the caster (superfine) sugar for sprinkling, if you like, to give the loops a warm, spicy flavour.

Cook's Tip
If you don't have a piping bag, you could fry teaspoons of mixture in the same way. Don't try to fry too many fritters at a time as they swell a little during cooking.

kheer Energy 379kcal/1591kJ; Protein 9.3g; Carbohydrate 58.9g, of which sugars 43.5g; Fat 12.8g, of which saturates 6.4g; Cholesterol 28mg; Calcium 270mg; Fibre 0.5g; Sodium 90mg.
sweet fried loops Energy 87kcal/362kJ; Protein 0.9g; Carbohydrate 5.5g, of which sugars 0.7g; Fat 7g, of which saturates 0.9g; Cholesterol 8mg; Calcium 10mg; Fibre 0.2g; Sodium 3mg.

Ground Rice Pudding

This delicious and light ground rice pudding is the perfect end to a spicy meal. It can be served either hot or cold.

Serves 4–6

50g/2oz/½ cup coarsely ground rice
4 green cardamom pods, crushed
900ml/1½ pints/3¾ cups semi-skimmed (low-fat) milk
90ml/6 tbsp sugar
15ml/1 tbsp rose water
15ml/1 tbsp crushed pistachio nuts, to garnish

1 Place the ground rice in a pan with the cardamom pods.

2 Add 600ml/1 pint/2½ cups of the milk and bring to the boil over a medium heat, stirring occasionally.

3 Add the remaining milk and stir over a medium heat for about 10 minutes, or until the rice mixture thickens to the consistency of a creamy chicken soup.

4 Stir in the sugar and rose water and continue to cook for a further 2 minutes.

5 Garnish with the pistachio nuts and serve.

Variation
For an even richer version of this pudding, you could add 40g/1½oz ground almonds to the rice at step 1.

Cook's Tip
Rose water is a distillation of scented rose petals which has the intense fragrance and flavour of roses. It is a popular flavouring in Indian cooking. Use it cautiously, adding just enough to suit your taste.

Black Rice Pudding

This unusual rice pudding, flavoured with fresh root ginger, is quite delicious. When cooked, black rice still retains its husk and has a nutty texture. Serve in small bowls, with a little coconut milk or cream poured over each helping.

Serves 6

115g/4oz/generous ½ cup black glutinous rice
475ml/16fl oz/2 cups water
1cm/½in piece fresh root ginger, bruised
50g/2oz/¼ cup soft dark brown sugar
50g/2oz/¼ cup white sugar
300ml/½ pint/1¼ cups coconut milk or cream, to serve

1 Put the black glutinous rice in a sieve (strainer) and rinse well under cold running water.

2 Drain and put in a large pan, with the water. Bring to the boil and stir to prevent the rice from settling on the base of the pan. Cover and cook for about 30 minutes.

3 Add the ginger and both the brown and white sugar.

4 Cook for a further 15 minutes, adding a little more water if necessary, until the rice is cooked and porridge-like.

5 Remove the ginger and serve warm, in bowls, topped with coconut milk or cream.

Cook's Tip
Although black glutinous rice looks similar to wild rice, which is the seed of a rush plant, it is in fact a true rice. It has a particularly nutty flavour that is ideal for puddings and cakes. Long cooking makes the pudding thick and creamy, as the rice is naturally sticky.

ground rice pudding Energy 158kcal/670kJ; Protein 5.8g; Carbohydrate 29.4g, of which sugars 22.7g; Fat 2.6g, of which saturates 1.6g; Cholesterol 9mg; Calcium 190mg; Fibre 0g; Sodium 65mg.
black rice pudding Energy 249kcal/1044kJ; Protein 4g; Carbohydrate 42.5g, of which sugars 14.4g; Fat 7g, of which saturates 5.5g; Cholesterol 0mg; Calcium 33mg; Fibre 1.4g; Sodium 78mg.

Baked Rice Pudding

Black glutinous rice, also known as black sticky rice, has long dark grains and a nutty taste reminiscent of wild rice. This baked pudding has a distinct character and flavour all of its own, as well as an intriguing appearance.

Serves 4–6

175g/6oz/scant 1 cup white or black glutinous rice
30ml/2 tbsp soft light brown sugar
475ml/16fl oz/2 cups coconut milk
250ml/8fl oz/1 cup water
3 eggs
30ml/2 tbsp white sugar

1 Combine the glutinous rice and brown sugar in a pan. Pour in half the coconut milk and the water.

2 Bring to the boil, reduce the heat to low and simmer, stirring occasionally, for 15–20 minutes, or until the rice has absorbed most of the liquid. Preheat the oven to 150°C/300°F/Gas 2.

3 Spoon the rice mixture into a single, large ovenproof dish or divide it among individual ramekins. Beat the eggs with the remaining coconut milk and sugar in a bowl.

4 Strain the egg mixture into a jug (pitcher), then pour it evenly over the par-cooked rice in the dish or ramekins.

5 Place the dish or individual ramekins in a roasting pan. Carefully pour in enough hot water to come halfway up the sides of the dish or ramekins.

6 Cover with foil and bake for about 35–60 minutes, or until the custard has set. Serve warm or cold.

Cook's Tip

Throughout South-east Asia, black glutinous rice is usually used for sweet dishes, whereas its white counterpart is more often used in savoury recipes.

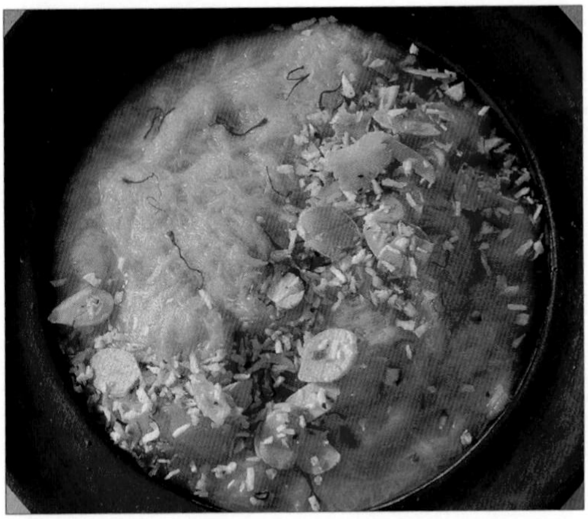

Traditional Indian Vermicelli

Indian vermicelli, made from wheat, is much finer than Italian vermicelli pasta and has a good texture in desserts. It is available from most Asian stores. This is an interesting version of rice pudding.

Serves 4

115g/4oz/1 cup Indian vermicelli
1.2 litres/2 pints/5 cups water
2.5ml/½ tsp saffron threads
15ml/1 tbsp sugar
60ml/4 tbsp low-fat fromage frais or Greek (US strained plain) yogurt, to serve

To decorate

15ml/1 tbsp shredded fresh or desiccated (dry unsweetened shredded) coconut
15ml/1 tbsp flaked (sliced) almonds
15ml/1 tbsp chopped pistachio nuts
15ml/1 tbsp sugar

1 Crush the vermicelli sticks in your hands and place in a pan.

2 Pour the water over the vermicelli, add the saffron and bring to the boil. Boil rapidly, uncovered, for about 5 minutes.

3 Stir in the sugar and continue cooking vigorously until the water has evaporated. Press in a sieve (strainer), if necessary, to remove any excess liquid.

4 Place the vermicelli in a serving dish and decorate with the coconut, almonds, pistachio nuts and sugar. Serve with fromage frais or yogurt.

Variation

You can use a variety of fruits instead of nuts to garnish this dessert. Try a few soft fruits such as blackberries, raspberries or strawberries, if they are in season, or add some chopped dried apricots or sultanas (golden raisins).

baked rice Energy 297kcal/1252kJ; Protein 8.8g; Carbohydrate 54.3g, of which sugars 21.5g; Fat 5.2g, of which saturates 1.4g; Cholesterol 143mg; Calcium 71mg; Fibre 0g; Sodium 185mg.
Indian vermicelli Energy 126kcal/527kJ; Protein 3.7g; Carbohydrate 27.5g, of which sugars 5g; Fat 0.2g, of which saturates 0g; Cholesterol 0mg; Calcium 21mg; Fibre 0g; Sodium 8mg.

Coconut Rice Pudding

This rice pudding is often accompanied by fruits in syrup, or sautéed bananas or pineapple.

Serves 4–6

90g/3½oz/½ cup pudding rice
600ml/1 pint/2½ cups coconut milk
300ml/½ pint/1¼ cups full-fat (whole) milk
75g/2¾oz/scant ½ cup caster (superfine) sugar
25g/1oz/2 tbsp butter, plus extra for greasing
45ml/3 tbsp grated fresh or desiccated (dry unsweetened shredded) coconut, toasted
1 small, ripe pineapple
30ml/2 tbsp sesame oil
5cm/2in piece of fresh root ginger, peeled and grated
shavings of toasted coconut, to decorate

1 Preheat the oven to 150°C/300°F/Gas 2. Grease an ovenproof dish. In a bowl, mix the rice with the coconut milk, milk and 50g/2oz/¼ cup of the sugar and pour it into the ovenproof dish.

2 Dot pieces of butter over the top and put into the oven.

3 After 30 minutes, take the dish out and gently stir in the toasted coconut. Return it to the oven for a further 1½ hours, or until almost all the milk is absorbed and a golden skin has formed on top of the pudding.

4 Using a sharp knife, peel the pineapple and remove the core, then cut the flesh into bitesize cubes.

5 Towards the end of the cooking time, heat the oil in a large wok or heavy pan. Stir in the ginger, stir-fry until it becomes aromatic, then add the pineapple cubes, turning them over to sear on both sides. Sprinkle the ingredients with the remaining sugar and continue to cook until the pineapple is slightly caramelized in texture.

6 Serve the pudding spooned into bowls and topped with the hot, caramelized pineapple and toasted coconut.

Fruit Vermicelli Pudding

This tasty dessert is prepared by Muslims early in the morning of Eid-ul-Fitr, the feast after the 30 days of Ramadan.

Serves 4–6

75g/3oz/6 tbsp ghee
115g/4oz/1 cup Indian vermicelli, coarsely broken
25g/1oz/¼ cup flaked (sliced) almonds
25g/1oz/¼ cup pistachio nuts, slivered
25g/1oz/¼ cup cuddapah nuts or almonds
50g/2oz/⅓ cup sultanas (golden raisins)
50g/2oz/⅓ cup dates, stoned (pitted) and thinly sliced
1.2 litres/2 pints/5 cups full cream (whole) milk
60ml/4 tbsp soft dark brown sugar
1 sachet saffron powder

1 Heat 50g/2oz/4 tbsp of the ghee in a frying pan and sauté the vermicelli until golden brown. (If you are using the Italian variety, sauté it for a little longer.) Remove and set aside.

2 Heat the remaining ghee in a separate pan and fry the almonds, pistachio and cuddapah nuts, sultanas and dates over a medium heat until the sultanas swell. Add the nuts and fruit to the vermicelli and mix gently.

3 Heat the milk in a large, heavy pan and add the sugar. Bring to the boil, add the vermicelli mixture and let the liquid return to the boil, stirring constantly.

4 Reduce the heat and simmer until the vermicelli is soft and you have a fairly thick pudding. Stir in the saffron powder and cook for 1 minute more. Serve hot or cold.

Cook's Tip
Cuddapah nuts taste a little like a combination of almonds and pistachio nuts and are also known as almondettes. If you can't locate them use extra almonds for this dish.

coconut rice pudding Energy 259kcal/1087kJ; Protein 5.8g; Carbohydrate 34g, of which sugars 19.9g; Fat 11.5g, of which saturates 8.2g; Cholesterol 19mg; Calcium 152mg; Fibre 1g; Sodium 153mg.
fruit vermicelli Energy 461kcal/1919kJ; Protein 11.2g; Carbohydrate 43.8g, of which sugars 28.4g; Fat 27.4g, of which saturates 14g; Cholesterol 63mg; Calcium 278mg; Fibre 1.2g; Sodium 114mg.

Pancakes Filled with Sweet Coconut

Traditionally, the pale green colour used for the pancake batter was obtained from the juice squeezed from fresh pandanus leaves. Green food colouring can be used instead.

Makes 12–15

175g/6oz/¾ cup soft dark brown sugar
450ml/¾ pint/scant 2 cups water
1 pandanus leaf, stripped through with a fork and tied into a knot
175g/6oz/2 cups desiccated (dry unsweetened shredded) coconut
vegetable oil, for frying
salt

For the pancake batter
225g/8oz/2 cups plain (all-purpose) flour, sifted
2 eggs, beaten
2 drops of edible green food colouring
few drops of vanilla extract
450ml/15fl oz/scant 2 cups water
45ml/3 tbsp groundnut (peanut) oil

1 Dissolve the sugar in the water with the pandanus leaf, in a pan over gentle heat, stirring all the time. Increase the heat and allow to boil gently for 3–4 minutes, until the mixture just becomes syrupy. Do not let it caramelize.

2 Put the coconut in a karahi or wok with a pinch of salt. Pour over the prepared sugar syrup and cook over a very gentle heat, stirring from time to time, until the mixture becomes almost dry; this will take 5–10 minutes. Set aside until required.

3 To make the batter, blend together the flour, eggs, food colouring, vanilla extract, water and oil either by hand or in a food processor.

4 Brush an 18cm/7in frying pan with oil and cook 12–15 pancakes. Keep the pancakes warm. Fill each pancake with a generous spoonful of the sweet coconut mixture, roll up and serve immediately.

Coconut Pancakes

These light and sweet pancakes are often served as street food by the hawkers in Bangkok. They make a delightful coconut-flavoured dessert.

Makes 8

75g/3oz/⅔ cup plain (all-purpose) flour, sifted
60ml/4 tbsp rice flour
45ml/3 tbsp caster (superfine) sugar
50g/2oz/⅔ cup desiccated (dry unsweetened shredded) coconut
1 egg
275ml/9fl oz/generous 1 cup coconut milk
vegetable oil, for frying
lime wedges and maple syrup, to serve

1 Place the plain flour, rice flour, sugar and coconut in a bowl, stir to mix and then make a small well in the centre. Break the egg into the well and pour in the coconut milk.

2 With a whisk or fork, beat the egg into the coconut milk and then gradually incorporate the surrounding dry ingredients, whisking constantly until the mixture forms a batter. The mixture will not be entirely smooth, because of the coconut, but there shouldn't be any large lumps.

3 Heat a little oil in a 13cm/5in non-stick frying pan. Pour in about 45ml/3 tbsp of the mixture and spread to a thin layer with the back of a spoon. Cook over a high heat for about 30–60 seconds, until bubbles appear on the surface of the pancake, then turn it over and cook the other side until golden.

4 Slide the pancake on to a plate and keep it warm in a very low oven. Make more pancakes in the same way. Serve warm, with lime wedges for squeezing and maple syrup for drizzling.

Variation
Serve with honey instead of maple syrup, if you like.

pancakes filled w. coconut Energy 200kcal/836kJ; Protein 2.6g; Carbohydrate 21.9g, of which sugars 8.8g; Fat 11.7g, of which saturates 4.4g; Cholesterol 24mg; Calcium 33mg; Fibre 1.3g; Sodium 49mg.
coconut pancakes Energy 200kcal/837kJ; Protein 2.6g; Carbohydrate 21.9g, of which sugars 8.8g; Fat 11.7g, of which saturates 4.4g; Cholesterol 24mg; Calcium 33mg; Fibre 1.3g; Sodium 49mg.

Kulfi with Cardamom

The delicious, traditional Indian ice cream, kulfi, is always made with sweetened full cream milk and is a lovely refreshing way to end an Indian meal. Making kulfi is easy if you use yogurt pots or dariole moulds.

Serves 6

2 litres/3 ½ pints/9 cups creamy milk
12 cardamoms
175g/6oz/scant 1 cup caster (superfine) sugar
25g/1oz/¼ cup blanched almonds, chopped
toasted flaked (sliced) almonds and cardamoms, to decorate

1 Place the milk and cardamom pods in a large, heavy pan. Bring to the boil, then simmer vigorously until reduced by one-third.

2 Strain the milk into a bowl, discarding the cardamoms, then stir in the caster sugar and chopped almonds until the sugar is dissolved. Leave to cool.

3 Pour the mixture into a freezerproof container, cover and freeze until almost firm, stirring every 30 minutes.

4 When almost solid, pack the ice cream into six kulfi moulds or clean yogurt pots. Return to the freezer until required, removing the pots about 10 minutes before serving and turning out the individual ices. Decorate with toasted almonds and cardamoms before serving.

Variation

Rose water is also a traditional flavouring for kulfi. Add 15ml/1 tbsp to the recipe, if you like.

Cook's Tip

Use a large pan for reducing the milk as there needs to be plenty of room for it to bubble up.

Leche Flan

Serve this Filipino dessert hot or cold with whipped cream or crème fraîche.

Serves 8

5 large eggs
30ml/2 tbsp caster (superfine) sugar
few drops vanilla extract
400g/14oz can evaporated milk
300ml/½ pint/1 ¼ cups milk
5ml/1 tsp finely grated lime rind
strips of lime rind, to decorate

For the caramel

225g/8oz/generous 1 cup sugar
120ml/4fl oz/½ cup water

1 To make the caramel, put the sugar and water in a heavy pan. Stir to dissolve the sugar, then boil without stirring until the caramel is golden.

2 Quickly pour into eight individual ramekins, rotating them to coat the sides. Leave to set.

3 Preheat the oven to 150°C/300°F/Gas 2. Beat the eggs, sugar and vanilla extract in a bowl.

4 Mix the evaporated milk and fresh milk in a pan. Heat to just below boiling point, then pour on to the egg mixture, stirring all the time. Strain the custard mixture into a jug (pitcher) and add the grated lime rind. Leave the custard to cool. Pour into the caramel-coated ramekins.

5 Place the ramekins in a roasting pan and pour in enough warm water to come halfway up the sides of the dishes.

6 Transfer the roasting pan to the oven and cook the custards for 35–45 minutes or until just set. They will just shimmer when the ramekins are gently shaken.

7 Serve the custards in their ramekin dishes. Alternatively, invert them on to serving plates. Break up the caramel into smaller pieces and use to decorate the custards. The custards can be served warm or cold, decorated with strips of lime rind.

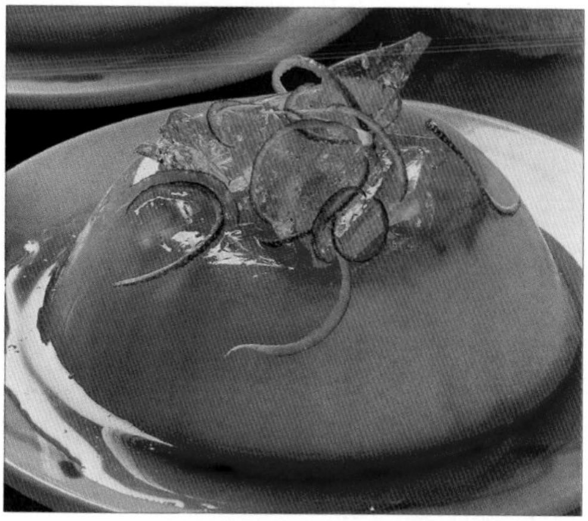

kulfi Energy 272kcal/1147kJ; Protein 15g; Carbohydrate 25.2g, of which sugars 24.9g; Fat 13.3g, of which saturates 4.9g; Cholesterol 22mg; Calcium 467mg; Fibre 0.8g; Sodium 228mg.
leche flan Energy 229kcal/967kJ; Protein 9.3g; Carbohydrate 36.4g, of which sugars 36.4g; Fat 6.2g, of which saturates 2.7g; Cholesterol 130mg; Calcium 211mg; Fibre 0g; Sodium 121mg.

Steamed Coconut Custard

This popular dessert migrated to India from South-east Asia. Coconut milk makes marvellous custard. Here it is cooked with cellophane noodles and chopped bananas, a combination that works very well.

Serves 8
25g/1oz cellophane noodles
3 eggs
400ml/14fl oz can coconut milk
75ml/5 tbsp water
25g/1oz/2 tbsp sugar
4 ripe bananas, peeled and cut into small pieces
salt
vanilla ice cream, to serve (optional)

1 Soak the cellophane noodles in a bowl of warm water for 5 minutes.

2 Beat the eggs in a bowl until pale. Whisk in the coconut milk, water and sugar.

3 Strain into a 1.75 litre/3 pint/7½ cup heatproof soufflé dish.

4 Drain the noodles well and cut them into small pieces with scissors. Stir the noodles into the coconut milk mixture, together with the chopped bananas. Add a pinch of salt and mix well.

5 Cover the dish with foil and place in a steamer for about 1 hour, or until set. A skewer inserted in the centre should come out clean. Serve hot or cold, on its own or topped with vanilla ice cream.

Cook's Tip
Cellophane noodles are translucent, thin dried noodles made from seaweed and mung bean flour. They make this dessert thick and creamy.

Steamed Custard in Nectarines

Steaming nectarines or peaches brings out their natural colour and sweetness, so this is a good way of making the most of under-ripe or less flavourful fruit.

Serves 4–6
6 nectarines
1 large (US extra large) egg
45ml/3 tbsp palm sugar (jaggery) or soft light brown sugar
30ml/2 tbsp coconut milk

1 Cut the nectarines in half. Using a teaspoon, scoop out the stones (pits) and a little of the surrounding flesh.

2 Lightly beat the egg, then add the sugar and the coconut milk. Beat until the sugar has dissolved.

3 Transfer the nectarines to a steamer and carefully fill the cavities three-quarters full with the custard mixture. Steam over a pan of simmering water for 5–10 minutes, until set.

4 Remove from the heat and leave to cool completely before transferring to plates and serving.

Variations
• *This recipe would also work well with peaches or pears. The pears might need a little longer to cook.*
• *A soft berry coulis would make a delicious accompaniment to the nectarines. Cook 350g/12oz/2 cups raspberries in a pan with 30ml/2 tbsp sugar and 15ml/1 tbsp water for about 10 minutes, or until the juices run. Press the raspberries through a fine sieve (strainer) to remove the seeds. Put a spoonful of coulis on to each plate beside the nectarines.*

Cook's Tip
Palm sugar, also known as jaggery, is made from the sap of certain Asian palm trees, such as coconut and palmyrah. If you buy it as a cake or large lump, grate it before use.

coconut custard Energy 110kcal/463kJ; Protein 3.3g; Carbohydrate 19.9g, of which sugars 16.2g; Fat 2.4g, of which saturates 0.7g; Cholesterol 71mg; Calcium 30mg; Fibre 0.6g; Sodium 82mg.
custard nectarines Energy 119kcal/507kJ; Protein 3.8g; Carbohydrate 25.2g, of which sugars 25.2g; Fat 1.1g, of which saturates 0.3g; Cholesterol 32mg; Calcium 24mg; Fibre 2.3g; Sodium 20mg.

Caramel Custard with Fresh Fruit

A creamy caramel dessert is a wonderful way to end a meal. It is light and delicious, and this recipe is very simple to make. Fresh fruit is the perfect accompaniment.

Serves 6
30ml/2 tbsp sugar
30ml/2 tbsp water

For the custard
6 eggs
4 drops vanilla extract
115g/4oz/generous ½ cup sugar
750ml/1¼ pints/3 cups semi-skimmed (low-fat) milk
fresh fruit, such as strawberries, blueberries, orange and banana slices, and raspberries, to serve

1 To make the caramel, place the sugar and water in a heavy pan and heat until the sugar has dissolved and the mixture is bubbling and pale gold in colour. Watch the sugar carefully, as it can quickly burn once it begins to caramelize. Pour carefully into a 1.2 litre/2 pint/5 cup soufflé dish. Leave the caramel to cool completely.

2 Preheat the oven to 180°C/350°F/Gas 4. To make the custard, break the eggs into a medium mixing bowl and whisk until frothy.

3 Stir the vanilla extract into the whisked eggs and gradually add the sugar. Add the milk in a steady stream, whisking constantly.

4 Pour the custard over the top of the caramel.

5 Cook the custard in the oven for 35–40 minutes. Remove from the oven and leave to cool for 30 minutes or until the mixture is set.

6 Loosen the custard from the sides of the dish with a knife. Place a serving dish upside-down on top of the soufflé dish and invert, giving a gentle shake if necessary to turn out the custard on to the serving dish.

7 Arrange any fresh fruit of your choice around the custard on the serving dish and serve immediately.

Egg Custard in Pumpkin

This unusual dessert has arrived in Malaysia from Thailand, where it is called sangkaya faktong and is traditionally made with ducks' eggs. It makes a spectacular dessert for a party. You do not specifically have to use either pumpkin or ducks' eggs to make this recipe. Any good-looking squash can be used as the 'bowl' for the custard, and hens' eggs are perfectly satisfactory.

Serves 4
150g/5oz palm sugar (jaggery)
6 large (US extra large) eggs
250ml/8fl oz/1 cup coconut cream
1 pumpkin, about 20cm/8in in diameter

1 Grate the palm sugar, if necessary. Beat the eggs lightly and whisk in the coconut cream and sugar. Cut off the top of the pumpkin and scoop out the seeds and fibres.

2 Pour in the frothy custard mixture, cover with the pumpkin top and place the pumpkin in a steamer.

3 Cover the steamer and steam for 25 minutes until the custard is set. Allow to cool.

4 Cut into slices to serve, but do not eat the pumpkin skin.

Variations
• *If you use only egg yolks (for this, increase the number to 8), the result will be an even richer and more luxurious custard. Fresh, tart blackcurrants work well as an accompaniment.*
• *If you would prefer to make a version of this dessert that is fully edible, you can cut the top off unripe nectarines and hollow them out, then fill them with the custard mix before steaming and cutting into soft slices.*

caramel custard Energy 197kcal/830kJ; Protein 10.6g; Carbohydrate 23.3g, of which sugars 23.3g; Fat 7.7g, of which saturates 2.9g; Cholesterol 198mg; Calcium 187mg; Fibre 0g; Sodium 125mg.
egg custard Energy 217kcal/907kJ; Protein 4.6g; Carbohydrate 16.3g, of which sugars 15.7g; Fat 15.4g, of which saturates 11.9g; Cholesterol 71mg; Calcium 71mg; Fibre 1.3g; Sodium 88mg.

Coconut Custard Pots

This traditional dessert can be baked or steamed, and the pots are popularly served as a topping for sweet sticky rice. The coconut custard also works well with a selection of fresh fruit, where it can be spooned over the top as desired. In terms of flavour, mangoes and tamarillos go particularly well with the custard and rice.

Serves 4

4 eggs
75g/3oz/6 tbsp soft light brown sugar
250ml/8fl oz/1 cup coconut milk
5ml/1 tsp vanilla, rose or jasmine extract
fresh mint leaves and icing (confectioners') sugar, to decorate (optional)
sliced fruit, to serve

1 Preheat the oven to 150°C/300°F/Gas 2. Whisk the eggs and sugar in a bowl until smooth. Add the coconut milk and extract and whisk well.

2 Strain the mixture into a jug (pitcher), then pour it into four individual heatproof glasses, ramekins or an ovenproof dish.

3 Stand the glasses, ramekins or dish in a roasting pan. Fill the pan with hot water to reach halfway up the sides of the ramekins or dish.

4 Bake for about 35–40 minutes, or until the custards are set. Test with a fine skewer or cocktail stick (toothpick).

5 Remove the roasting pan from the oven, lift out the ramekins or dish and leave to cool.

6 Decorate with the mint leaves and a dusting of icing sugar.

Cook's Tip
If you bake this in one large dish, you may need to extend the cooking time. Simply check the mixture has set before serving.

Coconut & Mandarin Custards

These scented custards with a fabulous melt-in-the-mouth texture are best served warm. However, they are also delicious served chilled, making them perfect for easy entertaining. If you prefer, make the praline the day before.

Serves 4

200ml/7fl oz/scant 1 cup coconut cream
200ml/7fl oz/scant 1 cup double (heavy) cream
2.5ml/½ tsp finely ground star anise
75ml/5 tbsp golden caster (superfine) sugar
15ml/1 tbsp very finely grated mandarin or orange rind
4 egg yolks

For the praline
175g/6oz/scant 1 cup caster (superfine) sugar
50g/2oz/½ cup roughly chopped mixed nuts

1 Make the praline. Place the sugar in a non-stick wok with 15–30ml/1–2 tbsp water. Cook over a medium heat until the sugar dissolves and turns light gold.

2 Remove the syrup from the heat and pour on to a baking sheet lined with baking parchment. Spread it out using the back of a spoon, then sprinkle the chopped nuts evenly over the top and leave to harden.

3 Meanwhile, place the coconut cream, double cream, star anise, sugar, mandarin or orange rind and egg yolks in a large bowl. Whisk to combine and pour the mixture into four lightly greased ramekins or small, heatproof bowls.

4 Place the ramekins or bowls in a large steamer, cover and place in a wok and steam over gently simmering water for 12–15 minutes, or until the custards are just set.

5 Carefully lift the custards from the steamer and leave to cool slightly for about 10 minutes. Meanwhile, break the hardened praline into rough pieces and serve it on top of, or alongside, the custards once the latter have cooled.

coconut custard Energy 433kcal/1792kJ; Protein 10.2g; Carbohydrate 7.8g, of which sugars 7.8g; Fat 40.5g, of which saturates 29g; Cholesterol 170mg; Calcium 168mg; Fibre 4.6g; Sodium 108mg.
coconut & mandarin Energy 643kcal/2688kJ; Protein 6.7g; Carbohydrate 71g, of which sugars 69.3g; Fat 38.9g, of which saturates 19.6g; Cholesterol 270mg; Calcium 100mg; Fibre 0.4g; Sodium 115mg.

Steamed Ginger Custards

Delicate and warming, ginger custard is a favourite among the Chinese. These individual custards are often served warm, straight from the steamer, and enjoyed as a mid-afternoon snack. They work just as well served as a chilled dessert, however.

Serves 4
115g/4oz fresh root ginger, chopped
400ml/14fl oz/1⅔ cups coconut milk
60ml/4 tbsp sugar
2 egg whites
shredded ginger, toasted, to serve (optional)

1 Using a mortar and pestle or food processor, grind the ginger to a fine paste. Press the ginger paste through a fine sieve (strainer) set over a bowl, or twist it in a piece of muslin (cheesecloth), to extract the juice.

2 Fill a wok one-third of the way up with water. Place a bamboo steamer in the wok, bring the water to the boil and reduce the heat to low.

3 In a bowl, whisk the coconut milk, sugar and egg whites with the ginger juice until the mixture is smooth and the sugar has dissolved.

4 Pour the mixture into four individual heatproof bowls and place them in the steamer. Cover and steam for 15–20 minutes, until the mixture sets.

5 Remove the bowls from the steamer and leave to cool. Cover them with clear film (plastic wrap) and place in the refrigerator overnight. Serve the custards chilled or at room temperature as desired.

Variation
Slice about 6 pieces of preserved (stem) ginger and add them to the coconut mixture before pouring into bowls for steaming. It will intensify the flavour of this sweet custard dessert.

Tapioca Pudding

This pudding, made from large pearl tapioca and coconut milk and served warm, is much lighter than the Western-style version. You can adjust the sweetness to your taste. Serve with lychees, or you could try the smaller, similar-tasting logans.

Serves 4
115g/4oz/⅔ cup tapioca
475ml/16fl oz/2 cups water
175g/6oz/¾ cup sugar
pinch of salt
250ml/8fl oz/1 cup coconut milk
250g/9oz prepared tropical fruits
finely shredded rind of 1 lime, to decorate

1 Soak the tapioca in warm water for 1 hour so that the grains swell. Drain.

2 Put the measured water in a pan and bring to the boil. Stir in the sugar and salt.

3 Add the coconut milk and tapioca and simmer for 10 minutes or until the tapioca turns transparent.

4 Serve warm, topped with tropical fruits and decorated with the finely shredded lime rind.

Cook's Tip
Sliced kiwi fruits, mangoes and strawberries would make a bright and tasty selection to serve with this pudding.

Variation
Serve this tapioca pudding with a refreshing peach salad for a change. Peel, stone (pit) and very thinly slice 8 peaches and put them in a serving bowl. Add 30ml/2 tbsp rose water, 20ml/4 tsp sugar, the juice of 1 lemon and 50ml/2fl oz/¼ cup freshly squeezed orange juice. Turn the peach slices in the syrup and chill well before serving.

ginger custards Energy 89kcal/380kJ; Protein 2g; Carbohydrate 20.8g, of which sugars 20.8g; Fat 0.4g, of which saturates 0.2g; Cholesterol 0mg; Calcium 50mg; Fibre 0.3g; Sodium 159mg.
tapioca pudding Energy 324kcal/1384kJ; Protein 1g; Carbohydrate 84.7g, of which sugars 57.2g; Fat 0.4g, of which saturates 0.2g; Cholesterol 0mg; Calcium 51mg; Fibre 1.8g; Sodium 74mg.

Coconut Cream Diamonds

Although commercially ground rice can be used for this dish, grinding jasmine rice yourself – in a food processor – gives a much better result.

Serves 4–6

75g/3oz/scant ½ cup jasmine rice, soaked overnight in 175ml/6fl oz/¾ cup water
350ml/12fl oz/1½ cups coconut milk
150ml/¼ pint/⅔ cup single (light) cream
50g/2oz/¼ cup caster (superfine) sugar
raspberries and fresh mint leaves, to decorate

For the coulis

75g/3oz/¾ cup blackcurrants, stalks removed
30ml/2 tbsp caster (superfine) sugar
75g/3oz/½ cup fresh or frozen raspberries

1 Put the rice and its soaking water into a food processor and process for a few minutes until the mixture is soupy. Heat the coconut milk and cream in a non-stick pan. When the mixture is on the point of boiling, stir in the rice mixture. Cook over a very gentle heat for 10 minutes, stirring constantly.

2 Stir the sugar into the coconut rice mixture and continue cooking for a further 10–15 minutes, or until the mixture is thick and creamy. Line a rectangular tin (pan) with baking parchment. Pour the coconut rice mixture into the pan, cool, then chill until the dessert is set and firm.

3 To make the coulis, put the blackcurrants in a bowl and sprinkle with the sugar. Set aside for 30 minutes. Transfer the blackcurrants and raspberries to a sieve (strainer) over a bowl. Using a spoon, press the fruit against the sieve so that the juices collect in the bowl. Taste the coulis and add more sugar if necessary.

4 Cut the coconut cream into diamonds. Spoon a little of the coulis on to each plate, arrange the diamonds on top and decorate with the raspberries and mint leaves.

Tapioca with Banana & Coconut

This is the type of dessert that everybody loves when they need a pick me up. Sweet and nourishing, the tapioca pearls are cooked in coconut milk and sweetened with bananas and sugar.

Serves 4

550ml/18fl oz/2½ cups water
40g/1½oz tapioca pearls
550ml/18fl oz/2½ cups coconut milk
90g/3½oz/½ cup sugar
3 ripe bananas, diced
salt

1 Pour the water into a pan and bring it to the boil. Stir in the tapioca pearls, reduce the heat and simmer for about 20 minutes, until translucent.

2 Pour in the coconut milk, then add the sugar and a pinch of salt. Cook gently for 30 minutes.

3 Stir in the diced bananas and cook them for 5–10 minutes until soft.

4 Spoon into individual warmed bowls and serve immediately while still hot.

Variations

Instead of adding the diced bananas to the warm tapioca mixture, try one of the following, adjusting the cooking time as needed so that the fruit is fully cooked:

- *Sliced rhubarb*
- *Small apple or pear, cut into wedges*
- *Nectarine or mango slices*

Cook's Tip

A pinch of salt added to this recipe enhances the flavour of the coconut milk and counterbalances the sweetness. You can try the recipe with sweet potato, taro root, yellow corn or rice.

coconut diamonds Energy 165kcal/696kJ; Protein 2.4g; Carbohydrate 28.1g, of which sugars 18.8g; Fat 5.2g, of which saturates 3.2g; Cholesterol 14mg; Calcium 59mg; Fibre 0.8g; Sodium 73mg.
tapioca Energy 226kcal/964kJ; Protein 1.5g; Carbohydrate 57.2g, of which sugars 45.9g; Fat 0.7g, of which saturates 0.4g; Cholesterol 0mg; Calcium 57mg; Fibre 0.9g; Sodium 154mg.

Sweet Rice Dumplings

These rice dumplings are filled with mung bean paste and then simmered in a ginger-infused syrup.

Serves 4–6

For the syrup
25g/1oz fresh root ginger, peeled and finely shredded
115g/4oz/generous ½ cup sugar

For the filling
40g/1½oz dried split mung beans, soaked for 6 hours and drained
25g/1oz/2 tbsp sugar

For the dough
225g/8oz/2 cups sticky glutinous rice flour
175ml/6fl oz/¾ cup boiling water

1 For the syrup, stir the ginger and sugar in a heavy pan over a low heat, until the sugar begins to brown. Remove from the heat and stir in 400ml/14fl oz/1⅔ cups water – it will bubble and spit. Return the pan to the heat and bring to the boil, stirring. Reduce the heat and simmer for 5 minutes.

2 For the filling, put the soaked mung beans in a pan with the sugar and add enough water to cover. Bring to the boil, stirring, until the sugar has dissolved. Simmer for 15–20 minutes until all the water has been absorbed or evaporated. Pound to a paste and leave to cool. Roll the filling into 16–20 balls.

3 To make the dough, put the flour in a bowl. Make a well in the centre and gradually pour in the water, drawing in the flour to form a dough. When cool enough to handle, knead the dough for a few minutes, until soft, smooth and springy.

4 Divide the dough in half and roll each half into a sausage, about 25cm/10in long. Divide each sausage into 8–10 pieces, and roll these into balls, then flatten them in your palm. Place a ball of bean filling in the centre of the dough and seal it by pinching and rolling the dough. Repeat with the remaining balls.

5 Cook the dumplings in a pan of boiling water for 2–3 minutes, until they rise to the surface. Heat the syrup in a heavy pan, drop in the cooked dumplings, and simmer for a further 2–3 minutes. Serve at room temperature, or chilled.

Mung Bean Dumplings

These sweet rice dumplings are often served with jasmine tea.

Serves 6

100g/3½oz/scant ½ cup split mung beans, soaked for 6 hours and drained
115g/4oz/generous ½ cup caster (superfine) sugar
300g/10½oz/scant 3 cups glutinous rice flour
50g/2oz/½ cup rice flour
1 medium potato, boiled in its skin, peeled and mashed
75g/3oz/6 tbsp sesame seeds
vegetable oil, for deep-frying

1 Put the mung beans in a large pan with half the caster sugar and pour in 450ml/¾ pint/scant 2 cups water. Bring to the boil, stirring constantly until all the sugar has dissolved. Reduce the heat and simmer gently for 15–20 minutes until the mung beans are soft. You may need to add more water if the beans are becoming dry, otherwise they may burn.

2 Once the mung beans are soft and all the water has been absorbed, reduce the beans to a smooth paste in a mortar and pestle or food processor and leave to cool.

3 In a large bowl, beat the flours and remaining sugar into the mashed potato. Add about 200ml/7fl oz/scant 1 cup water to bind the mixture into a moist dough. Divide the dough into 24 pieces, roll each one into a small ball, then flatten with the heel of your hand to make a disc and lay out on a lightly floured board.

4 Divide the mung bean paste into 24 small portions. Place one portion of bean paste in the centre of a dough disc. Fold over the edges of the dough and then shape into a ball. Repeat for the remaining dumplings.

5 Spread the sesame seeds on a plate and roll the dumplings in them to coat. Heat enough oil for deep-frying in a wok or heavy pan. When the oil is hot enough to brown a cube of bread in 45 seconds, fry the balls in batches until golden. Drain on kitchen paper and serve warm.

sweet rice dumplings Energy 231kcal/975kJ; Protein 2.7g; Carbohydrate 54.7g, of which sugars 24.5g; Fat 0.3g, of which saturates 0g; Cholesterol 0mg; Calcium 23mg; Fibre 0.9g; Sodium 4mg.
mung bean dumplings Energy 514kcal/2151kJ; Protein 10.4g; Carbohydrate 79.6g, of which sugars 20.9g; Fat 17.2g, of which saturates 2.2g; Cholesterol 0mg; Calcium 127mg; Fibre 5.1g; Sodium 13mg.

Sweet & Spicy Rice Fritters

These delicious little golden balls of rice are scented with sweet, warm spices and will fill the kitchen with wonderful aromas while you're cooking. To enjoy them at their best, serve piping hot, as soon as you've dusted them with sugar.

Serves 4

175g/6oz cooked basmati rice
2 eggs, lightly beaten
60ml/4 tbsp caster (superfine) sugar
a pinch of grated nutmeg
2.5ml/½ tsp ground cinnamon
a pinch of ground cloves
10ml/2 tsp vanilla extract
50g/2oz/½ cup plain (all-purpose) flour
10ml/2 tsp baking powder
a pinch of salt
25g/1oz desiccated (dry unsweetened shredded) coconut
sunflower oil, for deep-frying
icing (confectioners') sugar, to dust

1 Place the cooked rice, eggs, sugar, nutmeg, cinnamon, cloves and vanilla extract in a large bowl and whisk together by hand, or with an electric whisk, to combine.

2 Sift in the flour, baking powder and salt and add the coconut. Mix well until thoroughly combined.

3 Fill a wok one-third full of the oil and heat to 180°C/350°F or until a cube of bread, dropped into the oil, browns in 45 seconds. Alternatively, use a deep-fryer and follow the manufacturer's directions.

4 Very gently, drop tablespoonfuls of the mixture into the oil, one at a time, and fry for 2–3 minutes, or until golden. Carefully remove the fritters from the wok using a slotted spoon and drain well on kitchen paper.

5 Divide the fritters into four portions and serve them in bowls or on plates, or simply pile them up on a large platter.

6 Dust the fritters generously with some sifted icing sugar and serve immediately.

Coconut Rice Fritters

These delicious rice fritters can be served at any time and go especially well with a mug of steaming milky coffee or hot chocolate.

Makes 28

150g/5oz/⅔ cup long grain rice, cooked
30ml/2 tbsp coconut milk powder
45ml/3 tbsp sugar
2 egg yolks
juice of ½ lemon
75g/3oz desiccated (dry unsweetened shredded) coconut
vegetable oil, for deep-frying
icing (confectioners') sugar, for dusting

1 Place 75g/3oz of the cooked rice in a mortar and pound with a pestle until smooth and sticky. Alternatively, process in a food processor.

2 Pour the pounded rice into a bowl and mix in the remaining rice, the coconut milk powder, sugar, egg yolks and lemon juice.

3 Spread out the desiccated coconut on a tray or plate. With wet hands, divide the rice mixture into thumb-sized pieces and roll them in the coconut to make neat balls.

4 Heat the oil in a wok or deep-fryer to 180°C/350°F, or until a cube of bread browns in 45 seconds. Fry the coconut rice balls, three or four at a time, for 1–2 minutes, until the coconut is evenly browned.

5 As each fritter browns, lift it out, drain on kitchen paper and transfer to a plate. Dust the fritters with icing sugar. Place a wooden skewer in each one and serve.

Cook's Tip

To make a hot chocolate for two, prepare a syrup with 30ml/2 tbsp sugar and 120ml/4fl oz/½ cup water and melt 115g/4oz good-quality plain (semisweet) chocolate in it. Finally, whisk in 200ml/7fl oz/scant 1 cup evaporated milk over a low heat.

sweet & spicy fritters Energy 316kcal/1321kJ; Protein 6.6g; Carbohydrate 45.7g, of which sugars 16.3g; Fat 12.4g, of which saturates 4.8g; Cholesterol 95mg; Calcium 46mg; Fibre 1.3g; Sodium 38mg.
coconut rice fritters Energy 61kcal/254kJ; Protein 0.5g; Carbohydrate 3.5g, of which sugars 1.9g; Fat 5.1g, of which saturates 2.1g; Cholesterol 14mg; Calcium 4mg; Fibre 0.4g; Sodium 2mg.

Sago Pudding with Palm Syrup

Palm sugar, also known as jaggery, makes a sweet syrup to pour over this delicious sago and coconut pudding.

Serves 4

1 pandanus (screwpine) leaf, tied in a knot
250g/9oz pearl sago, picked over, washed and drained
400ml/14fl oz/1⅔ cups coconut milk, lightly beaten
salt

For the syrup

250ml/8fl oz/1 cup water
175g/6oz/¾ cup palm sugar (jaggery)

1 Bring a deep pan of water to the boil. Drop in the pandanus leaf and let the sago pour into the water through the fingertips of one hand, while you stir with a wooden spoon with the other, to prevent the pearls from sticking.

2 Boil for 5 minutes, then remove from the heat, cover the pan and leave the sago to steam for about 10 minutes – the pearls should be swollen and translucent. Drain the sago through a sieve (strainer) and rinse under running cold water.

3 Reserve the pandanus leaf and put the sago into a bowl. Stir in 15–30ml/1–2 tbsp of the coconut milk – enough to bind it together – with a pinch of salt. Spoon the sago into a lightly greased mould, or four separate moulds, packing it down gently, and leave it to set at room temperature.

4 Meanwhile, make the syrup. Put the water and palm sugar into a heavy pan and stir over a high heat until the sugar has dissolved. Bring to the boil and boil for 2 minutes. Drop in the reserved pandanus leaf, then simmer for 10 minutes.

5 Beat the rest of the coconut milk with a pinch of salt. Turn the mould, or individual moulds, upside down in a shallow bowl and slip them off the pudding. Spoon the coconut milk over the top, allowing it to flow down the sides and form a pool in the dish, and pour over the hot syrup. Serve immediately, while the syrup is still hot.

Pancakes with Red Bean Paste

In China, sweetened red beans are often used in desserts and sweetmeats because the rich colour is associated with good luck.

Serves 4

175g/6oz/scant 1 cup aduki beans, soaked overnight in cold water to cover
115g/4oz/1 cup plain (all-purpose) flour
1 large (US extra large) egg, lightly beaten
300ml/½ pint/1¼ cups semi-skimmed (low-fat) milk
5ml/1 tsp vegetable oil
75g/3oz/6 tbsp caster (superfine) sugar
2.5ml/½ tsp vanilla extract
fromage frais or natural (plain) yogurt, to serve (optional)

1 Bring 600ml/1 pint/2½ cups water to the boil in a pan. Drain the beans in a sieve (strainer), add them to the pan and boil rapidly for 10 minutes.

2 Skim the surface, lower the heat, cover the pan and simmer, stirring occasionally, for 40 minutes or until the beans are soft.

3 Sift the flour into a bowl, make a well in the centre and add the egg and half the milk, drawing in the flour. Whisk in the remaining milk to make a smooth batter. Set aside.

4 Heat a 20cm/8in non-stick omelette pan and brush lightly with the vegetable oil. When hot, add the batter to make eight thin pancakes, regreasing the pan as necessary. Cover with foil.

5 When the beans are soft and all the water has been absorbed, process them in a food processor until a smooth paste is produced. Add the sugar and vanilla extract and blitz until the sugar has dissolved.

6 Preheat the grill (broiler). Spread a little of the bean paste on the centre of each pancake and fold them into parcels, pressing down lightly with your fingers to flatten. Place on a baking sheet and grill (broil) for a few minutes until crisp and lightly toasted on each side. Serve with fromage frais or yogurt.

sago pudding Energy 416kcal/1777kJ; Protein 0.7g; Carbohydrate 109.4g, of which sugars 50.6g; Fat 0.4g, of which saturates 0.2g; Cholesterol 0mg; Calcium 59mg; Fibre 0.3g; Sodium 115mg.
pancakes w. bean paste Energy 368kcal/1562kJ; Protein 17.2g; Carbohydrate 69.1g, of which sugars 24.8g; Fat 4.5g, of which saturates 1.6g; Cholesterol 52mg; Calcium 183mg; Fibre 4.5g; Sodium 59mg.

Celebration Rice Cake

Not a dry snack from the health food store, but a sumptuous celebration gateau, made from Thai fragrant rice and cream, with a fruit topping.

Serves 8–10

225g/8oz/generous 1 cup fragrant rice, rinsed
1 litre/1¾ pints/4 cups milk
115g/4oz/scant ½ cup caster (superfine) sugar
6 green cardamom pods, crushed
2 bay leaves
300ml/½ pint/1¼ cups whipping cream
6 eggs, separated
red and white currants, sliced star fruit (carambola) and kiwi fruit, to decorate

For the topping

250ml/8fl oz/1 cup double (heavy) cream
150g/5oz/⅔ cup low-fat soft cheese
5ml/1 tsp vanilla extract
grated rind of 1 lemon
40g/1½oz/3 tbsp caster (superfine) sugar

1 Grease and line a 25cm/10in round, deep cake tin (pan).

2 Cook the rice in a pan of boiling unsalted water for 3 minutes, then drain, return to the pan and pour in the milk. Stir in the caster sugar, cardamoms and bay leaves. Bring to the boil, then lower the heat and simmer for 20 minutes, stirring occasionally. Cool, then remove the bay leaves and cardamom husks.

3 Preheat the oven to 180°C/350°F/Gas 4. Spoon the rice mixture into a bowl. Beat in the cream and then the egg yolks. Whisk the egg whites until they form soft peaks, then fold them into the rice mixture.

4 Spoon into the prepared tin and bake for 45–50 minutes until risen and golden brown. Chill overnight in the tin. Turn the cake out on to a large serving plate.

5 Whip the cream until stiff, then gently fold in the soft cheese, vanilla extract, lemon rind and sugar. Cover the top of the cake with the cream mixture, swirling it attractively. Decorate with red and white currants, sliced star fruit and kiwi fruit.

Golden Steamed Sponge Cake

Cakes are not traditionally served for dessert in China, but this light sponge is very popular and is often served on the dim sum trolley at lunchtime.

Serves 8

175g/6oz/1½ cups plain (all-purpose) flour
5ml/1 tsp baking powder
1.5ml/¼ tsp bicarbonate of soda (baking soda)
3 large (US extra large) eggs
115g/4oz/⅔ cup soft light brown sugar
45ml/3 tbsp walnut oil
30ml/2 tbsp golden (light corn) syrup
5ml/1 tsp vanilla extract

1 Sift the flour, baking powder and bicarbonate of soda into a bowl. Line an 18cm/7in diameter bamboo steamer or cake tin (pan) with baking parchment.

2 In a mixing bowl, whisk the eggs with the sugar until thick and frothy. Beat in the walnut oil and syrup, then set the mixture aside for about 30 minutes.

3 Add the sifted flour, baking powder and bicarbonate of soda to the egg mixture with the vanilla extract, and beat rapidly by hand or with an electric whisk to form a thick batter that is free from lumps.

4 Pour the batter into the paper-lined steamer or tin. Cover and steam over boiling water for 30 minutes or until the sponge springs back when gently pressed with a finger. Leave to cool for a few minutes before serving.

Variation

This cake is usually served on its own, cut into slabs or wedges. To dress it up a bit, add a scoop each of apricot compote and thick, creamy yogurt to each dessert plate. Alternatively, top it with a combination of mascarpone and cream cheese with some vanilla extract and decorate with walnut halves.

celebration rice cake Energy 492kcal/2047kJ; Protein 12.1g; Carbohydrate 41g, of which sugars 23.1g; Fat 31.9g, of which saturates 18.7g; Cholesterol 189mg; Calcium 197mg; Fibre 0g; Sodium 165mg.
golden steamed sponge cake Energy 150kcal/632kJ; Protein 4.4g; Carbohydrate 20g, of which sugars 3.3g; Fat 6.5g, of which saturates 1g; Cholesterol 71mg; Calcium 42mg; Fibre 0.7g; Sodium 37mg.

Avocado Fool

This sweet avocado dessert can also be served as a thick purée or blended with coconut milk until it is the consistency of thick pouring cream. This makes a delicious drink when a couple of ice cubes are stirred in.

Serves 2
1 avocado, stoned (pitted)
juice of ½ lime
30ml/2 tbsp sweetened condensed milk
30ml/2 tbsp coconut cream
a pinch of salt
fresh mint leaves, to decorate
½ lime, halved, to serve

1 Put the avocado flesh into a food processor or blender and purée it with the lime juice until well mixed.

2 Add the condensed milk, coconut cream and salt and process until the mixture is smooth and creamy.

3 Spoon the mixture into individual bowls or glasses and chill over ice.

4 Decorate with a few mint leaves and serve with lime wedges to squeeze over.

Cook's Tip
Avocados discolour quickly when cut and exposed to the air, so prepare them immediately before they are to be used. If you have used only half an avocado and don't want to throw away the other half, you can preserve the rest for a short while by leaving the stone (pit) in place and wrapping it very tightly in clear film (plastic wrap). Store in the refrigerator but use as soon as possible.

Variation
This recipe works equally well with other soft-fleshed fruit, such as bananas, mango and papaya.

Mango & Lime Fool

Canned mangoes are used here for convenience, but the dish tastes even better if made with fresh ones. Choose a variety like the voluptuous Alphonso mango, which is wonderfully fragrant and tastes indescribably delicious.

Serves 4
400g/14oz can sliced mango
grated rind of 1 lime
juice of ½ lime
150ml/¼ pint/⅔ cup double (heavy) cream
90ml/6 tbsp Greek (US strained plain) yogurt
fresh mango slices, to decorate (optional)

1 Drain the canned mango slices and put them in the bowl of a food processor.

2 Add the grated lime rind and the lime juice. Process until the mixture forms a smooth purée. Alternatively, mash the mango slices with a potato masher, then press through a sieve (strainer) into a bowl with the back of a wooden spoon. Stir in the lime rind and juice.

3 Pour the cream into a bowl and add the yogurt. Whisk until the mixture is thick and then quickly whisk in the mango mixture.

4 Spoon into four tall cups or glasses and chill for 1–2 hours. Just before serving, decorate each glass with fresh mango slices, if you like.

Cook's Tip
When mixing the cream and yogurt mixture with the mango purée, whisk just enough to combine, so as not to lose the lightness of the whipped cream mixture. If you prefer, fold the mixtures together lightly, so that the fool is rippled.

avocado fool Energy 152kcal/632kJ; Protein 2.3g; Carbohydrate 10.8g, of which sugars 10.1g; Fat 11.3g, of which saturates 3.1g; Cholesterol 5mg; Calcium 58mg; Fibre 1.7g; Sodium 57mg.
mango fool Energy 269kcal/1118kJ; Protein 2.8g; Carbohydrate 15.2g, of which sugars 14.9g; Fat 22.6g, of which saturates 13.8g; Cholesterol 51mg; Calcium 64mg; Fibre 2.6g; Sodium 26mg.

Mango Sorbet with Sauce

After a heavy meal, this delightful sorbet makes a very refreshing dessert. Mango is said to be one of the oldest fruits cultivated in India, having been presented by Lord Shiva to his beautiful wife, Parvathi.

Serves 4–6

900g/2lb mango pulp
2.5ml/½ tsp lemon juice
grated rind of 1 orange and 1 lemon
4 egg whites
50g/2oz/¼ cup caster (superfine) sugar
120ml/4fl oz/½ cup double (heavy) cream
50g/2oz/½ cup icing (confectioners') sugar

1 In a large, chilled bowl, mix half of the mango pulp with the lemon juice and the grated rind.

2 Whisk the egg whites until peaks form, then gently fold them into the mango mixture, with the caster sugar. Cover with clear film (plastic wrap) and place in the freezer for at least 1 hour.

3 Remove from the freezer and beat again. Transfer to an ice cream container, and freeze until fully set.

4 In a bowl, whip the double cream with the icing sugar and the remaining mango pulp. Cover and chill the sauce for 24 hours.

5 Remove the sorbet 10 minutes before serving. Scoop out individual servings and cover with a generous helping of mango sauce. Serve immediately.

Variation
Try this sorbet made with full-flavoured locally grown strawberries when in season for a delicious change.

Indian Ice Cream

Kulfi-wallahs (ice-cream vendors) have always made kulfi, and continue to this day, without using modern freezers. Kulfi is packed into metal cones sealed with dough and then churned in clay pots set in ice and salt until set. Try this method – it works extremely well in an ordinary freezer.

Serves 4–6

3 × 400ml/14fl oz cans evaporated milk
3 egg whites
350g/12oz/3 cups icing (confectioners') sugar
5ml/1 tsp ground cardamom
15ml/1 tbsp rose water
175g/6oz/1½ cups pistachio nuts, chopped
75g/3oz/½ cup sultanas (golden raisins)
75g/3oz/¾ cup flaked (sliced) almonds
25g/1oz/3 tbsp glacé (candied) cherries, halved

1 Remove the labels from the cans of evaporated milk and lay the cans down in a pan with a tight-fitting cover. Fill the pan with water to reach three-quarters up the cans. Bring to the boil, cover and simmer for 20 minutes. (Don't leave the cans of evaporated milk unattended. Top up the water if necessary; the pan must never boil dry.) When cool, remove the cans and chill in the refrigerator for 24 hours. Chill a large bowl too.

2 Whisk the egg whites in another large bowl until peaks form. Open the cans and empty the milk into the chilled bowl. Whisk until doubled in quantity, then fold in the whisked egg whites and icing sugar.

3 Gently fold in the remaining ingredients, cover the bowl with clear film (plastic wrap) and place in the freezer for 1 hour.

4 Remove the ice cream from the freezer and mix well with a fork. Transfer to a serving container and return to the freezer for a final setting. Remove from the freezer 10 minutes before serving.

mango sorbet Energy 206kcal/881kJ; Protein 6.1g; Carbohydrate 47g, of which sugars 46.4g; Fat 0.8g, of which saturates 0.4g; Cholesterol 0mg; Calcium 92mg; Fibre 5.9g; Sodium 91mg.
Indian ice cream Energy 746kcal/3136kJ; Protein 25.6g; Carbohydrate 96.3g, of which sugars 95.2g; Fat 31.4g, of which saturates 7.7g; Cholesterol 34mg; Calcium 624mg; Fibre 3g; Sodium 424mg.

Coconut & Lemon Grass Ice Cream

The combination of cream and coconut milk makes for a wonderfully rich ice cream. The lemon grass flavouring is very subtle, but quite delicious.

Serves 4

2 lemon grass stalks
475ml/16fl oz/2 cups double (heavy) cream
120ml/4fl oz/½ cup coconut milk
4 large (US extra large) eggs
105ml/7 tbsp caster (superfine) sugar
5ml/1 tsp vanilla extract

1 Cut the lemon grass stalks in half lengthways. Use a mallet or rolling pin to mash the pieces, breaking up the fibres so that all the flavour is released. Pour the cream and coconut milk into a pan. Add the lemon grass stalks and heat gently, stirring frequently, until the mixture starts to simmer.

2 Put the eggs, sugar and vanilla extract in a large bowl. Using an electric whisk, whisk until the mixture is becomes light and fluffy.

3 Strain the cream mixture into a heatproof bowl that will fit over a pan of simmering water. Whisk in the egg mixture, then place the bowl over the pan and continue to whisk until the mixture thickens. Remove it from the heat and leave to cool. Chill the coconut custard in the refrigerator for 3–4 hours.

4 Pour the mixture into a plastic tub or similar freezerproof container. Freeze for 4 hours, beating two or three times at hourly intervals with a fork to break up the ice crystals.

5 Alternatively, use an ice-cream maker. Pour the chilled mixture into the machine and churn until it is firm enough to scoop. Serve immediately, or scrape into a freezerproof container and place in the freezer. Allow the ice cream to soften in the refrigerator for 30 minutes before serving.

Mango Ice Cream

Canned mangoes are used to make a deliciously rich and creamy ice cream, with a delicate oriental flavour.

Serves 4–6

2 x 425g/15oz cans sliced mango, drained
50g/2oz/¼ cup caster (superfine) sugar
30ml/2 tbsp lime juice
45ml/3 tbsp hot water
15ml/1 tbsp powdered gelatine
350ml/12fl oz/1½ cups double (heavy) cream, lightly whipped
fresh mint sprigs, to decorate

1 Reserve four slices of mango for decoration and chop the remainder. Place the chopped mango pieces in a bowl with the caster sugar and lime juice.

2 Put the hot water in a small heatproof bowl and sprinkle over the gelatine. Place the bowl over a pan of gently simmering water and stir until the gelatine has dissolved. Pour on to the mango mixture and mix well.

3 Add the lightly whipped cream and fold into the mango mixture. Pour the mixture into a plastic freezer container and freeze until half frozen.

4 Place the half-frozen ice cream in a food processor or blender and process until smooth. Spoon back into the container and return to the freezer to freeze completely.

5 Remove from the freezer 10 minutes before serving and place in the refrigerator. Serve scoops of ice cream decorated with pieces of the reserved sliced mango and fresh mint sprigs.

Cook's Tips

- *Transferring the ice cream to the refrigerator for a short time before serving allows it to soften slightly, making scooping easier and helping the flavour to be more pronounced.*
- *Use a metal scoop to serve the ice cream, dipping the scoop briefly in warm water between servings. Or simply slice, if easier.*

coconut & lemon grass Energy 445kcal/1862kJ; Protein 4.4g; Carbohydrate 54g, of which sugars 54g; Fat 25g, of which saturates 13.9g; Cholesterol 244mg; Calcium 11mg; Fibre 0g; Sodium 164mg.
mango ice cream Energy 409kcal/1701kJ; Protein 1.4g; Carbohydrate 32.4g, of which sugars 32.3g; Fat 31.3g, of which saturates 19.5g; Cholesterol 80mg; Calcium 44mg; Fibre 0.9g; Sodium 17mg.

Coconut Sorbet

Deliciously refreshing and cooling, this tropical sorbet can be found in different versions all over South-east Asia. Other classic Asian sorbets include recipes made with lychees, pineapple, watermelon, and even a delicately-spiced version with lemon grass.

Serves 6

175g/6oz/scant 1 cup caster (superfine) sugar
120ml/4fl oz/½ cup coconut milk
50g/2oz/⅔ cup grated or desiccated (dry unsweetened shredded) coconut
a squeeze of lime juice

1 Place the sugar in a heavy pan and add 200ml/7fl oz/scant 1 cup water. Bring to the boil, stirring constantly, until the sugar has dissolved completely.

2 Reduce the heat and simmer for 5 minutes to make a syrup.

3 Stir the coconut milk into the sugar syrup, along with most of the coconut and the lime juice. Pour the mixture into a bowl or freezer container and freeze for 1 hour.

4 Take the sorbet out of the freezer and beat it with a fork, or blend it in a food processor, until it is smooth and creamy, then return it to the freezer and leave until frozen.

5 Before serving, remove the sorbet from the freezer and allow to stand at room temperature for 10–15 minutes to soften slightly.

6 Serve the sorbet in small bowls and decorate with the remaining grated coconut.

Cook's Tip

Light and refreshing, this sorbet is very welcome on a hot day, or as a palate refresher during a spicy meal. You could serve it in coconut shells, garnished with sprigs of fresh mint.

Coconut Ice with Ginger Syrup

This ice cream is delectable and very easy to make in an ice-cream maker, especially if you use the type with a bowl that is placed in the freezer to chill before the ice-cream mixture is added.

Serves 6

400ml/14fl oz can coconut milk
400ml/14fl oz can sweetened condensed milk
2.5ml/½ tsp salt
coconut shells (optional) and thinly pared strips of coconut, to serve

For the gula melaka sauce

150g/5oz/¾ cup palm sugar (jaggery) or muscovado (molasses) sugar
1cm/½in slice fresh root ginger, bruised
1 pandanus (screwpine) leaf (optional)

1 Chill the cans of coconut and condensed milk very thoroughly. In a bowl, mix the coconut milk with the condensed milk. Gently whisk together with the salt.

2 Pour the mixture into the frozen freezer bowl of an ice-cream maker (or follow the appliance instructions) and churn until the mixture has thickened. (This will take 30–40 minutes.)

3 Transfer the mixture to a lidded plastic tub, cover and freeze until the consistency is right for scooping. If you do not have an ice-cream maker, pour the mixture into a shallow container and freeze on the coldest setting.

4 When ice crystals form around the sides of the ice cream, beat the mixture, then return it to the freezer. Do this at least twice. The more you do it, the creamier the mixture will be.

5 Make the sauce. Dissolve the sugar in 150ml/¼ pint/⅔ cup water in a pan. Add the ginger and bring to the boil. Add the pandanus leaf, if using, and simmer for 3–4 minutes. Set aside.

6 Serve the ice cream in coconut shells or in a bowl. Sprinkle with the strips of coconut. Remove the pandanus leaf and ginger from the sauce and serve on the side.

coconut sorbet Energy 170kcal/717kJ; Protein 0.7g; Carbohydrate 32g, of which sugars 32g; Fat 5.2g, of which saturates 4.5g; Cholesterol 0mg; Calcium 23mg; Fibre 1.2g; Sodium 26mg.
coconut ice w. ginger syrup Energy 276kcal/1168kJ; Protein 6.9g; Carbohydrate 47g, of which sugars 47g; Fat 8.1g, of which saturates 5.1g; Cholesterol 28mg; Calcium 248mg; Fibre 0g; Sodium 347mg.

Star Anise Ice Cream

This syrup-based ice cream is flavoured with the clean, warming taste of star anise and is the perfect exotic treat to cleanse the palate.

Serves 6–8

500ml/17fl oz/2¼ cups double (heavy) cream
8 whole star anise
90g/3½oz/½ cup caster (superfine) sugar
4 large (US extra large) egg yolks
ground star anise, to decorate

1 In a heavy pan, heat the cream with the star anise to just below boiling point, then remove from the heat and leave to infuse (steep) until cool.

2 In another pan, dissolve the sugar in 150ml/¼ pint/⅔ cup water, stirring constantly. Bring to the boil for a few minutes to form a light syrup, then leave to cool for 1 minute.

3 Whisk the egg yolks in a bowl. Trickle in the hot syrup, whisking constantly, until the mixture becomes mousse-like. Pour in the infused cream through a sieve (strainer), and continue to whisk until well mixed.

4 Pour the mixture into a freezerproof container and freeze for 4 hours, beating twice with a fork or whisking with an electric mixer to break up the ice crystals. To serve, dust with a little ground star anise.

Cook's Tips

- *You can use an ice-cream maker with this recipe, if you have one. Simply pour in the mixture at the beginning of Step 4 and churn until smooth.*
- *Spices play an important role in many traditional Asian ice creams, with the lively tastes of cinnamon, clove, star anise and pandanus (screwpine) leaf all proving popular.*

Green Tea Ice Cream

In the past, the Japanese did not follow a meal with dessert, apart from some fruit. This custom is slowly changing and now many Japanese restaurants offer light desserts such as sorbet or ice cream. Here, ice cream is flavoured with matcha – the finest green powdered tea available.

Serves 4

500ml/17fl oz carton good-quality vanilla ice cream
15ml/1 tbsp matcha (powdered green tea)
15ml/1 tbsp lukewarm water from the kettle
seeds from ¼ pomegranate (optional)

1 Soften the ice cream by transferring it to the refrigerator for 20–30 minutes. Do not allow it to melt.

2 Mix the matcha powder and lukewarm water in a cup and stir well to make a smooth paste.

3 Put half the ice cream into a mixing bowl. Add the matcha liquid and mix thoroughly with a rubber spatula, then add the rest of the ice cream. You can stop mixing at the stage when the ice cream looks a marbled dark green and white, or continue mixing until the ice cream is a uniform pale green. Put the bowl into the freezer.

4 After 1 hour, the ice cream will be ready to serve. Scoop into individual glass cups. If you like, top with pomegranate seeds.

Cook's Tip/Variation

- *Matcha is the tea used in the Tea Ceremony, a special tea-making ritual integral to Japanese culture.*
- *Sweet aduki beans and French sweet chestnut purée can be used to make other Japanese-style ice creams. Use 30ml/2 tbsp soft cooked sweet aduki beans or 20ml/4 tsp chestnut purée per 100ml/3fl oz/scant ½ cup good-quality vanilla ice cream.*

star anise ice cream Energy 380kcal/1570kJ; Protein 2.3g; Carbohydrate 12.8g, of which sugars 12.8g; Fat 35.9g, of which saturates 21.5g; Cholesterol 170mg; Calcium 46mg; Fibre 0g; Sodium 18mg.
green tea ice cream Energy 269kcal/1120kJ; Protein 4.9g; Carbohydrate 21.1g, of which sugars 21g; Fat 18.9g, of which saturates 11.3g; Cholesterol 0mg; Calcium 126mg; Fibre 0g; Sodium 75mg.

Mango & Coconut Tofu Whip

This smooth dessert has a truly tropical taste. Few fruits are quite so luscious and sweet as mangoes and their slightly resinous flavour is superbly complemented by coconut cream. Add the magical texture of silken tofu and you will achieve perfection in a glass.

Serves 6
2 large ripe mangoes
200ml/7fl oz/scant 1 cup coconut cream
200g/7oz silken tofu
45ml/3 tbsp maple syrup
mint sprigs and strips of lime rind, to decorate

1 Using a sharp knife, peel and stone (pit) the mangoes and coarsely chop the flesh. Place the flesh in a blender or food processor with the coconut cream and silken tofu.

2 Add the maple syrup and process to a smooth, rich cream. Pour into serving glasses or bowls and chill for at least 1 hour before serving. Decorate with mint sprigs and strips of lime rind.

Cook's Tip
Make sure that you buy pure maple syrup for the best flavour.

Variations
- *Silken tofu can also be used to make a berry fruit fool. Tip a 200g/7oz packet of silken tofu into the bowl of a food processor and add 175g/6oz hulled strawberries, raspberries or blackberries. Process the mixture to a smooth purée, then scrape into a bowl and sweeten with a little honey, maple syrup or maize malt syrup.*
- *For a delectable tofu smoothie, blend 2 bananas with 400g/14oz silken tofu, sweeten with honey, and flavour with almond extract. For best results, cut up and freeze the tofu first.*

Lychee Sorbet

Sorbets are lovely alternatives to ice cream, especially for those who are watching their weight. They are easy to make and you can use any soft fruit. They make delightful taste cleansers between courses but are equally satisfying as a dessert at the end of a meal. Many kinds of tropical fruit make successful sorbets, including limes, mangoes and papayas, but fragrant lychee sorbet remains a favourite.

Serves 4
500g/1¼lb lychees, peeled and stoned (pitted)
500ml/17fl oz/generous 2 cups lychee syrup
juice of 2 limes
fresh mint leaves, to decorate

1 Process the lychees in a food processor with half the syrup until you get a smooth purée. Mix in the remaining syrup and the lime juice.

2 Pour into a large plastic container or ice cream tub, cover and place in the coldest part of the freezer.

3 Freeze the mixture for several hours until slushy. Return to the processor and blend until light and creamy. Return to the container and re-freeze until firm, preferably overnight.

4 Serve in individual bowls, decorated with a mint leaf or two.

Cook's Tip
Lychee syrup is available from supermarkets. If fresh lychees are not available you can make this sorbet using canned lychees and the syrup from the can. You can add 250ml/8fl oz/1 cup of single (light) cream or natural (plain) yogurt when processing the second time for an even smoother sorbet.

mango & coconut Energy 90kcal/382kJ; Protein 3.3g; Carbohydrate 16.5g, of which sugars 16.2g; Fat 1.7g, of which saturates 0.4g; Cholesterol 0mg; Calcium 197mg; Fibre 1.3g; Sodium 96mg.
lychee sorbet Energy 249kcal/1064kJ; Protein 1.4g; Carbohydrate 64.7g, of which sugars 64.7g; Fat 0.1g, of which saturates 0g; Cholesterol 0mg; Calcium 31mg; Fibre 0.9g; Sodium 4mg.

Rose-flavoured Lassi

Soothing and cooling, this Indian yogurt-based drink is an ideal partner to spicy food. Savoury lassi is often salty and flavoured with mint, whereas the sweet drink is fragrant with the traditional essences of rose or pandanus.

Serves 2

300ml/½ pint/1¼ cups natural (plain) yogurt
5–10ml/1–2 tsp rose extract
10ml/2 tsp sugar
6 ice cubes
rose petals, to decorate

1 In a jug (pitcher), beat the yogurt with 150ml/¼ pint/⅔ cup water, until smooth.

2 Add the rose essence and sugar, adjusting the sweetness to taste, and mix well.

3 Divide the ice cubes between two glasses and pour in the lassi. Decorate with a few rose petals and serve.

Pistachio Lassi

This delicate flavour of pistachio nuts combines beautifully with the yogurt to create a light drink that needs very little sweetening. Don't forget to allow a few pistachios for decoration.

Serves 4

8–12 pistachio nuts
300ml/½ pint/1¼ cups natural (plain) yogurt
5ml/1 tsp sugar, to taste

1 Chop four pistachio nuts roughly and set them aside for the decoration. Grind the remaining nuts as finely as you can. Pour the yogurt into a tall jug (pitcher) and add the sugar.

2 Whisk until frothy, then add 300ml/½ pint/1¼ cups water and the ground nuts. Whisk for 2 minutes. Pour into chilled glasses. Top with the chopped nuts and serve very cold.

Mango & Lime Lassi

Inspired by the classic Indian drink, this tangy, fruity blend is great for breakfast or as a delicious pick-me-up at any time of day. Soft, ripe mango blended with yogurt and sharp, zesty lime and lemon juice makes a wonderfully thick, cooling drink that's packed with energy. It can also be enjoyed as a mellow soother when you need to unwind.

Makes 2 tall glasses

1 mango
finely grated rind and juice of 1 lime
15ml/1 tbsp lemon juice
5–10ml/1–2 tsp caster (superfine) sugar
100ml/3½fl oz/scant ½ cup natural (plain) yogurt
mineral water
1 extra lime, halved, to serve

1 Peel the mango and cut as much flesh as you can from the stone (pit). Discard the pit and put the mango flesh into a blender or food processor and add the lime rind and juice.

2 Add the lemon juice, sugar and natural yogurt. Whizz until the mixture is completely smooth, stopping blending to scrape down the sides of the bowl once or twice, if necessary.

3 Test the consistency is correct – if the smoothie thickly coats the back of a spoon it will be too thick to drink. Stir in a little mineral water to thin it down.

4 Serve immediately, with half a lime on the side of each glass so that more juice can be squeezed in, if desired.

Cook's Tip/Variation

If you don't have a blender or food processor you can still make smoothies by stewing fruit gently in a pan, then mashing it with a fork until it makes a fine purée. Chill this, and add it to yogurt or milk, or fruit juice, if you prefer a non-dairy option. Either shake them together in a screw top jar or use a whisk, then press the drink through a seive.

rose-flavoured lassi Energy 104kcal/438kJ; Protein 7.7g; Carbohydrate 16.5g, of which sugars 16.5g; Fat 1.5g, of which saturates 0.8g; Cholesterol 2mg; Calcium 288mg; Fibre 0g; Sodium 125mg.
pistachio lassi Energy 106kcal/442kJ; Protein 5.6g; Carbohydrate 7.5g, of which sugars 7.3g; Fat 6.3g, of which saturates 1.1g; Cholesterol 1mg; Calcium 154mg; Fibre 0.6g; Sodium 115mg.
mango & lime lassi Energy 79kcal/334kJ; Protein 2.7g; Carbohydrate 17g, of which sugars 17g; Fat 0.5g, of which saturates 0.3g; Cholesterol 1mg; Calcium 102mg; Fibre 0.4g; Sodium 43mg.

Rainbow Drink

Thirst-quenching and appetizing, rainbow drinks are a delightful South-east Asian speciality.

Serves 4

50g/2oz dried split mung beans, soaked for 4 hours and drained
50g/2oz red aduki beans, soaked for 4 hours and drained
25g/1oz/2 tbsp sugar
crushed ice, to serve
15g/½oz jellied agar-agar, soaked in warm water for 30 minutes and shredded into long strands, to decorate

For the syrup

300ml/½ pint/1¼ cups coconut milk
50g/2oz/¼ cup sugar
25g/1oz tapioca pearls

1 Put the mung beans and aduki beans into two separate pans and divide the sugar between them. Pour in enough water to cover and, stirring all the time, bring it to the boil. Reduce the heat and leave both pans to simmer for about 15 minutes, stirring from time to time, until the beans are tender but not mushy – you may have to add more water. Drain the beans, leave to cool and chill separately in the refrigerator.

2 In a heavy pan, bring the coconut milk to the boil. Reduce the heat and stir in the sugar, until it dissolves. Add the tapioca pearls and simmer for about 10 minutes, until they become transparent. Leave to cool and chill in the refrigerator.

3 Divide the mung beans among four tall glasses, add some crushed ice, then the aduki beans and more ice. Pour the coconut syrup over the top and decorate with strands of agar agar. Serve immediately with straws and long spoons.

Cook's Tip

Many variations of rainbow drinks are served throughout South-east Asia in tall clear glasses in markets, restaurants and bars. They usually combine ingredients such as lotus seeds, taro, sweet potato, and tapioca pearls with exotic fruits. Tapioca pearls are also used in the iced drink known as bubble tea, which has become popular on the US West Coast.

Tea & Fruit Punch

This delicious punch can be served hot or cold. White wine or brandy may be added to taste.

Makes 4

600ml/1 pint/2½ cups water
1 cinnamon stick
4 cloves
12.5ml/2½ tsp Earl Grey tea leaves
175g/6oz/scant 1 cup sugar
450ml/¾ pint/scant 2 cups tropical soft drink concentrate
1 lemon, sliced
1 small orange, sliced
½ cucumber, sliced

1 Bring the water to the boil in a pan with the cinnamon stick and cloves. Remove from the heat and add the tea leaves. Leave to brew for about 5 minutes. Stir and strain into a large bowl, add the sugar and stir until dissolved. Leave to cool.

2 Add the soft drink concentrate and chill for 2–3 hours. Place the fruit and cucumber in a chilled bowl and pour over the tea mix.

3 Chill for a further 24 hours before serving.

Almond Sherbet

Traditionally, this drink was always made in the month of Ramadan to break the Muslim fast. It should be served chilled.

Serves 4

50g/2oz/½ cup ground almonds
600ml/1 pint/2½ cups semi-skimmed (low-fat) milk
10ml/2 tsp sugar, or to taste

1 Put the ground almonds into a serving jug (pitcher).

2 Pour in the semi-skimmed milk and add the sugar; stir to mix.

3 Taste for sweetness and adjust as necessary. Serve very cold in long glasses. Chilling the glasses first helps to keep the drink cold and adds a sense of occasion.

soya milk w. pandanus Energy 384kcal/1584kJ; Protein 34.8g; Carbohydrate 9.6g, of which sugars 9.6g; Fat 19.2g, of which saturates 3.6g; Cholesterol 0mg; Calcium 156mg; Fibre 0g; Sodium 384mg.
tea & fruit punch Energy 277kcal/1184kJ; Protein 0.3g; Carbohydrate 73.6g, of which sugars 73.4g; Fat 0g, of which saturates 0g; Cholesterol 0mg; Calcium 30mg; Fibre 0g; Sodium 48mg.
almond sherbet Energy 155kcal/651kJ; Protein 7.8g; Carbohydrate 10.5g, of which sugars 10.2g; Fat 9.5g, of which saturates 2.2g; Cholesterol 9mg; Calcium 211mg; Fibre 0.9g; Sodium 67mg.

Sweet Soya Milk with Pandanus

In the streets and markets of many Asian cities, freshly made soya milk is sold daily. Often infused with pandanus leaves, or ginger, and served hot or chilled, it is a sweet and nourishing drink, enjoyed by children and adults. If you can't find pandanus leaves, which are available in some Asian markets, replace them with a vanilla pod (bean).

Makes 1.2 litres/2 pints/ 5 cups

225g/8oz/1 ¼ cups soya beans, soaked overnight and drained
1.5 litres/2½ pints/6 cups water
2 pandanus (screwpine) leaves, slightly bruised
15ml/2 tbsp sugar

1 Put a third of the soya beans into a blender with a third of the water. Blend until thick and smooth. Pour the purée into a bowl and repeat with the rest of the beans and water.

2 Strain the purée through a fine sieve (strainer) set over a bowl to extract the milk. Discard the solids remaining in the sieve. Line the sieve with a piece of muslin (cheesecloth), then strain the milk again.

3 Pour the milk into a pan and bring it to the boil. Stir in the pandanus leaves with the sugar, until it has dissolved. Return the milk to the boil, reduce the heat and simmer for 10 minutes.

4 Remove the pandanus leaves, then ladle the hot milk into cups and serve. You can also leave it to cool, then pour it into a tall jug (pitcher) and chill in the refrigerator.

Variation
To make ginger-flavoured soya milk, stir in 25g/1oz grated fresh root ginger with the sugar. Bring the liquid to the boil and simmer for 10 minutes, then remove from the heat and leave to infuse (steep) for 20 minutes more.

Spiced Lassi

Lassi, or buttermilk, is prepared by churning yogurt with water and then removing the fat. To make this refreshing drink without churning, use low-fat natural yogurt instead.

Serves 4

450ml/¾ pint/scant 2 cups natural (plain) low-fat yogurt
300ml/½ pint/1 ¼ cups water
2.5cm/1in piece fresh root ginger, finely crushed
2 fresh green chillies, finely chopped
2.5ml/½ tsp ground cumin
salt and ground black pepper
a few fresh coriander (cilantro) leaves, chopped, to garnish

1 In a bowl, whisk the yogurt and water until well blended. The consistency should be that of full cream (whole) milk. Adjust by adding more water if necessary.

2 Add the ginger, chillies and ground cumin.

3 Season with the salt and black pepper, and mix well.

4 Pour into four serving glasses and chill. Garnish with chopped coriander before serving.

Cook's Tip
Lassi is often drunk with hot and spicy curries as it refreshes the palate well.

Variation
If you prefer an unspiced and cooler version, try Rose Water Lassi. Blend 300ml/½ pint/1 ¼ cups natural (plain) yogurt with 60ml/4 tbsp caster (superfine) sugar, 400ml/14fl oz/1⅔ cups water and 15ml/1 tbsp rose water in a food processor or blender. Pour into individual glasses or a jug (pitcher) and add fresh mint leaves to decorate, if you like.

spiced lassi Energy 74kcal/311kJ; Protein 6.3g; Carbohydrate 9.8g, of which sugars 8.5g; Fat 1.6g, of which saturates 0.6g; Cholesterol 1mg; Calcium 221mg; Fibre 0g; Sodium 95mg.
rainbow drink Energy 188kcal/800kJ; Protein 6.3g; Carbohydrate 42.1g, of which sugars 25g; Fat 0.5g, of which saturates 0.2g; Cholesterol 0mg; Calcium 55mg; Fibre 2.5g; Sodium 87mg.

Index

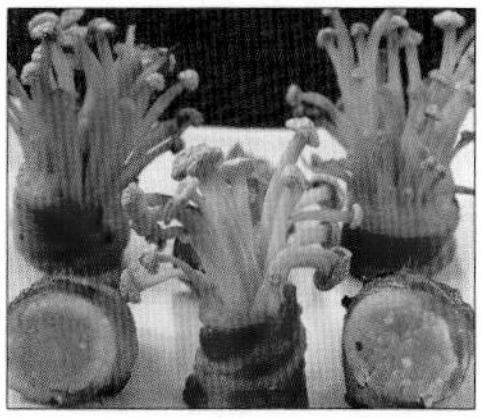